Child and Adolescent Psychopathology

Child and Adolescent Psychopathology

Edited By
Theodore P. Beauchaine
Stephen P. Hinshaw

WILEY

John Wiley & Sons, Inc.

Contents

List of Contributors

Robert F. Asarnow, Ph.D.
Department of Psychiatry and
   Biobehavioral Sciences
UCLA
Los Angeles, California

Theodore P. Beauchaine, Ph.D.
Department of Psychology
University of Washington
Seattle, Washington

Joseph C. Blader, Ph.D.
Department of Psychiatry &
   Behavioral Science
Stony Brook State University of
   New York
Stony Brook, New York

Sandra A. Brown, Ph.D.
Department of Psychology and
   Psychiatry
Veterans Affairs San Diego
   Healthcare System
La Jolla, California

Sara J. Bufferd
Department of Psychology
University at Stony Brook
Stony Brook, New York

Cynthia M. Bulik, Ph.D.
Department of Psychiatry
University of North Carolina at
   Chapel Hill
Chapel Hill, North Carolina

Gabrielle A. Carlson, M.D.
Department of Psychiatry &
   Behavioral Science
Stony Brook State University of
   New York
Stony Brook, New York

Dante Cicchetti, Ph.D.
Institute of Child Development
   and Department of Psychiatry
University of Minnesota
Minneapolis, Minnesota

James Coan, Ph.D.
Department of Psychology
University of Virginia
Charlottesville, Virginia

Pamela M. Cole
Department of Psychology
Pennsylvania State University
University Park, Pennsylvania

Nicole A. Crocker, B.A.
Department of Psychology
San Diego State University
San Diego, California

Sheila E. Crowell, M.A.
Department of Psychology
University of Washington
Seattle, Washington

Geraldine Dawson, Ph.D.
Department of Psychology
University of Washington
Seattle, Washington

Thomas J. Dishion, Ph.D.
Child and Family Center
University of Oregon
Eugene, Oregon

Margaret W. Dyson
Department of Psychology
University at Stony Brook
Stony Brook, New York

Susan Faja, M.S.
Department of Psychology
University of Washington
Seattle, Washington

Susanna L. Fryer, M.S.
Department of Psychology
San Diego State University
San Diego, California

Lisa M. Gatzke-Kopp, Ph.D.
Department of Psychology
University of Washington
Seattle, Washington

Sarah E. Hall
Department of Psychology
Pennsylvania State University
University Park, Pennsylvania

Kristina D. Hiatt, Ph.D.
Department of Psychology
University of Oregon
Eugene, Oregon

Stephen P. Hinshaw, Ph.D.
Department of Psychology
University of California
Berkeley, California

Jerome Kagan, Ph.D.
Department of Psychology
Harvard University
Cambridge, Massachusetts

Claudia L. Kernan, Ph.D.
Department of Psychiatry and
    Biobehavioral Sciences
Los Angeles, California

Daniel N. Klein, Ph.D.
Department of Psychology
University at Stony Brook
Stony Brook, New York

Benjamin B. Lahey
Department of Health Studies
University of Chicago
Chicago, Illinois

Mark F. Lenzenweger, Ph.D.
Department of Psychology
State University of New York at
    Binghamton
Binghamton, New York

Sarah N. Mattson, Ph.D.
Department of Psychology
San Diego State University
San Diego, California

Emily Neuhaus, M.A.
Department of Psychology
University of Washington
Seattle, Washington

Joel Nigg, Ph.D.
Department of Psychology
Michigan State University
East Lansing, Michigan

Molly Nikolas, M.A.
Department of Psychology
Michigan State University
East Lansing, Michigan

Thomas G. O'Connor, Ph.D.
Department of Psychiatry
University of Rochester Medical
    Center
Rochester, New York

Bruce D. Perry, M.D., Ph.D.
The ChildTrauma Academy
Houston, Texas

Sir Michael Rutter
Social, Genetic, and Developmental
    Psychiatry Centre,
London, England

Katherine E. Shannon, M.S.
Department of Psychology
University of Washington
Seattle, Washington

Wendy K. Silverman, Ph.D.
Department of Psychology
Florida International University
Miami, Florida

Eric Stice, Ph.D.
Oregon Research Institute
Eugene, Oregon

Dana C. Torpey
Department of Psychology
University at Stony Brook
Stony Brook, New York

Everett Waters
Department of Psychology
State University of New York at
    Stony Brook
Stony Brook, New York

Carl F. Weems, Ph.D.
Department of Psychology
University of New Orleans
New Orleans, Louisiana

Preface

By almost any metric chosen, societal costs of mental illness are staggering. According to the World Health Organization (WHO, 2007), 5 of the 10 leading causes of disability worldwide are mental disorders, with 285 million people affected by either depression, Schizophrenia, or an alcohol/drug use condition (and many more, of course, indirectly affected as family members). Mental disorders account for nearly 900,000 suicides per year globally, and over 1 billion lost days of work per year in the United States. It is therefore of little surprise that most of us have either a family member, friend, or colleague who suffers from a mental disorder.

These statistics suggest that elucidating the causes of mental illness should be an international priority. Although most who study psychopathology would undoubtedly agree with this statement, until quite recently a deep understanding of the roots of mental illness was precluded by our inability to observe genetic and neural vulnerabilities that contribute to psychiatric disturbance. As a result, most of what we learned about mental illness was obtained through observation and classification of symptoms. Useful in the early stages of research on psychopathology, symptom classification often tells us little about underlying processes—be they biological or environmental—that lead to a particular disorder. This is an important limitation because a thorough understanding of the processes through which mental disorders emerge can be critical to the development of effective treatments.

In the past decade and a half or so, major advances in psychiatric genetics and neuroscience have moved us beyond an exclusive reliance on behavioral symptoms as markers of psychopathology, providing new and important insights into the etiology of many disorders. As we describe in Chapter 3, it is now clear that behavioral traits—including those that predispose to psychopathology—almost always arise from complex interactions between biological vulnerabilities and exposure to environmental risks across development. For example, heritable disorders such as Schizophrenia are affected strongly by environmental experiences, and the effects of environmentally transmitted risks such as child maltreatment are moderated by genes and other biological predispositions (Chapter 20). Moreover, recent research has revealed that the expression of several genes implicated in behavior regulation can be altered by environmental input, findings that obscure traditional boundaries between nature and nurture.

Scientific advances such as these make it an exciting and challenging time to be a student of psychopathology. The current proliferation of research findings is both astounding and humbling, stretching our capacity to integrate new information into our thinking. This shift in the scientific landscape—from a relatively static view of psychopathology based on specific clusters of behavior to a dynamic view of disorders emerging from complex interactions between vulnerabilities and risks across time—served as the impetus for this book. To date, most graduate-level psychopathology texts have been organized around symptom-based approaches to classifying mental illness, with limited consideration of the genetic and neural substrates of behavior, or of the unfolding of interactions between biological vulnerabilities and environmental risk across time. Our main objective in first proposing and then editing this book was to organize a text around the developmental psychopathology perspective, which emphasizes complex transactions between individuals and their environments over time (Chapter 1), at all relevant levels of analysis including genetic, neural, behavioral, and social (Chapter 2).

The first three chapters of this book outline a foundation for understanding mental illness within a developmental psychopathology framework. Chapter 1 provides a brief historical account of developmental psychopathology, outlines differences between the developmental psychopathology perspective and traditional approaches to research on mental illness, and defines a number of important terms that appear throughout later chapters. Chapter 2 emphasizes the importance of understanding psychopathology not so much as clusters of related symptoms but rather as the end result of dynamic and complex transactions operating across multiple levels of analysis. Chapter 3 outlines basic principles of research on the genetics of psychopathology and explains why genes cannot be considered without also considering environments.

Following these introductory chapters, Part I: Risk Factors for Psychopathology describes a number of vulnerability traits that often contribute to the later emergence of mental illness. Importantly, none of these traits necessarily results in psychopathology, and many individuals who are affected by such vulnerabilities learn to cope with them, leading gratifying and productive lives. Nevertheless, such individuals are much more likely than others to develop mental illness when exposed to significant environmental risk.

Part II: Externalizing Behavior Disorders includes chapters covering the major classes of externalizing or disruptive conditions outlined in the *Diagnostic and Statistical Manual of Mental Disorders–Fourth Edition*. These include Attention-Deficit/Hyperactivity Disorder (Chapter 11), Oppositional Defiant Disorder and Conduct Disorder (Chapter 12), Antisocial Personality Disorder (Chapter 13), and alcohol and drug abuse/dependence (Chapter 14). Even though we have organized the externalizing disorders around the *DSM-IV* framework, it is important to note that recent research supports a spectrum model of externalizing psychopathology, with common genetic vulnerability observed across this spectrum. Nevertheless, the *DSM-IV* is the predominant classification scheme for mental illness, and any student of psychopathology should be familiar with this system.

Part III: Internalizing Behavior Disorders is also organized around the *DSM-IV* perspective, and includes chapters describing anxiety disorders (Chapter 15), depressive disorders (Chapter 16), and borderline personality development (Chapter 17). Of course, it could be argued that Borderline Personality Disorder contains an admixture of internalizing and externalizing symptoms, revealing again that problems related to mental disorders do not fit into neat categories and that the search for underlying mechanisms is of paramount importance. As with externalizing disorders, it is important to note that common genetic vulnerability predisposes individuals to mental illness across the internalizing spectrum.

Finally, Part IV: Other Psychological Disorders includes chapters describing common forms of psychopathology that are not readily subsumed within either the internalizing or externalizing spectra. These include Bipolar Disorder (Chapter 18), autism spectrum disorders (Chapter 19), Schizophrenia (Chapter 20), and eating disorders (Chapter 21).

Some readers may note that certain disorders that are often covered in graduate psychopathology texts are not included in this book. For example, we do not address developmental disabilities or Mental Retardation. In omitting these disorders, we are not implying that they are unimportant. Rather, the proliferation of literature addressing developmental disabilities makes it difficult to cover the topic adequately in a text that already includes 21 chapters. Thus, we were left with a difficult choice, and we decided not to delimit coverage of the conditions summarized previously. We refer interested readers to other sources (e.g., Jacobson, Mulick, & Rojahn, 2007) for excellent coverage of developmental disabilities and Mental Retardation.

Without further preamble, we now invite you to join in the quest for deepened understanding of mental disorders and conditions that originate in childhood and adolescence. We hope that the emphasis in this volume on biological and genetic substrates—and the interactions of these with environmental contexts—will challenge your preconceived notions as to what is *biological* and what is *environmental* in relation to normal and atypical development and psychopathology. We hope as well that our coverage will propel a new generation of investigators, clinicians, and policymakers to pursue the daunting but essential goal of explaining, treating, and preventing the devastation that so often attends to psychopathology.

THEODORE P. BEAUCHAINE, PH.D.
STEPHEN P. HINSHAW, PH.D.

REFERENCES

Jacobson, J. W., Mulick, J. A., & Rojahn, J. (Eds.). (2007). *Handbook of intellectual and developmental disabilities*. New York: Springer.

World Health Organization. (2007). *Mental health*. Retrieved October 9, 2007, from source.

Foreword

This engaging and thought-provoking volume on child psychopathology is refreshingly different from traditional texts on the mental disorders of childhood. Although a few chapters pay passing tribute to the all-encompassing theories of pioneers such as Freud, Piaget, or Erikson, there is an implicit acceptance that they provide a hopelessly inadequate portrayal of what development is all about. Indeed, it was the failure of these *big* theories that provided a crucial impetus for the emergence of developmental psychopathology (DP). But, six other innovations in this exciting text warrant emphasis.

First, whilst providing a mass of well-summarized factual evidence on both neuroscience and clinical disorders, the editors and authors have not been afraid to question and criticize the prevailing dogma. As a result, the book provides not just a state-of-the-art summary of current knowledge and understanding, but also a thoughtful look at how approaches could, and should, develop in the years ahead. Second, whilst rightly rejecting crude simplistic biological reductionism, there is an overt acceptance that, if we are to understand the workings of the mind, we must appreciate the functioning of the brain as it operates over the course of development and the interconnections between brain and mind (the biggest challenge of all).

Third, whilst emphasizing that development is a biological phenomenon involving both change and continuity, it also involves the operation of thought processes as reflected in the cognitive and affective processing of experiences, together with personal agency with respect to how individuals respond to the challenges that they face. Fourth, there is an explicit recognition that experiences (both physical and psychosocial; both prenatal and postnatal) bring about changes in the organism. That is, as some have put it, they "get under the skin," and it is essential that we investigate the processes by which this comes about, together with the resultant effects.

Fifth, throughout the volume, there is the repeated emphasis that we cannot be content with determining the degree to which mental disorders are due to genetic, environmental, and developmental influences.

Instead, we must understand the interdependence and co-action of these three domains.

Sixth, there is, throughout the whole of the book, a detailed, well-informed, and up-to-date discussion of genetic concepts and findings. There is an appropriate appreciation of the pervasiveness of genetic influences but, equally, a rejection of genetic determinism. Rather, the importance of gene–environment interplay is discussed in relation to how it affects both exposure to, and susceptibility to, environmental hazards. There are reminders, as well, that gene effects are dependent on gene expression, and that the influences on expression include environmental features.

It has been argued, in my view correctly, that DP is not a theory. Rather, it is a conceptualization that should both guide research and inform clinical and developmental thinking. The book admirably succeeds in that purpose. Readers will learn an immense amount about risk and protective factors, about development, about clinical disorders, and about neuroscience, but most of all they will be helped in how to think about the issues as they will arise in the future and not just as they face us today. As the preface indicates, there is no attempt to cover the whole of developmental psychopathology. Instead, there is a focus on a selected sample of key topics chosen to illustrate some of the most important issues as they apply to mental disorders in childhood.

The book, whilst providing informed guidance on the official classification schemes and approaches to diagnosis, is straightforward in pointing out the numerous arbitrary rules and assumptions. Over the years, huge progress has been made in sorting out the differences and similarities among disorders. These strengths are explained but readers are encouraged to think about how things might, and ought to, change as new evidence comes in.

I presume that the prime goal of the editors, and authors, was to provide a clear, interesting, evidence-based approach to childhood psychopathology. Clearly, that goal is well achieved but, for me, the greater attraction of the volume is that it encourages readers to think about the issues in a constructive fashion that should help them in the years ahead to accommodate and integrate new research findings and, by so doing, to ensure that clinical progress continues.

MICHAEL RUTTER
Professor of Developmental Psychopathology
Institute of Psychiatry, Kings College, London UK

PART I

THE DEVELOPMENTAL PSYCHOPATHOLOGY APPROACH TO UNDERSTANDING BEHAVIOR

CHAPTER 1

Developmental Psychopathology as a Scientific Discipline: Relevance to Behavioral and Emotional Disorders of Childhood and Adolescence

STEPHEN P. HINSHAW

A wealth of information has accumulated in recent years about the causes, correlates, and underlying mechanisms of child and adolescent mental disorders. At the same time, treatment strategies are becoming increasingly evidence based. The major goal of this volume is to provide up-to-date, conceptually and developmentally derived information about (a) risk factors for child and adolescent psychopathology and (b) the major conditions and disorders that come to clinical attention. Intervention strategies are not emphasized herein, as such information would require a set of chapters fully as long as the present contents. For a recent compendium of evidence-based treatments for child and adolescent disorders, see Silverman and Hinshaw (2008).

To contextualize and put into perspective why this topic area is so important, it is necessary to consider the levels of impairment and pain linked with child and adolescent psychopathology. Think, for instance, of the hopelessness and despair associated with depression in youth; the major limitations on life choices—and the sheer loneliness—so often imposed by many forms of Anxiety Disorder; the disorganization and chaos related to Bipolar Disorder; the personal, family, school, and peer-related disruptions incurred by dysregulated attention and impulse control; the havoc wreaked by severely aggressive behavior on individuals and even entire communities; or the isolation and lost opportunities linked to Autism and other Pervasive Developmental Disorders. Similar portraits pertain to eating disorders, substance use and abuse, schizophrenia-spectrum conditions, and the beginnings of personality disorders. Overall, the personal and family confusion, grief, emptiness, and lost opportunities incurred by conditions such as these are deeply felt by all who are affected.

Furthermore, emotional and behavioral problems in children and adolescents are distressingly prevalent and often lead to serious impairments in such crucial life domains as academic achievement, interpersonal competencies, and independent living skills (for thorough accounts, see Mash & Barkley, 2003; Wolfe & Mash, 2006). These conditions incur massive pain for individuals, families, and communities at large, triggering major economic burdens for caregivers, school districts, and health care systems. From a developmental perspective, not only are the major child and adolescent disturbances likely to persist across the lifespan, but the majority of mental disturbances experienced by adults have their origins in childhood and adolescence (Kessler, Berglund, Demler, Jin, & Walters, 2005).

Over and above the clinical and policy-related concerns raised by child and adolescent psychopathology, during the past century these conditions have begun to engage serious scientific efforts aimed at understanding their etiology, individual-level and systems-related maintaining factors, and empirically supported prevention and intervention efforts. After millennia of professional and scientific neglect of childhood psychopathology, we have now entered a time of rapid progress. The study of child and adolescent disorders is a major endeavor, and increasingly sophisticated efforts have begun to bear fruit in terms of scientific advances.

Conceptual bases for integrating developmental processes into the study of child and adolescent psychopathology have been present for several centuries, spanning fields such as embryology, systems theory, philosophy, and genetics (Cicchetti, 2006; Gottlieb & Willoughby, 2006). Yet it is only in the past several decades that developmental psychopathology (DP) has taken formal shape as a perspective on behavioral and emotional disturbance throughout the lifespan, and as a major conceptual guidepost for the study of both normal and atypical development (for initial efforts, see Achenbach, 1974; Sroufe & Rutter, 1984). During this period, DP has exerted a major force on clinical child psychology, child psychiatry, developmental psychology, mental health services research, and a number of other disciplines in the behavioral and neurological sciences. New courses have been formed at major universities, journals have been created, and governmental agencies have taken on the DP moniker to define their missions. It is remarkable how pervasive the DP perspective has become, galvanizing a host of clinical and scientific efforts.

In the book that follows, a key objective is to bring to life the core tenets and principles of DP into a guide for students, clinicians, and scholars that can facilitate deepened understanding of the major forms of child and adolescent behavioral and emotional disturbance. To meet this aim, we have asked leaders in the field to present up-to-date material that is at once developmentally based, clinically relevant, and directly inclusive of the types of psychobiological formulations that are gaining ascendancy in the entire mental health enterprise. Thus, our intention is to supplement the kinds of developmental, process-oriented constructs typically linked to DP with appreciation of core findings in behavioral and molecular genetics, neural pathways, and brain plasticity that have risen to prominence in recent years.

In our instructions to the volume's contributors, we asked explicitly for coverage of historical context, epidemiologic factors, diagnostic issues, sex differences, cultural variables, developmental processes, and important psychobiological mechanisms that could illuminate the pathology under discussion. In providing these guidelines, we were clear that emphasis on neural and neurophysiological processes must not be reductionistic. Indeed, psychosocial and family factors—which served as the predominant modality throughout much of the last century—interact and transact with biological risk variables to produce both maladaptation and healthy adaptation throughout development (for a compendium of integrative work focusing on adolescents, see Romer & Walker, 2007). Thus, we asked contributors to consider multilevel models, emphasizing transaction across a range of individual and contextual factors in the formation of psychopathology. Indeed, it is important to note that modern views of behavioral and molecular genetics have placed into sharp relief the unique and interactive roles that environmental and cultural forces exert on development (e.g., Cicchetti & Curtis, 2006; Rutter, Pickles, Murray, & Eaves, 2001).

Given page limitations and the desire for focused rather than exhaustive coverage, each chapter is relatively brief, with the goal of providing cogent, recent, and incisive commentary on conceptual issues, clinically relevant material, neuroscientific advances, and interactive models. It is our sincere hope that readers will use these contributions as a springboard for further exploration of conceptual frameworks, empirical research on etiology and mechanisms, and implications for prevention and treatment. Above all, we hope to provide a window into the integration of genetic, biological, psychological, and contextual forces that conspire to create costly and impairing patterns of maladaptive development. The utter complexity of the enterprise is daunting and challenging; despite the considerable advances that have been made, the road ahead is long.

KEY DP CONCEPTS AND PRINCIPLES

What characterizes a truly developmental view of psychopathology, as opposed to the kinds of descriptive, symptom-focused presentations that still dominate most classification systems and that still permeate all too many texts and articles? As discussed in key treatises (e.g., Cicchetti & Cohen, 2006; Mash & Dozois, 2003; Rutter & Sroufe, 2000; Sameroff, Lewis, & Miller, 2000), several core points are commonly viewed as central to the DP perspective. These include the necessity of (a) interweaving studies of normal development and pathological functioning into a true synthesis; (b) examining the developmental continuities and discontinuities of traits, behavior patterns, emotional responses, and disorders; (c) evaluating evidence across multiple levels of analysis (from genes to cultures, including the intermediate levels of individuals, families, schools, and neighborhoods); (d) incorporating distinct perspectives, including clinical and developmental psychology, child and adolescent psychiatry, genetics, neurology, public health, philosophy of science, and many others, into a truly multidisciplinary effort; (e) exploring both risk and protective factors and their interplay, so that competence, strength, and resilience as well as pathology and impairment can be understood; (f) involving reciprocal, transactional models of influence in the field's causal models, through which linear patterns of association and causation are replaced by probabilistic, dynamic, nonlinear, and complex conceptual models; and (g) capturing the importance of social and cultural context in understanding the function and meaning of behavioral and emotional patterns.

Three related principles bear emphasis. The first is that multiple pathways to pathology exist. Indeed, disparate routes may lead to a common condition or outcome, exemplifying the construct of *equifinality*. For example, aggressive behavior could result from physical abuse, from a heritable tendency toward disinhibition, from injury to the frontal lobes, from coercive parenting interchanges with the developing child, from prenatal and perinatal risk factors acting in concert with early experiences of insecure attachment or parental rejection, or from different combinations of these vulnerabilities and risk factors (e.g., Raine, Brennan, & Mednick, 1997). In other words, separate causal influences may well yield similar clinical endstates. In addition, the concept of *multifinality* pertains when a given risk factor or initial state leads to disparate outcomes during the course of development across different individuals. For instance, abuse

[handwritten margin note: DP perspective core principles]

*[handwritten note: *Equifinality — different routes lead to the same disorder]*

*[handwritten note: *Multifinality — The same routes may lead to a different disorder]*

may or may not lead to severe maladaptation, depending on a host of intervening factors; extremes of inhibited temperament may produce shyness and social withdrawal, but other, healthier outcomes are also possible, depending on the presence or absence of additional risk or protective factors (for discussion, see Cicchetti & Rogosch, 1996).

Second, DP models place strong emphasis on person-centered research designs, in which the typical practice of examining global effects of one or more risk/protective variables across an entire sample or population is supplemented by consideration of unique subgroups—whether defined by genotypes, personality variables, socialization practices, neighborhoods, or other key factors—and their unique developmental journeys across the lifespan (see Bergman, von Eye, & Magnusson, 2006). Another way of putting this is that developmental continuities and discontinuities may well differ across homogeneous subgroups of participants. Even in variable-centered research, key moderator variables and mediator processes must always be considered (e.g., Hinshaw, 2002; Howe, Reiss, & Yuh, 2002; Kraemer et al., 2001), to ensure that (a) results are applicable to subsets of participants grouped on the basis of the moderator variable of interest (male versus female participants, those from different ethnic groups, or those with different patterns of comorbidity) and (b) underlying mechanisms of change, gleaned from mediator variables, are considered explicitly.

Third, given the rapid growth in recent years of genetic and genomic models as well as brain imaging methods, DP researchers in the twenty-first century must pay increasing attention to the role of the brain, and to neuroscientific principles in general, in order to account for the wide range of extant pathologies and their devastating impacts (see Cicchetti & Curtis, 2006). Clearly, we have come a long way from the mid-twentieth century, when biological and temperamental factors were virtually ignored in accounts of child development and psychopathology. To put into perspective just what a brain-based view entails, consider the following mathematical calculation: Adults have a "best estimate" of approximately 100 billion neurons in their brains; children are probably born with even higher numbers. Indeed a major developmental "task" over the earliest years of postnatal development is the pruning and migration of such neurons and their synaptic connections into a working, functional, and efficient brain.

As to the rate of neural development during the 40 weeks of human gestation, one can calculate the following quotient: Divide 200 billion (a fair estimate of the number of neurons with which an infant is born) by the number of seconds in 40 weeks. The result—of dividing 2 times 10 to the 11th power by this denominator, which is 2.4192 times 10 to the 7th power (i.e., the number of seconds)—is the astonishing figure that, on average, the embryo and fetus are producing around 8,000 new neurons *every sec-*

ond throughout the entire course of prenatal development. This average is not constant, of course, given that the neural tube and brain do not even form for some weeks; thus, in some crucial periods, this figure is far higher (see Giedd et al., 2006, for additional information on the precise timing of neural development across pregnancy and childhood).

Given such a staggering rate of development, a key question involves the joint influence of genes, hormones, nutrition, life experiences, and contextual influences on the plasticity of the brain's development—that is, the ultimate fate of this vast number of neurons—across childhood and adolescence. The number of potential synapses associated with any given neuron is large, making for an incalculably vast number of possible interconnections. Without transactional processes, multilevel models, computational frameworks, and a host of new information and technology related to developmental neuroscience, we will not be able to solve the problem of gaining deep understanding of relevant mechanisms (see also Romer & Walker, 2007).

All of the issues, terms, concepts, and principles described in the previous paragraphs have been stated and restated across a large number of articles, chapters, and books that promote and explicate DP models. Indeed, detailed discussion of any one of them could easily fill a volume unto itself. The challenge for the current chapter is to encapsulate these tenets, in order to foreshadow and illuminate the content of the remaining chapters on specific risk factors and specific disorders. In addition, explanations of these concepts too often remain at a rather global and abstract level, leaving unresolved precisely what they suggest for the investigation and treatment of behavioral and emotional disorders. In the following section, I therefore try to bring a number of these precepts to life. Note that in Chapter 2 Dante Cicchetti provides a treatise on the importance of investigating multiple levels of analysis in the DP enterprise. Because of this full coverage immediately following the current chapter, this topic is not emphasized herein, although integrating across multiple levels of analysis is essential to all work in DP (for a series of papers on this topic, see Cicchetti & Dawson, 2002).

NORMAL AND ATYPICAL DEVELOPMENT ARE MUTUALLY INFORMATIVE

As opposed to the study of discrete, mutually exclusive categories of *disorder*, DP models emphasize that phenomena defined as abnormal represent aberrations in normal developmental pathways and processes—and, accordingly, that without understanding typical development, the study of pathology will remain incomplete and decontextualized. For example, illuminating the nature of Attention-Deficit/Hyperactivity Disorder (ADHD)

DP model - emphasize the adnormal aberations in normal develpment requires thorough understanding of the normative development of attention, impulse control, and self-regulation (Nigg, 2006; Nigg, Hinshaw, & Huang-Pollack, 2006). Similarly, investigations of Autism must take into account the development of interpersonal awareness and empathy, which typically takes place over the first several years of life, to gain understanding of the devastating consequences of failure to attain such development (Dawson & Toth, 2006). Additional examples exist across all forms of disordered emotion and behavior. Although considered set-breaking at the outset of modern DP conceptions, this point is now taken for granted: Few would doubt the wisdom of understanding developmental sequences and processes associated with healthy outcomes as extremely relevant to the elucidation of pathology.

Intriguingly, however, the process is conceptualized as a two-way street, with the view that investigations of pathological conditions—sometimes referred to as *adaptational failures* in DP conceptualizations (e.g., Sroufe, 1997)—can and should provide a unique perspective on normal developmental mechanisms. In other words, it is posited explicitly that the study of disrupted developmental progressions can facilitate our understanding of what is normative.

This core tenet of DP—that mutual interplay between the study of normality and pathology, along with the perspective that progress in each domain depends on progress in the other—is now widespread. One of the best examples comes from neurology, which has a long tradition of utilizing the study of disrupted neural systems for enhancing understanding of healthy brain functioning and vice versa. For instance, "split-brain" patients (those who have had their cerebral hemispheres separated to provide relief from intractable seizures) provide unprecedented insights into normative brain processes and into the separable functions subserved by the right versus left hemispheres. This separation of functions becomes particularly evident with the severing of the large, interconnective structure known as the *corpus callosum* (see discussion in Gazzaniga, Ivry, & Mangun, 1998). Such induced hemispheric separation throws into sharp relief the typical interhemispheric communication and collaboration that takes place. Other neuroscience examples abound (see Cicchetti & Curtis, 2006; for a specific example, the study of phenylketonuria, or PKU, has implications for elaborating the normative development of executive functions; Diamond, Prevor, Callender, & Druin, 1997).

But how accurate is this perspective for DP? In other words, outside of neurological formulations, can investigations of pathology inform normal development? To reiterate, it is now commonly accepted that the more we know about basic emotion, cognition, attention, memory, social awareness, self-regulation, and the like, the greater the benefit for investigations

→ understanding abnormal helps us understand normal

→ understanding normal helps us understand abnormal

of psychopathology. Almost no forms of mental disorder constitute clearly demarcated, qualitatively distinct categories or taxa, so processes applying to individuals near the peak of the bell curve are likely to apply to those further out on the continuum as well. Indeed, nearly all forms of mental pathology appear consistent with a quantitative, dimensional perspective (Beauchaine, 2003), emphasizing the need for flow of information from normal developmental pathways to pathological functioning.

Yet regarding the other direction, what has been learned about normal developmental processes from studies of child and adolescent psychopathology? I have pondered this question for some time, prompted by a probing inquiry during a colloquium discussion from my eminent Berkeley colleague Alison Gopnik. My initial take was that we have *not* gained the kinds of dramatic insights about typical psychological development from studies of child and adolescent psychopathology that have been realized in neurology. Part of the reason is that pathological functioning is almost always multifaceted and complex, which makes it quite difficult to pinpoint areas of specific dysfunction that could inform how normal development occurs in their absence. In other words, there are few equivalents to the surgical procedures of creating lesions in certain brain tracts or to single-gene forms of pathology such as PKU.

Yet consider the work on Autism by Baron-Cohen (2000; see also Baron-Cohen, Leslie, & Frith, 1985, and the review in Dawson & Toth, 2006). Relevant findings suggest that the lack of social connectedness experienced by individuals with Autism may relate to a failure in attainment of a basic *theory of mind*, which deals with the developing realization that other humans have mental states that differ from one's own. Most normal 4- and 5-year-olds can master theory-of-mind tests, suggesting that basic social understanding is predicated on a domain-specific cognitive module that, once operative, occurs almost automatically. On the other hand, a high percentage of youth with Autistic Disorder, even those with high levels of intellectual functioning, do not "pass" such psychological tests, revealing that they have not come to the normally automatic realization that fellow humans have different minds and different psychological perspectives from their own.

Intriguingly, however, a number of individuals with high-functioning Autism can eventually learn to pass the kinds of experimental tests used to test for theory of mind. Through effortful processing, they can and do deduce that other children and adults have a different understanding than they do. Yet this theory-of-mind ability does not mean that their social interactions automatically become smooth and effortless. Indeed, the laborious kinds of calculations and inferences made by people with high-functioning Autism to understand interpersonal dynamics are not usually accompanied by smooth, effortless social interactions (e.g., Grandin, 2006). A key implication is that "normal" social-cognitive and social functioning is highly automatic and intuitive, qualitatively distinct from the ability to deduce social situations analytically in Autism—which is time consuming, not perceived as very skillful by peers, and probably quite different from the way the process works in typically developing individuals. Thus, disruptions in social cognition and social performance by persons with Autism may help to clarify the automatic and highly developed nature of the social cognitions and processes that underlie skilled interpersonal performance in normal development.

Another example pertains to work on the reward sensitivity of individuals with ADHD (e.g., Sagvolden, Johansen, Aase, & Russell, 2005). Here, considerable evidence reveals that, in people with this condition, withholding of rewards leads to rather sudden decrements in task performance, presumably related to a dopaminergically mediated problem with responding during extinction. In other words, ADHD is associated with large performance decrements when rewards are suddenly stopped. This insight may help to understand the mechanisms—largely mediated by subcortical, dopaminergic brain structures—by which typically developing individuals can maintain behavior during extinction, with mutual enhancement of the understanding of basic developmental processes and mechanisms underlying dysregulated attention and impulse control.

A third instance, noted extremely briefly, pertains to the horrific "experiments of nature" that occur when infants and toddlers are subjected to brutal institutionalization and lack of human contact during the earliest years of development (for review, see O'Connor, 2006). Intensive study of this topic has revealed essential information about rates of recovery during placement into stable homes, implications for attachment theory, the development of specific symptom patterns (e.g., inattention and over-activity as opposed to aggression; see Kreppner, O'Connor, Rutter, & the English and Romanian Adoptees Study Team, 2001), and the presence of social and cognitive "catch-up"—all of which are extremely informative about the normal-range development of secure relationships, emotional and behavioral functioning, and cognitive performance. I urge readers to seek other parallels regarding the ways in which knowledge about pathological functioning might elucidate normative processes.

DEVELOPMENTAL CONTINUITIES AND DISCONTINUITIES

With this principle, it is commonly asserted that DP models must emphasize both continuous and discontinuous processes at work in the development of pathology. What precisely does this mean? Taking the specific example of externalizing and antisocial behavior, it is well known from a number of longitudinal investigations that antisocial behaviors show strong stability across time—meaning that correlations are substantial between early measures of aggressive and antisocial tendencies and those made at later times. In other words, the rank order remains relatively preserved, such that the most aggressive individuals at early points in development remain highly aggressive, compared to others, across development. But does this mean that the precise forms of externalizing, antisocial behavior remain constant? Clearly not, given that those children with extremes of temper tantrums and defiance during the toddler and preschool years are not especially likely to exhibit high rates of tantrums during adolescence. Rather, they have a high likelihood of displaying physical aggression in grade school, covert antisocial behaviors in preadolescence, and various forms of delinquency by their teen years, followed by adult manifestations of antisocial behavior after adolescence (e.g., Moffitt, 1993). In short, continuities exist, but these are *heterotypic* in nature, as the actual form of the underlying antisocial trait changes form with development.

Another important consideration is that patterns of continuity may differ considerably across separable subgroups with different developmental patterns or trajectories. Not all highly aggressive or antisocial children remain so, as some are prone to desist with the transition to adolescence. Others, however—the so-called "early starter" or "life-course-persistent" subgroup—maintain high rates through at least early adulthood, although, as noted in the paragraph above, the specific forms of the antisocial actions may well change with development. In addition, a large subset does not display major externalizing problems in childhood but instead shows a sharp increase with adolescence (for a review, see Moffitt, 2006). Understanding such continuities and discontinuities in the form of homogeneous subgroups is likely to yield greater understanding than mere plots of overall curves or "growth." Sophisticated statistical strategies (for example, growth mixture modeling) are increasingly used to aid and abet this search for separable trajectories or classes defined on patterns of change of the relevant dependent variable (Muthén et al., 2002).

Multiple Levels of Analysis

As noted previously, extensive coverage of this topic is found in Chapter 2. In short, the greatest potential for progress in the DP field is made when investigators travel back and forth between "micro" and "macro" levels—including intermediate steps or pathways—to understand the mechanisms that underlie the development of adjustment and maladjustment. The essential task for the next generations of DP investigators is to link events at the level of the gene (e.g., genetic polymorphisms; transcription and translation) to neurotransmission and neuroanatomical development, and subsequently into individual differences in temperament, social cognition, and emotional response patterns. At the same time, such bottom-up conceptions must be supplemented by top-down understanding of the ways in which family interaction patterns, peer relations, school factors, and neighborhood/community variables influence the developing, plastic brain, even at the level of gene expression. Overall, progress in understanding pathological behavior will require multidisciplinary efforts in which investigators ranging from geneticists and biochemists, scientists focusing on individual pathology, experts on family and neighborhood processes, examiners of clinical service systems, and public health officials must work collaboratively and in increasingly diversified ways. The phenomena under consideration are too complex, too dynamic, and too multifaceted to be understood by an exclusive focus on psychobiological processes, family factors, peer processes, or cultural factors in isolation. Performing the necessary kinds of investigations often mandates large-scale, complex, and interdisciplinary work, necessitating collaborations across traditional disciplinary boundaries.

RISK AND PROTECTIVE FACTORS

The key focus of a discipline such as DP—with the term *psychopathology* embedded in its title—is to discover the nature of behavioral and emotional problems, syndromes, and disorders. Many different definitional schemes have been invoked to define and explain psychopathological functioning, with none able to provide a complete picture (see Hinshaw, 2007, Chapter 1). Indeed, it is clear that biological vulnerabilities, psychological handicaps, environmental potentiators, and cultural-level norms all play a major role in defining and understanding behavioral manifestations that are considered abnormal and/or pathological in a particular social context. Risk factors (and constitutional vulnerabilities) are those antecedent variables that predict such dysfunction, and the ultimate goal is to discover those risk variables that are both malleable and potentially causal of the disorder in question (Kraemer et al., 1997; see also Kraemer et al., 2001).

Yet disordered behavior is not uniform, and risk factors are not inevitable predictors. For most individuals with diagnosable forms of psychopathology, symptoms and impairments tend to wax and wane over time. It is often difficult to know when dysfunction precisely begins; it is also quite

Risk Factors – antecedent variables which predict dysfunction
↳ not inevitable

normative for periods of serious problems to be followed by healthier adjustment. In fact, the myth that mental disturbance is uniformly debilitating, handicapping, and permanent is a key reason for the continuing stigmatization of mental illness (Hinshaw, 2006, 2007).

Furthermore, and crucially, not all individuals who experience risk factors for disorder develop subsequent pathology. *Resilience* is the term often used to define unexpectedly good outcomes, or competence, despite the presence of adversity or risk (Luthar, 2006; Luthar, Cicchetti, & Becker, 2000; for a major research example, see Werner & Smith, 1982). Indeed, the concept of *multifinality*, noted previously, directly implies that, depending on a host of biological, environmental, and contextual factors, variegated outcomes may well emanate from common risk factors, with the distinct possibility of resilience and positive adaptation in some cases.

DP is therefore centrally involved in the search for what have been called *protective factors*—those variables and processes that mitigate risk and promote more successful outcomes than would be expected in the presence of risk factors. Controversy surrounds the construct of resilience, the nature of protective factors, and the definitions of competent functioning (see Masten, Burt, & Coatsworth, 2006). In fact, some have claimed that there is no need to invoke a set of special, mysterious processes that are involved in resilience, given that a certain percentage of any sample exposed to a risk factor will show better-than-expected outcomes and that protective factors are all too often simply the opposite poles of what we typically think of as risk variables or vulnerabilities (e.g., higher rather than lower IQ; easier rather than more difficult temperament; warm and structured rather than cold and lax parenting). Still, it is crucial to examine processes that may be involved in promoting competence and strength rather than disability and despair, given that such processes may be harnessed for prevention efforts and may provide key conceptual leads toward the understanding of both pathology and competence.

In short, gaining understanding of why some children born into poverty fare well in adolescence and adulthood, why some individuals with genetic alleles that tend to confer risk for pathological outcomes do not evidence psychopathology, why some youth with difficult temperamental features develop into highly competent adults, and why some people who lack secure attachments or enriching environments during their early years nonetheless show academic and social competence is essential for knowledge of both health and maladjustment. It is not just a luxury but a necessity to investigate positive developmental outcomes, given the general inseparability of health and pathology. Competence can shed light on the pathways that deflect away from pathology and, in so doing, may pro-

Protective Factors - variables that mitigate risk : promote successful outcomes

↳ build resilience

vide otherwise hidden insights into necessary developmental components of adjustment versus maladjustment (Luthar, 2006; Masten et al., 2006).

RECIPROCAL, TRANSACTIONAL MODELS

Linear models of causation, in which static psychological variables are assumed to respond in invariant ways to the influence of risk or protective factors, are not adequate to the task of explaining psychopathology and its development (see detailed explication in Richters, 1997, who highlights that very different explanatory systems are needed to deal with "open systems," such as human beings). Pathways to adolescent and adult functioning are marked by reciprocal patterns or chains, in which children influence parents, teachers, and peers, who in turn shape the further individual development of the child. Such mutually interactive processes themselves propel themselves over time, leading to what are termed *transactional models*. Furthermore, some developmental processes appear to operate via cascading, escalating chains (Masten et al., 2006), whereas others may, as just noted, be dampened or altered by mediating, protective factors. Dynamic systems models are clearly needed to help explicate core developmental phenomena (see Granic & Hollenstein, 2006).

To be specific: It is now well known that a great many cognitive and personality outcomes are at least moderately heritable, meaning that genetic factors explain a sizable proportion of individual differences in the trait, attribute, or disorder in question. But via gene–environment correlations, environments (genetically associated with the trait in question) may amplify the expression of the trait, and individuals may seek or evoke environmental responses that further promote the trait's unfolding. Furthermore, as noted explicitly in the chapter of Beauchaine and Neuhaus (this volume, Chapter 5), early maturing brain regions that give rise to expression of key emotional and behavioral characteristics may influence the developmental maturation of other, later-maturing regions; environmental events and factors may actually aid in the "turning on" of genes that further reinforce similar neural and behavioral actions. In addition, certain genotypes may become expressed only in the context of certain environmental factors, signifying the operation of gene–environment interactions (Rutter, Moffitt, & Caspi, 2006; see also Chapter 2 for further elucidation). Finally, processes of development may operate in highly nonlinear ways, requiring a new set of tools and conceptual models for understanding change processes (Granic & Hollenstein, 2006). Sensitive data-analytic strategies and innovative research designs are crucial tools for fostering greater understanding of such nonlinear phenomena.

Transactional Models = biofeedback / Brofenbrenner

CONTEXT MATTERS

A key tenet of DP is that family, school-related, neighborhood, and wider cultural contexts are central for the unfolding of aberrant as well as adaptive behavior. This point cannot be overemphasized: What may have been adaptive genetic effects at one point in human evolutionary history may be maladaptive in current times, given major environmental and cultural changes that render certain genetically mediated traits far less advantageous than previously (e.g., the storage of fat in times of uncertain meals and sudden need for survival-related activity; the presence of undue anxiety in relation to certain feared stimuli when conditions have markedly changed with respect to indoor, sedentary lifestyles). There are few absolutes in terms of behavior patterns that are inherently maladaptive or risk factors that inevitably yield dysfunction; the cultural setting and context are all-important for defining and creating healthy versus unhealthy adaptation.

Similarly, key environmental factors (such as parenting styles) are not always uniformly positive or uniformly negative in terms of their developmental effects. Deater-Deckard and Dodge (1997) have shown, for example, that harsh, authoritarian parenting predicts antisocial behavior in white, middle-class children but not necessarily in African-American families. Many forms of mental disorder are present at roughly equivalent rates across multiple cultures, revealing key evidence for universality; but the effects of risk or protective factors often differ markedly depending on their developmental timing, the family and social contexts in which they are experienced by the developing child, and the niche or *space* that exists in a given culture for their expression and resolution (see, for example, Serafica & Vargas, 2006). In short, the DP perspective tells us clearly that setting and context are all-important (Cicchetti, 2006).

Environmental factors not always uniform in terms of developmental effects

EQUIFINALITY AND MULTIFINALITY

As suggested earlier, there is overwhelming evidence that multiple pathways exist to both health and illness. It is a myth to think that all individuals displaying symptoms of a given mental disorder "got there" through similar mechanisms and processes. We know, for instance, that the broad syndrome of depression may emanate from heritable risks in some cases, from severe life losses and stressors in others, from the interaction of the two in a great many more, and from other early or contemporaneous risk factors in still others. ADHD is substantially heritable, but the constituent symptomatology may also emerge from low birthweight, severe early deprivation, or effects of teratogens like nicotine or tobacco in utero (Barkley, 2006; Gatzke-Kopp & Shannon, this volume). In short, *equifinality*—

the presence of multiple pathways leading to apparently similar outcome states—clearly operates with regard to the major entitites of mental disturbance that we now recognize (see Cicchetti & Rogosch, 1996).

In parallel, although inhibited temperament in infancy and toddlerhood is clearly predictive of risk for subsequent social anxiety, there is far from a 1:1 correspondence. Other risk and protective factors, including the presence of childrearing environments that gently but firmly "push" the child out of inhibited, withdrawn behavior patterns, may deflect any inevitable association between early inhibition and later internalizing conditions (see Kagan, 1997; Kagan, this volume, Chapter 6). Similarly, child maltreatment does not lead to a uniform set of outcomes but may instead yield a range of subsequent behavioral and emotional patterns even when the type or severity of abuse is held constant (Cicchetti & Valentino, 2006). Hence, through processes of *multifinality*, complex causal chains of influence render the operation of early risk factors as probabilistic rather than deterministic.

Thus, although the presence of multiple risk factors is clearly linked to lowered chances of recovery, the DP model emphasizes malleability, flexibility, and plasticity in development. The core issues in this regard involve, first, the attempt to disentangle the many potential developmental influences that may tip the individual toward health and competence versus disorder and failure; and second, the necessity of incorporating what is termed *probabilistic epigenesis* (Gottlieb & Willoughby, 2006) into causal models. This term means that genes do not provide a one-way causal influence on neural structures and behavior, largely because of highly interactive, reciprocal, and bidirectional influences with epigenetic factors (e.g., other brain structures and products, behavioral patterns, environmental influences). Here we see that several DP principles—for example, nonlinear causal patterns, reciprocal/transactional models, and the importance of context—are closely linked together. In an elegant musical metaphor, Boyce (2006) presents the notion of *symphonic causation* to illustrate the confluence of biological and contextual influences on development.

Symphonic Causation = nature And Nurture

Psychobiological Principles and Discoveries

The genomic era is upon us, and advances in brain imaging research have made the developing brain far more accessible to scientific view than ever before (see Giedd et al., 2006; Rende & Waldman, 2006). Although it is mistaken, as noted previously, to give primacy to any given level of analysis in a DP perspective—brain, contextual, or other—we have asked contributors to pay particular attention to psychobiological factors and processes in their coverage.

Part of the reason is historical: Family systemic and environmental views dominated the field for much of the twentieth century, and recent work on a range of psychobiological processes is not always featured in reviews and texts (see Boyce, 2006). Another issue has to do with explanatory power, as we now know that without understanding the potential effects of genes, physiological processes, and biological risk factors on psychopathology we have little hope of understanding the most severe forms of disorder. Because the brain is remarkably plastic and because context influences biological unfolding, we have—as noted throughout this chapter—asked authors to emphasize contextualization of the psychobiological perspectives they present. In fact, reductionistic accounts of (a) the primacy of single genes, (b) the inevitable predictability of later functioning from early temperament, or (c) the placement of psychopathology completely inside brightly colored brain images are as short-sighted as the exclusively environmental accounts of psychopathology that dominated a half-century ago—e.g., the blaming of Autism on emotional refrigeration by parents or Schizophrenia by schizophregenic mothers.

SUMMARY

All of the previous points converge on the core theme that the development of psychopathological functioning is multidetermined, complex, interactive, transactional, and in most instances nonlinear. It would be hard to imagine otherwise, given the staggering complexity of the brain and the myriad influences, ranging from the microsocial to the macrosocial, that impinge on the developing infant, toddler, and child. For those who like problems and solutions wrapped in neat packages, the study of DP will undoubtedly be a frustrating, if not unfathomable, endeavor. On the other hand, for those who are intrigued by the diverse clinical presentations of various pathological conditions in childhood and adolescence; those who are fascinated with how much remains to be learned about antecedent conditions and maintaining factors; those who are possessed by an intense "need to know" about the underlying mechanisms of eating disorders, conduct disturbance, substance abuse, anxiety and depression, Bipolar Disorder, Pervasive Developmental Disorders, ADHD, and other child and adolescent conditions; and those who realize the need to consider healthy outcomes and competence as well as maladaptation, the DP perspective is a necessary guide to and framework for the rapidly growing scientific enterprise linking normal and atypical development. Longitudinal, multilevel investigations are often required to gain the types of knowledge needed to understand psychopathology (and competence) from a developmental perspective, with potentially high yield for basic developmental science; for elucidation of highly impairing behavioral, emotional, and developmental conditions; and for informing prevention and intervention efforts. The study of DP is ever expanding, engaging scientists from multiple disciplines and perspectives. Progress is emerging quickly, but the territory to explore is vast.

A GUIDE TO THE BOOK'S CONTENTS

Immediately following this introduction, Dante Cicchetti (Chapter 2) provides a multiple-levels-of-analysis framework for DP. This chapter is a true companion to the present one, as the multilevel framework is one of the central tenets in the field of developmental psychopathology. Linking genes to phenotypes—and understanding the key mediating steps of the process, which include the role of context and environment in shaping such linkages—is essential to gain understanding of both disordered functioning and strength, competency, and resilience. And in Chapter 3, Ted Beauchaine, Stephen Hinshaw, and Lisa Gatzke-Kopp discuss a number of core themes related to genetic factors and mechanisms underlying psychopathology, with a key focus on how these genetic factors interact with environments to increase risk for psychopathology. This chapter is explicit that it is no longer sensible to speak of nature versus nurture but rather that an integrated, dynamic conception of biology-environment interplay is the current paradigm of interest.

Part I of the book features research on risk factors, those antecedent variables that help to set in motion the chains, pathways, or cascades of processes that emanate in psychopathological functioning. Bruce Perry (Chapter 4) elucidates the multiple ways that child abusive experiences set the stage for later maladaptation—although as emphasized, the risk is not absolute. Indeed, the concept of multifinality emphasizes that some children with high levels of maltreatment may nonetheless show resilient behavior. Next, Ted Beauchaine and Emily Neuhaus (Chapter 5) provide a richly contextualized perspective on the construct of impulsivity, alternately termed *disinhibition*. They highlight psychobiological, environmental, and interactive mechanisms that yield impulsive behavioral styles, which incur great risk for escalating impairments. Chapter 6 (Jerome Kagan) is a witty and engaging account of behavioral inhibition and its consequences for a range of internalizing behavior patterns. Emphasizing genetic risk factors, environmental potentiation of such risk, and the fascinating picture of heterotypic continuity across development in the face of inhibited temperament, Kagan's work strongly accentuates core DP principles and criticizes biological/genetic reductionism in accounting for all outcomes related to inhibited temperament. In Chapter 7, Susanna Fryer, Nicole

Crocker, and Sarah Mattson provide up-to-date information on teratogens—substances transmitted from a pregnant mother to her embryo or fetus—and their potential to promote dysfunction in the developing organism. This work emphasizes, once again, the probabilistic rather than the deterministic nature of this risk factor: maladaptive outcomes are not all or none in the face of this set of risk factors. Lisa Gatzke-Kopp and Kate Shannon write about various forms of brain injury (Chapter 8), with emphasis on risk for dysfunction and potential recovery. Of necessity, this chapter covers the specific "pathogens" of physical trauma and hypoxia, the construct of neural plasticity, and the potential for genetic factors to interact with trauma in the development of maladaptation. Chapter 9, written by Jim Coan and John Allen, features affective style, the patterns of emotion-related responding that may set the stage for maladaptive development. This dense, rich chapter challenges readers to consider levels of analysis not often dealt with in accounts of psychopathology. In Chapter 10, Pamela Cole and Sarah Hall discuss the "hot" topic of emotion regulation and, particularly, dysregulation, with its implications for disordered outcomes. In their view, emotions are inherently activating and organizing, but if attempts at their regulation are insufficient, if emotions are displayed in context-inappropriate fashion, or if emotions change either too quickly or too slowly, implications for dysfunction become apparent.

In Part II, the emphasis is on the externalizing (or disruptive) behavior disorders, those in which the salient symptomatology impinges on the personal space, rights, and integrity of others. Chapter 11, written by Joel Nigg and Molly Nikolas, features coverage of the core processes of inattention, impulsivity, and hyperactivity that characterize ADHD, and provides an intellectually rich account of key psychological and psychobiological processes and of both genetic and often-neglected environmental risk factors for this condition. Explicitly embracing the core tenets of DP, they emphasize the great need for integrated theoretical models in future work on this prevalent and distressing disorder. Chapter 12, by Benjamin Lahey, presents a comprehensive, multilevel, integrative view of the development of aggressive and antisocial behavior, with specific reference to the diagnostic categories of Oppositional Defiant Disorder and Conduct Disorder. A key issue for this domain of inquiry is the sheer number of pertinent risk factors, spanning intraindividual, familial, and wider contextual variables; Lahey's integrative account is a welcome antidote to the often-overwhelming feel of literature in this area. Kristi Hiatt and Tom Dishion, in Chapter 13, discuss principles and concepts underlying the development of antisocial personality, taking a lifespan perspective featuring interplay among the myriad risk factors (individual, parental, peer-related, neighborhood-level) that together yield adult antisocial behavior and, in some cases, psychopathy. It provides a fine counterpoint and complement to Chapter 13. Chapter 14, by Sandy Brown, discusses developmental trajectories of alcohol and substance problems, emphasizing inherited, cognitive, and social risk and protection, providing an elegantly integrated model of the development of substance use disorders in adolescence.

Next, Part III features internalizing conditions. Chapter 15, by Carl Weems and Wendy Silverman, covers the range of anxiety disorders, providing an integrative perspective on their origins and maintenance. Building from dimensional conceptions of anxiety and fear, they emphasize genetic and psychophysiological factors, social learning and cognitive processes, social and interpersonal variables, and interactions across these levels. Daniel Klein, Dana Torpey, Sara Bufferd, and Margaret Dyson (Chapter 16) review comprehensively known risk factors for and developmental issues related to child and adolescent depression. Covering the wide-ranging precursors to depressive outcomes (e.g., maladaptive cognitive patterns, stress reactivity, genetic vulnerability, disrupted parent-child relationships, to name some of the more salient), they provide an integrative developmental model. In Chapter 17 Sheila Crowell, Ted Beauchaine, and Mark Lenzenweger provide essential commentary on Borderline Personality Disorder, self-injurious behavior, and their developmental antecedents. With the understanding that research in this domain is rather limited, these authors emphasize potential genetic and neural risk factors, the clear role of parenting disruptions, and their interactions, concluding that Borderline Personality Disorder and intentional self-injury constitute extremes of impulse control problems, particularly in relation to severe stressors. Note that the placement of this chapter in Part III is somewhat arbitrary, given the admixture of dysphoric, internalizing features and disinhibited, externalizing symptoms involved in these behavior patterns.

Finally, the coverage in Part IV focuses on several additional, extremely important disorders. Bipolar Disorder—also representing an extreme blend of externalizing and internalizing features—is the topic of Chapter 18, written by Joseph Blader and Gabrielle Carlson. This detailed chapter lays out the complex interactions and transactions (and strong heritability) of Bipolar Disorder, dealing directly with core developmental issues related to assessment, diagnosis, and symptom presentation. Chapter 19 features Autism spectrum conditions; its authors are Geraldine Dawson and Susan Faja. Major psychobiological theorizing is occurring in relation to Autism spectrum disorders; this chapter presents a balanced perspective on the most promising of the latest conceptual models. Schizophrenia can and does exist in children, with major increases in prevalence throughout adolescence. In Chapter 20, Robert Asarnow and Claudia Kernan tackle the important developmental issues related to, and the strong psychobiologic roots of, schizophrenia-spectrum conditions, emphasizing developmental continuities and discontinuities. Finally, Chapter 21, authored by Eric Stice and Cindy Bulik, covers the eating disorders of Anorexia Nervosa, Bulimia Nervosa, and Binge Eating Disorder, once again featuring complex, interactive processes spanning psychobiological and psychosocial factors in such conditions while providing strong emphasis on a developmental neuroscience perspective.

The study of atypical development is fascinating, complex, and clinically relevant, with the potential for elucidating the processes by which normal development occurs. Progress in this field is accumulating rapidly, but there is still a huge distance to travel, given the almost unfathomable complexity of developmental processes and pathways that exist.

Recall the discussion, earlier in this chapter, of the prenatal rate of development of neurons. How does this unfathomable number of neurons, and the incalculable number of synapses that are shaped before and well after birth, produce consciousness, attentional deployment, memory, emotion regulation, and both healthy and atypical developmental patterns? Which models do we still need to construct if we are to begin to answer such questions with accuracy? These are among the most important issues in all of science, and the amount that needs to be learned is staggering. Yet with the tools of DP—and the new techniques and conceptual models that are necessary to develop to keep up the momentum—additional progress is in sight.

We wish you well as you begin your journey into the many aspects of developmental psychopathology and into the key risk factors for and manifestations of child and adolescent mental disorders that are presented in the following chapters. Smooth, packaged, easily digestible accounts are not found within these pages, as the kinds of reciprocal, interactive, cascading, and integrative models needed to facilitate further understanding are far from simple or linear. Yet, for the next generation of investigators, clinicians, and policy-makers—who, we hope, will carry with them an appreciation of the systemic models and transactional processes embedded in DP conceptualizations—there can be no more fascinating venture.

REFERENCES

Achenbach, T. M. (1974). *Developmental psychopathology*. New York: Ronald Press.

Barkley, R. A. (2006). *Attention deficit hyperactivity disorder: A handbook for diagnosis and treatment* (3rd ed.). New York: Guilford.

Baron-Cohen, S. (2000). Theory of mind and autism: A fifteen-year review. In S. Baron-Cohen, H. Tager-Flusberg, & D. J. Cohen (Eds.). *Understanding other minds: Perspectives from developmental cognitive neuroscience* (2nd ed., pp. 3–20). Oxford, UK: Oxford University Press.

Baron-Cohen, S., Leslie, A. M., & Frith, U. (1985). Does the autistic child have a "theory of mind"? *Cognition, 21,* 37–46.

Beauchaine, T. P. (2003). Taxometrics and developmental psychopathology. *Development and Psychopathology, 15,* 501–527.

Bergman, L. R., von Eye, A., & Magnusson, D. (2006). Person-oriented research strategies in developmental psychopathology. In D. Cicchetti & D. J. Cohen (Eds.), *Developmental psychopathology. Vol. 1: Theory and method* (2nd ed., pp. 850–888). New York: Wiley.

Boyce, T. (2006). Symphonic causation and the origins of childhood psychopathology. In D. Cicchetti & D. J. Cohen (Eds.), *Developmental psychopathology. Vol. 2: Developmental neuroscience* (2nd ed., pp. 797–817). New York: Wiley.

Cicchetti, D. (2006). Developmental psychopathology. In D. Cicchetti & D. J. Cohen (Eds.), *Developmental psychopathology. Vol. 1: Theory and method* (2nd ed., pp. 1–23). New York: Wiley.

Cicchetti, D., & Cohen, D. J. (Eds.). (2006). *Developmental psychopathology.* New York: Wiley.

Cicchetti, D., & Curtis, W. J. (2006). The developing brain and neural plasticity: Implications for normality, psychopathology, and resilience. In D. Cicchetti & D. J. Cohen (Eds.), *Developmental psychopathology. Vol. 2: Developmental neuroscience* (2nd ed., pp. 1–64). New York: Wiley.

Cicchetti, D., & Dawson, G. (Eds.). (2002). Multiple levels of analysis. *Development and psychopathology, 14,* Special Issue.

Cicchetti, D., & Rogosch, F. (1996). Equifinality and multifinality in developmental psychopathology. *Development and Psychopathology, 8,* 597–600.

Cicchetti, D., & Valentino, K. (2006). An ecological-transactional perspective on child maltreatment: Failure of the average expectable environment and its influence on child development. In D. Cicchetti & D. J. Cohen (Eds.), *Developmental psychopathology. Vol. 3: Risk, disorder, and adaptation,* (2nd ed., pp. 317–357). New York: Wiley.

Dawson, G., & Toth, K. (2006). Autism spectrum disorders. In D. Cicchetti & D. J. Cohen (Eds.), *Developmental psychopathology. Vol. 3: Risk, disorder, and adaptation* (2nd ed., pp. 317–357). New York: Wiley.

Deater-Deckard, K., & Dodge, K. A. (1997). Externalizing behavior problems and discipline revisited: Nonlinear effects and variation by culture, context, and gender. *Psychological Inquiry, 8,* 161–175.

Diamond, A., Prevor, M. B., Callender, G., & Druin, D. P. (1997). Prefrontal cortex cognitive deficits in children treated early and continuously for PKU. *Monographs of the Society for Research in Child Development, 62* (Serial No. 4).

Gazzaniga, M. S., Ivry, R. B., & Mangun, G. R. (1998). *Cognitive neuroscience: The biology of the mind.* New York: Norton.

Giedd, J. N., Shaw, P., Wallace, G., Gogtay, N., & Lenroot, R. K. (2006). Anatomic brain imaging studies of normal and abnormal brain development in children and adolescents. In D. Cicchetti & D. J. Cohen (Eds.), *Developmental psychopathology. Vol. 2: Developmental neuroscience* (2nd ed., pp. 127–196). New York: Wiley.

Gottlieb, G., & Willoughby, M. T. (2006). Probabilistic epigenesis of psychopathology. In D. Cicchetti & D. J. Cohen (Eds.), *Developmental psychopathology. Vol. 1: Theory and method* (2nd ed., pp. 673–700). New York: Wiley.

Granic, I., & Hollenstein, T. (2006). A survey of dynamics systems methods for developmental psychopathology. In D. Cicchetti & D. J. Cohen (Eds.), *Developmental psychopathology. Vol. 1: Theory and method* (2nd ed., pp. 889–930). New York: Wiley.

Grandin, T. (2006). *Thinking in pictures: And other reports from my life with Autism* (2nd ed.). New York: Vintage.

Hinshaw, S. P. (2002). Intervention research, theoretical mechanisms, and causal processes related to externalizing behavior patterns. *Development and Psychopathology, 14,* 789–818.

Hinshaw, S. P. (2006). Stigma and mental illness: Developmental issues and future prospects. In D. Cicchetti & D. J. Cohen (Eds.), *Developmental psychopathology. Vol. 3: Risk, disorder, and adaptation* (2nd ed., pp. 317–357). New York: Wiley.

Hinshaw, S. P. (2007). *The mark of shame: Stigma of mental illness and an agenda for change.* New York: Oxford University Press.

Howe, G. W., Reiss, D., & Yuh, J. (2002). Can prevention trials test theories of etiology? *Development and Psychopathology, 14,* 673–694.

Kagan, J. (1997). Temperament and the reactions to unfamiliarity. *Child Development, 68,* 139–143.

Kessler, R. C., Berglund, P., Demler, O., Jin, R., & Walters, E. E. (2005). Lifetime prevalence and age-of-onset distributions of DSM-IV disorders in the National Comorbidity Survey replication. *Archives of General Psychiatry, 62,* 593–602.

Kraemer, H. C., Kazdin, A. E., Offord, D. R., Kessler, R. C., Jensen, P. S., & Kupfer, D. J. (1997). Coming to terms with the terms of risk. *Archives of General Psychiatry, 54,* 337–343.

Kraemer, H. C., Stice, E., Kazdin, A., Offord, D., & Kupfer, D. (2001). How do risk factors work together? Mediators, moderators, and independent, overlapping, and proxy risk factors. *American Journal of Psychiatry, 158,* 848–856.

Kreppner, J. M., O'Connor, T. G., Rutter, M., & the English and Romanian Adoptees Study Team. (2001). Can inattention/overactivity be a deprivation disorder? *Journal of Abnormal Child Psychology, 29,* 513–528.

Luthar, S. S. (2006). Resilience in development: A synthesis of research across five decades. In D. Cicchetti & D. J. Cohen (Eds.), *Developmental psychopathology. Vol. 3: Risk, disorder, and adaptation* (2nd ed., pp. 739–795). New York: Wiley.

Luthar, S. S., Cicchetti, D., & Becker, B. (2000). The construct of resilience: A critical evaluation and guidelines for future work. *Child Development, 71,* 543–562.

Mash, E. J., & Barkley, R. A. (Eds.). (2003). *Child psychopathology* (2nd ed.). New York: Guilford.

Mash, E. J., & Dozois, D. J. A. (2003). Child psychopathology: A developmental-systems perspective. In E. J. Mash & R. A. Barkley (Eds.), *Child psychopathology* (2nd ed., pp. 3–71). New York: Guilford.

Masten, A. S., Burt, K. B., & Coatsworth, J. D. (2006). Competence and psychopathology in development. In D. Cicchetti & D. J. Cohen (Eds.), *Developmental psychopathology. Vol. 3: Risk, disorder, and adaptation* (2nd ed., pp. 696–738). New York: Wiley.

Moffitt, T. E. (1993). "Life-course-persistent" and "adolescence-limited" antisocial behavior: A developmental taxonomy. *Psychological Review, 100,* 674–701.

Moffitt, T. E. (2006). Life course persistent versus adolescence limited antisocial behavior. In D. Cicchetti & D. J. Cohen (Eds.), *Developmental psychopathology. Vol. 3: Risk, disorder, and adaptation* (2nd ed., pp. 570–598). New York: Wiley.

Muthén, B. O., Brown, C. H., Masyn, K., Jo, B., Khoo, S. T., Yang, C. C., et al. (2002). General growth mixture modeling for randomized prevention trials. *Biostatistics, 3,* 459–475.

Nigg, J. T. (2006). *What causes ADHD? Understanding what goes wrong and why.* New York: Guilford Press.

Nigg, J. T., Hinshaw, S. P., & Huang-Pollack, C. (2006). Disorders of attention and impulse regulation. In D. Cicchetti & D. J. Cohen (Eds.), *Developmental psychopathology. Vol. 3: Risk, disorder, and adaptation* (2nd ed., pp. 358–403). New York: Wiley.

O'Connor, T. G. (2006). The persisting effects of early experiences on psychological development. In D. Cicchetti & D. J. Cohen (Eds.), *Developmental psychopathology. Vol. 3: Risk, disorder, and adaptation* (2nd ed., pp. 202–234). New York: Wiley.

Raine, A., Brennan, P., & Mednick, S. A. (1997). Interaction between birth complications and early maternal rejection in predisposing individuals to adult violence: Specificity to serious, early-onset violence. *American Journal of Psychiatry, 154,* 1265–1271.

Rende, R., & Waldman, I. (2006). Behavioral and molecular genetics and developmental psychopathology. In D. Cicchetti & D. J. Cohen (Eds.), *Developmental psychopathology. Vol. 2: Developmental neuroscience* (2nd ed., pp. 427–464). New York: Wiley.

Richters, J. E. (1997). The Hubble Hypothesis and the developmentalist's dilemma. *Development and Psychopathology, 9,* 193–229.

Romer, D., & Walker, E. F. (Eds.). (2007). *Adolescent psychopathology and the developing brain.* New York: Oxford University Press.

Rutter, M., Moffitt, T. E., & Caspi, A. (2006). Gene-environment interplay and psychopathology: Multiple varieties but real effects. *Journal of Child Psychology and Psychiatry, 47,* 226–261.

Rutter, M., Pickles, A., Murray, R., & Eaves, L. (2001). Testing hypotheses on specific environmental causal effects on behavior. *Psychological Bulletin, 127,* 291–324.

Rutter, M., & Sroufe, L. A. (2000). Developmental psychopathology: Concepts and challenges. *Development and Psychopathology, 12,* 265–296.

Sagvolden, T., Johansen, E. B., Aase, H., & Russell, V. A. (2005). A dynamic developmental theory of attention-deficit/hyperactivity disorder (ADHD) predominantly hyperactive/impulsive and combined types. *Behavioral and Brain Sciences, 28,* 397–419.

Sameroff, A. J., Lewis, M., & Miller, S. M. (Eds.). (2000). Handbook of developmental psychopathology (2nd ed.). New York: Kluwer Academic/Plenum.

Serafica, F. C., & Vargas, L. A. (2006). Cultural diversity in the development of child psychopathology. In D. Cicchetti & D. J. Cohen (Eds.), *Developmental psychopathology. Vol. 1: Theory and method* (2nd ed., pp. 588–626). New York: Wiley.

Silverman, W., & Hinshaw, S. P. (2008). Evidence-based psychosocial treatments for children and adolescents. The ten year update. *Journal of Clinical Child and Adolescent Psychology, 37(2), Special Issue.*

Sroufe, L. A. (1997). Psychopathology as an outcome of development. *Development and Psychopathology, 9,* 251–268.

Sroufe, L. A., & Rutter, M. (1984). The domain of developmental psychopathology. *Child Development, 55,* 17–29.

Werner, E., & Smith, R. (1982). *Vulnerable but invincible: A study of resilient children.* New York: McGraw-Hill.

Wolfe, D. A., & Mash, E. J. (Eds.) (2006). *Behavioral and emotional disorders in adolescents.* New York: Guilford.

CHAPTER 2

A Multiple-Levels-of-Analysis Perspective on Research in Development and Psychopathology

DANTE CICCHETTI

lthough there exists some definitional divergence about what constitutes a developmental psychopathology perspective to uncovering pathways to adaptive and maladaptive outcomes in high-risk individuals, it is generally agreed that developmental psychopathologists should investigate functioning through the examination of multiple domains and multiple levels of analysis (Cicchetti, 1984, 1990, 1993; Cicchetti & Blender, 2004; Cicchetti & Dawson, 2002; Institute of Medicine,1989; Pennington, 2002; Rutter & Sroufe, 2000; Sroufe & Rutter, 1984). Indeed, since its inception as a scientific discipline over a quarter of a century ago, developmental psychopathology has been conceptualized as an interdisciplinary field (Cicchetti, 1984, 1990). The roots of the discipline can be traced to three theories of development, each of which was influenced by Western philosophy and embryology: Freudian psychoanalytic theory, Wernerian organismic theory, and Piagetian structural theory (Cicchetti, 1990; Kaplan, 1967). In addition, developmental psychopathology can trace its history back to research conducted within diverse disciplines, including genetics; embryology; the neurosciences; clinical, developmental, and experimental psychology; psychiatry; psychoanalysis; and sociology. In an early statement about the science of developmental psychopathology, Cicchetti (1990) asserted that such a perspective "should bridge fields of study . . . contribute greatly to reducing the dualisms that exist between . . . the behavioral and biological sciences, and . . . between basic and applied research" (p. 20). Developmental psychopathology transcends traditional disciplinary boundaries and emphasizes the criticality of moving beyond descriptive facts to a process-level comprehension of normal and abnormal development. The developmental psychopathology perspective provides a broad, integrative framework within which the contributions of separate disciplines can be fully realized in the broader context of understanding individual development and functioning (Cicchetti, 1984).

GOALS OF THE CHAPTER

In this chapter, I provide an overview of progress that has been made in the field of developmental psychopathology during the nearly 3 decades in which it has been an increasingly sophisticated, emergent discipline. Next, I describe how a multiple-levels-of-analysis approach holds great potential for advancing knowledge of development and psychopathology. I then illustrate how a multiple-levels approach to gene–environment interaction can enhance our understanding of developmental pathways to maladaptation and psychopathology. Subsequently, using child maltreatment as an illustrative exemplar, I present evidence demonstrating that early adverse experiences can exert harmful effects on neurobiological structure and functioning. The reciprocal relation between social experiences and neurobiological development provides yet another example of the power of a multiple-levels approach. In the penultimate section, I urge researchers to adopt this multilevel perspective in research on the determinants of resilient functioning. Finally, I call upon researchers to adopt a multiple-levels approach to the design, implementation, and evaluation of preventive interventions.

WHAT WE HAVE LEARNED

In a relatively short period of time, the field has witnessed the occurrence of major advances in understanding the complexity of causality, the interaction of risk and protective factors, the heterogeneity of disorder, and the importance of developmental processes and mechanisms. It is now widely understood that singular, linear cause rarely obtains (Sameroff & Chandler, 1975). Individual risk factors seldom are powerful enough to exert sufficient influence to result in psychopathology, and when they appear to have such effects, it is highly likely that they are surrogates for multiple, unobserved influences. Much more commonly, adequate prediction of either disturbance or resilience necessitates the consideration of multiple risks and protective factors and their interplay. Moreover, the consequences of any risk factor depend on a myriad of other aspects embedded in the developmental context. For example, Lynch and Cicchetti (1998) reported that impoverished children residing in communities high in violence fare far worse than those living in communities that are less violent. Even abused and neglected children, who typically have an array of difficulties in addition to their maltreatment experiences, differed in their functioning depending on the level of community violence present in their lives, with maltreated children who lived in settings high in violence exhibiting the most difficulties.

In addition, a particular vulnerability may not pose risk in the context of a protective condition. For example, Suomi (2000) has discovered that, relative to the long (l) allele, the short (s) allele in the serotonin transporter gene promoter region confers no detectable liability for rhesus monkeys reared by nurturant foster mothers; in fact, such animals become leaders of the group. Yet the same gene polymorphism may confer vulnerability for anxiety and behavioral pathology in monkeys raised without adults. To cite two additional interesting examples, male sex, a risk factor for conduct disorders, is a protective factor for eating disorders (i.e., Anorexia Nervosa, Bulimia Nervosa). In addition, Baldwin, Baldwin, and Cole (1990) found that in high-risk families from low-SES backgrounds levels of restriction and control in parenting (i.e., authoritarian parenting practices) were related to successful child outcomes and that such parenting practices were higher than in low-risk families showing child success. Accordingly, controlling forms of parenting may be a protective factor for one group but not for another.

These examples also illustrate the probabilistic rather than causal status of risk factors. It is now common knowledge that the same risk factors may be associated with different outcomes (multifinality) and that subgroups of individuals manifesting similar problems arrive at them from different beginnings (equifinality). This understanding has proven to be critical because it highlights the need for process-oriented research investigations. This attention to diversity in origins, processes, and outcomes in understanding developmental pathways does not suggest that prediction is futile as a result of the many potential individual patterns of adaptation. There are constraints on how much diversity is possible, and not all outcomes are equally likely (Cicchetti & Rogosch, 1996; Sroufe, Egeland, & Kreutzer, 1990). Furthermore, specificity of prediction can be enhanced with knowledge of differential mechanisms in disparate subgroups.

Finally, there has been an explosion in our knowledge of developmental neurobiology, the area of neuroscience that focuses on factors regulating the development of neurons, neuronal circuitry, and complex neuronal organization systems, including the brain (Cicchetti & Cannon, 1999; Nelson & Jeste, in press). Furthermore, advances in the field of molecular genetics have contributed to the understanding of neurological disease. These accomplishments have helped to engender renewed excitement for the potential contributing role that molecular genetics can make in discovering pathways to the development of psychopathology and resilience (Cicchetti & Blender, 2006; Moffitt, Caspi, & Rutter, 2006; Plomin & Rutter, 1998; Rutter, 2006).

The integrative nature of a developmental approach to psychopathology was articulated by Eisenberg (1977), who stated that development "constitutes the crucial link between genetic determinants and environmental variables and between physiogenic and psychogenic causes" (p. 225). Development thus encompasses "not only the roots of behavior in prior maturation as well as the residual of earlier stimulation, both internal and external, but also the modulations of that behavior by the social fields of the experienced present" (p. 225). Not surprisingly, given the intimate link between the study of normality and psychopathology, similar depictions of normative developmental processes have been espoused in the literature.

For example, Gottlieb (1991) conceived of development as a process "characterized by an increase of complexity of organization . . . at all levels of analysis . . . as a consequence of horizontal and vertical coactions among the organisms' parts, including organism-environment coactions" (p. 7). According to Gottlieb (1991; Gottlieb & Halpern, 2002), outcomes of development, be they organic, neural, or behavioral, occur as a function of at least two specific components of coaction (e.g., person-person, organism-organism, organism-environment, cell-cell, gene-gene, nucleus-cytoplasm). Gottlieb theorizes that the cause of development is the relationship between two or more components, not the components themselves. Accordingly, genes alone do not cause development any more than environmental enrichment by itself can cause development. Indeed, the phenotype *is* the interaction of the genotype with its surrounding environment, both internal and external.

Gottlieb's (1992) conceptualization is one of a fully interrelated coactional system in which the activity of genes themselves can be affected through the cytoplasm of the cell and by events originating at any other level of the system, including the external environment. For example, external environmental factors, such as social interactions, traumatic experiences such as domestic violence and child maltreatment, and the like, can cause hormones to be secreted—which, in turn, can result in the activation of DNA transcription inside the nucleus of the cell (i.e., "turning genes *effected by, but not controlled by past experiences*

on"). Environmental conditions may interact with an individual's genetic make-up to alter processes such as the timing of the initiation of transcription for a specific gene, the durations for which it does so, or whether the gene will ultimately be translated or expressed.

In Gottlieb's viewpoint, horizontal coactions take place at the same level of analysis, whereas vertical coactions occur at different levels of analysis. As such, vertical coactions are capable of influencing developmental organization from either lower-to-higher (bottom-up) or higher-to-lower (top-down) levels of the developing system. The probabilistic epigenesis perspective thus implies that individuals are neither unaffected by earlier experiences nor immutably controlled by them. Change in developmental course is thought to be possible as a result of new experiences, reciprocal interactions between levels of the developing person, and the individual's active self-organizing strivings for adaptation (see also Cicchetti & Tucker, 1994). Thus, epigenesis is viewed as probabilistic rather than predetermined, with the bidirectional and transactional nature of genetic, neural, behavioral, and environmental influences over the life course capturing the essence of probabilistic experiences. Because development is a dynamic process, assertions about causality must include a temporal dimension that specifies and describes when the experience or coactions occurred (Gottlieb & Halpern, 2002).

Thus, a *developmental analysis* presupposes change and novelty, highlights the critical role of timing in the appearance and organization of behavior, underscores multiple determination, and cautions against expecting invariant relations between causes and outcomes across the life course (Cacioppo & Tassinary, 1990; Cairns, 1998; Cicchetti, 1990; Kaplan, 1967; Sroufe, 1997). A developmental analysis is as applicable to the study of the gene or cell as it is to the investigation of the individual, family, or society (Cicchetti, 1990; Fishbein, 1976). Consequently, developmental psychopathologists must be cognizant of normal pathways of development, discover deviations from these pathways, articulate the developmental transformations that occur as individuals progress through these maladaptive courses, and identify the factors and mechanisms that may deflect an individual out of a particular pathway and onto a more or less adaptive course (Sroufe, 1989; Zigler & Glick, 1986).

MULTIPLE LEVELS OF ANALYSIS

Advances in scientific knowledge that have occurred over the past several decades have brought about a dramatic increase in our understanding of the multiple biological and psychological processes that contribute to the development of normality, psychopathology, and resilience. One outgrowth of these advances in understanding developmental processes has been that, in order to grasp fully the complexity inherent to the examination of the normal and abnormal human mind, it is critical that a multiple-levels-of-analysis approach and an interdisciplinary perspective be incorporated into the research methods of developmental psychopathologists. As the history of science attests, there are questions that are best examined using the conceptual and methodological tools of a single disciplinary perspective. For example, basic knowledge from research in separate disciplines is necessary before an interdisciplinary perspective can be implemented. Much of the success of modern neuroscience can be attributed to the incorporation of several previously independent disciplines (neuroanatomy, neurochemistry, neuropharmacology, molecular biology, and cognitive psychology) into a unified field (Albright, Jessell, Kandel, & Posner, 2000; Cicchetti & Posner, 2005).

In contrast, many of the answers to scientific questions that confront developmental psychopathologists are not as effectively approached by a single investigator or through a unitary disciplinary model. Rather, these questions can be most effectively addressed through an integrative interdisciplinary perspective (Pellmar & Eisenberg, 2000).

Calls for interdisciplinary research and a multiple-levels-of-analysis approach have been gaining momentum in scientific laboratories across the country (Cacioppo et al., 2000; Cicchetti, 2002; Cicchetti & Blender, 2004; Cicchetti & Posner, 2005; Kendler, 2005; Nelson & Bloom, 1997; Nelson et al., 2002). The sophisticated and comprehensive portrayals of adaptation and maladaptation that ensue will serve not only to advance scientific understanding, but also to inform efforts to prevent and ameliorate psychopathology (Cicchetti & Hinshaw, 2002; Hinshaw, 2002; Ialongo et al., 2006).

Most of the extant knowledge about the causes, correlates, courses, and consequences of psychopathology has been gleaned from research investigations that focused on relatively narrow domains of variables. Based on the questions presently at the forefront of research on development and psychopathology, future investigations increasingly will need to employ research designs and strategies that examine multiple domains of variables, both inside and outside the developing person (Cicchetti & Hinshaw, 2003; Cicchetti & Richters, 1997; Richters, 1997). Such research, by its very nature, must be interdisciplinary.

Because each level of analysis both informs and constrains all other levels of analysis, scientists conducting their work at each level will need to develop theories that are consistent across levels (Cicchetti & Dawson, 2002). When disciplines function in isolation, they run the risk of creating theories that are incorrect because vital information from other disciplines either has been ignored or is unknown. It is critical that an integrative framework be developed that incorporates all levels of analysis in the development of psychopathology.

Consistent with the writings of Cacioppo and his colleagues (Cacioppo & Bernston, 1992; Cacioppo et al., 2000), I use the term *level of analysis* to refer to the different scales into which behavior or the brain can be represented. The ultimate criterion of what constitutes a level of organization is its utility in elucidating the understanding of a particular biological or psychological phenomenon. Thus, levels can vary in organization from the molecular to the cellular, the tissue, the organ, the system, the organism, the physical environment, and the sociocultural context (Cacioppo et al., 2000; Gottlieb, 1992).

In recognition of the potential that a multilevel integrative perspective has for augmenting the understanding of mental illness, the National Advisory Mental Health Council's Workgroup on Basic Sciences recommended that research that integrates or translates levels of analysis—from genetic, to molecular, to cellular, to systems, to complex overt behavior—be accorded high priority by the National Institute of Mental Health (Cicchetti & Valentino, 2007). Indeed, a number of the critical principles inherent to a developmental psychopathology approach—such as the mutual interplay between the study of normality and psychopathology, multiple pathways to individual outcomes (equifinality) and diverse outcomes among individuals emanating from the same pathway (multifinality), and the attainment of unexpected competence despite adversity (resilience)—can make their fullest contribution to understanding developmental process through the application of a multiple-levels-of-analysis framework (Cicchetti & Blender, 2004, 2006).

In the next section, the concept of gene–environment interaction is examined in order to provide an illustration of how a multiple-level-of-analysis approach can augment our understanding of developmental pathways to mental disorder or resilience.

GENE–ENVIRONMENT INTERACTION

→ Seperate into component parts

Behavior-genetics designs offer strategies to disaggregate genetic and environmental contributions to psychopathological development at the etiologic level. Investigation of both sources of influence conjointly contributes to a more powerful means of delineating processes of pathogenesis than does either source alone. These designs capitalize on contrasts of different family contexts in which varying degrees of genetic similarity and/or environmental similarity can be compared. For example, in adoption studies, the development of siblings (who share 50% of their genetic makeup) who are reared in different families is contrasted with the development of siblings reared in the same family. Contrasts allow for differentiation of the degree of heritable versus environmental contributions to behavioral outcomes. Families of remarried parents with children from prior partnerships provide another family situation in which contrasts can be made of similarities and differences between genetically unrelated stepsiblings versus full siblings raised in the same family environment. Cross-fostering designs involve adoption of children of parents with a specified psychopathology into families in which the adoptive parents do not have the disorder under study; the approach involves examination of whether the adoptees have the same degree of risk for pathological development as do offspring reared by parents with the disorder.

Twin studies capitalize on the difference in degree of shared genetic makeup between monozygotic (MZ) twins, which is 100%, versus dizygotic (DZ) twins, who overlap 50% of their genes. Given the same rearing environments, greater similarity (concordance) between MZ twins as compared to DZ twins implies greater genetic influence. Behavior-genetics designs using twin samples contrast correlations between MZ and DZ twins to establish heritability estimates, as well as estimates of the degree of environmental influence.

Quantitative genetics provides an important approach for differentiating whether psychopathology constitutes an extreme mode of functioning on a normal distribution or a disordered condition that is discontinuous from normal variation in adaptation. For example, is clinical depression an extreme of normal sadness or a distinct disease entity? If quantitative (dimensional) data are obtained on probands, probands/relatives, and the population at large, then it is possible to assess the extent to which the genetic and environmental etiologies of abnormality differ from the genetic and environmental etiologies of normality. If group familiality differs from individual familiality, then this would provide strong evidence that the etiology of the disorder in question differs from the etiology of the normal distribution of variability. If, on the other hand, the two types of familiality are similar, then the results would be consistent with the hypothesis that psychopathology is etiologically part of the normal distribution (see Plomin, Rende, & Rutter, 1991; Rende & Plomin, 1995, for elaboration).

In these quantitative behavior-genetics models, continuously distributed phenotypes were posited and mental illnesses were thought to arise from many genes (known as polygenic determinism), each of which exerts a very small effect on the mental disorder investigated. In other words, behavior geneticists adhered to the belief that many genes plus environ-

Quantitative Genetics — is psychopathy an extreme level on a normal distribution, or is it a condition seperate from normal variations?

ments, in an additive fashion, were involved in the etiology of mental disorders (Gottesman & Shields, 1972; Rende & Waldman, 2006).

Influenced by the upsurge of interest in molecular genetics within the social and neurosciences, developmental psychopathologists have begun to investigate how the interdependence between an identified variation in the DNA sequence of a particular gene and a well-defined and appropriately measured environmental pathogen can exert impact upon behavioral outcomes (Moffitt et al., 2006; Plomin & Crabbe, 2000; Plomin & Rutter, 1998; Rende & Waldman, 2006; Rutter, 2006). Before the advent of molecular genetics approaches, most research in the area of genetics and psychopathology was conducted within the field of behavior genetics, with its assumption that genetic and environmental influences operate in an additive fashion. An additional supposition is that gene–environmental (G–E) effects are so infrequent and trivial that their presence could be ignored in quantitative behavior-genetic analyses (Moffitt et al., 2006). Such core assumptions from quantitative behavior genetics were carried over into the much newer field of psychiatric molecular genetics.

The perpetuation of the belief that additive effects predominate in the relation between genes and mental illnesses has contributed to a scientific strategy wherein single genes were examined in relation to specific mental disorders, but without consideration of the impact of different environmental circumstances on different forms of the same gene. Thus, the investigation of the interaction between measured genes and environments is a recent empirical phenomenon (Moffitt et al., 2006; Rutter, 2006).

Recently, the assumptions of behavior genetics have been challenged and researchers in the field of developmental psychopathology have been exhorted to examine G–E effects (Moffitt et al., 2006; Rutter, 2006). A number of cogent arguments support the position that G–E effects occur more frequently than heretofore assumed. As such, G–E effects play an important role in comprehending the development of mental health and disorder.

One of the most compelling reasons for encouraging increased research on G–E interactions in the field of developmental psychopathology is gleaned from the human and animal literature on behavioral responses to environmental challenges. Consistent with a developmental psychopathology perspective, heterogeneity (multifinality) is characteristic of the response to even the most pernicious and hazardous traumas, including the array of environmental risk factors for mental disorder (Cicchetti & Rogosch, 1996; Moffitt et al., 2006; Rutter, 2006). In other words, even in the face of extreme stress, individuals differ markedly with respect to their ultimate outcomes.

In empirical research guided by diathesis-stress models of psychopathology (Gottesman & Shields, 1972), as well as investigations of the deter-

G–E = gene/environmental effects

minants of resilient functioning in the face of serious adversity, it has been shown that individual differences in response to environmental risks are associated with preexisting individual variations that are under genetic influence (Cicchetti & Blender, 2006; Curtis & Cicchetti, 2003; Moffitt et al., 2006; Plomin et al., 2001; Rutter, 2006). Accordingly, in instances where there is individual variation among the psychological responses of humans to environmental risk factors for psychopathology, it is highly likely that G–E may be operating in some fashion.

EMERGING EMPIRICAL EVIDENCE OF G–E AND PSYCHOPATHOLOGY

Caspi et al. (2002) examined how genetic factors contribute to why some maltreated children grow up to develop antisocial personality characteristics, whereas other maltreated children do not. In this longitudinal investigation of males who were studied from birth to adulthood, it was discovered that a functional polymorphism in the promoter region of the gene encoding the neurotransmitter metabolizing enzyme monoamine oxidase A (MAOA) moderated the effect of maltreatment, which was defined broadly to include physical abuse and other serious and stressful experiences at home. MAOA degrades several biological amines including dopamine (DA), norepinephrine (NE), and serotonin (5-HTT). The link between child maltreatment and antisocial behavior was far less pronounced among males with high MAOA activity than among those with low MAOA activity. In other words, the functional polymorphism (high versus low activity) regulated the extent to which the MAOA gene was expressed.

Maltreated children grow up in extremely stressful environments (Cicchetti & Valentino, 2006). The results of the Caspi et al. (2002) investigation were the first to demonstrate that a G–E interaction helps to explain why some maltreated children, but not others, develop antisocial behavior via the effect that stressful experiences such as child abuse and neglect exert on neurotransmitter system development. Specifically, the probability that child maltreatment eventuated in adult antisocial behavior was greatly increased at low levels of MAOA expression. Because maltreatment was a clearly but broadly defined and well-measured environmental pathogen, the ability of Caspi and colleagues (2002) to detect a G–E interaction in the development of psychopathology was strengthened.

Foley and colleagues (2004) investigated the link between the MAOA polymorphism, adverse childhood environments, and resulting conduct disorder in adolescents. Consistent with the findings of Caspi et al. (2002), Foley et al. (2004) also found that the alleles resulting in low MAOA activity increased risk for conduct disorder only in the presence of an adverse childhood environment. Likewise, Kim-Cohen et al. (2006) replicated and extended the results of Caspi et al. (2002) through their demonstration that the MAOA polymorphism moderated the development of mental health problems after exposure to physical abuse in children.

To date, not all attempts at replicating the findings of Caspi et al. (2002) have reached similar conclusions. For example, Beitchman and colleagues (2004) found that persistent, pervasive, child-onset aggression was influenced by the MAOA polymorphism, but in an opposite way than obtained in the aforementioned studies. Specifically, clinically aggressive boys were more likely to have the allele that results in high MAOA activity; however, these boys had not been identified as maltreated.

A meta-analysis of existing published studies addressing the moderating effects of MAOA on relations between child maltreatment and psychopathology conducted by Kim-Cohen and colleagues (2006) demonstrated that across all studies, males who had the genotype conferring low as opposed to high MAOA activity were significantly more likely to develop mental health difficulties in the context of stressful environments. The results of this meta-analysis provide strong support for the hypothesis that the MAOA gene confers vulnerability to environmental stressors such as child abuse and neglect, and that this biological process begins to unfold during early childhood (cf. Kim-Cohen et al., 2006).

In another seminal investigation, Caspi et al. (2003) discovered that a functional polymorphism in the promoter region of the serotonin transporter (5-HTT) gene moderated the influence of stressful life events on the development of depression by early adulthood. Those with one or two copies of the short (s) allele of the 5-HTT promoter polymorphism exhibited more depressive symptoms, depressive disorders, and suicidality than individuals homozygous for the long (l) allele, but only when confronted with high life stress during adolescence.

This study, a large-scale prospective investigation of a representative birth cohort, provides additional evidence of a G–E interaction in which an individual's response to environmental insults is moderated by his or her genetic makeup. In addition, consistent with a G–E hypothesis, adult depression was predicted by the interaction between the s allele in the 5-HTT gene-linked-polymorphic region and child maltreatment that occurred during the first decade of life (Caspi et al., 2003). Child maltreatment predicted adult depression only among individuals carrying an s allele (i.e., s/s or s/l), but not among l/l homozygotes.

Kaufman and colleagues (2004) conducted a study with children that was a downward extension of the investigation of Caspi et al. (2003). The Kaufman et al. (2004) finding—that in maltreated children the s allele in the 5-HTT gene-linked polymorphic region confers vulnerability to depression only in individuals with a history of significant life stress—replicates the G–E interaction found in Caspi et al. (2003) with adults. Furthermore, the results of the Kaufman et al. study demonstrate that social support, in concert with the aforementioned genetic factor, additionally moderates the risk for depression in maltreated children. Specifically, maltreated children who were homozygous for the s allele and who had a dearth of social supports had depressive symptoms that were nearly twice as high as maltreated children with the s/s genotype and positive social supports. The latter group of maltreated children had levels of depressive symptoms that were comparable to those of nonmaltreated children in the comparison group with the same s/s genotype. Thus, the risk for depression in maltreated children was moderated by the interaction of genetic and environmental factors.

The multiple-levels-of-analysis perspective that characterizes molecular G–E research on psychopathology has moved beyond the behavior-genetics focus on heritability coefficients and additive models and has begun to address complex dynamic developmental questions such as "how do genetic and environmental factors transact throughout development in the course of disorder 'X'?" and "what factors cause which genes to turn on and off during specific phases of the epigenetic course?" In contrast to findings emanating from quantitative behavior-genetic research in which mental illnesses are thought to originate from many genes, each accounting for a small amount of variance, G–E research suggests that at least for some multifactorial mental disorders, a small number of genes with effects that are contingent on exposure to specific environmental pathogens may be sufficient for increasing the risk for development of some forms of psychopathology.

Future G–E investigations should examine brain endophenotypes that may be intermediate between the MAOA gene and antisocial behavior and the 5-HTT gene and depression. Endophenotypes are constructs beneath the observable surface, such as psychophysiological parameters, posited to underlie mental disorders or psychopathological symptoms. Endophenotypes are thought to be more directly influenced by the genes relevant to the disorder than are the manifest symptoms (Hanson & Gottesman, 2007). For example, the incorporation of assessments of the HPA axis functioning into research on G–E interactions could further enhance the predictive efficiency of such investigations. Maltreated children who demonstrate stress-induced neuroendocrine dysregulation (i.e., hyper- or hypocortisolism), have a paucity of social supports, and possess the s/s genotype for the 5-HTT gene, may be even more likely to develop Depressive Disorder than has been the case in previous studies. Delineation of stress-sensitive neural processes may pave the way for the formulation of pharmacological and behavioral prevention and intervention efforts to ameliorate the harmful impact that early stressful experiences exert on neurobiological development.

HOW EARLY ADVERSE EXPERIENCES AFFECT BRAIN DEVELOPMENT AND FUNCTION: ILLUSTRATION FROM THE STUDY OF CHILD MALTREATMENT

The notion of an average expectable environment for promoting normal development proposes that there are species-specific ranges of environmental conditions that facilitate normative developmental processes. Humans, like all species, develop within a normal reaction range when presented with an average expectable environment (Gottesman, 1963). For infants, the expectable environment includes protective, nurturant caregiver(s) and a larger social group in which the child will be socialized (Davies, Winter, & Cicchetti, 2006). For older children, the normative environment includes a supportive family, a peer group, and continued opportunities for exploration and mastery of the environment. Variations within this range of environments afford opportunities for individuals to dynamically engage in the construction of their own experiences (Scarr & McCartney, 1983). When environments fall outside the expectable range, however, normal development is impeded (Cicchetti & Lynch, 1995).

The investigation of child maltreatment—perhaps the greatest failure of the caregiving environment to provide the expectable experiences that are necessary to promote normal developmental processes—presents researchers with a vital opportunity to examine the effects of adverse social experiences on brain development and functioning. Until recently, the majority of our knowledge about the pathways, developmental trajectories, and ultimate consequences of psychopathology in maltreated children has been informed by investigations that have focused on psychological processes and outcomes. Researchers have now begun to embark on a multiple-levels-of-analysis approach to child maltreatment.

As research on the developmental sequelae of child maltreatment continues to burgeon, examination of the multifaceted neurobiological systems affected should provide insights into some of the mediators and moderators linking maltreatment to socioemotional and cognitive outcomes. Furthermore, because mechanisms of neural plasticity and synaptic pruning cause the brain's anatomical differentiations to be dependent on stimulation from the environment, it is clear that, in addition to genetic information, the cytoarchitecture of the cerebral cortex is shaped by input from the social environment (Cicchetti & Tucker, 1994).

Children who are endowed with normal brains may encounter a number of experiences (including child maltreatment) that may not only exert a negative impact on brain structure and function but also contribute to distorting these children's experiences of the world (Black et al., 1998; Cicchetti, 2002; Pollak, Cicchetti, & Klorman, 1998). Perturbations that occur during brain development can potentiate a cascade of maturational and structural changes that eventuate in neural systems proceeding along trajectories that deviate from those generally followed in normal neurobiological development. Consequently, early stresses may condition young neural networks to produce cascading effects through later development, possibly constraining the child's flexibility to adapt to challenging situations with new strategies rather than with old conceptual and behavioral prototypes. Accordingly, early psychological trauma such as that experienced by maltreated children may eventuate not only in emotional sensitization (Maughan & Cicchetti, 2002), but also in pathological sensitization of neuronal-physiological reactivity (Cicchetti & Tucker, 1994; Pollak et al., 1998). Such early developmental abnormalities may lead to the development of aberrant neural circuitry and compound themselves into enduring forms of psychopathology (Cicchetti & Cannon, 1999).

Children may be especially vulnerable to the effects of pathological experiences during periods of rapid creation or modification of neuronal connections (synapses) (Black et al., 1998). Pathological experiences may become part of a reinforcing cycle, as alterations in brain structure distort the child's processing of experience, with subsequent alterations in cognitive or social interactions causing additional pathological experience and added brain pathology (Black et al., 1998; Cicchetti & Tucker, 1994).

Numerous interconnected neurobiological systems are affected by the various stressors associated with child maltreatment (DeBellis, 2001). Moreover, each of these neurobiological systems influences, and is influenced by, multiple domains of psychological and biological development. Furthermore, in keeping with the concept of multifinality, the neurobiological development of maltreated children is not affected in the same way in all individuals, and not all maltreated children exhibit anomalies in brain structure or function. In the following I review the existing evidence on the effects of maltreatment on neurobiological structure and function. This research has examined different components of brain structure and function, each representing fairly distinct neural systems.

Neurobiological Structure: Neuroimaging

Over the past decade, neuroimaging investigations have begun to be conducted with children and adolescents who have been maltreated. In a magnetic resonance imaging (MRI) study, DeBellis and colleagues (1999) conducted an in-depth volumetric analysis of the entire brain of a group of hospitalized maltreated children and adolescents and a group of medically and psychiatrically well, nonmaltreated comparison participants. Consistent with the literature on child maltreatment, most of the children and adolescents who had experienced maltreatment had comorbid mental disorders, including Posttraumatic Stress Disorder (PTSD), Major Depressive Disorder, and Attention-Deficit/Hyperactivity Disorder (ADHD).

In contrast to the findings of reduced hippocampal volume in investigations of adults who retrospectively reported histories of abuse during childhood (Bremner et al., 1997), DeBellis et al. (1999) did not find reduced hippocampal volumes in the children and adolescents who had experienced maltreatment. Moreover, DeBellis and colleagues (2001) examined hippocampal volumes longitudinally in order to ascertain whether child maltreatment alters the development of the hippocampus during puberty. DeBellis and colleagues (2001) used MRI to scan the brains of maltreated and nonmaltreated children drawn from demographically comparable low-socioeconomic-status (SES) backgrounds on two occasions, once when they were prepubertal and then 2 to 3 years later. MRI scans revealed no differences between maltreated and nonmaltreated children in the volume of the brain areas measured—the temporal lobes, the amygdala, and the hippocampus—at either time period of assessment.

However, after controlling for intracranial volume and SES, DeBellis and colleagues (1999) discovered a number of unexpected structural brain anomalies in their sample of maltreated children and adolescents. These included smaller intracranial and cerebral volumes, smaller corpus callosum areas, and larger lateral ventricles than in the group of nonmaltreated participants. In addition, these investigators found a significant positive correlation between increased cranial volumes and age of onset of PTSD trauma (meaning that the older the child when trauma occurred, the larger the structures in question), and a significant negative correlation with the duration of maltreatment that led to a PTSD diagnosis (meaning that the shorter the period of maltreatment, the larger the structures). These results suggest that there may be sensitive periods and dose effects for stress-related alterations in brain development. Likewise, the finding that enlarged lateral ventricles were correlated positively with the duration of the maltreatment experienced suggests that there may have been neuronal loss associated with the severe stress of child maltreatment.

Teicher and colleagues (2004) investigated the corpus callosum in children who had been abused or neglected to ascertain whether there were structural abnormalities in its regional anatomy. The corpus callosum connects the left and right hemispheres and is the major myelinated tract in the brain. Regional corpus callosum area was measured by MRI in three groups of children: those who were abused and neglected, those admitted for psychiatric evaluation, and healthy controls. Teicher et al. found that the total area of the corpus callosum of the children who had experienced abuse and neglect was smaller than that of children evaluated for psychiatric problems and healthy controls. The latter two groups of children did not differ from each other. Child neglect was associated with a 15% to 18% reduction in corpus callosum regions. Among girls, corpus callosum reductions were most strongly associated with sexual abuse. These findings are congruent with the earlier assertion that negative early experiences can adversely affect neurobiological development. Of course, before one can conclude with confidence that these neurobiological anomalies are sequelae of child maltreatment, one needs to conduct prospective longitudinal investigations of children at high risk for being maltreated.

NEUROBIOLOGICAL FUNCTIONING I: ACOUSTIC STARTLE

Startle expression in humans and laboratory animals is affected by emotional factors, a connection that may be grounded in the evolutionary value of startle for immediate protection. The disturbances of anxiety and traumatization observed in childhood maltreatment (Cicchetti & Lynch, 1995), and the sensitivity of the startle reflex to these conditions, suggest a utility of examining startle patterns in maltreated children toward possible identification of an objective physiological marker of traumatization severity. In our laboratory, Klorman et al. (2003) investigated acoustic startle to a range of auditory intensities to identify possible abnormalities in response magnitude, onset latency, and habituation.

The acoustic startle reflex is an obligatory response to a sudden and unexpected stimulus that is marked by the cessation of ongoing behaviors and by a particular series of protective behaviors (Davis, 1984). The eyeblink is the most sensitive and consistent startle response across individuals, and this is the response that is most often measured in studies of this reflex. The startle eyeblink in humans is measured by electromyographic activity detected by electrodes overlying the obicularis oculi muscle, located below each eye.

Klorman et al. (2003) examined acoustic startle to 24 randomly ordered 50-millisecond binaural white noise burst probes of 70, 85, 100, and 115 decibels while children were watching silent cartoons. Participants were maltreated and nonmaltreated children matched for age, sex, and socioeconomic status (see Klorman et al., 2003). Maltreated boys' startle blinks had smaller amplitude and slower onset latency and were less affected by increasing probe loudness than were those of comparison boys. Among maltreatment subtypes, this pattern was most salient for physically abused boys. There were not enough physically abused girls to detect any potential differences from comparison children. The results for maltreated boys are consistent with those of Ornitz and Pynoos (1989) for diminished startle responses among children with PTSD. These investigators suggested that startle diminution in traumatized children may reflect cortically mediated attentional dysfunction, which affects brainstem mechanisms for startle responses.

Findings obtained from physically abused boys are consistent with those of Cicchetti and Rogosch (2001a). These investigators discovered that children who experienced physical abuse displayed a greater suppression of cortisol and significantly less variation in hypothalamic-pituitary-adrenal (HPA) axis functioning than did maltreated children who were sexually abused, emotionally abused, or neglected. Although startle responsiveness and cortisol regulation are linked to separate but interconnected neurobiological systems, in both the Klorman et al. (2003) and the Cicchetti and Rogosch (2001a) investigations, physically abused children exhibited diminished physiological responses. Physically abused children are often exposed to threat and danger so their smaller responses to startle and their suppression of cortisol may reflect allostatic load, the cumulative long-term effect of physiologic responses to stress (Davies et al., 2007; McEwen & Stellar, 1993). Repetitive social challenges in a child's environment, such as those engendered by physical abuse, can cause disruptions in basic homeostatic and regulatory processes that are essential to the maintenance of optimal physical and mental health (Repetti, Taylor, & Seeman, 2002).

Neurobiological Functioning II: Neuroendocrine Regulation

Incidents of child maltreatment, such as sexual, physical, and emotional abuse, as well as neglect, may engender massive stress in vulnerable children. Acute threat and emotional distress, as is found in instances of child maltreatment, may activate the locus coeruleus, the major noradrenergic-containing nucleus in the brain, and the sympathetic nervous system (SNS), eventuating in the biological changes accompanying the "fight or flight" reaction (Gunnar & Vazquez, 2006; Kaufman & Charney, 2001). Stressful experiences such as child maltreatment may potentiate the increased production of corticotrophin-releasing hormone (CRH) in the central amygdala and in the hypothalamus. CRH from the amygdala causes increased SNS activity, thereby promoting heightened behavioral and attentional arousal (Kaufman & Charney, 2001). CRH from the paraventricular nucleus of the hypothalamus, in concert with other hormones such as vasopressin, stimulate the production of adrenocorticotropic hormone (ACTH) in the anterior pituitary. The ACTH that is secreted into circulation selectively stimulates cells of the adrenal cortex to produce and release cortisol, a potent steroid hormone that impacts nearly all organs and tissues of the body (Gunnar & Vazquez, 2006; Lopez, Akil, & Watson, 1999). Cortisol, through negative feedback inhibition on the hypothalamus, pituitary, and additional brain structures, such as the hippocampus, suppresses the HPA axis, thereby bringing about restoration of basal levels of cortisol. Among its many influences, cortisol affects the central neural processes that are implicated in cognition, memory, and emotion.

The capacity to elevate cortisol in response to acute trauma is critical for survival. Brief elevations in corticosteroids following acute stressors appear to enhance the individual's ability to manage stressful experiences competently, both physiologically and behaviorally. However, chronic hyperactivity of the HPA axis (hypercortisolism) may eventuate in the accelerated loss or metabolism of hippocampal neurons, the inhibition of neurogenesis, lags in the development of myelination, abnormalities in synaptic pruning, and impaired affective and cognitive abilities (Gould et al., 1998; Sapolsky, 1992). Moreover, the elimination of glucocorticoids also can damage neurons (Gunnar & Vazquez, 2001; Heim, Ehlert, & Hellhammer, 2000). Hypocortisolism, in which individuals who are experiencing chronic stressors such as ongoing maltreatment, manifests in reduced adrenocortical secretion, reduced adrenocortical reactivity, and/or enhanced negative feedback inhibition of the HPA axis (Gunnar & Vazquez, 2001; Heim et al., 2000). Consequently, it is in an organism's best interests to avoid both chronic glucocorticoid hypersecretion and hyposecretion (Sapolsky, 1996).

A number of investigations have been conducted that reveal atypical physiological processes in maltreated children. Noradrenergic, dopaminergic, serotonergic, and glucocorticoid systems, which are all activated by stress, are affected by child maltreatment. For example, abnormal noradrenergic activity, as evidenced by lower urinary norepinephrine (NE), has been found in children who have been abused and neglected (Rogeness, 1991). Additionally, neglected children often exhibit lower levels of dopamine-beta-hydroxylase (DBH), an enzyme involved in the synthesis of NE, than do abused children or normal comparisons (Rogeness & McClure, 1996). Neglected children also have lower systolic and diastolic blood pressure, both of which are functions mediated in part by the NE system.

Furthermore, several investigations have shown that girls who have experienced sexual abuse display augmented morning cortisol levels, implicating altered glucocorticoid functioning in the HPA axis. Moreover, sexually abused girls excrete significantly more of the dopamine (DA) metabolite homovanallic acid (DeBellis et al., 1994; Putnam et al., 1991). These findings, along with others in the literature, suggest that sexual abuse is associated with enduring alterations of biological stress systems.

An additional example of how child maltreatment affects neuroendocrine regulation has been provided in a study conducted in our laboratory. Cicchetti and Rogosch (2001a) found substantial elevations in the morning cortisol levels of maltreated children who had been both physically and sexually abused, as well as neglected or emotionally maltreated. Moreover, many of the children in this multiple-abuse group also had cortisol levels that were elevated in both the morning and the afternoon. In contrast to the findings of the multiple-abuse group, a subgroup of children who had been physically abused showed only a marginally significant linkage with lower morning cortisol, relative to nonmaltreated children. In addition, this physically abused subgroup of children displayed a significantly smaller decrease in cortisol from morning to afternoon. This pattern suggests less diurnal variation for the physically abused group of children. Finally, no differences in patterns of cortisol regulation were obtained between the neglected and the emotionally maltreated groups of children and the comparison group of nonmaltreated children.

The divergent patterns of cortisol regulation for the varying subgroup configurations of maltreated children suggest that it is highly unlikely *multifinality* that the brains of all children are uniformly affected by the experience of maltreatment. Not all maltreated children displayed dysregulation of the hypothalamic-pituitary-adrenal (HPA) axis. The group of children who experienced sexual and physical abuse, in combination with neglect or emotional maltreatment, exhibited patterns akin to hypercortisolism. In addition, the pattern of HPA-axis functioning in children in the physically abused subgroup is suggestive of hypocortisolism (Gunnar & Vazquez, 2001).

The children in the multiple-abuse group had experienced chronic maltreatment across a range of developmental periods. This multifaceted assault on cognitive, social, emotional, and biological systems is likely to contribute to these children's expectations of continued adversity. In essence, the pervasiveness of negative experiences results in these children's construction of their worlds as marked by fear and a hypersensitivity to future maltreatment.

The development of behavior problems and psychopathology that often accompany stress-induced hyper- and hypocortisolism are partially a consequence of hormonal effects on gene expression (Cicchetti & Rogosch, 2001b; Cicchetti & Walker, 2001). Investigations have documented the role of stress hormones, such as cortisol, in the expression of genes (Watson & Gametchu, 1999). When stress hormones bind to nuclear receptors, these hormones can trigger DNA transcription and protein synthesis of particular genes. In turn, the resulting proteins influence neuronal structure and function, including neuronal growth, neurotransmitter synthesis, receptor density and sensitivity, and neurotransmitter reuptake.

NEUROBIOLOGICAL FUNCTIONING III: BRAIN EVENT-RELATED POTENTIALS AND EMOTION PROCESSING

Attachment systems have been theorized to be constructed to (a) permit flexible responses to environmental circumstances, (b) influence emotion regulation, and (c) function through mental representations (*internal working models*) that children hold of themselves and of their relationships with others. Cicchetti and Tucker (1994) proffered the hypothesis that these representations may be reflected through physiological activity as well as behavior. In our laboratory, we have focused on one type of physiological reaction, the event-related potential (ERP). The ERP is an index of central nervous system functioning thought to reflect the underlying neurological processing of discrete stimuli. ERPs also enable researchers to monitor neural activity associated with cognitive processing in real time.

In our laboratory, we have conducted several experiments in which we examined ERPs of maltreated and nonmaltreated children in response to a variety of emotion-eliciting stimuli that were presented as facial displays. The stimuli used in the experiments were photographs of prototypic facial expressions (e.g., happy, sad, fear, anger, neutral). The maltreated and nonmaltreated children were of comparable cognitive maturity and low-SES backgrounds.

The first two experiments investigated school-aged maltreated and nonmaltreated children (Pollak et al., 1997; Pollak et al., 2001), and the third experiment studied toddlers who had experienced maltreatment in the first year of life plus a group of nonmaltreated toddlers (Cicchetti & Curtis, 2005).

In each of these studies, the ERPs of maltreated youngsters showed an increased amplitude to facial displays of anger compared to other facial displays, whereas the ERPs of the nonmaltreated youngsters were comparable across all emotion conditions. The results of these ERP experiments suggest that the experiences that maltreated children encountered during their development caused particular stimuli to become personally meaningful, based in part upon the stored mental representations that have been associated with that particular stimulus over time. Accordingly, prior experiences of maltreated children are reflected in their psychophysiological responses. Moreover, maltreatment also appears to affect children's interpretations and comprehension of particular emotional displays. Specifically, neglected children, who often suffer from an extremely limited emotional environment, have more difficulty discriminating among emotional expressions than do nonmaltreated children or physically abused children (Pollak et al., 2000). Furthermore, physically abused children, who are often exposed to impending threat, display a response bias for angry facial expressions (Pollak et al., 2000; Pollak & Sinha, 2002) and are more likely than other maltreated children to impute negative intentions to ambiguous situations (Teisl & Cicchetti, in press). This pattern is known in the literature as the *hostile attribution bias* (see Dodge, Pettit, & Bates, 1997). Such selectivity in responding may allow maltreated children to use behavioral responses that are adaptive to address the challenges presented by their environments; however, responding in this fashion may provide maladaptive solutions when employed outside of the maltreating situation and may contribute to their social-cognitive difficulties and increased risk for behavior problems and psychopathology (Cicchetti & Valentino, 2006).

RESILIENCE: A MULTIPLE-LEVELS-OF-ANALYSIS PERSPECTIVE

Understanding how individuals overcome significant adversity and function adaptively has captured the imagination and interest of humanity throughout the ages; however, it has been only a little more than 3 decades since the systematic empirical study of the phenomenon that is today known as *resilience* began. The roots of work on resilience can be traced back to prior research in diverse areas, including investigations of Schizophrenia, poverty, and responses to trauma (Luthar, Cicchetti, & Becker, 2000; Masten, 2001).

Before the early 1970s, scientific investigations of children from high-risk environments, as well as those with mental disorders, portrayed the developmental course of such individuals as deterministic, inevitably eventuating in maladaptive and psychopathological outcomes (Luthar et al., 2000). As researchers discovered that not all high-risk children evinced the dire consequences that existing theories of psychopathology predicted, comprehending the processes through which children at risk did not develop psychopathology became viewed as important for informing theoretical viewpoints on the development of pathology (Cicchetti & Garmezy, 1993).

Resilience is a dynamic developmental process that has been operationalized as an individual's attainment of positive adaptation and competent functioning despite the experience of chronic stress or detrimental circumstances, or exposure to prolonged or severe trauma (Cicchetti

& Garmezy, 1993; Luthar et al., 2000). Resilience is multidimensional in nature, exemplified by findings that high-risk individuals may manifest competence in some domains and contexts, whereas they may exhibit problems in others.

Despite the growing attention paid to discovering the processes through which individuals at high risk do not develop maladaptively, the empirical study of resilience has focused primarily on detecting the psychosocial determinants of the phenomenon (Curtis & Cicchetti, 2003). For research on resilience to grow in ways that are commensurate with the complexity inherent to the construct, efforts to understand underlying processes will be facilitated by the increased implementation of multidisciplinary investigations designed within a developmental psychopathology framework. Research of this nature would entail a consideration of biological, psychological, and environmental/contextual processes from which varied pathways to resilience (equifinality) might eventuate, as well as those that result in diverse outcomes among individuals who have achieved resilient functioning (multifinality).

The role of biological factors in resilience is suggested by evidence on neurobiological and neuroendocrine function in relation to stress reactivity (Gunnar & Vazquez, 2006), by behavior-genetics research on nonshared environmental effects (Rende & Waldman, 2006), and by molecular genetics research that may reveal the genetic elements that serve a protective function for individuals experiencing significant adversity (Cicchetti & Blender, 2004).

To provide an example gleaned from the molecular genetics research reviewed earlier, it is conceivable that the gene encoding high MAOA activity, and the l/l allelic variant of the 5-HTT gene, may confer protection against the development of antisocial behavior in males who have been maltreated, and against the development of depression in individuals who have been maltreated (Caspi et al., 2002; Caspi et al., 2003; Kaufman et al., 2004). Consequently, the negative developmental sequelae associated with child maltreatment are not inevitable.

Children who develop in a resilient fashion despite having experienced significant adversity play an active role in constructing, seeking, and receiving the experiences that are developmentally appropriate for them. To date, research investigations that search for mechanisms of G–E interaction have yet to address the role that genetic factors may play in influencing how children who are developing in a resilient fashion have actively transformed their social environment (a process known as *evocative gene–environment correlation;* see Rende & Waldman, 2006; Scarr & McCartney, 1983). At the neurobiological level, different areas of the brain may attempt to compensate; on another level, individuals may seek out new experiences in areas where they have strength (Black et al., 1998; Cicchetti & Tucker, 1994). The effects of social experiences, such as child abuse and neglect, on brain biochemistry and microstructure may be either pathological or adaptive. Thus, neither early neurobiological anomalies alone nor aberrant experiences alone should be considered as determining the ultimate fate of the individual.

IMPLICATIONS OF A MULTIPLE-LEVELS-OF-ANALYSIS PERSPECTIVE FOR PREVENTIVE INTERVENTIONS

The time has come to incorporate neurobiological measures and molecular genetic techniques into the design and implementation of interventions to promote resilient functioning or to repair positive adaptations gone awry (Cicchetti & Gunnar, 2008). The inclusion of neurobiological and molecular genetics assessments into the design and evaluation of interventions aimed at fostering resilience enables scientists to discover whether the various components of multifaceted interventions each exert a differential impact on separate brain systems. If assessments of biological systems are routinely included in the measures used in resilience-facilitating interventions, then we will be in a position to discover whether the nervous system has been modified by experience.

The dearth of attention to biological processes in prevention evaluation may stem in part from beliefs that biological processes are not malleable or are less amenable to positive change as a result of experience. Evidence for neurobiological change in response to changes in the environment may be less apparent in normative populations where there is likely greater stability in supportive milieus. Although adversity and trauma are known to be detrimental to biological systems, how preventive interventions may contribute to recovery or repair of biological sequelae is little understood. Given that a multiple-levels perspective posits that there are bidirectional transactions between different levels of organismic organization and that experience influences biology, it is important to consider how changes in experience and behavioral functioning resulting from preventive interventions may alter biological processes.

The inclusion of a neurobiological and molecular genetics framework into the conceptualization of preventive interventions offers considerable promise for expansion of knowledge regarding complexity of the developmental process. Determining the multiple levels at which change is engendered through preventive interventions will provide more insights into the mechanisms of change, the extent to which neural plasticity may be promoted, and the interrelations between biological and psychological processes in resilience and psychopathology.

CONCLUSION

In this chapter, I have argued that it is imperative that researchers in developmental psychopathology adapt a multiple-levels-of-analysis approach to the study of both deviant and adaptive functioning. New programs of research must take into account both normal and abnormal developmental processes in examining psychopathology, and intervention studies must be undertaken in order to more fully establish the characteristics of and processes underlying the relation among genetics, neurobiology, and psychopathology.

In order to ensure that future generations of scholars in developmental psychopathology are knowledgeable about a multiple-levels-of-analysis perspective, undergraduate, graduate, and medical school programs in clinical and developmental psychology, neuroscience and molecular genetics, pediatrics, and psychiatry should encourage students to take coursework in a broad spectrum of areas (Cicchetti & Toth, 1991; Pellmar & Eisenberg, 2000). These might include courses in basic neurobiology, neuroendocrinology, immunology, molecular genetics, and developmental processes, as well as courses on brain imaging technologies, molecular genetics laboratory methods, neuroendocrine and immunological assay techniques, and other tools involved in assessing neurobiological and genetic processes.

Finally, students in basic science areas, such as neuroscience and molecular genetics, should be encouraged to gain exposure to the fundamentals of normative and atypical developmental processes. Furthermore, specific interdisciplinary programs for both students and faculty, spanning interest areas from clinical intervention to basic neuroscience, would help to foster communication and collaborative research endeavors among the fields of molecular genetics, developmental neuroscience, and developmental psychopathology (see, e.g., Cicchetti & Posner, 2005). The power embodied by cross-disciplinary collaborations that utilize multiple-levels-of-analysis methodologies promises to significantly strengthen our capacity to decrease the burden of mental illness for individuals as well as for society at large.

REFERENCES

Albright, T. D., Jessell, T. M., Kandel, E. R., & Posner, M. I. (2005). Neuroscience: A century of progress and the mysteries that remain. *Neuron, 25*, S1–S55.

Baldwin, A. L., Baldwin, C. P., & Cole, R. (1990). Stress-resistant families and stress-resistant children. In J. Rolf, A. Masten, D. Cicchetti, K. Nuechterlein, & S. Weintraub (Eds.), *Risk and protective factors in the development of psychopathology* (pp. 257–280). New York: Cambridge University Press.

Beitchman, J. H., Mik, H. M., Ehtesham, S., Douglas, L., & Kennedy, J. L. (2004). MAOA and persistent, pervasive childhood aggression. *Molecular Psychiatry, 9*(6), 546–547.

Black, J. E., Jones, T. A., Nelson, C. A., & Greenough, W. T. (1998). Neuronal plasticity and the developing brain. In N. E. Alessi, J. T. Coyle, S. I. Harrison, & S. Eth (Eds.), *Handbook of child and adolescent psychiatry* (pp. 31–53). New York: Wiley.

Bremner, J. D., Randall, P., Vermetten, E., Staib, L., Bronen, R. A., Mazure, C. J., et al. (1997). Magnetic resonance imaging-based measurement of hippocampal volume in posttraumatic stress disorder related to childhood physical and sexual abuse: A preliminary report. *Biological Psychiatry, 41,* 23–32.

Cacioppo, J. T., & Berntson, G. G. (1992). Social psychological contributions to the decade of the brain: The doctrine of multilevel analysis. *American Psychologist, 47,* 1019–1028.

Cacioppo, J. T., Berntson, G. G., Sheridan, J. F., & McClintock, M. K. (2000). Multilevel integrative analysis of human behavior: Social neuroscience and the complementing nature of social and biological approaches. *Psychological Bulletin, 126,* 829–843.

Cacioppo, J. T., & Tassinary, L. G. (1990). Inferring psychological significance from physiological signals. *American Psychologist, 45*(1), 16–24.

Cairns, R. B. (1998). The making of developmental psychology. In W. Damon & R. M. Lerner (Eds.), *Handbook of child psychology. Vol. 1: Theoretical models of human development* (5th ed., pp. 25–106). New York: Wiley.

Caspi, A., McClay, J., Moffitt, T., Mill, J., Martin, J., Craig, I. W., et al. (2002). Role of genotype in the cycle of violence in maltreated children. *Science, 297,* 851–854.

Caspi, A., Sugden, K., Moffitt, T. E., Taylor, A., Craig, I. W., Harrington, H. L., et al. (2003). Influence of life stress on depression: Moderation by a polymorphism in the 5-HTT gene. *Science, 301,* 386–389.

Cicchetti, D. (1984). The emergence of developmental psychopathology. *Child Development, 55,* 1–7.

Cicchetti, D. (1990). A historical perspective on the discipline of developmental psychopathology. In J. Rolf, A. Masten, D. Cicchetti, K. Nuechterlein, & S. Weintraub (Eds.), *Risk and protective factors in the development of psychopathology* (pp. 2–28). New York: Cambridge University Press.

Cicchetti, D. (1993). Developmental psychopathology: Reactions, reflections, projections. *Developmental Review, 13,* 471–502.

Cicchetti, D. (2002). How a child builds a brain: Insights from normality and psychopathology. In W. Hartup & R. Weinberg (Eds.), *Minnesota Symposia on Child Psychology. Vol. 32: Child psychology in retrospect and prospect* (pp. 23–71). Mahwah, NJ: Erlbaum.

Cicchetti, D., & Blender, J. A. (2006). A multiple-levels-of-analysis perspective on resilience: Implications for the developing brain, neural plasticity, and preventive interventions. *Annals of the New York Academy of Sciences, 1094,* 471–502.

Cicchetti, D., & Blender, J. A. (2004). A multiple-levels-of-analysis approach to the study of developmental processes in maltreated children. *Proceedings of the National Academy of Sciences, 101*(50), 17325–17326.

Cicchetti, D., & Cannon, T. D. (1999). Neurodevelopmental processes in the ontogenesis and epigenesis of psychopathology. *Development and Psychopathology, 11,* 375–393.

Cicchetti, D., & Curtis, W. J. (2005). An event-related potential (ERP) study of processing of affective facial expressions in young children who have experienced maltreatment during the first year of life. *Development and Psychopathology, 17*(3), 641–677.

Cicchetti, D., & Dawson, G. (Eds.). (2002). Multiple levels of analysis [Special Issue]. *Development and Psychopathology, 14*(3), 417–666.

Cicchetti, D., & Garmezy, N. (Eds.). (1993). Milestones in the development of resilience [Special Issue]. *Development and Psychopathology, 5*(4), 497–774.

Cicchetti, D., & Gunnar, M. R. (Eds.). (2008). Integrating biological measures into the design and evaluation of preventative interventions[Special Issue]. *Development and Psychopathology, 20*(3).

Cicchetti, D., & Hinshaw, S. P. (Eds.). (2002). Prevention and intervention science: Contributions to developmental theory [Special Issue]. *Development and Psychopathology, 14*(4), 667–981.

Cicchetti, D., & Lynch, M. (1995). Failures in the expectable environment and their impact on individual development: The case of child maltreatment. In D. Cicchetti & D. J. Cohen (Eds.), *Developmental psychopathology. Vol. 2: Risk, disorder, and adaptation* (pp. 32–71). New York: Wiley.

Cicchetti, D., & Posner, M. I. (Eds.). (2005). Integrating cognitive and affective neuroscience and developmental psychopathology [Special Issue]. *Development and Psychopathology, 17,* 569–891.

Cicchetti, D., & Richters, J. E. (Eds.). (1997). Conceptual and scientific underpinnings of research in developmental psychopathology [Special Issue]. *Development and Psychopathology, 9*(2), 189–471.

Cicchetti, D., & Rogosch, F. A. (1996). Equifinality and multifinality in developmental psychopathology. *Development and Psychopathology, 8,* 597–600.

Cicchetti, D., & Rogosch, F. A. (2001a). Diverse patterns of neuroendocrine activity in maltreated children. *Development and Psychopathology, 13,* 677–694.

Cicchetti, D., & Rogosch, F. A. (2001b). The impact of child maltreatment and psychopathology upon neuroendocrine functioning. *Development and Psychopathology, 13,* 783–804.

Cicchetti, D., & Toth, S. L. (1991). The making of a developmental psychopathologist. In J. Cantor, C. Spiker, & L. Lipsitt (Eds.), *Child behavior and development: Training for diversity* (pp. 34–72). Norwood, NJ: Ablex.

Cicchetti, D., & Tucker, D. (1994). Development and self-regulatory structures of the mind. *Development and Psychopathology, 6,* 533–549.

Cicchetti, D., & Valentino, K. (2007). Toward the application of a multiple-levels-of-analysis perspective to research in development and psychopathology. In A. Masten (Ed.), *Minnesota Symposia on Child Psychology, 34* (pp. 243–284). Mahwah, NJ: Lawrence Erlbaum.

Cicchetti, D., & Valentino, K. (2006). An ecological transactional perspective on child maltreatment: Failure of the average expectable environment and its influence upon child development. In D. Cicchetti & D. J. Cohen (Eds.), *Developmental psychopathology. Vol 3: Risk, disorder, and adaptation* (2nd ed., pp. 129–201). New York: Wiley.

Cicchetti, D., & Walker, E. F. (Eds.). (2001). Stress and development: Biological and psychological consequences [Special Issue]. *Development and Psychopathology, 13*(3), 413–753.

Curtis, W. J., & Cicchetti, D. (2003). Moving research on resilience into the 21st century: Theoretical and methodological considerations in examining the biological contributors to resilience. *Development and Psychopathology, 15*, 773–810.

Davies, P. T., Sturge-Apple, M. L., Cicchetti, D., & Cummings, E. M. (in press). The role of adrenocortical functioning in pathways between interparental conflict and child maladjustment. *Developmental Psychology, 43*, 918–930.

Davies, P. T., Winter, M. A., & Cicchetti, D. (2006). The implications of emotional security theory for understanding and treating childhood psychopathology. *Development and Psychopathology, 18*(3), 707–736.

Davis, M. (1984). The mammalian startle response. In R. C. Eaton (Ed.), *Neural mechanisms of startle behavior* (pp. 287–351). New York: Plenum.

DeBellis, M. D. (2001). Developmental traumatology: The psychobiological development of maltreated children and its implications for research, treatment, and policy. *Development and Psychopathology, 13*, 539–564.

DeBellis, M. D., Hall, J., Boring, A. M., Frustaci, K., & Moritz, G. (2001). A pilot longitudinal study of hippocampal volumes in pediatric maltreatment related Posttraumatic Stress Disorder. *Society of Biological Psychiatry, 50*, 305–309.

DeBellis, M. D., Keshavan, M. S., Casey, B. J., Clark, D. B., Giedd, J., Boring, A. M., et al. (1999). Developmental traumatology: Biological stress systems and brain development in maltreated children with PTSD: Pt. II The relationship between characteristics of trauma and psychiatric symptoms and adverse brain development in maltreated children and adolescents with PTSD. *Biological Psychiatry, 45*, 1271–1284.

DeBellis, M. D., Leffer, L., Trickett, P. K., & Putnam, F. W. (1994). Urinary catecholamine excretion in sexually abused girls. *Journal of the American Academy of Child and Adolescent Psychiatry, 33*, 320–327.

Dodge, K., Pettit, G., & Bates, J. E. (1997). How the experience of early physical abuse leads children to become chronically aggressive. In D. Cicchetti & S. L. Toth (Eds.), *Rochester Symposium on Developmental Psychopathology. Vol. 8: Trauma: Perspectives on theory, research and intervention* (pp. 263–288). Rochester, NY: University of Rochester Press.

Eisenberg, L. (1977). Development as a unifying concept in psychiatry. *British Journal of Psychiatry, 131*, 225–237.

Fishbein, H. (1976). *Evolution, development, and children's learning.* Pacific Palisades, CA: Goodyear Publishing.

Foley, D. L., Eaves, L. J., Wormley, B., Silberg, J. L., Maes, H. H., Kuhn, J., et al. (2004). Childhood adversity, monoamine oxidase: A genotype, and risk for conduct disorder. *Archives of General Psychiatry, 61*(7), 738–744.

Gottesman, I: I. (1963). Genetic aspects of intelligent behavior. In N. R. Ellis (Ed.), *Handbook of mental deficiency: Psychological theory and research* (pp. 253–296). New York: McGraw-Hill.

Gottesman, I., & Shields, J. (1972). *Schizophrenia and genetics: A twin study vantage point.* New York: Academic Press.

Gottlieb, G. (1991). Experiential canalization of behavioral development: Theory. *Developmental Psychology, 27,* 4–13.

Gottlieb, G. (1992). *Individual development and evolution: The genesis of novel behavior.* New York: Oxford University Press.

Gottlieb, G., & Halpern, C. T. (2002). A relational view of causality in normal and abnormal development. *Development and Psychopathology, 14*(3), 421–436.

Gould, E., Tanapat, P., McEwen, B. S., Flugge, G., & Fuchs, E. (1998) Proliferation of granule cell precursors in the dentate gyrus of adult monkeys is diminished by stress. *Proceedings of the National Academy of Sciences, 95*(6), 3168–3171.

Gunnar, M. R., & Vazquez, D. M. (2001). Low cortisol and a flattening of expected daytime rhythm: Potential indices of risk in human development. *Development and Psychopathology, 13,* 515–538.

Gunnar, M. R., & Vazquez, D. M. (2006). Stress neurobiology and developmental psychopathology. In D. Cicchetti & D. Cohen (Eds.), *Developmental psychopathology. Vol. 2: Developmental neuroscience* (2nd ed., pp. 533–577). New York: Wiley.

Hanson, D. R., & Gottesman, I. I. (2007). Choreographing genetic, epigenetic, and stochastic steps in the dances of developmental psychopathology. In A. Master (Ed.), Multiple dynamics in developmental psychopathology: Pathways to the future. *Minnesota Symposia on Child Psychology, 34* (pp. 27–43). Mahwah, NJ: Erlbaum.

Heim, C., Ehlert, U., & Hellhammer, D. H. (2000). Invited review: The potential role of hypocortisolism in the pathophysiology of stress-related bodily disorders. *Psychoneuroendocrinology, 25,* 1–35.

Hinshaw, S. P. (2002). Intervention research, theoretical mechanisms, and causal processes related to externalizing behavior patterns. *Development and Psychopathology, 14*(4), 789–818.

Ialongo, N., Rogosch, F. A., Cicchetti, D., Toth, S. L., Buckley, J., Petras, H., & Neiderhiser, J., (2006). A developmental psychopathology approach to the prevention of mental health disorders. In D. Cicchetti & D. Cohen (Eds.), *Developmental psychopathology. Vol. 1: Theory and method* (2nd ed., pp. 968–1018). New York: Wiley.

Institute of Medicine. (1989). *Research on children and adolescents with mental behavioral and developmental disorders.* Washington, DC: National Academy Press.

Kaplan, B. (1967). Meditations on genesis. *Human Development, 10,* 65–87.

Kaufman, J., & Charney, D. (2001). Effects of early stress on brain structure and function: Implications for understanding the relationship between child maltreatment and depression. *Development and Psychopathology, 13,* 451–471.

Kaufman, J., Yang, B., Douglas-Palumberi, H., Houshyar, S., Lipschitz, D., Krystal, J., et al. (2004). Social supports and serotonin transporter gene moderate depression in maltreated children. *Proceedings of the National Academy of Sciences of the United States of America, 101*(49), 17316–17321.

Kendler, K. S. (2005). Toward a philosophical structure for psychiatry. *The American Journal of Psychiatry, 162*(3), 433–440.

Kim-Cohen, J., Caspi, A., Taylor, A., Williams, B., Newcombe, R., Craig, I. W., & Moffitt, T. E. (2006). MAOA, maltreatment, and gene–environment interaction predicting children's mental health: new evidence and a meta-analysis. *Molecular Psychiatry 11,* 903–913.

Klorman, R., Cicchetti, D., Thatcher, J. E., & Ison, J. R. (2003). Acoustic startle in maltreated children. *Journal of Abnormal Child Psychology, 31,* 359–370.

Lopez, J. F., Akil, H., & Watson, S. J. (1999). Neural circuits mediating stress. *Biological Psychiatry, 46,* 1461–1471.

Luthar, S. S., Cicchetti, D., & Becker, B. (2000). The construct of resilience: A critical evaluation and guidelines for future work. *Child Development, 71,* 543–562.

Lynch, M., & Cicchetti, D. (1998). An ecological-transactional analysis of children and contexts: The longitudinal interplay among child maltreatment, community violence, and children's symptomatology. *Development and Psychopathology, 10,* 235–257.

Masten, A. S. (2001). Ordinary magic: Resilience processes in development. *American Psychologist, 56*(3), 227–238.

Maughan, A., & Cicchetti, D. (2002). The impact of child maltreatment and interadult violence on children's emotion regulation abilities. *Child Development, 73,* 1525–1542.

McEwen, B. S., & Stellar, E. (1993). Stress and the individual mechanisms leading to disease. *Archives of Internal Medicine, 153,* 2093–2101.

Moffitt, T. E., Caspi, A., & Rutter, M. (2006). Measured gene-environment interactions in psychopathology: Concepts, research strategies, and implications for research, intervention, and public understanding of genetics. *Perspectives on Psychological Science, 1*(1), 5–27.

Nelson, C. A., & Bloom, F. E. (1997). Child development and neuroscience. *Child Development, 68,* 970–987.

Nelson, C. A., Bloom, F. E., Cameron, J. L., Amaral, D., Dahl, R. E., & Pine, D. (2002). An integrative, multidisciplinary approach to the study of brain-behavior relations in the context of typical and atypical development. *Development and Psychopathology, 14,* 499–520.

Nelson, C. A., & Jeste, S. (in press). Neurobiological perspectives on developmental psychopathology. In M. Rutter, D. Bishop, D. Pine, S. Scott, J. Stevenson, E. Taylor, & A. Thapar (Eds.), *Textbook on child and adolescent psychiatry* (5th ed.). London: Blackwell Publishing.

Ornitz, E. M., & Pynoos, R. S. (1989). Startle modulation in children with posttraumatic stress disorder. *American Journal of Psychiatry, 146,* 866–870.

Pellmar, T. C., & Eisenberg, L. (Eds.). (2000). *Bridging disciplines in the brain, behavioral, and clinical sciences.* Washington, DC: National Academy Press.

Pennington, B. F. (2002). *The development of psychopathology: A neuroscience approach.* New York: Guilford.

Plomin, R., & Crabbe, J. (2000). DNA. *Psychological Bulletin, 126*(6), 806–828.

Plomin, R., DeFries, J. C., McClearn, G. E., & McGuffin, P. (2001). *Behavior genetics.* New York: Worth.

Plomin, R., Rende, R., & Rutter, M. (1991). Quantitative genetics and developmental psychopathology. In D. Cicchetti & S. L. Toth (Eds.), *Rochester Symposium on Developmental Psychopathology. Vol. 2: Internalizing and externalizing expressions of dysfunction* (pp. 155–202). Hillsdale, NJ: Lawrence Erlbaum.

Plomin, R., & Rutter, M. (1998). Child development, molecular genetics, and what to do with genes once they are found. *Child Development, 69,* 1223–1242.

Pollak, S. D., Cicchetti, D., Hornung, K., & Reed, A. (2000). Recognizing emotion in faces: Developmental effects of child abuse and neglect. *Developmental Psychology, 36,* 679–688.

Pollak, S. D., Cicchetti, D., & Klorman, R. (1998). Stress, memory, and emotion: Developmental considerations from the study of child maltreatment. *Development and Psychopathology, 10,* 811–828.

Pollak, S. D., Cicchetti, D., Klorman, R., & Brumaghim, J. (1997). Cognitive brain event-related potentials and emotion processing in maltreated children. *Child Development, 68,* 773–787.

Pollak, S. D., Klorman, R., Thatcher, J. E., & Cicchetti, D. (2001). P3b reflects maltreated children's reactions to facial displays of emotion. *Psychophysiology, 38,* 267–274.

Pollak, S. D., & Sinha, P. (2002). Effects of early experience on children's recognition of facial displays of emotion. *Developmental Psychology, 38,* 784–791.

Putnam, F. W., Trickett, P. K., Helmers, K., Dorn, L., & Everett, B. (1991). *Cortisol abnormalities in sexually abused girls.* Paper presented at the 144th annual meeting of the American Psychiatric Association.

Rende, R., & Plomin, R. (1995). Nature, nurture, and the development of psychopathology. In D. Cicchetti & D. Cohen (Eds.), *Developmental psychopathology. Vol. 1: Theory and methods* (pp. 291–314). New York: Wiley.

Rende, R., & Waldman, I. (2006). Behavioral and molecular genetics and developmental psychopathology. In D. Cicchetti & D. Cohen (Eds.), *Developmental psychopathology. Vol. 2: Developmental neuroscience* (2nd ed., pp. 427–464). New York: Wiley.

Repetti, R., Taylor, S., & Seeman, T. (2002). Risky families: Family social environments and the mental and physical health of offspring. *Psychological Bulletin, 128,* 330–366.

Richters, J. E. (1997). The Hubble hypothesis and the developmentalist's dilemma. *Development and Psychopathology, 9,* 193–229.

Rogeness, G. A. (1991). Psychosocial factors and amine systems. *Psychiatry Research, 37*(2), 215–217.

Rogeness, G. A., & McClure, E. B. (1996). Development and neurotransmitter-environmental interactions. *Development and Psychopathology, 8*(1), 183–199.

Rutter, M. J. (2006). *Genes and behaviour: Nature-nurture interplay.* London: Blackwell Publishing.

Rutter, M., & Sroufe, L. A. (2000). Developmental psychopathology: Concepts and challenges. *Development and Psychopathology, 12,* 265–296.

Sameroff, A. J., & Chandler, M. J. (1975). Reproductive risk and the continuum of caretaking casualty. In F. D. Horowitz (Ed.), *Review of child development research. Vol. 4.* (pp. 187–244). Chicago: University of Chicago Press.

Sapolsky, R. M. (1992). *Stress, the aging brain, and the mechanisms of neuron death.* Cambridge, MA: MIT Press.

Sapolsky, R. M. (1996). Stress, glucocorticoids, and damage to the NS: The current state of confusion. *Stress, 1*, 1–19.

Scarr, S., & McCartney, K. (1983). How people make their own environments: A theory of genotype–environment effects. *Child Development, 54*, 424–435.

Sroufe, L. A. (1997). Psychopathology as an outcome of development. *Development and Psychopathology, 9*, 251–268.

Sroufe, L. A. (1989). Pathways to adaptation and maladaptation: Psychopathology as a developmental deviation. In D. Cicchetti (Ed.), *Rochester Symposium on Developmental Psychopathology. Vol. 1: The emergence of a discipline* (pp. 13–40). Hillsdale, NJ: Erlbaum.

Sroufe, L. A., Egeland, B., & Kreutzer, T. (1990). The fate of early experience following developmental change: Longitudinal approaches to individual adaptation in childhood. *Child Development, 61*, 1363–1373.

Sroufe, L. A., & Rutter, M. (1984). The domain of developmental psychopathology. *Child Development, 55*, 17–29.

Suomi, S. (2000). Parents, peers, and the process of socialization in primates. In J. Borkowski, S. Ramey, & M. Bristol-Power (Eds.), *Parenting and your child's world* (pp. 265–279). Hillsdale, NJ: Erlbaum.

Teicher, M. H., Dumont, N., Ito, Y., Vaituzis, A. C., Giedd, J., & Andersen, S. (2004). Childhood neglect is associated with reduced corpus callosum area. *Biological Psychiatry, 56*, 80–85.

Teisl, M., & Cicchetti, D. (in press). Physical abuse, cognitive and emotional processes, and aggressive/disruptive behavior problems. *Social Development.*

Watson, C., & Gametchu, B. (1999). Membrane-initiated steroid actions and the proteins that mediate them. *Proceedings of the Society for Experimental Biology and Medicine, 220*, 9–19.

Zigler, E., & Glick, M. (1986). *A developmental approach to adult psychopathology.* New York: Wiley.

CHAPTER 3

Genetic and Environmental Influences on Behavior

THEODORE P. BEAUCHAINE, STEPHEN P. HINSHAW,
AND LISA GATZKE-KOPP

HISTORICAL CONTEXT

Theories regarding the causes of abnormal behavior span the entirety of written history. In the Second Century A.D., for example, Galen—extending the writings of Hippocrates—attributed temperamental characteristics to individual differences in four bodily humors. According to his account of human behavior, melancholia—or depression—resulted from an excess of black bile, whereas emotional volatility resulted from an excess of yellow bile. Although Galen's theory placed the locus of mental illness within the individual, other historically influential accounts of psychopathology emphasized the role of environment in shaping behavior. Perhaps the most prominent of these is Freud's psychoanalytic theory, which attributed the causes of mental illness to intrapsychic conflicts among the id, ego, and superego. According to Freud, both the ego and superego derived their relative strength or weakness almost exclusively from early experience.

Although extracted from very different historical epochs, these examples reflect a clear difference in beliefs about the importance of nature versus nurture in the development of mental illness. Until the Twentieth Cen-

*Preparation of this chapter was supported by grants MH63699 and MH067192 from the National Institute of Mental Health.

tury, such differences in opinion were irresolvable because formal scientific methods had not been applied to the study of psychopathology and because appropriate technological and methodological tools had not been developed to effectively parse the relative contributions of heritable and environmental influences on individual differences in behavior. Toward the end of the century, however, advances in molecular genetics, along with refinements in both behavioral genetics and statistical modeling, provided the means for resolving long-standing questions about the etiological substrates of psychopathology (see, e.g., Rende & Waldman, 2006). Yet despite these breakthroughs, disagreements over the relative contributions of genes and environment in explaining psychopathology lingered (Albee & Joffe, 2004; Beauchaine et al., in press; Joffe, 2004). Indeed, preferred explanations for individual differences in behavior have waxed and waned between genes and environment several times during the past 50 years, often influenced as much by political considerations as by scientific innovation (see Rutter, Moffitt, & Caspi, 2006).

In the past decade, a more balanced perspective has emerged. Theoretical advances, the capacity to conduct genome-wide scans, and more widespread use of advanced statistical methods have revealed that both genetic and environmental influences play significant roles in the expression of all behavioral traits—including those linked to psychopathology—and that the nature-versus-nurture question is misleading because it forces us to choose between influences that are mutually important. In fact, although genetic and environmental influences have often been treated as separate by researchers, a growing body of research indicates that each affects the other, oftentimes interdependently (Moffitt, Caspi, & Rutter, 2006; Rutter, 2002, 2007). It has long been known, for example, that impulsivity is a highly heritable trait (e.g., Cadoret, Leve, & Devor, 1997; Hinshaw, 2002, 2003; see also Beauchaine & Neuhaus, this volume, Chapter 5), conferring risk for a host of behavioral disorders including delinquency, antisocial behavior, and both alcohol and substance dependencies (Krueger et al., 2002). However, recent research demonstrates that impulsive boys are especially likely to develop these conditions in neighborhoods with high rates of drug use, violence, and criminality (Lynam et al., 2000) or when maltreated by caretakers (Jaffee et al., 2005). Furthermore, at-risk individuals may evoke reactions from others that exacerbate inherited liabilities (e.g., O'Connor, Deater-Deckard, et al., 1998). Thus, the combination of both genetically mediated vulnerability and environmental risk results in worse outcomes than either factor alone. When vulnerability and risk interact in such a way, studying either in isolation causes us to underestimate their combined importance (Beauchaine et al., in press).

Our primary objective in writing this chapter is to provide an integrated account of the interplay of biological and environmental influences on psychopathology across the lifespan. We focus on broad conceptual issues; findings specific to particular forms of psychopathology can be found in later chapters. Our approach is influenced heavily by the seminal work of Rutter and others who have written extensively about the mutual interplay of genes and environment in shaping human development and behavior (see, e.g., Rutter, 2002, 2007; Rutter, Moffitt, & Caspi, 2006).

THE DEVELOPMENTAL PSYCHOPATHOLOGY PERSPECTIVE

As outlined in the two previous chapters, the contents of this book are organized around the *developmental psychopathology* perspective, an approach to the study of mental illness that has emerged primarily in the last 25 years. This framework is advantageous for studying the emergence of behavior disorders because it integrates the strengths of numerous other disciplines, including psychiatric genetics, child clinical psychology, child psychiatry, developmental psychology, epidemiology, and clinical neuroscience, among others. Developmental psychopathologists seek to characterize the course of mental illness as precisely as possible and at as many levels of analysis as possible. Levels of analysis refer to different systems through which a psychopathological trait is expressed, spanning genes to behavior to broad cultural factors (see Cicchetti, this volume, Chapter 2).

The advantage of a multiple-levels-of-analysis approach to understanding psychopathology is exemplified in research on Schizophrenia, an oftentimes progressively degenerative disorder in which afflicted individuals experience delusions, exhibit odd behaviors, and typically become isolated and avolitional (see Asarnow & Kernan, this volume, Chapter 20). Although Schizophrenia is transmitted through a number of genes (see Gottesman & Gould, 2003), the exact number of high-risk alleles (or their combinations) required for behavioral expression of the disorder remains to be determined. Yet identifying all such genes will not result in a full understanding of the disorder, because genes do not affect behavior directly (see Rutter, Moffitt, & Caspi, 2006). Rather, they code for variations in protein expression that lead to structural and functional variations in the central nervous system and the rest of the body. In the case of Schizophrenia, genetic liability is marked within the central and peripheral nervous systems by neuromotor abnormalities, eye tracking dysfunction, and abnormal activity in the prefrontal cortex during working memory tasks—whether or not the at-risk individual has developed the disorder (Callicott et al., 2003; Erlenmeyer-Kimling, Golden, & Cornblatt, 1989; Glahn et al., 2003; Lenzenweger, McLachlan, & Rubin, 2007; Ross, 2003).

Despite these clear biological substrates, environmental influences have profound effects on the expression of Schizophrenia. In fact, protective familial environments can improve the course of the disorder and in some cases prevent the onset of illness (e.g., Asarnow & Kernan, this volume, Chapter 20; Cornblatt, 2001; Cornblatt et al., 1999). This example illustrates the importance of incorporating information from genetic, neurological, behavioral, and environmental levels of analysis toward understanding the complexity of debilitating conditions such as Schizophrenia. Specifying the determinants of psychopathology across all relevant levels of analysis and understanding the interactions and transactions across such levels are therefore primary objectives of developmental psychopathology research (see Cicchetti, this volume, Chapter 2).

TERMINOLOGICAL AND CONCEPTUAL ISSUES

GENOTYPES, PHENOTYPES, AND ENDOPHENOTYPES

Our main goals in writing this chapter are to describe the interactive roles of biology and environment in shaping behavior, including psychopathology, and to present important principles for interpreting more specific findings presented in later chapters. Toward addressing these objectives, we first consider important distinctions between *genotypes, phenotypes*, and *endophenotypes*, important constructs in genetics research. Although our descriptions are necessarily brief, they provide a foundation for understanding the remainder of the contents of this volume.

Genotype.   As most readers are undoubtedly aware, the word *genotype* refers to the genetic make-up of an individual, either at a particular genetic locus or across the entire genome. Genetic information is contained in one's DNA, which guides the synthesis of messenger RNA through a process called *transcription*. In turn, messenger RNA guides the production of polypeptides through a process called *translation*. These polypeptides are the building blocks of proteins, or *gene products*. Through transcription, translation, and a number of other complex *gene-regulation* processes, variations in gene expression affect both the structure and function of the brain and all body systems. Among other important influences, genetic polymorphisms (i.e., variants in specific alleles of genes) give rise to individual differences in the synthesis, reuptake, and catalysis of neurotransmitters subserving mood, self-regulation, and motivation.

In the traditional view, all genetic variation was assumed to be fully inherited and fixed across the lifespan. It was also believed that heritable genetic variation encoded psychiatric disorders directly, through either single or multiple loci—assumptions referred to as *monogenic* and *polygenic determinism*, respectively. These assumptions imply (at least for serious mental disorders) that particular genes or patterns of genes always result in psychopathology, regardless of environmental input (see Rutter, Moffitt, & Caspi, 2006). However, it is now recognized that a number of intervening influences—many of which fall under environmental control—affect gene transcription, translation, and promotion, thereby altering gene expression. Although we discuss some of these intervening influences in later sections, for now it is sufficient to state that (a) both genes and environment are implicated in the expression of almost all forms of psychopathology, (b) there are no genes "for" particular behaviors or disorders, (c) environments can alter gene expression, and (d) many people who are genetically vulnerable never develop mental illness (see Kendler, 2005; Plomin, 1989).

Phenotype.   The word *phenotype* refers to observable characteristics—both physical and behavioral—that result from the interplay between an organism's genes and the environment. The phenotype concept stems from early work in Mendelian genetics, where the physical characteristics of an organism are reliable, outwardly measurable indications of the underlying genotype. In Mendel's experiments on flower color and pea pod shape, phenotypes were dictated almost exclusively by inherited pairs of dominant and recessive genes, with very limited environmental influence except in cases of severe deprivation (Hartl & Jones, 2002). In contrast, assumedly polygenic traits such as most forms of psychopathology are influenced by many genes, so the correspondence between genotype (at the level of a specific genetic locus) and phenotype is far from 1:1. Furthermore, with multiple genetic influences, there are many opportunities for both gene-gene interactions and environmental regulation of gene expression. As a result, there is limited correspondence between genotypes and phenotypes, which presents formidable obstacles for psychiatric genetics, a topic to which we return in later sections.

Endophenotype.   As defined by Gottesman and Gould (2003), endophenotypes are "measurable components unseen by the unaided eye along the pathway between disease and distal genotype" (p. 636). In other words, endophenotypes are biological and behavioral manifestations of genetic vulnerability that require careful measurement to be detected. Because such markers fall along the causal chain between genotype and pheno-

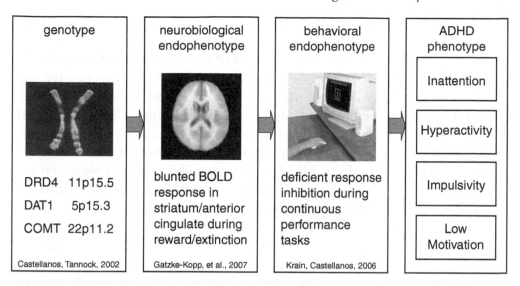

Figure 3.1. Relations among putative genotypes, endophenotypes, and phenotypes for ADHD. Note that endophenotypes can be identified at many levels of analysis, including neurobiological and behavioral, and that many additional genetic, endo-phenotypic, and phenotypic indicators of ADHD have been specified that are not depicted here. DRD4 = dopamine type 4 receptor gene; DAT = dopamine transporter gene; COMT = catechol-o-methyl-transferase gene; BOLD = blood oxygen level dependent (a means of inferring brain activation in functional magnetic resonance imaging [fMRI] research). Adapted from Beauchaine & Marsh (2006).

type, they lie closer to the genetic substrates of psychiatric illness than readily observable behaviors (see Coan & Allen, this volume, Chapter 9; Gould & Gottesman, 2006; Lenzenweger, 2004). This closer proximity to genes makes carefully chosen endophenotypes quite valuable to psychiatric geneticists in their attempts to identify specific alleles associated with psychopathology (see e.g., Beauchaine & Marsh, 2006; Castellanos & Tannock, 2002; Skuse, 2001). Figure 3.1 depicts two levels of endophenotype along the causal chain between the genetic substrates of impulsivity and the expression of Attention-Deficit/Hyperactivity Disorder (ADHD). On the far left are candidate genes associated with impulsivity. These genes are expressed at multiple endophenotypic levels, including neurobiological and behavioral. At the neurobiological level, impulsive individuals exhibit abnormal brain responses in the striatum and anterior cingulate cortex during conditions of reward and extinction, respectively (Durston et al., 2003; Gatzke-Kopp et al., 2007). These neural differences are likely to give rise to difficulties in inhibiting prepotent behaviors during response-inhibition tasks—a behavioral endophenotype (see Krain & Catellanos, 2006). On the far right are some of the readily observable symptoms (phenotypes) of ADHD.

PSYCHIATRIC GENETICS

Broadly speaking, there are two objectives of psychiatric genetics research. The first is to parse variability in behavioral traits (e.g., impulsivity, aggression, anxiety) into portions accounted for by (a) heritable mechanisms, (b) environmental mechanisms, and sometimes (c) gene × environment interactions. This is accomplished through *behavioral genetics* research. The second objective is to identify specific genetic alleles that confer vulnerability for psychopathology, which is accomplished though *molecular genetics* research. We describe these different approaches in the following pages, beginning with behavioral genetics.

BEHAVIORAL GENETICS

Traditionally, behavioral genetics studies have been used to divide sources of variance in behavior into three broad classes, including *additive genetic effects*, *shared environmental effects*, and *nonshared environmental effects*. Additive genetic effects encompass all sources of variance in a behavioral trait that are accounted for by heritable mechanisms within a population. Although potentially confusing, these *genetic effects* can arise from both genetic and nongenetic (although heritable) sources. For example, some genes are activated ("turned on") among offspring only when their mothers are exposed to particular environments, oftentimes prenatally (see Rutter, Moffitt, & Caspi, 2006). Such *maternal programming* effects may increase risk for or protect against the emergence of psychopathology through mechanisms to be described. These effects are not purely genetic, yet they are subsumed within the additive genetic component in behavioral genetics studies. Accordingly, to avoid confusion in this chapter we refer to *heritable effects* on behavior when the source of heritability cannot be unambiguously attributed to genes, reserving the term *genetic* for effects that are clearly attributable to genes.

After heritable effects are accounted for, the remaining variance in behavior is partitioned into shared environmental effects—which are attributable to common experiences of individuals (usually twins) who are reared together—and nonshared environmental effects, which are attributable to unique environmental experiences of individuals (again, usually twins) who are reared apart.[1] In the shorthand of behavioral genetics, heritable effects are denoted *A*, shared environmental effects are denoted

---

1. Thorough descriptions of genetically informative research designs are beyond the scope of this chapter. Interested readers are referred to Rende and Waldman (2006) for a more comprehensive account of behavioral and molecular genetics in developmental psychopathology research.

C, and nonshared environmental effects are denoted *E*. When squared, each term signifies a percentage of variance accounted for. In theory, these sources sum to 1.0, accounting for all variance in behavior ($A^2 + C^2 + E^2 = 1.0$). For example, averaged across many behavioral genetics studies, with participants ranging in age from early childhood through adulthood (Cadoret et al., 1997), heritable effects account for 44% of the variance in aggression (A^2; also denoted h^2), shared environmental effects account for 17% of the variance (C^2), and nonshared environmental effects account for 38% of the variance (E^2). Within rounding error, these sources add to 1.0, and indicate that both heredity and environment make important contributions to the expression of aggression and violence.

Several caveats should be considered in any discussion of the behavioral genetics of psychopathology. First, behavioral genetics studies demonstrate that heritability coefficients increase across the lifespan for almost all forms of psychopathology that have been assessed at different points in development. For example, twin studies indicate small heritability coefficients for symptoms of depression in childhood (Lemery & Doelger, 2005; Rice, Harold, & Thapar, 2002), yet larger heritability coefficients during adolescence (Scourfield et al., 2003). By adulthood, most studies yield substantial heritability coefficients for major depression, with nonsignificant environmental effects (Sullivan, Neale, & Kendler, 2000).

Similarly, heritability coefficients for antisocial behavior among males and eating disorders among females show increases across the lifespan (Hicks et al., 2007; Klump, McGue, & Iacono, 2000; Lyons et al., 1995). Moreover, although environmental characteristics affect the initiation of smoking and drinking, both smoking maintenance and heavy drinking patterns are accounted for almost entirely by heritable effects (e.g., Boomsma et al., 1994; Koopsman et al., 1999; Koopsman, van Doornen, & Boomsma, 1997; McGue et al., 2001; Viken et al., 1999).

Psychopathology researchers have offered a number of potential explanations for these increasing heritability coefficients. These include suggestions that the nature of psychopathology may be different among children than among adults (e.g., Klein et al., this volume, Chapter 16), that different genetic factors operate in childhood versus adolescence (Jacobson, Prescott, & Kendler, 2000), and that differences in heritability may indicate diverse equifinal pathways to psychopathology (e.g., Silberg, Rutter, & Eaves, 2001; Silberg, Rutter, Neale, & Eaves, 2001).

Although these mechanisms may well be operative, important artifactual influences should also be considered. For example, as we have noted elsewhere (Beauchaine et al., in press), developmental increases in heritability are a mathematical necessity in twin and adoption studies whenever there are individual differences in age of onset, even when the underlying causes of psychiatric disturbance are very similar across members of a population. This situation is illustrated in Figure 3.2, which depicts 10 hypothetical monozygotic twin pairs, all of whom are at high genetic risk for psychiatric disturbance. Even when reared in very similar environments, phenotypic variation among twins is observed due to stochastic (chance or random) effects (Wong, Gottesman, & Petronis, 2005). As a result, concordance rates must rise across development.

In addition, heritable vulnerabilities and environmental risk factors sometimes interact to affect both age of onset and severity of psychopathology. For example, in many cases genetic liability is insufficient to result in Schizophrenia. Rather, vulnerability is translated into illness only when coupled with significant environmental risk (Gottesman & Gould, 2003). When heritable vulnerabilities (G) and environmental risk factors (E) mutually influence the course of psychopathology, a heritability × environment (G × E) interaction is observed (see the following). Importantly, G × E interactions cannot be disentangled from pure heritability effects in behavioral genetics studies *unless* the specific environmental variable that interacts with heritability is measured. In most behavioral genetics studies, effects of environment are inferred, not measured. Under such conditions, G × E interactions are subsumed within the heritability (G) coefficient (see, e.g., Rutter, 2007). Thus, developmental increases in the heritability of psychopathology in part reflect the cumulative effects of unmeasured G × E interactions.

In recent years, increasingly sophisticated efforts to specify G × E interactions have appeared in the literature. These studies, some of which are described in the following pages, suggest that G × E interactions are much more common that previously thought (e.g., Caspi et al., 2002, 2003; Seeger et al., 2004). Consequently, behavioral genetics studies in which specific environmental influences are not measured may well overestimate the main effects of heritability on emerging psychopathology—an effect that magnifies across development as environmental insults accumulate. The likely end result may be a literature-wide overestimation of the main effects of genes in the pathogenesis of psychopathology.

In addition, behavioral genetics studies are almost always conducted with large samples recruited through twin registries. Ideally, these samples are representative of the population from which they are drawn. As a result, behavioral genetics analyses parse mostly *normal variation* in individual differences. This variation is analyzed by building structural models to evaluate linear associations between heritable influences and behavior, and between environmental influences and behavior. However, linear associations do not always represent processes that operate at the extremes of a distribution—the very region where psychopathology is represented (Beauchaine, 2003). According to most definitions, psychopathology is limited to the upper (or lower) extremes of a distribution, usually

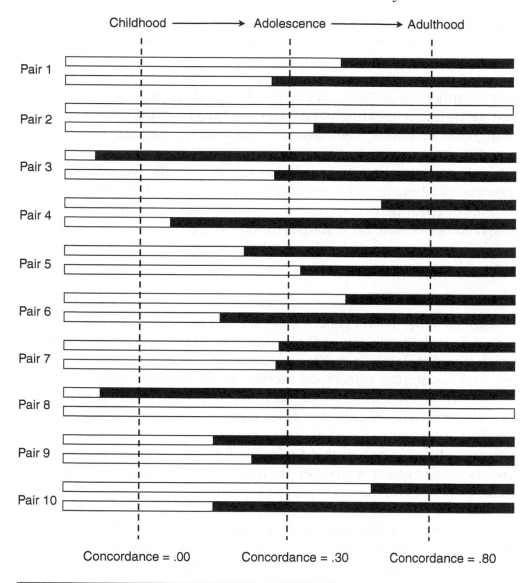

Figure 3.2. Hypothetical distribution of age of onset (solid bars) for psychiatric disturbance across 10 monozygotic twin pairs, all of whom are at high genetic risk. Concordance rates are determined from the proportion of twin pairs who are both afflicted. Because of differences in age of onset, concordance rates necessarily increase in adulthood. Although dichotomous outcomes are used here, the same argument applies to continuously assessed traits. Adapted from Beauchaine et al. (in press).

defined as behavior surpassing the 95th or 98th percentiles (or below the 2nd or 5th percentiles). Mechanisms of behavior can be quite different at the extremes of a distribution than in the middle of the distribution. Thus, gene-behavior and environment-behavior relations among those with psychopathology can be swamped in behavioral genetics analyses by normative variation in individual differences, thereby going undetected. Although this limitation is not specific to behavioral genetics, it has received very little attention in the literature.

Finally, behavioral genetics studies are nonspecific, providing broad information about heritable versus environmental risk but yielding no information about particular genes that contribute to the phenotype being analyzed. As a result, these studies cannot be used to identify disease processes or mechanisms of psychiatric disturbance.

Molecular Genetics

In contrast to behavioral genetics, molecular genetics studies identify specific gene polymorphisms that underlie phenotypic variation. There are two types of molecular genetics approaches: linkage and association studies. Linkage studies scan broad sections of the genome, requiring large samples of families with two or more children affected by psychopathology. Genetic data are collected from family members, and searches are conducted for genetic *markers* with known chromosomal locations. For example, the gene responsible for cystic fibrosis was found by "linking" the disease to a genetic variant on the long arm of chromosome 7 within affected families. This discovery was followed by several subsequent linkage analyses that identified the specific location (see Bolsover et al., 1997).

In child psychopathology research, linkage analyses have been applied to families of sibling pairs with autism to identify susceptibility loci for the disorder. These studies specify chromosomes 7 and 9 as likely locations of autism susceptibility genes, with additional markers on chromosomes 4 and 11 for females and males, respectively (Schellenberg et al., 2006). Specification of multiple susceptibility loci indicates that autism is a polygenic disorder. Although these studies provide important insights into the pathogenesis of autism, specific genes or combinations of genes that are necessary for developing the disorder have yet to be identified conclusively. Nevertheless, information obtained from linkage studies can narrow the list of candidate genes considerably. Linkage studies have also been used to identify several susceptibility loci for externalizing behavior disorders (see, e.g., Jain et al., 2007).

In contrast to linkage studies, association studies begin with a specific candidate gene that is suspected of conferring risk for a psychiatric disorder. Allelic frequencies of this gene are then compared among those with and without the disorder. Association studies can detect gene effects that account for far less variance in behavior than linkage studies can detect. However, well-articulated theories are required to identify candidate genes for analysis. As described in Chapter 5, for example, specific neural theories of impulsivity implicate the mesolimbic and mesocortical dopamine (DA) systems (Beauchaine & Neuhaus, this volume). Given that impulsivity is a highly heritable trait that confers risk for almost all externalizing disorders (Krueger et al., 2002), genes involved in the synthesis, turnover, and break down of DA should be associated with at least some of these conditions. Consistent with this supposition, association studies have identified several candidate alleles involved in DA neurotransmission, including variations in the DRD4 gene (chromosome 11p15.5) and the DAT1 gene (chromosome 5p15.3), among others (Benjamin et al., 1996; Castellanos & Tannock, 2002; Galili-Weisstub & Segman, 2003).

Even though molecular genetics studies are far more specific than behavioral genetics studies, they are not without limitations. Perhaps the biggest of these is the small amount of variance in behavior that most candidate genes account for. For example, although behavioral genetics studies routinely yield heritability coefficients that explain 80% or more of the variance in impulsivity (e.g., Levy et al., 1997; Price et al., 2001; Sherman, Iacono, & McGue, 1997), specific genes identified in molecular genetics studies account for an almost negligible fraction of this effect. Furthermore, nonreplications across studies are common. In part, this nonreplication is due to the assumedly polygenic nature of most psychiatric disorders, including ADHD (Swanson & Castellanos, 2002). Nevertheless, considerable work remains toward mapping the genetic substrates of almost all behavioral traits that confer vulnerability to psychopathology (see also Kagan, this volume, Chapter 6).

HETEROGENEITY OF PHENOTYPES

A formidable obstacle to identifying the genetic substrates of psychopathology is heterogeneous phenotypes, which derive from at least two sources (see Rende & Waldman, 2006; Skuse, 2001). First, criteria used for symptom assessment and participant selection often differ across studies. For example, different research laboratories studying the genetics of antisocial behavior sometimes define the construct differently. Some prefer more broad definitions that include both aggressive and nonaggressive antisocial activities, whereas others confine their definitions to overtly aggressive and violent offenses. In general, narrower definitions yield higher heritability coefficients in behavioral genetics studies and more replicable candidate alleles in molecular genetics studies (e.g., Eley, Lichtenstein, & Moffitt, 2003; Waldman et al., 1998). Presumably, this finding stems from the fact that narrow phenotypes identify individuals with more similar genetic vulnerabilities.

Second, two individuals can meet the same or very similar symptom criteria despite traversing quite different pathways to psychopathology, a phenomenon known as *equifinality* (Beauchaine & Marsh, 2006). For example, some cases of depression are influenced more by biological vulnerability and less by environmental risk, whereas others are influenced less by biological vulnerability and more by environmental risk (Beauchaine, 2003; Cicchetti, & Rogosch, 2002; Harrington, Rutter, & Fombonne, 1996). Yet different combinations of liability and risk can give rise to very similar behavioral syndromes. Evidence suggests that melancholia—a severe form of depression with a particularly insidious course—is more heritable and results from different genetic vulnerabilities than other forms of mood disorder (Eaves et al., 2005; Willeit et al., 2003). Melancholia also emerges as a discrete subtype of depression in taxometric analyses (Ambrosini et al., 2002; Beach & Amir, 2003), is associated with especially high risk of suicide (e.g., Carroll, Greden, & Feinberg, 1980), and confers greater risk for intergenerational transmission of both internalizing and externalizing disorders than other subtypes of depression (Shannon et al., 2007).

Despite these indications that melancholia is distinct from other mood disorders, until quite recently most genetic studies of depression—both behavioral and molecular—lumped all participants who met DSM-IV criteria for major depression into a single group for analysis, with no effort to stratify by subtype. One consequence of admixing participants with different etiologies is to water down and obscure genetic linkages to and associations with specific depression subtypes—resulting in small effect sizes and results that are difficult to replicate (see Castellanos & Tannock, 2002; Skuse, 2001). This pattern has led several psychiatric geneticists to advocate for the use of carefully chosen endophenotypes to differentiate between subgroups with distinct heritable vulnerabilities. In the case of melancholia, abnormal hypothalamic-pituitary-adrenal axis reactivity has emerged as a promising endophenotype (see, e.g., Coryell & Schlesser, 2001). This example illustrates why tightened definitions of psychopathology may be required in order to specify genetic vulnerabilities more precisely.

GENE–ENVIRONMENT INTERDEPENDENCE

Gene–environment interdependence occurs when heritable and environmental influences either correlate or interact with one another to explain more variance in behavior than their combined main effects (Rutter, 2007). There are several forms of gene–environment interdependence, each of which is outlined briefly in the following. More comprehensive accounts can be found in Moffitt et al. (2006), Rutter (2002, 2006, 2007), and Rutter, Moffitt, and Caspi (2006).

GENE × ENVIRONMENT INTERACTION

As mentioned previously, gene × environment interactions (G × E) refer to situations in which environments moderate the effects of genes on behavior, or in which genes moderate the effects of environments on behavior.[2] For example, Caspi et al. (2003) demonstrated that polymorphisms in the promoter region of the serotonin transporter gene (5-HTTLPR) moderate the effects of stressful life events—including maltreatment between ages 3 and 11—on adult depression. Individuals with two copies of the short allele (s/s homozygous) are more likely to experience adult depression following child adversity than individuals with two copies of the long allele (l/l homozygous). Those who are heterozygous (s/l) are at intermediate risk. Similar findings for the 5-HTTLPR gene have since been reported by others (Eley et al., 2004; Kaufman et al., 2004; see also Klein et al., this volume). Polymorphisms in the 5-HTTLPR gene (s/s) also moderate the effects of stressful life events on the development of drinking and drug use (Covault et al., 2007).

Importantly, although the main effect of maltreatment in predicting depression in the Caspi et al. (2003) study was significant, the main effect of 5-HTTLPR variation was not. Thus, had the gene–environment interaction not been assessed, variation in the 5-HTTLPR allele would have appeared to be unrelated to adult depression. This example argues strongly for assessing biology–environment interactions in psychopathology research, and illustrates how failure to asses interaction effects can lead to incorrect inferences about the importance of heritability (or of environmental influences) in the expression of psychopathology (see Beauchaine et al.,

---

2. Deciding whether genes moderate the effects of environment on behavior or whether environments moderate the effects of genes on behavior is dictated largely by theoretical considerations. For example, Caspi et al. (2002) demonstrated that children who are maltreated become violent later in life only if they carry a specific variable number tandem repeat (VNTR) in the promoter region of the monoamine oxidase A (MAOA) gene. One could conceptualize this as a case of genetic variation moderating the effect of maltreatment, or as a case of maltreatment moderating the effect of genetic variation. From an analytic standpoint, the decision is arbitrary because the mathematics are identical across models. Either way, the effect of one variable differs as a function of the other—the statistical definition of interaction. In the present example, our preference is to consider genetic variation the predictor and environment the moderator because genetic variation precedes maltreatment.

in press; Crowell et al., in press; Rutter, 2007). Of note, heritable traits can also be moderated by less pernicious environmental influences, including social contexts, religious experiences, marriage, and neighborhood risk, among other factors (Rutter, Moffit, & Caspi, 2006).

GENE–ENVIRONMENT CORRELATION

Gene–environment correlation (rGE) refers to situations in which (a) heritable traits of parents affect their child's exposure to adverse (or beneficial) environments, or (b) heritable traits of children affect their own exposure to various environments. Such correlations come in three forms, including *passive, active,* and *evocative* (Plomin, DeFries, & Loehlin, 1977).

Passive rGE. Passive rGEs occur when genetic factors that are common to both a parent and a child influence parenting behaviors. This can be associated with either positive or negative outcomes. For example, intelligent parents may purchase more books to read to their children than do parents of lower intelligence. In this case, a genetic advantage is correlated with environmental opportunity. Parents can also confer both genetic vulnerability to their offspring and provide risky rearing environments. For instance, twin studies indicate that genes play a significant role in the intergenerational transmission of depression from mothers to children (e.g., Rice, Harold, & Thapar, 2005), yet overwhelming evidence also demonstrates that maternal depression adversely affects parenting (Lovejoy et al., 2000; Rutter, 1990).

Although it is tempting to infer a passive rGE as the mechanism of intergenerational transmission of depression, rGEs cannot be disentangled from shared environmental effects in ordinary behavioral genetics designs (for a discussion of the difference between rGEs and shared environmental effects, see Rutter, Moffit, and Caspi, 2006). Rather, sophisticated analyses of data collected from twin pairs of *parents* are required. No such studies have been conducted to demonstrate a passive rGE for maternal depression. However, Neiderhiser et al. (2004) used a twin parent design to identify a passive rGE for positive but not negative aspects of maternal parenting behavior in a normative sample. Because these are the only conclusive data that demonstrate a passive rGE for parenting behavior, further research is needed to determine the importance of rGEs as a mechanism of intergenerational transmission of psychopathology.

Active rGE. Active rGEs occur when a child's heritable vulnerabilities influence his or her selection of environments. For example, a primary neural substrate of inherited impulsivity is deficient mesolimbic DA activity (see Gatzke-Kopp & Beauchaine, 2007; Sagvolden et al., 2005). This DA dysregulation predisposes to sensation-seeking behaviors, including early initiation and sustained use of substances, association with delinquent peers, and other high-risk activities (see Brown, this volume, Chapter 14). Thus, genetically vulnerable children and adolescents seek out risky environments and experiences. Importantly, some of these high-risk activities, particularly exposure to alcohol and strong stimulants, (a) amplify existing functional deficiencies in mesolimbic structures and (b) confer additional functional deficiencies in later developing mesocortical structures (e.g., Beauchaine et al., in press; Catlow & Kirstein, 2007). In this manner, active *r*GEs associated with externalizing behaviors can feed back to exacerbate pre-existing heritable compromises in motivation and self-control. Similar active *r*GEs have been described for other traits such as anxiety (Fox, Hane, & Pine, 2007).

Evocative rGE. Evocative *r*GEs occur when genetically influenced behaviors elicit reactions from others that interact with and exacerbate existing vulnerabilities. One behavioral trait that can evoke environmental risk is impulsivity. Impulsive children present with challenging behaviors that elicit and reinforce ineffective parenting, which in turn amplifies risk for progression of ADHD to more serious externalizing behaviors (Patterson, DeBaryshe, & Ramsey, 1989; Patterson, DeGarmo, & Knutson, 2000). O'Connor, Deater-Deckard, et al. (1998) reported an evocative *r*GE in a sample of children at high genetic risk for externalizing behaviors who were adopted at birth. Despite being raised by adoptive parents, these children received more negative, coercive parenting than those in a matched control group. Because the adoptive parent's behaviors could not be explained by shared genetic risk with the child, these data provide strong evidence for an evocative *r*GE. In the study of the parenting behaviors of twin mothers described previously, Neiderhiser et al. (2004) reported a similar evocative effect.

Of note, the same inherited deficiencies described previously in neural systems of self-control predispose children and adolescents to externalizing behaviors, which evoke negative responses from others. These negative responses can then, in turn, amplify the externalizing behaviors that elicited them. Over time, evoked cycles of negativity may affect developing neural systems through mechanisms of neural plasticity, with potential long-term consequences for adjustment (see Beauchaine et al., in press; Pollak, 2005). In this manner, evocative *r*GEs may amplify and solidify behavior patterns that were once malleable (see also Fishbein, 2000).

EPIGENETIC EFFECTS

Although underappreciated until quite recently, accumulating evidence suggests that a range of both endogenous and exogenous influences—including trauma and adverse rearing conditions faced early in life—can alter gene expression, with later consequences for brain development and behavior. The term *epigenesis* refers to changes in gene expression that result from alterations in DNA structure (as opposed to sequence) (Hartl & Jones, 2002). These genetic changes are mediated primarily by environmentally triggered methylation processes. For example, Weaver et al. (2004) reported epigenetically induced genetic variation in hippocampal glucocorticoid receptors among rat pups that experienced high levels of maternal caretaking behaviors, including licking, grooming, and arched-back nursing, compared with pups experiencing low levels of these behaviors. This epigenetic effect transmits adaptive variations in stress responding to offspring (see Meany, 2007). Rat pups reared in high-risk environments where such maternal caretaking behaviors are altered have more reactive hypothalamic-pituitary-adrenocortical responses, and are consequently more fearful, leaving them better prepared for the high-risk environment they are likely to face as they mature.[3]

Although epigenetic changes in gene expression clearly occur in humans, demonstrating clear-cut effects on behavior is difficult because it requires random assignment of groups to different environments (e.g., impoverished versus enriched; see Rutter, 2007), an ethically indefensible practice. Nevertheless, some recent models of antisocial behavior include epigenetic mechanisms of vulnerability (e.g., Tremblay, 2005). Furthermore, mammals are particularly susceptible to environmentally triggered alterations in gene expression (Hartl & Jones, 2002), and increasingly divergent patterns of DNA methylation emerge over the lifespans of monozygotic twins (Fraga et al., 2005). These findings suggest that epigenetic processes that activate and deactivate genes may be implicated in the development of psychopathology (see Kramer, 2005; Rutter, 2005; Rutter, Moffitt, & Caspi, 2006). For example, brain-derived neurotrophic factor (BDNF), which is involved in the differentiation of DA neurons in developing mesolimbic structures, may be susceptible to paternally mediated epigenetic effects that confer risk for ADHD and other externalizing behaviors (Kent et al., 2005).

---

3. It is important to note that these variations in maternal behavior do not necessarily reflect low levels of care or model adversity or neglect. Low licking and grooming mothers spent just as much time in proximity to and nursing their pups. Nevertheless, the nature of their interactions was different.

GENETICS OF COMORBIDITY

The term *comorbidity* refers to the co-occurrence of more than one assumedly independent psychiatric disorder within an individual. Although many subtypes and causes of comorbidity have been described (see Klein & Riso, 1993), two broad forms are important for this discussion. *Homotypic comorbidity* refers to the co-occurrence of multiple externalizing disorders within an individual or the co-occurrence of multiple internalizing disorders within an individual. For example, externalizing disorders including ADHD, Oppositional Defiant Disorder (ODD), Conduct Disorder (CD), Antisocial Personality Disorder (ASPD), and substance use disorders (SUDs) often co-occur, particularly as development proceeds from childhood through adulthood (Lewinsohn et al., 2004; Nadder et al., 2002). Comorbidity of internalizing disorders, including depression, dysthymia, and the anxiety disorders is also high (Angold & Costello, 1993; Brady & Kendall, 1992; Cloninger, 1990; Donaldson et al., 1997; Ferdinand et al., 2007).

In contrast to homotypic comorbidity, *heterotypic comorbidity* refers to the co-occurrence of at least one externalizing disorder and at least one internalizing disorder within an individual (e.g., CD and depression). This form of comorbidity is more perplexing because many (though not all) symptoms appear to overlap minimally (see Kopp & Beauchaine, 2007). For example, depression includes symptoms of sadness, anhedonia, and feelings of guilt or worthlessness, whereas CD is characterized by sensation seeking, lying, property destruction, and aggression. Yet despite these apparently distinct presentations, rates of comorbidity of CD and depression are much higher than expected by chance (Angold & Costello, 1993; Capaldi, 1991; Essau, 2003).

BEHAVIORAL GENETICS OF COMORBIDITY

Comorbid disorders have often been treated as distinct yet co-occurring conditions with different etiologies (see Beauchaine, 2003; Kopp & Beauchaine, 2007). Yet recent behavioral genetics studies suggest common heritable substrates for both homotypic and heterotypic comorbidity. We describe some of this evidence in the following.

Homotypic comorbidity. Behavioral genetics analyses indicated that most disorders within the externalizing spectrum share a common heritable vulnerability, with similar findings reported for disorders within the internalizing spectrum (Baker et al., 2007; Kendler et al., 2003; Krueger et al., 2002; see also Krueger & Markon, 2006). For example, in a recent behavioral genetics analysis of 1,048 participants in the Minnesota Twin Family Study, about 80% of the variance in disinhibition, conduct problems, antisocial personality, alcohol dependence, and drug dependence was accounted for by a single impulsivity trait (Krueger et al., 2002). Yet each specific category of externalizing behavior was influenced strongly by environmental effects. This pattern of results suggests that trait impulsivity arising primarily from heritable predispositions may manifest as one or more of several symptom clusters depending on the moderating effects of factors such as environment, cognitive ability, and personality predispositions across development (see Beauchaine & Neuhaus, this volume, Chapter 5). Similarly, much of the covariation among internalizing disorders is accounted for by common heritable effects (see Eley, Bolton, et al., 2003; Krueger & Markon, 2006).

Heterotypic comorbidity.   Behavioral genetics studies also suggest common heritability across internalizing and externalizing disorders. For example, O'Connor, McGuire, and colleagues (1998) reported that 45% of the covariation between depressive and antisocial symptoms was accounted for by a common genetic liability among 10- to 18-year-old twins. Similar findings have since been reported by others in both adolescent and adult samples (Burcusa, Iacono, & McGue, 2003; Kendler et al., 2003). Such findings offer an explanation of comorbidity not as diagnostic co-occurrence, but rather as covariation of related syndromes stemming from common latent genetic vulnerabilities.

Molecular Genetics of Comorbidity

Homotypic comorbidity.   Recall that molecular genetics studies benefit from and in some cases require sound theory to guide the search for candidate genes. As noted previously, modern accounts of impulsivity, which confers vulnerability across the externalizing spectrum (Krueger at al., 2002), implicate mesolimbic DA dysfunction (Beauchaine & Neuhaus, this volume, Chapter 5). In fact, aberrant neural responding in the mesolimbic DA system, including the ventral tegmental area and its projections to the nucleus accumbens, the caudate, and the putamen, is a core neural substrate of risk for all or most externalizing behaviors (Gatzke-Kopp & Beauchaine, 2007; Gatzke-Kopp et al., 2007). Furthermore, studies using both positron emission tomography (PET) and functional magnetic resonance imaging (fMRI) indicate that inadequately low levels of neural activity in the DA-mediated primary reward centers of the brain predispose to sensation-seeking, irritability, negative affectivity, and low motivation—core symptoms of externalizing psychopathology (Gatzke-Kopp & Beauchaine, 2007; Durston, 2003; Laakso et al., 2003; Leyton et al., 2002; Scheres et al., 2007; Vaidya et al., 1998).

As described previously, these findings suggest that genes involved in the synthesis, catalysis, and reuptake of DA should be candidates in molecular genetics studies of externalizing behavior patterns. In Chapter 5 we summarize studies implicating numerous genes involved in DA neurotransmission (e.g., DAT1, DrD4, dopamine-β-hydroxylase, monamine oxydase, catechol-o-methyl transferase) in the expression of impulsivity and related externalizing psychopathology (Beauchaine & Neuhaus, this volume). Thus, central DA dysfunction may account for much of the shared vulnerability for externalizing disorders. In contrast, vulnerability for internalizing disorders is conferred largely through trait anxiety, which has been linked closely with serotonin neurotransmission (Gray & McNaughton, 2000; see also Kagan, this volume, Chapter 6).

Heterotypic Comorbidity. Studies of overlapping vulnerabilities for conduct problems and depression provide potential insights into why heterotypic comorbidity is so common. It is important to note that, at symptom level, both disorders are characterized by negative affectivity, irritability, and anhedonia. Neurally, these symptoms are subserved by the same DA deficiencies described previously (and detailed in Chapter 5) for externalizing disorders (Bogdan & Pizzagalli, 2006; Forbes, Shaw, & Dahl, 2007; Keedwell, Andrew, Williams, Brammer, & Phillips, 2005; Nestler & Carlezon, 2006; Shankman, Klein, Tenke, & Bruder, 2007). In fact, neuroimaging studies reveal blunted activation within DA-mediated brain regions during reward tasks among both children and adolescents with conduct problems and among those with depression (Epstein et al., 2006; Forbes et al., 2006; Gatzke-Kopp et al., 2007; Scheres et al., 2007; Vaidya et al., 1998). Thus, both externalizing and internalizing disorders appear to share a common neural deficiency that accounts at least in part for overlap in symptoms. This conclusion is consistent with results outlined previously from behavioral genetics studies indicating a common heritable vulnerability for depression and antisocial behavior (Burcusa et al., 2003; Kendler et al., 2003).

Importantly, deficiencies in DA-mediated reward circuitry are moderated by other biologically influenced traits to affect behavior. One such trait is behavioral inhibition (see Fig. 3.3), which differentiates between those who present principally with CD and those who present principally with depression (Beauchaine & Neuhaus, this volume, Chapter 5). In this model, high trait anxiety potentiates depression among those with blunted reward systems, whereas low trait anxiety potentiates delinquency. Trait anxiety is modulated by an entirely different (primarily serotonergic)

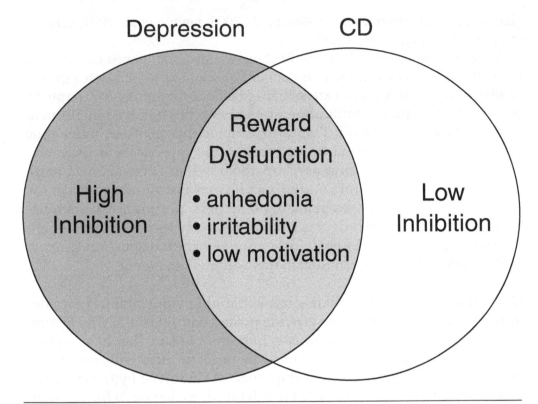

Figure 3.3. Symptom overlap for depression and conduct disorder. Both disorders are characterized by heritable deficiencies in dopaminergically mediated reward dysfunction, leading to common symptoms. However, the disorders are differentiated by heritable individual differences in behavioral inhibition. Adapted from Beauchaine et al., in press.

neural network, often referred to as the *septo-hippocampal system* (Gray & McNaughton, 2000). This example points out that two heritable traits may interact to affect behavioral outcomes (i.e., a trait–trait interaction; see Derryberry, Reed, & Pilkenton-Taylor, 2003).

GENETICS OF CONTINUITY

Whereas *homotypic continuity* describes the unfolding of a single class of behavioral/emotional disturbance over time (e.g., aggression, anxiety), *heterotypic continuity* refers to the sequential development of different internalizing or different externalizing behaviors or disorders across the lifespan (see Ferdinand et al., 2007; Rutter, Kim-Cohen, & Maughan, 2006). For example, delinquent adult males are likely to have traversed a developmental pathway that began with hyperactive/impulsive behaviors in toddlerhood, followed by ODD in preschool, early onset CD in elementary school, SUDs in adolescence, and ASPD in adulthood (see Loeber & Hay, 1997; Loeber & Keenan, 1994; Lynam, 1996, 1998).[4] Developmental trajectories of internalizing disorders in which infant reactivity and early shyness mark liability for later anxiety and depression have also been described (Kagan, this volume, Chapter 6; Kagan et al., 2007; see also Rutter, Kim-Cohen, & Maughan, 2006).

Few studies have addressed either the behavioral genetics or the molecular genetics of heterotypic continuity. Although some inferences can be offered from the cross-sectional studies previously outlined addressing homotypic comorbidity, longitudinal studies are required to make strong statements about the stability of behavior disorders over time, or about the heritable versus environmental bases of behavioral stability (see Rutter, Kim-Cohen, & Maughan, 2006). In one such behavioral genetics analysis, heritable factors accounted for much of the stability in antisocial behavior, depressive symptoms, and their co-occurrence over a 3-year interval among 10- to 18-year-olds (O'Connor, Neiderhiser, et al., 1998). Although molecular genetics studies addressing heterotypic continuity have not appeared in the literature to date, it is quite likely that many of the genes that predispose an individual to early ADHD also predispose the same individual to conduct problems and SUDs in later life, consistent with findings from studies implicating common genes for different externalizing disorders (see previous discussion).

As indicated in the latter sections of this chapter, even though much progress has been made toward specifying the behavioral and molecular genetic bases of psychopathology, considerable work remains on questions of comorbidity and continuity (for an extended discussion, see Rutter, Kim-Cohen, & Maughan, 2006). Nevertheless, investigations conducted to date suggest that mechanisms of both comorbidity and continuity are likely to result from broad vulnerability *traits* such as impulsivity and anxiety. This supposition is consistent with recent behavioral genetics approaches that have identified general internalizing and externalizing heritable vulnerabilities that account for more variance in psychopathology than do clusters of symptoms specific to any single disorder (e.g., Kendler et al., 2003; Krueger et al., 2002; Skuse, 2001).

---

4. This statement should not be taken to imply that all or even most children with ADHD go on to develop later antisocial behavior. Although children with ADHD are at high risk for more serious externalizing conduct later in life, many do not make this progression. Nevertheless, most antisocial adult males began as hyperactive-impulsive preschoolers.

SUMMARY AND CONCLUSIONS

Despite expanded acknowledgment of the importance of both genes and environments in the development of psychopathology, much work remains toward uncovering specific mechanisms through which "nature" and "nurture" interact to affect behavior. Although behavioral genetics studies parse phenotypic variance into amounts that can be attributed to heritability versus environment, one must keep in mind that genes are not measured in such studies. Rather, phenotypic similarities between related individuals are used to model purported genetic effects. The considerable distance between genotypes and phenotypes, along with various interdependencies among genotypes, phenotypes, and environments, can lead to inflated and misleading estimates of heritability. Furthermore, molecular genetics studies aimed at identifying specific allelic variations associated with psychological dysfunction often fail to account for environmental moderators of genetic vulnerability. More mechanistic studies, including experiments with animals, can uncover complex patterns of environmentally mediated gene expression and function. Such epigenetic processes, although underappreciated until quite recently, can produce phenotypic variation in genetically identical individuals.

Although epigenetic processes are difficult to study in humans, they should nevertheless be included in emerging models of developmental psychopathology. Even though most researchers now reject dichotomizing genetic and environmental influences on behavior (i.e., nature versus nurture), continued use of such terms contributes to an artificial fractionation of fluid and interdependent processes. As research progresses, the boundaries between nature and nurture will continue to dissolve as we increase our understanding of the interplay between heritable and experiential factors affecting psychopathology. Given the mutual interdependence of genes and environments in affecting behavior, it is no longer tenable to study psychopathology from strictly biological or strictly environmental perspectives (Beauchaine et al., in press; Rutter, Moffitt, & Caspi, 2006). Accordingly, the next generation of mental health professionals must be facile in their thinking about psychopathology across all relevant levels of analysis, including genes, neural systems, environments, and social systems, among others (Cicchetti, this volume, Chapter 2). Breakthroughs in the understanding of and treatment of psychopathology are unlikely to occur by considering any of these systems in isolation.

REFERENCES

Albee, G. W., & Joffe, J. M. (2004). Mental illness is NOT "an illness like any other." *Journal of Primary Prevention, 24,* 419–436.

Ambrosini, P. J., Bennett, D. S., Cleland, C. M., & Haslam, N. (2002). Taxonicity of adolescent melancholia: A categorical or dimensional construct? *Journal of Psychiatric Research, 36,* 247–256.

Angold, A., & Costello, E. J. (1993). Depressive comorbidity in children and adolescents: Empirical, theoretical, and methodological issues. *American Journal of Psychiatry, 150,* 1779–1791.

Baker, L. A., Jacobson, K. C., Raine, A., Lozano, D. I., & Bezdjian, S. (2007). Genetic and environmental bases of child antisocial behavior: A multi-informant twin study. *Journal of Abnormal Psychology, 116,* 219–235.

Beach, S. R. H., & Amir, N. (2003). Is depression taxonic, dimensional, or both? *Journal of Abnormal Psychology, 112,* 228–236.

Beauchaine, T. P. (2003). Taxometrics and developmental psychopathology. *Development and Psychopathology, 15,* 501–527.

Beauchaine, T. P., & Marsh, P. (2006). Taxometric methods: Enhancing early detection and prevention of psychopathology by identifying latent vulnerability traits. In D. Cicchetti & D. Cohen (Eds.) *Developmental psychopathology. Vol. 1: Theory and method* (2nd ed., pp. 931–967). Hoboken, NJ: Wiley.

Beauchaine, T. P., Neuhaus, E., Brenner, S. L., & Gatzke-Kopp, L. (in press). Ten good reasons to consider biological variables in prevention and intervention research. *Development and Psychopathology.*

Benjamin, J., Lin, L., Patterson, C., Greenberg, B. D., Murphy, D. L., & Hamer, D. H. (1996). Population and familial association between the D4 dopamine receptor gene and measures of novelty seeking. *Nature Genetics, 12,* 81–84.

Bogden, R., & Pizzagalli, D. (2006). Acute stress reduces reward responsiveness: Implications for depression. *Biological Psychiatry, 60,* 1147–1154.

Bolsover, S. R., Hyams, J. S., Jones, S., Shepard, E. A., & White, H. A. (1997). *From genes to cells.* New York: Wiley-Liss.

Boomsma, D. I., Koopsman, J. R., Van Doornen, L. J., & Orlebeke, J. F. (1994). Genetic and social influences on starting to smoke: A study of Dutch adolescent twins and their parents. *Addiction, 89,* 219–226.

Brady, E. U., & Kendall, P. C. (1992). Comorbidity of anxiety and depression in children and adolescents. *Psychological Bulletin, 111,* 244–255.

Burcusa, S. L., Iacono, W. G., & McGue, M. (2003). Adolescent twins discordant for major depressive disorder: Shared familial liability to externalizing and other internalizing disorders. *Journal of Child Psychology and Psychiatry, 44,* 997–1005.

Cadoret, R. J., Leve, L. D., & Devor, E. (1997). Genetics of aggressive and violent behavior. *Psychiatric Clinics of North America, 20,* 301–322.

Callicott, J. H., Egan, M. F., Mattay, V. S., Bertolino, A., Bone, A. D., Verchinksi, B., et al. (2003). Abnormal fMRI response of the dorsolateral prefrontal cortex in cognitively intact siblings of patients with schizophrenia. *American Journal of Psychiatry, 160,* 709–719.

Carroll, B. J., Greden, J. R., & Feinberg, M. (1980). Suicide, neuroendocrine dysfunction and CSF 5-HIAA concentrations in depression. In B. Angrist (Ed.), *Proceedings of the 12th CINP Congress* (pp. 307–313). Oxford: Pergamon Press.

Capaldi, D. M. (1991). Co-occurrence of conduct problems and depressive symptoms in early adolescent boys: I. Familial factors and general adjustment at Grade 6. *Development and Psychopathology, 3,* 277–300.

Caspi, A., McClay, J., Moffitt, T., Mill, J., Martin, J., Craig, I. W., et al. (2002). Role of genotype in the cycle of violence in maltreated children. *Science, 297,* 851–854.

Caspi, A., Sugden, K., Moffitt, T. E., Taylor, A., Craig, I. W., Harrington, H., et al. (2003). Influence of life stress on depression: Moderation by a polymorphism in the 5-HTT gene. *Science, 301,* 386–389.

Castellanos, F. X., & Tannock, R. (2002). Neuroscience of attention-deficit/hyperactivity disorder: The search for endophenotypes. *Nature Reviews Neuroscience, 3,* 617–628.

Catlow, B. J., & Kirstein, C. L. (2007). Cocaine during adolescence enhances dopamine in response to a natural reinforcer. *Neurotoxicology and Teratology, 29,* 57–65.

Cicchetti, D., & Rogosch, F. A. (2002). A developmental psychopathology perspective on adolescence. *Journal of Consulting and Clinical Psychology, 70,* 6–20.

Cloninger, C. R. (1990). Comorbidity of anxiety and depression. *Journal of Clinical Psychopharmacology, 10,* 43S–46S.

Cornblatt, B. A. (2001). Predictors of schizophrenia and preventive intervention. In A. Breier & P. Tran (Eds.), *Current issues in the psychopharmacology of schizophrenia* (pp. 389–406). Philadelphia: Lippincott Williams & Wilkins.

Cornblatt, B. A., Obuchowski, M., Roberts, S., Pollack, S., & Erlenmeyer-Kimling, L. (1999). Cognitive and behavioral precursors of schizophrenia. *Developmental Psychopathology, 11,* 487–508.

Coryell, W., & Schlesser, M. (2001). The dexamethasone suppression test and suicide prediction. *American Journal of Psychiatry, 158,* 748–753.

Covault, J., Tennen, H., Armeli, S., Conner, T. S., Herman, A. I., Cillessen, A., et al. (2007). Interactive effects of the serotonin transporter 5-HTTLPR polymorphism and stressful life events on college student drinking and drug use. *Biological Psychiatry, 61,* 609–616.

Crowell, S. E., Beauchaine, T. P., McCauley, E., Smith, C. J., Vasilev, C. A., & Stevens, A. L. (in press). Parent-child interactions, peripheral serotonin, and intentional self-injury in adolescents. *Journal of Consulting and Clinical Psychology.*

Derryberry, D., Reed, M. A., & Pilkenton-Taylor, C. (2003). Temperament and coping: Advantages of an individual differences perspective. *Development and Psychopathology, 15,* 1049–1066.

Donaldson, S. K., Klein, D. N., Riso, L. P., & Schwartz, J. E. (1997). Comorbidity between dysthymic and major depressive disorders: A family study analysis. *Journal of Affective Disorders, 42,* 103–111.

Durston, S. (2003). A review of the biological bases of ADHD: What have we learned from imaging studies? *Mental Retardation & Developmental Disabilities Reviews, 9,* 184–195.

Durston, S., Tottenham, N. T., Thomas, K. M., Davidson, M. C., Eigsti, I-M., Yang, Y., et al., (2003). Differential patterns of striatal activation in young children with and without ADHD. *Biological Psychiatry, 53,* 871–878.

Eaves, L., Erkanli, A., Silberg, J., Angold, A., Maes, H. H., & Foley, D. (2005). Application of Bayesian inference using Gibbs sampling to item-response theory modeling of multi-symptom genetic data. *Behavior Genetics, 35,* 765–780.

Eley, T., Bolton, D., O'Connor, T., Perrin, S., Smith, P., & Plomin, R. (2003). A twin study of anxiety-related behaviors in preschool children. *Journal of Child Psychology and Psychiatry, 44,* 945–960.

Eley, T., Lichtenstein, P., & Moffitt, T. E. (2003). A longitudinal behavioral genetic analysis of the etiology of aggressive and nonaggressive antisocial behavior. *Development & Psychopathology, 15,* 383–402.

Eley, T. C., Sugden, K., Corsico, A., Gregory, A. M., Sham, P., McGuffin, P., et al. (2004). Gene-environment interaction analysis of serotonin system markers with adolescent depression. *Molecular Psychiatry, 9,* 908–915.

Epstein, J., Hong, P., Kocsis, J. H., Yang, Y., Butler, T., & Chusid, J. (2006). Lack of ventral striatal response to positive stimuli in depressed versus normal subjects. *American Journal of Psychiatry, 163,* 1784–1790.

Erlenmeyer-Kimling, L., Golden, R. R., & Cornblatt, B. A. (1989). A taxometric analysis of cognitive and neuromotor variables in children at risk for schizophrenia. *Journal of Abnormal Psychology, 98,* 203–208.

Essau, C. A. (2003). Epidemiology and comorbidity. In C. A Essau (Ed.), *Conduct and oppositional defiant disorders: Epidemiology, risk factors, and treatment* (pp. 33–59). Mahwah, NJ: Erlbaum.

Ferdinand, R. F., Dieleman, G., Ormel, J., & Verhulst, F. C. (2007). Homotypic versus heterotypic continuity of anxiety symptoms in adolescents: Evidence for distinction between DSM-IV subtypes. *Journal of Abnormal Child Psychology, 35,* 325–333.

Fishbein, D. (2000). The importance of neurobiological research to the prevention of psychopathology. *Prevention Science, 1,* 89–106.

Forbes, E. E., May, J. C., Siegle, G. J., Ladouceur, C. D., Ryan, N. D., Carter, C. S., et al. (2006). Reward-related decision-making in pediatric major depressive disorder: An fMRI study. *Journal of Child Psychology and Psychiatry, 47,* 1031–1040.

Forbes, E. E., Shaw, D. S., & Dahl, R. E. (2007). Alterations in reward-related decision making in boys with recent and future depression. *Biological Psychiatry, 61,* 633–639.

Fox, N. A., Hane, A. A., & Pine, D. S. (2007). Plasticity for affective neurocircuitry: How the environment shapes gene expression. *Current Directions in Psychological Science, 16,* 1–5.

Fraga, M. F., Ballestar, E., Paz, M. F., Ropero, S., Setien, F., Ballestar, M. L., et al. (2005). Epigenetic differences arise during the lifetime of monozygotic twins. *Proceedings of the National Academy of Sciences, 102,* 10604–10609.

Galili-Weisstub, E., & Segman, R. H. (2003). Attention deficit hyperactivity disorder: Review of genetic association studies. *Israeli Journal of Psychiatry and Related Sciences, 40,* 57–66.

Gatzke-Kopp, L. M., & Beauchaine, T. P. (2007). Central nervous system substrates of impulsivity: Implications for the development of attention-deficit/hyperactivity disorder and conduct disorder. In D. Coch, G. Dawson, & K. Fischer (Eds.), *Human behavior and the developing Brain: Atypical development* (pp. 239–263). New York: Guilford.

Gatzke-Kopp, L. M., Beauchaine, T. P., Shannon, K. E., Chipman-Chacon, J., Fleming, A. P., Crowell, S. E., et al. (2007). Neurological correlates of reward responding in adolescents with conduct disorder and/or attention-deficit/hyperactivity disorder. Manuscript submitted for publication.

Glahn, D. C., Therman, S., Manninen, M., Huttunen, M., Kapiro, J., Lönnqvist, J., et al. (2003). Spatial working memory as an endophenotype for schizophrenia. *Biological Psychiatry, 53,* 624–626.

Gottesman, I. I., & Gould, T. D. (2003). The endophenotype concept in psychiatry: Etymology and strategic intentions. *American Journal of Psychiatry, 160,* 636–645.

Gould, T. D., & Gottesman, I. I. (2006). Psychiatric endophenotypes and the development of valid animal models. *Genes Brain and Behavior, 5,* 113–119.

Gray, J. A., & McNaughton, N. (2000). *The neuropsychology of anxiety* (2nd ed.). New York: Oxford University Press.

Harrington, R., Rutter, M., & Fombonne, E. (1996). Developmental pathways in depression: Multiple meanings, antecedents, and endpoints. *Development and Psychopathology, 8,* 601–616.

Hartl, D. L., & Jones, E. W. (2002). *Essential genetics: A genomics perspective.* Boston: Jones & Bartlett.

Hicks, B. M., Blonigen, D. M., Kramer, M. D., Krueger, R. F., Patrick, C. J., Iacono, W. G., et al. (2007). Gender differences and developmental change in externalizing disorders from late adolescence to early adulthood: A longitudinal twin study. *Journal of Abnormal Psychology, 116,* 433–447.

Hinshaw, S. P. (2002). Is ADHD an impairing condition in childhood and adolescence? In P. S. Jensen & J. R. Cooper (Eds.), *Attention deficit hyperactivity disorder* (pp. 5-1–5-21). Kingston, NJ: Civic Research Institute.

Hinshaw, S. P. (2003). Impulsivity, emotion regulation, and developmental psychopathology: Specificity vs. generality of linkages. *Annals of the New York Academy of Sciences, 1008,* 149–159.

Jacobson, K. C., Prescott, C. A., & Kendler, K. S. (2000). Genetic and environmental influences on juvenile antisocial behavior based on two occasions. *Psychological Medicine, 30,* 1315–1325.

Jaffee, S. R., Caspi, A., Moffitt, T. E., Dodge, K. A., Rutter, M., Taylor, A., et al. (2005). Nature × nurture: Genetic vulnerabilities interact with physical maltreatment to promote conduct problems. *Development and Psychopathology, 17,* 67-84.

Jain, M., Palacio, L. G., Castellanos, F. X., Palacio, J. D., Pineda, D., Restrepo, M. I., et al. (2007). Attention-deficit/hyperactivity disorder and comorbid disruptive behavior disorders: Evidence of pleiotropy and new susceptibility loci. *Biological Psychiatry, 61,* 1329–1339.

Joffe, J. M. (2004). Mental disorders: Should our emphasis be on biological or psychosocial factors? An introduction to the special issue. *Journal of Primary Prevention, 24*, 415–418.

Kagan, J., Snidman, N., Kahn, V., & Towsley, S. (2007). The preservation of two infant temperaments into adolescence. *Monographs of the Society for Research in Child Development, 72*, 1–75.

Kaufman, J., Yang, B., Douglas-Palumberi, H., Houshyar, S., Lipschitz, D., Krystal, J. H., et al. (2004). Social supports and serotonin transporter gene moderate depression in maltreated children. *Proceedings of the National Academy of Sciences, 101*, 17316–17421.

Keedwell, P., Andrew, C., Williams, S., Brammer, M., & Phillips. M. (2005). The neural correlates of anhedonia in major depressive disorder. *Biological Psychiatry, 58*, 843–853.

Kendler, K. S. (2005). 'A gene for . . .' The nature of gene action in psychiatric disorders. *American Journal of Psychiatry, 162*, 1243–1252.

Kendler, K. S., Prescott, C. A., Myers, J., & Neale, M. C. (2003). The structure of genetic and environmental risk factors for common psychiatric and substance use disorders in men and women. *Archives of General Psychiatry, 60*, 929–937.

Kent L., Green, E., Hawi, Z., Kirley, A., Dudbridge, F., Lowe, N., et al. (2005). Association of the paternally transmitted copy of common valine allele of the Val66-Met polymorphism of the brain-derived neurotrophic factor (BDNF) gene with susceptibility to ADHD. *Molecular Psychiatry, 10*, 939–943.

Klein, D. N., & Riso, L. P. (1993). Psychiatric disorders: Problems of boundaries and comorbidity. In C. G. Costello (Ed.), *Basic issues in psychopathology* (pp. 19–66). New York: Guilford.

Klump, K. L., McGue, M., & Iacono, W. G. (2000). Differential heritability of eating attitudes and behaviors in prepubertal versus pubertal twins. *International Journal of Eating Disorders, 33*, 287–292.

Koopsman, J. R., Slutzke, W. S., Heath, A. C., Neale, M. C., & Boomsma, D. I. (1999). The genetics of smoking initiation and quantity smoked in Dutch adolescent and young adult twins. *Behavior Genetics, 29*, 383–393.

Koopsman, J. R., van Doornen, L., & Boomsma, D. I. (1997). Association between alcohol use and smoking in adolescent and young adult twins: A bivariate genetic analysis. *Alcoholism: Clinical and Experimental Research, 21*, 537–546.

Kopp, L. M., & Beauchaine, T. P. (2007). Patterns of psychopathology in the families of children with conduct problems, depression, and both psychiatric conditions. *Journal of Abnormal Child Psychology, 35*, 301–312.

Krain, A. L., & Castellanos, F. X. (2006). Brain development and ADHD. *Clinical Psychology Review, 26*, 433–444.

Kramer, D. A. (2005). Commentary: Gene-environment interplay in the context of genetics, epigenetics, and gene expression. *Journal of the American Academy of Child and Adolescent Psychiatry, 44*, 19–27.

Krueger, R. F., Hicks, B. M., Patrick, C. J., Carlson, S. R., Iacono, W. G., & McGue, M. (2002). Etiologic connections among substance dependence, antisocial behavior, and personality: Modeling the externalizing spectrum. *Journal of Abnormal Psychology, 111*, 411–424.

Krueger, R. F., & Markon, K. E. (2006). Reinterpreting comorbidity: A model-based approach to understanding and classifying psychopathology. *Annual Review of Clinical Psychology, 2,* 111–133.

Laakso, A., Wallius, E., Kajander, J., Bergman, J., Eskola, O., Solin, O., et al. (2003). Personality traits and striatal dopamine synthesis capacity in healthy subjects. *American Journal of Psychiatry, 160,* 904–910.

Lemery, K. S., & Doelger, L. (2005). Genetic vulnerabilities to the development of psychopathology. In B. L. Hankin & J. R. Z. Abela (Eds.), *Development of psychopathology: A vulnerability-stress perspective* (pp. 161–198). Thousand Oaks, CA: Sage.

Lenzenweger, M. F. (2004). Consideration of the challenges, complications, and pitfalls of taxometric analysis. *Journal of Abnormal Psychology, 113,* 10–23.

Lenzenweger, M. F., McLachlan, G., & Rubin, D. B. (2007). Resolving the latent structure of schizophrenia endophenotypes using expectation-maximization-based finite mixture modeling. *Journal of Abnormal Psychology, 116,* 16–29.

Levy, F., Hay, D. A., McStephen, M., Wood, C., & Waldman, I. (1997). Attention-deficit hyperactivity disorder: A category or a continuum? Genetic analysis of a large-scale twin study. *Journal of the American Academy of Child and Adolescent Psychiatry, 36,* 737–744.

Lewinsohn, P. M., Shankman, S. A., Gau, J. M., & Klein, D. N. (2004). The prevalence and co-morbidity of subthreshold psychiatric conditions. *Psychological Medicine, 34,* 613–622.

Leyton, M., Boileau, I., Benkelfat, C., Diksic, M., Baker, G., & Dagher, A. (2002). Amphetamine-induced increases in extracellular dopamine, drug wanting and novelty seeking: A PET / [11C]Raclopride study in healthy men. *Neuropsychopharmacology, 27,* 1027–1035.

Loeber, R., & Hay, D. (1997). Key issues in the development of aggression and violence from childhood to early adulthood. *Annual Review of Psychology, 48,* 371–410.

Loeber, R., & Keenan, K. (1994). Interaction between conduct disorder and its comorbid conditions: Effects of age and gender. *Clinical Psychology Review, 14,* 497–523.

Lovejoy, M. C., Graczyk, P. A., O'Hare, E., & Neuman, G. (2000). Maternal depression and parenting behavior: A meta-analytic review. *Clinical Psychology Review, 20,* 561–592.

Lynam, D. R. (1996). The early identification of chronic offenders: Who is the fledgling psychopath? *Psychological Bulletin, 120,* 209–234.

Lynam, D. R. (1998). Early identification of the fledgling psychopath: Locating the psychopathic child in the current nomenclature. *Journal of Abnormal Psychology, 107,* 566–575.

Lynam, D. R., Caspi, A., Moffitt, T. E., Wikström, P. H., Loeber, R., & Novak, S. (2000). The interaction between impulsivity and neighborhood context on offending: The effects of impulsivity are stronger in poorer neighborhoods. *Journal of Abnormal Psychology, 109,* 563–574.

Lyons, M. J., True, W. R., Eisen, S. A., Goldberg, J., Meyer, J. M., Faraone, S. V., et al. (1995). Effects of genes and environment on antisocial traits. *Archives of General Psychiatry, 52,* 906–915.

McGue, M., Iacono, W. G., Legrand, L. N., & Elkins, I. (2001). Origins and consequences of age at first drink. II. Familial risk and heritability. *Alcoholism: Clinical and Experimental Research, 25,* 1166–1173.

Meany, M. J. (2007). Maternal programming of defensive responses through sustained effects on gene expression. In D. Romer & E. F. Walker (Eds.), *Adolescent psychopathology and the developing brain* (pp. 148–172). Oxford: Oxford University Press.

Moffitt, T. E., Caspi, A., & Rutter, M. (2006). Measured gene-environment interactions in psychopathology: Concepts, research strategies, and implications for research, intervention, and public understanding of genetics. *Perspectives on Psychological Science, 1,* 5–27.

Nadder, T. S., Rutter, M., Silberg, J. L., Maes, H. H., & Leaves, L. J. (2002). Genetic effects on the variation and covariation of attention deficit-hyperactivity disorder (ADHD) and oppositional-defiant disorder / conduct disorder (ODD / CD) symptomatologies across informant and occasion of measurement. *Psychological Medicine, 32,* 39–53.

Neiderhiser, J. M., Reiss, D., Pedersen, N. L., Lichtenstein, P., Spotts, E. L., Hansson, K. et al. (2004). Genetic and environmental influences on mothering of adolescents: A comparison of two samples. *Developmental Psychology, 40,* 335–351.

Nestler, E., & Carlezon, W. Jr., (2006). The mesolimbic dopamine reward circuit in depression. *Biological Psychiatry, 59,* 1151–1159.

O'Connor, T. G., Deater-Deckard, K., Fulker, D., Rutter, M., & Plomin, R. (1998). Genotype-environment correlations in late childhood and adolescence: Antisocial behavior problems and coercive parenting. *Developmental Psychology, 34,* 970–981.

O'Connor, T. G., McGuire, S., Reiss, D., Hetherington, E., & Plomin, R. (1998). Co-occurrence of depressive symptoms and antisocial behavior in adolescence: A common genetic liability. *Journal of Abnormal Psychology, 107,* 27–37.

O'Connor, T. G., Neiderhiser, J. M., Reiss, D., Hetherington, E. M., & Plomin, R. (1998). Genetic contributions to continuity, change, and co-occurrence of antisocial and depressive symptoms in adolescence. *Journal of Child Psychology and Psychiatry, 39,* 323–336.

Patterson, G. R., DeBaryshe, B. D., & Ramsey, E. (1989). A developmental perspective on antisocial behavior. *American Psychologist, 44,* 329–335.

Patterson, G. R., DeGarmo, D. S., & Knutson, N. M. (2000). Hyperactive and antisocial behaviors: Comorbid or two points in the same process? *Development and Psychopathology, 12,* 91–107.

Plomin, R. (1989). Environment and genes. *American Psychologist, 44,* 105–111.

Plomin, R., DeFries, J. C., & Loehlin, J. C. (1977). Genotype-environment interaction and correlation in the analysis of human behavior. *Psychological Bulletin, 84,* 309–322.

Pollak, S. D. (2005). Early adversity and mechanisms of plasticity: Integrating effective neuroscience with developmental approaches to psychopathology. *Development and Psychopathology, 17,* 735–752.

Price, T. S., Simonoff, E., Waldman, I., Asherson, P., & Plomin, R. (2001). Hyperactivity in pre-school children is highly heritable. *Journal of the American Academy of Child and Adolescent Psychiatry, 40,* 1342–1364.

Rende, R., & Waldman, I. (2006). Behavioral and molecular genetics and developmental psychopathology. In D. Cicchetti & D. Cohen (Eds.), *Developmental psychopathology. Vol. 2: Developmental neuroscience* (2nd ed., pp. 427–464). Hoboken, NJ: Wiley.

Rice, F., Harold, G. T., & Thapar, A. (2002). The genetic aetiology of childhood depression: A review. *Journal of Child Psychology and Psychiatry, 43*, 65–79.

Rice, F., Harold, G. T., & Thapar, A. (2005). The link between depression in mothers and offspring: An extended twin analysis. *Behavior Genetics, 35*, 565–577.

Ross, R. G. (2003). Early expression of a pathophysiological feature of schizophrenia: Saccadic intrusions into smooth-pursuit eye movements in school-age children vulnerable to schizophrenia. *Journal of the American Academy of Child and Adolescent Psychiatry, 42*, 468–476.

Rutter, M. (1990). Commentary: Some focus and process considerations regarding effects of parental depression on children. *Developmental Psychology, 26*, 60–67.

Rutter, M. (2002). The interplay of nature, nurture, and developmental influences. *Archives of General Psychiatry, 59*, 996–1000.

Rutter, M. (2005). Environmentally mediated risk for psychopathology: Research strategies and findings. *Journal of the American Academy of Child and Adolescent Psychiatry, 44*, 3–18.

Rutter, M. (2006). *Genes and behavior: Nature-nurture interplay explained.* Oxford: Blackwell.

Rutter, M. (2007). Gene-environment interdependence. *Developmental Science, 10*, 12–18.

Rutter, M., Kim-Cohen, J., & Maughan, B. (2006). Continuities and discontinuities in psychopathology between childhood and adult life. *Journal of Child Psychology and Psychiatry, 47*, 276–295.

Rutter, M., Moffitt, T. E., & Caspi, A. (2006). Gene-environment interplay and psychopathology: Multiple varieties but real effects. *Journal of Child Psychology and Psychiatry, 47*, 226–261.

Sagvolden, T., Johansen, E. B., Aase, H., & Russell, V. A. (2005). A dynamic developmental theory of attention-deficit/hyperactivity disorder (ADHD) predominantly hyperactive/impulsive and combined subtypes. *Behavioral and Brain Sciences, 28*, 397–468.

Schellenberg, G. D., Dawson, G., Sung, Y. J., Estes, A., Munson, J., Rosenthal, E., et al. (2006). Evidence for multiple loci from a genome scan of autism kindreds. *Molecular Psychiatry, 11*, 1049–1060.

Scheres, A., Milham, M. P., Knutson, B., & Castellanos, F. X. (2007). Ventral striatal hyporesponsiveness during reward anticipation in attention-deficit/hyperactivity disorder. *Biological Psychiatry, 61*, 720–724.

Scourfield, J., Rice, F., Thapar, A., Harold, G. T., Martin, N., & McGuffin, P. (2003). Depressive symptoms in children and adolescents: Changing aetiological influences with development. *Journal of Child Psychology and Psychiatry, 44*, 968–976.

Seeger, G., Schloss, P., Schmidt, M. H., Rüter-Jungfleisch, A., & Henn, F. A. (2004). Gene-environment interaction in hyperkinetic conduct disorder (HD + CD) as indicated by season of birth variations in dopamine receptor (DRD4) gene polymorphism. *Neuroscience Letters, 366,* 282–286.

Shankman, S. A., Klein, D. N., Tenke, C. E., & Bruder, G. E. (2007). Reward sensitivity in depression: A biobehavioral study. *Journal of Abnormal Psychology, 116,* 95–104.

Shannon, K. E., Beauchaine, T. P., Brenner, S. L., Neuhaus, E., & Gatzke-Kopp, L. (2007). Familial and temperamental predictors of resilience in children at risk for conduct disorder and depression. *Development & Psychopathology, 19,* 701–727.

Sherman, D., Iacono, W., & McGue, M. (1997) Attention deficit hyperactivity disorder dimensions: A twin study of inattention and impulsivity hyperactivity. *Journal of the American Academy of Child and Adolescent Psychiatry, 36,* 745–753.

Silberg, J. L., Rutter, M., & Eaves, L. (2001). Genetic and environmental influences on the temporal association between earlier anxiety and later depression in girls. *Biological Psychiatry, 49,* 1040–1049.

Silberg, J., Rutter, M., Neale, M., & Eaves, L. (2001). Genetic moderation of environmental risk for depression and anxiety in girls. *British Journal of Psychiatry, 179,* 116–121.

Skuse, D. H. (2001). Endophenotypes in child psychiatry. *British Journal of Psychiatry, 178,* 395–396.

Sullivan, P. F., Neale, M. C., & Kendler, K. S. (2000). Genetic epidemiology of major depresssive disorder: Review and meta-analysis. *American Journal of Psychiatry, 157,* 1552–1562.

Swanson, J. M., & Castellanos, F. X. (2002). Biological bases of ADHD—Neuroanatomy, genetics, and pathophysiology. In P. S. Jensen & J. R. Cooper (Eds.), *Attention deficit hyperactivity disorder* (pp. 7-1–7-20). Kingston, NJ: Civic Research Institute.

Tremblay, R. E. (2005). Towards an epigenetic approach to experimental criminology: The 2004 Joan McCord Prize Lecture. *Journal of Experimental Criminology, 1,* 397–415.

Vaidya, C., Austin, G., Kirkorian, G., Ridlehuber, H. W., Desmond, J. E., Glover, G., et al. (1998). Selective effects of methylphenidate in attention deficit hyperactivity disorder: A functional magnetic resonance study. *Proceedings of the National Academy of Sciences, 95,* 14494–14499.

Viken, R. J., Kaprio, J., Koskenvuo, M., & Rose, R. J. (1999). Longitudinal analyses of the determinants of drinking and of drinking to intoxication in adolescent twins. *Behavior Genetics, 29,* 455–461.

Waldman, I. D., Rowe, D. C., Abramowitz, A., Kozel, S. T., Mohr, J. H., Sherman, S. L., et al. (1998). Association and linkage of dopamine transporter gene and attention-deficit hyperactivity disorder in children: Heterogeneity owing to diagnostic subtype and severity. *American Journal of Human Genetics, 63,* 1767–1776.

Weaver, I. C. G., Cervoni, N., Champagne, F. A., D'Alessio, A. C., Sharma, S., Seckl, J. R., et al. (2004). Epigenetic programming by maternal behavior. *Nature Neuroscience, 7,* 847–854.

Willeit, M., Praschak-Rieder, N., Neumeister, A., Zill, P., Leisch, F., Stastny, J., et al.

(2003). A polymorphism (5-HTTLPR) in the serotonin transporter promoter gene is associated with DSM-IV depression subtypes in seasonal affective disorder. *Molecular Psychiatry, 8,* 942–946.

Wong, A. H. C., Gottesman, I. I., & Petronis, A. (2005). Phenotypic differences in genetically identical organisms: The epigenetic perspective. *Human Molecular Genetics, 14,* 11–18.

PART II

RISK FACTORS FOR PSYCHOPATHOLOGY

Child Maltreatment: A Neurodevelopmental Perspective on the Role of Trauma and Neglect in Psychopathology

BRUCE D. PERRY

INTRODUCTION

The purpose of this chapter is to examine potential mechanisms underlying the well-documented, complex relationships between maltreatment in childhood and the subsequent development of psychopathology. Thousands of studies over the last 50 years have described various aspects of these associations. Maltreatment in childhood increases risk for virtually every DSM-IV disorder, from symptoms related to autism-spectrum conditions to Achizophrenia, Attention-Deficit/Hyperactivity Disorder (ADHD), Major Depression, substance abuse disorders, and Post-traumatic Stress Disorder (PTSD). Although many of these conditions are significantly heritable, maltreatment can nevertheless contribute to the symptom expression and severity of each form of disorder. The developmental psychopathology perspective underscores the notion that all psychiatric conditions—even those with large genetic components—are shaped and maintained by the interaction of genetic vulnerabilities and environmental risk factors (see, e.g., Rutter, 2004), and few such risk factors are as powerful as maltreatment in childhood.

Yet the mechanisms underlying maltreatment-related increase in risk of neuropsychiatric problems are not fully determined. The key question addressed in this chapter, from a neurodevelopmental perspective, is as follows: How can maltreatment—abuse or neglect—contribute or lead to psychopathology? This neurodevelopmental "lens" provides significant insight into the sometimes confusing interrelationships between psychopathology, DSM-IV diagnoses, and developmental maltreatment. A neurodevelopmental perspective is meant to complement other theoretical and experimental views and can provide useful clues to the mechanisms underlying the origins of neuropsychiatric problems.

The primary premise of a neurodevelopmental perspective is that the human brain mediates all emotional, social, cognitive, and behavioral functioning. Neuropsychiatric disorders and psychopathology therefore must involve altered functioning of systems in the brain. The specific nature of dysfunction (e.g., anxiety versus inattention versus affect regulation versus thought disorder) is determined by which neural networks and brain areas are altered—and by a host of environmentally mediated consequences of the trauma. This chapter provides an overview of key neurodevelopmental processes and important neural networks that are affected by neglect or abuse and suggests mechanisms that may underlie neuropsychiatric problems related to such maltreatment. One major conclusion is that we can make plausible interpretations of the effects of abuse and neglect if we understand how these experiences influence the developing brain. *Simply stated, neglect results in dysfunctions in the neural systems that do not receive appropriately timed and patterned stimulation, and abuse/trauma results in alterations in brain systems that mediate the stress response.*

As just highlighted, two major forms of maltreatment are reviewed in this chapter: neglect and trauma. Although often co-occurring, these two types of maltreatment are distinctly different in the impact they have on the developing brain and on the development of psychopathology. Defined from a neurobiological perspective, *neglect* is the absence of an experience or pattern of experiences required to express an underlying genetic potential in a key developing neural system. In contrast, *trauma* is an experience or pattern of experiences that activate the stress-response systems in such an extreme or prolonged fashion as to cause alterations in the regulation and functioning of these systems. Both neglect- and trauma-related abnormalities in neurodevelopment may potentiate psychopathology, although the specific types and their severity will depend on a host of interacting neural and environmental events.

Maltreatment can have a negative impact on development in several ways. It may be the primary mediator of psychopathology, when these abnormal experiences directly alter developing neural systems. For example, neglect may precipitate an attachment disorder, and trauma may yield

PTSD. In addition, either form may play an exacerbating or expressing role for neuropsychiatric syndromes in individuals with genetic vulnerabilities (e.g., Major Depression, Schizophrenia). And finally, symptoms and problems caused by maltreatment can be disrupting factors for subsequent developmental opportunities (e.g., the negative impact of neglect-related attachment problems on social development, trauma-related hypervigilance on academic functioning). Often these secondary and tertiary effects are as devastating as the primary maltreatment-related pathology. In order to better understand the potential mechanisms by which maltreatment can cause or exacerbate psychopathology it is crucial to consider the core processes and principles of neurodevelopment.

NEURODEVELOPMENT

The brain develops extremely rapidly in utero and in the first years of life (see also Hinshaw, this volume). During this time important molecular processes are taking place that, if disrupted, can result in abnormal organization and function. Depending upon the nature, timing, and frequency of maltreatment, all of these processes can be influenced by chaos, threat, trauma, and neglect.

MOLECULAR PROCESSES OF NEURODEVELOPMENT

Neurogenesis. The vast majority of cell birth or neurogenesis takes place in utero. Relatively few neurons are created after birth, although researchers have demonstrated neurogenesis in the mature brain (Gould et al., 1999; Nelson, de Haan, & Thomas, 2006). Neurogenesis may be influenced by maternal substance use, especially alcohol use and abuse during pregnancy (see also Fryer, Crocker, & Mattson, this volume; Gatzke-Kopp & Shannon, this volume). Such exposure can have a devastating impact on fetal brain growth and result in profound psychopathology later in life (Bookstein et al., 2002).

Migration. As neurons are born and the brain grows, neurons move. Some neurons settle in the brainstem and others in the cortex, for example. Cortical cell migration and fate mapping (the neurodevelopmental process through which neurons migrate to their eventual target) are some of the most well-studied processes in developmental neuroscience (Rakic, 1981, 1996). It is clear that both genetic and environmental factors play important roles in determining a neuron's final location. Migration takes place primarily during the intrauterine and immediate perinatal period but continues throughout childhood and to a much lesser degree into adulthood. A host of intrautcrine and perinatal insults—experiences such as infection, lack of oxygen, exposure to alcohol and various psychotropic drugs—can alter migration of neurons and have a profound impact on the expression of genetic potentials for a host of functions (see Perry, 1988).

Differentiation.   Neurons can mature to thousands of unique structures, producing any of over 100 neurotransmitters (e.g., norepinephrine, dopamine, serotonin, acetylcholine, GABA, glutamate, CRF, Substance P). Developing neurons differentiate in response to chemical, often neurochemical, signals. Therefore, any experience that alters neurochemical, hormonal, or micro-environmental signals (e.g., extreme activation of the stress response) during development can change the ways in which certain neurons differentiate, thereby altering the functional capacity of the neural networks in which these neurons reside (e.g., Rutledge, Wright, & Duncan, 1974).

Apoptosis.   More neurons are born than are required to make a functional system. Redundant neurons, when unable to adequately "connect" into an active neural network, die (Kuan et al., 2000). Neurons that make synaptic connections with other neurons and have an adequate level of stimulation survive, whereas neurons with little activity reabsorb. This is an example of the important principle of activity-dependent development (see following discussion). Clearly, understimulation from neglect could increase apoptosis, or cell death, beyond normative levels.

Arborization.   As neurons differentiate, they send out short, fiber-like receptive processes called *dendrites.* These are the "receiving" sites of neurotransmission from presynaptic neurons. The density of these dendritic branches is related to the frequency and intensity of incoming signals. Arborization allows neurons to receive, process, and integrate complex patterns of input. Dendritic density may be one of the most experience-sensitive physical features of a neuron (Diamond et al., 1966; Greenough, Volkmar, & Juraska, 1973).

Synaptogenesis.   The most experience-sensitive feature of a neuron is the synapse. Developing neurons generate projections that become axons, which form synaptic junctions with the dendrites of other neurons. A continuous dynamic of synaptic neurotransmission regulates the activity chains of neurons that allow all brain function. During development, neurons "find" and connect with the appropriate target neurons. This process is guided by certain growth factors and cellular adhesion molecules that attract or repel a specific growth cone to appropriate target neurons. Furthermore, this process is influenced by neurotransmission. For example, altering levels of dopamine during those time periods that nigrostriatal cells are developing alters receptor expression and synaptogenesis (Wainwright et al., 1995). During the first 8 months of life there is an eight-fold increase in synaptic density while developing neurons in the brain are "seeking" their appropriate connections (Huttenlocher, 1979, 1994). This explosion of synaptogenesis allows the brain to have the flexibility to organize and function with a wide range of potential. Due to the rapid and important neural changes taking place in this first year, this is also a time of remarkable vulnerability to trauma and neglect.

Synaptic sculpting.   The synapse, which constitutes the region of interconnection between a presynaptic neuron's axon terminal and the postsynaptic neuron's dendrite, is a dynamic structure. With regular episodic release of neurotransmitter, occupation of receptors, release of growth factors, shifts of ions in and out of cells, and laying down of new microtubules and other structural molecules, the synapse is continually changing. A key determinant in this synaptic sculpting process is the activity of neurotransmission. When there is a consistent, active process of neurotransmitter release, synaptic connections are strengthened through physical changes that make the pre- and postsynaptic neurons grow more tightly interconnected, forging more-efficient neurotransmission between these two neurons. When there is little activity, the synaptic connection dissolves. Synaptic sculpting is a "use it or lose it" process (see following discussion). Dynamic synaptic sculpting continues through the entire life cycle, but the rate of sculpting decreases with age. This powerful activity-dependent process appears to be the molecular basis of learning and memory and is therefore at the core of neurodevelopment.

Myelination.   Specialized glial cells wrap around axons and thereby create more-efficient electrochemical transduction down the neuron. This process allows a neural network to function more rapidly and efficiently, thereby providing for more complex functioning (e.g., walking depends upon the myelination of neurons in the spinal cord for efficient, smooth regulation of neuromotor functioning). Myelination begins in the first year of life but continues in many key areas throughout childhood, with a major burst in key cortical areas taking place in adolescence. Final myelination of key cortical tracts can take place as late as age 30. This process may be affected by abuse and neglect. For example, neglect involving substantial malnutrition can negatively influence myelination.

The neurodevelopmental processes previously described are sensitive to *signals* from neurotransmitters, neuromodulators, neurohormones, ions, growth factors, cellular adhesion molecules, and other morphogens. Disruption of the pattern, timing, or intensity of these cues can lead to abnormal neurodevelopment and potentiate psychopathology. The *specific* form of psychopathology depends upon the timing of the insult (e.g., an in utero insult during the development of the brainstem has different effects from an age-2 insult during the active development of the cortex), the nature of the insult (e.g., a lack of sensory stimulation from neglect will potentiate different outcomes from abnormally persisting activation of the stress response from trauma), and the pattern of the insult (e.g., different effects will emanate from a discrete single event, a chronic experience with a chaotic pattern, or an episodic event with a regular pattern). Experience, good and bad, shapes the neuroarcheology of the individual's brain (see Perry, 2001a). The effects of maltreatment are therefore extremely dependent upon the state of development of the child and the stage of neurodevelopment. Several key principles help to explain key findings of developmental maltreatment.

PRINCIPLES OF NEURODEVELOPMENT

Nature and nurture.   Neurodevelopment is the product of genetic potential and how that potential is expressed as a function of the timing, nature, and pattern of experience. Genetic differences in key neural factors are related to the functioning of the stress-response systems, for example. Yet the way these genetic vulnerabilities are expressed remain sensitive to developmental experiences of trauma (Caspi et al., 2002, 2003).

The impact of experience on neurodevelopment shifts across the lifespan. In the just-fertilized ovum, chemical processes driving development are genetically determined sequences of molecular events. By birth, however, the brain has developed to the point where environmental cues mediated by the senses play a major role in neural differentiation, arborization, and synaptogenesis, helping to create functional neural networks. By adolescence, the majority of the changes that are taking place in the brain are determined by experience, not genes. The languages, beliefs, cultural practices, and complex cognitive and emotional functioning (e.g., self-esteem) by this age are largely experience-based.

Sequential development.   In general, the brain develops in a sequential and hierarchical fashion, organizing itself from least (brainstem) to most (cortex) complex regions. These different areas develop, organize, and become fully functional at different times during childhood. At birth, for example, brainstem areas responsible for regulating cardiovascular and respiratory functions must be intact for the infant to survive, and any malfunction is immediately observable. In contrast, cortical areas responsible for abstract cognition are not fully functional until adulthood.

This principle is important in understanding the role of the stress response in shaping future neurodevelopment. As described in detail in the following, the monoamine neurons originating in the brainstem and diencephalon, which are present at birth, send direct connections into all other brain areas (see Fig. 4.1). If these systems are poorly organized or dysregulated themselves, they can dysregulate and disorganize later-developing parts of the brain (see also Beauchaine & Neuhaus, this volume). The "higher" and more complex areas (e.g., limbic and cortical) have not yet organized. The final organization of these important areas (and all of the functions

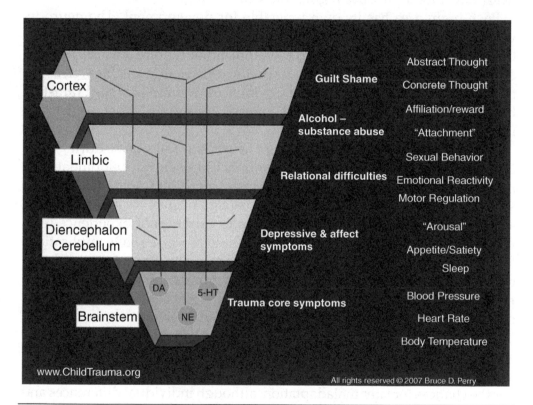

Figure 4.1. Brain organization and monoamine systems: The human brain has a hierarchical organization. The multiple parallel systems in the brain are organized in various brain regions with the most simple in the brainstem and the most complex in the cortex. Although this diagram is somewhat simplified, it is clear that functional complexity correlates with the organizational complexity of the brain, with the most simple regulatory functions mediated by the lower less complex brainstem and the most complex functions—those that confer uniquely human properties—are in the cortex. The brainstem and diencephalic-originating monoamine systems (DA: dopamine; NE: norepinephrine; 5-HT: serotonin) project up (and down) throughout the brain.

mediated by them) are influenced by the pattern, intensity, and nature of stimulation coming from their constituent adrenergic, noradrenergic, serotonergic, and dopaminergic neurons.

Trauma results in profound alterations in the pattern of activation in these stress-mediating neural systems. Such changed activation in turn creates patterned, repetitive neuronal signals in a distributed and diverse set of brain systems, influencing the organization and function of these higher brain areas. The result can be compromised function and psychopathology. Traumatic stress, for example, can influence cortically mediated (e.g., cognition), limbic-mediated (e.g., affect regulation), diencephalic-mediated (e.g., fine motor regulation, startle response), and brainstem-mediated (e.g. heart rate, blood pressure regulation) functioning.

Each brain area has its own timetable for development. The neurodevelopmental processes described previously are most active in different brain areas at different times and therefore either require (critical periods) or are sensitive to (sensitive periods) organizing experiences, as well as the neurotrophic cues related to these experiences. Neurons for the brainstem have to migrate, differentiate, and connect, for example, before neurons for the cortex do so.

Disruptions of experience-dependent neurochemical signals during early life may lead to major abnormalities or deficits in neurodevelopment. Disruption of critical neurodevelopmental cues can result from (a) lack of sensory experience during sensitive periods (e.g., neglect) or (b) atypical or abnormal patterns of necessary cues due to extremes of experience (e.g., traumatic stress; see Perry, 2001a, 2001b). These processes have implications for understanding psychopathology related to maltreatment. In the development of socio-emotional and cognitive functioning, for example, early life nurturing appears to be critical. If such nurturing is absent for the first 3 years of life but the child is then adopted and begins to receive attention, love, and care, these positive experiences may not be sufficient to overcome already acquired disorganization of the neural systems mediating socio-emotional and cognitive functioning. The longer the period of deprivation, the stronger the chances for later maladaptation, although individual differences and apparent resilience in response to severe early deprivation are also apparent (e.g., Beckett et al., 2006; Rutter & O'Connor, 2004).

Activity-dependent neurodevelopment. As described in detail in the previous paragraphs, the brain organizes in a use-dependent fashion. If a child is neglected—if he or she hears few words, has few relational opportunities, and/or has little physical comfort and love—the rapidly organizing networks in the brain that mediate language, social affiliation, and attachment do not receive sufficient patterned, repetitive activation to develop normally. The result may be a neglect-related set of deficits in the domains in which the neglect occurred. (Croft et al., 2007; O'Connor et al., 2000; Perry, 2002; Rutter et al., 2007).

Sensitive and critical windows. Because of sequential and activity-dependent development of the brain, there are times during which developing neural systems are more sensitive to experience than they are at other times. In healthy development, that sensitivity allows the brain to efficiently organize in response to the unique demands of a given environment. If a child is born into a hunter–gatherer clan in New Guinea as opposed to a suburban English family, for example, different genes can be expressed, and different neural networks can be organized to best fit that family, culture, and environment. For most functions, this sensitivity passes with time. Acquisition of language with full fluency after a certain age becomes more difficult; formation of key relational and attachment capacities after the first 5 years of life becomes difficult if these initial years were characterized by disorganized, absent, or abusive primary caregivers.

Sensitive periods are different for each brain area and neural system and, as a result, for different functions. The sequential development of the brain and the sequential unfolding of the genetic map for development mean that sensitive periods for neural systems (and the functions they mediate) occur when that area is most actively organizing. The brainstem must organize key systems by birth; therefore, the sensitive period for those brainstem-mediated functions is during the prenatal period. A variety of in utero experiences may influence the development of the key stress-mediating neurotransmitter systems that originate in the brainstem. For example, prenatal exposure to psychoactive drugs may disrupt normal development of brainstem catecholamines (Perry, 1988). In animal models, brief prenatal and perinatal stress can cause altered development of hippocampal organization and the hypothalamic-pituitary-adrenal axis, which remain changed throughout life, at least in animal models (Plotsky & Meaney, 1993). The neocortex, in contrast, has systems and functions organizing throughout childhood and into adulthood. The sensitive periods for these cortically mediated functions are therefore likely to be very long.

The primary implication is that early childhood trauma or maltreatment has a disproportionately large capacity to cause dysfunction in comparison with similar trauma or neglect later in life (see Rutter et al., 1998; Rutter et al., 1999). The younger a child is, the more likely he or she is to have enduring and pervasive problems following trauma and neglect. Neglect in the first years of life can have a devastating impact even if a child is removed from the neglectful environment (Perry, 2002; Perry, 2006). The longer a child remains in a neglectful environment, the more vulnerable he or she becomes (e.g., Rutter et al., 1998, 1999; O'Connor et al., 2000; Perry, 2006).

A major consequence of these principles is that the organizing brain of an infant or young child is more malleable than a mature brain. Although experience may alter the behavior of an adult, experience literally provides the organizing framework for an infant and child. Because the brain is most plastic (receptive to environmental input) in early childhood, the child is most sensitive to experience—both good and bad—at this time. In parallel, the brain may also be most amenable to corrective and therapeutic experiences that occur early in life.

THE NEURODEVELOPMENTAL IMPACT OF NEGLECT

Deprivation during the sensitive period of a given neural system results in insufficient patterned, repetitive activity to stimulate adequate organization. The deprived developing neural network may therefore have altered neural microarchitecture, which may involve problems in cell migration, synaptogenesis, and dendritic sprouting. The result is a neural system that is less functionally capable. These sequelae of deprivation and neglect can take multiple forms. In some rare cases, a single domain of functioning is influenced. Our group has worked with several children who were raised with cognitive stimulation and physical and emotional warmth, but they were physically restrained for multiple years and, therefore, were unable to sit, stand, or walk. But such isolated forms of neglect or restraint are rare. Most neglect takes the form of chaotic, mistimed, and inconsistent experiences related to the primary caregiver's isolation, personal chaos, incompetence, ignorance, domestic violence, substance abuse, or psychopathology. The end result can manifest as delays in motor, self-regulatory, affective, and cognitive functioning, often in combination. A common manifestation of this form of neglect is in speech and language acquisition: If the infant or toddler hears few words, the developing speech and language systems are negatively influenced (Huttenlocher et al., 2002).

The earlier and more pervasive the neglect, the more devastating the developmental problems for the child. Indeed, a chaotic, inattentive, and ignorant caregiver can produce Pervasive Developmental Delay (PDD; DSM-IV-TR) in a young child (Rutter et al., 1999). Yet the very same inattention for the same duration at age 10 is likely to have very different and less severe impacts than such insensitivity and neglect during the first years of life.

Studies of the neurodevelopmental impact of neglect are not as common as those on the effects of trauma. Yet animal studies, descriptive reports with severely neglected children, and some recent studies with adopted children following neglect document some aspects of the neurodevelopmental impact of neglect.

Animal Studies

Hubel and Weisel's landmark studies on development of the visual system using sensory deprivation techniques helped define the concepts of critical and sensitive period (Hubel & Wiesel, 1963). In hundreds of other studies, extremes of sensory deprivation (Hubel & Wiesel, 1970; Greenough et al.,1973) or sensory enrichment (Greenough & Volkmar, 1973; Diamond, Krech, & Rosenzweig, 1964; Diamond et al., 1966) have been studied. These include disruptions of visual stimuli (Coleman & Riesen, 1968), environmental enrichment (Altman & Das, 1964; Cummins & Livesey, 1979), touch (Ebinger, 1974; Rutledge et al., 1974), and other factors that alter the typical experiences of development (Uno et al., 1989; Plotsky & Meaney, 1993; Meaney et al., 1988).

Findings from these investigations generally demonstrate that the brains of animals reared in enriched environments are larger, more complex, and functionally more flexible than the brains of those raised under deprivation. Indeed, associations exist between the density of dendritic branching and the complexity of an environment (Diamond & Hopson, 1998). Rats raised in enriched environments have higher densities of various neuronal and glial microstructures, including a 30% higher synaptic density in the cortex, compared to rats raised in environmentally deprived settings (Bennett et al., 1964; Altman & Das, 1964). Furthermore, animals raised in the wild have from 15% to 30% larger brain mass than their domestically reared offspring (Darwin, 1868; Rohrs, 1955; Rohrs & Ebinger, 1978; Rehkamper, Haase, & Frahm, 1988).

Animal studies suggest that critical periods exist during which specific sensory experiences are required for optimal organization and development of parts of the brain mediating specific functions (e.g., visual input during the development of the visual cortex). Although these phenomena have been examined in great detail for the primary sensory modalities in animals, few studies have examined the issues of critical or sensitive periods in humans. Existing evidence suggests that humans tend to have longer periods of sensitivity and that the concept of critical period may not be as useful (Perry, 2006). Yet altered emotional, behavioral, cognitive, social, and physical functioning have been demonstrated in humans following specific types of neglect. For obvious ethical reasons, most of these findings come from descriptive clinical rather than experimental studies.

NEGLECT IN EARLY CHILDHOOD

The majority of clinical reports on neglect have focused on institutionalized children or feral children. As early as 1833, with the famous Kaspar Hauser, feral children were described (Heidenreich, 1834). Hauser was abandoned as a young child and raised from early childhood (likely around age 2) until age 17 in a dungeon, experiencing relative sensory, emotional, and cognitive neglect. His emotional, behavioral, and cognitive functioning was, as one might expect, extremely primitive and delayed.

In the early 1940s, Spitz described the impact of neglectful caregiving on children in foundling homes (orphanages). Most significantly, he demonstrated that children raised in fostered placements with more attentive and nurturing caregiving had superior physical, emotional, and cognitive outcomes to those in the orphanage settings (Spitz, 1945, 1946).

Dennis (1973) described a series of findings from children raised in a Lebanese orphanage. These children were raised in an institutional environment devoid of individual attention, cognitive stimulation, emotional affection, or other enrichment. Prior to 1956 all of these children remained at the orphanage until age 6, at which time they were transferred to another institution. Evaluation of these children at age 16 demonstrated a mean IQ of approximately 50. When adoption became common, children adopted prior to age 2 had a mean IQ of 100 by adolescence, while children adopted between ages 2 and 6 had IQ values of approximately 80 (Dennis, 1973). This apparent graded recovery is consistent with the known principles of neurodevelopment described previously: The older a child was at time of adoption, (i.e., the longer the child experienced neglect), the more pervasive and resistant to recovery were the deficits.

Money and Annecillo (1976) reported the impact of change in placement on children with psychosocial dwarfism (failure to thrive). In this preliminary study, 12 of 16 children removed from neglectful homes recorded remarkable increases in IQ and other aspects of emotional and behavioral functioning. Furthermore, they reported that the longer the child was out of the abusive home, the higher the increase in IQ. Indeed, in some cases IQ increased by 55 points.

A more recent report on a group of 111 Romanian orphans (Rutter & English and Romanian Adoptees study team, 1998; Rutter et al., 1999) adopted prior to age 2 from institutional settings, characterized by extremes of emotional and physical deprivation, demonstrated similar findings. Approximately one-half of the children were adopted prior to age 6 months and the other half between 6 months and 2 years. At the time of adoption, these children had significant delays. Four years after being placed in stable and enriching environments, they were reevaluated. Although both groups improved, the group adopted at a younger age had significantly greater improvements in all domains. Children in both groups were at much greater risk for meeting diagnostic criteria for Autism-Spectrum Disorder, a finding that sheds light on the evolving relationships between early life trauma, neglect, and subsequent development of severe neuropsychiatric problems (Read et al., 2001).

These observations are consistent with the clinical experiences of the Child Trauma Academy, which has worked with over 1,000 maltreated children for the last 15 years. In a group of 200 children under the age of 6 at time of removal, significant developmental delays were seen in more than 85%. Yet the severity of these developmental problems increased with age of removal, suggesting again that the longer the child was in the neglectful environment—the earlier and more pervasive the neglect—the more indelible and pervasive the deficits. Note, however, that we have recorded increases in IQ of over 40 points in more than 60 children following removal from neglectful environments and placement in consistent, predictable, nurturing, and enriching environments (Perry, 2002), revealing the plasticity of the developing brain.

Neurobiological Findings

All of these reported developmental problems—language, fine and large motor delays, impulsivity, disorganized attachment, dysphoria, attention and hyperactivity, and a host of others described in these neglected children—are caused by abnormalities in the brain. Despite this obvious statement, very few studies have examined directly any aspect of neurobiology in neglected children. One early clue in humans derives from the case of Kasper Hauser (see previous discussion). On autopsy, Hauser's brain was notable for small cortical size and few, nondistinct cortical gyri—all consistent with cortical atrophy (Simon, 1978).

Our group has examined various aspects of neurodevelopment in neglected children (Perry, 2005; Perry & Pollard, 1997). Globally neglected children had smaller frontal-occipital circumference (FOC), a measure of head size and in young children a reasonable measure of brain size. Neuroimaging demonstrated that 64.7% of the brain scans were abnormal in the children with global neglect and 12% were abnormal in children following chaotic neglect. The majority of the findings were "enlarged ventricles" or "cortical atrophy" (Fig. 4.2). Once the children were removed from the neglectful settings, recovery of function and relative brain-size was observed. The degree of recovery over a 1-year period, however, was inversely proportional to age at which the child was removed from neglecting caregivers. In other words, as suggested previously, the less

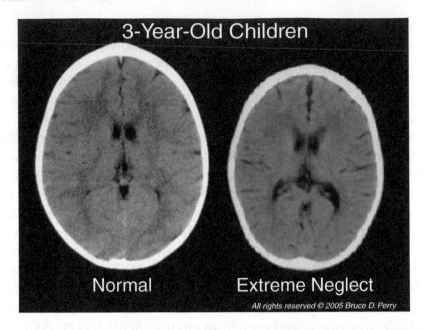

3-Year-Old Children

Normal   Extreme Neglect

Figure 4.2. Impact of neglect on brain development: These images illustrate the impact of neglect on the developing brain. The CT scan on the left is from a healthy 3-year-old child with an average head size (50th percentile). The image on the right is from a 3-year-old child following total global neglect during early childhood. The brain is significantly smaller than average and has abnormal development of cortical, limbic, and midbrain structures.

time in the sensory-depriving environment, the more robust the recovery (Perry, 2005).

In the study of Romanian orphans previously described, 38% had FOC values below the third percentile (greater than 2 SD from the norm) at the time of adoption. In the groups adopted before 6 months versus after 6 months, 3%, and 13%, respectively, had persistently low FOCs 4 years later (Rutter & English and Romanian Adoptees study team, 1998; O'Connor et al., 2000). Strathearn (2001) has followed extremely low birth weight infants and shown that when these infants end up in neglectful homes, they have a significantly smaller head circumference at 2 and 4 years, despite having no significant difference in other growth parameters.

Studies from other groups report similar altered neurodevelopment in neglected children. Teicher has reported altered corpus callosum development in such children (Teicher et al., 2004). Moreover, altered brain-related measures (e.g., salivary cortisol) have been demonstrated in children adopted following neglect (Gunnar et al., 2001). Chugani and colleagues have demonstrated decreased metabolic activity in the orbital frontal gyrus, the infralimbic prefrontal cortex, the amygdale and head of the hippocampus, the lateral temporal cortex, and in the brainstem in a group of Romanian orphans (Chugani et al., 2001).

THE NEURODEVELOPMENTAL IMPACT OF TRAUMA

Although widely distributed, the brain's stress-mediating systems are well characterized; they involve both the central and autonomic nervous systems, as well as neuroendocrine and neuroimmune responses. Thus, stress-related neural networks permeate the entire brain. Consequently, localizing use-dependent alterations in the organization and functioning of neural systems due to abnormal patterns of stress activation can lead to dozens of psychopathological problems, with sequelae that may be more difficult to isolate than in cases of neglect.

The human brain is continually sensing, processing, storing, perceiving, and acting in response to information from the external and internal environments. This continuous monitoring process is especially sensitive to input that may indicate threat. The environment in which we live—external as "sensed" by our five senses and internal by a set of specialized neurons throughout the body (e.g., glucose or sodium sensitive neurons)—is always changing. Our physiology and neurophysiology are characterized by continuous processes of modulation, regulation, compensation, and activation, all designed to keep our body's systems in some state of equilibrium or homeostasis. Whenever incoming information from either inside or outside the body alters this homeostasis (Perry & Pollard, 1998), or indicates similarity to a pattern of activity previously associated with threat (Perry, 2001b), the brain initiates compensatory, adaptive responses to reestablish homeostasis or to take the necessary actions to survive.

SEQUENTIAL PROCESSING OF THREAT-RELATED NEURAL ACTIVITY

This process begins when our senses transform energy (e.g., light, sound, pressure) into patterned activity of sensory neurons. The first "stops" for sensory input from the outside environment (e.g., light, sound, taste, touch, smell) and from inside the body (e.g., glucose levels, temperature) are the lower, "regulatory" areas of the brain (see following discussion). These neural patterns of activity created by sensory input first come into the brain *separately*—visual input comes into one nucleus, auditory another, olfactory another, and so on. The source nuclei for primary sensory input are in lower parts of the brain that cannot be perceived consciously. In the following sections an overview of key brain systems, beginning with the brainstem and working "up" through the cortex, will give a sense of the various loci of traumatic experiences on brain development and functioning.

BRAINSTEM AND DIENCEPHALON

Neural input from our senses connects directly to the lower areas of the CNS in the brainstem, diencephalon, and hypothalamus. For example, our internal organs relay information to the amygdala and locus coeruleus, directly or through the nucleus paragigantocellularis and nucleus tractus solitaries (Elam, Thoren, & Svensson, 1986; Nauta & Whitlock, 1956; Saper, 1982). Other primary sensory input from visual, auditory, tactile, and olfactory systems connect directly into these lower brain nuclei where the process of sorting, integrating, interpreting, storing (if appropriate), and responding to these incoming signals begins.

These brainstem and diencephalic nuclei project to the thalamus, which begins the process of integrating this information, relaying sensory information to the primary sensory receptive areas of the cortex. These primary sensory regions project to adjacent cortical association areas. A feedback process involves projections from key cortical areas back to the lower parts of the brain; visual, auditory, and somatosensory cortical association areas send projections to the hippocampus, amygadala, orbitofrontal cortex, entorhinal cortex, cingulate gyrus, and other brain structures. This reciprocal processing allows the brain to sort, process, and "act" on the threat-related signals from the body and the external world.

The reticular activating system.   Key to this entire process is the role of an array of important neurotransmitter networks: the monoamine systems— epinephrine, norepinephrine, dopamine, and serotonin. These systems have key nuclei (clusters of cell bodies) that send direct axonal projections to virtually all other areas of the brain and periphery to influence the autonomic neurons that leave the brain and influence heart, lung, gut, skin, and the rest of the organs of the body. Historically, this network has been referred to as the *reticular activating system* (RAS), although contemporary accounts usually subdivide the RAS into its constituent parts.

The RAS is a network of ascending, arousal-related neural systems in the brain that consists of locus ceruleus noradrenergic neurons, dorsal raphe serotonergic neurons, cholinergic neurons from the lateral dorsal tegmentum, and mesolimbic and mesocortical dopaminergic neurons, among others. Much of the original research on arousal, fear, and response to stress and threat was conducted using various lesion models of the RAS (Moore & Bloom, 1979). The RAS appears to be an integrated neurophysiological system involved in arousal, anxiety, and modulation of limbic and cortical processing (Munk et al., 1996). Working together, the brainstem monoamine systems in the RAS provide the flexible and diverse functions necessary to modulate stress, distress, and trauma. A key component of the RAS is the locus coeruleus.

The locus ceruleus. The locus ceruleus is involved in initiating, maintaining, and mobilizing the total body response to threat (Aston-Jones et al., 1986). A bilateral grouping of norepinephrine-containing neurons originating in the pons, the locus ceruleus sends diverse axonal projections to virtually all major brain regions and thus functions as a general regulator of noradrenergic tone and activity (Foote, Bloom, & Aston-Jones, 1983). The locus ceruleus plays a major role in determining the *valence,* or value, of incoming sensory information. In response to novel or potentially threatening information, it increases its activity (Abercrombie & Jacobs, 1987, 1988). The ventral tegmental nucleus also plays a part in regulating the sympathetic nuclei in the pons/medulla (Moore & Bloom, 1979). Acute stress results in an increase in locus ceruleus and ventral tegmental nucleus activity and the release of catecholamines throughout the brain and the rest of the body. These brainstem catecholamine systems (locus ceruleus and ventral tegmental nucleus) play a critical role in regulating arousal, vigilance, affect, behavioral irritability, locomotion, attention, and sleep, as well as the startle response and the response to stress (Levine, Litto, & Jacobs, 1990; Morilak, Fornal, & Jacobs, 1987a, 1987b, 1987c).

Hypothalamus and thalamus. Sensory thalamic areas receive input from various afferent sensory systems. At this level, "feeling" begins. Although thalamic nuclei are important in the stress response, these regions have been studied primarily as "way stations" that transmit important arousal information from the RAS to key limbic, subcortical, and cortical areas involved in sensory integration and perception of threat-related information (Castro-Alamancos & Connors, 1996). The neuroendocrinological— and likely neuroimmunological—afferent and efferent wings of the threat response are mediated by hypothalamic and other anatomically related nuclei. Studies have demonstrated important roles for various hypothalamic nuclei and hypothalamic neuropeptides in the stress response in animals (Bartanusz et al., 1993; Miaskowski et al., 1988; Rosenbaum et al., 1988) and humans (Young & Lightman, 1992).

THE LIMBIC SYSTEM

The central role of the subcortical network of brain structures in emotion was hypothesized by Papez (1937) and elaborated by MacLean, who coined the term *limbic system*. This subcortical network is responsible for a range of emotion- and relational-related functions. Among the key sub-components of the limbic system are two brain areas known to be intimately involved in the stress response: the amygdala and hippocampus.

Amygdala. The amygdala has emerged as the key brain region responsible for the processing, interpretation, and integration of emotionally relevant information (Clugnet & LeDoux, 1990). Just as the locus ceruleus plays a central role in orchestrating arousal, the amygdala plays a central role in the processing afferent and efferent connections related to emotional functioning (LeDoux et al., 1988; Pavlides, Watanabe, & McEwen, 1993; Phillips & LeDoux, 1992). The amygdala receives input directly from the sensory thalamus, the hippocampus (via multiple projections), the entorhinal cortex, and the sensory association and polymodal sensory association areas of the cortex, as well as from various brainstem arousal systems via the RAS (Selden et al., 1991). The amygdala processes and determines the emotional valence of simple sensory input, complex multisensory perceptions, and complex cognitive abstractions, even responding specifically to complex socially relevant stimuli. In turn, the amygdala orchestrates the organism's response to this emotional information by sending projections to brain areas involved in motor (behavioral), autonomic nervous system, and neuroendocrine areas of the CNS (Davis, 1992a, 1992b; LeDoux et al., 1988). In a series of landmark studies, LeDoux and colleagues demonstrated the key role of the amygdala in "emotional" memory (LeDoux et al., 1990). Animals, including humans, store emotional as well as cognitive information, and the storage of emotional information is critically important in both normal and abnormal regulation of anxiety. The "site" at which anxiety is perceived is the amygdala (Davis, 1992a). It is in these limbic areas that the patterns of neuronal activity associated with threat— and mediated by the monoamine neurotransmitter systems of the reticular activating system—become "fear."

Hippocampus. This brain area is involved in the storage of various kinds of sensory information and is very sensitive to "stress" activation (Pavlides et al., 1993; Phillips & LeDoux, 1992; Sapolsky, Krey, & McEwen, 1984). The hippocampus appears to be critical in the storage and recall of cognitive and emotional memory (Selden et al., 1991). Any emotional state related to arousal or threat may alter hippocampal functioning, changing the efficiency and nature of hippocampal storage and retrieval. Threat alters the ability of the hippocampus and connected cortical areas to "store" certain types of cognitive information (e.g., verbal) but does not affect the storage of other types (e.g., nonverbal).

Hormonal signals affect heterogeneous corticosteroid nuclear receptors in the hypothalamic-pituitary-adrenal (HPA) axis. Stressful life events such as isolation increase HPA axis activity (McEwen, 2001). The hippocampus, amygdala, and medial prefrontal cortex (PFC) are limbic structures that are targets for (and modulators of) adrenal steroids. Glucocorticoids can result in neurotoxic damage to the hippocampus with suppression of neurogenesis (McEwen, 2001; Sapolsky, 2000). Exposure to stress results in release of corticotrophin-releasing hormone (CRH), adrenocorticotropic hormone (ACTH), and cortisol via activation of the HPA axis. Such exposure can promote partial resistance to feedback inhibition of cortisol release, with consequent increases in plasma cortisol levels and decreases in glucocorticoid receptors (Sapolsky & Plotsky, 1990). Glucocorticoid receptors are present in the brain in high density in areas relevant to stress and anxiety such as the hypothalamus, hippocampus, serotonergic, and noradrenergic cell bodies on both neurons and glia. Based on animal studies, mineralocorticoid expression is high in limbic regions such as the hippocampus, septum, and amygdala (Reul and de Kloet, 1985; Veldhuis & De Kloet, 1982).

Animal studies suggest that stress experienced during critical years of development can have long-lasting effects on the HPA axis (Caldji et al., 1998, 2000). For instance, rats that experience in utero stress or early maternal deprivation have increased corticosterone concentrations when exposed to stress. Early postnatal stress is associated with changes in basal concentrations of hypothalamic CRH, mRNA, hippocampal glucocorticoid receptor mRNA, and median eminence CRH, in addition to stress-induced CRH, cortocosterone, and ACTH release (Levine, Atha, & Wiener, 1993a; Levine, Wiener, & Coe, 1993b; Stanton, Gutierrez, & Levine, 1988). Adults with PTSD and nonhuman primates with early adverse experiences have elevated CRH concentrations and decreased cortisol levels in the cerebrospinal fluid (Coplan et al., 1996). Finally, a number of studies indicate the crucial role of corticotrophin-releasing factor (CRF) and the sensitivity of CRF receptors in mediating stress reactivity in humans (Kehne, 2007).

CORTEX

The quality and intensity of any emotional response, including anxiety, are dependent on subjective interpretation or cognitive appraisal of the specific situation eliciting the response (Maunsell, 1995; Singer, 1995). Most theories addressing the etiology of anxiety disorders focus on the process by which stimuli are "mislabeled" as being threat-related, thereby inducing a fear response and anxiety in situations where no true threat exists. How individuals "cortically interpret" the limbic-mediated activity (i.e., their internal state) associated with arousal plays a major role in their subjective sense of anxiety (Gorman et al., 1989). Klüver-Bucy syndrome, which results from damage to or surgical ablation of the temporal lobes, is characterized by absence of fear in response to current and previously threatening cues (Klüver & Bucy, 1937). The general disinhibition characteristic of this syndrome suggests loss of the capacity to interpret incoming threat-related cues from lower brain areas.

HETEROGENEITY OF ADAPTIVE RESPONSES TO THREAT: HYPERAROUSAL AND DISSOCIATION

Individual responses to threat can vary tremendously, which is not surprising considering the vast distribution of neural functions that are available to the stress-response network. Indeed, this network involves the entire brain, and, indirectly, the whole body, allowing responses to potential threats to be appropriate and proportional to needs. Specific adaptive changes taken by the brain to respond to the incoming threat-related signals vary depending upon many factors; different elements of the widely distributed neural system are recruited and others are shut down to conserve energy and focus the body's response to threat. Under normal circumstances (i.e., a normal stress-response capability), the responses are graded and proportional to the level of perceived threat. Thus, when the threat is mild, moderate activation of key systems takes place, leading to adaptive responses; yet when threat is extreme or ongoing, intense and prolonged activation occurs. Furthermore, adaptive responses to threat are specific to the nature of the threat—either preparing to flee or fight or preparing to be overwhelmed and injured. In cases of abnormal development or sensitivity of the stress-response systems (see following), responses to potential threat may well become inappropriate and out of proportion. Trauma can render the system overactive and overly reactive.

Two major interrelated response patterns—hyperarousal and dissociation—have been described (Perry et al., 1995). The hyperarousal response is well characterized, and was described originally as the *fight or flight response* (Cannon, 1914). As described previously, incoming signals activate the locus ceruleus, which initiates a cascade of neural activation recruiting key limbic and cortical areas to focus on and respond to the threat. These neural and neuroendocrine activations prepare the body to fight or flee. Cortisol and adrenaline course through the body, the heart rate escalates, and glycogen is mobilized from muscles. All distracting information is tuned out.

However, when either fighting or fleeing is not possible, the brain may recruit a different set of neural systems, using avoidant, dissociative adaptations. Dissociation is a mental mechanism through which one withdraws attention from external events and focuses on internal experience. Dissociation may involve a distorted sense of time, a detached feeling that one is "observing" something happen as if it is unreal, a sense that one is watching a movie of one's life. In extreme cases, especially if the trauma is repetitive and painful (e.g., sexual abuse), the child may withdraw into an elaborate fantasy world in which he or she may assume special powers or strengths. Like the alarm response, this "defeat" or dissociative response is graded. The intensity of the dissociation typically varies with the intensity and duration of the traumatic event.

The neurobiology of dissociation is related to but somewhat different from that of hyperarousal. Both use the monoamine systems in the brainstem and diencephalon, but somewhat different elements of these complex networks are recruited. In animals, the "defeat" response has a distinct neurobiology that is similar to dissociation response in humans, at levels of both neurobiology and phenomenology (Henry, Stephens, & Ely, 1986; Heinsbroek et al., 1991; Miczek, Thompson, & Tornatzky, 1990). As with the hyperarousal/fight or flight response, dissociation involves brainstem-mediated CNS activation, which results in increases in circulating epinephrine and associated stress steroids (Glavin, 1985; Henry et al. 1993; Herman et al., 1982). A major CNS difference, however, is that in dissociation, vagal tone increases, decreasing blood pressure and heart rate (occasionally resulting in fainting) despite increases in circulating epinephrine. In addition, there appears to be an increased relative importance of dopaminergic systems, primarily mesolimbic and mesocortical (Kalivas, 1985; Kalivas, Richardson-Carlson, & Van Orden, 1986; Kalivas et al., 1988; Abercrombie et al., 1989). These dopaminergic systems are intimately involved in reward processes (see Beauchaine & Neuhaus, this volume), as well as affective valence and affect modulation (e.g., cocaine-induced euphoria). In some cases, they are co-localized with endogenous opioids mediating pain and other sensory processing. In turn, opioid systems are involved in altering perception of pain, sense of time, place, and reality. Indeed, most opiate agonists can induce dissociative responses. Of primary importance in mediating the freeze-or-surrender dissociative response are endogenous opioid systems (Abercrombie & Jacobs, 1988).

For most children and adults, the adaptive response to an acute trauma involves a mixture of hyperarousal and dissociation. During the trauma, a child feels threatened and arousal systems are activated. With increased threat, the child moves along the arousal continuum. At some point along this continuum, the dissociative response is activated, resulting in the host of protective mental (e.g., decreases in the perception of anxiety and pain) and physiological responses (decreased heart rate) that characterize this response.

Whatever the adaptive response during trauma, the key issue for subsequent psychopathology is how long these systems are activated. The longer and more intense the activation, the more likely there will be molecular changes that lead to long-term functional changes. Extreme, long-lived trauma can cause alterations that lead to sensitized, dysfunctional neural networks; essentially the state of fear can become a persisting trait of anxiety. What were once adaptive neurobiological states can become, over time, maladaptive traits (Perry et al., 1995).

TRAUMA ALTERS STRESS-MEDIATING NEURAL NETWORKS

The clinical impact of traumatic stress on the developing child has been well documented. The simplest documentations are studies examining the development of obvious trauma-related psychopathology such as PTSD (for review see Perry, 1994, 2001b; Glaser, 2000; Teicher et al., 2002; DeBellis & Thomas, 2003; Bremner, 2003). The increased incidence of PTSD following trauma has been well documented. Table 4.1 summarizes the key factors that appear to be related to the development of trauma-specific psychopathology.

Traumatic stress results in altered measures of brain function and brain-mediated functioning in children. These include measures of hippocampal function, adrenergic receptor functioning, hippocampal and cortical structural development, cardiovascular functioning, and emotional, social, and behavioral functioning (Perry, 1998; Teicher et al., 1994, 1997; De Bellis et al., 1994, 1997, 1999a, 1999b, 2001, 2002; Scaer et al., 2001; Carrion et al., 2001, 2002a). Magnetic resonance imaging (MRI) has revealed reductions in hippocampal volume (Bremner et al., 1997; Stein et al., 1997; Bremner et al., 2003), alterations in the size of the cerbellar vermis (Anderson et al., 2002), and altered amygdala volumes (Driessen et al., 2000; Schmahl et al., 2003). Furthermore, sexually abused girls demonstrate neuroendocrine abnormalities as adolescents (Putnam, 1998).

Functioning of monoamine systems in adults is influenced by developmental trauma (Perry, 1994, 2001a, 2001b). Furthermore, developmental trauma appears to influence the expression of at least one genetic vulnerability marker for depression. A study of a polymorphism for the promoter region of the serotonin transporter (5-HTT) gene indicated that childhood maltreatment increased risk of depression in early adulthood for persons with the common short allele compared to persons with the long allele (see also Klein, Torpey, & Buffard, this volume). The short allele is associated with lower transcriptional efficiency of the promoter (Caspi et al., 2002, 2003).

Table 4.1.

Risk and attenuating factors for the development of psychopathology following trauma.

	Event-Related Factors	Individual Characteristics	Family and Social Factors
Increase Risk (*Prolong the intensity or duration of the acute stress response*)	• Multiple or repeated event (in this case, ongoing threat) • Physical injury to child • Involves physical injury or death to loved one, particularly mother • Dismembered or disfigured bodies seen • Destroys home, school, or community • Disrupts community infrastructure (as Katrina) • Perpetrator is family member • Long duration, difficult recovery (as in Katrina)	• Female • Age (younger more vulnerable) • Subjective perception of physical harm • History of previous exposure to trauma • No cultural or religious anchors • No shared experience with peers (experiential isolation) • Low IQ • Pre-existing neuropsychiatric disorder (especially anxiety related)	• Trauma directly impacts caregivers • Anxiety in primary caregivers • Continuing threat and disruption to family • Chaotic, overwhelmed family • Physical isolation • Distant caregiving • Absent caregivers
Decrease Risk (*Decrease intensity or duration of the acute stress response*)	• Single event • Perpetrator is stranger • No disruption of family or community structure • Short duration (e.g., tornado)	• Cognitively capable of understanding abstract concepts • Healthy coping skills • Educated about normative posttraumatic responses • Immediate posttraumatic interventions • Strong ties to cultural or religious belief system	• Intact, nurturing family supports • Nontraumatized caregivers • Caregivers educated about normative posttraumatic responses • Strong family beliefs • Mature and attuned parenting skills

The most overwhelming evidence for the impact of developmental trauma on stress-related neural networks comes from a retrospective epidemiological study of 17,000 adults. Over the last 10 years the Adverse Childhood Experience (ACE) studies have been reporting on increased risk of a host of emotional, social, behavioral, and physical health problems following abuse and related traumatic experiences in childhood (Anda et al.,1991, 2001; Dube et al., 2001a, 2001b, 2002a, 2002b, 2003a, 2003b). These findings converge with evidence from neurobiology about numerous effects of childhood stress on brain and physical systems (Glaser, 2000; Anda et al., 2006). This series of epidemiological studies examined the relationship between adverse childhood experiences, including child abuse, on a wide range of functioning in adult life. The findings are consistent with the view that developmental trauma influences the stress-response systems, and, therefore, can have destructive impact on all of the neural systems and functions that are interconnected to this widely distributed network (see Fig. 4.1).

Among the ACE findings are a graded increase in risk (i.e., more abuse translates into higher risk) for affective symptoms and panic attacks, memory problems, hallucinations, poor anger control, perpetuation of partner violence, unhealthy sexual behavior (early intercourse, promiscuity, sexual dissatisfaction), suicide, substance abuse, alcohol use and abuse, and smoking. In addition, there is a significant increase in risk for a range of physical health problems and mortality following adverse childhood experiences (Felitti et al., 1998).

Taken together, there is little doubt that developmental trauma alters key neural systems involved in the stress response, resulting in a host of neuropsychiatric and related functional problems—which may be contributed to and compounded by disrupted family systems, poverty, and other contextual risk factors within which abuse and neglect are so often embedded.

SUMMARY

All of the major molecular processes involved in brain development can be negatively influenced by abuse. With either neglect or trauma, the timing (the earlier in life the more impact), intensity, pattern, and duration of the maltreatment can alter virtually every brain system and brain area. The result is that in any given child, the individual history of maltreatment produces a unique pattern of altered neural systems and resulting psychopathology, exemplifying the developmental psychopathology concept of multifinality. As a result, maltreatment may be the Great Impostor. Depending on the age, nature, and pattern of maltreatment, a child may develop symptoms that mimic dozens of traditional DSM-IV diagnoses—from autism to ADHD to depression to "learning disorder." Furthermore, a genetically vulnerable child may develop a pathological phenotype while a hardier child may not.

This complexity poses a fundamental challenge to any attempts to create simple over-inclusive descriptive categories of psychopathology. Future classification of human psychopathology will need to incorporate a more neurodevelopmentally informed perspective in order to accurately understand the mechanisms that underlie neuropsychiatric symptoms in a given child or adult. This more mechanism-focused classification would approximate the current model of diagnostic classification in other areas of medicine where there is a more direct connection between the disease process and the pathophysiology. The hope and the promise is that understanding the mechanisms underlying psychopathology will lead to more effective interventions, and ultimately to more important changes in practice, programs, and policies that will help prevent the development of abuse-related psychopathology.

REFERENCES

Abercrombie, E. D., & Jacobs, B. L. (1987). Single-unit response of noradrenergic neurons in the locus coeruleus of freely moving cats. I. Acutely presented stressful and non-stressful stimuli. *Journal of Neuroscience, 7*, 2837–2847.

Abercrombie E. D., & Jacobs B. L. (1988). Systemic naloxone administration potentiates locus coeruleus noradrenergic neuronal activity under stressful but not non-stressful conditions. *Brain Research, 441*, 362–366.

Abercrombie E. D., Keefe K. A., DiFrischia D.S., & Zigmond, M. J. (1989). Differential effects of stress on in vivo dopamine release in striatum, nucleus accumbens and medial frontal cortex. *Journal of Neurochemistry, 52*, 1655–1658.

Altman, J., & Das, G. D. (1964). Autoradiographic examination of the effects of enriched environment on the rate of glial multiplication in the adult rat brain. *Nature, 204*, 1161–1165.

Anda, R. F., Chapman, D. P., Felitti, V. J., Edwards, V. E., Williamson, D. F., Croft, J. P., et al. (2002a). Adverse childhood experiences and risk of paternity in teen pregnancy. *Obstetrics and Gynecology, 100*, 37–45.

Anda, R. F., Croft, J. B., Felitti, V. J., Nordenberg, D., Giles, W. H., Williamson, D. F., et al. (1999). Adverse childhood experiences and smoking during adolescence and adulthood. *Journal of the American Medical Association, 282*, 1652.

Anda, R. F., Felitti, V. J., Chapman, D. P., Croft, J. B., Williamson, D. F., Santelli

J., et al. (2001). Abused boys, battered mothers, and male involvement in teen pregnancy. *Pediatrics, 107*(2), e19.

Anda, R. F., Felitti, R. F., Walker, J., Whitfield, C., Bremner, D. J., Perry, B. D., et al. (2006). The enduring effects of childhood abuse and related experiences: A convergence of evidence from neurobiology and epidemiology, *European Archives of Psychiatric and Clinical Neuroscience, 256*, 174–186.

Anderson, C. M., Teicher, M. H., Polcari, A., & Renshaw, P. I. (2002). Abnormal T2 relaxation time in the cerebellar vermis of adults sexually abused in childhood: Potential role of the vermis in stress-enhanced risk for drug abuse. *Psychoneuroendocrinology, 27*, 231–244.

Aston-Jones, G., Ennis, M., Pieribone, V. A., Nickell, W. T., & Shipley, M. T. (1986). The brain nucleus locus coeruleus: Restricted afferent control of a broad efferent network. *Science 234*, 734–737.

Bartanusz, V., Jezova, D., Bertini, L. T., Tilders, F. J., Aubry, J. M., & Kiss, J. Z. (1993). Stress-induced increase in vasopressin and corticotropin-releasing factor expression in hypophysiotrophic paraventricular neurons. *Endocrinology, 132*, 895–902.

Beckett, C., Maughan, B., Rutter, M., Castle, J., Colvert, E., Groothues, C., et al. (2006). Do the effects of early severe deprivation on cognition persist into early adolescence? Findings from the English and Romanian Adoptees Study. *Child Development, 77*, 696–711.

Bennett, E. L., Diamond, M. L., Krech, D., & Rosenzweig, M. R. (1964). Chemical and anatomical plasticity of the brain. *Science, 146*, 610–619.

Bennett, A. J., Lesch, K. P., Heils, A., Long, J. C., Lorenz, J. G., Shoaf, S. E., et al. (2002). Early experience and serotonin transporter gene variation interact to influence primate CNS function. *Molecular Psychiatry, 7*, 118–122.

Bookstein, F. L., Streissguth, A. P., Sampson, P. D., Connor, P. D., & Barr, H. M. (2002). Corpus callosum shape and neuropsychological deficits in adult males with heavy fetal alcohol exposure. *NeuroImage, 15*, 233–251.

Bremner, J. D. (2003). Long-term effects of childhood abuse on brain and neurobiology. *Child and Adolescent Psychiatric Clinics of North America, 12*, 271–292.

Bremner, J. D., Randall, P., Vermetten, E., Staib, L., Bronen, R. A., Mazure, C., et al. (1997). Magnetic image resonance-based measurement of hippocampal volume in posttraumatic stress disorder related to childhood physical and sexual abuse: A preliminary report. *Biological Psychiatry, 41*, 23–32.

Bremner, J. D., Vythilingam, M., Vermetten, E., Southwick, S. M., McGlashan, T., Nazeer, A., Khan, S., Vaccarino, L., Soufer, R., Garg, P. K., Ng, C. K., Staib, L. H., Duncan, J. S., & Charney, D. S. (2003). MRI and PET study of deficits in hippocampal structure and function in women with childhood sexual abuse and posttraumatic stress disorder. *American Journal of Psychiatry 160*, 924–932.

Caldji, C., Francis, D., Sharma, S., Plotsky, P. M., & Meaney, M. J. (2000). The effects of early rearing environment on the development of GABA and central benzodiazepine receptor levels and novelty-induced fearfulness in the rat. *Neuropsychopharmacology, 22*, 219–229.

Caldji, C., Tannenbaum, B., Sharma, S., Francis, D., Plotsky, P. M., & Meaney, M. J.

(1998). Maternal care during infancy regulates the development of neural systems mediating the expression of fearfulness in the rat. *Proceedings of the National Academy of Sciences, 95,* 5335–5340.

Cannon, W. B. (1914). The emergency function of the adrenal medulla in pain and the major emotions. *American Journal of Physiology, 33,* 356–372.

Carrion, V. G., Weems, C. F., Eliez, S., Patwardhan, A., Brown, W., Ray, R., et al. (2001). Attenuation of frontal asymmetry in pediatric posttraumatic stress disorder. *Biological Psychiatry, 50,* 943–951.

Carrion, V. G., Weems, C. F., Ray, R., Glaser, B., Hessl, D., & Reiss, A. L. (2002a). Diurnal salivary cortisol in pediatric posttraumatic stress disorder. *Biological Psychiatry 51,* 575–582.

Caspi, A., McClay, J., Moffitt, T. E., Mill, J., Martin, J., Craig, I. W., et al. (2002). Role of genotype in the cycle of violence in maltreated children. *Science, 297,* 851–854.

Caspi, A., Sugden, K., Moffitt, T. E., Taylor, A., Craig, I. W., Harrington, H., et al. (2003). Influence of life stress on depression: Moderation by a polymorphism in the 5-HTT gene. *Science, 301,* 386–389.

Castro-Alamancos, M. A., & Connors, B. W. (1996). Short-term plasticity of a thalamocortical pathway dynamically modulated by behavioral state. *Science, 272,* 274–277.

Chugani, H. T., Behen, M. E., Muzik, O., Juhasz, C., Nagy, F., & Chugani, D. C. (2001). Local brain functional activity following early deprivation: A study of post-institutionalized Romanian orphans. *Neuroimage, 6,* 1290–1301.

Clugnet, M. C., & LeDoux, J. E. (1990). Synaptic plasticity in fear conditioning circuits: Induction of LTP in the lateral nucleus of the amygdala by stimulation of the medial geniculate body. *Journal of Neuroscience, 10,* 2818–2824.

Coleman, P. D., & Riesen, A. H. (1968). Environmental effects on cortical dendritic fields: I. Rearing in the dark. *Journal of Anatomy, 102,* 363–374.

Coplan, J. D., Andrews, M. W., Rosenblum, L. A., Owens, M. J., Friedman, S., Gorman, J. M., et al. (1996). Persistent elevations of cerebrospinal fluid concentrations of corticotropin-releasing factor in adult nonhuman primates exposed to early-life stressors: Implications for the pathophysiology of mood and anxiety disorders. *Proceedings of the National Academy of Sciences, 93,* 1619–1623.

Croft, C., Beckett, C., Rutter, M., Castle, J., Colvert, E., Groothues, C., et al. (2007). Early adolescent outcomes of institutionally-deprived and non-deprived adoptees. II: Language as a protective factor and a vulnerable outcome. *Journal of Child Psychology and Psychiatry, 48,* 31–44.

Cummins, R. A., & Livesey, P. (1979). Enrichment-isolation, cortex length, and the rank order effect. *Brain Research, 178,* 88–98.

Darwin, C. (1868). The variations of animals and plants under domestication. London: J. Murray.

Davis, M. (1992a). The role of the amygdala in fear and anxiety. *Annual Review of Neuroscience, 15,* 353–375.

Davis, M. (1992b). The role of the amygdala in fear-potentiated startle: Implications for animal models of anxiety. *Trends in Pharmacological Science, 13,* 35–41.

De Bellis, M. D., Hall, J., Boring, A. M., Frustaci, K., & Moritz, G. (2001). A pilot study of hippocampal volumes in pediatric maltreatment-related posttraumatic stress disorder. *Biological Psychiatry, 50,* 305–309.

De Bellis, M. D., Baum, A. S., Birmaher, B., Keshavan, M. S., Eccard , C. H., Boring, A. M., et al. (1999a). A. E. Bennett Research Award. Developmental traumatology. Part I: Biological stress systems. *Biological Psychiatry, 45,* 1259–1270.

De Bellis, M. D., Baum, A. S., Birmaher, B., & Ryan, N. D. (1997). Urinary catecholamine excretion in childhood overanxious and posttraumatic stress disorders. *Annals of the New York Academy of Science, 821,* 451–455.

De Bellis, M. D., Chrousos, G. P., Dorn, L. D., Burke, L., Helmers, K., Kling, M. A., et al. (1994). Hypothalamic-pituitary-adrenal axis dysregulation in sexually abused girls. *Journal of Clinical Endocrinology and Metabolism, 78,* 249–255.

De Bellis, M. D., Keshavan, M. S., Clark, D. B., Casey, B. J., Giedd, J. N., Boring, A. M., et al. (1999b). A. E. Bennett Research Award. Developmental traumatology. Part II: Brain development. *Biological Psychiatry, 45,* 1271–1284.

De Bellis, M. D., Keshavan, M. S., Shifflett, H., Iyengar, S., Beers, S. R., Hall, J., et al. (2002). Brain structures in pediatric maltreatment-related posttraumatic stress disorder: A sociodemographically matched study. *Biological Psychiatry, 52,* 1066–1078.

De Bellis, M., & Thomas, L. (2003). Biologic findings of post-traumatic stress disorder and child maltreatment. *Current Psychiatry Reports, 5,* 108–117.

Dennis, W. (1973). *Children of the Creche.* New York: Appleton-Century-Crofts.

Diamond, M. C., & Hopson, J. (1998). *Magic trees of the mind: How to nurture your child's intelligence, creativity, and healthy emotions from birth through adolescence.* New York: Dutton.

Diamond, M. C., Krech, D., & Rosenzweig, M. R. (1964). The effects of an enriched environment on the histology of the rat cerebral cortex. *Comparative Neurology, 123,* 111–119.

Diamond, M. C., Law, F., Rhodes, H., Lindner, B., Rosenzweig, M. R., Krech, D., et al. (1966). Increases in cortical depth and glia numbers in rats subjected to enriched environments. *Comparative Neurology, 128,* 117–126.

Dube, S. R., Anda, R. F., Felitti, V. J., Chapman, D., Williamson, D. F., & Giles, W. H. (2001a). Childhood abuse, household dysfunction and the risk of attempted suicide throughout the life span: findings from the Adverse Childhood Experiences Study. *Journal of the American Medical Association, 286,* 3089–3096.

Dube, S. R., Anda, R. F., Felitti, V. J., Croft, J. B., Edwards, V. J., & Giles, W. H. (2001b). Growing up with parental alcohol abuse: Exposure to childhood abuse, neglect and household dysfunction. *Child Abuse and Neglect, 25,* 1627–1640.

Dube, S. R., Anda, R. F., Felitti, V. J., Edwards, V. J., & Croft, J. B. (2002a). Adverse childhood experiences and personal alcohol abuse as an adult. *Addictive Behaviors, 27,* 713–725.

Dube, S. R., Anda, R. F., Felitti, V. J., Edwards, V. J., & Williamson, D. F. (2002b).

Exposure to abuse, neglect and household dysfunction among adults who witnessed intimate partner violence as children. *Violence and Victims, 17,* 3–17.

Dube, S. R., Felitti, V. J., Chapman, D. P., Giles, W. H., & Anda, R. F. (2003a). Childhood abuse, neglect and household dysfunction and the risk of illicit drug use: the Adverse Childhood Experience Study. *Pediatrics, 111,* 564–572.

Dube, S. R., Felitti, V. J., Dong, M., Giles, W. H., & Anda, R. F. (2003b). The impact of adverse childhood experiences on health problems: Evidence from four birth cohorts dating back to 1900. *Preventive Medicine, 37,* 268–277.

Driessen, M., Herrmann, J., Stahl, K., Zwaan, M., Meier, S., Hill, A., et al. (2000). Magnetic resonance imaging volumes of the hippocampus and the amygdala in women with borderline personality disorder and early traumatization. *Archives of General Psychiatry, 57,* 1115–1122.

Ebinger, P. (1974). A cytoachitectonic volumetric comparison of brains in wild and domestic sheep. *Zeitschrift fur Anatomie und Entwicklungsgeschichte, 144,* 267–302.

Elam, M., Thoren, P., & Svensson, T. H. (1986). Locus coeruleus neurons and sympathetic nerves: Activation by visceral afferents. *Brain Research, 375,* 117–125.

Epstein, J. N., Saunders, B. E., Kilpatrick, D. G., & Resnick, H. S. (1998). PTSD as a mediator between childhood rape and alcohol use in adult women. *Child Abuse and Neglect 22,* 223–234.

Felitti, V. J., Anda, R. F., Nordenberg, D., Williamson, D. F., Spitz, A. M., Edwards, V., et al. (1998). Relationship of childhood abuse and household dysfunction to many of the leading causes of death in adults. The Adverse Childhood Experiences Study. *American Journal of Preventive Medicine, 14,* 245–258.

Foote, S. L., Bloom, E., & Aston-Jones, G. (1983). Nucleus locus coeruleus: New evidence of anatomical and physiological specificity. *Physiology and Behavior, 63,* 844–914.

Francis, D. D., Caldji, C., Champagne, F., Plotsky, P. M., & Meaney, M. J. (1999). The role of corticotropin-releasing factor-norepinephrine systems in mediating the effects of early experience on the development of behavioral and endocrine responses to stress. *Biological Psychiatry, 46,* 1153–1166.

Francis, D. D., Young, L. J., Meaney, M. J., & Insel, T. R. (2002). Naturally occurring differences in maternal care are associated with the expression of oxytocin and vasopression (V1a) receptors: Gender differences. *Journal of Neuroendocrinology, 14,* 349–353.

Glaser, D. (2000). Child abuse and neglect and the brain: A review. *Journal of Child Psychology and Psychiatry, 41,* 97–116.

Glavin, G. B. (1985). Stress and brain noradrenaline: A review. *Neuroscience Biobehavioral Reviews, 9,* 233–243.

Gorman, J. M., Liebowitz, M. R., Fyer, A. J., & Stein, J. (1989). A neuroanatomical hypothesis for panic disorder. *Am J Psychiatry 146,* 148–156.

Gould, E., Reeves, A. J., Graziano, M. S. A., & Gross, C. G. (1999). Neurogenesis in the neocortex of adult primates. *Science, 286,* 548–552.

Greenough, W. T., & Volkmar, F. R. (1973). Pattern of dendritic branching in occipital cortex of rats reared in complex environments. *Experimental Neurology, 40*, 491–504.

Greenough, W. T., Volkmar, F. R., & Juraska, J. M. (1973). Effects of rearing complexity on dendritic branching in frontolateral and temporal cortex of the rat. *Experimental Neurology, 41*, 371–378.

Gunnar, M. R., Morison, S. J., Chisholm, K., & Schuder, M. (2001). Salivary cortisol levels in children adopted from Romanian orphanages. *Development and Psychopathology, 13*, 611–628.

Heidenreich, F. W. (1834). Kaspar Hausers verwundung, krankeit und liechenoffnung. *Journal der Chirurgie und Augen-Heilkunde, 21*, 91–123.

Heim, C., & Nemeroff, C. B. (2001). The role of childhood trauma in the neurobiology of mood and anxiety disorders: Preclinical and clinical studies. *Biological Psychiatry, 49*, 1023–1039.

Heim, C., Newport, D. J., Bonsall, R., Miller, A. H., & Nemeroff, C. B. (2001). Altered pituitary-adrenal axis responses to provocative challenge tests in adult survivors of childhood abuse. *American Journal of Psychiatry, 158*, 575–581.

Heim, C., Newport, D. J., Heit, S., Graham, Y. P., Wilcox, M., Bonsall, R., et al. (2000). Pituitary-adrenal and autonomic responses to stress in women after sexual and physical abuse in childhood. *Journal of the American Medical Association, 284*, 592–597.

Heinsbroek, R. P. W., van Haaren, F., Feenstra, M. P. G., Boon P., van de Poll, N. E. (1991). Controllable and uncontrollable footshock and monoaminergic activity in the frontal cortex of male and female rats. *Brain Research 551*, 247–255.

Henry, J. P., Stephens, P. M., & Ely, D. L. (1986). Psychosocial hypertension and the defense and defeat reactions. *Journal of Hypertension, 4*, 687–697.

Henry, J. P., Liu, Y. Y., Nadra, W. E., Qian, C. G., Mormede, P., Lemaire, V., et al. (1993). Psychosocial stress can induce chronic hypertension in normotensive strains of rats. *Hypertension, 21*, 714–723.

Herman, J. P., Guillonneau, D., Dantzer, R., Scatton, B., Semerdjian-Rouquier, L., LeMoal, M. (1982). Differential effects of inescapable footshocks and of stimuli previously paired with inescapable footshocks on dopamine turnover in cortical and limbic areas of the rat. *Life Science, 30*, 2207–2214.

Hubel, D. H., & Wiesel, T. N. (1963). Receptive fields of cells in striate cortex of very young, visually inexperienced kittens. *Journal of Neurophysiology, 26*, 994–1002.

Hubel, D. H., & Wiesel, T. N. (1970). The period of susceptibility to the physiological effects of unilateral eye closure in kittens. *Journal of Physiology, 206*, 419–436.

Huttenlocher, J., Vasilyeva, M., Cymerman, E., & Levine, S. C. (2002). Language input and child syntax. *Cognitive Psychology, 45*, 337–374.

Huttenlocher, P. R. (1979). Synaptic density in human frontal cortex: Developmental changes and effects of aging. *Brain Research, 163*, 195–205.

Huttenlocher, P. R. (1994). Synaptogenesis in human cerebral cortex. In G. Dawson & K. W. Fischer (Eds.), *Human behavior and the developing brain* (pp. 35–54). New York: Guilford.

Kalivas, P. W. (1985). Sensitization to repeated enkephalin administration into the ventral tegmental area of the rat, II: Involvement of the mesolimbic dopamine system. *Journal of Pharmacology and Experimental Therapeutics, 235,* 544–550.

Kalivas, P. W., Duffy, P., Dilts, R., & Abhold, R. (1988). Enkephalin modulation of A10 dopamine neurons: A role in dopamine sensitization. *Annals of the New York Academy of Sciences, 537,* 405–414.

Kalivas, P. W., Richardson-Carlson, R., & Van Orden, G. (1986). Cross sensitization between foot shock stress and enkephalin-induced motor activity. *Biological Psychiatry, 21,* 939–950.

Kehne, J. (2007). The CRF1 receptor, a novel target for the treatment of depression, anxiety, and stress-related disorders. *CNS and Neurological Disorders—Drug Targets, 6,* 182–196.

Kendler, K. S., Bulik, C. M., Silberg, J., Hettema, J. M., Myers, J., & Prescott, C. A. (2000). Childhood sexual abuse and adult psychiatric and substance abuse disorders in women: An epidemiological and co-twin control analysis. *Archives of General Psychiatry, 57,* 953–959.

Klüver, H., & Bucy, P. C. (1937). "Psychic blindness" and other symptoms following bilateral temporal lobectomy in rhesus monkeys. *American Journal of Physiology, 119,* 352–353.

Kuan, C. Y., Roth, K. A., Flavell, R. A., & Rakic, P. (2000). Mechanisms of programmed cell death in the developing brain. *Trends in Neuroscience, 23,* 291–297.

LeDoux, J. E., Cicchetti, P., Xagoraris, A., & Romanski, L. M. (1990). The lateral amygdaloid nucleus: Sensory interface of the amygdala in fear conditioning. *Journal of Neuroscience, 10,* 1062–1069.

LeDoux, J. E., Iwata, J., Cicchetti, P., & Reis, D. J. (1988). Different projections of the central amygdaloid nucleus mediate autonomic and behavioral correlates of conditioned fear. *Journal of Neuroscience, 8,* 2517–2529.

Levine, E. S., Litto, W. J., & Jacobs, B. L. (1990). Activity of cat locus coeruleus noradrenergic neurons during the defense reaction. *Brain Research, 531,* 189–195.

Levine, S., Atha, K., & Wiener, S. G. (1993a). Early experience effects on the development of fear in the squirrel monkey. *Behavioral and Neural Biology, 60,* 225–233.

Levine, S., Wiener, S. G., & Coe, C. L. (1993b). Temporal and social factors influencing behavioral and hormonal responses to separation in mother and infant squirrel monkeys. *Psychoneuroendocrinology, 18,* 297–306.

Maunsell, J. H. (1995). The brain's visual world: Representation of visual targets in cerebral cortex. *Science, 270,* 764–769.

McEwen, B. S. (2001). From molecules to mind: Stress, individual differences, and the social environment. *Annals of the New York Academy of Sciences, 935,* 42–49.

Meaney, M. J., Aitken, D. H., van Berkal, C., Bhatnagar, S., & Sapolsky, R. M. (1988). Effect of neonatal handling on age-related impairments associated with the hippocampus. *Science, 239,* 766–768.

Miaskowski, C., Ong, G. L., Lukic, D., & Haldar, J. (1988). Immobilization stress affects oxytocin and vasopressin levels in hypothalamic and extrahypothalamic sites. *Brain Research, 458,* 137–141.

Miczek, K. A., Thompson, M. L., & Tornatzky, W. (1990). Subordinate animals: Behavioral and physiological adaptations and opioid tolerance. In M. Brown, G. Koob, & C. Rivier (Eds.), *Stress: Neurobiology and neuroendocrinology* (pp. 323–357). New York: Marcel Dekker.

Money, J., & Annecillo, C. (1976). IQ changes following change of domicile in the syndrome of reversible hyposomatotropinism (psychosocial dwarfism): Pilot investigation. *Psychoneuroendocrinology, 1,* 427–429.

Moore, R. Y., & Bloom, F. E. (1979). Central catecholamine neuron systems: Anatomy and physiology of the norepinephrine and epinephrine systems. *Annual Review of Neuroscience, 2,* 113–168.

Morilak, D. A., Fornal, C. A., & Jacobs, B. L. (1987a). Effects of physiological manipulations on locus coeruleus neuronal activity in freely moving cats. I: Thermoregulatory challenge. *Brain Research, 422,* 17–23.

Morilak, D. A., Fornal, C. A., & Jacobs, B. L. (1987b). Effects of physiological manipulations on locus coeruleus neuronal activity in freely moving cats. II: Cardiovascular challenge. *Brain Research, 422,* 24–31.

Morilak, D. A., Fornal, C. A., & Jacobs, B. L. (1987c). Effects of physiological manipulations on locus coeruleus neuronal activity in freely moving cats. III: Glucoregulatory challenge. *Brain Research, 422,* 32–39.

Munk, M. H., Roelfsema, P. R., Konig, P., Engel, A. K., & Singer, W. (1996). Role of reticular activation in the modulation of intracortical synchronization. *Science 272,* 271–274.

Nauta, W. J., & Whitlock, D. G. (1956). Subcortical projections from the temporal neocortex in Macaca mulatta. *Journal of Comparative Neurology, 106,* 183–212.

Nelson, C. A., de Haan, M., & Thomas, K. M. (2006). *Neuroscience of cognitive development.* Hoboken, NJ: Wiley.

O'Connor, C., Rutter, M., & English and Romanian Adoptees Study Team. (2000). Attachment disorder behavior following early severe deprivation: Extension and longitudinal follow-up. *Journal of the American Academy of Child and Adolescent Psychiatry, 39,* 703–712.

Papez, J. W. (1937). A proposed mechanism of emotion. *Archives of Neurology and Psychiatry 38,* 725–740.

Pavlides, C., Watanabe, Y., & McEwen, B. S. (1993). Effects of glucocorticoids on hippocampal long-term potentiation. *Hippocampus 3,* 183–192.

Perry, B. D. (1988). Placental and blood element neurotransmitter receptor regulation in humans: Potential models for studying neurochemical mechanisms underlying behavioral teratology. *Progress in Brain Research, 73,* 189–206.

Perry, B. D. (1994). Neurobiological sequelae of childhood trauma: Post-traumatic stress disorders in children. In M. Murberg (Ed.), *Catecholamines in post-traumatic stress disorder: Emerging concepts* (pp. 253–276). Washington, DC: American Psychiatric Press.

Perry, B. D. (2001a). The neurodevelopmental impact of violence in childhood. In

D. Schetky & E. P. Benedek (Eds.), *Textbook of child and adolescent forensic psychiatry* (pp. 221–238). Washington, DC: American Psychiatric Press.

Perry, B. D. (2001b). The neuroarcheology of childhood maltreatment: The neurodevelopmental costs of adverse childhood events. In K. Franey, R. Geffner, & R. Falconer (Eds.), *The cost of maltreatment: Who pays? We all do* (pp. 15–37). San Diego, CA: Family Violence and Sexual Assault Institute.

Perry, B. D. (2002). Childhood experience and the expression of genetic potential: What childhood neglect tells us about nature and nurture. *Brain and Mind, 3,* 79–100.

Perry, B. D. (2006). The neurosequential model of therapeutics: Applying principles of neuroscience to clinical work with traumatized and maltreated children. In N. B. Webb (Ed.), *Working with traumatized youth in child welfare* (pp. 27–52). New York: Guilford.

Perry, B. D., & Pollard, R. (1997). Altered brain development following global neglect in early childhood. *Proceedings from the Society for Neuroscience Annual Meeting* (New Orleans), (abstract).

Perry, B. D., & Pollard, R. (1998). Homeostasis, stress, trauma, and adaptation: A neurodevelopmental view of childhood trauma. *Child and Adolescent Psychiatric Clinics of North America, 7,* 33–51.

Perry, B. D., Pollard, R., Blakely, T., Baker, W., & Vigilante, D. (1995). Childhood trauma, the neurobiology of adaptation and 'use-dependent' development of the brain: How "states" become "traits." *Infant Mental Health Journal, 16,* 271–291.

Phillips, R. G., & LeDoux, J. E. (1992). Differential contribution of amygdala and hippocampus to cued and contextual fear conditioning. *Behavioral Neuroscience, 106,* 274–285.

Plotsky, P. M., & Meaney, M. J. (1993). Early, postnatal experience alters hypothalamic corticotropin releasing factor (CRF) mRNA, median eminence CRF content and stress-induced release in adult rats. *Molecular Brain Research, 18,* 195–200.

Putnam, F. W. (March, 1998). Developmental pathways in sexually abused girls. Presented at Psychological Trauma: Maturational Processes and Psychotherapeutic Interventions. Harvard Medical School, Boston.

Rakic, P. (1981). Development of visual centers in the primate brain depends upon binocular competition before birth. *Science, 214,* 928–931.

Rakic, P. (1996). Development of cerebral cortex in human and non-human primates. In M. Lewis (Ed.), *Child and adolescent psychiatry: A comprehensive textbook.* (pp. 9–30). New York: Williams and Wilkins.

Read, J., Perry, B. D., Moskowith, A., & Connolloy, J. (2001). The contribution of early traumatic events to schizophrenia in some patients: A traumagenic neurodevelopmental model. *Psychiatry, 64,* 319–345.

Rehkamper, G., Haase, E., & Frahm, H. D. (1988). Allometric comparison of brain weight and brain structure volumes in different breeds of the domestic pigeon, columbia livia f. d. *Brain Behavior and Evolution, 31,* 141–149.

Reul, J. M., & de Kloet, E. R. (1985). Two receptor systems for corticosterone in rat brain: Microdistribution and differential occupation. *Endocrinology, 117,* 2505–2511.

Rohrs, M. (1955). Vergleichende untersuchungen an wild- und hauskatzen. *Zoologischer Anzeiger, 155,* 53–69.

Rohrs, M., & Ebinger, P. (1978). Die beurteilung von hirngrobenunterschieden zwischen wild- und haustieren. *Journal of Zoological Systematics and Evolutionary Research, 16,* 1–14.

Rosenbaum, J. F., Biederman, J., Gersten, M., Hirshfeld, D. R., Meminger, S. R., Herman J. B., et al. (1988). Behavioral inhibition in children of parents with panic disorder and agoraphobia: A controlled study. *Archives of General Psychiatry, 45,* 463–470.

Rutledge, L. T., Wright, C., & Duncan, J. (1974). Morphological changes in pyramidal cells of mammalian neocortex associated with increased use. *Experimental Neurology, 44,* 209–228.

Rutter, M. (2004). Environmentally Mediated Risks for Psychopathology: Research Strategies and Findings. *Journal of the American Academy of Child & Adolescent Psychiatry, 44,* 3–18.

Rutter, M., Andersen-Wood, L., Beckett, C., Bredenkamp, D., Castle, J., Grootheus, C., et al. (1999). Quasi-autistic patterns following severe early global privation. *Journal of Child Psychology and Psychiatry, 40,* 537–549.

Rutter, M., Colvert, E., Kreppner, J., Beckett, C., Castle, J., Groothues, C., et al. (2007). Early adolescent outcomes for institutionally-deprived and non-deprived adoptees. I: Disinhibited attachment. *Journal of Child Psychology and Psychiatry, 48,* 17–30.

Rutter, M., & English and Romanian Adoptees Study Team. (1998). Developmental catch-up, and deficit, following adoption after severe global early privation. *Journal of Child Psychology and Psychiatry, 39,* 465–476.

Rutter, M., & O'Connor, T. G. (2004). Are there biological programming effects for psychological development? Findings from a study of Romanian adoptees. *Developmental Psychology, 40,* 81–94.

Saper, C. B. (1982). Convergence of autonomic and limbic connections in the insular cortex of the rat. *Journal of Comparative Neurology, 210,* 163–173.

Sapolsky, R. M. (2000). Glucocorticoids and hippocampal atrophy in neuropsychiatric disorders. *Archives of General Psychiatry, 57,* 925–935.

Sapolsky, R. M., Krey, L. C., & McEwen, B. S. (1984). Glucocorticoid-sensitive hippocampal neurons are involved in terminating the adrenocortical stress response. *Proceedings of the National Academy of Sciences, 81,* 6174–6177.

Saplosky, R. M., & Plotsky, P. M. (1990). Hypercortisolism and its possible neural bases. In *Biological Psychiatry, 27,* 937–945.

Schmahl, C. G., Vermetten, E., Elzinga, B. M., & Bremner, J. D. (2003). Magnetic resonance imaging of hippocampal and amygdala volume in women with childhood abuse and borderline personality disorder. *Psychiatry Research, 122,* 193–198.

Selden, N. R., Everitt, B. J., Jarrard, L. E., & Robbins, T. W. (1991). Complementary roles for the amygdala and hippocampus in aversive conditioning to explicit and contextual cues. *Neuroscience, 42,* 335–350.

Singer, W. (1995).Development and plasticity of cortical processing architectures. *Science, 270,* 758–764.

Simon, N. (1978). Kaspar Hauser. *Journal of Autism and Childhood Schizophrenia, 8,* 209–217.

Spitz, R. A. (1945). Hospitalism: An inquiry into the genesis of psychiatric conditions in early childhood. *Psychoanalytic Study of the Child, 1,* 53–74.

Spitz, R. A. (1946). Hospitalism: A follow-up report on investigation described in Volume I, 1945. *Psychoanalytic Study of the Child, 2,* 113–117.

Strathearn, L. L., Gray, P. H., O'Callaghan, M. J., & Wood, D. W. (submitted). Cognitive neurodevelopment in extremely low birth weight infants: Nature vs. nurture revisited.

Strathearn, L., Gray, P. H., O'Callaghan, F., & Wood, D. O. (2001). Childhood neglect and cognitive development in extremely low birth weight infants: A prospective study. *Pediatrics, 108,* 142–151.

Stanton, M. E., Gutierrez, Y. R., & Levine, S. (1988). Maternal deprivation potentiates pituitary-adrenal stress responses in infant rats. *Behavioral Neuroscience, 102,* 692–700.

Stein, M. B., Koverola, C., Hanna, C., Torchia, M. G., & McClarty, B. (1997). Hippocampal volume in women victimized by childhood sexual abuse. *Psychological Medicine, 27,* 1–9.

Teicher, M. H., Andersen, S. L., Polcari, A., Anderson, C. M., & Navalta, C. P. (2002). Developmental neurobiology of childhood stress and trauma. *Psychiatric Clinics of North America, 25,* 397–426.

Teicher, M. H., Ito, Y., Glod, C. A., Andersen, S. L., Dumont, N., & Ackerman, E. (1997). Preliminary evidence for abnormal cortical development in physically and sexually abused children using EEG coherence and MRI. *Annals of the New York Academy of Sciences, 821,* 160–175.

Teicher, M.H., Ito, Y., Glod, C. A., Schiffer, F., & Ackerman, E. (1994). Possible effects of early abuse on human brain development, as assessed by EEG coherence. *American Journal of Neuropsychopharmacology, 33,* 52.

Teicher, M. H., Dumont, N. L., Ito, Y., Vaituzis, C., Giedd, J. N., & Andersen, S. L. (2004). Childhood neglect is associated with reduced corpus callosum area. *Biological Psychiatry, 56,* 80–85.

Uno, H., Tarara, R., Else, J., Suleman, M. A., & Sapolsky, R. M. (1989). Hippocampal damage associated with prolonged and fatal stress in primates. *Journal of Neuroscience, 9,* 1705–1711.

Veldhuis, H. D., & De Kloet, E. R. (1982). Significance of ACTH4-10 in the control of hippocampal corticosterone receptor capacity of hypophysectomized rats. *Neuroendocrinology, 34,* 374–380.

Wainwright, M. S., Perry, B. D., Won, L. A., O'Malley, K. L., Wang, W-Y., & Heller, A. (1995). Immortalization of murine striatal neurons by somatic cell fusion with the N18TG2 neuroblastoma: Characterization of cell lines expressing a variety of dopamine receptors and cholinergic markers. *Journal of Neuroscience, 15,* 676–688.

Young, W. S., III, & Lightman, S. L. (1992). Chronic stress elevates enkephalin expression in the rat paraventricular and supraoptic nuclei. *Molecular Brain Research, 13,* 111–117.

CHAPTER 5

Impulsivity and Vulnerability to Psychopathology

THEODORE P. BEAUCHAINE AND EMILY NEUHAUS

T erms such as *impulsive, disinhibited,* and *hyperactive*—which are sometimes but not always used interchangeably in the psychopathology literature—have long been applied to individuals with deficient control over their behaviors. Although some degree of these behavioral problems may be normal for young children, those who display extreme impulsivity are vulnerable to a host of maladaptive outcomes, as are those who fail to acquire age-appropriate self-regulation skills as they mature. Indeed, trait impulsivity may underlie several disorders falling along the externalizing spectrum, including Attention-Deficit/Hyperactivity Disorder (ADHD), Conduct Disorder (CD), Antisocial Personality Disorder (ASPD), and many substance abuse and substance dependence disorders (see Barkley, 1997; Krueger et al., 2002).

According to developmental psychopathology models of externalizing behavior, extreme impulsivity expressed in the preschool years may represent the first stage in a trajectory that can progress—via potentiating and mediating variables—to early onset delinquency and other antisocial behavior patterns (Beauchaine, Gatzke-Kopp, & Mead, 2007; Campbell, Shaw, & Gilliom, 2000; Hinshaw, Lahey, & Hart, 1993; Patterson, DeGarmo,

Preparation of this chapter was supported by grants MH63699 and MH067192 from the National Institute of Mental Health. We thank Lisa Gatzke-Kopp for her helpful contribution.

& Knutson, 2000). In other cases, temperamental disinhibition marks the beginning stages of a developmental trajectory that also culminates in depression and internalizing psychopathology (Hirshfeld-Becker et al., 2002). Thus, impulsivity observed very early in life may indicate considerable risk for a wide range of adverse, multifinal outcomes.

HISTORICAL CONTEXT

As with nearly all psychological phenomena, ideas about the nature and etiology of disinhibition have evolved considerably over the nineteenth and twentieth centuries. Early neurobiological theories of behavioral control focused on frontal regions of the brain. These theories derived largely from observations of altered behavior among those who suffered from traumatic brain injuries, such as Phineas Gage. In 1848, Gage, a railroad foreman, suffered a severe brain injury when an iron rod—propelled by a blasting charge—penetrated his eye socket, exiting through the frontal part of his skull. Despite a full recovery of motor and sensory functions, Gage's personality transformed radically as a result of his injury (Macmillan, 1992). Whereas Gage had been "quiet and respectful" prior to the accident, he became "gross, profane, coarse, and vulgar to such a degree that his society was intolerable to decent people" (*American Phrenological Journal and Repository of Science, Literature, and General Intelligence*, 1851, cited in Macmillan, 1992, p. 86). He was further described as "impatient of restraint or advice when it conflicts with his desires, at times pertinaciously obstinate, yet capricious and vacillating, devising many plans of future operation, which are no sooner arranged than they are abandoned in turn for others appearing more feasible" (Harlow, 1868, cited in Macmillan, 2004, p. 182). Thus, the most striking result of Gage's injuries was marked behavioral disinhibition that contrasted starkly with the socially appropriate demeanor he had displayed previously.

Consistent with theories of the time, explanations of Gage's behavior relied upon two assumptions. First, particular brain regions located in the frontal lobe were assumed to support specific behavioral traits. When these regions were damaged, those traits were no longer supported. In Gage's case, the shift in behavior was attributed to the rod having injured the "regions of the organs of BENEVOLENCE and VENERATION" (*American Phrenological Journal and Repository of Science, Literature, and General Intelligence*, 1851, cited in Macmillan, 1992, p. 86). Second, it was assumed that competing factors were at work within the mind, with behavior resulting from the equilibrium established between them. When this equilibrium was disrupted by damage to parts of the brain, the changing balance affected behavior. In the absence of the inhibiting influence of the damaged areas, the balance between Gage's "intellectual faculties and his animal propensities" was destroyed (Harlow, 1868, cited in Macmillan, 2004, p. 182), resulting in disinhibited behavior. As later sections of this chapter will demonstrate, this theme—that behavior derives from a relative equilibrium between self-gratifying and cautious motivations—has influenced most major theories of impulsivity, and continues to do so today.

Twentieth-century conceptualizations of impulsivity and disinhibition continued to look toward physiology as the cause of such behaviors, and toward imbalances in competing neurobiological systems. Eppinger and Hess (1915) argued that vagotonia, an imbalance within the autonomic nervous system favoring the parasympathetic division over the sympathetic division, might account for a number of medical and psychological phenomena. They described vagotonia as an "abnormal irritability of all or only a few autonomic nerves" (p. 39), including the tenth cranial (vagal) nerve, and portrayed it as a chronic disposition as opposed to an acute disorder. Occurring more frequently in young individuals, vagotonia was hypothesized to cause neurasthenia, hysteria, and nervousness. Eppinger and Hess described patients with vagotonia as "hasty and precipitous" (p. 40), foreshadowing the links that would later be made between the condition and hyperactivity. Although the vagotonia hypothesis has since been refuted (see Beauchaine, 2001), by the mid twentieth century, it was a candidate cause of restlessness and hyperactivity in children, and was considered a possible predictor of later antisocial behavior (e.g., Venables, 1988). More recent sources indicate compromised sympathetic *and* parasympathetic functioning in impulsive children and adolescents (Beauchaine, Katkin, Strassberg, & Snarr, 2001; Beauchaine et al., 2007; Crowell et al., 2006).

At approximately the same time that the vagotonia hypothesis emerged, the encephalitis epidemics of 1918 spawned a group of children who displayed marked impulsivity, hyperactivity, inattention, aggression, and impairments in judgment (Carlson & Rapport, 1989; Schachar, 1986). Neurologists of the time attributed these behaviors to organic sequelae of encephalitic infection, and eventually the term *minimal brain dysfunction* (MBD) was created to describe not only these children, but children with learning disabilities and other problems (Hässler, 1992). Theories regarding which regions of the brain that were injured varied, but it was assumed that impulsivity and hyperactivity were caused by brain damage of some sort, even among children with no documented history of head trauma or illness (Lyon, Fletcher, & Barnes, 2003). Although the problem behaviors included under MBD shifted over the next few decades, variations of the term and concept remained popular until recently (Hässler, 1992). It was not until the DSM-III emerged in 1980 (APA, 1980) that the category of MBD began to be dropped, and children with learning difficulties were distinguished officially from those with behavioral difficulties (Lyon et al., 2003).

TERMINOLOGICAL AND CONCEPTUAL ISSUES

Despite the centrality of trait disinhibition to current theories of ADHD, CD, antisocial behavior, and substance abuse and substance dependence disorders, the construct lacks a consistent operational definition. Traditionally, impulsivity has been defined by behavioral symptoms, although some researchers have attempted to refine these definitions based on results from neuropsychological tests. For example, reaction time during verbal tasks has been used to assess the degree of "short-circuiting of analytic or reflective thought processes" (Oas, 1985, p. 141). Alternatively, errors in maze solving have been suggested to reflect impulsivity, as they may represent lack of attention to detail as well as carelessness and lack of planning (Porteus, 1965). Perseverative errors during set-shifting tasks such as the Wisconsin Card Sorting Test have also been attributed to impulsivity (e.g., Avila et al., 2004), as have errors due to overly quick responding and lack of reflection during match-to-sample tasks such as the Matching Familiar Figures Test (Oas, 1984). Among the most popular measures of impulsivity in neuropsychology are drawing tasks such as the Bender Gestalt (Bender, 1938) and the Draw-A-Person test (Koppitz, 1968). In such tests, impulsivity is assessed by scoring drawings on the basis of variables such as completion time, overall quality, omissions, asymmetry, detailing, and shading (Oas, 1984).

Although measures such as these may provide a means of operationalizing impulsivity, they do not speak to the neural mechanisms underlying the construct, nor do they fully explain relations between impulsivity and psychopathology. Many of these formulations describe impulsivity in highly cognitive terms, likening it to executive functions such as inhibitory control (the ability to interrupt an ongoing action or prevent a prepotent reaction; Kenemans et al., 2005) and effortful control (the ability to control attentional processes and behavior to inhibit a dominant response in favor of a nondominant response; Rothbart & Bates, 1998), two closely related constructs. Although it remains to be determined how cognitive constructs such as these relate to behavioral or trait disinhibition, they are likely to show some overlap, as different measures of inhibitory and effortful control correlate with various facets of impulsivity and problem behavior (e.g., Enticott, Ogloff, & Bradshaw, 2006; Murray & Kochanska, 2002).

More recent models of disinhibition integrate multiple components of the trait, suggesting several alternative brain mechanisms that may be responsible for impulsive behavior, exemplifying equifinality. Nigg (2000, 2005), for example, has suggested that disinhibition results from dysfunction in at least one of two inhibitory systems. He distinguishes between motivational inhibition, which results from behavioral suppression in the context of anxiety-provoking cues, and executive inhibition, or the deliberate process of stopping or suppressing a response that is prepotent but task-inappropriate. Barkley (1997) has also characterized disinhibition as faulty inhibition, positing a hierarchical inhibitory structure in which behavioral inhibition consists of three subprocesses (inhibition of prepotent responses, stopping ongoing responses, and controlling interfering stimuli), each supporting a number of executive functions that allow for effective goal-directed behavior.

Impulsivity has also been described as "behavior that is socially inappropriate or maladaptive and is quickly emitted without forethought" (Oas, 1985, p. 142). This behavioral rather than neuropsychological definition has a number of strengths. Although it is distinct from the more heavily cognitive formulations of disinhibition, it does not rule out cognitively mediated mechanisms. Furthermore, it emphasizes disinhibition as a maladaptive trait, distinguishing it from other qualities such as spontaneity that are frequently viewed more positively. Finally, it does not include causal assumptions regarding the etiology of disinhibition, allowing for both psychological and biological factors to contribute to the trait.

At present, the most widely used definition of impulsivity/disinhibition is likely to be the one described in the DSM-IV (APA, 2000). As a component of ADHD, impulsivity is demonstrated by "impatience, difficulty in delaying responses, blurting out answers before questions have been completed, difficulty awaiting one's turn, and frequently interrupting or intruding on others" (p. 86). Similarly, Sagvolden, Johansen, Aase, and Russell (2005) describe impulsivity as taking action without forethought and failing to plan ahead, linking it to such related concepts as risk taking, novelty seeking, sensation seeking, overrapid responding, and susceptibility to the pull of immediate rewards (see also Hirshfeld-Becker et al., 2002). These behaviors are considered pathological when they are performed to the point that they interfere with social, academic, and/or occupational functioning, consistent with Oas's (1985) theme of disinhibition as maladaptive and socially inappropriate.

ETIOLOGICAL FORMULATIONS

HETEROGENEITY IN THE IMPULSIVITY PHENOTYPE

As should be apparent from the previous discussion, the behavioral (phenotypic) expression of impulsivity may derive from one or more of several sources (see also Sonuga-Barke, 2005). Well-characterized influences on impulsive behavior include brain injuries, which may result from head trauma, hypoxia, or other central nervous system insults (Gatzke-Kopp & Shannon, this volume, Chapter 8); exposure to teratogenic agents such as alcohol, stimulant drugs of abuse, and lead (Fryer, Crocker, & Mattson, this volume, Chapter 7); early traumatic experiences including social deprivation, child abuse, and neglect (Lucas et al., 2004; Poeggel et al., 1999); or genetic vulnerabilities that give rise to deficient executive control over behavior (Nigg & Nikolas, this volume, Chapter 11). Although this list is certainly not exhaustive, it illustrates the heterogeneous nature of broad behavioral traits such as impulsivity (see Beauchaine & Marsh, 2006).

Rather than describing each of these mechanisms in detail, we begin by focusing on particular neurobiological substrates of disinhibition that (a) give rise to individual differences in impulsivity that are temperamental, present very early in life, and emerge before ADHD can be diagnosed; (b) are supported by voluminous literatures derived from both animal models and humans; and (c) confer vulnerability to externalizing disorders across the lifespan, particularly in the context of high-risk environments characterized by violence, trauma, and emotional lability. This focus on temperamental impulsivity is consistent with our main objective in writing this chapter—to describe early onset disinhibition as a *vulnerability* for later psychopathology. Readers should note, however, that it may be difficult in clinical practice to distinguish between children who are impulsive due to an inherited temperamental trait versus children who are impulsive due to other etiological influences such as prenatal stimulant exposure.

Most modern accounts of temperamental disinhibition emphasize structural and functional abnormalities in phylogenetically old brain regions including the mesolimbic dopamine system and the basal ganglia, overlapping neural networks that mature very early in life and are likely to subserve individual differences in impulsivity among young children (see Beauchaine et al., 2001; Gatzke-Kopp & Beauchaine, 2007; Sagvolden et al., 2005). Accordingly, heritable compromises in the functioning of these brain regions and associated risk for psychopathology provide the foundations of this chapter. In contrast, frontal theories of disinhibition are not considered foundational because these brain regions mature very late in adolescence, and are therefore less likely to underlie the early expression of impulsivity (Halperin & Schulz, 2006). Nevertheless, the neurodevel-opment of frontal regions may be affected—through mechanisms of neu-ral plasticity, programming, and pruning—by early experiences that are themselves a product of impulsivity (Beauchaine, Neuhaus, Brenner, & Gatzke-Kopp, in press; Sagvolden et al., 2005). In other words, heritable compromises in the functioning of early maturing brain regions that give rise to impulsivity are likely to alter the neurodevelopment of later ma-turing brain regions that are responsible for executive functioning and planning—especially in high-risk environments. This model highlights the interactive nature of the brain in affecting behavior, and of behavior in affecting subsequent brain development. Recognition and description of such transactions between the individual and the environment are tenets of the developmental psychopathology perspective (see Cicchetti, 2006; Hinshaw, this volume, Chapter 1; Sroufe & Rutter, 1984; Rutter & Sroufe, 2000). In later sections, we therefore describe neurodevelopmental mecha-nisms through which early impulsivity may potentiate vulnerability for deficient executive functioning later in life.

TEMPERAMENTAL IMPULSIVITY AND CENTRAL DOPAMINE FUNCTIONING

Theories advanced to explain individual differences in impulsivity have long focused on the mesolimbic dopamine (DA) system, including the ven-tral tegmental area and its projections to the nucleus accumbens (Swartz, 1999), and on other dopaminergic networks within the central nervous sys-tem (Castellanos, 1999; Gatzke-Kopp & Beauchaine, 2007, Kalivas & Na-kamura, 1999; Sagvolden et al., 2005). Many of these theories follow from seminal research on reinforcement motivation and substance dependence conducted with rodents and nonhuman primates. This research has dem-onstrated that (a) electrical and pharmacological stimulation of dopamin-ergically mediated mesolimbic structures is reinforcing, such that trained animals will engage in prolonged periods of operant behaviors (e.g., lever pressing) to obtain these incentives (see Milner, 1991); (b) neural activity increases within mesolimbic structures during both reward anticipation and reward-seeking behaviors, and following administration of DA ago-nists (see Knutson et al., 2001; Phillips, Blaha, & Fibiger, 1989); and (c) DA antagonists attenuate—and in extreme cases block—the rewarding prop-erties of food, water, and stimulant drugs of abuse (e.g., Rolls et al., 1974).

Based largely on this set of observations, several authors have offered theories of impulsivity and personality that explain individual differences in approach behavior as variations in activity of mesolimbic structures. The most renowned of these theories is probably that offered by Gray (1987a, 1987b), in which he proposed a mesolimbic behavioral approach system (BAS) as the neural substrate of appetitive motivation. Soon afterward, clinical scientists interested in impulsivity coopted dopaminergic theories of approach motivation to explain the unbridled reward-seeking behaviors observed in ADHD, CD, and related externalizing disorders (e.g., Fowles, 1988; Rogeness, Javors, & Plizka, 1992; Quay, 1993).

Although these early theories correctly identified mesolimbic neural structures implicated in the expression of impulsivity, most researchers at the time subscribed to the face-valid assumption that excessive dopaminergic activity led to impulsive behavior. In other words, they assumed a positive correspondence between neural responding and behavior. This assumption is evident in the formulation of measures such as the BIS/BAS scales (Carver & White, 1994), which presuppose a direct relation between impulsive behaviors and BAS activity (see Brenner, Beauchaine, & Sylvers, 2005). However, several clear and consistent findings present intractable problems for theories linking excessive mesolimbic DA activity to impulsivity.

First, several studies have indicated reduced sympathetic nervous system (SNS)–linked cardiac reactivity to reward among impulsive preschoolers, middle-schoolers, and adolescents (Beauchaine et al., 2001, 2007; Crowell et al., 2006). These findings are significant because SNS-linked cardiac reactivity to incentives serves as a peripheral index of central DA responding (Brenner et al., 2005), and because infusions of DA into mesolimbic structures produce SNS-mediated increases in cardiac output (van den Buuse, 1998). Thus, reduced cardiac reactivity to reward among impulsive children and adolescents is likely to mark attenuated DA responding— directly opposite to expectations based on the excessive DA theory.

Second, studies using both single photon emission computed tomography (SPECT) and positron emission tomography (PET) demonstrate that the primary mechanism of action of methylphenidate and related DA agonists is increased neural activity in the striatum, a structure located within the mesolimbic reward pathway (e.g., Vles et al., 2003; Volkow et al., 2002). Thus, pharmacological interventions that *increase* mesolimbic DA activity by inhibiting reuptake *decrease* hyperactivity, impulsivity, and related aggressive behaviors (e.g., Hinshaw et al., 1989; MTA Cooperative Group, 1999). Theories of excessive DA as a mechanism of impulsivity predict the opposite effect (i.e., increasing striatal DA activity should exacerbate impulsivity).

Finally, infusions of DA into mesolimbic structures are experienced as pleasurable, and individual differences in central DA expression have been linked with trait-positive affectivity (see Ashby, Isen, & Turken, 1999; Berridge, 2003; Forbes & Dahl, 2005). In contrast, PET studies indicate that low levels of striatal DA activity are associated with trait irritability

(Laakso et al., 2003). When interpreted in the context of positive relations between externalizing behaviors and both negative affectivity and irritability (e.g., Martel & Nigg, 2006; Mick et al., 2005), these findings suggest diminished rather than excessive DA functioning among at least some impulsive individuals.

These converging sources of evidence for reduced DA functioning as a neural substrate of impulsivity have led to a reformulation of first-generation models. We and others have suggested that underactivation of striatal DA leads to increased behavioral responding, which functions to raise activation levels within the mesolimbic system (Beauchaine et al., 2007; Gatzke-Kopp & Beauchaine, 2007; Sagvolden et al., 2005). Thus, what has been assumed to be reward hypersensitivity is more likely to be reward *insensitivity*, which results in increased impulsive and perseverative responding to up-regulate a chronically aversive mood state—the affective consequence of an underactive mesolimbic DA system (Ashby et al., 1999; Forbes & Dahl, 2005; Laakso et al., 2003). In addition to the literature previously cited, this interpretation is supported by research indicating (a) associations between low basal DA activity and blunted DA reactivity and a propensity to use DA agonist drugs of abuse (De Witte et al., 2003; Laine et al., 2001; Martin-Soelch et al., 2001; Martinez et al., 2007); (b) significant correlations between blunted DA responses to amphetamine administration and the personality trait of novelty seeking (Leyton et al., 2002); and (c) recent neuroimaging studies indicating reduced striatal activity during reward tasks among children and adolescents with ADHD and CD (Durston et al., 2003; Vaidya et al., 1998). Thus, accumulating evidence now supports the hypothesis that trait impulsivity results at least in part from abnormally low central DA activity.

GENETICS AND HERITABILITY

Behavioral Genetics of Impulsivity

There are two general approaches to studying the genetic bases and heritability of any behavioral trait—behavioral genetics and molecular genetics. Behavioral genetics studies are used to parse variability in behavior into heritable (both genetic and nongenetic) and nonheritable (environmental) components. Overwhelming evidence indicates that impulsivity is among the most highly heritable of all behavioral traits. Behavior genetics studies comparing concordance rates of impulsivity and ADHD for monozygotic and dizygotic twins produce heritability estimates (h^2) approaching .8, indicating that as much as 80% of the variance in impulsive behavior is accounted for by genetic factors (e.g., Price et al., 2001; Sherman, Iacono, & McGue, 1997). Levy and colleagues (1997), for example, found evidence of high heritability for ADHD, both as a diagnostic syndrome and as a continuously distributed trait. Furthermore, Krueger et al. (2002) identified a common vulnerability for a wide range of externalizing symptoms including disinhibition, conduct problems, antisocial personality, alcohol dependence, and drug dependence among a sample of 1,048 participants in the Minnesota Twin Family Study. This vulnerability for externalizing disorders, which is likely to reflect trait impulsivity (Beauchaine & Marsh, 2006), was 81% heritable. However, each specific category of externalizing behavior was influenced strongly by environmental effects. This finding is important because it demonstrates that a common genetic vulnerability can result in divergent multifinal outcomes depending on environmental experiences, a point to which we return in the following sections.

Molecular Genetics of Impulsivity

In contrast to behavioral genetics, molecular genetics, including both linkage and association studies, are designed to identify specific genes that contribute to the expression of a trait or disorder. Linkage studies search for genetic markers with known chromosomal locations among large numbers of families with two or more affected children. Using this approach, the gene responsible for cystic fibrosis was found by "linking" the disease to a DNA variant on the long arm of chromosome 7 within afflicted families. This discovery was followed by a number of additional linkage studies that specified the location on chromosome 7 in greater detail (see Bolsover et al., 1997). Because linkage analyses scan broad sections of the genome, the approach works best when very few genes with large effects contribute to a behavioral trait or disease—a rare precondition for psychiatric disorders, which are usually polygenically determined.

In contrast to linkage studies, genetic association studies begin with a candidate gene that is thought to play an etiological role in the expression of a disorder. Using this approach, allelic frequencies of specific genetic polymorphisms are compared among those with and without the condition under study. Association studies can be used to detect genes that account for much smaller amounts of variance in behavior. Given well-articulated theories specifying altered DA functioning as a pathophysiological determinant of impulsivity (see previous discussion), association studies are well suited for use with this behavioral trait (Galili-Weisstub & Segman, 2003).

Not surprisingly, association studies far outnumber linkage studies of impulsivity and ADHD. Although results from these studies have been mixed—with limited effect sizes and a number of nonreplications—both the DRD4 gene (chromosome 11p15.5) and the DAT1 gene (chromosome 5p15.3) appear to be implicated in the pathophysiology of impulsivity (Benjamin et al., 1996; Castellanos & Tannock, 2002; Galili-Weisstub & Segman, 2003). The DRD4 gene codes for DA receptors are located throughout the central and peripheral nervous systems. The DAT1, or dopamine transporter gene, regulates synaptic levels of DA, and is the principal target of psychostimulants used to treat ADHD (Grace, 2002). Although other DA genes have been studied, evidence for their roles in the pathophysiology of impulsivity is less consistent (see also Nigg, this volume, Chapter 11).

Finally, in addition to genes that are involved directly in DA expression, association studies have also been conducted to evaluate the effects of genes that are involved in the synthesis and metabolism of DA, as these processes also influence synaptic activity and reuptake. Candidate genes include those that encode for dopamine-β-hydroxylase (DBH), which converts DA to norepinephrine; and both monamine oxydase (MAO) and catechol-o-methyl transferase (COMT), enzymes involved in DA degradation. Association studies involving these genes have been few and conflicting, yet polymorphisms in the MAO gene (Xp11.23-11.4) have been associated with high risk for antisocial behavior among adult males who were maltreated as children (Caspi et al., 2002), reflecting a possible gene–environment interaction in externalizing behavior.

To summarize, behavioral genetics studies of trait impulsivity indicate impressively high heritability estimates and suggest that disinhibition contributes to a number of externalizing behavior patterns. Yet despite this high heritability, candidate genes identified to date account for very little variance in impulsive behavior. This suggests that considerable work remains in the attempt to understand the genetic bases of impulsivity, a state of affairs that extends to research on most behavioral traits (see, e.g., Kagan, this volume, Chapter 6).

IMPULSIVITY AND VULNERABILITY TO PSYCHOPATHOLOGY

In developmental psychopathology, a distinction is often made between vulnerabilities and risk factors for psychiatric disorders (Luthar, 2006). Vulnerabilities are usually assumed to be biologically based traits that render individuals susceptible to psychopathology, whereas risk factors are environmental influences that interact with vulnerabilities to potentiate psychopathology. For example, it is now known that distressing experiences (risk factors) elicit Posttraumatic Stress Disorder only in genetically predisposed (vulnerable) individuals (e.g., Orr et al., 2003; Stein, Jang, Taylor, Vernon, & Livesley, 2002). Although the distinction between vulnerabilities and risk factors breaks down when we consider the interactive roles that genetically determined traits play in eliciting specific environments (evocative effects), and that environments play in the expression of genes (see Moffitt, 2005; Shannon et al., 2007), we maintain traditional use of the terms in upcoming sections, where we outline factors that amplify the likelihood of psychopathology among impulsive and therefore vulnerable individuals.

Before proceeding, however, it should be noted that temperamental impulsivity is usually not enough—except in perhaps the most extreme cases—to result in psychopathology in the absence of additional vulnerabilities and/or risk factors. Research with impulsive preschoolers indicates that at least half progress into later childhood without developing significant behavior problems (see Campbell et al., 2000). In the sections to follow we summarize several additional vulnerabilities and risk factors that interact with temperamental disinhibition to increase the probability of later psychopathology.

Behavioral Inhibition

In addition to impulsivity, a second well-characterized temperamental trait is behavioral *inhibition*. This term refers to a general tendency to be wary in novel situations, to be "slow to warm up," and to avoid overly stimulating environments. Kagan, Reznick, and Snidman (1988) identified a group of 3-year-olds who displayed high degrees of behavioral inhibition in unfamiliar laboratory settings. These children avoided approaching and interacting with unfamiliar children and adults, remained in close proximity to their mothers, and ceased vocalizing in the presence of strangers. When they were reassessed at age 7, they remained quiet, cautious, and socially avoidant. Thus, like trait impulsivity, behavioral inhibition can be detected very early in life and is stable (although not invariant) across development. It is also mediated largely by genetic factors (see Kagan, this volume, Chapter 6).

It has often been assumed that trait inhibition and impulsivity mark extremes along a continuum of behavioral control. Yet the neural substrates of the two traits are almost completely nonoverlapping. In contrast to impulsivity, behavioral inhibition, which renders individuals vulnerable to anxiety disorders, is mediated by the septo-hippocampal system, a primarily serotonergic network (see Gray & McNaughton, 2000). Moreover, the two systems evolved to subserve distinct functions: approach behaviors promote survival by ensuring engagement in activities such as eating, drinking, and copulating; whereas avoidance behaviors promote survival by reducing exposure to danger. In fact, Gray and others (Gray & McNaughton, 2000; McNaughton & Corr, 2004) have argued convincingly that the functional role of the septo-hippocampal system is to *suppress* approach behaviors under conditions of threat.

This conceptualization—with approach tendencies being actively suppressed by avoidance tendencies—is supported by a large literature on experiments with animals, and has direct implications for psychopathology (see Beauchaine, 2001; Beauchaine et al., 2007). Given that the approach and avoidance systems operate with substantial independence, one can be high or low on either or both dimensions. A person who is temperamentally impulsive due to a heritable DA deficiency may be protected from severe psychopathology *if* he or she is also high on behavioral inhibition. Although this might seem implausible at first glance, symptoms of anxiety are not uncommon among impulsive children with ADHD (Angold, Costello, & Erkanli, 1999; MTA Cooperative Group, 1999), and in the absence of additional comorbidities, such children are more responsive to behavioral interventions than their nonanxious counterparts (Jensen et al., 2001). This greater sensitivity to environmental cues is precisely what would be expected from a more responsive septo-hippocampal system.

In contrast, an impulsive person who is low on trait anxiety may be especially vulnerable to developing more serious externalizing disorders. Psychopathy, a behavior pattern characterized by manipulation of others, superficial charm, callousness, and lack of remorse, is probably the most intractable form of externalizing conduct (see Lykken, 2006). As several authors have noted, psychopaths exhibit excessive approach behaviors that are *coupled with* a disturbing lack of anxiety and fear (see Fowles & Dindo, 2006). Thus, their impulsive tendencies are not inhibited by impending consequences because they are very low on behavioral inhibition. As a result, the condition is largely unresponsive to treatment.

Given that temperamental impulsivity and inhibition are both largely heritable, individuals with psychopathy appear to be "doubly vulnerable" to psychopathology. This situation might best be considered a trait × trait interaction, with two largely independent heritable attributes contributing to behavioral functioning (see also Derryberry, Reed, & Pilkenton-Taylor, 2003). Although such models are rare in psychopathology research, recent advances in molecular genetics make it much easier to study interactions among underlying genes that potentiate psychiatric morbidity.

ENVIRONMENTAL RISK

There is also considerable evidence that environmental risk can lead to more severe psychopathology among impulsive children, including those with ADHD. These children are more likely than their non-ADHD peers to develop Oppositional Defiant Disorder (ODD), Conduct Disorder (CD), and Antisocial Personality Disorder (Barkley, 2003). Longitudinal studies suggest that, for many children, hyperactivity/impulsivity constitutes the first stage in a trajectory that progresses—via mediating risk factors—to antisocial behaviors, eventually culminating in early onset delinquency. We outline some of these risk factors in the following sections.

Parenting. One of the most thoroughly studied environmental correlates of externalizing behavior is parenting. Numerous studies have demonstrated that the parents of impulsive and aggressive children are more negative, lax, verbose, and overreactive in their discipline practices than the parents of control children (Arnold et al., 1993; Barkley, Karlsson, & Pollard, 1985). In a longitudinal study of impulsive boys, Patterson et al. (2000) demonstrated that the relation between hyperactivity and antisocial behavior was mediated fully by coercive parental discipline. Thus, hyperactivity led to more serious externalizing behaviors only when parents consistently nagged their children and were explosive in their discipline practices. Similarly, Beiderman et al. (1996) demonstrated that hyperactive children who developed Conduct Disorder were more likely to be reared by antisocial parents than hyperactive children who did not develop Conduct Disorder.

Consistent with these findings, research has demonstrated that coercive family interaction patterns—in which both children and their parents escalate aversive behaviors and negative affect in order to assert their respective wills—promote physical aggression, conduct problems, and delinquency (Snyder et al., 1994; Snyder, Schrepferman, & St. Peter, 1997). Developmental models suggest that these repeated episodes of negative affective and behavioral escalation, which are enacted thousands of times in the families of at-risk children, promote emotion dysregulation and emotional lability, which in turn increase risk for more severe conduct problems and other adverse outcomes (Beauchaine et al., 2007; Crowell, Beauchaine, & Lenzenweger, this volume). Moreover, interventions that successfully reduce such parenting behaviors also reduce delinquency (e.g., Martinez & Forgatch, 2001). Although these findings have been interpreted by some as evidence of direct environmental effects, it is possible that heritable genetic vulnerabilities are driving the coercive behaviors observed by both parties. Such genetic versus environmental hypotheses cannot be disambiguated without true experiments in which impulsive children are assigned randomly to coercive and noncoercive caretakers—an ethically indefensible practice. Nevertheless, in a randomized clinical trial, Hinshaw et al. (2000) found that reductions in negative/ineffective discipline in parents of youth with ADHD mediated school-based reductions in disruptive behavior and improvements in social skills, with effects most pronounced for families receiving the multimodal combination of medication and intensive behavior therapy.

Child abuse and neglect. Although associated with parenting practices (Azar, 2002), a second risk factor that we consider separately is child abuse and neglect. Those who study child maltreatment have traditionally considered social mechanisms of risk and intergenerational transmission (see Cicchetti & Valentino, 2006). We have therefore included child abuse and neglect under environmental risk factors. However, evidence also suggests that genetic and temperamental factors play roles in determining who engages in child abuse and neglect, and in influencing the likelihood that a person who suffers abuse will become a future offender (Farrington et al., 2001). Although the direction of effects is unclear, maltreated children are more impulsive than nonmaltreated children (Famularo, Kinscherff, & Fenton, 1992). Furthermore, behavior genetics studies indicate that physical abuse often plays a direct role in the development of antisocial behavior among children at risk (Trouton, Spinath, & Plomin, 2002). Abuse is also more likely to lead to Conduct Disorder among children who are genetically vulnerable—as determined in part by impulsive characteristics of family members (Jaffee et al., 2004). Thus, impulsive children may be at higher risk for child abuse and neglect, which then amplifies risk for conduct problems and delinquency. As noted previously, one possible mechanism for this effect is a gene × environment interaction involving a polymorphism of the MAO gene, which is associated with high risk for antisocial behavior among males who were maltreated as children (Caspi et al., 2002). This variant in MAO is likely to affect behavior in part through altered DA turnover.

Neighborhood effects. A third environmental risk factor that has received increasing attention in recent years is neighborhood context. For example, Lynam et al. (2000) found that impulsive boys, as assessed by a number of neuropsychological tests and self-report measures, were at higher risk than nonimpulsive boys for engaging in both status offenses and violent crimes, yet only when they lived in neighborhoods of low socioeconomic status (SES) and high delinquency. No such effects were observed in high SES neighborhoods. Although others have failed to replicate this finding (Vazsonyi, Cleveland, & Wiebe, 2006), several ongoing studies are examining the relation between impulsivity and neighborhood context in offending, so much more will be known in the upcoming decade. Regardless of the outcome of these efforts, the Lynam et al. finding exemplifies a trait × environment interaction and illustrates the importance of environmental opportunities in the expression of temperamental risk.

Epigenetic and Other Experience-Dependent Effects

Epigenetic effects.   Epigenetic effects refer to alterations in gene expression that result from changes in DNA structure rather than changes in DNA sequence (Hartl & Jones, 2002). Such alterations are mediated by methylation processes that are triggered by environmental events. For example, Weaver et al. (2004) demonstrated epigenetically transmitted differences in the glucocorticoid receptor gene promoter in the hippocampi of rat pups that received high levels of maternal licking, grooming, and arched-back nursing compared with pups that experienced low levels of these maternal behaviors. This epigenetic effect transmits adaptive variations in stress responding to offspring. Rat pups reared in hazardous environments where maternal behaviors are compromised have more reactive hypothalamic-pituitary-adrenocortical responses, and are consequently more fearful and wary. Thus, they are better prepared for the hazardous environment that they are likely to face.

Although epigenetic effects on psychopathology have only begun to be studied, mammals are particularly susceptible to such alterations in gene expression (Hartl & Jones, 2002), and increasingly divergent patterns of DNA methylation emerge over the lifetimes of monozygotic twin pairs (Fraga et al., 2005). Accordingly, several authors have emphasized the importance of epigenetic effects for child psychopathology research (e.g., Kramer, 2004; Rutter, 2005). Yet demonstrating these effects among humans is difficult, as it requires random assignment of groups to contrasted environments (e.g., impoverished versus enriched). Nevertheless, theoretical models of antisocial behavior that include epigenetic effects have begun to appear (Tremblay, 2005). Furthermore, recent evidence suggests that the expression of brain-derived neurotrophic factor (BDNF), which is involved in the differentiation of DA neurons in developing mesolimbic structures and has been implicated in the pathogenesis of impulsivity, may be susceptible to paternally mediated epigenetic effects (Kent et al., 2005). In addition, although the precise mechanism remains to be described, the DRD4*7 allele, which has been linked with ADHD (see previous discussion), is less likely to be transmitted to offspring born in the autumn and winter months than to offspring born in the spring or summer (Seeger et al., 2004). Although these findings are preliminary, the study of epigenetic effects will almost certainly accelerate in the upcoming decade. A greater understanding of the processes and timing of these effects may help in formulating targeted interventions for vulnerable children.

Neural plasticity. In addition to epigenetic effects, several other mechanisms of neural programming exist, some of which are relevant for models linking early impulsivity to later psychopathology. Neural plasticity refers to experience-dependent functional changes in neural networks, including their efficiency, sensitivity, and time course of responding (Pollak, 2005). Such experience-dependent changes occur in several neural systems including mesolimbic DA structures. For example, Lucas et al. (2004) reported decreased DA transporter densities in mesolimbic brain regions of male rats that were exposed repeatedly to more dominant males in a stress-inducing paradigm. Similarly, repeated episodes of maternal separation early in the lives of rat pups produce long-term decreases in DA transporter expression (Meaney, Brake, & Gratton, 2002). Of particular significance, these effects result in greater sensitivity to the behavioral effects of cocaine and amphetamines later in life. Although similar experiments clearly cannot be conducted with humans, these findings illustrate the exquisite sensitivity of the mesolimbic DA system to early experience, and suggest the possibility that experience-dependent changes in DA functioning may predispose affected individuals to stimulant use.

Perhaps more troubling, strong stimulants themselves induce experience-dependent changes in neural functioning that are similar to those observed following stress exposure. Through this mechanism, alterations in DA expression lead to sensitization and addiction to stimulant drugs of abuse including nicotine, amphetamines, and cocaine (e.g., Saal et al., 2003; Taylor & Jentsch, 2001; Thomas et al., 2001). Chronic elevation of DA neural firing in the nucleus accumbens by strong stimulants has two other problematic effects. First, it down-regulates basal DA activity (Scafidi et al., 1996), which is likely to exacerbate impulsive tendencies that emerge from mesolimbic hyporesponding (see previous discussion). Second, it suppresses the strength of connections from the mesolimbic system to the prefrontal cortex (Thomas et al., 2001), which may alter development of executive functioning and long-term planning. In normally developing adolescents, mesolimbic structures are recruited during reward-seeking behaviors in much in the same way as observed among children. In contrast, adults depend more on frontal regions in responding to reward tasks (Galvin et al., 2006). This shift reflects a developmental migration from dependence on "bottom-up" neural processing in phylogenetically old limbic structures to "top-down" neural processing in phylogenetically newer cortical structures. Once developed, these frontal (mesocortical) structures inhibit reward-related behaviors when it is advantageous to do so (Taylor & Jentsch, 2001). Environmental risks including stress and drug exposure may prevent this maturational process from unfolding, resulting in an underdeveloped mesocortical DA system that predisposes the individual to further stimulant use and abuse (Prasad, Hochstatter, & Sorg, 1999), and to the potential long-term sequelae of early impulsivity, including conduct problems, delinquency, and antisocial personality development.

Implications for Learning.   As many readers are probably aware, the same mesolimbic and mesocortical structures that have been discussed in this chapter are also recruited for associative learning processes (see Berridge & Robinson, 2003; Sagvolden et al., 2005). Thus, alterations in DA responding that arise from genetic, epigenetic, and experience-dependent effects are likely to influence the efficiency of knowledge acquisition. This might occur through at least three mechanisms: (1) sensation-seeking tendencies that reduce motivation for learning "mundane" information; (2) reduced efficacy of associative learning due to dampened activation of mesolimbic structures; and (3) compromised executive functioning. Although we do not have space to review the learning literature in further detail, these findings underscore the importance of early intervention for impulsive children who may be on an externalizing trajectory.

SYNTHESIS AND FUTURE DIRECTIONS

This chapter describes (a) heritable biological mechanisms of vulnerability that lead to impulsivity among affected children, (b) environmental risk factors that can potentiate vulnerability, leading to more serious externalizing behaviors that are especially difficult to treat, and (c) the potential importance of gene × environment interactions. Although discussion of environmental, epigenetic, and experience-dependent risk factors for delinquency is sobering, it is worth repeating that only about half of impulsive preschool children develop more serious externalizing behaviors (Campbell et al., 2000). Furthermore, progress over the past decade in the specification of mechanisms through which impulsive behaviors escalate has been truly astounding.

Modern neuroscientific methods have provided insights into the development of externalizing behaviors that were unimaginable just a few years ago (Beauchaine et al., in press). When considered in conjunction with findings using more traditional approaches, it becomes apparent that some children face a cascade of cumulative vulnerability and risk that is increasingly difficult to reverse across development. In the worst cases, impulsive children are reared by impulsive parents who, in addition to conferring genetic liability, transmit risk through inconsistent and stressful caretaking during infancy, child maltreatment, and coercive, labile parenting. Further accumulation of risk may occur via exposure to violence in high-risk neighborhoods, early escalation of substance use, low motivation, and learning difficulties. By middle childhood and adolescence, exposure to stimulant drugs of abuse compromises the development of executive functions and self-regulation, compounding problem behaviors.

In contrast, an impulsive child who is reared in a maximally protective environment faces few or none of these additional risk factors, and may develop both psychological and biological resilience given enriched educational experiences and competent parenting that teaches strong emotion-regulation skills (Beauchaine et al., 2007; Raine et al., 2001; see also Cole, this volume, Chapter 10). Parenting interventions have proven quite effective in reversing risk for conduct problems, especially when delivered early in childhood (Beauchaine, Webster-Stratton, & Reid, 2005; Nock, 2003). Thus, there is reason to be optimistic. It is our hope that our knowledge of risk and resilience will continue to grow, and that science will affect public policy so that more children on externalizing trajectories receive preventive services.

REFERENCES

American Phrenological Journal and Repository of Science, Literature, and General Intelligence. (1851). Issue 13.

American Psychiatric Association. (1980). *Diagnostic and statistical manual of mental disorders* (3rd ed.). Washington, DC: Author.

American Psychiatric Association. (2000). *Diagnostic and statistical manual of mental disorders* (4th ed., text revision). Washington, DC: Author.

Angold, A., Costello, E. J., & Erkanli, A. (1999). Comorbidity. *Journal of Child Psychology and Psychiatry, 40,* 57–87.

Arnold, D. S., O'Leary, S. G., Wolff, L. S., & Acker, M. M. (1993). The Parenting Scale: A measure of dysfunctional discipline practices. *Psychological Assessment, 5,* 137–144.

Ashby, F. G., Isen, A. M., & Turken, A. U. (1999). A neuropsychological theory of positive affect and its influence on cognition. *Psychological Review, 106,* 529–550.

Avila, C., Cuenca, I., Félix, V., Parcet, M. A., & Miranda, A. (2004). Measuring impulsivity in school-aged boys and examining its relationship with ADHD and ODD ratings. *Journal of Abnormal Child Psychology, 32,* 295–304.

Azar, S. (2002). Parenting and child maltreatment. In M. H. Bornstein (Ed.), *Handbook of parenting. Vol. 4: Social conditions and applied parenting* (2nd ed., pp. 361–388). Mahwah, NJ: Erlbaum.

Barkley, R. A. (1997). Behavioral inhibition, sustained attention, and executive functions: Constructing a unifying theory of ADHD. *Psychological Bulletin, 121,* 65–94.

Barkley, R. A. (2003). Attention-deficit/hyperactivity disorder. In E. J. Mash &

R. A. Barkley (Eds.), *Child psychopathology* (2nd ed., pp. 75–143). New York: Guilford.

Barkley, R. A., Karlsson, J., & Pollard, S. (1985). Effects of age on the mother-child interactions of ADD-H and normal boys. *Journal of Abnormal Child Psychology, 13,* 631–637.

Beauchaine, T. P. (2001). Vagal tone, development, and Gray's motivational theory: Toward an integrated model of autonomic nervous system functioning in psychopathology. *Development and Psychopathology, 13,* 183–214.

Beauchaine, T. P., Neuhaus, E., Brenner, S. L., & Gatzke-Kopp, L. M. (in press). Ten good reasons to consider biological variables in prevention and intervention research. *Development and Psychopathology.*

Beauchaine, T. P., Gatzke-Kopp, L., & Mead, H. K. (2007). Polyvagal theory and developmental psychopathology: Emotion dysregulation and conduct problems from preschool to adolescence. *Biological Psychology, 74,* 174–184.

Beauchaine, T. P., Katkin, E. S., Strassberg, Z., & Snarr, J. (2001). Disinhibitory psychopathology in male adolescents: Discriminating conduct disorder from attention-deficit/hyperactivity disorder through concurrent assessment of multiple autonomic states. *Journal of Abnormal Psychology, 110,* 610–624.

Beauchaine, T. P., & Marsh, P. (2006). Taxometric methods: Enhancing early detection and prevention of psychopathology by identifying latent vulnerability traits. In D. Cicchetti & D. Cohen (Eds.), *Developmental psychopathology. Vol. 1: Theory and method* (2nd ed., pp. 931–967). Hoboken, NJ: Wiley.

Beauchaine, T. P., Webster-Stratton, C., & Reid, M. J. (2005). Mediators, moderators, and predictors of one-year outcomes among children treated for early-onset conduct problems: A latent growth curve analysis. *Journal of Consulting and Clinical Psychology, 73,* 371–388.

Beiderman, J., Faraone, S. V., Milberger, S., Jetton, J. G., Chen, L., Mick, F., et al. (1996). Is childhood oppositional defiant disorder a precursor to adolescent conduct disorder? Findings from a four-year follow-up of children with ADHD. *Journal of the American Academy of Child and Adolescent Psychiatry, 35,* 1193–1204.

Benjamin, J., Lin, L., Patterson, C., Greenberg, B. D., Murphy, D. L., & Hamer, D. H. (1996). Population and familial association between the D4 dopamine receptor gene and measures of novelty seeking. *Nature Genetics, 12,* 81–84.

Bender, L. (1938) *A visual-motor Gestalt test and its clinical use.* New York: American Orthopsychiatric Association.

Berridge, K. C. (2003). Pleasures of the brain. *Brain and Cognition, 52,* 106–128.

Berridge, K. C., & Robinson, T. E. (2003). Parsing reward. *Trends in Neuroscience, 26,* 507–513.

Bolsover, S. R., Hyams, J. S., Jones, S., Shepard, E. A., & White, H. A. (1997). *From genes to cells.* New York: Wiley-Liss.

Brenner, S. L., Beauchaine, T. P., & Sylvers, P. D. (2005). A comparison of psychophysiological and self-report measures of BAS and BIS activation. *Psychophysiology, 42,* 108–115.

Campbell, S. B., Shaw, D. S., & Gilliom, M. (2000). Early externalizing behavior problems: Toddlers and preschoolers at risk for later maladjustment. *Development and Psychopathology, 12,* 467–488.

Carlson, G. A., & Rapport, M. D. (1989). Diagnostic classification issues in attention-deficit hyperactivity disorder. *Psychiatric Annals, 19,* 576–583.

Carver, C. S., & White, T. L. (1994). Behavioral inhibition, behavioral activation, and affective responses to impending reward and punishment: The BIS/BAS scales. *Journal of Personality and Social Psychology, 67,* 319–333.

Caspi, A., McClay, J., Moffitt, T. E., Mill, J., Martin J., Craig, I. W., et al. (2002). Role of genotype in the cycle of violence in maltreated children. *Science, 297,* 851–854.

Castellanos, F. X. (1999). The psychobiology of attention-deficit/hyperactivity disorder. In H. C. Quay & A. E. Hogan (Eds.), *Handbook of disruptive behavior disorders* (pp. 179–198). New York: Kluwer/Plenum Publishers.

Castellanos, F. X., & Tannock, R. (2002). Neuroscience of attention-deficit/hyperactivity disorder: The search for endophenotypes. *Nature Neuroscience, 3,* 617–628.

Cicchetti, D. (2006). Development and psychopathology. In D. Cicchetti & D. J. Cohen (Eds.), *Developmental psychopathology. Vol. 1: Theory and method* (2nd ed., pp. 1–24). New York: Wiley.

Cicchetti, D., & Valentino, K. (2006). An ecological-transactional perspective on child maltreatment: Failure of the average expected environment and its influence on child development. In D. Cicchetti & D. J. Cohen (Eds.), *Developmental psychopathology. Vol. 3: Risk, disorder, and adaptation* (2nd ed., pp. 129–201). New York: Wiley.

Crowell, S., Beauchaine, T. P., Gatzke-Kopp, L., Sylvers, P., Mead, H., & Chipman-Chacon, J. (2006). Autonomic correlates of attention-deficit/hyperactivity disorder and oppositional defiant disorder in preschool children. *Journal of Abnormal Psychology, 115,* 174–178.

De Witte, P., Pinto, E., Ansseau, M., & Verbanck, P. (2003). Alcohol and withdrawal: From animal research to clinical issues. *Neuroscience and Biobehavioral Reviews, 27,* 189–197.

Derryberry, D., Reed, M. A., & Pilkenton-Taylor, C. (2003). Temperament and coping: Advantages of an individual differences perspective. *Development and Psychopathology, 15,* 1049–1066.

Durston, S., Tottenham, N. T., Thomas, K. M., Davidson, M. C., Eigsti, I-M., Yang, Y., et al. (2003). Differential patterns of striatal activation in young children with and without ADHD. *Biological Psychiatry, 53,* 871–878.

Enticott, P. G., Ogloff, J. R. P., & Bradshaw, J. L. (2006). Associations between laboratory measures of executive inhibitory control and self-reported impulsivity. *Personality and Individual Differences, 41,* 285–294.

Eppinger, H., & Hess, L. (1915). *Vagotonia; A Clinical study in negative neurology* (W. M. Kraus & S. E. Jelliffe, Trans.). New York: The Nervous and Mental Disease Publishing Company. (Original work published 1910).

Famularo, R., Kinscherff, R., & Fenton, T. (1992). Psychiatric diagnoses of maltreated children: Preliminary findings. *Journal of the American Academy of Child and Adolescent Psychiatry, 31,* 863–867.

Farrington, D. P., Jolliffe, D., Loeber, R., Stouthamer-Loeber, M., & Kalb, L. M. (2001). The concentration of offenders in families, and family criminality in predicting boys' delinquency. *Journal of Adolescence, 24,* 579–596.

Forbes, E. E., & Dahl, R. E. (2005). Neural systems of positive affect: Relevance to understanding child and adolescent depression? *Development and Psychopathology, 17,* 827–850.

Fowles, D. C. (1988). Psychophysiology and psychopathology: A motivational approach. *Psychophysiology, 25,* 373–391.

Fowles, D. C., & Dindo, L. (2006). A dual-deficit model of psychopathy. In C. J. Patrick (Ed.), *Handbook of psychopathy* (pp. 14–34). New York: Guilford.

Fraga, M. F., Ballestar, E., Paz, M. F., Ropero, S., Setien, F., Ballestar, M. L., et al. (2005). Epigenetic differences arise during the lifetime of monozygotic twins. *Proceedings of the National Academy of Sciences, 102,* 10604–10609.

Galili-Weisstub, E., & Segman, R. H. (2003). Attention deficit hyperactivity disorder: Review of genetic association studies. *Israeli Journal of Psychiatry and Related Sciences, 40,* 57–66.

Galvin, A., Hare, T. A., Parra, C. E., Penn, J., Voss, H., Glover, G., & Casey, B. J. (2006). Earlier development of the accumbens relative to orbitofrontal cortex might underlie risk-taking behavior in adolescents. *Journal of Neuroscience, 26,* 6885–6892.

Gatzke-Kopp, L., & Beauchaine, T. P. (2007). Central nervous system substrates of impulsivity: Implications for the development of attention-deficit/hyperactivity disorder and conduct disorder. In D. Coch, G. Dawson, & K. Fischer (Eds.), *Human behavior and the developing brain: Atypical development* (pp. 239–263). New York: Guilford.

Grace, A. A. (2002). Dopamine. In K. L. Davis, D. Charney, J. T. Coyle, & C. Nemeroff (Eds.), *Neuropsychopharmacology: The fifth generation of progress* (pp. 119–132). Nashville, TN: American College of Neuropsychopharmacology.

Gray, J. A. (1987a). The neuropsychology of emotion and personality. In S. M. Stahl, S. D. Iversen, & E. C. Goodman (Eds.), *Cognitive neurochemistry* (pp. 171–190). Oxford, England: Oxford University Press.

Gray, J. A. (1987b). Perspectives on anxiety and impulsivity: A commentary. *Journal of Research in Personality, 21,* 493–509.

Gray, J. A., & McNaughton, N. (2000). *The neuropsychology of anxiety* (2nd ed.). New York: Oxford University Press.

Halperin, J. M., & Schulz, K. P. (2006). Revisiting the role of the prefrontal cortex in the patho-physiology of attention-deficit/hyperactivity disorder. *Psychological Bulletin, 132,* 560–581.

Harlow, J. M. (1868). Recovery from the passage of an iron bar through the head. *Publications of the Massachusetts Medical Society, 2,* 327–347.

Hartl, D. L., & Jones, E. W. (2002). *Essential genetics: A genomics perspective* (3rd ed.). Boston: Jones and Bartlett Publishers.

Hässler, F. (1992). The hyperkinetic child: A historical review. *Acta Paedopsychiatrica, 55,* 147–149.

Hinshaw, S. P., Henker, B., Whalen, C. K., Erhardt, D., & Dunnington, R. E. (1989). Aggressive, prosocial, and nonsocial behavior in hyperactive boys: Dose effects of methylphenidate in naturalistic settings. *Journal of Consulting and Clinical Psychology, 57,* 636–643.

Hinshaw, S. P., Lahey, B. B., & Hart, E. L. (1993). Issues of taxonomy and comorbidity in the development of conduct disorder. *Development and Psychopathology, 5,* 31–49.

Hinshaw, S. P., Owens, E. B., Wells, K.C., Kraemer, H.C., Abikoff, H.B., Arnold, L.E., et al. (2000). Family processes and treatment outcome in the MTA: Negative/ineffective parenting practices in relation to multimodal treatment. *Journal of Abnormal Child Psychology, 28,* 555–568.

Hirshfeld-Becker, D. R., Biederman, J., Faraone, S. V., Violette, H., Wrightsman, J., & Rosenbaum, J. F. (2002). Temperamental correlates of disruptive behavior disorders in young children: Preliminary findings. *Biological Psychiatry, 50,* 563–574.

Jaffee, S. R., Caspi, A., Moffitt, T. E., Polo-Tomas, M., Price, T. S., & Taylor, A. (2004). The limits of child effects: Evidence for genetically mediated child effects on corporal punishment but not on physical maltreatment. *Developmental Psychology, 40,* 1047–1058.

Jensen, P. S., Hinshaw, S. P., Kraemer, H. C., Lenora, N., Newcorn, J. H., Abikoff, H. B., et al. (2001). ADHD comorbidity findings from the MTA study: Comparing comorbid subgroups. *Journal of the American Academy of Child and Adolescent Psychiatry, 40,* 147–158.

Kalivas, P. W., & Nakamura, M. (1999). Neural systems for behavioral activation and reward. *Current Opinion in Neurobiology, 9,* 223–227.

Kagan, J., Reznick, J. S., & Snidman, N. (1988). Biological bases of childhood shyness. *Science, 240,* 167–171.

Kenemans, J. L., Bekker, E. M., Lijffijt, M., Overtoom, C. C. E., Jonkman, L. M., & Verbaten, M. N. (2005). Attention deficit and impulsivity: Selecting, shifting, and stopping. *International Journal of Psychophysiology, 58,* 59–70.

Kent L., Green, E., Hawi, Z., Kirley, A., Dudbridge, F., Lowe, N., et al. (2005). Association of the paternally transmitted copy of common valine allele of the Val66-Met polymorphism of the brain-derived neurotrophic factor (BDNF) gene with susceptibility to ADHD. *Molecular Psychiatry, 10,* 939–943.

Knutson, B., Fong, G. W., Adams, C. M., Varner, J. L., & Hommer, D. (2001). Dissociation of reward anticipation and outcome with event-related fMRI. *Brain Imaging, 12,* 3683–3687.

Koppitz, E. M. (1968). *Psychological evaluation of children's human figure drawings.* New York: Grune & Stratton.

Kramer, D. A. (2004). Commentary: Gene-environment interplay in the context of genetics, epigenetics, and gene expression. *Journal of the American Academy of Child and Adolescent Psychiatry, 44,* 19–27.

Krueger, R. F., Hicks, B. M., Patrick, C. J., Carlson, S. R., Iacono, W. G., & McGue, M. (2002). Etiologic connections among substance dependence, antisocial behavior, and personality: Modeling the externalizing spectrum. *Journal of Abnormal Psychology, 111,* 411–424.

Laakso, A., Wallius, E., Kajander, J., Bergman, J., Eskola, O., Solin, O., Ilonen, T., Salokangas, R. K. R., Syvälahti, E., & Hietala, J. (2003). Personality traits and striatal dopamine synthesis capacity in healthy subjects. *American Journal of Psychiatry, 160,* 904–910.

Laine, T., Ahonen, A., Räsänen, P., & Tiihonen, J. (2001). Dopamine transporter density and novelty seeking among alcoholics. *Journal of Addictive Diseases, 20,* 95–100.

Levy, F., Hay, D. A., McStephen, M., Wood, C., & Waldman, I. (1997). Attention-deficit hyperactivity disorder: A category or a continuum? Genetic analysis of a large-scale twin study. *Journal of the American Academy of Child and Adolescent Psychiatry, 36,* 737–744.

Leyton, M., Boileau, I., Benkelfat, C., Diksic, M., Baker, G., & Dagher, A. (2002). Amphetamine-induced increases in extracellular dopamine, drug wanting and novelty seeking: A PET/[¹¹C]Raclopride study in healthy men. *Neuropsychopharmacology, 27,* 1027–1035.

Lucas, L., Celen, Z., Tamashiro, K., Blanchard, R., Blanchard, D., Markham, C., Sakai, R., & McEwen, B. (2004). Repeated exposure to social stress has long term effects on indirect markers of dopaminergic activity in brain regions associated with motivated behavior. *Neuroscience, 124,* 449–457.

Luthar, S. S. (2006). Resilience in development: A synthesis of research across five decades. In D. Cicchetti & D. Cohen (Eds.), *Developmental Psychopathology. Vol. 3: Risk, disorder, and adaptation* (2nd ed., pp. 739–795). Hoboken, NJ: Wiley.

Lykken, D. T. (2006). Psychopathic personality. In C. J. Patrick (Ed.), *Handbook of psychopathy* (pp. 3–13). New York: Guilford.

Lynam, D., Caspi, A., Moffitt, T. E., Wikström, P-O. H., Loeber, R., & Novak, S. (2000). The interaction between impulsivity and neighborhood context on offending: The effects of impulsivity are stronger in poorer neighborhoods. *Journal of Abnormal Psychology, 109,* 563–574.

Lyon, G. R., Fletcher, J. M., & Barnes, M. C. (2003). Learning disabilities. In E. J. Mash & R. A. Barkley (Eds.), *Child psychopathology* (2nd ed., pp. 520–586). New York: Guilford.

Macmillan, M. (1992). Inhibition and the control of behavior: From Gall to Freud via Phineas Gage and the frontal lobes. *Brain and Cognition, 19,* 72–104.

Macmillan, M. (2004). Inhibition and Phineas Gage: Repression and Sigmund Freud. *Neuro-Psychoanalysis, 6,* 181–192.

Martel, M. N., & Nigg, J. T. (2006). Child ADHD and personality/temperament traits of reactive and effortful control, resiliency, and emotionality. *Journal of Child Psychology and Psychiatry, 47,* 1175–1183.

Martin-Soelch, C., Leenders, K. L., Chevalley, A. F., Missimer, J., Künig, G., Magyar, S., et al. (2001). Reward mechanisms in the brain and their role in dependence: Evidence from neurophysiological and neuroimaging studies. *Brain Research Reviews, 36,* 139–149.

Martinez, C. R., & Forgatch, M. S. (2001). Preventing problems with boys' noncompliance: Effects of a parent training intervention for divorcing mothers. *Journal of Consulting and Clinical Psychology, 69,* 416–428.

Martinez, D., Narendran, R., Foltin, R. W., Slifstein, M., Hwang, D., Broft, A., et al. (2007). Amphetamine-induced dopamine release: Markedly blunted in cocaine dependence and predictive of the choice to self-administer cocaine. *American Journal of Psychiatry, 164,* 622–627.

McNaughton, N., & Corr, P. J. (2004). A two-dimensional neuropsychology of defense: Fear/anxiety and defensive distance. *Neuroscience and Biobehavioral Reviews, 28,* 285–305.

Meaney, M. J., Brake, W., & Gratton, A. (2002). Environmental regulation of the development of mesolimbic dopamine systems: a neurobiological mechanism for vulnerability to drug abuse? *Psychoneuroendocrinology, 27,* 127–138.

Mick, E., Spencer, T., Wozniak, J., & Biederman, J. (2005). Heterogeneity of irritability in attention-deficit/hyperactivity disorder subjects with and without mood disorders. *Biological Psychiatry, 58,* 576–582.

Milner, P. M. (1991). Brain stimulation reward: A review. *Canadian Journal of Psychology, 45,* 1–36.

Moffitt, T. E. (2005). A new look at behavioral genetics in developmental psychopathology: Gene-environment interplay in antisocial behaviors. *Psychological Bulletin, 131,* 533–554.

MTA Cooperative Group. (1999). A 14-month randomized clinical trial of treatment strategies for attention-deficit/hyperactivity disorder. *Archives of General Psychiatry, 56,* 1073–1086.

Murray, K. T., & Kochanska, G. (2002). Effortful control: Factor structure and relation to externalizing and internalizing behaviors. *Journal of Abnormal Child Psychology, 30,* 503–514.

Nigg, J. T. (2000). On inhibition/disinhibition in developmental psychopathology: Views from cognitive and personality psychology and a working inhibition taxonomy. *Psychological Bulletin, 126,* 220–246.

Nigg, J. T. (2005). Reinforcement gradient, response inhibition, genetic versus experiential effects, and multiple pathways to ADHD. *Behavioral and Brain Sciences, 28,* 437–438.

Nock, M. K. (2003). Progress review of the psychosocial treatment of child conduct problems. *Clinical Psychology Science and Practice, 10,* 1–28.

Oas, P. (1984). Validity of the Draw-A-Person and Bender Gestalt tests as measures of impulsivity with adolescents. *Journal of Consulting and Clinical Psychology, 52,* 1011–1019.

Oas, P. (1985). The psychological assessment of impulsivity: A review. *Journal of Psychoeducational Assessment, 3,* 141–156.

Orr, S. P., Metzger, L. J., Lasko, N. B., Macklin, M. L., Hu, F. B., Shalev, A. Y., et al. (2003). Physiologic responses to sudden, loud tones in monozygotic twins discordant for combat exposure: Association with posttraumatic stress disorder. *Archives of General Psychiatry, 60,* 283–288.

Patterson, G. R., DeGarmo, D. S., & Knutson, N. (2000). Hyperactive and antisocial behaviors: Comorbid or two points in the same process? *Development and Psychopathology, 12,* 91–106.

Phillips, A. G., Blaha, C. D., & Fibiger, H. C. (1989). Neurochemical correlates of brain stimulation reward measured by exvivo and invivo analyses. *Neuroscience and Biobehavioral Reviews, 13,* 99–104.

Poeggel, G., Lange, E., Hase, C., Metzger, M., Gulyaeva, N., & Braun, K. (1999). Maternal separation and early social deprivation in Octodon degus: Quantitative changes in nicotinamide adenine dinucleotide phosphate-diaphorase-reactive neurons in the prefrontal cortex and nucleus accumbens. *Neuroscience, 94,* 497–504.

Pollak, S. (2005). Early adversity and mechanisms of plasticity: Integrating affective neuroscience with developmental approaches to psychopathology. *Development and Psychopathology, 17,* 735–752.

Porteus, S. D. (1965). *Porteus maze tests: Fifty years application.* Palo Alto, CA: Pacific Books.

Prasad, B. M., Hochstatter, T., & Sorg, B. A. (1999). Expression of cocaine sensitization: Regulation by the medial prefrontal cortex. *Neuroscience, 88,* 765–774.

Price, T. S., Simonoff, E., Waldman, I., Asherson, P., & Plomin, R. (2001). Hyperactivity in pre-school children is highly heritable. *Journal of the American Academy of Child and Adolescent Psychiatry, 40,* 1342–1364.

Quay, H. C. (1993). The psychobiology of undersocialized aggressive conduct disorder: A theoretical perspective. *Development and Psychopathology, 5,* 165–180.

Raine, A., Venables, P. H., Dalais, C., Mellingen, K., Reynolds, C., & Mednick, S. A. (2001). Early educational and health enrichment at age 3–5 years is associated with increased autonomic and central nervous system arousal and orienting at age 11 years: Evidence from the Mauritius Child Health Project. *Psychophysiology, 38,* 254–266

Rogeness, G., Javors, M., & Pliszka, S. (1992). Neurochemistry and child and adolescent psychiatry. *Journal of the American Academy of Child and Adolescent Psychiatry, 31,* 765–781.

Rolls, E. T., Rolls, B. J., Kelly, P. H., Shaw, S. G., Wood, R. J., & Dale, R. (1974). The relative attenuation of self-stimulation, eating, and drinking produced by dopamine receptor blockade. *Psychopharmacologia, 38,* 219–230.

Rothbart, M. K., & Bates, J. E. (1998). Temperament. In W. Damon (Series Ed.) & N. Eisenberg (Vol. Ed.), Handbook of child psychology. Vol. 3: Social, emotional, and personality development (pp. 105–176). New York: Wiley.

Rutter, M. (2005). Environmentally mediated risk for psychopathology: Research strategies and findings. *Journal of the American Academy of Child and Adolescent Psychiatry, 44,* 3–18.

Rutter, M., & Sroufe, L. A. (2000). Developmental psychopathology: Concepts and Challenges, *Development and Psychopathology, 12,* 265–296.

Saal, D., Dong, Y., Bonci, A., & Malenka, R. C. (2003). Drugs of abuse and stress trigger a common synaptic adaptation in dopamine neurons. *Neuron, 37,* 577–582.

Sagvolden, T., Johansen, E. B., Aase, H., & Russell, V. A. (2005). A dynamic developmental theory of attention-deficit/hyperactivity disorder (ADHD) predominantly hyperactive/impulsive and combined subtypes. *Behavioral and Brain Sciences, 28,* 397–468.

Scafidi, F. A., Field, T. M., Wheeden, A., Schanberg, S., Kuhn, C., Symanski, R., et al. (1996). Cocaine-exposed preterm neonates show behavioral and hormonal differences. *Pediatrics, 97,* 851–855.

Schachar, R. (1986). Hyperkinetic syndrome: Historical development of the concept. In E. A. Taylor (Ed.), *The overactive child* (pp. 19–40). London: MacKeith.

Seeger, G., Schloss, P., Schmidt, M. H., Rüter-Jungfleisch, A., & Henn, F. A. (2004). Gene-environment interaction in hyperkinetic conduct disorder (HD + CD) as indicated by season of birth variations in dopamine receptor (DRD4) gene polymorphism. *Neuroscience Letters, 366,* 282–286.

Shannon, K. E., Beauchaine, T. P., Brenner, S. L., Neuhaus, E., & Gatzke-Kopp, L. (2007). Familial and temperamental predictors of resilience in children at risk for conduct disorder and depression. *Development and Psychopathology, 19,* 701–727.

Sherman, D., Iacono, W., & McGue, M. (1997). Attention deficit hyperactivity disorder dimensions: A twin study of inattention and impulsivity hyperactivity. *Journal of the American Academy of Child and Adolescent Psychiatry, 36,* 745–753.

Snyder, J., Edwards, P., McGraw, K., Kilgore, K., & Holton, A. (1994). Escalation and reinforcement in mother-child conflict: Social processes associated with the development of physical aggression. *Development and Psychopathology, 6,* 305–321.

Snyder, J., Schrepferman, L., & St. Peter, C. (1997). Origins of antisocial behavior: Negative reinforcement and affect dysregulation of behavior as socialization mechanisms in family interaction. *Behavior Modification, 21,* 187–215.

Sonuga-Barke, E. J. S. (2005). Causal models of attention-deficit/hyperactivity disorder: From common simple deficits to multiple developmental pathways. *Biological Psychiatry, 57,* 1231–1238.

Sroufe, L. A., & Rutter, M. (1984). The domain of developmental psychopathology. *Child Development, 55,* 17–29.

Stein, M. B., Jang, K. L., Taylor, S., Vernon, P. A., & Livesley, W. J. (2002). Genetic and environmental influences on trauma exposure and posttraumatic stress disorder symptoms: A twin study. *American Journal of Psychiatry, 159,* 1675–1681.

Swartz, J. R. (1999). Dopamine projections and frontal systems function. In B. L. Miller & J. L. Cummings (Eds.), *The human frontal lobes: Functions and disorders* (pp. 159–173). New York: Guilford.

Taylor, J. R., & Jentsch, J. D. (2001). Stimulant effects on striatal and cortical dopamine systems involved in reward-related behavior and impulsivity. In M. V. Salanto, A. F. T. Arnsten, & F. X. Castellanos (Eds.), *Stimulant drugs and ADHD: Basic and clinical neuroscience* (pp. 104–133). New York: Oxford University Press.

Thomas, M. J., Beurrier, C., Bonci, A., & Malenka, R. C. (2001). Long-term depression in the nucleus accumbens: A neural correlate of behavioral sensitization to cocaine. *Nature Neuroscience, 4,* 1217–1223.

Tremblay, R. E. (2005). Towards an epigenetic approach to experimental criminology: The 2004 Joan McCord Prize Lecture. *Journal of Experimental Criminology, 1,* 397–415.

Trouton, A., Spinath, F. M., & Plomin, R. (2002). Twins Early Development Study (TEDS): A multivariate, longitudinal genetic investigation of language, cognition and behavior problems in childhood. *Twin Research, 5,* 444–448.

van den Buuse, M. (1998). Role of the mesolimbic dopamine system in cardiovascular homeostasis: Stimulation of the ventral tegmental area modulates the effect of vasopressin in conscious rats. *Clinical Experimental Pharmacology and Physiology, 25,* 661–668.

Vaidya, C., Austin, G., Kirkorian, G., Ridlehuber, H. W., Desmond, J. E., Glover, G., et al. (1998). Selective effects of methylphenidate in attention deficit hyperactivity disorder: A functional magnetic resonance study. *Proceedings of the National Academy of Sciences, 95,* 14494–14499.

Vazsonyi, A. T., Cleveland, H. H., & Wiebe, R. P. (2006). Does the effect of impulsivity on delinquency vary by level of neighborhood disadvantage? *Criminal Justice and Behavior, 33,* 511–541.

Venables, P. H. (1988). Psychophysiology and crime. In T. E. Moffit & S. A. Mednick (Eds.), *Biological contributions to crime causation* (pp. 3–13). Boston: Martinus Nijhoff.

Vles, J., Feron, F., Hendriksen, J., Jolles, J., van Kroonenburgh, M., & Weber, W. (2003). Methylphenidate down-regulates the dopamine receptor and transporter system in children with attention deficit hyperkinetic disorder. *Neuropediatrics, 34,* 77–80.

Volkow, N. D., Fowler, J. S., Wang, G., Ding, Y., & Gatley, S. J. (2002). Mechanism of action of methylphenidate: Insights from PET imaging studies. *Journal of Attention Disorders, 6,* S31–S43.

Weaver, I. C. G., Cervoni, N., Champagne, F. A., D'Alessio, A. C., Sharma, S., Seckl, J. R., et al. (2004). Epigenetic programming by maternal behavior. *Nature Neuroscience, 7,* 847–854.

CHAPTER 6

Behavioral Inhibition as a Risk Factor for Psychopathology

JEROME KAGAN

HISTORICAL CONTEXT

The explicit as well as the implicit meanings of psychopathology, like most words with implications for functioning in a society, have undergone serious changes as a result of historical events. However, the pace of these changes has accelerated over the past 200 years. Americans and Europeans during the early decades of the nineteenth century restricted the category of *psychopathological* to a small number of deviant profiles that either prevented individuals from carrying out their expected responsibilities or disrupted community harmony. Most of these people were regarded as biologically different from the majority of the population. This frame of mind is easy to understand. Most early nineteenth century families lived in small communities and implemented relatively similar child-rearing practices. Hence, if a 15-year-old became unusually aggressive, suicidal, or fearful, it was reasonable to conclude that the causal conditions must have a foundation in the person's constitution. Historical contexts in ancient Greece, Rome, and China led to different conceptions of causal conditions.

Freud introduced three seminal alterations in the existing perspective as the twentieth century began. First, he inserted the vague notion of anxiety, conceived as a derivative of libidinal energy, between the biology that was the presumed foundation of symptoms and the individual's behaviors and emotions. Second, he insisted that the child's early experiences,

157

especially within the family, made an important contribution to psychological dispositions. Finally, Freud argued that anyone exposed to certain early experiences was potentially vulnerable to acquiring an intense level of anxiety. Thus, everyone was at risk for a mental illness. The latter revolutionary idea happened to be concordant with a growing egalitarian ethic among Americans, who were trying to assimilate the recent increase in European immigrants. When this ethical idea was married to the emphasis on environmental causation promoted by Freud and the early behaviorists, psychologists and physicians wanted to learn more about a child's early socialization experiences.

Importantly, at the center of this curiosity was the intuition that a mother's care for and love of her infants and children were the most important protections against future pathology. American husbands at the beginning of the nineteenth century awarded their wives more dignity and power than men in most cultures. Carl Degler (1981) has speculated that husbands traveling with their families by wagon train from eastern towns over the Appalachians to settle the Midwest and territories beyond were forced by the isolation and dangers to treat their wives as companions. These events came together to persuade two generations of psychologists and psychiatrists—from about 1900 to 1960—of the certain truth that individuals who developed a mental illness, including those with autism, must have suffered childhood experiences, especially within their families, that brought about their symptoms.

The narrative changed when a confident cohort of neuroscientists and molecular biologists appeared on the horizon armed with novel methods that made genes and molecules, and their effects on a material brain, the major culprits in pathology. This suggestion found a receptive audience because, in addition to the belief in the psychological power of a mother's love, Americans were also friendly to the premise that material entities, the misshapen forms of which could cause anomalies, lay at the foundation of all natural phenomena. This materialistic perspective catapulted biological processes to an alpha position, over the complaints of psychoanalysts and developmental psychologists. The shiny side of this assumption was the implication that if scientists could discover ways to undo or correct the material malformations that caused pathology, more rapid cures that did not require psychotherapy or dramatic social reorganization might be possible. This is the state of affairs at present.

EMOTIONS AS RISK FACTORS

Investigators who believed in the importance of biological processes recognized that alcohol dependents, criminals, depressives, and agoraphobics did not possess their maladaptive characteristics as young children. Therefore, they must have been born with a biological predisposition, or encountered unusually stressful conditions, rendering them especially vulnerable to emotionally arousing experiences that were handled more effectively by the majority. This conceptualization defines the concept of a *risk factor*. However, there are three relatively independent kinds of risk factors.

One category of risk refers to the experiences of childhood that provoke excessive uncertainty, anger, sadness, shame, or guilt, with parental abuse, neglect, marital divorce, and harsh parental socialization often nominated as the most significant conditions. These psychosocial risk factors constituted the primary candidates as precursors of psychopathology for much of the twentieth century.

A second category of risk derives from the historical and cultural settings in which children develop, although this factor is often ignored. In order to discuss the importance of sociocultural factors, I note that two criteria must be met before an individual is assigned to a category of psychopathology. For one, the profile must be statistically deviant. Over 60% of Americans live in dense urban and suburban communities with strangers and, as a result, experience frequent bouts of anger, either because a stranger violates one of their ethical norms or frustrates them more directly on highways, in movie queues, or on buses (for example) by playing loud music. Thus, anger at another is an expected and common emotion in contemporary life and is not treated as a sign of pathology. In addition, the symptoms must compromise the individual's capacity for pleasure, hinder his or her ability to assume expected responsibilities, or interfere with the lives of others. Note that this latter criterion renders the local culture a risk factor. An American 20-year-old who tries to hang himself because he hoped to ascend to heaven would be classified as delusional and placed under medical supervision, not only because the behavior was deviant, but also because his belief violated community premises. However, a Palestinian 20-year-old about to blow himself up on a Jerusalem bus might be regarded by his family and community as a martyr with no need for medical care. Sixteenth-century Roman Catholic cardinals were convinced that Martin Luther was mentally disturbed. However, the peasants he saved from spending their limited resources on the purchase of indulgences celebrated Luther's courage.

The third category of risk, which is the main theme of this chapter, is represented by biological biases, either inherited or derived from conditions existing prenatally or during the early years of life, that render a child susceptible to psychopathology following particular experiences. The combination of biological vulnerabilities—called a *diatheses*—and untoward experiences—often referred to as *stressors*—increase the probability that a child will develop a profile of emotions and actions that interferes with his or her competence to carry out appropriate assignments, therefore warranting the designation *psychopathological*. Many of these biological biases are called *temperaments*.

TEMPERAMENTS

Temperamental biases are biologically based foundations for clusters of feelings and actions that appear during early childhood and are sculpted by the environment into a large but limited number of profiles that ultimately define a personality. Extreme levels of extraversion, conscientiousness, and impulsivity, for example, are the joint products of a personal history and a temperamental bias. It is generally assumed, but not yet proven, that the biological foundations for most but not all human temperaments are heritable neurochemical profiles. This hypothesis, which was anticipated 75 years ago (e.g., McDougall, 1908; Rich, 1928), was present in early form in the writing of the ancients who posited melancholic, sanguine, choleric, and phlegmatic temperamental types derived from the balance of the four body humors within each person.

Genes, Neurochemistry, and Temperament

Recent research provides a preliminary scaffolding for speculations regarding the possible neural bases for human temperaments. There are at least 150 different molecules that, along with the density and location of their receptors, have the potential to influence the emotions and behaviors that define human temperaments. These molecules include norepinephrine, dopamine, epinephrine, serotonin, corticotropin releasing hormone (CRH), glutamate, gamma aminobutyric acid (GABA), opioids, vasopressin, oxytocin, prolactin, monoamine oxidase (MAO), neuropeptide S, and the sex hormones androgen and estrogen (Hartl & Jones, 2005). The genes that code for these molecules and their receptor distributions and densities often have a number of polymorphisms (variations within a DNA sequence called an *allele*) in one or more of the gene's exons, or in the regulatory sequences that moderate the exons, called *promoters* and *enhancers*. Promoters control the effectiveness of the transcription of the exon into messenger RNA; enhancers determine where and when the transcriptions will occur.

If each gene—consisting of exons, introns, enhancers, and promoters—were capable of influencing brain chemistry and had on average five polymorphisms, there would be about 3^{750} possible neurochemical combinations that could function as the foundation of a temperamental bias (Irizarry & Galbraith, 2004). Even if a majority of these neurochemical profiles have no relevance for any temperament profile, the large number of remaining patterns implies that future scientists will discover many new temperaments that have yet to be characterized.

Some polymorphisms appear to be related to the temperamental bias called *behavioral inhibition*. For example, many relaxed (compared with irritable) 2-year-olds possess the longer variant in the promoter region of the gene that transcribes the serotonin transporter molecule (5-HTTLPR) (Auerbach et al., 1999). Many very shy school-age children and prepubertal rhesus monkeys who tend to avoid novelty possess the two short forms of 5-HTTLPR (Battaglia et al., 2005; Bethea et al., 2004). Furthermore, many 1-year-olds with extreme levels of avoidant behavior to a stranger possess two short alleles of 5-HTTLPR, as well as the longer seven-repeat polymorphism of the gene for the DRD4 receptor. By contrast, many of the least avoidant children have the two long forms of the gene for 5-HTTLPR along with the seven-repeat polymorphism of DRD4 (Lakatos et al., 2003). However, these relations are not always replicated across laboratories. One reason is that scientists usually measure only one polymorphism rather than several (Arbelle et al., 2003).

INTERACTION WITH EXPERIENCE

The postnatal environment is always influential and we should expect interactions between a polymorphism and experience with respect to a phenotype. A child's social class and the differential experiences it represents are often significant interacting factors. Research has indicated that upper-middle-class adults with 2 or 5 rather than 7 repeats of the gene for the DRD4 receptor are high in novelty seeking, yet surprisingly, individuals from economically disadvantaged backgrounds with the same polymorphisms are not (Lahti et al., 2006; Eley et al., 2004; Caspi et al., 2003; Kaufman et al., 2004).

The presence of the short allele of 5-HTTLPR explained only 2% of the variance in the self-reported distress of a large sample of German adults. Distress was predicted best by a combination of sex (women more than men) and employment (unemployed rather than employed) (Grabe et al., 2005). Such findings suggest that investigators who are trying to predict depression or anxiety would do far better if they relied on demographic features than on genetic markers, even though the combination of genetic markers and psychological features predicts criminality and depression with greater accuracy for a small proportion of the population.

NONHERITABLE FACTORS

Some neurochemical profiles that influence temperament could be the result of nonheritable alterations in brain chemistry. A female fetus lying next to her dizygotic (fraternal) twin brother is affected by the androgens secreted by him, and is likely as an older child to have a higher pain threshold (Morley-Fletcher et al., 2003). Season of conception has a modest association with behaviors and moods related to behavioral inhibition. Conceptions during the early fall months in the Northern Hemisphere (and conceptions during February through April in the Southern Hemisphere) predict extreme shyness in children (Gortmaker et al., 1997). Melatonin, secreted by the pineal gland, is a likely cause of this outcome. Humans secrete larger amounts of melatonin when the hours of daylight are decreasing, and the change in melatonin to light onset is heritable. A pregnant mother's secretion of high levels of melatonin could affect fetal brain development in diverse ways because this molecule binds to receptors in many sites, including the hypothalamus (Thomas et al., 2002). It also contributes to cell death (Ciesla, 2001) and suppresses dopamine release (Zisapel, 2001).

To summarize, if we regard each gene that contributes to a temperamental bias as a word in a sentence whose letters could be rearranged, and the meaning of the sentence is analogous to a temperament, there will be many opportunities for a rearrangement of letters to change the meaning of a sentence. Some alterations such as *ran* for *run* will have little effect on meaning. But spelling *hate* as *mate* or *rape* as *race* changes meaning more dramatically. Because current laboratory assays can only evaluate a small proportion of the very large number of relevant polymorphisms, contemporary scientists resemble children who can only read six words trying to read a Harry Potter novel. It is likely that when scientists are able to measure many more alleles that affect mood and/or behavior, they will discover that combinations of genes and rearing environments are the best predictors of the psychological variations that define human temperaments and pathologies. Of course, the complexity of the coming task is daunting.

The immaturity of our current understanding of the relations among genes, brain chemistry, experience, and behavior frustrates any attempt to posit a relation between a particular gene or physiological profile on the one hand, and a temperamental bias on the other. Thus, every current definition of temperament has to be based on behavior, observed directly or described by an informant on a questionnaire or in an interview. Although future investigators will add biological measures to behavioral data, a psychological component will always be a part of the definition because the concept *temperament* is an inherently psychobiological construct.

REACTION TO UNFAMILIARITY

Two of the most extensively studied temperamental biases in children older than 1 year are defined by the contrast between a restrained, cautious, avoidant reaction to unfamiliar persons, objects, events, or places—called *inhibited*—and an affectively spontaneous approach—called *uninhibited* (Asendorpf, 1989, 1991; Bates, 1989; Kagan, 1994). The behaviors usually displayed to unfamiliar events are moderately stable over time, relatively easy to measure, and show variation within every animal species studied (Schneirla, 1959; Scott & Fuller, 1965; Wirtschafter, 2005).

My colleagues and I, who introduced the concepts of inhibited and uninhibited 20 years ago, have discovered that behavioral signs of each of these biases are moderately stable from the second to the fifth year—and modestly associated with peripheral biological measurements in theoretical accord with the presumed physiological foundations for the two temperaments (Kagan, Reznick, & Snidman, 1988). Middle-class, Caucasian, 2-year-olds who show consistent avoidance of and distress to unfamiliar people, procedures, and situations (which was the original definition of inhibited), preserve some form of these tendencies over the next few years, along with greater sympathetic tone in the cardiovascular system. These features appear to be heritable because identical twins are more similar in displays of this profile during early childhood than are fraternal twins (Kagan & Saudino, 2001; Bartels et al., 2004). Furthermore, inhibited children are more likely to be born to families in which one or both parents have or had an anxiety disorder (Rosenbaum et al., 1991; Merikangas et al., 2003), and inhibited children born to a parent diagnosed with Panic Disorder are more likely to have a distinct polymorphism in the region of the CRH gene (Smoller et al., 2005).

Research by other scientists affirms these conclusions. There is modest preservation of teacher-rated fearfulness from kindergarten to the sixth grade (Cote et al., 2002), and boys who are described by their mothers as very shy during late childhood marry, became fathers, and establish careers later in life than their less shy peers (Caspi, Elder, & Bem, 1988). Rubin, Burgess, and Hastings (2002) distinguish between children in peer groups who play alone and show signs of timidity (called *reticent*), and children who play alone, but display no signs of anxiety or uncertainty (called *solitary-passive*). Although both types preserve their respective behavior pattern, the former, who more often stare at other children while alone, resemble inhibited children (Coplan et al., 1994).

It should not be surprising that inhibited behavior is subject to environmental modification. Two-year-olds who are reticent in a laboratory setting preserve that style only if they have intrusive, protective, hypercritical mothers (Rubin et al., 2002). Placement in daycare before the second birthday can also reduce the preservation of shy behavior (Fox et al., 2001).

It must be remembered that temperamental biases are subordinate to the more important influences of culture, class, and historical context on the behaviors classified as shy or timid. Temperament has its greatest influence on behavioral inhibition among children who live in a particular culture at a particular time. Hence, variation in timid or bold behavior among children growing up in contemporary middle-class American homes should be due, in large measure, to their temperaments because their culture and historical era are controlled.

High- and low-reactive infants.   My laboratory has been studying a large longitudinal cohort of 16-week-old Caucasian infants born to middle-class families. The explicit aim of our work was to discover infant behaviors that might predict the inhibited and uninhibited profiles that appear in the second year. The central hypothesis guiding the infant assessments was that variation in the excitability of the amygdala and its projections to other brain regions, particularly to motor and autonomic targets, would be important for the development of inhibited and uninhibited behavioral profiles. This hypothesis does not exclude the possibility that other brain circuits are also relevant.

The amygdala consists of a number of neuronal clusters, called the *basolateral, cortical, medial,* and *central areas,* each with a distinctive set of connections, neurochemistries, and functions. Each cluster in the amygdala projects to at least 15 different sites and receives input from roughly the same number of regions, resulting in about 600 known amygdala connections (Stefanacci & Amaral, 2002). The threshold of excitability in each of the amygdala clusters is influenced by a large number of molecules, including GABA, glutamate, opioids, CREB, norepinephrine, dopamine, vasopressin, and oxytocin (Kirsch et al., 2005). The balance among the molecules determines the neural state within each of the components of this structure.

A primary function of the amygdala is to react to unfamiliar or unexpected events (Fitzgerald et al., 2006). There is reasonable support for the suggestion that a young infant with an excitable amygdala is more likely than others to become inhibited several years later. Newborn infants whose rate of sucking increases dramatically following an unexpected change in taste sensation from water to a sweet taste are more inhibited during the second year than infants who show a minimal increase in sucking rate following a change in taste (La Gasse, Gruber, & Lipsitt, 1989). The unexpected change in taste quality activates the central nucleus of the amygdala, which is followed by activation of the motor centers that control sucking. Infants with a more excitable central nucleus should therefore have a greater increase in sucking rate. Furthermore, activation of the amygdala in many animal species is accompanied by limb movements, arching of the back, and distress cries (Pitkanen, 2000).

The complete corpus of data implies that young infants who inherit a neurochemistry that renders one or more areas of the amygdala excitable should display more vigorous motor activity, especially arches of the back, and more frequent crying to unfamiliar or highly stimulating events, compared with infants who have a neurochemistry that renders the amygdala less excitable. This hypothesis is in accord with Rothbart's (1989) emphasis on variation in reactivity as an infant temperamental quality. We coded the frequency of limb movements, arching of the back, fretting, crying, babbling, smiling, and heart rate in our sample of over 500 healthy, 16-week-old Caucasian, middle-class infants during a 45-minute battery consisting of several unfamiliar events. Twenty percent of the infants were classified as high-reactive because they showed high levels of motor activity and crying; 40% were classified as low-reactive because they showed very little motor activity and crying. We have followed these two groups through 15 years of age.

High- and low-reactives during the childhood years. When these children were seen in the laboratory at 14 and 21 months, the high-reactives were more timid, shy, and fearful to unfamiliar social and nonsocial incentives than the low-reactives. At 7 years of age, the high-reactives were more likely to exhibit anxious symptoms (Kagan & Snidman, 2004). At 11 years of age, the high-reactives were both quieter and emotionally more subdued during a laboratory session and showed four biological signs that are indirect indices of a more excitable amygdala.

Moreover, the high-reactives displayed, in their resting EEGs, greater activation of the right compared with the left hemisphere. Left-hemisphere activation, especially in the frontal area, is more likely when individuals are in a happy, relaxed state. Individuals who show left-hemisphere activation more often report a sanguine mood, have a bias to detect pleasant features in pairs of words, and show less anxiety than the smaller proportion who display greater activation in the right frontal area (Davidson, Jackson, & Kalin, 2000; Davidson, 2003; Fox, Calkins, & Bell, 1994; Fox et al., 2005). Because the amygdala projects ipsilaterally to the frontal cortex, greater activity in the right amygdala should lead to greater activation in the right frontal area (Cameron, 2002). Moreover, visceral feedback from the body to the central nucleus of the amygdala is greater to the right than to the left amygala, and the right amygdala of rats becomes more active than the left following exposure to a cat (Adamec, Blundell, & Burton, 2005). Therefore, children who experience more frequent visceral activity, which is transmitted to the brain, should have a more active right amygdala and display right, rather than left, frontal activation.

In addition, high-reactives showed a larger brain-stem auditory-evoked response from the inferior colliculus. Because the amygdala primes the inferior colliculus, this result suggests that high-reactives possess a more excitable amygdala (Brandao, Coimbra, & Osaki, 2001). High-reactives also showed larger N400 waveforms to discrepant visual scenes (for example, a baby's head on an animal's body) and greater sympathetic rather than parasympathetic tone in the cardiovascular system (Kagan & Snidman, 2004). These results are in accord with reports of others (Fox et al., 2005; Schmidt et al., 1999).

This sample was again evaluated when they were 15 years old in a laboratory setting and via a long interview at home. As was true at the earlier ages, the 15-year-olds who had been high-reactives smiled less often than low-reactives and showed more restless activity during the interview. Moreover, more high- than low-reactives showed greater right than left frontal activation, a larger waveform from the inferior colliculus, a larger ERP waveform to discrepancy, and greater sympathetic tone at both 11 and 15 years of age.

Sources of worry.   Several questions posed during the interview asked each adolescent to nominate the targets of their primary worries. Although most adolescents reported concerns that centered on the quality of their performance at school and in extracurricular activities, more high-reactives confessed to worrying over encountering unfamiliar people, places, or situations, as well as the inability to know what might happen in the future. Two-thirds of high-reactives, but only one-fifth of low-reactives, nominated one or more of these latter worries. Every 1 of the 11 high-reactive adolescents who had become so distressed during the final episode of the 4-month infant assessment that the session had to be terminated nominated unfamiliarity as a serious source of worry. Some verbatim excerpts illustrate their concerns with unpredictable situations: "In a crowd I feel isolated and left out, I don't know what to pay attention to because it is all so ambiguous"; "I worry about the future, over not knowing what will happen next"; "I wanted to be a doctor but decided against it because I felt it would be too much of a strain"; "I like being alone and, therefore, horses are my hobby. I don't have to worry about fitting in with others when I am with my horses"; "I get nervous before every vacation because I don't know what will happen." Similar statements were rare among the low-reactives.

The high-reactives were also less likely on a Q-sort procedure to rank the item "most of the time I'm happy" as characteristic of their personality, and were more likely to rank items describing themselves as serious, not easy-going, and wishing for a more relaxed mood as more characteristic of their personalities.

Youth in contemporary America are trying to establish their personal philosophy at a time when there is little if any consensus on the meaning of life or its origin. This state of affairs creates high levels of uncertainty in some adolescents. As a result, those with a temperamental bias that renders them vulnerable to worry about obligations that deserve unquestioned loyalty should try to find a belief system that mutes their private angst. A religious commitment is one effective strategy because it provides a partial answer to this question and assures each believer of his/her essential virtue and value when disappointments, failures, and frustrations occur. The interview data revealed that 45% of the adolescents who had been high-reactive infants regarded themselves as very religious, compared with only 25% of the low-reactives. This result cannot be explained as caused by parental religiosity.

Relation of Temperament to Psychopathology

The temperamental bias called *high-reactivity* has some implications for particular psychiatric symptoms. A clue to the symptoms that high-reactives might develop is revealed by the worries they confessed to during the interview, compared with the worries expressed by low-reactives. Low-reactive individuals often worry about such matters as the potential for inadequate performance in school, on the athletic field, or on the stage; each represents a realistic concern with clear features. Most adolescents know their level of talent in varied domains and the performance qualities that others will evaluate as satisfactory. They understand that a poor school performance can affect their future, and appreciate that study and practice can decrease the probability of a grade or athletic performance lower than the one they desired. Hence, these worries do not have a great deal of ambiguity, and the adolescent has some control over the outcome. As a result, the intensity of uncertainty is muted to some degree.

In contrast, worries about future encounters with strangers, places, or novel challenges—typical for high-reactives—are much more ambiguous. In addition, the ability to control the outcome of the encounters is compromised, and serious failure is therefore possible. Adolescents with these worries cannot be certain of the qualities others will judge or how they will react, and they believe there is not much they can do to reduce the probability of an incorrect or socially inappropriate response. Therefore, the level of uncertainty is considerably higher than it is among those who are concerned only with quality of performance.

One prototypic high-reactive adolescent girl who had been very inhibited in her second year of life told the interviewer she does not like spring because the weather is so unpredictable. One high-reactive boy reported feeling anxious in dyadic interactions because he was acutely aware of all the things he could say, but was uncertain as to which statements might be interpreted as undesirable. A high-reactive male diagnosed with Social Anxiety Disorder had displayed frequent arches of the back and a chronically unhappy facial expression during his infant evaluation at 4 months and had a fear score in the second year in the top 20% of the distribution. During the second year of life he screamed when a stranger entered the playroom, when a blood pressure cuff was applied, and when a clown unexpectedly opened the door of the room while he was on the couch with his mother. Years later, he missed many days during his senior year of high school because of extreme social anxiety. However, rather than present a timid persona, which is characteristic of this temperamental category, he had become an angry young man who peppered his interview replies with obscenities, and denied guilt, happiness, or any hope for his future.

The distinction between concern over adequate performance versus worrying over coping with future unfamiliar situations resembles Freud's contrast between realistic and neurotic anxiety. Adults who are high on anxiety sensitivity report heightened concern over future feelings of uncertainty that are not under their personal control (Floyd, Garfield, & LaSota, 2005) and more intensely unpleasant feelings during the first few minutes of a carbon dioxide (CO_2) challenge (Feldner et al., 2006). A large sample of middle-class adults diagnosed with Social Phobia contained two different subgroups. The group that was anxious over meeting strangers reported anhedonia and a depressed mood. In contrast, the group that was anxious over the quality of their public performances reported high levels of physiological arousal (Hughes et al., 2006). A survey of the fears of college students from seven different societies revealed minimal cultural or sex differences in the prevalence of realistic fears (e.g., dangerous animals), but significant cultural and sex differences in the incidence of less realistic fears (e.g., small animals) (Davey et al., 1998). The self-reported unrealistic fears of monozygotic twins and their spouses (an accident while boating or walking in a dark place) had higher heritability values than more realistic fears of illness, a car accident, or criticism for a mistake (Sundet et al., 2003). Thus, this temperament seems to have a greater influence on the frequency of less realistic, less probable threats.

All adolescents meet new people, visit unfamiliar places, and are unable to control future events. Thus, it is appropriate to ask why high-reactives are most likely to name these events as a primary source of worry. One possible answer is that they are more susceptible to the sensations resulting from unexpected visceral feedback from targets in the autonomic nervous system. When these sensations pierce consciousness, they create uncertainty because their origin is ambiguous. This psychological state resembles the state evoked when as children they encountered unfamiliar objects, people, or situations. The amygdala participates in both psychological states. The state created by unexpected visceral feedback can function as a conditioned stimulus to provoke the state of uncertainty that usually accompanies encounters with unfamiliar people or settings. Phrased a little differently, the feeling generated by the unexpected visceral feedback is uncontrollable, and its origin ambiguous; hence, it resembles the feeling evoked when the child anticipated a future encounter with strangers or unfamiliar places.

High-reactive youth in our culture are biased to interpret the feeling evoked by the visceral feedback as implying that they are worried about future encounters with strangers and new places because these events are the most frequent novelties in their lives, and because the folk theory they learned implied that their uncertainty was due to a compromise in their psychological characteristics. Members of other cultures might impose different interpretations on the same visceral feedback. Cambodian refugees living in Massachusetts, for example, interpret an unexpected bout of tachycardia as implying a weak heart produced by a loss of energy following lack of sleep or diminished appetite (Hinton et al., 2005a, 2005b).

If the uncertainty produced by unexpected visceral feedback over unfamiliar events were frequent or were intense during childhood, the amygdala-hippocampal pathway could become sensitized—the technical term is *kindled*—and these children might remain vulnerable to anxiety over the anticipation of unfamiliar contexts for a long time (Pape & Stork, 2003). Rat strains differ in the ease of amygdala kindling due in part to inherited neurochemical profiles (Kelly et al., 2003). It is possible that encounters with the unfamiliar generate a more salient psychobiological state in high- than in low-reactives because of their inherited neurochemistry. Oxytocin, which mutes excitatory flow from the amygdala to the brainstem, might be one influential molecule (Huber, Veinante, & Stoop, 2005). Adults given oxytocin intranasally show less activation of the amygdala to faces with fearful or angry expressions than those given a placebo (Kirsch et al., 2005). Hence, an inherited compromise in oxytocin function could render children more vulnerable to anxiety over the unfamiliar.

However, if the source of unfamiliarity were the color, taste, and viscosity of liquids with a bitter taste, rather than strangers or visits to new cities, high-reactives might develop serious worries over drinking liquids with a novel color and viscosity, and psychiatrists would have invented a category called *drinking anxiety disorder*. Some individuals do develop phobias of foods with unfamiliar qualities. Social anxiety, which is the most likely risk outcome for high-reactives, is relatively frequent in our culture because strangers and new places are more common than unfamiliar liquids. Pious medieval Christians who suffered a misfortune after violating an ethical norm worried excessively over God's wrath. The Saulteaux Indians of Manitoba worry about contracting a serious disease because illness is a sign that they violated an ethical norm on sexual, aggressive, or sharing behavior with others (Hallowell, 1941).

Social anxiety is a natural phenomenon, but it is especially salient in societies such as our own in which unfamiliar settings are frequent and social acceptance is a primary motive. A temperament can render individuals vulnerable to some form of anxiety; history and culture supply the specific target of this emotional family. In contemporary America, occupational and social failure have replaced the seven traditional sins of pride, anger, envy, avarice, sloth, gluttony, and lust as bases for anxiety, shame, and guilt.

Segments of a society can become vulnerable to anxiety over the validity of their ethical beliefs when historical changes in the economy or social structure alter the legitimacy of traditional norms. Individuals who wish to remain loyal to the older mores often support counterreformation efforts that restore the traditional ideology. The witch craze of late–fifteenth century Europe, for example, was brought on in part by the desire among older citizens to restore women, who were beginning to enter the work force, to their traditional roles as homemakers and mothers.

New ideas that have ethical implications can be as powerful elicitors of anxiety or anger as unexpected or unfamiliar events are for animals, even though the physiological mechanisms are not always the same. Worry over the large number of abortions performed on unmarried adolescents does not require the basolateral nucleus of the amygdala, whereas a rat's acquisition of conditioned freezing to a stimulus that signaled electric shock does. Thus, scientists should not treat classically conditioned responses in animals as an appropriate model for all forms of human anxiety disorder (See Phelps, 2006, for a different view). Classical-conditioning mechanisms might be a fruitful model for some human phobias (for example, fear of large animals or of particular foods). These models are less likely to illuminate the reasons for anxiety over the future, contracting illness because violations of ethical imperatives to share food with relatives, or a feeling of unacceptability by others because of self-identification with a stigmatized social category.

Social phobia.   Although high-reactives are more likely than others to become shy, introverted adults, most will not meet criteria for a psychiatric diagnosis of Social Phobia. Only one of every two adults who scored in the 90th percentile on a scale for self-reported shyness received a diagnosis of Social Phobia (Chavira, Stein, & Malcarne, 2002). Furthermore, less than 15% of chronically shy children developed Social Anxiety Disorder (Prior et al., 2000; Biederman et al., 2001). Conversely, about one-half of adults with Social Phobia did not remember being excessively shy as young children, although they may have distorted their recollections of their childhood personality (Cox, McPherson, & Enns, 2005).

Depression. The development of serious depression was not frequent in our sample, but it did occur most often among high-reactive girls. Five of the nine cases of clinical depression in the sample of 15-year-olds occurred among high-reactive girls (this frequency represents 16% of high-reactive girls but only 8% of girls from other temperamental groups). The small number of adolescents from a sample of over 500 Canadian children ages 6 to 14 who experienced an increase in depressed mood between 11 and 14 years were a subsample of girls who, when they were 6 years old, had been described by their mothers as unusually reactive to frustration, pain, or disappointment (Brendgen et al., 2005). A few high-reactive girls developed both serious anxiety to the unfamiliar plus depression. Of the many possible explanations of this fact, one might involve less effective binding of the serotonin transporter molecule within the amygdala, a condition associated with greater amygdalar activity. Depressed adults show a lower binding potential of the serotonin transporter molecule within the amygdala (Parsey et al., 2006a, b), and adults with the short form of the allele of 5-HTTLPR show greater activity in the right amygdala to the unexpected appearance of fearful or angry faces (Hariri, Drabant, & Weinberger, 2006).

Anhedonia. The neurochemistry of high-reactives could interfere with the intensity or frequency of subjective feelings of pleasure that often occur when a person receives an unexpected or larger-than-anticipated desirable experience. This state is mediated in part by the discharge of dopamine-producing neurons that accompany the anticipation of a desired event (Schultz, 2006). Furthermore, CRH neurons, usually activated by the anticipation of threat and present in dopamine-producing brain sites, can suppress the release of dopamine to imminent reward (Austin, Rhodes, & Lewis, 1997). There also appears to be an association between an introverted personality and polymorphisms of the COMT gene, which affects the efficiency of dopamine degradation in the synapse (Stein et al., 2005; Golimbet et al., 2005).

Perhaps one reason why high-reactive adolescents do not like new activities (whether risky or not), even though they promise excitement, is that these youth fail to experience pleasure when they anticipate visiting a new city, meeting a new person, or engaging in a novel activity. This profile should render them reluctant to seek out new events (Netter, 2006).

This argument is supported by a study of 111 college students who initially filled out a questionnaire measuring social anxiety and then rated their mood on each of 21 consecutive days. The students with high scores on the social anxiety scale were least likely to report pleasurable experiences and more likely to confess to a melancholic mood across the 3 weeks (Kashdan & Steger, 2006).

Some Caveats.   Verbal reports of moods and actions, usually without any direct behavioral observations or biological evidence, represent the usual information that clinicians use in arriving at diagnoses of mental illness. This epistemology resembles the basis for diagnosing physical illness in the eighteenth century, before assays of blood, urine, and X-rays were possible. But the meaning and therefore the validity of every conclusion cannot be separated from the evidence used to arrive at the inference. The same is true of single variables in a research study. A single measure, whether self-report, behavioral, or biological, rarely has an unequivocal meaning. Greater right compared with left frontal activation in the EEG represents only one component of a brain state that is necessarily integrated with other features of the person's biology, past experience, and immediate context to create one of many possible psychological states. Our data also illustrate the ambiguity of verbal replies to questions as simple as "Are you happy most of the time?" because this self-report had different correlates in children with different temperaments. Hence, it is likely that the self-reports of more complex psychological states are equally ambiguous.

Accordingly, investigators should not treat similar answers on a questionnaire or in an interview as having the same transparent meaning (Schienle et al., 2006). Adults instructed to worry about issues they had previously told an investigator were serious sources of concern showed activation of frontal sites (measured by PET), but less activity in the amygdala and the insula, and no change in heart rate or skin conductance. This finding suggests that some self-reports of anxiety are cognitive judgments (Hoehn-Saric et al., 2005). Investigators should not assume that a verbal report of an emotional state reflects the same biological or psychological condition in all respondents who offer the same description.

A single variable, such as the meaning of the word *missed* in a sentence, cannot have a single meaning because most self-reports, behaviors, or biological reactions are the result of more than one condition. The foundations of many currently popular psychopathological constructs, not just anxiety, are associated with more than one set of causal conditions. In other words, there is usually more than one pathway to a given psychiatric disorder—a phenomenon termed *equifinality* in the development and psychopathology literature. A person could be classified as impulsive because of a life history that led to minimal concern with quality of performance or because of a biology that compromised frontal lobe function. A prolonged period of apathy could be provoked by loss of a loved one or a neurochemistry characterized by compromised norepinephrine function. Two photographs of the Washington monument, one made with a traditional camera and the other with a digital camera, appear very similar despite the distinctly different mechanisms that produced the two pictures. Mice can develop the same phenotype of light-colored fur as a function of two different polymorphisms (Hoekstra et al., 2006).

THE CELEBRATION OF BIOLOGICAL ETIOLOGY

Although the evidence indicates that almost all psychopathological profiles are a joint function of a biologically based diathesis and environmental experience, there is currently more enthusiasm and financial support for research that probes the biological rather than the environmental contributions to these profiles. This situation was reversed a half-century earlier, and I end this chapter by addressing some reasons for the current bias.

First, American and European scientists prefer materialistic explanations of natural phenomena. Genes, neurons, transmitters, and circuits are material entities whose forms can be observed or imagined. Neither feelings nor thoughts, which the Greeks and Descartes assigned to the soul, possess this quality. Second, anxiety, depression, criminality, and alcohol dependence are more prevalent among those who are poor and/or belong to an ethnic minority. However, investigators who claim that the child-rearing practices of the parents of these patients made a contribution to the symptoms might provoke, in the current political climate, accusations that they held prejudicial attitudes toward the socially disadvantaged. No one is supposed to blame a victim for his/her circumstances.

Third, theoretical advances in every discipline often follow the introduction of new, more powerful methods. Investigators studying the importance of the social environment continue to use the traditional methods of questionnaires, interviews, and only, occasionally, behavioral observations. These scientists have not invented more sensitive ways to measure the psychological consequences of experience. In contrast, geneticists, molecular biologists, and neuroscientists enjoy many new technologies. Furthermore, these technologies are more easily implemented with rats and mice than with humans. As a result, scientists seeking research funds, and acceptance from respected colleagues, rationalize the use of rodents as a useful model for many forms of mental illness in humans.

However, these investigators typically probe the biological rather than the experiential contributions to a behavioral or biological outcome that is presumed to share essential features with some form of human pathology. The problem with this assumption is that there is no experimental manipulation with mice that could simulate the effects of being an economically disadvantaged member of an ethnic minority, a homely child rejected by peers, a child with less well-educated parents who cannot read, or a parent who believes that she was responsible for her child's current difficulties. Thus, materialism, a reluctance to blame the victim, and powerful biological techniques that can be used more effectively with animals than with humans came together to create the current imbalance in the study of the causes and cures for human psychopathology.

Obviously, the current emphasis on the biological contribution has considerable value, but it has the disadvantage of failing to raise public consciousness over the psychological contributions of peers and adults who interact with the children who might become patients, and motivates a single-minded approach to finding drugs or psychotherapeutic treatments that are directed only at the patients rather than urging clinicians to combine these treatments with the strategies that might alter the social context. Every river is capable of becoming polluted and losing its capacity to sustain life. However, ecologists do not attribute an inherent flaw to a river that has become polluted. Rather, they urge changes in the practices of industry and agriculture that are the root causes of the pollution. Psychiatrists and psychologists should adopt a similar strategy when they deal with anxiety, mood, and character disorders. The current Zeitgeist among neurobiologists and like-minded psychiatrists and psychologists is too friendly to a view of causality, reminiscent of Leibniz, which assumes that certain brain states automatically provoke particular mental states. Clinicians and scientists should be more receptive to Newton's argument that an apple falls from a tree when the gravitational force on the apple exceeds that of the force that holds the fruit to the branch on which it rests (Hall, 1980).

REFERENCES

Adamec, R. E., Blundell, J., & Burton, P. (2005). Neural circuit changes mediating a lasting bias and behavioral response to predator stress. *Neuroscience and Biobehavioral Reviews, 29,* 1225–1241.

Arbelle, S., Benjamin, J., Golin, M., Kremer, I., Belmaker, R. H., & Ebstein, R. P. (2003). Relation of shyness in grade school children to the genotype for the long form of the serotonin transporter promoter region polymorphism. *American Journal of Psychiatry, 160,* 671–676.

Asendorpf, J. B. (1989). Shyness as a final pathway for two different kinds of inhibition. *Journal of Personality and Social Psychology, 57,* 481–492.

Asendorpf, J. B. (1991). Development of inhibited children's coping with unfamiliarity. *Child Development, 62,* 1460–1474.

Auerbach, J., Geller, V., Lezer, S., Shinwell, E., Belmaker, R. H., & Levin, J. (1999). Dopamine D4 receptor (D4DR) and serotonin transporter promoter (5-HTTLPR) polymorphisms in the determination of temperament in 2-month-old infants. *Molecular Psychiatry, 4,* 369–373.

Austin, M. C., Rhodes, J. L., & Lewis, D. A. (1997). Differential distribution of corticotropin-releasing hormone immunoreactive axons in monoaminergic nuclei of the human brainstem. *Neuropsychopharmacology, 17,* 326–341.

Bartels, M., van den Oord, E. J., Hudziak, J. J., Rietveld, M. J., van Beijsterveldt, C. E., & Boomma, D. I. (2004). Genetic and environmental mechanisms underlying stability and change in problem behaviors at ages 3, 7, 10, and 12. *Developmental Psychology, 40,* 852–867.

Bates, J. E. (1989). Concepts and measures of temperament. In J. A. Kohnstamm, J. E. Bates, & M. K. Rothbart (Eds.), *Temperament and childhood* (pp. 3–26). New York: Wiley.

Battaglia, M., Ogliari, A., Zanoni, A., Citterio, A., Pozzoli, U., Giorda, R., et al. (2005). Influence of the serotonin transporter promoter gene and shyness on children's cerebral responses to facial expressions. *Archives of General Psychiatry, 62,* 85–94.

Bethea, C. L., Streicher, J. M., Coleman, K., Pau, F. K., Moessner, R., & Cameron, J. L. (2004). Anxious behavior and fenfluramine-induced prolactin secretion in young rhesus macaques with different alleles of the serotonin reuptake transporter polymorphism (5HTTLPR). *Behavior Genetics, 34,* 295–307.

Biederman, J., Hirshfeld-Becker, D. R., Rosenbaum, J. F., Herot, C., Friedman, D., Snidman, N., et al. (2001). Further evidence of association between behavioral inhibition and social anxiety in children. *American Journal of Psychiatry, 158,* 1673–1679.

Brandao, M. L., Coimbra, N. C., & Osaki, M. Y. (2001). Changes in the auditory-evoked potentials induced by fear-evoking stimulation. *Physiology and Behavior, 72,* 365–372.

Brendgen, M., Wanner, B., Morin, A. J. S., & Vitaro, F. (2005). Relations with parents and with peers, temperament, and trajectories of depressed mood during early adolescence. *Journal of Abnormal Child Psychology, 33,* 579–594.

Cameron, O. G. (2002). *Visceral sensory neuroscience.* New York: Oxford University Press.

Caspi, A., Elder, G. H., & Bem, D. J. (1988). Living away from the world. *Developmental Psychology, 24,* 824–831.

Caspi, A., Sugden, K., Moffitt, T. E., Taylor, A., Craig, I. W., Harrington, H., et al. (2003). Influence of life stress on depression: moderation by a polymorphism in the 5-HTT gene. *Science, 301,* 386–389.

Chavira, D. A., Stein, M. B., & Malcarne, V. L. (2002). Scrutinizing the relationship between shyness and social phobia. *Journal of Anxiety Disorders, 16,* 585–598.

Ciesla, W. (2001). Can melatonin regulate the expression of prohormone convertase 1 and 2 gene via monomeric and dimeric forms of RZR/ROR nuclear receptor, and can melatonin influence the processes of embryogenesis or carcinogenesis by disturbing the proportion of cAMP and cGMP concentrations? Theoretic model of controlled apoptosis. *Medical Hypotheses, 56,* 181–193.

Coplan, R. J., Rubin, K. H., Fox, N. A., Calkins, S. D., & Stuart, S. L. (1994). Being alone, playing alone, and acting alone. *Child Development, 65,* 129–137.

Cote, S., Tremblay, R. E., Nagin, D., Zoccolillo, M., & Vitaro, F. (2002). The development of impulsivity, fearfulness, and helpfulness during childhood. *Journal of Child Psychology and Psychiatry, 43,* 609–618.

Cox, B. J., MacPherson, P. S., & Enns, M. W. (2005). Psychiatric correlates of childhood shyness in a nationally representative sample. *Behavior Research and Therapy, 43,* 1019–1027.

Davey, G. C., McDonald, A. S., Hirisave, U., Prabhu, G. G., Iwawaki, S., Jim, C. I., Merckelbach, H., de Jong, P. J., Leung, P. W., & Reimann, B. C. (1998). A cross-cultural study of animal fears. *Behavior Research and Therapy, 36,* 735–750.

Davidson, R. J. (2003). Right frontal brain activity, cortisol, and withdrawal behavior in 6-month-old infants. *Behavioral Neuroscience, 117,* 11–20.

Davidson, R. J., Jackson, D. L., & Kalin, N. H. (2000). Emotion, plasticity, context, and regulation. *Psychological Bulletin, 126,* 890–909.

Degler, C. N. (1981). *At odds.* New York: Oxford University Press.

Eley, P. C., Sugden, K., Corsico, A., Gregory, A. M., Shaw, P., McGuffin, P., et al. (2004). Gene-environment interaction analysis of serotonin system markers with adolescent depression. *Molecular Psychiatry, 9,* 908–915.

Feldner, M. T., Zvolensky, M. J., Stickle, T. R., Bonn-Miller, M. O., & Leen-Feldner, E. W. (2006). Anxiety sensitivity-physical concerns as a moderator of the emotional consequences of emotion suppression during biological challenge: An experimental test using individual growth curve analysis. *Behavior Research and Therapy, 44,* 249–272.

Fitzgerald, D. A., Angstadt, M., Jelsone, L. M., Nathan, P. J., & Phan, K. L. (2006). Beyond threat. *Neuroimage, 30,* 1441–1448.

Floyd, M., Garfield, A., & LaSota, M. T. (2005). Anxiety sensitivity and worry. *Personality and Individual Differences, 38,* 1223–1229.

Fox, N. A., Henderson, H. A., Rubin, K. H., Calkins, S. D., & Schmidt, L. A. (2001). Continuity and discontinuity of behavioral inhibition and exuberance. *Child Development, 72,* 1–21.

Fox, N. A., Calkins, S. D., & Bell, M. A. (1994). Neural plasticity and development in the first two years of life. *Development and Psychopathology, 6,* 677–696.

Fox, N. A., Henderson, H. A., Marshall, T. J., Nichols, K. E., & Ghera, M. N. (2005). Behavioral inhibition: Linking biology and behavior within a developmental framework. In S. Fiske, A. Kazdin, & D. Schacter (Eds.), *Annual Review of Psychology, 56,* 235–262.

Golimbet, V. E., Gritsenko, I. K., Alfimova, M. V., & Ebstein, R. P. (2005). Polymorphic markers of the dopamine D4 receptor gene promoter region and personality traits in mentally healthy individuals from the Russian population. *Genetika, 41,* 966–972.

Gortmaker, S. L., Kagan, J., Caspi, A., & Silva, P. A. (1997). Daylength during pregnancy and shyness in children. *Developmental Psychobiology, 31,* 107–114.

Grabe, H. J., Lange, M., Wolff, B., Volzke, H., Lucht, M., Freyberger, H. J., et al.

(2005). Mental and physical distress is modulated in the 5-HT transporter gene interacting with social stressors and chronic disease burden. *Molecular Psychiatry, 10,* 1020–1024.

Hall, A. R. (1980). *Philosophers at war.* New York: Cambridge University Press.

Hallowell, A. I. (1941). The social function of anxiety in a primitive society. *American Sociological Review, 6,* 869–891.

Hariri, A. R., Drabant, E. M., & Weinberger, D. R. (2006). Imaging genetics: Perspectives from studies of genetically driven variation in serotonin function and corticolimbic affective processing. *Biological Psychiatry, 59,* 888–897.

Hartl, D., & Jones, E. W. (2005). *Genetics* (6th ed.). Boston: Jones & Bartlett.

Hinton, D. E., Pich, V., Safren, S. A., Pollack, M. H., & McNally, R. J. (2005a). Anxiety sensitivity in traumatized Cambodian refugees. *Behavioral Research and Therapy, 43,* 1631–1643.

Hinton, D. E., Pich, V., Chhean, D., Pollack. M. H., & McNally, R. J. (2005b). Sleep paralysis among Cambodian refugees: Association with PTSD diagnosis and severity. *Depression and Anxiety, 22,* 47–51.

Hoehn-Saric, R., Lee, J., McLeod, D., & Wong, D. (2005). Effect of worry on regional cerebral blood flow in nonanxious subjects. *Psychiatry Research: Neuroimaging, 140,* 259–269.

Hoekstra, H. E., Hirschmann, R. J., Bundey, R., Insel, P., & Crossland, J. (2006). A single amino acid mutation contributes to adaptive beach mouse color pattern. *Science, 313,* 101–104.

Huber, D., Veinante, P., & Stoop, R. (2005). Vasopressin and oxytocin excite distinct neuronal populations in the central amygdala. *Science, 308,* 245–248.

Hughes, A. A., Heimberg, R. G., Coles, M. E., Gibb, B. E., Liebowitz, M. R., & Schneier, F. R. (2006). Relations of the factors of the tripartite model of anxiety and depression to types of social anxiety. *Behaviour Research and Therapy, 44,* 1629–1641.

Irizarry, Y., & Galbraith, S. J. (2004). Complex disorders reloaded: causality, action, reaction, cause and effect. *Molecular Psychiatry, 9,* 431–432.

Kagan, J. (1994). *Galen's prophecy.* New York: Basic Books.

Kagan, J., Reznick, J. S., & Snidman, N. (1988). Biological bases of childhood shyness. *Science, 240,* 167–171.

Kagan, J., & Saudino, K. J. (2001). Behavioral inhibition and related temperaments. In R. N. Emde and J. K. Hewitt (Eds.), *Infants early childhood* (pp. 111–122). New York: Oxford University Press.

Kagan, J., & Snidman, N. (2004). *The long shadow of temperament.* Cambridge, MA: Harvard University Press.

Kashdan, T. B., & Steger, M. F. (2006). Expanding the topography of social anxiety. *Psychological Science, 17,* 120–128.

Kaufman, J., Yang, B. Z., Douglas-Palumberi, H., Houssyar, S., Lipschitz, D., Krystal, J. H., et al. (2004). Social supports and serotonin transporter gene modulate depression in maltreated children. *Proceedings of the National Academy of Sciences, 101,* 17316–17321.

Kelly, O., McIntosh, J., McIntyre, D., Merali, Z., & Anisman, H. (2003). Anxiety in rats selectively bred for fast and slow kindling rates: situation-specific outcomes. *Stress, 6,* 289–295.

Kirsch, P., Esslinger, C., Chen, Q., Mier, D., Lis, S., Siddhanti, S., et al. (2005). Oxytocin modulates neural circuitry for social cognition and fear to humans. *Journal of Neuroscience, 49,* 11489–11493.

La Gasse, L., Gruber, C., & Lipsitt, L. P. (1989). The infantile expression of avidity in relation to later assessments. In J. S. Reznick (Ed.), *Perspectives on behavioral inhibition* (pp. 159–176). Chicago: University of Chicago Press.

Lahti, J., Raikkonen, K., Ekelund, J., Peltonen, L., Raitakari, O. T., & Keltikangas-Jarvinen, L. (2006). Socio-demographic characteristics moderate the association between DRD4 and novelty seeking. *Personality and Individual Differences, 40,* 533–543.

Lakatos, K., Nemoda, Z., Birkas, E., Ronai, Z., Kovacs, E., Ney, K., et al. (2003). Association of D4 dopamine receptor gene and serotonin transporter promoter polymorphism with infants' response to novelty. *Molecular Psychiatry, 8,* 90–98.

McDougall W. (1908). *Introduction to social psychology.* London: Methuen.

Merikangas, K. R., Lieb, R., Wittchen, H. U., & Avenevoli, S. (2003). Family and high-risk studies of social anxiety disorder. *Acta Psychiatrica Scandinavia Supplement, 417,* 28–37.

Morley-Fletcher, S., Polanza, P., Parolaro, D., Vigaro, D., & Laviola, G. (2003). Intra-uterine position has long term influences on brain mu-opioid receptor densities and behavior in mice. *Psychoneuroendocrinology, 28,* 386–400.

Netter, P. (2006). Dopamine challenge tests as an indicator of psychological traits. *Human Psychopharmacology, 21,* 91–99.

Pape, H. C., & Stork, O. (2003). Genes and mechanisms in the amygdala involved in the formation of fear memory. *Annals of the New York Academy of Sciences, 985,* 92–105.

Parsey, R. V., Hastings, R. S., Oquendo, M. A., Hu, X., Goldman, D., Huang, Y., et al. (2006a). Effect of a triallelic functional polymorphism of the serotonin-transporter-linked promoter region on expression of serotonin transporter in the human brain. *American Journal of Psychiatry, 163,* 48–51.

Parsey, R. V., Hastings, R. S., Oquendo, M. A., Huang, Y. Y., Simpson, N. Arcement, J., et al. (2006b). Lower serotonin transporter binding potential in the human brain during major depressive episodes. *American Journal of Psychiatry, 163,* 52–58.

Phelps, E. A. (2006). Emotion and cognition. In S. T. Fiske, A. E. Kazdin, & D. L., Schacter (Eds.), *Annual Review of Psychology 57,* 27–53.

Pitkanen, A. (2000). Connectivity of the rat amygdaloid complex. In J. P. Aggleton (Ed.), *The amygdala* (2nd ed.). New York: Oxford University Press.

Prior, M., Smart, D., Sanson, A., & Oberklaid, F. (2000). Does shy-inhibited temperament in childhood lead to anxiety problems in adolescence? *Journal of the American Academy of Child and Adolescent Psychiatry, 39,* 461–468.

Rich, G. J. (1928). A biochemical approach to the study of personality. *Journal of Abnormal and Social Psychology, 23,* 158–179.

Rosenbaum, J. F., Biederman, J., Hirshfeld, D. R., Bolduc, E. A., Faraone, S. V., Kagan, J., et al. (1991). Further evidence of an association between behavioral inhibition and anxiety disorders: results from a family study of children from a non-clinical sample. *Journal of Psychiatric Research, 25,* 49–65.

Rothbart, M. K. (1989). Temperament in childhood. In J. A. Kohnstamm, J. E. Bates, & M. K. Rothbart (Eds.), *Temperament in childhood* (pp. 59–76). New York: Wiley.

Rubin, K. H., Burgess, K. B., & Hastings, D. D. (2002). The stability and social behavioral consequences of toddlers' inhibited temperament and parenting behaviors. *Child Development, 73,* 483–495.

Schmidt, L. A., Fox, N. A., Schulkin, J., & Gold, P. W. (1999). Behavioral and psychophysiological correlates of self-presentation in temperamentally shy children. *Developmental Psychobiology, 35,* 119–135.

Schienle, A., Schafer, A., Hermann, A., Walter, B., Stark, R., & Vaitl, D. (2006). fMRI responses to pictures of mutilation and contamination. *Neuroscience Letters, 393,* 174–178.

Schneirla, T. C. (1959). An evolutionary and developmental theory of biphasic processes approach and withdrawal. In M. R. Jones (Ed.), *Nebraska Symposium on Motivation* (pp. 1–44). Lincoln: University of Nebraska Press.

Schultz, W. (2006). Reward and addiction. In S. T. Fiske, A. E. Kazdin, & D. L. Schacter (Eds.), *Annual Review of Psychology, 57,* 87–116.

Scott, J. P., & Fuller, J. (1965). *Genetics and the social behavior of the dog.* Chicago: University of Chicago Press.

Smoller, J. W., Yamaki, L. H., Fagerness, J. A., Biederman, J., Racette, S., Laird, N. M., et al. (2005). The corticotropin-releasing hormone gene and behavioral inhibition in children at risk for panic disorder. *Biological Psychiatry, 15,* 1485–1492.

Stefanacci, L. & Amaral, D. G. (2002). Some observations on cortical input for the macaque amygdala. *Journal of Comparative Neurology, 451,* 301–323.

Stein, M. B., Fallin, M. D., Schork, N. J., & Gelernter, J. (2005). COMT polymorphisms and anxiety-related personality traits. *Neuropsychopharmacology, 30,* 2092–2102.

Sundet, J. M., Skre, I., Okkenhaug, J. J., & Tambs, K. (2003). Genetic and environmental causes of the interrelationships between self-reported fears. A study of a non-clinical sample of Norwegian identical twins and their families. *Scandinavian Journal of Psychology, 44,* 97–106.

Thomas, L., Purvis, C. C., Drew, J. E., Abramovich, D. R., & Williams, L. M. (2002). Melatonin receptors in human fetal brain: 2-[(125)I] iodomelatonin binding and MT1 gene expression. *Journal of Pineal Research, 33,* 218–224.

Wirtschafter, D. (2005). Cholinergic involvement in the cortical and hippocampal Fos expression induced in the rat by placement in a novel environment. *Brain Research, 1051,* 57–65.

Zisapel, N. (2001). Melatonin-dopamine interactions: from basic neurochemistry to a clinical setting. *Cellular and Molecular Neurobiology, 21,* 605–616.

CHAPTER 7

Exposure to Teratogenic Agents as a Risk Factor for Psychopathology

SUSANNA L. FRYER, NICOLE A. CROCKER, AND SARAH N. MATTSON

INTRODUCTION

teratogen is an agent that causes birth defects by altering the course of typical development. Examples of human teratogens exist in several classes of substances including drugs of abuse (e.g., alcohol, cocaine, nicotine), prescription medications (e.g., retinoic acid, valproic acid), environmental contaminants (e.g., pesticides, lead, methylmercury), and diseases (e.g., varicella, herpes simplex virus, rubella). Pregnant women are exposed to teratogens for a variety of reasons. Some women may be unaware of the teratogenic capability of certain substances; or, in the case of diseases such as varicella, even if awareness exists, exposure prevention may not be possible. Similarly, with conditions such as seizure disorder or severe depression, termination of pharmacologic treatment during pregnancy may not be advisable. Furthermore, given that about half of pregnancies in the United States are unplanned, and given that preg-

Acknowledgments: Preparation of this chapter was supported in part by National Institute on Alcohol Abuse and Alcoholism Grant numbers AA010820, AA010417, and AA016051. We gratefully acknowledge the assistance and support of the Center for Behavioral Teratology, San Diego State University.

nancy detection may not occur until fetal development is well underway, many teratogenic exposures occur prior to pregnancy recognition (Henshaw, 1998). As an example, over 130,000 pregnant women per year in the United States consume alcoholic beverages at levels that pose a teratogenic exposure risk to their fetuses (Lupton, Burd, & Harwood, 2004), and 10% of women who know they are pregnant report drinking alcohol during pregnancy (Centers for Disease Control and Prevention, 2004). These rates exist despite 3 decades of research on the effects of alcohol-induced birth defects and the presence of government-mandated labels on alcoholic beverages that warn of the association between drinking during pregnancy and harmful fetal effects. Thus, teratogenic exposures are common, and birth defects that can result from prenatal exposures constitute a major public health concern.

Behavioral teratogens are agents that cause changes in function (e.g., cognitive, affective, sensorimotor, social) when individuals are exposed during gestation (Vorhees, 1986). Behavioral teratogens can cause damage to the fetus even in the absence of gross physical or structural abnormalities that may occur with physical teratogens. The effects of behavioral teratogens may be subtle and are not necessarily easily recognizable at birth. The purpose of research aimed at identifying and characterizing the effects of behavioral teratogens is to determine the degree and nature of behavioral dysfunction attributable to fetal exposure to drugs or other agents. The hope is that identifying substances that can act as behavioral teratogens and increasing public awareness of teratogenic effects can reduce exposure to teratogens and resulting fetal damage.

As noted previously, the effects of teratogenic exposures are diverse and may include structural damage to the fetus, cognitive impairments, and emotional dysfunction. This chapter will focus on the association between teratogenic exposure and the development of mental illness. The etiology of psychopathology is complicated by gene–environment interactions (cf. Rutter, 2005), in which only certain genotypes are activated by certain environmental risks. Gene–environment correlation is also possible, to the extent that genes predisposing to maternal substance abuse may be accentuated by maladaptive child-rearing environments. In short, it is difficult to pinpoint the multifaceted etiology of psychopathology to single genetic or environmental causes. Rather, the complex behaviors that comprise psychopathology manifest in an emergent fashion from a continuous interplay between an individual's genetic expression patterns and his or her environment. For example, certain individuals may be genetically predisposed toward the development of mental illness, yet nongenetic factors, such as perinatal complications, early childhood experiences, and socioeconomic factors, may also be involved in the development of psychopathology. Factors such as family placement (e.g., being raised in a biological, foster, or adoptive home) (Viner & Taylor, 2005), socioeconomic status (SES) (Rutter, 2003), and general intelligence (Dykens, 2000) are potential sources of variance in mental health outcome that may be of particular concern in evaluating the mental health status in individuals with teratogenic exposures.

Alcohol will be the main focus of this chapter, as it is both an archetypal and a widely studied behavioral teratogen. The association between psychopathology and fetal exposure to nicotine, stimulant drugs, methylmercury, and lead will be discussed more briefly, as the effects of these exposures on mental health outcome are less well studied.

HISTORICAL CONTEXT

Knowledge of birth defects and their association with teratogenic exposure has evolved over the course of history. Early depictions, including carvings and drawings, indicate knowledge of birth defects as early as 6,500 BCE, and early written records indicate beliefs that birth defects were caused by various factors including witchcraft. Birth defects were also thought to portend adverse events. More recently, it was thought that the fetus was afforded significant protection by the uterus, and it was not until 1941 that an association between prenatal exposure to the rubella virus and subsequent birth defects was reported in the scientific literature. Even so, it took the experience with thalidomide in the mid-twentieth century to confirm the association between teratogens and birth defects (Vorhees, 1986).

Similarly, an association between gestational alcohol exposure and deleterious fetal effects was described anecdotally for centuries. Some contend that the association was documented in Greek and Roman mythology, and the Bible. Yet throughout the majority of the twentieth century alcohol was not recognized as a human teratogen. In fact, for much of the century, alcohol was used by physicians to treat premature labor, in a procedure referred to as an *ethanol drip*. Perhaps in part due to this medical usage, the first descriptions in the scientific literature of alcohol as a human teratogen were met with considerable resistance. Instead, it was posed that the constellation of symptoms identified as Fetal Alcohol Syndrome (FAS) were due to other factors such as inadequate prenatal nutrition or genetics ("Effect of alcoholism at time of conception," 1946). Because of their ability to control confounding factors, preclinical animal models were crucial in establishing the causal role of alcohol in bringing about central nervous system (CNS) abnormalities. After over 30 years of research on alcohol teratogenesis, prenatal alcohol exposure is now recognized as a major public health concern. As an example of this increased public awareness, in 1989 the United States Government passed the Alcoholic Beverage Warning Label Act, which mandates that alcoholic beverages contain labels that warn of alcohol's capability to cause harmful effects on the developing fetus. In addition, in February 2005, the U.S. Surgeon General issued an updated "Advisory on Alcohol Use and Pregnancy." This advisory recommended that (a) pregnant women should not drink alcohol, (b) pregnant women who have already consumed alcohol during pregnancy should stop drinking to minimize further risk, and (c) women who are considering pregnancy or who might become pregnant should also abstain from alcohol (http://www.hhs.gov/surgeongeneral/pressreleases/sg02222005.html). Despite this progress, women continue to drink during pregnancy, and much work remains to be done to address this phenomenon.

FETAL ALCOHOL SPECTRUM DISORDERS

Since the first descriptions of FAS appeared in the scientific literature (Jones & Smith, 1973; Jones et al., 1973; Lemoine et al., 1968), the pattern of birth defects associated with maternal alcohol consumption has been studied extensively. FAS is characterized by a triad of presenting symptoms: (a) pre- and/or postnatal growth deficiency, (b) dysmorphic facial features (short palpebral fissures, indistinct philtrum, and a thin upper lip), and (c) central nervous system (CNS) dysfunction. Although CNS dysfunction is required for the diagnosis of FAS, cognitive deficits and behavioral abnormalities are commonly observed following prenatal alcohol exposure even in the absence of the growth deficiency and facial stigmata required for clinical recognition of FAS (e.g., Mattson et al., 1997, 1998).

Given the variable clinical presentation of individuals with histories of gestational alcohol exposure, the term *Fetal Alcohol Spectrum Disorders* (FASD) is now used to describe the range of effects attributable to prenatal exposure (Bertrand, Floyd, & Weber, 2005). These effects may range from complete manifestation of FAS (i.e., meeting all diagnostic criteria) to subtle neurobehavioral or physical defects. The umbrella term FASD includes both dysmorphic (i.e., FAS) and nondysmorphic cases of prenatal alcohol exposure, and encompasses historical terms such as Fetal Alcohol Effects (FAE), partial FAS, Alcohol-Related Birth Defects (ARBD), and Alcohol-Related Neurodevelopmental Disorder (ARND). It should be noted that FASD is a nondiagnostic term and that the narrower conception of FAS is currently the only medically defined diagnosis that addresses the effects of prenatal alcohol exposure. Refining the diagnostic criteria that characterize FASD remains a major research priority (Riley et al., 2003).

Birth defects caused by maternal alcohol use constitute a serious public health concern, both in the United States and internationally. Incidence rates of FAS average about 1 case per 1,000 live births (Bertrand et al., 2005), making FAS the leading preventable cause of Mental Retardation (Pulsifer, 1996). Moreover, it is estimated that more subtle birth defects due to prenatal alcohol exposure occur more frequently, as the combined rate for dysmorphic (i.e., FAS) and nondysmorphic FASD cases has been conservatively estimated at 9.1 cases per 1,000 live births (Sampson et al., 1997). The costs of fetal alcohol effects pose a heavy burden on society: By 1998, costs for FAS alone in the United States were estimated to have reached 4 billion dollars annually (Lupton et al., 2004). Costs related to FASD are bound to be considerably higher.

General Psychopathology Inventories

Although the cognitive deficits associated with fetal alcohol effects have been studied extensively, the literature focused on the mental health outcomes of those with FASD is less developed but growing quickly. In one longitudinal investigation, behavior associated with psychopathology was rated in children with FAS, a large portion of whom were mentally retarded (Steinhausen, Nestler, & Spohr, 1982; Steinhausen, Willms, & Spohr, 1993, 1994). Increased rates of many maladaptive behaviors were observed, including stereotypies, sleeping problems, tics, head and body rocking, peer relationship difficulties, and phobic behaviors. Moreover, an index of psychopathological behavior, created from the sum of symptom scores, correlated with degree of dysmorphology (Steinhausen et al., 1982). A follow-up report demonstrated the persistence of symptoms through late childhood, including hyperkinetic behaviors, sleep disturbances, abnormal habits, stereotyped behaviors, and emotional disorders (Steinhausen & Spohr, 1998).

A more recent study used *Diagnostic and Statistical Manual of Mental Disorders–IV* (DSM-IV; American Psychiatric Association, 1994, 2000) criteria to evaluate psychopathology in a sample of 23 children with histories of heavy prenatal alcohol exposure, ages 5 to 13 (O'Connor et al., 2002). Two of the study participants met full criteria for FAS and six other children had physical anomalies thought to be attributable to alcohol exposure. Based on psychiatric interview, 87% of the sample (20 out of 23) met criteria for at least one of the psychiatric disorders examined, with mood disorders being the most common (including both major depressive and bipolar disorders). These data also suggested comparable mental health outcomes regardless of the severity of fetal alcohol effects; nondysmorphic individuals were as likely to have clinically significant psychopathology as those children with hallmark facial features of FAS. Notably, in an effort to focus on the development of psychiatric illness in children with FASD independent of Mental Retardation, children with an intelligence quotient (IQ) below 70 were excluded from this study. Also, as is frequently the case in a sample of children with FASD, family placement varied, with 3 children living with their biological mothers, 14 living in adopted homes, and 6 children residing in foster care. As previously discussed, factors such as general intelligence, SES, and family placement are important sources of variance in mental health outcomes and must be considered when interpreting data associating psychopathology with teratogenic exposure. In addition, the authors noted that, because the sample was clinically referred, the high rates of observed psychopathology may not generalize to the entire alcohol-exposed population (O'Connor et al., 2002). In any case, these data underscore previous findings of high rates of psychiatric disorders in children with FASD (Steinhausen et al., 1993) and confirm that mental health problems can occur independently of the various intellectual disabilities and dysmorphic features associated with FAS per se.

Increased rates of psychopathology have also been documented in adult samples, suggesting that the psychiatric symptoms observed in children with FASD do not dissipate with time. One study used a structured, DSM-IV based psychiatric interview to evaluate mental health in 25 nonmentally retarded, clinically referred young adults with histories of prenatal alcohol exposure. Twenty-three of the participants (92%) met criteria for a DSM-IV Axis I disorder. Alcohol or drug dependencies were the most common diagnoses, followed by Major Depressive Disorder (Famy, Streissguth, & Unis, 1998). Even though the O'Connor and Famy studies are limited by small sample sizes and lack of comparison groups, they nonetheless suggest markedly high rates of psychiatric disorders in clinical FASD samples. Moreover, a recent study with an increased sample size and inclusion of a control group demonstrated similarly high rates of overall psychiatric disorders in the alcohol-exposed group (Fryer et al., 2007). Still, data from future studies with increased sample sizes and clinical comparison groups will be a helpful addition to the literature attempting to characterize the mental healthcare needs of alcohol-exposed individuals.

It bears repeating that because these studies involve participants who were identified due to clinically significant problems or recognition of fetal alcohol effects, results may not generalize to the entire alcohol-exposed population. That is, these studies select against individuals who were exposed to alcohol prenatally but experience few or no psychiatric or behavioral symptoms. Although retrospective studies are important in characterizing those individuals most in need of clinical services, studies that identify participants prospectively (i.e., at or near the time of teratogenic exposure) can increase the external validity of research findings that suggest a link between prenatal alcohol exposure and psychopathology. Also, prospective studies typically enable better control of confounding factors, because environmental and demographic information can be collected more accurately nearer to the time of exposure.

The Seattle Study on Alcohol and Pregnancy, a large-scale population-based study of alcohol's behavioral teratogenicity, uses a prospective study design. Streissguth and colleagues initially identified 1,529 pregnant women in the mid-1970s and collected information about their use of alcohol, cigarettes, caffeine, and other recreational and prescription drugs (Barr et al., 2006). Importantly, these pregnancies were not considered high risk, and all women received prenatal care. A cohort of 500 mother-infant pairs was selected—oversampling for alcohol use—and followed into adulthood. Of this birth cohort, 400 young adults, including individuals with and without prenatal alcohol exposure, were interviewed at about age 25 using Structured Clinical Interviews for DSM-IV (both Axis I and Axis II). The purpose of this study was to determine whether the high rates of psychiatric illness observed in clinical samples of individuals with FASD would be replicated in a nonclinical, community sample.

The odds of developing Axis I somatoform and substance use disorders and Axis II paranoid, passive-aggressive, and antisocial traits were at least doubled in individuals who had been exposed to one or more binge-drinking episodes versus those who had not. Substance use disorders and Axis II passive-aggressive and antisocial personality traits remained at least a twofold risk in alcohol-exposed individuals, even after controlling for confounding factors including prenatal nicotine or marijuana exposure, family placement, low SES, poor maternal nutrition, breastfeeding, and family history of psychiatric problems and alcoholism. The authors note that, given the epidemiological focus of their study, including thorough control of many other factors that may predict mental health, prenatal alcohol exposure is likely to play a causal role in the observed increase in the disorders noted.

In summary, the consensus from these global mental health outcome studies suggests that individuals with fetal alcohol exposure histories suffer from substantial psychiatric illness. Moreover, the diversity of study methodologies (e.g., encompassing both prospective and retrospective subject ascertainment, longitudinal versus cross-sectional design, targeting different portions of the age span) supports the generalizability of the association between FASD and increased psychopathology.

DISRUPTIVE BEHAVIOR DISORDERS

A review of available literature suggests that certain types of psychopathology are more likely than others to follow gestational alcohol exposure. Among these are disorders in the disruptive behavior spectrum (i.e., Attention-Deficit/Hyperactivity Disorder [ADHD], Oppositional Defiant Disorder, Conduct Disorder). For instance, in a recent study examining psychopathology in a retrospectively ascertained sample of children with heavy prenatal alcohol exposure, group differences between alcohol-exposed versus typically developing peers were observed in terms of ADHD, Oppositional Defiant Disorder, Conduct Disorder, depressive disorders, and specific phobias (Fryer et al., 2007). The group difference in the ADHD category was by far the largest effect. This finding is consistent with previous research suggesting that increased ADHD rates are among the most notable psychopathological outcomes within the FASD population (Burd et al., 2003; Streissguth et al., 1996).

In addition to the increased rates of ADHD in this population, the association between prenatal alcohol exposure and attention deficits, considered dimensionally, is well documented. Converging evidence from psychopathological outcome studies (Steinhausen & Spohr, 1998; Steinhausen et al., 1993), case reports (Lemoine et al., 1968), and developmental cognitive studies (Coles et al., 2002; Mattson & Riley, 1998) corroborate the widespread presence of attention problems in the FASD population. More specifically, studies have shown that deficits on measures of attention associated with prenatal alcohol exposure occur independently of general intelligence deficits; they are also persistent (Brown et al., 1991; Streissguth et al., 1995). A recent study also suggests that children with FASD can be distinguished from nonexposed peers based on scores from standard psychological measures of attention (Lee, Mattson, & Riley, 2004). Test results from two frequently used attention measures (the Freedom from Distractibility Index from the Wechsler Intelligence Scale for Children–III and the Attention Problems Scale from the Child Behavior Checklist [CBCL, Achenbach, 1991]) classified children as alcohol-exposed versus comparison with over 90% accuracy. In summary, attention deficits are hallmark features of prenatal alcohol exposure, and although these deficits are obviously not exclusive markers of FASD, data suggest that their presence may be useful as markers of alcohol teratogenic effects.

Increased delinquent behavior has also been reported in alcohol-exposed youths (Schonfeld, Mattson, & Riley, 2005; Streissguth et al., 1996). However, factors such as amount of exposure (Lynch et al., 2003) and home placement (biological, foster, or adoptive) (Schonfeld et al., 2005) are likely to moderate the relation between prenatal alcohol exposure and delinquency. For example, an investigation of a low-SES community sample did not find an increased rate of delinquency when alcohol-exposed youth were compared to either nonexposed peers (also low SES) or a special education comparison group (Lynch et al., 2003). Rather, within this sample, delinquency was related to environmental and behavioral variables such as low parental supervision, adolescent life stress, and self-reported drug use. In terms of family placement, higher rates of delinquent behavior were endorsed by alcohol-exposed adolescents in biological and foster homes versus those in adoptive homes (Schonfeld et al., 2005). However, given the relatively small sample size of the alcohol-exposed group ($n = 27$), further research is indicated to confirm this family placement finding. Still, such results underscore the importance of controlling for environmental influences when assessing the relation between teratogenic exposures and mental health outcomes.

Regardless of potential moderating or mediating factors, individuals with prenatal alcohol exposure are significantly overrepresented in the criminal justice system (Boland et al., 1998; Fast & Conry, 2004), although corrections staff are largely unaware of this phenomenon (Burd et al., 2004). One of the few systematic FASD screens of a delinquent group undertaken by a forensic psychiatric facility in Canada revealed that 23% of juvenile detainees were exposed to significant amounts of alcohol prenatally (Fast, Conry, & Loock, 1999). Of the 67 individuals who were identified as having birth defects related to alcohol exposure, only 3 individuals had been given an alcohol-related diagnosis prior to the screen. Overall, the association between prenatal alcohol exposure and disruptive behavior appears to be reliable and persistent, and is evident at relatively low exposure levels. For example, when researchers in the Seattle project, described previously, conducted psychosocial assessments of 14-year-old exposed offspring, misbehaviors were among the outcomes most strongly associated with alcohol exposure. Examples of the types of delinquent behaviors most correlated with alcohol exposure were self-reported antisocial behaviors (e.g., fighting), parent-reported misbehavior as measured by the CBCL Delinquent Behavior scale, and adolescent use of nicotine, alcohol, and other drugs (Carmichael Olson et al., 1997). In summary, FASD are associated with significantly elevated rates of both Conduct Disorder and Oppositional Defiant Disorder (Fryer et al., 2007), higher levels of adult antisocial personality traits (Barr et al., 2006), and legal problems (Fast et al., 1999; Streissguth et al., 1996). Whether this association is direct—or is potentially mediated by a more proximal linkage between FASD and early appearing attentional/impulse control problems as well as learning difficulties, which themselves predict later conduct problems—is indeterminate (e.g., Hinshaw, 1992).

Mood Disorders

Psychopathology associated with alcohol teratogenesis is not limited to the disruptive behavior spectrum. In particular, elevated rates of depressive disorders have also been noted in children with FASD, based on psychiatric parent interviews (Fryer et al., 2007; O'Connor et al., 2002). Also, depressive features are noted on parent questionnaires (Roebuck, Mattson, & Riley, 1999). The potential link between fetal alcohol exposure and depression has been less frequently investigated than the relation with disruptive psychopathology, although research is increasingly focusing on this important topic. Moreover, data examining child and adolescent psychopathology rates indicate that the comorbidities among disruptive behavior disorders and mood disorders are high in the general population (Angold, Costello, & Erkanli, 1999). As with the general population, psychiatric comorbidities are common among children with FASD. Thus, some degree of overlap among those needing services for problems such as mood and disruptive disorders is to be expected.

One longitudinal study examined the relation between prenatal alcohol exposure, negative infant affect, and subsequent symptoms of childhood depression (O'Connor, 2001). Results indicated that gestational alcohol exposure was a significant risk factor for developing depressive features at 6 years of age, both as a direct effect and as an indirect effect, mediated through the pathway of negative infant affect. Interestingly, the authors note that the association between alcohol exposure and depressive symptoms may be moderated by factors such as sex and maternal depression status, as girls whose mothers had high levels of depression were among those most affected in the sample (O'Connor & Kasari, 2000). More recent work identified prenatal alcohol exposure as a possible etiological factor in the development of childhood-onset depression and suggested this association may be mediated by the quality and nature of mother-child interactions (O'Connor & Paley, 2006).

SES is another possible influence on the association between FASD and internalizing outcomes; it emerged as a significant covariate in explaining parent ratings of child internalizing behaviors on the CBCL (Mattson & Riley, 2000). It should be noted, however, that in this study, which included a lower IQ control group, there were no between-group differences on withdrawn behaviors, somatic complaints, or anxious/depressed behaviors, although a significant overall effect of prenatal alcohol exposure on the internalizing summary scale was observed. This suggests that, at least in the context of parent ratings of behavior, larger and clearer effects are associated with externalizing behaviors. Regardless, because the internalizing problems associated with the depressive disorders may be more difficult to recognize than externalizing behaviors, recognition of an increased risk of depressive disorders is of clinical significance.

ADAPTIVE DYSFUNCTION

As might be expected in a population characterized by cognitive impairments and increased rates of mental illness, adaptive dysfunction has been documented in individuals with prenatal alcohol exposure histories (Streissguth et al., 1991; Whaley, O'Connor, & Gunderson, 2001). The Seattle study found that as alcohol-exposed individuals reached adulthood, their overall adaptive abilities were equivalent to those of a typically developing 7-year-old, with social skills showing the most severe detriment (Streissguth et al., 1991). Importantly, this adaptive dysfunction occurred independently of general intelligence detriments (Thomas et al., 1998). In addition, deficits in adaptive functioning may relate to mental health disabilities in this population. One study of children and adults with FASD revealed that mental health problems had the highest prevalence compared to other negative consequences studied, such as legal trouble and disrupted schooling (Streissguth et al., 1996). In fact, mental health problems occurred in the alcohol-exposed sample at a two-fold rate compared to other negative outcomes of interest. Over 400 heavily exposed individuals with FASD were studied, and 94% of the sample experienced mental health problems based on caretaker report.

POSSIBLE MECHANISMS OF ACTION

Because of the infeasibility of controlling for confounding factors such as maternal nutrition and timing and dose of alcohol exposure in humans, research focused on identifying mechanisms of alcohol teratogenesis is typically derived from preclinical animal models of FASD and in vitro tissue culture studies. It is unlikely that the variable and wide-ranging effects associated with prenatal alcohol exposure are produced via a single process or pathway. Rather, a multitude of possible mechanisms for causing the pathology associated with FASD have been identified, including the following: oxidative stress, changes in glucose metabolism, mitochondrial damage, abnormal growth factor activity, dysregulation of developmental gene expression, anomalous cell adhesion, and abnormalities in the development and regulation of neurotransmitter systems (e.g., excitotoxicity) (Goodlett & Horn, 2001). The majority of these potential mechanisms may result in CNS damage by inducing either necrotic or apoptotic cell death, although disturbance to normal cell division and maturation could also be operative. Unfortunately, pinpointing the exact mechanisms through which alcohol exerts teratogenic effects in any given individual is complicated by a host of factors, including variations in timing, dose, and pattern of exposure, maternal characteristics, and fetal genetic factors. Further complicating matters, mechanisms of damage are likely to vary by brain region and cell type (Goodlett, Horn, & Zhou, 2005). Despite these complexities, mechanistic studies have been invaluable in clarifying alcohol's negative effects on the developing fetus, and will likely continue to be of great utility in the future, particularly in the development of prevention and treatment efforts, which are lacking for this population. With regard to treating the psychopathology associated with FASD, preclinical studies can inform intervention efforts by refining our understanding of the structural and functional CNS deficits that may contribute to mental illness in this population. Such translational research is crucial to developing effective, evidence-based treatments.

In summary, the extant literature indicates that prenatal alcohol exposure is associated with clinically significant psychopathology. Moreover, certain psychiatric sequelae, such as those occurring with disruptive behavior disorders, antisocial traits, substance use disorders, and depressive disorders appear to be more prevalent in individuals with FASD than in comparison populations. As discussed previously, etiologic pathways are likely to be complex, and it is not always possible to disentangle the direct effects of prenatal alcohol exposure from important correlates. Ultimately, this body of research suggests that alcohol teratogenesis should be considered as a possible etiological factor contributing to mental illness, and individuals with histories of prenatal alcohol exposure should be referred for psychiatric evaluation.

PSYCHOPATHOLOGY RELATED TO OTHER PRENATAL EXPOSURES

In comparison to alcohol, much less is known about the effects of other potential teratogens on behavioral and psychopathological outcomes. This section will describe research findings related to prenatal nicotine, stimulant drugs, methylmercury, and lead exposures.

NICOTINE

Perhaps because of the high frequency of fetal cigarrette smoke exposure, the effects of gestational nicotine exposure on resulting offspring have been studied fairly extensively, although less is known about behavioral and psychopathological outcomes. It is estimated that nearly a quarter of pregnant women in the United States continue to smoke during pregnancy (National Institute on Drug Abuse, 1996). With regard to psychopathology, the most commonly reported effects include increases in antisocial or delinquent behavior and ADHD.

Several studies have focused on the effects of nicotine exposure on antisocial and / or delinquent behavior. Converging data from criminal records (Brennan, Grekin, & Mednick, 1999; Gibson, Piquero, & Tibbetts, 2000; Piquero et al., 2002; Rantakallio et al., 1992; Räsänen et al., 1999), parental report of child behavior (Maughan et al., 2001; Wasserman et al., 2001), and structured psychiatric clinical interviews (Wakschlag et al., 1997; Wakschlag et al., 2002; Wakschlag et al., 2006; Weissman et al., 1999) support a relation between prenatal nicotine exposure and increased delinquency. Importantly, the relation between conduct problems in offspring and fetal nicotine exposure remains after controlling for genetic factors and parental antisocial behavior (Maughan et al., 2004), although it is essential to consider additional moderating factors to discern the multifaceted etiology of misconduct.

The relation between prenatal nicotine exposure and the development of ADHD is also supported by several studies. Offspring exposed to nicotine during gestation are at increased risk for ADHD symptoms (Batstra, Hadders-Algra, & Neeleman, 2003; Fried, Watkinson, & Gray, 1992; Mick et al., 2002; Naeye & Peters, 1984; Rodriguez & Bohlin, 2005; Romano et al., 2006), and some research suggests that the effects of fetal nicotine exposure on attention are independent of those associated with antisocial behaviors (Button, Thapar, & McGuffin, 2005) and genetic transmission (Thapar et al., 2003). In a study comparing a large sample of boys diagnosed with ADHD to their peers, increased rates of maternal smoking were documented retrospectively in the ADHD group (Milberger et al., 1996). Importantly, the relation remained significant after controlling for SES, parental IQ, and parental ADHD diagnosis. Similarly, a case-control study estimated that maternal smoking was associated with a three-fold increase in developing a hyperkinetic disorder, although other predictive factors such as SES and family psychiatric history partially weakened this association (Linnet et al., 2005). In spite of this evidence, the relation between nicotine exposure and disruptive psychopathology is not universally accepted, and some researchers have contested the degree of risk once confounding factors are controlled (Hill et al., 2000; Knopik et al., 2005; Silberg et al., 2003).

Prenatal nicotine exposure is also associated with other indicators of disruptive behavior, such as increases in dimensional measures of externalizing behavior, delinquency, and ADHD-like symptoms (Fergusson, 1999; Griesler, Kandel, & Davies, 1998; Orlebeke, Knol, & Verhulst, 1997; Williams et al., 1998). In some samples, these effects survive statistical control of potentially confounding influence including child variables (e.g., sex, ethnicity), maternal variables (e.g., education, age, emotional responsiveness), socioeconomic status, and parental histories of substance use and criminality (Fergusson, Horwood, & Lynskey, 1993). There is some evidence that teratogenic exposure may interact with genetic factors in producing psychological outcome; a polymorphism of the dopamine transporter gene has been associated with increases in hyperactive/impulsive and oppositional behaviors, but only in those children who were prenatally exposed to nicotine (Kahn et al., 2003). Although the etiology of such behaviors is clearly multifaceted, this study identifies one potential mechanism of how environment–gene interactions may increase psychopathological risk.

The association between disruptive, externalizing behavior and prenatal nicotine exposure appears to manifest in offspring at a young age. Assessments of toddlers whose mothers smoked during pregnancy reveal higher rates of negative conduct, including aggressive, oppositional, and/or hyperactive behaviors even after controlling for socioeconomic and child-rearing variables (Brook, Brook, & Whiteman, 2000; Day et al., 2000; Linnet et al., 2006). Poor peer relations and increased tantrums have also been described among toddlers exposed to nicotine, while covarying the effects of other drug exposures such as alcohol, marijuana, and cocaine (Faden & Graubard, 2000). Maternal smoking during pregnancy was also identified as a risk factor for persisting generalized behavioral problems, as measured by the CBCL Total Problems summary score, in a large sample of low weight, premature offspring assessed at 3, 5, and 8 years of age (Gray, Indurkhya, & McCormick, 2004). Finally, although the disruptive disorders are the most commonly studied, a smaller body of literature suggests that higher rates of substance use problems and depression are also associated with nicotine exposure (Brennan et al., 2002; Fergusson, Woodward, & Horwood, 1998; Weissman et al., 1999).

In summary, prenatal nicotine exposure appears to pose an increased risk for psychiatric symptoms, although other important explanatory variables such as concurrent prenatal exposures and family history likely contribute to the association. Most notably, increased antisocial behavior (including criminality) and attention deficits have been identified as probable sequelae of prenatal nicotine exposure. Future research with greater control of confounding variables will be useful in further defining the role that prenatal nicotine exposure plays in the development of psychiatric symptoms.

STIMULANT DRUGS

The teratogenic effects of other drugs of abuse are less studied than those of alcohol and nicotine, but there is some evidence that prenatal exposure to stimulants may be associated with subtle neurobehavioral alterations. Although early depictions of fetal cocaine exposure in the popular media were somewhat exaggerated, more recent research has attempted to clarify this issue. Regarding psychopathology, increased levels of aggressive behavior have been reported in cocaine-exposed children (Bendersky, Bennett, & Lewis, 2006; Griffith, Azuma, & Chasnoff, 1994; Linares et al., 2006; Sood et al., 2005), although the moderating effects of sex and comorbid alcohol exposure are important to consider (Nordstrom Bailey et al., 2005). With regard to sex, one study suggested that teacher ratings of behavioral problems manifest in boys more than girls with prenatal cocaine exposure (Delaney-Black et al., 2004).

Prenatal cocaine exposure may also relate to increased infant irritability and lability (Behnke et al., 2002; Richardson, 1998). Still, it is not clear whether these behaviors observed in infancy correlate directly with increased psychopathology later in life. One follow-up study of 6-year-olds did not find effects of prenatal cocaine exposure on teacher ratings of child behavior after controlling for the influences of race, child IQ, school grade, and fetal exposure to alcohol, marijuana, and tobacco (Richardson, Conroy, & Day, 1996). These findings suggest that the neurobehavioral effects of cocaine teratogenesis are subtle and may manifest differently as a factor of the exposed child's age and may interact with other risk factors. Interestingly, cognitive deficits, including deficits in attention, have been associated with prenatal cocaine exposure (Bandstra et al., 2001; Heffelfinger et al., 2002; Noland et al., 2005; Savage et al., 2005). Yet the relation of these deficits to the development of ADHD remains unclear.

Despite the effects noted previously, many studies have failed to find a sizable association between prenatal cocaine exposure and the development of psychopathological symptoms such as behavioral problems (Accornero et al., 2002; Azuma & Chasnoff, 1993; Bennett, Bendersky, & Lewis, 2002; Frank et al., 2001; Messinger et al., 2004; Phelps, Wallace, & Bontrager, 1997; Warner et al., 2006), depressive symptoms (O'Leary et al., 2006), and poor impulse control (Bendersky & Lewis, 1998). Rather, research has suggested that postnatal variables such as the mother's recent drug use, level of mental functioning, and depressive symptoms may be better predictors of mental health status in cocaine-exposed children than exposure-related variables per se.

In a previously discussed study that focused on alcohol exposure and development of depressive features in children, exposure to cocaine was associated with negative infant affect, but not with subsequent development of depressive features (O'Connor & Paley, 2006). Nicotine, marijuana, and caffeine were also examined in this sample. They were not associated with childhood depression, although it is unclear whether exposure to these other drugs occurred at rates high enough to afford adequate statistical power to detect effects, were they to exist.

Regarding amphetamine and methamphetamine, there is some indication that prenatal exposure is associated with increased risk for neurobehavioral detriments. However, there is not sufficient research to draw conclusions and, to date, little research has examined whether these exposures increase risk for psychopathology (Center for the Evaluation of Risks to Human Reproduction, 2005). One longitudinal study in which pregnant women were recruited prospectively indicated a relation between amphetamine abuse during pregnancy and aggression and maladjustment in offspring, who were assessed repeatedly throughout childhood and adolescence (Billing et al., 1994; Billing et al., 1988; Eriksson, Jonsson, & Zetterström, 2000). In a recent study of 1,632 pregnant women, 5.2% reported methamphetamine use in pregnancy (Arria et al., 2006), suggesting a sizable public health risk of this exposure. Additional research is sorely needed.

Possible Mechanisms of Action

As with the study of FASD, preclinical animal models of gestational stimulant drug exposure have been invaluable in elucidating the role of drugs of abuse on the developing CNS. In particular, monoaminergic systems have been implicated as targets of such exposure (cf. Mayes, 2002; Middaugh, 1989), although factors such as age and sex may be important moderators of outcome (Glatt et al., 2000). Atypical development of monoamine transmission may help to explain the attention and arousal dysfunction observed in prenatal exposure cases to stimulants. For example, one possible causal model of arousal dysregulation following prenatal cocaine exposure is impairment in the ability to switch between executively versus automatically driven arousal (Mayes, 2002), functions subserved by the prefrontal cortex that rely on intact dopamine and norepinephrine transmission systems. Due to cocaine's effects on the developing monoaminergic system (e.g., uncoupling of the D_1 receptor), it is possible that the normal balance between dopaminergically mediated and noradrenergically mediated arousal-regulatory systems is disrupted, leading to hyperarousal (Mayes, 2002). As with the case of alcohol, the mechanisms through which stimulant drugs affect prenatal development are likely to be multifaceted, but the distillation of such mechanisms can greatly inform intervention efforts.

In summary, it appears that the behavioral effects of prenatal stimulant exposure are less pronounced than those associated with alcohol and nicotine teratogenesis and that environmental factors related to caregivers may be especially important to consider in stimulant-exposure cases. Ultimately, more research is needed to clarify whether exposure to stimulants increases the risk for developing psychopathology.

Methylmercury and Lead

Methylmercury toxicity has also been associated with neurobehavioral deficits, as a result of both developmental and prenatal exposure (Mendola et al., 2002). However, there is little existing evidence that low-level exposures are associated with marked alterations of the course of typical behavioral development (Davidson et al., 2004; Myers et al., 2003). Much of the research on methylmercury exposure derives from one longitudinal study of relatively low levels of exposure resulting from fish consumption (for review, see Davidson et al., 2006). Results from this investigation fail to indicate an association between prenatal methylmercury exposure and later adverse developmental outcomes in offspring. However, in another cohort exposed to methylmercury through maternal consumption of whale meat, mercury-related cognitive deficits were found (Grandjean et al., 1997). Although developmental outcome studies of prenatal exposure to methylmercury have revealed inconsistent findings (e.g., Spurgeon, 2006), only a few have examined behavior. Of the studies in which a behavioral measure was used, prenatal exposure to methylmercury was not related to negative behavioral outcomes (reviewed in Myers & Davidson, 1998). Thus, although existing data do not suggest a link between methylmercury teratogenesis and psychopathology, more research is needed to confirm this preliminary conclusion, particularly in cases with higher exposure levels.

In considering teratogenic exposure to lead, it is often difficult to differentiate between prenatal and postnatal exposure, given the likelihood of continued environmental exposure after birth (Burns et al., 1999; Needleman et al., 2002; Wasserman et al., 1998). Research that has attempted to disambiguate the effects of timing of lead exposure suggests that postnatal lead exposure may be more influential than prenatal exposure (Bellinger, 1994; Leviton et al., 1993). However, there is some evidence for increased rates of delinquency in children exposed prenatally to lead. More specifically, the Cincinnati Lead Study, which identified a cohort of pregnant women prospectively in order to examine the effects of lead toxicity on child development, found increased rates of both self- and parent-reported delinquency and antisocial behavior associated with prenatal lead exposure (Dietrich et al., 2001). This relation was independent of birth weight, parental IQ, quality of home environment, and SES. Interestingly, adolescent marijuana use was also associated significantly with delinquent and antisocial outcome measures. This finding underscores a common theme: Fetal exposures to teratogenic agents are not necessarily the sole or direct cause of mental illness. Rather, it seems teratogenic exposures act in concert with other risk factors, and a combination of interacting determinants is often necessary to lead to the development of psychopathological behavior.

CONCLUSIONS

Available data underscore the need for clinicians to take thorough prenatal exposure histories and to consider the possible influence of teratogenic effects when assessing and treating psychiatric symptoms. The examples discussed in this chapter demonstrate that teratogenic exposure may increase the risk for psychopathology, and suggest that such exposure should be considered as a possible factor in the etiology of several common psychiatric disorders. Also, it may be that individuals with teratogenic exposures, such as alcohol, may not respond in the same manner as other mental health patients to psychotherapeutic and/or pharmacological treatment methods (O'Connor et al., 2002). Thus, taking an accurate prenatal history could be important for determining the most effective treatment.

RISK AND PROTECTIVE FACTORS

Although complete prevention of teratogenic exposure is clearly ideal, this may not always be possible or practical. In addition, given the multifactorial nature of the etiology of psychiatric illness, it is important to identify factors that may prevent or limit the development of mental health problems in the face of teratogenic exposure. Such protective factors can form the cornerstone of effective mental health intervention and prevention efforts. An equally important task is to identify variables that increase the likelihood of developing psychopathology in cases of teratogenic exposures. Once identified, it is hoped that exposure to such risk factors can be minimized. For example, in the case of alcohol, potential aspects that may protect individuals against a negative mental health outcome status include disability service eligibility; a nurturing, stable home (Streissguth et al., 1996); and early identification and treatment of children (Streissguth et al., 2004). More specifically, based on caregiver interviews, children that were reared in more stable home settings were three- to four-fold less likely to have experienced the majority of adverse life events examined (i.e., disrupted schooling, legal trouble, substance abuse, inappropriate sexual behaviors) (Streissguth et al., 2004). This is an important point to underscore, as it highlights the interactive nature of gene– and biology–environment relationships that drive the development of psychopathology. Thus, a stable and nurturing home has been identified as one potential and salient environmentally mediated pathway to protect children with prenatal alcohol exposure from developing psychopathological behavior.

FUTURE RESEARCH DIRECTIONS

Insufficient data exist to determine conclusively whether an association exists between all known teratogenic exposures and psychopathology. Furthermore, the behavioral teratogenicity of many additional compounds, such as common prescription medications, remains virtually unknown. However, the effect of prenatal alcohol exposure on the development of psychiatric symptoms provides clear evidence that teratogenic exposure can increase the risk of developing psychopathology. More research is needed in order to provide pregnant women and their health care providers with adequate information and thus to promote the health of both the mother and her child. In particular, future studies might focus on developing a profile of potential mental health problems for exposed individuals, while also distilling factors that may prevent development of mental health problems in these children. In order to promote factors that protect against mental illness, and to deliver interventions effectively, valid early detection methods and increased awareness of teratogenic exposures, especially among pediatric healthcare providers, are necessary.

REFERENCES

Accornero, V. H., Morrow, C. E., Bandstra, E. S., Johnson, A. L., & Anthony, J. C. (2002). Behavioral outcome of preschoolers exposed prenatally to cocaine: Role of maternal behavioral health. *Journal of Pediatric Psychology, 27,* 259–269.

Achenbach, T. M. (1991). *Manual for the child behavior checklist/4-18 and 1991 profile.* Burlington: University of Vermont Department of Psychiatry.

American Psychiatric Association. (1994). *Diagnostic and statistical manual of mental disorders* (4th ed.). Washington, DC: American Psychiatric Association.

American Psychiatric Association. (2000). *Diagnostic and statistical manual of mental disorders* (4th ed. text revision). Washington, DC: American Psychiatric Association.

Angold, A., Costello, E. J., & Erkanli, A. (1999). Comorbidity. *Journal of Child Psychology and Psychiatry and Allied Disciplines, 40,* 57–87.

Arria, A. M., Derauf, C., LaGasse, L. L., Grant, P., Shah, R., Smith, L., et al. (2006). Methamphetamine and other substance use during pregnancy: Preliminary estimates from the Infant Development, Environment, and Lifestyle (IDEAL) study. *Maternal and Child Health Journal, 10,* 293–302.

Azuma, S. D., & Chasnoff, I. J. (1993). Outcome of children prenatally exposed to cocaine and other drugs: A path analysis of three-year data. *Pediatrics, 92,* 396–402.

Bandstra, E. S., Morrow, C. E., Anthony, J. C., Accornero, V. H., & Fried, P. A. (2001). Longitudinal investigation of task persistence and sustained attention in children with prenatal cocaine exposure. *Neurotoxicology and Teratology, 23,* 545–559.

Barr, H. M., Bookstein, F. L., O'Malley, K. D., Connor, P. D., Huggins, J. E., & Streissguth, A. P. (2006). Binge drinking during pregnancy as a predictor of psychiatric disorders on the structured clinical interview for DSM-IV in young adult offspring. *American Journal of Psychiatry, 163,* 1061–1065.

Batstra, L., Hadders-Algra, M., & Neeleman, J. (2003). Effect of antenatal exposure to maternal smoking on behavioural problems and academic achievement in childhood: Prospective evidence from a Dutch birth cohort. *Early Human Development, 75,* 21–33.

Behnke, M., Eyler, F. D., Garvan, C. W., Wobie, K., & Hou, W. (2002). Cocaine exposure and developmental outcome from birth to 6 months. *Neurotoxicology and Teratology, 24,* 283–295.

Bellinger, D. (1994). Teratogen update: Lead. *Teratology, 50,* 367–373.

Bendersky, M., Bennett, D., & Lewis, M. (2006). Aggression at age 5 as a function of prenatal exposure to cocaine, gender, and environmental risk. *Journal of Pediatric Psychology, 31,* 71–84.

Bendersky, M., & Lewis, M. (1998). Prenatal cocaine exposure and impulse control at two years. *Annals of the New York Academy of Sciences, 846,* 365–367.

Bennett, D. S., Bendersky, M., & Lewis, M. (2002). Children's intellectual and emotional-behavioral adjustment at 4 years as a function of cocaine exposure, maternal characteristics, and environmental risk. *Developmental Psychology, 38,* 648–658.

Bertrand, J., Floyd, R. L., & Weber, M. K. (2005). Guidelines for identifying and referring persons with fetal alcohol syndrome. *Morbidity and Mortality Weekly Report, 54,* 1–14.

Billing, L., Eriksson, M., Jonsson, B., Steneroth, G., & Zetterström, R. (1994). The influence of environmental factors on behavioural problems in 8-year-old children exposed to amphetamine during fetal life. *Child Abuse and Neglect, 18,* 3–9.

Billing, L., Eriksson, M., Steneroth, G., & Zetterström, R. (1988). Predictive indicators for adjustment in 4-year-old children whose mothers used amphetamine during pregnancy. *Child Abuse and Neglect, 12,* 503–507.

Boland, F. J., Burrill, R., Duwyn, M., & Karp, J. (1998). *Fetal alcohol syndrome: Implications for correctional service.* Ottawa: Correctional Service of Canada.

Brennan, P. A., Grekin, E. R., & Mednick, S. A. (1999). Maternal smoking during pregnancy and adult male criminal outcomes. *Archives of General Psychiatry, 56,* 215–219.

Brennan, P. A., Grekin, E. R., Mortensen, E. L., & Mednick, S. A. (2002). Relationship of maternal smoking during pregnancy with criminal arrest and hospitalization for substance abuse in male and female adult offspring. *American Journal of Psychiatry, 159,* 48–54.

Brook, J. S., Brook, D. W., & Whiteman, M. (2000). The influence of maternal smoking during pregnancy on the toddler's negativity. *Archives of Pediatrics & Adolescent Medicine, 154,* 381–385.

Brown, R. T., Coles, C. D., Smith, I. E., Platzman, K. A., Silverstein, J., Erickson, S., & Falek, A. (1991). Effects of prenatal alcohol exposure at school age. II. Attention and behavior. *Neurotoxicology and Teratology, 13,* 369–376.

Burd, L., Klug, M. G., Martsolf, J. T., & Kerbeshian, J. (2003). Fetal alcohol syndrome: Neuropsychiatric phenomics. *Neurotoxicology and Teratology, 25,* 697–705.

Burd, L., Selfridge, R. H., Klug, M. G., & Bakko, S. A. (2004). Fetal alcohol syndrome in the United States corrections system. *Addiction Biology, 9,* 169–176.

Burns, J. M., Baghurst, P. A., Sawyer, M. G., McMichael, A. J., & Tong, S.-L. (1999). Lifetime low-level exposure to environmental lead and children's emotional and behavioral development at ages 11–13 years. The Port Pirie cohort study. *American Journal of Epidemiology, 149,* 740–749.

Button, T. M. M., Thapar, A., & McGuffin, P. (2005). Relationship between antisocial behaviour, attention-deficit hyperactivity disorder and maternal prenatal smoking. *British Journal of Psychiatry, 187,* 155–160.

Carmichael Olson, H., Streissguth, A. P., Sampson, P. D., Barr, H. M., Bookstein, F. L., & Thiede, K. (1997). Association of prenatal alcohol exposure with behavioral and learning problems in early adolescence. *Journal of the American Academy of Child and Adolescent Psychiatry, 36,* 1187–1194.

Center for the Evaluation of Risks to Human Reproduction. (2005). *NTP-CERHR monograph on the potential human reproductive and developmental effects of amphetamines* (05-4474): National Toxicology Program, U.S. Department of Health and Human Services.

Centers for Disease Control and Prevention. (2004). Alcohol consumption among women who are pregnant or who might become pregnant—United States, 2002. *Morbidity and Mortality Weekly Report, 53,* 1178–1181.

Coles, C. D., Platzman, K. A., Lynch, M. E., & Freides, D. (2002). Auditory and visual sustained attention in adolescents prenatally exposed to alcohol. *Alcoholism: Clinical and Experimental Research, 26,* 263–271.

Davidson, P. W., Myers, G. J., Shamlaye, C., Cox, C., & Wilding, G. E. (2004). Prenatal exposure to methylmercury and child development: Influence of social factors. *Neurotoxicology and Teratology, 26,* 553–559.

Davidson, P. W., Myers, G. J., Weiss, B., Shamlaye, C. F., & Cox, C. (2006). Prenatal methyl mercury exposure from fish consumption and child development: A review of evidence and perspectives from the Seychelles child development study. *NeuroToxicology, 6,* 1106–1109.

Day, N. L., Richardson, G. A., Goldschmidt, L., & Cornelius, M. D. (2000). Effects of prenatal tobacco exposure on preschoolers' behavior. *Journal of Developmental and Behavioral Pediatrics, 21,* 180–188.

Delaney-Black, V., Covington, C., Nordstrom, B., Ager, J., Janisse, J., Hannigan, J. H., et al. (2004). Prenatal cocaine: Quantity of exposure and gender moderation. *Journal of Developmental and Behavioral Pediatrics, 25*, 254–263.

Dietrich, K. N., Ris, M. D., Succop, P. A., Berger, O. G., & Bornschein, R. L. (2001). Early exposure to lead and juvenile delinquency. *Neurotoxicology and Teratology, 23*, 511–518.

Dykens, E. M. (2000). Psychopathology in children with intellectual disability. *Journal of Child Psychology and Psychiatry and Allied Disciplines, 41*, 407–417.

Effect of alcoholism at time of conception. (1946). *Journal of the American Medical Association, 132*, 419.

Eriksson, M., Jonsson, B., & Zetterström, R. (2000). Children of mothers abusing amphetamine: Head circumference during infancy and psychosocial development until 14 years of age. *Acta Paediatrica, 89*, 1474–1478.

Faden, V. B., & Graubard, B. I. (2000). Maternal substance use during pregnancy and developmental outcome at age three. *Journal of Substance Abuse, 12*, 329–340.

Famy, C., Streissguth, A. P., & Unis, A. S. (1998). Mental illness in adults with fetal alcohol syndrome or fetal alcohol effects. *American Journal of Psychiatry, 155*, 552–554.

Fast, D. K., & Conry, J. (2004). The challenge of fetal alcohol syndrome in the criminal legal system. *Addiction Biology, 9*, 161–166.

Fast, D. K., Conry, J., & Loock, C. A. (1999). Identifying fetal alcohol syndrome among youth in the criminal justice system. *Journal of Developmental and Behavioral Pediatrics, 20*, 370–372.

Fergusson, D. M. (1999). Prenatal smoking and antisocial behavior. *Archives of General Psychiatry, 56*, 223–224.

Fergusson, D. M., Horwood, L. J., & Lynskey, M. T. (1993). Maternal smoking before and after pregnancy: Effects on behavioral outcomes in middle childhood. *Pediatrics, 92*, 815–822.

Fergusson, D. M., Woodward, L. J., & Horwood, L. J. (1998). Maternal smoking during pregnancy and psychiatric adjustment in late adolescence. *Archives of General Psychiatry, 55*, 721–727.

Frank, D. A., Augustyn, M., Knight, W. G., Pell, T., & Zuckerman, B. (2001). Growth, development, and behavior in early childhood following prenatal cocaine exposure. *Journal of the American Medical Association, 285*, 1613–1625.

Fried, P. A., Watkinson, B., & Gray, R. (1992). A follow-up study of attentional behavior in 6-year-old children exposed prenatally to marijuana, cigarettes, and alcohol. *Neurotoxicology and Teratology, 14*, 299–311.

Fryer, S. L., McGee, C. L., Matt, G. E., Riley, E. P., & Mattson, S. N. (2007). Evaluation of psychopathological conditions in children with heavy prenatal alcohol exposure. *Pediatrics, 119*, e733–741.

Gibson, C. L., Piquero, A. R., & Tibbetts, S. G. (2000). Assessing the relationship between maternal cigarette smoking during pregnancy and age at first police contact. *Justice Quarterly, 17*, 519–542.

Glatt, S. J., Bolaños, C. A., Trksak, G. H., & Jackson, D. (2000). Effects of prenatal cocaine exposure on dopamine system development: A meta-analysis. *Neurotoxicology and Teratology, 22*, 617–629.

Goodlett, C. R., & Horn, K. H. (2001). Mechanisms of alcohol-induced damage to the developing nervous system. *Alcohol Research and Health, 25,* 175–184.

Goodlett, C. R., Horn, K. H., & Zhou, F. C. (2005). Alcohol teratogenesis: Mechanisms of damage and strategies for intervention. *Experimental Biology and Medicine, 230,* 394–406.

Grandjean, P., Weihe, P., White, R. F., Debes, F., Araki, S., Yokoyama, K., et al. (1997). Cognitive deficit in 7-year-old children with prenatal exposure to methylmercury. *Neurotoxicology and Teratology, 19,* 417–428.

Gray, R. F., Indurkhya, A., & McCormick, M. C. (2004). Prevalence, stability, and predictors of clinically significant behavior problems in low birth weight children at 3, 5, and 8 years of age. *Pediatrics, 114,* 736–743.

Griesler, P. C., Kandel, D. B., & Davies, M. (1998). Maternal smoking in pregnancy, child behavior problems, and adolescent smoking. *Journal of Research on Adolescence, 8,* 159–185.

Griffith, D. R., Azuma, S. D., & Chasnoff, I. J. (1994). Three-year outcome of children exposed prenatally to drugs. *Journal of the American Academy of Child and Adolescent Psychiatry, 33,* 20–27.

Heffelfinger, A. K., Craft, S., White, D. A., & Shyken, J. (2002). Visual attention in preschool children prenatally exposed to cocaine: Implications for behavioral regulation. *Journal of the International Neuropsychological Society, 8,* 12–21.

Henshaw, S. K. (1998). Unintended pregnancy in the United States. *Family Planning Perspectives, 30,* 24–29, 46.

Hinshaw, S. P. (1992). Externalizing behavior problems and academic underachievement in childhood and adolescence: Causal relationships and underlying mechanisms. *Psychological Bulletin, 111,* 127–155.

Hill, S. Y., Lowers, L., Locke-Wellman, J., & Shen, S. (2000). Maternal smoking and drinking during pregnancy and the risk for child and adolescent psychiatric disorders. *Journal of Studies on Alcohol, 61,* 661–668.

Jones, K. L., & Smith, D. W. (1973). Recognition of the fetal alcohol syndrome in early infancy. *Lancet, 2,* 999–1001.

Jones, K. L., Smith, D. W., Ulleland, C. N., & Streissguth, A. P. (1973). Pattern of malformation in offspring of chronic alcoholic mothers. *Lancet, 1,* 1267–1271.

Kahn, R. S., Khoury, J., Nichols, W. C., & Lanphear, B. P. (2003). Role of dopamine transporter genotype and maternal prenatal smoking in childhood hyperactive-impulsive, inattentive, and oppositional behaviors. *Journal of Pediatrics, 143,* 104–110.

Knopik, V. S., Sparrow, E. P., Madden, P. A. F., Bucholz, K. K., Hudziak, J. J., Reich, W., et al. (2005). Contributions of parental alcoholism, prenatal substance exposure, and genetic transmission to child ADHD risk: A female twin study. *Psychological Medicine, 35,* 625–635.

Lee, K. T., Mattson, S. N., & Riley, E. P. (2004). Classifying children with heavy prenatal alcohol exposure using measures of attention. *Journal of the International Neuropsychological Society, 10,* 271–277.

Lemoine, P., Harousseau, H., Borteyru, J.-P., & Menuet, J.-C. (1968). Les enfants de parents alcooliques. Anomalies observees. A propos de 127 cas [children of alcoholic parents. Abnormalities observed in 127 cases]. *Ouest Medical, 21,* 476–482.

Leviton, A., Bellinger, D., Allred, E. N., Rabinowitz, M., Needleman, H., & Schoenbaum, S. (1993). Pre- and postnatal low-level lead exposure and children's dysfunction in school. *Environmental Research, 60,* 30–43.

Linares, T. J., Singer, L. T., Kirchner, H. L., Short, E. J., Min, M. O., Hussey, P., & Minnes, S. (2006). Mental health outcomes of cocaine-exposed children at 6 years of age. *Journal of Pediatric Psychology, 31,* 85–97.

Linnet, K. M., Obel, C., Bonde, E., Thomsen, P. H., Secher, N. J., Wisborg, K., & Henriksen, T. B. (2006). Cigarette smoking during pregnancy and hyperactive-distractible preschoolers: A follow-up study. *Acta Paediatrica, 95,* 694–700.

Linnet, K. M., Wisborg, K., Obel, C., Secher, N. J., Thomsen, P. H., Agerbo, E., & Henriksen, T. B. (2005). Smoking during pregnancy and the risk for hyperkinetic disorder in offspring. *Pediatrics, 116,* 462–467.

Lupton, C., Burd, L., & Harwood, R. (2004). Cost of fetal alcohol spectrum disorders. *American Journal of Medical Genetics Part C: Seminars in Medical Genetics, 127,* 42–50.

Lynch, M. E., Coles, C. D., Corley, T., & Falek, A. (2003). Examining delinquency in adolescents differentially prenatally exposed to alcohol: The role of proximal and distal risk factors. *Journal of Studies on Alcohol, 64,* 678–686.

Mattson, S. N., & Riley, E. P. (1998). A review of the neurobehavioral deficits in children with fetal alcohol syndrome or prenatal exposure to alcohol. *Alcoholism: Clinical and Experimental Research, 22,* 279–294.

Mattson, S. N., & Riley, E. P. (2000). Parent ratings of behavior in children with heavy prenatal alcohol exposure and IQ-matched controls. *Alcoholism: Clinical and Experimental Research, 24,* 226–231.

Mattson, S. N., Riley, E. P., Gramling, L. J., Delis, D. C., & Jones, K. L. (1997). Heavy prenatal alcohol exposure with or without physical features of fetal alcohol syndrome leads to IQ deficits. *Journal of Pediatrics, 131,* 718–721.

Mattson, S. N., Riley, E. P., Gramling, L. J., Delis, D. C., & Jones, K. L. (1998). Neuropsychological comparison of alcohol-exposed children with or without physical features of fetal alcohol syndrome. *Neuropsychology, 12,* 146–153.

Maughan, B., Taylor, A., Caspi, A., & Moffitt, T. E. (2004). Prenatal smoking and early childhood conduct problems: Testing genetic and environmental explanations of the association. *Archives of General Psychiatry, 61,* 836–843.

Maughan, B., Taylor, C., Taylor, A., Butler, N., & Bynner, J. (2001). Pregnancy smoking and childhood conduct problems: A causal association? *Journal of Child Psychology and Psychiatry, 42,* 1021–1028.

Mayes, L. C. (2002). A behavioral teratogenic model of the impact of prenatal cocaine exposure on arousal regulatory systems. *Neurotoxicology and Teratology, 24,* 385–395.

Mendola, P., Selevan, S. G., Gutter, S., & Rice, D. (2002). Environmental factors associated with a spectrum of neurodevelopmental deficits. *Mental Retardation and Developmental Disabilities Research Reviews, 8,* 188–197.

Messinger, D. S., Bauer, C. R., Das, A., Seifer, R., Lester, B. M., Lagasse, L. L., et al. (2004). The maternal lifestyle study: Cognitive, motor, and behavioral outcomes of cocaine-exposed and opiate-exposed infants through three years of age. *Pediatrics, 113,* 1677–1685.

Mick, E., Biederman, J., Faraone, S. V., Sayer, J., & Kleinman, S. (2002). Case-control study of attention-deficit hyperactivity disorder and maternal smoking, alcohol use, and drug use during pregnancy. *Journal of the American Academy of Child and Adolescent Psychiatry, 41,* 378–385.

Middaugh, L. D. (1989). Prenatal amphetamine effects on behavior: Possible mediation by brain monoamines. *Annals of the New York Academy of Sciences, 562,* 308–318.

Milberger, S., Biederman, J., Faraone, S. V., Chen, L., & Jones, J. (1996). Is maternal smoking during pregnancy a risk factor for attention deficit hyperactivity disorder in children? *The American Journal of Psychiatry, 153,* 1138–1142.

Myers, G. J., & Davidson, P. W. (1998). Prenatal methylmercury exposure and children: Neurologic, developmental, and behavioral research. *Environmental Health Perspectives, 106* (Suppl 3), 841–847.

Myers, G. J., Davidson, P. W., Cox, C., Shamlaye, C. F., Palumbo, D., Cernichiari, E., et al. (2003). Prenatal methylmercury exposure from ocean fish consumption in the Seychelles child development study. *Lancet, 361,* 1686–1692.

Naeye, R. L., & Peters, E. C. (1984). Mental development of children whose mothers smoked during pregnancy. *Obstetrics and Gynecology, 64,* 601–607.

National Institute on Drug Abuse. (1996). *National pregnancy & health survey: Drug use among women delivering livebirths, 1992* (Vol. Publication No. 96-3819). Rockville, MD: National Institutes of Health.

Needleman, H. L., McFarland, C., Ness, R. B., Fienberg, S. E., & Tobin, M. J. (2002). Bone lead levels in adjudicated delinquents. A case control study. *Neurotoxicology and Teratology, 24,* 711–717.

Noland, J. S., Singer, L. T., Short, E. J., Minnes, S., Arendt, R. E., Kirchner, H. L., & Bearer, C. (2005). Prenatal drug exposure and selective attention in preschoolers. *Neurotoxicology and Teratology, 27,* 429–438.

Nordstrom Bailey, B., Sood, B. G., Sokol, R. J., Ager, J., Janisse, J., Hannigan, J. H., et al. (2005). Gender and alcohol moderate prenatal cocaine effects on teacher-report of child behavior. *Neurotoxicology and Teratology, 27,* 181–189.

O'Connor, M. J. (2001). Prenatal alcohol exposure and infant negative affect as precursors of depressive features in children. *Infant Mental Health Journal, 22,* 291–299.

O'Connor, M. J., & Kasari, C. (2000). Prenatal alcohol exposure and depressive features in children. *Alcoholism: Clinical and Experimental Research, 24,* 1084–1092.

O'Connor, M. J., & Paley, B. (2006). The relationship of prenatal alcohol exposure and the postnatal environment to child depressive symptoms. *Journal of Pediatric Psychology, 31,* 50–64.

O'Connor, M. J., Shah, B., Whaley, S., Cronin, P., Gunderson, B., & Graham, J. (2002). Psychiatric illness in a clinical sample of children with prenatal alcohol exposure. *The American Journal of Drug and Alcohol Abuse, 28,* 743–754.

O'Leary, C. C., Frank, D. A., Grant-Knight, W., Beeghly, M., Augustyn, M., Rose-Jacobs, R., et al. (2006). Suicidal ideation among urban nine and ten year olds. *Journal of Developmental and Behavioral Pediatrics, 27,* 33–39.

Orlebeke, J. F., Knol, D. L., & Verhulst, F. C. (1997). Increase in child behavior problems resulting from maternal smoking during pregnancy. *Archives of Environmental Health, 52,* 317–321.

Phelps, L., Wallace, N. V., & Bontrager, A. (1997). Risk factors in early child development: Is prenatal cocaine/poly-drug exposure a key variable? *Psychology in the Schools, 34,* 245–252.

Piquero, A. R., Gibson, C. L., Tibbetts, S. G., Turner, M. G., & Katz, S. H. (2002). Maternal cigarette smoking during pregnancy and life-course-persistent offending. *International Journal of Offender Therapy and Comparative Criminology, 46,* 231–248.

Pulsifer, M. B. (1996). The neuropsychology of mental retardation. *Journal of the International Neuropsychological Society, 2,* 159–176.

Rantakallio, P., Läärä, E., Isohanni, M., & Moilanen, I. (1992). Maternal smoking during pregnancy and delinquency of the offspring: An association without causation? *International Journal of Epidemiology, 21,* 1106–1113.

Räsänen, P., Hakko, H., Isohanni, M., Hodgins, S., Järvelin, M.-R., & Tiihonen, J. (1999). Maternal smoking during pregnancy and risk of criminal behavior among adult male offspring in the northern Finland 1966 birth cohort. *American Journal of Psychiatry, 156,* 857–862.

Richardson, G. A. (1998). Prenatal cocaine exposure. A longitudinal study of development. *Annals of the New York Academy of Sciences, 846,* 144–152.

Richardson, G. A., Conroy, M. L., & Day, N. L. (1996). Prenatal cocaine exposure: Effects on the development of school-age children. *Neurotoxicology and Teratology, 18,* 627–634.

Riley, E. P., Guerri, C., Calhoun, F., Charness, M. E., Foroud, T. M., Li, T.-K., et al. (2003). Prenatal alcohol exposure: Advancing knowledge through international collaborations. *Alcoholism: Clinical and Experimental Research, 27,* 118–135.

Rodriguez, A., & Bohlin, G. (2005). Are maternal smoking and stress during pregnancy related to ADHD symptoms in children? *Journal of Child Psychology and Psychiatry, 46,* 246–254.

Roebuck, T. M., Mattson, S. N., & Riley, E. P. (1999). Behavioral and psychosocial profiles of alcohol-exposed children. *Alcoholism: Clinical and Experimental Research, 23,* 1070–1076.

Romano, E., Tremblay, R. E., Farhat, A., & Côté, S. (2006). Development and prediction of hyperactive symptoms from 2 to 7 years in a population-based sample. *Pediatrics, 117,* 2101–2110.

Rutter, M. (2003). Poverty and child mental health: Natural experiments and social causation. *Journal of the American Medical Association, 290,* 2063–2064.

Rutter, M. (2005). Environmentally mediated risks for psychopathology: Research strategies and findings. *Journal of the American Academy of Child and Adolescent Psychiatry, 44,* 3–18.

Sampson, P. D., Streissguth, A. P., Bookstein, F. L., Little, R. E., Clarren, S. K., Dehaene, P., et al. (1997). Incidence of fetal alcohol syndrome and prevalence of alcohol-related neurodevelopmental disorder. *Teratology, 56,* 317–326.

Savage, J., Brodsky, N. L., Malmud, E., Giannetta, J. M., & Hurt, H. (2005). Attentional functioning and impulse control in cocaine-exposed and control children at age ten years. *Journal of Developmental and Behavioral Pediatrics, 26,* 42–47.

Schonfeld, A. M., Mattson, S. N., & Riley, E. P. (2005). Moral maturity and delinquency after prenatal alcohol exposure. *Journal of Studies on Alcohol, 66,* 545–555.

Silberg, J. L., Parr, T., Neale, M. C., Rutter, M., Angold, A., & Eaves, L. J. (2003).

Maternal smoking during pregnancy and risk to boys' conduct disturbance: An examination of the causal hypothesis. *Biological Psychiatry, 53,* 130–135.

Sood, B. G., Nordstrom Bailey, B., Covington, C., Sokol, R. J., Ager, J., Janisse, J., et al. (2005). Gender and alcohol moderate caregiver reported child behavior after prenatal cocaine. *Neurotoxicology and Teratology, 27,* 191–201.

Spurgeon, A. (2006). Prenatal methylmercury exposure and developmental outcomes: Review of the evidence and discussion of future directions. *Environmental Health Perspectives, 114,* 307–312.

Steinhausen, H.-C., Nestler, V., & Spohr, H.-L. (1982). Development and psychopathology of children with the fetal alcohol syndrome. *Journal of Developmental and Behavioral Pediatrics, 3,* 49–54.

Steinhausen, H.-C., & Spohr, H.-L. (1998). Long-term outcome of children with fetal alcohol syndrome: Psychopathology, behavior and intelligence. *Alcoholism: Clinical and Experimental Research, 22,* 334–338.

Steinhausen, H.-C., Willms, J., & Spohr, H.-L. (1993). Long-term psychopathological and cognitive outcome of children with fetal alcohol syndrome. *Journal of the American Academy of Child and Adolescent Psychiatry, 32,* 990–994.

Steinhausen, H.-C., Willms, J., & Spohr, H.-L. (1994). Correlates of psychopathology and intelligence in children with fetal alcohol syndrome. *Journal of Child Psychology and Psychiatry and Allied Disciplines, 35,* 323–331.

Streissguth, A. P., Aase, J. M., Clarren, S. K., Randels, S. P., LaDue, R. A., & Smith, D. F. (1991). Fetal alcohol syndrome in adolescents and adults. *Journal of the American Medical Association, 265,* 1961–1967.

Streissguth, A. P., Barr, H. M., Kogan, J., & Bookstein, F. L. (1996). *Final report: Understanding the occurrence of secondary disabilities in clients with fetal alcohol syndrome (FAS) and fetal alcohol effects (FAE).* Seattle, WA: University of Washington Publication Services.

Streissguth, A. P., Bookstein, F. L., Barr, H. M., Sampson, P. D., O'Malley, K., & Young, J. K. (2004). Risk factors for adverse life outcomes in fetal alcohol syndrome and fetal alcohol effects. *Journal of Developmental and Behavioral Pediatrics, 25,* 228–238.

Streissguth, A. P., Bookstein, F. L., Sampson, P. D., & Barr, H. M. (1995). Attention: Prenatal alcohol and continuities of vigilance and attentional problems from 4 through 14 years. *Development and Psychopathology, 7,* 419–446.

Thapar, A., Fowler, T., Rice, F., Scourfield, J., van den Bree, M., Thomas, H., et al. (2003). Maternal smoking during pregnancy and attention deficit hyperactivity disorder symptoms in offspring. *American Journal of Psychiatry, 160,* 1985–1989.

Thomas, S. E., Kelly, S. J., Mattson, S. N., & Riley, E. P. (1998). Comparison of social abilities of children with fetal alcohol syndrome to those of children with similar IQ scores and normal controls. *Alcoholism: Clinical and Experimental Research, 22,* 528–533.

Viner, R. M., & Taylor, B. (2005). Adult health and social outcomes of children who have been in public care: Population-based study. *Pediatrics, 115,* 894–899.

Vorhees, C. V. (1986). Principles of behavioral teratology. In E. P. Riley & C. V. Vorhees (Eds.), *Handbook of behavioral teratology* (pp. 23–48). New York: Plenum Press.

Wakschlag, L. S., Lahey, B. B., Loeber, R., Green, S. M., Gordon, R. A., & Leventhal, B. L. (1997). Maternal smoking during pregnancy and the risk of conduct disorder in boys. *Archives of General Psychiatry, 54,* 670–676.

Wakschlag, L. S., Pickett, K. E., Cook, E., Jr., Benowitz, N. L., & Leventhal, B. L. (2002). Maternal smoking during pregnancy and severe antisocial behavior in offspring: A review. *American Journal of Public Health, 92,* 966–974.

Wakschlag, L. S., Pickett, K. E., Kasza, K. E., & Loeber, R. (2006). Is prenatal smoking associated with a developmental pattern of conduct problems in young boys? *Journal of the American Academy of Child and Adolescent Psychiatry, 45,* 461–467.

Warner, T. D., Behnke, M., Hou, W., Garvan, C. W., Wobie, K., & Eyler, F. D. (2006). Predicting caregiver-reported behavior problems in cocaine-exposed children at 3 years. *Journal of Developmental and Behavioral Pediatrics, 27,* 83–92.

Wasserman, G. A., Liu, X., Pine, D. S., & Graziano, J. H. (2001). Contribution of maternal smoking during pregnancy and lead exposure to early child behavior problems. *Neurotoxicology and Teratology, 23,* 13–21.

Wasserman, G. A., Staghezza-Jaramillo, B., Shrout, P., Popovac, D., & Graziano, J. (1998). The effect of lead exposure on behavior problems in preschool children. *American Journal of Public Health, 88,* 481–486.

Weissman, M. M., Warner, V., Wickramaratne, P. J., & Kandel, D. B. (1999). Maternal smoking during pregnancy and psychopathology in offspring followed to adulthood. *Journal of the American Academy of Child and Adolescent Psychiatry, 38,* 892–899.

Whaley, S. E., O'Connor, M. J., & Gunderson, B. (2001). Comparison of the adaptive functioning of children prenatally exposed to alcohol to a nonexposed clinical sample. *Alcoholism: Clinical and Experimental Research, 25,* 1018–1024.

Williams, G. M., O'Callaghan, M., Najman, J. M., Bor, W., Andersen, M. J., Richards, D., & U. C. (1998). Maternal cigarette smoking and child psychiatric morbidity: A longitudinal study. *Pediatrics, 102,* e11.

CHAPTER 8

Brain Injury as a Risk Factor for Psychopathology

LISA M. GATZKE-KOPP AND KATHERINE E. SHANNON

HISTORICAL CONTEXT

The 1848 accident of railroad worker Phineas Gage has become legendary in psychology and neuroscience, appearing commonly in introductory textbooks. Gage attained fame after surviving an extraordinary accident involving an explosion that turned a three-foot-long iron rod into a projectile that passed completely through the frontal portion of his skull and brain. Merely surviving such an accident is uncommon, but more remarkable was his apparent recovery of memory, communication, and most other basic mental functions. However, reports from those close to Gage indicate that the injury resulted in a permanent change in his personality, and led to self-destructive and socially inappropriate behaviors resulting from poor judgment (see Macmillan, 2002). Continued fascination with this story over the past 150 years follows from its demonstration that the brain is responsible for more than our ability to walk in a coordinated fashion or to learn to speak a foreign language. Although the brain does serve these functions, it is also responsible for the most fundamental aspects of our individuality. This story illustrates both the importance of brain function for cardinal components of psychological

Acknowledgments: Work on this chapter was supported by Grant R01 MH63699, awarded to Theodore P. Beauchaine by the National Institute of Mental Health.

health, and that this organ—and all of its associated functions—is vulnerable to injury.

Gage's story is an incontrovertible and obvious example of brain injury, but recently scientists' understanding of the conditions and mechanisms of brain injury has expanded with respect to traumatic force occurring without skull penetration, referred to as *closed head injury*. The prevalence of closed head injuries and the extent of ensuing sequelae continue to be a prominent focus of medical research. This is especially true in the area of minor head injuries, commonly known as *concussions*. A concussion is usually defined as neurological impairment occurring in response to traumatic force that results in biomechanical strain on central nervous system (CNS) tissue. Impairment can consist of any of a range of symptoms across one or more domains including the following: (a) cognitive: confusion, poor concentration, inability to follow directions or answer questions, amnesia, or loss of consciousness; (b) medical: headaches, nausea, or vomiting; (c) sensory: dizziness, poor coordination or loss of balance, alterations in vision or hearing (seeing stars or hearing ringing); and (d) psychological: irritability, changes in personality, or emotions inappropriate for their context (McCrory et al., 2005).

Concussions were long believed to be transient physical states with complete resolution of symptoms expected within 3 months. Because symptoms resolved, it was believed that no permanent changes in either behavior or physiology characterized concussion victims (Gaetz, Goodman, & Weinberg, 2000). Yet research in the past 15 years has uncovered significant and concerning effects of mild head injuries, particularly when such injuries are experienced repeatedly. Repetitive injuries are common among athletes at both the amateur and professional levels, from adolescence through adulthood, and consequently organized sports have become a focus of both research and policy developments with regard to brain injury. Evidence of enduring effects of repeated concussions became evident among boxers, with forcible impact to the head being a defining feature of the sport (Chappell et al., 2006). Other high-contact sports such as football, hockey, and even soccer, where head-to-head contact can occur as athletes compete to strike the ball, are associated with high concussion prevalences (Delaney, Puni, & Rouah, 2006).

Accordingly, researchers have worked to provide decision-making guidelines to physicians regarding returning an athelete to play after concussion. Following from extensive research, recommendations have gone beyond sideline assessments of concussive symptoms to include baseline administration of standardized neuropsychological tests prior to participation in the sport, giving physicians an individualized basis for comparison of function postinjury. Neuropsychological assessment improves sensitivity when used in conjunction with symptom reports and provides an objective measure of function that is not reliant on the honest reporting of the player who may be highly motivated or under extreme pressure to return to play quickly (Van Kampen et al., 2006).

Research has also established the importance of nontraumatic brain injuries. Much attention has been paid to the condition of low birth weight (LBW) in children as a marker of risk for developing psychopathology. LBW is defined as weight less than 2500g, although sometimes a distinction is made between low birth weight that often results from premature birth and low weight for gestational age, defined as a weight below the 10th percentile for a given gestational age, which is a more specific indication of intrauterine growth restriction (World Health Organization, 1992). These conditions are robustly associated with adverse psychological outcomes ranging from reductions in IQ and cognitive disabilities, to the development of emotional and behavioral disorders (Buka, Lipsitt, & Tsuang, 1992). The criteria for LBW are objective, and are easily and reliably measured. The convenience of this indicator has contributed to its popularity in research applications. However, the fact that LBW is an indicator of otherwise unspecified maldevelopment makes it difficult to identify specific sequelae. A wide range of factors such as exposure to chemical teratogens, exposure to maternal cortisol, restricted blood flow through the umbilical artery, micro- and macro-nutrient deficiency, and insufficient oxygen supply can all contribute to restrictions in uterine growth and premature birth, resulting in clinically low birth weight (Ashdown-Lambert, 2005; Jaddoe & Witteman, 2006; Luther et al., 2005). All of these factors may confer vulnerability that is distinct from other potential contributions to birth weight. For instance, exposure to maternal smoking is associated with LBW and may have different psychological sequelae than maternal undernutrition. Because a discussion of these individual contributions to birth weight is beyond the scope of this chapter, and because teratogenic exposure is discussed elsewhere in this volume (see Fryer, Crocker, & Mattson), the discussion in this chapter will be limited to distinct mechanisms associating low birth weight with neuronal damage following from restrictions of oxygen or blood supply to neurons (hypoxia and ischemia, respectively). These effects are known to result in extensive cell death (Arpino et al., 2005; Vannucci, 2000) and are likely to be a fairly common mechanism associated with many factors leading to low birth weight.

The developments in research over the past several decades have highlighted the fact that injury to the brain can occur at any time during development, ranging from relatively inconspicuous forms of injury that may even escape detection, to penetrating forces such as the example with Gage. This multifarious vulnerability of the CNS makes addressing the topic insurmountable in a single chapter. As such, we focus on the most common and basic injurious factors resulting in brain cell death: traumatic injury resulting from blunt force and severe cellular oxygen deprivation (hypoxia). In this chapter, we review basic brain injury mechanisms, discuss specific developmental aspects of brain injury, and consider how injury contributes to the development of psychopathology.

PREVALENCE

Each year an estimated 475,000 children between the ages of 0 and 14 years receive medical attention for a traumatic brain injury, of whom fewer than 1 percent die. An unknown number of additional individuals sustain injuries that are unreported and receive no medical attention (Langlois, Rutland-Brown, & Thomas, 2004). Such injuries result from falls, sport-related accidents, motor vehicle accidents, or abuse. Abuse represents a larger proportion of the injury etiologies among infants and toddlers, with approximately 25 percent of brain injury patients in this age range having been shaken or forcibly struck by a caretaker (Bruce, 1996; Duhaime et al., 1998). In this context, it is important to note that the brain can sustain injury without experiencing traumatic force. Factors resulting in even mild levels of oxygen desaturation—including medical conditions such as congenital heart disease, sleep-disordered breathing, and severe or poorly treated asthma, as well as accidents such as near-drownings or carbon monoxide poisoning—can result in cell death (Bass et al., 2004; Hori, 1985). The extent of hypoxic injury in response to such events is difficult to quantify and may go unrecognized in mild cases, making the prevalence of such injuries difficult to estimate.

Epidemiological data indicate that certain individuals are more susceptible to brain injuries, with rates of occurrence higher in males and among individuals of lower socioeconomic status (Bruns & Hauser, 2003). Researchers reviewing medical charts across more than 70 hospitals found that children with high levels of impulsivity, such as those with Attention-Deficit/Hyperactivity Disorder (ADHD), are more likely to sustain injuries to all areas of the body, with head injuries being no exception. Furthermore, these hyperactive/impulsive children were more likely to have sustained more severe injuries (DiScala et al., 1998). However, prospectively conducted studies have frequently failed to report this association (see Davidson, 1987), and others have suggested that the apparent link is due in large part to poor parental supervision commonly experienced by externalizing children (Schwebel, Hodgens, & Sterling, 2006). Given these conflicting findings, debate continues with regard to whether or not impulsivity is a risk factor for head injuries or whether head injuries and externalizing behaviors are multifinal consequences of other environmental risks.

MECHANISMS OF BRAIN INJURY

Trauma

Traumatic brain injury (TBI) is defined as a change in brain function that manifests as confusion, altered level of consciousness, coma, seizure, acute sensory or motor neurological deficit, neuropsychological deficit, or behavioral change, resulting from any blunt or penetrating force to the head (Bruns & Hauser, 2003). TBI occurs when the rapid deceleration of the brain against the bony inner surface of the skull leads to tissue compression, resulting in neuronal and vascular damage (Finnie & Blumbergs, 2002). The nature of the mechanical force applied to the head produces different types of tissue damage, most commonly classified as *focal* or *diffuse* (Gennarelli & Meaney, 1996). Focal tissue damage occurs most often in injuries resulting from a translational force applied along the linear axis of the brain (Yeates, 2000). Under conditions insufficient to penetrate the skull, the force results in a localized deformation of the bone and compression of the underlying tissue (Gennarelli & Meaney, 1996). When the brain compresses against the skull, small hemorrhages develop on the gyral surfaces of the brain, causing a contusion or focal tissue damage (Finnie & Blumbergs, 2002). Such injuries also result in contrecoup contusions, constituting compressive tissue damage at regions remote from the initial contact point. This occurs when the force applied to the head causes the brain to rebound, contacting the skull a second time at a point opposite the initial contact (Gennarelli & Meaney, 1996). These types of injuries can result in significant tissue damage, most commonly without a loss of consciousness (Gennarelli & Meaney, 1996). Given the degree of tissue damage that can occur without a consequent loss of consciousness, this neurological indicator (i.e., unconsciousness) is a poor surrogate for radiological assessment (Schutzman & Greenes, 2001).

In contrast to focal damage caused by translational injuries, diffuse damage results from rotational forces, producing angular movement around the brain's center of gravity. This occurs when the head strikes against a broad object, such as the interior of a car, diffusing the force across the surface of the skull (Gennarelli & Meaney, 1996). The rotational force produces a shearing strain on the brain, tearing axonal tissue. By destroying axons, afferent and efferent activity can be interrupted in any brain region. The destruction of axonal communications between regions can produce the same functional impairments as direct focal damage in the disrupted region. For instance, a disruption in the connection between the frontal cortex and subcortical structures can produce frontally mediated impairment without observable damage to the frontal lobe (Schnider & Gutbrod, 1999). In fact, axonal damage is frequently undetectable by standard neuroimaging protocols, requiring specialized imaging techniques such as diffusion tensor imaging (Ashwal, Holshouser, & Tong, 2006). Because of the disruption in connections between anatomical regions, these types of injuries often lead to widespread damage and can affect deeper anatomical structures than are vulnerable to focal contusions. It is diffuse axonal injuries that lead to concussive symptoms, and these injuries represent the most common form of head injury in clinical practice (Gennarelli & Meaney, 1996).

Regardless of the form of injury, TBI severity is most commonly classified into categories of mild, moderate, or severe based on acute neurological impairment using the Glasgow Coma Scale (GCS; Teasdale & Jennett, 1974). Past epidemiological estimates of hospitalized brain-injured patients indicate that as many as 80 percent suffered injuries classified as mild based on GCS ratings (Kraus & Nourjah, 1988). Mild injuries can include loss of consciousness, concussive symptoms, and the need for short-term hospitalization, but may also present with such mild sequelae as to be dismissed by the victim (Gabriel & Turner, 1996; Rimel et al., 1981). Although these injuries are generally considered to be uncomplicated, imparting no lasting damage, evidence suggests that damage may exist at a microscopic level not easily revealed through clinical neuroimaging techniques (Zhang et al., 2003). The acquisition of small lesions that result from mild injury may be especially dangerous if they accumulate over time through repeated injury exposure, such as may occur among athletes (Collins et al., 2003). Clinical observations indicate that repeated trauma is relatively common among individuals presenting with mild head injury (Rimel et al., 1981).

In addition to the primary effects of damage in response to the biomechanical strain placed on the tissue, secondary injuries frequently evolve from brain trauma. Most commonly edema, or swelling, occurs at the site of focal injuries, increasing intracranial pressure and restricting blood flow, which leads to metabolic failures that result in cell death (Bigler, 2001b). This type of cell death, described in further detail in the section addressing hypoxia, can lead to apoptosis, or the signaling of one cell to induce death in neighboring cells. Secondary brain injury in response to trauma develops over time, and can occur in those whose injuries are initially classified as mild and whose clinical evaluations in the immediate aftermath of the injury appear normal (Schutzman & Greenes, 2001). Because of the extent of secondary injuries, tissue damage is often more global than local. Studies of both children and adults indicate that reductions in total grey and white matter follow even mild injuries and appear to increase linearly with injury severity (Bigler, 2001a; Wilde et al., 2005). Because the brain can sustain microscopic damage that is not structurally visible, and because secondary injuries can exacerbate the extent of the primary injury over time, standard medical neuroimaging techniques can underestimate the extent of injury (Schnider & Gutbrod, 1999). Imaging techniques to assess both primary and secondary injuries are being developed at a rapid pace, and research suggests that these techniques offer unique advantages in prognosis. The use of magnetic resonance spectroscopy allows for the assessment of metabolic function of neurochemical activity indicative of secondary injuries. Furthermore, in comparison with traditional techniques, susceptibility weighted and diffusion weighted imaging offer distinct advantages in the assessment of secondary injuries resulting from hemorrhagic injuries. As research addresses the application of these techniques in pediatric populations, their utilization in clinical practice is likely to improve the assessment of both diagnosis and prognosis (Ashwal et al., 2006).

Hypoxia

Hypoxia refers to a reduction in the supply of oxygen necessary for normal cellular function and can occur through both respiratory and circulatory failures (Nyakas, Buwalda, & Luiten, 1996). Normal blood oxygen saturation levels in children are observed at 92 to 100 percent, with risk for hypoxia existing at lower levels (Uliel et al., 2004). Hypoxia leads to brain damage through both acute and protracted pathways. The acute reduction in oxygen available to the cell inhibits metabolic processes and results in a release of neurotransmitters having an excitotoxic effect, resulting in toxic accumulation of calcium in the cell (Golan & Huleihel, 2006). Following this necrotic tissue damage, the cytotoxic process induces a stress response that propagates a chemical signal initiating the self-destructive process known as *apoptosis* (programmed cell death in neighboring cells). The extended activation of programmed cell death can occur up to several weeks beyond the original hypoxic insult. It is the accumulation of cell loss over these several weeks that ultimately leads to behavioral deficits (Golan & Huleihel, 2006). Although research has focused on medical interventions that may be capable of arresting this process and alleviating the damage induced by acute hypoxic events, such procedures are not medically available at present.

Hypoxia occurring in conjunction with a variety of medical conditions can cause adverse neurological effects (Bass et al., 2004). However, the majority of hypoxic events occur pre- and perinatally. Consequently, these models have dominated the study of hypoxia, with far less attention paid to the effects of acute hypoxic events later in life. Hypoxia is a common complication of compromised pregnancies and can result from a variety of etiologies including premature birth and placental insufficiency (Vannucci, 2000). Hypoxia is also a complication of restricted blood flow to the umbilical artery, which occurs during episodes of maternal alcohol consumption (Mukherjee & Hodgen, 1982) and maternal smoking (Socol et al., 1982; see also Fryer, Crocker, & Mattson, this volume). In cases of prenatal hypoxic exposure, infants are often characterized by low birth weight for their gestational age, an overt indication of maldevelopment (McClure et al., 2005). In addition to prenatal damage, hypoxia can also occur during the birthing process. Prolonged labor or complications during delivery restrict oxygen flow to the fetus. In addition, birth complications may be accompanied by respiratory difficulties requiring resuscitation upon delivery. Hypoxic damage ranks among the top 10 causes of death in neonates (Martin et al., 2005) and is a common complication in babies born preterm (prior to week 37 of gestation). The incidence of preterm birth is an increasingly frequent occurrence, accounting for 12.3 percent of U.S. births in 2003 (Martin et al., 2005). Although survival of infants born preterm has increased dramatically in recent years, no reduction in the neurological sequelae of hypoxia among such infants has been observed (Inder & Volpe, 2000). Thus, the increasing survival of preterm infants represents an increase in the number of children likely to suffer functional deficits affecting neuropsychological and neurobehavioral health.

The regions of tissue damage and resultant behavioral implications in response to hypoxia are dependent on a wide range of factors, complicating clinical efforts to generate a prognosis (Golan & Huleihel, 2006). Factors such as developmental maturation of the neural tissue, duration and degree of hypoxic exposure, and the degree of neuroprotective factors intrinsic to an individual are difficult to identify and quantify in clinical practice. As expected, sequelae following hypoxia are variable and range from mild or subtle impairments in cognition and behavior, to deficits in motor coordination, and in extreme cases to the development of cerebral palsy. The additional presence of ischemia (reduced blood supply resulting in deficient nutritional supply to the cell) results in more severe atrophy of brain regions including the motor cortex, hippocampus, and striatum. Indeed, there is a greater likelihood of severe deficits in motor function in these areas than with hypoxia in the absence of ischemia (Decker & Rye, 2002). When extreme and overt compromise is evident—resulting in such conditions as motor disabilities, cerebral palsy, and even epilepsy—the extent of damage is revealed readily with neuroimaging techniques. Using magnetic resonance imaging, white matter damage is the most commonly identified pathology in infants suffering hypoxia prenatally, with additional reductions in overall cortical gray matter (Robinson, 2005).

However, more subtle variations in neurochemical function affecting cellular communication exist in response to hypoxia that are insufficient to produce gross structural damage. For instance, researchers have found decrements in dopamine receptors in the striatum following experimental induction of hypoxia/ischemia, despite the normal structural appearance of the region (Zouakia et al., 1997). Striatal cells are the most vulnerable to cell death resulting from mild hypoxia (Rothstein & Levison, 2005). Subtle neurochemical disruptions are thought to result in psychological and behavioral disturbances, such as ADHD, which are observed with higher frequency in cases of fetal hypoxia, even in the absence of marked neurological dysfunction (Nyakas et al., 1996). Such findings are consistent with theories identifying striatal mesolimbic dopamine deficiency as a primary etiological contribution to the development of ADHD (Gatzke-Kopp & Beauchaine, in press; Sagvolden et al., 2005; see also Beauchaine & Neuhaus, this volume).

DEVELOPMENTAL CONSIDERATIONS

Although brain injury has been studied extensively, both epidemiologically and through experimental animal models, researchers have begun to acknowledge that injuries sustained by children confer different vulnerabilities than similar injuries sustained by adults. Rodent models of dopaminergic lesions demonstrate that the same DA-depleting lesion that produces severe motor impairment in mature rats can result in motor hyperactivity when induced in juvenile rats (Davids et al., 2003). In human case studies, children experiencing frontal lobe damage experience greater loss of psychosocial function than adults who sustained similar injuries (Anderson et al., 1999).

Developmental factors affect the nature and degree of injury sustained, and the degree of functional recovery likely to follow. Children's relatively large heads and weaker neck muscles increase their vulnerability to rotational movements implicated in diffuse axonal injuries. Furthermore, the greater flexibility of their skulls allows force to be distributed over greater surface area, favoring diffuse over focal injuries (Anderson et al., 2005).

The developmental state of the tissue is also implicated in the extent of damage these mechanical forces have on the brain. Unlike any other organ in the human body, brain development is substantially incomplete at birth with developmental changes continuing well into the postnatal period through adolescence and early adulthood (Johnson, 1999; Nowakowski & Hayes, 2002; Sowell et al., 1999). Developmental changes taking place in the brain differ between tissues types. White matter develops its characteristic white appearance only after birth as the axons connecting cells across anatomical regions become encased in myelin to increase speed and efficiency of signal conduction (Andersen, 2003). Although this process is greatest in the first 2 years of life, myelination continues to take place throughout childhood and adolescence, with an approximately linear increase in white matter observed throughout the brain over time (Giedd et al., 1999). The overall lower level of axonal myelination in children increases the susceptibility of these fibers to shearing strain and makes children more vulnerable to diffuse injuries (Lea & Faden, 2001).

Gray matter development consists of processes that refine synaptic relationships between neurons. Immature brains contain an excess of neurons. As some of these neurons are used, they form connections with other neurons, developing efficient circuits. Neurons that are not used are eliminated. Despite the elimination taking place, the brain continues to grow through early childhood. This growth is due in part to arborization, or branching of neurons to increase the number of neighboring cells with which they communicate directly. In longitudinal analyses of normal participants, repeated neuroimaging protocols throughout childhood and adolescence show that gray matter develops at different rates across each of the four lobes (Giedd, 2004), with regions of the frontal lobe continuing to develop well into adulthood (Diamond, 2002). Gray matter tissue in children is more susceptible to secondary injuries in response to trauma, such as edema (Aldrich et al., 1992). This susceptibiliy is likely to be related to the immaturity of neurochemical receptors in young brains, which increases vulnerability to excitotoxic damage associated with hypoxia and contributes to extensive apoptotic cell death (Lea & Faden, 2001).

Despite these anatomical characteristics that confer increased vulnerability following brain trauma, the relative immaturity of the brain at birth is also an asset in human development, as it confers plasticity and allows for a phenomenon known as *experience-dependent development*. Research indicates that the structure of neural tissue is not determined entirely by genetic or chemical signals taking place during development, and that specialization can emerge out of necessity (Johnson, 1999). During early stages of brain development, the brain is widely activated in response to sensory stimulation. During this time, brain cells are plastic, or flexible; they establish connections with other cells and develop specialized function only in response to environmental stimuli. When anatomy is compromised through injury prior to the specialization of cortical tissue, alternate brain regions may assume the responsibilities of the lost tissue. For instance, portions of the auditory cortex can be induced to respond to visual stimuli when the visual cortex is damaged prior to the specialization of cortical tissue (Johnson, 1999). Efficient and restricted localization of neural function, characteristic of adult brains, develops over time in accordance with synaptic input, within the confines of functional neuroanatomy. However, once specialization takes place, flexibility is diminished and accommodation is less likely to take place in response to tissue loss (Knudsen, 2004).

The idea that functional recovery occurs more readily in the younger brain is known as the *Kennard principle,* named after Margaret Kennard, whose research first identified the compensatory ability of infantile brains as compared to adult brains (Kolb & Gibb, 2001). Given that developmental processes such as pruning continue in the human brain through about 16 years of age (Johnston, 2004), it would appear that opportunities for plasticity would be high through nearly all of childhood. In fact, children do show resilient recovery of function, exemplified by the recovery of language by the right hemisphere following resection of the left hemisphere (Boatman et al., 1999). However, scientists soon observed that there were limits to plasticity and that functional recovery was far from absolute. Early damage often carries with it a substantial cost. Even when recovery occurs for some basic functions, it can be at the expense of other abilities (Luciana, 2003). In rodents, early brain tissue damage results in neural organizational compensations that allow for recovery of motor control not seen in animals damaged in adulthood, but this comes at the expense of diminished cognitive functioning (Kolb & Gibb, 2001). Furthermore, evidence of brain dysfunction may develop over time in cases where function appears normal in the immediate aftermath of an injury (McGrath et al., 2000).

With respect to pediatric injuries, functional recovery may be hindered by the very plasticity that it relies upon. Plasticity results from the dynamics of the affected system's utilization of stimulus input to establish functional and organizational activity. However, over the course of development, the experiences required for input at later developmental stages build upon successful acquisition of skills at earlier developmental stages (Nowakowski & Hayes, 2002). Because human development builds upon previous experience, damage to the brain that results in an inability to acquire basic psychological functions will affect all higher-order processing dependent on that initial component (Bachevalier & Loveland, 2003; Black et al., 1998). This argument negates the view that increased plasticity in childhood is predictive of full recovery, instead supporting the position that extensive damage in childhood effectively prevents the acquisition of new skills necessary to traverse the developmental landscape. Research demonstrates that the younger the injury is sustained, the less severe the injury need be to result in life-long impact on cognitive functioning (Anderson et al., 2005). An analogy to consider is a developmental ladder. If damage occurs that eliminates rungs from the ladder, the person is unlikely to climb beyond the damaged portion. The lower on the ladder the damage occurs, the lower overall height can be achieved.

Resolution to the contradictory predictions offered by theories of increased plasticity versus successive acclimation of skills may be informed by considering brain development in a regional rather than a global manner. For instance, research indicates that cognitive skills are most vulnerable when undergoing rapid development (Ewing-Cobbs et al., 2004). This effect may be observed because damage occurring prior to this developmental flourishing allows time for alternative brain regions to be recruited, and damage occurring later allows for the preservation of successive skills that were acquired prior to the injury. Given this hypothesis, the developmental time point of maximal vulnerability is likely to shift across different brain regions and associated cognitive developments in accordance with developmental patterns of brain maturation.

BRAIN INJURY AND THE FRONTAL LOBE

Regionally, the temporal and frontal lobes are especially vulnerable to damage, and are compromised most frequently among children with focal lesions (Levin et al., 1989; Mendelsohn et al., 1992; Wilde et al., 2005). The susceptibility of these regions is a consequence of their proximal location to the jagged inner surface of the skull, which produces the greatest vulnerability along the ventral surface (Schnider & Gutbrod, 1999). In addition, these regions readily sustain contrecoup contusions regardless of the initial site of impact (Gennarelli & Meaney, 1996). Although many brain regions are developmentally stable at adult levels by adolescence, maturational changes in the frontal region continue through adolescence and into early adulthood, reflecting emotional and cognitive development also documented across this age range (Sowell et al., 1999). This protracted maturation indicates that the prefrontal region may be developmentally vulnerable longer than other anatomical sites. The functions attributed to the frontal lobe are critical to mental health, and their compromise is consequently of substantial clinical importance. This anatomical region is frequently divided into dorsal and orbital cortical subregions, which have unique psychological functions (Duncan & Owen, 2000).

DORSOLATERAL PREFRONTAL CORTEX

The dorsolateral and middorsal corticies respond to a wide array of cognitive demands requiring problem solving and executive functioning (Duncan & Owen, 2000). The dorsolateral prefrontal cortex is integral to this system and operates through a network of interconnected structures including the dorsal caudate, global pallidus, dorsomedial thalamic nucleus, and cerebellum (Heyder, Suchan, & Daum, 2004). As such, the integrity of this network is necessary for working memory, decision making, problem solving, cognitive flexibility, behavioral inhibition, and abstract reasoning—functions that are necessary to develop and attain long-term goals (Anderson & Catroppa, 2005; Levin & Hanten, 2005). Such skills represent a critical component of development and are crucial in allowing children to adapt to changing developmental demands. These skills begin to emerge in preschool and undergo rapid development during this period (Diamond, 2002). Because these cortical regions are not well developed in young children, however, damage is less likely to reveal immediate behavioral deficits, whereas such damage would be readily detected among adults. In other words, it may appear in the immediate aftermath of injury that behavioral deficits are minimal in children, because the functions associated with this region have not yet fully developed and therefore cannot be lost. However, the interrupted developmental progression in self-control is likely to reveal itself over time, as these children fail to acquire skills that are developing in their peers (Eslinger, Biddle, & Grattan, 1997).

ORBITOFRONTAL CORTEX

In contrast to executive function deficits, damage in the orbitofrontal region is associated with social/emotional functioning important in interpersonal relationships, including the ability to read social and emotional cues from others and to use this information in a self-regulatory manner (Bachevalier & Loveland, 2003). Damage in this region is also associated with an inability to develop and/or use internal cues of potential punishment to guide behavior (Damasio, Tranel, & Damasio, 1990). Interestingly, behavioral and personality deficits associated with damage in this region frequently exist in the absence of neuropsychological deficits (Schnider & Gutbrod, 1999). Hemispheric localization of orbitofrontal lesions is influential in the clinical presentation of symptoms. Lesions localized to the left hemisphere are associated with depressive symptoms, apathy, emotional blunting, and an inability to plan for the future, whereas right-hemisphere lesions are associated with hyperactivity, disinhibition, socially inappropriate behavior, irritability, and a pathological lack of empathy (Schnider & Gutbrod, 1999). When damage extends across both hemispheres, characteristics of both syndromes coexist (Schnider & Gutbrod, 1999).

As would be expected from the previous discussion, damage in the orbitofrontal region acquired by children results in more extensive deficits in social behavior than lesions acquired in adulthood (Anderson et al., 1999; Bachevalier & Loveland, 2003). Anderson and colleagues (1999) describe two striking case studies of individuals who sustained significant orbitofrontal damage before age 16 months. In both cases, recovery and function appeared very positive in the immediate aftermath of the lesion, and cognitive and motoric development proceeded normally. However, many years later these individuals were brought to medical attention because of their significant psychopathological behaviors. These individuals were insensitive to punishment, unresponsive to future consequences, and, unlike adults with similar damage, they showed extensive impairment in moral and social reasoning. The increased deficits in comparison to adult-onset lesions indicate impairment in the acquisition of normal social behavior leading to more global dysfunction.

THE ROLE OF GENES IN BRAIN INJURY

In addition to factors including developmental state and injury severity, marked individual differences in functional and structural deficits endured in response to brain injury may be controlled by genetic factors (Blackman, Worley, & Strittmatter, 2005). Individual differences in genotype appear to have a moderating effect on the functional consequences of brain injury. One such gene identified is the Apolipoprotein E (ApoE) gene, which has at least three well-characterized allelic variants. The ε4 allele of the ApoE gene has garnered much attention in conferring risk for the development of Alzheimer's disease. Extensive research on the function of the ApoE proteins indicates a role in neurologic repair, with variability between alleles implicated in the degree of neural damage suffered from oxidative, circulatory, and traumatic type injuries over the lifespan (Blackman et al., 2005). Specifically, in contrast to the ε2 and possibly ε3 alleles, the ε4 allele appears less effective in conferring neuroprotection and leads to increased damage due to postinjury inflammation, edema, and excitotoxicity (Aono et al., 2002; Laskowitz et al., 1998; Laskowitz et al., 1997; Lee et al., 2004; Lynch et al., 2002). Thus, genes appear to be critical in the degree of pathological response to brain injury, establishing the potential for important gene–environment interactions applicable to psychological function.

Interestingly, research examining ApoE ε4 in children has been contradictory. The few studies available indicate a neuroprotective function of ε4 as opposed to ε2, the opposite finding from studies with adults (Blackman et al., 2005). This differential effect may relate, in part, to the fact that preliminary studies have focused on mental development under adverse conditions of malnourishment rather than traumatic injury, as researched in adults (Oria et al., 2005). Clearly, much more research is needed to determine if the ε4 allele has protective effects under certain environmental conditions and/or if these effects are dependent on the developmental state of the nervous system.

Research also indicates the potential for genotypes to interact with environmental trauma exposure in ways that produce specific psychiatric outcomes. A range of perinatal traumatic factors, many of which are thought to contribute to hypoxic damage in neonates, have been associated repeatedly with later development of schizophrenia (Rosso & Cannon, 2003). In a study of patients with schizophrenia, their nonaffected siblings, and controls, Cannon and colleagues (2002) found that a history of fetal hypoxia was associated with a distinct pattern of brain abnormalities visible on magnetic resonance images in patients with schizophrenia and in a high genetic risk sample, but not in the control sample. These researchers suggest that one component of the genetic risk for schizophrenia might be a heightened sensitivity to hypoxic events, leading to an initial diathesis for schizophrenia in individuals who experience hypoxia during neural development (Cannon et al., 2002). Reaction to hypoxia is regulated by enzymes categorized as hypoxia-inducible factors, which are destroyed in the presence of oxygen, but which in the absence of oxygen regulate gene transcription of a wide array of genes affecting stress responsivity, metabolism, signal transduction, protein synthesis, and cell-cycle regulation, including programmed cell death (Stenzel-Poore et al., 2003; Wenger, 2002). These gene products can have injurious or protective functions depending on the context and severity of the hypoxic insult.

Testing the theory that hypoxia-regulated genes contribute to the pathogenesis of schizophrenia, researchers identified all genetic variants that have been associated with the disorder in at least two published studies. Findings indicate that as many as 50 percent of reported schizophrenia-related genes are regulated by hypoxia/ischemia. Furthermore, animal models indicate that these genes are likely to be expressed during development and thus may contribute to the pathogenesis of schizophrenia (Schmidt-Kastner et al., 2006). In contrast, these authors found that only 21 percent of genes associated with autism, a disorder not commonly associated with hypoxia, were regulated by oxidative stress. The authors postulate that faulty genes responding to oxidative stress may confer risk by producing defective gene products normally serving neuroprotective functions. This finding integrates previously independent literatures regarding genetic and perinatal risk factors for schizophrenia.

It is of interest that the disorders most commonly associated with hypoxic injury are those for which disrupted dopamine signaling is considered to be of primary etiology (ADHD and schizophrenia). This finding is consistent with the wide range of effects of hypoxia on all classes of dopamine receptors (Chen et al., 1997). Although the theorized disruptions in dopamine differ considerably between ADHD and schizophrenia, the vulnerability of the dopaminergic system to hypoxic insult may result in behavioral disruption in individuals whose dopaminergic function is genetically compromised (McAllister et al., 2005).

CLINICAL CONSIDERATIONS

Brain injury can play a causal role in the pathogenesis of specific psychological disorders by compromising neural systems directly. Changes in behavior and personality are common in response to brain injury as a consequence of the high prevalence of orbitofrontal damage. However, deficits in personality and behavior often exist without concurrent evidence of impairment in other domains, making assessment of injury-related outcomes difficult to quantify (Schnider & Gutbrod, 1999). Low-grade hypoxia may also contribute directly to the development of psychopathology. In animal experiments, intermittent hypoxia results in attenuation of extracellular dopamine in the nigrostriatal region, which is implicated in behavioral hyperactivity and increased responding to novelty (Decker et al., 2005). This suggests a link between hypoxic damage and ADHD. This research is consistent with the frequent observation of ADHD in children exposed to hypoxic conditions (Nyakas et al., 1996). Additionally, neuronal sensitivity to hypoxia results in learning disabilities (Inder & Volpe, 2000; Nyakas et al., 1996). Interestingly, evidence suggests that male and female brains differ in the degree of vulnerability to ischemia / hypoxia-induced damage, with females showing less severe pathological outcomes (Du et al., 2004; Hurn, Vannucci, & Hagberg, 2004). This observation is consistent with the increased incidence of ADHD and possibly learning disorders in males, conditions associated with hypoxic exposure.

Although psychological symptoms may develop as a direct result of dysfunction in the damaged area, brain injury also contributes to psychopathology in an indirect manner through the exacerbation of preexisting pathology, a reaction of the child and / or his or her family to the child's loss of function when damage is extensive, or a reaction to the injurious situation such as the development of posttraumatic stress disorder (Middleton,

2001). Such responses are especially likely when considering that factors such as low socioeconomic status and poor family functioning increase the risk of sustaining a brain injury (Bruce, 1996), and that brain-injured patients show higher levels of premorbid psychological and behavioral disturbances (Cattelani et al., 1998). Premorbid functioning not only affects the probability of sustaining an injury, but it also contributes significantly to the development of adverse outcomes postinjury (Donders & Strom, 2000). Among adults, socioeconomic status is a better predictor of long-term psychiatric and social functioning than the severity of head injury (Hoofien et al., 2002). Among children, measures of family functioning prior to injury are more predictive of cognitive and behavioral functioning 1 year following the injury than is injury severity. High family functioning mitigates the effects of brain injury, whereas poor functioning exacerbates these effects (Yeates et al., 1997). These factors moderate the development of depression in postinjury children (Kirkwood et al., 2000). Brain injury establishes vulnerability, and when such vulnerability is met with additional environmental risks, the likelihood of developing psychopathology is greatly increased.

Identifying the impact of brain injury on psychopathological development is important because it has implications for treatment. For instance, research suggests that when ADHD emerges after traumatic brain injury it is less likely to respond to methylphenidate treatment than ADHD that follows a traditional developmental course (Jin & Schachar, 2004). When brain injury is identified, treatment should focus not only on the child's level of functioning but also on the quality of the familial environment. Because premorbid functioning is frequently compromised, dysfunctional family systems may already be in place, limiting the potential effectiveness of the family to cope with the injury and contribute to successful recovery. These factors are especially important to consider given that head injuries may result from abuse or neglect, implicating a deficient recovery environment. In addition, brain-injured patients may also suffer academic difficulties due to the increased rate of learning disorders in this group. This is especially true of males, who consistently show increased rates of disability, increased behavior problems, lower IQ scores, lower developmental achievement scores, and increased rates of learning disorders and utilization of special education services in comparison to females (Aylward, 2002).

Assessing the role that head injuries play in the development of psychopathology is extremely challenging because brain injury can be difficult to detect in cases where it exists primarily at a microscopic or neurochemical level (with normal structural appearance). Furthermore, a long interval between the acquisition of injury and the onset of psychopathology may obscure the causal relation between the injury and later behavior. As many as 75 percent of infants surviving acute perinatal asphyxia are classified as *nonimpaired* because they fail to show neurological indicators of encephalopathic damage in the weeks after injury. However, impairments in cognitive, memory, and socioemotional behavior often are not evident until later in life when the child fails to meet increasing developmental demands (de Haan et al., 2006). Even cases of mild insults may produce lasting alterations in development, which may take years to recognize (Gronwall, Wrightson, & McGinn, 1997). In addition, mild damage, such as the low-grade hypoxia associated with snoring, may result in reductions in attention and intelligence, despite the fact that children continue to score within the normal range and are thus overlooked medically (Blunden et al., 2000). Therefore, careful consideration of potential contributions of brain injury to presenting psychological symptoms should be undertaken so that appropriate comprehensive treatment plans can be developed.

FUTURE DIRECTIONS

Although children with acute brain injuries present and are treated in medical settings, the impact of their injuries may have life-long consequences, including psychopathology. Severe injury affects multiple domains of functioning and presents serious challenges to both the child and his or her caretakers. However, brain injuries can also be subtle, as in mild TBI or hypoxia. Such injuries may be difficult to detect despite the fact that they often potentiate psychopathology. In addition to the environmental and genetic factors that are becoming increasingly well characterized in the development of psychopathology, early brain injury should not be overlooked, particularly as an environmental potentiator of genetic susceptibility in at-risk individuals. Because injuries can be difficult to detect and sequelae may take years to manifest, the association with injury and psychopathological outcomes may be overlooked in clinical practice. However, brain injury as an etiological factor may be important in informing treatment strategies and, as such, should be assessed adequately.

Research aimed at addressing these challenges involves improving the ability to assess brain damage resulting from concussions. Assessment currently focuses on the reporting of symptoms, supported by neuropsychological profiles. However, neuropsychological testing has a multitude of shortcomings including practice effects, mediocre reliability and sensitivity, poor norms for many measures, and the finding that individuals can return to baseline performance while still showing active symptoms of concussion (Randolph, McCrea, & Barr, 2005). Furthermore, ongoing maturation of the brain and cognitive abilities may render baseline neuropsychological testing inadequate for application to children. The "return to baseline" goal may therefore be inappropriate for younger athletes (Buzzini & Guskiewicz, 2006). Given these inadequacies, an emphasis has been placed on identifying psychophysiological profiles that can identify damage more accurately. Neuroimaging techniques capable of assessing metabolic processes indicative of secondary injuries as well as techniques capable of imaging diffuse axonal injuries are being developed and have the promise to greatly improve assessment of the extent of damage. In addition, studies using event-related potential methodologies have identified psychophysiological deficits that correlate with symptom severity and show higher sensitivity than neuropsychological tests (Gaetz et al., 2000; Lavoie et al., 2004). While further research on the genetics of brain injury may also assist in identifying individuals at high risk, it more importantly may help in characterizing the biological processes involved in injury and developing appropriate pharmaceutical approaches to arresting these processes and reducing the severity of their impact.

REFERENCES

Aldrich, E. F., Eisenberg, H. M., Saydjari, C., Luerssen, T. G., Foulkes, M. A., Jane, J. A., et al. (1992). Diffuse brain swelling in severely head-injured children. A report from the NIH Traumatic Coma Data Bank. *Journal of Neurosurgery, 76*, 450–454.

Andersen, S. L. (2003). Trajectories of brain development: Point of vulnerability or window of opportunity? *Neuroscience and Biobehavioral Reviews, 27*, 318.

Anderson, S. W., Bechara, A., Damasio, H., Tranel, D., & Damasio, A. R. (1999). Impairment of social and moral behavior related to early damage in human prefrontal cortex. *Nature Neuroscience, 2*, 1032–1037.

Anderson, V., & Catroppa, C. (2005). Recovery of executive skills following paediatric traumatic brain injury (TBI): A 2 year follow-up. *Brain Injury, 19*, 459–470.

Anderson, V., Catroppa, C., Morse, S., Haritou, F., & Rosenfeld, J. (2005). Functional plasticity of vulnerability after early brain injury? *Pediatrics, 116*, 1374–1382.

Aono, M., Lee, Y., Grant, E. R., Zivin, R. A., Pearlstein, R. D., Warner, D. S., et al. (2002). Apo-lipoprotein E protects against NMDA excitotoxicity. *Neurobiology of Disease, 11*, 214–220.

Arpino, C., D'Argenzio, L., Ticconi, C., Di Paolo, A., Stellin, V., Lopez, L., et al. (2005). Brain damage in preterm infants: Etiological pathways. *Annali dell'Istituto superiore di sanita, 41*, 229–237.

Ashdown-Lambert, J. R. (2005). A review of low birth weight: Predictors, precursors, and morbidity outcomes. *Journal of the Royal Society of Health, 125*, 76–83.

Ashwal, S., Holshouser, B. A., & Tong, K. (2006). Use of advanced neuroimaging techniques in the evaluation of pediatric traumatic brain injury. *Developmental Neuroscience, 28,* 309–326.

Aylward, G. P. (2002). Cognitive and neuropsychological outcomes: More than IQ scores. *Mental Retardation and Developmental Disabilities Research Reviews, 8,* 234–240.

Bachevalier, J., & Loveland, K. A. (2003). Early orbitofrontal-limbic dysfunction and autism. In D. Cicchetti & W. Walker (Eds.), *Neurodevelopmental mechanisms in psychopathology* (pp. 215–236). New York: Cambridge University Press.

Bass, J. L., Corwin, M., Moore, C., Nishida, H., Parker, S., Schonwald, A., et al. (2004). The effect of chronic or intermittent hypoxia on cognition in childhood: A review of the evidence. *Pediatrics, 114,* 805–816.

Bigler, E. D. (2001b). Quantitative magnetic resonance imaging in traumatic brain injury. *The Journal of Head Trauma Rehabilitation, 16,* 117–134.

Bigler, E. D. (2001a). The lesion(s) in traumatic brain injury: Implications for clinical neuropsychology. *Archives of Clinical Neuropsychology, 16,* 95–131.

Black, J. E., Jones, T. A., Nelson, C. A., & Greenough, W. T. (1998). Neuronal plasticity and the developing brain. In N. Alessi, J. Coyle, S. Harrison, & S. Eth (Eds.), *The handbook of child and adolescent psychiatry, Volume 6* (pp. 31–53). New York: Wiley.

Blackman, J. A., Worley, G., & Strittmatter, W. J. (2005). Apolipoprotein E and brain injury: Implications for children. *Developmental Medicine & Child Neurology, 47,* 64–70.

Blunden, S., Lushington, K., Kennedy, D., Martin, J., & Dawson, D. (2000). Behavior and neurocognitive performance in children aged 5–10 years who snore compared to controls. *Journal of Clinical and Experimental Neuropsychology, 22,* 554–568.

Boatman, D., Freeman, J., Vining, E., Pulsifer, M., Miglioretti, D., Minahan, R., et al. (1999). Language recovery after left hemispherectomy in children with late-onset seizures. *Annals of Neurology, 46,* 579–586

Bruce, D. A. (1996). Pediatric head injury. In R. Wilkins & S. Rengachary (Eds.), *Neurosurgery* (2nd ed.; pp. 2709–2715). New York: McGraw-Hill.

Bruns, J., & Hauser, A. (2003). The epidemiology of traumatic brain injury: A review. *Epilepsia, 44* (Suppl. 10), 2–10.

Buka, S. L., Lipsitt, L. P., & Tsuang, M. T. (1992). Emotional and behavioral development of low-birthweight infants. In S. Friedman & M. Sigman (Eds.), *The psychological development of low birthweight children.* (pp. 187–214). New Jersey: Ablex Publishing.

Buzzini, S. R. R., & Guskiewicz, K. M. (2006). Sport-related concussion in the young athlete. *Current Opinion in Pediatrics, 18,* 376–382.

Cannon, T. D., van Erp, T. G. M., Rosso, I. M., Huttunen, M., Lonnqvist, J., Pirkola, T., et al. (2002). Fetal hypoxia and structural brain abnormalities in schizophrenic patients, their siblings, and controls. *Archives of General Psychiatry, 59,* 35–41.

Cattelani, R., Lombardi, F., Brianti, R., & Mazzucchi, A. (1998). Traumatic brain injury in childhood: Intellectual, behavioral, and social outcome into adulthood. *Brain Injury, 12,* 283–296.

Chappell, M. H., Ulug, A. M., Zhang, L., Heitger, M. H. Jordan, B. D., Zimmerman, R. D., et al. (2006). Distribution of microstructural damage in the brains of professional boxers: A diffusion MRI study. *Journal of Magnetic Resonance Imaging, 24,* 537–542.

Chen, Y., Hillesfors-Berglund, M., Herrera-Marschitz, M., Bjelke, B., Gross, J., Andersson, K., et al. (1997). Perinatal asphyxia induces long-term changes in dopamine D_1, D_2, and D_3 receptor binding in the rat brain. *Experimental Neurology, 146,* 74–80.

Collins, M. W., Lovell, M. R., Iverson, G. L., Cantu, R. C., Maroon, J. C., & Field, M. (2003). Cumulative effects of concussion in high school athletes. *Neurosurgery, 53,* 247–248.

Damasio, A. R., Tranel, D., & Damasio, H. (1990). Individuals with sociopathic behavior caused by frontal damage fail to respond autonomically to social stimuli. *Behavioral Brain Research, 41,* 81–94.

Davids, E., Zhang, K., Tarazi, F. I., & Baldessarini, R. J. (2003). Animal models of attention-deficit/hyperactivity disorder. *Brain Research Reviews, 42,* 1–21.

Davidson, L. L. (1987). Hyperactivity, antisocial behavior and childhood injury: a critical analysis of the literature. *Journal of Developmental and Behavioral Pediatrics, 8,* 335–340.

Decker, M. J., Jones, K. A., Solomon, I. G., Keating, G. L., & Rye, D. B. (2005). Reduced extracellular dopamine and increased responsiveness to novelty: Neurochemical and behavioral sequelae of intermittent hypoxia. *Sleep, 28,* 165–167.

Decker, M. J., & Rye, D. B. (2002). Neonatal intermittent hypoxia impairs dopamine signaling and executive functioning. *Sleep and Breathing, 6,* 205–210.

de Haan, M., Wyatt, J. S., Roth, S., Vargha-Khadem, F., Gadian, D., & Mishkin, M. (2006). Brain and cognitive-behavioral development after asphyxia at term birth. *Developmental Science, 9,* 350–358.

Delaney, J. S., Puni, V., & Rouah, F. (2006). Mechanisms of injury for concussions in university football, ice hockey, and soccer: A pilot study. *Clinical Journal of Sports Medicine, 16,* 162–165.

Diamond, A. (2002). Normal development of prefrontal cortex from birth to young adulthood: Cognitive functions, anatomy, and biochemistry. In D. Stuss, & R. Knight (Eds.), *Principles of frontal lobe function* (pp. 466–503). New York: Oxford University Press.

DiScala, C., Lescohier, I., Barthel, M., & Li, G. (1998). Injuries to children with attention deficit hyperactivity disorder. *Pediatrics, 102,* 1415–1421.

Donders, J., & Strom, D. (2000). Neurobehavioral recovery after pediatric head trauma: Injury, pre-injury, and post-injury issues. *The Journal of Head Trauma Rehabilitation, 15,* 792–803.

Du, L. N., Bayi, H., Lai, Y. C., Zhang, X. P., Kochanek, P. M., Watkins, S. C., et al. (2004). Innate gender-based proclivity in response to cytotoxicity and programmed cell death pathway. *Journal of Biological Chemistry, 279,* 38563–38570.

Duhaime, A-C., Christian, C. W., Rorke, L. B., & Zimmerman, R. A. (1998). Non-accidental head injury in infants—The "shaken-baby syndrome." *The New England Journal of Medicine, 338,* 1822–1829.

Duncan, J., & Owen, A. M. (2000). Common regions of the human frontal lobe recruited by diverse cognitive demands. *Trends in Neuroscience, 23,* 475–483.

Eslinger, P. J., Biddle, K. R., & Grattan, L. M. (1997). Cognitive and social development in children with prefrontal cortex lesions. In N. Krasnegor, G. Lyon, & P. Goldman-Rakic (Eds.), *Development of the prefrontal cortex: Evolution, neurobiology, and behavior.* (pp. 295–335). Baltimore: Paul H. Brooks Publishing Co.

Ewing-Cobbs, L., Prasad, M. R., Landry, S. H., Kramer, L., & DeLeon, R. (2004). Executive functions following traumatic brain injury in young children: A preliminary analysis. *Developmental Neuropsychology, 26,* 487–512.

Finnie, J. & Blumbergs, P. (2002). Traumatic brain injury. *Veterinary Pathology, 39,* 679–689.

Gabriel, E., & Turner, D. (1996). Minor head injury management and outcome. In R. Wilkin & S. Rengachary (Eds.) *Neurosurgery* (2nd ed.; pp. 2723–2726). New York: McGraw-Hill.

Gaetz, M., Goodman, D., & Weinberg, H. (2000). Electrophysiological evidence for the cumulative effects of concussion. *Brain Injury, 14,* 1077–1088.

Gatzke-Kopp, L. M., & Beauchaine, T. P. (in press). Central nervous system substrates of impulsivity: Implications for the development of attention-deficit/hyperactivity disorder and conduct disorder. In D. Coch, G. Dawson, & K. Fischer (Eds.), *Human behavior and the developing brain: Atypical development.* New York: Guilford.

Gennarelli, T. A., & Meaney, D. F. (1996). Mechanisms of primary head injury. In R. Wilkin & S. Rengachary (Eds.) *Neurosurgery* (2nd ed.; pp. 2611–2621). New York: McGraw-Hill.

Giedd, J. N. (2004). Structural magnetic resonance imaging of the adolescent brain. *Annals of the New York Academy of Sciences, 1021,* 77–85.

Giedd, J. N., Blumenthal, J., Jeffries, N. O., Castellanos, F. X., Liu, H., Zijdenbos, A., et al. (1999). Brain development during childhood and adolescence: A longitudinal MRI study. *Nature Neuroscience, 2,* 861–863.

Golan, H., & Huleihel, M. (2006). The effect of prenatal hypoxia on brain development: Short- and long-term consequences demonstrated in rodent models. *Developmental Science, 9,* 338–349.

Gronwall, D., Wrightson, P., & McGinn, V. (1997). Effect of mild head injury during the preschool years. *Journal of the International Neuropsychological Society, 3,* 592–597.

Heyder, K., Suchan, B., & Daum, I. (2004). Cortico-subcortical contributions to executive control. *Acta Psychologica, 115,* 271–289.

Hoofien, D., Vakil, E., Gilboa, A., Donovick, P. J., & Barak, O. (2002). Comparison of the predictive power of socioeconomic variables, severity of injury and age on long-term outcome of traumatic brain injury: Sample-specific variables versus factors as predictors. *Brain Injury, 16,* 9–27.

Hori, T. (1985). Pathophysiology analysis of hypoxaemia during acute severe asthma. *Archives of Diseases in Childhood, 60,* 640–643.

Hurn, P. D., Vannucci, S. J., & Hagberg, H. (2004). Adult or perinatal brain injury: Does sex matter? *Stroke, 36,* 193–195.

Inder, T. E., & Volpe, J. J. (2000). Mechanisms of perinatal brain injury. *Seminars in Neonatology, 5,* 3–16.

Jaddoe, V., & Witteman, J. (2006). Hypotheses on the fetal origins of adult diseases: Contributions of epidemiological studies. *European Journal of Epidemiology, 21,* 91–102.

Jin, C., & Schachar, R. (2004). Methylphenidate treatment of attention-deficit/hyperactivity disorder secondary to traumatic brain injury: A critical appraisal of treatment studies. *CNS Spectrums, 9,* 217–226.

Johnson, M. H. (1999). Cortical plasticity in normal and abnormal cognitive development: Evidence and working hypotheses. *Development and Psychopathology, 11,* 419–437.

Johnston, M. V. (2004). Clinical disorders of brain plasticity. *Brain and Development, 26,* 73–80.

Kirkwood, M., Janusz, J., Yeates, K. O., Taylor, H. G., Wade, S. L., Stancin, T., et al. (2000). Prevalence and correlates of depressive symptoms following traumatic brain injuries in children. *Child Neurology, 6,* 195–208.

Knudsen, E. I. (2004). Sensitive periods in the development of the brain and behavior. *Journal of Cognitive Neuroscience, 16,* 1412–1425.

Kolb, B., & Gibb, R. (2001). Early brain injury, plasticity and behavior. In C. Nelson & M. Luciana (Eds.), *Handbook of developmental cognitive neuroscience* (pp. 175–190). Cambridge MA: MIT Press.

Kraus, J. F., & Nourjah, P. (1988). The epidemiology of mild, uncomplicated brain injury. *Journal of Trauma, 28,* 1637–1643.

Langlois, J. A., Rutland-Brown, W., & Thomas, K. E. (2004). *Traumatic brain injury in the United States: Emergency department visits, hospitalizations, and deaths.* Centers for Disease Control and Prevention, National Center for Injury Prevention and Control. Atlanta, GA.

Laskowitz, D. T., Matthew, W. D., Bennett, E. R., Schmechel, D., Herbstreith, M. H., Goel, S., et al. (1998). Endogenous apolipoprotein E suppresses LPS-stimulated microglial nitric oxide production. *NeuroReport, 9,* 615–618.

Laskowitz, D. T., Sheng, H., Bart, R. D., Joyner, K. A., Roses, A. D., & Warner, D. S. (1997). Apolipoprotein E-deficient mice have increased susceptibility to focal cerebral ischemia. *Journal of Cerebral Blood Flow & Metabolism, 17,* 753–758.

Lavoie, M. E., Dupuis, F., Johnston, K. M., Leclerc, S., & Lassonde, M. (2004). Visual P300 effects beyond symptoms in concussed college athletes. *Journal of Clinical and Experimental Neuropsychology, 26,* 55–73.

Lea, P. M., & Faden, A. I. (2001). Traumatic brain injury: Developmental differences in glutamate receptor response and the impact on treatment. *Mental Retardation and Developmental Disabilities Research Reviews, 7,* 235–248.

Lee, Y., Aono, M., Laskowitz, D., Warner, D. S., & Pearlstein, R. D. (2004). Apolipoprotein E protects against oxidative stress in mixed neuronal-glial cell cultures by reducing glutamate toxicity. *Neurochemistry International, 44,* 107–118.

Levin, H. S., Amparo, E. G., Eisenberg, H. M., Miner, M. E., High, W. M., Ewing-Cobbs, L., et al. (1989). Magnetic resonance imaging after closed head injury in children. *Neurosurgery, 24,* 223–227.

Levin, H. S., & Hanten, G. (2005). Executive functions after traumatic brain injury in children. *Pediatric Neurology, 33,* 79–93.

Luciana, M. (2003). Cognitive development in children born preterm: Implications for theories of brain plasticity following early injury. *Development and Psychopathology, 15,* 1017–1047.

Luther, J. S., Redmer, D. A., Reynolds, L., & Wallace, J. (2005). Nutritional paradigms of ovine fetal growth restriction: Implications for human pregnancy. *Human Fertility, 8,* 179–187.

Lynch, J. R., Pineda, J. A., Morgan, D., Zhang, L., Warner, D. S., Benveniste, H., et al. (2002). Apolipoprotein E affects the central nervous system response to injury and the development of cerebral edema. *Annals of Neurology, 51,* 113–117.

Macmillan, M. (2002). *An odd kind of fame: Stories of Phineas Gage.* Cambridge, MA: MIT Press.

Martin, J. A., Kochanek, K. D., Strobino, D. M., Guyer, B., & MacDorman, M. F. (2005). Annual summary of vital statistics—2003. *Pediatrics, 115,* 619–634.

McAllister, T. W., Rhodes, C. H., Flashman, L. A., McDonald, B. C., Belloni, D., & Saykin, A. J. (2005). Effect of the dopamine D2 receptor T allele on response latency after mild traumatic brain injury. *American Journal of Psychiatry, 162,* 1749–1751.

McClure, M. M., Peiffer, A. M., Rosen, G. D., & Fitch, R. H. (2005). Auditory processing deficits in rats with neonatal hypoxic-ischemic injury. *International Journal of Developmental Neuroscience, 23,* 351–362.

McCrory, P., Johnston, K., Meeuwisse, W., Aubry, M., Cantu, R., Dvorak, J., et al. (2005). Summary and agreement statement of the 2nd international conference on concussion in sport, Prague 2004. *British Journal of Sports Medicine, 39,* 196–204.

McGrath, M. M., Sullivan, M. C., Lester, B. M., & Oh, W. (2000). Longitudinal neurological follow-up in neonatal intensive care unit survivors with various neonatal morbidities. *Pediatrics, 106,* 1397–1405.

Mendelsohn, D., Levin, H. S., Bruce, D., Lilly, M., Harward, H., Culhane, K. A., et al. (1992). Late MRI after head injury in children: Relationship to clinical features and outcome. *Child Nervous System, 8,* 445–452.

Middleton, J. A. (2001). Practitioner review: psychological sequelae of head injury in children and adolescents. *Journal of Child Psychology and Psychiatry, 42,* 165–180.

Mukherjee, A. B., & Hodgen, G. D. (1982). Maternal ethanol exposure induces transient impairment of umbilical circulation and fetal hypoxia in monkeys. *Science, 218,* 700–702.

Nowakowski, R. S., & Hayes, N. L. (2002). General principles of CNS development. In M. Johnson, Y. Munakata, & R. Gilmore (Eds.), *Brain development and cognition: A reader* (2nd ed.; pp. 57–82). Malden, MA: Blackwell.

Nyakas, C., Buwalda, B., & Luiten, P. G. M. (1996). Hypoxia and brain development. *Progress in Neurobiology, 49,* 1–51.

Oria, R. B., Patrick, P. D., Zhang, H., Lorntz, B., De Castro Costa, C. M., Brito, G. A. C., et al. (2005). APOE4 protects the cognitive development in children with heavy diarrhea burdens in northeast Brazil. *Pediatric Research, 57,* 310–316.

Randolph, C., McCrea, M., & Barr, W. B. (2005). Is neuropsychological testing useful in the management of sport-related concussion? *Journal of Athletic Training, 40,* 139–154.

Rimel, R. W., Giordani, B., Barth, J. T., Boll, T. J., & Jane, J. A. (1981). Disability caused by minor head injury. *Neurosurgery, 9,* 221–228.

Robinson, S. (2005). Systematic prenatal insults disrupt telencephalon development: Implications for potential interventions. *Epilepsy & Behavior, 7*, 345–363.

Rosso, I. M., & Cannon, T. D. (2003). Obstetric complications and neurodevelopmental mechanisms in schizophrenia. In D. Cicchetti & E. Walker (Eds.), *Neurodevelopmental mechanisms in psychopathology* (pp. 111–137). New York: Cambridge University Press.

Rothstein, R. P., & Levison, S. W. (2005). Gray matter oligodendrocyte progenitors and neurons die caspase-3 mediated deaths subsequent to mild perinatal hypoxic/ischemic insults. *Developmental Neuroscience, 27*, 149–159.

Sagvolden, T., Johansen, E. B., Aase, H., & Russell, V. A. (2005). A dynamic developmental theory of attention-deficit/hyperactivity disorder (ADHD) predominantly hyperactive/impulsive and combined subtypes. *Behavioral and Brain Sciences, 28*, 397–468.

Schmidt-Kastner, R., van Os, J., Steinbusch, H. W. M., & Schmitz, C. (2006). Gene regulation by hypoxia and the neurodevelopmental origin of schizophrenia. *Schizophrenia Research, 84*, 253–271.

Schnider, A., & Gutbrod, K. (1999). Traumatic brain injury. In D. Cicchetti & E. Walker (Eds.), *The human frontal lobes: Functions and disorders* (pp. 487–506). New York: Guilford.

Schutzman, S. A., & Greenes, D. S. (2001). Pediatric minor head trauma. *Annals of Emergency Medicine, 37*, 64–74.

Schwebel, D. C., Hodgens, J. B., & Sterling, S. (2006). How mothers parent their children with behavior disorders: implications for unintentional injury risk. *Journal of Safety Research, 37*, 167–173.

Socol, M. L., Manning, F. A., Murata, Y., & Druzin, M. L. (1982). Maternal smoking causes fetal hypoxia: Experimental evidence. *American Journal of Obstetrics and Gynecology, 15*, 214–218.

Sowell, E. R., Thompson, P. M., Holmes, C. J., Jernigan, T. L., & Toga, A. W. (1999). In vivo evidence for post-adolescent brain maturation in frontal and striatal regions. *Nature Neuroscience, 2*, 859–861.

Stenzel-Poore, M. P., Stevens, S. L., Xiong, Z., Lessov, N. S., Harrington, C. A., Mori, M., et al. (2003). Effect of ischaemic preconditioning on genomic response to cerebral ischaemia: similarity to neuroprotective strategies in hibernation and hypoxia-tolerant states. *The Lancet, 362*, 1028–1037.

Teasdale, G., & Jennett, B. (1974). Assessment of coma and impaired consciousness. A practical scale. *Lancet, 2*, 81–84.

Van Kampen, D. A., Lovell, M. R., Pardini, J. E., Collins, M. W., & Fu, F. H. (2006). The "value added" of neurocognitive testing after sports-related concussion. *American Journal of Sports Medicine, 34*, 1630–1635.

Vannucci, R. C. (2000). Hypoxic-schemic encephalopathy. *American Journal of Perinatology, 17*, 113–120.

Uliel, S., Tauman, R., Greenfield, M., & Sivan, Y. (2004). Normal polysomnographic respiratory values in children and adolescents. *Chest, 125*, 872–878.

Wenger, R. H. (2002). Cellular adaptation to hypoxia: O_2-sensing protein hydroxylases, hypoxia-inducible transcription factors, and O_2-regulated gene expression. *The FASEB Journal, 16*, 1151–1162.

Wilde, E. A., Hunter, J. V., Newsom, M. R., Scheibel, R. S., Bigler, E. D., Johnson, J. L., et al. (2005). Frontal and temporal morphometric findings on MRI in children after moderate to severe traumatic brain injury. *Journal of Neurotrauma, 22,* 333–344.

World Health Organization. (1992). *Low birth weight: A tabulation of available information.* Geneva: World Health Organization.

Yeates, K. O. (2000). Closed-head injury. In K. Yeates, M. Ris, & H. Taylor (Eds.), *Pediatric neuropsychology: Research, theory, and practice* (pp. 92–116). New York: Guilford.

Yeates, K. O., Taylor, H. G., Drotar, D., Wade, S. L., Klein, S., Stancin, T., et al. (1997). Preinjury family environment as a determinant of recovery from traumatic brain injuries in school-age children. *Journal of the International Neuropsychological Society, 3,* 617–630.

Zhang, L. J., Ravdin, L. D., Relkin, N., Zimmerman, R. D., Jordan, B., Lathan, W. E., et al. (2003). Increased diffusion in the brain of professional boxers: A preclinical sign of traumatic brain injury? *American Journal of Neuroradiology, 24,* 52–57.

Zouakia, A., Guilloteau, D., Zimmer, L., Besnard, J. C., & Chalon, S. (1997). Evolution of dopamine receptors in the rat after neonatal hypoxia-ischemia: Autoradiographic studies. *Life Sciences, 60,* 151–162.

CHAPTER 9

Affective Style and Risk for Psychopathology

JAMES A. COAN AND JOHN J. B. ALLEN

In the attempt to identify causal mechanisms of vulnerability to psychopathology, psychophysiological markers are highly valued for the important links they provide among social, behavioral, psychological, and cellular levels of analysis (Anderson & Scott, 1999). The promise of such markers lies in their potential to serve as objectively measurable individual differences related to underlying mechanisms of risk. Often referred to as *endophenotypes* (see Gottesman & Gould, 2003; Iacono, 1998), psychophysiological markers of vulnerability may stem from genetic factors, environmental pressures, or gene–environment interactions (Gould & Gottesman, 2006). In the history of research on vulnerability to psychopathology, the search for reliable endophenotypes is a common theme. Potential markers such as low urinary levels of the noradrenaline metabolite MHPG (e.g., Fawcett & Maas, 1972), abnormal responses to the dexamethasone suppression test (e.g., Carroll, 1982), and reduced latency to the first period of rapid eye movement (REM) sleep (e.g., Kupfer, 1995) have met with varied success as indicators of vulnerability to diverse forms of psychopathology, yet each comes with shortcomings, suggesting strongly that better markers are needed (Berman, Narasimhan, & Charney, 1997).

One promising candidate for such a marker is the degree of asymmetry in neural activity across the frontal cortex, observed either at rest or during critical emotional challenges. This asymmetry in neural activity is indexed by the difference in brain activation between the right and left hemispheres at any given cortical region. Frontal hemisphere asymmetries in neural activity have—in numerous laboratories and across diverse experimental contexts—been associated with various forms of psychopathology and with more normative expressions of emotion and motivation (Coan & Allen, 2004). The dominant index of such hemispheric differences is *frontal EEG asymmetry*, often a single score representing the disparity in *alpha power* between corresponding left- and right-sided electroencephalographic (EEG) leads placed on the scalp over the frontal cortex. Insofar as individual differences in this measure predict (a) behavioral patterns of emotional responding and (b) the presence or absence of psychopathology, EEG asymmetry appears to mark the psychological construct of *affective style*, a predisposition to react to the environment with a positive versus negative emotional valence (see Davidson, 1998a; Hagemann, 2004).

Although EEG asymmetry often corresponds with affective style, which we describe in further detail in the following, it should not be treated as equivalent to affective style. As a general rule of thumb, neurophysiological markers should never be conflated with psychological constructs. Rather, physiological measures are tools for understanding the neural bases of behavior. Such measures rarely if ever capture the complexity of psychological predispositions and responses (see, e.g., Davidson, 2004a).

Affective style describes individual differences in emotional and/or motivational predispositions to respond to environmental events. As instantiated in the "glass-is-half-full versus glass-is-half-empty" aphorism, some people are predisposed to respond to environmental events with predominantly positive affectivity, whereas others are predisposed to respond to the same environmental events with predominantly negative affectivity. Considerable research over the past decade has identified some of the neural correlates of affective style, including both central dopamine functioning (e.g., Ashby, Isen, & Turken, 1999; Carver, 2004; Laakso et al., 2003) and septo-hippocampal functioning (e.g., Corr, 2004; Gray & McNaughton, 2000). The former system comprises neural structures within the mesocorticolimbic reward pathway (see, e.g., Berridge & Robinson, 2003), whereas the latter includes interconnections with the amygdala, a structure implicated in the processing of nearly all emotion cues (see, e.g., Davidson, 2002, 2004a). Negative affective style may confer risk for psychopathology, particularly depression (Davidson, 1994, 1998a, 2000), but also anxiety (Davidson, 2002; Heller et al., 1997; Nitschke et al., 1999), hypomania (Harmon-Jones et al., 2002), and conduct problems (Rybak et al., 2006).

Although frontal EEG asymmetry has been the focus of considerable research on affective style, it is not a sole indicator. Other biological markers of affective style and closely related motivational constructs include cardiac psychophysiology (see Brenner, Beauchaine, & Sylvers, 2005) and certain event-related potential components of the EEG (see Luu, Collins, & Tucker, 2000). Nevertheless, our focus here is on EEG asymmetry, which is the most widely studied marker of affective style.

The empirical association between frontal EEG asymmetry and affective style suggests that the measure may serve as a useful endophenotypic marker of vulnerability for certain forms of psychopathology. This constitutes a major assumption of the chapter that follows in which we (a) explain the association between frontal EEG asymmetry and affective style; (b) discuss the differences and similarities among three types of endophenotypic markers; and (c) review the literature supporting frontal EEG asymmetry as an endophenotypic marker of vulnerability for psychopathology.

CONCEPTUAL MODELS OF AFFECTIVE STYLE

As alluded to previously, affective style refers to a trait-like predisposition to respond in emotionally characteristic ways to environmental cues, particularly cues containing affective information (e.g., Davidson, 1992a). The diversity of observations regarding associations among motivational constructs, emotional responses, and frontal EEG asymmetries long ago suggested the need for an organizational model, and to date at least two prominent models of affective style have emerged (Van Honk & Schutter, 2006). The *valence model* references positive and negative affectivity—trait predispositions to engage in positive versus negative affect, respectively (cf., Gray & Watson, 2007). This model suggests that individuals predisposed to relatively greater left frontal brain activity respond to environmental demands with increased probability of positive affect, or decreased probability of negative affect. By contrast, individuals predisposed to relatively greater right-frontal activity are thought to show the reverse pattern, responding to environmental demands with an increased probability of negative affect, and a decreased probability of positive affect. A substantial literature either supports or partially supports the valence model. For example, infants who cry following maternal separation tend toward relatively greater right-frontal activity measured at rest than infants who do not cry following separation (Davidson & Fox, 1989; Fox, Bell, & Jones, 1992). In addition, individuals with greater resting right-frontal activity tend to respond with greater negative affect when negative film clips are presented, and individuals with greater resting left frontal activity tend to respond with greater positive affect when positive films are presented (Tomarken, Davidson, & Henriques, 1990; Wheeler, Davidson, & Tomarken, 1993).

More recently, a *motivational model* has been proposed (Davidson, 1992b; Harmon-Jones & Allen, 1998) based on accumulating evidence that tendencies toward relatively greater left frontal activity are also associated with (a) trait-like hostility and anger, (b) negatively valenced affective states (Harmon-Jones, 2001; Harmon-Jones & Allen, 1998), and (c) general behavioral activation (reward-seeking) tendencies (e.g., Brenner et al., 2005; Coan & Allen, 2003; Harmon-Jones & Allen, 1997; Sutton & Davidson, 1997). These findings are consistent with the motivational model of frontal EEG asymmetry and affective style, which states that individuals predisposed to relatively greater left frontal activity than right respond to environmental demands with an increased probability of approach-oriented affect (e.g., both joy and anger), or a decreased probability of withdrawal or passive-avoidance related affect (e.g., fear, sadness). By contrast, individuals predisposed to relatively greater right-frontal activity than left are thought to respond to environmental demands with an increased probability of withdrawal or passive-avoidance related affect, or a decreased probability of approach-oriented affect.

The motivational model enjoys a great deal of empirical support, in part because it can accommodate earlier research supporting the valence model. Indeed, several theorists have noted similarities between the motivational model of frontal EEG asymmetry and other motivational models of behavior, particularly that of Gray (1972; 1987), which specifies distinct behavioral inhibition and behavioral activation systems (the BIS and the BAS, respectively; see also Beauchaine & Neuhaus, this volume). According to Gray, the BAS responds to incentives and guides organisms toward attaining desirable stimuli through approach behaviors, and toward evading undesirable stimuli through active avoidance behaviors. In contrast, the BIS increases arousal and attention and inhibits prepotent approach or avoidance behaviors to resolve goal conflict between competing motivations (Corr, 2004; Gray & McNaughton, 2000). Frontal EEG asymmetries appear to correspond in part with scales developed by Carver and White (1994) to measure dispositional BIS and BAS tendencies in humans. As measured by the Carver and White scales, the BAS and BIS appear to correspond with frontal EEG asymmetries in ways that are highly similar (but not identical) to the motivational model of affective style (Coan & Allen, 2003; Harmon-Jones & Allen, 1997; Sutton & Davidson, 1997). At least three independent investigations confirm that individuals who show a propensity for relatively greater left frontal activity than right while at rest tend to score higher on the BAS scale (Coan & Allen, 2003; Harmon-Jones & Allen, 1997; Sutton & Davidson, 1997).

Attempts to associate right-frontal activity with the BIS have been less successful. Although Sutton and Davidson (1997) observed a correspondence between right-frontal activity and BIS scores, neither Harmon-Jones and Allen (1997) nor Coan and Allen (2003) were able to do so.

AFFECTIVE STYLE, EEG ASYMMETRIES, AND PSYCHOPATHOLOGY

The theory of affective style suggests that individual differences in response to environmental challenges (e.g., an argument with a friend or parent, a disappointment) can be explained in part by emotional reactivity and engagement, and in part by predispositions toward approach versus withdrawal behavior (which affect emotional reactivity and engagement). Some individuals are more likely to engage actively with or otherwise approach environmental challenges, whereas others are more likely to withdraw from or avoid environmental challenges. Davidson (1998a) has proposed that these differences are probably insufficient to explain the presence or absence of psychopathology. Rather, affective style likely represents a diathesis, or vulnerability, that does not usually manifest as psychopathology without sufficient environmental stress (see also Beauchaine & Hinshaw, this volume). This is a classic moderator formulation (Coan & Allen, 2004) in which affective style alters the effect of environmental challenges on individual functioning. Thus, it is the *interaction* between affective style (vulnerability) and environmental risk that leads either to psychopathology or mental health. Neither affective style nor environmental experience is likely to be a strong determinant of psychopathology in isolation.

Any diathesis/stress model of psychopathology involves a number of assumptions, many of which have not been tested for affective style. Within the model proposed by Davidson (1998a), the first among these is the assumption that affective style is a stable, trait-like phenomenon, and that the markers used to assesses it (frontal EEG asymmetry) are stable as well. Apart from this important issue, one may ask what kind of *marker* of psychopathology frontal EEG asymmetry constitutes. Recently, Allen, Urry, Hitt, and Coan (2004) proposed that the extent to which frontal EEG asymmetries represent episode, liability, or genetic vulnerability markers (cf., Iacono & Ficken, 1989) of psychopathology remains uncertain.

If frontal EEG asymmetries serve as *episode markers,* one would expect to see specific patterns of frontal EEG asymmetry in the presence of diagnosable psychopathology, but not when the condition remits. Such a marker would be very useful for delimiting pathology onset or remission, suggesting when treatment may be needed or no longer needed, or identifying individuals with similar etiologies or prognoses. Episode marker criteria run counter to diathesis/stress models of psychopathology. Indeed, the diathesis/stress model of affective style presupposes that frontal EEG asymmetries function as nonspecific *liability markers*—which are present and measurable both prior to and following remission of psychopathology. If frontal EEG asymmetries represent liability markers, they should be relatively independent of situational factors affecting mood and emotion.

Although a large literature has characterized personality traits such as positive and negative affectivity as both stable and moderately to highly heritable (e.g., Finkel & McGue, 1997), the literature to date is relatively silent on the question of genetic explanations for affective style. Stability does not necessarily imply genetic control. A given individual's tendency toward one pattern of affective style versus another may be stable throughout much of his or her lifetime, regardless of whether the predisposition stems from strong genetic influences or early experiences. In either case, a person's affective style and resulting pattern of frontal EEG asymmetry, if a genuine liability marker, would be useful for identifying those who are at greater risk for psychopathology than others in the general population. It remains possible, however, to distinguish liability markers from *genetic vulnerability markers,* which are a special class of liability marker that are entirely under genetic control.

Genetic vulnerability markers satisfy the same criteria as liability markers, with a few additional requirements. If frontal EEG asymmetries mark genetic vulnerability, they should be relatively independent of situational factors, yet characterize most persons with a given disorder (e.g., depression). In addition, they should be present in both depressed and nondepressed individuals, and demonstrate heritability within the normal population. Note, however, that they need not predict future depression, because genetic alleles may be linked to pathology only in the presence of certain environmental circumstances. In other words, even if frontal EEG asymmetries mark genetic vulnerability, it is not the case that a given individual's affective style is *sufficient* to cause psychopathology.

To date, the degree to which frontal EEG asymmetry functions best as an episode, liability, or genetic vulnerability marker for psychopathology is not yet resolved. Thus far, it is clear that frontal EEG asymmetry does not characterize all psychopathologic individuals (Reid et al., 1998). Nevertheless, many of the extant data are consistent with the proposition that frontal EEG asymmetry indexes vulnerability for psychopathology in at least a subset of individuals who are at risk for certain pathological conditions, including depression and anxiety.

Table 9.1 provides an overview of studies consistent with frontal EEG asymmetry as an episode, liability, and genetic vulnerability marker of

Table 9.1.

Characteristics of Psychophysiological Markers as Applied to Frontal EEG Asymmetry and Depression

Episode	Liability	Genetic
Characterizes most depressed persons (sensitivity)[1,8,9,12,-14,16]	Characterizes most depressed persons (sensitivity)[1,8,9,12,-14,16]	Characterizes most depressed persons (sensitivity)[1,8,9,12,-14,16]
Differentiates depressed from nondepressed (specificity)[1,-6,8,9,10,12,15-17]	Differentiates depressed from nondepressed, not only in episode but in remission as well[1,9,11]	Differentiates depressed from nondepressed, not only in episode but in remission as well[1,9,11]
Changes with variations in clinical state[-2,-8,15]	Demonstrates stability in both depressed and nondepressed individuals[1,2,-8,18]	Demonstrates stability in both depressed and nondepressed individuals[1,2,-8,18]
	Predicts the future development of depression in individuals currently not depressed[NA]	Predicts the future development of depression in individuals currently not depressed[NA]
		Is heritable within the normal population[3,4,17]
		Is more common in depressed persons with a strong family history of depression than those without a such a history[NA]
		Is more prevalent in families of depressed individuals than in families of nondepressed individuals[6,7,12]
		Identifies those family members at risk for depression[NA]

[1]Allen, Iacono, Depue, & Arbisi, 1993
[2]Allen, Urry, Hitt, & Coan, 2002
[3]Anokhin, Heath & Myers, 2006
[4]Coan, 2003
[5]Davidson, Marshall, Tomarken, & Henriques, 2000
[6]Dawson, Frey, Panagiotides, Osterling, & Hessl, 1997
[7]Dawson, Frey, Panagiotides et al., 1999a
[8]Debener et al., 2000
[9]Gotlib, Ranganath, & Rosenfeld, 1998
[10]Heller, Nitschke, Etienne, & Miller, 1997
[11]Henriques & Davidson, 1990

[12]Henriques & Davidson, 1991
[13]Jones, Field, Fox, Lundy, & Davalos, 1997
[14]Reid, Duke, & Allen, 1998
[15]Rosenfeld, Baehr, Baehr, Gotlib, & Ranganath, 1996
[16]Schaffer, Davidson, & Saron, 1983
[17]Smit, Posthuma, Boomsma & de Geus, 2007
[18]Tomarken, Davidson, Wheeler, & Kinney, 1992
[19]Wiedemann et al., 1999
[NA]No Data Currently Available

Note: Numerical superscripts refer to studies listed. Positive numbers indicate that the study is consistent with the characteristic, and negative numbers indicate the study is inconsistent with the characteristic. NA = None Available. List of characteristics is after that of Iacono & Ficken (1989).

depression. Importantly, none of these studies *confirms* that frontal EEG asymmetry is an episode, liability, or genetic vulnerability marker.

Frontal EEG Asymmetry As an Episode Marker

The efficiency of any variable as an episode marker depends on two factors—*sensitivity* and *specificity*. A sensitive biomarker is present in nearly all people who exhibit a disorder. In contrast, a specific biomarker is present only in people with the disorder, and not in people without the disorder.

Sensitivity.   In attempting to classify depressed versus nondepressed individuals, frontal EEG asymmetry has often but not always demonstrated reasonable sensitivity. For example, setting an arbitrarily but objective cutpoint of perfect symmetry in frontal activity (left activity = right activity), relatively greater right-frontal brain activity has characterized 69% (Henriques & Davidson, 1991), 83% (Schaffer, Davidson, & Saron, 1983), and in one study 100% (Allen et al., 1993) of depressed persons. Relatively greater right- than left-frontal activity also characterizes individuals suffering from seasonal depression (Allen et al., 1993), college students with high scores on the Beck Depression Inventory (BDI) (Schaffer et al., 1983), and individuals diagnosed with Unipolar Depression (Debener et al., 2000; Gotlib, Ranganath, & Rosenfeld, 1998; Henriques & Davidson, 1991).

Yet this pattern of moderate to high sensitivity is not always replicated. Reid et al. (1998) analyzed two independent samples (one diagnosed via interview, the other defined psychometrically), and did not find the expected pattern of relatively greater right- than left-frontal activity among depressed individuals.

Specificity.   One can also ask how specific frontal EEG asymmetry is as a marker of psychopathology. Most who study frontal EEG asymmetry and psychopathology attempt to separate depressed individuals from nondepressed controls, but some have sought to distinguish anxious from nonanxious controls (Davidson et al., 2000; Heller, Etienne, & Miller, 1995; Wiedemann et al., 1999). In both cases, relatively greater right-frontal (sometimes described as relatively less left-frontal) activity corresponds with symptoms of both depression and anxiety. A recent meta-analysis by Thibodeau, Jorgensen, and Kim (2006) revealed that effect sizes concerning both forms of psychopathology lie in the moderate range—indicating substantial overlap in asymmetry scores for depressed/anxious people versus normal controls—which argues against strong specificity.

To date, no studies have evaluated receiver operating characteristic (ROC) curves for measures of lateral asymmetry. Such reports are needed to establish the sensitivity and specificity of these scores vis-à-vis depression and/or anxiety. Nevertheless, the data previously presented suggest that sensitivity is moderate, with insufficient evidence for specificity.

Because relatively greater right-frontal brain activity has been associated with anxiety as well as depression (Davidson et al., 2000; Heller et al., 1997; Wiedemann et al., 1999), frontal EEG asymmetries favoring the right may indicate a general predisposition toward internalizing psychopathology. Some have suggested that the specificity of frontal EEG asymmetries may be improved by taking a more nuanced view of asymmetry patterns. For example, Heller and colleagues (Heller & Nitschke, 1998; Heller et al., 1997) have proposed that more complex patterns of cortical brain function may distinguish depression from anxiety, and even specific forms of anxiety. These authors distinguish between *anxious apprehension*, which they describe as a primarily worry-based and ruminative concern for the future characterized by negative expectations, and *anxious arousal*, which they describe as primarily the experience of somatic panic symptoms such as muscle tension and rapid heart rate. In drawing these distinctions, they proposed that anxious apprehension should be characterized by relatively greater *left*-frontal activity by virtue of its orientation toward scanning the environment. It should be noted, however, that depression and anxiety (a) share common genetic vulnerability and (b) are often comorbid within individuals (see, e.g., Brady & Kendall, 1992; Krueger & Markon, 2006). Thus, efforts to parse lateral asymmetries into depression- and anxiety-specific patterns face a formidable challenge.

FRONTAL EEG ASYMMETRY AS A LIABILITY MARKER

If frontal EEG asymmetry functions as a liability marker, we would expect that—as with episode markers—it demonstrate sensitivity in characterizing depressed persons from nondepressed controls, and from those with other forms of psychopathology. Unlike episode markers, however, one should also expect individual differences in the measure to be stable, not only across time and situations, but also across episodes of psychopathology. That is, one should expect frontal EEG asymmetry to differentiate clinical from nonclinical samples, not only during actual clinical episodes but also during periods of remission. Finally, if frontal EEG asymmetry represents a liability marker, it should be possible to predict later psychopathology in individuals of nonclinical status who subsequently experience a significant life stressor. In other words, those who carry the liability should be susceptible to psychopathology following adverse events.

In any discussion of the stability of a construct or measure, it should be noted that the term *stability* has several meanings. One is the preservation of rank order of a trait or measure in a given sample over time. That is, do those high on the measure remain high (and those low remain low)—even if the overall level of the scores rises or falls? Another meaning has to do with the preservation of the actual score across time. We comment on the connotation of stability in the following text.

To date, only two studies have examined the stability of frontal EEG asymmetries during treatment of depression. Allen et al. (1993) found correlations in frontal asymmetry scores over 2 weeks ranging from .70 to .77 among individuals treated with light therapy for seasonal depression. More recently, Allen, Urry, Hitt, and Coan (2004) examined stability in a nonmedicated sample of depressed individuals engaged in a nonpharmacological treatment. Across three measurement occasions separated by 4-week intervals, intraclass correlations (ICCs) at the frontal sites averaged .56. Across five measurement occasions, the same ICC was .61. Although individuals in this study made substantial improvements in their clinical status, within-sample individual differences were moderately stable. An earlier examination of 15 depressed patients undergoing pharmacotherapy generated no evidence of systematic mood-dependent changes in frontal EEG asymmetry across 2 weeks of treatment, despite the fact that depressed patients as a group showed the expected pattern of relatively greater right-frontal resting activity (Debener et al., 2000). However, most of the patients in this investigation were receiving antidepressants, benzodiazepines, or both, raising the question of whether such medications influenced asymmetry scores. No studies have addressed this question.

Clinical status notwithstanding, the test-retest stabilities of individual differences in frontal EEG asymmetry range from acceptable to good. For example, Tomarken and colleagues observed an average test-retest correlation across 3 weeks of .66 in a nonclinical sample of undergraduate university students (Tomarken et al., 1992). In addition, Hagemann and colleagues observed that across four occasions of measurement, approximately 60% of the variance in frontal EEG asymmetry was accounted for by a stable latent trait (Hagemann et al., 2002).

Thus, the limited data suggest that individual differences in frontal EEG asymmetry are relatively independent of clinical status. At the very least, there is little evidence to suggest that occasion-specific variation is related to diagnostic status or even mood. Yet some exceptions have been reported for children and adolescents. For example, in one study of depressed adolescents, music and massage therapy appeared to attenuate the pattern of relatively greater right-frontal activity observed in the depressed group (Jones & Field, 1999). Indeed, massage therapy can reduce right-frontal asymmetries in 1-month-old infants (Jones, Field, & Davalos, 1998). Although these findings are striking, it is less clear that the changes in frontal

EEG asymmetry actually covaried with alterations in clinical state or mediated the effects of therapy on clinical state (cf., Coan & Allen, 2004).

Differentiation during remission.   In three studies, individuals who were formerly depressed continued to demonstrate relatively greater right-frontal activity when compared to never-depressed controls (Allen et al., 1993; Gotlib et al., 1998; Henriques & Davidson, 1990). For example, Henriques and Davidson (1990) observed, in six normal-mood but previously depressed individuals, evidence of less left- than right-frontal activity compared to eight never-depressed controls, leading them to suggest that frontal EEG asymmetries provide a state-independent marker of depression risk. In the Allen et al. (1993) study of Seasonal Affective Disorder, individuals suffering from depressive symptoms continued to display a pattern of less left- than right-frontal activity compared with controls, even after bright-light-induced remission of symptoms. Later, Gotlib et al. (1998) observed that a group consisting of both currently and previously depressed individuals showed less left- than right-frontal activity compared with never-depressed controls. Moreover, statistical tests of the difference in frontal EEG asymmetry between current and previously depressed individuals were not significant. These authors argued that frontal EEG asymmetry served as a state-independent marker of risk for psychopathology, particularly depression. Interestingly, and contrary to both predictions and past empirical evidence, Gotlib et al. (1998) also observed that frontal EEG asymmetry was not related to susceptibility to a negative mood induction, reports of depressogenic cognitive styles, or attentional biases for negative stimuli.

These last observations do not necessarily invalidate the liability marker hypothesis, but they do appear to run counter to the specific predictions of the diathesis/stress model of affective style and psychopathology, which states that it is the interaction between vulnerabilities reflecting (and possibly supporting) affective style and negative environmental stimuli that results in psychopathology. However, none of these studies measure stressors directly and, under such conditions, no diathesis-stress interaction would be found.

Frontal EEG asymmetry as a moderator of affect.   The diathesis/stress model of affective style (Davidson, 1998a) specifies at least two depressogenic elements in producing psychopathology—affective vulnerability and negative environmental challenges. According to this formulation, frontal EEG asymmetries reflect affective dispositions that either enhance or diminish emotional responses preferentially for some but not other classes of stimuli, with consequences for the development of psychopathology. Differential effects of one variable (affective responding) across different levels or types of another variable (eliciting stimuli) is a defining feature of statistical moderation (Baron & Kenny, 1986; Kraemer et al., 2001; see also Coan & Allen, 2004).

In early work in this area, Davidson and Fox (1989) observed a greater probability of crying in response to maternal separation among infants who had relatively greater right resting frontal activity. Fox, Bell, and Jones (1992) later reported that this pattern of results was modestly stable over a 5-month assessment period. Among adults, affective responses to negative emotional film clips are more negative for individuals with a propensity for relatively greater right-frontal activity (Tomarken et al., 1990; Wheeler et al., 1993). Interestingly, responses to *positive* emotional film clips were observed by Wheeler et al. (1993) to be more positive among individuals with a propensity for relatively greater left-frontal activity.

Unfortunately, attempts to replicate such observations have not always succeeded, perhaps in part due to methodological inconsistencies across laboratories. This point is exemplified in the work of Hagemann and colleagues (1998), who were not able to replicate any of the findings of Tomarken et al. (1990) or Wheeler et al. (1993). Unlike the earlier studies, which used film clips as affective stimuli, Hagemann et al. (1998) used normed, emotionally charged images. Although they did observe that individuals with a propensity for greater left-frontal activity at rest tended to respond more positively to positively valenced images, this was only observed when using a particular EEG reference point (Cz) with several methodological shortcomings (see following discussion for more information about the EEG referencing; Allen, Coan, & Nazarian, 2004a; Hagemann, Naumann, & Thayer, 2001).

Although the results described previously are consistent with a moderator formulation of affective responding, almost no studies have tested the statistical interaction between lateral asymmetry and stimulus type in predicting outcome variables. One exception includes the work of Henderson, Fox, and Rubin (2001), who modeled frontal EEG asymmetries recorded at 9 months of age as a moderator of behaviorally rated negative affectivity in predicting social wariness by the age of 4. In this work, infants who showed a high level of negative affect at 9 months were more likely to be socially wary at 4 years *if* at age 9 months they also showed relatively greater right-frontal activity at rest. Tests of statistical interactions have rarely been applied to more clinically relevant outcomes. One instance includes work by Bruder and colleagues, who observed that frontal EEG asymmetry moderated treatment response to fluoxetine among individuals suffering from depression (2001). That is, individuals with relatively greater left- than right-frontal activity were more responsive to fluoxetine.

In summarizing the evidence for the status of frontal EEG asymmetry as a liability marker for psychopathology, it is apparent that (a) frontal EEG asymmetries demonstrate trait-like stability across time in depressed participants and nondepressed controls; and (b) variations in frontal EEG asymmetry observed across measurement occasions do not vary with clinical state. Finally, although explicit tests of moderation have been evaluated for affect and social-regulation effects that are plausibly related to psychopathology, no explicit tests of the diathesis/stress model have been conducted with regard to the development of diagnosable mental illness.

Frontal EEG Asymmetry As a Marker of Genetic Vulnerability

Weak evidence for frontal EEG asymmetry as a marker of genetic vulnerability derives in part from studies finding relatively greater right- than left-frontal activity in young infants of depressed mothers (Dawson et al., 1997, 1999b; Jones et al., 1997). For example, Dawson et al. (1997) observed that infants of depressed mothers exhibited a pattern of right-frontal asymmetry compared with infants of nondepressed mothers. This pattern of frontal EEG asymmetry distinguished between infants whose mothers were diagnosed with major depression and those whose mothers had subthreshold symptoms. Dawson and colleagues have also observed infants of depressed mothers to exhibit relatively greater right- than left-frontal activity during interactions with both their mothers and familiar experimenters (Dawson et al., 1999a, 1999b). Field et al. (1995) have observed similar effects, reporting that infants of depressed mothers showed relatively greater right- than left-frontal activity when compared with those of nondepressed mothers.

Importantly, such studies, although consistent with genetic effects, cannot disentangle genetic predispositions from other heritable (e.g., epigenetic, programming) effects. Moreover, the few empirical investigations of the heritability of frontal EEG asymmetry suggest that, despite its trait-like properties, heritability is modest. For example, Coan (2003) found that 22% of the variance in EEG asymmetry was heritable in young-adult females, but virtually none of the variance was heritable in young-adult males. Similarly, in a study of 73 monozygotic and 50 dizygotic female twins, Anokhin et al. (2006) estimated that approximately 27% of frontal EEG asymmetry over the mid-frontal regions was heritable. In contrast, the authors of another recent study reported heritability coefficients of .61 and .57 for young-adult females and males, respectively (Smit et al., 2007). These estimates are derived from behavior genetics analyses, which detect additive and nonadditive heritable effects, but cannot identify interactive effects. Future efforts, with large samples and molecular genetics assessments of specific candidate genes will be needed to examine whether frontal EEG asymmetry reflects the influences of specific alleles.

METHODOLOGICAL ISSUES IN FRONTAL EEG ASYMMETRY RESEARCH

There are many methodological complexities underlying the measurement of frontal EEG asymmetry that are likely to contribute to the aforementioned inconsistencies in observed effects across laboratories. As such, individuals interested in frontal EEG asymmetry may find a brief review of major methodological issues useful. Comprehensive coverage of measurement, data reduction, and data analysis can be found elsewhere (see Allen, Coan, & Nazarian, 2004).

ALPHA POWER AND NEURAL ACTIVITY/ACTIVATION

One of the most formidable hurdles for new readers of this literature concerns the inverse relation between neural activity in the *alpha range* (8 to 13 Hz) and cortical processing. A good deal of evidence suggests that when alpha power (i.e., alpha amplitude) is high, active cortical processing is low (Allen, Coan, & Nazarian, 2004a), although not all frequencies in the alpha band show this relationship uniformly (Oakes et al., 2004). Thus, greater left-frontal alpha power suggests less left-frontal brain activity. It is customary for researchers to assume this inverse relationship and to speak primarily in terms of cortical activity, thereby performing a mental alpha power/cortical activity translation for the reader. Confusingly, however, this is not always the practice among researchers.

Another source of confusion concerns the frequent use of the terms *activity* and *activation* as if they are interchangeable when referring to EEG measures of alpha power. In this chapter, *activity* refers to the inverse of alpha power during tonic (resting) EEG measurement. By contrast, *activation* refers to the difference between two conditions of EEG measurement (e.g., resting versus task). It is worth noting that the overwhelming majority of studies using EEG are designed to measure cortical activity, not cortical activation.

ASYMMETRY SCORES

The most common index of frontal EEG asymmetry is the asymmetry score. As stated previously, this is simply the difference in alpha power between the right and left hemispheres at any given cortical region. A closer look at this score, however, reveals several complexities. First, alpha power tends to be positively skewed, and is frequently natural log (ln)-transformed before the difference score is computed. Typically, ln(alpha power) over the left hemisphere is subtracted from ln(alpha power) over the right hemisphere. Interpreted in terms of alpha, higher scores on this scale indicate relatively greater right-frontal alpha power and lower scores indicate relatively greater left-frontal alpha. Expressed in terms of activity, higher scores indicate relatively greater left-frontal activity and lower scores indicate relatively greater right-frontal activity. However one wishes to interpret the score, zero indicates symmetry. Because the asymmetry score is so frequently used, it is often difficult to know which hemisphere (or whether one hemisphere more than the other) is responsible for observed hemispheric differences.

REFERENCE SCHEME

One difficult methodological quandary facing frontal EEG asymmetry research regards the selection of an appropriate *reference site*. Any EEG recording represents the difference in electrical potentials between an active site and a reference. The ideal reference is inactive, providing investigators with estimates of spectral power that reflect activity at the site of interest. One such reference, for example, derives from the average electrical activity of the earlobes, or of the mastoid bones just behind the ear; another involves the average of all EEG recording sites.

Many reference montages exist, and as Reid et al. (1998) and others (Coan, Allen, & McKnight, 2006; Hagemann, Naumann, & Thayer, 2001) have noted, data derived from one reference scheme often do not correlate well with data derived using another. Thus, reference schemes often do not "agree" about what the brain is doing, raising concerns over the interpretation of findings and about standardization across laboratories. Worse yet, it is difficult to be certain which reference scheme provides the "best" measure of EEG, although empirical and rational arguments tend to conclude that the Cz or vertex (top and middle of the head) may be the most problematic option (Allen, Coan, & Nazarian, 2004a; Hagemann et al., 2001).

Unfortunately, the overwhelming majority of studies in this area depend on the Cz reference scheme (Coan & Allen, 2004). On the one hand, frequent use of the Cz reference could be partially responsible for misleading results and inconsistencies in this literature. On the other hand, the fact that so many significant effects have been obtained *despite* this problem may indicate that the size of many effects has been underestimated (Coan, Allen, & McKnight, 2006). The issue of the optimal or standard reference scheme in EEG recording awaits resolution. Until that time, interested readers are advised to be aware of the reference scheme used in any report of frontal EEG asymmetry.

THE FUTURE OF AFFECTIVE STYLE AND FRONTAL EEG ASYMMETRY RESEARCH

The future of research on affective style and frontal EEG asymmetry as a vulnerability marker is naturally somewhat unclear. Nevertheless, in the remainder of this chapter we offer speculations—recommendations perhaps—on what is likely or ought to follow the work that has already been conducted.

THE NEURAL GENERATORS OF FRONTAL EEG ASYMMETRY

Identification of the neural structures underlying the manifestation of alpha asymmetries at the scalp is likely to greatly increase our understanding of affective style, as well as of links between affective style and risk for psychopathology. To date, theories of the most likely neural generators of frontal EEG asymmetries have targeted the dorsolateral prefrontal cortex (dlPFC) and the ventrolateral prefrontal cortex (vlPFC) (Craig, 2005; Davidson, 2004b). A large literature now implicates these and other prefrontal (and limbic) regions in depression, anxiety, and conduct problems. For example, components of the right dlPFC may interact with paralimbic structures in linking depressogenic cognitions to negative moods and behaviors (e.g., Mayberg et al., 1999; Teasdale et al., 1999), and individuals with unilateral left-hemisphere damage to the prefrontal cortex have long been observed to experience more depressive symptoms than those with damage to the right hemisphere (e.g., Gainotti, 1972).

Dysfunctions of the medial orbitofrontal cortex appear to be common to a variety of anxiety disorders, from simple phobias to Obsessive-Compulsive Disorder and Posttraumatic Stress Disorder (Rauch et al., 1997); and increased activity specifically in left orbitofrontal and ventrolateral prefrontal cortices have been observed in both anticipatory anxiety and anxious apprehension (Chua et al., 1999; Engels et al., 2007). In contrast, converging evidence from a variety of sources implicate the right dlPFC in threat-related vigilance (*anxious arousal*, cf., Engels et al., 2007) and avoidance motivation (Coan, Schaefer, & Davidson, 2006; Damasio et al., 2000; Kalin et al., 1998; Kalin et al., 2001; Tranel, Bechara, & Denburg, 2002). In one recent study of the neural correlates of cognitive-behavioral therapy (CBT) for spider phobia, researchers reported that spider phobic individuals showed significant activation in the right dlPFC during the presentation of spider films (Paquette et al., 2003). Moreover, these researchers observed decreased activation in right dlPFC during film presentation at a follow-up assessment, presumably as a function of the CBT intervention targeting avoidance motivation.

Prefrontal dysfunctions are now widely implicated in aggressive, impulsive, and even criminal behavior (Raine et al., 1998), and some evidence suggests this dysfunction may be lateralized. Examples include observations that bilateral or right-hemisphere (but not left-hemisphere) lesions of the ventromedial prefrontal and orbitofrontal cortices are associated with impulsivity and aggression (Anderson et al., 1999), and that violent criminals show lower ratios of lateral and medial prefrontal to subcortical glucose metabolism in the right hemisphere during continuous-performance tasks compared with controls (Raine et al., 1998).

As methods for detailing specific functional relationships between neural structures and affective style grow more sophisticated and affordable, researchers interested in using frontal EEG asymmetry as an index of affective style and risk for psychopathology will do well to link those asymmetries to the neural structures that underlie them.

Emotion-Regulation Capabilities Versus Dispositions

Despite progress in the measurement of frontal EEG asymmetry, noteworthy inconsistencies in findings across laboratories remain (e.g., Allen, Coan, & Nazarian, 2004; Coan & Allen, 2004; Davidson, 1998b; Hagemann, 2004; Hagemann et al., 1998; Reid et al., 1998). If the potential of frontal EEG asymmetry as a vulnerability marker for psychopathology is to be realized, such inconsistencies must be resolved. One potential reason for these inconsistencies, recently discussed by Coan and colleagues (Coan, Allen, & McKnight, 2006), concerns the conditions under which frontal EEG asymmetries are typically recorded.

Individual differences in frontal EEG asymmetry are usually obtained under "resting" conditions, during which participants are instructed to relax, rest their eyes, or focus their attention on a fixation point, for the purpose of estimating of their "true" or absolute level of frontal EEG asymmetry. Fundamental individual dispositions are thought to manifest in the absence of strong contextual demands. The currently dominant model of frontal EEG asymmetry and affective style—what Coan and colleagues (Coan, Allen, & McKnight, 2006) have called the *dispositional model*—assumes that, all else being equal, individuals have a single true asymmetry score that accurately reflects their affective style and that is independent of situational factors, such as the particular demands of a given emotional situation. According to this perspective, if under optimal resting conditions (or other conditions in which situational influences on frontal EEG asymmetry are perfectly controlled or eliminated), a person manifests relatively greater right- than left-frontal cortical activity, that person is assumed to possess a disposition to respond across most situations with withdrawal-related affect. This withdrawal-related affective predisposition might place such individuals at increased risk for psychopathology.

Coan, Allen, and McKnight (2006) proposed that overreliance on this traditional dispositional model of frontal EEG asymmetry might be responsible for inconsistencies both within and across laboratories in assessing the role of frontal EEG asymmetry in emotion and psychopathology. This is the case because measures of frontal EEG asymmetry taken at rest are uncontrolled. The uncontrolled nature of such tasks allows for a great deal of variability in participant cognitive and emotional states—variability that may attenuate meaningful associations between frontal EEG asymmetry, emotion, and psychopathology. Such uncontrolled sources of variance could derive from, for example, the quality of a person's previous night of sleep, level of hunger, alcohol consumption, or relationship status. When uncontrolled sources of variance such as these are allowed to contribute to a given estimate of frontal EEG asymmetry, it may become more difficult to detect the signal of interest, such as relatively greater right prefrontal activity (putatively withdrawal motivation) that may indicate risk for affective psychopathology.

Accordingly, Coan, Allen, and McKnight (2006) argued that the resting condition is not optimal for assessing individual differences in frontal EEG asymmetry that are relevant to affective style and risk for psychopathology. Overreliance on the resting condition leaves open the question of how individual differences in brain systems implicated in the development of psychopathology actually manifest under stressful conditions—conditions thought to contribute critically to psychopathology in diathesis-stress formulations. For example, although an individual may indeed be at risk for psychopathology, an endophenotypic marker of that risk may only manifest in the presence of relevant stimuli (cf., Allen & Di Parsia, 2002). Put another way, a person at risk for depression may manifest relatively greater right-frontal activity during an evaluative social situation, but not during a pleasant reunion with an old friend or, as in the ideal form of the resting task, when in a passive, neutral state.

To deal with this problem, Coan, Allen, and McKnight (2006) proposed a *capability model* of frontal EEG asymmetry that conceptualized affective styles as emotion-regulatory abilities instead of more passive emotional predispositions. The practical consequence of this conceptualization is that the optimal measurement of individual differences in frontal EEG asymmetry is likely to require carefully controlled emotional challenges that expose individual capabilities for regulating emotional responses. In support of this position, Coan, Allen, and McKnight (2006) provided empirical evidence that individual differences in frontal EEG asymmetry are (a) more pronounced during emotional challenges than at "rest," (b) more resistant to measurement error during emotional challenges than during resting tasks, and (c) more reliable in their association with criterion measures during emotional challenges than at rest.

Coan, Allen, and McKnight (2006) noted that a pressing methodological issue related to the capability model concerns the recording conditions under which individual differences in frontal EEG asymmetry are most reliable and "diagnostic" (cf., Mischel, Shoda, & Mendoza-Denton, 2002). That is, the field must identify which classes of stimuli or experimental recording situations, outside of the resting situation, provide access to individual differences in frontal EEG asymmetry most aligned with affective style and risk for psychopathology. There are many possibilities related to this question. Apart from, for example, the simple distinction between the resting task and some emotional task, it may be that the most meaningful and predictive individual differences in frontal EEG asymmetry manifest during the anticipation of emotional stimuli (e.g., Shankman et al., 2007; Zinser et al., 1999). Alternatively, the recovery period following an emotional stimulus may be of primary importance. A related point, explored in more detail in the following, concerns the analysis of *change* in frontal EEG asymmetry.

FRONTAL EEG ASYMMETRY AND EVERYDAY EXPERIENCE

In recent years, great strides have been made in *experience sampling*—the assessment of daily emotional experience and responding. Diary methods are now routinely used to track daily affect, both generally and in specific situations (Bolger, Davis, & Rafaeli, 2003). With such tools, assessments of individual differences in emotional responding have reached unprecedented levels of detail, and have been applied to a wide variety of life situations, from exchanges in the workplace (Conway & Briner, 2002), to marital interactions (Laurenceau, Barrett, & Rovine, 2005), feelings of loneliness (Hawkley et al., 2003), and responses to parental demands (Almeida, Wethington, & Chandler, 1999). Moreover, recent developments in experience sampling may ease costs attributable to data-collection materials (e.g., hand-held computers) and subject burden (e.g., Kahneman, Krueger, Schkade, Schwarz, & Stone, 2004).

To date, no studies have used experience sampling in testing affective models of frontal EEG asymmetry. Doing so would offer a great deal more insight into the degree to which the emotion-regulatory capabilities frontal EEG asymmetries are thought to index actually manifest in ordinary life situations. In turn, such findings may lead to insights into the role of affective style in the development of psychopathology. Tests of the diathesis-stress model might be optimized with measures of affective responses to specific situations occurring in real time, and relatively free of strict experimental control. For example, individual differences in frontal EEG asymmetry recorded during laboratory emotional challenges emphasizing social evaluation may moderate associations between current social support levels and psychopathology. If individual differences in EEG asymmetry indeed interact with situational demands to influence the likelihood of psychopathology, the circle of measured affective responses and situational demands must be widened to include situations that occur naturally outside of the specific constraints of the laboratory. Experience sampling methods offer this possibility.

FRONTAL EEG ASYMMETRY AND TIME

A related point concerns the analysis of time. Most studies of individual differences in frontal EEG asymmetry related to risk for psychopathology use mean levels of brain activity, often collapsed across 8-minute resting conditions. Some studies of state EEG asymmetry appeal to "change" scores between some emotional challenge and a resting condition. Although it is tempting to interpret scores computed in this way as actual measures of change across time, this is only true in instances in which one condition directly follows another. Otherwise, such "change" scores are simply difference scores—mean differences in amplitude attributable to different experimental situations. Davidson (1998a) has outlined the need for including time information in the study of frontal EEG asymmetry as well as other affective measures potentially related to psychopathology. He identified at least three components that need to be better understood, which may lead to a more informed science of the neural markers of risk for psychopathology. These components were referred to as *rise time to peak, peak amplitude*, and *recovery time*. Individual differences in any of these parameters could be meaningfully implicated in emotional responding and risk for psychopathology.

The rise time to peak refers to the speed with which a given response, in this instance frontal EEG asymmetry, changes from some initial value to a peak level of activation in response to an experimental situation. At the very least, the computation of the rise time to peak assumes a measured initial value and a peak value. Theoretically, the change score referred to previously would provide a measure of rise time to peak if indeed the initial value always preceded the peak value, and some experimental situation was instantiated between the two measurements. Other options for measuring rise time to peak may exist as well, and newer analyses (e.g., multilevel modeling), as well as improvements in data-collection hardware and software, make more sophisticated approaches to understanding the rise time to peak tenable. These may include, for example, multiple samples of alpha power throughout the period of stimulus presentation, and the modeling of these multiple samples to include time (e.g., slopes indexing change). To date, no researchers have pursued this strategy.

Individual differences in the peak amplitude of frontal EEG asymmetry—the maximum degree of change in the measure in response to some experimental situation—are likely to be found and likely to be meaningful. This point is closely related to the issue raised by Coan, Allen, and McKnight. (2006) in their description of the capability model, which states that individual differences in frontal EEG asymmetries are likely to reflect emotion-regulation capabilities that may in turn be optimally meaningful when measured in the context of an emotional challenge. Interest in peak amplitude raises similar questions about the widespread dependence upon resting tasks as well, because resting tasks preclude identification of anything like a peak amplitude measure of frontal EEG asymmetry. Interestingly, Davidson (1998) also described the possibility of measuring individual differences in *activation threshold*—the quantity of stimulus required to cause a given individual to respond. Stimulus thresholds could be similarly framed in terms of a capability model of frontal EEG activity, and may indeed hold significant consequences for our understanding of psychopathology risk. Moreover, and as with peak amplitude, stimulus thresholds are irrelevant in the context of resting measurement.

Finally, recovery times following the peak amplitude of a response are essentially the same as rise times to peak, but in the opposite direction, following rather than preceding the peak amplitude. Although recovery times of EEG asymmetry per se have not been examined, EEG asymmetry has predicted the duration of affective responses assessed via affectively modulated EMG startle (Jackson et al., 2003). As with both rise times and peak amplitudes, recovery times may hold essential information about individual risk for psychopathology. Indeed, it is possible that some of these parameters have more consequences for some forms of psychopathology than others. For example, depressed individuals may "hold on" to particular patterns of activation for longer time periods than controls. All of these parameters could, with sufficient sampling across time, be measured in the context of a single model, using MLM and other data-analytic procedures. These possibilities are all quite rich and remain to be examined in future work.

SOCIOCULTURAL SITUATIONS AND FACTORS

It could be said that the most common context within which emotional behavior occurs, and occurs most intensely, is interpersonal (Roberts, Tsai, & Coan, 2007). There is little doubt that frontal EEG asymmetries are implicated in social responding. Numerous findings now indicate that relatively greater right-frontal activity is associated with greater social inhibition (Fox et al., 1995), lower sociability (Schmidt & Fox, 1994), higher levels of shyness (Schmidt, 1999), and intense social fear (Davidson et al., 2000). Missing from many of these studies, however, is how frontal EEG asymmetries function in social bonding, social support and caretaking, and attachment (e.g., Fox & Davidson, 1991). Increasing evidence suggests that emotional behavior is tightly linked to the formation of attachment bonds and the social regulation of emotion (Coan, Schaefer, & Davidson, 2006; Insel & Fernald, 2004). Increased attention to the role of prefrontal asymmetries in these processes stands to benefit both the study of interpersonal behavior and frontal EEG asymmetry, and, indeed, both are increasingly implicated in the etiology of many forms of psychopathology, some quite severe.

Related to social behavior are sociodemographic factors about which very little is known from the perspective of frontal EEG asymmetry and affective style. An important recent exception to this concerns the relationship between frontal EEG asymmetry and socioeconomic status (SES) (Tomarken et al., 2004). In this work, higher SES corresponded with relatively greater left-frontal brain activity at rest. Interestingly, SES has long-been implicated in the development of psychopathology (Leventhal & Brooks-Gunn, 2000; Truong & Ma, 2006). Tomarken and colleagues (2004) noted that explanations for the relationship between frontal EEG asymmetry and SES may include a variety of stressors associated not only with low SES, but also increased risk for psychopathology, including decreased levels of maternal warmth, peer-group instability, fewer opportunities for social support, or decreased cognitive stimulation. We note that many of these additional risk factors—any one or combination of which may be related to frontal EEG asymmetry in determining psychopathology—lie in the interpersonal domain. By expanding attention to a wider variety of social processes and sociodemographic factors, the role of frontal EEG asymmetry in psychopathology might be further clarified.

CONCLUDING REMARKS

Frontal EEG asymmetry—a putative measure of affective style—is implicated in emotional responding and psychopathology. Thus far, the status of frontal EEG asymmetries as a marker of risk for psychopathology is uncertain, but an increasing body of evidence suggests it may indeed function as a liability marker of risk for depression and anxiety. Although preliminary evidence suggests it may ultimately serve as a marker of genetically influenced risk for these disorders (i.e., an endophenotype), the probability of this latter possibility does not seem strong. In any case, if frontal EEG asymmetry is ultimately going to offer clinical utility, it will have to be understood in much greater depth, and a large number of questions regarding its optimal measurement conditions will need to be resolved. Among the measurement issues for which resolution may be particularly important concerns the conditions under which individual differences in frontal EEG asymmetry are optimally measured—measurement conditions that constitute *diagnostic situations*. The identification of such situations is going to require researchers in this area to creatively expand their methodological explorations. Several steps may facilitate these goals, including: (a) working toward understanding the neural generators of frontal EEG asymmetries manifest in scalp recordings; (b) conceptualizing individual differences in frontal EEG asymmetry as reflecting capabilities for emotion regulation in specific situations rather than dispositions to respond in a particular way across situations; (c) using experience sampling techniques for the purpose of understanding the role of frontal EEG asymmetries in every day emotional responding, or in response to specific kinds of environmental events; (d) attending to the time course of responding in frontal EEG asymmetry; and (e) paying greater attention to the function of frontal EEG asymmetries in social contexts, including consideration of sociodemographic factors.

When discussing the role of frontal EEG asymmetry as both a measure of affective style and a marker of risk, a valid objection is that such a marker would have little practical value even if all methodological difficulties were resolved and a frontal EEG asymmetry measure of great specificity and sensitivity resulted. Admittedly, the procedure is far too cumbersome to be used, for example, in some way analogous to tests for scoliosis, given en masse to grade school children across the United States, in some kind of effort to screen for potential depression risk. The costs of simple EEG assessments have, however, decreased dramatically in the last decade, just as computing and analysis power has advanced exponentially. Although frontal EEG asymmetry may never serve practically as a screening instrument to preempt the initial onset of psychopathology, it may yet prove very useful as an assessment of severity, prognosis, or risk for relapse, even in the near future. Moreover, if validated as an indicator of risk, further examinations may discover well-validated correlates of frontal EEG asymmetry that themselves are well-suited to screening and prospective identification of large numbers of at-risk individuals. Finally, the potential of such findings for influencing theory both with regard to normative affective style and to the development of psychopathology is likely in any case to be great. It is with these thoughts in mind that the future of research in this area is anticipated with great enthusiasm.

REFERENCES

Allen, J. J., Iacono, W. G., Depue, R. A., & Arbisi, P. (1993). Regional electroencephalographic asymmetries in bipolar seasonal affective disorder before and after exposure to bright light. *Biological Psychiatry, 33,* 642–646.

Allen, J. J. B., Coan, J. A., & Nazarian, M. (2004). Issues and assumptions on the road from raw signals to metrics of frontal EEG asymmetry in emotion. *Biological Psychology, 67,* 183–218.

Allen, J. J. B., Urry, H. L., Hitt, S. K., & Coan, J. A. (2004). The stability of resting frontal electroencephalographic asymmetry in depression. *Psychophysiology, 41,* 269–280.

Allen, N. B., & Di Parsia, P. (2002). Effects of mood induction on startle modulation by social threat in individuals with and without a history of depression. *Psychophysiology, 39,* S5.

Almeida, D. M., Wethington, E., & Chandler, A. L. (1999). Daily transmission of tensions between marital dyads and parent-child dyads. *Journal of Marriage & Family, 61,* 49–61.

Anderson, N. B., & Scott, P. A. (1999). Making the case for psychophysiology during the era of molecular biology. *Psychophysiology, 36,* 1–13.

Anderson, S. W., Bechara, A., Damasio, H., Tranel, D., & Damasio, A. R. (1999). Impairment of social and moral behavior related to early damage in the human prefrontal cortex. *Nature Neuroscience, 2,* 1032–1037.

Ashby, F. G., Isen, A. M., & Turken, A. U. (1999). A neuropsychological theory of positive affect and its influence on cognition. *Psychological Review, 106,* 529–550.

Baron, R. M., & Kenny, D. (1986). The moderator-mediator variable distinction in social psychological research: Conceptual, strategic, and statistical considerations. *Journal of Personality and Social Psychology, 51,* 1173–1182.

Berman, R. M., Narasimhan, M., & Charney, D. S. (1997). Treatment-refractory depression: definitions and characteristics. *Depression and Anxiety, 5,* 154–164.

Berridge, K. C., & Robinson, T. E. (2003). Parsing reward. *Trends in Neuroscience, 26,* 507–513.

Bolger, N., Davis, A., & Rafaeli, E. (2003). Diary methods: Capturing life as it is lived. *Annual Review of Psychology, 54,* 579–616.

Brady, E. U., & Kendall, P. C. (1992). Comorbidity of anxiety and depression in children and adolescents. *Psychological Bulletin, 111,* 244–255.

Brenner, S. L., Beauchaine, T. P., & Sylvers, P. D. (2005). A comparison of psychophysiological and self-report measures of BAS and BIS activation. *Psychophysiology, 42,* 108–115.

Bruder, G. E., Stewart, J. W., Tenke, C. E., McGrath, P. J., Leite, P., Bhattacharya, N., et al. (2001). Electroencephalographic and perceptual asymmetry differences between responders and nonresponders to an SSRI antidepressant. *Biological Psychiatry, 49,* 416–425.

Carroll, B. J. (1982). The dexamethasone suppression test for melancholia. *British Journal of Psychiatry, 140,* 292–304.

Carver, C. S. (2004). Negative affects deriving from the behavioral approach system. *Emotion, 4,* 3–22.

Carver, C. S., & White, T. L. (1994). Behavioral inhibition, behavioral activation, and affective responses to impending reward and punishment: The BIS/BAS Scales. *Journal of Personality & Social Psychology, 67,* 319–333.

Chua, P., Krams, M., Toni, I., Passingham, R., & Dolan, R. (1999). A functional anatomy of anticipatory anxiety. *NeuroImage, 9,* 563–571.

Coan, J. A. (2003). *The heritability of trait frontal EEG asymmetry and negative emotionality: Sex differences and genetic nonadditivity.* Unpublished doctoral dissertation, University of Arizona.

Coan, J. A., & Allen, J. J. B. (2003). Frontal EEG asymmetry and the behavioral activation and inhibition systems. *Psychophysiology, 40,* 106–114.

Coan, J. A., & Allen, J. J. B. (2004). Frontal EEG asymmetry as a moderator and mediator of emotion. *Biological Psychology, 67,* 7–49.

Coan, J. A., Allen, J. J. B., & Harmon-Jones, E. (2001). Voluntary facial expression and hemispheric asymmetry over the frontal cortex. *Psychophysiology, 38,* 912–925.

Coan, J. A., Allen, J. J. B., & McKnight, P. E. (2006). A capability model of individual differences in frontal EEG asymmetry. *Biological Psychology, 72,* 198–207.

Coan, J. A., Schaefer, H. S., & Davidson, R. J. (2006). Lending a hand: Social regulation of the neural response to threat. *Psychological Science, 17,* 1032–1039.

Conway, N., & Briner, R. B. (2002). A daily diary study of affective responses to psychological contract breach and exceeded promises. *Journal of Organizational Behavior, 23,* 287–302.

Corr, P. J. (2004). Reinforcement sensitivity theory and personality. *Neuroscience and Biobehavioral Reviews, 28,* 317–332.

Craig, A. D. (2005). Forebrain emotional asymmetry: A neuroanatomical basis? *Trends in Cognitive Science, 9,* 566–571.

Damasio, A. R., Grabowski, T. J., Bechara, A., Damasio, H., Ponto, L. L. B., Parvizi, J., et al. (2000). Subcortical and cortical brain activity during the feeling of self-generated emotions. *Nature Neuroscience, 3,* 1049–1056.

Davidson, R. J. (1992a). Emotion and affective style: Hemispheric substrates. *Psychological Science, 3,* 39–43.

Davidson, R. J. (1992b). Prolegomenon to the structure of emotion: Gleanings from neuropsychology. *Cognition and Emotion, 6,* 245–268.

Davidson, R. J. (1994). Asymmetric brain function, affective style, and psychopathology: The role of early experience and plasticity. *Development and Psychopathology, 6,* 741–758.

Davidson, R. J. (1998a). Affective style and affective disorders: Perspectives from affective neuroscience. *Cognition & Emotion, 12,* 307–330.

Davidson, R. J. (1998b). Anterior electrophysiological asymmetries, emotion, and depression: Conceptual and methodological conundrums. *Psychophysiology, 35,* 607–614.

Davidson, R. J. (2000). Affective style, psychopathology, and resilience: Brain mechanisms and plasticity. *American Psychologist, 55,* 1196–1214.

Davidson, R. J. (2002). Anxiety and affective style: Role of prefrontal cortex and amygdala. *Biological Psychiatry, 51,* 68–80.

Davidson, R. J. (2004a). Affective style: Causes and consequences. In J. T. Cacioppo & G. G. Berntson (Eds.), *Essays in social neuroscience* (pp. 77–91). Cambridge: MIT Press.

Davidson, R. J. (2004b). What does the prefrontal cortex "do" in affect: Perspectives in frontal EEG asymmetry research. *Biological Psychology, 67,* 219–234.

Davidson, R. J., Ekman, P., Saron, C. D., Senulis, J. A., & Friesen, W. V. (1990). Approach/withdrawal and cerebral asymmetry: Emotional expression and brain physiology. Vol. I: *Journal of Personality and Social Psychology, 58,* 330–341.

Davidson, R. J., & Fox, N. A. (1989). Frontal brain asymmetry predicts infants' response to maternal separation. *Journal of Abnormal Psychology, 98,* 127–131.

Davidson, R. J., Marshall, J. R., Tomarken, A. J., & Henriques, J. B. (2000). While a phobic waits: regional brain electrical and autonomic activity in social phobics during anticipation of public speaking. *Biological Psychiatry, 47,* 85–95.

Dawson, G., Frey, K., Panagiotides, H., Osterling, J., & Hessl, D. (1997). Infants of depressed mothers exhibit atypical frontal brain activity: A replication and extension of previous findings. *Journal of Child Psychology and Psychiatry & Allied Disciplines, 38,* 179–186.

Dawson, G., Frey, K., Panagiotides, H., Yamada, E., Hessl, D., & Osterling, J. (1999a). Infants of depressed mothers exhibit atypical frontal electrical brain activity during interactions with mother and with a familiar, nondepressed adult. *Child Development, 70,* 1058–1066.

Dawson, G., Frey, K., Self, J., Panagiotides, H., Hessl, D., Yamada, E., et al. (1999b). Frontal brain electrical activity in infants of depressed and nondepressed mothers: Relation to variations in infant behavior. *Development and Psychopathology, 11,* 589–605.

Debener, S., Beauducel, A., Nessler, D., Brocke, B., Heilemann, H., & Kayser, J. (2000). Is resting anterior EEG alpha asymmetry a trait marker for depression? Findings for healthy adults and clinically depressed patients. *Neuropsychobiology, 41,* 31–37.

Depue, R. A., & Iacono, W. G. (1989). Neurobehavioral aspects of affective disorders. *Annual Review of Psychology, 40,* 457–492.

Depue, R. A., Krauss, S. P., & Spoont, M. R. (1987). A two-dimensional threshold model of seasonal bipolar affective disorder. In D. Magnusson & A. Ohman (Eds.), *Psychopathology: An interactional perspective* (pp. 95–123). Orlando, FL: Academic Press.

Engels, A. S., Heller, W., Mohanty, A., Herrington, J. D., Banich, M. T., Webb, A. G., et al. (2007). Specificity of regional brain activity in anxiety types during emotion processing. *Psychophysiology, 44,* 352–363.

Fawcett, J., & Maas, J. W. (1972). Depression and MHPG excretion. Response to dextro-amphetamine and tricyclic antidepressants. *Archives of General Psychiatry, 26,* 246–251.

Field, T., Fox, N., Pickens, J., & Nawrocki, T. (1995). Relative right frontal EEG activation in 3- to 6-month-old infants of "depressed" mothers. *Developmental Psychology, 31,* 358–363.

Finkel, D., & McGue, M. (1997). Sex differences and nonadditivity in heritability of the Multidimensional Personality Questionnaire Scales. *Journal of Personality & Social Psychology, 72,* 929–938.

Fox, N. A., Bell, M. A., & Jones, N. A. (1992). Individual differences in response to stress and cerebral asymmetry. *Developmental Neuropsychology, 8,* 161–184.

Fox, N. A., & Davidson, R. J. (1991). Hemispheric specialization and attachment behaviors: Developmental processes and individual differences in separation protest. In J. L. Gewirtz & W. M. Kurtines (Eds.), *Intersection points in attachment research* (pp. 147–164). Hillsdale, NJ: Erlbaum.

Fox, N. A., Rubin, K. H., Calkins, S. D., Marshall, T. R., Coplan, R. J., Porges, S. W., et al. (1995). Frontal activation asymmetry and social competence at four years of age. *Child Development, 66,* 1770–1784.

Gainotti, G. (1972). Emotional behavior and hemispheric side of the lesion. *Cortex, 8,* 41–55.

Gotlib, I. H., Ranganath, C., & Rosenfeld, J. P. (1998). Frontal EEG alpha asymmetry, depression, and cognitive functioning. *Cognition and Emotion, 12,* 449–478.

Gottesman, I. I., & Gould, T. D. (2003). The Endophenotype concept in psychiatry: Etymology and strategic intentions. *American Journal of Psychiatry, 160,* 636–645.

Gould, T. D., & Gottesman, I. I. (2006). Psychiatric endophenotypes and the development of valid animal models. *Genes Brain and Behavior, 5,* 113–119.

Gray, J. A. (1972). The psychophysiological basis of introversion-extraversion: A modification of Eysenck's theory. In V. D. Nebylitsyn & J. A. Gray (Eds.), *The biological bases of individual behavior* (pp. 182–205). San Diego: Academic Press.

Gray, J. A. (1987). *The psychology of fear and stress* (2nd ed.). Cambridge, UK: Cambridge University Press.

Gray, J. A. (1994). Three fundamental Emotion Systems. In P. Ekman & R. J. Davidson (Eds.), *The nature of emotion* (pp. 243–247). New York: Oxford University Press.

Gray, J. A., & McNaughton, N. (2000). *The neuropsychology of anxiety* (2nd ed.). New York: Oxford University Press.

Gray, E. K., & Watson, D. (2007). Assessing positive and negative affect via self report. In J. A. Coan & J. J. B. Allen (Ed.), *Handbook of Emotion Elicitation and Assessment* (pp. 171–183). New York: Oxford University Press.

Hagemann, D. (2004). Individual differences in anterior EEG-asymmetry: Methodological problems and solutions. *Biological Psychology, 67,* 157–182.

Hagemann, D., Naumann, E., Becker, G., Maier, S., & Bartussek, D. (1998). Frontal brain asymmetry and affective style: a conceptual replication. *Psychophysiology, 35,* 372–388.

Hagemann, D., Naumann, E., & Thayer, J. F. (2001). The quest for the EEG reference revisited: A glance from brain asymmetry research. *Psychophysiology, 38,* 847–857.

Hagemann, D., Naumann, E., Thayer, J. F., & Bartussek, D. (2002). Does resting electroencephalograph asymmetry reflect a trait?: An application of latent state-trait theory. *Journal of Personality and Social Psychology, 82,* 619–641.

Harmon-Jones, E. (2006). Unilateral right-hand contractions cause contralateral alpha power suppression and approach motivational affective experience. *Psychophysiology, 43,* 598–603.

Harmon-Jones, E., Abramson, L. Y., Sigelman, J., Bohlig, A., Hogan, M. E., & Harmon-Jones, C. (2002). Proneness to hypomania/mania symptoms or depression symptoms and asymmetrical frontal cortical responses to an anger-evoking event. *Journal of Personality and Social Psychology, 82,* 610–618.

Harmon-Jones, E., & Allen, J. J. B. (1997). Behavioral activation sensitivity and resting frontal EEG asymmetry: Covariation of putative indicators related to risk for mood disorders. *Journal of Abnormal Psychology, 106,* 159–163.

Harmon-Jones, E., & Allen, J. J. B. (1998). Anger and frontal brain activity: EEG asymmetry consistent with approach motivation despite negative affective valence. *Journal of Personality and Social Psychology, 74,* 1310–1316.

Hawkley, L. C., Burleson, M. H., Berntson, G. G., & Cacioppo, J. T. (2003). Loneliness in everyday life: Cardiovascular activity, psychosocial context, and health behaviors. *Journal of Personality and Social Psychology, 85,* 105–120.

Heller, W., Etienne, M. A., & Miller, G. A. (1995). Patterns of perceptual asymmetry in depression and anxiety: implications for neuropsychological models of emotion and psychopathology. *Journal of Abnormal Psychology, 104,* 327–333.

Heller, W., & Nitschke, J. B. (1998). The puzzle of regional brain activity in depression and anxiety: The importance of subtypes and comorbidity. *Cognition and Emotion, 12,* 421–447

Heller, W., Nitschke, J. B., Etienne, M. A., & Miller, G. A. (1997). Patterns of regional brain activity differentiate types of anxiety. *Journal of Abnormal Psychology, 106,* 376–385.

Henderson, H. A., Fox, N. A., & Rubin, K. H. (2001). Temperamental contributions to social behavior: The moderating roles of frontal EEG asymmetry and gender. *Journal of the American Academy of Child and Adolescent Psychiatry, 40,* 68–74.

Henriques, J. B., & Davidson, R. J. (1990). Regional brain electrical asymmetries discriminate between previously depressed and healthy control subjects. *Journal of Abnormal Psychology, 99,* 22–31.

Henriques, J. B., & Davidson, R. J. (1991). Left frontal hypoactivation in depression. *Journal of Abnormal Psychology, 100,* 535–545.

Iacono, W. G. (1998). Identifying psychophysiological risk for psychopathology: Examples from substance abuse and schizophrenia research. *Psychophysiology, 35,* 621–637.

Iacono, W. G., & Ficken, J. W. (1989). Research strategies employing psychophysiological measures: Identifying and using psychophysiological markers. In G. Turpin (Ed.), *Handbook of clinical psychophysiology* (pp. 45–70). New York: Wiley.

Insel, T. R., & Fernald, R. D. (2004). How the brain processes social information: Searching for the social brain. *Annual Review of Neuroscience, 27,* 697–722.

Jackson, D. C., Mueller, C. J., Dolski, I., Dalton, K. M., Nitschke, J. B., Urry, H. L. et al. (2003). Now you feel it, now you don't: Frontal brain electrical asymmetry and individual differences in emotion regulation. *Psychological Science, 14,* 612–617.

Jones, N. A., & Field, T. (1999). Massage and music therapies attenuate frontal EEG asymmetry in depressed adolescents. *Adolescence, 34,* 529–534.

Jones, N. A., Field, T., & Davalos, M. (1998). Massage therapy attenuates right frontal EEG asymmetry in one-month-old infants of depressed mothers. *Infant Behavior and Development, 21,* 527–530.

Jones, N. A., Field, T., Davalos, M., & Pickens, J. (1997). EEG stability in infants / children of depressed mothers. *Child Psychiatry and Human Development, 28,* 59–70.

Jones, N. A., & Fox, N. A. (1992). Electroencephalogram asymmetry during emotionally evocative films and its relation to positive and negative affectivity. *Brain and Cognition, 20,* 280–299.

Kahneman, D., Krueger, A. B., Schkade, D. A., Schwarz, N., & Stone, A. A. (2004). A Survey Method for Characterizing Daily Life Experience: The Day Reconstruction Method. *Science, 306,* 1776–1780.

Kalin, N. H., Larson, C., Shelton, S. E., & Davidson, R. J. (1998). Asymmetric frontal brain activity, cortisol, and behavior associated with fearful temperament in rhesus monkeys. *Behavioral Neuroscience, 112,* 286–292.

Kalin, N. H., Shelton, S. E., Davidson, R. J., & Kelley, A. E. (2001). The primate amygdala mediates acute fear but not the behavioral and physiological components of anxious temperament. *Journal of Neuroscience, 21,* 2067–2074.

Kraemer, H. C., Stice, E., Kazdin, A., Offord, D., & Kupfer, D. (2001). How do risk factors work together? Mediators, moderators, and independent, overlapping, and proxy risk factors. *American Journal of Psychiatry, 158,* 848–856.

Krueger, R. F., & Markon, K. E. (2006). Reinterpreting comorbidity: A model-based approach to understanding and classifying psychopathology. *Annual Review of Clinical Psychology, 2,* 111–133.

Kupfer, D. J. (1995). Sleep research in depressive illness: Clinical implications—A tasting menu. *Biological Psychiatry, 38,* 391–403.

Laakso, A., Wallius, E., Kajander, J., Bergman, J., Eskola, O. Solin, O., Ilonen, T., Salokangas, R. K. R., Syvälahti, E., & Hietala, J. (2003). Personality traits and striatal dopamine synthesis capacity in healthy subjects. *American Journal of Psychiatry, 160,* 904–910.

Laurenceau, J.-P., Barrett, L. F., & Rovine, M. J. (2005). The Interpersonal Process Model of Intimacy in Marriage: A Daily-Diary and Multilevel Modeling Approach. *Journal of Family Psychology, 19,* 314–323.

Leventhal, T., & Brooks-Gunn, J. (2000). The neighborhoods they live in: The effects of neighborhood residence on child and adolescent outcomes. *Psychological Bulletin, 126,* 309–337.

Luu, P., Collins, P., & Tucker, D. M. (2000). Mood, personality, and self-monitoring: Negative affect and emotionality in relation to frontal lobe mechanisms of error monitoring. *Journal of Experimental Psychology General, 129,* 43–60.

Lykken, D. T., Tellegen, A., & Iacono, W. G. (1982). EEG spectra in twins: Evidence for a neglected mechanism of genetic determination. *Physiological Psychology, 10,* 60–65.

Mayberg H. S., Liotti M., Brannan S. K. , McGinnis S., Mahurin, R. K., Jerabek P. A., et al. (1999). Reciprocal limbic-cortical function and negative mood: Converging PET findings in depression and normal sadness. *American Journal of Psychiatry. 156*, 675–682.

Mischel, W., Shoda, Y., & Mendoza-Denton, R. (2002). Situation-behavior profiles as a locus of consistency in personality. *Current Directions in Psychological Science, 11*, 50–54.

Nitschke, J. B., Heller, W., Palmieri, P. A., & Miller, G. A. (1999). Contrasting patterns of brain activity in anxious apprehension and anxious arousal. *Psychophysiology, 36*, 628–637.

Oakes, T. R., Pizzagalli, D. A., Hendrick, A. M., Horras, K. A., Larson, C. L., Abercrombie, H. C., et al. (2004). Functional coupling of simultaneous electrical and metabolic activity in the human brain. *Human Brain Mapping, 21*, 257–270.

Paquette, V., Levesque, J., Mensour, B., Leroux, J. M., Beaudoin, G., Bourgouin, P., et al. (2003). "Change the mind and you change the brain": Effects of cognitive-behavioral therapy on the neural correlates of spider phobia. *Neuroimage, 18*, 401–409.

Raine, A. J., Meloy, J. R., Bihrle, S., Stoddard, J., LaCasse, L., & Buchsbaum, M. S. (1998). Reduced prefrontal and increased subcortical brain functioning assessed using positron emission tomography in predatory and affective murderers. *Behavioral Sciences and the Law, 16*, 319–332.

Rauch, S. L., Savage, C. R., Alpert, N. M., Fischman, A. J., & Jenike, M. A. (1997). The functional neuroanatomy of anxiety: A study of three disorders using positron emission tomography and symptom provocation. *Biological Psychiatry, 42*, 446–452.

Reid, S. A., Duke, L. M., & Allen, J. J. B. (1998). Resting frontal electroencephalographic asymmetry in depression: inconsistencies suggest the need to identify mediating factors. *Psychophysiology, 35*, 389–404.

Roberts, N. A., Tsai, J. L., & Coan, J. A. (2007). Emotion elicitation using dyadic interaction tasks. In J. A. Coan & J. J. B. Allen (Eds.), *Handbook of emotion elicitation and assessment* (pp. 106–123). New York: Oxford University Press.

Rybak, M., Crayton, J. W., Young, I. J., Herba, E., & Konopka, L. M. (2006). Frontal alpha power asymmetry in aggressive children and adolescents with mood and disruptive behavior disorders. *Journal of Clinical EEG & Neuroscience, 37*, 16–24.

Schaffer, C. E., Davidson, R. J., & Saron, C. (1983). Frontal and parietal electroencephalogram asymmetry in depressed and nondepressed subjects. *Biological Psychiatry, 18*, 753–762.

Schmidt, L. A. (1999). Frontal brain electrical activity in shyness and sociability. *Psychological Science, 10*, 316–320.

Schmidt, L. A., & Fox, N. A. (1994). Patterns of cortical electrophysiology and autonomic activity in adults' shyness and sociability. *Biological Psychology, 38*, 183–198.

Shankman, S. A., Klein, D. N., Tenke, C. E., & Bruder, G. E. (2007). Reward sensitivity in depression: A biobehavioral study. *Journal of Abnormal Psychology, 116*, 95–104.

Smit, D. J. A., Posthuma, D., Boomsma, D. I., & De Geus, E. J. C. (2007). The relation between frontal EEG asymmetry and the risk for anxiety and depression. *Biological Psychology, 74*, 26–33.

Stassen, H. H., Bomben, G., & Hell, D. (1998). Familial brain wave patterns: Study of a 12-sib family. *Psychiatric Genetics, 8,* 141–153.

Stassen, H. H., Lykken, D. T., & Bomben, G. (1988). The within-pair EEG similarity of twins reared apart. *European Archives of Psychiatry and Neurological Sciences, 237,* 244–252.

Sutton, S. K., & Davidson, R. J. (1997). Prefrontal brain asymmetry: A biological substrate of the behavioral approach and inhibition systems. *Psychological Science, 8,* 204–210.

Teasdale, J. D., Howard, R. J., Cox, S, G., Ha, Y., Brammer, M. J., Williams, S. C. R., & Checkley, S. A. (1999). Functional MRI study of the cognitive generation of affect. *American Journal of Psychiatry, 156,* 209–215.

Thibodeau, R., Jorgensen, R. S., & Kim, S. (2006). Depression, anxiety, and resting frontal EEG asymmetry: A meta-analytic review. *Journal of Abnormal Psychology, 115,* 715–729.

Tomarken, A. J., Davidson, R. J., & Henriques, J. B. (1990). Resting frontal brain asymmetry predicts affective responses to films. *Journal of Personality and Social Psychology, 59,* 791–801.

Tomarken, A. J., Davidson, R. J., Wheeler, R. E., & Kinney, L. (1992). Psychometric properties of resting anterior EEG asymmetry: Temporal stability and internal consistency. *Psychophysiology, 29,* 576–592.

Tomarken, A. J., Dichter, G. S., Garber, J., & Simien, C. (2004). Resting frontal brain activity: Linkages to maternal depression and socio-economic status among adolescents. *Biological Psychology, 67,* 77–102.

Tranel, D., Bechara, A., & Denburg, N. L. (2002). Asymmetric functional roles of right and left ventromedial prefrontal cortices in social conduct, decision-making, and emotional processing. *Cortex, 38,* 589–612.

Truong, K. D., & Ma, S. (2006). A systematic review of relations between neighborhoods and mental health. *Journal of Mental Health Policy and Economics, 9,* 137–154.

Turkheimer, E. (1998). Heritability and biological explanation. *Psychological Review, 105,* 782–791.

Van Honk, J., & Schutter, D. J. J. G. (2006). From affective valence to motivational direction: The frontal asymmetry of emotion revised. *Psychological Science, 17,* 963–965.

Wheeler, R. E., Davidson, R. J., & Tomarken, A. J. (1993). Frontal brain asymmetry and emotional reactivity: A biological substrate of affective style. *Psychophysiology, 30,* 82–89.

Wiedemann, G., Pauli, P., Dengler, W., Lutzenberger, W., Birbaumer, N., & Buchkremer, G. (1999). Frontal brain asymmetry as a biological substrate of emotions in patients with panic disorders. *Archives of General Psychiatry, 56,* 78–84.

Zinser, M. C., Fiore, M. C., Davidson, R. J., & Baker, T. B. (1999). Manipulating smoking motivation: Impact on an electrophysiological index of approach motivation. *Journal of Abnormal Psychology, 108,* 240–254.

CHAPTER 10

Emotion Dysregulation As a Risk Factor for Psychopathology

PAMELA M. COLE AND SARAH E. HALL

Emotion regulation is of keen interest in all areas of contemporary psychological science and practice. Emotions play a role in all aspects of human functioning. They are studied in labs, in homes and in public, in the workplace and the classroom, and in the sports arena and the playground. This widespread interest is understandable when we appreciate the basic nature of emotion. Emotions fuel actions that are aimed at maintaining and regaining our well-being. They do so by enabling us to evaluate and cope with events around us—abilities that are critical to survival. Although the modern world differs sharply from that in which emotions first evolved, the continuing importance of emotions for survival is obvious. For example, in the first months of life, infant cries virtually ensure the immediate aid of adults, and infant smiles are central building blocks in the developing relationship between infant and caregiver.

Despite the significance of emotion for human adaptation, it also plays a central role in psychopathology. The concept of emotion regulation helps us understand how emotions, which are so essential for adapting behavior to circumstances, are also implicated in psychological dysfunction. This concept helps us to distinguish the type of emotional responses we have from the ways in which we modulate those responses. Each class of emotion has an important role in maintaining well-being in a complex and ever-changing environment. If well-regulated, emotions support healthy, competent psychological functioning. In clinical work, however, we are keenly aware of patterns of emotion regulation that have acquired a maladaptive quality, such that emotions seem to interfere with functioning. We believe in such cases it is the manner in which emotions are regulated that compromises emotional functioning such that the ability to form and maintain good relationships or to engage in productive activity is impaired. A pattern of emotion regulation is maladaptive when it has a clear cost to the individual.

Keen interest in emotion regulation, particularly from the viewpoint of developmental psychopathology, has led to a growing body of empirical work aimed at documenting individual differences in emotion regulation that distinguish between the development of psychopathology and emotional competence. This is the approach we adopt in studying emotion regulation. We assume that early forms of emotion dysregulation can signal risk for psychopathology, and that early identification of such risk will contribute to a scientific basis for determining when intervention is needed. How does a daycare provider, a parent, or a teacher know if an irritable child is going through a "phase" or is at risk and in need of specialized care? What is the best way to intervene? We also assume, given the plasticity of the brain and behavior in early childhood, that early intervention may prevent later serious clinical outcomes.

In pursuit of these goals, questions arise about the nature of emotion regulation and dysregulation. This is a particularly thorny problem for practitioners and researchers who rely on observations of children to judge the quality of their emotion regulation. Behavioral observations provide the most readily available information for those who care for young children. In this chapter, we focus on the qualities of emotion dysregulation that are observed in children and relate them to adults with psychological problems, from both research and diagnostic perspectives. We discuss what is known about how emotion regulation develops among emotionally competent children and how children who have or are at risk for psychopathology differ. We hope this discussion provides a clinically informed approach to the study of the development of emotion dysregulation.

EMOTION AND EMOTION REGULATION

EMOTION

Before embarking on a discussion of emotion dysregulation, it is wise to clarify our understanding of the nature of emotion. We subscribe to the view that emotions comprise two integrated processes: appraisal and action preparation, which constitute a kind of psychological radar and response readiness system, respectively (e.g., Arnold, 1960; Barrett & Campos, 1987; Ekman & Davidson, 1994; Frijda, 1986; Lazarus, 1991). Appraising is the radar through which we evaluate circumstances in regard to their significance for our well-being. Action preparation is the readiness to respond in a particular manner that enables us to act to regain or maintain well-being. As opposed to the stereotypic view that emotions are disorganizing—compromising reasonable action—we, along with many others, believe that emotions are designed to organize adaptive responses to shifting environmental circumstances (Barrett & Campos, 1987; Frijda, 1986; Lazarus, 1991). Emotions are adaptive because they permit very rapid detection of circumstances that threaten our well-being and permit us to act on our own behalf without delay. Yet at the same time, human beings are also well-equipped to regulate reactions such that the readiness to respond alone does not dictate action.

The appraisal and action preparation processes that define emotion are continual, not occasional states of arousal (Izard, 1971). Emotions are often regarded as periodic states because they are not always observable or even felt consciously. Even when relying on behavioral observations to study emotion, we must appreciate that these ways of understanding emotion are limited in the degree to which they penetrate the full realm of emotional functioning. Emotions are not entities residing within a person that occasionally materialize; rather, emotions are best conceptualized as ongoing processes of relating to changing environments (both actual and perceived) in terms of their significance for well-being (e.g., Barrett & Campos, 1987). Advances in affective neuroscience suggest that emotional functioning is supported by a set of active, dynamic, ongoing processes reflecting organismic adjustments to situational changes (Davidson, 2000), and that these ongoing processes usually operate out of conscious awareness (e.g., LeDoux, 1986).

This view regards emotions as inherently regulatory. Emotions motivate and ready particular types of action that are aimed at specific ways of changing the relation of the person to the environment. As emotions change, other psychological processes are influenced, such as attention and aspects of cognition, in addition to the potentiation of particular kinds of action (Frijda, 1986; Levenson, 2003). Evidence for the regulatory influences of emotion is growing. Emotions focus attention (e.g., Fenske & Raymond, 2006; Hajcak, Molnar, George, Bolger, Koola, & Najas, 2007), facilitate or limit memory processes (e.g., Hamann, 2001; Isen, Shalker, Clark, & Karp, 1978; Ochsner & Schacter, 2000), and facilitate specific motor activities (e.g., Hajcak et al., 2007).

In addition to regulating other processes, emotions are inherently self-regulatory. This is readily observed in the physiological systems that support emotions. The central nervous system is a dynamic, self-organizing biological system, a fact that has become increasingly evident in affective neuroscience research on emotion (Davidson, 2000). As neural transmission from the limbic system—a set of phylogenically older brain regions involved in the generation of emotion—proceeds "forward" through cortical pathways to the prefrontal and orbitofrontal cortices, a set of phylogenically newer brain regions that support regulatory processes (e.g., self-monitoring, effortful reallocation of attention, response inhibition, planning), the brain's neurocircuitry provides ongoing feedback to these and other key areas of the brain. Moreover, studies using functional magnetic resonance imaging (fMRI), eye blink startle, positron emission tomography (PET), and electrophysiology (EEG and ERP) to study these areas of the central nervous system suggest that individuals with psychopathology regulate emotion differently than do nonsymptomatic persons. The extant evidence, however, does not fully explain the complex neural mechanisms that underlie emotion regulation.

Like the central nervous system, the autonomic nervous system, which plays an important role in action readiness, is a self-regulatory system. During a change in emotional state (e.g., an angry or fearful response), neural information directs the heart to increase its rate of output, pumping blood to other muscles and bringing increased oxygen to them, thereby fortifying their readiness to contract. This increased cardiac output, which is facilitated by reduced parasympathetic and increased sympathetic activation of the autonomic system, is crucial in readying action. Indeed, the vagus nerve of the parasympathetic nervous system plays a crucial role in regulating the cardiovascular response. As we breathe, heart rate fluctuates in response to cyclic activation and deactivation of parasympathetic input, which is under control of the vagus nerve. Vagal tone is an index of this heart rate variability. In response to a perceived threat to well-being, there is vagal withdrawal. The coordinated but somewhat independent functioning of the sympathetic and parasympathetic systems is viewed as a set of cardiovascular concomitants of emotion regulation. Evidence indicates that individuals with greater heart rate variability (higher vagal tone) are more emotionally well-regulated (Porges, 2001), perhaps because they have greater autonomic control over emotional responding. Indeed, there is evidence suggesting that higher vagal tone is associated with less negative emotional responses to laboratory challenges (Calkins & Dedmon, 2000; Calkins & Keane, 2004). Perhaps more importantly, children with high vagal tone appear to be buffered from some of the negative sequelae of being reared in adverse familial environments (El-Sheikh, 2005; El-Sheikh, Harger, & Whitson, 2001; Katz & Gottman, 1995, 1997; Shannon et al., in press). In sum, being emotional entails continual processes of evaluating the meaning of, and readying responses to, ever-changing circumstances, a set of processes that both regulate other psychological systems and are inherently self-regulatory.

EMOTION REGULATION

The contemporary view of emotion that we have detailed creates a challenge for defining emotion regulation (Cole, Martin, & Dennis, 2004). How—if at all—does emotion regulation differ from emotional responses (Cicchetti, Ackerman, & Izard, 1995; Campos, Frankel, & Camras, 2004)? This is a particular challenge when we rely on behavioral observations to gauge the adaptiveness of children's emotion regulation. At this level of analysis, the inherent regulatory operations that underlie emotion expression and emotion-related behavior are inaccessible to observation. The facial expression we observe is a product of both a response to changing circumstances and the inherent regulation of the response at levels that are beyond the individual's awareness and ordinary observation.

Despite the limitations of inferring emotion regulation from behavior, there is clinical utility in having behavioral methods to gauge the quality of emotion regulation, even as we appreciate the complexity of unobserved emotional processes. We conceptualize emotion regulation as *changes* in an initial emotional response (i.e., the initial response to circumstances that are perceived to matter for well-being; Cole et al., 2004). If an emotion reflects a change in the relation of the individual to circumstances, then emotion regulation refers to the modulation of that response. As an emotional response unfolds, psychological processes can be recruited to modulate the initial response—we can shift attention, recall memories that intensify or reduce the emotion, reappraise the situation, or take instrumental action. These may alter the temporal dynamics of the emotion or change the emotion (Davidson, 2000; Thompson, 1994). Such inferences require rigorous scientific methods. Although they do not reveal the whole nature of emotion, behavioral observations are one method for inferring emotion regulation and dysregulation.

We cannot infer problems in the regulation of emotion solely on the basis of the valence, intensity, or duration of an emotional response. The ability to have quick, intense, and sustained emotion is part of the adaptive nature of emotions. It is the capacity to *regulate* emotional responses that allows us to vary and modulate a response to a situation. Appropriate inferences about emotion regulation can be gleaned from meticulous observations of behavior, including examination of temporal sequences (e.g., observed emotion, behavior, changes in observed emotion), convergence of information based on multiple levels of measurement (behavioral, self-report, and physiological), and strategic manipulations of situational context (Cole et al., 2004). Ultimately, evidence from laboratory studies of physiological processes, along with field and lab research of children's emotion-related behavior in context, have the potential to provide a fuller picture of emotional development and of the trajectories that lead to emotional competence and disorder. This is especially true for the study of emotion regulation in early childhood, a period of rapid neurological and behavioral development when patterns of emotion regulation are being established (e.g., Gunnar & Quevedo, 2007).

In sum, despite the complex nature of emotion, it is possible to conceptualize emotion regulation as changes in initial responses to circumstances that involve the recruitment of other processes (attentional, cognitive, social, and behavioral) to modulate the response (Cole et al., 2004; Gross, 1998). Mental health and emotional competence involve both emotional responsiveness to situations and regulation of emotional responses such that behavior accords to social standards (Eisenberg et al., 1993, 1997; Saarni, 1999).

EMOTION DYSREGULATION

Given the adaptive nature of emotion, it might seem paradoxical that emotion dysregulation figures prominently in contemporary conceptualizations of psychopathology. The view that emotions disrupt or interfere with rationality and propriety is a classical one seen in philosophical treatises of several ancient cultures. Modern science makes a compelling case that emotions are neither irrational nor disruptive by nature. They are organizing, regulated processes. Fear, anger, sadness, joy, interest, guilt, and other emotions are all advantageous for dealing with the complexity of a social world that is constantly changing and often challenging. There is adaptive value in intense or sustained emotion; the elegance of the emotion system is that it has multiple points at which emotional responses can be modified, without the necessity of awareness (Frijda, 1986; Levenson, 2003). Nonetheless, individuals can develop patterns of emotion regulation that appear emotionally dysregulated.

We all have times when our emotions get the better of us. Within a developmental psychopathology framework, such common instances of feeling emotionally "out of control" provide a point of contrast with atypical functioning. The contrast is important because we need to understand variations in typical emotional functioning and how they differ from the emotional symptoms that disrupt and compromise lives. Emotional symptoms are stable patterns of emotion regulation that have particular problematic features *even as they serve the goals of achieving an immediate sense of well-*

being. For instance, by being hostile, the person with Borderline Personality Disorder fends off feeling rejected. In this and other clinical examples, emotions are not unregulated (Cole, Michel, & Teti, 1994); rather, they are regulated in a manner that limits psychological discomfort in some way, but at the expense of relationships, productive activity, or future developmental goals. Such problematic patterns develop when biology and circumstances conspire to override a person's ability to regulate emotions in ways that achieve individual goals for well-being (within situational constraints) and promote the longer-term goals of becoming a competent, healthy person. For example, sustained exposure to stress in early childhood appears to dysregulate the physiological stress response, perhaps depleting the capacity of the organism to maintain a high state of action readiness (e.g., Gunnar & Quevedo, 2007). Emotion dysregulation then refers to dysfunctional or maladaptive patterns of emotion regulation. How then do we distinguish emotion regulation from emotion dysregulation?

EMOTION DYSREGULATION FROM A CLINICAL PERSPECTIVE

Emotion dysregulation is a salient feature of psychopathology (Berenbaum, Raghavan, Le, Vernon, & Gomez, 2003; Cicchetti, Ackerman, & Izard, 1995; Cole, Michel et al., 1994; Gross & Muñoz, 1995; Keenan, 2000). Its prominence is evident in contemporary conceptualizations of many major psychological disorders, including Conduct Disorder, depression, anxiety disorders, Bipolar Disorder, Borderline Personality Disorder, and eating disorders (e.g., Barkley, 1997; Beauchaine, Gatze-Kopp, & Mead, 2007; Gotlib, Joormann, Minor, & Cooney, 2006; Kovacs et al., 2006; Leibenluft, Charney, & Pine, 2003; Linehan, 1993; Mennin, Heimberg, Turk, & Fresco, 2002; Overton, Selway, Strongman, & Houston, 2005). Emotion dysregulation is also evident in the symptom criteria and associated features of disorders identified in the *Diagnostic and Statistical Manual of Mental Disorders–Fourth Edition* (DSM-IV-TR; American Psychiatric Association, 2000; see Table 10.1), even though the system does not theorize about the role of emotion in psychopathology.

The prominence of emotion dysregulation in psychopathology has led many researchers to explore developmental links between early emotional functioning and later symptoms of psychopathology (e.g., Calkins, Dedmon, Gill, Lomax, & Johnson, 2002; Cole, Zahn-Waxler, Fox, Usher, & Welsh, 1996; Gilliom, Shaw, Beck, Schonberg, & Lukon, 2002; Maughan & Cicchetti, 2002). In general, higher levels of negative emotion are associated with concurrent and later adjustment problems and psychopathology.

Table 10.1.

Symptoms of Disorders that Involve Emotional Processes (DSM-IV; APA, 2000)

	Ineffective Strategies	Emotion-Behavior Sequences	Context Inappropriateness	Aberrations of Change
Pervasive developmental disorders	Giggling, weeping for no apparent reason, excessive fearfulness in face of danger	Aggression motivated by distress	Absence of emotional reaction, lack of fear to real dangers	
Disruptive behavior disorders	Being angry/resentful/spiteful/vindictive, poor frustration tolerance, irritability, temper outbursts	Aggression, hostile behavior toward authorities	Lack of guilt/remorse, callousness, little empathy/concern for others, misperceiving others' intentions as hostile/threatening	Being touchy or easily annoyed by others, mood lability
Substance use disorders	Anxiety, depression, extreme anger	Belligerence, aggressive behavior	Inappropriate laughter and grandiosity, affective blunting, paranoid ideation	Mood lability, anhedonia, dysphoria
Schizophrenia			Inappropriate affect, affective flattening	Anhedonia
Mood disorders	Prolonged dysphoria or irritability. Persistent elevated mood	Hostile feelings or behavior	Excessive/inappropriate guilt, diminished interest or pleasure, indiscriminant enthusiasm	Depressed mood, worthlessness, hopelessness, mood lability, abnormal mood

Anxiety-related disorders	Persistent fear, discomfort, anxiety, worry, difficulty controlling these emotions, fear of humiliation or embarrassment	Avoidance	Unreasonable fear, apathy	Marked, excessive, persistent fear
Posttraumatic Stress Disorder	Intense fear/helplessness, poor affect modulation, excessive guilt, shame, despair, feeling constantly threatened	Efforts to avoid feelings associated with the trauma, hostility	Emotional numbing, diminished interest, restricted range of affect (e.g., unable to have loving feelings)	Intense distress at exposure to cues, outbursts of anger
Eating disorders	Intense fear of gaining weight, depressed mood, irritability, feelings of ineffectiveness, depressive symptoms (e.g., low self-esteem), anxiety symptoms	Social withdrawal, binge eating triggered by dysphoric mood states, vomiting to reduce fear of gaining weight	Overly restrained emotional expression	
Personality disorders	Excessive social anxiety, irritability, intense anger, difficulty controlling anger	Hostility, problems in relationships	Pervasive distrust, restricted range of emotions, emotional coldness, flatness, and detachment, lack of empathy, inappropriate anger, need for excessive admiration	Affective instability, marked reactivity of mood, rapidly shifting and shallow emotions

Relations between particular patterns of emotion dysregulation and specific forms of psychopathology, however, remain to be specified. Specificity in predicting such relations will depend upon recognizing that emotion dysregulation is not a matter of "greater" negative emotion. From a clinical perspective, other features constitute emotion dysregulation.

Saarni (1999) provides a conceptual framework for defining emotional competence (see also Halberstadt, Denham, & Dunsmore, 2001; Mayer & Salovey, 2004). In this view, competence includes the ability to experience a full range of emotions, responsiveness to others' emotional states, valuing one's own and others' emotions, appreciating the need to regulate emotion and the ability to do so in ways that fit situational constraints, and a sense of emotional self-efficacy. Emotional dysregulation can be distinguished from the patterns of emotion regulation that constitute emotional competence when we consider the symptoms associated with various forms of psychopathology. As can be gleaned from Table 10.1, emotion dysregulation involves emotional responses with the following characteristics:

a. emotions endure and regulatory attempts are ineffective,
b. emotions interfere with appropriate behavior,
c. emotions that are expressed or experienced are context inappropriate, and
d. emotions either change too abruptly or too slowly.

These qualities are not mutually exclusive. Because they are based on observation, a particular observable symptom could be produced by several or different aspects of dysregulation. As a group, these characteristics share qualities of being unpredictable, inappropriate, and maladaptive. Thus, dysregulation stems not from the fact of being very angry, sad, anxious, ashamed, guilty, proud, or happy, but from deviations from the typical manner in which strong or enduring emotions are regulated (see Cole, Dennis, Martin, & Hall, in press, for a clinical example).

CHARACTERISTICS OF EMOTIONAL DYSREGULATION

Emotions Are Enduring and Regulatory Attempts Are Ineffective

Intense and even enduring emotions are not necessarily dysfunctional, as long as they are regulated effectively. One partner in a couple may sustain strong anger for several days due to something the other partner did; he may even actively work to stay angry in order to emphasize the perceived seriousness of the problem. If the couple has a good relationship, the other partner will come to see how great the concern is; through both mutual and self-regulatory behavior the anger is resolved.

On the other hand, symptoms such as prolonged irritability, sad mood, generalized anxiety, and mania differ from more typical instances of sustained emotion. These symptoms reflect sustained emotion that is unresponsive to efforts to modulation; the reasons for this are likely to be diverse and include lack of skillfulness in executing a regulatory strategy, dysregulation of biological systems that support emotion, and secondary or partial gains for sustaining the prolonged emotion. The sustained emotion is not *un*regulated. Rather, the strategies a person uses to modify the emotion are either ineffective (e.g., avoiding novel situations reduces anxiety but is not ideal in many situations) or are typically effective but used ineffectively (e.g., distraction to stop depressive thinking cannot be maintained long enough to alter mood).

A variety of regulatory strategies can be used to modify the temporal and intensive dynamics of an emotional response—reducing its intensity, shortening its duration, or shifting from one emotion to another (Davidson, 2000; Thompson, 1994). A long list of strategies can be gleaned from the clinical, developmental, and social psychology literatures. Active problem-solving, cognitive reappraisal, exercise, information-seeking, and support-seeking are among the adaptive strategies; avoidance, denial, emotion suppression, rumination, substance use, aggression, and venting are among the less optimal responses (e.g., Folkman & Lazarus, 1980; Grolnick, Bridges, & Connell, 1996; Gross, 1998; Hayes, Wilson, Gifford, Follette, & Strosahl, 1996; Rothbart, Ziaie, & O'Boyle, 1992). Strategies can be grouped as: (a) self-directed efforts to modify internal state (e.g., attention redirection, reappraisal, self-soothing); (b) outward-directed efforts to alter circumstances (e.g., active problem-solving, information and support seeking); and (c) responsiveness to the efforts of others to soothe, redirect, or discourage the emotions of the target person or alter the circumstances for the person. Mentally healthy, emotionally competent individuals are assumed to have a repertoire of strategies from which to choose; to be able to select among them and deploy them effectively and flexibly to fit personal needs and situational constraints; and to be responsive to the regulatory efforts of others (Halberstadt et al., 2001; Lazarus, 1991; Saarni, 1999). Even a less optimal strategy, such as denial, used selectively can be adaptive (Lazarus, 1991).

Developmental considerations.   Caregivers intervene to help infants and young children maintain and regain calm and pleasant states. In so doing, they are promoting the development of self-regulation of emotion (Diener & Mangelsdorf, 1999; Kopp, 1989; Sroufe, 1996; Thompson, 1994), even accounting for individual differences in infant temperament (Calkins, 1994).

Ordinarily, by the time children enter school, they are able to deal with a range of challenges (frustrations, disappointments) and they do not become overly dysregulated by them. Many children, however, face unusual adverse circumstances (e.g., maltreatment, parental psychopathology) that threaten their emotional development, including their ability to effectively regulate emotions (Gunnar & Quevedo, 2007; Maughan & Cicchetti, 2002).

There is evidence of age-related increases in the number and type of strategies children attempt over the first 5 years of life (Grolnick et al., 1996; Mangelsdorf, Shapiro, & Marzolf, 1995; Rothbart et al., 1992; Stansbury & Sigman, 2000), which are assumed to account for parallel decreases in the frequency and intensity of negative emotion. There is, however, limited research on the *effectiveness* of children's emotion regulation strategies, despite the potential importance of this aspect of emotion regulation. Infants spontaneously engage in behaviors that reduce their negative emotion, but these are limited in effectiveness. For instance, infants' efforts to self-comfort or to focus attention when frustrated serve to reduce their distress (Crockenberg & Leerkes, 2004; Stifter & Braungart, 1995), but typically these are momentary reductions and the child becomes upset again if the situation is unchanged. Although much more research is needed, preliminary evidence suggests several factors that influence self-regulatory effectiveness in early childhood. These include the intensity of the initial emotional response (Little & Carter, 2005; Stifter & Braungart, 1995), the availability of the child's caregiver (Diener & Mangelsdorf, 1999), and the type of emotion that is felt (Buss & Goldsmith, 1998; Diener & Mangelsdorf, 1999). For instance, very young children's self-distraction and active problem solving are associated with decreases in anger, but not in fear (Buss & Goldsmith, 1998).

With older children and adolescents, there are also few studies of strategy effectiveness. However, research suggests that shifting attention away from a source of distress effectively decreases negative emotion and/or promotes recovery of calm or positive emotions (Reijntjes, Stegge, Meerum Terwogt, Kamphuis, & Telch, 2006; Silk, Steinberg, & Morris, 2003). It is noteworthy that, across the course of infancy to adolescence, strategic deployment of attention—such as focusing on a problem or engaging in distraction—consistently aids modulation of even intense emotion (Silk et al., 2003). Indeed, the NICHD Study of Early Child Care indicated that high negative emotionality in infancy is associated with *better* school readiness if the children also have attentional control skills (Belsky, Friedman, & Hsieh, 2001).

Individual differences. In both early and middle childhood, children with externalizing problems do not regulate frustration as well as children without any symptoms (e.g., Calkins & Dedmon, 2000; Cole, Zahn-Waxler, & Smith, 1994; Eisenberg et al., 2001; Gilliom et al., 2002), which is taken to indicate that they have less adaptive or less effective strategies. When strategies are assessed, children with externalizing problems are less likely to use purportedly effective strategies, such as self-distraction and active problem solving (e.g., Calkins & Dedmon, 2000; Calkins et al., 2002; Eisenberg et al., 2001; Melnick & Hinshaw, 2000). There is, however, very little evidence to call upon to understand whether children who are at risk for any form of psychopathology attempt effective strategies without success.

A particularly interesting longitudinal study provides the most compelling evidence for the clinical importance of effective strategies in the face of high levels of negative emotion. Three-year-old boys with oppositional defiant symptoms who shift attention away from a source of frustration, and seek information about what they can do, show immediate decreases in anger (Gilliom et al., 2002). Moreover, the strategies they use predict their later adjustment. Reliance on attention shifting at age 3 predicts greater cooperativeness and fewer externalizing symptoms at age 6, whereas reliance on information seeking predicts assertiveness. In a different study, 4- to 7-year-old daughters of depressed mothers, a group of children who are at risk for later psychopathology, engaged in less active distraction and less active efforts to strategize than children whose mothers were asymptomatic (Silk, Shaw, Skuban, Oland, & Kovacs, 2006). Finally, school-age children and adolescents who have high levels of anxiety, sadness, or anger report using strategies that are less effective in modulating emotion. These children are also less confident that they can use adaptive strategies effectively (Burwell & Shirk, 2007; Suveg & Zeman, 2004; Zeman, Shipman, & Suveg, 2002).

More empirical evidence is needed to determine whether children with specific symptoms or diagnosable conditions merely deploy different strategies or whether they also have fewer strategies available, use less mature or appropriate strategies, or use strategies less effectively or less flexibly. Nevertheless, the research does suggest that (a) attention shifting, problem-focused information seeking and instrumental, appropriate efforts to work out a problem are effective, at least in the short term, in regulating children's emotions; (b) greater reliance on these strategies is associated with better adjustment in infants, toddlers, preschoolers, school-age children, preadolescent children, and adolescents; and (c) children with symptoms of anxiety, depression, and behavior disorders are less likely to use these strategies and may lack confidence that they can use them effectively. With a repertoire of effective strategies that are deployed flexibly to match situational demands, a person should not experience enduring emotion that is disabling. Rather, this person should be able to feel intensely for as long as needed when the situation requires it. Moreover, intense or enduring emotion is likely to be associated with behavior that is socially and situationally appropriate, our second feature of emotion dysregulation.

EMOTIONS INTERFERE WITH APPROPRIATE BEHAVIOR

Emotions, as stated previously, are defined in part by readiness to act in a particular manner—approaching an obstacle with force (anger), approaching a goal with eagerness and openness (joy), withdrawing from a situation (fear), and relinquishing a goal (sadness), to name a few. This aspect of emotions is a crucial part of their adaptive function—they quickly (and without the necessity of awareness) ready us to intervene on the environment to maintain and regain individual well-being. The world, however, is complex, and many situations involve multiple and sometimes conflicting goals and social constraints. Emotionally competent, mentally healthy children who feel strong emotions generally behave such that their actions take into account these situational constraints. That is, although emotion makes certain actions aimed at preserving well-being likely, the behaviors that are enacted to achieve goals can be either appropriate or inappropriate. Moreover, actions can be understandable and effective in the short run (a child hits another child to get a toy), but if they become a stable pattern they interfere with the goals of development—such as forming good friendships and learning self-control—that are essential to becoming a competent, healthy person (Cicchetti et al., 1995; Cole, Michel et al., 1994). A poignant illustration is that of incest victims who dissociate from their overwhelming emotions; initially this regulatory strategy is not linked to symptoms but it has detrimental effects on long-term mental health (e.g., Marx & Sloan, 2002). In sum, patterns of regulation of both positive and negative emotions are dysregulated when they lead to behavior that violates social standards or compromise developmental goals.

Developmental considerations.   Negative emotions are not dysregulated when they lead to appropriate behavior, particularly action that resolves a problem in a way that serves the well-being of the individual and of others. Intense negative affect in infants, for example, maintains proximity to the caregiver and elicits responsive caregiving (Gianino & Tronick, 1988). Approximately midway through the second year of life, toddlers' intense negative emotions are more resistant to caregiver regulatory efforts and lead to behaviors—including tantrums and defiance—that upset caregivers but are common at this age (Potegal & Davidson, 2003).

Yet even in young children, negative emotions can organize appropriate behavior. We examined typically developing children's emotion-behavior temporal sequences in frustrating situations, finding a close relation between sustained frustration and disruptive behavior at 18 and 24 months of age. By age 36 months, however, this association was no longer present (Hall & Cole, 2007). Some children are able to remain focused and on-task despite being frustrated. Moreover, as building frustration is modulated in typically developing 3- to 4-year-olds, anger is followed by *appropriate* action, such as task persistence and flexible problem solving (Dennis et al., 2007). In sum, an emotion-behavior sequence in which emotion organizes behavior that is developmentally and socially appropriate is distinct from a sequence that results in actions that are socially inappropriate and/or create risk for the developmental pathway to socioemotional competence and mental health.

Individual differences.   Emotion-behavior sequences should differentiate typically developing children from those at risk for psychopathology. Research, however, has tended to focus only on correlations between the frequency of negative emotions and behaviors and not on how emotions organize or disorganize behavior. Nonetheless, there is some evidence indicating the value of this means of approaching emotion dysregulation. Anger is more likely to lead to inappropriate behavior in school-aged children with behavior problems whereas anger does not in children without symptoms (Casey, 1996). In this study, children were exposed to background anger as they played with another child; 86.7% of school-aged children with Oppositional Defiant Disorder either stopped playing (i.e., shut down) or became disruptive, whereas 60% of control children continued to work productively on the task.

Emotions about emotions.   One aspect of the emotional process by which an initial emotional response leads to inappropriate behavior is the emotional reactions we can have to our initial emotional responses. This aspect of emotional dynamics is often conceptualized by clinicians, but less often by researchers. Adults with depression and anxiety, for example, feel guilty or self-critical about being despondent or irritable. As part of our discussion about emotion-behavior sequences we briefly focus on this aspect of emotional functioning.

Consider that certain children and youth with serious misconduct cannot tolerate feeling vulnerable (see Cole, Hall, & Radzioch, in press). They typically grew up in families of high conflict or stress (e.g., domestic violence). These experiences contribute to their feeling acutely vulnerable in early childhood, but unlike typical children, their parents do not help them deal with their emotional responses and indeed are often the source of the distress. These children regulate their intense vulnerable emotions as best they can, but they cannot resolve them. Many seem to avoid feeling them as they get older. They instead become angry, even hostile, when feelings of vulnerability (e.g., sadness, rejection, anxiety) are evoked.

Unfortunately, we know very little concerning emotions about emotions in either typically developing or at-risk children. The nearest evidence comes from developmental research on emotion understanding. Saarni (1999) points out that the emotionally competent person is aware of all emotions (does not selectively attend to certain emotions), appreciates the mixed emotions that often occur, and realizes that one can be unaware of emotions (see also Halberstadt et al., 2001; Southam-Gerow & Kendall, 2002). There is a body of developmental work on the understanding of mixed emotions that can provide a point of departure for a deeper understanding of the development of emotional dysregulation.

By about age 8 to 9 years, typically developing children have a fairly differentiated understanding of multiple emotions, including mixed and opposite emotions (Pons, Harris, & de Rosnay, 2004; Wintre & Vallance, 1994; Harter & Whitesell, 1989). The understanding that one emotion influences another emotion, however, appears to be fairly sophisticated, not appearing until the preadolescent period (Donaldson & Westerman, 1986). Adolescents who do not acknowledge mixed emotions tend to endorse repressive coping styles (Sincoff, 1992), and adolescents with externalizing and internalizing disorders have different patterns of talking about real and imagined emotion (O'Kearney & Dadds, 2005). Those with externalizing problems have a less complex and differentiated understanding of their emotional responses, compared to internalizing and asymptomatic youth. Internalizing youth, on the other hand, are less differentiated in explaining their emotional responses to fear-eliciting circumstances. They also refer to sadness in anger-eliciting contexts and are more likely to invoke cognitive states (e.g., being confused) than their externalizing and nonsymptomatic counterparts.

In sum, the study of temporal emotion-behavior sequences helps us examine the effects of emotion on behavior, an important aspect of emotion dysregulation. Moreover, understanding how typically developing children behave appropriately under conditions of intense or sustained emotion is important to understanding typical and atypical development and linking early emotion dysregulation to specific clinical outcomes. Finally, in considering how the unfolding of an emotional response influences behavior, we need basic and applied developmental work on emotions about emotions.

EMOTIONS THAT ARE CONTEXT INAPPROPRIATE

A third feature of emotion dysregulation involves the fit between an emotional response and the situation in which it occurs. In contrast to the previous discussion of inappropriate action that results from an emotional response, here we focus on the appropriateness of the emotional responses themselves, both experienced and expressed. Emotion expression is behavior, but we include it here given the focus on the emotional response. The emphasis in this section is on emotional responses that deviate from how most individuals would feel in a given context.

In considering the context appropriateness of an emotional response, there are three points to keep in mind. First, positive as well as negative emotions can be contextually inappropriate, as when a person enjoys causing harm to someone. Second, situations alone do not dictate our emotional responses. In fact, the emotion theories that guide our thinking emphasize that emotions reflect the personal meanings of our circumstances; emotional responses to the same situation can and do vary between individuals. Nonetheless, there are contexts that tend to elicit emotions from a particular emotion family—such as anger-frustration-irritation—which provide a means of examining atypical emotional responses in children. Third, a major source of individual differences in appraising situations, one that is quite relevant to developmental psychopathology, is the child's developmental level. A child's ability to understand a situation and appreciate its complexity will influence whether he or she finds a specific situational context frightening or funny, frustrating or inconsequential.

Developmental considerations. There is debate about how early we can see specific emotions emerge because each type of emotion requires the ability to engage in particular appraisals. Infant emotional expressions may reflect undifferentiated distress (Bridges, 1931; Lewis & Haviland-Jones, 2000; Sroufe, 1996). Most developmental scientists agree that a set of specific emotions—joy, anger, sadness, and fear—are discernible by the end of the first year (Bennett, Bendersky, & Lewis, 2005; Camras, Oster, Campos, & Bakeman, 2003; Sroufe, 1996). By that time, infant emotional expressions conform to social expectations and are reliably interpreted by trained research staff and caregivers (Malatesta & Haviland, 1982).

Being able to generate such context-appropriate emotions is one skill underlying emotional competence. Another is the ability to modulate the expression of context-appropriate emotions in ways that conform to social standards (Denham, 1998; Lewis, 1993; Saarni, 1999). As early as age 3 years, typically developing children spontaneously attempt to modulate disappointment (anger and sadness) according to social standards (Cole,

1986). Skill at expressive control, as well as pressure to conform, increases with age. By middle childhood, parents complain that they are no longer sure what their children are feeling. Children too report feeling distinct social pressure about when and to whom they express specific emotions. For example, one study indicated that children are willing to reveal sadness to a parent but not to a peer and anger to a peer more than to a parent (Zeman & Garber, 1996). The ability to articulate display rules and convincingly dissemble or mask felt emotion is relatively well-developed by middle childhood (Feldman, Jenkins, & Popoola, 1979; Harris, 1995; Saarni, 1979, 1982). In sum, early in life, there is evidence of context-appropriate emotion and, as early as age 3, of emerging skills at modulating emotional expression to conform to social expectations. This suggests a basis for studying context-inappropriate emotion.

Individual differences in context-inappropriate emotion can be conceptualized in three different ways. We discuss the inappropriate expression of an emotion that may fit the situational context, emotional responses that are atypical in the context, and lack of emotional responsiveness to an evocative situation. Each is in contrast to typical, appropriate emotional reactions to situations.

Socially inappropriate emotion expression.   An expressed emotion is inappropriate when it violates social or cultural norms for the situation, such as laughing when someone is hurt or expressing anger at a mistake that was clearly accidental. The emotional response may be understandable in the context but its expression is rude or inconsiderate or disrespectful. The expression of socially inappropriate emotion is related to a variety of risk factors and psychological problems, including maltreatment (Shields & Cicchetti, 1998), anxiety (Suveg & Zeman, 2004; Weisbrot, Gadow, DeVincent, & Pomeroy, 2005, 2005), and disruptive behavior problems (Casey, 1996; Cole, Zahn-Waxler et al., 1994). In contrast, the ability to modulate expression of a felt emotion according to social standards is associated with social competence and adaptive functioning. Preschoolers (e.g., Garner & Power, 1996; Liew, Eisenberg, & Reiser, 2004) and school-aged children (McDowell, O'Neill, & Parke, 2000) who are able to appear positive when disappointed have more emotion understanding and are more socially competent.

Although this type of context-inappropriate emotion signals general risk for psychopathology, there is a need for greater specificity in linking aspects of the emotional response and particular types of psychopathology. For example, might the inappropriate expression of fear predict a different outcome than the inappropriate expression of anger? A related question is whether certain ways of modulating emotion expression might be preferable. Gross (1998), for example, has indicated that suppressing an emotional expression may have negative implications for health in contrast to an actual reappraisal of a situation. Cole, Zahn-Waxler et al. (1994) found that preschool-aged girls with high levels of oppositional behavior, in contrast to girls who were asymptomatic, tended not to reveal disappointment when the social pressure for expression modulation ended. Research on children's expressive control has not explored these potentially important aspects of emotion regulation.

In studying this form of context-inappropriate emotion, it is also important to consider mechanisms that link socially inappropriate emotional expression to psychopathology. Inappropriate expression of emotion may involve lack of social awareness, disregard for social display rules (and the effect of one's emotions on others), or inability to regulate expression even when the individual wishes to do so. Moreover, a consistent pattern of expressing socially inappropriate emotion interferes with relationships (e.g., Halberstadt et al., 2001).

Atypical emotional responses to specific contexts.   The second form of context-inappropriate emotion involves emotional responses that are not those typically felt in a given situation. This form is different from that just described in which situation-congruent emotions are expressed inappropriately. In this section, the emphasis is on emotional responses that are incongruent with the context, such as feeling sadness or fear in response to a situation that is typically enjoyable for most people or feeling joy in situations that anger or disturb most people. Excessive distrust, laughter in situations that are troubling, and emotional reactions that occur for no apparent reason are symptoms that embody this emotion-context mismatch. These atypical emotional responses may involve deviant forms of emotional reactivity or distorted attributions. An example of the latter is seen in the hostile attributional bias—in which malevolent intent is attributed to interpersonal behavior that is ambiguous as to its intention—a bias that leads to context-inappropriate anger (Crick & Dodge, 1994). Although there are a number of symptoms of major disorders that can be construed as context-inappropriate emotion, there is little research that addresses their development. There is work, however, that suggests a link between emotions that are not typical to a context and risk for psychopathology.

Aggressive, disruptive children and youth are usually thought of as having difficulty regulating anger. However, some of them respond with positive emotions to situations in which other children feel angry, anxious, or subdued. For example, oppositional preschoolers and their mothers have a higher rate of laughing at the other's anger than dyads in which the child is not symptomatic (Cole, Teti, & Zahn-Waxler, 2003). This finding is interesting in light of evidence that some children and youth who are aggressive or have externalizing behavior problems enjoy misbehaving. They may not be focused on the negative consequences of misbehavior (harm to the other, damaged relationships, punishment); rather, they may derive a sense of mastery or power from their misconduct (see Cole, Hall et al., in press, for a case study).

Positive emotion in the face of wrong-doing may be linked to the fact that aggressive and externalizing children identify more positive and fewer negative consequences of their aggressive behavior (Boldizar, Perry, & Perry, 1989; Slaby & Guerra, 1988), and are less accurate in perceiving peers' negative emotions, particularly with regard to others' vulnerable emotions, such as sadness and fear (Blair & Coles, 2000; Casey, 1996). These findings suggest that many externalizing children and youth have context-inappropriate emotions, including feeling proud about their aggressive acts or deriving pleasure from the suffering of the victim. What is unknown is the timing and conditions under which this type of inappropriate emotional response develops and whether it is linked to the lack of remorse and empathy that is associated with psychopathy and severe Conduct Disorder.

Context-inappropriate emotion has also been linked to risk for anxiety symptoms. Toddlers who react with fear to situations that other children find interesting and enjoyable (e.g., a puppet show) may be exhibiting dysregulated fear (Buss, 2007). Preliminary evidence suggests that this mismatch between a minimally threatening or pleasurable context and a fearful response may indicate risk for the development of anxiety symptoms (see also Kagan, this volume). Similarly, a link between depression and emotion-context mismatch has been suggested in the adult clinical literature. Adults with Major Depressive Disorder report higher levels of sadness than controls while watching films that generally evoke happy emotions (Rottenberg, Gross, & Gotlib, 2005). This type of finding makes it quite interesting to note that infants who react to a blocked goal with sadness, rather than frustration, have higher cortisol responses (Lewis & Ramsay, 2005). The potential links between such individual differences in early childhood and adulthood and the development of anxiety and mood disorders require intensive study.

Emotional unresponsiveness.   The third form of context-inappropriate emotion that constitutes a form of emotion dysregulation is being emotionally unresponsive to situations that usually evoke emotional responses. Emotional inexpressivity and flat affect are key characteristics of several disorders including Schizophrenia, Depressive Disorder, and Posttraumatic Stress Disorder. Various types of inexpressivity in children—including an apparent lack of positive expressiveness, empathy, and guilt—are linked to childhood psychopathology, including conduct problems and internalizing symptoms (Cole et al., 1996; Frick, Lilienfeld, Ellis, Loney, & Silverthorn, 1999; Hayden, Klein, & Durbin, 2005; Hayden, Klein, Durbin, & Olino, 2006). Included in this category of emotional dysregulation is not only being emotionally unresponsive to one particular type of context but also more generalized flatness of affect.

Emotional unresponsiveness to situations that typically make children respond with anger and related emotions (anger, frustration, irritation) is sometimes linked with disruptive behavior problems or general difficulties with emotion regulation. These include being unresponsive (absence of sympathy, empathy, or guilt) when harm comes to others (Eisenberg, Fabes, Murphy, Karbon, Smith, & Maszk, 1996; Frick et al., 1999; Liew, Eisenberg, Losoya, Fabes, Guthrie, & Murphy, 2003), to stories about another child's sadness, fear, and anger (Cole et al., 1996), and, in oppositional girls, after a personal disappointment (Cole, Zahn-Waxler et al., 1994). The emotional unresponsiveness of these children may have a biological basis, as they fail to show the same physiological responsiveness to emotional stimuli as normal children (Fung et al., 2005) and have brain structure abnormalities that are linked with deficits in emotional responding (Raine et al., 2003). Emotional unresponsiveness to situations that typically elicit positive emotions in children, on the other hand, has been linked with internalizing problems. Preschoolers who express low levels of positive emotion during enjoyable tasks are likely to exhibit disruptive behavior symptoms at preschool age but, a few years later, to display a depressive style of thinking (e.g., helplessness, negative self-view; Hayden et al. , 2005, 2006). Similarly, the absence of positive affect distinguishes depressed preschoolers from those who have no symptoms (Luby, Belden, & Spitznagel, 2006).

General emotional unresponsiveness and flatness of affect are associated with adult psychopathology. Emotional inexpressivity predicts self-harm among female college students (Gratz, 2006), a finding consistent with the idea that parasuicidal behavior is a means of creating sensation or feeling in individuals who have lost the ability to experience emotion as a normal response to their environment (see Crowell, Beauchaine, & Lenzenweger, this volume). Similarly, adult survivors of incest often report feeling emotionally "numb" (Cole, Michel et al., 1994), an emotional reaction that serves a protective purpose during the abuse but that marks dysregulated emotional functioning in the longer term. This interpretation is consistent with work on experiential avoidance, in which individuals consistently and actively attempt to limit their experience of negative emotions (Hayes et al., 1996). Although most individuals occasionally avoid experiences of negative emotions (e.g., avoiding the discussion of a sad event), attempts to avoid negative emotion become problematic when they reflect a global, established pattern. Such a pattern often interferes with the ability to work productively and be emotionally responsive in relationships, consequences that paradoxically increase stress and thus the likelihood of feeling distressed (Hayes et al., 1996; Marx & Sloan, 2002). Experiential avoidance has been linked to a variety of disorders, including depression, anxiety, Obsessive-Compulsive Disorder, Agoraphobia, substance abuse, and Borderline Personality Disorder (Hayes et al., 1996, 2004).

In sum, context-inappropriate emotion can be associated with emotional dysregulation. It includes socially inappropriate emotional expressions, mismatches between emotional responses and situational context, and emotional unresponsiveness to particular or a range of situations. This aspect of emotional dysregulation appears to be important to understanding the development of psychopathology, but research on both typical and atypical development in relation to context-inappropriate emotion is quite limited.

EMOTIONS CHANGE TOO ABRUPTLY OR TOO SLOWLY

The final quality of emotional dysregulation that we discuss is deviance in how emotional responses change. In research involving the coding of facial expressions of emotion, participants are often exposed to standard emotional evocative stimuli or circumstances and no particular demand to mask emotion. In both children and adults, and appreciating considerable variation across individuals and situations, we typically see a relatively gradual rise of emotional response, a peak level of intensity, and a relatively gradual return to a "neutral" expression. In addition, in quasinaturalistic task procedures (e.g., toy removal), there are usually periods of neutral expression marked by periodic emotion "episodes." This pattern is in contrast to emotions that linger (the person does not recover within the typical time period) or change frequently. We posit that the quality of emotional change may be important in understanding emotion dysregulation, although there is little work to inform this discussion. Poor emotional recovery (e.g., unrelenting dysphoria or anxiety) and lability (i.e., emotions or moods that change quickly and unpredictably) are symptomatic of a few forms of serious psychopathology.

Developmental considerations. Young infants are said to be emotionally labile, switching emotions quickly (Camras, 1994). For example, most infants switch quickly from distressed crying to laughter when a parent distracts them with an object. Defined in this manner, lability appears to be normal in infancy and is presumed to decline with age (Gerson et al., 1996), a supposition supported by the finding that 6-month-olds change facial expressions significantly less frequently than 3-month-olds (Malatesta & Haviland, 1982). However, periods of hormonal change, such as adolescence and menopause, are also thought to involve emotional lability (e.g., Gerson et al., 1996), although evidence that adolescents are more labile than children is equivocal (Larson & Lampman-Petraitis, 1989). One source of confusion may be the different ways that the term *lability* is used. In referring to children's emotional responses to situations, lability refers to two qualities: (a) unpredictable, intense, and rapid onset of emotions (i.e., high emotional reactivity), and (b) rapid or frequent changes in emotion during emotional episodes (e.g., switching from crying to laughing). In adults, lability describes mood changes. Moods are extended periods of time in which there is a predominant emotional tone (happy, down) that is not linked to situational changes.

Individual differences. Emotional lability has been linked to psychopathology, although there is very limited evidence that is informed by emotion theories or developmental models. Hospitalized adolescents are more labile than outpatient and asymptomatic adolescents (Gerson et al., 1996). Self-reported lability is associated with adolescent depressive symptoms and problem behaviors (Larsen, Raffaelli, Richards, & Ham, 1990; Silk et al., 2003), and, in adults, affective lability is associated with Borderline Personality Disorder (Koenigsburg et al., 2002). Lability in childhood may predict the development of later disorders, such as Bipolar Disorder (see Blader & Carlson, this volume; Fergus et al., 2003; Kochman et al., 2005).

Major and unpredictable changes in mood state are the key feature of Bipolar Disorder in adults. There is consensus that the presentation of the disorder is markedly different in children. Specifically, children who have Bipolar Disorder may be intensely and unpredictably reactive (e.g., respond suddenly with intense anger to a situation that is not that frustrating) as well as being generally irritable (Leibenluft et al., 2003). Seen less commonly in children are mood swings between periods of depression and euphoria, the classic form of Bipolar Disorder in adults. Lability defined by these specific types of mood swings predicts the severity of symptoms and poor treatment outcomes in adults (Benazzi, 2004; Wehr, Sack, Rosenthal, & Cowdry, 1988). Rapid cycling, in which manic and depressive states change frequently in the course of a year, has been implicated in childhood Bipolar Disorder (e.g., Geller et al., 1995, 2002; see also Balder & Carlson, this volume, for an alternative perspective). Some researchers have identified children with a cyclothymic temperament, marked by emotional reactivity and lability. Children and adolescents with this disposition are at risk for developing later and more severe Bipolar Disorder, including psychotic symptoms and comorbidity with disruptive behavior disorders (Kochman et al., 2005). It is unclear whether early lability is a causal factor or a signal of the development of Bipolar Disorder but, it is clear that there is a critical need to understand lability in the context of both normal and atypical development.

Emotional responses that resist change.   Generally, emotional lability is not contrasted with prolonged emotions and moods that resist change. We place them together to underscore the value of appreciating the temporal dynamics of emotions rather than their valence or intensity. Normally, emotional responses develop and resolve in short periods of time. Moods are enduring, emotionally valenced states, but even these tend not to be prolonged to the point of impairing a person's functioning. When emotions and moods resist change, it is cause for concern.

Developmental considerations.   A hallmark of emotional health is being able to recover from a negative emotion (Davidson, 2000). There is surprisingly little known about this ability in studies of emotion regulation despite the increasing emphasis on positive emotion (Frederickson, 2001). Aggressive kindergartners have difficulty shifting to a positive emotional state after a difficult task (Wilson, 2003). Yet we know very little about the development of this ability and the significance of individual differences in latency to regain a calm or content state after being upset or to evince joy in a pleasurable activity after being distressed. It is also worth noting that emotion regulation requires effort that may tap and potentially deplete psychological resources (Baumeister, Bratslavsky, Murven, & Tice, 1998). Nonetheless, the ability to experience positive emotion after being frustrated seems to restore the ability to self-regulate (Tice, Baumeister, & Zhang, 2004).

Individual differences.   Resistance to emotional change is a feature of mood disorders as well as anxiety disorders. In depression, for example, prolonged sadness or irritability is a central symptom in adults or children. The inability to resolve anger and sadness is a main complaint of loved ones who try, unsuccessfully, to soothe the distress of a depressed child or encourage him or her to feel better. There may well be a relation between these mood symptoms and anhedonic symptoms, in which activities that a person previously enjoyed are no longer fun or interesting. Similarly, in anxiety disorders such as Generalized Anxiety Disorder (GAD), individuals remain anxious or worried even when immediate danger to the well-being has subsided. There is a need for research that dissects the degree to which ineffective emotion regulation strategies, emotions about emotions, and low positive emotionality contribute to or become associated with the development of depressive and anxious symptoms. In our studies of how preschool age children with oppositional symptoms handle disappointment, we find that they openly express anger in situations in which asymptomatic children smile (Cole, Zahn-Waxler et al., 1994). Even more interesting is what happens when the experimenter leaves the room. The anger of oppositional children continues and even intensifies, whereas the anger of asymptomatic children is expressed as soon as the experimenter leaves the room, then dissipates while they wait.

SUMMARY AND CONCLUSIONS

Emotional dysregulation is a central aspect of many forms of psychopathology. Dysregulation is not simply a matter of being more emotionally negative. In this chapter, we discussed four ways that patterns of emotion regulation appear as emotion dysregulation: enduring emotion when strategies are ineffective, emotions that lead to inappropriate behavior, emotion expression and experience that is contextually inappropriate, and aberrations in the quality of how emotions change, including both lability and slow recovery. These are not mutually exclusive categories. Yet each is associated with specific types of symptoms. There is very limited research to address when any aspect of emotional dysregulation signals emerging psychopathology and when it is a correlate or product of psychopathology. Nonetheless, there is accumulating evidence that early emotional difficulties precede the emergence of symptoms and disorders and therefore may signal risk for emerging psychopathology. It therefore seems especially important to have a clinically informed conceptualization of emotion dysregulation and to use it to design studies that examine how skillful emotion regulation develops typically, how children with and without specific disorders differ, and the conditions that lead to the development of both appropriate effective emotion regulation and problematic dysregulation. Such research will be particularly valuable if specific aspects of dysregulation and specific symptoms are more closely linked. Moreover, this research has promise not only for understanding disorders of childhood but also for understanding the emergence of disorders that are more often regarded as adult psychopathology, such as personality disorders, which are thought to have their origins in early childhood emotional experience (Linehan, 1993; Rogosch & Cicchetti, 2005). There is a critical need for early identification and mental health intervention crisis in childhood (Tolan &

Dodge, 2005). A clinically informed, developmentally informed examination of emotion regulation and dysregulation can play a critical role in addressing the needs of children.

REFERENCES

American Psychiatric Association. (2000). *Diagnostic and statistical manual of mental disorders. Text revision* (4th ed., *DSM-IV-TR*). Washington, DC: American Psychiatric Association.

Arnold, M. B. (1960). *Emotion and personality.* New York: Columbia University Press.

Barkley, R. A. (1997). *ADHD and the nature of self-control.* New York: Guilford.

Barrett, K. C., & Campos, J. J. (1987). Perspectives on emotional development II: A functionalist approach to emotions. In J. D. Osofsky, (Ed.), *Handbook of infant development* (2nd ed., pp. 555–578). Oxford, England: Wiley.

Baumeister, R. F., Bratslavsky, E., Murven, M., & Tice, D. M. (1998). Ego depletion: Is the active self a limited resource? *Journal of Personality and Social Psychology, 74,* 1252–1265.

Beauchaine, T. P., Gatze-Kopp, L., & Mead, H. K. (2007). Polyvagal theory and developmental psychopathology: Emotion dysregulation and conduct problems from preschool to adolescence. *Biological Psychology, 74,* 174–184.

Belsky, J., Friedman, S. L., & Hsieh, K. (2001). Testing a core emotion-regulation prediction: Does early attentional persistence moderate the effect of infant negative emotionality on later development? *Child Development, 72,* 123–133.

Benazzi, F. (2004). Inter-episode mood lability in mood disorders: Residual symptom or natural course of illness? *Psychiatry and Clinical Neurosciences, 58,* 480–486.

Bennett, D. S., Bendersky, M., & Lewis, M. (2005). Does the organization of emotional expression change over time? Facial expressivity from 4 to 12 months. *Infancy, 8,* 167–187.

Berenbaum, H., Raghavan, C., Le, H., Vernon, L. L., & Gomez, J. J. (2003). A taxonomy of emotional disturbances. *Clinical Psychology: Science and Practice, 10,* 206–226.

Blair, R. J. R., & Coles, M. (2000). Expression recognition and behavioural problems in early adolescence. *Cognitive Development, 15,* 421–434.

Boldizar, J. P., Perry, D. G., & Perry, L. C. (1989). Outcome values and aggression. *Child Development, 60,* 571–579.

Bridges, K. M. B. (1931). *The social and emotional development of the pre-school child.* Oxford, England: Kegan Paul.

Burwell, R. A., & Shirk, S. R. (2007). Subtypes of rumination in adolescence: Associations between brooding, reflection, depressive symptoms, and coping. *Journal of Clinical Child and Adolescent Psychology, 36,* 56–65.

Buss, K. A., & Goldsmith, H. H. (1998). Fear and anger regulation in infancy: Effects on the temporal dynamics of affective expression. *Child Development, 69,* 359–374.

Buss, K. A. (May, 2007). *Adjustment in kindergarten for toddlers with dysregulated fear profiles*. Paper presented at the annual meeting of the Association for Psychological Science, Washington, D.C.

Calkins, S. D. (1994). Origins and outcomes of individual differences in emotion regulation. In N. A. Fox (Ed.), The development of emotion regulation: Biological and behavioral considerations. *Monographs of the Society for Research in Child Development, 59* (2-3, Serial No. 240), 53–72.

Calkins, S. D., & Dedmon, S. E. (2000). Physiological and behavioral regulation in two-year-old children with aggressive/destructive behavior problems. *Journal of Abnormal Child Psychology, 28*, 103–118.

Calkins, S. D., & Keane, S. P. (2004). Cardiac vagal regulation across the preschool period: Stability, continuity, and implications for child adjustment. *Developmental Psychobiology, 45*, 101–113.

Calkins, S. D., Dedmon, S. E., Gill, K. L., Lomax, L. E., & Johnson, L. M. (2002). Frustration in infancy: Implications for emotion regulation, physiological processes, and temperament. *Infancy, 3*, 175–197.

Campos, J. J., Frankel, C. B., & Camras, L. A. (2004). On the nature of emotion regulation. *Child Development, 75*, 377–394.

Camras, L. (1994). Two aspects of emotional development: Expression and elicitation. In P. Ekman & R. J. Davidson (Eds.), *The nature of emotion: Fundamental questions* (pp. 347–351). New York: Oxford University Press.

Camras, L. A., Oster, H., Campos, J. J., & Bakeman, R. (2003). Emotional facial expressions in European-American, Japanese, and Chinese infants. In P. Ekman, J. J. Campos, R. J. Davidson, & F. B. M. de Waal (Eds.), Emotions inside out: 130 years after Darwin's *The expression of the emotions in man and animals. Annals of the New York of Sciences: Vol. 1000* (pp. 135–151). New York: New York University Press.

Casey, R. J. (1996). Emotional competence in children with externalizing and internalizing disorders. In M. Lewis (Ed.), *Emotional development in atypical children* (pp.161–183). Hillsdale, NJ: Erlbaum.

Cicchetti, D., Ackerman, B. P., & Izard, C. E. (1995). Emotions and emotion regulation in developmental psychopathology. *Development and Psychopathology, 7*, 1–10.

Cole, P. M. (1986). Children's spontaneous control of facial expression. *Child Development, 57*, 1309–1321.

Cole, P. M., Dennis, T., Martin, S. E., & Hall, S. E. (in press). Emotion regulation and the early development of psychopathology. In S. Jung, et al. (Eds.), *Regulating emotions*. Malden, MA: Blackwell.

Cole, P. M., Hall, S. E, & Radzioch, A. M. (in press). Emotional dysregulation and the development of serious misconduct. In S. Olson & A. Sameroff, *Regulatory processes in the development of behavior problems: Biological, behavioral, and social-ecological interactions*. New York: Cambridge University.

Cole, P. M., Martin, S. E., & Dennis, T. A. (2004). Emotion regulation as a scientific construct: Methodological challenges and directions for child development research. *Child Development, 75*, 317–333.

Cole, P. M., Michel, M. K., & Teti, L. O. (1994). The development of emotion regulation and dysregulation: A clinical perspective. In N. A. Fox (Ed.), The development of emotion regulation: Biological and behavioral considerations. *Monographs of the Society for Research in Child Development, 59* (2-3, Serial No. 240), 73–100.

Cole, P. M., Teti, L. O., & Zahn-Waxler, C. (2003). Mutual emotion regulation and the stability of conduct problems between preschool and school age. *Development and Psychopathology, 15,* 1–18.

Cole, P. M., Zahn-Waxler, C., Fox, N. A., Usher, B. A., & Welsh, J. D. (1996). Individual differences in emotion regulation and behavior problems in preschool children. *Journal of Abnormal Psychology, 105,* 518–529.

Cole, P. M., Zahn-Waxler, C., & Smith, K. D. (1994). Expressive control during a disappointment: Variation related to preschoolers' behavior problems. *Developmental Psychology, 30,* 835–846.

Crick, N. R., & Dodge, D. K. (1994). A review and reformulation of social information-processing mechanisms in children's social adjustment. *Psychological Bulletin, 115,* 74–101.

Crockenberg, S. C., & Leerkes, E. M. (2004). Infant and maternal behaviors regulate infant reactivity to novelty at 6 months. *Developmental Psychology, 40,* 1123–1132.

Davidson, R. J. (2000). Affective style, psychopathology, and resilience: Brain mechanisms and plasticity. *American Psychologist, 55,* 1196–1214.

Denham, S. A. (1998). *Emotional development in young children.* New York: Guilford.

Dennis, T. A., Wiggins, C. N., Cole, P. M., Myftaraj, L., Cushing, A., Zalewski. M. T., & Cohen, L. H. (2007). Functional relations between preschool age children's emotions and their regulatory behaviors. Unpublished manuscript, City University of New York—Hunter College.

Diener, M. L., & Mangelsdorf, S. C. (1999). Behavioral strategies for emotion regulation in toddlers: Associations with maternal involvement and emotional expressions. *Infant Behavior and Development, 22,* 569–583.

Donaldson, S. K., & Westerman, M. A. (1986). Development of children's understanding of ambivalence and causal theories of emotions. *Developmental Psychology, 22,* 655–662.

Eisenberg, N., Cumberland, A., Spinrad, T. L., Fabes, R. A., Shepard, S. A., Reiser, M., et al. (2001). The relations of regulation and emotionality to children's externalizing and internalizing problem behavior. *Child Development, 72,* 1112–1134.

Eisenberg, N., Fabes, R. A., Bernzweig, J., Karbon, M., et al. (1993). The relations of emotionality and regulation to preschoolers' social skills and sociometric status. *Child Development, 64,* 1418–1438.

Eisenberg, N., Fabes, R. A., Murphy, B., Karbon, M., Smith, M., & Maszk, P. (1996). The relations of children's dispositional empathy-related responding to their emotionality, regulation, and social functioning. *Developmental Psychology, 32,* 195–209.

Eisenberg, N., Fabes, R. A., Shepard, S. A., Murphy, B. C., Guthrie, I. K., Jones, S., et al. (1997). Contemporaneous and longitudinal prediction of children's social functioning from regulation and emotionality. *Child Development, 68,* 642–664.

Ekman, P., & Davidson, R. J. (1994). *The nature of emotion: Fundamental questions.* New York: Oxford University Press.

El-Sheikh, M. (2005). Does poor vagal tone exacerbate child maladjustment in the context of parental problem drinking? A longitudinal examination. *Journal of Abnormal Psychology, 114,* 735–741.

El-Sheikh, M., Harger, J., & Whitson, S. M. (2001). Exposure to interparental conflict and children's adjustment and physical health: The moderating role of vagal tone. *Child Development, 72,* 1617–1636.

Feldman, R. S., Jenkins, L., & Popoola, O. (1979). Detection of deception in adults and children via facial expressions. *Child Development, 50,* 350–355.

Fenske, M, J., & Raymond, J. E. (2006). Affective influences of selective attention. *Current Directions in Psychological Science, 15,* 312–316.

Fergus, E. L., Miller, R. B., Luckenbaugh, D. A., Leverich, G. S., Findling, R. L., Speer, A. M., et al. (2003). Is there progression from irritability/dyscontrol to major depressive and manic symptoms? A retrospective community survey of parents of bipolar children. *Journal of Affective Disorders, 77,* 71–78.

Folkman, S., & Lazarus, R. S. (1980). Coping and emotion. In N. L. Stein, B. Leventhal, & T. Trabasso (Eds.), *Psychological and biological approaches to emotion* (pp. 313–332). Hillsdale, NJ: Erlbaum.

Frederickson, B. L. (2001). The role of positive emotions in positive psychology: The broaden-and-build theory of positive emotions. *American Psychologist, 56,* 218–226.

Frick, P. J., Lilienfeld, S. O., Ellis, M., Loney, B., & Silverthorn, P. (1999) The association between anxiety and psychopathy dimensions in children. *Journal of Abnormal Child Psychology, 27,* 383–392.

Frijda, N. H. (1986). *The emotions: Studies in emotion and social interaction.* New York: Cambridge University Press.

Fung, M. T., Raine, A., Loeber, R., Lynam, D. R., Steinhauer, S. R., Venables, P. H., & Stouthmaer-Loeber, M. (2005). Reduced electrodermal activity in psychopathy-prone adolescents. *Journal of Abnormal Psychology, 114,* 187–196.

Garner, P. W., & Power, T. G. (1996). Preschoolers' emotional control in the disappointment paradigm and its relation to temperament, emotional knowledge, and family expressiveness. *Child Development, 67,* 1406–1419.

Geller, B., Sun, K., Zimerman, B., Luby, J., Frazier, J., & Williams, M. (1995). Complex and rapid-cycling in bipolar children and adolescents: A preliminiary study. *Journal of Affective Disorders, 34,* 259–268.

Geller, B., Craney, J. L., Bolhofner, K., Nickelsburg, M. J., Williams, M., & Zimerman, B. (2002). Two-year prospective follow-up of children with a prepubertal and early adolescent bipolar disorder phenotype. *American Journal of Psychiatry, 159,* 927–933.

Gerson, A.C., Gerring, J. P., Freund, L., Joshi, P., Capozzoli, J., Brady, K., et al. (1996). The Children's Affective Lability Scale: A psychometric evaluation of reliability. *Psychiatry Research, 65,* 189–197.

Gianino, A., & Tronick, E. Z. (1988). The mutual regulation model: The infant's self and interactive regulation and coping and defensive capacities. In T. M. Field, P. M. McCabe, & N. Schneiderman (Eds.), *Stress and coping across development* (pp. 47–68). Hillsdale, NJ: Erlbaum.

Gilliom, M., Shaw, D. S., Beck, J. E., Schonberg, M. A., & Lukon, J. L. (2002). Anger regulation in disadvantaged preschool boys: Strategies, antecedents, and the development of self-control. *Developmental Psychology, 34,* 222–235.

Gotlib, I. H., Joormann, J., Minor, K. M., & Cooney, R. E. (2006). Cognitive and biological functioning in children at risk for depression. In T. Canli (Ed.), *Biology of personality and individual differences* (pp. 353–382). New York: Guilford.

Gratz, K. L. (2006). Risk factors for deliberate self-harm among female college students: The role and interaction of childhood maltreatment, emotional inexpressivity, and affect intensity/reactivity. *American Journal of Orthopsychiatry, 76*, 238–250.

Grolnick, W. S., Bridges, L. J., & Connell, J. P. (1996). Emotion regulation in two-year-olds: Strategies and emotional expression in four contexts. *Child Development, 67*, 928–941.

Gross, J. J., (1998). The emerging field of emotion regulation: An integrative review. *Review of General Psychology, 2*, 271–299.

Gross, J. J., & Muñoz, R. F. (1995). Emotion regulation and mental health. *Clinical Psychology: Science and Practice, 2*, 151–164.

Gunnar, M., & Quevedo, K. (2007). The neurobiology of stress and development. *Annual Review of Psychology, 58*, 145–173.

Hajcak, G., Molnar, C., George, M. S., Bolger, K., Koola, J., & Nahas, Z. (2007). Emotion facilitates action: A transcranial magnetic stimulation study of motor cortex excitability during picture viewing. *Psychophysiology, 44*, 91–97.

Halberstadt, A. G., Denham, S. A., & Dunsmore, J. C. (2001). Affective social competence. *Social Development, 10*, 79–119.

Hall, S. E., & Cole, P. M. (2007). Toddlers' emotional self-regulation: Stability and change across time. Poster presented at the meeting of the Society for Research in Child Development. Boston, MA.

Hamann, S. (2001). Cognitive and neural mechanisms of emotional memory. *Trends in Cognitive Sciences, 5*, 394–400.

Harris, P. L. (1995). Children's awareness and lack of awareness of mind and emotion. In D. Cicchetti & S. L. Toth (Eds.), *Emotion, cognition, and representation. Rochester symposium on developmental psychopathology* (pp. 35–57). Rochester, NY: University of Rochester Press.

Harter, N. R., & Whitesell, S. (1989). Children's reports of conflict between simultaneous opposite-valence emotions. *Child Development, 60*, 673–682.

Hayden, E. P., Klein, D. N., & Durbin, C. E. (2005). Parent reports and laboratory assessments of child temperament: A comparison of their associations with risk for depression and externalizing disorders. *Journal of Psychopathology and Behavioral Assessment, 27*, 89–100.

Hayden, E. P., Klein, D. N., Durbin, C. E., & Olino, T. M. (2006). Positive emotionality at age three predicts cognitive styles in seven-year-old children. *Development and Psychopathology, 18*, 409–423.

Hayes, S. C., Wilson, K. G., Gifford, E. V., Follette, V. M., & Strosahl, K. D. (1996). Experiential avoidance and behavioral disorders: A functional dimensional approach to diagnosis and treatment. *Journal of Consulting and Clinical Psychology, 64*, 1152–1168.

Hayes, S .C., Strosahl, K., Wilson, K. G., Bissett, R. T., Pistorello, J., Toarmino, D., et al. (2004). Measuring experiential avoidance: A preliminary test of a working model. *Psychological Record, 54*, 553–578.

Isen, A. M., Shalker, T. E., Clark, M., & Karp, L. (1978). Affect, accessibility of material in memory, and behavior: A cognitive loop? *Journal of Personality and Social Psychology, 36*, 1–12.

Izard, C. E. (1971). *The face of emotion*. East Norwalk, CT: Appleton-Century-Crofts.

Katz, L. F., & Gottman, J. M. (1995). Vagal tone protects children from martial conflict. *Development and Psychopathology, 7*, 83–92.

Katz, L. F., & Gottman, J. M. (1997). Buffering children from marital conflict and dissolution. *Journal of Clinical Child Psychology, 26*, 157–171.

Keenan, K. (2000). Emotion dysregulation as a risk factor for child psychopathology. *Clinical Psychology: Science and Practice, 7*, 418–434.

Kochman, F. J., Hantouche, E. G., Ferrari, P., Lencrenon, S., Bayart, D., & Akiskal, H. S. (2005). Cyclothymic temperament as a prospective predictor of bipolarity and suicidality in children and adolescents with major depressive disorder. *Journal of Affective Disorders, 85*, 181–189.

Koenigsburg, H. W., Harvey, P. D., Mitropoulou, V., Schmeidler, J., New, A. S., Goodman, M., et al. (2002). Characterizing affective instability in borderline personality disorder. *American Journal of Psychiatry, 159*, 784–788.

Kopp, C. B. (1989). Regulation of distress and negative emotions: A developmental view. *Developmental Psychology, 25*, 343–354.

Kovacs, M., Sherrill, J., George, C. J., Pollock, M., Tumuluru, R. V., & Ho, V. (2006). Contextual emotion-regulation therapy for childhood depression: Description and pilot testing of a new intervention. *Journal of the American Academy of Child & Adolescent Psychiatry, 45*, 892–903.

Larsen, R. W., Raffaelli, M., Richards, M. H., & Ham, M. (1990). Ecology of depression in late childhood and early adolescence: A profile of daily states and activities. *Journal of Abnormal Psychology, 99*, 92–102.

Larson, R., & Lampman-Petraitis, C. (1989). Daily emotional states as reported by children and adolescents. *Child Development, 60*, 1250–1260.

Lazarus, R. S. (1991). *Emotion and adaptation*. New York: Oxford University Press.

LeDoux, J. E. (1986). Sensory systems and emotion: A model of affective processing. *Integrative Psychiatry, 4*, 237–243.

Leibenluft, E., Charney, D. S., & Pine, D. S. (2003). Researching the pathophysiology of pediatric bipolar disorder. *Biological Psychiatry, 53*, 1009–1020.

Levenson, R. W. (2003). Blood, sweat, and fears: The autonomic architecture of emotions. In P. Ekman, J. J. Campos, R. J. Davidson, & F. B. M. De Waal (Eds.), Emotions inside out: 130 years after Darwin's: The expression of the emotions in man and animals (pp. 348–366). *Annals of the New York Academy of Sciences*, Vol. 1000. New York: New York University.

Lewis, M. (1993). The emergence of human emotions. In M. Lewis & J. M. Haviland (Eds.), *Handbook of emotions* (pp. 223–235). New York: Guilford.

Lewis, M., & Haviland-Jones, J. M. (2000). *Handbook of emotions* (2nd ed.). New York: Guilford.

Lewis, M., & Ramsay, D. (2005). Infant emotional and cortisol responses to goal blockage. *Child Development, 76*, 518–530.

Liew, J., Eisenberg, N., Losoya, S. H., Fabes, R. A., Guthrie, I. K., & Murphy, B. C.

(2003). Children's physiological indices of empathy and their social-emotional adjustment: Does caregivers' expressivity matter? *Journal of Family Psychology, 17,* 584–597.

Liew, J., Eisenberg, N., & Reiser, M. (2004). Preschoolers' effortful control and negative emotionality, immediate reactions to disappointment, and quality of social functioning. *Journal of Experimental Child Psychology, 89,* 298–313.

Linehan, M. M. (1993). *Cognitive-behavioral treatment of borderline personality disorder.* New York: Guilford.

Little, C., & Carter, A. S. (2005). Negative emotional reactivity and regulation in 12-month-olds following emotional challenge: Contributions of maternal-infant emotional availability in a low-income sample. *Infant Mental Health Journal, 26,* 354–368.

Luby, J. L., Belden, A. C., & Spitznagel, E. (2006). Risk factors for preschool depression: The mediating role of early stressful life events. Journal of Child Psychology and Psychiatry, 47, 1292–1298.

Malatesta, C. Z., & Haviland, J. M. (1982). Learning display rules: The socialization of emotion expression in infancy. *Child Development, 53,* 991–1003.

Mangelsdorf, S. C., Shapiro, J. R., & Marzolf, D. (1995). Developmental and temperamental differences in emotion regulation in infancy. *Child Development, 66,* 1817–1828.

Marx, B. P., & Sloan, D. M. (2002). The role of emotion in the psychological functioning of adult survivors of childhood sexual abuse. *Behavior Therapy, 33,* 563–577.

Maughan, A., & Cicchetti, D. (2002). Impact of child maltreatment and interadult violence on children's emotion regulation abilities and socioemotional adjustment. *Child Development, 73,* 1525–1542.

Mayer, J. D., & Salovey, P. (2004). What is emotional intelligence? In P. Salovey, M. A. Brackett, & J. D. Mayer (Eds.), *Emotional intelligence.* Port Chester, NY: Dude.

McDowell, D. J., O'Neill, R., & Parke, R. D. (2000). Display rule application in a disappointing situation and children's emotional reactivity: Relations with social competence. *Merrill-Palmer Quarterly, 46,* 306–324.

Melnick, S. M., & Hinshaw, S. P. (2000). Emotion regulation and parenting in AD/HD and comparison boys: Linkages with social behaviors and peer preference. *Journal of Abnormal Child Psychology, 28,* 73–86.

Mennin, D. S., Heimberg, R. G., Turk, C. L., & Fresco, D. M. (2002). Applying an emotion regulation framework to integrative approaches to generalized anxiety disorder. *Clinical Psychology: Science and Practice, 9,* 85–90.

Ochsner, K. N., & Schacter, D. L. (2000). A social cognitive neuroscience approach to emotion and memory. In J. Borod (Ed.), *The neurophysiology of emotion* (pp. 163–193). New York: Oxford University.

O'Kearney, R., & Dadds, M. R. (2005). Language for emotions in adolescents with externalizing and internalizing disorders. *Development and Psychopathology, 17,* 529–548.

Overton, A., Selway, S., Strongman, K., & Houston, M. (2005). Eating disorders—the regulation of positive as well as negative emotional experience. *Journal of Clinical Psychology in Medical Settings, 12,* 39–56.

Pons, F., Harris, P. L., & de Rosnay, M. (2004). Emotion comprehension between 3 and 11 years: Developmental periods and hierarchical organization. *European Journal of Developmental Psychology, 1*, 127–152.

Porges, S. W. (2001). The polyvagal theory: Phylogenetic substrates of a social nervous system. *International Journal of Psychophysiology, 42*, 123–146.

Potegal, M., & Davidson, R. J. (2003). Temper tantrums in young children. Vol. 1: Behavioral composition. *Journal of Developmental & Behavioral Pediatrics, 24*, 140–147.

Raine, A., Lencz, T., Taylor, K., Hellige, J. B., Bihrle, S., Lacasse, L., Lee, M., Iishikawa, S., & Colletti, P. (2003). Corpus callosum abnormalities in psychopathic antisocial individuals. *Archives of General Psychiatry, 60*, 1134–1142.

Reijntjes, A., Stegge, H., Meerum Terwogt, M., Kamphuis, J. H., & Telch, M. J. (2006). Emotion regulation and its effects on mood improvement in response to an in vivo peer rejection challenge. *Emotion, 6*, 543–552.

Rogosch, F. A., & Cicchetti, D. (2005). Child maltreatment, attention networks, and potential precursors to borderline personality disorder. *Development and Psychopathology, 17*, 1071–1089.

Rothbart, M. K., Ziaie, H., & O'Boyle, C. G. (1992). Self-regulation and emotion in infancy. In N. Eisenberg & R. A. Fabes (Eds.), *Emotion and its regulation in early development* (pp. 7–23). San Francisco, CA: Jossey-Bass.

Rottenberg, J., Gross, J. J., & Gotlib, I. H. (2005). Emotion context insensitivity in major depressive disorder. *Journal of Abnormal Psychology, 114*, 627–639.

Saarni, C. (1979). Children's understanding of display rules for expressive behavior. *Developmental Psychology, 15*, 424–429.

Saarni, C. (1999). *The development of emotional competence.* New York: Guilford.

Shannon, K. E., Beauchaine, T. P., Brenner, S. L., Neuhaus, E., & Gatzke-Kopp, L. (in press). Familial and temperamental predictors of resilience in children at risk for conduct disorder and depression. *Development and Psychopathology.*

Shields, A., & Cicchetti, D. (1998). Reactive aggression among maltreated children: The contributions of attention and emotion dysregulation. *Journal of Clinical Child Psychology, 27*, 381–395.

Silk, J. S., Shaw, D. S., Skuban, E. M., Oland, A. A., & Kovacs, M. (2006). Emotion regulation strategies in offspring of childhood-onset depressed mothers. *Journal of Child Psychology and Psychiatry, 47*, 69–78.

Silk, J. S., Steinberg, L., & Morris, A. S. (2003). Adolescents' emotion regulation in daily life: Links to depressive symptoms and problem behavior. *Child Development, 74*, 1869–1880.

Sincoff, J. B. (1992). Ambivalence and defense: Effects of a repressive style on normal adolescents' and young adults' mixed feelings. *Journal of Abnormal Psychology, 101*, 251–256.

Slaby, R. G., & Guerra, N. G. (1988). Cognitive mediators of aggression in adolescent offenders. Vol. I: Assessment. *Developmental Psychology, 24*, 580–588.

Southam-Gerow, M. A., & Kendall, P. C. (2002). A preliminary study of the emotion understanding of youths referred for treatment of anxiety disorders. *Journal of Clinical Child Psychology, 29*, 319–327.

Sroufe, L. A. (1996). *Emotional development: The organization of emotional life in the early years.* New York: Cambridge University Press.

Stansbury, K., & Sigman, M. (2000). Responses of preschoolers in two frustrating episodes: Emergence of complex strategies for emotion regulation. *Journal of Genetic Psychology, 161,* 182–202.

Stifter, C. A., & Braungart, J. M. (1995). The regulation of negative reactivity in infancy: Function and development. *Developmental Psychology, 31,* 448–455.

Suveg, C., & Zeman, J. (2004). Emotion regulation in children with anxiety disorders. *Journal of Clinical Child and Adolescent Psychology, 33,* 750–759.

Thompson, R. A. (1994). Emotion regulation: A theme in search of definition. In N. A. Fox (Ed.), The development of emotion regulation: Biological and behavioral considerations. *Monographs of the Society for Research in Child Development, 59* (2-3, Serial No. 240), 25–52.

Tice, D. M., Baumeister, R. F., & Zhang, L. (2004). The role of emotion in self-regulation: Differing role of positive and negative emotions. In P. Philippot & R. S. Feldman (Eds.), *The regulation of emotion* (pp. 213–226). Mahwah, NJ: Erlbaum.

Tolan, P. J., & Dodge, K. A. (2005). Children's mental health as a primary care and concern: A system for comprehensive support and service. *American Psychologist, 60,* 601–614.

Wehr, T. A., Sack, D. A., Rosenthal, N. E., & Cowdry, R. W. (1988). Rapid cycling affective disorder: Contributing factors and treatment responses in 51 patients. *American Journal of Psychiatry, 145,* 179–184.

Weisbrot, D. M., Gadow, K. D., DeVincent, C. J., & Pomeroy, J. (2005). The presentation of anxiety in children with pervasive developmental disorders. *Journal of Child and Adolescent Psychopharmacology, 15,* 477–496.

Wilson, B. J. (2003). The role of attentional processes in children's prosocial behavior with peers: Attention shifting and emotion. *Development and Psychopathology, 15,* 313–329.

Wintre, M. G., & Vallance, D. D. (1994). A developmental sequence in the comprehension of emotions: Intensity, multiple emotions, and valence. *Developmental Psychology, 30,* 509–514.

Zeman, J., & Garber, J. (1996). Display rules for anger, sadness, and pain: It depends on who is watching. *Child Development, 67,* 957–973.

Zeman, J., Shipman, K., & Suveg, C. (2002). Anger and sadness regulation: *Journal of Clinical Child and Adolescent Psychology, 31,* 393–398.

PART III

EXTERNALIZING BEHAVIOR DISORDERS

CHAPTER 11

Attention-Deficit/ Hyperactivity Disorder

JOEL NIGG AND MOLLY NIKOLAS

HISTORICAL CONTEXT

Few child difficulties generate as much controversy and concern in our society as problems with attention and impulse control, especially Attention-Deficit/Hyperactivity Disorder (ADHD; American Psychiatric Association, 1994, 2000). Such concern is fueled in part by dramatically rising rates of medication treatments for children in the United States (Robison et al., 1999), combined with inadequate mental health services. The debate is important: ADHD is a highly impairing syndrome affecting a large number of children.

The disorder has been in the medical literature in the United States since the beginning of the 20th Century; treatment with stimulant medication began mid-century. Stimulant treatment rates rose markedly in the second half of the twentieth century, sparking controversy and, in the 1970s, lawsuits. Treatment rates rose markedly again from 1990 to the present. This was attributable in part to changes in educational policy that facilitated identification of children with ADHD in the United States. It has also been influenced by a widening definition of the ADHD phenotype. In *DSM-III* (APA, 1980), the condition was labeled Attention Deficit Disorder (ADD with two types: with and without hyperactivity). These subtypes were

Acknowledgments: Work on this chapter was supported by NIMH grants MH63146 and MH59105 to Joel Nigg.

eliminated and the condition was renamed as ADHD in the *DSM-III-R* (APA, 1987). In *DSM-IV* (APA, 1994), the name was retained but subtypes were reintroduced in modified form: a Predominantly Inattentive Type (ADHD-PI, similar to *DSM-III* ADD without hyperactivity), a Predominantly Hyperactive-Impulsive Type (ADHD-PH, unprecedented in previous nomenclatures), and a Combined Type (ADHD-C).

Appropriate breadth and delineation of the phenotype has been a persistent concern. For instance, historically, motor control problems were a part of the overinclusive term *minimal brain dysfunction*, used mid-century. They were removed in *DSM-III-R* and *DSM-IV*, and moved to the diagnostic category of Developmental Coordination Disorder. However, data continue to appear on motor control problems, clumsiness, and motor output in ADHD (Piek, Pitcher, & Hay, 1999). Traditionally considered a disorder of childhood, by the end of the twentieth century it had become clear that ADHD persists into adolescence and adulthood in many cases (Mannuzza & Klein, 2000). Accordingly, data on adults with ADHD are now of great interest.

In this chapter, we emphasize mechanistic theories about within-child psychological and/or cognitive dysfunction in ADHD and a multilevel perspective on etiology. We conclude by emphasizing that ADHD is not a unitary syndrome but reflects important heterogeneity among affected children. For more detailed discussions of ADHD see Barkley (2006), Nigg (2006a), and Nigg, Hinshaw, and Huang-Pollock (2006).

TERMINOLOGICAL AND CONCEPTUAL ISSUES

Despite continued public controversy, there is substantial evidence for the validity of ADHD with regard to factor structure, impairment, and family patterns (Faraone et al., 2005). It is important to note that symptom domains are divided into distinct dimensions—in the *DSM-IV*, these are (a) inattentive-disorganized, and (b) hyperactive-impulsive. Despite some debate as to whether impulsivity and hyperactivity should count as one dimension or as separate subdimensions, the two-factor solution has received strong support in terms of divergent external validity, with inattentive behaviors uniquely associated with academic problems and hyperactive/impulsive behaviors aggregating with disruptive tendencies in school and home settings (Lahey & Willcutt, 2002). These two symptoms domains may have partially distinct etiological inputs, a point to which we return subsequently.

Less clear is whether it is more accurate to view ADHD as a discrete syndrome, or as reflecting extreme standing on a normal, varying trait. Evidence is mounting that the syndrome reflects extreme standing on a continuously varying trait in the population (Willcutt, Pennington, & DeFries, 2000). Clinicians still need to make diagnostic decisions, however, and the cut points in the *DSM-IV* have empirical support at most efficiently identifying impaired children in need of services. However, when we consider models of etiology, a dimensional model is likely to be most useful.

In addition, the subtypes proposed in *DSM-IV* have not attained strong empirical support. ADHD-C describes children who are both inattentive-disorganized and impulsive-hyperactive. Most research on ADHD pertains to this group of children, who comprise the bulk of clinical referrals. ADHD-PH is still largely unstudied, and many children in this classification are preschoolers (Lahey et al., 1994). Work on ADHD-PI also is less advanced, and fewer conclusions can be drawn than about ADHD-C. A particular focus is whether ADHD-C and ADHD-PI are distinct conditions or whether ADHD-PI is essentially a mild version of ADHD-C (Milich, Balentine, & Lynam, 2001). Lahey et al. (2005) followed preschoolers with ADHD for 8 years; a majority of children failed to meet criteria for ADHD on at least one assessment, yet many met criteria again at a later wave. A substantial percentage (37% of ADHD-C and 50% of ADHD-PI) met criteria for a different subtype at least twice during the eight assessments. Furthermore, family studies assessing whether ADHD subtypes "breed true" have yielded mixed results. In a recent meta-analysis, Stawicki, Nigg, and von Eye (2006) concluded that reliable familial separation of the combined and inattentive types exists, but with only a weak effect, most likely because the ADHD-PI group includes some children with subthreshold ADHD-C.

As a result, efforts to refine the ADHD phenotype and the subtyping scheme continue. For example, latent class analyses of population samples suggest potential modifications to the current nosology, with subtypes defined somewhat differently (Hudziak et al., 1998; Neuman et al., 2001; Rasmussen et al., 2004). These studies identified three mild and three severe classes of ADHD; the clinical classes exhibited heritability, familial clustering, differential patterns of cormorbidity, and stability across informants. However, the clinical utility and developmental course of these empirically derived classes remain important questions if they are to influence the current diagnostic system. Future refinement of the phenotype is possible in *DSM-V*.

Note that studies of ADHD sometimes use the *DSM-IV* criteria, sometimes the International Classification of Disease–10th Edition (ICD-10) criteria for hyperkinetic disorder, and sometimes merely extreme rating scale scores. However, we use the term *ADHD* throughout to avoid tedious cataloguing of differences in phenotype definition across studies.

DIAGNOSTIC ISSUES AND *DSM-IV* CRITERIA

Table 11.1 lists *DSM-IV* features of ADHD, ICD-10 symptoms of hyperkinetic disorder, and the current diagnostic algorithms in use to define this disorder. Although the symptom lists are similar, several distinctions can be seen between ADHD and hyperkinetic disorder, reflecting ongoing differences in how this syndrome is defined in Europe and the United States. The most important difference is that the two systems have different rules about comorbid disorders as rule-outs, with ICD-10 being more restrictive and *DSM-IV* being more inclusive. Additional criteria include onset by age 7 years, cross-situational display, and impairment.

Whereas guidelines about age of onset lack consistent empirical support (Kordon, Kahl, & Wahl, 2006), guidelines requiring cross-situational impairment have strong empirical support. Failure to assess impairment is likely to inflate prevalence estimates (Gordon et al., 2005) and inclusion of both parent and teacher standardized ratings enhances assessment validity (Pelham, Fabiano, & Massetti, 2005). Thus, accurate assessment requires a careful history, data from multiple informants with normed rating scales, distinguishing ADHD from normal developmental variation and the several medical and psychiatric conditions that feature inattention and impulse control problems (e.g., anxiety and mood disorders, sleep and health-related disorders, some learning disorders), and, when possible, direct observation. Consideration of functional adjustment in multiple domains can further assist with treatment tailoring (Pelham et al., 2005).

PREVALENCE

Two population-based national surveys in the United States yielded an incidence of 6.8% among children ages 6 to 11 (Pastor & Reuben, 2002; but note that fully half of these also had received a diagnosis of learning disability) and of 6.6% among adults recalling childhood symptoms (Kessler et al., 2006; 4.4% of adults showed current ADHD). Our recent review of five available studies of local prevalence rates that used either structured clinical interviews or multiple informants (Nigg, 2006a) arrived at a total of 6.8%: 2.9% for ADHD-C, 3.2% for ADHD-PI, and 0.6% for ADHD-PH. Polanczyk et al. (2007) reviewed 102 studies and arrived at a worldwide prevalence estimate of 5.3% (6.3% in North America) for all subtypes. Thus, multiple approaches converge rather consistently on a prevalence across all subtypes of 6 to 7% in the United States, and just over 5% worldwide. Despite their convergence, these may be high estimates. Few studies

Table 11.1.
Diagnostic Criteria for ADHD in DSM-IV and ICD-10

1. Fails to give close attention to details or makes careless mistakes in school-work, work, or other activities.
2. Has difficulty sustaining attention on tasks or play activities.
3. Does not seem to listen when spoken to directly.
4. Does not follow through on instructions and fails to finish schoolwork, chores, or work duties.
5. Has difficulty organizing tasks and activities (ICD-10: . . . is often impaired in organizing tasks).
6. Avoids, dislikes, or is reluctant to engage in tasks that require sustained mental effort such as homework.
7. Loses things necessary for tasks or activities (e.g., toys, school assignments, pencils, books, tools).
8. Is easily distracted by extraneous stimuli (ICD-10: . . . by external stimuli).
9. Is forgetful in daily activities (ICD-10: . . . in the course of daily activities).
10. Fidgets with hands or feet or squirms in seat (ICD-10: . . . on seat).
11. Leaves seat in classroom or in other situations in which remaining seated is expected.
12. Runs about or climbs excessively in situations in which it is inappropriate.
13. Has difficulty playing or engaging in leisure activities quietly (ICD-10: is often unduly noisy in playing or has difficulty in engaging quietly in leisure activities).
14. Is "on the go" or often acts as if "driven by a motor" (ICD-10: exhibits a persistent pattern of excessive motor activity that is not substantially modified by social context or demands).
15. Talks excessively (ICD-10 . . . "without appropriate response to social con-straints").
16. Blurts out answers before the questions have been completed.
17. Has difficulty awaiting turn (ICD-10: fails to wait in lines or await turns in games or group situations).
18. Interrupts or intrudes on others (e.g., butts into conversations or games).

NB: Each behavior must occur "often" and must persist for at least 6 months to a degree that is maladaptive and inconsistent with developmental level.

Subtypes:

DSM-IV ADHD-C: 6 items from items 1–9, plus 6 items from items 10–18.

DSM-IV ADHD-PI: 6 items from items 1–9.

DSM-IV ADHD-HI: 6 items from items 10–18.

ICD-10 Hyperkinetic Disorder: 6 items from 1–9, plus 3 items from 10–14, plus 1 item from 16–18.

Source: Adapted from the *DSM-IV* (APA, 1994) and ICD-10 (WHO, 1993).

used full *DSM-IV* criteria. Prevalence rates are much lower for ICD-10 criteria, typically around 1%. Finally, although administrative prevalence (case identification) has risen, whether there are changes in actual population incidence remains unstudied and unknown.

RISK FACTORS AND ETIOLOGICAL FORMULATIONS

We now turn to etiological approaches, emphasizing both (a) within-child correlates that may elucidate etiology and help explain the behavioral problems observed, and (b) risk factors that may contribute to the disorder, perhaps via these internal mechanisms. We bypass a range of psychological mechanisms such as self-esteem and locus of control, and instead focus primarily on neurally mediated models.

ETIOLOGY I: GENETIC INFLUENCES ON LIABILITY TO ADHD

It has long been established that ADHD "runs in families," with a two- to four-fold increased risk among first-degree relatives. How much of this familial similarity is due to genes versus common family experiences? Over a dozen behavioral genetic (twin and/or adoption) studies of ADHD have established that in parent ratings, (a) substantial portions of liability are carried by genetic variation, with heritability estimated from .6 to as high as .8 or .9, (b) nonshared environment effects are modest to small, and (c) shared environment effects are negligible. Heritability estimates are somewhat lower, however, when teacher ratings are examined, although the heritability of a latent variable for shared parent and teacher agreement was .78 in a large Dutch sample (Derks et al., 2006). Relatively few studies have examined twin concordance of ADHD diagnoses derived from full clinical evaluation or the combining of parent and teacher input on symptoms and impairment.

Yet the variation in results for teacher versus parent ratings raises questions of rater bias (known as contrast effects) as an influence on heritability estimates. Contrast bias (parents emphasizing differences more in dizygotic [DZ] than monozygotic [M2] twins) inflates heritability estimates of activity levels in preschoolers (Saudino, 2003); these effects in ADHD ratings appear to depend on what rating scale is used (Hay et al., 2007). Rietveld et al. (2004) reported on a longitudinal study of a large sample of twins in Europe, with maternal CBCL ratings at four age points (3, 7, 10, and 12 years). Even with rater contrast effects controlled, heritability was above .7 at each age. Simonoff et al. (1998) confirmed maternal contrast effects, but also noted biases in teacher ratings due to twin confusion (known as correlated errors), especially for MZ twins. Many twins have the same teacher, and teachers have more difficulty differentiating between MZ twins. When these effects are accounted for, heritability is between .6 and .7. In sum, the heritability of ADHD is around .7. Nonshared environmental effects account for the remainder of variance in ADHD liability. Thus, the field has moved rapidly into molecular genetic studies of ADHD.

With regard to molecular genetics, two approaches are commonly used to seek genes that contribute to risk for ADHD: genome-wide scans and candidate gene studies. Genome-wide scans attempt to identify chromosomal regions throughout the entire genome that may contain genes for ADHD. Initial genome-wide scans for ADHD yielded nonreplication of findings, suggesting this search will not be straightforward and will require large pooled samples. Examination of pooled data across the two major samples reported to date found common linkages to chromosome 5p13 (Ogdie et al., 2006). Furthermore, fine mapping of this region indicates a strong signal at this locus on chromosome 5—the same region to which the dopamine transporter gene has been mapped (Hebebrand et al., 2006). It remains to be seen whether this finding will replicate in new samples.

Candidate gene studies focus largely on specific genes, identified a priori and thought to influence relevant neural transmission systems. Most of the focus has been on dopaminergic and noradrenergic systems, in part because psychostimulants are believed to achieve their therapeutic effects by altering catecholamine neural transmission. The dopamine (DA) transporter gene (DAT1, *SLC6A3*), located on chromosome 5p15.3, influences reuptake of DA in the synapse. The 10-repeat allele of a tandem repeat polymorphism in the 3′ untranslated region of the gene has been studied extensively; a recent meta-analysis of 9 studies indicates a small, but significant, association with ADHD (odds ratio = 1.13; Faraone et al., 2005).

Dopamine receptor genes have also received considerable attention in the ADHD genetics literature, particularly the D4 receptor (DRD4), which is expressed in the prefrontal-striatal circuits implicated in neural models of ADHD (see the following). The 7-repeat allele of a tandem repeat polymorphism in exon III was associated with ADHD in recent meta-analyses of 18 studies (pooled odds ratio = 1.45; Faraone et al., 2005). Other DA receptor genes have also been examined for association with ADHD, but initial findings for the D2, D3, and D5 receptor gene have been mixed, leaving conclusions uncertain.

Dopaminergic precursor genes have also been examined in relation to ADHD. As opposed to transporter and receptor genes, the precursor genes code for enzymes that aid in the synthesis and conversion of dopamine before it is released into the synapse. The dopamine beta-hydroxylase gene

(DBH) codes for an enzyme that aids in the presynaptic conversion of dopamine to norepinephrine. The TaqI A2 allele of intron 5 of DBH was associated with ADHD in initial studies (Kirley et al., 2002; Roman et al., 2002). The tyrosine hydroxylase (TH) gene codes for a rate-limiting enzyme in the synthesis of DA, but a marker in the promoter region of the TH gene was not associated with ADHD in studies to date (Barr et al., 2000).

The noradrenergic alpha-2a receptor gene (ADRA2A) is expressed in the prefrontal cortex and thought to be involved in working memory. Although several initial studies in specialized samples were negative for association with ADHD, a more recent study examining other markers (Park et al., 2005) found an association between the inattentive and hyperactive symptom domains and the *DraI* polymorphism of ADRA2A in a U.S. sample, although the test for association with the actual disorder failed to reach significance. This did not replicate in a sample of Han Chinese children with ADHD (Wang et al., 2006).

Considerable interest has also accrued in the serotonin (5-HT) system and ADHD, as well as other disorders (see other chapters in this volume). Overtransmission of the "long" allele of a 44-bp insertion/deletion polymorphism of the 5-HT transporter gene (5-HTT, *SLC6A4*) has been reported for children with ADHD (Kent et al., 2002; Manor et al., 2001), although comorbid conditions such as ODD and CD were not well-controlled for. Additionally, initial evidence has also been found for an association between the G allele of the 5-HT HTR1B receptor and ADHD (Hawi et al., 2002). The gene for TH, the enzyme crucial to 5-HT synthesis, has been associated with aggression and impulsivity, but not ADHD (Li et al., 2006).

Overall, the most well-replicated gene findings account for only a fraction of genetic influence on ADHD, but nonetheless converge with imaging and neuropsychological data in suggesting involvement of prefrontal and striatal neural networks. Note that as a complex disorder, ADHD is likely to be influenced by several genes, each of small to moderate effect, interacting with one another and, potentially, with environmental factors (see also Beauchaine & Neuhaus, this volume); thus, genes cannot be used to diagnose ADHD.

Etiology II: Environmental Risks and Triggers

There are many possible environmental contributors to ADHD. Inadequate schooling, rapid societal tempo, and family stress have been alleged to increase the incidence of ADHD. Many of these sociological ideas are interesting but untested (or untestable). After considering the conceptual context for environmental etiologies in ADHD, we review biological and psychosocial influences that warrant deeper study. Evaluation of environmental influences on ADHD must consider the nature of ADHD etiology noted earlier: shared environment effects are very small, and nonshared effects are modest. Yet, these simple variance partitionings do not tell the whole story.

First, we must consider gene–environment correlations. For instance, if a parent has an impulsive temperament, passes the genetic risk onto her child, but then also provides a chaotic home environment that is correlated with her genotype, that chaotic environment may be a route of expressing the genetic influence, even though it emerges as part of the heritability term in behavior genetic studies. Genetically informative studies of socialization effects are needed to clarify gene–environment correlations.

These effects signify potential epigenetic influences. The development of the child's self-control, which rests on genetically influenced liability, depends on and interacts with socialization in a reciprocal and transactional manner. Yet a child's readiness, in the form of trait-like characteristics such as self-control and language ability, is crucial to his or her ability to benefit from typical social interchanges. Such characteristics influence caregivers and at times make it more difficult for the child to learn social rules (Johnston & Mash, 2001), perhaps triggering a recursive loop in which the child inadvertently contributes to counterproductive socialization experiences. The preschool years are an especially critical time for these socialization dynamics, during the period that language, deliberate effortful control, and affect regulation develop rapidly via interchanges with caregivers. Various kinds of family stressors may therefore be related to ADHD symptoms, perhaps because they disrupt the ability of caregivers to participate fully in this developmental dialectic. In turn, various characteristics of caregivers can influence children's behavior both via genetic mediation and through direct socialization influences. Despite these recursive loops, most data on child-parenting effects have suggested child effects on caregivers in ADHD. For example, in their classic study, Barkley and Cunningham (1979) found that when hyperactive children were switched from placebo to medication, their mothers' negative/controlling behaviors were dramatically reduced.

Second, certain types of gene–environment interactions *inflate* the heritability term in twin studies (Purcell, 2002). That is, some experiential effects may differentially activate genetic risk. Such interactive experiential triggers are of unknown effect size in ADHD. We therefore highlight potential environmental effects when triggers are widespread in the population and present intriguing directions, even though most of these need further study.

With regard to possible environmental potentiators of genetic liability, the biological context, both pre- and postnatally, is fertile ground. For example, low birth weight (< 2500 grams) is a specific risk factor for inattention/hyperactivity but not other behavior problems at age 6 (Breslau & Chilcoate, 2000). However, low birth weight is multiply determined by factors such as maternal health and nutrition, maternal smoking, maternal weight, low SES, stress, and other factors, making identification of specific biological mechanisms difficult (see also Gatzke-Kopp & Shannon, this volume). On the other hand, an extensive literature indicates that some prenatal teratogens increase risk of ADHD (see Fryer, Crocker, & Mattson, this volume). For example, alcohol exposure, at least for women in the United States at moderate levels of drinking (Jacobson et al., 2004; Mick et al., 2002), increases risk of offspring ADHD. However, these children may have a somewhat distinct neuropsychological profile from typical ADHD, with particular problems in visual attention and mathematics. Maternal smoking during pregnancy has been related to ADHD in numerous studies (Linnet et al., 2003), though it remains unclear whether this effect is attributable in large part to genetic effects (that is, GE correlation) or to effects on temperament that lead to oppositional-defiant behavior (for a review see Nigg, 2006b). Effects of other drug exposures are less clear, as are effects of maternal stress during pregnancy (Linnet et al., 2003).

Postnatal exposures to certain toxins are known routes to hyperactivity in some instances. Particularly well studied are effects of lead exposure, which even at low levels can contribute to later ADHD symptoms (Chiodo, Jacobson, & Jacobson, 2004: Nigg et al., in press). These findings are of particular public health concern, because the levels of lead being studied remain common in the United States and epidemic in many nations in the world. Numerous other toxins could potentially contribute to ADHD, but are to date insufficiently studied to draw firm conclusions (see Nigg, 2006a).

At all stages of development, short- and long-term effects of dietary insufficiencies have been a major question in the field for decades. Because of the well-documented adverse effects of the typical Western diet regarding such diseases such as obesity and diabetes, the domain seems relevant. However, establishing dietary contributors to ADHD has proven difficult. Widely touted claims that sugar or caffeine intake influence ADHD have not been convincing (Castellanos & Rapoport, 2002). Likewise, early claims that allergic reactions or intolerances to food additives contribute to ADHD appeared to have been disproved by the early 1980s (Kavale & Forness, 1983). Nevertheless, this last issue continues to be revisited. A recent meta-analysis (Schab & Trinh, 2004) identified 15 more recent studies with double-blind, placebo-controlled designs, yielding an aggregate significant effect. However, effects were confined to parental ratings, raising questions about effectiveness of the placebo controls even in these well-designed studies. More recently, a host of other dietary theories have begun to receive investigation. In all, continued study of dietary effects, perhaps acting in concert with genetic susceptibility in a subgroup of children, remains relevant to a complete understanding of this behavioral syndrome.

Many other experiential factors have been hypothesized to influence ADHD, from general sociological claims such as "faster pace of life" to more testable effects of early electronic media on brain development. Although no conclusive evidence has been reported, it remains possible that important discoveries will emerge in regard to experiential triggers.

MECHANISMS I. NEURAL IMAGING FINDINGS

Whether we discuss genetic contributors to liability or environmental triggers, these effects are presumably expressed in the brain. Thus, isolation of causal mechanisms suggests that we consider brain circuitry and their associated abilities. We first consider neuroimaging findings before turning to psychological functioning in ADHD.

Brain imaging studies provide an emerging picture of neural correlates of ADHD. Although this literature remains limited by (a) small samples, (b) varying methods, (c) difficulties in imaging subcortical structures, (d) a shortage of theoretical, hypothesis-driven research, and (e) inconsistent control for total brain volume, understanding of brain mechanisms is beginning to emerge. Major findings to date are summarized in Table 11.2. Children with ADHD taken as a group evidence a 5% reduction in overall brain volume and a 12% reduction in volume of key frontal and subcortical structures. The four main regions implicated are the prefrontal cortices (crucial to complex, planned behavior, keeping goals in mind, and overriding inappropriate responses), the basal ganglia/striatum (a group of subcortical structures important in response control), the cerebellum (important in temporal information processing and motor control), and the corpus callosum (involved in integrating information for efficient responding). The most compelling evidence points to a neural circuit that links the prefrontal cortex and a subcortical region known as the striatum, a circuit thought to be important in response control. Additionally, notably smaller structural sizes are noted in the cerebellum (especially the cerebellar vermis), a region important for temporal information processing and executive functioning, which is connected via long fiber projections to the prefrontal cortex. Casey et al. (1997) found that smaller right-frontal structures were associated with more response inhibition errors on a go/no-go task in children with ADHD, suggesting the functional importance of these findings.

Table 11.2.
Summary of Brain Imaging Findings in ADHD

Structure	Key Findings
Prefrontal Cortex	reduced right > left asymmetry, with relatively smaller right side; reduced dorsolateral prefrontal cortex volume; under-activation of right medial prefrontal cortex and ventrolateral prefrontal cortex to challenge
Dorsal Anterior Cingulate Cortex	few structural studies of this region; functional studies indicate possible hypoactivation during challenge tasks, need replication
Basal Ganglia	reduced volume of the caudate, but not putamen; decreased volume of the pallidum; reduced size of globus pallidus in preliminary studies; hypoactivation of left caudate during executive task performance; reduced blood flow to the putamen in reflexometric MRI study
Cerebellum	reduced size of vermis, especially posterior-inferior lobules; overall decreased right cerebellar volumes
Corpus Callossum	smaller rostrum (anterior and inferior region); abnormalities of the posterior regions linked to temporal and parietal cortices in the splenium
Exploratory Findings	decreased volume of the parietal lobe; reduced occipital gray and white matter; significantly larger posterior lateral ventricles bilaterally
Caveats	insufficient data on subregions of key structures; insufficient control of confounds; lack of data on key subcortical regions

Data from Giedd et al., 2001; Castellanos, 2001; Swanson & Castellanos, 2002; Seidman et al., 2005.

These findings are consistent with a formulation that a key mechanism in ADHD is reduction in health of neural circuits involved in cognitive control and complex integration of behavior based on contextual cues. Note, however, that these structural effects, although statistically moderate to large in size, are no larger than those observed for cognitive or neuropsychological measures. In the case of structural changes, the 10 to 12% reductions noted equate to an effect size of ½ to ¾ of a standard deviation. Thus, at an individual level, many if not most children with ADHD do not show abnormal structural magnetic resonance imaging (MRI) scans; as a result, brain scans provide no diagnostic utility at present. Instead, imaging findings provide clues to mechanisms at the group level and may eventually identify a subgroup of children with subtle brain alterations. Initial longitudinal data (Castellanos et al., 2002) suggest that these volumetric reductions are present early in life, and are stable yet nonprogressive (regardless of medication treatment). That finding is consistent with the idea of either inherited or early acquired brain alterations, rather than a progressive developmental process or delay.

Functional magnetic resonance imaging studies (fMRI) have indicated that the dorsal anterior cingulate cortex, which plays an important role in attention, cognition, and decision making, is hypoactive in ADHD, and that there are altered activation patterns in the striatum, including the left caudate (Durston et al., 2003; Rubia et al., 1999). Results are less consistent for the lateral frontal cortex. Nonetheless, these results seem to confirm that the same regions with altered size are also showing hypoactivation (see Gatzke-Kopp & Beauchaine, in press, for a review). Activation studies are just beginning to be conducted on key subcortical incentive-response regions such as the nucleus accumbens and the cerebellum. A meta-analysis of 16 fMRI studies of ADHD revealed consistent brain-activation deficits in virtually all regions of the prefrontal cortex, as well as other brain regions (Dickstein et al., 2006). These findings support abnormal functioning in fronto-striatal as well as frontal-parietal neural circuitry in ADHD.

In addition, a growing electrophysiological literature has suggested that ADHD is associated with slow wave brain activity and poor early alerting to stimuli (for an overview, see Banaschewski & Brandeis, 2007). The future is likely to see extensive use of these methodologies in understanding ADHD and marking treatment responses.

MECHANISMS II. PERFORMANCE STUDIES OF NEUROPSYCHOLOGIAL AND COGNITIVE ABILITIES

In understanding the psychological mechanisms that are involved (and that might correspond to what is known about neural findings), four key functional systems in the brain are implicated in ADHD: (a) nonexecutive attention and arousal, (b) executive functioning and cognitive control, (c) motivation and reinforcement, and (d) temporal information processing.

Attention can be defined as the facilitated processing of one piece or source of information over others—in other words, the ability to focus or filter information. Usually considered a cognitive process, attention can be influenced by emotion as well (as when anxiety narrows attentional focus). Attentional selection (whether by location, movement, timing, or other features) is influenced both by bottom-up stimulus-driven processes that are relatively automatic and early developing, and by top-down goal-driven processes that are strategic, relatively deliberate, related to the concept of executive control, and later developing. In contrast, a posterior network involved in reflexive orienting and perceptual filtering is apparently not involved in ADHD-C (Huang-Pollock & Nigg, 2003; Huang-Pollock,

Nigg, & Carr, 2005; Sergeant & van der Meere, 1988), though its role in ADHD-PI remains unclear.

On the other hand, aspects of a system responsible for attentional alerting (immediate focus of attention on something important, related to the older concept of *arousal*) and vigilance (maintaining the alert state over time, also called *sustained attention*) are salient for ADHD. This system involves a right-lateralized network of neural structures that include the noradrenergic system originating in the locus coeruleus, the cholinergic system of the basal forebrain, the intralaminar thalamic nuclei, the right prefrontal cortex (Posner & Peterson, 1990), and possibly the ascending reticular activating system (related to wakefulness). Sustained attention (vigilance) appears to be affected only under certain task conditions (such as different event rates), potentially implicating a process known as activation or response readiness (Sergeant, Oosterlaan, & van der Meere, 1999). In contrast, abnormalities in the alerting function in ADHD are apparent in the form of (a) poor signal detection on continuous-performance tasks (Losier, McGrath, & Klein, 1996); (b) a tendency to respond too slowly on "fast as you can" reaction-time tasks (apparently due to an excess of extremely slow responses, suggesting failures of alertness), and (c) excess slow-wave activity in brain EEG observations (Barry, Clarke, & Johnstone, 2003).

Cognitive control (related to the older but widely used term, *executive function*) refers to strategic allocation of both attention and response. When in the service of a later goal held in mind we suppress an unwanted thought (I am anxious but I focus on the exam question), or behavior (I am eager to interrupt but I want to keep my New Year's resolution not to), we engage in cognitive control. Children must use this ability to study first and play later, to pay attention in class even when other children are talking, to keep track of their materials when returning home from school, and to wait their turn. Such behaviors depend on dopaminergic and noradrenergic circuits in dorsolateral and orbital-prefrontal cortices and their projections to and from the basal ganglia and parietal cortex. These circuits track whether what has occurred is consistent with expectations—and adjust behavior accordingly. Yet also relevant are prefrontal-cerebellar circuits, which may be important for determining if the timing of events is consistent with what was expected and then modulating behavior (Nigg & Casey, 2005). We parse this broad domain into (a) working memory (which depends on maintaining attentional control); (b) response suppression (executive inhibition); and (c) shifting (involving parietal activity).

Working memory refers to a limited capacity system for keeping something in mind while doing something else, such as remembering a phone number while completing a conversation. It is supported by simple passive storage or *short-term* memory (holding something in mind for a moment).

Table 11.3.

Summary of Neuropsychological Findings in ADHD

Domain	Status	Meta-Analytic Effect Size
Attention		
Perceptual selection	4	na
Reflexive orienting	4	$d=.20$
Alerting/Vigilance System	1	$d=.75$
Cognitive Control/Executive functioning		
Interference Control	4	$d=.20$
Working Memory Verbal	2	$d=.45$
Working Memory Spatial	1	$d=1.0$
Planning	2	$d=.55$
Response Inhibition	1	$d=.60$
Set Shifting	2	$d=.50$
Activation	3	na
Motivational Response		
Reactive (anxious) inhibition	4	na
Reward response (approach)	2	na
Motor and Temporal Response		
Motor control	2	na
Temporal processing	2	na

Ratings of status: 1 = replicated deficit, substantial in size (reliably larger than .50 based on number of studies, confidence interval around pooled effect size); 2 = deficit probably exists, but aggregate effects are modest in size (not reliably larger than .50) or consistent results rely on a small number of studies (so pooled effect size has wide confidence interval); 3 = possible deficit but findings are mixed across different indicators, and positive findings rest on small number of studies; 4 = spared (or effect is too trivial in size to be clinically meaningful). Na = not available or not applicable. Effect sizes are rounded-off estimates. Reprinted from Nigg, 2006, where a detailed review is also available.

It includes separate neural loops for handling verbal information (the left-lateralized phonological loop) and spatial information (right lateralized). Most of the 20 or so studies on working memory and ADHD have taken place in the last decade and were evaluated in two recent meta-analyses (Martinussen et al., 2005; Willcutt et al., 2005). Both reviews pegged effects for verbal working memory and storage in the small to medium range, at d =.43 (Martinussen et al., 2005) to d =.54 (Willcutt et al., 2005). In contrast to these modest effects, spatial working-memory weaknesses were medium to large, in the range of d =.72 (Willcutt et al., 2005) to d =1.06 (Martinussen et al., 2005). Effects were nearly as large for short-term memory (d =.85 in Martinussen et al., 2005). The small number of studies included (6 to 8) must be kept in mind, but results indicate a meaningful ADHD effect for spatial tasks.

Response suppression (executive inhibition) refers to the ability to interrupt a response during dynamic moment-to-moment behavior. Although often conceptually associated with impulsivity, this ability may be equally or more related to inattention-disorganization, in that maintaining focused behavior requires continually suppressing alternative behaviors that may be activated by context. Imagine a *check-swing* in baseball as an index of keeping behavior immediately responsive to a rapidly changing context (Logan, 1994). Several experimental computer-based paradigms, brain imaging results, and brain-injury studies converge on links between this ability and a right-lateralized neural circuit involving the inferior frontal gyrus and, subcortically, the caudate, a structure in the basal ganglia. Key measurement paradigms include the go/no-go task, the antisaccade task (an eye-movement experiment), and the Logan (1994) stopping task. All converge on some ADHD-related weakness in this ability. Nearly 30 studies have been conducted on the stopping task alone, making it perhaps the most heavily studied paradigm in ADHD. Willcutt et al. (2005) reviewed 27 of these studies and noted a composite effect size for ADHD versus control of d =.61 (a medium effect size).

Set shifting refers to shifting one's mental focus within a task such as sorting by color versus sorting by number; whereas *task switching* refers to alternating tasks, such as counting objects versus naming objects. These abilities involve attentional networks in the parietal cortex (particularly for set shifting) and likely involve executive control and perhaps cerebellar control for task switching. Most neuropsychological studies of ADHD appear to involve set shifting, using tasks such as the Wisconsin Card Sort, and these yield only small to medium ADHD effects that do not replicate well (d =.46 across 24 studies; Willcutt et al., 2005). On the other hand, task-switching paradigms have only recently begun to be examined in ADHD.

Overall, difficulties in cognitive control are relevant to ADHD. They appear to be right-lateralized, involving in particular spatial working memory (and the dorsolateral prefrontal cortex) and response suppression (and inferior right prefrontal cortex and projection zones). In contrast, other executive abilities, such as verbal working memory and set shifting, exhibit smaller weaknesses, suggesting that they are less likely to be core mechanisms.

MOTIVATION, APPROACH, AND REINFORCEMENT RESPONSE

The central motivational processes involved in ADHD have been approached from both a temperament perspective (for reviews see Nigg, 2006b; Rothbart & Bates, 1998) and an experimental perspective, examining response to reinforcement. We begin with temperament, synthesizing several models to focus on two key traits.

Withdrawal or reactive control is anchored in limbic structures including the amygdala, the hippocampus, and their interconnections. This form of control implements reactions of anxiety and fear that trigger spontaneous inhibition of behaviors in response to novelty or threat. A rich literature suggests that this reactive control of behavior is related to anxiety and anxiety disorders (Kagan & Snidman, 2004). Low response on this system (failure of fear response) appears to be related to psychopathy (Blair et al., 2006) and perhaps Conduct Disorder (CCD), but not with ADHD. As reviewed in detail by Nigg (2001), experimental paradigms designed to elicit caution in response to potential punishment cues do not yield a reliable set of responses in relation to ADHD.

Approach, or willingness to seek incentive or reward / reinforcement, is associated with speed of reinforcement learning. It is conceptualized as related to the appetitive, dopaminergic systems, including the nucleus accumbens and ascending limbic-frontal dopaminergic networks. At the level of the autonomic nervous system, it is linked with sympathetic activation during the performance of rewarded behaviors. One crucial index is heart-rate acceleration in response to incentives (Beauchaine, 2001). Goldsmith, Lemery, and Essex (2004) followed children from birth through first grade, with multisource temperament measures and parent and teacher ratings of ADHD symptoms. Observational data linked hyperactivity / impulsivity primarily with high approach, though magnitudes of associations were modest (rs in the .2 to .3 range). Other studies of personality and temperament have yielded mixed results for this trait (Nigg et al., 2002), although cross-sectional ratings of children suggest it is related to hyperactivity / impulsivity but not inattention (Martel & Nigg, 2006).

Another line of work has considered ADHD from the viewpoint of reinforcement response—mechanistic activation levels in the appetitive and reinforcement learning systems of the midbrain ascending DA network. These neurons appear to signal unexpected responses to the PFC and to be heavily involved in reinforcement learning, as well as in triggering cognitive control in a bottom-up process. Relying heavily on a series of elegant animal studies, Sagvolden et al. (2005) suggested that ADHD may be linked to a weakened reinforcement-delay gradient—that is, as the time to wait for an outcome increases, children with ADHD lose interest in earning the reward more precipitously than do other children. The result is difficulty in learning and in unlearning behaviors that are linked to reinforcers. Human studies to evaluate this theory are needed. A large literature on reward response in ADHD has yielded complex findings that are difficult to link to any one theory. A comprehensive review by Luman, Oosterlaan, and Sergeant (2005) concluded that ADHD is associated with (a) increased weighting of near-term over long-term (but larger) reward, (b) possible positive response to high-intensity reinforcement, and (c) lack of physiological response (e.g., heart-rate acceleration) to potential rewards. However, comorbid conditions, notably Conduct Disorder, have not been adequately considered in this literature.

Temporal Information Processing and Motor Control

In recent years the field has focused increasingly on temporal information processing. This idea emanates both from (a) recent theories of executive functioning, which emphasize the importance of temporal integration for both behavioral control (Barkley, 1997) and for learning and modulation of behavior (Nigg & Casey, 2005), and from (b) imaging findings of cerebellar alterations, as noted earlier. The cerebellum is now thought to be involved not only in learning of complex motor behaviors, but also in timing of behavior and temporal dependent learning. In short, the mind's internal "clock" may depend on the cerebellum. Implications of faulty time perception for behavioral control are extensive (Barkley, 1997). Toplak et al. (2005) reviewed some 20 extant studies and concluded that ADHD is associated with poor time estimation and poor time reproduction. Although more work in this area is needed, the implications for a complete understanding of neurobiology in ADHD are substantial. Problems in cerebellar functioning and temporal information processing could contribute to poor reinforcement learning, poor executive functioning, and even poor motor coordination.

DEVELOPMENTAL PROGRESSION

Despite questions about the appropriate age-of-onset criterion (if any) for diagnosing ADHD, the early school years are the modal age of case identification. It may be possible to identify ADHD in children as young as age 3 (Lahey et al., 1998; see also Campbell, 2002), although this is controversial. Even earlier in development, it is likely that the consolidation of regulatory capacities in the toddler years, and the influence of temperament in the first year of life, may interact with the social environment to shape vulnerability to ADHD (Nigg et al., 2006; see also Beauchaine & Neuhaus, this volume). However, diagnostic prediction from these temperamental precursors remains uncertain, and many at-risk toddlers do not go on to develop ADHD.

Some of the variation in subtype status is related to normal developmental trajectories. That is, motoric hyperactivity is more pronounced in preschool, and tends to decline with time, whereas problems with inattention can become more pronounced with age as peers undergo rapid maturation of prefrontal cortical structures and accompanying cognitive abilities at the same time that school demands intensify. Many children with ADHD-PI during preschool develop ADHD-C (or remit) as they enter the school years. Correspondingly, the inattentive type becomes more common later in childhood and through adolescence (Hart et al., 1995). Moreover, heterotypic continuity is not well addressed in the diagnostic system. That is, most behavioral symptoms are designed to describe school-age children; corresponding criteria for adolescence or adulthood are lacking (although this issue is beginning to be addressed by empirical work by Achenbach [1991], Conners [1997] and others). Adult findings are emerging; but they suggest a syndrome with clinical validity in terms of impairment and cognitive deficits (Murphy, Barkley, & Bush, 2001; Nigg, Stavro et al., 2005).

COMORBIDITY

ADHD is likely to exist in concert with one or more disruptive behavior disorders (Oppositional Defiant Disorder, Conduct Disorder), anxiety disorders, and learning disorders, providing possible clues to heterogeneity. In particular, consistent with the nosology in ICD-10, when ADHD co-occurs with clinically significant aggression or with major internalizing (anxious, depressed) features, it may constitute a substantially different condition than when it exists alone (e.g., Jensen et al., 2001).

Figure 11.1 illustrates patterns of comorbidity for boys with ADHD-C in the large, multisite, multimodal treatment study of ADHD (hereafter referred to as the MTA). As can be seen, even after accounting for Oppositional Defiant Disorder (the most frequently co-occurring condition), half of the children had at least one additional *DSM-IV* syndrome. Thus, clinical assessment must include comorbid disorders in case formulation. Similarly, a complete nosological account of heterogeneity must take in to account patterns of comorbid problems. It is important to recognize that many studies of etiology have not adequately considered comorbid conditions. Thus, degree of specificity of many of these effects to ADHD versus other disorders remains under dispute.

SEX DIFFERENCES

As with most psychiatric/developmental disorders of childhood onset, ADHD shows a male preponderance, on the order of 2.5:1 (Pastor &

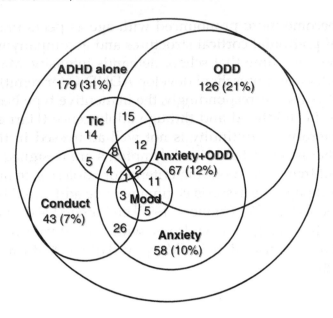

Figure 11.1. Patterns of comorbidity in the MTA study

Reuben, 2002; Polanczyk et al., 2007), which drops noticeably, to only 1.6:1, by adulthood (Kessler et al., 2006), perhaps due to later onset in girls or to stronger persistence of the Inattentive Type in females. However, boys are referred for treatment at much higher rates than girls. In addition, the larger sex difference in childhood may be an artifact of criteria that were developed based on male samples. Girls may be more likely to display inattentive behaviors, yet whether they show a greater number of comorbid internalizing problems is controversial. Studies of clinically referred girls and boys with ADHD indicate that they show comparable levels of impairment in academic and social functioning, but girls with the disorder may have greater intellectual deficits (Gaub & Carlson, 1997). In community samples, however, girls are less likely to have comorbid externalizing problems than boys, and they do not show greater intellectual impairment (Gaub & Carlson, 1997). With regard to cognitive and biological correlates, girls with ADHD show similar patterns of impairments in executive functioning and cognitive control as their male counterparts (Hinshaw et al., 2002; Rucklidge & Tannock, 2001). In a major series of clinical cases, girls and boys with ADHD showed similar patterns of impairment on measures of set-shifting and interference control, and both groups performed significantly worse than sex-matched controls (Seidman et al., 2005). In the same sample at Massachusetts General Hospital, Doyle et al. (2005) reported patterns of neuropsychological impairment in family members of girls with ADHD similar to those in the relatives of boys with the disorder. These types of data suggest important similarities between manifestation of ADHD in boys and girls and suggest that the same construct is being captured.

However, key issues remain. It is unclear whether sex-specific cutoffs should be considered when diagnosing ADHD in girls (see Hinshaw & Blachman, 2005). Girls are less active and disruptive than boys overall, yet symptom counts used to diagnose ADHD are the same for both sexes. Hence, it is possible that some impaired girls are missed by current criteria. Second, other evidence suggests that girls may have greater resistance to the etiological factors that cause ADHD. In a twin study, Rhee, Waldman, Hay, and Levy (1999) found evidence consistent with this differential threshold model, suggesting that girls with ADHD need more risk genes before manifesting ADHD. Further research that incorporate studies of hormonal and other sex-specific effects in early development will be important to a complete understanding of ADHD. Despite recent advances, ADHD in girls remains less well understood than in boys, and the apparent equalizing of prevalence in adolescence and adulthood is not well explained.

CULTURAL CONSIDERATIONS

A metaregression analysis by Polanczyk et al. (2007) included data from over 170,000 participants in 102 studies on all populated continents (though the majority of studies have been conducted in North America and Europe), with a pooled worldwide prevalence rate of 5.29%. Crossnationally, significant variation exists: Prevalence was highest in South America (11.8%) and Africa (8.5%) and lowest in the Middle East (2.4%), though these differences were nonsignificant after adjustment for methodology differences. Few studies were available in these regions, so confidence intervals were too wide to enable differentiation across regions. Continents with enough data for narrow confidence intervals all had similar prevalences (North America, 6.3%; Europe, 4.7%; Oceania, 4.6%; Asia, 3.7%). Within-country data were not analyzed due to the reduced N of available studies. Thus, additional local incidence data will be important to etiological theories. For example, if lead exposure, anemia, or malnutrition contribute to ADHD, then incidence should be higher in nations with higher exposures, unless these effects are countered by alternative etiologies in developed nations (e.g., higher rates of surviving children with low birth weight). That said, rates of stimulant treatment are higher in the United States than in many nations due to differences in historical approach, laws, and professional practice. Nevertheless, several complexities are worthy of comment.

First, ADHD-related behaviors may not have the same meaning in the eyes of teachers and parents across cultural groups. For example, Mann et al. (1992) and Mueller et al. (1995) found that clinicians of different cultures rated the same child actors at significantly different symptom levels, even when faced with identical behaviors (independent of race of the child). On the other hand, Epstein et al. (2005) found that teacher's ratings of excess ADHD symptoms in African American children were consistent with behavioral observations of the same classrooms. This main effect of race was partially due to the fact that African American children were more often in classrooms where the average child had more misbehavior. The paucity of research on these issues represents a gaping hole in our knowledge base.

Second, it is unclear to what extent the ADHD syndrome has similar internal validity across ethnic or cultural groups, or under what conditions this might change. Reid et al. (1998) examined the factor loadings of ADHD symptoms in African American and Euro-American children in the United States. Although the general two-factor symptom structure was preserved across groups, the item loadings differed, suggesting that the syndrome might have a different meaning in the two groups. It is not difficult to imagine how the same behavior could have different meanings across racial groups in the United States (for instance, one might speculate that an African American child more often may be socialized to call out in groups, whereas a European American child may be socialized to remain quiet or wait his or her turn in large groups). Different meanings across nations are also plausible. Still, countering such suppositions, the major review by Rohde et al. (2005) concluded that studies in nondeveloped nations yield similar factor structures, treatment responses, prevalences, and biological correlates as do studies in developed nations, supporting the crosscultural validity of ADHD. Likewise, Yang, Schaller, and Parker (2000) found similar factor loadings in Taiwan and the United States. Such evidence raises the question of when, if at all, racially or culturally specific norms should be included in the assessment of ADHD. Again, a paucity of research signifies ripe opportunities for future investigators in this area to clarify local variation or boundary conditions, if any, on the crosscultural validity of ADHD and thus to provide a more differentiated map of construct validity.

Third, in addition to the fact that treatment rates differ across nations, approaches to treatment may be different across cultural groups even within the United States. Substantial data suggest that non-White children are treated with stimulants and receive health care for ADHD-related problems at far lower rates than White children (Ray et al., 2006). Data are lacking as to the important issue of whether this discrepancy leads to excess poor outcomes among minority children. These differences in services may reflect reduced access to care, or they may reflect distinct attitudes toward the diagnostic and treatment infrastructure. Further empirical work is needed on such issues as costs, access to care, attitudes and beliefs, and differential outcomes.

PROTECTIVE FACTORS

Aside from obvious and global protections such as strong prenatal care and avoidance of early risk factors (e.g., severe trauma, low birth weight), little is known about protective factors against ADHD. However, some clues have come from recent studies of risk–experience interactions. For example, when children are exposed to environmental contaminants early in life (typically prenatally), effects on intellectual and ADHD outcomes are moderated by family context (those that breast fed, a proxy for more well-prepared parents, did not show associations of exposure to later problem outcome; Jacobson & Jacobson, 2003). Similarly, Tully et al. (2004) found that parental warmth moderated the effect of low birth weight on ADHD outcome. This result is consistent with Breslau and Chilcoat's (2000) finding that the effect of low birth weight on ADHD was smaller in suburban than urban communities, suggesting that additional family resources or better health care may have prevented these risk factors from having their full effect.

Second, recent findings regarding biological, genetic, and cognitive protective factors suggest that children exposed to multiple indicators of adversity (low SES, parental Axis I disorders, marital conflict, family stress)—but who are below clinical cutoffs for ADHD symptoms (classified as the *resilient group*)—are more effective in neuropsychological response inhibition and have fewer *risk* catecholamine genotypes (defined by a count of risk markers across three catecholamine genes expressed in the brain) (Nigg et al., 2007). Notably, higher IQ did not serve as such a protective factor.

Third, what about secondary protection? That is, once a child has ADHD, what are protective factors that prevent the worst outcomes? Here, we are on firmer empirical footing, although protective factors often appear to be simply the converse of risk factors. These include (a) stronger reading ability, (b) absence of aggressive behavior, and (c) positive peer relations (for a review, see Barkley, 2006). Additionally, effective parenting may have some effect in reducing persistence of ADHD from preschool into childhood (Campbell, 2002).

THEORETICAL SYNTHESIS

ADHD is a syndrome that reflects multiple developmental pathways and causal processes. A range of early risks during development apparently affects a minority of these children via neural injury (e.g., prenatal substance exposure)—effects that could be preventable (if society so desired) through adequate prenatal care and reduction in exposure to environmental toxins. A percentage may represent extreme temperaments interacting with a society demanding tight conformity to indoor, desk-type work in childhood. However, findings of neuropsychological weaknesses in these children argue against this subgroup's constituting the modal group. Another unknown percentage is likely to reflect the confluence or interaction of vulnerable constitution (genetic liability) and environmental risks (e.g., contaminants or teratogens). Identifying such interactions is a major objective.

The primary internal mechanism driving ADHD appears to involve various types of breakdown in the striatal-prefrontal neural circuitry that supports cognitive control. However, whether the primary element here is a problem in top-down control, or in bottom-up signaling of the need for control, remains in debate. One possible resolution to this debate lies in the idea that both are involved in distinct aspects of the disorder. Sonuga-Barke (2005) suggested a dual-pathway approach. Within the framework advanced here, it may be that that the inattentive-disorganized symptom domain reflects breakdowns in top-down control mechanisms (anchored in a frontal-striatal neural circuit), whereas hyperactivity-impulsivity reflects breakdowns in bottom-up signaling, perhaps involving reactive control or motivational response processes (anchored in frontal-limbic circuitry). Additional pathways have been suggested (Nigg, 2006a, b). Thus, more than one mechanism may lead to ADHD, and multiple influences may converge to create the full syndrome. For example, we noted previously that distinct external correlates accompany ADHD with and without aggression.

What remains to be clarified is the extent to which distinct etiological influences (e.g., lead exposure, teratogens) operate independently of or interactively with genetic susceptibility. One promising model is that genes confer susceptibility to ADHD and that a range of biological and perhaps experiential stressors in the pre- and postnatal environment set the vulnerable child on a course toward ADHD. In other instances, ADHD may reflect an extreme temperament (e.g., high approach, activity level, extraversion) that plays out in recursive loops in a particular socialization context to lead to the requisite set of symptoms. Defining and mapping of these distinct routes and pathways is an exciting challenge for researchers in the coming generation.

In summary, ADHD is a complex syndrome, with substantial genetic influence that involves early departures from normal maturation of prefrontal-subcortical and cerebellar brain circuitry. In many instances, this pathway may reflect activating effects of early pre- or perinatal insult; in other instances, it may reflect an extreme genotype. These child characteristics serve as a liability or vulnerability to ADHD. Effects are then likely to be mediated through socialization (genotype-experience correlations), to culminate in breakdowns or failure in the learning of self-regulation and cognitive control, which in turn manifest as persistent problems with adaptation and regulation of cognition and motor control—that is, symptoms of ADHD.

FUTURE DIRECTIONS

Key issues for future directions can be summed up in three broad domains. First, how will the phenotype best be defined, and how will heterogeneity and specificity issues be resolved? This clarification will require a shift from variable-centered to person-centered approaches, and greater attention to mechanistic variability within ADHD samples. Nearly all biological and genetic findings are nonspecific—that is, similar genes, neural regions, and cognitive problems are seen in other disorders. This nonspecificity suggests that either very subtle differences in neural effects are extremely important or, more likely, that these neural or temperamental susceptibilities are shaped by particulars of the learning environment that are yet to be fully specified. The critical roles of integration of functions and of socialization in the development of regulatory control supports this supposition.

Second, what are the specific etiologies of the expected subgroups currently defined as having ADHD? Most research has focused on specifying within-child mechanisms, but these are not adequately linked with causes (be it specific genotype, specific perinatal or toxic events, or specific epigenetic processes in socialization). Thus, whereas genetic work on ADHD is in its infancy, as it progresses its integration with likely experiential etiologies will be essential. These include both direct gene–environment interactions (such as effects of low level lead or low birth weight on genetically vulnerable children) and epigenetic effects in which the nature of the socialization environment or the nature of biological insult may alter or instantiate expression of genetic liability.

Third, what are key moderators of the meaning and outcome of these behaviors? Here, we can point particularly to the need to understand cultural variation in the meaning of the behaviors and their external correlates, as we map validity with greater precision. Relatedly, it is clear that this syndrome, like many child psychopathologies, will not be fully understood without an adequate explanation of sex differences in incidence and risk. More generally, interactions with widespread societal risk factors also remain unknown. Distinct neuropsychological and temperamental pathways are emerging, and a key goal for the next generation of research is to map those to specific etiologies.

Finally, and following from this emphasis on etiology, in addition to identifying prevention opportunities, there remains a need to identify long-term treatments that can alter the developmental course for these children, so that self-regulation is more easily at their command. Current treatments ameliorate symptoms but it is not clear that they reverse the developmental course of regulatory problems. A better understanding of the early dynamics of etiology and mechanism may be helpful in this regard.

In conclusion, ADHD is an important and fascinating syndrome, with multiple routes to its final endpoint. Despite controversies about misdiagnosis, which may emanate from inadequate mental health services, the multiple impairments and strong psychobiological underpinnings seen worldwide in these children argue against the idea that ADHD is merely a cultural construct. Furthermore, the complexity of the syndrome's mechanisms and causes is becoming tractable. Still, these effects are likely interacting with poorly understood biological activators and, perhaps, cultural moderators. Their understanding will require describing experiential and genetic effects in integrative studies. The study and treatment of ADHD are characterized by energy and optimism on the part of researchers and practitioners, as their efforts begin to show promise of bearing further fruit.

REFERENCES

Achenbach, T. (1991). *Manual for the Young Adult Self Report and Young Adult Behavior Checklist*. Burlington, VT: University of Vermont Psychiatry.

American Psychiatric Association. (1980). *Diagnostic and statistical manual of mental disorders*. (3rd ed.) Washington, DC: Author

American Psychiatric Association (1987). *Diagnostic and statistical manual of mental disorders* (3rd ed., rev.) Washington, DC: Author.

American Psychiatric Association (1994). *Diagnostic and statistical manual of mental disorders* (4th ed.) Washington, DC: Author.

American Psychiatric Association (2000). *Diagnostic and statistical manual of mental disorders* (4th ed., text revision). Washington, DC: Author.

Banaschewski, T., & Brandeis, D. (2007). Annotation: What electrical brain activity tells us about brain function that other techniques cannot tell us—A child psychiatric perspective. *Journal of Child Psychology and Psychiatry, 48,* 415–435.

Barkley, R. A. (1997). Behavioral inhibition, sustained attention, and executive function: Constructing a unified theory of ADHD. *Psychological Bulletin, 121,* 65–94.

Barkley, R. A. (2006). *Attention-deficit hyperactivity disorder: A handbook for diagnosis and treatment* (3rd ed.). New York: Guilford.

Barkley, R. A., & Cunningham, C. (1979). The effects of methylphenidate on the mother-child interactions of hyperactive children. *Archives of General Psychiatry, 36,* 201–208.

Barr, C. L., Wigg, K. G., Bloom, S., Schachar, R., Tannock, R., Roberts, W., et al. (2000). Further evidence from haplotype analysis for linkage of the dopamine D4 receptor gene and attention-deficit hyperactivity disorder. *American Journal of Medical Genetics, 96,* 262–267.

Barry, R. J., Clarke, A. R., & Johnstone, S. J. (2003). A review of electrophysiology in attention-deficit/hyperactivity disorder: I. Qualitative and quantitative electroencephalography. *Clinical Neurophysiology, 114,* 171–183.

Beauchaine, T. P. (2001). Vagal tone, development, and Gray's motivational theory: Toward an integrated model of autonomic nervous system functioning in psychopathology. *Development and Psychopathology, 13,* 183–214.

Blair, R. J., Peschardt, K. S., Budhani, S., Mitchell, D. G., & Pine, D. S. (2006). The development of psychopathy. *Journal of Child Psychology and Psychiatry, 47,* 262–276.

Breslau, N., & Chilcoat, H.D. (2000). Psychiatric sequelae of low birth weight at 11 years of age. *Biological Psychiatry, 47,* 1005–1011.

Campbell, S. B. (2002). *Behavior problems in preschool children* (2nd ed.). New York: Guilford.

Casey, B. J., Castellanos, F. X., Giedd, J. N., & Marsh, W. L. (1997). Implication of right frontostriatal circuitry in response inhibition and attention/deficit hyperactivity disorder. *Journal of the American Academy of Child and Adolescent Psychiatry, 36,* 374–383.

Castellanos, F. X., Lee, P. P., Sharp, W., Jeffries, N. O., Greenstein, D. K., Clasen, L. S., et al. (2002). Developmental trajectories of brain volume abnormalities in children and adolescents with attention-deficit/hyperactivity disorder. *Journal of the American Medical Association, 288,* 1740–1748.

Castellanos, F. X., & Rapoport, J. L. (2002). Effects of caffeine on development and behavior in infancy and childhood: A review of the published literature. *Food and Chemical Toxicology, 40,* 1235–1242.

Chiodo, L. M., Jacobson, S. W., & Jacobson, J. L. (2004). Neurodevelopmental effects of postnatal lead exposure at very low levels. *Neurotoxicology and Teratology, 26,* 259–264.

Connors, C. K. (1997). *Connors' Rating Scales–Revised.* Toronto, Ontario, Canada: Multi-Health Systems, Inc.

Derks, E. M., Hudziak, J. J., van Beijsterveldt, C. E. M., Dolan, C. V., & Boomsma, D. I. (2006). Genetic analysis of maternal and teacher ratings on attention problems in 7-year-old Dutch twins. *Behavior Genetics, 36,* 833–844.

Dickstein, S. G., Bannon, K., Castellanos, F. X., & Milham, M.P. (2006). The neural correlates of attention deficit hyperactivity disorder: An ALE meta-analysis. *Journal of Child Psychology and Psychiatry, 47*, 1051–1062.

Doyle, A. E., Biederman, J., Seidman, L. J., Rske-Nielsen, J. J., & Faraone, S. V. (2005). Neuropsychological functioning in relatives of girls with and without ADHD. *Psychological Medicine, 35*, 1121–1132.

Durston, S., Tottenham, N. T., Thomas, K. M., Davidson, M. C., Eisgsti, I. M., Yang, Y., et al. (2003). Differential patterns of striatal activation in young children with and without ADHD. *Biological Psychiatry, 53*, 871–878.

Epstein, J. N., Willoughby, M., Valencia, E. Y., Tonev, S. T., Abikoff, H. B., Arnold, L. E., et al. (2005). The role of children's ethnicity in the relationship between teacher ratings of attention-deficit/hyperactivity disorder and observed classroom behavior. *Journal of Consulting and Clinical Psychology, 73*, 424–434.

Faraone, S. V., Perlis, R. H., Doyle, A. E., Smoller, J. W., Goralnick, J. J., Holmgren, M.A., et al. (2005). Molecular genetics of attention-deficit hyperactivity disorder. *Biological Psychiatry, 57*, 1313–1323.

Gatzke-Kopp, L., & Beauchaine, T. P. (in press). Central nervous system substrates of impulsivity: Implications for the development of attention-deficit/hyperactivity disorder and conduct disorder. In D. Coch, G. Dawson, & K. Fischer (Eds.), *Human behavior and the developing brain: Atypical development.* New York: Guilford.

Gaub, M., & Carlson, C. (1997). Gender differences in ADHD: A meta-analysis and critical review. *Journal of the American Academy of Child and Adolescent Psychiatry, 36*, 1036–1045.

Goldsmith, H. H., Lemery, K. S., & Essex, M. J. (2004). Temperament as a liability factor for childhood behavior disorders: The concept of liability. In L. Dilalla (Ed.), *Behavior genetics principles: Perspectives in development, personality, and psychopathology* (pp. 19–39). Washington DC: APA Press.

Gordon, M., Shtshel, K., Faraone, S., Barkely, R., Lewandowski, L., Hudziak, J., et al. (2005). Symptoms versus impairment: The case for respecting *DSM-IV*'s criterion D. *ADHD Report, 13*, 1–9.

Hart, E. L., Lahey, B. B., Loeber, R., Applegate, B., & Frick, P. J. (1995). Developmental changes in attention-deficit hyperactivity disorder in boys: A four year longitudinal study. *Journal of Abnormal Child Psychology, 23*, 729–750.

Hawi, Z., Dring, M., Kirley, A., Foley, D., Kent, L., Craddock, N., et al. (2002). Serotonergic system and attention deficit hyperactivity disorder (ADHD): A potential susceptibility locus at the 5-HT (1B) receptor gene in 273 nuclear families from multi-centre sample. *Molecular Psychiatry, 7(7)*, 718–725.

Hawi, Z., Lowe, N., Kirley, A., Gruenhage, F., Nothen, M., Greenwood, T., et al. (2003). Linkage disequilibrium mapping at DAT1, DRD5, and DBH narrows the search for ADHD susceptibility alleles at these loci. *Molecular Psychiatry, 8*, 299–308.

Hay, D. A., Bennett, K. S., Levy, F., Sergeant, J. A., & Swanson, J. M. (2007). A twin study of ADHD rated by *DSM-IV* and the Strengths and Weaknesses of ADHD and Normal Behaviors (SWAN) scale. *Biological Psychiatry, 61*, 700–705.

Hebebrand, J., Dempfle, A., Saar, K., Thiele, H., Herpertz-Dahlmann, B., Linder, M., et al. (2006). A genome-wide scan for attention/deficit hyperactivity disorder in 155 German sib-pairs. *Molecular Psychiatry, 11*, 196–205.

Hinshaw, S. P., & Blachman, D. R. (2005). Attention-deficit/hyperactivity disorder. In D. Bell-Dolan, S. Foster, & E. J. Mash (Eds.), *Handbook of behavioral and emotional problems in girls* (pp. 117–147). New York: Kluwer Academic/Plenum.

Hinshaw, S. P., Carte, E. T., Sami, N., Treauting, J. J., & Zupan, B. A. (2002). Preadolescent girls with attention-deficit hyperactivity disorder. Vol. II: Neuropsychological performance in relation to subtypes and individual classification. *Journal of Consulting and Clinical Psychology, 70,* 1099–1111.

Huang-Pollock, C. L., & Nigg, J. T. (2003). Searching for the attention deficit in attention deficit hyperactivity disorder: The case of visuospatial orienting. *Clinical Psychology Review, 23,* 801–830.

Huang-Pollock, C. L., Nigg, J. T., & Carr, T. H. (2005). Deficient attention is hard to find: Applying the perceptual load model of selective attention to attention deficit hyperactivity disorder subtypes. *Journal of Child Psychology and Psychiatry, 46,* 1211–1218.

Hudziak, J. K., Heath, A. C., Madden, P. F., Reich, W., Bucholz, K., Slutske, W., et al. (1998). Latent class and factor analysis of *DSM-IV* ADHD: A twin study of female adolescents. *Journal of the American Academy of Child and Adolescent Psychiatry, 37,* 848–857.

Jacobson J. L., & Jacobson, S. W. (2003). Prenatal exposure to polychlorinated biphenyls and attention at school age. *Journal of Pediatrics, 143,* 780–788.

Jacobson, S. W., Jacobson, J. L., Sokol, R. J., Chiodo, L. M., & Corobana, R. (2004). Maternal age, alcohol abuse history, and quality of parenting as moderators of the effects of prenatal alcohol exposure on 7.5 year intellectual function. *Alcoholism: Clinical and Experimental Research, 28,* 1732–1745.

Jensen, P. S., Hinshaw, S. P., Kraemer, H. C., Lenora, N., Newcorn, J. H., Abikoff, H. B., et al. (2001). ADHD comorbidity findings from the MTA study: Comparing comorbid subgroups. *Journal of the American Academy of Child and Adolescent Psychiatry, 40,* 147–158.

Johnston, C., & Mash, E. J. (2001). Families of children with Attention-Deficit/Hyperactivity Disorder: Review and recommendations for future research. *Clinical Child & Family Psychology Review, 4,* 183–207.

Kagan, J., & Snidman, N. (2004). *The long shadow of temperament.* Cambridge, MA: Harvard University Press.

Kavale, K. A., & Forness, S. R. (1983). Hyperactivity and diet treatment: A meta-analysis of the Feingold hypothesis. *Journal of Learning Disabilities, 16,* 324–330.

Kent, L., Doerry, U., Hardy, E., Parmar, R., Gingell, K., Hawi, Z., et al. (2002). Evidence that variation at the serotonin transporter gene influences susceptibility to attention deficit hyperactivity disorder (ADHD): Analysis and pooled analysis. *Molecular Psychiatry, 7,* 908–912.

Kessler, R. C., Adler, L., Barkley, R., Biederman, J., Conners, C. K., Demler, O., et al. (2006). The prevalence and correlates of adult ADHD in the United States: results from the National Comorbidity Survey Replication. *American Journal of Psychiatry, 163,* 716–723.

Kirley, A., Hawi, Z., Daly, G., McCarron, M., Mullins, C., Millar, N., et al. (2002). Dopaminergic system genes in ADHD: Toward a biological hypothesis. *Neuropsychopharmacology, 27,* 607–619.

Kordon, A., Kahl, K. G., & Wahl, K. (2006). A new understanding of attention-deficit disorders—Beyond the age-at-onset criterion of *DSM-IV*. *European Archives of Psychiatry and Clinical Neuroscience, 256* (S1), i47–i54.

Lahey, B. B., Applegate, B., McBurnett, K., Biederman, J., Greenhill, L. L., Hynd, G., et al. (1994). *DSM-IV* field trials for attention deficit hyperactivity disorder in children and adolescents. *American Journal of Psychiatry, 151,* 1673–1685.

Lahey, B. B., Pelham, W. E., Stein, M. A., Loney, J., Trapani, C., Nugent, K., et al., (1998). Validity of *DSM-IV* attention-deficit/hyperactivity disorder for younger children. *Journal of the American Academy of Child and Adolescent Psychiatry, 37,* 695–702.

Lahey, B. B., Pelham, W. E., Loney, J., Trapani, C., Nugent, K., et al. (2005). Instability of the *DSM-IV* subtypes of ADHD from preschool through elementary school. *Archives of General Psychiatry, 62,* 695–702.

Lahey, B. B., & Willcutt, E. G. (2002). Validity of the diagnosis and dimensions of attention deficit hyperactivity disorder. In P.S. Jensen & J.R. Cooper (Eds.), *Attention deficit hyperactivity disorder: State of the science, best practices* (pp. 1–1 to 1–23). Kingston, NJ: Civic Research Institute.

Li, J., Wang, Y., Zhou, R., Wang, B., Zhang, H., Yang, L., et al. (2006). No association of attention-deficit hyperactivity disorder with genes of the serotonergic pathway in Han Chinese subjects. *Neuroscience Letters, 430,* 172–175.

Linnet, K. M., Dalsgaard, S., Obel, C., Wisborg, K., Henrisken, T. B., Rodriguez, A., et al. (2003). Maternal lifestyle factors in pregnancy risk of attention deficit hyperactivity disorder and associated behaviors: Review of the current evidence. *American Journal of Psychiatry, 160,* 1028–1040.

Logan, G. (1994). A user's guide to the stop signal paradigm. In D. Dagenbach & T. Carr (Eds.), *Inhibition in language, memory, and attention* (pp.189–239). San Diego: Academic Press.

Losier, B. J., McGrath, P. J., & Klein, R. M. (1996). Error patterns on the continuous performance test in non-medicated and medicated samples of children with and without ADHD: A meta-analytic review. *Journal of Child Psychology and Psychiatry, 37,* 971–988.

Luman, M., Oosterlaan, J., & Sergeant, J. A. (2005). The impact of reinforcement contingencies on AD/HD: A review and theoretical appraisal. *Clinical Psychology Review, 25,* 183–213.

Mann, E. M., Ikeda, Y., Mueller, C. W., Takahashi, A., Tao, K., Humris, E., et al. (1992). Cross-cultural differences in rating hyperactive-disruptive behaviors in children. *American Journal of Psychiatry, 149,* 1539–1542.

Mannuzza, S., & Klein, R. G. (2000). Long-term prognosis in attention-deficit/hyperactivity disorder. *Child and Adolescent Psychiatric Clinics of North America, 9,* 711–726

Manor, I., Eisenberg, J., Tyano, S., Sever, Y., Cohen, H., Ebstein, R. P., et al. (2001). Family-based association study of the serotonin transporter promoter region polymorphism (5-HTTLPR) in attention deficit hyperactivity disorder. *American Journal of Medical Genetics, 105,* 91–95.

Martel, M., & Nigg, J. T. (2006). Temperamental regulation, control, and resiliency in relation to ADHD symptoms in children. *Journal of Child Psychology and Psychiatry, 47,* 1175–1183.

Martinussen, R., Hayden, J., Hogg-Johnson, S., & Tannock, R. (2005). A meta-analysis of working memory impairments in children with attention deficit hyperactivity disorder. *Journal of the American Academy of Child and Adolescent Psychiatry, 44,* 377–384.

Mick, E., Biederman, J., Faraone, S.V., Sayer, J., & Kleinman, S. (2002). Case-control study of attention-deficit hyperactivity disorder and maternal smoking, alcohol use, and drug use during pregnancy. *Journal of the American Academy of Child and Adolescent Psychiatry, 41,* 378–385.

Milich, R., Balentine, A., & Lynam, D. (2001). ADHD combined type and ADHD predominantly inattentive type are distinct and unrelated disorders. *Clinical Psychology: Science and Practice, 8,* 463–488.

Mueller, C. W., Mann, E. M., Thanapum, S., Humris, E., Ikeda, Y., Takahashi, A., et al. (1995). Teacher's ratings of disruptive behavior in five countries. *Journal of Clinical Child Psychology, 24,* 434–442.

Murphy, K. R., Barkley, R. A, & Bush, T. (2001). Executive functioning and olfactory identification in young adults with attention-deficit hyperactivity disorder. *Neuropsychology, 15,* 211–220.

Neuman, R. J ., Heath, A., Reich, W., Bucholz, K. K., Madden, P. A. F., Sun, L. S., et al. (2001). Latent class analysis of ADHD and comorbid symptoms in a population sample of adolescent female twins. *Journal of Child Psychology and Psychiatry, 42,* 933–942.

Nigg, J. T. (2001). Is ADHD an inhibitory disorder? *Psychological Bulletin, 126,* 240–246.

Nigg, J. T. (2006a). *What causes ADHD? Understanding what goes wrong and why.* New York: Guilford.

Nigg, J. T. (2006b). Temperament and developmental psychopathology. *Journal of Child Psychology and Psychiatry, 47,* 395–422.

Nigg, J. T., & Casey, B. J. (2005). An integrative theory of attention-deficit/hyperactivity disorder based on the cognitive and affective neurosciences. *Development and Psychopathology, 17,* 785–806.

Nigg, J. T., Hinshaw, S. P., & Huang-Pollack, C. (2006). Disorders of attention and impulse regulation. In D. Cicchetti & D. Cohen (Eds.), *Developmental psychopathology* (2nd ed., pp. 358–403). New York: Wiley.

Nigg, J. T., John, O. P., Blaskey, L. G., Huang-Pollock, C. L., Willcutt, E. G., Hinshaw, S. P., & Pennington, B. (2002). Big five dimensions and ADHD symptoms: Links between personality traits and clinical symptoms. *Journal of Personality and Social Psychology, 83*(2), 451–469.

Nigg, J. T., Knottnerus, G. M., Martel, M. M., Nikolas, M., Cavanaugh, K., Karmaus, W., & Rappley, M. D. (in press). Low blood lead levels associated with clinically diagnosed attention deficit hyperactivity disorder (ADHD) and mediated by weak cognitive control. *Biological Psychiatry.*

Nigg, J. T., Nikolas, M., Friderici, K., Park, L., & Zucker, R. A. (2007). Genotype and neuropsychological response inhibition as resilience promoters for ADHD, ODD, and CD under conditions of psychosocial adversity. *Development and Psychopathology, 19*(3), 767–786.

Nigg, J. T., Stavro, G., Ettenhofer, M., Hambrick, D., Miller, T., & Henderson, J.M. (2005). Executive functions and ADHD in adults: Evidence for selective effects on ADHD symptom domains. *Journal of Abnormal Psychology, 114,* 706–717.

Nigg, J. T., Willcutt, E., Doyle, A. E., & Sonuga-Barke, J. S. (2005). Causal heterogeneity in ADHD: Do we need neuropsychologically impaired subtypes? *Biological Psychiatry, 57,* 1224–1230.

Ogdie, M. N., Bakker, S. C., Fischer, S. E., Francks, C., Yang, M. H., Cantor, R. M., et al. (2006). Pooled genome-wide linkage data on 424 ADHD ASPs suggest genetic heterogeneity and a common risk locus at 5p13. *Molecular Psychiatry, 11,* 5–8.

Park, L., Nigg, J. T., Waldman, I., Nummy, K. A., Huang-Pollock, C., Rappley, M., et al. (2005). Association and linkage of α-2A adrenergic receptor gene polymorphisms with childhood ADHD. *Molecular Psychiatry, 10,* 572–580.

Pastor, P. N., & Reuben, C. A. (2002). Attention-deficit disorder and learning disability: United States, 1997–98. National Center for Health Statistics. *Vital Health Statistics, 10,* 206.

Pelham, W. E., Fabiano, G. A., & Massetti, G. A. (2005). Evidence based assessment of attention-deficit hyperactivity disorder in children and adolescents. *Journal of Clinical Child and Adolescent Psychology, 34,* 449–476.

Piek, J. P., Pitcher, T. M., & Hay, D. A. (1999). Motor coordination and kinaesthesia in boys with attention deficit hyperactivity disorder. *Developmental Medicine and Child Neurology, 37,* 976–984.

Polanczyk, G., Silva de Lima, M., Lessa Horta, B., Biederman, J., & Rohde, L. A. (2007). The worldwide prevalence of Attention-Deficit/Hyperactivity Disorder: A systematic review and meta-regression analyses. *American Journal of Psychiatry, 164*(6), 464–474.

Posner, M., & Petersen, S. (1990). The attention system of the human brain. *Annual Review of Neuroscience, 13,* 25–42.

Purcell, S. (2002). Variance components models for gene-environment interactions in twin analysis. *Twin Research, 5,* 444–471.

Rasmussen, E. R., Neuman, R. J., Heath, A. C., Levy, F., Hay, D. A., & Todd, R. D. (2004). Familial clustering of latent classes and *DSM-IV* defined attention-deficit hyperactivity disorder (ADHD) subtypes. *Journal of Child Psychology and Psychiatry, 45,* 589–598.

Ray, G. T., Levine, P., Croen, L. A., Bokhari, F. A., Hu, T. W., & Habel, L. A. (2006). Attention-deficit/hyperactivity disorder in children: excess costs before and after initial diagnosis and treatment cost differences by ethnicity. *Archives of Pediatric and Adolescent Medicine, 160,* 1063–1069.

Reid, R., DuPaul, G. J., Power, T. J., Anastopoulos, A. D., Rogers-Adkinson, D., Noll, M. B., et al. (1998). Assessing culturally different students for attention deficit hyperactivity disorder using behavior rating scales. *Journal of Abnormal Child Psychology, 26,* 187–198.

Rhee, S. W., Waldman, I. D., Hay, D. A., & Levy, F. (1999). Sex differences in genetic and environmental influences on *DSM-III-R* attention deficit/hyperactivity disorder. *Journal of Abnormal Psychology, 108,* 24–41.

Rietveld, M. J., Hudziak, J. J., Bartels, M., van Beijsterveldt, C. E., & Boomsma, D. I. (2004). Heritability of attention problems in children: Longitudinal results from a study of twins age 3–12. *Journal of Child Psychology and Psychiatry, 45,* 577–588.

Robison, L. M., Sclar, D. A., Skaer, T. L., & Galin, R. S. (1999). National trends in the prevalence of attention-deficit/hyperactivity disorder and the prescribing of methylphenidate among school age children: 1990–1995. *Clinical Pediatrics, 38,* 209–217.

Rohde, L. A., Szobot, C., Polanczyk, G., Schmitz, M., Martins S., & Tramontina, S. (2005). Attention-deficit/hyperactivity disorder in a diverse culture: do research and clinical findings support the notion of a cultural construct for the disorder? *Biological Psychiatry, 57,* 1436–1441.

Roman, T., Schmitz, M., Polanczyk, G., Eizirik, M., Rohde, L.A., & Hutz, M.H. (2002). Further evidence for the association between attention-deficit hyperactivity disorder and the dopamine beta-hydroxylase gene. *American Journal of Medical Genetics, 114,* 154–158.

Rothbart, M. K., & Bates, J. E. (1998). Temperament. In W. Damon (Series Ed.) and N. Eisenberg (Vol. Ed.), *Handbook of child psychology. Vol 3: Social, emotional, and personality development* (pp. 105–176). New York: Wiley.

Rubia, K., Overmeyer, S., Taylor, E., Brammer, M., Williams, S. C. R., Simmons, A., et al. (1999). Hypofrontality in attention-deficit hyperactivity disorder during higher order motor control: A study with functional MRI. *American Journal of Psychiatry, 156,* 891–896.

Rucklidge, J. J., & Tannock, R. (2001). Psychiatric, psychosocial, and cognitive functioning of female adolescents with ADHD. *Journal of the American Academy of Child and Adolescent Psychiatry, 40,* 530–540.

Sagvolden, T., Johansen, E. B., Aase, H., & Russell, V. A. (2005). A dynamic developmental theory of attention/deficit hyperactivity disorder (ADHD) predominantly hyperactive-impulsive and combined subtypes. *Behavioral and Brain Sciences, 28,* 397–419.

Saudino, K. J. (2003). Parent ratings of infant temperament: Lessons from twin studies. *Infant Behavior and Development, 26,* 118–120.

Schab, D. W., & Trinh, N. T. (2004). Do artificial food colors promote hyperactivity in children with hyperactive syndromes? A meta-analysis of double-blind placebo-controlled trails. *Journal of Developmental and Behavioral Pediatrics, 25,* 423–434.

Seidman, K. J., Biederman, J., Monteaux, M. C., Valera, E., Doyle, A. E., & Faraone, S. V. (2005). Impact of gender and age on executive functioning: Do girls and boys with and without attention-deficit hyperactivity disorder differ neuropsychologically in the preteen and teenage years? *Developmental Neuropsychology, 27,* 79–105.

Sergeant, J. A., Oosterlaan, J., & van der Meere, J. (1999). Information processing and energetic factors in attention-deficit/hyperactivity disorder. In H. C. Quay & A.E. Hogan (Eds.), *Handbook of disruptive behavior disorders* (pp. 75–104). New York: Kluwer/Plenum.

Sergeant, J. A., & van der Meere, J. J. (1988). What happens after a hyperactive child commits an error? *Psychological Research, 24,* 157–164.

Simonoff, E., Pickles, A., Hervas, A., Silberg, J. L., Rutter, M., & Eaves, L. (1998). Genetic influences on childhood hyperactivity: Contrast effects imply parental rating bias, not sibling interaction. *Psychological Medicine, 28,* 825–837.

Sonuga-Barke, E. J. S. (2005). Causal models of attention/deficit hyperactivity disorder: From common simple deficits to multiple developmental pathways. *Biological Psychiatry, 57,* 1231–1238.

Stawicki, J. A., Nigg, J. T., & von Eye, A. (2006). Family psychiatric history evidence on the nosological relations of *DSM-IV* ADHD Combined and Inattentive subtypes: New data and meta-analysis. *Journal of Child Psychology and Psychiatry, 47,* 935–945.

Toplak, M. E., Rucklidge, J. J., Hetherington, R., John, S., & Tannock, R. (2005). Time perception deficits in attention-deficit hyperactivity disorder and comorbid reading difficulties in child and adolescent samples. *Journal of Child Psychology and Psychiatry, 44,* 1–16.

Tully, L. A., Arseneault, L., Caspi, A., Moffitt, T. E., & Morgan, J. (2004). Does maternal warmth moderate the effects of birth weight on twins' attention-deficit/hyperactivity disorder (ADHD) symptoms and low IQ? *Journal of Consulting and Clinical Psychology, 72,* 218–226.

Wang, B., Wang, Y., Zhou, R., Li, J., Qian, Q., Yang, L., Guan, L., et al. (2006). Possible association of the alpha-2A adrenergic receptor (ADRA2A) with symptoms of attention-deficit hyperactivity disorder. *American Journal of Medical Genetics, 141,* 130–134.

Willcutt, E. G., Doyle, A. E., Nigg, J. T., Faraone, S. V., & Pennington, B. F. (2005). Validity of the executive function theory of ADHD: A meta-analytic review. *Biological Psychiatry, 57,* 1336–1346.

Willcutt, E. G., Pennington, B. F., & DeFries, J. C. (2000). Etiology of inattention and hyperactivity/impulsivity in a community sample of twins with learning difficulties. *Journal of Abnormal Psychology, 28,* 149–159.

Yang, K. N., Schaller, J. L., & Parker, R. (2000). Factor structures of Taiwanese teachers' ratings of ADHD: a comparison with U.S. studies. *Journal of Learning Disabilities, 33,* 72–82.

CHAPTER 12

Oppositional Defiant Disorder, Conduct Disorder, and Juvenile Delinquency

BENJAMIN B. LAHEY

INTRODUCTION

Children and adolescents who persistently violate laws and important social rules are seriously impaired in their social relationships and at risk for a range of serious consequences, including incarceration and violent death (Moffitt et al., 2001; Loeber & Stouthamer-Loeber, 1998). Such antisocial behavior also harms others in a variety of significant ways, from the loss of property to death by homicide (Loeber et al., 2005).

DEFINITION OF TERMS

A number of constructs have been developed to conceptualize and label antisocial behavior in youth. The term *juvenile delinquency* is used in the criminal justice system to refer to children and adolescents who have broken a law. This is a very broad term that refers to anything from sneaking into a movie without a ticket to homicide. In the *Diagnostic and Statistical Manual of Mental Disorders–Fourth Edition* (DSM-IV; American Psychiatric Association, 1994), two diagnoses are directly relevant to antisocial behav-

Acknowledgment: Preparation of this chapter was supported in part by grants R01 MH070025 and R01 MH53554 from the National Institute of Mental Health.

ior in youth. *Conduct Disorder* (CD) refers to engaging in at least 3 from a list of 15 antisocial behaviors within 12 months. CD only partially overlaps with delinquency for three reasons. First, not all juvenile crimes are symptoms of CD (e.g., selling drugs, receiving stolen property). Second, some symptoms of CD do not necessarily violate laws (e.g., bullying, staying out late without permission). Third, CD describes youth who frequently engage in a variety (i.e., at least three) of antisocial behaviors in a relatively short time frame, whereas a youth could be considered to be delinquent on the basis of a single criminal act.

The DSM-IV diagnosis of *Oppositional Defiant Disorder* (ODD) is also related to antisocial behavior in youth. ODD is defined as frequently engaging in at least 4 disruptive interpersonal behaviors, including arguing with adults, actively defying adult requests, and spiteful or vindictive behavior, for at least 6 months. ODD often severely impairs the social relationships of children and adolescents (Lahey et al., 1994) and is intimately linked to CD.

It is important to note that many investigators believe the DSM-IV diagnoses of ODD and CD reflect the (at least somewhat) arbitrary dichotomization of what are probably continua in nature (Boyle et al., 1996; Lahey et al., 1994). That is, youth do not suddenly shift from *normality* to *abnormality* when they engage in their fourth ODD symptom or their third CD symptom. Rather, the more symptoms of ODD or CD that a youth exhibits, the more serious the consequences for the youth and others. Another reason for caution regarding DSM-IV diagnostic definitions is that Rowe, Maughan, Costello, and Angold (2005) noted a large "hole" in the diagnosis of ODD. In the tenth edition of the International Classification of Diseases (ICD-10; World Health Organization, 1993) ODD is defined by the same symptoms as in DSM-IV, but in a different way. In ICD-10, if a youth does not meet diagnostic criteria for either ODD or CD, the total number of ODD plus CD symptoms is counted. If there are four such ODD + CD symptoms, the youth meets criteria for ODD. Rowe et al. found that this large group of youth was as impaired in their social functioning as youth who met DSM-IV criteria for ODD. It is not surprising that youth who exhibit three symptoms of ODD and one or two symptoms of CD (i.e., falling short of the diagnostic criteria for either disorder) would be impaired.

Although there are important differences between the constructs of juvenile delinquency, ODD, and CD, it will often be necessary to refer collectively to all three constructs in this chapter for the sake of brevity and clarity. For this purpose, the terms *conduct problems* and *antisocial behavior* refer collectively to juvenile delinquency, ODD, and CD. Similarly the term *youth* refers collectively to both children and adolescents in this chapter.

COMORBIDITY

One cannot view any form of psychopathology as if it were separate from all other forms. Youth who meet diagnostic criteria for any mental disorder are considerably more likely than chance to meet criteria for many other mental disorders (Angold, Costello, & Erkanli, 1999; Nottelmann & Jensen, 1995; Lahey et al., 2004). That is, co-occurrence of symptoms and diagnoses (or comorbidity) is the rule, not the exception. ODD and CD very often co-occur with each other, and both disorders often co-occur with Attention-Deficit/Hyperactivity Disorder (ADHD; Angold et al., 1999; Lahey, Miller, Gordon, & Riley, 1999). In addition, ODD and CD often co-occur with depression (Angold et al., 1999; Lahey et al., 2002; Rowe, Maughan, & Eley, 2006).

Some investigators view comorbidity as a problem for taxonomies of mental disorders (Rutter, 1997), whereas others view comorbidity as the inevitable result of the nearly ubiquitous correlations among symptoms of different disorders (Lahey, Applegate et al., 2004; Lahey et al., in press). In the latter view, comorbidity is informative rather than problematic. For example, CD is impairing and requires intervention regardless of whether it occurs alone or in the presence of symptoms of other disorders. On the other hand, a youth who meets criteria for CD and another disorder such as major depression may well need treatment for each disorder. In addition, viewing comorbidity as informative facilitates the study of both the overlapping and distinct causal influences on different forms of psychopathology.

DEVELOPMENTAL PERSPECTIVE AND NEED TO CONSIDER SEX DIFFERENCES

It is not possible to discuss any mental disorder without taking a *developmental perspective*. We humans are in a constant process of developmental change. The person we are today largely reflects the person we were yesterday, and predicts the person we will be tomorrow reasonably well, but people *change* over developmental time. The pace of this change is often too slow to notice, but if you doubt the need for a developmental perspective, pull out your photo albums and see what you were like as an infant, a second grader, a high school sophomore, and a college sophomore. It is almost as striking as seeing a caterpillar become a butterfly. More to the point, developmental changes in behavior are as profound as physical changes.

In this chapter, conduct problems are considered from four different developmental perspectives: (a) developmental trajectories of conduct problems; (b) age differences in the prevalence of conduct problems;

(c) childhood characteristics that predict later conduct problems; and (d) the adolescent and adult outcomes of childhood conduct problems.

Just as one cannot study conduct problems without taking developmental change into account, it also is necessary to consider potential differences between females and males when considering the development of conduct problems. Although conduct problems are prevalent and problematic in both sexes, they are considerably more common in males (Lahey et al., 2006; Moffitt et al., 2001). Because the sex difference in the prevalence of conduct problems is large, it will be necessary for the field to understand the causes of sex differences to fully understand the causes of conduct problems themselves. For the same reason, a theory of the origins of conduct problems that does not explain the origins of sex differences would be incomplete, if not inaccurate, for one or both sexes.

DEVELOPMENTAL TRAJECTORIES OF CONDUCT PROBLEMS

Many theorists (Farrington, 1991; Hinshaw, Lahey, & Hart, 1993; Loeber, 1988; Moffitt, 1993; Patterson, Reid, & Dishion, 1992; Quay, 1987) have suggested that one can only understand youth conduct problems by distinguishing between different *developmental trajectories* of conduct problems. In this context, a *trajectory* is a more or less distinct temporal pattern of conduct problems that each youth engages in from early childhood through adolescence. For example, two 17-year-olds arrested for shoplifting might have had very different developmental trajectories. One may have exhibited no symptoms of CD as a child and had never broken a law until skipping school and shoplifting for the first time at age 17. The other 17-year-old might have continuously met criteria for CD since early childhood, shoplifted dozens of times before, and committed many other crimes since middle childhood. Such differences in developmental trajectories may reveal a great deal about differences in the causes of those conduct problems.

Moffitt (1993, 2003) proposed that youth who follow two different trajectories engage in delinquency for entirely different reasons. According to Moffitt, a relatively small number of youth follow a *childhood-onset* (or *life-course persistent*) trajectory in which they exhibit symptoms of ADHD, ODD, and CD in childhood and engage in persistent conduct problems through adolescence and into adulthood. A larger group of youth follow an *adolescent-onset* (or *adolescence-limited*) trajectory in which they engage in relatively few conduct problems during childhood, first break laws during adolescence, and often desist from offending in early adulthood. Adolescent delinquency is common, but the exact numbers depend on how juvenile delinquency is defined. Approximately between 10 to 21% engage in what Moffitt (1993) refers to as adolescent-onset delinquency, whereas 5 to 14% of youth exhibit childhood-onset delinquency (Lahey et al., 2006; Moffitt et al., 2001).

Moffitt (1993, 2003) hypothesized that the conduct problems of youth on the childhood-onset trajectory are caused by a combination of early neurodevelopmental deficits and inadequate parenting and adverse so-cial influences, whereas adolescent-onset conduct problems are caused by peer influences during the transition to adulthood. That is, the causes of delinquency for youth on these two different trajectories are hypothesized to be qualitatively different. For this reason, Moffitt has argued that stud-ies of the causes of delinquency that do not distinguish these trajectories will produce disinformation that does not apply to either trajectory. In considering developmental trajectories, it also is important to note that many children who engage in high levels of childhood conduct problems are well behaved during adolescence (Coté et al., 2006; Moffitt et al., 1996; Raine et al., 2005). It is important to keep this large group of disruptive children whose behavior improves over time in mind when the risk factors and precursors to conduct problems are discussed.

ARE THERE SEX DIFFERENCES IN DEVELOPMENTAL TRAJECTORIES?

Essentially equal numbers of females and males exhibit adolescent-onset delinquency, but males outnumber females about 3:1 in the childhood-onset trajectory (Lahey et al., 2006; Moffitt et al., 2001). Silverthorn and Frick (1999) suggested that females rarely follow the childhood-onset trajectory and follow a trajectory unique to girls. Although this hypothesis stimu-lated research that clarified the nature of sex differences in delinquency, it has not been supported (Coté et al., 2001; Lahey et al., 2006; Moffitt et al., 2001). It seems like that girls follow both delinquency trajectories as Mof-fitt (1993, 2003) defines them; there are simply fewer girls on a childhood-onset trajectory.

ALTERNATIVE TO QUALITATIVE DEVELOPMENTAL TRAJECTORY MODELS

Lahey and Waldman (2003, 2005) suggested a different view of develop-mental trajectories. They agree with Moffitt (1993, 2003) that adolescent delinquents with high or low levels of childhood conduct problems tend to be antisocial for different reasons, but hypothesize that there is a *contin-uum* of such differences rather than two qualitatively distinct trajectories.

That is, there is not one group of adolescent delinquents who were holy terrors as children and another distinct group who were childhood angels. Rather, among adolescent delinquents, there is a continuum ranging from those who were very well behaved as children to those who were very poorly behaved from the toddler years onward, with every gradation in levels and consistency of childhood behavior problems in between. It only appears that there are two distinct groups of adolescent delinquents when researchers arbitrarily divide them into two such groups. Nonetheless, because the notion of two distinct developmental trajectories is a convenient and useful heurism, Moffitt's dichotomous terms are often used in this chapter for simplicity.

RELATIONS BETWEEN ODD, CD, AND DEVELOPMENTAL TRAJECTORIES OF DELINQUENCY

It is important to keep in mind that nearly all studies of developmental trajectories have examined delinquent behavior rather than ODD or CD. Thus, there currently is not enough information to know how many youth in Moffitt's two developmental trajectories of delinquency would meet diagnostic criteria for ODD or CD. Because most definitions of delinquency require only the commission of a single delinquent act, and because CD requires a variety of antisocial behaviors during the past 12 months, many delinquents do not meet criteria for CD. One study of CD suggested that most clinic-referred adolescents who meet criteria for CD reported that their CD behaviors began in childhood (i.e., had a childhood onset), with only a small percent reporting an adolescent onset of CD (Lahey et al., 1998). In a stronger longitudinal study of a representative sample of girls, Coté, Zoccolillo, Tremblay, Nagin, and Vitaro (2001) found that nearly all adolescent females who met criteria for CD had childhood-onset CD. These studies tentatively suggest that the great majority of youth who meet criteria for CD follow what Moffitt (1993, 2003) would define as a childhood-onset trajectory. More evidence is needed, but it is quite possible that most youth who meet criteria for CD have risk factors and outcomes similar to those of childhood-onset delinquency. On the other hand, there may be a group of youth who meet criteria for CD who have later ages of onset and who share risk factors and outcomes with adolescent-onset delinquency. Indeed, DSM-IV distinguishes between childhood- and adolescent-onset CD based on this premise. Unfortunately, the validity of these subtypes has not been studied extensively in large longitudinal studies (Lahey et al., 1998). There also is evidence that most youth on a childhood-onset trajectory of delinquency met criteria for ODD during childhood (Lahey et al., 2006), but more remains to be learned.

AGE, SEX, AND PREVALENCE
OF CONDUCT PROBLEMS

Another way to think about conduct problems developmentally is to consider the marked age differences in the numbers of youth who meet diagnostic criteria for ODD and CD from early childhood through adolescence. Although it is difficult to estimate the exact prevalence of ODD and CD in the general population for both technical and substantive reasons, there is good evidence that ODD is more prevalent than CD during early childhood, but by adolescence the numbers of youth who meet criteria for ODD and CD are close to equal (Lahey, Miller et al., 1999; Loeber et al., 2000; Maughan et al., 2004). This is because the prevalence of ODD either stays constant or declines somewhat from early childhood through adolescence (Lahey et al., 2000; Maughan et al., 2004), whereas the prevalence of CD increases from early childhood through adolescence. The age-related increase in the prevalence of CD is much greater in boys than girls, which means that the sex difference in CD is greatest during late adolescence (Lahey et al., 2000; Maughan et al., 2004; Moffitt et al., 2001). Boys appear to be somewhat more likely to meet criteria for ODD at all ages (Lahey et al., 2000; Maughan et al., 2004).

Rates of delinquency increase steeply with age until they peak at 16 or 17 years of age and then decline with increasing age almost as steeply, a developmental pattern known as the *age-crime curve* (Hirschi & Gottfredson, 1983). Because of the age-crime curve, more than half of all crime is juvenile crime. This curve is consistent with Moffitt's (1993, 2003) view that youth on a childhood-onset trajectory are joined by the larger number of youth on an adolescent-onset trajectory, swelling the total number of adolescents who engage in delinquency. Males are more likely to engage in delinquency than females at all ages, but, like the diagnosis of CD, the sex difference in delinquency is greatest when males are at the peak of their age-crime curve at 16 or 17 years of age (Farrington, & Painter, 2004; Moffitt et al., 2001; Lahey et al., 2006). Current evidence is sketchy, but the age-crime curve might be flatter for females, with an earlier peak (Farrington, & Painter, 2004; Moffitt et al., 2001; Lahey et al., 2006).

CHILD CHARACTERISTICS THAT
PREDICT CD AND DELINQUENCY

Many emotional and behavioral characteristics of children predict later CD and delinquency. In some cases, these behavioral characteristics are viewed as *developmental precursors* that appear to be "juvenile forms" of later conduct problems. Other childhood characteristics do not resemble later conduct problems but are still useful predictors of future serious conduct problems. Knowledge of these predictive child characteristics makes it possible to study children who will develop a disorder *before* the disorder emerges, facilitating both studies of early causes and efforts to prevent conduct problems.

PREDICTIVE CHILD CHARACTERISTICS

The following aspects of early child behavior predict serious conduct problems during later childhood and adolescence to a statistically significant extent. It should be kept in mind, however, that none predicts adolescent antisocial behavior with a high degree of certainty.

1. *Temperament.* Several aspects of young children's dispositions to respond to their environments predict later conduct problems. These include a tendency for young children to resist control by adults (Keily et al., 2001), a tendency to respond to threats and frustrations with negative emotions (Gilliom & Shaw, 2004), daring sensation seeking (Gilliom & Shaw, 2004; Raine et al., 1998), low levels of prosocial behavior (Coté et al., 2002), and impulsivity and lack of persistence (Henry et al., 1996).

2. *ODD and ADHD.* Although ODD is an important problem in its own right, it also may function as a developmental precursor to CD. ODD behaviors typically emerge earlier in childhood than most, but not all CD behaviors, and ODD predicts meeting criteria for CD in the future (Lahey, McBurnett, & Loeber, 2000; Rowe et al., 2002). The percentage of children with ODD who go on to meet criteria for CD is not known precisely, but is fairly high; conversely, it is likely that many children with ODD never meet criteria for CD (Lahey, McBurnett, & Loeber, 2000; Rowe et al., 2002). Some studies suggest that ADHD in early childhood also is an independent developmental precursor to later conduct problems (Mannuzza et al., 2004; Mannuzza et al., 1991; Mannuzza et al., 1993). In contrast, other longitudinal studies indicate that childhood ADHD does not predict future antisocial behavior when childhood CD is controlled (Lahey, McBurnett, & Loeber, 2000). The hypothesis that childhood ADHD predicts later Antisocial Personality Disorder is plausible, as Antisocial Personality Disorder is defined partly by impulsivity and irresponsibility—which are similar to key symptoms of ADHD—but the support for this hypothesis is quite inconsistent. One possible explanation for these confusing findings is that it is the *combination* of both childhood ADHD and CD that

is the developmental precursor to adult Antisocial Personality Disorder (Hinshaw et al., 1993; Lynam, 1998). More evidence is needed, however.

3. *Early shyness and anxiety*. There is evidence that shyness and fearfulness in early childhood—in the absence of early conduct problems—predicts *decreased* risk of later conduct problems (Graham & Rutter, 1973; Kohlberg, Ricks, & Snarey, 1984; Mitchell & Rosa, 1981; Moffitt et al., 2002; Sanson et al., 1996). In addition, delinquents with higher levels of anxiety are less likely to commit future crimes (Quay & Love, 1977). These findings are puzzling, as other studies show that anxiety disorders co-occur with conduct problems at greater than chance rates (Loeber & Keenan, 1994; Zoccolillo, 1992). It is possible that anxiety is heterogeneous and some aspects of anxiety foster conduct problems whereas other aspects inhibit conduct problems (Lahey & Waldman, 2003). In addition, children with conduct problems who are socially withdrawn are at increased risk for persistent and serious conduct problems (Blumstein, Farrington, & Moitra, 1985; Kerr et al., 1997). It seems likely, however, that what is meant by "socially withdrawn" in these studies refers to lack of interaction with other children, perhaps due to lack of interest in others or rejection by others, and not to fearful shyness (Rutter & Giller, 1983).

4. *Childhood cognitive skills and language*. Children with lower cognitive ability scores are more likely to develop conduct problems (Elkins et al., 1997; Fergusson, Horwood, & Ridder, 2005; Ge, Donnellan, & Wenk, 2001; Kratzer & Hodgins, 1999; Lynam, Moffitt, & Stouthamer-Loeber, 1993; Moffitt & Silva, 1988). This does not appear to be an artifact of the lower socioeconomic status (SES) of children with lower ability scores, the greater likelihood that more intelligent youths will avoid detection of their antisocial behavior, or lower test motivation (Lynam et al., 1993; Moffitt & Silva, 1988). At this time it is not clear if deficits in specific cognitive abilities are associated with conduct problems or if conduct problems are related to lower general intelligence. There is some evidence, however, that a specific cluster of executive function, memory, and language abilities may be associated with early onset conduct problems, even controlling for general intelligence (Giancola et al., 1996; Raine et al., 2005; Seguin, Boulerice, Harden, Tremblay, & Pihl, 1999).

5. *Lower verbal intelligence* is correlated with slower language development in early childhood (Sparks, Ganschow, & Thomas, 1996). This is important because slow language development is associated with the development of conduct problems (Baker & Cantwell, 1987; Beitchman et al., 2001; Cohen et al., 1998; Stattin & Klackenberg-Larsson,

1993). Keenan and Shaw (1997) suggested that slowly developing language makes the process of parents socializing their toddler's behavior more difficult and more frustrating on both sides. Toddlers with better language skills can communicate their needs better and are more likely understand the rules and requests of adults, both of which facilitate socialization. Language development is slower on average in boys, which may be one reason why boys exhibit more conduct problems from age 4 on (Keenan & Shaw, 1997).

Note on toddler conduct problems: Tremblay (2003) has suggested that the majority of children hit, kick, bite, and take things as soon as they can walk. Thus, it is possible that conduct problems begin so early in life that some of them actually emerge *at the same time* as ADHD and ODD, which perhaps have been viewed incorrectly as developmental precursors. This has three potentially important implications. First, perhaps the field should study toddler conduct problems rather than early developmental precursors such as temperament. For example, we need to know if toddler conduct problems are so common that they do not predict future serious conduct problems as well as ODD and perhaps ADHD. Second, Tremblay's observations imply that the "age of onset" of many conduct problems is very difficult to determine. (If toddlers engage in conduct problems, is the age of onset of conduct problems 12 to 18 months for everyone?) Therefore, it may be more informative to focus on the *level* of conduct problems during early childhood rather than attempting to define the age of onset (Lahey & Waldman, 2003). Third, Tremblay's views should stimulate research on the characteristics of young children who fail to show expected declines in early conduct problems with increasing age.

DEVELOPMENTAL TRAJECTORIES AND CHILD CHARACTERISTICS THAT PREDICT SERIOUS CONDUCT PROBLEMS

Importantly, all of the findings previously reviewed on characteristics of children that predict later conduct problems apply to childhood-onset delinquency—and, therefore, may apply to most youth who meet criteria for CD—but *not* to adolescent-onset delinquency. That is, youth on a childhood-onset delinquency trajectory exhibit higher levels of difficult temperament, ADHD, and ODD and lower levels of fearful shyness during childhood than either youth on an adolescent-onset delinquency trajectory or nondelinquent youth. In contrast, youth on an adolescent-onset delinquency trajectory do not exhibit higher mean levels of these predictive child characteristics than nondelinquent youth (Lahey et al., 2006; Moffitt et al., 2001; Raine et al., 2005).

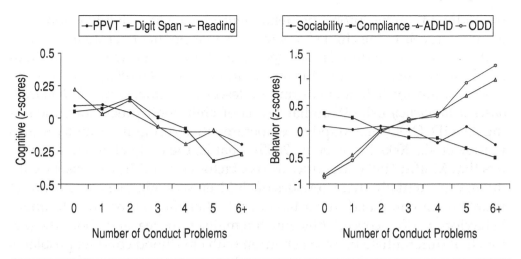

Figure 12.1. Association between the mean number of conduct problems at school entry and early childhood risk correlates among youth with mean self-reported adolescent delinquency scores more than 1 standard deviation above the mean. Figure reprinted from Lahey et al. (2006).

It is revealing to examine childhood characteristics that predict future conduct problems while viewing developmental trajectories as continua (Lahey & Waldman, 2003) rather than as the two distinct groups defined by Moffitt (1993). A large longitudinal study of the offspring of a nationally representative sample of mothers found that adolescents who engaged in high levels of delinquency varied considerably in their levels of the childhood characteristics that predict later delinquency (Lahey et al., 2006). As shown in Figure 12.1, youth who were highly delinquent during adolescence and who exhibited increasingly higher levels of childhood conduct problems had more increasingly lower scores on cognitive ability tests (left panel of Fig. 12.1), were progressively less sociable with interviewers and less compliant with adult instructions, and exhibited increasingly higher levels of ADHD and ODD symptoms.[1] Thus, two qualitatively distinct trajectory groups did not emerge; rather, at each progressively higher number

---

1. Scores on the three cognitive ability measures were based on first administrations of the Peabody Picture Vocabulary Test–Revised (PPVT; Dunn & Dunn, 1981) across 3 to 8 years, the Digit Span scale of the Wechsler Intelligence Scales for Children–Revised (Wechsler, 1974) across 7 to 9 years of age, and the Peabody Individual Achievement Test Reading Subtest (Dunn, & Markwardt, 1970) across ages 5 to 9 years. Sociability ratings were made by interviewers during the cognitive assessments between 2 to 6 years of age and compliance with adult instructions was rated by mothers during 2 to 6 years to define early child compliance). Mothers rated ADHD and ODD symptoms at 4 to 7 years (Peterson & Zill, 1986). To minimize sample bias, each risk correlate was adjusted for sex, family income, race-ethnicity, and maternal age at first birth (see Lahey et al., 2006, for more details).

of childhood conduct problems, delinquent adolescents exhibited more maladaptive levels of the child characteristics that predict later delinquency.

A provocative finding is that preadolescent children who exhibit high
levels of conduct problems during childhood, *regardless of whether they improve* (i.e., are not delinquent during adolescence) *or go on to exhibit childhood-
onset delinquency* exhibit similar levels of childhood precursors, including ADHD, ODD, maladaptive temperament, and cognitive ability scores
(Lahey et al., 2006; Raine et al., 2005). That is, the early child characteristics that Moffitt (1993) identifies as risk factors for childhood-onset delinquency are actually characteristics of children with high levels of conduct
problems in childhood, regardless of whether they go on to delinquent
behavior in adolescence. Thus, much remains to be learned about the factors that differentiate between children with childhood conduct problems
who improve or go on to engage in adolescent delinquency.

SEX DIFFERENCES IN CHILD CHARACTERISTICS THAT PREDICT SERIOUS CONDUCT PROBLEMS

Why are females less likely to exhibit adolescent delinquency than males?
One possible reason is that, on average, girls exhibit lower levels of the
child characteristics that predict future delinquency than boys (Lahey et al.,
2006; Moffitt et al., 2001). It is also possible that some of these child characteristics predict adolescent delinquency somewhat better in boys, but the evidence is inconclusive (Lahey et al., 2006; Moffitt et al., 2001). Keep in mind,
however, that the predictive child characteristics (e.g., ADHD and ODD)
are associated only with childhood-onset delinquency trajectory (and with
childhood conduct problems in non-delinquents). Although there are 3
times as many boys as girls on the childhood-onset delinquency trajectory,
there are few sex differences among those youth who are on the childhood-
onset delinquency trajectory in their predictive childhood characteristics
(Lahey et al., 2006; Moffitt et al., 2001). The possible exception is that chronic
childhood physical aggression may predict delinquency better in boys
(Broidy et al., 2003).

ADOLESCENT AND ADULT OUTCOMES OF CHILDHOOD ODD AND CD

Another way to understand conduct problems in developmental terms is
to examine the mental health outcomes of children and adolescents with
conduct problems later in life. Although ODD and CD are important because they cause serious impairment during childhood, they also are im-

portant because they increase the likelihood of other serious mental disorders in adolescence and adulthood. It is crucial to remember that not all children with high levels of childhood conduct problems persist in them or develop other problems (i.e., will follow a life-course persistent trajectory); many children with childhood behavior problems outgrow them and do not develop serious mental disorders (Moffitt et al., 1996).

The diagnosis of CD in childhood increases risk for criminal behavior in adolescence and adulthood (Fergusson et al., 2005; Kjelsberg, 2002) and for adult Antisocial Personality Disorder (Lahey et al., 2005; Maughan & Rutter, 2001). Antisocial Personality Disorder is a pernicious syndrome characterized by irresponsible behavior, persistent crime, and aggression and violence. Children with CD who are from low-income families and exhibit higher numbers of nonaggressive symptoms are particularly at risk for adult Antisocial Personality Disorder (Lahey et al., 2005). Nonetheless, the majority of children and adolescents with CD (perhaps 60 to 70%) do not progress to Antisocial Personality Disorder and serious criminality (Lahey et al., 2005; Maughan & Rutter, 2001).

It is also clear that adolescents who engage in high levels of delinquent behavior are at increased risk for criminal behavior during early adulthood (Piquero, Brame, & Moffitt, 2005), even though many adolescents cease to engage in criminal behavior during early adulthood. Crime is not the only adverse outcome associated with CD and serious adolescent delinquency, however: Antisocial adolescents are also at increased risk for reduced education, substance dependence, early parenthood, poor work records, dependence on welfare, unsuccessful family relationships, incarceration and criminal records, dangerous driving, and accidental injuries and early death (Loeber et al., 1998, 2005; Moffitt et al., 2001). Moffitt et al. (1996) hypothesized that many of these outcomes of adolescent conduct problems reduce the youth's chances for success in noncriminal arenas and "ensnare" youth in an antisocial future. Unfortunately, this cogent hypothesis has not yet been extensively tested.

Childhood ODD is associated with increased risk for later depressive disorders, whereas CD appears to indirectly increase risk for depression by causing stressful life events—such as expulsion from school, peer rejection, and incarceration—that precipitate depression (Burke et al., 2005; Little & Garber, 2005; Patterson & Stoolmiller, 1991). Children who meet criteria for CD also are at increased risk for adolescent drug and alcohol abuse (Marshal & Molina, 2006). This is important because the risk of suicide is greatest among adolescents with comorbid CD, depression, and substance abuse (Brent et al., 2002; Fombonne et al., 2001).

The adolescent and adult outcomes of serious conduct problems are quite poor for both males and females (Bardone et al., 1996; Bardone et al.,

1998; Moffitt et al., 2001). However, there are sex differences in the extent to which females and males are impaired in each specific area of adult functioning associated with youth conduct problems (Moffitt et al., 2001). Males are particularly likely to exhibit criminal behavior, work problems, and substance abuse, whereas females are more likely to experience depression, suicidal behavior, and poor physical health.

RISK FACTORS AND CAUSES OF CONDUCT PROBLEMS

An important goal for the twenty-first century is to move from cataloging lists of risk factors for conduct problems to understanding causal mechanisms (Lahey, Moffitt, & Caspi, 2003). There are many ways of doing this, but the field of behavior genetics provides a particularly helpful framework (Rutter, 2006). It is possible to use genetically informative samples to distinguish genetic from environmental causes (Rutter, 2006). For example, samples of both identical (monozygotic) twins, who share all of their segregating genes, and fraternal (dizygotic twins), who share 50% of their segregating genes on average, are genetically informative. When certain assumptions are met, finding that monozygotic twin pairs resemble each other on a trait more than dizygotic twin pairs suggests genetic influences on the trait (Rutter, 2006).

Rhee and Waldman (2002) conducted a meta-analytic review of many twin and adoption studies of conduct problems. They found that genetic influences account for 41% of the variation in broadly defined antisocial behavior among individuals in the population. For the diagnosis of CD in particular, the proportion of variance attributable to genes is 50%. A small proportion (11%) of the variance in CD is attributable to aspects of the environment that siblings share in common and make them more similar (e.g., the family's financial resources), with the remainder (39%) attributable to unshared aspects of the environment that make siblings different (e.g., only one sibling being abused) and to measurement error. There is similar evidence that the early childhood characteristics that predict later serious conduct problems, including difficult temperament and ODD, are substantially influenced by genes (Saudino, 2005; Simonoff, 2001).

Thus, there is strong evidence that a substantial proportion of the causal influences on conduct problems is genetic. It is very unlikely, however, that genes influence complex human traits such as conduct problems in simple and direct ways. Rather, genes influence human behavior through complex interplays with the environment (Rutter, 2006). By understanding something of the interplay between genes and environments, we will be in a better position to evaluate what is known about possible genetic and environmental influences later in the chapter.

GENE–ENVIRONMENT CORRELATIONS

Genetic and environmental influences on conduct problems are usually not independent, but are correlated in three ways (Plomin, DeFries, & Loehlin, 1977; Rutter, 2006). *Passive gene–environment correlation* occurs because children with conduct problems often have antisocial parents with mental health problems (Lahey et al., 1988, 1989; Nagin, Pogarsky, & Farrington, 1997). If the same genes increase the likelihood that both parents and their children will be antisocial, gene–environment correlation will exist. Passive gene–environment correlation is very important because children who are genetically at risk for conduct problems often will be raised by antisocial mothers who are unlikely to provide the kinds of skilled child rearing that could attenuate the development of conduct problems in the children.

Evocative gene–environment correlation occurs when the child's genetically influenced behavior changes the social environment, and, in turn, the changed social environment influences the development of conduct problems. Several inappropriate methods of parenting are associated with conduct problems in children (Patterson et al., 1992). Unfortunately, young children with ODD and early conduct problems tend to *evoke* exactly the kinds of coercive, harsh, rejecting, and inconsistent parenting behaviors that are thought to contribute to the development of their conduct problems (Anderson, Lytton, & Romney, 1986; Ge et al., 1996; Sanson & Prior, 1999). In this way, genes that influence the child's temperament and ODD become evocatively correlated with adverse parenting environments.

Active gene–environment correlation occurs when the child's *selection* of environments is partly influenced by genes. For example, some children selectively form friendships with delinquent peers who foster their delinquent behavior. Because there is evidence that association with delinquent peers is partly genetically influenced (Rowe & Osgood, 1984), this appears to be an instance of active gene–environment correlation.

GENE–ENVIRONMENT INTERACTIONS

There also are two kinds of evidence that conduct problems are influenced by gene–environment *interactions* (G×E). First, genetic influences on conduct problems apparently can be muted by favorable social learning environments. Evidence for this kind of G×E comes from adoption studies, which show that the adopted-away offspring of antisocial biological parents have fewer conduct problems when they are raised by well-adjusted adoptive parents than by antisocial adoptive parents (Bohman, 1996; Cadoret et al., 1995). Second, there is growing evidence that different individuals respond in different ways to the same experiences partly because of differences in their genes. Findings on this kind of G×E will be summarized in the following section on molecular genetics.

FACTORS THAT MIGHT BE ENVIRONMENTAL CAUSES OF CONDUCT PROBLEMS

In this section, findings on aspects of the child's environment that could be causes of conduct problems is reviewed. It is important to keep in mind that correlation does not imply causation; conduct problems may be correlated with a variable that is not causally related to it.

Prenatal and perinatal factors.   A number of pregnancy and birth factors are correlated with the development of serious conduct problems (Brennan, Grekin, & Mednick, 2003):

1. *Birth weight and birth complications.* Birth complications (e.g., lack of oxygen to the fetus during labor) and low birth weight and are correlated with future conduct problems (Brennan et al., 2003), particularly in disorganized families with few resources (Arseneault et al., 2002). This could indicate that better-functioning families provide environments that lessen the negative effects of birth complications. Usually, however, it is not possible to determine if birth factors have a causal effect because of the host of genetic and environmental variables that are correlated with them. Nonetheless, studies of genetically informative samples have provided evidence that at least some perinatal factors have a causal effect on risk for conduct problems (Raz, Shah, & Sander, 1996). For example, because monozygotic twins share all of their segregating genes, and share all aspects of the environment that are common to twins, finding differences between monozygotic twins in their conduct problems that are related to a birth factor would provide strong evidence that it plays a causal role. For example, van Os, Wichers, Danckaerts, Van Gestel, Derom, and Vlietinck (2001) found that the monozygotic twin with the lower birth weight was more likely to develop conduct problems. This suggests that birth weight plays a causal role, perhaps because low birth weight is associated with alterations in brain systems involved in risk for conduct problems (Brennan et al., 2003). Other studies suggest that birth complications interact with genetic risk for conduct problems (Wichers et al., 2002). There is also inconsistent evidence that correlation between birth com-

plications and conduct problems could be stronger in male offspring (Brennan et al., 2003). All of these issues require greater study.

2. *Maternal cigarette smoking and substance use during pregnancy.* Women who smoke, drink alcohol, or use drugs such as cocaine during pregnancy are considerably more likely to have children who develop conduct problems, even when other maternal characteristics known to be associated with conduct problems in their children are controlled (Brennan et al., 2003; Wakschlag et al., 2002). This suggests that toxic substances in tobacco or carbon monoxide, all of which cross the placental barrier to the fetus, could affect fetal brain development in ways that increase risk. The difficulty with this research is that women who smoke during pregnancy differ from women who do not smoke in many ways, including ways that have not been controlled in previous studies. A large study that controlled extraneous genetic and environmental factors has raised questions about causal effects of prenatal exposure to smoking. Like other studies, D'Onofrio, Van Hulle, Waldman, Rodgers, Harden, Rathouz, and Lahey (in press) found that women who smoked more on average during their pregnancies gave birth to children with more conduct problems. On the other hand, when mothers who smoked during one pregnancy smoked less (or not at all) during their other pregnancies, the level of conduct problems in their offspring did not vary with their level of smoking during each pregnancy. If smoking during pregnancy were causal, differences in child conduct problems related to the amount of maternal smoking would have been found both between and within families. Instead, the findings suggest that smoking during pregnancy is correlated with child conduct problems because of some other characteristic of mothers that has yet to be identified. Thus, even if maternal smoking proves not to be causal, it provides an important clue. Regardless of what maternal characteristic accounts for the apparent effect of maternal smoking, it is robustly related to conduct problems. Further findings by D'Onofrio, Van Hulle, Waldman, Rodgers, Harden, Rathouz, and Lahey (in press) suggest that it is an environmental factor, but much more research is needed.

There is much stronger evidence that maternal alcohol use during pregnancy plays a causal role in the conduct problems offspring. In the same sample used to study maternal cigarette smoking, D'Onofrio, Van Hulle, Waldman, Rodgers, Rathouz, and Lahey (in press) found a linear dose-response effect of maternal drinking. That is, the greater the amount of alcohol consumed, including even moderate levels of drinking, the greater the risk of conduct problems was in the offspring. Because this effect of alcohol was clear even when mothers drank at different levels during the pregnancies of their multiple children, these results strongly suggest (but do not prove by themselves) that there is an adverse causal effect of drinking alcohol during pregnancy. If a causal effect of maternal alcohol consumption is confirmed, this would mean that a preventable environmental cause of conduct problems had been discovered.

Socioeconomic status (SES).   Children and adolescents from families with lower incomes and less parental education are more likely to exhibit serious conduct problems (Coté et al., 2006; Lahey, Miller et al., 1999; Lahey & Waldman, 2003). This could be because poverty creates circumstances that foster conduct problems. Alternatively, antisocial parents who live in poverty because they did not succeed educationally and occupationally might transmit conduct problems to their offspring through genetic and environmental mechanisms that are unrelated to poverty itself—or both explanations could be correct (Dohrenwend et al., 1992; Miech et al., 1999). There is evidence that lower SES is more strongly associated with childhood-onset delinquency than adolescent-onset delinquency (Lahey et al., 2006; Moffitt et al., 2001). It is not clear if there are sex differences in the magnitude of the association between SES and conduct problems, however (Lahey et al., 2006; Moffitt et al., 2001).

Parental characteristics, family characteristics, and parenting.   Many studies have found that a set of correlated characteristics of parents are related to conduct problems in their offspring. Risk for conduct problems is highest among the children of mothers and fathers with histories of antisocial behavior and substance abuse, mothers with lower intelligence, and mothers who first gave birth at younger ages (Lahey, Miller et al., 1999; Lahey et al., 2003, 2006; Moffitt et al., 2001). In addition, women who have multiple partners and/or have discordant partner relationships are more likely to have children with conduct problems (Keenan, Loeber, & Green, 1999; Lahey, Miller et al., 1999). However, it is not known why these characteristics of parents and families are related to risk for offspring conduct problems. According to social learning theory (Patterson et al., 1992), these and other parent and family characteristics cause child conduct problems by disrupting parenting. There is some support for this view (Jaffee et al., 2006), but surprisingly little is known about this topic. Furthermore, there is robust evidence that inadequate supervision and inconsistent, coercive, and punitive discipline—including physical and sexual abuse and neglect—are correlated with offspring conduct problems (Lahey, Miller et al., 1999; Patterson, & Stouthamer-Loeber, 1984). It is also clear that interventions that change these aspects of parenting behavior reduce child conduct problems (Beauchaine, Webster-Stratton, & Reid, 2005; Nock, 2003). To use an old saw, however, this does not necessarily mean than deficient parenting causes child conduct problems, any more than the fact that aspirin relieves headaches means that headaches are caused by aspirin deficiency. Nonetheless, evidence from studies of parent training provide potentially important clues about the origins of conduct problems that should be followed in future studies.

Deviant peer influence and gang membership. Two robust findings suggest the importance of peers in the origins of juvenile delinquency. First, almost all crime committed by adolescents is committed in the company of other youth (Conger & Simons, 1997). Second, association with delinquent peers is perhaps the strongest correlate of adolescent delinquency (Conger & Simons, 1997). Some evidence from longitudinal studies indicates that developing friendships with delinquent peers leads to increases in delinquency in youth who had not previously been delinquent (Keenan, Loeber, & Zhang, 1995), which suggests a causal influence. More can be learned from studies of membership in antisocial gangs, which is a special case of delinquent peer influence. Although it is clear that engaging in conduct problems during childhood increases the likelihood that a male child will join an antisocial gang (Lahey, Gordon et al., 1999), drug selling, violent behavior, and vandalism all increase sharply when a youth joins a gang, compared to before gang entry and after leaving the gang (Gordon et al., 2004). Again, this temporal pattern suggests, but does not prove, a causal effect of peer influence. In Moffitt's (1993, 2003) model, peer influence is particularly important for delinquent adolescents who did not engage in high levels of conduct problems when children, but much remains to be learned about peer influences. In particular, little is currently known about sex differences in peer influences on delinquency.

Neighborhoods and urbanicity. Juvenile delinquency is far more common among youth who live in neighborhoods that are characterized by poverty and social disorganization (Loeber et al., 1998). Sampson, Raudenbush, and Earls (1997) suggested that the most important aspects of high-crime neighborhoods are a lack of social connectedness among neighbors and the absence of working together to supervise youth and reduce crime. Tuvblad, Grann, and Lichtenstein (2006) found that the proportion of variance in adolescent conduct problems attributable to environmental influences was lower, and the proportion attributable to environmental influences shared by siblings was greater, in such high-risk neighborhoods. If replicated, this interaction provides support for the hypothesis that neighborhood factors play a causal role in the origins of conduct problems.

In addition, juvenile crime is highly concentrated in high-density cities (Laub, 1983). European studies have found that youth living in big cities report rates of delinquent behavior that are twice that of rural youth (Rutter et al., 1975; Wichström, Skogen, & Oia, 1996), but evidence from North America is inconsistent (Costello et al., 1996; Offord et al., 1987). More research on this important topic is needed.

STUDIES OF NEUROPHYSIOLOGICAL MECHANISMS

It is important to relate individual differences in behavior to variations in the anatomy and physiology of neural systems because it can link what is known about conduct problems to everything that is known about those neural systems. The first physiological studies examined correlations between conduct problems and peripheral makers of neural activity. The most consistent and robust finding is that lower resting heart rate predicts adolescent conduct problems (Ortiz & Raine, 2004). Low resting heart rate is interesting partly because it also is related to the temperamental trait of fearless stimulation-seeking (Raine, 2002). In addition, there is evidence that higher autonomic arousal is inversely related to conduct problems and positively related to recovery from childhood conduct problems (Lahey et al., 1993; Popma et al., 2006; Quay, 1993; Raine, Venables, & Williams, 1995). Similarly, individual differences in hypothalamic-pituitary-adrenal (HPA) activity may be related to conduct problems (McBurnett et al., 2000, 2005; Popma et al., 2006).

Recent advances in brain imaging have allowed studies relating brain anatomy and physiology to conduct problems. These studies suggest that structural and functional deficits of the prefrontal cortex are related to serious conduct problems (Ishikawa & Raine, 2003; Raine, 2002). This suggests the hypothesis that impaired development of the prefrontal cortex, which continues to develop through adolescence, is a major factor in the origins of serious conduct problems (Ishikawa & Raine, 2003; Raine, 2002). There are some intriguing links among these research literatures, which could lead to a more integrated theory of neural mechanisms in the future. Low resting heart rate may be correlated with conduct problems because the prefrontal cortex plays a role in regulating autonomic arousal (Raine, 2002). It is also interesting that there is evidence that maternal alcohol consumption during pregnancy might cause smaller offspring frontal cortex size (Brennan et al., 2003). Maternal alcohol use in pregnancy and delivery complications also have been linked to HPA axis reactivity (Brennan et al., 2003). One frontier of biological research is studies to explore possible causal links between malnutrition during pregnancy and offspring antisocial behavior (Raine, 2002).

PROGRESS IN MOLECULAR GENETICS

In the last 5 years, the ice has been broken in the search for gene variants that increase risk for conduct problems. Although it is likely that some of the first replicated findings in this area will be refined or refuted in the future, enough has been learned to summarize early progress in the molecular genetics of conduct problems. These findings are exciting both in supporting hypotheses regarding the role of specific neurotransmitter systems in conduct problems and in fleshing out hypotheses regarding gene–environment interplay (Rutter, 2006).

Caspi et al., (2002) reported an interaction between childhood maltreatment and a variant of the gene that encodes the enzyme, monoamine oxidase-A (MAO-A). MAO-A is of interest because regulates the availability of several neurotransmitters, including serotonin, dopamine, and norepinephrine, all of which have been implicated in animal studies as being involved in aggression (Rutter, Moffitt, & Caspi, 2006). Because one genetic polymorphism codes for or either low or high levels of MAO-A activity, it influences activity in all of the neural systems in which MAO-A plays a role. Caspi et al., (2002) found that childhood maltreatment predicted the development of serious conduct problems regardless of MAO-A genotype, but maltreated children with the low-activity MAO-A genotype exhibited significantly higher levels of conduct problems than maltreated children without that genotype. This genetic moderation of the apparent effect of maltreatment has been replicated in two studies (Foley et al., 2004; Nilsson et al., 2006), and another study closely replicated the pattern of differences but the interaction did not reach statistical significance (Haberstick et al., 2005). A study of a clinic-referred sample did not replicate the finding (Young et al., 2006), but a meta-analysis of all existing studies confirmed the role of MAO-A in interaction with childhood maltreatment in predicting serious antisocial behavior (Kim-Cohen et al., 2006). Thus, it seems increasingly likely that the Caspi et al., (2002) findings will stand up to future attempts at replication.

It should be noted that the Caspi et al., (2002) findings could reflect gene–gene interaction instead of G×E. That is, a different gene (or genes) that is passed from parent to child (manifested in the parent as risk for harsh discipline and in the child as risk for aggressive conduct problems) could interact with the MAO-A gene to result in the observed increased risk for serious conduct problems in maltreated children, even if childhood maltreatment had no causal environmental effect. On the other hand, evidence from two other types of studies, which are not subject to the same alternative explanation, support Caspi et al., (2002) hypothesis of G–E. First, Newman et al., (2005) found that rhesus monkeys randomly assigned to be raised with or without their mothers were more aggressive if they had the analogous low-activity MAO-A genotype when raised in isolation. Second, imaging studies of humans have shown that persons with the low-activity MAO-A genotype exhibit a pattern of greater arousal in the amygdala and less arousal of prefrontal cortex that is associated with aggression when presented with emotion-provoking stimuli (Meyer-Lindberg & Weinberger, 2006; Meyer-Lindberg et al., 2006).

The MAO-A gene is not the only gene that is related to variations in the neural systems related to aggression, of course. Catechol-O-methyl transferase (COMT) is an enzyme involved in the breakdown of synaptic dopamine, epinephrine, and norepinephrine that has been linked with variations in frontal cortex functioning. Thapar et al. (2005) found that a genotype of the COMT gene is associated with increased risk for childhood conduct problems. They also found evidence of GxE because the association between low birth weight and conduct problems was stronger among children with the high-risk COMT genotype. There also are several findings relating conduct problems to variants in the gene encoding the dopamine transporter, which reuptakes dopamine from the synapse (Lee et al., in press, 2006; Young et al., 2002), and of an interaction between maternal insensitivity and variants of the D4 receptor for dopaminergic neurons (Bakermans-Kranenburg & van Ijzendoorn, 2006). In addition, there is a report linking the serotonin transporter gene to oppositional and aggressive behavior (Haberstick, Smolen, & Hewitt, 2006). A vast amount undoubtedly remains to be learned about GxE, but the field of the molecular genetics of conduct problems is already producing cogent findings.

TOWARD A THEORETICAL SYNTHESIS

Lahey and Waldman (2003, 2005) proposed a theoretical model that integrates current findings on the development of serious conduct problems. Other theoretical models of antisocial behavior in youth are presented in Lahey, Moffitt, and Caspi (2003). In the Lahey and Waldman model, children are born with individual differences in dispositions to respond socially and emotionally to the environment. Variations in these dispositions among children in the population are influenced by genes and prenatal influences and are shaped by the postnatal environment from birth onward. Across many studies, three dispositions have been identified as being related to conduct problems, although the definitions and labels of the dispositions vary somewhat across studies:

1. *Prosociality versus callousness.* Children who care about the feelings of other children and want to please adults are less likely to develop

serious conduct problems than children who callously disregard the wishes and feelings of others (e.g., Frick, 2006; Messer et al., 2006). In the Lahey and Waldman (2003, 2005) model, this is because the natural consequences of common early childhood misbehaviors such as hitting and taking things from others (e.g., seeing the other child cry) are *punishing* to children who care about the feelings of the other child, but are either neutral or *reinforcing* to more callous children. These individual differences lead to reinforcement histories that increase or decrease the likelihood of future antisocial behavior. Callous children are particularly likely to acquire a pattern of planful, goal-directed aggression (Frick, 2006; Kempes et al., 2006).

2. *Daring sensation seeking versus fearful inhibition.* Children who find novelty and danger to be attractive and exciting are more likely to develop conduct problems than children who react fearfully to novel, loud, and risky situations (Biederman et al., 2001; Raine et al., 1998; Quay, 1965). Lahey and Waldman (2003, 2005) hypothesized that involvement in fights and engaging in transgressions that could lead to apprehension and punishment is reinforcing to daring children, but punishing to less daring children.

3. *Negative emotionality versus emotional stability.* Children who react with intense negative emotions to even minor frustrations and threats are hypothesized to be at high risk for conduct problems (Lahey & Waldman, 2003, 2005). When adults attempt to control or discipline highly emotional children, their children are likely to respond with intensely oppositional, defiant, and coercive responses, often prompting the adults to back down from their requests. The net result is negative reinforcement that increases the likelihood of future oppositional-defiant behavior by the child (Patterson et al., 1992). In addition, negative emotional responses to minor frustrations and provocations from other children (e.g., someone is playing with a toy that the child wants to play with) increase the likelihood of reacting in an antisocial manner (e.g., grabbing the toy), leading to negative reinforcement of the antisocial behavior through the removal of the frustration or threat (i.e., the aggressive child gets the toy).

Thus, in a multitude of such ways, individual differences in these three early socioemotional dispositions are hypothesized to increase or decrease the likelihood that a child will learn childhood-onset conduct problems and persist in them as he or she interacts with the social environment. In addition, slowly developing cognitive skills and language are hypothesized to interfere with socialization and thereby influence risk for conduct problems (Keenan & Shaw, 1997; Lahey & Waldman, 2003, 2005). Lahey and Waldman (2003, 2005) posit that the three dispositions and cognitive ability play less of a role in the development of adolescent-onset conduct problems. On the other hand, the inverse of these predispositions (prosociality, fearfulness, calm response to frustration and threat, and higher intelligence) may protect adolescents from the development of delinquent behavior in the absence of a childhood history of conduct problems.

At a different level of analysis, individual differences in these predispositions and abilities can be understood as individual differences in brain structure and function that are caused by the same genetic and environmental influences. Genes are hypothesized to influence conduct problems partly because they influence neural systems related to the dispositions and abilities that influence the likelihood that conduct problems will develop. Genes also are hypothesized to influence the environments that foster or reduce the likelihood of conduct problems and interact with those environments. Thus, this theoretical model, and others like it, can and should incorporate variables at biological, environmental, and behavioral levels of analysis.

The Lahey and Waldman (2003, 2005) model was advanced partly to integrate the vast accumulation of empirical findings on the origins of antisocial behavior in youth, but also to stimulate empirical tests that can refute its hypotheses. Many tests will be required, but an early prospective test confirmed the prediction that children high in both negative emotionality and daring are at increased risk for the child conduct problems (Gilliom & Shaw, 2004). Prosociality was not measured in that study, however. In addition, Waldman, Van Hulle, Applegate, Pardini, Frick, and Lahey (2006) confirmed a key prediction regarding the mediation of genetic influences by finding that half of the genetic influences on child and adolescent conduct disorder were shared with the dispositions, particularly with negative emotionality and low prosociality. The ultimate goal of such models is advanced understanding of the causes of conduct problems and to facilitate early prevention.

REFERENCES

American Psychiatric Association. (1994). *Diagnostic and statistical manual of mental disorders, Fourth Edition.* Washington, DC: American Psychiatric Association.

Anderson, K. E., Lytton, H., & Romney, D. M. (1986). Mothers' interactions with normal and conduct-disordered boys: Who affects whom? *Developmental Psychology, 22,* 604–609.

Angold, A., Costello, E. J., & Erkanli, A. (1999). Comorbidity. *Journal of Child Psychology and Psychiatry, 40,* 57–87.

Arseneault, L., Tremblay, R., Boulerice, B., & Saucier, J. (2002). Obstetrical complications and violent delinquency: Testing two developmental pathways. *Child Development, 73,* 496–508.

Baker, L., & Cantwell, D. P. (1987). A prospective psychiatric follow-up of children with speech/language disorders. *Journal of the American Academy of Child and Adolescent Psychiatry, 26,* 546–553.

Bakermans-Kranenburg, M. J., & van Ijzendoorn, M. H. (2006). Gene-environment interaction of the dopamine D4 receptor (DRD4) and observed maternal insensitivity predicting externalizing behavior in preschoolers. *Developmental Psychobiology, 48,* 406–409.

Bardone, A. M., Moffitt, T., Caspi, A., & Dickson, N. (1996). Adult mental health and social outcomes of adolescent girls with depression and conduct disorder. *Development and Psychopathology, 8,* 811–829.

Bardone, A. M., Moffitt, T. E., Caspi, A., Dickson, N., Stanton, W. R., & Silva, P. A. (1998). Adult physical health outcomes of adolescent girls with conduct disorder, depression, and anxiety. *Journal of the American Academy of Child and Adolescent Psychiatry, 37,* 594–601.

Beauchaine, T. P., Webster-Stratton, C., & Reid, M. J. (2005). Mediators, moderators, and predictors of one-year outcomes among children treated for early-onset conduct problems: A latent growth curve analysis. *Journal of Consulting and Clinical Psychology, 73,* 371–388.

Beitchman, J. H., Wilson, B., Johnson, C. J., Atkinson, L., Young, A., Adlaf, E., Escobar, M., & Douglas, L. (2001). Fourteen-year follow-up of speech/language-impaired and control children: Psychiatric outcome. *Journal of the American Academy of Child and Adolescent Psychiatry, 40,* 75–82.

Biederman, J., Hirshfeld-Becker, D. R., Rosenbaum, J. F., Herot, C., Friedman, D., Snidman, N., et al. (2001). Further evidence of association between behavioral inhibition and social anxiety in children. *American Journal of Psychiatry, 158,* 1673–1679.

Blumstein, A., Farrington, D. P., & Moitra, S. (1985), Delinquency careers: Innocents, desisters, and persisters. In M. Tonry & N. Morris (Eds.), *Crime and justice.* Chicago: University of Chicago Press.

Bohman, M. (1996). Predispositions to criminality: Swedish adoption studies in retrospect. In G. R. Bock & J. A. Goode (Eds.), *Genetics of criminal and antisocial behavior.* Chichester, England: Wiley.

Boyle, M. H., Offord, D. R., Racine, Y., Szatmari, P., Fleming, J. E., & Sanford, M. (1996). Identifying thresholds for clasifying childhood psychiatric disorder: Issues and prospects. *Journal of the American Academy of Child and Adolescent Psychiatry, 35,* 1440–1448.

Brennan, P. A., Grekin, E. R., & Mednick, S. (2003). Prenatal and perinatal influences on conduct disorder and serious delinquency. In B. B. Lahey, T. E. Moffitt, & A. Caspi (Eds.), *Causes of conduct disorder and serious delinquency* (pp. 319–344). New York: Guilford.

Brent, D. A., Oquendo, M., Birmaher, B., Greenhill, L., Kolko, D., Stanley, B., et al. (2002). Familial pathways to early-onset suicide attempt: Risk for suicidal behavior in offspring of mood-disordered suicide attempters. *Archives of General Psychiatry, 59,* 801–807.

Broidy, L. M., Nagin, D. S., Tremblay, R. E., Bates, J. E., Brame, B., Dodge, K. A., et al. (2003). Developmental trajectories of childhood disruptive behaviors and adolescent delinquency: A six-site, cross-national study. *Developmental Psychology, 39,* 222–245.

Burke, J. D., Loeber, R., Lahey, B. B., & Rathouz, P. J. (2005). Developmental transitions among affective and behavioral disorders in adolescent boys. *Journal of Child Psychology and Psychiatry, 46,* 1200–1210.

Cadoret, R. J., Yates, W. R., Troughton, E., Woodward, G., & Stewart, M. A. (1995). Genetic-environmental interaction in the genesis of aggressivity and conduct disorders. *Archives of General Psychiatry, 52,* 916–924.

Caspi, A., McClay, J., Moffitt, T., Mill, J., Martin, J., Craig, I. W., et al. (2002). Role of genotype in the cycle of violence in maltreated children. *Science, 297,* 851–854.

Cohen, N. J., Menna, R., Vallance, D. D., Barwick, M. A., Im, N., & Horodezky, N. B. (1998). Language, social cognitive processing, and behavioral characteristics of psychiatrically disturbed children with previously identified and unsuspected language impairments. *Journal of Child Psychology and Psychiatry, 39,* 853–864.

Conger, R. D., & Simons, R. L. (1997). Life-course contingencies in the development of adolescent antisocial behavior: A matching law approach. In T. Thornberry (Ed.), *Developmental theories of crime and delinquency* (pp. 55–100). New Brunswick, NJ: Transaction Publishers.

Costello, E. J., Angold, A., Burns, B. J., Stangl, D. K., Tweed, D. L., Erkanli, A., et al. (1996). The Great Smoky Mountains Study of youth: Goals, design, methods, and the prevalence of *DSM-III-R* disorders. *Archives of General Psychiatry, 53,* 1129–1136.

Coté, S., Tremblay, R. E, Nagin, D. S., Zoccolillo, M., & Vitaro, F. (2002). Childhood behavioral profiles leading to adolescent conduct disorder: risk trajectories for boys and girls. *Journal of the American Academy of Child and Adolescent Psychiatry, 41,* 1086–1094.

Coté, S. M., Vaillancourt, T., Le Blanc, J. C., Nagin, D. S., & Tremblay, R. E. (2006). The development of physical aggression from toddlerhood to pre-adolescence: A nationwide longitudinal study of Canadian children. *Journal of Abnormal Child Psychology, 34,* 71–85.

Coté, S., Zoccolillo, M., Tremblay, R. E., Nagin, D., & Vitaro, F. (2001). Predicting girls' conduct disorder in adolescence from childhood trajectories of disruptive behaviors. *Journal of the American Academy of Child and Adolescent Psychiatry, 40,* 678–684.

D'Onofrio, B. M., Van Hulle, C. A., Waldman, I. D., Rodgers, J. L., Harden, K. P., Rathouz, P. J., et al. (in press). Smoking during pregnancy and offspring externalizing problems: An exploration of genetic and environmental confounds. *Development and Psychopathology.*

D'Onofrio, B. M., Van Hulle, C. A., Waldman, I. D., Rodgers, J. L., Rathouz, P. J., & Lahey, B. B. (in press). *Causal inferences regarding exposure to prenatal alcohol and childhood conduct problems. Archives of General Psychiatry.*

Dohrenwend, B. P., Levav, I., Shrout, P. E., Schwartz, S., Naveh, G., Link, B. G., et al. (1992). Socioeconomic status and psychiatric disorders: The causation-selection issue. *Science, 255,* 946–952.

Dunn, L. M., & Dunn, L. M. (1981). *Peabody Picture Vocabulary Test-Revised*. Circle Pines, MN: American Guidance Service.

Dunn, L. M., & Markwardt, F. C. (1970). *Peabody Individual Achievement Test Manual*. Circle Pines, MN: American Guidance Service.

Elkins, I., Iacono, W., Doyle, A., & McGue, M. (1997). Characteristics associated with the persistence of antisocial behavior: Results from recent longitudinal research. *Aggression and Violent Behavior, 2*, 101–124.

Farrington, D. P. (1991). Antisocial personality from childhood to adulthood. *The Psychologist, 4*, 389–394.

Farrington, D. P., & Painter, K. A. (2004). *Gender differences in offending: Implications for risk-focused prevention*. London: Home Office.

Fergusson, D. M., Horwood, L. J., & Ridder, E. M. (2005). Show me the child at seven: The consequences of conduct problems in childhood for psychosocial functioning in adulthood. *Journal of Child Psychology and Psychiatry, 46*, 837–849.

Foley, D. L., Eaves, L. J., Wormley, B., Silberg, J. L., Maes, H. H., Kuhn, J., et al. (2004). Childhood adversity, monoamine oxidase a genotype, and risk for conduct disorder. *Archives of General Psychiatry, 61*, 1–7.

Fombonne, E., Wostear, G., Cooper, V., Harrington, R., & Rutter, M. (2001). The Maudsley long-term follow-up of child and adolescent depression: 2. Suicidality, criminality and social dysfunction in adulthood. *British Journal of Psychiatry, 179*, 218–223.

Frick, P. J. (2006). Developmental pathways to conduct disorder. *Child and Adolescent Psychiatric Clinics of North America, 15*, 311–331.

Ge, X., Conger, R. D., Cadoret, R. J., Neiderhiser, J. M., Yates, W., Troughton, E., et al. (1996). The developmental interface between nature and nurture: A mutual influence model of child antisocial behavior and parent behaviors. *Developmental Psychology, 32*, 574–589.

Ge, X., Donnellan, M. B., & Wenk, E. (2001). The development of persistent criminal offending in males. *Criminal Justice and Behavior, 26*, 731–755.

Giancola, P. R., Martin, C. S., Tarter, R. E., Pelham, W. E., & Moss, H. B. (1996). Executive cognitive functioning and aggressive behavior in preadolescent boys at high risk for substance abuse/dependence. *Journal of Studies on Alcohol, 57*, 352–359.

Gilliom, M., & Shaw, D. S. (2004). Codevelopment of externalizing and internalizing problems in early childhood. *Development and Psychopathology, 16*, 313–333.

Gordon, R. A., Lahey, B. B., Kawai, E., Loeber, R., Stouthamer-Loeber, M., & Farrington, D. P. (2004). Antisocial behavior and youth gang membership: Selection and socialization. *Criminology, 42*, 55–87.

Graham P., & Rutter, M. (1973). Psychiatric disorders in the young adolescent: A follow-up study. *Proceedings of the Royal Society of Medicine, 66*, 1226–1229.

Haberstick, B., Lessem, J., Hopfer, C., Smolen, A., Ehringer, M., Timberlake, D., et al. (2005). Monoamine oxidase A (MAO-A) and antisocial behaviors in the presence of childhood and adolescent maltreatment. *American Journal of Medical Genetics: Neuropsychiatric Genetics, 135*, 59–64.

Haberstick, B. C., Smolen, A., & Hewitt, J. K. (2006). Family-based association test of the 5HTTLPR and aggressive behavior in a general population sample of children. *Biological Psychiatry, 59*, 836–843.

Henry, B., Caspi, A., Moffitt, T. E., & Silva, P. A. (1996). Temperamental and familial predictors of violent and nonviolent criminal convictions: Age 3 to age 18. *Developmental Psychology, 32*, 614–623.

Hinshaw, S. P., Lahey, B. B., & Hart, E. L. (1993). Issues of taxonomy and comorbidity in the development of conduct disorder. *Development and Psychopathology, 5*, 31–50.

Hirschi, T., & Gottfredson, M. (1983). Age and the explanation of crime. *American Journal of Sociology, 89*, 552–584.

Ishikawa, S. S., & Raine, A. (2003). Prefrontal deficits and antisocial behavior: A causal model. In B. B. Lahey, T. E. Moffitt, & A. Caspi (Eds.), *Causes of conduct disorder and juvenile delinquency* (pp. 277–304). New York: Guilford.

Jaffee, S. R., Belsky, J., Harrington, H., Caspi, A., Moffitt, T. E. (2006). When parents have a history of conduct disorder: How is the caregiving environment affected? *Journal of Abnormal Psychology, 115*, 309–319.

Keenan, K., Loeber, R., & Green, S. (1999). Conduct disorder in girls: A review of the literature. *Clinical Child and Family Psychology Review, 2*, 3–19.

Keenan, K., Loeber, R., & Zhang, Q. (1995). The influence of deviant peers on the development of boys' disruptive and delinquent behavior: A temporal analysis. *Development and Psychopathology, 7*, 715–726.

Keenan, K., & Shaw, D. (1997). Developmental and social influences on young girls' early problem behavior. *Psychological Bulletin, 121*, 95–113.

Keily, M., Bates, J., Dodge, K., & Pettit, G. (2001). Effects of temperament on the development of externalizing and internalizing behaviors over 9 years. In F. Columbus (Ed.), *Advances in psychology research* (Vol. 6, pp. 255–288). Hauppauge, NY: Nova Science Publishers.

Kempes, M., Matthys, W., Maassen, G., van Goozen, S., & van Engeland, H. (2006). A parent questionnaire for distinguishing between reactive and proactive aggression in children. *European Child and Adolescent Psychiatry, 15*, 38–45.

Kerr, M., Tremblay, R.E., Pagani-Kurtz, L., & Vitaro, F. (1997). Boy's behavioral inhibition and the risk of later delinquency. *Archives of General Psychiatry, 54*, 809–816.

Kim-Cohen, J., Caspi, A., Taylor, A., Williams, B., Newcombe, R., Craig, I. W., & Moffitt, T. E. (2006). MAOA, maltreatment, and gene-environment interaction predicting children's mental health: New evidence and a meta-analysis. *Molecular Psychiatry, 11*, 903–913.

Kjelsberg, E. (2002). *DSM-IV* conduct disorder symptoms in adolescents as markers of registered criminality. *European Child and Adolescent Psychiatry, 11*, 2–9.

Kohlberg, L., Ricks, D., & Snarey, J. (1984). Childhood development as a predictor of adaptation in adulthood. *Genetic Psychology Monographs, 110*, 91–172.

Kratzer, L., & Hodgins, S. (1999). A typology of offenders: A test of Moffitt's theory among males and females from childhood to age 30. *Criminal Behaviour and Mental Health, 9*, 57–73.

Lahey, B. B., Applegate, B., Barkley, R. A., Garfinkel, B., McBurnett, K., Kerdyk, L., et al. (1994). *DSM-IV* field trials for oppositional defiant disorder and conduct disorder in children and adolescents. *American Journal of Psychiatry, 151,* 1163–1171.

Lahey, B. B., Applegate, B., Waldman, I. D., Loft, J. D., Hankin, B. L., & Rick, J. (2004). The structure of child and adolescent psychopathology: Generating new hypotheses. *Journal of Abnormal Psychology, 113,* 358–385.

Lahey, B. B., Gordon, R. A., Loeber, R., Stouthamer-Loeber, M., & Farrington, D. P. (1999). *Journal of Abnormal Child Psychology, 27,* 261–276.

Lahey, B. B., Hart, E. L., Pliszka, S., & Applegate, B. (1993). Neurophysiological correlates of conduct disorder: A rationale and a review of research. *Journal of Clinical Child Psychology, 22,* 141–153.

Lahey, B. B., Loeber, R., Burke, J. D., & Applegate, B. (2005). Predicting future antisocial personality disorder in males from a clinical assessment in childhood. *Journal of Consulting and Clinical Psychology, 73,* 389–399.

Lahey, B. B., Loeber, R., Burke, J., Rathouz, P. J., & McBurnett, K. (2002). Waxing and waning in concert: Dynamic comorbidity of conduct disorder with other disruptive and emotional problems over 17 years among clinic-referred boys. *Journal of Abnormal Psychology, 111,* 556–567.

Lahey, B. B., Loeber, R., Quay, H. C., Applegate, B., Shaffer, D., & Waldman, I. (1998). Validity of *DSM-IV* subtypes of conduct disorder based on age of onset. *Journal of the American Academy of Child & Adolescent Psychiatry, 37,* 435–442.

Lahey, B. B., McBurnett, K., & Loeber, R. (2000). Are attention-deficit hyperactivity disorder and oppositional defiant disorder developmental precursors to conduct disorder? In A. Sameroff, M. Lewis, & S. Miller (Eds.), *Handbook of developmental psychopathology* (2nd ed., pp. 431–446). New York: Plenum.

Lahey, B. B., Miller, T. L., Gordon, R. A., & Riley, A. (1999). Developmental epidemiology of the disruptive behavior disorders. In H. Quay & A. Hogan (Eds.), *Handbook of the disruptive behavior disorders* (pp. 23–48). New York: Plenum.

Lahey, B. B., Moffitt, T. E., & Caspi, A. (Eds.). (2003). *Causes of conduct disorder and serious delinquency.* New York: Guilford.

Lahey, B. B., Piacentini, J. C., McBurnett, K., Stone, P. A., Hartdagen, S., & Hynd, G. W. (1988). Psychopathology in the parents of children with conduct disorder and hyperactivity. *Journal of the American Academy of Child and Adolescent Psychiatry, 27,* 163–170.

Lahey, B. B., Rathouz, P. J., Applegate, B., Van Hulle, C. A., Garriock, H. A., Urbano, R. C., Chapman, D. A., Krueger, R. F., & Waldman, I. D. (in press). Testing structural models of *DSM-IV* symptoms of common forms of child and adolescent psychopathology. *Journal of Abnormal Child Psychology.*

Lahey, B. B., Russo, M. F., Walker, J. L., & Piacentini, J. C. (1989). Personality characteristics of the mothers of children with disruptive behavior disorders. *Journal of Consulting and Clinical Psychology, 57,* 512–515.

Lahey, B. B., Schwab-Stone, M., Goodman, S. H., Waldman, I. D., Canino, G., Rathouz, P. J., et al. (2000). Age and gender differences in oppositional behavior and conduct problems: A cross-sectional household study of middle childhood and adolescence. *Journal of Abnormal Psychology, 109,* 488–503.

Lahey, B. B., Van Hulle, C. A., Waldman, I. D., Rodgers, J. L., D'Onofrio, B. M., Pedlow, S., et al. (2006). Testing descriptive hypotheses regarding sex differences in the development of conduct problems and delinquency. *Journal of Abnormal Child Psychology, 34,* 737–755.

Lahey, B. B., & Waldman, I. D. (2003). A developmental propensity model of the origins of conduct problems during childhood and adolescence. In B. B. Lahey, T. E. Moffitt, & A. Caspi (Eds.), *Causes of conduct disorder and serious delinquency* (pp. 76–117). New York: Guilford.

Lahey, B. B., & Waldman, I. D. (2005). A developmental model of the propensity to offend during childhood and adolescence. In D. P. Farrington (Ed.), *Advances in criminological theory* (Vol. 13, pp. 15–50). Piscataway, NJ: Transaction Publishers.

Laub, J. (1983). Urbanism, race, and crime. *Journal of Research in Crime and Delinquency, 20,* 183–198.

Lee, S. S., Lahey, B. B., Waldman, I., Van Hulle, C. A., Rathouz, P., Pelham, W. E., et al. (2007). Association of dopamine transporter genotype with disruptive behavior disorders in an eight-year longitudinal study of children and adolescents. *American Journal of Medical Genetics Part B: Neuropsychiatric Genetics, 144,* 310–317.

Lee, S. S., Rathouz, P. J., Van Hulle, C. A., Waldman, I. D., Cook, E., & Lahey, B. B. (2006). *Heterosis in the association of DAT1 with delinquency.* Manuscript under review.

Loeber, R. (1988). Natural histories of conduct problems, delinquency, and associated substance abuse: Evidence for developmental progressions. In B. B. Lahey & A. E. Kazdin (Eds.), *Advances in clinical child psychology,* Volume 11. New York: Plenum.

Loeber, R., Burke, J. D., Lahey, B. B., Winters, A., & Zera, M. (2000). Oppositional defiant and conduct disorder: A review of the past 10 years, Part I. *Journal of the American Academy of Child and Adolescent Psychiatry, 39,* 1468–1484.

Loeber, R., Farrington, D. P., Stouthamer-Loeber, M., & Van Kammen, W. (1998). *Antisocial behavior and mental health problems.* Mahway, NJ: Erlbaum.

Loeber, R., Green, S. M., Keenan, K., & Lahey, B. B. (1995). Which boys will fare worse? Early predictors of the onset of conduct disorder in a six-year longitudinal study. *Journal of the American Academy of Child and Adolescent Psychiatry, 34,* 499–509.

Loeber, R., & Keenan, K. (1994). Interaction between conduct disorder and its comorbid conditions: Effects of age and gender. *Clinical Psychology Review, 14,* 497–523.

Loeber, R., Pardini, D., Homish, D. L., Wei, E. H., Crawford, A. M., Farrington, D.P., et al. (2005). The prediction of violence and homicide in young men. *Journal of Consulting and Clinical Psychology, 73,* 1074–1088.

Loeber, R., & Stouthamer-Loeber, M. (1998). Development of juvenile aggression and violence: Some common misconceptions and controversies. *American Psychologist, 53,* 242–259.

Little, S. A., & Garber, J. (2005). The role of social stressors and interpersonal orientation in explaining the longitudinal relation between externalizing and depressive symptoms. *Journal of Abnormal Psychology, 114,* 432–443.

Lynam, D. R. (1998). Early identification of the fledgling psychopath: Locating the psychopathic child in the current nomenclature. *Journal of Abnormal Psychology*, *107*, 566–575.

Lynam, D., Moffitt, T., & Stouthamer-Loeber, M. (1993). Explaining the relation between IQ and delinquency: Class, race, test motivation, school failure or self-control? *Journal of Abnormal Psychology*, *102*, 187–196.

Mannuzza, S., Klein, R. G., Abikoff, H., & Moulton, J. L. (2004). Significance of childhood conduct problems to later development of conduct disorder among children with ADHD: A prospective follow-up study. *Journal of Abnormal Child Psychology*, *32*, 565–573.

Mannuzza, S., Klein, R.G., Bessler, A., Malloy, P., & LaPadula, M. (1993). Adult outcome of hyperactive boys: Educational achievement, occupational rank, and psychiatric status. *Archives of General Psychiatry*, *50*, 565–576.

Mannuzza, S., Klein, R. G., Bonagura, N., Malloy, P., Giampino, T. L., & Addalli, K. A. (1991). Hyperactive boys almost grown up: Replication of psychiatric status. *Archives of General Psychiatry*, *48*, 77–83.

Marshal, M. P., & Molina, B. S. G. (2006). Antisocial behaviors moderate the deviant peer pathway to substance use in children with ADHD. *Journal of Clinical Child and Adolescent Psychology*, *35*, 216–226.

Maughan, B., Rowe, R., Messer, J., Goodman, R., & Meltzer, H. (2004). Conduct disorder and oppositional defiant disorder in a national sample: Developmental epidemiology. *Journal of Child Psychology and Psychiatry*, *45*, 609–621.

Maughan, B., & Rutter, M. (2001). Antisocial children grown up. In J. Hill & B. Maughan (Eds.), *Conduct disorders in childhood and adolescence* (pp. 507–552). New York: Cambridge University Press.

McBurnett, K., Lahey, B. B., Rathouz, P. J., & Loeber, R. (2000). Low salivary cortisol and persistent aggression in boys referred for disruptive behavior. *Archives of General Psychiatry*, *57*, 38–43.

McBurnett, K., Raine, A., Stouthamer-Loeber, M., Loeber, R., Kumar, A. M., Kumar, M., et al. (2005). Mood and hormone responses to psychological challenge in adolescent males with conduct problems. *Biological Psychiatry*, *57*, 1109–1116.

Messer, J., Goodman, R., Rowe, R., Meltzer, H., & Maughan, B. (2006). Preadolescent conduct problems in girls and boys. *Journal of the American Academy of Child and Adolescent Psychiatry*, *45*, 184–191.

Miech, R. A., Caspi, A., Moffitt, T. E., Wright, B. R. E., & Silva, P. A. (1999). Low socioeconomic status and mental disorders: A longitudinal study of selection and causation during young adulthood. *American Journal of Sociology*, *104*, 1096–1131.

Mitchell, S., & Rosa, P. (1981). Boyhood behavior problems as precursors of criminality: A fifteen year study. *Journal of Child Psychology and Psychiatry*, *22*, 19–33.

Moffitt, T. E. (1993). Adolescence-limited and life-course-persistent antisocial behavior: A developmental taxonomy. *Psychological Review*, *100*, 674–701.

Moffitt, T. E. (2003). Life-course persistent and adolescence-limited antisocial behavior: A research review and a research agenda. In B. B. Lahey, T. E. Moffitt & A. Caspi (Eds.), *Causes of conduct disorder and juvenile delinquency* (pp. 49–75). New York: Guilford.

Moffitt, T. E., Caspi, A., Dickson, N., Silva, P., & Stanton, W. (1996). Childhood-onset versus adolescent-onset antisocial conduct problems in males: Natural history from ages 3 to 18 years. *Development and Psychopathology, 8,* 399–424.

Moffitt, T. E., Caspi, A., Harrington, H., Milne, B. J. (2002). Males on the life-course-persistent and adolescence-limited antisocial pathways: Follow-up at age 26 years. *Development and Psychopathology, 14,* 179–207.

Moffitt, T. E., Caspi, A., Rutter, M., & Silva, P. (2001). *Sex differences in antisocial behavior.* Cambridge, UK: Cambridge University Press.

Moffitt, T. E., & Silva, P. A. (1988). IQ and delinquency: A direct test of the differential detection hypothesis. *Journal of Abnormal Psychology, 97,* 330–333.

Meyer-Lindenberg, A., Buckholtz, J. W., Kolachana, B., Hariri, A. R., Pezawas, L., Blasi, G., et al. (2006). Neural mechanisms of genetic risk for impulsivity and violence in humans. *Proceedings of the National Academy of Sciences, 103,* 6269–6274.

Meyer-Lindenberg, A., & Weinberger, D. R. (2006). Intermediate phenotypes and genetic mechanisms of psychiatric disorders. *Nature Reviews Neuroscience, 7,* 818–827.

Nagin, D. S., Pogarsky, G., & Farrington, D. P. (1997). Adolescent mothers and the criminal behavior of their children. *Law and Society Review, 31,* 137–162.

Newman, T. K., Syagailo, Y. V., Barr, C. S., Wendland, J. R., Champoux, M., Graessle, M., et al. (2005). Monoamine oxidase A gene promoter variation and rearing experience influences aggressive behavior in rhesus monkeys. *Biological Psychiatry, 57,* 167–172.

Nilsson, K. W., Sjoberg, R. L., Damberg, M., Leppert, J., Ohrvik, J., Alm, P. O., et al. (2006). Role of monoamine oxidase A genotype and psychosocial factors in male adolescent criminal activity. *Biological Psychiatry, 59,* 121–127.

Nock, M. K. (2003). Progress review of the psychosocial treatment of child conduct problems. *Clinical Psychology: Science and Practice, 10,* 1–28.

Nottelmann, E. D., & Jensen, P. S. (1995). Comorbidity of disorders in children and adolescents: Developmental perspectives. In T. H. Ollendick & R. J. Prinz (Eds.), *Advances in clinical child psychology* (Vol. 17, pp. 109–155). New York: Plenum.

Offord, D. R., Boyle, M. H., Szatmari, P., Rae-Grant, N., Links, P. S., Cadman, D. T., Byles, J. A., Crawford, J. W., Blum, H. M., Byrne, C., Thomas, H., Woodward, C. A. (1987). Ontario Child Health Study: II. Six-month prevalence of disorder and rates of service utilization. *Archives of General Psychiatry, 44,* 832–836.

Ortiz, J., & Raine, A. (2004). Heart rate level and antisocial behavior in children and adolescents: A meta-analysis. *Journal of the American Academy of Child and Adolescent Psychiatry, 43,* 154–162.

Patterson, G. R., Reid, J. B., & Dishion, T. J. (1992). *Antisocial boys.* Eugene, OR: Castalia.

Patterson, G. R., & Stoolmiller, M. (1991). Replications of a dual failure model for boys' depressed mood. *Journal of Consulting and Clinical Psychology, 59,* 491–498.

Patterson, G. R., & Stouthamer-Loeber, M. (1984). The correlation of family management practices and delinquency. *Child Development, 55,* 1299–1307.

Peterson, J. L., & Zill, N. (1986). Marital disruption, parent-child relationships, and behavior problems in children. *Journal of Marriage and the Family, 48,* 295–307.

Piquero, A. R., Brame, R., & Moffitt, T. E. (2005). Extending the study of continuity and change: Gender differences in the linkage between adolescent and adult offending. *Journal of Quantitative Criminology, 21*, 219–243.

Plomin, R., DeFries, J. C., & Loehlin, J. C. (1977). Genotype-environment interaction and correlation in the analysis of human behavior. *Psychological Bulletin, 84*, 309–322.

Popma, A., Jansen, L. M. C., Vermeiren, R., Steiner, H., Raine, A., Van Goozen, S. H. M., et al. (2006). *Psychoneuroendocrinology, 31*, 948–957.

Quay, H. C. (1987). Patterns of delinquent behavior. In H. C. Quay (Ed.), *Handbook of juvenile delinquency* (pp. 118–138). New York: Wiley.

Quay, H. C. (1965). Psychopathic personality as pathological stimulation-seeking. *American Journal of Psychiatry, 122*, 180–183.

Quay, H. C. (1993). The psychobiology of undersocialized aggressive conduct disorder: A theoretical perspective. *Development and Psychopathology, 5*, 165–180.

Quay, H. C., & Love, C. T. (1977). The effect of a juvenile diversion program on rearrests. *Criminal Justice and Behavior, 4*, 377–396.

Raine, A. (2002). The role of prefrontal deficits, low autonomic arousal and early health factors in the development of antisocial and aggressive behavior in children. *Journal of Child Psychology and Psychiatry, 43*, 417–434.

Raine, A., Moffitt, T. E., Caspi, A., Loeber, R., Stouthamer-Loeber, M., & Lynam, D. (2005). Neurocognitive impairments in boys on the life-course persistent antisocial path. *Journal of Abnormal Psychology, 114*, 38–49.

Raine, A., Reynolds, C., Venables, P. H., Mednick, S. A., & Farrington, D. P. (1998). Fearlessness, stimulation-seeking, and large body size at age 3 years as early predispositions to childhood aggression at age 11 years. *Archives of General Psychiatry, 55*, 745–751.

Raine, A., Venables, P. H., & Williams, M. (1995). High autonomic arousal and electrodermal orienting at age 15 years as protective factors against criminal behavior at age 29 years. *American Journal of Psychiatry, 152*, 1595–1600.

Raz, S., Shah, F., & Sander, C. J. (1996). Differential effects of perinatal hypoxic risk on early developmental outcome: A twin study. *Neuropsychology, 10*, 429–436.

Rhee, S. H., & Waldman, I. D. (2002). Genetic and environmental influences on antisocial behavior: A meta-analysis of twin and adoption studies. *Psychological Bulletin, 128*, 490–529.

Rowe, D. C., & Osgood, D. W. (1984). Heredity and sociology theories of delinquency: A reconsideration. *American Sociological Review, 49*, 526–540.

Rowe, R., Maughan, B., Costello, E. J., & Angold, A. (2005). Defining oppositional defiant disorder. *Journal of Child Psychology and Psychiatry, 46*, 1309–1316.

Rowe, R., Maughan, B., & Eley, T. C. (2006). Links between antisocial behavior and depressed mood: The role of life events and attributional style. *Journal of Abnormal Child Psychology, 34*, 293–302.

Rowe, R., Maughan, B., Pickles, A., Costello, E. J., & Angold, A. (2002). The relationship between *DSM-IV* oppositional defiant disorder and conduct disorder: Findings from the Great Smoky Mountains Study. *Journal of Child Psychology and Psychiatry, 43*, 365–373.

Rutter, M. (1997). Comorbidity: Concepts, claims and choices. *Criminal Behaviour and Mental Health, 7*, 265–285.

Rutter, M. (2006). *Genes and behavior: Nature-nurture interplay explained.* Malden, MA: Blackwell.

Rutter, M., & Giller, H. (1983). *Juvenile delinquency: Trends and perspectives.* Harmondsworth, UK: Penguin.

Rutter, M., Moffitt, T. E., & Caspi, A. (2006). Gene–environment interplay and psychopathology: Multiple varieties but real effects. *Journal of Child Psychopathology and Psychiatry, 47,* 226–261.

Rutter, M., Yule, B., Quinton, D., Rowlands, O., Yule, W., & Berger, M. (1975). Attainment and adjustment in two geographical areas: III—Some factors accounting for area differences. *British Journal of Psychiatry, 126,* 520–33.

Sampson, R. J., Raudenbush, S. W., & Earls, F. (1997). Neighborhoods and violent crime: A multilevel study of collective efficacy. *Science, 277,* 918–924.

Sanson, A., Pedlow, R., Cann, W., Prior, M., & Oberklaid, F. (1996). Shyness ratings: Stability and correlates in early childhood. *International Journal of Behavioral Development, 19,* 705–724.

Sanson, A., & Prior, M. (1999). Temperament and behavioral precursors to oppositional defiant disorder and conduct disorder. In H. Quay & A. Hogan (Eds.), *Handbook of the disruptive behavior disorders* (pp. 397–417). New York: Kluwer Academic/Plenum.

Saudino, K. J. (2005). Behavioral genetics and child temperament. *Journal of Developmental and Behavioral Pediatrics, 26,* 214–223.

Seguin, J. R., Boulerice, B., Harden, P. W., Tremblay, R. E., Pihl, R. O. (1999). Executive functions and physical aggression after controlling for attention deficit hyperactivity disorder, general memory and IQ. *Journal of Child Psychology and Psychiatry, 40,* 1197–1208.

Shaw, D. S., Gilliom, M., Ingoldsby, E. M., & Nagin, D. S. (2003). Trajectories leading to school-age conduct problems. *Developmental Psychology, 39,* 189–200.

Silverthorn, P., & Frick, P. J. (1999). Developmental pathways to antisocial behavior: The delayed-onset pathway in girls. *Development and Psychopathology, 11,* 101–126.

Simonoff, E. (2001). Gene-environment interplay in oppositional defiant and conduct disorder. *Child and Adolescent Psychiatric Clinics of North America, 10,* 351–374.

Sparks, R., Ganschow, L., & Thomas, A. (1996). Role of intelligence tests in speech/language referrals. *Perceptual and Motor Skills, 83,* 195–204.

Stattin, H., & Klackenberg-Larsson, I. (1993). Early language and intelligence development and their relationship to future criminal behavior. *Journal of Abnormal Psychology, 102,* 369–378.

Thapar, A., Langley, K., Fowler, T., Rice, F., Turic, D., Whittinger, N., et al. (2005). Catechol O-methyltransferase gene variant and birth weight predict early-onset antisocial behavior in children with attention-deficit/hyperactivity disorder. *Archives of General Psychiatry, 62,* 1275–1278.

Tremblay, R. E. (2003). Why socialization fails: The case of chronic physical aggression. In B. B. Lahey, T. E. Moffitt, A. Caspi (Eds.), *Causes of conduct disorder and juvenile delinquency* (pp. 182–226). New York: Guilford.

Tuvblad, C., Grann, M., & Lichtenstein, P. (2006). Heritability for adolescent antisocial behavior differs with socioeconomic status: gene-environment interaction. *Journal of Child Psychology and Psychiatry, 47,* 734–743.

van Os, J., Wichers, M. Danckaerts, M., Van Gestel, S., Derom, C., & Vlietinck, R. (2001). A prospective twin study of birth weight discordance and child problem behavior. *Biological Psychiatry, 501,* 593–599.

Wakschlag, L. S., Pickett, K. E., Cook, E., Benowitz, N. L., & Leventhal, B. L. (2002). Maternal smoking during pregnancy and severe antisocial behavior in offspring. Are they causally linked? *American Journal of Public Health, 92,* 966–974.

Waldman, I. D., Van Hulle, C. A., Applegate, B., Pardini, D., Frick, P. J., & Lahey, B. B. (2006). *Genetic influences on youth conduct disorder are mediated largely through socioemotional dispositions relevant to callous-unemotional traits.* Manuscript under review.

Wechsler, D. (1974). *Wechsler Intelligence Scales for Children–Revised.* New York: Psychological Corporation.

Wichers, M. C., Purcell, S., Danckaerts, M., Derom, C., Derom, R., Vlietinck, R., et al. (2002). Prenatal life and post-natal psychopathology: Evidence for negative gene-birth weight interaction. *Psychological Medicine, 32,* 1165–1174.

Wichström, L., Skogen, K., & Oia, T. (1996). Increased rate of conduct problems in urban areas: What is the mechanism? *Journal of the American Academy of Child and Adolescent Psychiatry, 35,* 471–479.

World Health Organization (1993). ICD-10 *Classification of mental and behavioural disorders: Diagnostic research criteria.* Geneva: World Health Organization.

Young, S., Smolen, A., Corley, R., Krauter, K., DeFries, J., Crowley, T., et al. (2002). Dopamine transporter polymorphism associated with externalizing behavior problems in children. *American Journal of Medical Genetics Part B: Neuropsychiatric Genetic, 114,* 144–149.

Young, S. E., Smolen A., Hewitt, J. K., Haberstick, B., Stallings, M., Corley, R., et al. (2006). Interaction between MAO-A genotype and maltreatment in the risk for conduct disorder: Failure to confirm in adolescent patients. *American Journal of Psychiatry, 163,* 1019–1025.

Zoccolillo, M. (1992). Co-occurrence of conduct disorder and its adult outcomes with depressive and anxiety disorders: A review. *Journal of the American Academy of Child and Adolescent Psychiatry, 31,* 547–556.

CHAPTER 13

Antisocial Personality Development

KRISTINA D. HIATT AND THOMAS J. DISHION

Many children and adolescents show episodes of problem behavior at some point in their development. Many of these youth will eventually assume adult responsibilities, develop prosocial skills, and desist from problem behaviors. Unfortunately, some youth fail to make this transition away from antisocial behavior, and instead show a consistent pattern of criminal, impulsive, and irresponsible behaviors well into adulthood. In this chapter, we address current knowledge and understanding of the development of persistent antisocial behavior, which is termed Antisocial Personality Disorder (ASPD) when in adulthood.

HISTORICAL PERSPECTIVE

Throughout history, societies have been faced with individuals who routinely and persistently engage in behavior that violates societal norms and the rights of others. Even a small number of these individuals can incur extremely large costs because of their disproportionate involvement in crime and violence (e.g., Farrington, Barnes, & Lambert, 1986), their major burden on healthcare systems due to multiple problem behaviors (Miller, 2004), and their failure to maintain consistent employment, fulfill obligations to friends and family, and behave in a trustworthy manner. Accordingly, virtually all societies have struggled with prevention, management, and rehabilitation of severely antisocial individuals.

Historically, there have been two predominant philosophical perspectives on the origins of antisocial behavior: Antisocial qualities are either considered to be innate and characterological, or acquired through poor socialization. Hobbes, in *Leviathan* (Rogers & Schulman, 1651/2003), argued that antisocial tendencies are innate, and, consequently, that prosocial behaviors conducive to group living require careful training and socialization. In contrast, Rousseau (Friedlander, 1762/2004) proposed that children are prosocial by nature but that their natural goodness is transformed into antisocial behavior through the misguided efforts of adults. Similarly, John Locke (Anstey, 2003) proposed that children are a tabula rasa with respect to good and evil and that all behaviors are outcomes of experience and learning.

Current perspectives on antisocial behavior tend to blend these two poles of thought, with antisocial behavior viewed as the result of interactions between individual vulnerabilities (e.g., difficult temperament, limitations in cognitive abilities) and poor socialization experiences (e.g., coercive parenting, neglect, deviant peers). Inherent in this transactional or diathesis-stress perspective is the idea that the same outcome (e.g., persistent antisocial behavior) may be due, across individuals, to a relatively greater contribution of either internal vulnerabilities or environmental risks. Thus, an individual with relatively few vulnerabilities may require a severely maladaptive environment to become antisocial, whereas relatively minor environmental deficiencies may promote antisocial behavior in an individual with stronger vulnerabilities. From this perspective, there are multiple pathways to persistent antisocial behavior (signifying equifinality), and divergent outcomes for youth who begin life with key risk factors for such behavior (signifying multifinality). Strategies for prevention and intervention should be tailored accordingly, to address the specific risk factors that may be operating for individual youth.

Early approaches to antisocial behavior were concerned primarily with managing individuals who broke the law. Consequently, much of our knowledge of antisocial behavior comes from professional fields such as juvenile justice, corrections, social work, and criminology. The role of psychology is relatively recent. Healy (1926) published the first psychologically oriented treatise on the etiology and treatment of antisocial behavior. Influenced heavily by the psychodynamic theory of that time, his thinking emphasized internal, intraindividual factors in the etiology of crime, especially lack of cognitive abilities (i.e., "dull thinking") and problematic parenting.

Despite his focus on personality, Healy noted that peers are often a proximal factor in the commission of antisocial acts, and the influence of environmental factors was underscored by his publication of quasiexperimental findings showing that rates of recidivism vary as a function of the correctional strategy used (Healy & Bronner, 1936). In Chicago, where institutionalization was the dominant strategy, failure rates reached 70%, whereas in Boston, where foster care was the pervasive practice, recidivism was only 27%. Aware of the limitations of quasiexperimental strategies, the authors suggested tentatively that institutionalization may not be the ideal solution for diverting youth from lives of crime. This suggestion has gone largely unheeded, despite later studies using random assignment and solid measurement procedures that produced essentially the same results (Chamberlain & Reid, 1998; Eddy & Chamberlain, 2000).

Current approaches to studying adolescent and adult antisocial behavior are usually oriented toward identifying developmental processes through longitudinal studies, a strategy that began to be applied in earnest to the domain of antisocial behavior in the late 1970s and early 1980s. Modern studies represent a fusion of the seminal works of Robins (1966), who demonstrated the continuity of antisocial behavior, with the life-course perspective of Elder (1985). Earlier work by Glueck and Glueck (1950), which emphasized the contribution of family and contextual factors, had been largely rejected by many sociologists. However, a new generation of young sociologists (e.g., Sampson & Laub, 1993) resurrected the Glueck data set and reanalyzed the findings using modern statistical techniques. The results suggested that family variables should be a central focus for theories about the development of antisocial behavior in children. A review of research findings by Loeber and Dishion (1983) also provided a strong empirical base for emphasizing family variables. The 1970s and 1980s also witnessed the emergence of improved methodologies for studying social interactions within close relationships. The relationship dynamics within which antisocial behaviors are embedded have provided practical insights that have influenced intervention practices (e.g., Forgatch & DeGarmo, 1999; Henggeler et al., 1998).

In addition to the increased focus on relationship dynamics, modern statistical techniques allow us to examine the effects of broad social contexts (e.g., schools, neighborhoods) on the development of antisocial behavior. Furthermore, advances in neuroscience and genetics have allowed for greater specification of individual differences that may be critical in understanding the development of persistent antisocial behavior (see Viding, 2004).

TERMINOLOGICAL, CONCEPTUAL, AND DIAGNOSTIC ISSUES

Broadly speaking, *antisocial behavior* refers to activities that violate societal norms, laws, and / or the rights of others. Such behaviors may include both criminal (e.g., theft, fraud, assault, driving while intoxicated, illicit drug use) and noncriminal acts (e.g., deceitfulness, irresponsibility). In childhood and adolescence, violations of family rules and expectations through disobedience and defiance also fall under the rubric of antisocial behavior and are generally referred to as *conduct problems* or *disruptive behaviors* (milder forms may be termed *oppositional/defiant*). Antisocial behavior that leads to contact with the legal system is usually referred to as *delinquent* behavior in children and adolescents, and as *criminal* behavior in adults.

When antisocial behavior persists across time and situations, it is often considered pathological and can result in the diagnosis of a disruptive behavior disorder. Among children and adolescents, persistent antisocial behavior may lead to a *Diagnostic and Statistical Manual of Mental Disorders* (*DSM-IV*; APA, 2000) diagnosis of Oppositional Defiant Disorder (ODD) or Conduct Disorder (CD; see Lahey, this volume). In individuals 18 or older, persistent antisocial behavior may lead to a diagnosis of ASPD. The development of ASPD is the main focus of this chapter.

Current *DSM-IV* diagnostic criteria for ASPD include a pervasive pattern of disregard for and violation of the rights of others, as indicated by three (or more) of the following: (a) failure to conform to social norms with respect to lawful behaviors as indicated by repeatedly performing acts that are grounds for arrest; (b) deceitfulness, as indicated by repeated lying, use of aliases, or conning others for personal pleasure or profit; (c) impulsivity or failure to plan ahead; (d) irritability and aggressiveness, as indicated by repeated physical fights or assaults; (e) reckless disregard for safety of self or others; (f) consistent irresponsibility, as indicated by repeated failure to sustain consistent work behavior or honor financial obligations; and (g) lack of remorse, as indicated by being indifferent to or rationalizing having hurt, mistreated, or stolen from another. As with all personality disorders, the individual must be at least 18 years of age (Criterion B). There must also be evidence of Conduct Disorder (CD) before the age of 15 years (Criterion C), and the antisocial behavior must not occur exclusively during the course of Schizophrenia or manic episodes.

ASPD is very common among criminal offenders (Widiger & Corbitt, 1995). However, many criminals do not have ASPD. For example, individuals who commit isolated crimes (e.g., a single episode of theft, assault, drug use, or even murder) and who do not have a broader history of irresponsible or antisocial behavior would not meet criteria for ASPD. Antisocial personality refers specifically to individuals with a persistent pattern of antisocial behavior (criminal or not) over an extended period of time (and beginning before the age of 15 years).

Aggressive and violent antisocial behavior is of great societal concern, but it is not uniquely related to antisocial personality. Aggression has many contributing causes, and isolated acts of aggression or violence can occur without a significant history of antisocial behavior (e.g., crimes of passion). Furthermore, some persistently aggressive and violent individuals may not be considered to have an antisocial personality, such as a man who gets into weekly fist fights at the local bar but does not cause serious harm and otherwise behaves lawfully and responsibly. On the other hand, risk of aggression and violence is greater among people with ASPD than among people without ASPD, perhaps because many individuals with ASPD also have personality traits that place them at greater risk for repeated aggression and violence.

ASPD overlaps to some degree with the terms *dyssocial personality, sociopathy,* and *psychopathy.* Dyssocial personality disorder is the diagnostic term for persistent adult antisocial behavior used in the World Health Organization's International Classification of Diseases (ICD-10) diagnostic manual. Although similar to *DSM-IV* ASPD in many respects, dyssocial personality diagnoses do not require a history of Conduct Disorder in childhood or adolescence.

Sociopathy is a historically prevalent term that has no defined diagnostic criteria and is not formally used in clinical psychology or psychiatry. The original *DSM* (APA, 1952) included diagnostic criteria for sociopathic personality disturbance, antisocial reaction, which was revised and renamed Antisocial Personality Disorder in the second edition of the *DSM* (APA, 1968).

Psychopathy refers to a subtype of ASPD that is based on the clinical descriptions of Cleckley (1941) and emphasizes affective and interpersonal traits (e.g., callousness, shallow affect, lack of interpersonal connectedness, superficial charm) in addition to chronic antisocial behavior. Accordingly, most individuals with psychopathy also meet criteria for ASPD. However, the relation between ASPD and psychopathy is not transitive, as only a small subset of individuals with ASPD meet criteria for psychopathy. Psychopathy is diagnosed routinely in forensic settings and is the focus of considerable research, but it is not included as a diagnosis in the *DSM-IV.* In forensic settings, psychopathy is typically assessed using a semistructured interview and rating system known as the Psychopathy Checklist–Revised (PCL-R; Hare, 1991, 2003). The PCL-R has at least two correlated factors (Harpur, Hakstian, & Hare, 1988; Harpur, Hare, & Hakstian, 1989): an interpersonal/affective factor (e.g., superficial charm, exaggerated self-worth, lying, manipulation, lack of guilt, shallow affect, callousness, failing to accept responsibility for own actions), which is commonly associated with Cleckley's (1941) original characterization of psychopathic personality; and an unstable and socially deviant lifestyle factor (e.g., need for stimulation, parasitic lifestyle, lack of meaningful goals, unstable employment, unstable romantic relationships, a wide variety of criminal behavior), which overlaps substantially with ASPD as defined by the *DSM-IV*. These two factors are moderately to highly correlated ($r = .50$ or greater), and high scores on both factors are traditionally required for a clinical diagnosis of psychopathy (Hare, 1991).

Originally, the *DSM* construct of ASPD was rooted in personality, with diagnostic criteria drawn from the construct of psychopathy (Cleckley, 1941). In its earliest instantiation, ASPD required not only persistent antisocial behavior but also specific personality features such as lack of emotional depth, lack of remorse or guilt, and shallow interpersonal relationships. However, it became clear that practitioners were unable to reliably infer the personality traits described by Cleckley in the course of standard clinical assessments. As early versions of the *DSM* were revised to improve diagnostic reliability, there was an increased focus on observable behavioral criteria (i.e., antisocial acts) rather than inferred personality characteristics. This focus on greater reliability was most clearly evidenced in *DSM-III* (APA, 1980), which equated ASPD with persistent antisocial behavior, irrespective of personality traits. Personality characteristics returned to some extent in the *DSM-IV*; psychopathic personality features are specifically referenced in the "Associated Features and Disorders" section of the *DSM-IV* text, and current diagnostic criteria include some subjective features such as lack of remorse. Nevertheless, current ASPD criteria can be (and often are) met on the basis of antisocial behavior alone.

There continues to be active debate over the *DSM* ASPD construct, and whether it should remain behavioral and objective or include some or all of the personality characteristics of psychopathy. As defined by the *DSM*, ASPD is very common in criminal populations, with up to 80% of incarcerated individuals meeting criteria for the diagnosis (Widiger & Corbitt, 1995). Accordingly, those with the disorder are heterogeneous with respect to personality, attitudes, and motivations for engaging in criminal behavior, and a diagnosis of ASPD has limited utility for making differential predictions of institutional adjustment, response to treatment, or behavior following release from prison. In contrast, psychopathy is present in only a small subset of criminal offenders and has substantial predictive validity (e.g., institutional adjustment, recidivism rates) within forensic populations (e.g., Hare et al., 2000).

Specifically, individuals with psychopathy have a particularly pernicious criminal course, and suggestions abound that they have a more homogeneous set of psychophysiological and biological risk factors (see later section on individual differences).

Although current *DSM-IV* criteria for ASPD identify a heterogeneous group of individuals with persistent antisocial behavior, there are some benefits to the present approach. First, diagnostic reliability in clinical settings has improved. Second, ASPD diagnoses may be informative and discriminating when used with community populations, despite the lack of discrimination among individuals in forensic settings. However, even in community samples, those who meet criteria for ASPD are heterogeneous in terms of etiologic and maintenance factors, suggesting that clinicians may need to further differentiate individuals using other diagnostic methods in order to determine the most appropriate treatments. In addition, research investigators and forensic psychologists must continue to use specialized diagnostic instruments (e.g., the PCL-R) to identify subgroups of particular interest within the ASPD category.

In the remainder of this chapter, we review current knowledge and theories regarding the development of persistent adult antisocial behavior. Most of the existing work defines adult antisocial behavior in ways that are compatible with *DSM-IV* ASPD diagnostic criteria, although the criteria used often vary across studies. This chapter follows the *DSM* model in emphasizing antisocial behavior as the outcome of interest, irrespective of personality or other individual differences. This approach allows an overview of the factors that have been associated with adult antisocial behavior across individuals, while recognizing that different pathways may ultimately prove to be more or less relevant for particular subgroups within the broad ASPD category.

PREVALENCE

The 2001–2002 National Epidemiologic Survey on Alcohol and Related Conditions (N = 43,093) indicated a lifetime prevalence rate of 3.63% for ASPD, with the risk being 3 times greater among men than among women (Compton et al., 2005; Grant et al., 2004). For comparison, the lifetime prevalence of adult antisocial behavior only (not meeting the childhood CD criterion) was 12.3%, and the prevalence of retrospectively reported CD in childhood without antisocial behavior in adulthood was 1.1% (Compton et al., 2005). Estimates of ASPD prevalence within incarcerated populations range from 49 to 80% (Widiger & Corbitt, 1995).

RISK FACTORS

Because of the marked continuity of childhood-onset and adolescent conduct problems and later antisocial behavior, many if not all of the risk factors for child and adolescent conduct problems are relevant to the development of adult ASPD. Thus, factors associated with childhood and adolescent CD, such as child vulnerabilities (e.g., negative emotionality, "difficult" temperament, prenatal or perinatal complications), family risk (e.g., large family size, antisocial parent), parenting risk (e.g., harsh and inconsistent discipline, poor monitoring), peer risk (e.g., peer rejection, deviant peers), and sociocultural risk (e.g., high delinquency neighborhood or school), all contribute risk for ASPD (see also Beauchaine & Neuhaus, this volume; Gatzke-Kopp & Shannon, this volume). This overlap is due to both the natural continuity of antisocial behavior and the diagnostic requirement of CD prior to age 15.

Accordingly, childhood conduct problems are perhaps the best single predictor of adult ASPD. Lahey, Loeber, Burke, and Applegate (2005) followed a clinical sample of boys with behavior problems and found that 54% of those who received a CD diagnosis at the time of entry into the study (ages 7 to 12 years) met criteria for ASPD at age 18 or 19, compared with 27% of those who did not meet criteria for CD. Interestingly, these effects were moderated by family socioeconomic status (SES). Children with CD who were from higher SES families were far less likely to meet criteria for ASPD as young adults (20%) compared to those from lower SES families (65%). Childhood aggression alone is also predictive of adult ASPD. Petras et al. (2004) found that 27% of boys with consistently high levels of teacher-rated aggression in elementary school met ASPD criteria at age 19 to 20, compared to 11% of boys with stable low aggression in elementary school. Boys with increasing levels of aggression from Grades 1 to 5 were also at risk for ASPD (25.6%).

In general, earlier onset of conduct problems is associated with greater risk of persistence into adulthood (Moffitt, 1993, 2006). Data from the NIMH Epidemiological Catchment Area (ECA) survey of more than 8,000 adults indicated a 12.4-fold increase in risk for adult antisocial behavior among those with childhood-onset (before age 13) conduct problems compared to a 5.5-fold increase among those with adolescent-onset (age 13 or later) conduct problems, relative to those with no history of conduct problems (Ridenour et al., 2002).

Although earlier onset is typically associated with poorer outcomes, these data and others (e.g., Moffitt et al., 2002) also make clear that adolescent-onset conduct problems are themselves associated with increased risk of adult ASPD. In Moffitt and colleagues' longitudinal study of a New Zealand birth cohort, 34% of men with adolescent-onset conduct problems were convicted in adult criminal court by age 26, compared with 55% of men with childhood-onset conduct problems. Despite this difference in criminal conviction rates, comparable percentages from each group met criteria for ASPD (which includes a broader range of antisocial behaviors) at age 26 (Moffitt et al., 2002).

However, not all youth with conduct problems continue to show antisocial behavior in adulthood. Data from multiple large-scale longitudinal studies reveal that only about 50% of boys with childhood conduct problems develop adult ASPD (Moffitt et al., 2002; Patterson & Yoerger, 1999; Robins, 1966). Although those who do not become antisocial adults remain at risk for other forms of psychopathology in adulthood (Moffitt, 2006; Robins, 1966; Wiesner, Kim, & Capaldi, 2005), their desistence from antisocial behavior underscores the importance of identifying (a) early risk factors that are differentially associated with persistent antisocial behavior, and (b) the developmental and transactional processes that maintain and promote antisocial behavior in adolescence and adulthood, as well as those that may promote desistence.

With regard to early risk factors, many researchers have proposed that childhood abuse and neglect may be particularly important in the etiology of antisocial personality styles and persistent adult antisocial behavior. Luntz and Widom (1994) found that 20% of boys who were abused or neglected before age 12 met criteria for ASPD 20 years later, compared with only 10% of controls. Similarly, maltreatment in adolescence is associated with increased risk of adult antisocial behavior (Smith, Ireland, & Thornberry, 2005), and childhood abuse and neglect are associated with higher psychopathy scores among young adults (Weiler & Widom, 1996). Childhood physical abuse appears to have a stronger relationship with adult antisocial behavior than either childhood neglect or emotional abuse (Cohen, Brown, & Smailes, 2001). The effects of abuse and neglect may be mediated by other environmental risk factors, such as other stressful life events, rather than being associated directly with later adjustment (Horwitz et al., 2001). In addition, recent data suggest important interactions between early maltreatment and genetic vulnerabilities (Caspi et al., 2002, discussed in the following; see also Cicchetti, this volume).

Neurobiological risk factors may play a greater role in ASPD than in childhood- or adolescence-limited antisocial behavior. Minor physical anomalies (MPAs), such as low-seated ears, adherent ear lobes, and furrowed tongues, are associated with increased risk of antisocial behavior, perhaps because they are indicators of fetal maldevelopment or prenatal/perinatal trauma (e.g., anoxia, infection). When combined with an adverse home environment, MPAs are associated with increased risk of violence and aggression in adulthood (Mednick & Kandel, 1988; Brennan, Mednick, & Raine, 1997). Raine, Venables, and Williams (1995) found that physiological arousal and reactivity at age 14 years was related to the persistence of antisocial behavior through age 29 years. Those who desisted between early adolescence and adulthood had higher electrodermal and cardiovascular arousal and higher electrodermal orienting at age 14 than did those who persisted, suggesting that normal autonomic arousal may serve as a protective factor against persistent antisocial behavior. Consistent with this conjecture, Shannon, Beauchaine, Brenner, Neuhaus, and Gatzke-Kopp (in press) recently reported that children with antisocial fathers were protected from developing conduct problems if they had normal autonomic arousal patterns.

Antisocial behavior tends to run in families (e.g., Farrington et al., 1996). Although some of this familial transmission can be explained through behavioral or environmental learning (e.g., Dishion, Owen, & Bullock, 2004; Patterson & Dishion, 1988), genetic factors are also at play. Behavioral genetic studies suggest that antisocial behavior that persists from early adolescence through adulthood may have a stronger genetic basis than other forms of antisocial behavior (see Moffitt, 2006). As with other behavioral traits, there is also evidence that the influence of genes increases from childhood to adulthood, whereas the influence of environmental factors becomes weaker (Jacobson, Prescott, & Kendler, 2002). Most genetic risk for antisocial behavior appears to operate through general predisposing vulnerabilities such as temperament (e.g., negative affectivity, impulsivity) that confer broad risk for psychopathology—especially externalizing behaviors—rather than specific risk for ASPD (e.g., Krueger et al., 2002).

Recent molecular genetics work has also revealed clear gene–environment interactions in the development of antisocial behavior problems. Caspi and colleagues (Caspi et al., 2002) examined the interaction between exposure to maltreatment and polymorphisms in the monoamine oxidase-A (MAO-A) gene, which encodes an enzyme that metabolizes all monoamines, including both dopamine and serotonin. Outcome measures were juvenile and adult antisocial behavior. Among individuals with the low MAO-A activity genotype, childhood maltreatment greatly increased the risk of antisocial behavior (85% showed some form of antisocial behavior). However, childhood maltreatment had relatively little impact on risk of adult antisocial behavior among those with the high MAO-A activity allele. These findings indicate that some children are more genetically vulnerable than others to coercive, harsh discipline practices characteristic of maltreating families, and could have important implications for prevention and treatment.

DEVELOPMENTAL PROGRESSION

There is now general consensus that there is a synergistic interplay between the individual and the environment, and that liabilities in both domains are necessary to account for long-term patterns of antisocial behavior (Dishion & Patterson, 2006). In addition to the gene–environment interactions previously discussed, the ways individuals respond to and interact with their environments throughout development play a critical role in the persistence of antisocial behavior into adulthood. As individuals age and new developmental challenges are faced, the relative importance of particular transactions and relationships changes. At the earliest ages, child–caregiver interactions are likely to be of utmost importance. As the individual grows older, relationships with institutions and communities (e.g., schools and teachers) strengthen, and peers and romantic partners increase in influence. Other factors such as the work community become influential in adulthood. The individual's transactions with these and other settings throughout development have the potential to shape and modify the course of antisocial behavior.

Longitudinal studies that follow at-risk individuals from childhood to adulthood are ideal for examining the developmental progression of antisocial behavior. Accordingly, a number of longitudinal studies of antisocial behavior are currently being conducted with children and adolescents. However, many of these studies began fairly recently and the participants have not yet reached adulthood.

The quality of the parent-child relationship, from infancy onward, is a natural candidate for influencing risk for persistent antisocial behavior. The handful of longitudinal studies that have followed children into adulthood confirm that parenting factors contribute to persistence of antisocial behavior in adulthood. For example, the Cambridge Study in Delinquent Development (Farrington, 2005), a longitudinal study of 411 London boys from ages 10 to adulthood, indicated that low parental involvement in middle childhood is associated with persistent antisocial behavior in adulthood. Johnson, Smailes, Cohen, Kasen, and Brook (2004) found that adult antisocial behavior in the offspring of antisocial parents was largely mediated by the quality of parenting received in childhood and adolescence. Data from the Oregon Youth Study (see Patterson, 1982) show that coercive parent–child interactions (see following; and see Beauchaine & Neuhaus, this volume) in childhood predict persistence of antisocial behavior to adolescence and adulthood (Patterson, Reid, & Dishion, 1992). Thus, parenting factors do appear to be associated with the development of antisocial behavior in adulthood. It should be noted, however, that deficiencies in parent–child interactions may be bidirectional, and few studies have attempted to differentiate common genetic effects (i.e., shared genes that predispose the parent to poor parenting and the child to antisocial behavior) from parenting effects per se. Nevertheless, the effectiveness of interventions that reduce coercive interactions and improve family management in reducing child and adolescent antisocial behavior suggests that parenting may contribute independently to the development of antisocial behavior (Beauchaine, Webster-Stratton, & Reid, 2005; Connell et al., in press; Dishion, Patterson, & Kavanagh, 1992; Forgatch, 1991; Forgatch, Bullock, & Patterson, 2004; Martinez & Forgatch, 2001).

As children become adolescents, peer relationships increase in importance. Studies of the developmental precursors and sequelae of peer experiences in childhood and adolescence lead to the conclusion that peer relationships play a critical role in the maintenance, amplification, and continuity of antisocial behavior from adolescence to adulthood. Peer rejection in childhood accounts for adult antisocial behavior after controlling for composite measures of antisocial behavior and academic functioning in childhood and adolescence (Nelson & Dishion, 2004). Direct observations of friendships suggest that many youth adapt to peer rejection by formulating friendships that support deviance (Dishion, Nelson & Yasui, 2005). Dishion, Nelson, Winter, and Bullock (2004) found that boys with a combination of well-organized peer interactions (low "entropy") and high levels of deviancy training (i.e., peer reinforcement of antisocial attitudes and behaviors) at age 14 were most likely to engage in substance use and antisocial behavior in adulthood (age 26), suggesting that adolescents who organize their relationships around deviance are the most at risk for long-term maintenance of antisocial behavior. Similarly, Piehler and Dishion (in press) found that friendships that were both more mutual and more deviant predicted high levels of antisocial behavior by age 18 as defined by arrests and self-report. It seems that deviancy training can be thought of as a specialized social skill that can be used to select friends and through which antisocial behavior is amplified and maintained. We found that 30 minutes of videotaped interactions with "best friends" rendered a deviancy training score that was stable over a 5-year period from age 14 to 18, even when a vast majority (88%) of the youth brought in different friends for the videotaped interaction at different assessment waves. Deviancy training predicts multiple forms of problem behavior in young adulthood (Patterson, Dishion, & Yoerger, 2000). These data have led to articulation of a deviancy training model of antisocial behavior (see following discussion on Etiological Formulations) and suggest that deviancy training is an active maladaptation that leads to further entrenchment in a deviant lifestyle.

Substance use and abuse also plays an important role in the continuity of antisocial behavior from adolescence to adulthood. Although minor delinquent offenses typically precede the initiation of drug use (e.g., Moffitt et al., 1996; Taylor et al., 2002), substance use itself increases the frequency of delinquent and antisocial behaviors (e.g., Zhang, Wieczorek, & Welte, 1997). Furthermore, a lack of drug or alcohol problems is associated with the desistence of childhood conduct problems (Moffitt et al., 1996; Zucker et al., 1996).

Numerous sociocultural variables correlate with improvement in adult antisocial behavior, including marriage (Farrington, 1995), good social integration (Reiss, Grubin, & Meux, 1996), parenthood and increased family responsibilities (Black, Baumgard, & Bell, 1995), academic success (Robins & Regier, 1991), and stable employment (Farrington, 1995; Robins, 1966). What is difficult to know from such correlational evidence is whether certain individuals with antisocial behavior patterns "migrate" or self-select into these advantageous ecologies or whether these sociocultural influences independently predict desistence.

Although there is evidence that supportive romantic relationships are associated with transitioning away from deviant behavior in early adulthood (Quinton et al., 1993), this is not always the case. In some cases, antisocial individuals may partner with other antisocial individuals. Such assortative mating can lead to amplification of antisocial behavior (Caspi & Herbener, 1990; Quinton et al., 1993). Recent follow-up studies of adolescent males suggest that marriage and continued involvement in deviant peer groups can go hand in hand, contributing to the persistence, rather than desistence, of antisocial behavior (Shortt et al., 2003).

In general, symptoms of ASPD diminish with age in adulthood (Mulder et al., 1994; Robins & Regier, 1991). Desistence is particularly pronounced between the ages of 45 and 64 (Black et al., 1995). In a community sample of women, Mulder et al. (1994) found that no one aged 45 or older met ASPD criteria. The reasons for the decline in antisocial behavior with age have not been investigated systematically, but are likely to include both social and biological factors, such as increased attachment to social institutions (marriage, employment) (see Sampson & Laub, 1993), and decreased impulsivity and sensation seeking (see Reio & Choi, 2004; Giambra, Camp, & Grodsky, 1992).

ETIOLOGICAL FORMULATIONS

Although many risk factors have been linked to the development and maintenance of persistent conduct problems and ASPD, less is known about the causal status of individual vulnerabilities, the mechanisms through which they operate, or how they interact with environmental risk factors. For example, poor parenting is associated with persistent antisocial behavior, but this could occur through any number of mechanisms. Poor parenting might cause the development of antisocial behavior; poor parenting might be evoked by the child's antisocial behavior (evocative effects); or both poor parenting and child antisocial behavior might be caused by a third variable such as low SES or temperament. Understanding the causal status of risk factors is critical to effective early identification and prevention. Although relatively little is known about the etiological role of different vulnerabilities and risk factors, there are a number of models of ASPD development that have gained preliminary support and are helping to guide etiological research. The most prominent models address three primary levels of analysis: (a) individual differences, (b) environmental/relational factors, and (c) transactional processes.

INDIVIDUAL DIFFERENCES

As discussed earlier, ASPD is an extremely heterogeneous diagnostic category. The diagnosis of ASPD is based primarily upon overt behaviors without regard to causes or context. As a result, seemingly very different individuals can receive the same diagnosis, and a single etiological model is unlikely to account for all ASPD individuals. Accordingly, many researchers have sought to define subtypes of ASPD and develop etiological models that are specific to the unique characteristics of each subtype.

Psychopathy. Arguably the longest-standing and most empirically supported subtype of ASPD, *psychopathy* refers to a personality type characterized by distinct affective, behavioral, and interpersonal traits (see previous discussion). As noted previously, psychopathy accounts for a relatively small subset of individuals with ASPD—about 15 to 25% (Hare, 1991). Compared to individuals with ASPD only, psychopathic individuals are at heightened risk for recidivism and violent offending (Hare et al., 2000). In addition to their unique clinical and prognostic correlates, individuals with psychopathy differ from other ASPD individuals with respect to physiology, neuropsychology, attention, emotion, and behavior (see Hiatt & Newman, 2006, for a review). There are several well-established etiological theories and models of psychopathy. These include Newman's (e.g., Newman, 1998; Newman & Wallace, 1993) response-modulation hypothesis, Lykken's (1995) low-fear hypothesis, and Blair's (e.g, Blair, 2002) amygdala/orbital-frontal deficit model. Although these models are quite different in the specific processes implicated, they all suggest that the primary cause of psychopathy is biological or temperamental, is present at or near birth, and persists throughout the life course, driving the clinical symptoms.

Early onset versus adolescent onset. Another widely supported etiological distinction is between early onset and adolescent-onset antisocial behavior. This distinction was offered by Moffitt and colleagues (e.g., Moffitt, 1993, 2006), who referred to early onset cases as life-course persistent (LCP) and to adolescent-onset cases as adolescence limited (AL). Moffitt explained the LCP pathway using a diathesis-stress model that highlights individual vulnerabilities. She proposed that LCP antisocial individuals can be distinguished from their AL counterparts on a host of neurological, cognitive, and temperamental factors that are present at or near birth. These factors are proposed to interact with criminogenic environments to initiate and maintain antisocial behavior throughout the lifecourse. Although LCP and AL individuals may show similar rates of antisocial behavior in adolescence, AL individuals are expected to desist from offending earlier and are viewed as being at lower risk for ASPD in adulthood.

Patterson and colleagues proposed a somewhat different distinction between early onset and adolescent-onset pathways of antisocial behavior. Patterson, DeBaryshe, and Ramsey (1989) proposed that *early starters* are characterized by a developmental pathway of coercive parenting, school failure, and early antisocial behavior, whereas *late starters* are characterized by poor parental monitoring, oppositionality, and deviant peer involvement starting in adolescence. Patterson et al. argue that late starters typically exhibit marginal levels of social adaptation in the elementary school years (e.g., poor academic and social skills), making them more vulnerable to perturbations in parental monitoring and supervision.

The distinction between early onset and adolescent-onset pathways has been supported by numerous empirical studies showing different constellations of risk factors for the two groups (Jeglum-Bartusch et al., 1997; Moffitt, 1990; Moffitt & Caspi, 2001; Patterson, DeGarmo, & Knutson, 2000). However, Moffitt and colleagues' assertion that adolescent-onset antisocial behavior is near-normative and resolves by adulthood has not received consistent support. As noted earlier, adolescent-onset antisocial behavior is associated with substantially increased risk of ASPD in adulthood, although still smaller than the risk incurred by the early onset group (e.g., Mamorstein & Iacono, 2005; Moffitt et al., 2002). Accordingly, Moffitt (2003) has revised predictions for the AL group by proposing that recovery from antisocial behavior may be delayed if the antisocial behaviors exhibited in adolescence attract "snares" such as a criminal record, incarceration, or school drop-out that interfere with a return to prosocial behavior.

Environmental and Relationship Factors

Coercive parenting. Patterson's (1982) coercion model focuses specifically on contributions of parent-child interactions to child ASB. According to this model, antisocial behavior persists because it is rewarded, either through escape from an aversive situation (negative reinforcement, escape conditioning) or through acquisition of desired outcomes (positive reinforcement). Coercive interactions between the parent and child consist of a cycle of intrusive demands, compliance refusals, escalating distress and negative affect, and finally withdrawal of the demand. A high rate of coercive behavior between the parent and child sets the stage for more serious antisocial behavior. Furthermore, the impact of contextual variables, such as divorce, poverty, and neighborhood risk on child outcomes is proposed to be mediated by their impact on parenting practices. According to this model, the individual with early onset delinquency is trained by family members to engage in high rates of overt antisocial behavior, at the expense of well-developed social and self-regulatory skills. Patterson's coercion model has received considerable empirical support (see Dishion & Patterson, 2006; Snyder & Stoolmiller, 2002) with respect to childhood and adolescent antisocial behavior, but it has not yet been directly examined with regard to adult ASPD outcomes.

Peer influences. Dishion and colleagues have highlighted the critical role of peer relationships in the persistence or desistance of antisocial behavior in later childhood and adolescence. They posit peers as a major proximal cause of antisocial behavior, beginning in early childhood and accelerating in influence during early adolescence. Three different pathways are relevant: (a) antisocial behavior interferes with positive peer relations, depriving children of the positive benefits of peer learning and confining them within marginal social niches; (b) children may act as models and a source of reinforcement for antisocial behavior; and (c) as children develop friendship networks, support for ASB is established by providing both reinforcement and opportunity for such behavior within networks of deviant peers.

As previously mentioned, Dishion and colleagues have found that well-organized deviant peer interactions in adolescence are associated with higher levels of antisocial behavior at ages 18 (Piehler & Dishion, in press) and 26 (Nelson & Dishion, 2004). The association between friendship patterns and persistent antisocial behavior fits the classic definition of a *maladaptation* in developmental psychopathology frameworks. That is, youth adapt to failure in school and among peers by formulating their own social niches, which reinforce the very traits that led to failure and rejection. Not only are deviant peer relationships highly correlated with antisocial be-havior, but randomized intervention trials that aggregate high-risk adoles-cents in treatment groups often show increases in problem behavior, rather than the hoped-for decreases (Dishion, McCord, & Poulin, 1999; Dodge, Dishion, & Lansford, 2006).

Social bonding.   Sampson and Laub (e.g., 2005) propose that attenuated bonds to society play a primary role in criminal risk. Their model em-phasizes social connections throughout development, with different social institutions changing in importance over time (e.g., parenting and attach-ment in childhood, schooling and peers in adolescence, marital stability and employment in adulthood). An individual's degree of investment and connection to each of these domains is seen as an important predictor of criminal persistence and desistance. Consistent with this model, Sampson and Laub (1990) found that job stability and marital attachment in adult-hood were related to changes in antisocial behavior across a wide variety of outcomes, with stronger ties to work and family predicting lower rates of crime and deviance.

TRANSACTIONAL PROCESSES

Transactional models focus upon the bidirectional effects between indi-viduals and their social environments. Outcomes are viewed as a func-tion of the dynamic interactions between the individual and his or her environment over time. Thus, neither individual characteristics alone nor environmental characteristics alone can explain course or outcome. Trans-actional elements play a role in most current models of antisocial behavior (e.g., Beauchaine, Gatzke-Kopp, & Mead, 2007; Farrington, 2005; Dishion & Patterson, 2006; Moffitt, 1993), although they are more explicit in some models than others. For illustrative purposes, we describe Thornberry's (2005) transactional model in some detail.

Thornberry (2005) proposed that the onset, course, and desistance/per-sistence of antisocial behavior do not break down into discrete etiological patterns. Rather, they are seen as a continuum of possibilities based upon the relative influences of particular risk factors. Interactions between in-dividual characteristics, ineffective parenting, and position in the social structure are used to explain different phenotypic patterns of antisocial behavior. Severity and course are related both to cumulative load in each risk domain and to the relative degree of risk in each domain. Very early onset externalizing behaviors are hypothesized to result from "the intense coupling of difficult temperament, ineffective parenting, and structural adversity" (p.168). When these risk factors are less tightly coupled, or in cases where these vulnerabilities and risks are intermixed with strengths, antisocial behavior is expected to be delayed or avoided.

Antisocial behavior that begins in early or mid-adolescence is seen as dominated by peer relationships, whereas onset in late adolescence or early adulthood is hypothesized to result from "a combination of developmental challenges, individual characteristics, and structural position" (Thornberry, 2005, p. 171). Some individuals with social and cognitive skill deficits are insulated from antisocial behavior in childhood because of highly structured family and school supports. When these supports are removed or weakened in the transition to adulthood, individual vulnerability increases. Overall, Thornberry argues that, as the age of onset increases, the strength of the causal factors associated with antisocial behavior diminishes, such that they are "less numerous, less extreme, and less intertwined. Because of that, they are also less likely to be highly stable over time" (p. 176).

Advances in understanding the multivariate interplay of environmental influences has been dramatically improved by innovation in quantitative models of development. For example, Patterson (1993) provided the first use of latent growth-curve modeling to predict both initial levels of antisocial behavior and growth over time. The analysis revealed that antisocial behavior could be likened to a *chimera* in that it changed in form and function over time. Harsh, conflictual, and coercive parenting seemed to account for the onset and maintenance of chronic behavior problems in childhood, whereas deviant peer involvement predicted growth in the problem behavior to new and more dangerous forms.

COMORBIDITY

In child and adolescent samples, ADHD frequently co-occurs with conduct disorders and appears to increase risk for persistent antisocial and criminal behavior (e.g., Barkley et al., 1990; Biederman et al., 1996; Mannuzza et al., 2004; see also Beauchaine & Neuhaus, this volume). Epidemiological studies indicate that 30 to 50% of children with ADHD also meet criteria for ODD and/or CD. However, the evidence is mixed as to whether ADHD alone (i.e., in the absence of conduct problems) places children at risk for later criminality (e.g., Langley & Thapar, 2006; Satterfield & Schell, 1997; Thapar et al., 2006).

In adulthood, substance abuse is the most prominent comorbid condition. Nearly all *DSM-IV* substance use disorders are highly comorbid with adult antisocial behavior, with odds ratios of 2.5 to 8.8 (Compton et al., 2005). Patterns of comorbidity are essentially the same for individuals with full ASPD and those who exhibit adult antisocial behavior only (no history of childhood CD) (Compton et al., 2005). Similarly, Robins and Regier (1991) reported that men with ASPD are 3 times as likely to abuse alcohol and 5 times as likely to abuse drugs as those without ASPD. For women, these comorbidity rates are even higher. Women with ASPD show 10 to 13 times the risk for alcohol abuse (Mulder et al., 1994; Robins & Regier, 1991) and 12 times the risk for drug abuse (Robins & Regier, 1991) compared to women without ASPD. Substance Use Disorder may either precede (Martens, 2000) or follow (Ross, Glaser, & Germanson, 1988) the development of ASPD. Evidence indicates that the comorbidity between ASPD and Substance Use Disorder emanates in large part from common genetic risk, although environmental factors also play a substantial role (Kendler et al., 2003; Krueger et al., 2002; Young et al., 2006).

Although externalizing syndromes are the most common comorbid disorders, individuals with ASPD also have an increased risk of anxiety disorders (e.g., Goodwin & Hamilton, 2003, Grant et al., 2004) and depression (e.g., Grant et al., 2004).

SEX DIFFERENCES

A prominent sex difference is found in the population prevalence of ASPD, with men being 2 to 3 times more likely to receive a diagnosis (APA, 2000; Hesselbrock, Meyer, & Keener, 1985; Flynn et al., 1996; Mulder et al., 1994). Despite this difference in prevalence, the prognosis and correlates of ASPD appear to be similar for both men and women (see Cale & Lilienfeld, 2002). Nevertheless, some studies have found sex differences in the correlates of persistent antisocial behavior. In a combined analysis of four different longitudinal samples, Broidy et al. (2003) found that childhood physical aggression predicted adolescent offending among boys but not among girls. More generally, Broidy et al. found that girls' delinquency was relatively difficult to predict from childhood risk factors.

CULTURAL CONSIDERATIONS

As noted previously, sociocultural factors may contribute substantial risk for antisocial behavior. Family and neighborhood-level risk factors, such as poverty, unemployment, single parenthood, and low income, often co-occur with ethnic minority status. Thus, ethnic and cultural differences in crime and antisocial behavior are amplified by socioeconomic and neighborhood risk factors.

In addition, risk factors for antisocial behavior may operate differently across ethnic groups. For example, Deater-Deckard and colleagues (1996) found that physical spanking correlated with higher rates of problem behavior among European American youth but not among African American youth. Dishion and Bullock (2001) found that observed relationship quality between parent and child was higher among high-risk African American boys than among successful African American boys. This paradoxical finding has yet to be explained by current etiological theories of ASPD. Nevertheless, family management interventions appear to work equally well across ethnic groups (Connell, Dishion, & Deater-Deckard, 2006; Dishion, Nelson, & Kavanagh, 2003; Gross et al., 2003; Henggeler et al., 1998).

Inequalities in the perception and interpretation of—as well as the reaction to—antisocial behavior across ethnic groups may also have a substantial impact on the course of antisocial behavior. Studies suggest that, compared to European American children, African American children receive more negative feedback for their school behavior and performance (Alexander & Entwisle, 1988), are more likely to be retained a grade in school (Meisels, 1992), and are more likely to be placed into special education classes for emotional disturbance (Wang, Reynolds, & Walberg, 1986). Perhaps most notable is the discrepancy between self-reported antisocial behavior as compared to arrest and rearrest rates among African American and European American adolescents (Elliott, 1994). Although self-reported rates of antisocial behavior are similar for both ethnic groups, arrest and rearrest rates are dramatically higher among African Americans. These findings suggest that similar behaviors may evoke harsher responses from society among African American as opposed to European American youth. Harsher societal responses (e.g., expulsion versus detention; juvenile detention versus probation) may further entrench minority youth in an antisocial lifestyle by limiting access to prosocial opportunities. There is a pressing need for further examination of cultural and ethnic contributions to antisocial behavior and greater understanding of the sociocultural factors that initiate and maintain criminal involvement in minority populations.

THEORETICAL SYNTHESIS AND FUTURE DIRECTIONS

Although there has been considerable progress in understanding the development of persistent and severe patterns of antisocial behavior, there is a need for continued research to clarify linkages across levels of analysis,

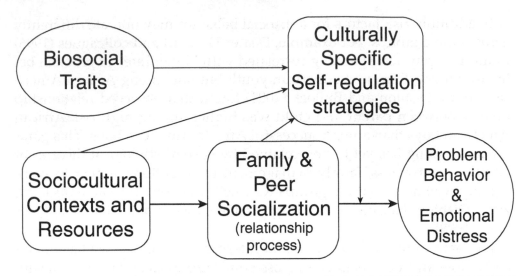

Figure 13.1. A model for self regulation in the development of problem behavior. Adapted from Dishion & Patterson, 2006.

from the genome to the community. Thankfully, some of this research is currently underway, following increasing appreciation and support for transactional models that examine concurrent influences and interactions. We offer Figure 13.1 as a summary of the existing literature on antisocial behavior from adolescence to adulthood. Rather than list all possible risk factors, we consider research on the broader domains with a known linkage to antisocial behavior.

RELATIONSHIP DYNAMICS

It is well established that parent-child and peer-child interactions are relevant to the development and progression of antisocial behavior. Historically, the majority of the research has focused on parent socialization processes in childhood and the later development of ASPD (e.g., Loeber & Dishion, 1983). Recent years have seen an increased focus on the parenting of adolescents and the continuance of problem behavior from adolescence to adulthood. Interventions that target parenting have been shown to reduce problem behavior in both children (e.g., Webster-Stratton & Taylor, 2001) and adolescents (Connell et al., in press).

Peer relationships may be especially relevant to understanding the progression from adolescent antisocial behavior to adult ASPD. As youth develop peer groups and romantic relationships, the extent to which these relationships are organized around deviance is a strong predictor of continued antisocial behavior across adolescence and early adulthood

(Shortt et al., 2003; Dishion, Nelson, & Bullock, 2004). In adolescence, there is growing evidence that a combination of parental disengagement and youth involvement with deviant peers greatly increases the risk of persistent antisocial behavior (Dishion, Nelson, & Bullock, 2004). Deviancy training among peers also has important implications for the design of interventions. Aggregating high-risk adolescents in treatment groups may be counterproductive, as peer reinforcement of antisocial behavior outweighs the effects of treatment (Dishion et al., 1999). These findings have been replicated in a variety of settings, suggesting a need for a greater focus on prevention programs that bring together heterogenous youth rather than treatment groups that target high-risk youth exclusively (Dishion & Dodge, 2005).

Given the importance of parent and peer relationships in the persistence and escalation of antisocial behavior, examination of parent and peer relationship dynamics will be important for further specifying pathways to ASPD. For example, analyses which attempt to confirm the differential prognoses of early versus late starters may benefit from inclusion of parent and peer dynamics. We hypothesize that, for many youth, the risk for ASPD depends largely upon parent involvement and the quality of peer networks that evolve in adolescence. Compared to late starters, early starters may experience greater parental disengagement in adolescence and may develop peer groups that are more tightly organized around antisocial and deviant behaviors.

Recent methodological advances have created new opportunities for the analysis of parent and peer relationships. The dynamic systems framework may prove to be particularly useful. This approach allows for examination of change and stability in systems (e.g., dyadic relationships) over time, and has been applied to parent–child and peer–peer interactions observed in the laboratory. Using dynamic systems methods, it is possible to examine relationship patterns in real time (e.g., moment-to-moment observations) and developmental time (e.g., days, weeks, years). The dynamic systems approach can produce measures such as stable relationship patterns (*attractors*), abrupt changes in the system (*phase transitions*), and the overall predictability of the system (*entropy*). Granic and Hollenstein (2003) provide an excellent review of dynamic systems strategies as they might be applied to understanding deviance and adjustment.

Relationship measures derived from a dynamic systems approach may be even more valuable when combined with measures of the content or valence of the interaction. For example, predictable relationship patterns (low entropy) may be associated with either positive or negative adjustment depending upon the content of the interaction. Dishion and colleagues (2004) found that low entropy predicted positive future adjustment when the content of the interaction was prosocial, but predicted negative future adjustment (antisocial behavior 10 years later) when the content of the interaction was antisocial. Furthermore, antisocial youth with well-organized relationships (low entropy) were at greater risk for future antisocial behavior than similarly deviant youth with poorly organized peer relationships (high entropy).

Identification of key relationship patterns may also be improved by "perturbing" the system. For example, rigid negativity in parent-child relationships is predictive of poor adjustment but may not be noticeable unless the system is challenged. Thus, it may be necessary to stress the dyad in order to observe patterns of interest (e.g., by asking the parent to resolve a dispute with the child during the interaction) (Granic & Lamey, 2002).

These and other methodological and analytic innovations for examining relationship dynamics are invigorating social interaction research and may play a key role in differentiating patterns of antisocial behavior and creating a better understanding of the pathways that lead to persistent antisocial behavior and adult ASPD (Dishion & Snyder, 2004).

Self-Regulation

Another promising direction for research is the study of intraindividual factors that moderate vulnerability or resilience to risks such as deviant peers in adolescence. Self-regulation may be a critical moderator of relationship dynamics (see Cole, this volume). Two studies of adolescents have now shown that youth with good self-regulatory skills (i.e., high effortful control) are less vulnerable to deviant peer influences with respect to the continuity and maintenance of antisocial behavior in adolescence (Goodnight et al., 2006; Dishion & Connell, in press). Effortful control (Rothbart et al., 2003) also seems to protect youth against the development of ASPD and major depression. There is ongoing research into the genetic and neurobiological components of self-regulatory abilities (e.g., Rothbart et al., 2003), and there are promising directions for future links across levels of analysis.

One relatively overlooked area of research in the domain of self-regulation involves cultural differences. There has been very little attention to cultural factors in the development of self-regulation in children and adolescents. Early cross-cultural work by Whiting & Edwards (1988) suggested that children in cultures that required chores and supervised participation in the adult community were more prosocial. By way of extension, one might hypothesize the cultural rituals that involve daily routines within the context of the extended family and community could function to promote high levels of self-regulation among adolescents, which in turn may protect against negative peer influences and help prevent the development of ASPD. Future research would do well to define and measure culturally specific self-regulatory factors that may account for why some risk factors promote antisocial behavior in some ethnic cultures and not others (e.g., Deater-Deckard & Dodge, 1997). For example, self-regulatory skills may be embedded in beliefs and social cognitions such as expectations of fairness and future events, and the meaning associated with both parent and peer relationships.

BIOSOCIAL FACTORS

Informed, theoretically driven inclusion of genetic and neurobiological (e.g., functional magnetic resonance imaging) measurements in longitudinal research is likely to greatly advance our understanding of antisocial behavior development. Genetic factors, in particular, have shown remarkable person–environment interactions and are in need of further investigation and inclusion in developmental and transactional models. A critical further step is to link these gene–environment interactions with behavioral and physiological measures, to better understand the mechanisms and processes through which they lead to adaptive or maladaptive outcomes, and to identify targets for intervention (Lewis & Stieben, 2004; Tucker, Derryberry, & Luu, 2000; Steinberg et al., 2006; Rueda, Posner, & Rothbart, 2004). Interactions among risk factors will likely be the rule, rather than the exception, in explaining antisocial behavior. It has become increasingly clear that many risk factors have marginal effects in isolation but substantial effects in conjunction with particular environmental or individual characteristics.

SOCIOCULTURAL FACTORS

There is extensive evidence that disrupted neighborhoods, schools, and communities increase the risk of antisocial behavior among youth (e.g., Eamon & Mulder, 2005; Ingoldsby et al., 2006; Lynam et al., 2000). However, much of this risk is mediated by parenting and peer factors. In addition, some individuals seem to be less negatively influenced by impoverished social environments. An exciting direction for future research is to systematically apply and evaluate systems-level policies and interventions for improving sociocultural contexts and reducing antisocial behavior. Commonly held community standards for behavior can have a substantial impact on rates of antisocial behavior. One obvious setting for system-level intervention is the public school system. Research by Kellam and colleagues suggests that systematic interventions that improve the behavior-management practices of teachers in the first grade can have far-reaching effects on children up to adolescence (Kellam et al., 1998; Ialongo et al., 2001). A school-wide approach to improving school behavior management and academic instruction has been designed and tested by Horner and colleagues (Horner, Day, & Day, 1997; Crone & Horner, 2003). However, there has yet to be an experiment with random assignment of a large number of schools to school-wide (as opposed to classroom-specific) training in behavior management and academic instruction, in order to determine the impact on the reduction of antisocial behavior.

Defining Disorder(s)

Cutting across each of these future directions is a need to carefully define and measure the syndrome of interest with regard to adult antisocial behavior, and to improve our understanding of which risk and protective factors, and which developmental pathways, are most relevant for different forms of antisocial behavior. The *DSM-IV* conceptualization of ASPD provides a starting point for research by identifying a broad group of individuals with a persistent pattern of antisocial behavior, but future research will need to build upon the ASPD construct to examine such issues as (a) whether ASPD is different in nature from less severe or persistent forms of antisocial behavior, and (b) whether the development (and treatment) of persistent antisocial behavior can be better understood by disaggregating ASPD into more homogenous groupings.

SUMMARY

The past several decades have seen great progress in understanding persistent antisocial behavior, due in large part to several large-scale, long-term longitudinal research projects that have documented the progression of antisocial behavior from childhood to adulthood. However, there is still much work to be done to separate correlates from causes, to illuminate the complex and interactive processes among risk and protective factors, to improve early identification of children at risk for long-term behavior problems, and to improve the efficacy of treatments and interventions. Progress in understanding antisocial behavior will come from research that becomes both more specific, by improving diagnostic specificity and examining individual differences at the level of genetics and neurobiology, and more general, by using increasingly sophisticated analytic techniques to examine complex interactions across multiple domains and developmental periods.

REFERENCES

Alexander, K. L., & Entwisle, D. R. (1988). Achievement in the first 2 years of school: Patterns and processes. *Monographs of the Society for Research in Child Development, 53,* 157.

American Psychiatric Association (1952). *Diagnostic and statistical manual of mental disorders.* Washington, DC: Author.

American Psychiatric Association (1968). *Diagnostic and statistical manual of mental disorders* (2nd ed.). Washington, DC: Author.

American Psychiatric Association (1980). *Diagnostic and statistical manual of mental disorders* (3rd ed.). Washington, DC: Author.

American Psychiatric Association (1994). *Diagnostic and statistical manual of mental disorders* (4th ed.). Washington, DC: Author.

American Psychiatric Association (2000). *Diagnostic and statistical manual of mental disorders* (4th ed., text revision). Washington, DC: Author.

Anstey, P. (2003). *The philosophy of John Locke: New perspectives.* New York: Routledge Publishing.

Barkley, R. A., Fischer, M., Edelbrock, C. S., & Smallish, I. (1990). The adolescent outcome of hyperactive children diagnosed by research criteria. *Journal of the American Academy of Child and Adolescent Psychiatry, 29,* 546–557.

Beauchaine, T. P., Gatzke-Kopp, L., & Mead, H. K. (2007). Polyvagal theory and developmental psychopathology: Emotion dysregulation and conduct problems from preschool to adolescence. *Biological Psychology, 74,* 174–184.

Beauchaine, T. P., Webster-Stratton, C., & Reid, M. J. (2005). Mediators, moderators, and predictors of one-year outcomes among children treated for early-onset conduct problems: A latent growth curve analysis. *Journal of Consulting and Clinical Psychology, 73,* 371–388.

Biederman, J., Faraone, S., Milberger, S., Guite, J., Mick, E., Chen, L., et al. (1996). A prospective 4-year follow-up study of attention-deficit hyperactivity and related disorders. *Archives of General Psychiatry, 53,* 437–446.

Black, D. W., Baumgard, C. H., & Bell, S. E. (1995). A 16- to 45-year follow-up of 71 men with antisocial personality disorder. *Comprehensive Psychiatry, 36,* 130–140.

Blair, R. J. R. (2002). Neuro-cognitive models of acquired sociopathy and developmental psychopathy. In J. Glicksohn (Ed.), *The neurobiology of criminal behavior* (pp. 157–186). Dordrecht, Netherlands: Kluwer Academic Publishers.

Brennan, P. A., Mednick, S. A., & Raine, A. (1997). Biosocial interactions and violence: A focus on perinatal factors. In A. Raine, P. A. Brennan, D. Farrington, & S. A. Mednick (Eds.), *Biosocial bases of violence* (pp. 163–174). New York: Plenum.

Broidy, L. M., Tremblay, R. E., Brame, B., Fergusson, D., Horwood, J. L., Laird, R. D., et al. (2003). Developmental trajectories of childhood disruptive behaviors and adolescent delinquency: A six-site, cross-national study. *Developmental Psychology, 39,* 222–245.

Cale, E. M., & Lilienfeld, S. O. (2002). Sex differences in psychopathy and antisocial personality disorder: A review and integration. *Clinical Psychology Review, 22,* 1179–1207.

Caspi, A., & Herbener, E. S. (1990). Continuity and change: Assortative marriage and the consistency of personality in adulthood. *Journal of Personality and Social Psychology, 58,* 250–258.

Caspi, A., McClay, J., Moffitt, T., Mill, J., Martin, J., Craig, I. W., et al. (2002). Role of genotype in the cycle of violence in maltreated children. *Science, 297,* 851–854.

Chamberlain, P., & Reid, J. (1998). Comparison of two community alternatives to incarceration for chronic juvenile offenders. *Journal of Consulting and Clinical Psychology, 6,* 624–633.

Cleckley, H. (1941). *The mask of sanity.* Oxford, UK: Mosby.

Cohen, P., Brown, J., & Smailes, E. (2001). Child abuse and neglect and the development of mental disorders in the general population. *Development and Psychopathology, 13,* 981–999.

Compton, W. M., Conway, K. P., Stinson, F. S., Colliver, J. D., & Grant, B. F. (2005). Prevalence, correlates, and comorbidity of *DSM-IV* antisocial personality syndromes and alcohol and specific drug use disorders in the United States: Results from the National Epidemiologic Survey on Alcohol and Related Conditions. *Journal of Clinical Psychiatry, 66,* 677–685.

Connell, A. M., Dishion, T. J., & Deater-Deckard, K. (2006). Variable- and person-centered approaches to the analysis of early adolescent substance use: Linking peer, family, and intervention effects with developmental trajectories. [Special Issue]. *Merrill-Palmer Quarterly, 52*(3), 421–448.

Connell, A., Dishion, T., Yasui, M., & Kavanagh, K. (in press). An ecological approach to family intervention to reduce adolescent problem behavior: Intervention engagement and longitudinal change. In S. Evans (Ed.), *Advances in school-based mental health, Vol. 2.* Kingston, NJ: Civic Research Institute.

Crone, D. A., & Horner, R. H. (2003). *Building positive behavior support systems in schools: Functional behavioral assessment.* New York: Guilford.

Deater-Deckard, K., & Dodge, K. A. (1997). Externalizing behavior problems and discipline revisited: Nonlinear effects in variation by culture, context, and gender. *Psychological Inquiry, 8,* 161–175.

Deater-Deckard, K., Dodge, K. A., Bates, J. E., & Pettit, G. S. (1996). Physical discipline among African American and European American mothers: Links to children's externalizing behaviors. *Developmental Psychology, 32,* 1065–1072.

Dishion, T. J., & Bullock, B. M. (2001). Parenting and adolescent problem behavior: An ecological analysis of the nurturance hypothesis. In J. G. Borkowski, S. L. Ramey, & M. Bristol-Power (Eds.), *Parenting and the child's world: Influences on academic, intellectual, and social-emotional development* (pp. 231–249). Mahwah, NJ: Erlbaum.

Dishion, T. J., & Connell, A. (2006). *Adolescents' resilience as a self-regulatory process: Promising themes for linking intervention with developmental science* (pp. 125–138). New York: New York Academy of Sciences.

Dishion, T. J., & Dodge, K. A. (2005). Peer contagion in interventions for children and adolescents: Moving toward an understanding of the ecology and dynamics of change. *Journal of Abnormal Child Psychology, 33*(3), 395–400.

Dishion, T. J., McCord, J., & Poulin, F. (1999). When interventions do harm: Peer groups and problem behavior. *American Psychologist, 54,* 755–764.

Dishion, T. J., Nelson, S. E., & Bullock, B. M. (2004). Premature adolescent autonomy: Parent disengagement and deviant peer process in the amplification of problem behavior. In J. Kiesner & M. Kerr (Eds.), Peer and family processes in the development of antisocial and aggressive behavior [Special Issue]. *Journal on Adolescence, 27,* 515–530.

Dishion, T. J., Nelson, S. E., & Kavanagh, K. (2003). The family check-up for high-risk adolescents: Preventing early-onset substance use by parent monitoring. In J. E. Lochman & R. Salekin (Eds.), Behavior oriented interventions for children with aggressive behavior and/or conduct problems [Special issue]. *Behavior Therapy, 34,* 553–571.

Dishion, T. J., Nelson, S. E., Winter, C. E., & Bullock, B. M. (2004). Adolescent friendship as a dynamic system: Entropy and deviance in the etiology and course of male antisocial behavior. *Journal of Abnormal Child Psychology, 32,* 651–663.

Dishion, T. J., Nelson, S. E., & Yasui, M. (2005). Predicting early adolescent gang involvement from middle school adaptation. *Journal of Clinical Child and Adolescent Psychology, 34,* 62–73.

Dishion, T. J., Owen, L. D., & Bullock, B. M. (2004). Like father, like son: Toward a developmental model for the transmission of male deviance across generations. *European Journal of Developmental Psychology, 1,* 105–126.

Dishion, T. J., & Patterson, G. R. (2006). The development and ecology of antisocial behavior in children and adolescents. In D. Cicchetti & D. J. Cohen (Eds.), *Developmental psychopathology. Vol. 3: Risk, disorder, and adaptation* (2nd ed., pp. 503–541). Hoboken, NJ: Wiley.

Dishion, T. J., Patterson, G. R., & Kavanagh, K. A. (1992). An experimental test of the coercion model: Linking theory, measurement, and intervention. In J. McCord & R. Tremblay (Eds.), *The interaction of theory and practice: Experimental studies of intervention* (pp. 253–282). New York: Guilford.

Dishion, T. J., & Snyder, J. (2004). An introduction to the special issue on advances in process and dynamic system analysis of social interaction and the development of antisocial behavior. *Journal of Abnormal Child Psychology, 32,* 575–578.

Dodge, K. A., Dishion, T. J., & Lansford, J. E. (2006). *Deviant peer influences in programs for youth: Problems and solutions.* New York: Guilford.

Eamon, M. K., & Mulder, C. (2005). Predicting antisocial behavior among Latino young adolescents: An ecological systems analysis. *American Journal of Orthopsychiatry, 75,* 117–127.

Eddy, J. M., & Chamberlain, P. (2000). Family management and deviant peer association as mediators of the impact of treatment conditions on youth antisocial behavior. *Journal of Consulting and Clinical Psychology, 68,* 857–863.

Elder, G. H. Jr. (1985). *Life course dynamics: Trajectories and transitions, 1968–1980.* Ithaca, NY: Cornell University Press.

Elliott, D. S. (1994). Serious violent offenders: Onset, developmental course, and termination—The American Society of Criminology 1993 presidential address. *Criminology, 32,* 1–21.

Farrington, D. P. (1995). The twelfth Tizard lecture. The development of offending and antisocial behavior from childhood: Key findings from the Cambridge study in delinquent development. *Journal of Child Psychology and Psychiatry, 36,* 929–964.

Farrington, D. P. (2005). The integrated cognitive antisocial potential (ICAP) theory. In D. P. Farrington (Ed.), Integrated developmental and life-course theories of offending (pp. 73–92). New Brunswick, NJ: Transaction.

Farrington, D. P., Barnes, G. C., & Lambert, S. (1996). The concentration of offending in families. *Legal and Criminological Psychology, 1*(Part 1), 47–63.

Flynn, P. M., Craddock, S. G., Luckey, J. W., Hubbard, R. L., & Dunteman, G. H. (1996). Comorbidity of antisocial personality and mood disorders among psychoactive substance-dependent treatment clients. *Journal of Personality Disorders, 10,* 56–67.

Forgatch, M. S. (1991). The clinical science vortex: Developing a theory for antisocial behavior. In D. J. Pepler & K. H. Rubin (Eds.), *The development and treatment of childhood aggression* (pp. 291–315). Hillsdale, NJ: Erlbaum.

Forgatch, M. S., Bullock, B. M., & Patterson, G. R. (2004). From theory to practice: Increasing effective parenting through role-play. In H. Steiner (Ed.), *Handbook of mental health interventions in children and adolescents: An integrated developmental approach* (pp. 782–813). San Francisco, CA: Jossey-Bass.

Forgatch, M. S., & DeGarmo, D. S. (1999). Parenting through change: An effective prevention program for single mothers. *Journal of Consulting and Clinical Psychology, 67,* 711–724.

Friedlander, E. (2004). *J. J. Rousseau: An afterlife of words.* Cambridge, MA: Harvard University Press (Original work published 1762).

Giambra, L. M., Camp, C. J., & Grodsky, A. (1992). Curiosity and stimulation seeking across the adult life span: Cross-sectional and 6- to 8-year longitudinal findings. *Psychology and Aging, 7,* 150–157.

Glueck, S., & Glueck, E. (1950). *Unraveling juvenile delinquency.* Oxford, England: Commonwealth Fund.

Goodnight, J. A., Bates, J. E., Newman, J. P., Dodge, K. A., & Pettit, G. S. (2006). The interactive influences of friend deviance and reward dominance on the development of externalizing behavior during middle adolescence. *Journal of Abnormal Child Psychology, 34*(5), 573–583.

Goodwin, R. D., & Hamilton, S. P. (2003). Lifetime comorbidity of antisocial personality disorder and anxiety disorders among adults in the community. *Psychiatry Research, 117,* 159–166.

Granic, I., & Hollenstein, T. (2003). Dynamic systems methods for models of developmental psychopathology. *Development and Psychopathology, 15,* 641–669.

Granic, I., & Lamey, A.V. (2002). Combining dynamic systems and multivariate analyses to compare the mother-child interactions of externalizing subtypes. *Journal of Abnormal Child Psychology, 39,* 265–283.

Grant, B. F., Hasin, D. S., Stinson, F. S., Dawson, D. A., Chou, S. P., Ruan, W. J., & Pickering, R. P. (2004). Prevalence, correlates, and disability of personality disorders in the United States: Results from the National Epidemiologic Survey on Alcohol and Related Conditions. *Journal of Clinical Psychiatry, 65,* 948–958.

Gross, D., Fogg, L., Webster-Stratton, C., Garvey, C., Julion, W., & Grady, J. (2003). Parent training of toddlers in day care in low-income urban communities. *Journal of Consulting and Clinical Psychology, 71,* 261–278.

Hare, R. D. (1991). *The Hare Psychopathy Checklist–Revised.* Toronto: Multi-Health Systems.

Hare, R. D. (2003). *The Hare PCL–R,* 2nd ed. Toronto: Multi-Health Systems.

Hare, R. D., Clark, D., Grann, M., & Thornton, D. (2000). Psychopathy and the predictive validity of the PCL–R: An international perspective. *Behavioral Sciences and the Law, 18,* 623–645.

Harpur, T. J., Hakstian, A. R., & Hare, R. D. (1988). Factor structure of the Psychopathy Checklist. *Journal of Consulting and Clinical Psychology, 56,* 741–747.

Harpur, T. J., Hare, R. D., & Hakstian, A. R. (1989). Two-factor conceptualization of psychopathy: Construct validity and assessment implications. *Psychological Assessment, 1,* 6–17.

Healy, W. (1926). Preventing delinquency among children. *Proceedings and Addresses of the National Educational Association, 64,* 113–118.

Healy, W., & Bronner, A. F. (1936). *New light on delinquency and its treatment.* New Haven, CT: Yale University Press.

Henggeler, S. W., Schoenwald, S. K., Borduin, C. M., Rowland, M. D., & Cunningham, P. B. (1998). *Multisystemic treatment of antisocial behavior in children and adolescents.* New York: Guilford.

Hesselbrock, M. N., Meyer, R. E., & Keener, J. J. (1985). Psychopathology in hospitalized alcoholics. *Archives of General Psychiatry, 42,* 1050–1055.

Hiatt, K. D., & Newman, J. P. (2006). Understanding psychopathy: The cognitive side. In C. J. Patrick (Ed.), *Handbook of psychopathy* (pp. 334–352). New York: Guilford.

Horner, R. H, Day, H. M., & Day, J. R. (1997). Using neutralizing routines to reduce problem behaviors. *Journal of Applied Behavior Analysis, 30,* 601–614.

Horwitz, A. V., Widom, C. S., McLaughlin, J., & White, H. R. (2001). The impact of childhood abuse and neglect on adult mental health: A prospective study. *Journal of Health and Social Behavior, 42,* 184–201.

Ialongo, N., Poduska, J., Werthhamer, L., & Kellam, S. (2001). The distal impact of two first-grade preventive interventions on conduct problems and disorder in early adolescence. *Journal of Emotional and Behavioral Disorders, 9,* 146–160.

Ingoldsby, E. M., Shaw, D. S., Winslow, E., Schonberg, M., Gilliom, M., & Criss, M. M. (2006). Neighborhood disadvantage, parent-child conflict, neighborhood peer relationships, and early antisocial behavior problem trajectories. *Journal of Abnormal Child Psychology, 34,* 303–319.

Jacobson, K. C., Prescott, C. A., & Kendler, K. S. (2002). Sex differences in the genetic and environmental influences on the development of antisocial behavior. *Development and Psychopathology, 14,* 395–416.

Jeglum-Bartusch, D. R., Lynam, D. R., Moffitt, T. E., & Silva, P. A. (1997). Is age important? Testing a general versus a developmental theory of antisocial behavior. *Criminology, 35,* 13–48.

Johnson, J. G., Smailes, E., Cohen, P., Kasen, S., & Brook, J. S. (2004). Anti-social parental behaviour, problematic parenting, and aggressive offspring behaviour during adulthood: A 25-year longitudinal investigation. *British Journal of Criminology, 44,* 915–930.

Kellam, S. G., Mayer, L. S., Rebok, G. W., & Hawkins, W. E. (1998). Effects of improving achievement on aggressive behavior and of improving aggressive behavior on achievement through two preventive interventions: An investigation of causal paths. In B. P. Dohrenwend (Ed.), *Adversity, stress, and psychopathology* (pp. 486–505). New York: Oxford University Press.

Kendler, K. S., Prescott, C. A., Myers, J., & Neale, M. C. (2003). The structure of genetic and environmental risk factors for common psychiatric and substance use disorders in men and women. *Archives of General Psychiatry, 60,* 929–937.

Krueger, R. F., Hicks, B. M., Patrick, C. J., Carlson, S. R., Iacono, W. G., & McGue, M. (2002). Etiologic connections among substance dependence, antisocial behavior, and personality: Modeling the externalizing spectrum. *Journal of Abnormal Psychology, 111,* 411–424.

Lahey, B. B., Loeber, R., Burke, J. D., & Applegate, B. (2005). Predicting future antisocial personality disorder in males from a clinical assessment in childhood. *Journal of Consulting and Clinical Psychology, 73,* 389–399.

Langley, K., & Thapar, A. (2006). COMT gene variant and birth weight predict early-onset antisocial behavior in children with Attention Deficit Hyperactivity Disorder. *Directions in Psychiatry, 26,* 219–225.

Lewis, M. D., & Stieben, J. (2004). Emotion regulation in the brain: Conceptual issues and directions for developmental research. *Child Development, 75,* 371–376.

Loeber, R., & Dishion, T. (1983). Early predictors of male delinquency: A review. *Psychological Bulletin, 94,* 68–99.

Luntz, B. K., & Widom, C. S. (1994). Antisocial personality disorder in abused and neglected children grown up. *American Journal of Psychiatry, 151,* 670–674.

Lykken, David T. (1995). *The antisocial personalities.* Hillsdale, NJ: Erlbaum.

Lynam, D. R., Caspi, A., Moffit, T. E., Wikstrom, P. O., Loeber, R., & Novak, S. (2000). The interaction between impulsivity and neighborhood context on offending: The effects of impulsivity are stronger in poorer neighborhoods. *Journal of Abnormal Psychology, 109,* 563–574.

Mannuzza, S., Klein, R. G., Abikoff, H., & Moulton, J. L., III (2004). Significance of childhood conduct problems to later development of conduct disorder among children with ADHD: A prospective follow-up study. *Journal of Abnormal Child Psychology, 32,* 565–573.

Mamorstein, N., & Iacono, W. G. (2005). Longitudinal follow-up of adolescents with late-onset antisocial behavior: A pathological yet overlooked group. *Journal of the American Academy of Child & Adolescent Psychiatry, 44,* 1284–1291.

Martens, W. H. J. (2000). Antisocial and psychopathic personality disorders: Causes, course, and remission—a review article. *International Journal of Offender Therapy and Comparative Criminology, 44,* 406–430.

Martinez, C. R., Jr. & Forgatch, M. S. (2001). Preventing problems for boys' noncompliance: Effects of a parent training intervention for divorcing mothers. *Journal of Consulting and Clinical Psychology, 69,* 416–428.

Martinez, C. R., Jr., & Forgatch, M. S. (2002). Adjusting to change: Linking family structure transitions with parenting and boys' adjustment. *Journal of Family Psychology, 16,* 107–117.

Mednick, S. A., & Kandel, E. S., (1988). Congenital determinants of violence. *Bulletin of the American Academy of Psychiatry and the Law, 16,* 101–109.

Meisels, S. J. (1992). Doing harm by doing good: Iatrogenic effects of early childhood enrollment and promotion policies. *Early Childhood Research Quarterly, 7,* 155–174.

Miller, T. R. (2004). The social costs of adolescent problem behavior. In A. Biglan, P. A. Brennan, S. L. Foster, & H. D. Holder (Eds.), *Helping adolescents at risk: Prevention of multiple problem behaviors.* New York: Guilford.

Moffitt, T. E. (1990). Juvenile delinquency and Attention Deficit Disorder: Boys' developmental trajectories from age 3 to age 15. *Child Development, 61,* 893–910.

Moffitt, T. E. (1993). Adolescence-limited and life-course-persistent antisocial behavior: A developmental taxonomy. *Psychological Review, 100,* 674–701.

Moffitt, T. E. (2003). Life-Course-Persistent and Adolescence-Limited antisocial behavior: A 10-year research review and a research agenda. In B. Lahey, T. E. Moffitt, & A. Caspi (Eds.), *Causes of conduct disorder and juvenile delinquency* (pp. 49–75). New York: Guilford.

Moffitt, T. E. (2006). The new look of behavioral genetics in developmental psychopathology: Gene-environment interplay in antisocial behaviors. *Psychological Bulletin, 131,* 533–554.

Moffitt, T. E., & Caspi, A. (2001). Childhood predictors differentiate life-course persistent and adolescence-limited antisocial pathways among males and females. *Development and Psychopathology, 13,* 355–375.

Moffitt, T. E., Caspi, A., Dickson, N., Silva, P., & Stanton, W. (1996). Childhood-onset versus adolescent-onset antisocial conduct problems in males: Natural history from ages 3 to 18 years. *Development and Psychopathology, 8,* 399–424.

Moffit, T. E., Caspi, A., Harrington, H., & Milne, B. J. (2002). Males on the life-course-persistent and adolescence-limited antisocial pathways: Follow-up at age 26 years. *Development and Psychopathology, 14,* 179–207.

Mulder, R. T., Wells, J. E., Joyce, P. R., & Bushnell, J. A. (1994). Antisocial women. *Journal of Personality Disorders, 8,* 279–287.

Nelson, S. E., & Dishion, T. J. (2004). From boys to men: Predicting adult adaptation from middle childhood sociometric status. *Development and Psychopathology, 16,* 441–459.

Newman, J. P. (1998). Psychopathic behavior: An information processing perspective. In D. J. Cooke, R. D. Hare, & A. Forth (Eds.), *Psychopathy: Theory, research, and implications for society* (pp. 81–104). Dordrecht, Netherlands: Kluwer.

Newman, J. P., & Wallace, J. F. (1993). Diverse pathways to deficient self-regulation: Implications for disinhibitory psychopathology in children. *Clinical Psychology Review, 13,* 699–720.

Patterson, G. R. (1982). *A social learning approach: Vol. 3: Coercive family process.* Eugene, OR: Castalia.

Patterson, G. R. (1993). Orderly change in a stable world: The antisocial trait as a chimera. *Journal of Consulting and Clinical Psychology, 61,* 911–919.

Patterson, G. R., DeBaryshe, B. D., & Ramsey, E. (1989). A developmental perspective on antisocial behavior. *American Psychologist, 44,* 329–335.

Patterson, G. R., DeGarmo, D. S., & Knutson, N. (2000). Hyperactive and antisocial behaviors: Comorbid or two points in the same process? *Development and Psychopathology, 12,* 91–106.

Patterson, G. R., & Dishion, T. J. (1988). Multilevel family process models: Traits, interactions, and relationships. In R. Hinde & J. Stevenson-Hinde (Eds.), *Relationships within families: Mutual influences* (pp. 283–310). Oxford: Clarendon.

Patterson, G. R., Dishion, T. J., & Yoerger, K. (2000). Adolescent growth in new forms of problem behavior: Macro- and micro-peer dynamics. *Prevention Science, 1,* 3–13.

Patterson, G. R., Reid, J. B., & Dishion, T. J. (1992). *A social interactional approach. Vol. 4: Antisocial boys.* Eugene, OR: Castalia.

Patterson, G. R., & Yoerger, K. (1999). Intraindividual growth in covert antisocial behavior: A necessary precursor to chronic and adult arrests? *Criminal Behaviour and Mental Health, 9,* 86–100.

Petras, H., Schaeffer, C. M., Ialongo, N., Hubbard, S., Muthen, B., et al. (2004). When the course of aggressive behavior in childhood does not predict antisocial outcomes in adolescence and young adulthood: An examination of potential explanatory variable. *Development and Psychopathology, 16,* 919–941.

Piehler, T. F., & Dishion, T. J. (in press). Interpersonal dynamics within adolescent friendship: Dyadic mutuality and deviant talk and patterns of antisocial behavior. *Child Development.*

Quinton, D., Pickles, A., Maughan, B., & Rutter, M. (1993). Partners, peers, and pathways: Assortative pairing and continuities in conduct disorder. *Developmental Psychology, 5,* 763–783.

Raine, A., Venables, P. H., & Williams, M. (1995). High autonomic arousal and electrodermal orienting at age 15 years as protective factors against criminal behavior at age 29 years. *American Journal of Psychiatry, 152,* 1595–1600.

Reio, T. G., Jr., & Choi, N. (2004). Novelty seeking in adulthood: Increases accompany decline. *Journal of Genetic Psychology, 165,* 119–133.

Reiss, D., Grubin, D., & Meux, C. (1996). Young "psychopaths" in special hospital: Treatment and outcome. *British Journal of Psychiatry, 168,* 99–104.

Ridenour, T. A., Cottler, L. B., Robins, L. N., Compton, W. M., Spitznagel, E. L., Cunningham-Williams, R. M. (2002). Test of the plausibility of adolescent substance use playing a casual role in developing adulthood antisocial behavior. *Journal of Abnormal Psychology, 111,* 144–155.

Robins, L. N. (1966). *Deviant children grown up: A sociological and psychiatric study of sociopathic personality.* Baltimore: Williams & Wilkins.

Robins, L. N., & Regier, D. A. (1991). *Psychiatric disorders in America: The Epidemiologic Catchment Area Study.* New York: Free Press.

Rogers, G., & Schulman, K. (2003). *Leviathan/Thomas Hobbes: A critical edition.* Bristol: Thoemmes Continuum. (Original work published 1651).

Ross, H. E., Glaser, F. B., & Germanson, T. (1988). The prevalence of psychiatric disorders in patients with alcohol and other drug problems. *Archives of General Psychiatry, 45,* 1023–1031.

Rothbart, M. K., Ellis, L. K., Rueda, M., and Posner, M. I. (2003). Developing mechanisms of temperamental effortful control. *Journal of Personality, 71,* 1113–1143.

Rueda, M. R., Posner, M. I., & Rothbart, M. K. (2004). Attentional control and self-regulation. In R. F. Baumeister & K. D. Vohs (Eds.), *Handbook of self-regulation: Research, theory, and applications* (pp. 283–300). New York: Guilford.

Sampson, R. J., & Laub, J. H. (1990). Crime and deviance over the life curse: The salience of adult social bonds. *American Sociological Review, 55,* 609–627.

Sampson, R. J., & Laub, J. H. (1993). *Crime in the making: Pathways and turning points through life.* Cambridge, MA: Harvard University Press.

Sampson, R. J., & Laub, J. H. (2005). A life-course view of the development of crime. *Annals of the American Academy of Political and Social Science, 602,* 12–45.

Satterfield, J. H., & Schell, A. (1997). A prospective study of hyperactive boys with conduct problems and normal boys: Adolescent and adult criminality. *Journal of the American Academy of Child and Adolescent Psychiatry, 36,* 1726–1735.

Shannon, K. E., Beauchaine, T. P., Brenner, S. L., Neuhaus, E., & Gatzke-Kopp, L. (2007). Familial and temperamental predictors of resilience in children at risk for conduct disorder and depression. *Development and Psychopathology, 19,* 701–727.

Shortt, J. W., Capaldi, D. M., Dishion, T. J., Bank, L., & Owen, L. D. (2003). The role of adolescent friends, romantic partners, and siblings in the emergence of the adult antisocial lifestyle. *Journal of Family Psychology, 17,* 521–533.

Smith, C. A., Ireland, T. O., & Thornberry, T. P. (2005). Adolescent maltreatment and its impact on young adult antisocial behavior. *Child Abuse and Neglect, 29,* 1099–1119.

Snyder, J., & Stoolmiller, M. (2002). Reinforcement and coercion mechanisms in the development of antisocial behavior: The family. In J. B. Reid, G. R. Patterson, & J. Snyder (Eds.), *Antisocial behavior in children and adolescents: A developmental analysis and model for intervention* (pp. 65–100). Washington, DC: American Psychological Association.

Steinberg, L., Dahl, R., Keating, D., Kupfer, D. J., Masten, A. S., & Pine, D. S. (2006). The study of developmental psychopathology in adolescence: Integrating affective neuroscience with the study of context. In D. Cicchetti & D. J. Cohen (Eds.), *Developmental psychopathology. Vol. 2: Developmental neuroscience* (2nd ed., pp. 710–741). Hoboken, NJ: Wiley.

Taylor, J., Malone, S., Iacono, W. G., McGue, M. (2002). Development of substance dependence in two delinquency subgroups and nondelinquents from a male twin sample. *Journal of the American Academy of Child & Adolescent Psychiatry, 41,* 386–393.

Thapar, A., van den Bree, M., Fowler, T., Langley, K., & Whittinger, N. (2006). Predictors of antisocial behaviour in children with attention deficit hyperactivity disorder. *European Child & Adolescent Psychiatry, 15,* 118–125.

Thornberry, T. P. (2005). Explaining multiple patterns of offending across the life course and across generation. *Annals of the American Academy of Political and Social Science, 602,* 156–195.

Tucker, D. M., Derryberry, D., & Luu, P. (2000). Anatomy and physiology of human emotion: Vertical integration of brainstem, limbic, and cortical systems. In J. C. Borod (Ed.), *The neuropsychology of emotion* (pp. 56–79). New York: Oxford University Press.

Viding, E. (2004). On the nature and nurture of antisocial behavior and violence. In J. Devine, J. Gilligan, K. A. Miczek, R. Shaikh, & D. Pfaff (Eds.), *Youth violence: Scientific approaches to prevention* (pp. 267–277). New York: New York Academy of Sciences.

Wang, M. C., Reynolds, M. C., & Walberg, H. J. (1986). Rethinking special education. *Educational Leadership, 44,* 26–31.

Webster-Stratton, C., & Taylor, T. (2001). Nipping early risk factors in the bud: Preventing substance abuse, delinquency, and violence in adolescence through interventions targeted at young children (0 to 8 Years). *Prevention Science, 2,* 165–192.

Weiler, B. L., & Widom, C. S. (1996). Psychopathy and violent behaviour in abused and neglected young adults. *Criminal Behaviour and Mental Health, 6,* 253–271.

Whiting, B. B., & Edwards, C. P. (1988). *Children of different worlds: The formation of social behavior.* Cambridge: Harvard University Press.

Widiger, T. A., & Corbitt, E. (1995). Antisocial personality disorder. In W. J. Livesley (Ed.), *The* DSM-IV *personality disorders* (pp. 103–134). New York: Guilford.

Wiesner, M., Kim, H. K., & Capaldi, D. M. (2005). Developmental trajectories of offending: Validation and prediction to young adult alcohol use, drug use, and depressive symptoms. *Development and Psychopathology, 17,* 251–270.

Young, S. E., Rhee, S. H., Stallings, M. C., Corley, R. P., & Hewitt, J. K. (2006). Genetic and environmental vulnerabilities underlying adolescent substance use and problem use: General or specific? *Behavior Genetics, 36,* 603–615.

Zhang, L., Wieczorek, W. F., & Welte, J. W. (1997). The impact of age of onset of substance use on delinquency. *Journal of Research in Crime and Delinquency, 34,* 253–268.

Zucker, R. A., Ellis, D. A., Fitzgerald, H. E., Bingham, C. R., & Sanford, D. P. (1996). Other evidence for at least two alcoholisms. Vol. II: Life course variation in antisociality and heterogeneity of alcoholic outcome. *Development and Psychopathology, 8,* 831–848.

CHAPTER 14

Prevalence of Alcohol and Drug Involvement During Childhood and Adolescence

SANDRA A. BROWN

Alcohol and drug use is a salient concern during adolescence. National surveys in the United States indicate that alcohol is consistently the drug of choice for teens. By the time teens are in the 12th grade, 4 out of 5 have begun drinking alcohol and 50% have consumed alcohol in the past month (Johnston et al., 2006). Increasingly, youth consume alcohol in a particularly hazardous fashion (Brown et al., in press). According to the National Epidemiological Survey of Alcohol and Related Conditions (NESARC; Grant & Dawson, 1997), adolescents drink alcohol half as often as adults but consume 4.9 drinks per occasion, whereas the mean consumption of adults is 2.6 drinks.

Although the majority of youth who initiate alcohol, tobacco, or other substance involvement do so in mid- to late-adolescence, a small portion begin drinking alcohol in childhood. Only recently has the extent of children's alcohol consumption been evaluated through national surveys (see Donovan, in press, for review). These surveys include the Partnership Attitude Tracking Study (PATS; grades four through six), the National Survey of Parents and Youth (NSPY; youth ages 9 to 18 years), and the Health Behavior in School-Aged Children (HBSC; ages 11, 13, and 15 years) and PRIDE surveys (youth to sixth graders). Furthermore, 39 of 50 states have had statewide surveys of alcohol and drug involvement that included youth in sixth grade or younger.

Using the lowest level of exposure to alcohol, as measured by ever having tasted alcohol, the HBSC survey indicates that 62% of boys and 58% of girls have sampled alcohol by sixth grade. The HBSC survey also ranked the United States 16th among 28 countries evaluated (Currie et al., 2000). When children are queried as to whether they have ever had more than a sip of alcohol, as in the PATS surveys, rates more than double between grades four (9 to 10 year olds) and six (11 to 12 years olds). For example, 10% of fourth graders and 29% of sixth graders report having had more than a sip of alcohol. According to NSPY and the National Institute of Alcohol Abuse and Alcoholism, 6% of 9 year olds and 15 % of 12 year olds have had a drink of alcohol. Recent drinking is often considered an indicator of regular drinking and a precursor to heavier substance involvement and other behavioral problems of adolescence. Several statewide surveys and one national survey (HBSC) have assessed how often children drink. Results suggest that approximately 8% of sixth-grade boys and 7% of sixth-grade girls drink alcohol on at least a weekly basis. As Donovan (in press) notes in his review of childhood alcohol exposure, it is clear from national surveys that substantial numbers of children have experience with alcohol. Rates of personal exposure to alcohol increase dramatically in the upper elementary school years (grades four to six) with boys more likely to display early alcohol experimentation than girls.

The greatest escalation in alcohol involvement occurs between 12 and 15 years of age. Multiple national surveys indicate that use of alcohol—by far the most commonly used drug of children and adolescents—increases dramatically during this period. According to the Monitoring the Future (MTF) study (Johnston et al., 2006), by eighth grade 41% of students report lifetime drinking, which rises to 63% by tenth grade. The prevalence of prior 30 day use is 17% for eighth graders and 33% for tenth graders.

It is during this period that quantity of alcohol consumption is first measured in national surveys. For example, MTF results indicate that 20% of eighth graders and 42% of tenth graders report being drunk on at least one occasion in their lifetimes (Johnston et al., 2006). The rate of binge drinking (five or more drinks in a row) in the prior 2 weeks rises from 19% in eighth grade to 42% in tenth grade. Thus, the majority of early adolescents who drink alcohol do so episodically and often to excess. As described later in this chapter, such high doses of alcohol early in adolescence appear to have adverse effects on health and multiple developmental systems.

As youth progress into middle and late adolescence, alcohol and other drug involvement continues to escalate, as does intensity of use. By 12th grade (modal age = 18 years), almost 80% of youth report having ingested alcohol at least once and nearly 60% have been drunk at least once (Johnston et al., 2006). Among high school seniors, 50% report using alcohol in the past 30 days, 31% report being drunk, and 28% report 5 or more drinks per occasion during the prior 2 weeks. By contrast, rates of daily drinking remain low (3%), highlighting the heavy, episodic nature of youth involvement with alcohol and other substances.

As youth transition into late adolescence, they experience important changes in roles (e.g., jobs, college, military), relationships (e.g., romantic involvements, sexual relations), and physical contexts (e.g., living independently away from family). During this age range, their involvement with alcohol and drugs escalates to the highest levels observed at any point during the lifespan (Brown et al., in press). As noted previously, the prevalence of alcohol use tends to be higher among boys than girls in late childhood, but this difference diminishes during late adolescence. However, the intensity of alcohol use continues to be greater for boys across adolescence and young adulthood (Li, Hewitt, & Grant, 2004).

The second most commonly used drug among adolescents is nicotine, with over 60% of high school seniors reporting any lifetime use. Approximately one-third of seniors indicate smoking cigarettes in the last month. Cigarette use among adults has decreased over the last decade, yet nicotine use among adolescents has been more resistant to reductions in prevalence.

Exposure to other illicit substances is not uncommon among adolescents. Approximately half of high school seniors report lifetime use of a drug other than alcohol or cigarettes (Johnston et al., 2006). Marijuana is the most widely used illicit substance by adolescents. Half of high school seniors report lifetime use of marijuana. One in five seniors has smoked marijuana in the prior month. The greatest increase in use of any substance among adolescents over the last decade has been MDMA (Ecstasy). Seven percent of high school seniors reported use of Ecstasy in 1997; by 2001 that number had increased to 11.7%. Over the last decade, greater access and availability have been linked with trends for increased use of hard drugs (e.g., opiates, cocaine, crack), while hallucinogens and inhalants displayed marked decreases.

These prevalence rates in national school-based samples may underestimate actual prevalence. Indeed, adolescents with problematic substance involvement have higher rates of truancy, suspensions, and expulsions (Brown, Mott, & Stewart, 1992), meaning that the youth most at risk for substance use may not be available in school surveys. Furthermore, among adolescents involved in substance abuse treatment programs, over half report not attending school immediately preceding admission to treatment (Brown et al., 1994).

Youth in treatment programs are also more likely to use multiple substances in significantly greater quantities than in community-based samples (Abrantes, Brown, & Tomlinson, 2003). Alcohol, marijuana, amphetamines, and cigarettes are the most frequently used substances among adolescents receiving treatment, with 75% indicating weekly use of marijuana prior to substance abuse intervention (Abrantes et al., 2003). One in five youth in treatment also report abuse of prescription medications, either by consuming more than the prescribed dose or by acquiring prescription medications for recreational use.

Although it is useful to ascertain normative changes in alcohol and drug involvement, from a developmental perspective it is even more important to understand trajectories in patterns of substance involvement over time and to appreciate individual differences in the behavioral, cognitive, and social patterns and consequences associated with longitudinal patterns of use. A number of longitudinal studies spanning middle- to late-adolescence have recently evaluated patterns of substance involvement among youth. All of these studies show marked variability in alcohol involvement. For example, different trajectories of alcohol involvement during adolescence include abstention, stable moderate use, fling (short-term heavy) use, excess use that diminishes over time, chronic problematic use, and late-onset heavy use with rapid escalation to problems (e.g., Muthen & Muthen, 2000; Schulenberg, O'Malley, Bachman, Wadsworth, & Johnston, 1996; Tucker, Orlando, & Ellickson, 2003). Although estimates vary across studies, it appears that half of all youth display low-risk alcohol use trajectories and approximately one-third exhibit stable moderate alcohol consumption with intermittent or time-limited problems across adolescence and emerging adulthood (Chassin, Pitts, & Prost, 2002). Fling drinkers constitute about 10% of youth who exhibit heavy or problematic consumption only during the late-adolescent to early adult years (Schulenberg et al., 1996). Approximately 10% of youth display heavy drinking in early to middle adolescence but decrease their use around age 18. These dramatic changes over time are linked to environmental changes in exposure and contingencies, anticipatory role shifts, and personal change efforts (Brown, in press; Kypri et al., 2004).

ABUSE AND DEPENDENCE: CRITERIA AND DIAGNOSTIC ISSUES

Substance use disorders (SUDs) in adolescence involve the self-administration of any substance that induces long-term changes in mood, perception, or brain functioning (Brown, Aarons, & Abrantes, 2001; Bukstein, 1995). In general, substances are used initially by youth in social settings to produce a change in affective state or consciousness. Although almost all abused substances can lead to psychological dependence, some also produce physical dependence. *Psychological dependence* refers to the subjective feeling of needing the substance to function adequately. *Physical dependence* occurs when physiological and psychological adaptations to the substance occur. *Tolerance*—the need to ingest larger amounts of a substance for an effect once obtained at a lower dose—exemplifies such an adaptation. Another aspect of physical dependence involves the experience of adverse physiological symptoms—referred to as *withdrawal*—when consumption of an abused substance is ended abruptly.

Indicators of SUDs among adolescents often involve physical, socioemotional, and health changes. Such changes include deterioration in appearance (e.g., rapid weight loss, unusual breath and body odors, cuts and bruises); blood-shot eyes, very large or small pupils, and watery or blank stares; increased energy or lethargy, insomnia or excessive sleep; clinically significant levels of depression or anxiety; deviant behaviors that were not evident in childhood; decreases in school grades; changes in social activities or peer groups; chronic coughing or sniffing; skin boils or sores; nasal bleeding; and evidence of intravenous drug use (needle tracks) or inhalation (perforated nasal septum) (Brown & Abrantes, 2005).

Diagnostic criteria for alcohol and other substance use disorders appear in the *Diagnostic and Statistical Manual of Mental Disorders–Fourth Edition* (American Psychiatric Association, 2000). These criteria are listed in Table 14.1. Two types of substance use disorders (abuse and dependence) are characterized by a maladaptive pattern of use and symptoms that result in clinical impairment or distress. These diagnoses are mutually exclusive, with abuse typically considered less severe and less chronic than dependence. Substance dependence diagnoses are also characterized as to whether physiological dependence occurs—that is, with versus without evidence of tolerance or withdrawal.

According to the National Household Survey on Drug Abuse, 7.8% of adolescents ages 12 to 17 meet criteria for substance abuse or dependence, with prevalence rates increasing from early to late adolescence (Substance Abuse and Mental Health Services Administration, 1999). The largest increase in dependence is in the age range of 18 to 20. The prevalence of SUDs among youth ages 13 to 18 has been examined in multiple sectors of public service care including mental health, alcohol and drug, child welfare, juvenile justice, and severely emotionally disturbed groups in schools (Aarons et al., 2001). Using *DSM-IV* lifetime rates of SUDs, 35% of adolescents within these systems of care meet diagnostic criteria for either substance abuse or substance dependence. Alcohol and marijuana

Table 14.1.

DSM-IV criteria for Substance Use Disorders

Maladaptive pattern of substance use leading to clinically significant impairment or distress with:

Abuse manifested by one (or more) of the following, within a 12-month period:
  (1) recurrent use resulting in failure to fulfill major role obligations at work, school, or home
  (2) recurrent use in situations in which it is physically hazardous
  (3) recurrent substance-related legal problems
  (4) continued substance use despite persistent or recurrent social or interpersonal problems caused or exacerbated by the effects of the substance

Note: The symptoms have never met the criteria for Substance Dependence for this class of substance.

Dependence manifested by three (or more) of the following, occurring in the same 12-month period:
  (1) tolerance (a need for markedly increased amounts of the substance to achieve intoxication or desired effect or markedly diminished effect with continued use of the same amount of the substance)
  (2) characteristic withdrawal syndrome for the substance or the same (or a closely related) substance taken to relieve or avoid withdrawal symptoms
  (3) substance taken in larger amounts or over a longer period than intended
  (4) persistent desire or unsuccessful efforts to cut down or control substance use
  (5) a great deal of time is spent in activities necessary to obtain, use, or recover from effects of the substance
  (6) important social, occupational, or recreational activities given up or reduced because of substance use
  (7) continued use despite knowledge of having a persistent or recurrent physical or psychological problem that is likely to have been caused or exacerbated by the substance

* Adapted from American Psychiatric Association (1994). *Diagnostic and Statistical Manual of Mental Disorders*, 4th ed. Washington, DC: Author.

use disorders are the most prevalent, with the highest rates reported in mental health settings. Other illicit SUDs are more prevalent in juvenile justice settings.

As these figures indicate, alcohol and drug involvement progresses to the level of an SUD for a significant number of youth. Among adolescents, this progression occurs more rapidly than among adults. Adolescent SUDs are associated with a variety of developmentally significant impairments such as poor academic functioning (Chatlos, 1997), family problems (e.g., Dakof, 2000), health problems (Brown & Tapert, 2004a), morphological and functional neuroanatomical abnormalities (Tapert et al., 2004), and psychiatric comorbidity (Abrantes et al., 2003). Moreover, emerging evi-

dence from developmentally focused longitudinal studies ind[?]
SUDs during adolescence predict a wide range of adverse o[?]
adulthood.

DSM-IV criteria were developed based on extensive research with adults. Consequently, questions have been raised regarding the applicability of SUD diagnoses to children and adolescents. Although consistent use of *DSM-IV* criteria to diagnose SUDs enhances communication between clinicians and researchers (Connors, 1995), there are several significant limitations to the current system, as current criteria do not account for developmental differences between adults and adolescents (Brown et al., 2001). For example, withdrawal symptoms and physiological depen-dence are less prevalent among children and adolescents than among adults (Kaminer, 1994; Stewart & Brown, 1995). Instead, cognitive and affective withdrawal features are much more prevalent among youth than are physiological symptoms. Consequently, clinicians should not rely on physiological symptoms to determine dependence in adolescents.

In addition, application of *DSM-IV* criteria for SUDs can result in no diagnosis, even when youth exhibit multiple substance use problems. Because there is no overlap between dependence and abuse symptoms, it is possible for an individual to exhibit multiple substance-related problems (e.g., two dependence symptoms) and not meet criteria for either abuse or dependence. In contrast, youth with only one abuse symptom can meet criteria for substance abuse. Pollock and Martin (1999) found that 31% who had alcohol dependence symptoms did not meet criteria for either abuse or dependence. Furthermore, when these adolescents were evaluated 1 year later, they exhibited outcomes more comparable to abusers than nonabusers. Similarly, among those receiving treatment in publicly funded substance abuse programs, 18% did not meet *DSM-IV* criteria for a SUD even though all exhibited multiple alcohol and/or drug problems sufficient to merit hospitalization (Aarons et al., 2001). Consequently, *DSM-IV* abuse and dependence criteria may not be sensitive enough to identify substance use problems among some adolescents.

Thus, alternative approaches to the *DSM-IV* have been suggested, including some that assess use continuously rather than discretely (Angold et al., 1999; Lewinsohn et al., 2000). More recently, item response theory and clustering approaches have been used to demonstrate the advantages of a continuum incorporating both abuse and dependence symptoms to reflect the normal developmental progression of the disorder (Harrison, Fulkerson, & Beebe, 1998). Further work will be necessary to determine the validity of using *DSM* criteria for making diagnoses of adolescent substance abuse or dependence.

HISTORICAL CONTEXT AND ETIOLOGICAL FORMULATIONS

Considerable research has been devoted to understanding the onset of SUDs and the progression to abuse and dependence among youth. A number of models seek to explain youth externalizing behavior more generally, whereas other models address SUDs specifically. Early etiological theories of substance use among adolescents focused on the interplay of person and environment and included the theory of planned behavior (TPB), social learning theory (SLT), problem behavior theory (PBT), and the domain model. More recent models incorporate genetic, neurobiological, neurophysiological, and neuropsychological factors.

ENVIRONMENTAL MODELS

Theory of planned behavior (TPB). This theory, a derivative of the theory of reasoned action (Ajzen & Fishbein, 1980), has been used to explain why youth engage in various addictive behaviors. In this cognitive and behavioral theory, attitudes about using substances, perceived social norms of alcohol/drug use, and self-efficacy for coping in potential use situations influence youths' intentions to use substances. Behavioral intention, in turn, influences substance use decisions and behavior. Substance-specific attitudes result from underlying expectations about personal consequences associated with substance use and the value placed on these consequences (Ajzen & Fishbein, 1980; Goldman et al., 1991; Petraitis, Flay, & Miller, 1995). Normative beliefs about substance use are determined by perceived use rates of others, the perception that others prefer the adolescent in question to use a substance, and personal motivation to please others. Self-efficacy about substance use refers to whether the adolescent feels control over his or her own behaviors in use situations. Two types of self-efficacy related to substance use intentions are described in this model: substance use self-efficacy, or the ability to successfully obtain and use substances, and refusal self-efficacy, or the ability to resist perceived pressures to use (Ajzen, 1988, 2001). Although support for TPB has been demonstrated for experimental substance use, causal links between substance-specific beliefs and substance uses may be more bidirectional, as proposed in other cognitively oriented models (e.g., expectancy theory).

Social learning theory (SLT). Initially developed by Akers (1977) and subsequently refined by Bandura (1986), SLT focuses on relations between perceived contingencies and substance use. From this perspective, adolescents develop outcome expectations about the effects of substance use by observing (e.g., parents, peers, media) or by learning about the effects of substance use (e.g., discussions of use effects). SLT posits that positive social, personal, and physiological expectations, which result from attending to influential social role models, are predictive of adolescent substance use. Aspects of this model are salient in broader decision-making models of deviant youth (Brown et al., 2001).

Problem behavior theory (PBT). Problem behavior theory is a generalist model that considers substance involvement to be one of a number of deviant behaviors that typically co-occur among adolescents (Jessor & Jessor, 1977). From this perspective, adolescent deviant behavior reflects unconventionality. Thus, if an adolescent is prone to engage in one deviant behavior, he or she is likely to engage in others (see also Beauchaine, Hinshaw, & Gatzke-Kopp, this volume). Numerous studies support the high co-occurrence of multiple problems or delinquent behaviors, including marijuana and alcohol use, early and high-risk sexual behavior, illegal activity, truancy, and aggression. Individuals high on this risk-taking characteristic are less likely to engage in health-promoting behaviors (Jessor & Jessor, 1977). Furthermore, adolescents at risk for deviant behaviors are more detached from their parents, more influenced by their peers, less responsive to negative reinforcement, and show distinct neuroanatomical response patterns reflective of poorer executive functioning skills (e.g., Zucker et al., 2006).

Domain model. Huba and colleagues (Huba, Wingard, & Bentler, 1980) extended these models to focus on the interaction of biological, intrapersonal, interpersonal, and sociocultural factors in jointly influencing adolescent substance use behavior. Biological mechanisms include genetic susceptibility, physiological reactions to substance use, and general health. Psychological state, cognitive style, personality traits, and personal values comprise the intrapersonal domain; interpersonal factors of social support, modeling, social reinforcement, personal identity, and belonging also contribute to use decisions. Finally, sociocultural and environmental factors include social sanctions of substance use, degree of availability of substances, social expectations, and environmental stressors.

Behavioral Genetic, Neurobiological, and Integrated Perspectives

Behavioral genetics studies (see Beauchaine, Hinshaw, & Gatzke-Kopp, this volume) have consistently linked parental alcohol and drug dependence to risk for alcohol and drug dependence in offspring (e.g., Schuckit, 1988). Although associated risks (e.g., Conduct Disorder) may influence outcomes, differences in behavioral, cognitive, and neurological measures have been observed between offspring of alcoholics (family history positive, FHP) and offspring of nonalcoholics (family history negative, FHN). For example, when FHP adolescents are compared to FHN teens, they demonstrate greater impulsivity, rebelliousness (Knop et al., 1985), poorer response inhibition (Nigg et al., 2006), poorer neuropsychological performance (Tapert & Brown, 1999; Tarter & Edwards, 1988), and fewer physiological and subjective effects of alcohol predating exposure (Newlin, 1994). These preexisting vulnerabilities, which predispose FHP adolescents to problematic substance use, are consistent with behavioral genetics studies indicating that a substantial portion of risk for SUDs is heritable, and over half is nondrug specific (e.g., Kendler et al., 2003; Tsuang et al., 1998).

Multiple genetic pathways that are influenced by environmental risk factors and life experiences have been proposed. Cadoret and colleagues (1995) found support for a direct pathway from parental alcoholism to drug abuse and dependency in male offspring, and for an indirect pathway from parental Antisocial Personality Disorder to externalizing behaviors and eventually drug abuse and dependence. Schuckit, Smith, Anderson, and Brown (2004) reported that perceptions of lower response to alcohol among children who are offspring of alcoholics predate personal exposure, and they identified a pathway of genetic risk in which the effect of family history is mediated through low physiological responding, which in turn predicts higher use per drinking episode, developing eventually into patterns of alcohol dependence 20 years later (Schuckit et al., 2005).

In addition, molecular genetics research has identified a number of candidate liability genes affecting liver enzyme activity (e.g., Wall, Shea, Chan, & Carr, 2001), serotonin neurotransmission (e.g., Schuckit et al., 1999), and dopamine neurotransmission in the mesolimbic reward system (e.g., Limosin et al., 2003; Lu, Lee, Ko, & Lin, 2001). These findings are consistent with prominent animal models of abuse and dependence that implicate primary reward pathways (see, e.g., Robinson & Berridge, 2003). Several of these findings are described in more detail in the following.

Maturation theory.   Maturation theory (Tarter et al., 1999) is a recent heuristic model of the development of early onset SUDs. According to this model, deviations in somatic and neurological maturation, along with stressful and adverse environments, predispose children to difficulties in regulating affect and behavior. Children with difficult temperaments in infancy are predisposed to oppositional behaviors. Family conflict then leads to conduct problems, and in turn to SUDs (Dawes et al., 2000; Tarter et al., 1999). Maturation theory incorporates an epigenetic perspective in which, from the moment of conception, genetic and environmental interactions result in developmental sequences of events leading to increased risk for SUDs. Thus, no single genetic or nongenetic factor dominates risk for addictive disorders. Instead, clusters of vulnerabilities interact with environmental experiences to culminate in one of many phenotypic patterns of addiction.

Expectancy theory.   Expectancy theory (Goldman et al., 1991; Goldman & Rather, 1993) has emerged as an alcohol/drug-specific integrative model of youth substance involvement because it considers multiple system levels of potential influence on youth substance use as well as processes through which these systems interact over time in the context of development. Expectancies of the effects of alcohol and drugs are understood to reflect both content of cognitions (e.g., immediate and distal consequences of use), memories of prior use (that influence access to perceived consequences), and motivation (e.g., neural activation patterns).

Expectancies, which are influenced by both genetic and environmental factors, including learning experiences, are proximal to youth substance use decisions and are continually modified via acquisition of updated cognitive content, and adapted physiological and neuroanatomical responses (Anderson et al., 2005). Such modifications occur with each use experience or substance-related exposure to increase the likelihood of use in future high-risk situations. Thus, vulnerabilities present in childhood (e.g., genetic predispositions, temperament) affect learning processes by (a) influencing self-selection of environments, (b) directing attention to specific rewards, and (c) magnifying the subjective experience of the reward itself. In concert, this unfolding process builds a network of alcohol and drug expectancies that dominate adolescent use decisions.

RISK FACTORS

Given widespread use of alcohol over the course of adolescence and exposure to diverse substances during this period, there is great interest in discovering factors that increase risk for early onset use and predict escalation to frequent use or involvement with other substances, high-dose drinking, and/or emergence of associated problems. A broad range of risk factors has been identified, yet few are specific to alcohol/drugs. Clusters of co-occurring risk factors appear to facilitate progression of certain use trajectories (Tarter et al., 1999). These developmental trajectories may be viewed as a succession of intermediary phenotypes that, depending on the severity of alcohol/drug consequences, may reach the threshold for an SUD diagnosis. As is obvious from the diagnostic criteria for SUDs (see Table 14.1), a diagnosis of dependence (the endpoint phenotype) is multidimensional and developmentally variable. Because the phenotype varies across development, the significance of individual risk and protective factors change as youth traverse changing demands during adolescence.

The following summarizes generic and alcohol/drug-specific risk and protective factors for children and adolescents. Risk factors range from biogenetic (e.g., liver enzyme activity) to intraindividual (e.g., personality), interpersonal (e.g., family, peers), and environmental (e.g., community, cultural). Multiple risk factors often co-occur or are nested in certain contexts (families with alcohol/drug-dependent parents). Certain risks are dynamic in that they provoke other risks that shape developmental experiences. For example, youth with genetically influenced sensation-seeking tendencies seek out risky environments, which provide exposure to substance use and reinforcement for use, as well as involvement in other problematic behaviors. This exemplifies an evocative gene–environment correlation (see Beauchaine, Hinshaw, & Gatzke-Kopp, this volume).

Temperament, which is present early in life, may directly and indirectly influence substance involvement among adolescents (Sher, 1993; Windle, 1990). Several heritable temperamental traits have been associated with increased risk for adolescent substance use and substance use problems. In particular, difficult temperament (Windle, 1990), high sensation-seeking (Zuckerman, 1994), behavioral disinhibition (McGue et al., 2001), impulsivity (Baker & Yardley, 2002), aggression (Kuo et al., 2002), behavioral undercontrol (Colder & Chassin, 1993), and negative affectivity and antisocial patterns (Zucker et al., 2000) have been associated with early onset of use and problems throughout adolescence. For example, high novelty seeking and low harm avoidance at age 11 predict subsequent alcohol abuse (Cloninger, Sigvardsson, & Bohman, 1988). These risk factors result in lower inhibitory control over behavior and have neurochemical and neurophysiological substrates that influence youth decision making in both positive social situations, where teens have initial alcohol/drug exposure, and more distressing contexts such as high-risk relapse situations (Cyders et al., in press; Smith et al., in press). Other temperamental features such as trait anxiety and anxiety sensitivity influence youth motivation for alcohol, cigarette, and marijuana use (Comeau, Stewart, & Loba, 2001). Furthermore, genetically influenced individual differences in alcohol metabolism influence motivation-related expectancies and drinking behavior (McCarthy et al., 2001).

Childhood behavior problems. Substance use disorders and concomitant mental health problems may develop independently, one may cause or exacerbate the other, or common mechanisms may underlie both. Prospective studies have shown that disruptive behavior at early ages (e.g., hyperactivity, aggression, symptoms of Conduct Disorder) predicts early onset of substance involvement and more rapid progression to substance-related problems (Dobkin et al., 1995; Johnson et al., 1995).

High rates of comorbid mental health disorders with adolescent SUDs are present in both community and clinical samples. In a large community sample of 14- to 18-year-olds, two-thirds of adolescents who met diagnostic criteria for an SUD also met lifetime criteria for at least one other Axis I disorder (Lewinsohn, Rohde, & Seeley, 1995). The Methods for the Epidemiology of Child and Adolescent Mental Disorders (MECA) study obtained similar rates of comorbidity in a stratified community sample of youth, ages 9 to 18 (Kandel et al.,1997). Among weekly drinkers, two-thirds met criteria for a *DSM-IV* psychiatric disorder. Furthermore, among those who used illicit drugs three or more times in the past year, 85% of girls and 58% of boys met criteria for a nonalcohol-, nondrug-related Axis I disorder. In their review of community based samples, Armstrong & Costello (2002) found that 60% of adolescent substance users evidenced a comorbid disorder.

Rates of psychiatric disorders are substantially higher among substance-abusing adolescents who are in treatment (Abrantes et al., 2003; Greenbaum, Foster-Johnson, & Petrila, 1996). Adolescents in inpatient substance-abuse treatment report rates of Axis I mental health disorders ranging from 68% (Novins et al., 1996) to 82% (Stowell & Estroff, 1992). Conversely, one-third to one-half of adolescents admitted to acute-care psychiatric settings meet criteria for one or more SUD (Grilo et al., 1995).

Recent reviews addressing comorbid SUDs and psychiatric disorders (Brown & Abrantes, 2005; Cornelius et al., 2003) are consistent in identifying both externalizing disorders (Conduct Disorder, Attention-Deficit / Hyperactivity Disorder, and Oppositional Defiant Disorder) and internalizing disorders (depression, anxiety) among youth with SUDs. In addition, a history of physical and / or sexual abuse is also prevalent among adolescents with SUDs. For example, in a large multisite study of adolescents in drug treatment, 59% of girls and 39% of boys reported a history of physical and / or sexual abuse (Grella & Joshi, 2003).

Alcohol and drug expectancies. Alcohol and drug outcome expectancies—the anticipated effects of using a specific substance (Brown, 1993; Goldman et al., 1991)—develop through both direct and vicarious learning experiences with substances, including peer and parental modeling and media exposure. Expectancies (e.g., more global positive effects, increased social facilitation, enhancement of cognitive and motor performance) partially mediate the relationship between family histories of substance problems and substance involvement in offspring (Goldman & Rather, 1993; Sher,

1994; Zucker et al., 2006). Furthermore, expectancies predict both the progression from initiation of use to problematic use (Brown, 1993; Smith et al., 1995), and especially poor outcomes among adolescents (Vik, Brown, & Myers, 1997).

Furthermore, higher positive expectancies and lower negative expectancies are associated with extraversion (Anderson et al., 2005; Brown & Munson, 1987) and neuroanatomical activation patterns that indicate low response inhibition. Specifically, lower activation levels in the right inferior parietal, right middle frontal, and left superior and temporal regions as measured by functional magnetic resonance imaging (fMRI) during inhibition tasks predict more positive and lower negative expectancies. These regions are implicated in sustained and selective attention, inhibitory control, and risk-taking decision making (Anderson et al., 2005). In general, positive expectancies are related to accelerated substance involvement and substance-related problems, whereas negative outcome expectancies operate as a protective factor against the initiation of use (Brown, 1993).

Age of onset.   The age at which involvement with psychoactive substances is initiated has important epidemiological and developmental implications. Clearly, not all youth with exposure to psychoactive substances develop substance use disorders. However, age of first use is a reliable risk factor for the onset of substance use problems and later disorders. The National Household Survey on Drug Abuse showed that although 11.8% of adolescents whose first use of marijuana was before age 15 developed dependence, only 2.1% of those whose first use of marijuana was after age 17 developed dependence. Early onset of alcohol and marijuana use is also predictive of binge drinking in adolescence (D'Amico et al., 2001). According to the National Longitudinal Survey of Youth (NLSY), the odds of developing alcohol dependence decrease by 9% for each year that the onset of drinking is delayed (Grant, Stinson, & Harford, 2001). Among youth receiving treatment for substance use disorders, age of alcohol initiation has been reported at 11 years with progression to weekly alcohol use by age 13, while other drug use was initiated by age 13.7 years and progressed to regular use within a year (Brown et al., 1996). Among substance-abusing adolescents with comorbid psychopathology, the age of onset of drug initiation is earlier, with first use at 12.4 years and weekly use at 13.3 years (Abrantes et al., 2003).

Family influences.   Both disruptions in family relations and functioning and parental psychopathology are precursors, correlates, and consequences of adolescent SUDs. A family history (FH) of alcohol or drug dependence is associated with a four- to nine-fold risk of SUDs in male offspring, and a two- to three-fold risk in female offspring. This transmission appears to be nonspecific to SUDs, extending to delayed or deficient behavioral, emotional, and cognitive regulation (Tarter et al., 1999). A positive FH is also associated with elevated rates of comorbid mental health disorders and SUDs during adolescence and with altered neurocognitive and neurophysiological functioning during childhood and adolescence. For example, children with FH show (a) altered neural responses—as measured using electroencephalography—in response to novel stimuli, (b) different neural activation responses to memory tests, (c) blunted inferior parietal responses to inhibition tasks, and (c) lower executive functioning on neurocognitive tests (Brown & Tapert, 2004a; Schweinsburg et al., 2004; Tapert & Brown, 2000; Tapert et al., 2004b) compared to youth without such a family history.

Parental deviance and psychopathology may also confer risk for SUDs through lack of parental involvement and/or low levels of parent-child affection (Baer & Bray, 1999; Loukas et al., 2003; Sadava, 1987; Zucker et al., 2006). Inconsistent parental discipline, lower monitoring of behavior, excessive punishment, and permissiveness are all risk factors for SUDs among adolescents (Brody & Forehand, 1993; Chilcoat & Anthony, 1996; Gilvarry, 2000; Williams & Hine, 2002). In addition, family conflict is predictive of more disruptive behavior in children, which elevates risk for SUDs during adolescence (Loukas et al., 2003; Zucker et al., 2000). The extent to which parents monitor youth activities also influences the selection of peers (Brown et al., 1992; Chassin et al., 1993) and, consequently, future risk.

Peers. Peer influences are one of the most significant and consistent risk factors for adolescent substance involvement (Bates & Labouvie, 1995; Fergusson, Horwood, & Lynskey, 1995). Higher perceptions of peer use and more friends who engage in substance use and deviant behaviors (Barnes, Farrell, & Banerjee, 1994; Epstein & Botvin, 2002; Vik, Grizzle, & Brown, 1992) create greater access to substances and lead to the adoption of beliefs and values consistent with a drug-use lifestyle (Tapert, Stewart, & Brown, 1999). For example, Bryant and Zimmerman (2002) found that African American students who perceived negative school attitudes in their peers were more likely to initiate cigarette and marijuana use. Furthermore, associations with substance-abusing and deviant peers mediate the relationship between parental alcoholism, low socioeconomic status, and family conflict on the one hand, and substance abuse during adolescence on the other (Fergusson & Horwood, 1999). In addition to access and modeling, high-risk peers increase exposure to stressful situations and model maladaptive coping efforts (Richter, Brown, & Mott, 1991), each of which alter progression of substance involvement.

Stress. Stressful life experiences increase substantially during early and middle adolescence, as does heightened reactivity to stress, especially for girls (Arnett, 1999). Stressful life events are correlated with substance use and, when occurring in the context of economic adversity, predict progression of substance involvement over the course of adolescence (e.g. Pandina & Schuele, 1983; Wills, Vaccaro, & McNamara, 1992). For example, youth from alcohol-abusing families experience more life stress and rate stressful life events as more negative than youth from families with no parental alcohol or substance abuse (Brown, 1989). Consistent with a developmental framework, the stress–substance involvement association is bidirectional, as adolescent alcohol and drug use provokes substantial stress in the form of subsequent physical, academic, legal, family, peer, and emotional problems (Tate et al., 2007).

The impact of adolescent stress and addictive behaviors is depicted in Figure 14.1. Although stress may influence substance involvement directly (Wills et al., 1992), both moderating and mediating influences (e.g., self-

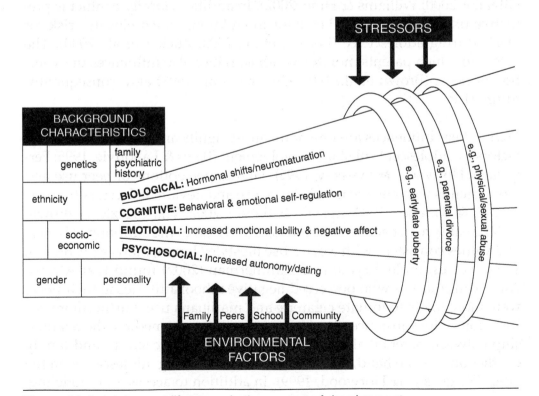

Figure 14.1. Adolescent life stress in the context of development.

regulation skills, coping repertoires, family support, peer behaviors) affect substance-use behavior over the course of adolescence (Dawes et al., 2000). Furthermore, cognitive, behavioral, and physiological responses to stress change over the course of adolescence, particularly in relation to the onset and progression of neurohormonal changes associated with puberty.

Neurocognitive functioning.   Evidence is emerging that processes underlying poor executive functions may predispose youth to SUDs. Executive functions mediate thinking, affect, motivation, and social judgment. Delayed or poorly developed executive functioning is observed among youth at greater risk of developing SUDs, including children of alcoholics (Hill et al., 1990), children with Conduct Disorder and ADHD (Kim, Kim, & Kwon, 2001; Lynam & Henry, 2001), and adolescents with attentional disorders (Pogge, Stokes, & Harvey, 1992; Sullivan & Rudnik-Levin, 2001). Executive functioning also negatively predicts age at first drink (Deckel, Bauer, & Hesselbrock, 1995), and among FH youth executive functioning predicts the number of drinks used per occasion (Deckel & Hesselbrock, 1996). Poorer executive functioning also elevates risk when combined with other risk factors, including maladaptive coping patterns (Giancola, Shoal, & Mezzich, 2001) and difficult temperament (Giancola & Parker, 2001). Finally, poor executive functioning is associated with reduced ability to appreciate abuse consequences (Blume, Marlatt, & Schmaling, 2000). It should be noted that deficiencies in executive functioning are not specific to SUDs. Rather, they increase risk for all externalizing behaviors.

Sleep difficulties.   Sleep problems measured between 3 and 5 years of age predict early onset of substance use at ages 12 to 14 (Zucker et al., 2004). Although these sleep abnormalities appear to reflect risk that is independent of other temperament and childhood behavior problems, the nature of this risk (genetic, physiologic dysregulation, etc.) has not been determined.

PROTECTIVE FACTORS

Protective factors are not simply the absence of risk characteristics. Rather, they are distinctive characteristics or circumstances associated with decreased likelihood of engaging in health-damaging behaviors, despite the presence of one or more significant risk factors (Jessor et al., 1995). Protective factors for substance use and associated problems among adolescents include certain temperamental traits, high intelligence, social support, involvement with conventional peers, religiosity, and low-risk taking (Brown et al., 2001; Gilvarry, 2000). Competence skills (e.g., decision making, self-efficacy) and psychological wellness are also protective agents against alcohol involvement across adolescence (Epstein & Botvin, 2002). A genetic deficiency in the Km aldehyde dehydrogenase (ALDH2) isoenzyme is associated with adverse reactions to alcohol. This genetic polymorphism is more prevalent in northern Asians (Chinese, Japanese, and Koreans) than in Caucasians, African Americans, and Native Americans, and results in adverse physiological response to alcohol-including flushing, tachycardia, hypotension, nausea, and vomiting (Luczak, Glatt, & Wall, 2006). These physiological responses act as a protective factor against the development of heavy drinking patterns by lowering the positive reinforcement value of alcohol. By disrupting both regular use and binge onset, ALDH2 polymorphisms and related expectancies may also act to deter progression to other drugs, although this remains to be examined.

DEVELOPMENTAL COURSE AND OUTCOMES

During adolescence, youth typically seek autonomy and independence from their parents. Across species, increases in exploration, risk-taking, and independence appear during adolescence. It is therefore not surprising that middle school and high school students explore new activities and experiment with substance use (Schinke, Botvin, & Orlandi, 1991). For example, several studies indicate that experimental alcohol and marijuana use in adolescence is not associated with more adverse outcomes or poorer adjustment in late adolescence or young adulthood (e.g., Newcomb & Bentler, 1988; Shelder & Block, 1990). By contrast, nonnormative use in the form of early onset, polysubstance involvement, and recurrent heavy drinking are associated with substance elevation in risk for SUDs (e.g., Grant & Dawson, 1997). As noted previously, the majority of youth who experiment with substances do not progress to substance dependence.

In the United States, initiation of substance use typically occurs in early to middle adolescence, with the use of gateway substances including cigarettes, alcohol, and marijuana (Kandel, Yamaguchi, & Chen, 1992), followed by other illegal drugs in late adolescence for a portion of gateway substance users. This sequence varies across different ethnic groups and among multiethnic adolescents (Chen et al., 2002). Binge drinking and more diversified substance involvement peaks during late adolescence and early adulthood (Chen & Kandel, 1995). Transitions out of the family of origin to independent and less restrictive living situations predict greater access to and acceptance of use of alcohol and other substances (Chassin & Ritter, 2001; Kypri et al., 2004). Transition to adult roles including work, marriage, and parenthood are associated with a decline in substance involvement and abuse/dependence symptoms (Chilcoat & Breslau, 1996;

Gotham, Sher, & Wood, 1997; Zucker et al., 2006). Thus, a portion of substance-abusing youth mature out of problematic use when anticipating or transitioning into adult responsibilities (Chassin & Ritter, 2001) or changing environments (Schulenberg, Maggs, & Hurrelmann, 1997).

Biological, individual, and environmental factors operate in concert to predict SUDs in adolescence. Although certain factors predict substance involvement during adolescence directly, mediators and moderators at multiple system levels influence the initiation and progression of adolescent substance involvement. Thus, a multitude of trajectories may lead to abuse and dependence among youth. Several broad developmental pathways to SUDs in adolescence have been proposed.

DEVIANCE PRONE PATHWAY

Zucker and colleagues (2000) have described a parental alcoholism / deviance proneness pathway that operates as a risk factor for behavioral difficulties among offspring. Behavior problems including Conduct Disorder elevate risk for early substance involvement and persistent deviant behaviors in adolescence. Because parental SUDs and psychopathology are associated with ineffective parenting, risk for behavioral and cognitive problems is elevated in offspring. These, in turn, result in emotional distress and affiliation with substance-using, deviant peers, and eventually the offspring's own substance involvement and problematic behaviors (Sher, 1994). A key feature of this model involves the child's reduced ability to self-regulate emotional distress and inhibit behaviors, which elevates risk for the development of substance-use problems in adolescence. Difficulties in self-regulation are reflected in higher-order executive functioning deficits that have been demonstrated in neuropsychological and neuroimaging studies of adolescent substance abusers (e.g., Anderson et al., 2005; De Bellis et al., 2000; Giancola & Parker, 2001). Although the primary emphasis among substance-abuse researchers has been on environmental mechanisms operating within high-risk families, genetic factors also contribute to heterotypic continuity among adolescents on the deviance-prone trajectory (see, e.g., Beauchaine et al., in press). Furthermore, genetic and environmental risk are likely to interact to reinforce one another in affecting SUD outcomes, reflecting a passive gene–environment correlation (see Beauchaine, Hinshaw, & Gatzke-Kopp, this volume; Rutter, 2007).

NEGATIVE AFFECTIVITY PATHWAY

A second developmental pathway to SUDs relates to deficient regulation of negative affect. This pathway appears to be associated with both exposure to environmental stressors and temperamental negative emotionality (Colder & Chassin, 1993, 1997; Cooper et al., 1995). Research suggests that substance use among those on this trajectory is also mediated by peer use and/or adolescent-onset deviant behavior, and is associated with an elevated incidence of comorbid internalizing disorders (Abrantes et al., 2003). Although the negative affectivity pathway has received support in both cross-sectional and crosscultural research (e.g., Rose et al., 1997), associations between negative affectivity and substance involvement have been modest in prospective high-risk studies (Chassin & Ritter, 2001). Only about one-fourth of those who evidence negative affectivity as children and who possess poor self-regulation and coping skills exemplify this trajectory (Colder & Chassin, 1993; Cooper et al., 1995).

ENHANCED REINFORCEMENT PATHWAY

Some youth are less sensitive to the effects of substances and consequently use substances more frequently and/or in greater quantities (Chassin & Ritter, 2001; Schuckit et al., 2004). This low response to alcohol is associated with higher positive reinforcement expectancies. The pathway appears to be genetically influenced and based on physiological response differences to the pharmacological effects of substances (e.g., Conrod, Peterson, & Pihl, 1997; Schuckit et al., 2004). Genetically influenced physiological and subjective responses appear to affect use decisions via expectancies, which develop in part as a result of individual reactions to alcohol (McCarthy et al., 2001). Thus, in addition to the physiological effects of substances, positive cognitions and outcome expectancies develop based on personal use of a substance and continued drinking. In turn, escalation to abuse occurs via the impact of both expectancies and continued use on decision making (Schuckit et al., 2004).

SEX, RACE, AND ETHNIC DIFFERENCES

SEX EFFECTS

Historically, prevalence rates of substance involvement have been higher for adolescent males than females. However, recent trends indicate few prevalence differences between male and female adolescents (Wallace et al., 2003). Increased alcohol and drug use among girls has resulted in convergence of prevalence rates during the adolescent years. Furthermore, NHSDA data demonstrate that among adolescents ages 12 to 17, rates of substance dependence do not differ between boys and girls (7.6% versus

8.0%, respectively). By contrast, both the volume of alcohol consumption and the prevalence of dependence remain higher among boys than girls, particularly in late adolescence. In addition, the impacts of alcohol vary by both sex and age. For example, early exposure to alcohol delays the onset of puberty for girls, but raises testosterone, aggression, and sexual behavior for males. In contrast, by late adolescence alcohol exposure reduces testosterone for males. There is some evidence that high-dose alcohol exposure as well as other drug exposure may more consistently produce deleterious cognitive effects for girls than boys (Brown & Tapert, 2004b).

RACE EFFECTS AND ETHNIC DIFFERENCES

Differences in prevalence rates of substance use across racial and ethnic groups have also been identified. For example, American Indian high school seniors have the greatest lifetime and 30-day prevalence rates for alcohol use (Wallace et al., 2002). In contrast, Asian American adolescents display the lowest prevalence rates of substance involvement, which may reflect both genetic protective factors and cultural influences (Luczak et al., 2006). White, Mexican American, Cuban American, and Puerto Rican high school seniors display comparable rates of substance use. African American use rates are somewhat lower than other ethnic groups. When sex and ethnic differences are examined concurrently, Native American girls display the highest rates of alcohol and drug use, whereas African American and Asian American girls demonstrate the lowest rates of substance involvement (Wallace et al., 2003).

DEVELOPMENTAL CONSIDERATIONS

BRAIN DEVELOPMENT

Until recently, the extent of human brain development during and after puberty was not fully appreciated. With the advent of structural and functional neuroimaging procedures and more cognitive science-based behavioral tests, a more complete understanding of adolescent brain development is emerging. Early adolescence is characterized by secondary and tertiary expanses of the cerebral cortex in prefrontal, parietal, and temporal regions (Giedd et al., 1999). Subcortical structures in the medial temporal lobe that are dense in sex-steroid receptors—particularly the amygdala and the hippocampus—exhibit substantial changes during this period (De Bellis & Keshavan, 2001; Sowell et al., 2004; Toga & Thompson, 2003). Throughout adolescence, there is a decrease in gray matter volume associated with dendritic pruning of synaptic connections (Giedd et al., 1999; Gogtay et al., 2004). Important functional changes also unfold as myelination proceeds from more posterior to anterior regions (Huttenlocher, 1990; Paus et al., 1999), with prefrontal regions maturing last (Huttenlocher & Dabholkar, 1997; Sowell et al., 1999). The higher-order association cortices undergo similar changes subsequent to primary sensory motor cortices. As a result of both synaptic refinement and mylenation, white matter volume increases, as does the density, organization, and integrity of white matter pathways (Barnea-Goraly et al., 2005; Giedd et al., 1999; Jernigan & Gamst, 2005). These structural and functional changes that unfold during adolescence contribute to maturing neurocognitive processes and increased regional specificity of processing during cognitive and behavior tasks. Some of these neuroanatomical changes appear to be both hormone and experience dependent.

Across species, brain responses during adolescence reflect an increased salience of and attention to social and affective cues (Nelson et al., 2002; Steinberg, 2004) that are matched to increases in social affiliative behaviors. Similarly, there are profound changes in circadian rhythm resulting in delayed sleepiness and later waking times for youth. During the academic year, late sleep onset but early rise for school may result in a cumulative sleep deficit and weekend catch-up efforts at recovery (Herman, 2005; Wolfson & Carskadon, 1998). Daytime sleepiness is associated with poorer academic performance, negative mood states, accidents, and use of addictive substances (Roehrs et al., 1994; Wolfson & Carskadon, 1998).

DEVELOPMENT OF EMOTIONAL AND BEHAVIORAL SELF-REGULATION

Early and middle adolescence is marked by emerging self-regulation and inhibitory control, which continue to develop in concert with neuromaturation into the mid-20s. *Self-regulation* is defined as the ability to control and plan behavior, and includes the ability to resist impulses to engage in behaviors with negative consequences (e.g., alcohol and substance use). Self-regulation increases over childhood and early adolescence, and appears stable during late adolescence (Raffaelli, Crockett, & Shen, 2005). Because late adolescent and adult responsibilities often include delayed reinforcement, impairments in control over behavioral impulses can have long-term prognostic significance for diverse aspects of functioning including SUDs. In fact, disinhibited behavior predicts SUD risk in late adolescence and early adulthood (Elkins, McGue, & Iacono, 2007; Windle et al., in press). As noted previously, neurobehavioral measures of disinhibition have also been associated with risk for both adolescent AUDs and SUDs. Self-regulating behavioral impulses is increasingly important for teens as many new social and environmental contexts involve access to alcohol/drugs, exposure to substance-using models (Bachanas et al., 2002), and social reinforcement for substance involvement.

Substantial increases in risk-taking and exploratory behavior are typically exhibited during adolescence. For many adolescents, this includes healthy activities such as sports, music, and the arts, but may also include high-risk behaviors such as unprotected sex, hazardous driving, or heavy drinking. In part, the greater risk-taking of youth is a consequence of attention to and cognitive processing of the social and emotional cues and of deficits in risk appraisal (Myers & Brown, 1994; Reyna & Farley, 2006). However, personal control over risk taking also reflects maturation of a cognitive-control network involved in planning and self-regulation (lateral prefrontal and parietal cortices), and a processing of social and emotional stimuli (limbic system including the amygdala, nucleus accumbens, and medial prefrontal cortex), which mature at different rates over the course of adolescence (Steinberg, 2004). Many of these same structures are implicated in prominent neural models of substance use (e.g., Robinson & Berridge, 2003), and with both elevated risk taking in social contexts and states of emotional arousal.

CHANGING COGNITIVE ABILITIES

Cognitive differences between adolescents and adults are often subtle and reflect executive functioning differences in planning and anticipation, as well as inhibition of prepotent behaviors, particularly in social or emotional contexts. As outlined previously, it is well established that executive functioning deficits are a risk factor for early substance-use onset. Emerging evidence also suggests that adolescent substance involvement may exacerbate these preexisting deficiencies. Metacognition, which refers to strategic self-monitoring aspects of executive functioning (Jarman, Vavrik, & Walton, 1995), develops throughout adolescence in conjunction with inhibitory control (Christ et al., 2001). Girls appear to develop several executive function and self-regulation skills earlier than boys (Raffaelli et al., 2005). Verbal processing develops by mid-adolescence in females, whereas boys may not achieve mature verbal processing until late adolescence (Levin et al., 1991). In contrast, boys develop skills in certain nonverbal tasks more rapidly than girls (Davies & Rose, 1999). These and other sex differences may underlie the different patterns of substance use for boys and girls described previously.

There is an increasing appreciation for the development and role of working memory during adolescence and alcohol-/substance-use related deficits in working memory for youth in this age range. Working memory, or the ability to maintain and manipulate information, is fundamental to critical tasks such as language comprehension and abstract reasoning (Baddeley, 1992, 2000; Gathercole, 1999). Verbal and spatial working memory abilities improve throughout childhood and adolescence (Gathercole et al., 2004; Luna et al., 2004), and spatial working memory continues to develop throughout adolescence (Luna et al., 2004). Older adolescents are more accurate and faster than younger adolescents on spatial working memory tasks (Kwon, Reiss, & Menon, 2002; Zald & Iacono, 1998). Although older youth activate similar brain regions as adults while performing working memory tasks (Casey et al., 1995; Thomas et al., 1999), they exhibit more frontal and parietal brain activation compared to younger adolescents (Klingberg, Forssberg, & Westerberg, 2002; Kwon et al., 2002; Schweinsburg, Nagel, & Tapert, 2005), and more widespread activation than adults (Klingberg et al., 2002; Kwon et al., 2002). Working memory differences have been demonstrated between youth with extensive alcohol and drug exposure and comparable community controls (Brown et al., 2000).

Decision-making skills are also critical to successful navigation of the shifting demands of adolescence including alcohol and substance use. Decision making involves multiple cognitive abilities that develop at different rates, including logical reasoning (Mueller, Overton, & Reene, 2001), management of reasoning biases (Klaczynski, 2000), and judgments of probable success (Klaczynski, 2001). Social judgment (Cauffman & Steinberg, 2000) and social problem solving (Hains & Ryan, 1983) improve from early adolescence to middle adolescence (Ormond et al., 1991). In general, adolescents have a larger gap between procedural knowledge (e.g., memory skills, goal-oriented planning) and factual knowledge than do adults, which may disadvantage their decision making, particularly for high-risk behaviors such as alcohol and drug use (Brown et al., in press). Practice in applying executive strategies can improve decision making and is important for adolescent alcohol/drug use because these decisions involve risk taking, social context selection, and the assessment of consequences. In this regard, although most adolescents perform similar to adults on standard judgment tasks, adolescents at risk for SUDs may have decision-making impairments in certain contexts (e.g., high arousal, social pressure), demonstrating greater risk taking when faced with real-life decision-making situations (Ernst et al., 2003).

Developmentally Dependent Effects

Evidence is mounting that alcohol and other addictive substances affect adolescents differently than they affect adults (Brown et al., in press; Windle et al., in press). Although few studies assessing biological sensitivity of children and adolescents to alcohol and drugs have been conducted, animal models have consistently shown marked differences in responses to and impacts of alcohol on younger animals compared to adults. First, adolescent animals appear to be less sensitive to the adverse effects of alcohol than adults (Casey et al., 1995; Zald & Iacono, 1998). Alcohol is less sedating, produces less motor impairment, less social and affective impairment, and fewer postintoxication (hangover) effects on adolescent animals than adult animals. Although no longer allowed, an early study in which high doses of alcohol were administered to youth (males ages 8 to 15 years) indicated little behavioral change in children relative to what would be expected for the same dose (blood alcohol concentration) among adults (Behar et al., 1983). Of note, reduced sensitivity to the effects of alcohol and other substances has been linked to subsequent increases in drinks per occasion and to long-term elevations in risk for the development of alcohol dependence among humans (Schuckit et al., 2004). Second, relative to adult animals, experimental studies with low doses of alcohol indicate that adolescent exposure results in greater social facilitation (Varlinskaya & Spear, 2002). Because most early alcohol and drug involvement is strongly influenced by social factors, these results suggest potential heightened reward value for alcohol and other substances during this developmental period. Third, there is evidence of greater long-term behavioral and brain impairment among adolescents compared with adults exposed to alcohol. In both animal and human studies, clear age-dependent effects are identified for semantic and figural memory (Acheson, Stein, & Swartzwelder, 1998; White & Swartzwelder, 2005). Additionally, animal studies demonstrate that early adolescent alcohol exposure is associated with increased tolerance, craving, and subsequent motor-impairing effects that can persist into adulthood. The greatest damage identified postmortem in animal studies is in frontal brain regions that control executive planning and reasoning processes (Crews et al., 2000) and that continue to mature after adolescence in humans.

In humans, adolescent drinking and drug use have been associated with physical problems (loss of consciousness), fragmentary to full black-out periods (memory loss), interpersonal conflict, reduced school involvement and success, and elevated rates of risky sexual behaviors, accidents, and injuries (see Brown & Tapert, 2004a; Brown et al., in press; Windle et al., in press). Of greatest concern are suicidal ideation, attempts, and completions following alcohol/drug exposure, and increased risk associated with ideation during periods of alcohol and/or drug intoxication (e.g., Hingson et al., 2005; Windle, Miller-Tutzauer, & Domenico, 1992).

DOUBLE DEVELOPMENTAL SYNTHESIS

Child and adolescent development involves substantial changes across systems ranging from biological, cognitive, social-emotional, and behavioral, varying with genetics, community, and cultural factors. Changes in any of these systems may influence a variety of aspects of early alcohol and other drug involvement (e.g., onset, escalation, problems). As should be clear from this review, exposure to alcohol and other drugs may directly or indirectly influence all important developmental system levels of functioning and may delay, promote, or disadvantage important aspects of normal development. These bidirectional, and in some cases synergistic, effects may produce short-term consequences that quickly resolve (hangovers). In other cases, such effects may alter developmental trajectories in ways that impact long-term adult functioning (e.g., SUDs, frontal lobe development).

Thus, understanding youth development and the development of alcohol and drug problems in adolescents requires both an appreciation for the processes and tasks of normative adolescent development, and knowledge of the impact and mechanisms of progression along the continuum of alcohol and drug dependence. Regardless of which etiological model of SUDs applies, core developmental processes and system-specific stages must be considered to account for the complex symptom matrix that youth with SUDs present. The joint consideration of both mechanisms of development and processes of adolescent addiction progression should facilitate better prediction of risk, optimal research paradigms, and creation of substance interventions for this prevalent adolescent disorder.

FUTURE DIRECTIONS FOR PREVENTION

Alcohol- and drug-prevention programs for youth are varied and extensive. These programs range from education-based school approaches (e.g., Moskowitz, 1983), to risk-reduction and skill-development programs (Botvin, 2000; Gorman, 1996), to community-wide applications (Perry et al., 1996). Among these, overall effectiveness is mixed, with some programs demonstrating modest improvements (e.g., Botvin's Life Skills Training), while others appear to actually accelerate onset and use rates in high-risk populations (e.g., DARE). Those with the largest, positive effect sizes typically operate across multiple reinforcement systems (e.g., individual, school, family, community/public policy; see Perry et al., 1996). Primary and early intervention effects involving peer leaders, motivational enhancement, improved accuracy of perceived social norms, challenges to outcome expectancies, and social practice appear most promising.

There is growing appreciation for considering development in the timing (e.g., primary prevention prior to typical onset of use), content (e.g., feature common social contextual features of initial and early use episodes), and process (e.g. consideration of cognitive development) of interventions. The application of neuroscience findings to interventions is a relatively new but promising endeavor.

Because the initiation or refusal to use alcohol and other drugs typically involves a social decision, prevention programs may target components of the decision-making process (Milgram, 1996), including accuracy of information available for consideration (Moskowitz, 1983), consequences of use (Snow et al., 1992), perceived social pressures to use (Ellickson, Bell, & McGuigan, 1993), generation of behavior alternatives (Snow et al., 1992), and problem-solving skills practice (Brown et al., 2001). Although prevention research is in its infancy regarding identification of specific cognitive functions that support high-level processes, such as decision making, executive functions may be a particularly fruitful focus. By creating concrete interventions to facilitate goal generation, negotiation of social contexts, increased variability in responses, and regulation of response initiation and inhibition, adolescents should have more intrapersonal resources for dealing with the risks they will face.

REFERENCES

Aarons, G. A., Brown, S. A., Hough, R. L., Garland, A. F., & Wood, P. A. (2001). Prevalence of adolescent substance use disorders across five sectors of care. *Journal of the American Academy of Child and Adolescent Psychiatry, 40*, 419–426.

Abrantes, A. M., Brown, S. A., & Tomlinson, K. L. (2003). Psychiatric comorbidity among inpatient substance abusing adolescents. *Journal of Child and Adolescent Substance Abuse, 13*, 83–101.

Acheson, S. K., Stein, R. M., & Swartzwelder, H. S. (1998). Impairment of semantic and figural memory by acute ethanol: Age-dependent effects. *Alcoholism: Clinical and Experimental Research, 22*, 1437–1442.

Ajzen, I. (1988). *Attitudes, personality, and behavior:* Homewood, IL: Dorsey Press.

Ajzen, I. (2001). Nature and operation of attitudes. *Annual Review Psychology, 52*, 27–58.

Ajzen, I., & Fishbein, M. (1980). *Understanding attitudes and predicting social behavior:* Englewood Cliffs, NJ: Prentice Hall.

Akers, R. L. (1977). *Deviant behavior: A social learning approach, 2nd ed.* Belmont, CA: Wadsworth.

American Psychiatric Association. (2000). *Diagnostic and Statistical Manual of Mental Disorders IV* (4th ed.). Washington, DC: American Psychiatric Association.

Anderson, K. G., Schweinsburg, A., Paulus, M. P., Brown, S. A., & Tapert, S. F.

(2005). Examining personality and alcohol expectancies using fMRI with adolescents. *Journal of Studies on Alcohol, 66*, 323–332.

Angold, A., Costello, E. J., Farmer, E., Burns, B. J., & Erkanli, A. (1999). Impaired but undiagnosed. *Journal of the American Academy of Child and Adolescent Psychiatry, 38*, 129–137.

Armstrong, T. D., & Costello, E. J. (2002). Community studies on adolescent substance use, abuse, or dependence and psychiatric comorbidity. *Journal of Consulting and Clinical Psychology, 70*, 1224–1239.

Arnett, J. J. (1999). Adolescent storm and stress, reconsidered. *American Psychologist, 54*, 317–326.

Bachanas, P. J., Morris, M. K., Lewis-Gess, J. K., Sarett-Cuasay, E. J., Flores, A. L., & Sirl, K. S., et al. (2002). Psychological adjustment, substance use, HIV knowledge, and risky sexual behavior in at-risk minority females: Developmental differences during adolescence. *Journal of Pediatric Psychology, 27*, 373–384.

Baddeley, A. (1992). Working memory. *Science, 255*, 556–559.

Baddeley, A. (2000). The episodic buffer: a new component of working memory? *Trends in Cognitive Science, 4*, 417–423.

Baer, P. E., & Bray, J. H. (1999). Adolescent individuation and alcohol use. *Journal of Studies on Alcohol Supplement, 13*, 52–62.

Baker, J. R., & Yardley, J. K. (2002). Moderating effect of gender on the relationship between sensation seeking-impulsivity and substance use in adolescents. *Journal of Child and Adolescent Substance Abuse, 12*, 27–43.

Bandura, A. (1986). *Social foundations of thought and action: A social cognitive theory.* Englewood Cliffs, NJ: Prentice Hall.

Barnea-Goraly, N., Menon, V., Eckert, M., Tamm, L., Bammer, R., Karchemskiy, A., et al. (2005). White matter development during childhood and adolescence: a cross-sectional diffusion tensor imaging study. *Cerebral Cortex, 15*, 1848–1854.

Barnes, G. M., Farrell, M. P., & Banerjee, S. (1994). Family influence on alcohol abuse and other problem behaviors among black and white adolescents in a general population sample. *Journal of Research on Adolescence, 4*, 183–201.

Bates, M. E., & Labouvie, E. W. (1995). Personality-environment constellation and alcohol use: A process-oriented study of intraindividual change during adolescence. *Psychology of Addictive Behaviors, 9*, 23–35.

Behar, D., Berg, C. J., Rapoport, J. L., Nelson, W., Linnoila, M., Cohen, M., & Al, E. (1983). Behavioral and psychological effects of ethanol in high-risk and control children: A pilot study. *Alcoholism: Clinical and Experimental Research, 7*(4), 404–410.

Beauchaine, T. P., Neuhaus, E., Brenner, S. L., & Gatzke-Kopp, L. (in press). Ten good reasons to consider biological variables in prevention and intervention research. *Development and Psychopathology.*

Blume, A. W., Marlatt, G. A., & Schmaling, K. B. (2000). Executive cognitive function and heavy drinking behavior among college students. *Psychology of Addictive Behaviors, 14*, 299–302.

Botvin, G. J. (2000). Preventing drug abuse in schools: Social and competence enhancement approaches targeting individual-level etiologic factors. *Addictive Behaviors, 25*, 887–897.

Brody, G. H., & Forehand, R. (1993). Prospective associations among family form, family process, and adolescents' alcohol and drug use. *Behaviour Research, and Therapy, 31,* 587–593.

Brown, S. A. (1989). Life events of adolescents in relation to personal and parental substance abuse. *American Journal of Psychiatry, 146,* 484–489.

Brown, S. A. (1993). Drug effect expectancies and addictive behavior change. *Experimental and Clinical Psychopharmacology, 1,* 55–67.

Brown, S. A., Aarons, G. A., & Abrantes, A. M. (2001). Adolescent alcohol and drug abuse. In C. E. Walker & M. C. Roberts (Eds.), *Handbook of clinical child psychology* (3rd ed., pp. 757–775). New York: Wiley.

Brown, S. A., & Abrantes, A. M. (2005). Substance use disorders. In D. A. Wolfe & E. J. Mash (Eds.), *Behavioral and emotional disorders in adolescents* (pp. 226–258). New York: Guilford.

Brown, S. A., Gleghorn, A., Schuckit, M. A., Myers, M. G., & Mott, M. A. (1996). Conduct disorder among adolescent alcohol and drug abusers. *Journal of Studies on Alcohol, 57,* 314–324.

Brown, S. A., McGue, M. K., Maggs, J., Schulenberg, J. E., Hingson, R., Swartzwelder, H. S., et al. (in press). A developmental perspective on alcohol and youth ages 16–20. *Pediatrics.*

Brown, S. A., Mott, M. A., & Stewart, M. A. (1992). Adolescent alcohol and drug abuse. In C. E. Walker & M. C. Roberts (Eds.), *Handbook of clinical child psychology* (2nd ed., pp. 677–693). New York: Wiley.

Brown, S. A., & Munson, E. (1987). Extroversion, anxiety and the perceived effects of alcohol. *Journal of Studies on Alcohol, 48,* 272–276.

Brown, S. A., Myers, M., Mott, M. A., & Vik, P. W. (1994). Correlates of success following treatment for adolescent substance abuse. *Applied and Preventive Psychology, 3,* 61–73.

Brown, S. A., & Tapert, S. F. (2004a). Adolescence and the trajectory of alcohol use: Basic to clinical studies. In R. E. Dahl & L. P. Spear (Eds.), Adolescent brain development: Vulnerabilities and opportunities. *Annals of the New York Academy of Sciences, 1021,* 234–244.

Brown, S. A., & Tapert, S. F. (2004b). Health consequences of adolescent alcohol involvement. In R. J. Bonnie & M. E. O'Connell (Eds.), *Reducing underage drinking: A collective responsibility* (pp. 383–401). Washington, DC: National Academy Press.

Brown, S. A., Tapert, S. F., Granholm, E., & Delis, D. C. (2000). Neurocognitive functioning of adolescents: Effects of protracted alcohol use. *Alcohol Clinical and Experimental Research, 24,* 164–171.

Bryant, A. L., & Zimmerman, M. A. (2002). Examining the effects of academic beliefs and behaviors on changes in substance use among urban adolescents. *Journal of Educational Psychology, 94,* 621–637.

Bukstein, O. G. (1995). *Adolescent substance abuse: Assessment, prevention, and treatment.* Hoboken, NJ: Wiley.

Cadoret, R. J., Yates, W. R., Troughton, E., Woodworth, G., & Stewart, M. A. (1995). Adoption study demonstrating two genetic pathways to drug abuse. *Archives of General Psychiatry, 52,* 42–52.

Casey, B. J., Cohen, J. D., Jezzard, P., Turner, R., Noll, D. C., & Trainor, R. J., et al. (1995). Activation of prefrontal cortex in children during a nonspatial working-memory task with fMRI. *Neuroimage, 2*, 221–229.

Cauffman, E., & Steinberg, L. (2000). (Im)maturity of judgment in adolescence: Why adolescents may be less culpable than adults. *Behavioral Sciences and the Law, 18*, 741–760.

Chassin, L., Pillow, D. R., Curran, P. J., Molina, B. S., & Barrera, M. (1993). Relation of parental alcoholism to early adolescent substance use: A test of three mediating mechanisms. *Journal of Abnormal Psychology, 102*, 3–19.

Chassin, L., Pitts, S. C., & Prost, J. (2002). Binge drinking trajectories from adolescence to emerging adulthood in a high-risk sample: predictors and substance abuse outcomes. *Journal of Consulting and Clinical Psychology, 70*, 67–78.

Chassin, L., & Ritter, J. (2001). Vulnerability to substance use disorders in childhood and adolescence. In R. E. Ingram & J. M. Price (Eds.), *Vulnerability to psychopathology* (pp. 107–134). New York: Guilford.

Chatlos, J. C. (1997). Substance use and abuse and the impact on academic difficulties. *Journal of the American Academy of Child and Adolescent Psychiatry, 6*, 545–568.

Chen, K., & Kandel, D. B. (1995). The natural history of drug use from adolescence to the mid-thirties in a general population sample. *American Journal of Public Health, 85*, 41–47.

Chen, X., Unger, J. B., Palmer, P., Weiner, M. D., Johnson, C. A., Wong, M. A., et al. (2002). Prior cigarette smoking initiation predicting current alcohol use: Evidence for a gateway drug effect among California adolescents from eleven ethnic groups. *Addictive Behaviors, 27*, 799–817.

Chilcoat, H., & Breslau, N. (1996). Alcohol disorders in young adulthood: Effects of transitions into adult roles. *Journal of Health and Social Behavior, 37*, 339–349.

Chilcoat, H. D., & Anthony, J. C. (1996). Impact of parent monitoring on initiation of drug use through late childhood. *Journal of the American Academy of Child and Adolescent Psychiatry, 35*, 91–100.

Christ, S. E., White, D. A., Mandernach, T., & Keys, B. A. (2001). Inhibitory control across the life span. *Developmental Neuropsychology, 20*, 653–669.

Cloninger, C. R., Sigvardsson, S., & Bohman, M. (1988). Childhood personality predicts alcohol abuse in young adults *Alcoholism: Clinical and Experimental Research, 12*, 494–505.

Colder, C., & Chassin, L. (1993). The stress and negative affect model of adolescent alcohol use and the moderating effects of behavioral under control. *Journal of Studies on Alcohol, 54*, 326–333.

Colder, C., & Chassin, L. (1997). Affectivity and impulsivity: Temperamental risk for adolescent alcohol involvement. *Psychology of Addictive Behaviors, 11*, 83–87.

Comeau, N., Stewart, S. H., & Loba, P. (2001). The relations of trait anxiety, anxiety sensitivity and sensation seeking to adolescents' motivations for alcohol, cigarette, and marijuana use. *Addictive Behaviors, 26*, 803–825.

Connors, G. J. (1995). Screening for alcohol problems. In J. P. Allen & M. Columbus (Eds.), *Assessing alcohol problems* (pp. 17–29). Bethesda, MD: National Institute of Health.

Conrod, P. J., Peterson, J. B., & Pihl, R. O. (1997). Disinhibited personality and sensitivity to alcohol reinforcement: Independent correlates of drinking behavior in sons of alcoholics. *Alcoholism Clinical and Experimental Research, 21,* 1320–1332.

Cooper, M. L., Frone, M. R., Russell, M., & Mudar, P. (1995). Drinking to regulate positive and negative emotions: A motivational model of alcohol use. *Journal of Personality and Social Psychology, 69,* 990–1005.

Cornelius, J. R., Salloum, I. M., Bukstein, O. B., & Clark, D. B. (2003). *Psychiatric comorbidity: Implications for treatment and clinical research.* In J. C. Soares & S. Gershon (Eds.), *Handbook of medical psychiatry* (pp. 553–561). New York: Marcel Dekker.

Crews, F. T., Braun, C. J., Hoplight, B., Switzer, R. C., III, & Knapp, D. J. (2000). Binge ethanol consumption causes differential brain damage in young adolescent rats compared with adult rats. *Alcoholism Clinical and Experimental Research, 24,* 1712–1723.

Currie, C., Hurrelmann, K., Settertobulte, W., Smith, R., & Todd, J., (Eds.) (2000). *Health behavior in school-aged children: A WHO cross-national study (HBSC) international report.* Copenhagen, Denmark: World Health Organization. Retrieved August 24, 2006 from http://www.hbsc.org/downloads/Int_Report_00.pdf.

Cyders, M. A., Smith, G. T., Spillane, N. S., Fischer, S., Annus, A. M., & Peterson, C. (in press). Integration of impulsivity and positive mood to predict risky behavior: Development and validation of a measure of positive urgency. *Psychological Assessment.*

D'Amico, E. J., Metrik, J., McCarthy, D. M., Appelbaum, M., Frissell, K. C., & Brown, S. A. (2001). Progression into and out of binge drinking among high school students. *Psychology of Addictive Behaviors, 15,* 341–349.

Dakof, G. A. (2000). Understanding gender differences in adolescent drug abuse: Issues of comorbidity and family functioning. *Journal of Psychoactive Drugs, 32,* 25–32.

Davies, P. L., & Rose, J. D. (1999). Assessment of cognitive development in adolescents by means of neuropsychological tasks. *Developmental Neuropsychology 15,* 227–248.

Dawes, M. A., Antelman, S. M., Vanyukov, M. M., Giancola, P., Tarter, R. E., Susman, E. J., et al. (2000). Developmental sources of variation in liability to adolescent substance use disorders. *Drug and Alcohol Dependence, 61,* 3–14.

De Bellis, M. D., Clark, D. B., Beers, S. R., Soloff, P. H., Boring, A. M., Hall, J., et al. (2000). Hippocampal volume in adolescent-onset alcohol use disorders. *American Journal Psychiatry, 157,* 737–744.

De Bellis, M. D., & Keshavan, M. S. (2001). Sex differences in brain maturation during childhood and adolescence. *Cerebral Cortex, 11,* 552–557.

Deckel, A. W., Bauer, L., & Hesselbrock, V. (1995). Anterior brain dysfunctioning as a risk factor in alcoholic behaviors. *Addiction, 90,* 1323–1334.

Deckel, A. W., & Hesselbrock, V. (1996). Behavioral and cognitive measurements predict scores on the MAST: a 3-year prospective study. *Alcoholism: Clinical Experimental Research, 20,* 1173–1178.

Dobkin, P. L., Tremblay, R. E., Masse, L. C., & Vitaro, F. (1995). Individual and peer characteristics in predicting boys' early onset of substance abuse: A seven-year longitudinal study. *Child Development, 66,* 1198–1214.

Donovan, J. E. (in press). Tween to Teen Project. Really underage drinkers: The epidemiology of children's alcohol use in the United States. *Prevention Science*.

Elkins, I. J., McGue, M., & Iacono, W. G. (2007). A prospective study of the effects of ADHD, conduct disorder, and gender on adolescent substance use and abuse: Dimensional and categorical approaches. *Archives of General Psychiatry*.

Ellickson, P. L., Bell, R. M., & McGuigan, K. (1993). Preventing adolescent drug use: Long-term results of a junior high program. *American Journal of Public Health, 83*, 856–861.

Epstein, J. A., & Botvin, G. J. (2002). The moderating role of risk-taking tendency and refusal assertiveness on social influences in alcohol use among inner-city adolescents. *Journal of Studies on Alcohol, 63*, 456–459.

Ernst, M., Grant, S. J., London, E. D., Contoreggi, C. S., Kimes, A. S., & Spurgeon, L. (2003). Decision making in adolescents with behavior disorders and adults with substance abuse. *American Journal of Psychiatry, 160*, 33–40.

Fergusson, D., Horwood, J., & Lynskey, M. (1995). The prevalence and risk factors associated with abusive or hazardous alcohol consumption in 16-year-olds. *Addiction, 90*, 935–946.

Fergusson, D. M., & Horwood, L. J. (1999). Prospective childhood predictors of deviant peer affiliations in adolescence. *Journal of Child Psychology and Psychiatry, 40*, 581–592.

Gathercole, S. (1999). Cognitive approaches to the development of short-term memory. *Trends in Cognitive Sciences, 3*, 410–419.

Gathercole, S. E., Pickering, S. J., Ambridge, B., & Wearing, H. (2004). The structure of working memory from 4 to 15 years of age. *Developmental Psychology, 40*, 177–190.

Giancola, P. R., & Parker, A. M. (2001). A six-year prospective study of pathways toward drug use in adolescent boys with and without a family history of a substance use disorder. *Journal of Studies on Alcohol, 62*, 166–178.

Giancola, P. R., Shoal, G. D., & Mezzich, A. C. (2001). Constructive thinking, executive functioning, antisocial behavior, and drug use involvement in adolescent females with a substance use disorder. *Experimental Clinical Psychopharmacology, 9*, 215–227.

Giedd, J. N., Blumenthal, J., Jeffries, N. O., Castellanos, F. X., Liu, H., Zijdenbos, A., et al. (1999). Brain development during childhood and adolescence: a longitudinal MRI study. *Natural Neuroscience, 2*, 861–863.

Gilvarry, E. (2000). Substance abuse in young people. *Journal of Child Psychology and Psychiatry, 41*, 55–80.

Gogtay, N., Giedd, J. N., Lusk, L., Hayashi, K. M., Greenstein, D., Vaituzis, A. C., et al. (2004). Dynamic mapping of human cortical development during childhood through early adulthood. *Proceedings of the National Academy of Sciences of the United States of America, 101*, 8174–8179.

Goldman, M. S., Brown, S. A., Christiansen, B. A., & Smith, G. T. (1991). Alcoholism and memory broadening the scope of alcohol-expectancy research. *Psychological Bulletin, 110*, 137–146.

Goldman, M. S., & Rather, B. C. (1993). *Substance use disorders: Cognitive models and architecture*. In P.C. Kendall & K. Dobson (Eds.), *Psychopathology and cognition* (pp. 245–292). New York: Academic Press.

Gorman, D. (1996). Do school-based social skills training programs prevent alcohol use among young people? *Addiction Research, 4,* 191–210.

Gotham, H., Sher, K., & Wood, P. (1997). Predicting stability and change in frequency of intoxication from the college years to beyond: Individual difference and role transition variables. *Journal of Abnormal Psychology, 106,* 619–629.

Grant, B. F., & Dawson, D. A. (1997). Age at onset of alcohol use and its association with *DSM-IV* alcohol abuse and dependence: Results from the National Longitudinal Alcohol Epidemiologic Survey. *Journal of Substance Abuse, 9,* 103–110.

Grant, B. F., Stinson, F. S., & Harford, T. C. (2001). Age of onset of alcohol use and *DSM-IV* alcohol abuse and dependence: A 12-year follow-up. *Journal of Substance Abuse, 13,* 493–504.

Greenbaum, P. E., Foster-Johnson, L., & Petrila, A. (1996). Co-occurring addictive and mental disorders among adolescents: Prevalence research and future directions. *American Journal of Orthopsychiatry, 66,* 52–60.

Grella, C. E., & Joshi, V. (2003). Treatment processes and outcomes among adolescents with a history of abuse who are in drug treatment. *Child Maltreatment: Journal of the American Professional Society on the Abuse of Children, 8,* 7–18.

Grilo, C. M., Becker, D. F., Walker, M. L., Levy, K. N., Edell, W. S., & McGlashan, T. H. (1995). Psychiatric comorbidity in adolescent inpatients with substance use disorder. *Journal of the American Academy of Child and Adolescent Psychiatry, 34,* 1085–1091.

Hains, A. A., & Ryan, E. B. (1983). The development of social cognitive-processes among juvenile delinquents and nondelinquent peers. *Child Development, 54,* 1536–1544.

Harrison, P. A., Fulkerson, J. A., & Beebe, T. J. (1998). *DSM-IV* substance use disorder criteria for adolescents: A critical examination based on statewide school survey. *American Journal of Psychiatry, 155,* 486–492.

Herman, J. (2005). Circadian rhythm disorders: Diagnosis and treatment. In S. Sheldon, R. Ferber, & M. Kryger (Eds.), *Principles and practice of pediatric sleep medicine* (pp. 101–111). Philadelphia: Elsevier/Saunders.

Hill, S. Y., Steinhauer, S., Park, J., & Zubin, J. (1990). Event-related potential characteristics in children of alcoholics from high density families. *Alcoholism: Clinical and Experimental Research, 14,* 6–16.

Hingson, R., Heeren, T., Winter, M., & Wechsler, H. (2005). Magnitude of alcohol-related mortality and morbidity among U.S. college students ages 18–24: Changes from 1998 to 2001. *Annual Review of Public Health, 26,* 259–279.

Huba, G. J., Wingard, J. A., & Bentler, P. M. (1980). Framework for an interactive theory of drug use. *NIDA Research Monograph, 30,* 95–101.

Huttenlocher, P. R. (1990). Morphometric study of human cerebral-cortex development. *Neuropsychologia, 28,* 517–527.

Huttenlocher, P. R., & Dabholkar, A. S. (1997). Regional differences in synaptogenesis in human cerebral cortex. *Journal of Comparative Neurology, 387,* 167–178.

Jarman, R. F., Vavrik, J., & Walton, P. D. (1995). Metacognitive and frontal lobe processes: At the interface of cognitive psychology and neuropsychology. *Genetic, Social, and General Psychology Monographs, 121,* 153–210.

Jernigan, T. L., & Gamst, A. C. (2005). Changes in volume with age-consistency and interpretation of observed effects. *Neurobiology of Aging, 26,* 1271–1274.

Jessor, R., & Jessor, S. L. (1977). *Problem behavior and psychosocial development:* New York: Academic Press.

Jessor, R., Van Den Bos, J., Vanderryn, J., Costa, F. M., & Turbin, M. (1995). Protective factors in adolescent problem behavior: Moderator effects and developmental change. *Developmental Psychology, 31,* 923–933.

Johnson, E. O., Arria, A. M., Borges, G., Ialongo, N., & Anthony, J. C. (1995). The growth of conduct problem behaviors from middle childhood to early adolescence: Sex differences and the suspected influence of early alcohol use. *Journal of Studies on Alcohol, 56,* 661–671.

Johnston, L. D., O'Malley, P. M., Bachman, J. G., & Schulenberg, J. E. (2006). *Monitoring the Future national survey results on drug use, 1975–2005. Vol. I: Secondary school students (NIH Publication No. 06-5883).* Bethesda, MD: National Institute on Drug Abuse.

Kaminer, Y. (1994). *Adolescent substance abuse: A comprehensive guide to theory and practice.* New York: Plenum.

Kandel, D. B., Johnson, J. G., Bird, H. R., Canino, G., Goodman, S. H., Lahey, B. B., et al. (1997). Psychiatric disorders associated with substance use among children and adolescents: Findings from the Methods for the Epidemiology of Child and Adolescent Mental Disorders (MECA) Study. *Journal of Abnormal Child Psychology, 25,* 121–132.

Kandel, D. B., Yamaguchi, K., & Chen, K. (1992). Stages of progression in drug involvement from adolescence to adulthood: Further evidence for the gateway theory. *Journal of Studies on Alcohol, 53,* 447–457.

Kendler, K. S., Prescott, C. A., Myers, J., & Neale, M. C. (2003). The structure of genetic and environmental risk factors for common psychiatric and substance use disorders in men and women. *Archives of General Psychiatry, 60,* 929–937.

Kim, M. S., Kim, J. J., & Kwon, J. S. (2001). Frontal P300 decrement and executive dysfunction in adolescents with conduct problems. *Child Psychiatry and Human Development, 32,* 93–106.

Klaczynski, P. A. (2000). Motivated scientific reasoning biases, epistemological beliefs, and theory polarization: A two-process approach to adolescent cognition. *Child Development, 71,* 1347–1366.

Klaczynski, P. A. (2001). Analytic and heuristic processing influences on adolescent reasoning and decision-making. *Child Development, 72,* 844–861.

Klingberg, T., Forssberg, H., & Westerberg, H. (2002). Increased brain activity in frontal and parietal cortex underlies the development of visuospatial working memory capacity during childhood. *Journal of Cognitive Neuroscience, 14,* 1–10.

Knop, J., Teasdale, T. W., Schulsinger, F., & Goodwin, D. W. (1985). A prospective study of young men at high risk for alcoholism: school behavior and achievement. *Journal of Studies on Alcohol, 46,* 273–278.

Kuo, P. H., Yang, H. J., Soong, W. T., & Chen, W. J. (2002). Substance use among adolescents in Taiwan: Associated personality traits, incompetence, and behavioral/emotional problems. *Drug and Alcohol Dependence, 67,* 27–39.

Kwon, H., Reiss, A. L., & Menon, V. (2002). Neural basis of protracted developmental changes in visuo-spatial working memory. *Proceedings of the National Academy of Sciences of the United States of America, 99,* 13336–13341.

Kypri, K., McCarthy, D. M., Coe, M. T., & Brown, S. A. (2004). Transition to independent living and substance involvement of treated and high-risk youth. *Journal of Child and Adolescent Substance Abuse, 13*, 85–100.

Levin, H. S., Culhane, K. A., Hartmann, J., Evankovich, K., Mattson, A. J., & Harward, H., et al. (1991). Developmental-changes in performance on tests of purported frontal-lobe functioning. *Developmental Neuropsychology, 7*, 377–395.

Lewinsohn, P. M., Rohde, P., & Seeley, J. R. (1995). Adolescent psychopathology. Vol. III: The clinical consequences of comorbidity. *Journal of the American Academy of Child and Adolescent Psychiatry, 34*, 510–519.

Lewinsohn, P. M., Solomon, A., Seeley, J. R., & Zeiss, A. (2000). Clinical implications of "subthreshold" depressive symptoms. *Journal of Abnormal Psychology, 109*, 345–351.

Li, T. K., Hewitt, B. G., & Grant, B. F. (2004). Alcohol use disorders and mood disorders: A National Institute on Alcohol Abuse and Alcoholism perspective. *Biological Psychiatry, 56*, 718–720.

Limosin, F., Loze, J. Y., Dubertret, C., Gouya, L., Ades, J., & Rouillon, F. (2003). Impulsiveness as the intermediate link between the dopamine receptor D2 gene and alcohol dependencies. *Psychiatric Genetics, 13*, 127–129.

Loukas, A., Zucker, R. A., Fitzgerald, H. E., & Krull, J. L. (2003). Developmental trajectories of disruptive behavior problems among sons of alcoholics: effects of parent psychopathology, family conflict, and child under control. *Journal of Abnormal Psychology, 112*, 119–131.

Lu, R. -B., Lee, J. -F., Ko, H. -C., & Lin, W. -W. (2001). Dopamine D2 receptor gene (DRD2) is associated with alcoholism with conduct disorder. *Alcoholism: Clinical and Experimental Research, 25*, 177–184.

Luczak, S. E., Glatt, S. J., & Wall, T. L. (2006). Meta-analyses of ALDH2 and ADH1B with alcohol dependence in Asians. *Psychological Bulletin, 132*, 607–621.

Luna, B., Garver, K. E., Urban, T. A., Lazar, N. A., & Sweeney, J. A. (2004). Maturation of cognitive processes from late childhood to adulthood. *Child Development, 75*, 1357–1372.

Lynam, D. R., & Henry, B. (2001). The role of neuropsychological deficits in conduct disorders. In J. Hill & B. Maughan (Eds.), *Conduct disorders in childhood and adolescence* (pp. 235–263). New York: Cambridge University Press.

McCarthy, D. M., Brown, S. A., Carr, L. G., & Wall, T. L. (2001). ALDH2 Status, alcohol expectancies and alcohol response: Preliminary evidence for a mediation model. *Alcoholism Clinical and Experimental Research, 25*, 1558–1563.

McGue, M., Iacono, W. G., Legrand, L. N., Malone, S., & Elkins, I. (2001). Origins and consequences of age at first drink. I. Associations with substance-use disorders, disinhibitory behavior and psychopathology, and P3 amplitude. *Alcoholism: Clinical and Experimental Research, 25*, 1156–1165.

Milgram, G. G. (1996). Responsible decision making regarding alcohol: A reemerging prevention/education strategy for the 1990s. *Journal of Drug Education, 26*, 357–365.

Moskowitz, J. M. (1983). Preventing adolescent substance abuse through drug education. *NIDA Research Monograph, 47*, 233–249.

Mueller, U., Overton, W. F., & Reene, K. (2001). Development of conditional reasoning: A longitudinal study. *Journal of Cognition and Development, 2*, 27–49.

Muthen, B. O., & Muthen, L. K. (2000). The development of heavy drinking and alcohol-related problems from ages 18 to 37 in a U.S. national sample. *Journal of Studies on Alcohol, 61,* 290–300.

Myers, M. G., & Brown, S. A. (1994). Smoking and health in substance abusing adolescents: A two-year follow-up. *Pediatrics, 93,* 561–566.

Nelson, C. A., Bloom, F. E., Cameron, J. L., Amaral, D., Dahl, R. E., & Pine, D. (2002). An integrative, multidisciplinary approach to the study of brain-behavior relations in the context of typical and atypical development. *Development and Psychopathology, 14,* 499–520.

Newcomb, M., & Bentler, P. (1988). *Consequences of teenage drug use: Impact on the lives of young adults.* Newbury Park: Sage.

Newlin, D. B. (1994). Alcohol challenge in high-risk individuals. In R. Zucker, G. Boyd, & J. Howard (Eds.), *The development of alcohol problems: Exploring the biopsychosocial matrix of risk* (DHHS Publication No. ADM 94-3495, pp. 47–68). Washington, DC: U.S. Government Printing Office.

Nigg, J. T., Wong, M. M., Martel, M. M., Jester, J. M., Puttler, L. I., Glass, J. M., et al. (2006). Poor response inhibition as a predictor of problem drinking and illicit drug use in adolescents at risk for alcoholism and other substance use disorders. *Journal of the American Academy of Child & Adolescent Psychiatry, 45,* 468–475.

Novins, D. K., Beals, J., Shore, J. H., & Manson, S. M. (1996). Substance abuse treatment of American Indian adolescents: Comorbid symptomatology, gender differences, and treatment patterns. *Journal of the American Academy of Child and Adolescent Psychiatry, 35,* 1593–1601.

Ormond, C., Luszcz, M. A., Mann, L., & Beswick, G. (1991). A metacognitive analysis of decision making in adolescence. *Journal of Adolescence, 14,* 275–291.

Pandina, R. J., & Schuele, J. A. (1983). Psychosocial correlates of alcohol and drug use of adolescent students and adolescents in treatment. *Journal of Studies on Alcohol, 44,* 950–973.

Paus, T., Zijdenbos, A., Worsley, K., Collins, D. L., Blumenthal, J., Giedd, J. N., et al. (1999). Structural maturation of neural pathways in children and adolescents: in vivo study. *Science, 283,* 1908–1911.

Perry, C. L., Williams, C. L., VeblenMortenson, S., Toomey, T. L., Komro, K. A., Anstine, P. S., et al. (1996). Project Northland: Outcomes of a communitywide alcohol use prevention program during early adolescence. *American Journal of Public Health, 86,* 956–965.

Petraitis, J., Flay, B. R., & Miller, T. Q. (1995). Reviewing theories of adolescent substance use: Organizing pieces of the puzzle. *Psychological Bulletin, 117,* 67–86.

Pogge, D. L., Stokes, J., & Harvey, P. D. (1992). Psychometric vs. attentional correlates of early onset alcohol and substance-abuse. *Journal of Abnormal Child Psychology, 20,* 151–162.

Pollock, N. K., & Martin, C. S. (1999). Diagnostic orphans: Adolescents with alcohol symptoms who do not qualify for *DSM-IV* abuse or dependence diagnoses. *American Journal of Psychiatry, 156,* 897–901.

Raffaelli, M., Crockett, L. J., & Shen, Y. L. (2005). Developmental stability and change in self-regulation from childhood to adolescence. *Journal of Genetic Psychology, 166,* 54–75.

Reyna, V. F., & Farley, F. (2006). Risk and rationality in adolescent decision making: Implications for theory, practice, and public policy. *Psychological Science, 17,* 1–44.

Richter, S. S., Brown, S. A., & Mott, M. A. (1991). The impact of social support and self-esteem on adolescent substance abuse treatment outcome. *Journal of Substance Abuse, 3,* 371–385.

Robinson, T. E., & Berridge, K. C. (2003). Addiction. *Annual Review of Psychology, 54,* 25–53.

Roehrs, T., Beare, D., Zorick, F., & Roth, T. (1994). Sleepiness and ethanol effects on simulated driving. *Alcoholism: Clinical Experimental Research, 18,* 154–158.

Rose, R. J., Kaprio, J., Pulkkinen, L., Koskenvuo, M., Viken, R. J., & Bates, J. E. (1997). FinnTwin 12 and FinnTwin 16: Longitudinal twin-family studies in Finland. *Behavioral Genetics, 27,* 603–604.

Rutter, M. (2007). Gene-environment interdependence. *Developmental Science, 10,* 12–18.

Sadava, S. W. (1987). *Interactionist theories.* In H. T. Blane & K. E. Leonard (Eds.), *Psychological theories of drinking and alcoholism* (pp. 90–130). New York: Guilford.

Schinke, S. P., Botvin, G. J., & Orlandi, M. A. (1991). *Substance abuse in children and adolescents: Evaluation and intervention.* Newbury Park, CA: Sage.

Schuckit, M. (1988). Reactions to alcohol in sons of alcoholics and controls. *Alcoholism: Clinical and Experimental Research, 12,* 465–470.

Schuckit, M. A., Mazzanti, C., Smith, T. L., Ahmed, U., Radel, M., Iwata, N., & Goldman, D. (1999). Selective genotyping for the role of 5HT2A, 5HT2C, and GABAα6 Receptors and the serotonin transporter in level of response to alcohol. *Biological Psychiatry, 45,* 647–651.

Schuckit, M. A., Smith, T. L., Anderson, K. G., & Brown, S. A. (2004). Testing the level of response to alcohol-social information processing model of the alcoholism risk: A 20-year prospective study. *Alcoholism: Clinical and Experimental Research, 28,* 1881–1889.

Schuckit, M. A., Smith, T. L., Danko, G. P., Anderson, K. G., Brown, S. A., Kuperman, S., et al. (2005). Evaluation of a "level of response to alcohol based" structural equation model in adolescents. *Journal of Studies on Alcohol, 66,* 174–185.

Schulenberg, J., Maggs, J. L., & Hurrelmann, K. (1997). *Health risks and developmental transitions during adolescence.* New York: Cambridge University Press.

Schulenberg, J., O'Malley, P. M., Bachman, J. G., Wadsworth, K. N., & Johnston, L. D. (1996). Getting drunk and growing up: trajectories of frequent binge drinking during the transition to young adulthood. *Journal of Studies on Alcohol, 57,* 289–304.

Schweinsburg, A. D., Nagel, B. J., & Tapert, S. F. (2005). fMRI reveals alteration of spatial working memory networks across adolescence. *Journal of the International Neuropsychological Society, 11*(5), 631–644.

Schweinsburg, A. D., Paulus, M. P., Barlett, V. C., Killeen, L. A., Caldwell, L. C., Pulido, C., et al. (2004). An fMRI study of response inhibition in youths with a family history of alcoholism. *Annals of the New York Academy of Science, 1021,* 391–394.

Shelder, J., & Block, J. (1990). Adolescent drug use and psychological health. *American Psychologist, 45,* 612–630.

Sher, K. J. (1993). Children of alcoholics and the intergenerational transmission of alcoholism: A biopsychosocial perspective. In J. S. Baer, G. A. Marlatt, & R. J. McMahon (Eds.), *Addictive behaviors across the lifespan* (pp. 3–33). Newbury Park, CA: Sage.

Sher, K. J. (1994). Individual-level risk factors. In R. Zucker, G. Boyd, & J. Howard (Eds.), *The development of alcohol problems: Exploring the biopsychosocial matrix of risk* (DHHS Publication No. ADM 94-2495, pp. 77–108). Washington, DC: U.S. Government Printing Office.

Smith, G. T., Fischer, S., Cyders, M. A., Annus, A. M., Spillane, N. S., & McCarthy, D. M. (in press). On the validity and utility of discriminating among impulsivity-like traits. *Assessment*.

Smith, G. T., Goldman, M. S., Greenbaum, P. E., & Christiansen, B. A. (1995). Expectancy for social facilitation from drinking: The divergent paths of high-expectancy and low-expectancy adolescents. *Journal of Abnormal Psychology, 104*, 32–40.

Snow, D. L., Tebes, J. K., Arthur, M. W., & Tapasak, R. C. (1992). Two-year follow-up of a social-cognitive intervention to prevent substance use. *Journal of Drug Education, 22*, 101–114.

Sowell, E. R., Thompson, P. M., Holmes, C. J., Jernigan, T. L., & Toga, A. W. (1999). In vivo evidence for post-adolescent brain maturation in frontal and striatal regions. *Nature Neuroscience, 2*, 859–861.

Sowell, E. R., Thompson, P. M., Leonard, C. M., Welcome, S. E., Kan, E., & Toga, A. W. (2004). Longitudinal mapping of cortical thickness and brain growth in normal children. *Journal of Neuroscience, 24*, 8223–8231.

Steinberg, L. (2004). Risk taking in adolescence: what changes, and why? *Annals of the New York Academy of the Sciences, 1021*, 51–58.

Stewart, D. G., & Brown, S. A. (1995). Withdrawal and dependency symptoms among adolescent alcohol and drug abusers. *Addiction, 90*, 627–635.

Stowell, R. J., & Estroff, T. W. (1992). Psychiatric disorders in substance-abusing adolescent inpatients: A pilot study. *Journal of the American Academy of Child and Adolescent Psychiatry, 31*, 1036–1040.

Substance Abuse and Mental Health Services Administration. (1999). *Treatment of adolescents with substance use disorders: Treatment improvement protocol (TIP), Series 32*. Rockville, MD: Department of Health and Human Services.

Sullivan, M. A., & Rudnik-Levin, F. (2001). Attention deficit/hyperactivity disorder and substance abuse: Diagnostic and therapeutic considerations. *Annals of the New York Academy of Sciences, 931*, 251–270.

Tapert, S. F., & Brown, S. A. (1999). Neuropsychological correlates of adolescent substance abuse: Four year outcomes. *Journal of the International Neuropsychological Society, 5*, 475–487.

Tapert, S. F., & Brown, S. A. (2000). Substance dependence, family history of alcohol dependence, and neuropsychological functioning in adolescence. *Addictions, 95*, 1043–1053.

Tapert, S. F., Schweinsburg, A. D., Barlett, V. C., Brown, S. A., Frank, L. R., Brown, G. G., et al. (2004). Blood oxygen level dependent response and spatial working memory in adolescents with alcohol use disorders. *Alcoholism: Clinical & Experimental Research, 28*, 1577–1586.

Tapert, S. F., Stewart, D. G., & Brown, S. A. (1999). *Drug abuse in adolescence.* In A. J. Goreczny & M. Hersen (Eds.), *Handbook of pediatrics and adolescent health psychology* (pp. 161–178). Needham Heights, MA: Allyn & Bacon.

Tarter, R., Vanyukov, M., Giancola, P., Dawes, M., Blackson, T., Mezzich, A., et al. (1999). Etiology of early age onset substance use disorder: A maturational perspective. *Development and Psychopathology, 11,* 657–683.

Tarter, R. E., & Edwards, K. (1988). Psychological factors associated with the risk for alcoholism. *Alcoholism: Clinical and Experimental Research, 12,* 471–480.

Tate, S. R., Patterson, K. A., Nagel, B. J., Anderson, K. G., & Brown, S. A. (2007). Addiction and stress in adolescents. In M. al'Absi (Ed.), *Stress and addiction: Biological and psychological mechanisms* (pp. 249–262). New York: Elsevier.

Thomas, K. M., King, S. W., Franzen, P. L., Welsh, T. F., Berkowitz, A. L., Noll, D. C., et al. (1999). A developmental functional MRI study of spatial working memory. *Neuroimage, 10,* 327–338.

Toga, A. W., & Thompson, P. M. (2003). Temporal dynamics of brain anatomy. *Annual Review of Biomedical Engineering, 5,* 119–145.

Tsuang, M. T., Lyons, M. J., Meyer, J. M., Doyle, T., Eisen, S. A., Goldberg, J., et al. (1998). Co-occurrence of abuse of different drugs in men: The role of drug-specific and shared vulnerabilities. *Archives of General Psychiatry, 55,* 967–972.

Tucker, J. S., Orlando, M., & Ellickson, P. L. (2003). Patterns and correlates of binge drinking trajectories from early adolescence to young adulthood. *Health Psychology, 22,* 79–87

Varlinskaya, E. I., & Spear, L. P. (2002). Acute effects of ethanol on social behavior of adolescent and adult rats: Role of familiarity of the test situation. *Alcoholism: Clinical and Experimental Research, 26,* 1502–1511.

Vik, P. W., Brown, S. A., & Myers, M. G. (1997). *Adolescent substance abuse problems:* In E. J. Mash & L. G. Terdal (Eds.), *Assessment of childhood disorders* (3rd ed., pp. 717–748). New York: Guilford.

Vik, P. W., Grizzle, K., & Brown, S. A. (1992). Social resource characteristics and adolescent substance abuse relapse. *Journal of Adolescent Chemical Dependency, 2,* 59–74.

Wall, T. L., Shea, S. H., Chan, K. K., & Carr, L. G.(2001). A genetic association with the development of alcohol and other substance use behavior in Asian Americans. *Journal of Abnormal Psychology, 110,* 173–178.

Wallace, J. M., Jr., Bachman, J. G., O'Malley, P. M., Johnston, L. D., Schulenberg, J. E., & Cooper, S. M. (2002). Tobacco, alcohol, and illicit drug use: Racial and ethnic differences among U.S. high school seniors, 1976–2000. *Public Health Reports, 117,* S67–S75.

Wallace, J. M., Jr., Bachman, J. G., O'Malley, P. M., Schulenberg, J. E., Cooper, S. M., & Johnston, L. D. (2003). Gender and ethnic differences in smoking, drinking and illicit drug use among American 8th, 10th and 12th grade students, 1976–2000. *Addiction, 98,* 225–234.

White, A. M., & Swartzwelder, H. S. (2005). Age-related effects of alcohol on memory and memory-related brain function in adolescents and adults. In M. Galanter (Ed.), *Recent developments in alcoholism. Volume 17: Alcohol problems in adolescents and young adults* (pp. 161–176). New York: Kluwer Academic/ Plenum Publishers.

Williams, P. S., & Hine, D. W. (2002). Parental behaviour and alcohol misuse among adolescents: A path analysis of mediating influences. *Australian Journal of Psychology, 54*, 17–24.

Wills, T. A., Vaccaro, D., & McNamara, G. (1992). The role of life events, family support, and competence in adolescent substance use: A test of vulnerability and protective factors. *American Journal of Community Psychology, 20*, 349–374.

Windle, M. (1990). Temperament and personality attributes of children of alcoholics. In M. Windle & J. S. Searles (Eds.), *Children of alcoholics: Critical perspectives* (pp. 129–167). New York: Guilford.

Windle, M., Miller-Tutzauer, C., & Domenico, D. (1992). Alcohol use, suicidal behavior, and risky activities among adolescents. *Journal of Research on Adolescence, 2*, 317–330.

Windle, M., Spear, L.P., Fuligini, A. J., Angold, A., Brown, J. D., Pine, D., & Smith, G. (in press). *Transitions into underage and problem drinking: Developmental processes and mechanisms between ages 10–15.*

Wolfson, A. R., & Carskadon, M. A. (1998). Sleep schedules and daytime functioning in adolescents. *Child Development, 69*, 875–887.

Zald, D. H., & Iacono, W. G. (1998). The development of spatial working memory abilities. *Developmental Neuropsychology, 14*, 563–578.

Zucker, R. A., Fitzgerald, H. E., Refior, S. K., Puttler, L. I., Pallas, D. M., & Ellis, D. A. (2000). The clinical and social ecology of childhood for children of alcoholics: Description of a study and implications for a differentiated social policy. In H. E. Fitzgerald, B. M. Lester, & B. S. Zuckerman (Eds.), *Children of addiction: Research, health, and public policy issues* (pp. 109–141). New York: Routledge Falmer.

Zucker, R. A., Jester, J. M., Fitzgerald, H. E., Puttler, L. I., & Wong, M. M. (2004). Predicting onset of drinking from behavior at three years of age: Influence of early child expectancies on parental alcohol involvement upon early first use. In J. E. Donovan et al. (Eds.), Really underage drinkers: Alcohol use among elementary students. *Alcoholism: Clinical and Experimental Research, 28*, 341–349.

Zucker, R. A., Wong, M. M., Clark, D. B., Leonard, K. E., Schulenberg, J. E., Cornelius, J. R., et al. (2006). Predicting risky drinking outcomes longitudinally: what kind of advance notice can we get? *Alcoholism: Clinical and Experimental Research, 30*, 243–252.

Zuckerman, M. (1994). *Behavioral expressions and biosocial bases of sensation seeking:* New York: Cambridge University Press.

PART IV

INTERNALIZING BEHAVIOR DISORDERS

CHAPTER 15

Anxiety Disorders

CARL WEEMS AND WENDY SILVERMAN

HISTORICAL CONTEXT

Interest in childhood anxiety can be traced as far back as ancient Greece, in the writings of Hippocrates, and in writings from the Middle Ages (Silverman & Treffers, 2001). Conceptions of childhood internalizing problems can also be found in writings from early America (e.g., Benjamin Rush), and many famous cases in the modern history of psychology pertain to childhood anxiety (e.g., Freud's case study of Little Hans and Watson's experiment with Albert; see Silverman & Treffers, 2001, for a review).

The systematic study of anxiety disorders in youth received a major impetus when this superordinate category was introduced as a primary class of child and adolescent disorders in the *Diagnostic and Statistical Manual of Mental Disorders–Third Edition* (DSM-III, American Psychiatric Association, 1980). In DSM-II (APA, 1968) there was only one specific childhood anxiety category, referred to as "Overanxious Reaction." DSM-III then introduced—and DSM-III-R (APA, 1987) retained—a new broad category entitled "Anxiety Disorders of Childhood and Adolescence." Within this broad category three subcategories were introduced: (1) Separation Anxiety Disorder, (2) Overanxious Disorder, and (3) Avoidant Disorder. In addition to these childhood-specific disorders, children could also receive

Acknowledgments: Writing of this chapter was supported in part by grants from the National Institute of Mental Health to Carl Weems (MH067572) and Wendy Silverman (MH63997).

447

diagnoses of other anxiety/phobic disorders classified among adults, with identical criteria used regardless of age.

Claims were soon made to the effect that the majority of new DSM-III categories and subcategories, including those relating to anxiety, were overrefined, untested, and excessive in number (see Silverman, 1992). It was also contended that the use of similar diagnostic criteria in children and adults was inconsistent with developmental changes in the expression of psychopathology across the lifespan. These were serious charges, and investigators were thus faced with the challenge of providing empirical data that would either support or refute the validity of each new diagnostic category. Hence, a great deal of time and energy was devoted toward establishing the basic requirements of a useful taxonomic scheme, including reliability, coverage, descriptive validity, and predictive validity (Blashfield, 1989). This work spurred concentrated efforts toward developing and evaluating structured interviewing procedures as a way to yield improved diagnoses (e.g., Silverman & Nelles, 1988; Silverman & Rabian, 1995).

With the latest version of the DSM (DSM-IV; APA, 1994, 2000), major changes were made. The broad category, "Anxiety Disorders of Childhood and Adolescence," as well as more specific subcategories (Overanxious Disorder and Avoidant Disorder) from DSM-III and DSM-III-R, were eliminated. Only one such category, Separation Anxiety Disorder, was retained as a distinct child anxiety disorder, under the broad category "Other Disorders of Childhood and Adolescence" (APA, 1994). Thus, in DSM-IV, with the exception of Separation Anxiety Disorder, the same sets of diagnostic criteria and subcategories of anxiety disorders apply to children and adults. The reader should not infer, however, that all scientists believe that this resolution is optimal. Indeed, some investigators still assert that the DSM-IV criteria were formulated in the absence of hard empirical data (Silverman, 1993).

TERMINOLOGICAL AND CONCEPTUAL ISSUES

At the outset it is important to delineate some basic ideas about what constitutes anxiety. We assume that anxiety is a higher-order feeling state (Damasio, 2003) produced by specific brain mechanisms responsible for basic emotion—primarily those brain systems involved in sympathetic arousal and fear responses, but also those involved with negative affect and behavioral avoidance. *Anxiety* is defined in this chapter as the product of a multicomplex response system, involving affective, behavioral, physiological, and cognitive components (e.g., Barlow, 2002; Lang, 1977). Worry, for example, is one component of the anxiety response system that can be viewed as a cognitive process preparing the individual to anticipate future danger. Fear, in contrast, is a part of the response system that fosters preparation for either freezing to avoid impending punishment or escaping as part of the fight/flight response (Barlow, 2002; Gray & McNaughton, 2000; Borkovec, Shadick, & Hopkins, 1991; Mathews, 1990).

A core defining feature of anxiety problems is dysregulation of the normal response system. Such dysregulation may involve intense and disabling worry that does not help anticipate true future danger—or intense fear reactions in the absence of true threat. An additional nonspecific core feature is the distress/impairment that may result from dysregulation in the anxiety response system, and the corresponding negative emotional states (e.g., being upset or overconcerned). For convenience we refer to these core features of anxiety problems as *anxious emotion*. These core features of anxiety problems may be expressed behaviorally (e.g., avoidance), cognitively (e.g., concentration difficulties), physiologically (e.g., dizziness, racing heart), or socially (e.g., academic impairment). Primary features of anxiety *cut across* all anxiety disorders represented in the DSM-IV and are therefore not specific to any particular diagnosis. In contrast, *secondary features* of anxiety are those aspects that *differentiate* the specific categories of anxiety disorders in the DSM-IV (APA, 1994). For example, worry about separation from parents is specific to Separation Anxiety Disorder, interpersonal concerns are specific to Social Anxiety Disorder, and uncued panic attacks are specific to Panic Disorder.

DIAGNOSTIC ISSUES AND DSM-IV CRITERIA

The conceptualization and classification of the anxiety disorders in the DSM-IV (1994, 2000) currently dominate the field. Anxiety disorders delineated in the DSM-IV include specific phobias, Social Anxiety Disorder, Generalized Anxiety Disorder, Separation Anxiety Disorder, Obsessive Compulsive Disorder, Panic Disorder, and Posttraumatic Stress Disorder (PTSD). These disorders can appear at any age, with the exception of Separation Anxiety Disorder, which as noted previously is diagnosed only if it emerges before age 18.

The DSM-IV (APA, 1994, 2000) provides criteria for making specific anxiety disorder diagnoses and for assisting differential diagnosis. The following summarizes key clinical features of each anxiety disorder: (1) Specific phobias are characterized by extreme and unreasonable fears of a specific object or situation such as dogs, loud noises, or the dark; (2) Social Anxiety Disorder is characterized by an extreme and unreasonable fear of being embarrassed or humiliated in front of other youths or adults. Children and adolescents with Social Anxiety Disorder may avoid such places as school, restaurants, and parties; (3) Generalized Anxiety Disorder is characterized by persistent and excessive worry about a number of events or activities. Youth may worry about their school performance, their social relationships, and their health or the health of others; they may seek constant reassurance and approval from others to help alleviate their worry; (4) Separation Anxiety Disorder is characterized by excessive worry concerning separation from home or loved ones. Key clinical features include unrealistic worry about harm to self or significant others during periods of separation, reluctance to sleep alone or be alone, physical complaints, and signs of distress in anticipation of separation. School refusal behavior is another common feature of Separation Anxiety Disorder; (5) Obsessive Compulsive Disorder (OCD) is characterized by recurrent thoughts or behavior patterns that are severe enough to be time consuming, distressful, and highly interfering. The most common obsessions in young people are repeated thoughts about contamination, repeated doubts, having things in a particular order, and aggressive or horrible impulses. Common compulsions are repeated washing, touching, checking, or repeating certain words or numbers; (6) Panic Disorder is characterized by sudden and severe attacks of anxiety. These attacks may consist of shortness of breath, heart palpitations, dizziness, upset stomach, sweating, and fear of dying or losing control. Youth with Panic Disorder may also show agoraphobia in which they avoid situations in which the attacks have occurred, such as shopping malls, theaters, and stadiums.

Finally, a child or adolescent who experiences a catastrophic or otherwise traumatic event may develop ongoing difficulties known as Posttraumatic Stress Disorder (PTSD; APA, 1994, 2000). The traumatic event must involve a situation in which someone's life has been threatened or severe injury has occurred. Following exposure to the trauma, the youth may exhibit agitated or confused behavior as well as intense fear, helplessness, anger, sadness, horror, and/or denial. Youth with PTSD usually avoid situations or places that remind them of the trauma. They also may become depressed, withdrawn, emotionally unresponsive, and detached from their feelings.

Research has consistently shown that the DSM anxiety disorders have high rates of comorbidity with one another (Costello, Egger, & Angold, 2004; Curry, March, & Hervey, 2004). Moreover, the only variables that distinguish among anxiety disorders are definitional (i.e., secondary features outlined previously such as social concerns in Social Anxiety Disorder and worries about separation in Separation Anxiety Disorder). Thus, discrimination among anxiety disorders is largely tautological (Weems & Stickle,

2005) in that "empirical support" for a specific disorder is often derived from the definitional criteria used to define the disorder in the first place. With the exceptions of OCD and possibly PTSD, there is little evidence that anxiety disorders are differentially related to treatment outcomes, although it is recognized that such null findings may be attributed in part to insufficient sample sizes (see Berman et al., 2000; see also Dadds et al., 2004; Saavedra & Silverman, 2001). Finally, longitudinal research on the stability of child and adolescent anxiety disorders has produced highly inconsistent results (e.g., Last et al., 1996; Newman et al., 1996). Such considerations point to the importance of the developmental psychopathology perspective in refining diagnostic criteria and improving the assessment of anxiety problems in childhood and adolescence.

PREVALENCE

Anxiety disorders in childhood and adolescence are quite prevalent and can cause significant psychosocial impairment (Bernstein & Borchardt, 1991; Bernstein, Borchardt, & Perwien, 1996; Silverman & Ginsburg, 1998). The most recent reviews (e.g., Costello et al., 2004) indicate that, among studies assessing current or short-term (3 month) prevalence for any anxiety disorder, rates are approximately 2% to 4%. Among studies assessing prevalence over 6 months, 12 months, or lifetime, prevalence rates are much higher, between 10% and 20%. Prevalence rates appear to vary somewhat by the type of anxiety disorder (see Silverman & Ginsburg, 1998).

RISK FACTORS AND ETIOLOGICAL FORMULATIONS

THEORETICAL FRAMEWORK

In terms of DSM-IV anxiety disorder symptoms, linkages between (a) normal development; (b) various biological, cognitive, behavioral, and social mechanisms; and (c) symptoms of anxiety and phobic disorders can be understood as stemming from interactions between biological (e.g., genes, neurobiology) and behavioral (e.g., parenting, exposure to trauma) factors that cause dysregulation of the normal anxiety response system and foster distress and impairment. These factors give rise to undifferentiated anxious emotion (the primary features of anxious emotion). Specific anxiety disorders are then shaped by biological, cognitive, behavioral, and social processes (Vasey & Dadds, 2001; Weems & Stickle, 2005). For example, genetic predispositions and early experiences may render a child vulnerable to elevated levels of anxiety and distress, sometimes termed *trait anxiety*. Additional, more specific experiences such as being socially teased by peers upon entry into school may foster the development of social anxiety; a frightening experience with a dog may result in an animal phobia; and biological vulnerability such as the experience of uncued physiological arousal may lead to Panic Disorder.

In understanding the etiology of childhood anxiety problems we use a developmental perspective that emphasizes the complex interactions among various influences. From this perspective, all behavior patterns among individuals have varying trajectories over time (Baltes, Reese, & Lipsitt, 1980; Baltes, Reese, & Nesselroade, 1988). Identifying symptom trajectories has been particularly useful in understanding such problem domains as Conduct Disorder (Moffitt, 1993, 2006) and may also be useful for studying anxiety disorders (Henry & Moffitt, 1991; Weems et al., 2002). Specific processes implicated in the origins of problematic anxiety include but are not limited to genetics, temperament, and psychophysiology (biological processes); operant, observational, and respondent learning (behavioral learning processes); information processing and stimuli/event interpretation (cognitive processes); attachment relations and sociability (social and interpersonal processes); and the interaction of these factors in various contexts (parent-child relationships, family, home, school, community). These domains are particularly relevant because treatment researchers have focused intervention efforts on biological systems (see Walkup, Labellarte, & Ginsburg, 2002), social family systems (see Ginsburg & Schlossberg, 2002), and cognitive and behavioral processes (Kendall, 1994; Silverman et al., 1999; see Silverman & Berman, 2001). Drawing from general developmental psychopathology models (e.g., Bronfenbrenner, 1977; Cicchetti & Rogosch, 1996), we now review specific processes that may influence individual pathways in the experience of anxiety.

BIOLOGICAL PROCESSES

Central nervous system.   The conceptions of a behavioral approach system (BAS) and a behavioral inhibition system (BIS) are a good starting point for understanding central nervous system structures involved in the anxiety response (Gray, 1994). The BAS is composed of brain structures that are involved in approach behaviors. These structures include dopaminergically mediated portions of the basal ganglia. Also involved are neocortical areas including the motor, sensorimotor, and prefrontal cortices (Gray, 1994). The BIS is composed of afferent (outgoing) projections through the noradrenergic fibers of the locus coeruleus and the serotonergic fibers from the median raphe (Gray, 1994; Gray & McNaughton, 2000). The BIS is important in the experience of anxiety in response to either novelty or impending punishment, whether real or perceived. Activation of the BIS is functional in that exposure to punishment, novel stimuli, and stimuli of innate fear lead to the inhibition of approach behavior. The combined function of the BAS and the BIS is to evaluate incoming stimuli regarding possible benefit versus possible punishment, and to activate approach or avoidance behaviors accordingly. Approach is generally associated with positive emotions and avoidance with negative emotions.

Theories regarding the circuits of the central nervous system that are involved in the anxiety response have also emphasized an important role of the amygdala (e.g., Davis, 1998; LeDoux, 2000). The amygdala is a collection of nuclei found in the anterior portion of the temporal lobes that function to evaluate the emotional significance of incoming stimuli after receiving input from relevant projections in the cortex, hippocampus, and thalamus. In turn, the amygdala projects to other anxiety response system–relevant brain structures in the frontal cortex (choice behavior), the hippocampus (memory consolidation), the striatum (approach/avoidance), and the hypothalamus and brain stem (autonomic responses, startle, corticosteroid response) (see Gordon & Hen, 2004; LeDoux, 2000). It is important to realize however, that no single structure, neurotransmitter, or gene controls the entire anxiety response system. It is the complex workings of several interrelated systems that give rise to anxious emotion.

As noted previously, negative affect is an important component of anxiety problems. In terms of the structural bases of negative affect, functional brain studies suggest that normal threat assessment and emotional learning may involve differential hemispheric activation. Electroencephalography (EEG) research has demonstrated increased right prefrontal and anterior temporal region activation in response to negative emotion, and increased left prefrontal activation in response to positive emotion (Davidson, 1998). Furthermore, Davidson (1998) and colleagues (Davidson et al., 2000) have shown that increased left prefrontal activation is associated with the ability to suppress startle responses to negative stimuli. Davidson et al. (2000) also have uncovered greater relative right than left prefrontal lobe activation in adults with social anxiety and depression. These findings have been replicated in infants (Davidson & Fox, 1989) and school-age children (8 to 11 years of age) who were diagnosed with anxiety disorders (Baving, Laucht, & Schmidt, 2002).

In addition, a number of specific neurotransmitters and neurotransmitter systems have been implicated in anxiety and anxiety-related behavior. In particular, both gamma aminobutyric acid (GABA) and serotonin (5-HT) have been foci of research on anxiety. This interest follows from findings that anti-anxiety (anxiolytic) medications such as benzodiazepines and selective serotonin reuptake inhibitors (SSRIs) modulate GABA and 5-HT neurotransmission. The noradrenergic system has also been implicated in anxiety disorders with a strong sympathetic component, such as Panic Disorder (Gordon & Hen, 2004).

Another theoretically important system is the hypothalamic-pituitary-adrenal (HPA) axis. Activation of the HPA axis often follows from fight-flight reactions in response to stress and fear, although its time course is considerably longer, spanning minutes to hours. Fear reactions are associated with elevations in the secretion of cortisol, a corticosteroid hormone produced by the adrenal cortex (see Gunnar, 2001). The HPA axis has therefore been implicated in the pathophysiology of anxiety disorders. The release of cortisol is controlled by the hypothalamus, where corticotropin-releasing hormone (CRH) is secreted. CRH then stimulates the pituitary gland, resulting in the release of adrenocorticotrophic hormone (ACTH), which in turn causes the adrenal cortex to release cortisol. Cortisol helps to regulate behavioral and emotional responding through a feedback loop to the pituitary and hypothalamus.

Cortisol secretion may underlie protective mechanisms upon exposure to danger; however, prolonged exposure to glucocorticoids such as cortisol may also be neurotoxic and related to anxiety problems. For example, animal studies have demonstrated hippocampal atrophy in rats and primates exposed to either psychological stress or elevated levels of glucocorticoids (see Sapolsky, 2000). Furthermore, maltreated children with PTSD symptoms and those diagnosed with PTSD demonstrate dysregulation in diurnal cortisol levels (Carrión et al., 2002; De Bellis et al., 1999a), and symptoms of Social Anxiety Disorder have been associated with heightened cortisol reactivity among clinic-referred youth (Granger, Weisz, & Kauneckis, 1994; see Gunnar, 2001, for a review). Moreover, youth who have experienced severe stressors are more likely to display reductions in cerebral volume and frontal lobe asymmetry, possibly due to effects of prolonged cortisol secretion (Carrión et al., 2001; De Bellis et al., 1999b). Recently, Carrión, Weems, and Reiss (in press) found that cortisol levels were associated with changes in the volume of the hippocampus in a small (n = 15) sample of youth ages 8 to 14 years who were exposed to traumatic stressors. Higher cortisol levels were related to decreases in hippocampal volume over a 1-year period. Finally, research on behavioral inhibition, a risk factor for later childhood anxiety disorders (see Kagan, this volume), has linked the construct with increased cortisol levels in very young children (e.g., Kagan, Reznick, & Snidman, 1987, 1988).

Genetic influences.   Evidence suggests that there is moderate genetic risk for symptoms of anxiety. Twin studies suggest that about 33% of the variance in childhood anxiety symptoms is accounted for by genetic influences (see Eley, 2001). Genetic influences may help to account for children's early anxious styles, including physiological reactivity and avoidance behaviors. It is important to note, however, that genes do not act directly on behavior. Genes code for proteins that in turn affect brain structures and regulative processes such as neurotransmitter receptors.

In addition to traditional behavior genetic studies, research on the molecular genetics of anxiety is emerging. Such investigations have focused on genes encoding components of the 5-HT and GABA systems. Results have been mixed, but the strongest findings have linked genes to anxiety-related traits such as behavioral inhibition and not to specific disorders. Such findings point to the importance of differentiating between primary and secondary features of anxiety. For example, the gene encoding the GABA-synthetic enzyme GAD65 has been associated with behavioral inhibition, a risk factor for anxiety disorders such as Panic Disorder, yet no genes encoding GABA receptors have been linked directly to Panic Disorder (see Gordon & Hem, 2004). One of the most promising lines of research suggests that polymorphisms in the promoter region of the gene for the 5-HT transporter (5-HTT) may also be associated with behavioral inhibition, particularly among individuals exposed to environmental risk (Fox et al., 2005).

Temperament theorists have drawn from genetic models, suggesting that anxiety problems stem from biological predispositions to react negatively to novelty (see Biederman et al., 1990, 1993; Kagan, Reznick, & Gibbons, 1989; Kagan et al., 1987, 1988). Temperamentally inhibited children display many of the same behavioral, affective, and physiological characteristics as children with anxiety disorders. These characteristics include avoidance and withdrawal from novelty, clinging or dependence on parents, fearfulness, and autonomic hyperarousal (Kagan et al., 1987). Such children are more likely than their peers to respond to potentially fearful situations (e.g., interactions with a stranger, separations from mother) with heightened physiological reactivity, which may result from a lower threshold of amygdalar and hypothalamic activity. In addition, research suggests that the genetic contribution to anxiety may increase with age, although similar findings hold for most behavioral traits (Eley, 2001). The idea that the genetic contribution to individual differences in anxiety increases with age points to the possibility that genetic vulnerability may unfold over time as environmental risks mount.

Psychophysiology. A growing body of research suggests that anxiety disorders in youth are characterized by differences in sympathetic arousal as expressed by increased heart rate, blood pressure, and electrodermal responding (e.g., Beidel, 1991; Carrión et al., 2002). Research on behavioral inhibition has also indicated that it is concurrently and longitudinally associated with elevated and stable heart rates in community-recruited samples of youth (Kagan et al., 1987, 1988). Data available from youth with elevated anxiety also suggest different physiological responses to anxiety-provoking stimuli. Beidel (1991) compared a community sample of 23 children with high test anxiety (mean age 9.8 years) and 15 children without test anxiety (mean age 9.6 years) and found significant group differences in pulse rate and systolic blood pressure during social evaluative tasks. More recently, Scheeringa, Zeanah, Myers, and Putnam (2004) found that young children (n = 62, ages 1.5 to 6 years) exposed to trauma and who either met criteria for or had symptoms of PTSD exhibited decreased heart periods (i.e., shorter interbeat intervals, signifying higher heart rates) compared to a matched control group who did not have symptoms of PTSD, during recall of trauma memories (an enacted traumatic event in the controls).

Weems, Zakem, Costa, Cannon, and Watts (2005) examined skin conductance and heart rate responses among youth exposed to a fear-eliciting stimulus (video of a large dog), and their relation to child- and parent-rated anxiety symptoms and cognitive bias in a community-recruited sample (n = 49). Results indicated that heart rate and skin conductance were associated with youth ratings of anxiety disorder symptoms and that the heart rate response was more strongly associated with anxiety symptoms than with skin conductance response. These responses were uniquely associated with youth-reported symptoms of anxiety but not with depression.

There are also salient individual differences in the absolute level of arousal that individuals comfortably tolerate. For example, research on anxiety sensitivity has shown that the absolute level of arousal symptoms is not crucial for anxiety problems to develop (Schmidt, Lerew, & Jackson, 1997). Anxiety sensitivity involves the belief that anxiety sensations (e.g., heart beat awareness, increased heart rate, trembling, shortness of breath) have negative social, psychological, and / or physical consequences (Reiss, 1991). One's interpretation of arousal symptoms appears to be especially important in influencing his or her experience of anxiety (Reiss, 1991; Weems et al., 1998). In other words, some individuals experience considerable negative affect and distress with relatively little physiological arousal.

BEHAVIORAL LEARNING PROCESSES

Proponents of behavioral conceptualizations of anxiety disorders have proposed respondent (classical or Pavlovian conditioning), vicarious (social modeling), and operant (Skinnerian conditioning) accounts of the acquisition of anxiety disorders. Limitations to early classical conditioning accounts involving the direct pairing of stimuli with aversive events (e.g., a large dog bites a child, resulting in a fear of dogs) have prompted theorists to posit multiple learning pathways to anxiety and phobic disorders (Bouton, Mineka, & Barlow, 2001). Rachman (1977) has posited three major pathways. It is important to recognize that there are multiple learning processes involved in the development of anxiety disorder because research suggests that most anxiety disorders do not result from a single exposure to a feared stimulus (Bouton et al., 2001).

The first is through classical aversive conditioning (Wolpe & Rachman, 1960). A large body of research suggests that exposure to traumatic events is associated with increased risk for anxiety disorders, particularly PTSD. Events that have been researched extensively as traumatic during childhood include experiences of child abuse, maltreatment, and exposure to community violence. Research indicates that between 25 and 55% of youth with past histories of physical and sexual abuse will meet criteria for a diagnosis of PTSD (Ackerman et al., 1998; Kiser et al., 1991). Research also suggests that exposure to natural disasters, such as an earthquake or hurricane, is associated with PTSD symptoms in youth (e.g., La Greca et al., 1996). Furthermore, the level of PTSD symptoms a child or adolescent experiences is related to the number of disaster exposure events that the youth experiences (La Greca, Silverman, & Wasserstein, 1998). In addition, however, vulnerabilities such as preexisting trait anxiety are risk factors for postdisaster PTSD, and predict symptoms beyond exposure to the stressful event (La Greca et al., 1998).

The second of Rachman's pathways is vicarious acquisition through observational learning or modeling. Via this pathway, children may acquire fears by observing the actions of salient others such as parents, caregivers, siblings, or friends (Bandura, 1982). For example, a child who sees his or her mother react fearfully to a dog may begin to model this reaction.

The third pathway is through verbal transmission of information. Through this mechanism, children may acquire fears by talking about fearful things with parents, caregivers, siblings, or friends. For example, the type of information (positive versus negative) youth receive about a potential fear stimulus (e.g., an animal) has been shown to change the valence of fear beliefs (Field, 2006; Field, Argyris, & Knowles, 2001; Field & Lawson, 2003).

Ollendick, Vasey, and King (2001) have suggested a fourth pathway to anxiety problems through operant conditioning. This account draws from the learning theory of Mowrer (e.g., Mowrer, 1960) in suggesting that, if a child learns to cope with normative anxiety and fear responses through avoidance of the anxiety or fear-provoking stimulus, then normal anxiety responses may be maintained at high levels and may eventually turn into problematic anxiety. Withdrawal from the stimulus may be negatively reinforced by reduction in anxiety after withdrawing, or avoidance may be positively reinforced by caregivers through approval of avoidance behaviors. Considerable evidence exists to support these learning pathways in childhood anxiety (see Ollendick et al., 2001, for a review).

Proponents of cognitive and information processing models propose various stages in cognition, such as encoding, interpretation, and recall, that may contribute to the etiology and maintenance of anxiety disorders (Vasey, Dalgleish, & Silverman, 2003). According to these models, anxious children have biased interpretations, judgments, and memories, as well as attentional selectivity (Vasey & MacLeod, 2001). In conjunction with biological and learning accounts, cognitive factors may foster or hamper learning acquisition, exacerbate biological predispositions, and maintain anxiety disorder symptoms. Selective attention, memory biases, and negative cognitive errors are three specific forms of biases that have begun to garner attention in terms of their relation to childhood anxiety symptoms. Selective attention involves focusing attention toward a category of stimuli (e.g., threatening stimuli) when such stimuli are placed in a context with other categories of stimuli (e.g., neutral or other nonthreatening stimuli). A predisposition for attending to and processing potentially threatening stimuli is thought to characterize anxious individuals and may serve to maintain anxiety by overallocating intellectual resources toward threat (Mathews, 1990).

Studies have also demonstrated a link between childhood anxiety problems and selective attention (e.g., Dalgleish et al., 2003; Vasey et al., 1995). Vasey et al. (1995) used a word dot-probe detection task with a sample of children and adolescents ages 9 to 17 who met diagnostic criteria for an anxiety disorder (n = 12) and control participants matched on age, sex, and intellectual ability (n = 12). Youth with anxiety disorders had shorter detection latencies for threat words. Similar results have been found among test-anxious youth (Vasey, El-Hag, & Daleiden, 1996), as well as among youth with Generalized Anxiety Disorder (Dalgleish et al., 2003). However, it is important to note that such studies do not inform us about causal or directional associations between such cognitive biases and anxiety.

Memory biases refer to a predisposition to recall threatening information (see Vasey & MacLeod, 2001). Similar to research on selective attention, evidence supporting a link between memory biases and anxiety problems in children and adolescents has been found (Daleiden, 1998; Moradi et al., 2000). Nevertheless, more research is needed to examine associations between both selective attention and memory biases and youth anxiety symptoms in order to determine whether these differences exist only in extremely impaired individuals. The majority of past research on youth anxiety has focused on comparing groups in the extremes of anxious psychopathology (i.e., those with diagnosed disorders compared to groups with no history of psychiatric diagnosis).

Negatively biased cognitions have long been implicated in emotional problems such as anxiety disorders (e.g., Beck, 1976). Research has shown that clinically anxious youth presented with ambiguous vignettes and then asked to explain what was happening in the story are more likely to provide interpretations indicating threat than nonanxious control youth (Barrett et al., 1996). A well-validated measure for assessing negative interpretive biases is the Children's Negative Cognitive Error Questionnaire (CNCEQ; Leitenberg, Yost, & Carroll-Wilson, 1986). Research using the CNCEQ suggests that cognitive biases are associated with symptoms of anxiety and can be assessed validly in both child and adolescent samples (Epkins, 1996; Leitenberg et al., 1986; Leung & Wong, 1998; Weems et al., 2001). Watts and Weems (in press) examined links among selective attention, memory bias, cognitive errors, and anxiety problems in a community sample of 81 youth ages 9 to 17. Parents completed measures of the child's anxiety symptoms. Selective attention, memory bias, and cognitive errors were each uniquely associated with childhood anxiety symptoms.

Models integrating the affective, cognitive, and physiological components of anxiety suggest that cognitive biases may exert their effect by exacerbating the negative feelings that heightened physiological responding can elicit. In other words, negative cognitive biases should not necessarily be correlated with physiological reactivity, but should interact with physiological responses to produce the negative affective states that are characteristic of anxiety disorder symptoms (see Alfano, Beidel, & Turner, 2002; Vasey & Dadds, 2001.) As noted previously, Weems et al. (2005) examined the physiological responses of youth exposed to a mildly phobic stimulus. Heart rate responses interacted with cognitive biases in predicting anxiety disorder symptoms.

A growing body of research has implicated anxiety sensitivity as a risk factor for panic attacks and Panic Disorder (e.g., Maller & Reiss, 1992; Schmidt et al., 1997, 1999). Once again, anxiety sensitivity involves the belief that anxiety sensations have negative social, psychological, and/or physical consequences (Reiss, 1991). Research with child and adolescent samples using the Childhood Anxiety Sensitivity Index (CASI; Silverman et al., 1991) has demonstrated that anxiety sensitivity in youth is related to fears, depression, and negative cognitive errors (Weems et al., 1998, 2001, 1997). In addition, results from nonclinical samples suggest that anxiety sensitivity discriminates adolescents who report panic attacks from those who do not (Lau, Calamari, & Waraczynski, 1996). Levels of anxiety sensitivity differentiate youth with Panic Disorder from youth with other anxiety disorders (Kearney et al., 1997). Finally, Hayward, Killen, Kraemer, and Taylor (2000) investigated predictors of panic attacks in a large sample (n =2,365) of adolescents (mean age 15.4 years) who were followed over a 4-year period. Anxiety sensitivity predicted the onset of panic attacks during the study period.

Several investigators and theorists have emphasized a key role for the construct of *control* in anxiety and anxiety disorders in youth (e.g., Capps et al., 1996; Cortez & Bugental, 1995; Granger et al., 1994; Muris et al., 2003; see Chorpita & Barlow, 1998; Weems & Silverman, 2006, for reviews). For example, Chorpita and Barlow (1998) described how early childhood experiences with diminished control may result in a cognitive style that increases the probability of interpreting events as out of one's control. Based on these findings, Chorpita and Barlow proposed a model in which perceived control (or lack thereof) may represent a psychological vulnerability for anxiety problems.

Barlow's (2002) model of anxiety suggests that a perceived lack of control over *external* threats (events, objects, situations that are fear producing) and/or negative *internal* emotional and bodily reactions are central to the experience of anxiety problems. That is, beliefs that anxiety-eliciting events and sensations are uncontrollable comprise part of what makes anxiety a "problem" for individuals with anxiety disorders. Nonpathological anxiety is differentiated from pathological anxiety both by subjective anxiety responses to the experience, and by the belief that the event is uncontrollable. Empirical support exists for the importance of control cognitions in youth (Ginsburg, Lambert, & Drake, 2004; Weems et al., 2003).

SOCIAL AND INTERPERSONAL PROCESSES

Interpersonal theories focus on children's relationships with others. Research suggests important peer (Bell-Dolan, Foster, & Christopher, 1995) and parenting (Berg, 1976) influences on childhood anxiety. Moreover, social contextual approaches suggest that factors such as poverty, parental psychopathology, exposure to trauma, and exposure to violence can exacerbate vulnerability to anxiety disorders. According to attachment theory, for example, a child's interactions with the environment are influenced by the underlying quality of the parent-child relationship, and a number of factors influence the quality of that relationship (e.g., poverty, parental psychopathology). Attachment theory suggests that human infants form enduring emotional bonds with their caretakers (Bowlby, 1977; Cassidy, 1999). When the child's caretakers are responsive, the resultant emotional bonds can provide a lasting sense of security that continues even when the caretaker is not present. However, an inconsistently responsive caretaker, a neglectful caretaker, or some other disruption in the parent-child bond may cause the child to become insecurely attached. Children with insecure attachments have particular difficulty during separations from their parents (Ainsworth, Blehar, Waters, & Wall, 1978).

The reactions of children with anxiety disorders such as Separation Anxiety Disorder (SAD) can be strikingly similar to those reported of insecurely attached children in the strange situation (Ainsworth et al., 1978). For example, children with SAD protest desperately when separation is imminent, cry and become agitated during separation, and may act angrily or aggressively toward the parent upon return. Warren, Huston, Egeland, and Sroufe (1997) found that children (n =172) classified as anxious/resistant in their attachment (assessed at 12 months of age) were more likely to have anxiety disorders at age 17, even when controlling for measures of temperament and maternal anxiety, than children classified with other types of attachment.

Overcontrolling parental behaviors are also thought to influence childhood anxiety, although it is indeterminate whether these patterns are maintaining factors or truly causal. For example, anxiety in either member of the mother-child dyad tends to elicit maternal overcontrol during interactions (Whaley, Pinto, & Sigman, 1999; Woodruff-Borden et al., 2002), and research indicates higher levels of maternal control in anxious mother-child dyads as opposed to control dyads (e.g., Siqueland, Kendall, & Steinberg, 1996; see also Silverman & Ginsburg, 1998). Costa and Weems (2005) tested a model of the association between maternal and child anxiety that includes mother and child attachment beliefs and children's perceptions of maternal control as mediators. The study was conducted with mothers and their children ages 6 to 17 (n = 88). Maternal anxiety was associated with child anxiety and maternal anxious attachment beliefs, whereas child anxiety was associated with maternal anxious attachment beliefs, child insecure attachment beliefs, and children's perceptions of maternal control. Maternal anxious attachment beliefs mediated the association between maternal and child anxiety. Taken together, research suggests that parents who exhibit overcontrolling, overinvolved, dependent, or intrusive behavior may (a) prevent youth from facing fear-provoking events, a developmentally important task that allows children to face fear; or (b) send the message that particular stimuli are threatening, which may reinforce a child's or adolescent's anxiety (Rapee, 1997; Rapee et al., 2000; Vasey & Ollendick, 2000).

An important point to be made here is that social-interpersonal models emphasize learning experiences wherein the behavior of the parent is learned by the child. In discussing mediation in this section, we have focused on possible behaviors of the parent or parent-child relationship that foster children's learning of anxious behaviors. Research is beginning to show that some of these processes may be influenced by genes. For example, in the Fox et al. (2005) study previously noted, neither genotype (i.e., the short allele for serotonin transporter) nor low social support predicted behavioral inhibition by itself. However, their interaction was predictive. These results suggest that, among children with relatively low social support, genotype status was associated with behavioral inhibition. Such findings point to the importance of the concept of gene–environment interactions in developmental psychopathology research on childhood anxiety.

DEVELOPMENTAL PROGRESSION

Research suggests that childhood anxiety disorders are associated with adult anxiety and depressive disorders (Pine et al., & Ma, 1998). As noted previously, however, results from prospective longitudinal studies of childhood anxiety disorders have indicated widely varying stability estimates, ranging from 4% to 80% (e.g., Keller et al., 1992; Last et al., 1996; March, Leonard, & Swedo, 1995; Newman et al., 1996; see Silverman & Ginsburg, 1998, for a review). These wide-ranging stability estimates may exist for many reasons, including the type of disorder, the informant, the sample, and the amount of time between evaluations. Interestingly, studies have shown similarly wide estimates even for the same anxiety disorder across similar time frames. For example, Last et al. (1996) found that 13.6% of youth with Social Phobia retained the diagnosis after 3 to 4 years, whereas Newman et al. (1996) found that 79.3% of youth with Social Phobia retained the diagnosis after 0 to 3 years. The main difference between these studies was the age of participants (5 to 18 in Last et al.; 11 to 21 in Newman et al.). Other possible sources of inconsistency include the types of assessment instruments used, sample variations, different definitions of impairment, and limited understanding and use of empirically derived developmental information regarding the classification of anxiety disorders (see Curry et al., 2004; Scheeringa, Peebles, Cook, & Zeanah, 2001).

Some authors posited specific age differences in the expression of phobic and anxiety disorders in youth (Westenberg, Siebelink, & Treffers, 2001; Warren & Sroufe, 2004). Drawing on stage theories (e.g., Loevinger, 1976), Westenberg et al. suggested that the predominant expression of fear and anxiety symptoms may be tied in part to sequential developmental challenges. For example, children ages 6 to 9 years have begun the process of individuation and are expressing autonomy from their parents. The developmental challenge is self-reliance, but this challenge is likely to give rise to concerns about separation from or loss of parents. In contrast, youth ages 10 to 13 years are gaining insight into mortality and broader world concerns. Finally, emerging social understanding and comprehension in adolescence may lead to a predominance of social and evaluative concerns (see Warren & Sroufe, 2004; Westenberg et al., 2001). In the models of both Westenberg et al. (2001) and Warren and Sroufe (2004), separation anxiety symptoms and animal fears are the predominant expression of anxiety in children ages 6 to 9, compared with generalized anxiety symptoms and fears concerning danger and death in children ages 10 to 13, and social anxiety symptoms and social/performance related fears in adolescents around ages 14 to 17.

Epidemiological data from community samples are fairly consistent with these predictions (see Costello et al., 2004), providing empirical evidence that the predominant expression of phobic and anxiety symptoms is tied to normative developmental milestones. Research in clinical samples also suggests that Separation Anxiety Disorder is more common in children, whereas Social Phobia is more common in adolescents (Weems et al., 1998, 1999). Research examining specific fear and anxiety symptoms dimensionally across age ranges also supports the notion of sequential developmental differences in the expression of symptoms (Chorpita et al., 2000; Ollendick, Matson, & Helsel, 1985; Ollendick, King, & Frary, 1989).

In terms of a priori tests of the developmental hypothesis, Westenberg, Siebelink, Warmenhoven, and Treffers (1999) reported that Separation Anxiety Disorder precedes Overanxious Disorder (using DSM-III-R criteria). Moreover, Westenberg, Drewes, Siebelink, and Treffers (2004) found that child self-rated fears of physical danger and punishment decrease with age, and self-rated fears of social and achievement evaluation increase with age, controlling for overall fears. Weems and Costa (2005) also tested this developmental theory and found that specific symptoms dominated at certain ages (e.g., separation anxiety in children 6 to 9 years, death and danger fears in youth 10 to 13 years, and social anxiety and fears of criticism in youth 14 to 17 years). These findings suggest that models of the etiology of childhood anxiety should consider differences across childhood and adolescence in developmental expression. This concept has been termed *heterotypic continuity* (e.g., Moffitt, 1993).

COMORBIDITY

As noted previously, comorbidity among the anxiety disorders in youth is substantial, with estimates as high as 50% in population studies (see Costello et al., 2004) and as high as 70% in clinical samples (Weems et al., 1998). Across studies, comorbidity of anxiety disorders with ADHD range from 0 to 21%, with Conduct Disorder and Oppositional Defiant Disorder from

3% to 13%, and with depression from 1% to 20% (Costello et al., 2004). In general, there is a high degree of association between depression and anxiety, and anxiety disorders often co-occur within individuals. Similar findings in community samples suggest that comorbidity is not just a function of referral biases. Moreover, rates of comorbidity exceed rates that would be predicted by intersecting base rates (see Curry et al., 2004).

CULTURAL CONSIDERATIONS

A large body of literature indicates cultural and ethnic differences in the expression of anxious symptoms. Research suggests that Latino children have higher levels of internalizing symptoms than white non-Latino children in terms of both anxious and somatic complaints (Ginsburg & Silverman, 1996; Pina & Silverman, 2004; Roberts, 1992; Varela et al., 2004a, b). Little is known about the mechanisms that may be responsible for this cultural variability. Researchers have focused on the effects that culture-specific socialization practices and family variables may have on emotion expression. For example, researchers have speculated that because Latino culture is characterized by a collectivistic ideal, emotions and willingness to express emotions will tend to be consistent with cultural norms (Triandis et al., 1985). In a collectivistic society, interdependence and subordination to the group are cultivated through strict social norms and expectations of conformity, self-restraint, and social inhibition. Thus, symptom elevations in anxiety reflect the societal emphasis on those particular mood states and behaviors (Weisz et al., 1987). From this perspective, individualistic cultures such as that in the United States, which emphasize autonomous, outgoing, self-promoting behaviors, should have more children with disruptive behavior problems because this type of expression is supported (Weisz et al., 1987). An alternative explanation for an association between collectivistic cultures and internalizing symptoms is that an emphasis on the control of emotions may stifle children's understanding and managing of their internal states (Varela et al., 2004a, b). From this perspective, the social constraints on expressing emotions such as anxiety lead to a failure to develop emotion-regulation skills, which leads to greater emotional difficulties.

SEX DIFFERENCES

Girls and women experience higher levels of anxiety and related symptoms than boys and men (Silverman & Carter, 2006). Epidemiological research has indicated a roughly 2:1 girl:boy ratio for anxiety disorders (Costello et al.,

2004). These findings are consistent with research on youth self-reports of fear, which show that girls report more fears than boys (Ginsburg & Silverman, 2000; Ollendick et al., 2001, 1985, 1989). Although these findings are consistent, the mechanisms responsible for the sex differences remain obscure. Research suggests that girls and women show higher heritability estimates for anxiety than boys and men (see Eley, 2001), with some developmental variation. That is, girls have higher heritability of anxiety symptoms in early adolescence (ages 11 to 13) than in late childhood (ages 8 to 10) or mid-adolescence (ages 14 to 16), with boys showing a decrease in heritability over time (e.g., Topolski, et al., 1997). However, genetic influences do not rule out socialization processes in the expression of symptoms—in girls' increased willingness to report certain types of symptoms (Ginsburg & Silverman, 2000; Rutter, Caspi, & Moffitt, 2003).

THEORETICAL SYNTHESIS AND FUTURE DIRECTIONS

This chapter has provided an overview of a developmental psychopathology approach to describing continuity and change in childhood anxiety disorders. This approach suggests that a comprehensive theory of anxiety disorders requires differentiation between primary and secondary features. Primary features of problematic anxiety are (a) dysregulation of the anxiety response system and (b) negative affect and distress/impairment that result from physiological arousal. Secondary features are aspects that distinguish the various DSM-IV (APA, 1994) anxiety disorders from one another (e.g., interpersonal concerns in Social Anxiety Disorder, uncued panic attacks in Panic Disorder). Significant advances have been made in understanding the developmental psychopathology of childhood anxiety disorders. Research has identified biological, behavioral, cognitive, interpersonal, and contextual processes important to understanding the origins of childhood anxiety.

The developmental psychopathology view can be summarized via a hypothetical child's emotional development into adulthood. This child may be behaviorally inhibited very early in life. This behavioral inhibition is likely to be the product of genetic risk factors (e.g., double short 5HTT allele), which may interact with environmental risks (e.g., low social support, parental reinforcement of avoidance). A child exposed to this combination of genetic vulnerability and environmental risk is likely to experience elevated anxiety (i.e., dysregulation of the anxiety response system and corresponding distress), which is in turn shaped by normative developmental processes and individual experiences. For example, the child with a propensity for elevated arousal and avoidance may live with parents who are unskilled in reducing the child's anxious responding, or who model withdrawn or anxious behaviors in social contexts. Such parents may themselves be anxious. The child may also be exposed repeatedly to socially challenging events that he or she is allowed to avoid. This avoidance may result in a failure to develop cognitive, social, and behavioral skills for facing social situations. Vulnerability to developing an anxiety disorder is high for this child, and the specific set of risk factors may potentiate social anxiety. Early in the child's life, the resultant dysregulation in the anxiety response system may manifest as Separation Anxiety Disorder. Later in development the dysregulation is more likely to result in Social Anxiety Disorder.

We encourage future research that tests the hypothesized factors of influence on shaping continuity and change in both primary and secondary features of anxiety. Our view emphasizes trajectories (versus purely diagnostic categorical approaches) of anxiety over time, throughout childhood and adolescence, to determine common pathways in anxious emotion. We also encourage research aimed at clarifying the role of the factors that are hypothesized to shape these pathways. We suggest that taking an approach that emphasizes the distinction between core and secondary features of anxious emotion will facilitate understanding of the basic developmental psychopathology of anxiety and also individual variation in expression of anxious emotion.

REFERENCES

Ackerman, P.T., Newton, J.E.O., McPherson, W.B., Jones, J.G., & Dykman, R.A. (1998). Prevalence of posttraumatic stress disorder and other psychiatric diagnoses in three groups of abused children (sexual, physical, and both). *Child Abuse and Neglect, 22,* 759–794.

Ainsworth, M. D., Blehar, M. C., Waters, E., & Wall, S. (1978). *Patterns of attachment: A psychological study of the strange situation.* Hillsdale, NJ: Erlbaum.

Albano, A. M., & Kendall, P. C. (2002). Cognitive behavioral therapy for children and adolescents with anxiety disorders: Clinical research advances. *International Review of Psychiatry, 14,* 129–134.

Alfano, C. A., Beidel, D. C., & Turner, S. C. (2002). Cognition in childhood anxiety: Conceptual methodological and developmental issues. *Clinical Psychology Review, 22,* 1208–1238.

American Psychiatric Association. (1968). *Diagnostic and statistical manual of mental disorders.* (2nd ed.) Washington, DC: Author.

American Psychiatric Association. (1980). *Diagnostic and statistical manual of mental disorders.* (3rd ed.) Washington, DC: Author.

American Psychiatric Association (1987). *Diagnostic and statistical manual of mental disorders* (3rd ed., rev.) Washington, DC: Author.

American Psychiatric Association (1994). *Diagnostic and statistical manual of mental disorders* (4th ed.) Washington, DC: Author.

American Psychiatric Association (2000). *Diagnostic and statistical manual of mental disorders* (4th ed., text revision). Washington, DC: Author.

Bandura, A. (1982). Self-efficacy mechanism in human agency. *American Psychologist 37*, 122–147.

Barlow, D. H. (2002). *Anxiety and its disorders: The nature and treatment of anxiety and panic.* (2nd ed.) New York: Guilford.

Baltes, P. B., Reese, H. W., & Lipsitt, L. P. (1980). Life-span developmental psychology. *Annual Review of Psychology, 31*, 65–110.

Baltes, P. B., Reese, H. W., & Nesselroade, J. R. (1988). *Life-span developmental psychology: An introduction to research methods.* Hillsdale, NJ: Erlbaum.

Barrett, P. M., Rapee, R. M., Dadds, M. M., & Ryan, S. M. (1996). Family enhancement of cognitive style in anxious and aggressive children. *Journal of Abnormal Child Psychology, 24*, 187–203.

Baving, L., Laucht, M., & Schmidt, M. H. (2002). Frontal brain activation in anxious school children. *Journal of Child Psychology and Psychiatry, 43*, 265–274.

Beck, A. T. (1976). *Cognitive therapy and the emotional disorders.* New York: International Universities Press.

Beidel, D.C. (1991). Determining the reliability of psychophysiological assessment in childhood anxiety. *Journal of Anxiety Disorders, 5*, 139–150.

Bell-Dolan, D. J., Foster, S. L., & Christopher, J. S. (1995). Girls' peer relations and internalizing problems: Are socially neglected, rejected, and withdrawn girls at risk? *Journal of Clinical Child Psychology, 24*, 463–473.

Bernstein, G.A., & Borchardt, C.M. (1991). Anxiety disorders of childhood and adolescence: A critical review. *Journal of the American Academy of Child and Adolescent Psychiatry, 30*, 519–532.

Bernstein, G. A., Borchardt, C. M., & Perwien, A. R. (1996). Anxiety disorders in children and adolescents: A review of the past 10 years. *Journal of the American Academy of Child and Adolescent Psychiatry, 35*, 1110–1119.

Berg, I. (1976). School phobia in the children of agoraphobic women. *British Journal of Psychiatry, 128*, 86–89.

Berman, S. L., Weems, C. F., Silverman, W. K., & Kurtines, W. M. (2000). Predictors of outcome in exposure based cognitive and behavioral interventions for phobic and anxiety disorders. *Behavior Therapy, 31*, 713–731.

Biederman, J., Rosenbaum, J. F., Bolduc-Murphy, E. A., Faraone, S. V., Chaloff, J., Hirshfeld, D. R., & Kagan, J. (1993). Behavioral inhibition as a temperamental risk factor for anxiety disorders. *Child and Adolescent Psychiatric Clinics of North America, 2*, 667–684.

Biederman, J., Rosenbaum, J. F., Hirshfeld, D., Faraone, V., Bolduc, E., Gersten, M., Meminger, S., & Reznick, S. (1990). Psychiatric correlates of behavioral inhibition in young children of parents with and without psychiatric disorders. *Archives of General Psychiatry, 47*, 21–26.

Blashfield, R.K. (1989). Alternative taxonomic models of psychiatric classification. In L. N. Robins & J. E. Barrett (Eds.), *The validity of psychiatric diagnosis* (pp. 19–31). New York: Raven Press.

Borkovec, T. D., Shadick, R., & Hopkins, M. (1991) The nature of normal worry and pathological worry. In R. M. Rapee & D. H. Barlow (Eds.), *Chronic anxiety: Generalized anxiety disorder and mixed anxiety-depression* (pp. 29–51). New York: Guilford.

Bouton, M. E., Mineka, S., & Barlow, D. H. (2001). A modern learning theory perspective on the etiology of panic disorder. *Psychological Review, 108*, 4–32.

Bowlby, J. (1977). The making and breaking of affectional bonds: Aetiology and psychopathology in the light of attachment theory. *British Journal of Psychiatry, 130*, 201–210.

Bronfenbrenner, U. (1977). Toward an experimental ecology of human development, *American Psychologist, 32*, 513–531.

Capps, L., Sigman, M., Sena R., Henker, B., & Whalen, C. (1996). Fear, anxiety, and perceived control in children of agoraphobic parents. *Journal of Child Psychology and Psychiatry, 37*, 445–452.

Carrión, V. G., Weems, C. F., Eliez, S., Patwardhan, A., Brown, W., Ray, R., & Reiss, A. L. (2001). Attenuation of frontal lobe asymmetry in pediatric PTSD. *Biological Psychiatry, 50*, 943–951.

Carrión, V. G., Weems, C. F., Ray, R., Glasser, B., Hessl, D., & Reiss, A. (2002). Diurnal salivary cortisol in pediatric Posttraumatic Stress Disorder. *Biological Psychiatry, 51*, 575–582.

Carrión, V. G., Weems, C. F., & Reiss, A. L. (in press). Stress predicts brain changes in children: A pilot longitudinal study on youth stress, PTSD, and the hippocampus. *Pediatrics.*

Cassidy, J. (1999). The nature of the child's ties. In J. Cassidy & P. Shaver (Eds.), *Handbook of attachment: Theory, research, and clinical applications.* (pp. 3–20). New York: Guilford.

Chorpita, B. F., & Barlow, D. H. (1998). The development of anxiety: The role of control in the early environment. *Psychological Bulletin, 124*, 3–21.

Chorpita, B.F., Yim, L., Moffitt, C., Umemoto, L.A., & Francis, S.E. (2000). Assessment of symptoms of *DSM-IV* anxiety and depression in children: A revised child anxiety and depression scale. *Behavior Research and Therapy, 38*, 835–855.

Cicchetti, D., & Rogosch, F. A. (1996). Equifinality and multifinality in developmental psychopathology. *Development and Psychopathology, 8*, 597–600.

Clark, L. A., & Watson, D. (1991a). Theoretical and empirical issues in differentiating depression from anxiety. In J. Becker & A. Kleinman (Eds.), *Psychosocial aspects of depression.* (pp. 39–65). Hillsdale, NJ: Erlbaum.

Clark, L. A., & Watson, D. (1991b). Tripartite model of anxiety and depression: Psychometric evidence and taxonomic implications. *Journal of Abnormal Psychology, 100*, 316–336

Clark, L. A., Watson, D., & Reynolds, S. (1995) Diagnosis and classification of psychopathology: Challenges to the current system and future directions. *Annual Review of Psychology, 46*, 121–153.

Costa, N. M., & Weems, C. F. (2005). Maternal and child anxiety: Do attachment beliefs or children's perceptions of maternal control mediate their association? *Social Development, 14*, 574–590.

Cortez, V. L., & Bugental, D. B. (1995). Priming of perceived control in young children as a buffer against fear-inducing events. *Child Development, 66*, 687–696.

Costello, E. J., Egger, H. L., & Angold, A. (2004). Developmental epidemiology of anxiety disorders. In T. H. Ollendick & J. S. March (Eds.). *Phobic and anxiety disorders in children and adolescents: A clinician's guide to effective psychosocial and pharmacological interventions* (pp. 61–91). New York: Oxford University Press.

Curry, J. F., March, J. S., & Hervey, A. S. (2004). Comorbidity of childhood and adolescent anxiety disorders. In T. H. Ollendick & J. S. March (Eds.), *Phobic and anxiety disorders in children and adolescents: A clinician's guide to effective psychosocial and pharmacological interventions* (pp. 116–140). New York: Oxford University Press.

Dadds, M. R., James, R. C., Barrett, P. M., & Verhulst (2004). Diagnostic issues. In T. H. Ollendick & J. S. March (Eds.), *Phobic and anxiety disorders in children and adolescents: A clinician's guide to effective psychosocial and pharmacological interventions* (pp. 3–33). London: Oxford University Press.

Daleiden, E. L. (1998). Childhood anxiety and memory functioning: A comparison of systemic and processing accounts. *Journal of Experimental Child Psychology, 68,* 216–235.

Dalgleish, T., Taghavi, M. R., Neshat-Doost, H. T., Moradi, A. R., Canterbury, R., & Yule, W. (2003). Patterns of processing bias for emotional information across clinical disorders: A comparison of attention, memory, and prospective cognition in children and adolescents with depression, generalized anxiety, and posttraumatic stress disorder. *Journal of Clinical Child and Adolescent Psychology, 32,* 10–21.

Damasio, A. (2003). *Looking for Spinoza: Joy, sorrow, and the feeling brain.* Orlando, FL: Harcourt.

Davidson, R. J., & Fox, N. A. (1989). Frontal brain asymmetry predicts infants' response to maternal separation. *Journal of Abnormal Psychology, 98,* 127–131.

Davidson, R. J. (1998). Affective style and affective disorders: Perspectives from affective neuroscience. *Cognition and Emotion, 12,* 307–320.

Davidson, R. J., Marshall, J. R., Tomarken, A. J., Henriques, J. B. (2000). While a phobic waits: regional brain electrical and autonomic activity in social phobics during anticipation of public speaking. *Biological Psychiatry, 47,* 85–95.

Davis, M. (1998). Are different parts of the Amygdala involved in fear versus anxiety? *Biological Psychiatry, 48,* 51–57.

De Bellis, M. D., Baum, A. S., Birmaher, B., Keshavan, M. S., Eccard, C. H., Boring, A. M., et al. (1999a). Developmental traumatology: I. Biological Stress Systems. *Biological Psychiatry, 45,* 1259–1270.

De Bellis, M. D., Keshavan, M. S., Clark, D. B., Casey, B. J., Giedd, J. N., Boring, A. M., et al. (1999b). Developmental traumatology: II. Brain development. *Biological Psychiatry, 45,* 1271–1284.

Eley, T. C. (2001). Contributions of behavioral genetics research: Quantifying genetic, shared environmental and nonshared environmental influences. In M. W. Vasey amd M. R. Dadds (Eds.), *The developmental psychopathology of anxiety* (pp. 45–59). London: Oxford University Press.

Epkins, C. C. (1996). Cognitive specificity and affective confounding in social anxiety and dysphoria in children. *Journal of Psychopathology and Behavioral Assessment, 18,* 83–101.

Field, A. P. (2006). Watch out for the beast: Fear information and attentional bias in children. *Journal of Clinical Child & Adolescent Psychology, 35*, 431–439.

Field, A. P., Argyris, N. G., & Knowles, K. A. (2001). Who's afraid of the big bad wolf: A prospective paradigm to test Rachman's indirect pathways in children. *Behavior Research and Therapy, 39*, 1259–1276.

Field, A.P., & Lawson, J. (2003). Fear information and the development of fears during childhood: Effects on implicit fear responses and behavioral avoidance. *Behavior Research and Therapy, 41*, 1277–1293.

Fox, N. A., Nichols, K. E., Henderson, H. A., Rubin, K., Schmidt, L., Hamer, D., Ernst, M., & Pine, D. S. (2005). Evidence for a gene-environment interaction in predicting behavioral inhibition in middle childhood. *Psychological Science, 16*, 921–926.

Ginsburg, G. S., Lambert, S. F., & Drake, K. L. (2004). Attributions of control, anxiety sensitivity, and panic symptoms among adolescents. *Cognitive Therapy and Research, 28*, 745–763.

Ginsburg, G. S., & Schlossberg, M. C. (2002). Family based treatment of childhood anxiety disorders. *International Review of Psychiatry, 14*, 143–154.

Ginsburg, G. S., & Silverman, W. K. (1996). Phobic and anxiety disorders in Hispanic and Caucasian youth. *Journal of Anxiety Disorders, 10*, 517–528.

Ginsburg, G. S., & Silverman, W. K. (2000). Gender role orientation and fearfulness in children with anxiety disorders. *Journal of Anxiety Disorders, 14*, 57–68.

Granger, D. A., Weisz, J. R., & Kauneckis, D. (1994). Neuroendocrine reactivity, internalizing behavior problems, and control related cognitions in clinic-referred children and adolescents. *Journal of Abnormal Psychology, 103*, 267–276.

Gray, J. A. (1982). *Neuropsychological theory of anxiety: An investigation of the septal-hippocampal system.* Cambridge: Cambridge University Press.

Gray, J. A., & McNaughton, N. (2000). *The neuropsychology of anxiety* (2nd ed.). New York: Oxford University Press.

Gunnar, M. (2001). Cortisol and anxiety. In M. W. Vasey & M. R. Dadds (Eds.), *The developmental psychopathology of anxiety.* London: Oxford University Press.

Hayward, C., Killen, J. D., Kraemer, H. C., & Taylor, C. (2000). Predictors of panic attacks in adolescents. *Journal of the American Academy Child and Adolescent Psychiatry, 39*, 207–214.

Henry, B., & Moffitt, T. E. (1991). Anxiety and cognitive task performance: A longitudinal perspective. *Child Study Journal, 21*, 167–183.

Kagan, J., Reznick, J. S., & Gibbons, J. (1989). Inhibited and uninhibited types of children. *Child Development, 60*, 838–845.

Kagan, J., Reznick, J. S., & Snidman, N. (1987). The physiology and psychology of behavioral inhibition. *Child Development, 58*, 1459–1473.

Kagan, J., Reznick, J. S., & Snidman, N. (1988). Biological bases of childhood shyness. *Science, 240*, 167–171.

Kearney, C. A., Albano, A. M., Eisen, A. R., Allan, W. D., & Barlow, D. H. (1997). The phenomenology of panic disorder in youngsters: An empirical study of a clinical sample. *Journal of Anxiety Disorders, 11*, 49–62.

Keller, M. B., Lavori, P. W., Wunder, J., Beardslee, W. R., Schwartz, C. E., & Roth, J. (1992). Chronic course of anxiety disorders in children and adolescents. *Journal of the American Academy of Child and Adolescent Psychiatry, 31*, 595–599.

Kendall, P. C. (1994). Treating anxiety disorders in children: Results of a random-ized clinical trial. *Journal of Consulting and Clinical Psychology, 62,* 200–210.

Kiser, L. J., Heston, J., Millsap, P. A., Pruitt, D. B. (1991). Physical and sexual abuse in childhood: Relationship with posttraumatic stress disorder. *Journal of the American Academy of Child and Adolescent Psychiatry, 30,* 776–783.

La Greca, A. M., Silverman, W. K., Vernberg, E. M., & Prinstein, M. (1996). Symp-toms of posttraumatic stress after Hurricane Andrew: A prospective study. *Journal of Consulting and Clinical Psychology, 64,* 712–723.

La Greca, A. M., Silverman, W. K., & Wasserstein, S. B. (1998). Children's pre-disaster functioning as a predictor of posttraumatic stress following Hurricane Andrew. *Journal of Consulting and Clinical Psychology, 66,* 883–892.

Lang, P. J. (1977). Imagery in therapy: An information processing analysis of fear. *Behavior Therapy, 8,* 862–886.

Last, C. G., Perrin, S., Hersen, M. & Kazdin, A. E. (1996). A prospective study of childhood anxiety disorders. *Journal of the American Academy of Child and Ado-lescent Psychiatry, 35,* 1502–1510.

Lau, J. J., Calamari, J. E., & Waraczynski, M. (1996). Panic attack symptomology and anxiety sensitivity in adolescents. *Journal of Anxiety Disorders, 10,* 355–364.

LeDoux, J. (2000). Emotion circuits in the brain. *Annual Review of Neuroscience, 23,* 155–184.

Leung, P. W. L., & Wong, M. M. T. (1998). Can cognitive errors differentiate be-tween internalizing and externalizing problems. *Journal of Child Psychology Psy-chiatry and Allied Disciplines, 39,* 263–269.

Leitenberg, H., Yost, L. W., & Carroll-Wilson, M. (1986). Negative cognitive errors in children: Questionnaire development, normative data, and comparisons be-tween children with and without self-reported symptoms of depression, low self-esteem, and evaluation anxiety. *Journal of Consulting and Clinical Psychol-ogy, 54,* 528–536.

Loevinger, J. (1976). *Ego development: Conceptions and theories.* San Fransisco: Josey-Bass.

March, J. S., Leonard, H. L., & Swedo, S. E. (1995). Obsessive-compulsive disorder. In J. S. March (Ed.), *Anxiety disorders in children and adolescents* (pp. 251–275). New York: Guilford.

Maller, R. G., & Reiss, S. (1992). Anxiety sensitivity in 1984 and panic attacks in 1987. *Journal of Anxiety Disorders, 6,* 241–247.

Mathews, A. (1990). Why worry? The cognitive function of anxiety. *Behaviour Re-search and Therapy, 28,* 455–468.

Moffitt, T. E. (1993). Adolescence–limited and life–course–persistent antisocial behavior: A developmental taxonomy. *Psychological Review, 100,* 674–701.

Moffit, T. E. (2006). Life-course-persistent versus adolescent-limited antisocial be-havior. In D. Cicchetti & D. J. Cohen (Eds.), *Developmental psychopathology, Vol 3. Risk, disorder, and adaptation* (2nd ed., pp. 570–598). Hoboken, NJ: Wiley.

Moradi, A. R., Taghavi, M. R., Neshat-Doost, H. T., Yule, W. & Dalgleish, T. (2000). Memory bias for emotional information in children and adolescents with post-traumatic stress disorder: A preliminary study. *Journal of Anxiety Disorders, 14,* 521–532.

Mowrer, O. H. (1960). *Learning theory and behavior.* New York: Wiley.

Muris, P., Schouten, E., Meesters, C., & Gijsbers, H. (2003). Contingency-competence-control-related beliefs and symptoms of anxiety and depression in a young adolescent sample. *Child Psychiatry and Human Development, 33*, 325–339.

Newman, D. L., Moffitt, T. E., Caspi, A., Magdol, L., Silva, P. A., & Stanton, W. R. (1996). Psychiatric disorder in a birth cohort of young adults: Prevalence, comorbidity, clinical significance, and new case incidence from ages 11–21. *Journal of Consulting and Clinical Psychology, 64*, 552–562.

Ollendick, T. H., King, N. J., & Frary, R. B. (1989). Fears in children and adolescents: Reliability and generalizability across gender, age, and nationality. *Behavior Research and Therapy, 27*, 19–26.

Ollendick, T. H., Langley, A. K., Jones, R. T., & Kephart, C. (2001). Fear in children and adolescents: Relations with negative life events, attributional style, and avoidant coping. *Journal of Child Psychology and Psychiatry, 42*, 1029–1034.

Ollendick, T. H., & March, J. S. (Eds.). (2004). *Phobic and anxiety disorders in children and adolescents: A clinician's guide to effective psychosocial and pharmacological interventions*. London: Oxford University Press.

Ollendick, T. H., Matson, J. L., & Helsel, W. J. (1985). Fears in children and adolescents: Normative data. *Behaviour Research and Therapy, 23*, 465–467.

Ollendick, T. H., Vasey, M. W., & King, N. J. (2001). Operant conditioning influences in childhood anxiety. In M. W. Vasey & M. R. Dadds (Eds.), *The developmental psychopathology of anxiety* (pp. 231–252). London: Oxford University Press.

Pina, A. A., & Silverman, W. K. (2004). Clinical phenomenology, somatic symptoms, and distress in Hispanic/Latino and Euro-American youths with anxiety disorders. *Journal of Clinical Child and Adolescent Psychology, 33*, 227–236.

Pine, D. S., Cohen, P., Gurley, D., Brook, J., & Ma, Y. (1998). The risk for early-adulthood anxiety and depressive disorders in adolescents with anxiety and depressive disorders. *Archives of General Psychiatry, 55*, 56–64.

Rachman, S. (1977). The conditioning theory of fear-acquisition: A critical examination. *Behavior Research and Therapy, 15*, 375–387.

Rapee, R. M. (1997). Potential role of childrearing practices in the development of anxiety and depression. *Clinical Psychology Review, 17*, 47–67.

Rapee, R. M., Craske, M. G., Brown, T. A., & Barlow, D. H. (1996). Measurement of perceived control over anxiety related events. *Behavior Therapy, 27*, 279–293.

Rapee, R. M., Wignall, A., Hudson, J. L., & Schniering, C. A. (2000). *Treating anxious children and adolescents*. Oakland, CA: New Harbinger Publications.

Reiss, S. (1991). Expectancy model of fear, anxiety, and panic. *Clinical Psychology Review, 11*, 141–153.

Rosenbaum, J. F., Biederman, J., & Gersten, M. (1988). Behavioral inhibition in children of parents with panic disorder and agoraphobia: A controlled study. *Archives of General Psychiatry, 45*, 463–470.

Rutter, M., Caspi, A., & Moffitt, T. E. (2003). Using sex differences in psychopathology to study causal mechanisms: Unifying issues and research strategies. *Journal of Child Psychology & Psychiatry and Allied Disciplines, 44*, 1092–1115.

Saavedra, L. M., & Silverman, W. K. (2001). What a difference two decades make: Classification of anxiety disorders in children. *International Journal of Psychiatry, 14*, 87–101.

Sapolsky, R. M. (2000). Glucocorticoids and hippocampal atrophy in neuropsy-chiatric disorders. *Archives of General Psychiatry, 57,* 925–935.

Schmidt, N. B., Lerew, D. R., & Jackson, R. J. (1997). The role of anxiety sensitivity in the pathogenesis of panic: Prospective evaluation of spontaneous panic at-tacks during acute stress. *Journal of Abnormal Psychology, 106,* 355–364.

Schmidt, N. B., Lerew, D. R., & Jackson, R. J. (1999). Prospective evaluation of anxiety sensitivity in the pathogenesis of panic: Replication and extension. *Journal of Abnormal Psychology, 108,* 532–537.

Scheeringa, M. S., Peebles, C. D., Cook, C. A., & Zeanah, C. H. (2001), Toward establishing procedural, criterion, and discriminant validity for PTSD in early childhood. *Journal of the American Academy of Child and Adolescent Psychiatry, 40,* 52–60.

Scheeringa, M. S., Zeanah, C. H., Myers, L., & Putnam, F. (2004). Heart period and variability findings in preschool children with post traumatic stress symptoms. *Biological Psychiatry, 55,* 685–691.

Schippell, P. L., Vasey, M. W., Cravens-Brown, L. M., & Bretveld, R. A. (2003) Sup-pressed attention to rejection, ridicule, and failure cues: A unique correlate of reactive but not pro-active aggression in youth. *Journal of Clinical Child and Adolescent Psychology, 32,* 40–55.

Silverman, W. K. (1992). Taxonomy of anxiety disorders in children. In G. D. Bur-rows, R. Noyes, & S. M. Roth (Eds.), *Handbook of anxiety.* (Vol. 5; pp. 281–308). Amsterdam: Elsevier Science Publishers.

Silverman, W. K. (1993). *DSM* and the classification of anxiety disorders in chil-dren and adults. In C. G. Last (Ed.), *Anxiety across the lifespan: A developmental perspective on anxiety and the anxiety disorders* (pp. 7–36). New York: Springer.

Silverman, W. K., & Berman, S. L. (2001). Psychosocial interventions for anxi-ety disorders in children: Status and future directions. In W. K. Silverman & P. D. A. Treffers (Eds.), *Anxiety disorders in children and adolescents: Research, as-sessment and intervention* (pp. 313–334). Cambridge, U. K.: Cambridge Univer-sity Press.

Silverman, W. K., & Carter, R. (2006). Anxiety disturbance in girls and women. In J. Worell & C. Goodheart (Eds.), *Handbook of girls' and women's psychological health* (pp. 60–68). New York: Oxford University Press.

Silverman, W. K., Fleisig, W., Rabian, B., & Peterson, R. A. (1991). Childhood anxi-ety sensitivity index. *Journal of Clinical Child Psychology, 20,* 162–168.

Silverman, W. K., & Ginsburg, G. (1998). Anxiety disorders. In T. H. Ollendick & M. Hersen (Eds.), *Handbook of child psychopathology* (3rd ed., pp. 239–268). New York: Plenum Press.

Silverman, W. K., Kurtines, W. M., Ginsburg, G. S., Weems, C. F., Rabian, B., & Serafini, L. T. (1999). Contingency management, self-control, and education support in the treatment of childhood phobic disorders: A randomized clinical trial. *Journal of Consulting and Clinical Psychology, 67,* 675–687.

Silverman, W. K., & Nelles, W. B. (1988). The Anxiety Disorders Interview Sched-ule for Children. *Journal of the American Academy of Child and Adolescent Psychia-try, 27,* 772–778.

Silverman, W. K., & Ollendick, T. H. (2005). Evidence-Based Assessment of Anxiety and Its Disorders in Children and Adolescents. *Journal of Clinical Child & Adolescent Psychology, 34,* 380–411.

Silverman, W. K., & Rabian, B. (1995). Test-retest reliability of the *DSM-III-R* anxiety disorders symptoms using the Anxiety Disorders Interview Schedule for Children. *Journal of Anxiety Disorders, 9,* 139–150.

Silverman, W. K., & Treffers, P. D. A. (Eds.). (2001). *Anxiety disorders in children and adolescents: Research, assessment and intervention.* Cambridge, UK: Cambridge University Press.

Siqueland, L., Kendall, P. C., & Steinberg, L. (1996). Anxiety in children: Perceived family environments and observed family interaction. *Journal of Clinical Child Psychology, 25,* 225–237.

Topolski, T. D., Hewitt, J. K., Eaves, L. J., Silberg J. L., Meyer, J. M., Rutter, M., et al. (1997). Genetic and environmental influences on child reports of manifest anxiety and symptoms of separation anxiety and overanxious disorders: A community-based twin study. *Behavior Genetics, 22,* 15–26.

Triandis, H. C., Leung, K., Villareal, M. J., & Clark, F. L. (1985). Allocentric versus idiocentric tendencies: Convergent discriminant validation. *Journal of Research in Personality, 19,* 395–415.

Varela, R. E., Vernberg, E. M., Sanchez-Sosa, J. J., Riveros, A., Mitchell, M., & Mashunkashey, J. (2004a). Anxiety reporting and culturally associated interpretation biases and cognitive schemas: A comparison of Mexican, Mexican American, and European American families. *Journal of Clinical Child and Adolescent Psychology, 33,* 237–247.

Varela, R. E., Vernberg, E. M., Sanchez-Sosa, J. J., Riveros, A., Mashunkashey, J., & Mitchell, M. (2004b). Parenting practices of Mexican, Mexican American, and European American families: Social context and cultural influences. *Journal of Family Psychology, 18,* 651–657.

Vasa, R. A., & Pine, D. S. (2004). Neurobiology. In T. L. Morris & J. S. March (Eds.). *Anxiety disorders in children and adolescents* (2nd ed.; pp. 3–26). New York: Guilford.

Vasey, M. W., & Dadds, M. R. (2001) (Eds.). *The developmental psychopathology of anxiety.* London: Oxford University Press.

Vasey, M. W., El-Hag, N., & Daleiden E. L. (1996). Anxiety and the processing of emotionally-threatening stimuli: Distinctive patterns of selective attention among high- and low-test anxious children. *Child Development, 67,* 1173–1185.

Vasey M. W., Daleiden E. L., Williams L. L., & Brown L. M. (1995). Biased attention in childhood anxiety disorders: A preliminary study. *Journal of Abnormal Child Psychology, 23,* 267–279.

Vasey, M. W., Dalgleish, T., & Silverman, W. K. (2003). Research on information processing factors in child and adolescent psychopathology: A critical commentary. *Journal of Clinical Child and Adolescent Psychology, 32,* 81–93.

Vasey, M. W., & MacLeod, C. (2001). Information-processing factors in childhood anxiety: A review and developmental perspective. In M. W. Vasey & M. R. Dadds (Eds.), *The developmental psychopathology of anxiety* (pp. 253–277). London: Oxford University Press.

Vasey, M. W., & Ollendick, T. H. (2000). Anxiety. In M. Lewis & A. Sameroff (Eds.),

Cognitive interference: Theory, methods, and findings (pp. 117–138). Hillsdale, NJ: Erlbaum.

Walkup, J. T., Labellarte, M. L., & Ginsburg, G. S. (2002). The pharmacological treatment of childhood anxiety disorders. *International Review of Psychiatry, 14,* 143–154.

Warren S. L., Huston L., Egeland B., & Sroufe L. A. (1997). Child and adolescent anxiety disorders and early attachment. *Journal of the American Academy of Child and Adolescent Psychiatry, 36,* 637–644.

Warren, S. L., & Sroufe, L. A. (2004). Developmental issues. In T. H. Ollendick & J. S. March (Eds.), *Phobic and anxiety disorders in children and adolescents: A clinician's guide to effective psychosocial and pharmacological interventions* (pp. 92–115). New York: Oxford University Press.

Watts, S. E., & Weems, C. F. (in press). Associations among selective attention, memory bias, cognitive errors and symptoms of anxiety in youth. *Journal of Abnormal Child Psychology.*

Weems, C. F. (2005). Childhood anxiety disorders: An overview of recent guides for professionals and parents. *Journal of Clinical Child and Adolescent Psychology, 34,* 772–778.

Weems, C. F., Berman, S. L., Silverman, W. K., & Saavedra, L. S. (2001). Cognitive errors in youth with anxiety disorders: The linkages between negative cognitive errors and anxious symptoms. *Cognitive Therapy and Research, 25,* 559–575.

Weems, C. F., & Costa, N. M. (2005). Developmental differences in the expression of childhood anxiety symptoms and fears. *Journal of the American Academy of Child and Adolescent Psychiatry, 44,* 656–663.

Weems, C. F., Hammond-Laurence, K., Silverman, W. K., & Ferguson, C. (1997). The relation between anxiety sensitivity and depression in children referred for anxiety. *Behavior Research and Therapy, 35,* 961–966.

Weems, C. F., Hammond-Laurence, K., Silverman, W. K., & Ginsburg, G. S. (1998). Testing the utility of the anxiety sensitivity construct in children and adolescents referred for anxiety disorders. *Journal of Clinical Child Psychology, 27,* 69–77.

Weems, C. F., Hayward, C., Killen, J. D., & Taylor, C. B. (2002). A longitudinal investigation of anxiety sensitivity in adolescence. *Journal of Abnormal Psychology, 111,* 471–477.

Weems, C. F., & Silverman, W. K. (2006). An integrative model of control: Implications for understanding emotion regulation and dysregulation in childhood anxiety. *Journal of Affective Disorders, 91,* 113–124.

Weems, C. F., Silverman, W. K., Rapee, R., & Pina, A. A. (2003). The role of control in childhood anxiety disorders. *Cognitive Therapy and Research, 27,* 557–568.

Weems, C. F., Silverman, W. K., Saavedra, L. S., Pina, A. A, & Lumpkin, P. W. (1999). The discrimination of children's phobias using the Revised Fear Survey Schedule for Children. *Journal of Child Psychology and Psychiatry and Allied Disciplines, 35,* 941–952.

Weems, C. F., & Stickle, T. R. (2005). Anxiety disorders in childhood: Casting a nomological net. *Clinical Child and Family Psychology Review, 8,* 107–134.

Weems, C. F., Zakem, A., Costa, N. M., Cannon, M. F., & Watts, S. E. (2005). Physiological response and childhood anxiety: Association with symptoms of anxiety disorders and cognitive bias. *Journal of Clinical Child and Adolescent Psychology, 34,* 712–723.

Weisz, J., Suwanlert, S., Chaiyasit, W., & Walter, B. (1987). Over- and under-controlled referral problems among children and adolescents from Thailand and the United States: The *Wat* and *Wai* of cultural differences. *Journal of Consulting and Clinical Psychology, 55,* 719–726.

Westenberg, P. M., Drewes, M. J., Siebelink, B. M., & Treffers, P. D. A. (2004). A developmental analysis of self-reported fears in late childhood through mid-adolescence: social-evaluative fears on the rise? *Journal of Child Psychology and Psychiatry, 45,* 481–496.

Westenberg, P. M., Siebelink, B. M., & Treffers, P. D. A. (2001), Psychosocial developmental theory in relation to anxiety and its disorders. In W. K. Silverman & P. D. A. Treffers (Eds.), *Anxiety disorders in children and adolescents: Research, assessment and intervention* (pp. 72–89). Cambridge, UK: Cambridge University Press.

Westenberg, P. M., Siebelink, B. M., Warmenhoven, N. J., & Treffers, P. D. A. (1999). Separation anxiety and overanxious disorders: Relations to age and level of psychosocial maturity. *Journal of the American Academy of Child and Adolescent Psychiatry, 38,* 1000–1007.

Whaley, S. E., Pinto, A., & Sigman, M. (1999). Characterizing interactions between anxious mothers and their children. *Journal of Consulting and Clinical Psychology, 67,* 826–836.

Wolpe, J., & Rachman, S. (1960). Psychoanalytic "evidence": A critique based on Freud's case of little Hans. *Journal of Nervous & Mental Disease, 131,* 135–148.

Woodruff-Borden, J., Morrow, C., Bourland, S., & Cambron, S. (2002). The behavior of anxious parents: Examining mechanisms of transmission of anxiety from parent to child. *Journal of Clinical Child and Adolescent Psychology, 31,* 364–374.

CHAPTER 16

Depressive Disorders

DANIEL N. KLEIN, DANA C. TORPEY, SARA J. BUFFERD,
AND MARGARET W. DYSON

HISTORICAL CONTEXT

Recognition of child and adolescent depressive disorders is relatively recent. Prior to the mid-1970s, it was thought that depression rarely occurred in children, in part because it was believed that children had not yet developed the cognitive capacity to experience symptoms such as guilt and hopelessness (Rie, 1966). In addition, many clinicians believed that to the extent that children did experience depression, it was expressed in behavioral disturbances such as conduct problems, hyperactivity, enuresis, and somatic concerns (i.e., *depressive equivalents* or *masked depression*) (Toolan, 1962). This began to change by the mid-to-late 1970s, with an important conference on childhood depression sponsored by the National Institute of Mental Health (Schulterbrandt & Raskin, 1977). In the late 1970s, Puig-Antich and colleagues (1978), Carlson and Cantwell (1980), and several other groups of investigators demonstrated that many children and adolescents met full adult criteria for Major Depressive Disorder (MDD). By the early 1980s, the concept of childhood depression was widely accepted.

TERMINOLOGICAL AND CONCEPTUAL ISSUES

Depressive disorders in youth constitute a significant social and public health problem. Depressed children and adolescents often exhibit significant impairment in family, school, and peer functioning, and some degree of impairment may persist after recovery from the depressive episode (Garber & Horowitz, 2002; Lewinsohn & Essau, 2002). Depressed adolescents are also at risk for school dropout and unplanned pregnancy. Moreover, depression is the leading risk factor for youth suicide, and may be a risk factor for the development of other disorders such as substance abuse (Birmaher, Arbelaez, & Brent, 2002).

Depression is a complex phenomenon, in a number of senses. First, the term can encompass (1) a mood *state;* (2) a clinical *syndrome* that can be caused by a variety of nonpsychiatric factors such as endocrine disorders, psychoactive drugs, and major stressors, such as bereavement; and (3) a psychiatric *disorder*. In the present chapter, we will focus on depressive disorders, emphasizing MDD, as that has been the focus of most of the research in this area.

Second, the processes that are responsible for the pathogenesis of MDD and other depressive disorders are unknown, although evidence for a number of factors will be discussed in this chapter. It is highly likely that the depressive disorders are *multifactorial* conditions, in the sense that they are caused by the combination of many etiological factors. Moreover, depressive disorders are probably *etiologically heterogeneous,* meaning that there are different subtypes of depression that are caused by different sets of etiological processes.

As a result, depressive disorders are characterized by both *equifinality* and *multifinality* (e.g., Cicchetti & Rogosch, 1996). Consistent with the idea of etiological heterogeneity, depression exhibits equifinality in that a variety of developmental pathways can lead to the same clinical syndrome. Depression is also characterized by multifinality in that it is unlikely that any set of etiological factors is entirely specific to depression. Rather, the same etiological factor may contribute to a variety of pathological and nonpathological outcomes depending on the presence or absence of other moderating variables (e.g., other risk and protective factors).

In this chapter, we will discuss the diagnosis and classification of depressive disorders in children and adolescents; briefly review their prevalence in community samples; summarize data on the course of juvenile depression and its comorbidity with other psychiatric disorders; discuss genetic, neurobiological, cognitive, interpersonal, and socioenvironmental factors that may contribute to the pathogenesis of depression; and consider the roles of sex and culture.

DIAGNOSIS AND CLASSIFICATION

The current edition of the *Diagnostic and Statistical Manual of Mental Disorders* (American Psychiatric Association, 2000) defines MDD in children and adolescents as a period of persisting depressed or irritable mood or loss of interest or pleasure that lasts at least 2 weeks and is accompanied by a variety of other symptoms, including low energy and fatigue; inappropriate feelings of guilt or worthlessness; difficulty thinking, concentrating, or making decisions; sleep disturbance (insomnia or hypersomia); appetite disturbance (eating too little or too much or significant weight loss or gain); psychomotor disturbance (retardation, which refers to extreme slowing in movement and speech, or agitation, which is extreme restlessness); and thoughts of death or suicidal thoughts or behavior. Dysthymic Disorder is a milder but more chronic condition, characterized by a period of depressed or irritable mood that is present for at least 50% of the time for at least 1 year and is accompanied by several other symptoms.

There are a number of controversies in the diagnosis and classification of depression in general, and in children and adolescents in particular. These include the continuity between child, adolescent, and adult depression; whether depression has discrete boundaries or shades continuously into normal mood states; the identification of more homogeneous subtypes; whether there are age-specific expressions of depression; the existence and manifestations of depression in very young children; and how to assess child and adolescent depression. We discuss each of these in turn below.

CONTINUITY

There is considerable evidence for continuity between adolescent and adult depression, yet the evidence for continuity between (a) prepubertal and (b) adolescent and adult depression is less consistent. Three lines of research that inform the issue of continuity include studies of the clinical presentation, longitudinal course, and familial aggregation of depression.

Depressed children, adolescents, and adults tend to exhibit similar symptoms although, as discussed in the following, there may be some developmental variations. Follow-up studies indicate that depressed adolescents are at high risk for developing episodes of MDD as adults (Lewinsohn et al., 1999; Weissman, Wolk, Goldstein et al., 1999). However, follow-up studies of prepubertal children have yielded mixed results, with some studies indicating that depressed children are at increased risk for depression in adulthood, and other studies failing to find evidence of increased risk, except in particular subgroups (Harrington et al., 1990; Weissman, Wolk, Wickramaratne et al., 1999). Finally, family studies have found significantly higher rates of MDD in the first-degree relatives of depressed adolescents than adolescents with other forms of psychopathology or adolescents with no history of psychiatric disorder (Klein et al., 2001). Family studies have also found higher rates of MDD in the relatives of depressed children than in the relatives of healthy children, but comparisons of rates of depression in relatives of depressed children and children with other psychiatric disorders have yielded inconsistent results (Kovacs et al., 1997; Puig-Antich et al., 1989). The possibility of discontinuity between prepubertal and postpubertal depression is further reinforced by differences in the ratio of males to females and in the role of genetic factors in childhood-onset depression compared to adolescent- and adult-onset depression (see following).

DISCRETENESS AND BOUNDARIES

The question of whether mood disorders are discrete entities or extremes along a continuum has been debated for much of the past century. This issue has implications for identifying etiological factors, defining disorders and subtypes, and optimizing the selection of assessment approaches and statistical models. Currently, Meehl's (1995) taxometric procedures are regarded as the best means of testing whether disorders are discrete or continuous. Only a few studies have applied these techniques to child and adolescent depression, with conflicting results (Hankin et al., 2005; Solomon et al., 2006); however, there is evidence that some subtypes of youth depression, such as Melancholia, may be taxonic (Ambrosini et al., 2002).

Even when disorders are not discrete, it may be necessary to establish cut-points on an underlying continuum to indicate when a phenomenon warrants clinical attention, as is done for hypertension (Kessler, 2002). Unfortunately, the distinctions among mood disorders and normal variations in mood, nonpathological dysphoria, and responses to major stressors are difficult to make, and can be influenced by a variety of sociocultural and economic factors. Some investigators believe that the boundaries in the *DSM-IV* are too broad and include many individuals with demoralization and transient stress responses. Given the major developmental transitions and emotional intensity that characterize adolescence (Arnett, 1999), it may be difficult to distinguish mood disorders from normal variations in mood during this period. Consistent with this possibility, Wickramaratne and Weissman (1998) reported that, whereas rates of depression in offspring of depressed versus nondepressed parents differed in childhood and young adulthood, there were no differences in adolescence, a period marked by significant increase in rates of depression regardless of parental diagnosis. Nevertheless, some investigators believe that the current boundaries for depressive disorders are too strict, pointing to evidence that subthreshold depressive symptoms are common in juveniles and adults and are often associated with functional impairment (e.g., Lewinsohn et al., 2000).

SUBTYPES

As depression is almost undoubtedly heterogeneous etiologically, there has been considerable effort expended in trying to delineate more homogeneous subtypes of adult mood disorders. In addition to the unipolar-bipolar distinction, subtypes have been proposed on the basis of symptoms (e.g., psychotic, melancholic, atypical) and course (e.g., age of onset, recurrent, chronic, seasonal pattern). Unfortunately, the issue of heterogeneity has largely been ignored in child and adolescent depression. Despite some intriguing findings (e.g., Ambrosini et al., 2002, and Luby, Mrakotosky, & Heffelfinger, 2004, for melancholia), the validity of distinct subtypes of depression in children and adolescents remains to be established.

AGE-SPECIFIC MANIFESTATIONS

Setting aside the issue of continuity regarding etiology, the question of whether the clinical presentations of MDD and DD differ as a function of developmental level is complex and still unresolved. The available literature suggests that the symptoms of MDD are fairly similar in school-aged children, adolescents, and adults, although hopelessness and some vegetative (i.e., disturbances in sleep and appetite) and motivational symptoms may be somewhat more frequent in adolescents than children (Weiss & Garber, 2003). Nonetheless, the manifestations of particular symptoms vary as a function of the child's level of cognitive and social development. For example, younger children may appear sad but have difficulty reporting their mood, and prepubertal children may lose interest in their friends and activities but are obviously unlikely to experience decreased libido. There have also been several studies exploring whether there are developmental differences in the structure of the depressive syndrome, although findings have been inconsistent (Weiss & Garber, 2003).

DEPRESSION IN VERY YOUNG CHILDREN

There has been little systematic research on depression in infants and preschool-aged children. Thus, it is unclear whether a syndrome comparable to that identified in school-aged children, adolescents, and adults exists in younger children. However, in an important series of papers, Luby and her colleagues (e.g., Luby et al., 2002, 2003) reported that MDD can be identified in preschool-aged children using modified *DSM-IV* criteria with a shorter duration requirement and provided preliminary evidence for its construct validity.

ASSESSMENT

A variety of structured and semistructured diagnostic interviews, symptom rating scales, and parent-, teacher-, and self-report questionnaires for depression in youth exist (see Klein, Dougherty, & Olino, 2005, for a review).

However, the concordance between evaluations conducted with different informants tends to be low, as it is for most areas of psychopathology (Achenbach, McConaughy, & Howell, 1987). This issue raises the question of which source(s) to rely on, and how (or whether) to combine data from different informants. Although there are no firm conclusions, some "rules of thumb" include (a) placing greater weight on self-reports of internalizing symptoms versus informants' reports of externalizing symptoms and (b) relying more on parents' reports for children than for adolescents (Klein et al., 2005).

EPIDEMIOLOGY

The best approach to estimating the prevalence of any disorder is to use representative community samples, as treatment-seeking samples are biased in a number of respects, including greater severity and comorbidity (see Goodman et al., 1998). There have been few epidemiological studies of the prevalence of depression in representative samples of preschool- and school-age children, but a greater number of such studies in adolescents are available.

Depression is fairly rare in preschool-aged children, with a 3 to 6 month prevalence of 1 to 2% (Egger et al., 2006). The point prevalence of MDD in school-aged children is also low, with most estimates ranging from 1 to 3% (Garber & Horowitz, 2002). For example, in the Great Smokey Mountain Study (Costello et al., 1996), which examined a representative community sample of 9-, 11-, and 13-year-olds, the 3-month prevalence of depressive disorders was 1.5%.

The prevalence of depression rises sharply in adolescence, approaching adult levels. Most estimates of point prevalence are in the 5 to 6% range, and estimates of lifetime prevalence fall in the 15 to 20% range (Costello et al., 2003; Lewinsohn & Essau, 2002). For example, in the Oregon Adolescent Depression Project, which assessed a large representative sample of high school students, the point prevalences of MDD and DD were 2.6% and 0.5%, respectively, and lifetime prevalences were 18.5% for MDD and 3.2% for DD (Lewinsohn et al., 1993).

Studies examining ethnic/racial differences in the prevalence of depression in youth have yielded inconsistent findings (Costello, Keeler, & Angold, 2001; Wight et al., 2005). The risk of depression appears to be greater for youth from lower socioeconomic status backgrounds, which might account for the inconsistent effects observed for race/ethnicity (Costello et al., 2001). There is some evidence suggesting cultural differences in the expression of depression, with somatic symptoms playing a greater role among Chinese American than Caucasian youth (Chen, Roberts, & Aday, 1998).

SEX DIFFERENCES

One of the best-established findings regarding child and adolescent depression is that rates of symptoms and diagnoses in males and females are similar in childhood, but between the ages of 12 and 15 the rate of depression in females exhibits a marked increase (Hankin & Abramson, 2001; Nolen-Hoeksema, 2002). A variety of explanations for the increased vulnerability to depression in adolescent girls have been considered, with most focusing on sex differences in the many biological, psychological, and social changes and challenges that occur during this period.

There has been some support for the role of hormones and pubertal timing. For example, in a longitudinal study of adolescent females, Angold, Costello, Erkanli, and Worthman (1999) found that increases in estrogen and testosterone levels were associated with the onset of depressive disorders. The biological changes in puberty appear to interact with broader social and environmental factors. For example, the physical changes associated with puberty may lead to greater dissatisfaction with one's body among girls than among boys, and there is evidence that body dissatisfaction predicts increases in depressive symptoms (Allgood-Merten, Lewinsohn, & Hops, 1990). Early maturing girls are at particularly high risk for depression compared to their peers (Ge, Conger, & Elder, 2001; Graber et al., 1997), perhaps because they are faced with expectations, pressures, and reactions that they are not ready for—and perhaps also because they lack the support of peers who are dealing with the same issues.

Another set of explanations suggest that the increased rate of depression in adolescent females is due to their experiencing higher levels of stress than males during the transition to adolescence. Both males and females report increases in the numbers of stressors from childhood to adolescence, and in many studies the increase is greater for females than males (e.g., Ge et al., 2001; Rudolph & Hammen, 1999). However, the sex differences in stress vary across types of life events, with females experiencing particularly high rates of interpersonal stressors compared to males (Shih et al., 2006).

A final set of explanations deals with the contention that females have greater vulnerabilities than males prior to adolescence, and these preexisting vulnerabilities interact with the stressors and challenges of adolescence to produce higher rates of depression in females (Nolen-Hoeksema, & Girgus, 1994). Indeed, there is evidence that adolescent females experience higher levels of depression than males in response to comparable levels of stress (Ge et al., 1994; Shih et al., 2006), suggesting preexisting differences in susceptibility. A number of vulnerabilities have been hypothesized. For example, due to a combination of biological and socialization processes, girls may have greater affiliative needs than boys, rendering them more vulnerable to interpersonal stressors (Cyranowski et al., 2000; Rudolph, Flynn, & Abaied, in press). There is also evidence that females are more likely to cope with adversity and dysphoric moods in a passive, ruminative way, while males are more likely to use active and avoidant strategies (Nolen-Hoeksema, 2002). As passive, ruminative coping is associated with depression, this tendency could contribute to the higher rate of depression among females as they confront challenges in adolescence (Nolen-Hoeksema, 2002).

COMORBIDITY

The majority of children and adolescents with MDD or DD also meet criteria for other psychiatric disorders. Although rates of comorbidity are high in adults, they tend to be even higher in children and adolescents (Rohde, Lewinsohn, & Seeley, 1991). In a meta-analysis of studies using community samples, Angold, Costello, and Erkanli (1999) reported that depressed children and adolescents were 8.2 times more likely than nondepressed youths to meet criteria for an anxiety disorder, 6.6 times more likely to meet criteria for Conduct Disorder, and 5.5 times more likely to meet criteria for Attention-Deficit/Hyperactivity Disorder. Juvenile depression also frequently co-occurs with substance use, eating, and developmental disorders (Angold et al., 1999). Rates of comorbidity are even higher in clinical samples (Kovacs, 1996).

It is unlikely that methodological issues such as sampling or rater biases account for these high comorbidity rates (Angold et al., 1999). However, comorbidity may be an indication that the boundaries in our classification system are drawn in the wrong places (Klein & Riso, 1993). In some cases, when depression co-occurs with another disorder, it may represent a distinct syndrome that differs from depressions that do not co-occur with the other disorder. For example, some investigators have argued that depressed children with comorbid Conduct Disorder represent a distinct subgroup, as there is evidence that they have lower rates of depression in their relatives and are less likely to experience depression as adults than depressed children without Conduct Disorder (Harrington et al., 1990).

Alternatively, comorbidity may be due to common etiological factors between the two disorders. For example, Clark and Watson (1991) have hypothesized that depressive and anxiety disorders have both common and unique etiological influences. In their tripartite model, they propose that the temperamental trait of negative emotionality (NE) predisposes to both depression and anxiety, increasing the likelihood that the two disorders will co-occur. A number of cross-sectional and longitudinal studies have confirmed that youths with depressive disorders and youths with anxiety disorders both report elevated levels of NE (e.g., Chorpita & Daleiden, 2002; Lonigan, Phillips, & Hooe, 2003).

Finally, comorbidity may reflect the causal influence of one disorder on another. For example, a number of studies have indicated that anxiety disorders/symptoms in children and adolescents predict subsequent depressive disorders/symptoms (e.g., Cole et al., 1998; Orvaschel, Lewinsohn, & Seeley, 1995). However, to the extent that anxiety has a causal influence on depression, the process appears to be complex. Thus, Eaves and Silburg (2003) recently reported that childhood anxiety influences the development of depression in adolescence through three distinct pathways: one in which genetic differences in anxiety predict later genetic differences in depression; a second in which the genes that affect early anxiety increase sensitivity to adverse life events, indirectly increasing the risk for depression (an example of *gene–environment interaction*, as discussed in the following); and a third in which the genes that increase risk for early anxiety increase exposure to depressogenic environmental influences (an example of *gene–environment correlation*, also discussed in the following). Moreover, a growing number of studies have revealed that the temporal relationship between anxiety and depression runs in both directions, with anxiety disorders predicting subsequent depressive disorders and depression predicting subsequent anxiety (Costello et al., 2003; Pine et al., 1998). Such findings once again point to the multiple etiologic pathways leading to depression in children and adolescents, exemplifying equifinality.

COURSE AND OUTCOME

Almost all children and adolescents with an episode of MDD recover from that episode, although many continue to experience subsyndromal (or residual) symptoms. The length of episodes varies. The mean duration of episodes of MDD is approximately 7 to 8 months in clinical samples, and episodes of DD last an average of 48 months (Birmaher et al., 2002; Kovacs, 1996). The majority of youths with DD experience superimposed episodes of MDD (a phenomenon referred to as *double depression*) (Kovacs, Akiskal, & Gatsonis, 1994). Rates of relapse and recurrence of MDD are high, with the majority of depressed juveniles experiencing another episode within several years (Birmaher et al., 2002; Kovacs, 1996). Long-term follow-up studies indicate that 40 to 70% of depressed adolescents experience a recurrence of MDD in adulthood (Fombonne et al., 2001; Lewinsohn et al., 1999; Weissman, Wolk, Goldstein et al., 1999). However, as noted earlier, the evidence for children with MDD is less consistent (Harrington et al., 1990; Weissman, Wolk, Wickramaratne et al., 1999).

Studies have identified a number of predictors of the duration of MDD episodes and the probability of recurrence. Variables that are associated with a longer time to recovery include an early age of onset, greater severity of depression, suicidality, double depression, the presence of comorbid anxiety or disruptive behavior disorders, depressotypic cognitions, and adverse family environments (Birmaher et al., 2002). Predictors of an increased risk of recurrence include greater severity, psychotic symptoms, suicidality, a prior history of recurrent MDD, double depression, the presence of subthreshold symptoms after recovery, a depressotypic cognitive style, recent stressful life events, adverse family environments, and a family history of MDD (particularly if it is recurrent) (Birmaher et al., 2002).

It is difficult to determine the relative importance of these prognostic factors, as there are few instances in which most of these variables have been included in the same study. However, in a study of a community sample of depressed adolescents, Lewinsohn, Rohde, Seeley, Klein, and Gotlib (2000) examined most of these variables as predictors of recurrence in young adulthood. They found that a prior history of recurrent MDD, a family history of recurrent MDD, personality disorder traits, and, for females only, greater conflict with parents were significant and independent predictors of subsequent recurrence.

Children and adolescents with MDD and DD are also at risk for developing manic and hypomanic episodes. The probability of *switching* to Bipolar Disorder is higher in patients with psychotic symptoms, psychomotor retardation, a family history of Bipolar Disorder, and/or a high familial loading for mood disorders (Geller, Fox, & Clark, 1994).

RISK FACTORS

GENETICS

The first step in investigating the role of genes in the etiology and pathogenesis of a disorder is to determine whether the disorder aggregates within families. There are two approaches to exploring the familial aggregation of depression in youth. The bottom-up approach starts with depressed children or adolescents and examines rates of mood disorders in their relatives. The top-down (or high risk) approach starts with depressed parents and examines rates of mood disorders in their offspring. Both bottom-up (Klein et al., 2001; Kovacs et al., 1997; Puig-Antich et al., 1989) and top-down (Klein, Lewinsohn et al., 2005; Weissman et al., 2006) studies indicate that depression in children and adolescents aggregates in families: Adult relatives of depressed youth and offspring of depressed parents are over two times more likely to have a mood disorder than the relatives of healthy controls (Rice, Harold, & Thapar, 2002).

Family studies have also addressed the specificity of the familial aggregation of youth depression. This addresses the question of whether a specific liability for mood disorders or a more general liability for psychopathology is transmitted. These results have been inconsistent, with some studies finding evidence for specificity of familial aggregation (e.g., Klein et al., 2001) but others indicating that the rates of a variety of nonmood disorders (e.g., anxiety disorders, disruptive behavior disorders, substance use disorders) are also elevated in the relatives of depressed youth and the offspring of depressed parents (e.g., Puig-Antich et al., 1987; Weissman et al., 2006). As noted earlier, the evidence for specificity of familial aggregation is somewhat greater for adolescents than children, raising the possibility that these may be different forms of disorder.

Disorders can run in families for a variety of reasons other than genes. Hence, twin and adoption studies are necessary to help determine whether familial aggregation is due to genetic or environmental factors. Unfortunately, there have not been any twin or adoption studies of depressive disorders in children or adolescents. However, a number of twin studies have examined the role of genetic factors in the transmission of depressive *symptoms*.

Modern twin studies use structural equation modeling to distinguish between additive genetic factors, shared environmental factors (aspects of the environment that make twins similar to one another), and unique environmental factors (aspects of the environment that make twins different from one another). Twin studies of depressive symptoms indicate that genetic factors play a modest role in youth depression (Lemery & Doelger, 2005; Rice et al., 2002). There is some evidence suggesting that genes play a greater role in adolescent than childhood depression, and a recent longitudinal twin study reported that new genetic influences on depression emerge as children grow older (Scourfield et al., 2003). At the same time, some studies have reported that shared environmental factors play a greater role in childhood than adolescent depression (Rice et al., 2002; Scourfield et al., 2003). These findings are consistent with the possibility that there are qualitative differences between child and adolescent depression. On the other hand, genetic effects on behavior tend to increase across the lifespan, regardless of the trait or disorder being studied (Lemery & Doelger, 2005). Thus, lower heritability coefficients for childhood depression cannot necessarily be interpreted as suggesting qualitative differences across development. Moreover, it is difficult to draw strong conclusions from twin studies because they have been limited to depressive symptoms, rather than diagnoses, and the magnitude of the genetic and environmental effects appear to vary as a function of the youth's sex, the informant (parent versus child report), and the assessment instrument (Lemery & Doelger, 2005; Rice et al., 2002).

Twin studies provide information regarding the role of genetic factors in a disorder, but cannot identify the particular genes involved. The two major approaches to identifying specific genes are linkage and association studies. Linkage studies examine the relationships between genetic markers with known chromosomal locations and the occurrence of disorder within families. *Linkage* between a genetic marker and a disorder suggests that the marker, or a gene that is in close proximity to it, contributes to the etiology of the disorder. This approach has been very successful in disorders that are caused by a single gene with large effects (e.g., Huntington's Disease), but may be less useful for disorders that are caused by many genes, none of which have major effects. Several genome-wide linkage studies are currently being conducted on adult depression; however, few consistent findings have emerged at this point (Levinson, 2006).

Association studies compare the frequencies of variants (or polymorphisms) of specific genes that are hypothesized to play a role in the pathophysiology of the disorder (candidate genes) between groups of depressed and nondepressed individuals. Most of these studies have also focused on adult depression. The majority have examined genes involved in the synthesis, release, and reuptake of the neurotransmitter serotonin (5-HT), although other genes such as brain-derived neurotrophic factor (BDNF), which has been implicated in brain plasticity and response to stress, are also being investigated. Association studies are more powerful than linkage studies in detecting genes with small effects. As it is likely that multiple genes with small effects (polygenic transmission) are involved in youth depression, association studies may ultimately be the more useful approach. Thus far, however, association studies have not produced well-replicated findings for depressive disorders (Levinson, 2006). One possible explanation is that, consistent with diathesis-stress models of psychopathology, individuals with a genetic predisposition may not develop a Depressive Disorder unless they experience significant environmental stress (Moffitt, Caspi, & Rutter, 2006). This suggests that it may be critical to take the environment into account in studying the role of genes in depression (and vice versa). Indeed, as discussed in the following, intriguing evidence is emerging suggesting the role of gene–environment interactions in the etiology of depression in both youths and adults.

The relationship between genetic and environmental factors is complex, and can include both gene–environment correlations and gene–environment interactions (Rutter, Moffitt, & Caspi, 2006). *Gene–environment correlation* refers to situations in which certain genotypes increase the risk of exposure to high-risk environments. There are three broad types of gene–environment correlations. *Passive gene–environment correlations* refer to the fact that children usually inherit their genes from the same people who raise them, so their genotypes and child-rearing environments are correlated. For example, depressed parents are less engaged and more hostile and critical of their children than nondepressed parents (Lovejoy et al., 2000). An adverse child-rearing environment, in turn, is a risk factor for later depression (Klein, 2006). *Evocative gene–environment correlations* refer to the possibility that the child's genes may be expressed in ways that tend to evoke certain reactions in others. For example, a child who is temperamentally inhibited and socially withdrawn may be more likely to be ignored by his/her peers, leading to loneliness and low self-esteem, and limiting opportunities to develop and practice social skills, all of which might increase risk for depression (Klein et al., in press). Finally, *active gene–environment correlations* refer to the fact that, as children grow older, they have increasing opportunities to choose their environments, such as peers and activities (*niche-picking*). There is evidence that some of the same genes that predispose to depression increase the likelihood that adolescents will experience higher rates of dependent life events (i.e., stressors that they help create), which in turn increases levels of depression (Silberg et al., 1999).

Genes may also interact with the environment by increasing susceptibility to environmental stress. For example, in a sample of female adolescent twins, Silberg et al. (2001) reported that stressful life events were associated with depressive symptoms only among girls with a high genetic vulnerability to depression. Recently, several studies have suggested gene–environment interactions for depression at the molecular level. In 2003, Caspi and colleagues reported that young adults with a short allele in the promoter region of the serotonin transporter gene (5-HTT-LPR) had an increased rate of depressive disorders, but only when exposed to stressful life events (Caspi et al., 2003). Since then, several studies have indicated similar findings for depressive symptoms in children and adolescents (Eley et al., 2004; Kaufman et al., 2004). Moreover, Kaufman et al. (2006) found that this effect depended on a gene–gene interaction between the 5-HTT-LPR polymorphism and a variant of the BDNF gene, such that children with the combination of both of these polymorphisms and a high level of environmental stress exhibited the greatest depression. The recent molecular genetic evidence for gene–environment interactions is very exciting, but it must be viewed cautiously as there have been some failures to replicate (Zammit & Owen, 2006), and statistical interactions are highly sensitive to the scaling of the variables and statistical models employed (Eaves, 2006). In addition, the findings are paradoxical in that the high-risk short allele of the 5-HTT-LPR gene produces fewer transporter molecules, which should reduce serotonin uptake activity. However, many antidepressant medications that are used to treat depression (i.e., the selective serotonin reuptake inhibitors) are also believed to operate by reducing serotonin uptake (Levinson, 2006).

The growing evidence that genes influence sensitivity to the environment has been paralleled by emerging findings indicating that the environment also influences the expression and regulation of genes (epigenetics). For example, studies of rodents and primates have demonstrated that maternal behavior and separation can have lasting effects on neuroendocrine stress response (Frances et al., 1999) and neurotransmitter systems that are also dysregulated in depression (Bremner & Vermetten, 2001) (see following). Similarly, women with a history of abuse in childhood exhibit abnormalities in neuroendocrine and autonomic responses to laboratory stressors (Heim et al., 2000). Most important in this context, however, Weaver et al. (2004) recently demonstrated that the persisting effects of the early rearing environment on neurobiological stress reactivity are mediated by changes in gene expression. Specifically, they found that the maternal behavior in rats influences the methylation of a key binding site on the rat pup's glucocorticoid receptor gene that regulates expression of that receptor, thereby influencing long-term neuroendocrine stress reactivity. Thus, while early experience does not actually alter DNA sequences, it appears to have a significant and persisting impact on the regulation and expression of genes.

Finally, genes do not have direct effects on behavior. Rather, pathways from genes to disorders include a number of intermediate biological and behavioral variables (or endophenotypes). One of the pathways from genes to depression may be mediated by child temperament. Two temperamental traits that have been linked to depression are the previously noted construct of high negative emotionality (NE) (i.e., propensity to sad, fearful, anxious, and/or irritable affect, particularly in response to stress) and low positive emotionality (PE) (i.e., decreased levels of joy and exuberance; social introversion; low appetitive drive/approach behavior). Evidence suggests several linked findings: Offspring of depressed parents have lower levels of PE and higher levels of NE than the offspring of nondepressed parents; NE and MDD have shared genetic influences; low PE and high

NE may lead to a variety of cognitive and interpersonal problems that increase the risk of depression; and low PE and high NE in children predict the subsequent development of depression (Klein et al., in press).

MALADAPTIVE PARENTING AND ABUSE

A number of studies have indicated associations between maladaptive parenting, including abuse, and child and adolescent depression. In clinical samples, depressed adolescents report lower levels of care and warmth, communication and sharing, and more tension in their relationships with their mothers and fathers than do psychiatric controls (Puig-Antich et al., 1993; Rey, 1995). Similarly, in community samples, depressive symptoms and disorders are associated with adolescents' reports of lower levels of parental warmth and care and higher levels of parental intrusiveness (Martin et al., 2004; Patton et al., 2001). Moreover, these problems often continue after depressive symptoms have remitted (Puig-Antich et al., 1985).

Children's reports on interview and questionnaire measures are consistent with observational data. For example, parents of depressed children exhibit higher levels of expressed emotion (EE), characterized by criticism and emotional overinvolvement, when discussing their child, than do parents of nonaffectively ill children (Asarnow et al., 2001). Although much of these data are cross-sectional or retrospective, longitudinal studies have shown that maladaptive parenting predicts later increases in depressive symptoms (Duggal et al., 2001; Stice, Ragan, & Randall, 2004).

There is intriguing evidence that childhood-onset and adolescent-onset depressions may be associated with somewhat different aspects of parenting and the family context. Thus, in a long-term prospective longitudinal study, Duggal et al. (2001) reported that a broad index of family adversity, including abuse, family stress, and low levels of early emotional support, predicted depressive symptoms in childhood, whereas depressive symptoms in adolescence were associated specifically with early lack of emotional support.

Physical, sexual, and emotional abuse are also associated with depressive symptoms in children. However, each of these forms of maltreatment may have different effects. For example, in a longitudinal study, Kim and Cicchetti (2006) found that physical abuse and neglect were associated with greater initial levels of depression, but that the effects of emotional maltreatment on depression were more persistent. It should be noted as well that there are clear effects of physical abuse on externalizing behavior (see review of Coie & Dodge, 1998). Finally, in addition to having a direct effect on youth depression, maladaptive parenting and abuse may influence a variety of other processes that further increase risk for mood disorders, including increased neurobiological and behavioral response to stress (Heim et al., 2000), cognitive vulnerabilities (Alloy et al., 2006), low self-esteem (Kim & Cicchetti, 2006), and interpersonal deficits (Rudolph et al., in press).

BIOLOGICAL FACTORS

There is a growing literature on the neurobiological correlates of depression in children and adolescents. Although there are many conflicting findings, it appears that the neurobiology of depression in children and adolescents is similar to that in adults in some respects but different in other respects. To the extent that there are differences between adult and youth depression, it is unclear whether they reflect differences in etiology and pathophysiology or differences in the maturation of the neurobiological systems. In addition, insofar as child and adolescent depression are associated with neurobiological abnormalities, it has not been determined whether they play an etiological role or are a concomitant or consequence of depression or of variables associated with depression, such as stress and comorbid psychiatric disorders.

Neuroendocrinology. Adult depression is often characterized by dysregulation of the hypothalamic pituitary adrenal (HPA) axis, which is a key stress-response system. A number of studies have examined cortisol, which is released by the adrenal glands, and growth hormone (GH), which is released by the pituitary, in depressed youth (Birmaher et al., 1996; Kaufman & Charney, 2003).

Adults with depression often exhibit increased basal levels of cortisol, abnormalities in the diurnal pattern of cortisol secretion (in which cortisol production is greatest in the early morning hours), and abnormal hormonal responses to pharmacological challenge agents such as dexamethasone. In contrast, depressed children and adolescents do not exhibit abnormalities in basal cortisol levels or the diurnal pattern of cortisol secretion. However, like depressed adults, but unlike healthy youths, many depressed children and adolescents fail to suppress cortisol production after ingesting the synthetic corticosteroid dexamethasone (Kaufman & Charney, 2003). In addition, depressed preschoolers exhibit a greater and more prolonged cortisol response to laboratory stress than do healthy and nondepressed psychiatric controls (Luby et al., 2003). Finally, elevations in morning cortisol predict the subsequent first onset of MDD in adolescents (Goodyer et al., 2000), suggesting that HPA axis dysregulation may predispose to the development of juvenile mood disorders.

Depressed youth also resemble depressed adults but differ from healthy controls in their hyposecretion of GH in response to GH-releasing hormone (Dahl et al., 2000). This may be a vulnerability marker, as it is evident following remission of symptoms (Dahl et al., 2000) and in children of depressed parents who are at risk for developing the disorder (Birmaher et al., 2000).

Sleep architecture.   Depressed adults exhibit a number of sleep abnormalities, including reduced rapid-eye-movement (REM) latency and increased REM density. Some studies have reported that depressed adolescents exhibit similar abnormalities (Birmaher et al., 1996; Kaufman & Charney, 2003), although conflicting results have also been reported (Bertocci et al., 2005). In contrast, the sleep architecture of depressed children does not differ from healthy controls (Birmaher et al., 1996; Kaufman & Charney, 2003).

Neurotransmitters.   Dysregulation of neurotransmitters, including serotonin and norepinephrine, has long been hypothesized to play a role in adult mood disorders. Studies using serotoninergic and noradrenergic precursors and direct and indirect agonists have provided some evidence for dysregulation in these systems in adults (Flores, Musselman, & De-Battista, 2004). However, the effects of serotonergic challenge agents on neuroendocrine measures such as prolactin levels in depressed children and adolescents tend to differ from the effects in depressed adults, with children exhibiting augmented, and adults blunted hormonal responses. In addition, depressed children and adolescents have a poorer response to serotonergic antidepressant medications than depressed adults, suggesting important discontinuity in serotonergic function. In contrast, some evidence suggests that both depressed children and adults exhibit blunted neuroendocrine responses to noradrenergic challenge agents compared to controls (Kaufman & Charney, 2003).

Structural and functional brain correlates.   Many studies of depressed adults have reported structural and functional abnormalities in parts of the brain circuitry that are involved in emotional reactivity and regulation, such as the prefrontal cortex, amygdala, and hippocampus. Only a few studies have used magnetic resonance imaging (MRI) to examine structural abnormalities in these areas in depressed children and adolescents, with inconsistent results. For example, Steingard et al. (2002) found significantly smaller frontal white matter volume and larger frontal gray matter volume in depressed adolescents than controls. In contrast, Nolan et al. (2002) found that depressed children and adolescents with a negative family history of MDD had significantly *larger* left prefrontal cortex white matter volumes than depressed youth with a family history of MDD and health controls. Depressed youth with a positive family history did not differ from controls on prefrontal cortical white or gray matter volume. Some studies have reported decreased amygdala volumes in depressed youth (e.g., Rosso et al., 2005), whereas others have not (e.g., MacMillan et al., 2003). Finally, most studies examining hippocampal volume have failed to find differences between depressed and nondepressed youths (e.g., MacMillan et al., 2003; Rosso et al., 2005). Unfortunately, these studies have used small samples, making replication difficult and increasing the chances of spurious findings.

Even fewer researchers have used functional MRI (fMRI) to examine brain function in depressed children and adolescents. Studies that are available suggest that there may be functional abnormalities in brain circuits involved in emotional processing and reactivity. For example, Thomas et al. (2001) found that in response to slides of faces with fearful expressions, children and adolescents with MDD exhibited decreased left amygdala activation and youths with anxiety disorders displayed increased right amygdala activation, compared to controls.

The findings of decreased amygdala volume and activation contrast with studies of adult depression, which typically report increased amygdala volume and increased activation in response to negative stimuli. (Davidson et al., 2002). However, there are too few neuroimaging studies of child and adolescent depression to draw conclusions at this point.

COGNITIVE FACTORS

A range of cognitive factors have been hypothesized to predispose to depression, including dysfunctional attitudes, negative inferential styles, attention and memory biases, and negative self-concepts. Although many of these theories are extensions from the adult literature, a number of studies have tested these factors in children and adolescents.

Beck (1967) proposed that people with depressogenic schemas, or mental representations, develop dysfunctional attitudes that may lead to a negative view of the self, world, and future. He suggested that individuals with such beliefs are at high risk for developing depression if they experience a stressful life event. Similarly, in the current version of helplessness-hopelessness theory, Abramson, Metalsky, and Alloy (1989) hypothesize that a negative life event, in conjunction with a negative inferential style (tending to see the causes of negative events as internal, stable, and global, and inferring negative characteristics about oneself because of the event) leads to helplessness, which causes at least some forms of depression.

A number of studies have confirmed associations between depressive cognitions and attributions and depressive symptoms in children and adolescents (Gladstone & Kaslow, 1995; Joiner & Wagner, 1995). However, studies examining whether such cognitions and attributions predict the development of depression, and whether they increase sensitivity to stressful life events, have been conflicting (see Hammen & Rudolph, 2003; Hankin & Abela, 2005).

Cognitive theories of depression suggest that depressed adults and youth exhibit attentional and memory biases for negative information and against positive information. Studies have generally revealed little evidence for attentional biases in depression (although see Joormann et al., 2007 for an important recent exception). However, there is support for memory biases in both adult and youth depression, particularly for self-relevant stimuli. For example, studies have indicated that children and adolescents with elevated levels of depressive symptoms recall fewer positive, and more negative, self-descriptive words than nondepressed youth (e.g., Cole & Jordan, 1995; Neshat-Doost et al., 1998).

Cognitive theories of youth depression have also emphasized the role of self-esteem, self-efficacy, and self-perceived competence. For example, Cole (1991) reported that low perceived competence in multiple domains (academic, social, sports, physical attractiveness, and behavioral conduct) is associated with depressive symptoms in children. However, longitudinal data indicate that, whereas children's underestimation of their competence (compared to others' ratings) predicts depressive symptoms over time, previous depression also predicts underestimation of competence (Hoffman et al., 2000).

Depressed children and adolescents clearly exhibit a variety of depressotypic cognitions. However, it is less certain whether these cognitive variables are predisposing factors, concomitants, or consequences of depression. One problem is the difficulty of observing depressive cognitive schemas in the nondepressed state. Thus, many cognitive theorists have hypothesized that depressogenic cognitions must be primed or activated in order to be observed (Persons & Miranda, 1992). This is typically accomplished by inducing negative mood states in vulnerable individuals, such as those with a previous history of, or familial risk for, depression. These studies have generally found that remitted depressed children and adolescents (Timbremont & Braet, 2004) and children of depressed mothers (Taylor and Ingram, 1999) exhibit greater levels of depressive cognitions after negative mood induction than controls.

PEER RELATIONSHIPS

A number of studies have documented that depressed children and adolescents have difficulties with peer (and for adolescents, romantic) relationships (Rudolph et al., in press). For example, children who report being less accepted by peers have higher levels of depressive symptoms than children who feel socially accepted. Peer and teacher reports also indicate that depressed children have deficits in social skills and difficulties with interpersonal relationships. Moreover, observational studies have reported that depressed children are more withdrawn, passive, and isolated, and more aggressive and hostile than their peers (Rudolph et al., in press).

The direction of the association between depression and interpersonal relationships is complex. Prospective studies have reported that difficulties with peer relationships predict increases in depression. For example, Schrepferman, Eby, Snyder, and Stropes (2006) found that low peer sociometric ratings in kindergarten and first grade were associated with increased depressive symptoms in third and fourth grade in both boys and girls, and that the observer's ratings of disengagement from peers on the playground also predicted later depression in girls. Similarly, examining young adolescents' relationships with their best friends, Allen et al. (2006) reported that a withdrawn, angry, or dependent pattern of behavior predicted increased levels of depressive symptoms 1 year later. On the other hand, depression also predicts decreases in peer support (Stice et al., 2004). Thus, it is likely that the association between depression and peer and romantic relationships is reciprocal and transactional. Indeed, in a longitudinal study with a middle school sample, Prinstein, Borelli, Cheah, Simon, and Aikins (2005) reported that depressive symptoms predicted less stability in friendships, while less positive friendships combined with excessive reassurance-seeking predicted increases in depressive symptoms.

LIFE STRESS

Stressful life events appear to play a substantial role in the development of depression in youth (Goodyer, 2001; Grant et al., 2003). Correlational studies have shown that negative life events are associated with depressive symptoms in young children, school-age children, and adolescents. In addition, prospective studies reveal that stressful life events often precede the onset and recurrence of depressive symptoms and episodes in adolescents (Cole et al., 2006; Goodyer et al., 2000; Patton et al., 2003), suggesting that they have a causal influence. Moreover, life events have been shown to predict the first onset of MDD in adolescents (Monroe et al., 1999). Overall, most depressed youth experienced a stressful life event within several months prior to the onset of their depression; however, the majority of children and adolescents who experience life stress do not become depressed (Goodyer, 2001). This is consistent with diathesis-stress models of psychopathology and with the recent studies of gene–environment interactions in depression discussed previously, and suggests that life events tend to trigger depression primarily in youths with an existing predisposition.

In some cases, depressed individuals contribute to the occurrence of the stressors that they experience. The stress-generation model (Hammen, 1991) suggests that depression and related features lead to impaired functioning, which increases the likelihood of self-generated stressful events; in turn, these *dependent* events can serve to exacerbate depressive symptoms. Studies provide support for the concurrent link between depressive symptoms and dependent stressors in children and adolescents (Rudolph & Hammen, 1999; Williamson et al., 1995), and longitudinal data reveal that depressive symptoms/disorders are associated with subsequent negative events (Cole et al., 2006; Patton et al., 2003). The stress-generation model is consistent with evidence for gene–environment correlations discussed earlier (Silberg et al., 1999), and helps to explain why a genetic predisposition for depression is associated with an increased rate of dependent life events.

Certain types of stressors, such as negative interpersonal life events, appear to be particularly potent risk factors for depression in youth (Rudolph & Hammen, 1999). Thus, events involving loss (Eley & Stevenson, 2000; Goodyer et al., 2000; Patton et al., 2003), disruption of important friendships (Eley & Stevenson, 2000; Prinstein et al., 2005), and romantic breakups (Monroe et al., 1999) have been linked with depression in children and adolescents. In addition, there is some evidence that individuals with particular personality styles are more vulnerable to specific types of life events. For example, adolescents with a *sociotropic* personality style, whose self-esteem is closely connected to the state of their interpersonal relationships, may be more prone to develop depression after an interpersonal stressor (Little & Garber, 2005).

PROTECTIVE FACTORS

Protective factors are variables that reduce risk in high-risk contexts. Thus, the protective factor alters (or moderates) the association between a high-risk environmental or biological context and an adverse outcome (Luthar, Cicchetti, & Becker, 2000). Identifying such factors could have important implications for prevention. Unfortunately, there has been little research on protective factors in youth depression. Moreover, most of the work that has been conducted focuses on variables that appear to be the absence or opposite of established risk factors, such as high self-esteem and self-efficacy, an "easy" temperament, and family and peer support (e.g., Denny et al., 2004). Demonstrating that a caring, involved parent is associated with decreased risk provides little information over and above existing evidence that parental rejection and neglect are associated with increased risk. Hence, in order to be useful, "protective factors" should be more than just the absence or opposite of established risk factors. For example, a protective factor might be a variable whose presence shifts a high-risk trajectory in a more positive direction, but whose absence has no influence on the risk trajectory.

CONCLUSIONS AND FUTURE DIRECTIONS

Given the current state of knowledge, it would be premature to attempt to offer a comprehensive theoretical model of the etiopathogenesis of depressive disorders in children and adolescents. However, enough is known to begin to outline some of the key features of such a model. First, youth depression is a multifactorial and etiologically heterogeneous condition, with multiple developmental pathways leading toward it and away from it. Few risk factors are specific to depression, and there may be considerable overlap with the etiologies of other psychiatric disorders, particularly the anxiety disorders, contributing to the comorbidity that is almost ubiquitous in youth depression.

There appear to be important differences between at least some forms of childhood-onset and adolescent-onset depression, as well as heterogeneity within both groups. Adolescent-onset depression exhibits considerable continuity with adult depression, whereas there is less continuity between childhood-onset depression and both adolescent and adult depression.

Genetic influences play an important role in youth depression, but it may be greater in adolescence than childhood. Conversely, parental and family influences may be more important for children, although it appears that early adversity can have effects on depression that persist into adulthood (e.g., Heim et al., 2000). The influence of genes appears to be complex and indirect, with multiple genes having small effects and operating through intermediate phenotypes such as temperament and susceptibility to stress. Genetic factors also appear to be mediated and moderated by a number of other factors such as gender, early adversity, comorbid psychopathology, dysregulation in key neurobiological pathways, cognitive biases, interpersonal difficulties, and both independent and self-generated life stressors. Finally, these risk factors also have independent effects on depression, and they may, in turn, be exacerbated by depression through reciprocal and transactional patterns.

For heuristic purposes, we will briefly outline one possible, but undoubtedly oversimplified, model of the etiopathogenesis of depression. The two major sets of distal causes include a genetic predisposition (which is probably graded and continuous, depending on the number of susceptibility genes that the individual possesses) and an adverse early environment (e.g., parental rejection, neglect, physical and sexual abuse). These two sets of distal causes often co-occur (i.e., passive gene–environment correlation), and may have additive or interactive effects; but in some cases they may also comprise independent pathways to depression. Genetic susceptibilities may be expressed in the form of temperamental vulnerabilities that, at the behavioral level, are reflected by low PE and/or high NE, and that are accompanied by dysregulation in a number of neurobiological systems. These temperamental vulnerabilities can also be influenced by environmental adversity, which can have lasting effects on behavioral and neurobiological stress-response systems. As the child enters the early school-age years, these temperamental vulnerabilities are elaborated cognitively, leading to the emergence of depressive cognitive schemas. At the same time, these temperamental, and eventually cognitive, vulnerabilities can lead to interpersonal deficits that in turn reinforce the depressive schemas and generate dependent stressors that may sensitize or kindle neurobiological stress-response systems. When these emotional/neurobiological/cognitive vulnerabilities and the level of dependent and independent environmental stressors combine, either additively or interactively, to exceed some hypothetical threshold, the emotional and cognitive precursors of depression escalate to the point of a diagnosable disorder. This can occur at virtually any point during the lifespan. However, it appears that, due to some combination of the distribution of liability in the population, the development of critical neurobiological, cognitive, and interpersonal systems, and the developmental challenges and transitions that emerge at this time, the period during which this escalation is most likely to occur is early adolescence. Moreover, it is particularly likely to occur in females, perhaps due to sex differences in preexisting vulnerability factors to a sharper increase in depression-relevant stressors (e.g., disturbances in interpersonal relationships) during this critical period.

A great deal of work is necessary on a number of fronts in order to advance our understanding of depression in children and adolescents. Research is needed to clarify the relationship between childhood- and adolescent-onset depression, delineate more homogeneous subtypes of depression, elucidate the reasons for comorbidity (particularly with anxiety disorders but also with disruptive conditions), and understand the expression of depression in early childhood. Genetically informative designs and prospective longitudinal studies of high-risk and community samples of infants and young children prior to the onset of depressive disorders are necessary in order to determine the processes and mechanisms involved in the pathogenesis of child and adolescent depression. It will be particularly important to identify endophenotypes for youth depression and to continue to trace the complex pathways between genes, neurobiology, and behavior. This will include elucidating the role of early adversity on neurobiological and psychosocial sources of risk, and the interactions between specific genes and specific environmental contexts. Finally, it is critical to develop a firmer understanding of the reasons for the sharp increase in depression among females in early adolescence.

We are in a period in which knowledge of genetics and neurobiology is growing rapidly, and stimulating interdisciplinary and cross-domain research. Together with a rapidly growing appreciation of the importance of a developmental psychopathology perspective, there are grounds for guarded optimism for progress in the area of child and adolescent depression.

REFERENCES

Abramson, L. Y., Metalsky, G. I., & Alloy, L. B. (1989). Hopelessness depression: A theory-based subtype of depression. *Psychological Review, 96,* 358–372.

Achenbach, T. M., McConaughy, S. H., & Howell, C. T. (1987). Child/adolescent behavioral and emotional problems: Implications of cross-informant correlations for situational specificity. *Psychological Bulletin, 101,* 213–232.

Allen, J. P., Insabella, G., Porter, M. R., Smith, F. D., Land, D., & Phillips, N. (2006). A social-interactional model for the development of depressive symptoms in adolescents. *Journal of Consulting and Clinical Psychology, 74,* 55–65.

Allgood-Merten, B., Lewinsohn, P. M., & Hops, H. (1990). Sex differences and adolescent depression. *Journal of Abnormal Psychology, 99,* 55–63.

Alloy, L. B., Abramson, L. Y., Smith, J. M., Gibb, B. E., & Neeren, A. M. (2006). Role of parenting and maltreatment histories in unipolar and bipolar mood disorders: Mediation by cognitive vulnerability to depression. *Clinical Child and Family Psychology Review, 9,* 23–64.

Ambrosini, P., Bennett, D., Cleland, C., & Haslam, N. (2002). Taxonicity of adolescent melancholia: A categorical or dimensional construct? *Journal of Psychiatric Research 36,* 247–256.

American Psychological Association. (2000). *Diagnostic and Statistical Manual of Mental Disorders* (4th ed., text revision). Washington, DC: American Psychological Association.

Angold, A., Costello, E. J., & Erkanli, A. (1999). Comorbidity. *Journal of Child Psychology & Psychiatry & Allied Disciplines, 40,* 57–87.

Angold, A., Costello, E. J., Erkanli, A., & Worthman, C. M. (1999). Pubertal changes in hormone levels and depression in girls. *Psychological Medicine, 29,* 1043–1053.

Arnett, J. J. (1999). Adolescent storm and stress, reconsidered. *American Psychologist, 54,* 317–326.

Asarnow, J. R., Tompson, M., Woo, S., & Cantwell, D. P. (2001). Is expressed emotion a specific risk factor for depression or a nonspecific correlate of psychopathology? *Journal of Abnormal Child Psychology, 29,* 573–583.

Beck, A. T. (1967). *Depression: Clinical, experimental, and theoretical aspects.* New York: Harper & Row.

Bertocci, M. A., Dahl, R. E., Williamson, D. E., Iosif, A. M., Birmaher, B., Axelson, D., et al. (2005). Subjective sleep complaints in pediatric depression: A controlled study and comparison with EEG measures of sleep and waking. *Journal of the American Academy of Child and Adolescent Psychiatry, 44,* 1158–1166.

Birmaher, B., Arbelaez, C., & Brent, D. (2002). Course and outcome of child and adolescent major depressive disorder. *Child and Adolescent Clinics of North America, 11,* 619–638.

Birmaher, B., Dahl, R. E., Williamson, D. E., Perel, J. M., Brent, D. A., Axelson, D. A., et al. (2000). Growth hormone secretion in children and adolescents at high risk for major depressive disorder. *Archives of General Psychiatry, 57,* 867–872.

Birmaher, B., Ryan, N. D., Williamson, D. E., Brent, D. A., Kaufman, J., Dahl, R. E., et al. (1996). Childhood and adolescent depression: A review of the past 10 years. Part I. *American Academy of Child and Adolescent Psychiatry, 35,* 1427–1439.

Bremner, J. D., & Vermetten, E. (2001). Stress and development: Biological and behavioral consequences. *Development and Psychopathology, 13,* 473–489.

Carlson, G. A., & Cantwell, D. P. (1980). Unmasking masked depression in children and adolescents. *American Journal of Psychiatry, 137,* 445–449.

Caspi, A., Sugden, K., Moffitt, T. E., Taylor, A., Craig, I., et al. (2003). Influence of life stress on depression: Moderation by a polymorphism on the 5-HTT gene. *Science, 301,* 386–389.

Chen, I. G., Roberts, R. E., & Aday, L. A. (1998). Ethnicity and adolescent depression: The case of Chinese Americans. *The Journal of Nervous and Mental Disease, 186,* 623–630.

Chorpita, B. F., & Daleiden, E. L. (2002). Tripartite dimensions of emotion in a child clinical sample: Measurement strategies and implications for clinical utility. *Journal of Consulting and Clinical Psychology, 70,* 1150–1160.

Cicchetti, D., & Rogosch, F. A. (1996). Equifinality and multifinality in developmental psychopathology. *Development and Psychopathology, 8,* 597–600.

Clark, L. A., & Watson, D. (1991). Tripartite model of anxiety and depression: evidence and taxonomic implications. *Journal of Abnormal Psychology, 100,* 316–336.

Coie, J. D., & Dodge, K. A. (1998). Aggression and antisocial behavior. In W. Damon & N. Eisenberg (Eds.), *Handbook of child psychology. Vol 3: Social, emotional, and personality development* (5th ed., pp. 779–862). Hoboken, NJ: Wiley.

Cole, D. A. (1991). Preliminary support for a competency-based model of depression in children. *Journal of Abnormal Psychology, 100,* 181–190.

Cole, D. A., & Jordan, A. E. (1995). Competence and memory: Integrating psychosocial and cognitive correlates of child depression. *Child Development, 66,* 459–473.

Cole, D. A., Nolen-Hoeksema, S., Girgus, J., & Paul, G. (2006). Stress exposure and stress generation in child and adolescent depression: A latent trait-state-error approach to longitudinal analyses. *Journal of Abnormal Psychology, 115,* 40–51.

Cole, D. A., Peeke, L. G., Martin, J. M., Truglio, R., & Seroczynski, A. D. (1998). A longitudinal look at the relation between depression and anxiety in children and adolescents. *Journal of Consulting and Clinical Psychology, 66,* 451–460.

Costello, E. J., Angold, A., Burns, B. J., Stangl, D. K., Tweed, D. L., Erkanli, A., & Worthman, C. M. (1996). The Great Smokey Mountain Study of Youth: Goals, designs, methods, and the prevalence of *DSM-III-R* disorders. *Archives of General Psychiatry, 53,* 1137–1143.

Costello, E. J., Keeler, G. P., & Angold, A. (2001). Poverty, race / ethnicity, and psychiatric disorder: A study of rural children. *American Journal of Public Health, 91,* 1494–1498.

Costello, E. J., Mustillo, S., Erkanli, A., Keeler, G., & Angold, A. (2003). Prevalence and development of psychiatric disorders in childhood and adolescence. *Archives of General Psychiatry, 60,* 837–844.

Cyranowski, J. M., Frank, E., Young, E., & Shear, M. K. (2000). Adolescent onset of the gender difference in lifetime rates of major depression: A theoretical model. *Archives of General Psychiatry, 57,* 21–27.

Dahl, R. E., Birmaher, B., Williamson, D. E., Dorn, L., Perel, J., Kaufman, J., et al. (2000). Low growth hormone response to growth hormone-releasing hormone in child depression. *Biological Psychiatry, 48,* 981–988.

Denny, S., Clark, T. C., Fleming, T., & Wall, M. (2004). Emotional resilience: Risk and protective factors for depression among alternative education students in New Zealand. *American Journal of Orthopsychiatry, 74,* 137–149.

Duggal, S., Carlson, E. A., Sroufe, L. A., & Egeland, B. (2001). Depressive symptomatology in childhood and adolescence. *Development and Psychopathology, 13,* 143–164.

Eaves, L. J. (2006). Genotype × environment interaction in psychopathology: Fact or artifact? *Twin Research, 9,* 1–8.

Eaves, L., & Silberg, J. (2003). Resolving multiple epigenetic pathways to adolescent depression. *Journal of Child Psychology and Psychiatry and Allied Disciplines, 44,* 1006–1014.

Frances, D. D., Caldji, C., Champagne, F., Plotsky, P. M., & Meaney, M. J. (1999). The role of corticotrophin-releasing factor-norepinephrine systems in mediating the effects of early experience on the development of behavioral and endocrine responses to stress. *Biological Psychiatry, 46,* 1153–1166.

Egger, H. L, Erkanli, A., Keeler, G., Potts, E., Walter, B. K., Angold, A. (2006). Test-Retest Reliability of the Preschool Age Psychiatric Assessment (PAPA). *Journal of the American Academy of Child and Adolescent Psychiatry. 45,* 538–549.

Eley, T. C., & Stevenson, J. (2000). Specific life events and chronic experiences differentially associated with depression and anxiety in young twins. *Journal of Abnormal Child Psychology, 28,* 383–394.

Eley, T. C., Sugden, K., Corsico, A., Gregory, A. M., Sham, P., McGuffin, P., et al. (2004). Gene-environment interaction analysis of serotonin system markers with adolescent depression. *Molecular Psychiatry, 9,* 908–915.

Flores, B.H., Musselman, D.L., & DeBattista, C. (2004). Biology of mood disorders. In A.F. Schatzberg & C.B. Nemeroff (Eds.), *American psychiatric textbook of psychopharmacology* (3rd ed., pp. 717–763). Washington, DC: American Psychiatric Association.

Fombonne, E., Wostear, G., Cooper, V., Harrington, R., & Rutter, M. (2001). The Maudsley long-term follow-up of child and adolescent depression. Vol. 1: Psychiatric outcomes in adulthood. *British Journal of Psychiatry, 179,* 210–217.

Garber, J., & Horowitz, J. L. (2002). Depression in children. In I. H. Gotlib & C. L. Hammen (Eds.), *Handbook of depression* (pp. 510–540). New York: Guilford.

Ge, X., Conger, R. D., & Elder, G. H., Jr. (2001). Pubertal transition, stressful life events, and the emergence of gender differences in adolescent depressive symptoms. *Developmental Psychology, 37,* 404–417.

Ge, X., Lorenz, F. O., Conger, R. D., Elder, G. H., & Simons, R. L. (1994). Trajectories of stressful life events and depressive symptoms during adolescence. *Developmental Psychology, 30,* 467–483.

Geller, B., Fox, L.W., & Clark, K.A. (1994). Rate and predictors of prepubertal bipolarity during follow-up of 6- to12-year-old depressed children. *Journal of the American Academy of Child and Adolescent Psychiatry, 33,* 461–468.

Gladstone, T. R. G., & Kaslow, N. J. (1995). Depression and attributions in children and adolescents: A meta-analytic review. *Journal of Abnormal Child Psychology, 23,* 597–606.

Goodman, S. H., Lahey, B. B., Fielding, B., Dulcan, M., Narrow, W., & Regier, D. (1998). Representativeness of clinical samples of youths with mental disorders: A preliminary population-based study. *Journal of Abnormal Psychology, 106,* 3–14.

Goodyer, I. M. (2001). Life events: Their nature and effects. In I. Goodyer (Ed.), *The depressed child and adolescent* (2nd ed., pp. 204–232). New York: Cambridge University Press.

Goodyer, I. M., Herbert, J., Tamplin, A., & Altham, P. M. (2000). Recent life events, cortisol, dehydroepiandrosterone and the onset of major depression in high-risk adolescents. *British Journal of Psychiatry, 177,* 499–504.

Graber, J. A., Lewinsohn, P. M., Seeley, J. R., & Brooks-Gunn, J. (1997). Is psychopathology associated with the timing of pubertal development? *Journal of the American Academy of Child and Adolescent Psychiatry, 36,* 1768–1776.

Grant, K. E., Compas, B. E., Stuhlmacher, A. F., Thurm, A. E., McMahon, S. D., & Halpert, J. A. (2003). Stressors and child and adolescent psychopathology: Moving from markers to mechanisms of risk. *Psychological Bulletin, 129,* 447–466.

Hammen, C. (1991). Generation of stress in the course of unipolar depression. *Journal of Abnormal Psychology, 100,* 555–561.

Hammen, C., & Rudolph, K. D. (2003). Childhood mood disorders. In E. J. Mash & R. A. Barkley (Eds.), *Child psychopathology* (pp. 233–278). New York: Guilford.

Hankin, B. L., & Abramson (2001). Development of gender differences in depression: An elaborated cognitive vulnerability-transactional stress theory. *Psychological Bulletin, 127,* 773–796.

Hankin, B. L., & Abela, J. R. Z. (2005). Depression from childhood through adolescence and adulthood: A developmental vulnerability and stress perspective. In *Development of psychopathology: A vulnerability-stress perspective* (pp. 245–288). Thousand Oaks, CA: Sage.

Hankin, B. L., Fraley, R. C., Lahey, B. B., & Waldman, I. D. (2005). Is depression best viewed as a continuum or discrete category? A taxometric analysis of childhood and adolescent depression in a population-based sample. *Journal of Abnormal Psychology, 114,* 96–110.

Harrington, R.C., Fudge, H., Rutter, M., Pickles, A., & Hill, J. (1990). Adult outcomes of childhood and adolescent depression. Vol. I: Psychiatric status. *Archives of General Psychiatry, 47,* 465–473.

Heim, C., Newport, J. D., Heit, S., Graham, Y. P., Wilcox, M., Bonsall, R., et al. (2000). Pituitary-adrenal and autonomic responses to stress in women after sexual and physical abuse in childhood. *Journal of the American Medical Association, 284,* 592–597.

Hoffman, K. B., Cole, D. A., Martin, J. M., Tram, J., & Seroczynski, A. D. (2000). Are the discrepancies between self-and others' appraisals of competence predictive or reflective of depressive symptoms in children and adolescents: A longitudinal study, Part II. *Journal of Abnormal Psychology, 109,* 651–662.

Joiner, T. E., & Wagner, K. D. (1995). Attributional style and depression in children and adolescents: A meta-analytic review. *Clinical Psychology Review, 15,* 777–798.

Joormann, J., Talbot, L., & Gotlib, I. H. (2007). Biased processing of emotional information in girls at risk for depression. *Journal of Abnormal Psychology, 116,* 135–143.

Kaufman, J., & Charney, D. (2003). The neurobiology of child and adolescent depression. In D. Cicchetti & E. Walker (Eds.), *Neurodevelopmental mechanisms in psychopathology* (pp. 461–490). Cambridge, U. K.: Cambridge University Press.

Kaufman, J., Yang, B., Douglas-Palumberi, H., Grasso, D., Lipschitz, D., Houshyar, S., et al. (2006). Brain-derived neurotrophic factor-5-HHTLPR gene interactions and environmental modifiers of depression in children. *Biological Psychiatry, 59,* 673–680.

Kaufman, J., Yang, B., Douglas-Palumberi, H., Houshyar, S., Lipschitz, D., Krystal, et al. (2004). Social supports and serotonin transporter gene moderate depression in maltreated children. *Proceedings of the National Academy of Sciences, 101,* 17316–17421.

Kessler, R. C. (2002). The categorical versus dimensional assessment controversy in the sociology of mental illness. *Journal of Health and Social Behavior, 43,* 171–188.

Kim, J., & Cicchetti, D. (2006). Longitudinal trajectories of self-system processes and depressive symptoms among maltreated and nonmaltreated children. *Child Development, 77,* 624–639.

Klein, D. N. (2006). Depression and childhood adversity and abuse. *Depression: Mind and Body, 2,* 89–93.

Klein, D. N., Dougherty, L. R., Laptook, R. S., & Olino, T. M. (in press). Temperament and risk for mood disorders in adolescents. In N. Allen & L. Sheeher (Eds.), *Adolescent emotional development and the emergence of depressive disorders.* Cambridge, England: Cambridge University Press.

Klein, D. N., Dougherty, L. R., & Olino, T. M. (2005). Toward guidelines for evidence-based assessment of depression in children and adolescents. *Journal of Child and Adolescent Clinical Psychology, 34,* 412–432.

Klein, D. N., Lewinsohn, P. M., Rohde, P., Seeley, J. R., & Olino, T. M. (2005). Psychopathology in the adolescent and young adult offspring of a community sample of mothers and fathers with major depression. *Psychological Medicine, 35*, 353–365.

Klein, D. N., Lewinsohn, P. M., Seeley, J. R., & Rohde, P. (2001). Family study of major depressive disorder in a community sample of adolescents. *Archives of General Psychiatry, 58*, 13–20.

Klein, D. N., & Riso, L. P. (1993). Psychiatric diagnoses: Problems of boundaries and co-occurrences. In C.G. Costello (Ed.), *Basic issues in psychopathology* (pp. 19–66). New York: Guilford.

Kovacs, M. (1996). Presentation and course of major depressive disorder during childhood and later years of the life span. *Journal of the American Academy of Child and Adolescent Psychiatry, 35*, 705–715.

Kovacs, M., Akiskal, A., & Gatsonis, C. (1994). Childhood-onset dysthymic disorder: Clinical features and prospective naturalistic outcome. *Archives of General Psychiatry, 51*, 365–374.

Kovacs, M., Devlin, B., Pollock, M., Richards, C., & Mukerji, P. (1997). A controlled family history study of childhood-onset depressive disorder. *Archives of General Psychiatry, 54*, 613–623.

Lemery, K. S., & Doelger, L. (2005). Genetic vulnerabilities to the development of psychopathology. In B. L. Hankin & J. R. Z. Abela (Eds.), *Development of psychopathology: A vulnerability-stress perspective* (pp. 161–198). Thousand Oaks, CA: Sage.

Levinson, D.F. (2006). The genetics of depression: A review. *Biological Psychiatry, 60*, 84–92.

Lewinsohn, P. M., & Essau, C. A. (2002). Depression in adolescents. In I. H. Gotlib & C. L. Hammen (Eds.), *Handbook of depression* (pp. 541–559). New York: Guilford.

Lewinsohn, P. M., Hops, H., Roberts, R. E., Seeley, J. R., Andrews, J. A. (1993). Adolescent psychopathology: I. Prevalence and incidence of depression and other *DSM-III-R* disorders in high school students. *Journal of Abnormal Psychology, 102*, 133–144.

Lewinsohn, P. M., Rohde, P., Klein, D. N., & Seeley, J. R. (1999). The natural course of adolescent major depressive disorder. Vol. I: Continuity into young adulthood. *Journal of the American Academy of Child and Adolescent Psychiatry, 38*, 56–63.

Lewinsohn, P. M., Rohde, P., Seeley, J. R., Klein, D. N., & Gotlib, I. H. (2000). The natural course of adolescent major depressive disorder: II. Predictors of depression recurrence in young adults. *American Journal of Psychiatry, 157*, 1584–1591.

Lewinsohn, P. M., Solomon, A., Seeley, J. R., & Zeiss, A. (2000). Clinical implications of "subthreshold" depressive symptoms. *Journal of Abnormal Psychology, 109*, 345–351.

Little, S. A., & Garber, J. (2005). The role of social stressors and interpersonal orientation in explaining the longitudinal relation between externalizing and depressive symptoms. *Journal of Abnormal Psychology, 114*, 432–443.

Lonigan, C. J., Phillips, B. M., & Hooe, E. S. (2003). Relations of positive and negative affectivity to anxiety and depression in children: Evidence from a latent variable longitudinal study. *Journal of Consulting and Clinical Psychology, 71*, 465–481.

Lovejoy, M. C., Graczyk, P. A., O'Hare, E., & Neuman, G. (2000). Maternal depression and parenting behavior: A meta-analytic review. *Clinical Psychology Review, 20,* 561–592.

Luby, J. L., Heffelfinger, A., Mrakotsky, C., Brown, K., Hessler, M., & Spitznagel, E. (2003). Alterations in stress cortisol reactivity in depressed preschoolers relative to psychiatric and no-disorder comparison groups. *Archives of General Psychiatry, 60,* 1248–1255.

Luby, J. L., Heffelfinger, A., Mrakotsky, C., Hessler, M. J., Brown, K. M., & Hildebrand, T. (2002). Preschool major depressive disorder: Preliminary validation for developmentally modified *DSM-IV* criteria. *Journal of the American Academy of Child and Adolescent Psychiatry, 41,* 928–937.

Luby, J. L., Mrakotsky, C., & Heffelfinger, A. (2004). Characteristics of depressed preschoolers with and without melancholia: Evidence for a melancholic depressive subtype in young children. *American Journal of Psychiatry, 161,* 1998–2004.

Luthar, S. S., Cicchetti, D., & Becker, B. (2000). The construct of resilience: A critical evaluation and guidelines for future work. *Child Development, 71,* 543–562.

MacMillan, S., Szeszko, P. R., Moore, G. J., Madden, R., Lorch, E., Ivey, J., et al. (2003). Increased amygdala: Hippocampal volume ratios associated with severity of anxiety in pediatric major depression. *Journal of Child and Adolescent Psychopharmacology, 13,* 65–73.

Martin, G., Bergen, H. A., Roeger, L., & Allison, S. (2004). Depression in young adolescents: Investigations using 2 and 3 factor versions of the Parental Bonding Instrument. *The Journal of Nervous and Mental Disease, 192,* 650–657.

Meehl, P. E. (1995). Bootstraps taxometrics: Solving the classification problem in psychopathology. *American Psychologist, 50,* 266–275.

Moffitt, T. E., Caspi, A., & Rutter, M. (2006). Measured gene-environment interactions in psychopathology: Concepts, research strategies, and implications for research, intervention, and public understanding of genetics. *Perspectives on Psychological Science, 1,* 5–27.

Monroe, S. M., Rohde, P., Seeley, J. R., & Lewinsohn, P. M. (1999). Life events and depression in adolescence: Relationship loss as a prospective risk factor for first onset of major depressive disorder. *Journal of Abnormal Psychology, 108,* 606–614.

Neshat-Doost, H. T., Taghavi, M. R., Moradi, A. R., Yule, W., & Dalgleish, T. (1998). Memory for emotional trait adjectives in clinically depressed youth. *Journal of Abnormal Psychology, 107,* 642–650.

Nolan, C. L., Moore, G. J., Madden, R., Farchione, T., Bartoi, M., Lorch, E., et al. (2002). Prefrontal cortical volume in childhood-onset major depression. *Archives of General Psychiatry, 59,* 173–179.

Nolen-Hoeksema, S. (2002). Gender differences in depression. In I. Gotlib & C. Hammen (Eds.), *Handbook of depression* (pp. 492–509). New York: Guilford.

Nolen-Hoeksema, S., & Girgus, J. S. (1994). The emergence of gender differences in depression during adolescence. *Psychological Bulletin, 115,* 424–443.

Orvaschel, H., Lewinsohn, P. M., & Seeley, J. R. (1995). Continuity of psychopathology in a community sample of adolescents. *Journal of the American Academy of Child and Adolescent Psychiatry, 32,* 1155–1163.

Patton, G. C., Coffey, C., Posterino, M., Carlin, J. B., & Bowes, G. (2003). Life events and early onset depression: Cause or consequence? *Psychological Medicine, 33,* 1203–1210.

Patton, G. C., Coffey, C., Posterino, M., Carlin, J. B., & Wolfe, R. (2001). Parental "affectionless control" in adolescent depressive disorder. *Social Psychiatry and Psychiatric Epidemiology, 36,* 475–480.

Persons, J. B., & Miranda, J. (1992). Cognitive theories of vulnerability to depression: Reconciling negative evidence. *Cognitive Therapy and Research, 16,* 485–502.

Pine, D. S., Cohen, P., Gurley, D., Brook, J., & Ma, Y. (1998). The risk for early-adulthood anxiety and depressive disorders in adolescents with anxiety and depressive disorders. *Archives of General Psychiatry, 55,* 56–64.

Prinstein, M. J., Borelli, J. L., Cheah, C. S. L., Simon, V. A., & Aikins, J. W. (2005). Adolescent girls' interpersonal vulnerability to depressive symptoms: A longitudinal examination of reassurance–seeking and peer relationships. *Journal of Abnormal Psychology, 114,* 676–688.

Puig-Antich, J., Blau, S., Marx, J., Greenhill, L. L., & Chambers, W. (1978). Prepubertal major depressive disorder: A pilot study. *Journal of the American Academy of Child Psychiatry, 17,* 696–707.

Puig-Antich, J., Goetz, D., Davies, M., Kaplan, T., Davies, S., et al. (1989). A controlled family history study of prepubertal major depressive disorder. *Archives of General Psychiatry, 46,* 406–418.

Puig-Antich, J., Kaufman, J., Ryan, N. D., Williamson, D. E., Dahl, R. E., Lukens, E., et al. (1993). The psychosocial functioning and family environment of depressed adolescents. *Journal of the American Academy of Child and Adolescent Psychiatry, 32,* 244–253.

Puig-Antich, J., Lukens, E., Davies, M., Goetz, D., Brennan-Quattrock, J., & Todak, G. (1985). Psychosocial functioning in prepubertal major depressive disorders. Vol. II: Interpersonal relationships after sustained recovery from affective episode. *Archives of General Psychiatry, 42,* 511–517.

Rey, J. M. (1995). Perceptions of poor maternal care are associated with adolescent depression. *Journal of Affective Disorders, 34,* 95–100.

Rice, F., Harold, G. T., & Thapar, A. (2002). The genetic aetiology of childhood depression: A review. *Journal of Child Psychology and Psychiatry, 43,* 65–79.

Rie, H. H. (1966). Depression in childhood: A survey of some pertinent contributions. *Journal of the American Academy of Child Psychiatry, 5,* 653–685.

Rohde, P., Lewinsohn, P. M., Seeley, J. R. (1991). Comorbidity of unipolar depression. Vol. II: Comorbidity with other mental disorders in adolescents and adults. *Journal of Abnormal Psychology, 100,* 214–222.

Rosso, I. M., Cintron, C. M., Steingard, R. J., Renshaw, P. F., Young, A. D., & Yurgelun-Todd, D. A. (2005). Amygdala and hippocampus volumes in pediatric major depression. *Biological Psychiatry, 57,* 21–26.

Rudolph, K. D., & Hammen, C. (1999). Age and gender as determinants of stress exposure, generation, and reactions in youngsters: A transactional perspective. *Child Development, 70,* 660–677.

Rudolph, K. D., Flynn, M., & Abaied, J. L. (in press). A developmental perspective on interpersonal theories of youth depression. In J. R. Z. Abela & B. L. Hankin (Eds.), *Child and adolescent depression: Causes, treatment, and prevention*. New York: Guilford.

Rutter, M., Moffitt, T. E., & Caspi, A. (2006). Gene-environment interplay and psychopathology: multiple varieties but real effects. *Journal of Child Psychology and Psychiatry, 47*, 226–261.

Schrepferman, L. M., Eby, J., Snyder, J., & Stropes, J. (2006). Early affiliation and social engagement with peers: Prospective risk and protective factors for childhood depressive behaviors. *Journal of Emotional and Behavioral Disorders, 14*, 50–61.

Schulterbrandt, J. G., & Raskin, A. (1977). *Depression in childhood: Diagnosis, treatment, and conceptual models*. New York: Raven Press.

Scourfield, J., Rice, F., Thapar, A., Harold, G. T., Martin, N., & McGuffin, P. (2003). Depressive symptoms in children and adolescents: Changing aetiological influences with development. *Journal of Child Psychology and Psychiatry, 44*, 968–976.

Shih, J. H., Eberhart, N. K., Hammen, C. L., & Brennan, P. A. (2006). Differential exposure and reactivity to interpersonal stress predict sex differences in adolescent depression. *Journal of Clinical Child and Adolescent Psychology, 35*, 103–115.

Silberg, J., Pickles, A., Rutter, M., Hewitt, J., Simonoff, E., Maes, H., et al. (1999). The influence of genetic factors and life stress on depression among adolescent girls. *Archives of General Psychiatry, 56*, 225–232.

Silberg, J., Rutter, M., Neale, M., & Eaves, L. (2001). Genetic moderation of environmental risk for depression and anxiety in adolescent girls. *British Journal of Psychiatry, 179*, 116–121.

Steingard, R. J., Renshaw, P. F., Hennen, J., Lenox, M., Cintron, C. B., Young, A. D., et al. (2002). Smaller frontal lobe white matter volumes in depressed adolescents. *Biological Psychiatry, 52*, 413–417.

Stice, E., Ragan, J., & Randall, P. (2004). Prospective relations between social support and depression: Differential direction of effects for parent and peer support? *Journal of Abnormal Psychology, 113*, 155–159.

Solomon, A., Ruscio, J., Seeley, Jr., & Lewinsohn, P. M. (2006). A taxometric investiagation of unipolar depression in a large community sample. *Psychological Medicine, 36*, 973–985.

Taylor, L., & Ingram, R. E. (1999). Cognitive reactivity and depressotypic information processing in children of depressed mothers. *Journal of Abnormal Psychology, 108*, 202–210.

Thomas, K. M., Drevets, W. C., Dahl, R. E., Ryan, N. D., Birmaher, B., Eccard, C. H., et al. (2001). Amygdala response to fearful faces in anxious and depressed children. *Archives of General Psychiatry, 58*, 1057–1063.

Timbremont, B., & Braet, C. (2004). Cognitive vulnerability in remitted depressed children and adolescents. *Behavior Research and Therapy, 42*, 423–437.

Toolan, J. M. (1962). Depression in children and adolescents. *American Journal of Orthopsychiatry, 32*, 404–415.

Weaver, I. C. G., Cervoni, N., Champagne, F. A., D'Alessio, A. C., Sharma, S.,

Seckl, J. R., Dymov, S., Szyf, M., & Meaney, M. J. (2004). Epigenetic programming by maternal behavior. *Nature Neuroscience, 7,* 847–854.

Weiss, B., & Garber, G. (2003). Developmental differences in the phenomenology of depression. *Development and Psychopathology, 15,* 403–430.

Weissman, M. M., Wolk, S., Goldstein, R. B., Moreau, D., Adams, P., et al. (1999). Depressed adolescents grown up. *Journal of the American Medical Association, 281,* 1707–1713.

Weissman, M. M., Wolk, S., Wickramaratne, P., Goldstein, R. B., Adams, P., et al. (1999). Children with prepubertal-onset major depressive disorder and anxiety grown up. *Archives of General Psychiatry, 56,* 794–801.

Weissman, M. M., Wickramaratne, P., Nomura, Y., Warner, V., Pilowsky, D., & Verdeli, H. (2006). Offspring of depressed parents: 20 years later. *American Journal of Psychiatry, 163,* 1001–1008.

Wickramaratne, P. & Weissman, M. M (1998). Onset of psychopathology in offspring by developmental phase and parental depression. *Journal of the American Academy of Child and Adolescent Psychiatry, 37,* 933–942.

Wight, R. G., Aneshensel, C. S., Botticello, A. L., & Sepulveda, J. E. (2005). A multilevel analysis of ethnic variation in depressive symptoms among adolescents in the United States. *Social Science & Medicine, 60,* 2073–2084.

Williamson, D. E., Birmaher, B., Anderson, B. P., Al-Shabbout, M., & Ryan, N. D. (1995). Stressful life events in depressed adolescents: The role of dependent events during the depressive episode. *Journal of the American Academy of Child and Adolescent Psychiatry, 34,* 591–598.

Zammit, S., & Owen, M. J. (2006). Stressful life events, 5HTT genotype, and risk of depression. *British Journal of Psychiatry, 188,* 199–201.

CHAPTER 17

The Development of Borderline Personality Disorder and Self-Injurious Behavior

SHEILA E. CROWELL, THEODORE P. BEAUCHAINE,
AND MARK F. LENZENWEGER

By definition, personality disorders are characterized by long-standing patterns of experience and behavior that are persistent and pervasive and that emerge in late adolescence or early adulthood (American Psychiatric Association [APA], 2000). Borderline Personality Disorder (BPD) is characterized by emotion dysregulation, impulsivity, identity disturbance, excessive fear and anger, and self-injurious behaviors (APA, 2000). Because only 5 of 9 specific criteria must be present for a BPD diagnosis, the disorder captures a very heterogeneous group of individuals. As a result, two people diagnosed with BPD might overlap on only one behavioral criterion.

According to current convention (APA, 2000), personality disorders cannot be diagnosed before age 18. As a result, the diagnosis of BPD among children and adolescents is controversial. Instead, researchers examining borderline features among youth often use the construct of *borderline pathology* (BP) to describe their samples (e.g., Guzder et al., 1996; Kernberg,

Acknowledgment: Work on this chapter was supported by Grants MH74196 to Sheila E. Crowell and MH63699 to Theodore P. Beauchaine from the National Institute of Mental Health. We express thanks to Patricia Loesche.

1990). As outlined in the following, this construct shares many of the features of BPD and may be a risk factor for the adult condition. Indeed, it is hard to imagine that precursors of the extremely difficult symptoms linked to BPD do not appear well before the age of 18 years. Yet despite burgeoning interest in the development and pathogenesis of BPD (see Lenzenweger & Cicchetti, 2005), the etiology of the disorder is not well delineated, and longitudinal research is desperately needed.

In this chapter, we first review the literature on BP and self-injurious behavior in childhood and adolescence, and then we discuss a biosocial developmental model of BPD. In accordance with the developmental psychopathology perspective, we assume that there are child and adolescent precursors of adult BPD and that identifying these precursors will allow for more effective prevention and treatment of the disorder. Before proceeding, however, it is critical to note that children and adolescents who engage in self-injurious behavior or show signs of BP do not necessarily represent the same populations as adults who engage in similar behaviors. Furthermore, although there is some overlap among children and adults who engage in self-inflicted injury and those who present with BP, these two populations are not identical, and the developmental trajectories for each are likely to be only partially overlapping. In other words, not all children who engage in intentional self-injury show signs of BP. Accordingly, we review the literatures on BPD and intentional self-injury separately.

HISTORICAL CONTEXT

BORDERLINE PERSONALITY DISORDER

Historically, the term *borderline* resulted from difficulties diagnosing individuals who did not fit into the standard psychiatric nomenclature of the early to mid twentieth century. Because these individuals were not clearly *psychotic* or *neurotic,* they were described as being on "the border line group of neuroses" (Stern, 1938, p. 467). In other words, early practitioners remained uncertain as to whether so-called *borderline* individuals would develop psychotic disorders, such as Schizophrenia; neurotic disorders, such as anxiety and depression; or whether they would vacillate between the two states (Knight, 1953). Following this initial description of borderline pathology, research focused on identifying concrete diagnostic criteria for BPD. Kernberg (1967) was among the first to identify borderline personality organization, a specific and stable personality pattern that could be differentiated from both the psychotic and neurotic conditions.

Soon thereafter, two important reviews (Gunderson & Singer, 1975; Spitzer, Endicott, & Gibbon, 1979) established the diagnostic criteria for BPD that would eventually be used in the DSM-III (APA, 1980).

Once the BPD diagnosis was outlined, research focused increasingly on the assessment and validity of the proposed DSM-III criteria. Diagnostic measures, including the International Personality Disorders Examination (IPDE; Loranger, 1999; Loranger et al., 1988) and the Millon Clinical Multiaxial Inventory (MCMI; Millon, 1983), emerged during this time. In addition, research addressing patterns of comorbidity, the validity of BPD, correlates of BPD, and behavioral and pharmacological treatments for the disorder expanded (e.g., Herman, Perry, & van der Kolk, 1989; Linehan, 1993; Loranger, Oldham, & Tulis, 1982; Soloff, 2000; Zanarini et al., 1998b). More recently, theory-driven experimental research has focused on dysfunctional psychosocial and biological underpinnings of BPD. In one early application of this type of research, Korfine & Hooley (2000) found that individuals with BPD were more likely than controls to remember borderline-relevant words (e.g., abandon, misunderstood, suicide) on a directed forgetting task. Similarly, a recent functional imaging study testing neurobiological theories of emotion dysregulation in BPD indicated support for theories of amygdala overactivation among adults with the disorder (Herpertz et al., 2001).

BORDERLINE PATHOLOGY IN CHILDHOOD

Although research on child BP evolved in parallel with the adult literature, existing research with youth is extremely limited in scope. Similar to the research on BPD in adults, exploration of BP in children began with clinical descriptions of those who could not be classified as either psychotic or neurotic (Geleerd, 1958; Weil, 1953). These clinical descriptions were followed by early attempts to identify diagnostic criteria for BP in childhood (e.g., Bemporad et al., 1982; Kernberg, Weiner, & Bardenstein, 2000; Vela, Gottlieb, & Gottlieb, 1983). Yet despite these preliminary efforts, relatively little agreement was reached regarding diagnostic criteria and neuropsychological correlates of the disorder (Vela et al., 1983). Furthermore, prospective studies using these preliminary diagnostic criteria showed that children with BP developed a wide range of Axis II disorders as adults, the most common being Antisocial Personality Disorder (ASPD)—not BPD (Lofgren et al., 1991). Although there is renewed interest in the developmental course of BPD (Lenzenweger & Cicchetti, 2005), there is a striking lack of developmental literature available compared with other psychological disorders. To date, the developmental research consists primarily of (a) retrospective reports from adults who meet criteria for BPD, and (b) research on correlates of childhood BP (see Paris, 2000, for a review).

Self-Inflicted Injury

Broadly defined, self-inflicted injury (SII) includes all volitional acts of self-injury, from repetitive self-mutilation to unsuccessful suicide attempts. This class of behavior has also been referred to as *parasuicide* (Kreitman, 1977), a term that has been debated because of an implied relation to completed suicide (Meuhlenkamp & Miller, 2004). At the broadest level, SII can be divided into SII with and without suicidal intent (e.g., Beautrais, Joyce, & Mulder, 1996; Zlotnick, Mattia, & Zimmerman, 1999), and most of the research literature has historically fallen into one of these two categories.

Initially, both suicidal and nonsuicidal self-injury were considered to result from the same unconscious mechanisms and drives (Zilboorg, 1936a, b). This perspective was summarized in an important methodological critique (Simpson, 1950), which identified suicide as a form of displacement of the desire to kill. In this same review, Simpson highlighted significant methodological barriers to conducting suicide research. These included the challenges of obtaining reliable statistics with regard to death by suicide, problems inherent in collecting data postmortem, and difficulties identifying those at risk for suicidal behavior prospectively given an unknown etiology and the infrequent occurrence of the behavior (see, e.g., Baldessarini, Finklestein, & Arana, 1983). Yet despite Simpson's efforts to identify variables predictive of suicide risk (e.g., family, religion, neighborhood, income, sex, age, race), there were several decades during which the literature consisted primarily of descriptive case reports (Flood & Seager, 1968; Mason, 1954). In striking contrast to the majority of the scientific literature, Offer and Barglow (1960) identified a subgroup of hospitalized youth who harmed themselves without suicidal intent. These authors were among the first to conclude that nonsuicidal self-mutilation is learned, and that the act of self-injury serves both instrumental and emotional functions.

Following this report, the literatures on suicidal and nonsuicidal SII began to diverge. However, researchers studying both nonsuicidal self-injury and suicide attempts rarely ascertained the suicidal intent of individuals. Rather, intent was often inferred from the lethality of the behavior. Thus, research on nonsuicidal self-injury focused primarily on individuals engaging in low-lethality behaviors, such as repetitive cutting, burning, or bruising (e.g., Simpson, 1975), whereas research on suicidal self-injury focused more on high-lethality behaviors such as hanging, gun injuries, and asphyxiation (e.g., Seiden, 1978). Unfortunately, as these two bodies of work evolved independently, researchers working in each area often neglected to identify important similarities and differences between the two populations (see Lester, 1972). During this same period, there was growing interest in identifying diagnostic criteria for "deliberate self-injury syndrome," which would be classified as an impulse control disorder (Kahan & Pattison, 1984). These efforts, later abandoned, were based on evidence that intentional self-harm was prevalent and often occurred independent of other Axis I and Axis II disorders. Currently, research on adolescent suicide and nonsuicidal SII is focused on (a) understanding the etiology of SII, (b) placing adolescent SII within a theoretical context, and (c) developing a standard of care for adolescents who engage in SII (e.g., Berman, Jobes, & Silverman, 2006; Gratz, 2003; Zlotnick et al., 1997). Thus, a broad understanding of adolescent SII is emerging, along with a standard of care for treatment.

TERMINOLOGICAL AND CONCEPTUAL ISSUES

BORDERLINE PERSONALITY DISORDER

Given consistent findings to suggest that borderline features do not reside on the border of other diagnoses, it is now widely agreed that the term borderline is incorrect, imprecise, and outdated (Loranger et al., 1982). These sentiments were already present when diagnostic criteria were being established for the *DSM-III* (APA, 1980). At that time, Spitzer et al. (1979) suggested that a more fitting label might be "unstable personality disorder," a label that was ultimately adopted by the ICD-10 Classification of Mental and Behavioural Disorders (World Health Organization, 1992). For pediatric populations, there has been some effort to replace the borderline label with the term *multiple complex developmental disorder* (MCDD; Cohen, Paul, & Volkmar, 1987). Similar to those with BP, youth diagnosed as MCDD are described as having dysregulated affect, intense anxiety, poor social skills, interpersonal deficits, and episodic thought disorder. However, there is no evidence to suggest that youth with MCDD are at risk for developing BPD as adults.

SELF-INFLICTED INJURY

As noted previously, there are a multitude of labels and definitions that have been used to describe intentional self-injurious behaviors. The most commonly used terms include deliberate self-harm, self-injury, parasuicide, self-mutilation (including non-suicidal scratching, stabbing, or cutting, or amputation), self-poisoning (for overdoses or the ingestion of toxic substances), suicidal behaviors, and suicide attempts (e.g., Comtois, 2002; Kreitman, 1977; Welch, 2001). The lack of definitional consensus exists despite repeated attempts to develop a standard nomenclature for suicidal behavior (see O'Carroll et al., 1996, for a review). For purposes of this review, we will use the following terms: (1) *suicide,* which will be used in cases where SII resulted in death; (2) *suicidal behavior* (SB), which includes unambivalent and ambivalent suicide attempts with suicidal intent; (3) *non-suicidal self-injury* (NSSI), which will be used where there is an absence of suicidal intent; and (4) *self-inflicted injury* (SII), which is the broadest term and will therefore be used when suicide intent was not sufficiently measured or when a sample consists of individuals who engage in both SB and NSSI.

DIAGNOSTIC ISSUES AND *DSM-IV* CRITERIA

DSM-IV criteria for BPD are presented in Table 17.1. According to the *DSM-IV-TR* (APA, 2000), the diagnosis of a personality disorder prior to age 18 should only be given when "maladaptive personality traits appear to be pervasive, persistent, and unlikely to be limited to a particular developmental stage or an episode of an Axis I disorder. (p. 387)" Thus, the clinical diagnosis of BPD, while occasionally used for individuals as young as 16, is rarely given to children and adolescents. To date, efforts to

Table 17.1.
Diagnostic Criteria for Borderline Personality Disorder
(American Psychiatric Association, 2000)

1. Frantic efforts to avoid real or imagined abandonment
2. A pattern of unstable and intense interpersonal relationships characterized by alternating between extremes of idealization and devaluation
3. Identity disturbance markedly and persistently unstable self-image or sense of self
4. Impulsivity in at least two areas that are potentially self-damaging (e.g., spending, sex, substance abuse, reckless driving, binge eating)
5. Recurrent suicidal behavior, gestures, or threats, or self-mutilating behavior
6. Affective instability due to a marked reactivity of mood (e.g., intense episodic dysphoria irritability or anxiety usually lasting a few hours and only rarely more than a few days)
7. Chronic feelings of emptiness
8. Inappropriate, intense anger or difficulty controlling anger (e.g., frequent displays of temper, constant anger, recurrent physical fights)
9. Transient, stress-related paranoid ideation or severe dissociative symptoms

identify BPD among youth have resulted in conflicting diagnostic criteria that are misleading in terms of their implied relation to BPD among adults (Bemporad et al., 1982; Vela et al., 1983). A further challenge inherent in applying the diagnosis of BPD to children is that the diagnostic criteria are not fully appropriate for youth. For example, youth often have not had a chance to develop a pattern of intense and unstable interpersonal relationships. Similarly, many youth are impulsive, emotionally unstable, and uncertain about their identities. Therefore, researchers working in this area have either modified the standard criteria (e.g., Goldman et al., 1992), or use adapted measures such as the Child Diagnostic Interview for Borderlines (C-DIB-R; e.g., Guzder et al., 1996). To the extent that the diagnosis of BP among youth could lead to improved treatment or prevention, it is important to identify and (when appropriate) diagnose high-risk youth.

PREVALENCE

BORDERLINE PERSONALITY DISORDER

There have been several epidemiologic studies of the prevalence of BPD among adults (e.g., Torgersen, Kringlen, & Cramer, 2001; Lenzenweger et al., in press; Samuels et al., 2002). These studies suggest rates of BPD ranging from 0.7% in Norway, to approximately .5% to 3.9% in the United States. The best U.S. population estimate for the prevalence of BPD of 1.4% comes from the recently completed NCS-R (Lenzenweger et al., 2007). In a community sample of children and adolescents, the prevalence of BPD was 11% at the first assessment (ages 9 to 19 years) and 7.8% at a follow-up assessment (ages 11 to 21 years; Bernstein et al., 1993). It is unclear why the prevalence of BPD was so unexpectedly elevated in this sample of youth compared with adults. Two possibilities for these unlikely prevalence rates include suboptimum diagnostic techniques and the difficulty of assessing borderline features given normative adolescent emotional lability.

SELF-INFLICTED INJURY

The true prevalence of SII among adolescents is difficult to measure epidemiologically. Although the prevalence of fatal SII can be established through examination of medical records and coroners' reports, data on nonfatal SII are much more challenging to track. Epidemiological data on SII that results in death suggest a complicated picture. Over the last 100 years, statistics indicate that suicide rates among adolescents have waxed and waned (Berman et al., 2006). Survey data on nonfatal SII indicate that every year approximately 17% of adolescents in the United States seriously consider suicide, 9% attempt suicide, and 3% make an attempt serious enough to warrant medical attention (Grunbaum et al., 2004).

SEX DIFFERENCES

Borderline Personality Disorder

Among clinical samples, approximately 70 to 80% of those who meet criteria for BPD are female (Swartz et al., 1990), yet this sex difference for adult BPD is not always observed in community samples (Lenzenweger et al., in press; Torgersen et al., 2001; Zimmerman & Coryell, 1990). Nevertheless, among a community sample of youth diagnosed with BPD, the disorder was more prevalent among girls than among boys (Bernstein et al., 1993). Thus, it is currently unclear whether a sex difference exists. Among clinical samples, elevated rates of borderline traits among females may be due to biases in the diagnostic criteria, sampling, or assessment instruments; differences in treatment seeking behaviors among women; or genuine differences between males and females in the expression of psychiatric illness (Corbitt & Widiger, 1995; Skodol & Bender, 2003). Some have hypothesized that BPD represents a female manifestation of Antisocial Personality Disorder (ASPD) and that sex differences are due to biases in diagnosis (Paris, 1997). There is some evidence to suggest that this is at least partly the case. First, the sex distributions of ASPD and BPD among clinical samples mirror one another, with approximately 80% of those with ASPD being male and 80% of those with BPD being female. There is also diagnostic overlap between the disorders, which are both characterized by impulsivity, anger/irritability, and aggression. Paris also identified several overlapping risk factors for the development of ASPD and BPD, including moderate to high heritability of traits common to both disorders (impulsivity, affective instability, cognitive deficits), reduced serotonin, family dysfunction, and histories of abuse. These same risk factors are also seen in adolescents who engage in SII (Brent et al., 2002; Brodsky et al., 2001; Crowell et al., 2005), and in adolescents with disruptive behavior disorders (Pollak, 2003).

Self-Inflicted Injury

Although NSSI and suicidal ideation are more common among females, suicide that results in death is more common among males. According to a recent review (Berman et al., 2006), the ratio of male to female *completed suicides* among adolescents ages 15 to 19 is 4.7:1. In contrast, the ratio of female to male *suicide attempts* is estimated to range from 2:1 to 3:1. Research suggests that these sex differences are due to (a) a higher likelihood of males to use more violent means of SII such as firearms, (b) greater exposure among males to risk factors for suicide (e.g., legal difficulties, financial problems, shame at failure), and (c) higher rates among males of comorbid psychiatric diagnoses, including substance abuse and Conduct Disorder (Brent et al., 1999; Gould et al., 1996; Shaffer et al., 1996).

RISK FACTORS AND ETIOLOGIC FORMULATIONS

Within the developmental psychopathology framework, BP and SII can be viewed as outcomes of multiple interacting risk factors, causal events, and transactional processes. This framework is particularly well suited for understanding the emergence of problems during adolescence and the continuity of these problems throughout development (Cicchetti & Rogosch, 2002). The concepts of multifinality and equifinality are particularly useful in understanding the development of BPD. Specifically, some youth with borderline features or SII may not develop BPD (i.e., multifinality), while others who develop BPD as adults likely have unique developmental trajectories, possibly not including borderline features or SII (i.e., equifinality).

So far, we have reviewed the literatures on the development of BPD and SII separately, highlighting the unique yet overlapping research histories of these two conditions. We have underscored the important point that BPD and SII are not equivalent—and that they do not necessarily co-occur within individuals. To the extent that they do, it is important to be mindful that self-injurious behavior is one of the criteria of BPD. Nonetheless, there is a substantial overlap of risk factors for BPD and SII, which suggests that their developmental progressions may be quite similar. Therefore, we discuss risk for the development of BPD and SII together within the broad categories of psychological risk, family characteristics, biological/neurochemical/genetic risk, and temperament/personality risk (for a more extensive review see Crowell et al., in press).

Psychological Risk Factors

Cross-sectional and longitudinal studies indicate that there are a number of comorbid disorders observed among individuals who meet criteria for BPD. In one longitudinal study (Zanarini et al., 2004a, b) the most common Axis I disorders found to co-occur with BPD were mood disorders (96.9%), anxiety disorders (89.0%), substance use disorders (62.1%), and eating disorders (53.8%). Comorbidity with Axis II disorders was highest for Cluster

C (anxious; 62.4%), followed by Cluster B (dramatic; 27.7%), then Cluster A (odd; 23.8%). Similarly, psychological autopsy studies of adolescent suicide victims have indicated that as many as 90% had an acute psychiatric disorder (Brent et al., 1999; Shaffer et al., 1996) or significant underlying psychiatric problems (Ernst et al., 2004). The most prevalent diagnoses observed among suicidal adolescents are mood disorders, Conduct Disorder, and substance use disorders (Berman et al., 2006).

An alternative to evaluating diagnostic categories as risk factors for BPD or ISI is to examine underlying core features or traits associated with the conditions, such as emotional dysregulation and impulsivity. For example, Paris (2005) has researched developmental precursors to BPD and identified behavioral dyscontrol as the first feature of borderline pathology to emerge, followed by emotion dysregulation (expressed as anxious and/or depressive features), which develops later. Indeed, the presence of both internalizing and externalizing symptoms predicts the continuation of Cluster B features from adolescence into adulthood (Crawford, Cohen, & Brook, 2001). These data are consistent with the Depue and Lenzenweger model discussed in the following (2001, 2005), which posits a central role for diminished neural constraint.

FAMILY PSYCHOPATHOLOGY AND FAMILY RISK FACTORS

There is a long history of research on psychopathology among the family members of individuals who meet criteria for BPD. Initially, this research addressed familial disorders on the Schizophrenia spectrum, followed by mood disorders, and more recently by impulse control disorders (see White et al., 2003, for a review). These studies reveal virtually no relation between BPD and Schizophrenia spectrum disorders, a possible relation between BPD and Major Depressive Disorder, and a significant familial aggregation of impulse control disorders among those diagnosed with BPD. Research also indicates that family psychopathology is a risk factor for suicide, NSSI, and SB (e.g., Brent et al., 1988, 1994). Findings suggest that at least half of adolescent suicide completers have a family history of psychiatric morbidity (Houston, Hawton, & Shepperd, 2001) and that the most common disorders found among first-degree relatives of suicide completers are mood disorders, substance use disorders, and Conduct Disorder/ASPD (e.g., Brent et al., 1999). Moreover, in addition to familial psychopathology, suicide victims are more likely to encounter significant familial stressors, including divorce, parent-child conflict, physical abuse, and frequent changes of residence (Brent et al., 1994). A family history of SII is also a risk factor, even when controlling for poor parent-child relationships and family psychopathology (e.g., Gould et al., 1996).

In addition to psychopathology within the family, histories of disrupted attachment relationships are quite common among individuals with BPD (e.g., Levy et al., 2005). In a recent review of 13 adult attachment studies, a consistent association was reported between BPD and insecure attachment, particularly the unresolved, preoccupied, and fearful subtypes (Agrawal et al., 2004). It should be noted that most people with insecure adult attachment classifications do not suffer from BPD. Nevertheless, according to Linehan's biosocial theory (1993), the development of BPD occurs in part due to an invalidating family environment in which parents respond inappropriately to or ignore the expression of children's private emotional experiences. That is, rather than validating the expression of emotional experiences, these parents punish or trivialize such expressions—which could clearly contribute to disturbed attachment relations.

An extremely invalidating environment is one that is characterized by neglect or by physical, emotional, or sexual abuse. Not surprisingly, abuse histories are related to increased risk for SII (Brent et al., 1999, 1994; Gould et al., 1996). Despite the retrospective nature of many studies relating abuse to SII, results are remarkably consistent with those from prospective studies, suggesting that adolescents and young adults with abuse histories are about 3 times more likely to engage in both NSSI and SB (Brown et al., 1999; Dube et al., 2001). The nature of the relation between childhood abuse and later BPD has been debated extensively. On one side, some investigators have noted that a high percentage of individuals with BPD report histories of neglect (92%), physical abuse (25 to 73%), and sexual abuse (40 to 76%) (Zanarini, 2000). Thus, many have described abuse as a critical risk factor and even a central etiological factor in the development of BPD (Herman & van der Kolk, 1987; Soloff, Lynch, & Kelly, 2002). In contrast, other researchers have criticized the retrospective nature of these reports and highlighted the importance of viewing no single event as causal in the pathogenesis of BPD (Zanarini et al., 1998a). The current consensus is that, even though histories of abuse are common among individuals with BPD, they are neither necessary nor sufficient for the development of the disorder (Zanarini et al., 1997).

SEXUAL ORIENTATION

Gay, lesbian, and bisexual (GLB) sexual orientations have been associated with heightened risk for self-reported suicide attempts among youth (e.g., Fergusson, Horwood, & Beautrais, 1999; Safren & Heimberg, 1999). However, much of the research on GLB youth is cross-sectional, retrospective, or conducted with relatively small sample sizes. Furthermore, many studies have not examined sexual orientation in conjunction with other established suicide risk factors, making it difficult to determine whether sexual minority status is associated with an increase in other risk factors (e.g., peer rejection, parent-child conflict), or whether it is a risk factor in its own right. Many of these methodological concerns were addressed in a longitudinal study of sexual orientation and suicide attempts among Norwegian youth (N = 2,924; Wichstrom & Hegna, 2003). This study included a large number of established risk factors and suggested that GLB sexual orientations remained significant risk factors for suicide attempts. In addition, crossgender roles uniquely predict suicidal behaviors independent of sexual orientation (Fitzpatrick et al., 2005). However, other data suggest that, although some sexual-minority youth are at risk for suicide, it is inappropriate to characterize the entire population as being at heightened risk (Savin-Williams & Ream, 2003). Thus, data linking sexual orientation to suicide risk do not establish a direct connection between sexual orientation and BPD. More likely, any observed links between sexual orientation and BPD are mediated through the stigma, shame, victimization, and social rejection that so often accompany sexual minority status in United States culture (see, e.g., Balsam, Rothblum, & Beauchaine, 2005). Accordingly, these mechanisms merit further study.

GENETIC, NEUROCHEMICAL, AND BIOLOGICAL RISK

Research on the development of BPD and SII suggests strong biological underpinnings for both conditions. Studies have consistently indicated a familial component to SII (Brent et al., 1996; Loranger et al., 1982). To date, over 20 controlled family studies have indicated at least a three-fold increase in risk of SII among relatives of individuals who themselves engaged in some form of self-injurious behavior (Baldessarini & Hennen, 2004). However, the specific mechanisms, whether genetic, environmental, or both, that contribute to SII independent of associated psychiatric disorders remain unknown (Mann, 2003). Research on the heritability of BPD has produced contradictory results, partially due to methodological differences between behavioral genetics studies but also due to the heterogeneity of the BPD phenotype (Skodol et al., 2002). In one of the largest and most methodologically sound twin studies to date, including 221 Norwegian twin pairs (Torgersen et al., 2000), the concordance rate for BPD was 38% among monozygotic twins and 11% among dizygotic twins, suggesting a strong genetic component. Another behavioral genetics study indicated that risk for affective instability and impulsivity was greater in the relatives of individuals diagnosed with BPD than in relatives of individuals with other disorders (Silverman et al., 1991). Thus, heritable traits, such as impulsive aggression and affective instability, may predispose individuals to BPD.

The familial nature of BPD is consistent with, although not proof of, an underlying biological / genetic contribution to the emergence of the disorder (Loranger et al., 1982).

Given consistent evidence that traits such as impulsivity and affective instability have heritable biological substrates, research on neurochemical risk has focused on neurotransmitter systems that are linked with the expression of such behaviors. Currently, research suggests that the neurotransmitter and neurochemical systems most likely to underlie impulsive behavior include serotonin, vasopressin, monoamine oxidase-A, and dopamine, whereas emotional dysregulation is more closely linked with acetylcholine, norepinephrine, and gamma-aminobutyric acid (see Crowell et al., in press). However, there is considerable variation in the amount of empirical support for the role of these neurotransmitters in BPD and SII. Although of clear theoretical interest, there is currently limited direct support for the role of vasopressin, monoamine oxidase-A, or gamma-aminobutyric acid in the expression of BPD or SII. Given space constraints, readers are therefore referred to the integrative review and model presented by Depue and Lenzenweger (2001, 2005).

Impulsivity: Serotonin and dopamine.   Evidence suggests that impulsive aggression is linked to specific genetic polymorphisms and functional impairments within the serotonin (5-HT) and dopamine (DA) systems. Deficits in central 5-HT have been consistently associated with mood disorders, suicidal behaviors, and aggression (Kamali, Oquendo, & Mann, 2002; Coccaro, 1989). Across numerous studies, individuals with personality disorders, including BPD, show a blunted prolactin response to fenfluramine challenge, suggesting reduced central 5-HT activity (e.g., Soloff, 2000). Genetic studies have focused on several 5-HT candidate genes including those that code for tryptophan hydroxylase (TPH; a rate limiting enzyme in the biosynthesis of 5-HT), the serotonin transporter (SERT), the 5-HT1b receptor, the 5-HT1a receptor, the 5-HT2a receptor, and others (Skodol et al., 2002). Although further work is needed, preliminary evidence suggests that individuals with BPD have fewer platelet SERT binding sites and that this variability is likely due to polymorphisms of the SERT gene (5-HTT; Greenberg et al., 1999). There have been conflicting findings on the relation between polymorphisms of the U and L alleles of the TPH gene and impulsive aggression (for a review see Gurvits et al., 2000). However, recent research supports a relation between BPD and TPH-1 (Zaboli et al., in press).

Similar to research on BPD, studies on the neurobiology of SII have focused primarily on serotonergic functioning. Although studies of 5-HT functioning among adults have conclusively supported a role for this neurotransmitter in SII (Mann, 2003), studies of adolescents are less common. Nevertheless, a recent postmortem study of suicide victims indicated higher levels of 5-HT2A receptors, 5-HT2A proteins, and mRNA expression in the prefrontal and hippocampal areas of adolescent suicide victims (Pandey et al., 2002). In another study, self-injuring adolescent girls had significantly lower peripheral serotonin levels compared with controls (Crowell et al., 2005).

Research on the genetics of 5-HT in ISI has focused on several candidate genes (e.g., 5-HTR1A, 5-HTR1B) and the serotonin transporter (SERT). The 5-HTR1A gene has been of interest in genetics studies based on findings of deficient 5-HT1A receptors in the midbrain and ventral PFC of depressed suicide victims (Arango et al., 2003). Similarly, research on the 5-HTR$_{1B}$ gene emerged based on findings that 5-HT$_{1B}$-knockout mice are impulsive, aggressive, and more likely to self-administer drugs and alcohol (Zhuang et al., 1999). However, research to date has produced conflicting results, with the gene coding for the serotonin transporter (SERT or 5-HTT) being the most promising link between 5-HT and self-injurious behavior. Research suggests that individuals with the short allele (i.e., SS or SL genotypes) are more likely than LL individuals to engage in suicidal behavior (Bondy, Buettner, & Zill, 2006; Anguelova, Benkelfat, & Turecki, 2003) or to have committed suicide by violent means (Lin & Tsai, 2004).

Although no studies have tested DA functioning directly in individuals diagnosed with BPD (Friedel, 2004), there is some consensus that DA dysfunction contributes to behavioral traits seen in the disorder. Nevertheless, the specific mechanism(s) of DA dysfunction remain(s) unresolved. Two reviews discussing DA dysfunction in BPD suggest hyperactivation in one or more DA systems within the CNS (Friedel, 2004; Skodol et al., 2002). However, empirical research with depressed adults (e.g., Epstein et al., 2006) and impulsive children and adolescents suggests that both traits are related to attenuated DA functioning (e.g., Bush et al., 1999; Vaidya et al., 1998). Furthermore, there is evidence of DA dysfunction among individuals at risk for suicide. For example, the authors of one study (Roy, Karoum, & Pollack, 1992) found that depressed suicide attempters had significantly reduced peripheral markers of DA (urinary homovanillic acid, dihydroxyphenylacetic acid, and total body output of DA) compared with depressed patients who had never attempted suicide. Moreover, patients who reattempted suicide during a 5-year follow-up had significantly smaller urinary outputs of homovanillic acid and total DA than patients who did not reattempt suicide, who had never attempted suicide, and than normal controls. This study confirmed earlier studies of reduced CSF homovanillic acid (Roy, Dejong, & Linnoila, 1989), suggesting that decreased DA neurotransmission may contribute to SB. A more recent study measuring postmortem homovanillic acid and dihydroxyphenylacetic acid confirmed that there is reduced DA turnover in the basal ganglia of depressed suicide victims (Bowden et al., 1997). Finally, data from challenge tests using apomorphine (a DA agonist) have indicated that, compared with controls, a smaller response is observed among depressed (Pitchot et al., 1992) and nondepressed (Pitchot, Hansenne, & Ansseau, 2001) suicide attempters and suicide victims (Pitchot, Reggers et al., 2001). In sum, these findings suggest that reduced DA functioning is characteristic of individuals who engage in SB.

Emotional lability: Acetylcholine and norepinephrine. Cholinergic neurons innervate several CNS structures that are involved in emotion regulation, including the amygdala, the hippocampus, the dorsal tegmental complex, and portions of both the striatum and the cingulate cortex. Moreover, the effectiveness of many antidepressant medications (including tricyclic and atypical antidepressants) may be due partly to the direct inhibitory effects on nicotinic acetylcholine receptors (NAChRs; Shytle et al., 2002). The primary theory of cholinergic dysfunction in mood disorders suggests that complex interactions between the cholinergic and adrenergic systems lead to some features of depression (see Shytle et al. for a review). Research also suggests that an imbalance in cholinergic versus adrenergic system activity could develop following prolonged exposure to stress, leading to chronic increases in heart rate, blood pressure, dysphoria, depression, anxiety, irritability, aggression, and hostility.

The norepinephrine (NE) system (also called the noradrenergic system) is believed to underlie individual reactivity to the environment, irritability, mood regulation, sociability, and affectivity (Gurvits et al., 2000). Increases of NE using reboxetine, a selective noradrenaline reuptake inhibitor, lead to increased social engagement and cooperation, and to reduced self-focus among typical volunteers (Tse & Bond, 2002). This quality of the NE system has led some to suggest that NE activity may interact with 5-HT activity to determine whether aggression is inwardly or outwardly directed (Gurvits et al., 2000). In other words, increased NE, which is associated with extraversion, alertness, and attention to external stimuli, may lead to outward aggression, whereas decreased NE may lead to social withdrawal. However, in one direct test, individuals who met criteria for BPD were not significantly different from typical controls on the clonidine NE challenge test (Paris et al., 2004).

In contrast, research with adult suicide victims with MDD has found reduced NE neurons in the locus coeruleus (Arango, Underwood, & Mann, 1996). Depressed suicide victims have heightened α2a-adrenocepter sensitivity in the frontal cortex (González-Maeso et al., 2002), reduced brainstem NE levels, and increased α2-adrenergic receptors in the brainstem (perhaps due to secondary upregulation as a consequence of lower NE levels; Ordway et al., 1994). Further observations supporting NE dysfunction include findings of increased tyrosine hydroxylase activity (the rate limiting enzyme of biosynthesis of NE) in the locus coeruleus of suicide victims (Zhu et al., 1999), which may be a consequence of chronic stress (e.g., Melia et al., 1992).

Other biological risk. Not only does chronic stress lead to NE depletion, but evidence suggests that chronic stress also leads to an elevated hypothalamic-pituitary-adrenal (HPA) axis response. Furthermore, there is increasing evidence that the HPA axis is involved in SB. This evidence comes from studies using the dexamethasone suppression test (DST), a challenge test of HPA axis reactivity. Although the DST is not a very useful indicator of depression in general because many who are depressed do not exhibit abnormal HPA axis functioning (see Beauchaine & Marsh, 2006), nonsuppression of cortisol in response to the DST among depressed individuals predicts heightened risk for future suicide. Coryell and Schlesser (2001) followed a group of depressed patients over 15 years and found that nonsuppressors were at 14-fold greater risk of death by suicide than those who suppressed cortisol in response to the DST. This finding is supported by meta-analytic results indicating that cortisol nonsuppression is predictive of later death by suicide (Lester, 1992). To date, however, there are no studies testing the DST among individuals diagnosed with BPD.

Many neuroanatomical studies of suicide risk and BPD have focused on the prefrontal cortex (PFC), particularly the ventromedial PFC, and its connections with the amygdala. One theory (see Mann, 2003) is that the PFC inhibits impulsive behavior by providing insight into consequences of future actions. Thus, deficits within the PFC likely contribute to suicidal and other impulsive behaviors through failure to inhibit aggressive impulses. The ventromedial PFC is rich in both DA- and 5-HT-modulated neurons and is densely connected with the basolateral amygdala, a limbic structure involved in processing emotional and social cues (Le Doux, 1992; Shaw et al., 2005). Changes in amygdala activation can be measured reliably in fMRI studies in which individuals are instructed to regulate emotional responses, and the PFC plays a role in modulating amygdala activity (e.g., Schaefer et al., 2002). Theories outlining the relation between frontolimbic dysfunction and BPD suggest that dysfunction of the neural circuitry of emotion regulation leads to impulsive aggression (e.g., Davidson, Putnam, & Larson, 2000). Thus, functional or structural abnormalities within these regions or their connections could lead to the core deficits seen in BPD.

Autonomic risk.   There is a rich theoretical literature linking autonomic nervous system (ANS) measures to the central nervous system substrates of various psychological conditions (for a review see Beauchaine et al., 2001). Of particular relevance to the development of BPD may be the functioning of the parasympathetic nervous system (PNS). PNS activity can be indexed by respiratory sinus arrhythmia (RSA), a marker of vagal influences on heart-rate fluctuations across the respiratory cycle (also referred to as *vagal tone;* Berntson et al., 1997). Both theoretical and empirical findings suggest that individual differences in RSA are associated with social affiliative behaviors and emotion-regulation capabilities, with reduced RSA conferring risk for psychopathology and heightened RSA buffering against risk (Beauchaine, 2001; Katz & Gottman, 1997). Thus, individuals at risk for BPD may also show reduced RSA under appropriate stimulus conditions. In support of this hypothesis, research suggests that self-injuring adolescents have reduced RSA compared with typical controls (Crowell et al., 2005).

Temperamental and personality risk.   Temperamental and personality characteristics that underlie BPD and SII likely reflect complex interactions among biological predispositions and environmental influences (see Depue & Lenzenweger, 2001, 2005). Evidence suggests that genetic factors account for 30 to 60% of the variance in adult personality traits (Carey & DiLalla, 1994). Yet despite the heritability of temperament and other traits related to BPD, evidence suggests that the disorder is not necessarily traitlike or enduring but rather is characterized by significant intraindividual change over time (Lenzenweger, Johnson, & Willett, 2004). Identifying personality or temperamental predictors of such change is critical because it could reveal systems that are most influential in the progression of the disorder and those that may be more malleable (Lenzenweger & Castro, 2005). One model of temperament that may be relevant to the development of BPD is the Depue-Lenzenweger (2001, 2005) neurobehavioral model. According to this model *agentic extraversion* is characterized by positive incentive motivation processes that are rooted in the mesolimbic DA system, *anxiety* involves tonic activity of the NE system, *nonaffective constraint* is driven by 5-HT, *fear* is rooted in phasic aspects of NE, and *affiliation* derives from oxytocin, vasopressin, and endogenous opiate activity.

Research suggests that BPD is most likely characterized by diminished agentic extraversion, increased anxiety, and diminished constraint (Lenzenweger et al., 2004). To place these terms within the context of this review, agentic extraversion (positive emotion) and anxiety (negative emotion) likely underlie emotion dysregulation processes, whereas nonaffective constraint is most likely related to impulsive features of BPD. Preliminary longitudinal data suggest combinations of these variables, such as higher agentic extraversion and lower nonaffective constraint, may be useful for predicting declines in BPD features across time (Lenzenweger & Castro, 2005). Thus, these data suggest that temperamental characteristics may be an important means of determining the course of BPD and potential targets for intervention efforts.

THEORETICAL SYNTHESIS AND DEVELOPMENTAL PROGRESSION

We now present a theoretical model of the developmental progression of BPD that incorporates many of the environmental and neurobiological risk factors outlined previously. This model focuses specifically on individuals with borderline features who present with SII. Therefore, the term BPD is used only to refer to individuals who have engaged in SII at some point of their development. Furthermore, because SII often emerges prior to BPD, the model incorporates a developmental framework for the emergence of SII first and BPD second. This model is outlined in the following and depicted in Figure 17.1.

A Biosocial Developmental Model of BPD

Our biosocial developmental model extends and elaborates on Linehan's (1993) theory. We explore the possibility that biological vulnerabilities for BPD are similar to many impulse control disorders, including Attention-Deficit/Hyperactivity Disorder and Conduct Disorder. This risk is likely to include an underactivated incentive motivational system (Beauchaine et al., 2001; Gatzke-Kopp & Beauchaine, in press; Depue & Lenzeneger, 2001, 2005). According to this model, SII may be one feature of BPD that emerges earlier than other features and may, in some cases, be a developmental precursor to the disorder (although see previous paragraphs for a discussion of multifinality).

As indicated in Figure 17.1, a child's inherited biological risk for the development of SII and later BPD most likely results from polymorphisms in one or more genes affecting 5-HT and DA expression. Such genetic risk, in turn, affects functioning within the 5-HT and DA systems, as well as the neuroanatomical structures that they innervate. This biological risk contributes to behavioral reactivity, impulsivity, oppositionality, and emotional

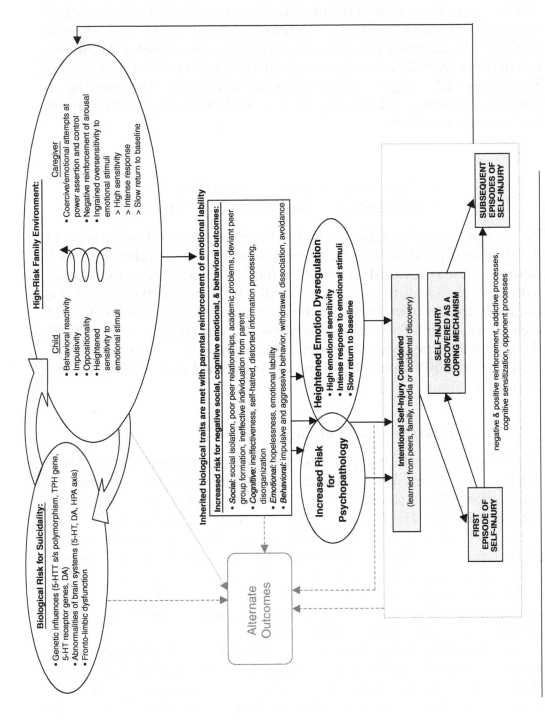

Figure 17.1. Developmental model of borderline personality and intentional self-injury

sensitivity that may be characteristic of children at risk for BPD and other impulse control problems. Within a high-risk family environment, these traits interact with the caregiver's unsuccessful attempts to manage and control a difficult child. This type of family environment is likely to be similar to that described by Patterson and colleagues as leading to the development of emotional lability among individuals at risk for Conduct Disorder and ASPD (Patterson, Chamberlain, & Reid, 1982; Patterson, DeBaryshe, & Ramsey, 1989; Patterson, Dishion, & Bank, 1984), although emotional invalidation is likely to play a more prominent role in the development of BPD (Linehan, 1993). Within such environments, repeated irritable exchanges between the child and the parent serve as training for coercive, emotionally labile interaction patterns. Thus, the core traits seen in BPD may be a consequence of reciprocal interactions between biological risk and environmental processes, sometimes but not always including trauma (see Kernberg & Caligor, 2005).

The complex interaction between characteristics of the child and the environment are thought to lead to an increase in risk factors for the development of BPD and SII, including social, cognitive, emotional, and behavioral instability. The increase in any combination of these risk factors is likely to increase risk for psychopathology in general, as well as for further emotion dysregulation. Among individuals at risk for the development of SII and BPD, it is probable that the overlap of extreme emotional dysregulation with a diagnosable psychiatric disorder leads to the discovery of SII as a means of coping with extreme emotional distress. It is the repeated iterations of the entire cycle that are believed to potentiate the development of BPD. In other words, repeated self-injury will negatively influence family functioning, which in turn affects the child's biological functioning. Together, these interacting risks lead to negative cognitive, emotional, behavioral, and social consequences, and increased risk for psychopathology and emotion dysregulation. Emotion dysregulation further contributes to the possibility that SII will develop as a coping mechanism and that further features of BPD will emerge.

Summary

Research to date on the development of SII and BPD is extremely limited. When compared with other psychological disorders, such as depression and ASPD, very little is known about the developmental trajectories leading to BPD. Moreover, those diagnosed with BPD represent a heterogeneous group of individuals, with unique life histories. It is currently unknown whether there are distinct subtypes within the BPD diagnosis.

Therefore, it is likely that the developmental model outlined here will only apply to some individuals who meet criteria for BPD in adulthood. More importantly, it is likely that many children with the risk factors previously described will not develop BPD, due to personal and/or environmental resilience. Historically, BPD is a disorder that has been characterized incorrectly and, as a consequence, been viewed as difficult or even impossible to treat. Given that there are now several empirically supported treatments for BPD (Linehan, 1993; Linehan et al., 2006; Clarkin et al., in press) it is critical that youth who might benefit from these treatments be identified for tertiary prevention (i.e., treatment). Moreover, it is necessary that theory-driven, longitudinal research be conducted on the development of BPD and self-inflicted injury among children and adolescents. This information could be used to identify risk factors or early manifestations of the disorder and, ultimately, in the service of secondary prevention efforts.

REFERENCES

Agrawal, H., Gunderson, J., Holmes, B., & Lyons-Ruth, K. (2004). Attachment studies with borderline patients: A review. *Harvard Review of Psychiatry, 12,* 94–104.

American Psychiatric Association. (1980). *Diagnostic and Statistical Manual of Mental Disorders* (3rd ed.). Washington, DC: Author.

American Psychiatric Association. (2000). *Diagnostic and Statistical Manual of Mental Disorders* (4th ed., text revision). Washington, DC: Author.

Anguelova, M., Benkelfat, C., & Turecki, G. (2003). A systematic review of association studies investigating genes coding for serotonin receptors and the serotonin transporter. Vol. II: Suicidal behavior. *Molecular Psychiatry, 8,* 646–653.

Arango, V., Huang, Y.-Y., Underwood, M. D., & Mann, J. J. (2003). Genetics of the serotonergic system in suicidal behavior. *Journal of Psychiatric Research, Brain Imaging, and Post-Mortem Studies in Affective Disorders, 37,* 375–386.

Arango, V., Underwood, M. D., & Mann, J. J. (1996). Fewer pigmented locus coeruleus neurons in suicide victims: Preliminary results. *Biological Psychiatry, 39,* 112–120.

Baldessarini, R. J., Finklestein, S., & Arana, G. W. (1983). The predictive power of diagnostic tests and the effect of prevalence of illness. *Archives of General Psychiatry, 40,* 569–573.

Baldessarini, R., & Hennen, J. (2004). Genetics of suicide: An overview. *Harvard Review of Psychiatry, 12,* 1–13.

Balsam, K. F., Rothblum, E. D., & Beauchaine, T. P. (2005). Victimization over the lifespan: A comparison of lesbian, gay, bisexual, and heterosexual siblings. *Journal of Consulting and Clinical Psychology, 73,* 477–487.

Beauchaine, T. P. (2001). Vagal tone, development, and Gray's motivational theory: Toward an integrated model of autonomic nervous system functioning in psychopathology. *Development and Psychopathology, 13,* 183–214.

Beauchaine, T. P., Katkin, E. S., Strassberg, Z., & Snarr, J. (2001). Disinhibitory psychopathology in male adolescents: Discriminating conduct disorder from attention-deficit/hyperactivity disorder through concurrent assessment of multiple autonomic states. *Journal of Abnormal Psychology, 110,* 610–624.

Beauchaine, T. P., & Marsh, P. (2006). Taxometric methods: Enhancing early detection and prevention of psychopathology by identifying latent vulnerability traits. In D. Cicchetti & D. Cohen (Eds.), *Developmental psychopathology* (2nd ed., pp. 931–967). Hoboken, NJ: Wiley.

Beautrais, A. L., Joyce, P. R., & Mulder, R. T. (1996). Risk factors for serious suicide attempts among youths aged 13 through 24 years. *American Academy of Child & Adolescent Psychiatry, 35,* 1174–1182.

Bemporad, J. R., Smith, H. F., Hanson, G., & Cicchetti, D. (1982). Borderline syndromes in childhood: Criteria for diagnosis. *American Journal of Psychiatry, 139,* 596–602.

Berman, A. L., Jobes, D. A., & Silverman, M. M. (2006). *Adolescent suicide: Assessment and intervention* (Second). Washington, DC: American Psychological Association.

Bernstein, D., Cohen, P., Velez, C., Schwab-Stone, M., Siever, L., & Shinsato, L. (1993). Prevalence and stability of the *DSM-III-R* personality disorders in a community-based survey of adolescents. *American Journal of Psychiatry, 150,* 1237–1243.

Berntson, G. G., Bigger, T. J., Eckberg, D. L., Grossman, P., Kaufmann, P. G., Malik, M., et al. (1997). Heart rate variability: Origins, methods, and interpretive caveats. *Psychophysiology, 34,* 623–648.

Bondy, B., Buettner, A., & Zill, P. (2006). Genetics of suicide. *Molecular Psychiatry, 11,* 336–351.

Bowden, C., Cheetham, S. C., Lowther, S., Katona, C. L. E., Crompton, M. R., & Horton, R. W. (1997). Reduced dopamine turnover in the basal ganglia of depressed suicides. *Brain Research, 769,* 135–140.

Brent, D., Perper, J. A., Goldstein, C. E., Kolko, D., Allan, M., Allman, C., et al. (1988). Risk factors for adolescent suicide: A comparison of adolescent suicide victims with suicidal inpatients. *Archives of General Psychiatry, 45,* 581–588.

Brent, D. A., Baugher, M., Bridge, J., Chen, T., & Chiappetta, L. (1999). Age- and sex-related risk factors for adolescent suicide. *Journal of the American Academy of Child & Adolescent Psychiatry, 38,* 1497–1505.

Brent, D. A., Bridge, J., Johnson, B. A., & Connolly, J. (1996). Suicidal behavior runs in families. A controlled family study of adolescent suicide victims. *Archives of General Psychiatry, 53,* 1145–1152.

Brent, D. A., Oquendo, M., Birmaher, B., Greenhill, L., Kolko, D., Stanley, B., et al. (2002). Familial pathways to early-onset suicide attempt: Risk for suicidal behavior in offspring of mood-disordered suicide attempters. *Archives of General Psychiatry, 59,* 801–807.

Brent, D. A., Perper, J. A., Moritz, G., Liotus, L., Schweers, J., Balach, L., et al. (1994). Familial risk factors for adolescent suicide: A case-control study. *Acta Psychiactra Scandinavia, 89,* 52–58.

Brodsky, B. S., Oquendo, M., Ellis, S., Haas, G. L., Malone, K. M., & Mann, J. J. (2001). The relationship of childhood abuse to impulsivity and suicidal behavior in adults with major depression. *American Journal of Psychiatry, 158,* 1871–1877.

Brown, J., Cohen, P., Johnson, J. G., & Smailes, E. M. (1999). Childhood abuse and neglect: Specificity of effects on adolescent and young adult depression and suicidality. *Journal of the American Academy of Child & Adolescent Psychiatry, 38,* 1490–1496.

Bush, G., Frazier, J. A., Rauch, S. L., Seidman, L. J., Whalen, P. J., Jenike, M. A., et al. (1999). Anterior cingulate cortex dysfunction in attention-deficit/hyperactivity disorder revealed by fMRI and the counting stroop. *Biological Psychiatry, 45,* 1542–1552.

Carey, G., & DiLalla, D. L. (1994). Personality and psychopathology: genetic perspectives. *Journal of Abnormal Psychology, 103,* 32–43.

Cicchetti, D., & Rogosch, F. A. (2002). A developmental psychopathology perspective on adolescence. *Journal of Consulting & Clinical Psychology, 70,* 6–20.

Clarkin, J. F., Levy, K. N., Lenzenweger, M. F., & Kernberg, O. F. (in press). Evaluating three treatments for Borderline Personality Disorder: A multiwave study. *American Journal of Psychiatry, 164,* 922–928.

Coccaro, E. F. (1989). Central serotonin and impulsive aggression. *British Journal of Psychiatry, 154,* 52–62.

Cohen, D., Paul, R., & Volkmar, F. (1987). Issues in the classification of pervasive developmental disorders and associated conditions. In D. J. Cohen & A. M. Donnellan (Eds.), *Handbook of autism and pervasive developmental disorders* (pp. 20–40). New York: Wiley.

Comtois, K. A. (2002). A review of interventions to reduce the prevalence of parasuicide. *Psychiatric Services, 53,* 1138–1144.

Corbitt, E. M., & Widiger, T. A. (1995). Sex differences among the personality disorders: An exploration of the data. *Clinical Psychology: Science and Practice, 2,* 225–238.

Coryell, W., & Schlesser, M. (2001). The dexamethasone suppression test and suicide prediction. *American Journal of Psychiatry, 158,* 748–753.

Crawford, T. N., Cohen, P., & Brook, J. S. (2001). Dramatic-erratic personality disorder symptoms. Vol. II: Developmental pathways from early adolescence to adulthood. *Journal of Personality Disorders, 15,* 336–350.

Crowell, S. E., Beauchaine, T. P., McCauley, E., Smith, C., Stevens, A. L., & Sylvers, P. D. (2005). Psychological, physiological, and serotonergic correlates of parasuicidal behavior among adolescent girls. *Development and Psychopathology, 17,* 1105–1127.

Davidson, R. J., Putnam, K. M., & Larson, C. L. (2000). Dysfunction in the neural circuitry of emotion regulation—A possible prelude to violence. *Science, 289,* 591–594.

Depue, R. A., & Lenzenweger, M. F. (2001). A neurobehavioral dimensional model. In W. J. Livesley (Ed.), *Handbook of personality disorders. Theory, research, and treatment* (pp. 136–176). New York: Guilford.

Depue, R. A., & Lenzenweger, M. F. (2005). A neurobehavioral dimensional model of personality disturbance. In M. F. Lenzenweger & J. F. Clarkin (Eds.), *Major theories of personality disorder* (2nd ed., pp. 391–454). New York: Guilford.

Dube, S. R., Anda, R. F., Felitti, V. J., Chapman, D. P., Williamson, D. F., & Giles, W. H. (2001). Childhood abuse, household dysfunction, and the risk of attempted suicide throughout the life span: Findings from the Adverse Childhood Experiences Study. *Journal of the American Medical Association, 286,* 3089–3096.

Epstein, J., Pan, H., Kocsis, J. H., Yang, Y., Butler, T., Chusid, J., et al. (2006). Lack of ventral striatal response to positive stimuli in depressed versus normal subjects. *American Journal of Psychiatry, 163,* 1784–1790.

Ernst, C., Lalovic, A., Lesage, A., Seguin, M., Tousignant, M., & Turecki, G. (2004). Suicide and no axis I psychopathology. *BMC Psychiatry, 4,* 7.

Fergusson, D. M., Horwood, L. J., & Beautrais, A. L. (1999). Is sexual orientation related to mental health problems and suicidality in young people? *Archives of General Psychiatry, 56,* 876–880.

Fitzpatrick, K. K., Euton, S. J., Jones, J. N., & Schmidt, N. B. (2005). Gender role, sexual orientation and suicide risk. *Journal of Affective Disorders, 87,* 35–42.

Flood, R. A., & Seager, C. P. (1968). A retrospective examination of psychiatric case records of patients who subsequently committed suicide. *British Journal of Psychiatry, 114,* 443–450.

Friedel, R. O. (2004). Dopamine dysfunction in borderline personality disorder: A hypothesis. *Neuropsychopharamcology, 29,* 1029–1039.

Gatzke-Kopp, L., & Beauchaine, T. P. (in press). Central nervous system substrates of impulsivity: Implications for the development of attention-deficit / hyperactivity disorder and conduct disorder. In D. Coch, G. Dawson, & K. Fischer (Eds.), *Human behavior, learning, and the developing brain: Atypical development.* New York: Guilford.

Geleerd, E. R. (1958). Borderline states in childhood and adolescence. *Psychoanalytic Study of the Child, 13,* 279–295.

Goldman, S., D'Angelo, E., DeMaso, D., & Mezzacappa, E. (1992). Physical and sexual abuse histories among children with borderline personality disorder. *American Journal of Psychiatry, 149,* 1723–1726.

González-Maeso, J., Rodríguez-Puertas, R., Meana, J. J., García-Sevilla, J. A., & Guimón, J. (2002). Neurotransmitter receptor-mediated activation of G-proteins in brains of suicide victims with mood disorders: selective supersensitivity of 2A-adrenoceptors. *Molecular Psychiatry, 7,* 755–767.

Gould, M. S., Fisher, P., Parides, M., Flory, M., & Shaffer, D. (1996). Psychosocial risk factors of child and adolescent completed suicide. *Archives of General Psychiatry, 53,* 1155–1162.

Gratz, K. L. (2003). Risk factors for and functions of deliberate self-harm: An empirical and conceptual review. *Clinical Psychology: Science and Practice, 10,* 192–205.

Greenberg, B. D., Tolliver, T. J., Huang, S.-J., Li, Q., Bengel, D., & Murphy, D. L. (1999). Genetic variation in the serotonin transporter promoter region affects serotonin uptake in human blood platelets. *American Journal of Medical Genetics, 88,* 83–87.

Grunbaum, J. A., Kann, L., Kinchen, S., Ross, J., Hawkins, J., Lowry, R., et al. (2004). Youth risk behavior surveillance: United States, 2003. *MMWR Surveillance Summaries, 53,* 1–96.

Gunderson, J. G., & Singer, M. T. (1975). Defining borderline patients: An overview. *American Journal of Psychiatry, 132,* 1–10.

Gurvits, I. G., Koenigsberg, H. W., & Siever, L. (2000). Neurotransmitter dysfunction in patients with borderline personality disorder. *Psychiatric Clinics of North America, 23,* 27–40.

Guzder, J., Paris, J., Zelkowitz, P., & Marchessault, K. (1996). Risk factors for borderline pathology in children. *Journal of the American Academy of Child and Adolescent Psychiatry, 35,* 26–33.

Herman, J. L., Perry, J. C., & van der Kolk, B. A. (1989). Childhood trauma in borderline personality disorder. *American Journal of Psychiatry, 146,* 490–495.

Herman, J. L., & van der Kolk, B. A. (1987). Traumatic antecedents of borderline personality disorder. In B. A. van der Kolk (Ed.), *Psychological trauma* (pp. 111–126). Washington, DC: American Psychiatric Press.

Herpertz, S. C., Dietrich, T. M., Wenning, B., Krings, T., Erberich, S. G., Willmes, K., et al. (2001). Evidence of abnormal amygdala functioning in borderline personality disorder: A functional MRI study. *Biological Psychiatry, 50,* 292–298.

Houston, K., Hawton, K., & Shepperd, R. (2001). Suicide in young people aged 15–24: A psychological autopsy study. *Journal of Affective Disorders, 63,* 159–170.

Kahan, J., & Pattison, E. M. (1984). Proposal for a distinctive diagnosis: The deliberate self-harm syndrome (DSH). *Suicide and Life-Threatening Behavior, 14,* 17–35.

Kamali, M., Oquendo, M. A., & Mann, J. J. (2002). Understanding the neurobiology of suicidal behavior. *Depression & Anxiety, 14,* 164–176.

Katz, L. F., & Gottman, J. M. (1997). Buffering children from marital conflict and dissolution. *Journal of Clinical Child Psychology, 26,* 157–171.

Kernberg, O. (1967). Borderline personality organization. *Journal of American Psychoanalytic Association, 15,* 641–685.

Kernberg, O., & Caligor, E. (2005). A psychoanalytic theory of personality disorders. In M. F. Lenzenweger & J. F. Clarkin (Eds.), Major theories of personality disorder (2nd ed.). New York: Guilford.

Kernberg, P. F. (1990). Resolved: Borderline personality exists in children under twelve. Affirmative. *Journal of the American Academy of Child and Adolescent Psychiatry, 29,* 478–482.

Kernberg, P. F., Weiner, A. S., & Bardenstein, K. K. (2000). *Personality disorders in children and adolescents.* New York: Basic Books.

Knight, R. P. (1953). Borderline states. *Bulletin of the Menninger Clinics, 17,* 1–12.

Korfine, L., & Hooley, J. M. (2000). Directed forgetting of emotional stimuli in borderline personality disorder. *Journal of Abnormal Psychology, 109,* 214–221.

Kreitman, N. (1977). *Parasuicide.* London: Wiley.

Le Doux, J. E. (1992). Emotion in the amygdala. In J. P. Aggleton (Ed.), *The amygdala: Neurobiological aspects of emotion, memory, and mental dysfunction* (pp. 339–351). New York: Wiley-Liss.

Lenzenweger, M. F., & Castro, D. D. (2005). Predicting change in borderline personality: Using neurobehavioral systems indicators within an individual growth curve framework. *Development and Psychopathology, 17,* 1207–1237.

Lenzenweger, M. F., & Cicchetti, D. (2005). Toward a developmental psychopathology approach to borderline personality disorder. *Development and Psychopathology, 17,* 893–898.

Lenzenweger, M. F., Johnson, M. D., & Willett, J. B. (2004). Individual growth curve analysis illuminates stability and change in personality disorder features: The longitudinal study of personality disorders. *Archives of General Psychiatry, 61,* 1015–1024.

Lenzenweger, M. F., Lane, M., Loranger, A. W., & Kessler, R. C. (in press). *DSM-IV* personality disorders in the National Comorbidity Survey Replication. *Biological Psychiatry, 62,* 553–564.

Lester, D. (1972). Self-mutilating behavior. *Psychological Bulletin, 78,* 119–128.

Lester, D. (1992). The dexamethasone suppression test as an indicator of suicide: A meta-analysis. *Pharmacopsychiatry, 25,* 265–270.

Levy, K. N., Meehan, K. B., Weber, M., Reynoso, J., & Clarkin, J. (2005). Attachment and borderline personality disorder: Implications for psychotherapy. *Psychopathology, 38,* 64–74.

Lin, P.,-Y., & Tsai, G. (2004). Association between serotonin transporter gene promoter polymorphism and suicide: Results of a meta-analysis. *Biological Psychiatry, 55,* 1023–1030.

Linehan, M. (1993). *Cognitive-behavioral treatment of borderline personality disorder.* New York: Guilford.

Linehan, M. M., Comtois, K. A., Murray, A. M., Brown, M. Z., Gallop, R. J., Heard, H. L., et al. (2006). Two-year randomized controlled trial and follow-up of dialectical behavior therapy vs. therapy by experts for suicidal behaviors and borderline personality disorder. *Archives of General Psychiatry, 63,* 757–766.

Lofgren, D., Bemporad, J., King, J., Lindem, K., & O'Driscoll, G. (1991). A prospective follow-up study of so-called borderline children. *American Journal of Psychiatry, 148,* 1541–1547.

Loranger, A. W. (1999). *International personality disorder examination:* DSM-IV *and* ICD-10 *interviews.* Odessa, FL: Psychological Assessment Resources, Inc.

Loranger, A. W., Oldham, J. M., & Tulis, E. H. (1982). Familial transmission of DSM-III borderline personality disorder. *Archives of General Psychiatry, 39,* 795–799.

Loranger, A. W., Susman, V. L., Oldham, J. M., & Russakoff, M. (1988). *The personality disorder examination (PDE) manual.* Yonkers, NY: DV Communications.

Mann, J. (2003). Neurobiology of suicidal behavior. *Nature Reviews Neuroscience, 4,* 819–828.

Mason, P. (1954). Suicide in adolescents. *Psychoanalytic Review, 41,* 48–54.

Melia, K. R., Rasmussen, K., Terwilliger, R. Z., Haycock, J. W., Nestler, E. J., & Duman, R. S. (1992). Coordinate regulation of the cyclic AMP system with firing rate and expression of tyrosine hydroxylase in the rat locus coeruleus: effects of chronic stress and drug treatments. *Journal Of Neurochemistry, 58,* 494–502.

Meuhlenkamp, J. J., & Miller, A. L. (2004). What is suicidal behavior? Definitional problems in research and practice. *APA Division 12, Section VII Newsletter, Fall/Winter 2004–2005,* 6–7.

Millon, T. (1983). *Millon clinical multiaxial inventory manual.* Minneapolis, MN: National Computer Systems.

O'Carroll, P. W., Berman, A. L., Maris, R. W., Moscicki, E. K., Tanney, B. L., & Silverman, M. M. (1996). Beyond the tower of Babel: A nomenclature for suicidology. *Suicide and Life-Threatening Behavior, 26,* 237–252.

Offer, D., & Barglow, P. (1960). Adolescent and young adult self-mutilation incidents in a general psychiatric hospital. *Archives of General Psychiatry, 3,* 194–204.

Ordway, G. A., Widdowson, P. S., Smith, K. S., & Halaris, A. (1994). Agonist binding to a2-adrenoceptors is elevated in the locus coeruleus from victims of suicide. *Journal of Neurochemistry, 63,* 617–624.

Pandey, G. N., Dwivedi, Y., Rizavi, H. S., Ren, X., Pandey, S., Pesold, C., et al. (2002). Higher expression of serotonin 5-HT 2a receptors in the post-mortem brains of teenage suicide victims. *American Journal of Psychiatry, 159,* 419–429.

Paris, J. (1997). Antisocial and borderline personality disorders: Two separate diagnoses or two aspects of the same psychopathology. *Comprehensive Psychiatry, 38,* 237–242.

Paris, J. (2000). Childhood precursors of borderline personality disorder. *Psychiatric Clinics of North America, 23,* 77–87.

Paris, J. (2005). The development of impulsivity and suicidality in borderline personality disorder. *Development and Psychopathology, 17,* 1091–1104.

Paris, J., Zweig-Frank, H., Ng Ying Kin, N. M. K., Schwartz, G., Steiger, H., & Nair, N. (2004). Neurobiological correlates of diagnosis and underlying traits in patients with borderline personality disorder compared with normal controls. *Psychiatry Research, 121,* 239–252.

Patterson, G. R., Chamberlain, P., & Reid, J. B. (1982). A comparative evaluation of a parent-training program. *Behavior Therapy, 13,* 638–650.

Patterson, G. R., DeBaryshe, B. D., & Ramsey, E. (1989). A developmental perspective on antisocial behavior. *American Psychologist, 44,* 329–335.

Patterson, G. R., Dishion, T. J., & Bank, L. (1984). Family interaction: A process model of deviancy training. *Aggressive Behavior, 10,* 253–267.

Pitchot, W., Hansenne, M., & Ansseau, M. (2001). Role of dopamine in non-depressed patients with a history of suicide attempts. *European Psychiatry, 16,* 424–427.

Pitchot, W., Hansenne, M., Moreno, A. G., & Ansseau, M. (1992). Suicidal behavior and growth hormone response to apomorphine test. *Biological Psychiatry, 15,* 1213–1219.

Pitchot, W., Reggers, J., Pinto, E., Hansenne, M., Fuchs, S., Pirard, S., et al. (2001). Reduced dopaminergic activity in depressed suicides. *Psychoneuroendocrinology, 26,* 331–335.

Pollak, S. D. (2003). Experience-dependent affective learning and risk for psychopathology in children. *Annals New York Academy of Sciences, 1008,* 102–111.

Roy, A., Dejong, J., & Linnoila, M. (1989). Cerebrospinal-fluid monoamine metabolites and suicidal-behavior in depressed-patients—A 5-year follow-up-study. *Archives of General Psychiatry, 46,* 609–612.

Roy, A., Karoum, F., & Pollack, S. (1992). Marked reduction in indexes of dopamine metabolism among patients with depression who attempt suicide. *Archives of General Psychiatry, 49,* 447–450.

Safren, S. A., & Heimberg, R. G. (1999). Depression, hopelessness, suicidality and related factors in sexual minority and heterosexual adolescents. *Journal of Consulting & Clinical Psychology, 67,* 859–866.

Savin-Williams, R. C., & Ream, G. L. (2003). Suicide attempts among sexual-minority male youth. *Journal of Clinical Child & Adolescent Psychology, 32,* 509–522.

Samuels, J. E., Eaton, W. W., Bienvenu, O. J., Brown, C., Costa, P. T., & Nestadt, G. (2002). Prevalence and correlates of personality disorders in a community sample. *British Journal of Psychiatry, 180,* 536–542.

Schaefer, S. M., Jackson, D. C., Davidson, R. J., Aguirre, G. K., Kimberg, D. Y., & Thompson-Schill, S. L. (2002). Modulation of amygdalar activity by the conscious regulation of negative emotion. *Journal of Cognitive Neuroscience, 15,* 913–921.

Seiden, R. H. (1978). Where are they now? A follow-up study of suicide attempters from the Golden Gate Bridge. *Suicide and Life-Threatening Behavior, 8,* 1–13.

Shaffer, D., Gould, M., Fisher, P., Trautman, P., Moreau, D., Kleinman, M., et al. (1996). Psychiatric diagnosis in child and adolescent suicide. *Archives of General Psychiatry, 53,* 339–348.

Shaw, P., Bramham, J., Lawrence, E. J., Morris, R., Baron-Cohen, S., & David, A. S. (2005). Differential effects of lesions of the amygdala and prefrontal cortex on recognizing facial expressions of complex emotions. *Journal of Cognitive Neuroscience, 17,* 1410–1419.

Shytle, R. D., Silver, A. A., Lukas, R. J., Newman, M. B., Sheehan, D. V., & Sanberg, P. R. (2002). Nicotinic acetylcholine receptors as targets for antidepressants. *Molecular Psychiatry, 7,* 525–535.

Silverman, J., Pinkham, L., Horvath, T., Coccaro, E., Klar, H., Schear, S., et al. (1991). Affective and impulsive personality disorder traits in the relatives of patients with borderline personality disorder. *American Journal of Psychiatry, 148,* 1378–1385.

Simpson, G. (1950). Methodological problems in determining the aetiology of suicide. *American Sociological Review, 15,* 658–663.

Simpson, M. A. (1975). The phenomenology of self-mutilation in a general hospital setting. *Canadian Psychiatric Association Journal, 20,* 429–434.

Skodol, A. E., & Bender, D. S. (2003). Why are women diagnosed borderline more than men? *Psychiatric Quarterly, 74,* 349–360.

Soloff, P. H. (2000). Psychopharmacology of borderline personality disorder. *Psychiatric Clinics of North America, 23,* 169–192.

Soloff, P. H., Lynch, K. G., & Kelly, T. M. (2002). Childhood abuse as a risk factor for suicidal behavior in borderline personality disorder. *Journal of Personality Disorders, 16,* 201–214.

Spitzer, R. L., Endicott, J., & Gibbon, M. (1979). Crossing the border into borderline personality and borderline schizophrenia. The development of criteria. *Archives of General Psychiatry, 36,* 17–24.

Stern, A. (1938). Psychoanalytic investigation of and therapy in the borderline group of neuroses. *Psychoanalytic Quarterly, 7,* 467–489.

Swartz, M., Blazer, D., George, L., & Winfield, I. (1990). Estimating the prevalence of borderline personality disorder in the community. *Journal of Personality Disorders, 4,* 257–272.

Torgersen, S., Kringlen, E., & Cramer, V. (2001). The prevalence of personality disorders in a community sample. *Archives of General Psychiatry, 58,* 590–596.

rgersen, S., Lygren, S., Oien, P. A., Skre, I., Onstad, S., Edvardsen, J., et al. (2000). A twin study of personality disorders. *Comprehensive Psychiatry, 41,* 416–425.

Tse, W., & Bond, A. (2002). Difference in serotonergic and noradrenergic regulation of human social behaviors. *Psychopharmacology, 159,* 216–221.

Vaidya, C. J., Austin, G., Kirkorian, G., Ridlehuber, H. W., Desmond, J. E., Glover, G. H., et al. (1998). Selective effects of methylphenidate in attention deficit hyperactivity disorders: A functional magnetic resonance study. *Proceedings of the National Academy of Sciences, 95,* 14494–14499.

Vela, R. M., Gottlieb, E. H., & Gottlieb, H. P. (1983). Borderline syndromes in childhood: A critical review. In K. S. Robson (Ed.), *The borderline child: Approaches to etiology, diagnosis, and treatment* (pp. 31–48). New York: McGraw-Hill.

Weil, A. P. (1953). Certain severe disturbances of ego development in childhood. *Psychoanalytic Study of the Child, 8,* 271–287.

Welch, S. S. (2001). A review of the literature on the epidemiology of parasuicide in the general population. *Psychiatric Services, 52,* 368–375.

White, C. N., Gunderson, J. G., Zanarini, M. C., & Hudson, J. I. (2003). Family studies of borderline personality disorder: A review. *Harvard Review of Psychiatry, 11,* 8–19.

Wichstrom, L., & Hegna, K. (2003). Sexual orientation and suicide attempt: A longitudinal study of the general Norwegian adolescent population. *Journal of Abnormal Psychology, 112,* 114–151.

World Health Organization. (1992). *The ICD-10 classification of mental and behavioural disorders: Clinical descriptions and diagnostic guidelines.* Geneva, Switzerland.

Zaboli, G., Gizatullin, R., Nilsonne, Å., Wilczek, A., Jönsson, E. G., Ahnemark, E., et al. (in press). Tryptophan hydroxylase-1 gene variants associate with a group of suicidal borderline women. *Neuropsychopharmacology.*

Zanarini, M., Williams, A., Lewis, R., Reich, R., Vera, S., Marino, M., et al. (1997). Reported pathological childhood experiences associated with the development of borderline personality disorder. *American Journal of Psychiatry, 154,* 1101–1106.

Zanarini, M. C. (2000). Childhood experiences associated with the development of borderline personality disorder. *Psychiatric Clinics of North America, 23,* 89–101.

Zanarini, M. C., Frankenburg, F. R., Dubo, E. D., Sickel, A. E., Trikha, A., Levin, A., et al. (1998a). Axis I comorbidity of borderline personality disorder. *American Journal of Psychiatry, 155,* 1733–1739.

Zanarini, M. C., Frankenburg, F. R., Dubo, E. D., Sickel, A. E., Trikha, A., Levin, A., et al. (1998b). Axis II comorbidity of borderline personality disorder. *Comprehensive Psychiatry, 39,* 296–302.

Zanarini, M. C., Frankenburg, F. R., Hennen, J., Reich, D. B., & Silk, K. R. (2004a). Axis I comorbidity in patients with borderline personality disorder: 6-Year follow-up and prediction of time to remission. *American Journal of Psychiatry, 161,* 2108–2114.

Zanarini, M. C., Frankenburg, F. R., Vujanovic, A. A., Hennen, J., Reich, D. B., & Silk, K. R. (2004b). Axis II comorbidity of borderline personality disorder: Description of 6-year course and prediction to time-to-remission. *Acta Psychiatrica Scandinavica, 110,* 416–420.

Zhu, M.-Y., Klimek, V., Dilley, G. E., Haycock, J. W., Stockmeier, C., Overholser, J. C., et al. (1999). Elevated levels of tyrosine hydroxylase in the locus coeruleus in major depression. *Biological Psychiatry, 46,* 1275–1286.

Zhuang, X., Gross, C., Santarelli, L., Compan, V., Trillat, A. C., & Hen, R. (1999). Altered emotional states in knockout mice lacking 5-HT1A or 5-HT1B receptors. *Neuropsychopharmacology, 21,* 52S–60S.

Zilboorg, G. (1936a). Considerations on suicide, with particular reference to that of the young. *Journal of Orthopsychiatry, 7,* 15–31.

Zilboorg, G. (1936b). Differential diagnostic types of suicide. *Archives of General Psychiatry, 35,* 270–291.

Zimmerman, M., & Coryell, W. H. (1990). Diagnosing personality disorders in the community. A comparison of self-report and interview measures. *Archives of General Psychiatry, 47,* 527–531.

Zlotnick, C., Donaldson, D., Spirito, A., & Pearlstein, T. (1997). Affect regulation and suicide attempts in adolescent inpatients. *Journal of the American Academy of Child & Adolescent Psychiatry, 36,* 793–798.

Zlotnick, C., Mattia, J. I., & Zimmerman, M. (1999). Clinical correlates of self-mutilation in a sample of general psychiatric patients. *Journal of Nervous and Mental Disease, 187,* 296–301.

PART V
OTHER PSYCHOLOGICAL DISORDERS

CHAPTER 18

Bipolar Disorder

JOSEPH C. BLADER AND GABRIELLE A. CARLSON

PHENOMENOLOGY AND IMPACT

Bipolar Disorder (BPD) describes a pattern of major mood disturbances over an extended period of time, which typically crystallizes in early adulthood. The phenomenology and course of BPD among adults provide a well-characterized template for the modern definition and understanding of this illness. Accordingly, this chapter first describes the adult presentation that typifies *classic* BPD. We then turn to the phenomenology as described in DSM-IV, with specific considerations for children and adolescents. In fact, controversy surrounds the entire topic of child and adolescent BPD, but we hope to provide some clarity on this fascinating yet misunderstood topic.

STANDARD BIPOLAR DISORDER IN ADULTHOOD

By most formal definitions, classic BPD comprises the following: (a) episodes of *depression;* interspersed, to greater or lesser degree, with (b) epi-

Acknowledgments: Preparation of this chapter was supported in part by grants from the U.S. National Institutes of Health (K23MH064975) and by the National Alliance for Research on Schizophrenia and Depression (Young Investigator Award).

Disclosures: Joseph C. Blader receives research support from Abbott Laboratories. Gabrielle A. Carlson receives research support from Bristol-Myers Squibb Co., Eli Lilly & Co., Otsuka America Pharmaceutical Inc., and Sanofi-aventis U.S., and has had an advisory or consulting relationship with Abbott Laboratories, Bristol-Myers Squibb Co., Eli Lilly & Co, Janssen Pharmaceutical, and Otsuka America Pharmaceutical.

sodes of *mania*; (3) intervals *between* episodes, with highly variable duration, mood state, and quality of functioning across patients; and (4) an overall course of psychiatric illness that is *chronic* (American Psychiatric Association [APA], 2000; Goodwin & Jamison, 2007; World Health Organization, 2004). A person who experiences episodes of both depression and mania today receives a diagnosis of Bipolar I Disorder, followed by *specifiers* that characterize the episode's polarity (most recent episode manic, most recent episode depressed, etc.), severity (e.g., with psychotic features), and course (e.g., rapid cycling), according to current nomenclature in the *Diagnostic and Statistical Manual of Mental Disorders* (DSM-IV; APA, 2000).

Within BPD, depressive episodes generally conform to the conventional signs and symptoms of major depression that develop among those with no history of bipolar illness (so-called "unipolar" depression; see Klein, Torpey, Bufferd, & Dyson, this volume) and are no less painful. The cardinal mood disturbance of a manic episode, in contrast, is seldom experienced by the person as disturbance at all—rather, one encounters an individual with near-boundless energy, enthusiasm, high self-regard, confidence, conviviality, and, not infrequently, creativity, charisma, and generosity, all of which may be quite uncharacteristic of the person at other times. Such a frame of mind might sound enviable. In mania, however, euphoric exuberance and misguided convictions about one's insights, abilities, entitlements and infallibility lead to severely disinhibited behavior. The combination of heightened motivation to brash pursuit of unrealistic aims, of drive toward immediate intense pleasures, and of diminished self-restraint is the essence of mania, which can lead to disastrous consequences.

Indeed, the conduct that ensues during manic episodes harms the individual, those close to him or her, and the broader community. Physically reckless, unprotected, impulsive conduct, and unrestrained and restless hedonistic behavior can lead to promiscuity, drug abuse, plundering of one's financial resources, gambling debt, and impulsive junkets that leave others ignorant of the person's whereabouts. Poor judgment and irresponsibility endanger one's occupational and family roles, and thus the well-being of dependents and colleagues. When contacts of the individual with BPD seem perplexed, or do not reciprocate enthusiasm, they risk being perceived as obstructionist or ungrateful. Social strife and rage are common results. Impatience with others' shortcomings or uncooperativeness, as well as the inevitable frustration of desires and goals unattained, often manifest as irritability.

A significant subgroup of affected persons also experience psychotic features (Kennedy et al., 2005; Müller-Oerlinghausen, Berghöfer, & Bauer, 2002). These often arise as unshakable delusions, which aggrandize to impossible extents one's abilities or even one's identity, and/or as hallucinations that reinforce one's elevated status (e.g., special messages from powerful or famous people or spirits). Paranoid or persecutory delusions focus on dangers associated with having a special mission or being the target of persons envious of one's special abilities or status (Keck et al., 2003). Psychotic delusions or hallucinations during a manic episode that emphasize one's importance or powers are called *mood-congruent* psychotic features; those that do not have a clear relationship to inflated worth (such as beliefs in thought insertion or that one really deserves punishment) are considered *mood-incongruent*.

A *mixed episode* occurs when an individual displays the features of major depression and mania simultaneously, typically an admixture of negative affect and behavioral activation (Bauer et al., 2005; Maj et al., 2003). This dysphoric state is not pleasurable, and irritability is the mood that predominates. Much has been written about whether the full syndrome or only some symptoms are necessary to define such mixed states. Distinguishing mixed episodes from agitated depressions, from very rapid cycling, or from severe mood lability is difficult, but the implications are considerable. A mixed episode is treated like a manic episode, whereas an agitated depression is a form of depression. Mistaking a mixed episode for a depression may prompt treatment with antidepressant medications, which can exacerbate the mania.

Outcomes for adults with BPD are diverse. The overall trend with age is for depressive episodes to become more frequent and longer in duration (Kupka et al., 2005; Suppes, Kelly, & Perla, 2005). In the best of cases, functioning between episodes of mood disturbance can be quite good (*full interepisode recovery*) and one can enjoy considerable social and occupational success. A person experiencing no current mood abnormality is called *euthymic*. The likelihood of this outcome increases with a stable, tolerant family and a social milieu that buffers a person from many stresses that would otherwise aggravate the impairment but is also firm about treatment adherence and lifestyle practices that may forestall relapses (Alloy et al., 2005; Johnson et al., 2003).

Less fortunate individuals experience an unstable, often unremitting course. They endure episodes that become longer and more frequent over time, and they may drift downward socially as interpersonal and occupational functioning become increasingly erratic and inadequate. Interepisode recovery is incomplete in such cases. Sources of social support may become either alienated or actively rejected by the increasingly irascible patient. Civil and criminal legal entanglements are common complications, as is drug abuse (Blader & Carlson, in press; Friedman et al., 2005; Quanbeck et al., 2005). Over time, a sizable proportion of individuals become permanently disabled (Judd et al., 2005); social marginalization and loneliness are common outcomes that further exacerbate the illness. The risk for suicide and age-adjusted mortality from all causes is quite high, particularly among those with earlier onset (Dilsaver et al., 1997; Ösby et al., 2001).

VARIATIONS FROM *STANDARD* BIPOLAR DISORDER IN ADULTHOOD

Other forms of bipolar disorder include the following diagnostic entities.

Hypomania differs from mania chiefly in terms of severity and level of impairment. That is, one can observe changes in activity level, impulse control, cognition, and mood that may yield real productivity (Judd et al., 2005). Such episodes may occur among individuals with histories of mania; hypomanic relapse without escalation into full-blown mania is a great relief. A person experiencing a hypomanic episode who has a history of mania would be diagnosed with Bipolar I Disorder, Most Recent Episode Hypomanic. However, a person with current hypomanic symptoms who had previously experienced a major depressive episode but not mania would, in the DSM-IV scheme, be eligible for diagnosis of Bipolar II Disorder, as would a currently depressed individual with history of hypomania. Some data indicate that hypomania is associated with greater lability—that is, more rapid intense mood shifts and more episodes, sometimes referred to as rapid cycling, where the total number of episodes exceeds four per year (Kupka et al., 2005; Papadimitriou et al., 2005).

Despite variability in the ratio of manic to depressive symptoms, current conceptualizations view all such mood cycling as manifestations of a single fundamental illness, namely BPD (Benazzi & Akiskal, 2005). The predecessor of this concept was Kraepelin's view that nearly all mood disorders are expressions of a single overarching illness, what he termed manic-depressive insanity.

DSM-IV CRITERIA AND DIAGNOSTIC ISSUES IN YOUTH

Four specific criteria constitute the DSM-IV symptoms of mania: (a) a *distinct period* of abnormally elevated, expansive, or irritable mood of at least 1 week duration of sufficient severity to warrant hospitalization; (b) co-occurrence of at least 3 other manic symptoms (4 if the main mood symptom is irritability); (c) significant impairment; and (d) symptoms not better accounted for by a drug of abuse or medication, or superimposed on Schizophrenia, a Schizophrenia Spectrum Disorder, or Psychotic Disorder, Not Otherwise Specified. An elevated mood is an exaggerated feeling of well-being that the person may describe as feeling "high," "ecstatic," or "on top of the world" (APA, 2000, p. 825). *Expansive* means "lack of restraint in expressing one's feelings, frequently with an overvaluation of one's significance or importance."

Adolescents are better equipped linguistically and experientially to articulate feelings of euphoria/elation than are children. Among children, mood is usually inferred from behavior. Hence, terms such as *silly* and *giddy* are used to describe a child's euphoria. However, it is not always clear when such behaviors indicate elation. Children may seek attention with silly antics for a variety of nonmanic reasons (Carlson & Meyer, 2006).

Extreme irritability (i.e., provocation to anger) is also a feature of mania, but because irritability is ubiquitous in children, the DSM-IV requires 4 rather than 3 of the other manic symptoms to establish the diagnosis. Mick, Spencer, Wozniak, and Biederman (2005) have distinguished the degree of explosiveness that accompanies a manic or mixed state from temper loss and anger often experienced by children with Attention-Deficit/Hyperactivity Disorder (ADHD), with parents more often endorsing ratings of "super-angry, grouchy, cranky" to characterize the former. Whether "super-angry" reflects a difference of degree or kind is not clear. Probably more germane to the identification of BPD is whether this mood state is sustained, occurs with a sufficiently long duration to be accompanied by other symptoms of mania, and represents a change from the child's usual state.

Other manic symptoms include the following.

Grandiosity, or the inflated appraisal of one's worth, power, knowledge, importance, or identity, is easily identified in an adult with mania. In children, inflated self-esteem may be hard to differentiate from excessive bragging to peers or from an immature belief set. For instance, a child, especially one with impaired social comprehension and concrete language, may interpret a compliment "you swim like a fish" to mean that he can swim across the ocean (Carlson & Meyer, 2006). Even in adolescents, who may feel that they can achieve greatness without finishing high school or are very popular without evidence to substantiate it, distinguishing truly inflated self-esteem from a defensive stance requires good clinical skills (Harrington & Myatt, 2003).

Decreased need for sleep is relatively straightforward when sleep time is replaced with energetic pursuit of nighttime activities and daytime fatigue is absent. Among children, one has to distinguish true decreased need for sleep from (a) highly prevalent bedtime struggles, especially among children with behavioral difficulties, and (b) true insomnia and night waking that typically occur among those with anxieties (Blader et al., 1997). This distinction can be accomplished by asking how difficult it is to arouse the child the next morning after a late bedtime, or how late on the weekend the child or teen sleeps in to catch up with the sleep deprivation.

Three other symptoms encompass increased motor behavior that characterizes mania:

Increased talkativeness and its close relative, *flight of ideas*, are reasonably pathognomic in those youth who are typically laconic or socially timid outside of manic episodes. Complicating matters is that, for children who may have BPD, new-onset volubility is very rare, and most "talkative" children considered for a BPD diagnosis have always been chatty. Also, one of the DSM-IV symptoms for ADHD is *talks excessively*, and distractible people are often "off topic," so sheer verbiage and even disconnectedness for many children considered for a BPD diagnosis is not that helpful in making a diagnosis. Adults may report rapid thoughts that accompany their rapid speech. Even children have articulated that they feel their brain is on over-drive (Goodwin & Jamison, p. 189), but it is not clear what to do with such a statement if the child speaks normally and quietly at the same time.

Distractibility that characterizes mania is similar to ADHD-related distractibility—it leads to impersistence in both conditions. This symptom lacks diagnostic specificity among youth who have always been distractible, so only a change or increase can be attributed to mania in these cases.

Increases in goal-directed activity in older individuals with BPD generally do have a focus and purpose, often of a rather grandiose nature, as noted earlier. A few children with BPD do get very excited about a project they intend to start or an invention that will reap millions of dollars. This type of activity must be differentiated from the more aimless but energetic *Brownian motion* intrinsic to ADHD. Still, like irritability, agitation is not specific to mania.

Finally, *excessive involvement in pleasurable activities* better conveys a BPD-specific abnormality for people who in the past have shown near-normal self-restraint and a characteristically circumspect approach to new undertakings. Among the vast majority of children considered for a BPD diagnosis, impulse-control deficiencies have been life-long, and such children start many short-lived activities with little deliberation at all.

One common research paradigm to evaluate symptom specificity for BPD incorporates children diagnosed with BPD and two comparison groups: children with ADHD and those with no diagnosis. This approach is limited by the fact that almost no one would confuse uncomplicated ADHD with BPD. Rather, the territory of greatest diagnostic controversy involves children with ADHD and the difficult behavior and irascibility highly characteristic of Oppositional Defiant Disorder (ODD) and other conduct problems. When the severity of ADHD symptoms and number of comorbidities is controlled, differences between so-called manic children and children with ADHD comorbid with ODD or Conduct Disorder (CD) largely disappear (Carlson, Bromet, & Jandorf, 1998). Only levels of depression distinguish the two groups.

One hazard of a definition of illness that is overly broad is a higher likelihood that it will improperly identify as *cases* people who actually have a different disorder. In other words, a broad definition may entail a reduction in *specificity*. The countervailing problem, of course, is that too narrow a definition may lack *sensitivity* and exclude real cases, thereby contributing to a misleading or incomplete account of etiology. The overarching question involves just what definitional criteria are necessary to define true cases of youth-onset BPD.

Current debate on delineation of Bipolar I Disorder focuses on the primacy of elation versus irritability. Leibenluft and colleagues (2003) have examined this question by proposing a subclassification scheme for children who may have BPD. The four categories they propose reflect how far clinical presentation departs from the current DSM-IV criteria, which were developed primarily with adults in mind.

1. First, a *narrow phenotype* has a symptom presentation, course, and episodicity fully aligned with current criteria for (adult) BPD, with the additional requirement that the mood abnormality be *euphoria* or that there be other signs of pathological grandiosity. They also define two *intermediate phenotypes*.
2. One intermediate phenotype encompasses manic episodes that last from 1 to 3 days, instead of the DSM-stipulated 4 (hypomania) to 7 (mania).
3. The other allows irritability to be the main mood aberration, so long as there is also evidence of well-demarcated episodes.
4. Their final category is a *broad phenotype* denoted as severe behavioral and mood dysregulation, which essentially encapsulates negative emotional reactivity and impulsivity.

Whether this is an accurate characterization of relatively discrete psychopathological entities remains uncertain. But as a provisional means to reduce heterogeneity in research samples it may prove quite useful, as it is clear that there are many more children and adolescents with mood disturbances that may be on the bipolar spectrum than are those with the classic, DSM-IV, adult-defined presentation.

HISTORICAL CONTEXT

The existence of a disturbance in which the same individual oscillates between extremes of excitement and melancholy was articulated very early in Western medical writings. Aretaeus (c. first to second centuries CE), a physician from Asia Minor who worked in Alexandria, often receives credit for the first linkage of these episodes to a single underlying illness (Angst & Marneros, 2001; Sedler, 1983). In modern times, Baillarger's (1809–1891) and Falret's (1794–1870) descriptions of a cyclical disturbance of depression and manic excitement established the entity in the emerging discipline of psychiatry. Emil Kraepelin (1856–1926) elaborated on these accounts, providing the designation *manic-depressive insanity* (Kraepelin, 1921). His goal was to distinguish forms of manic-depression, which were fundamentally disturbances of mood, from *dementia praecox*, which he regarded as involving fundamental disturbances of thought (as amended by Bleuler, the precursor of today's concept of *Schizophrenia*).

Our understanding of BPD in youth began with attempts to find youth versions of what Kraepelin had described. Child psychiatrists in the 1920s and 1930s concluded that Kraeplin's conception of manic-depression occurred among youth but that it was rare, appearing mostly in adolescents. In the 1950s, papers on youth manic-depression reported that the condition was indeed rare, with depression predominating, although an *alternate form* with more typical childhood behavioral psychopathology was proposed. Anthony and Scott (1960) reviewed the literature that examined classical manic-depressive psychosis in preadolescents, also concluding that it was exceptionally rare before age 11 (see Glovinsky, 2002, for a review).

Lithium's efficacy for the treatment of acute mania was established in the early 1950s, and its value as prophylaxis in preventing relapse was confirmed later. Youngerman and Canino (1978) reviewed 211 published studies and case reports of the use of lithium in youth and found 46 reports with enough detail to adequately characterize the patients and their responses. Of the 22 cases of children, only 2 had manic-depression and 2 had Atypical Mood Disorder. Twenty-four cases involving adolescents included 9 with manic-depression and 13 with Atypical Mood Disorder (the remaining 2 had other conditions). Response to lithium was poor in those without classic BPD.

This brief historical overview underscores the fact that classic manic-depression appears to be rarer in children than in adolescents. There has been a long-standing interest in trying to find a symptom constellation in younger children that is lithium responsive, but children with behavior problems (even those with a positive family history of bipolar illness) showed such a poor response to lithium USB IEEE 1284 C cable investigators were not inclined to examine the matter further.

Over the past 15 years or so, however, BPD among youth—and children in particular—has re-emerged as a topic of considerable interest, importance, and debate (Biederman et al., 1998). There is much uncertainty as to whether youth commonly diagnosed with ADHD plus severe ODD, by virtue of lifelong generalized impulsivity, obstreperous behavior, and bursts of intense rage, might better warrant a diagnosis of BPD. Indeed, the features of severe externalizing behavior accompanying ADHD-related symptomatology are similar, in many respects, to the wider phenotypes considered relevant to BPD (see previous discussion). We turn now to some of the conceptual issues that inform current work on this subject.

CONCEPTUAL ISSUES IN CHILD AND ADOLESCENT BIPOLAR DISORDER

TEMPORAL FACTORS: EPISODES AND ONSET

Apart from the prototypes of well-circumscribed periods in which one suffers from Major Depressive Disorder (MDD) or from mania, it is not always clear what constitutes an episode of affective illness. It is also controversial how essential to the definition of BPD such *episodicity* really is. As noted, among children, well-demarcated periods of abnormal mood and associated behavior are especially rare. Instead, some clinicians infer episodes from relatively brief periods of marked behavioral dyscontrol, often in the context of explosive angry outbursts or of silliness that seem excessive and situationally inappropriate. Current literature often refers to this form of affective oscillation as *ultradian* cycling, meaning that *cycles* appear many times within a single day (Geller & Tillman, 2005; Kramlinger & Post, 1996).

Similarly, the *onset* of psychopathology is difficult to define for many disorders of childhood. Should onset refer to the time during which a number of behavioral signs and symptoms first coalesce into the full syndrome that diagnostic criteria define? Or, should we take into account the first appearance of behavioral abnormalities that might be precursors of that syndrome? For children, the situation is further complicated because, for many behavioral disturbances, core aspects of temperament are noticeably extreme from very early in life. That is, there is no acute *break* or onset that is more characteristic of psychopathology first developing among older individuals.

SYMPTOM-RELATED TERMS AND CONCEPTS

Sustained mood versus transient affect versus emotion dysregulation.   One of the hallmarks of MDD is persistent negative affect that largely quashes both the capacity to experience pleasure (anhedonia) and the motivation to pursue experiences ordinarily found enjoyable (apathy). In fact, patients who do brighten when positive external events occur are said to have MDD with atypical features. Similarly, a striking characteristic of classic elated mania and hypomania is one's imperviousness to things that go badly.

However, among children diagnosed with BPD, such sustained disturbances of mood are infrequent. Rather, as ultradian cycling implies, their mood states are both transient and display a high degree of *reactivity*. That is, behavioral volatility is most often linked to some provocation or frustration and only rarely emerges "out of the blue." Likewise, *elation* may be precipitated by some exciting or highly stimulating event and is therefore not qualitatively inappropriate, though its expression may be excessive for the context.

The conceptual issue awaiting clarification is whether this sort of presentation among children derives from the same perturbation that drives BPD symptoms among older individuals, or whether it characterizes the emotional reactivity that accompanies deficits of executive function in other conditions. In ADHD, for example, undermodulated behavior occurs across a range of affective states and is thought to be the core deficit that leads to dysregulation of emotion. Temperament studies often find an *affective tone* factor that is distinct from *negative reactivity* (Sanson & Prior, 1999). In childhood BPD, it is uncertain if the chief abnormality concerns affective tone (i.e., dysphoria or elation highly disproportionate to environmental events) or reactivity (i.e., exaggerated and intense emotional responses to events that most other people would find bothersome or pleasant but with subdued reactions).

Temporal factors also define some important aspects of emotional function (Davidson, 1998; Thompson, 1990). A more gradual *ascent* may be more amenable to self-regulatory efforts in guiding behavior to deal adaptively with a provocation. By contrast, the volatility of children with BPD reflects in part their attainment of the *peak* of an emotional reaction faster than others in similar circumstances, which eventuates in more dyscontrolled behavior.

Impulsivity.   Deficient impulse control appears as a feature of numerous forms of psychopathology (e.g., ADHD, substance use and abuse disorders, early onset Conduct Disorder). BPD is somewhat different because many adults who develop the condition do not have histories of impulsive conduct; they may, in fact, seem highly deliberative when they are not experiencing a manic episode. A fair number, in fact, are quite lacking in spontaneity when not ill. So again, it is unclear whether impulsivity in mania shares a taproot with other types of disinhibitory psychopathology that are evident very early in life.

In ADHD, deficient inhibitory control is evident over several domains of functioning, such as cognition (e.g., distractibility, poor sustained attention), behavior (e.g., restlessness, overactivity, difficulty keeping conduct in conformity with situational constraints), and emotion (e.g., undermodulated emotional displays; Melnick & Hinshaw, 2000; see also Nigg & Nikolas, this volume). Impulse-control problems in mania arise, at least conceptually, from a heightened drive toward pleasurable pursuits, with risky conduct and impaired concentration viewed as *downstream* effects. Because ADHD and BPD may be comorbid in the same individual, however, differentiation is not always easy.

RISK FACTORS AND ETIOLOGICAL FORMULATIONS

DEPRESSION

Patients who develop BPD often experience depression as their first episode (Chengappa et al., 2003; Kutcher, Robertson, & Bird, 1998; Lewinsohn, Klein, & Seeley, 1995). Predicting who among depressed young people will develop a bipolar course becomes important in deciding treatment. Among adolescents with MDD, there are some factors that may increase the likelihood that BPD will evolve. These include precipitous onset of the depressive episode, psychotic features, psychomotor retardation, family history, and susceptibility to hypomania with antidepressant treatment (Strober & Carlson, 1982).

The conversion rate of adolescent unipolar MDD to BPD—a phenomenon called *switching*—is variable across studies and ranges from a low of 5.5% for Bipolar I and II over a 15 year follow up (Weissman et al., 1999) to a high of 49% (Geller et al., 2001). An earlier review (Kovacs, 1996) noted about 20% of adolescents with MDD developed a subsequent mania. For any given episode, mania usually develops between 1 and 6 months after the depressive episode, but manic onset may be later in some cases.

BIOLOGICAL SUSCEPTIBILITY FACTORS

Genetic markers. No matter how one defines BPD among youth, it seems safe to say that much of the liability has a genetic basis. First, in the case of classic (narrow phenotype) BPD, heritability estimates are as high as 80% (McGuffin et al., 2003), and early onset BPD may be even more firmly grounded in genetic risk. Bipolar Disorder heritability estimates exceed those for unipolar MDD (Craddock & Forty, 2006). Second, if the *broad phenotype* reflects a diathesis of deficient impulse control and affective instability, the heritability for these factors is also exceptionally high (Cates et al., 1993; Coccaro et al., 1997; Rietveld et al., 2004; Rujescu et al., 2002; Todd et al., 2001).

Different genome-scanning studies and meta-analyses have not yielded consistent conclusions about the genetic loci that confer susceptibility for BPD, even with fairly narrow definitions of the disorder. One analysis reported robust findings implicating chromosomes 13q and 22q (Badner & Gershon, 2002), while another reported modest effects for an entirely different set of regions on chromosomes 4q, 10q, 14q, and 18q (Lambert et al., 2005; Segurado et al., 2003), and in some populations 12q (Curtis et al., 2003). Still more recent attention has focused on chromosome 6q, with separate loci related to Schizophrenia and BPD, perhaps affecting the onset and course of illness (Kohn & Lerer, 2005). In an attempt at synthesis, recent work (MacQueen, Hajek, & Alda, 2005) has proposed that patterns of symptomatic overlap with other psychiatric disorders may signal BPD subgroups that share a specific constellation of genetic susceptibilities with these other conditions. That is, preliminary data suggest that genetic liability for BPD with prominent psychotic features may reside in part on chromosomal regions implicated in Schizophrenia (13q, 22q), whereas nonpsychotic mood lability and reactivity may be more strongly associated with 12q and 18q, which have been implicated in vulnerability for anxiety disorders.

Studies of specific genes with known cytochemical functions have also shown some overlap with both Schizophrenia and other mood disorders. For instance, the same polymorphisms of the catchol-0-methyltransferase (COMT) gene on chromosome 22q occur with heightened frequency among individuals affected with Schizophrenia and BPD. In some studies, brain-derived neurotrophic factor (BNDF) polymorphisms have been associated with risk for BPD and unipolar depression (Kremeyer et al., 2006; Levinson, 2006; Okada et al., 2006), a finding that has been replicated in children (Strauss et al., 2005).

Neurodevelopmental antecedents. Recent findings suggest that perinatal events, whether of genetic or adventitious origins, are associated with development of BPD in childhood. For instance, obstetrical complications were more prevalent among children diagnosed with BPD than controls— 54% versus 16% respectively (Pavuluri et al., in press). Given the clear association of such events with ADHD as well, comorbid impulsivity and attention problems should be considered in such studies. Indeed, after adjusting for family psychiatric histories, only prenatal maternal use of prescription and illicit drugs was associated with higher odds of the development of BPD. Larger studies involving adults do not indicate a major influence of perinatal problems, though wide variation in the definitions of such complications precludes a firm conclusion (Scott et al., 2006).

A study of 11- to 18-year-old psychiatric inpatients compared the neurodevelopmental status of youth who had BPD or unipolar depression with psychotic features (per ICD-10) to patients diagnosed with Nonpsychotic Unipolar Depressive Disorder (Sigurdsson et al., 1999). The former group had markedly higher rates of premorbid language, motor, and social developmental problems, leading the authors to conclude that such difficulties predispose more strongly to BPD than to depression. There were no differences in perinatal complications.

Disturbances of the sleep-wake cycle. There are some data to suggest that, at least among adults, circadian rhythms governing the sleep-wake cycle may be relevant to the development of BPD. It has been known for many years that sleep deprivation in some individuals with MDD provides symptomatic relief, and that resumption of sleep causes relapse in most cases. Moreover, some of these patients exhibit clear symptoms of hypomania with sleep deprivation (Giedke & Schwarzler, 2002). Regularizing sleep and wake times is widely seen as important to avoiding relapse of BPD (Frank et al., 1997). Some authors have therefore posited that a vulnerability toward circadian irregularity or desynchrony of a number of arousal-related physiological functions may hold etiological significance for BPD (Jones, 2001). This approach would comport with data that disturbed sleep patterns may contribute to affective and behavioral disorders among adolescents (Dahl, 2002). For a recent review, see Harvey, Mullin, and Hinshaw (2006).

Endophenotypes. An endophenotype is a heritable characteristic that is strongly associated with disease, yet is not a symptom of it. Endophenotypes form a subgroup of biomarkers. The broader category of biomarkers, though, also includes acquired precursors or concomitants of disease, so they do not necessarily have a genetic basis. Because endophenotypic characteristics are ideally detectable before the development of a disorder and can often be measured with far greater precision than clinical diagnoses, they are appealing for research on risk and genetic susceptibility. A more practical alternative tactic to large, longitudinal cohort studies involves comparing the unaffected relatives of people with a disorder to the relatives of unaffected controls, on the premise that the endophenotype would be more prevalent in the former group.

In BPD, this approach has suggested potential *cognitive* endophenotypes that emphasize impaired attentional control and other executive functions, based on the degree of deficit found among first-degree relatives of those with BPD (Hasler et al., 2006). Problems with sustained attention, which are particularly pathognomic of ADHD, were found among patients themselves, but not preferentially among their relatives, suggesting that sustained attention is more apt to be a concomitant of illness rather than an endophenotype (Clark, Kempton et al., 2005; Clark, Scarna, & Goodwin, 2005). Functional deficits related to attention and inhibitory control often implicate the dorsolateral prefontal cortex (DLPFC) and the ventrolateral prefrontal cortex (VLPFC) in ADHD (Halperin & Schulz, 2006; Pliszka et al., 2006). Some research suggests that functions subserved by VLPFC but not DLFPC are specifically deficient in patients with BPD and their relatives (Frangou et al., 2005).

Premorbid cognitive deficits common to Schizophrenia have not been found in adult or adolescent-onset bipolar patients (Cannon et al., 2002; Hollis, 2003; Zammit et al., 2004). Adequately controlled studies of childhood-onset BPD have not been conducted.

A propensity to construe ordinary troubles as catastrophes, to exaggerate and dwell on one's shortcomings or misfortunes, and to face the future with hopelessness and dread are highly prevalent cognitive features of depressive disorders (Beck, 1987). However, a manic analogue to *depressogenic* cognitions has yet to be confirmed (Alloy et al., 2005). Current efforts to evaluate positive self-dispositional cognitions along with the individual's attributions for them may advance this area (Jones, Mansell, & Waller, 2006).

Many children diagnosed with BPD exhibit aggressive behavior. A relationship between aggressive behavior and a tendency to overimpute hostility and threat to others whose real intentions are ambiguous has been shown (Burks et al., 1999). Depressed children also exhibit this effect (Quiggle et al., 1992), which might suggest that negative emotional reactivity biases cognitive appraisal, rather than the other way around. All the same, inaccurate appraisals, however initiated, may compromise emotional regulation if they feed rather than help to reduce emotional upset.

Recent work has suggested potential *anatomical* and *physiological* endophenotypes for BPD. The cingulate gyrus is a long rostral-caudal band of cortex at the base of the saggital fissure that integrates several components of the limbic system. Reductions in volume of the anterior portions of the cingulate have been reported in BPD patients and their unaffected close relatives (McDonald et al., 2004). Among patients themselves, different studies have suggested paucities of white matter, neuronal populations, and dendritic density (Harrison, 2002).

The amygdala is a distinct structure in the medial anterior portion of each temporal lobe that adjoins the hippocampus. Its role in motivation, emotional encoding, and response to threat has been thoroughly described, and it is a natural focus of interest for mood and anxiety disorders (see Kagan, this volume). Reduced amygdalar volume has been reported among the first-degree relatives, including children, of adults with BPD (Chang et al., 2005; Hajek, Carrey, & Alda, 2005). Among patients themselves, reduced amygdala volumes have been reported in BPD (Blumberg et al., 2005), but also in other disorders of affective instability (Rosso et al., 2005; Szeszko et al., 1999).

Scalp electroencephalographic (EEG) recordings taken while participants make simple responses to infrequent stimuli ordinarily show a large positive spike about 300 ms after stimulus presentation. This event-related potential (ERP), called the P300, is thought to reflect attentional and response-organizing activity. Patients with a number of psychiatric disorders that seem to have a common denominator of behavioral disinhibition (but also including Schizophrenia) show a reduced amplitude and a longer latency of P300 than do nonaffected individuals. Among adult probands, there is some evidence that right-lateralized P300 abnormalities might be an endophenotype for BPD (Pierson et al., 2000). In comparing children diagnosed with BPD to nondiagnosed control participants, the former exhibited reduced and delayed P300 only when response errors were penalized, suggesting that frustration disrupts attentional allocation in this disorder (Rich et al., 2005).

Experiential Susceptibility Factors

It is difficult to judge to what extent stressful life experiences contribute to the onset of BPD because (a) retrospective reports carry potential biases toward overidentification of events that may *explain* the illness; (b) even in prospective studies, many stressful events can arise as a consequence of behavioral disturbances that actually represent the simmering of the disorder; and (c) few studies include comparison groups. Moreover, most of the available data concern relapse rather than onset of BPD (Alloy et al., 2005). Among youth-onset BPD, however, efforts have been made to distinguish stressful life events that are independent of the patients' behavior. One investigation revealed higher rates of such independent stressful events in the families of youth with BPD than those with uncomplicated ADHD and no other diagnosis (Tillman et al., 2003).

Retrospective self-reports of child maltreatment are markedly elevated among adults with mood disorders, especially women (MacMillan et al., 2001). Among adults with BPD, several studies report high prevalence of severe childhood trauma, which is associated with a more pernicious course of illness (e.g., early onset, fewer remissions, suicidality; see Garno et al., 2005; Neria et al., 2005).

Psychotropic medications in therapeutic doses can elicit a manic-like episode in some individuals. Manic symptoms that first emerge during treatment with antidepressants are sometimes referred to as *medication-induced switching.* Currently, although medication-induced mania does not "count" toward a diagnosis of BPD, some contend that those who do *switch* have a vulnerability toward BPD and that exposure to the offending drugs may hasten progression of the illness. This important issue remains unsettled (Bauer et al., 2006). In children, activation on antidepressants or disinhibition on stimulants has been likened to switching but may be a function of young age rather than diagnosis (Carlson & Mick, 2003; Safer & Zito, 2006).

PATHOGENESIS

A time-tested approach to identifying mechanisms of mental illness is to ascertain the common characteristics of medications that improve the disorder. The dopamine hypothesis of Schizophrenia, and noradrenergic and serotonergic theories for depression and anxiety, for instance, derive from this tactic. There are inherent problems with this strategy, too detailed to discuss herein, with the key point that single-neurotransmitter models of psychopathology are almost undoubtedly too simplistic. Still, this approach can prove at least initially heuristic. Two potential mechanisms of action for antimanic drugs are under current consideration, which may bear on the development of BPD.

First, inositol is a constituent of phospholipase C, a complex on the interior surface of neuron membranes that breaks down when the synapse-facing G-protein-coupled receptor to which it is attached receives adequate neurotransmitter binding. The breakdown of phospholipase C constitutes a key component of the neuron's response to neurotransmission, setting in motion a number of cellular events. Lithium and other antimanic drugs share the capacity to inhibit free inositol, thereby down-regulating receptor production (Williams et al., 2002), which leads to the *inositol-depletion hypothesis* for their mechanism. It has been proposed, with some supporting evidence, that inositol-related intracellular cascades may be dysregulated in BPD (Silverstone et al., 2002).

Second, it has also been known for some time that lithium inhibits glycogen synthase kinase-3β (GSK3-b), an enzyme that regulates some intraneuronal signaling pathways. Recent evidence that valproic acid, an anticonvulsant effective in treating mania, also shares this property (Eickholt et al., 2005) has spurred interest in pathways that involve GSK3-b as perhaps influential in BPD (Einat & Manji, 2006).

PREVALENCE

The single-point prevalence of BPD among adults in the United States is generally agreed to be about 1 to 1.5%, with lifetime prevalence of disorders in the BPD spectrum in the range of 2.8 to 6.5% (Bauer & Pfennig, 2005; Kessler et al., 2006). Data from other countries are fairly similar, with a somewhat lower prevalence in East Asian countries (Weissman et al., 1996). However, community epidemiological surveys of teens show that application of the Bipolar I DSM-IV criteria yield prevalence estimates among adolescents in the range of 0.06% to 0.1% (Carlson & Kashani, 1988; Lewinsohn, Seeley, & Klein, 2003). One large epidemiological study involving 9- to 13-year-olds did not identify *any* children with BPD, in what would be viewed as a narrow phenotype (Costello et al., 1996).

Broader, subthreshhold criteria for BPD, with concurrent impairments, yield estimates of BPD-spectrum illness among adolescents of about 5% (Lewinsohn et al., 2003), a figure that resembles adult point-prevalence data for *soft* BPD-spectrum symptoms (Hirschfeld & Vornik, 2004; Kessler et al., 2005). When defined as the presence of any four manic symptoms, subthreshhold BPD prevalence rises to 13% (Carlson & Kashani, 1988). Estimates of the lifetime prevalence of severe mood dysregulation of the sort captured by the *broad juvenile BPD phenotype* are 3.3% among 9- to 19-year-olds, and 1.3% among children (Brotman et al., 2006). In short, whereas narrow-phenotype BPD is extremely rare in youth, broader conceptions of this condition are apparent prior to adulthood, even in preadolescents.

There is evidence that the rate of diagnoses of BPD in U.S. clinical settings has risen markedly in the past decade for children and adolescents (Blader & Carlson, in press; Harpaz-Rotem et al., 2005). It seems likely that this trend reflects a reclassification of chronically volatile, aggressive youngsters previously diagnosed with conduct-related problems, ADHD, or other mood disorders, rather than representing a true epidemic of BPD.

The consistently lower rate of clinically diagnosed BPD among youth in several European countries poses the possibility that BPD may be overdiagnosed in the United States, or perhaps underdiagnosed elsewhere (Meyer, Koßmann-Böhm, & Schlottke, 2004; Reichart et al., 2002; Soutullo et al., 2005). Whether his observation was prescient or specious, it is ironic that Kraepelin, in describing *manic temperament* among his early twentieth-century patients, wrote they " . . . are always beginning something new, make large plans and after a time drop them again . . . Others wish to become missionaries or to go to America" (Kraepelin, 1921, p. 127).

DEVELOPMENTAL PROGRESSION

Adolescent-onset BPD seems to show, unfortunately, the course of a particularly virulent illness (Lewinsohn et al., 2003), with high rates of serial hospitalizations, substance-abuse, suicide attempts or actual suicides, less robust response to lithium and divalproex, and generally worse interepisode functioning than adult-onset BPD (Birmaher et al., 2006; Goldstein et al., 2005; Lewinsohn et al., 2003; Wilcox & Anthony, 2004). In the short term, an appreciable number of youth seem to recover from the functional nadir of their index episode, but exacerbations and relapse are common (Birmaher et al., 2006). In addition, 20 to 25% of adolescents diagnosed with Bipolar II or Bipolar NOS progress to fulfill criteria for a more severe form of BPD (i.e., Bipolar I). Risk for adverse outcomes rises with earlier onset, presence of psychotic features, mixed episodes, and low socioeconomic resources (Birmaher et al., 2006). Among patients with BPD displaying psychotic features, those with onset prior to age 19 *and* who had ADHD as children had greater functional impairment at the end of a 24-month follow-up relative to those with early onset and no childhood psychopathology (Carlson et al., 2002).

Given the uncertainty about whether the typical childhood phenotype is best described as BPD at all, an obvious question regarding children with BPD symptoms is whether they will display features characteristic of adult BPD as they develop. To date, follow-ups of epidemiological samples do not suggest continuation of mania. In a longitudinal community study of adolescents followed into young adulthood, only 3 of 24 individuals who had originally met criteria for full or subthreshold BPD continued to meet the same criteria as young adults (Johnson et al., 2000). Hypomanic, cyclothymic, and subsyndromal manic symptoms in adolescence were not predictive of Bipolar I Disorder at young-adult follow-up (Lewinsohn, Klein, & Seeley, 2000). Rather, these early symptoms presaged elevated rates of MDD, personality disorders, and anxiety.

Results from longitudinal clinical studies have been mixed. Among 15 boys with ADHD who also met criteria for mania, only 1 was diagnosed with mania 6 years later (Hazell et al., 2003), although all continued to display marked functional impairments. By contrast, other longitudinal studies (Biederman et al., 2004; Geller et al., 2004) continue to show high rates of ADHD and mania from 4 to 7 years after baseline assessments. However, there is no evidence that these patients shed their externalizing symptoms and become uncomplicated cases of manic-depressive illness or classic Bipolar Disorder.

COMORBIDITY

Although few studies make the distinction, it is important to explicate whether one defines a comorbid condition as one that occurs contemporaneously with BPD, or as one that may appear before or following onset of BPD. Bipolar Disorder with childhood onset is typically superimposed on a history of ADHD (Biederman et al., 2005; Carlson, 1998; Pavuluri, Birmaher, & Naylor, 2005). Among adolescents, rates of comorbid ADHD drop to about 20 to 50% as precipitous onset of bipolar symptoms becomes more prevalent (Kafantaris et al., 1998). Retrospective studies of adults with BPD suggest still lower rates of premorbid ADHD: 15% among males and 5% among females (Nierenberg et al., 2005). However, childhood behavioral problems are more prevalent among adults with earlier onset of bipolarity (< 21 years of age) (Carlson, Bromet, & Sievers, 2000).

In one prospective study (Johnson et al., 2000), conduct-related disorders in adolescence conferred increased risk for BPD with early adult onset, yet only 7.4% of adults with BPD had a premorbid conduct-related disorder. On one level, this pattern of diminishing association between BPD and premorbid ADHD across age of onset seems to raise questions about whether BPD in distinct age cohorts really represents the same fundamental illness. On the other hand, the same condition may have a *developmental* form (i.e., early onset, insidious progression) and an *acquired* form (i.e., later onset, with a marked deviation from a relatively uneventful childhood). Childhood-onset Schizophrenia, even more strongly associated with premorbid developmental aberrations than its adult counterpart (Rapoport, Addington, & Frangou, 2005), and Type I versus Type II diabetes, provide illustrative precedents for this possibility.

Substance abuse is especially common among adolescents and adults with BPD, and it is the most prevalent secondary diagnosis among inpatients with the disorder (Blader & Carlson, in press). Community and clinical outpatient studies also show elevated rates of substance abuse, which worsens after the onset of BPD (Kessler et al., 1997). This onset in turn further increases risk for self-injurious behaviors (Goldstein et al., 2005; Lewinsohn et al., 2003). Using data from the Epidemiologic Catchment Area study, Carlson, Bromet, and Jandorf (1998) found that bipolar adults with comorbid substance abuse had demonstrated Conduct Disorder in adolescence, an association that was absent in Bipolar Disorder without such comorbid substance abuse.

Prevalence estimates of concurrently comorbid anxiety disorders vary considerably in child BPD. One research group (Dickstein et al., 2005) found that 77% of children who met *narrow* criteria for Bipolar I or II Disorder had at least one comorbid anxiety disorder. However, other investigators (Findling et al., 2001) reported significantly lower rates of anxiety disorders (12.5%) among children who met strict criteria for Bipolar I Disorder (yet here, anxiety symptoms were considered only if they persisted during periods of euthymia). As with adults, comorbid anxiety among youth with BPD is associated with greater functional impairment. Studies using retrospective reports to date onsets have yielded a mixed picture of how frequently anxiety and other mood disorders precede or follow BPD onset in youth (Dickstein et al., 2005; Masi et al., 2001; Tillman et al., 2003; Wagner, 2006).

Only very limited data address the appearance of BPD alongside developmental disorders. One study reported that about 20% of children diagnosed with mania also had comorbid Pervasive Developmental Disorder (Wozniak et al., 1997). Among a cohort of youth with a mean age of 12.8 years in a mood disorder specialty clinic, over 60% obtained parent ratings of autism-spectrum behaviors in the *likely autism-spectrum disorders* range (Towbin et al., 2005). Yet this method also showed that 48% of those with nonbipolar depressive or anxiety disorders fulfilled this criterion, meaning that generalizability of this finding is not assured.

Children with ADHD and multiple comorbidities, especially ODD/CD (aggression), learning disabilities, and pronounced negative affect, have long been known to be those who have the most indolent and severe course, with substance abuse and antisocial personality emerging into adolescence and young adulthood (Moffitt et al., 2002; Simonoff et al., 2004). Given that most children with prepubertal mania have precisely those problems (i.e., severe aggression, oppositional-defiance, negative affect, attentional and/or learning disabilities), it should not be surprising that their clinical picture remains stable and grim. What has not yet emerged from follow-up studies is whether the ultradian cycling diminishes with age, continuing as more muted emotional lability, or whether the cycles consolidate, become longer in duration, and truly are continuous with adult mixed/rapid cycling.

SEX DIFFERENCES

Epidemiological studies of BPD in adult populations have shown broadly similar rates for both sexes (Grant et al., 2005; Weissman et al., 1996), which also seems to be the case among adolescents (Johnson et al., 2000; Lewinsohn et al., 2003). However, these data may mask the tendency for males to have a greater likelihood of earlier onset, with more manic episodes of long duration. Females have a later onset (Kennedy et al., 2005) and are more likely to present with mixed and depressive episodes (Grant et al., 2005; Kennedy et al., 2005).

The sex composition of clinical samples of bipolar youth shows a preponderance of males among prepubertal outpatient children diagnosed with BPD (Biederman et al., 2005; Geller et al., 1998) as well as those admitted to inpatient care (~ 2:1) (Blader & Carlson, in press). Overall, then, males predominate among children diagnosed with BPD, sex ratios achieve approximate equality in adolescence, and females are more likely to experience mid-adult onset.

CULTURAL FACTORS

Within the United States, studies of racial patterns in clinical diagnoses have suggested some potential biases. African American individuals, especially men, are less likely to receive a diagnosis of BPD and more likely to receive a diagnosis of Schizophrenia or Schizoaffective Disorder than White patients (Kilbourne et al., 2005; Strakowski et al., 2003). Similar findings have emerged among adolescents (DelBello et al., 2001). Analysis of nationwide hospital discharges provides further evidence for this discrepancy, but also shows that African American children are more likely to be diagnosed with a conduct-problem disorder than are White children (Blader & Carlson, in press). Data from more recent years show a marked increase in the population-adjusted rates of BPD among African American individuals (Blader & Carlson, in press) that exceeds that found for Whites. Even so, there may be a trend to impute higher rates of psychotic features to Black patients, both adults and adolescents, the accuracy of which is uncertain (Patel, DelBello, & Strakowski, 2006). The extent to which nonracial cultural factors affect symptom expression in BPD is an interesting issue about which there is little empirical literature.

THEORETICAL SYNTHESIS AND FUTURE DIRECTIONS

Severe behavioral dyscontrol occasioned by affective instability, regardless of specific diagnosis, most often has a chronic course and confers risk for impairments that entail major personal and familial misfortune. The challenge for developmental psychopathology is to better elucidate the myriad ways these difficulties can develop early in life, which would enable the development of appropriate interventions.

Bipolar Disorder's signature features and course are well-characterized, and the fact that it develops frequently during middle to late adolescence makes it an important focus for developmental psychopathologists. Their perspective on multiple interactions over time among biological susceptibilities, other developmental factors, and social/environmental influences is essential for considering BPD in youth.

Beside *classic* BPD, which represents a qualitative change in behavior that occurs with well-delineated episodes, other forms of very early onset, chronic, and unremitting affective and behavioral volatility have been postulated to constitute a variant of BPD among youth. At this time, it remains uncertain whether these forms of impairment are (a) *developmental* versions of the same disease processes that underlie later-onset BPD, (b) separate types of illness that might involve perturbations of the same mechanisms of self-control and mood that are implicated in BPD, or (c) fundamentally different problems, such as severe ADHD with ODD, which demonstrates some phenotypic overlap with BPD.

A better detailed account of the underpinnings of impulse control, emotional states, affective regulation, and social adaptation, as well as the diverse ways that these areas can display dysfunction, will be pivotal to advancement of behavioral science. It is also imperative that a developmental framework inform the evolution of this knowledge.

REFERENCES

Akiskal, H. S. (1983). The bipolar spectrum: New concepts in classification and diagnosis. In L. Grinspoon (Ed.), *Psychiatry: The American Psychiatric Association annual review* (Vol. II, pp. 271–292). Washington, DC: American Psychiatric Press.

Alloy, L. B., Abramson, L. Y., Urosevic, S., Walshaw, P. D., Nusslock, R., & Neeren, A. M. (2005). The psychosocial context of bipolar disorder: Environmental, cognitive, and developmental risk factors. *Clinical Psychology Review, 25,* 1043–1075.

American Psychiatric Association. (2000). *Diagnostic and statistical manual of mental disorders* (4th ed., text revision). Washington, DC: American Psychiatric Press.

Angst, J., & Marneros, A. (2001). Bipolarity from ancient to modern times: Conception, birth and rebirth. *Journal of Affective Disorders, 67,* 3–19.

Anthony, E. J., & Scott, P. (1960). Manic-depressive psychosis in childhood. *Journal of Child Psychology and Psychiatry, 1,* 53–72.

Badner, J. A., & Gershon, E. S. (2002). Meta-analysis of whole-genome linkage scans of bipolar disorder and schizophrenia. *Molecular Psychiatry, 7,* 405–411.

Bauer, M., & Pfennig, A. (2005). Epidemiology of bipolar disorders. *Epilepsia, 46*(Suppl. 4), 8–13.

Bauer, M., Rasgon, N., Grof, P., Glenn, T., Lapp, M., Marsh, W., et al. (2006). Do antidepressants influence mood patterns? A naturalistic study in bipolar disorder. *European Psychiatry, 21,* 262–269.

Bauer, M. S., Simon, G. E., Ludman, E., & Unützer, J. (2005). 'Bipolarity' in bipolar disorder: Distribution of manic and depressive symptoms in a treated population. *British Journal of Psychiatry, 187,* 87–88.

Beck, A. T. (1987). Cognitive models of depression. *Journal of Cognitive Psychotherapy, 1,* 5–37.

Benazzi, F., & Akiskal, H. (2005). Irritable-hostile depression: Further validation as a bipolar depressive mixed state. *Journal of Affective Disorders, 84,* 197–207.

Biederman, J., Faraone, S. V., Wozniak, J., Mick, E., Kwon, A., & Aleardi, M. (2004). Further evidence of unique developmental phenotypic correlates of pediatric bipolar disorder: Findings from a large sample of clinically referred preadolescent children assessed over the last 7 years. *Journal of Affective Disorders, 82*(Suppl. 1), 45–58.

Biederman, J., Faraone, S. V., Wozniak, J., Mick, E., Kwon, A., Cayton, G. A., et al. (2005). Clinical correlates of bipolar disorder in a large, referred sample of children and adolescents. *Journal of Psychiatric Research, 39,* 611–622.

Biederman, J., Klein, R. G., Pine, D. S., & Klein, D. F. (1998). Resolved: Mania is mistaken for ADHD in prepubertal children [Debate Forum]. *Journal of the American Academy of Child and Adolescent Psychiatry, 37,* 1091–1099.

Birmaher, B., Axelson, D., Strober, M., Gill, M. K., Valeri, S., Chiappetta, L., et al. (2006). Clinical course of children and adolescents with bipolar spectrum disorders. *Archives of General Psychiatry, 63,* 175–183.

Blader, J. C., & Carlson, G. A. (in press). Increased rates of bipolar disorder diagnoses among U.S. child, adolescent, and adolescent inpatients, 1996–2004. *Biological Psychiatry.*

Blader, J. C., Koplewicz, H. S., Abikoff, H., & Foley, C. (1997). Sleep problems of elementary school children: A community survey. *Archives of Pediatrics and Adolescent Medicine, 151,* 473–480.

Blumberg, H. P., Fredericks, C., Wang, F., Kalmar, J. H., Spencer, L., Papademetris, X., et al. (2005). Preliminary evidence for persistent abnormalities in amygdala volumes in adolescents and young adults with bipolar disorder. *Bipolar Disorders, 7,* 570–576.

Brotman, M. A., Schmajuk, M., Rich, B. A., Dickstein, D. P., Guyer, A. E., Costello, E. J., et al. (2006). Prevalence, clinical correlates, and longitudinal course of severe mood dysregulation in children. *Biological Psychiatry, 60,* 991–997.

Burks, V. S., Laird, R. D., Dodge, K. A., Pettit, G. S., & Bates, J. E. (1999). Knowledge structures, social information processing, and children's aggressive behavior. *Social Development, 8,* 220–236.

Cannon, M., Caspi, A., Moffitt, T. E., Harrington, H., Taylor, A., Murray, R. M., et al. (2002). Evidence for early-childhood, pan-developmental impairment specific to schizophreniform disorder: Results from a longitudinal birth cohort. *Archives of General Psychiatry, 59,* 449–456.

Carlson, G. A. (1998). Mania and ADHD: Comorbidity or confusion. *Journal of Affective Disorders, 51,* 177–187.

Carlson, G. A., Bromet, E. J., Driessens, C., Mojtabai, R., & Schwartz, J. E. (2002). Age at onset, childhood psychopathology, and 2-year outcome in psychotic bipolar disorder. *American Journal of Psychiatry, 159,* 307–309.

Carlson, G. A., Bromet, E. J., & Jandorf, L. (1998) Conduct disorder and mania: What does it mean in adults. *Journal of Affective Disorders, 48,* 199–205.

Carlson, G. A., Bromet, E. J., & Sievers, S. (2000). Phenomenology and outcome of subjects with early- and adult-onset psychotic mania. *American Journal of Psychiatry, 157,* 213–219.

Carlson, G. A., & Goodwin, F. K. (1973). The stages of mania. A longitudinal analysis of the manic episode. *Archives of General Psychiatry, 28,* 221–228.

Carlson, G. A., & Kashani, J. H. (1988). Manic symptoms in a non-referred adolescent population. *Journal of Affective Disorders, 15,* 219–226.

Carlson, G. A., & Meyer, S. E. (2006). Phenomenology and diagnosis of bipolar disorder in children, adolescents, and adults: Complexities and developmental issues. *Development and Psychopathology, 18,* 939–969.

Carlson G.A., & Mick, E. (2003). Drug-induced disinhibition in psychiatrically hospitalized children. *Journal of Child and Adolescent Psychopharmacology, 13,* 153–63.

Cates, D. S., Houston, B. K., Vavak, C. R., Crawford, M. H., & Uttley, M. (1993). Heritability of hostility-related emotions, attitudes, and behaviors. *Journal of Behavioral Medicine, 16,* 237–256.

Chang, K., Karchemskiy, A., Barnea-Goraly, N., Garrett, A., Simeonova, D. I., & Reiss, A. (2005). Reduced amygdalar gray matter volume in familial pediatric bipolar disorder. *Journal of the American Academy of Child and Adolescent Psychiatry, 44,* 565–573.

Chengappa, K. N. R., Kupfer, D. J., Frank, E., Houck, P. R., Grochocinski, V. J., Cluss, P. A., et al. (2003). Relationship of birth cohort and early age at onset of illness in a bipolar disorder case registry. *American Journal of Psychiatry, 160,* 1636–1642.

Clark, L., Kempton, M. J., Scarna, A., Grasby, P. M., & Goodwin, G. M. (2005). Sustained attention-deficit confirmed in euthymic bipolar disorder but not in first-degree relatives of bipolar patients or euthymic unipolar depression. *Biological Psychiatry 57,* 183–187.

Clark, L., Scarna, A., & Goodwin, G. M. (2005). Executive function but not memory is impaired in first-degree relatives of bipolar I patients and in euthymic unipolar depression. *American Journal of Psychiatry, 162,* 1980–1982.

Coccaro, E. F., Bergeman, C. S., Kavoussi, R. J., & Seroczynski, A. D. (1997). Heritability of aggression and irritability: A twin study of the Buss-Durkee aggression scales in adult male subjects. *Biological Psychiatry, 41,* 273–284.

Costello, E. J., Angold, A., Burns, B. J., Stangl, D. K., Tweed, D. L., Erkanli, A., et al. (1996). The Great Smoky Mountains Study of Youth. Goals, design, methods, and the prevalence of *DSM-III-R* disorders. *Archives of General Psychiatry, 53,* 1129–1136.

Craddock, N., & Forty, L. (2006). Genetics of affective (mood) disorders. *European Journal of Human Genetics, 14,* 660–668.

Curtis, D., Kalsi, G., Brynjolfsson, J., McInnis, M., O'Neill, J., Smyth, C., et al. (2003). Genome scan of pedigrees multiply affected with bipolar disorder provides further support for the presence of a susceptibility locus on chromosome 12q23-q24, and suggests the presence of additional loci on 1p and 1q. *Psychiatric Genetics, 13,* 77–84.

Dahl, R. E. (2002). The regulation of sleep-arousal, affect, and attention in adolescence: Some questions and speculations. In M. A. Carskadon (Ed.), *Adolescent sleep patterns: Biological, social, and psychological influences* (pp. 269–284). New York: Cambridge University Press.

DelBello, M. P., Lopez-Larson, M. P., Soutullo, C. A., & Strakowski, S. M. (2001).

Effects of race on psychiatric diagnosis of hospitalized adolescents: A retrospective chart review. *Journal of Child and Adolescent Psychopharmacology, 11,* 85–103.

Dilsaver, S. C., Chen, Y.-W., Swann, A. C., Shoaib, A. M., Tsai-Dilsaver, Y., & Krajewski, K. J. (1997). Suicidality, panic disorder and psychosis in bipolar depression, depressive-mania and pure-mania. *Psychiatry Research, 73,* 47–56.

Eickholt, B. J., Towers, G. J., Ryves, W. J., Eikel, D., Adley, K., Ylinen, L. M. J., et al. (2005). Effects of valproic acid derivatives on inositol trisphosphate depletion, teratogenicity, glycogen synthase kinase-3β inhibition, and viral replication: A screening approach for new bipolar disorder drugs derived from the valproic acid core structure. *Molecular Pharmacology, 67,* 1426–1433.

Einat, H., & Manji, H. K. (2006). Cellular plasticity cascades: Genes-to-behavior pathways in animal models of bipolar disorder. *Biological Psychiatry, 59,* 1160–1171.

Frangou, S., Haldane, M., Roddy, D., & Kumari, V. (2005). Evidence for deficit in tasks of ventral, but not dorsal, prefrontal executive function as an endophenotypic marker for bipolar disorder. *Biological Psychiatry, 58,* 838–839.

Frank, E., Hlastala, S., Ritenour, A., Houck, P., Tu, X. M., Monk, T. H., et al. (1997). Inducing lifestyle regularity in recovering bipolar disorder patients: Results from the maintenance therapies in bipolar disorder protocol. *Biological Psychiatry, 41,* 1165–1173.

Friedman, S. H., Shelton, M. D., Elhaj, O., Youngstrom, E. A., Rapport, D. J., Packer, K. A., et al. (2005). Gender differences in criminality: Bipolar disorder with co-occurring substance abuse. *Journal of the American Academy of Psychiatry and the Law, 33,* 188–195.

Garno, J. L., Goldberg, J. F., Ramirez, P. M., & Ritzler, B. A. (2005). Impact of childhood abuse on the clinical course of bipolar disorder. *British Journal of Psychiatry, 186,* 121–125.

Geller, B., & Tillman, R. (2005). Prepubertal and early adolescent bipolar I disorder: Review of diagnostic validation by Robins and Guze criteria. *Journal of Clinical Psychiatry, 66*(Suppl. 7), 21–28.

Geller, B., Tillman, R., Craney, J. L., & Bolhofner, K. (2004). Four-year prospective outcome and natural history of mania in children with a prepubertal and early adolescent bipolar disorder phenotype. *Archives of General Psychiatry, 61,* 459–467.

Geller, B., Williams, M., Zimerman, B., Frazier, J., Beringer, L., & Warner, K. L. (1998). Prepubertal and early adolescent bipolarity differentiate from ADHD by manic symptoms, grandiose delusions, ultra-rapid or ultradian cycling. *Journal of Affective Disorders, 51,* 81–91.

Geller, B., Zimerman, B., Williams, M., Bolhofner, K., & Craney, L. L. (2001). Bipolar disorder at prospective follow-up of adults who had prepubertal major depressive disorder. *American Journal of Psychiatry, 158,* 125–127.

Giedke, H., & Schwarzler, F. (2002). Therapeutic use of sleep deprivation in depression. *Sleep Medicine Reviews, 6,* 361–377.

Glovinsky, I. (2002). A brief history of childhood-onset bipolar disorder through 1980. *Child and Adolescent Psychiatric Clinics of North America, 11,* 443–460.

Goldstein, T. R., Birmaher, B., Axelson, D., Ryan, N. D., Strober, M. A., Gill, M. K., et al. (2005). History of suicide attempts in pediatric bipolar disorder: Factors associated with increased risk. *Bipolar Disorders, 7,* 525–535.

Goodwin, F. K., & Jamison, K. R. (Eds.). (2007). *Manic-depressive illness: Bipolar and recurrent depression* (2nd ed.). New York: Oxford University Press.

Grant, B. F., Stinson, F. S., Hasin, D. S., Dawson, D. A., Chou, S. P., Ruan, W. J., et al. (2005). Prevalence, correlates, and comorbidity of bipolar I disorder and axis I and II disorders: Results from the National Epidemiologic Survey on Alcohol and Related Conditions. *Journal of Clinical Psychiatry, 66,* 1205–1215.

Hajek, T., Carrey, N., & Alda, M. (2005). Neuroanatomical abnormalities as risk factors for bipolar disorder. *Bipolar Disorders, 7,* 393–403.

Halperin, J. M., & Schulz, K. P. (2006). Revisiting the role of the prefrontal cortex in the pathophysiology of attention-deficit/hyperactivity disorder. *Psychological Bulletin, 132,* 560–581.

Hammen, C. (2007). Child and adolescent bipolar disorder. In F. K. Goodwin & K. R. Jamison (Eds.), *Manic-depressive illness: Bipolar and recurrent depression* (2nd ed.). New York: Oxford University Press.

Harpaz-Rotem, I., Leslie, D. L., Martin, A., & Rosenheck, R. A. (2005). Changes in child and adolescent inpatient psychiatric admission diagnoses between 1995 and 2000. *Social Psychiatry and Psychiatric Epidemiology, 40,* 642–647.

Harrington, R., & Myatt, T. (2003). Is preadolescent mania the same condition as adult mania? A British perspective. *Biological Psychiatry, 53,* 961–969.

Harrison, P. J. (2002). The neuropathology of primary mood disorder. *Brain, 125,* 1428–1449.

Harvey, A. G., Mullin, B. C., & Hinshaw, S. P. (2006). Sleep and circadian rhythms in children and adolescents with bipolar disorder. *Development and Psychopathology, 18,* 1147–1168.

Hasler, G., Drevets, W. C., Gould, T. D., Gottesman, I. I., & Manji, H. K. (2006). Toward constructing an endophenotype strategy for bipolar disorders. *Biological Psychiatry, 60,* 93–105.

Hazell, P. L., Carr, V., Lewin, T. J., & Sly, K. (2003). Manic symptoms in young males with ADHD predict functioning but not diagnosis after 6 years. *Journal of the American Academy of Child and Adolescent Psychiatry, 42,* 552–560.

Hirschfeld, R. M. A., & Vornik, L. A. (2004). Recognition and diagnosis of bipolar disorder. *Journal of Clinical Psychiatry, 65* (Suppl. 15), 5–9.

Hollis, C. (2003). Developmental precursors of child- and adolescent-onset schizophrenia and affective psychoses: Diagnostic specificity and continuity with symptom dimensions. *British Journal of Psychiatry, 182,* 37–44.

Johnson, L., Lundströem, O., Åberg-Wistedt, A., & Mathé, A. A. (2003). Social support in bipolar disorder: Its relevance to remission and relapse. *Bipolar Disorders, 5,* 129–137.

Jones, S., Mansell, W., & Waller, L. (2006). Appraisal of hypomania-relevant experiences: Development of a questionnaire to assess positive self-dispositional appraisals in bipolar and behavioural high risk samples. *Journal of Affective Disorders, 93,* 19–28.

Jones, S. H. (2001). Circadian rhythms, multilevel models of emotion and bipolar disorder—An initial step towards integration? *Clinical Psychology Review, 21,* 1193–1209.

Judd, L. L., Akiskal, H. S., Schettler, P. J., Endicott, J., Leon, A. C., Solomon, D. A., et al. (2005). Psychosocial disability in the course of bipolar I and II disorders: A prospective, comparative, longitudinal study. *Archives of General Psychiatry, 62,* 1322–1330.

Kafantaris, V., Coletti, D. J., Dicker, R., Padula, G., & Pollack, S. (1998). Are childhood psychiatric histories of bipolar adolescents associated with family history, psychosis, and response to lithium treatment? *Journal of Affective Disorders, 51,* 153–164.

Keck, P. E., Jr., McElroy, S. L., Havens, J. R., Altshuler, L. L., Nolen, W. A., Frye, M. A., et al. (2003). Psychosis in bipolar disorder: Phenomenology and impact on morbidity and course of illness. *Comprehensive Psychiatry, 44,* 263–269.

Kennedy, N., Boydell, J., Kalidindi, S., Fearon, P., Jones, P. B., van Os, J., et al. (2005). Gender differences in incidence and age at onset of mania and bipolar disorder over a 35-year period in Camberwell, England. *American Journal of Psychiatry, 162,* 257–262.

Kessler, R. C., Akiskal, H. S., Ames, M., Birnbaum, H., Greenberg, P., Hirschfeld, R. M. A., et al. (2006). Prevalence and effects of mood disorders on work performance in a nationally representative sample of U.S. workers. *American Journal of Psychiatry, 163,* 1561–1568.

Kessler, R. C., Berglund, P., Demler, O., Jin, R., Merikangas, K. R., & Walters, E. E. (2005). Lifetime prevalence and age-of-onset distributions of *DSM-IV* disorders in the National Comorbidity Survey Replication. *Arch Gen Psychiatry, 62,* 593–602.

Kessler, R. C., Crum, R. M., Warner, L. A., Nelson, C. B., Schulenberg, J., & Anthony, J. C. (1997). Lifetime co-occurrence of *DSM-III-R* alcohol abuse and dependence with other psychiatric disorders in the National Comorbidity Survey. *Archives of General Psychiatry, 54,* 313–321.

Kilbourne, A. M., Bauer, M. S., Han, X., Haas, G. L., Elder, P., Good, C. B., et al. (2005). Racial differences in the treatment of veterans with bipolar disorder. *Psychiatric Services, 56,* 1549–1555.

Kohn, Y., & Lerer, B. (2005). Excitement and confusion on chromosome 6q: The challenges of neuropsychiatric genetics in microcosm. *Molecular Psychiatry, 10,* 1062–1073.

Kovacs, M. (1996). Presentation and course of major depressive disorder during childhood and later years of the life span. *Journal of the American Academy of Child and Adolescent Psychiatry, 35,* 705–715.

Kraepelin, E. (1921). *Manic-depressive insanity and paranoia* (R. M. Barclay, Trans., G. M. Robertson, Ed.). Edinburgh: E. & S. Livingstone.

Kramlinger, K., & Post, R. (1996). Ultra-rapid and ultradian cycling in bipolar affective illness. *British Journal of Psychiatry, 168,* 314–323.

Kremeyer, B., Herzberg, I., Garcia, J., Kerr, E., Duque, C., Parra, V., et al. (2006). Transmission distortion of BDNF variants to bipolar disorder type I patients from a South American population isolate. *American Journal of Medical Genetics. Part B, Neuropsychiatric Genetics, 141,* 435–439.

Kupka, R. W., Luckenbaugh, D. A., Post, R. M., Suppes, T., Altshuler, L. L., Keck, P. E., Jr., et al. (2005). Comparison of rapid-cycling and non-rapid-cycling bipolar disorder based on prospective mood ratings in 539 outpatients. *American Journal of Psychiatry, 162,* 1273–1280.

Kutcher, S., Robertson, H. A., & Bird, D. (1998). Premorbid functioning in adolescent onset bipolar I disorder: A preliminary report from an ongoing study. *Journal of Affective Disorders, 51,* 137–144.

Lambert, D., Middle, F., Hamshere, M. L., Segurado, R., Raybould, R., Corvin, A., et al. (2005). Stage 2 of the Wellcome Trust UK-Irish bipolar affective disorder sibling-pair genome screen: Evidence for linkage on chromosomes 6q16-q21, 4q12-q21, 9p21, 10p14-p12 and 18q22. *Molecular Psychiatry, 10,* 831–841.

Leibenluft, E., Charney, D. S., Towbin, K. E., Bhangoo, R. K., & Pine, D. S. (2003). Defining clinical phenotypes of juvenile mania. *American Journal of Psychiatry, 160,* 430–437.

Levinson, D. F. (2006). The genetics of depression: A review. *Biological Psychiatry, 60,* 84–92.

Lewinsohn, P. M., Klein, D. N., & Seeley, J. R. (1995). Bipolar disorders in a community sample of older adolescents: Prevalence, phenomenology, comorbidity, and course. *Journal of the American Academy of Child and Adolescent Psychiatry, 34,* 454–463.

Lewinsohn, P. M., Klein, D. N., & Seeley, J. R. (2000). Bipolar disorder during adolescence and young adulthood in a community sample. *Bipolar Disorders, 2,* 281–293.

Lewinsohn, P. M., Seeley, J. R., & Klein, D. N. (2003). Bipolar disorders during adolescence. *Acta Psychiatrica Scandinavica, 108*(Suppl. 418), 47–50.

MacMillan, H. L., Fleming, J. E., Streiner, D. L., Lin, E., Boyle, M. H., Jamieson, E., et al. (2001). Childhood abuse and lifetime psychopathology in a community sample. *American Journal of Psychiatry, 158,* 1878–1883.

MacQueen, G. M., Hajek, T., & Alda, M. (2005). The phenotypes of bipolar disorder: Relevance for genetic investigations. *Molecular Psychiatry, 10,* 811–826.

Maj, M., Pirozzi, R., Magliano, L., & Bartoli, L. (2003). Agitated depression in bipolar I disorder: Prevalence, phenomenology, and outcome. *American Journal of Psychiatry, 160,* 2134–2140.

McDonald, C., Bullmore, E. T., Sham, P. C., Chitnis, X., Wickham, H., Bramon, E., et al. (2004). Association of genetic risks for schizophrenia and bipolar disorder with specific and generic brain structural endophenotypes. *Archives of General Psychiatry, 61,* 974–984.

McGuffin, P., Rijsdijk, F., Andrew, M., Sham, P., Katz, R., & Cardno, A. (2003). The heritability of bipolar affective disorder and the genetic relationship to unipolar depression. *Archives of General Psychiatry, 60,* 497–502.

Melnick, S. M., & Hinshaw, S. P. (2000). Emotion regulation and parenting in AD/HD and comparison boys: Linkages with social behaviors and peer preference. *Journal of Abnormal Child Psychology, 28,* 73–86.

Meyer, T. D., Koßmann-Böhm, S., & Schlottke, P. F. (2004). Do child psychiatrists in Germany diagnose bipolar disorders in children and adolescents? Results from a survey. *Bipolar Disorders, 6,* 426–431.

Mick, E., Spencer, T., Wozniak, J., & Biederman, J. (2005). Heterogeneity of irritability in attention-deficit/hyperactivity disorder subjects with and without mood disorders. *Biological Psychiatry, 58,* 576–582.

Moffitt, T. E., Caspi, A., Harrington, H., & Milne, B. J. (2002). Males on the life-course-persistent and adolescence-limited antisocial pathways: Follow-up at age 26 years. *Development and Psychopathology, 14,* 179–207.

Müller-Oerlinghausen, B., Berghöfer, A., & Bauer, M. (2002). Bipolar disorder. *Lancet, 359,* 241–247.

Neria, Y., Bromet, E. J., Carlson, G. A., & Naz, B. (2005). Assaultive trauma and illness course in psychotic bipolar disorder: findings from the Suffolk county mental health project. *Acta Psychiatrica Scandinavica, 111,* 380–383.

Nierenberg, A. A., Miyahara, S., Spencer, T., Wisniewski, S. R., Otto, M. W., Simon, N., et al. (2005). Clinical and diagnostic implications of lifetime attention-deficit/hyperactivity disorder comorbidity in adults with bipolar disorder: Data from the first 1000 STEP-BD participants. *Biological Psychiatry, 57,* 1467–1473.

Okada, T., Hashimoto, R., Numakawa, T., Iijima, Y., Kosuga, A., Tatsumi, M., et al. (2006). A complex polymorphic region in the brain-derived neurotrophic factor (BDNF) gene confers susceptibility to bipolar disorder and affects transcriptional activity. *Molecular Psychiatry, 11,* 695–703.

Ösby, U., Brandt, L., Correia, N., Ekbom, A., & Sparén, P. (2001). Excess mortality in bipolar and unipolar disorder in Sweden. *Archives of General Psychiatry, 58,* 844–850.

Papadimitriou, G. N., Calabrese, J. R., Dikeos, D. G., & Christodoulou, G. N. (2005). Rapid cycling bipolar disorder: Biology and pathogenesis. *International Journal of Neuropsychopharmacology, 8,* 281–292.

Patel, N. C., DelBello, M. P., & Strakowski, S. M. (2006). Ethnic differences in symptom presentation of youths with bipolar disorder. *Bipolar Disorders, 8,* 95–99.

Pavuluri, M. N., Birmaher, B., & Naylor, M. W. (2005). Pediatric bipolar disorder: A review of the past 10 years. *Journal of the American Academy of Child and Adolescent Psychiatry, 44,* 846–871.

Pavuluri, M. N., Henry, D. B., Nadimpalli, S. S., O'Connor, M. M., & Sweeney, J. A. (in press). Biological risk factors in pediatric bipolar disorder. *Biological Psychiatry.*

Pierson, A., Jouvent, R., Quintin, P., Perez-Diaz, F., & Leboyer, M. (2000). Information processing deficits in relatives of manic depressive patients. *Psychological Medicine, 30,* 545–555.

Pliszka, S. R., Glahn, D. C., Semrud-Clikeman, M., Franklin, C., Perez, R., III, Xiong, J., et al. (2006). Neuroimaging of inhibitory control areas in children with attention deficit hyperactivity disorder who were treatment naïve or in long-term treatment. *American Journal of Psychiatry, 163,* 1052–1060.

Quanbeck, C. D., Stone, D. C., McDermott, B. E., Boone, K., Scott, C. L., Frye, M. A., et al. (2005). Relationship between criminal arrest and community treatment history among patients with bipolar disorder. *Psychiatric Services, 56,* 847–852.

Quiggle, N. L., Garber, J., Panak, W. F., & Dodge, K. A. (1992). Social information processing in aggressive and depressed children. *Child Development, 63,* 1305–1320.

Rapoport, J. L., Addington, A. M., & Frangou, S. (2005). The neurodevelopmental model of schizophrenia: Update 2005. *Molecular Psychiatry, 10,* 434–449.

Reichart, C. G., Nolen, W. A., Wals, M., & Hillegers, M. H. J. (2002). Bipolar disorder in children and adolescents: A clinical reality? *Acta Neuropsychiatrica, 12,* 132–135.

Rich, B. A., Schmajuk, M., Perez-Edgar, K. E., Pine, D. S., Fox, N. A., & Leibenluft, E. (2005). The impact of reward, punishment, and frustration on attention in pediatric bipolar disorder. *Biological Psychiatry, 58,* 532–539.

Rietveld, M. J. H., Hudziak, J. J., Bartels, M., van Beijsterveldt, C. E. M., & Boomsma, D. I. (2004). Heritability of attention problems in children: Longitudinal results from a study of twins, age 3 to 12. *Journal of Child Psychology and Psychiatry, 45,* 577–588.

Rosso, I. M., Cintron, C. M., Steingard, R. J., Renshaw, P. F., Young, A. D., & Yurgelun-Todd, D. A. (2005). Amygdala and hippocampus volumes in pediatric major depression. *Biological Psychiatry, 57,* 21–26.

Rujescu, D., Giegling, I., Bondy, B., Gietl, A., Zill, P., & Möller, H.-J. (2002). Association of anger-related traits with SNPs in the TPH gene. *Molecular Psychiatry, 7,* 1023–1029.

Safer, D. J., & Zito, J. M. (2006). Treatment-emergent adverse events from selective serotonin reuptake inhibitors by age group: children versus adolescents. *Journal of Child and Adolescent Psychopharmacology, 16,* 159–69.

Sanson, A., & Prior, M. (1999). Temperament and behavioral precursors to oppositional defiant disorder and conduct disorder. In H. C. Quay & A. E. Hogan (Eds.), *Handbook of disruptive behavior disorders* (pp. 397–417). New York: Kluwer Academic / Plenum Publishers.

Schaffer, A., Cairney, J., Cheung, A., Veldhuizen, S., & Levitt, A. (2006). Community survey of bipolar disorder in Canada: Lifetime prevalence and illness characteristics. *Canadian Journal of Psychiatry, 51,* 9–16.

Scott, J., McNeill, Y., Cavanagh, J., Cannon, M., & Murray, R. (2006). Exposure to obstetric complications and subsequent development of bipolar disorder: Systematic review. *British Journal of Psychiatry, 189,* 3–11.

Sedler, M. J. (1983). Falret's discovery: The origin of the concept of bipolar affective illness. *American Journal of Psychiatry, 140,* 1127–1133.

Segurado, R., Detera-Wadleigh, S. D., Levinson, D. F., Lewis, C. M., Gill, M., Nurnberger, J. I., Jr., et al. (2003). Genome scan meta-analysis of schizophrenia and bipolar disorder, part III: Bipolar disorder. *American Journal of Human Genetics, 73,* 49–62.

Sigurdsson, E., Fombonne, E., Sayal, K., & Checkley, S. (1999). Neurodevelopmental antecedents of early-onset bipolar affective disorder. *British Journal of Psychiatry, 174,* 121–127.

Silverstone, P. H., Wu, R. H., O'Donnell, T., Ulrich, M., Asghar, S. J., & Hanstock, C. C. (2002). Chronic treatment with both lithium and sodium valproate may normalize phosphoinositol cycle activity in bipolar patients. *Human Psychopharmacology, 17,* 321–327.

Simonoff, E., Elander, J., Holmshaw, J., Pickles, A., Murray, R., & Rutter, M. (2004). Predictors of antisocial personality–Continuities from childhood to adult life. *British Journal of Psychiatry, 184,* 118–127.

Soutullo, C. A., Chang, K. D., Díez-Suárez, A., Figueroa-Quintana, A., Escamilla-Canales, I., Rapado-Castro, M., et al. (2005). Bipolar disorder in children and adolescents: International perspective on epidemiology and phenomenology. *Bipolar Disorders, 7,* 497–506.

Strakowski, S. M., Keck, P. E., Arnold, L. M., Collins, J., Wilson, R. M., Fleck, D. E., et al. (2003). Ethnicity and diagnosis in patients with affective disorders. *Journal of Clinical Psychiatry, 64,* 747–754.

Strauss, J., Barr, C. L., George, C. J., Devlin, B., Vetró, Á., Kiss, E., et al. (2005). Brain-derived neurotrophic factor variants are associated with childhood-onset mood disorder: Confirmation in a Hungarian sample. *Molecular Psychiatry, 10,* 861–867.

Strober, M., & Carlson, G. (1982). Bipolar illness in adolescents with major depression: Clinical, genetic, and psychopharmacologic predictors in a three- to four-year prospective follow-up investigation. *Archives of General Psychiatry, 39,* 549–555.

Suppes, T., Kelly, D. I., & Perla, J. M. (2005). Challenges in the management of bipolar depression. *Journal of Clinical Psychiatry, 66*(Suppl. 5), 11–16.

Szeszko, P. R., Robinson, D., Alvir, J. M. J., Bilder, R. M., Lencz, T., Ashtari, M., et al. (1999). Orbital frontal and amygdala volume reductions in obsessive-compulsive disorder. *Archives of General Psychiatry, 56,* 913–919.

Thompson, R. A. (1990). Emotion and self-regulation. In R. A. Thompson (Ed.), *Nebraska Symposium on Motivation, 1988* (Vol. 36; Socioemotional development: Current theory and research in motivation, pp. 367–467). Lincoln: University of Nebraska Press.

Tillman, R., Geller, B., Nickelsburg, M. J., Bolhofner, K., Craney, J. L., DelBello, M. P., et al. (2003). Life events in a prepubertal and early adolescent bipolar disorder phenotype compared to attention-deficit hyperactive and normal controls. *Journal of Child and Adolescent Psychopharmacology, 13,* 243–251.

Todd, R. D., Rasmussen, E. R., Neuman, R. J., Reich, W., Hudziak, J. J., Bucholz, K. K., et al. (2001). Familiality and heritability of subtypes of attention deficit hyperactivity disorder in a population sample of adolescent female twins. *American Journal of Psychiatry, 158,* 1891–1898.

Towbin, K. E., Pradella, A., Gorrindo, T., Pine, D. S., & Leibenluft, E. (2005). Autism spectrum traits in children with mood and anxiety disorders. *Journal of Child and Adolescent Psychopharmacology, 15,* 452–464.

Weissman, M. M., Bland, R. C., Canino, G. J., Faravelli, C., Greenwald, S., Hwu, H. G., et al. (1996). Cross-national epidemiology of major depression and bipolar disorder. *Journal of the American Medical Association, 276,* 293–299.

Weissman, M. M., Wolk, S., Wickramaratne, P., Goldstein, R. B., Adams, P., Greenwald, S., et al. (1999). Children with prepubertal-onset major depressive disorder and anxiety grown up. *Archives of General Psychiatry, 56,* 794–801.

Wilcox, H. C., & Anthony, J. C. (2004). Child and adolescent clinical features as forerunners of adult-onset major depressive disorder: Retrospective evidence from an epidemiological sample. *Journal of Affective Disorders, 82,* 9–20.

Williams, R. S., Cheng, L., Mudge, A. W., & Harwood, A. J. (2002). A common mechanism of action for three mood-stabilizing drugs. *Nature, 417,* 292–295.

World Health Organization. (2004). Chapter V, Mental and behavioural disorders. In *International statistical classification of diseases and related health problems* (10th rev., 2nd ed., Volume 1). Geneva: WHO Press.

Wozniak, J., Biederman, J., Faraone, S. V., Frazier, J., Kim, J., Millstein, R., et al. (1997). Mania in children with pervasive developmental disorder revisited. *Journal of the American Academy of Child and Adolescent Psychiatry, 36,* 1552–1559.

Youngerman, J., & Canino, I. A. (1978). Lithium carbonate use in children and adolescents. A survey of the literature. *Archives of General Psychiatry, 35,* 216–224.

Zammit, S., Allebeck, P., David, A. S., Dalman, C., Hemmingsson, T., Lundberg, I., et al. (2004). A longitudinal study of premorbid IQ score and risk of developing schizophrenia, bipolar disorder, severe depression, and other nonaffective psychoses. *Archives of General Psychiatry, 61,* 354–360.

CHAPTER 19

Autism Spectrum Disorders: A Developmental Perspective

GERALDINE DAWSON AND SUSAN FAJA

A utism spectrum disorders (ASDs) are a group of developmental disorders characterized by impairments in social and communication behavior and a restricted range of activities and interests. Despite significant advances in our understanding of ASD, the causes remain unknown, and, for many children with the disorder, effective treatments have yet to be discovered. In this chapter, we review current findings regarding early brain and behavioral development in autism, and provide a perspective that offers hope for improved outcomes for many individuals with the disorder.

HISTORICAL CONTEXT

Leo Kanner (1943) first characterized the difficulties associated with autism. In his seminal work, he described a variety of behaviors that have given rise to the modern diagnostic criteria, including lack of social reciprocity and emotional awareness, delays in communication and atypical use of lan-

Acknowledgments: Writing of this chapter was funded by grants from the National Institute of Child Health and Human Development (U19HD34565, P50HD066782, and R01HD-55741) and the National Institute of Mental Health (U54MH066399). Send correspondence to Geraldine Dawson at University of Washington, Box 357920, Autism Center, Seattle WA 98195.

guage, and repetitive interests and behaviors. At the same time in Austria, Hans Asperger described a high-functioning form of autism (Asperger, 1991) in which he compared the children studied to *absent-minded professors*. Asperger described the intense interests of these children and their abilities to provide lengthy descriptions of their interests.

Kanner (1943) included the following features in his description of autism: an inability to relate to people, language deviance characterized by delayed acquisition, echolalia, occasional mutism, pronoun reversals, literalness, excellent rote memory, repetitive and stereotyped play activities, and an obsessive desire for maintenance of sameness in the environment. Kanner also noted that the children began experiencing difficulties during infancy. The children's lack of obvious physical anomalies and good rote memory led Kanner to conclude that they were endowed with normal cognitive potential.

During the next few decades following Kanner's (1943) article, clinicians and researchers disagreed whether or not autism was a form of childhood Schizophrenia. This disagreement was related in part to Kanner's use of the term *autism*, which many investigators confused with Bleuler's (1950) descriptions of autistic detachment from reality found in patients with schizophrenia. Verification of differences between autism and childhood schizophrenia came from studies (e.g., Kolvin, 1971a) showing that the distribution of the onset of *childhood psychosis*, which included autism, is markedly bipolar and falls most frequently either before 3 years of age or in early adolescence. In addition, Kolvin (1971b) found differences between early and late onset childhood psychosis in parental social class, family history of schizophrenia, frequency of cerebral dysfunction, speech patterns, and intelligence quotient (IQ) level. Also, remissions and relapses were much more characteristic of late-onset childhood psychosis (i.e., schizophrenia). People with autism also rarely develop the delusions and hallucinations, which are hallmarks of schizophrenia.

TERMINOLOGICAL AND CONCEPTUAL ISSUES

Autism spectrum disorders include Autistic Disorder, Asperger's Disorder, and Pervasive Developmental Disorder, Not Otherwise Specified (PDD-NOS). In addition, two rare disorders are included under the current classification of Pervasive Developmental Disorder: Rett's Disorder and Childhood Disintegrative Disorder. ASDs are extremely heterogeneous in their presentation. The complex array of symptoms associated with autism has presented a significant challenge to investigators who seek to determine the core, underlying impairments and associated brain mechanisms in order to elucidate the etiology of autism and develop targeted interventions. Core impairments must be specific rather than broad and general, they must be unique to autism rather than a result of general developmental pathology, and they must be universal to all individuals with autism minimally at a certain point in development and ideally throughout development (Sigman and Capps, 1997). Given the heterogeneity of ASD, questions arise regarding the definition and measurement of a widely observed impairment across differing levels of intellect and throughout development. As a result of the heterogeneity, a variety of attempts to identify meaningful subgroups have been made.

DIAGNOSTIC ISSUES AND *DSM-IV* CRITERIA

The current diagnostic criteria include impairments in *social interaction:* (a) deficient regulation of social interaction by using nonverbal behaviors, (b) lack of developmentally appropriate peer relationships, (c) failure to share achievements, interests, or pleasure with others, and (d) lack of social or emotional reciprocity; *communication:* (a) delayed language without compensation by gestures, (b) impaired conversational ability, (c) repetitive, stereotyped, or idiosyncratic language, (d) absence of social imitative play or spontaneous make-believe play appropriate to the developmental stage; and, *repetitive or restricted behaviors or interests:* (a) preoccupation with abnormal interests that are repetitive or stereotyped, (b) rigid adherence to nonfunctional routines or rituals, (c) stereotyped, repetitive motor mannerisms, and (d) persistent preoccupation with parts of objects (American Psychiatric Association [APA], 2000). These symptoms typically appear before the age of 3. In order to receive a diagnosis of Autistic Disorder, a minimum of 6 of 12 symptoms must be present, while Asperger's Disorder and PDD-NOS require fewer symptoms or expression of symptoms in only two of three domains. Thus, autism may vary in its severity and individuals with strikingly different symptomatology may meet diagnostic criteria.

Infants at risk for autism are being identified at increasingly younger ages, yet many children continue to go undiagnosed until preschool (Coonrod & Stone, 2004; Howlin & Moore, 1997) or later (Mandell et al., 2002). Indeed, the core diagnostic criteria focus on behaviors observed in children aged 2 to 3 years and above (Sigman et al., 2004). Currently, autism screening tools exist for infants (e.g., The First Year Inventory; Reznick, Baranek, Reavis, Watson, & Crais, 2007) and toddlers (e.g., Modified-Checklist for Autism in Toddlers; Robins et al., 2001). In many cases, a diagnosis may be made reliably as early as 24 months (Lord et al., 2006). The mismatch between the age of diagnosis and the age at which diagnosis could potentially be made is problematic because it delays entry into early intervention programs and limits scientific knowledge of the early course of development.

PREVALENCE

Once believed to be a rare disorder, it is now estimated that ASD afflicts approximately 1 in 150 persons, a prevalence rate that is higher than that of Type 1 diabetes, blindness, Down syndrome, childhood cancer, and cystic fibrosis (Kuehn, 2007). Approximately one million individuals are affected in the United States, with an annual cost of $90 billion. The Center for Disease Control (CDC) conducted an epidemiological study with nearly 1,000 confirmed cases of 3- to 10-year-old children in metropolitan Atlanta (Yeargin-Allsopp et al., 2003) and found a prevalence rate of 3 to 4 per 1,000. More recently, the CDC released data suggesting a higher prevalence of 6 to 7 children per 1,000 (CDC, 2007), using a larger sample across multiple sites in the United States. The possibility of an autism epidemic has been raised due to increase in reported rates since the 1970s. Changes in prevalence data are, at least in part, likely a result of broadening diagnostic criteria with revisions to the *DSM*, methodological differences in prevalence research, and increasing awareness and use of ASD diagnoses.

RISK FACTORS AND ETIOLOGICAL FORMULATIONS

A developmental model of risk, risk processes, symptom emergence, and adaptation must be considered in autism, as illustrated in Figure 19.1. Genetic and environmental factors lead to abnormalities in brain development that contribute to altered patterns of interaction between the child and his or her environment. Such altered interactions, or risk processes, are hypothesized to disrupt critical input influencing the development of brain circuitry during early sensitive periods, thus serving as mediators of the effects of early susceptibilities on later outcome. Through these mediational processes, early susceptibilities contribute to outcome—the full autism syndrome. Thus, there is not a one-to-one correspondence between genetic or environmental factors and the occurrence of autism. Rather, there are individual differences in developmental pathways that children follow. These pathways can be explained in terms of interactions between early risk factors and the context in which the child develops. Although changes in developmental pathways are always possible, canalization con-

Vulnerabilities   Risk processes   Outcome

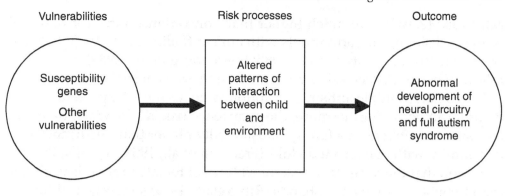

Figure 19.1. Experience-based risk processes in autism

strains the magnitude and quality of such changes. Thus, "the longer an individual continues along a maladaptive ontogenetic pathway, the more difficult it is to reclaim a normal developmental trajectory" (Cicchetti & Cohen, 1995, p. 7). The earlier risk for autism is detected and intervention begins, the greater the chance that intervention will alter abnormal developmental trajectories of individuals with ASD.

GENETIC RISK FACTORS

Twin studies provide strong evidence for genetic risk factors in autism. Concordance rates for monozygotic (MZ) twins are 69 to 95% (Bailey et al., 1995; Folstein & Rutter, 1977a, b; Ritvo et al., 1985; Steffenburg et al., 1989), whereas dizygotic (DZ) concordance rates range from 0 to 24%. When a broader ASD phenotype (e.g., language and / or social impairment) is used, concordance rates increase for both MZ (88 to 91%) and DZ (9 to 30%) twins (Bailey et al., 1995; Folstein & Rutter, 1977b; Steffenburg et al., 1989).

Sibling risk rates for ASD range from 2.8% to 7.0%, whereas rates in control families are much lower (August, Stewart, & Tsai, 1981; Bailey, Phillips, & Rutter, 1996; Smalley, Asarnow, & Spence, 1988). Nevertheless, 4.4 to 20.4% of siblings who do not meet criteria for ASD show a *lesser variant* of ASD, including difficulties such as severe social dysfunction and isolation (Bolton et al., 1994; Piven et al., 1990). To date, most studies have indicated that unaffected relatives, such as siblings and parents, show elevated rates of autism-related symptoms (Bailey et al., 1995, 1996; Folstein & Rutter, 1977b; Landa et al., 1992; Narayan, Moyes, & Wolff, 1990; Wolff, Naravan, & Moyes, 1988).

Although the mode of inheritance in autism is not completely understood, most cases of autism appear to be caused by multiple genes interacting epistatically. This conclusion is based on the fact that concordance rates for MZ twins are much higher than concordance rates for both DZ twins and siblings of individuals with autism (Bailey et al., 1995; Folstein & Rutter, 1977a, b; Ritvo et al., 1985; Steffenburg et al., 1989). The rapid falloff in risk with decreasing genetic relatedness is consistent with the hypothesis that multiple autism-susceptibility genes must be present for the disorder to occur. Furthermore, the recurrence risk is 35% when there are two affected siblings in a family, substantially higher than recurrence risk in a family with one affected child (Freeman et al., 1989). Finally, the observation that the recurrence risk for siblings of female probands is higher than for siblings of male probands (Ritvo et al., 1989) suggests multifactor inheritance. For multifactor traits, the recurrence risk is expected to be higher for relatives of the less common sex (Falconer, 1981), and males with autism outnumber females by 3–4 to 1 (Ritvo et al., 1989; Zahner & Pauls, 1987). A multifactor epistatic model with 2 to 10 contributing loci (Pickles et al., 1995) has been proposed.

Several genome-wide linkage studies of autism have been published (Auranen et al., 2002; Barrett et al., 1999; Buxbaum et al., 2001; Cantor et al., 2005; International Molecular Genetic Study of Autism Consortium, 1998, 2001; Lamb et al., 2005; Liu et al., 2001; McCauley et al., 2005; Philippe et al., 1999; Risch et al., 1999; Schellenberg et al., 2006; Shao et al., 2002; Stone et al., 2004; Yonan et al., 2003). Although no single region has been consistently associated with autism, a few signals for specific chromosomal regions have been identified in multiple studies. These include 1p (Auranen et al., 2002; Risch et al., 1999), 2q (Buxbaum et al., 2001; Lamb et al., 2005; Liu et al., 2001; Shao et al., 2002), 7q (Barrett et al., 1999; IMGSAC, 1998, 2001; Lamb et al., 2005; Schellenberg et al., 2006), 17q (Cantor et al., 2005; Lamb et al., 2005; Liu et al., 2001; McCauley et al., 2005), and 19q (Philippe et al., 1999; Shao et al., 2002), with the 2q, 7q, and 17q regions giving the strongest signals.

Over 100 genes have been tested as candidates for autism-susceptibility loci. Some of these candidate genes are promising. A positive association between autism and Engrailed 2 (EN-2) located on Chromosome 7 has been reported. In mice, EN-2 is expressed primarily in the cerebellum during nervous system development and is critical for cerebellar development (Cheh et al., 2006; Millen et al., 1994). Abnormalities in cerebellar development have been consistently demonstrated in individuals with autism, including reduced Purkinje cells in the cerebellar cortex (Bailey et al., 1998; Courchesne, 1997, 2004; Kemper & Bauman, 1998; Ritvo et al., 1986). Also targeting Chromosome 7q, the gene encoding the MET receptor tyrosine kinase was examined and a genetic association between the C allele in the promoter region of the MET gene was shown (Campbell et al., 2006). MET signaling is involved in neocortical and cerebellar development, immune function, and gastrointestinal repair. Finally, a collaboration among 50 institutions that pooled genetic data from 1,200 multiplex families found evidence of an association with neurexin 1, which is part of a family of genes that plays a role in the neurotransmitter glutamate, and autism (Szatmari et al., 2007). Glutamate is involved in both synaptogenesis and learning.

The serotonin transporter gene, SLC6A4, has been tested as a candidate gene in several studies that have yielded positive but not entirely consistent results (reviewed in Devlin et al., 2005). Elevated levels of platelet serotonin (5-HT) have been found in individuals with autism (Rolf et al., 1993). Serotonin is involved in guiding neuronal development, modulating sensory input and arousal, and in a variety of behaviors such as sleep, mood, aggression, impulsivity, and affiliation (Lucki, 1998). Serotonergic neurons innervate the limbic regions involved in emotional expression and social behavior. Devlin et al. (2005) investigated the impact of alleles at the 5-HTT-LPR and three other polymorphisms within SLC6A4 using a large family-based sample (390 families, 1,528 individuals). An excess transmission of the short allele of 5-HTT-LPR was found for individuals diagnosed with autism, both for the narrow diagnostic criteria and for the broader diagnosis of an ASD. A second study examined relations between variability in 5-HTT-LPR and early abnormalities in brain growth in autism. One of the most highly replicated biological findings in autism is enlargement of the cerebrum, especially early in life (discussed in more detail in the following). Combining samples of MRI data with DNA collected from young boys with ASD, the short (S) allele was strongly associated with increased cerebral cortical gray matter (Wassink et al., 2007).

Single-gene mutations have also been described in autism samples, including mutations of the neuroligin 3 and neuroligin 4 genes (Jamain et al., 2003), though these appear to be extremely rare causes of autism. Other single-gene disorders are associated with increased risk for autism or expression of an autistic-like phenotype, including Fragile X syndrome, Rett syndrome, Angelman syndrome, tuberous sclerosis, and neurofibromatosis (see Veenstra-VanderWeele & Cook, 2004, for review).

In summary, although there is strong evidence for genetic influences in autism, the role of susceptibility genes is complex. Evidence thus far indicates that multiple genes interact to increase susceptibility to autism by influencing gene expression or to encode functional changes in proteins that are part of complex regulatory networks. Studies are beginning to reveal specific genes that might lead to susceptibility for autism. As will be discussed in more detail in the following, the expression and effects of many genes are influenced by environmental factors, offering hope that early intervention can alter genetic expression, brain development, and behavioral outcome.

ENVIRONMENTAL RISK FACTORS

Concordance rates of less than 100% suggest that environmental factors are also involved in the etiology of autism; however, significant associations have not been found for many of the proposed sources of environmental risk. One area of investigation is the possible contribution of suboptimal conditions, or complications, with pregnancy, delivery, or early infancy to the development of autism. No single factor has emerged consistently, and individual adverse events appear to have minimal impact (Bolton et al., 1994, 1997; Bryson, Clark, & Smith, 1988; Cryan et al., 1996; Gillberg & Gillberg, 1983; Levy, Zoltak, & Saelens, 1988; Lord et al., 1991). It is possible that these factors may result from extant fetal abnormalities or genetic factors rather than play a causal role (Bolton et al., 1994, 1997). One exception that has been associated with autism is exposure to the teratogen thalidomide, with a rate of 33% of children exposed between the 20th and 24th day of pregnancy developing autism (Miller & Strömland, 1993).

Involvement of vaccinations during the first years of life, especially the measles-mumps-rubella (MMR) vaccination, has also been hypothesized as an environmental factor. Nonetheless, a number of epidemiological studies have failed to confirm an association between the MMR vaccine and autism (Wilson et al., 2003, for a review). A preservative containing ethyl mercury that was added to many vaccines, thimerosal, has also been examined as a possible risk factor. A recent review found no evidence of harm from thimerosal in vaccines (Ball, Ball, & Pratt, 2001), but thimerosal-free vaccines are now available for all routine childhood immunizations (Kimmel, 2002).

DEVELOPMENTAL PROGRESSION

BEHAVIORAL SYMPTOMS APPARENT IN INFANCY

Initial studies of the early course of autism focused on retrospective parent reports. Difficulties in social behavior, communication development, sensory peculiarities, and affective responses were reported (Dahlgren & Gillberg, 1989; De Giacomo & Fombonne, 1998; Hoshino et al., 1982; Ohta et al., 1987; Young, Brewer, & Pattison, 2003). Progress has been made in understanding the earliest symptoms of autism using complementary methods of retrospective videotape study and prospective research with high-risk infants. Infants at risk for autism show fewer behavioral symptoms at 6 months, but by 12 months core symptoms are apparent for many. In one study, infants who later developed autism were distinguished from typically developing children at 6 months by slightly lower frequency of attempts to seek physical contact, vocalizations, looking at faces, and smiling at others (Maestro et al., 2002). Displaying positive affect distinguished children at younger ages (Maestro et al., 2002; Werner et al., 2000), but less so by 12 months (Maestro et al., 2001; Mars, Mauk, & Dowrick, 1998). Zwaigenbaum and his coworkers (2005) have followed a large sample of infant siblings of children with autism and low-risk infants prospectively from the age of 6 months or younger, and prior to onset of parent concern. Infants were assessed using the Autism Observation Scale for Infants (Bryson et al., 2007) which measures visual attention, response to name, response to a brief still face, anticipatory responses, imitation, social babbling, eye contact and social smiling, reactivity, affect, ease of transitioning, and atypical motor and sensory behaviors. These markers did not distinguish groups at 6 months of age on the basis of their diagnostic classification at 24 months, yet a subset of the children who were later diagnosed exhibited impairments in responding to name or unusual sensory behaviors.

Emergence of increased symptoms between 6 and 12 months of age has been documented. First, failure to respond to name has been documented as a symptom by 8 to 10 months (Werner et al., 2000). Second, the rate of growth in visual attention differed by diagnostic group between 6 and 12 months, as measured by subtracting performance across time points (Zwaigenbaum et al., 2005). All infants whose visual attention performance declined later received an autism diagnosis, whereas none whose performance was similar or better at 12 months received a diagnosis. Finally, group differences emerged in the temperament of infant siblings. Parent ratings at 6 months suggested siblings who later developed autism had a lower activity level. By 12 months, these children exhibited more frequent and intense reactions to distress. They also spent more time fixating on a single object and were less active in their spontaneous visual exploration. At the time of diagnosis at 24 months, symptomatic siblings were less able to shift attention, exhibited less inhibitory control, and had diminished anticipatory and affective responses.

By 12 months, infants later diagnosed with autism are best distinguished from typical infants by reduced orienting when called by name, by decreased amount of time spent looking at the faces of others, and decreased social interest (Baranek, 1999; Osterling & Dawson, 1994, Osterling, Dawson, & Munson, 2002; Zwaigenbaum et al., 2005). Other behaviors that distinguished children with autism from typically developing children by 12 months include showing things to others and pointing to request or to share interest, social smiling, imitation, reactivity, and visual attention (Adrien et al., 1993; Maestro et al., 2002; Osterling & Dawson, 1994; Osterling et al., 2002; Werner & Dawson, 2005; Zwaigenbaum et al., 2005). In contrast, seeking physical contact, participating in social games, negative affective responses, object use, and symbolic play did not distinguish children with autism from controls (Baranek, 1999; Maestro et al., 2001; Osterling & Dawson, 1994; Osterling et al., 2002; Werner et al., 2000; Werner & Dawson, 2005). Finally, the presence of sensory-oriented behaviors is inconsistent (Baranek, 1999; Osterling & Dawson, 1994, Zwaigenbaum et al., 2005). In summary, specific behaviors related to social orienting and shared attention distinguish children with autism from typically developing infants by the end of the first year of life.

Changes in communication and cognitive development emerge between 12 and 24 months. Landa and Garrett-Mayer (2006) followed the cognitive development of high-risk infant siblings who later developed an autism spectrum disorder compared with language-delayed and unaffected groups. Infants did not differ at 6 months, but by 14 months children who received autism spectrum diagnoses differed from the unaffected group in gross and fine motor skills, receptive and expressive language, and overall intelligence on the Mullen scales (Mullen, 1995). The profile of performance distinguished children with ASDs from children with language delay by 24 months, with ability in the Visual Reception domain being significantly greater than Receptive Language ability for children with ASD. Detailed prospective examination of nine children who received autism spectrum diagnoses (Bryson, et al., 2007) suggests the presence of two diagnostic subgroups on the basis of the presence or absence of cognitive decline between 12 and 24 months. In children with cognitive loss, symptoms emerged earlier or were more severe. Given the observed cognitive impairments in ASD, an important question is what factors distinguish very young children with autism from children with other developmental delays. Two videotape investigations of infants between 9 and 12 months have used a comparison group with developmental delay (Baranek, 1999; Osterling et al., 2002). Again, looking at people and responding to name best distinguished infants with autism from infants with developmental delay without autism. These factors correctly classified 85% of the sample reported by Osterling and coworkers (2002).

Children who received a diagnosis were distinguished from at-risk siblings at 12 months by their language abilities, including receptive language and concurrent parent report of gesture use and understanding of words (Zwaigenbaum et al., 2005). Findings of language differences are of interest because communication differences were typically detected later in retrospective video analyses. By the second year of life, robust differences in social communication skills emerge. For example, sharing experiences, interests, and attention with others by pointing or showing objects distinguishes children with ASD (Maestro et al., 2001; Werner & Dawson, 2005). Pointing to request objects was also less frequent (Mars et al., 1998). Sullivan and colleagues (2007) examined the joint attention behavior of siblings of children with autism at 14 and 24 months. Compared with children who did not develop symptoms, children who later received a diagnosis of autism or its broader phenotype were distinguished by joint attention skills, and variation in this domain was predictive of future language ability. By age 2, children with autism are distinguished from controls by reduced ability to follow verbal instructions, babbling or making complex vocalizations, vocal imitation, and use of single words and phrases (Mars et al., 1998; Werner & Dawson, 2005).

The phenomenon of autistic regression has also been explored. It is estimated that 20% to 47% of children lose skills and develop autism symptoms after 1 to 2 years of seemingly more typical development (Davidovitch et al., 2000). Parental reports of regression during the second year of life are well documented (Goldberg et al., 2003; Lord, Shulman, & DiLavore, 2004; Ozonoff, Williams, & Landa, 2005; Werner & Dawson, 2005). Validation of these two different developmental courses, one with early onset during the first year of life and one with regression during the second year of life, comes from videotape studies (Osterling et al., 2002; Werner et al., 2000; Werner & Dawson, 2005). Werner and Dawson (2005) compared videotapes of two groups of infants with autism—those with parental reports of a regressive course and those with early onset—as well as a comparison group of typically developing infants. Infants with regression had similar joint attention behaviors and more frequent use of words or babbling compared with typical controls at 12 months. The frequency of these behaviors was significantly reduced in the early onset group. By 24 months, however, both groups of children with autism had fewer instances of word use or other vocalizations, declarative pointing, social gaze, and response to name than controls.

TODDLER-PRESCHOOL PERIOD

By the toddler-preschool period, at least five domains of social behavior are affected in autism. These include social orienting, joint attention, attention to emotional cues, motor imitation, and face processing. Each of these will be discussed briefly.

Social orienting. Dawson and her coworkers coined the term *social orienting impairment* to refer to the failure of young children with autism to spontaneously orient to naturally occurring social stimuli (Dawson, Meltzoff, Osterling, Rinaldi, & Brown, 1998). Mundy and Neal (2001) proposed that the developmental pathway of young children with autism is altered by this social orienting impairment because children are deprived of appropriate social stimulation. Very early in life, typical infants show remarkable sensitivity to social stimuli (Rochat, 1999). This early emerging sensitivity and attention to the social world is reflexive rather than voluntary. Very likely, the acquisition of subsequent social behaviors depends on this early propensity to devote attention to people (Rochat & Striano, 1999). As mentioned previously, one of the earliest and most basic social impairments in autism is a failure to orient to social stimuli and this almost certainly contributes to the later social and communicative impairments observed in the disorder (Dawson et al., 1998; Mundy & Neal, 2001). Dawson and colleagues demonstrated that, compared to children with Mental Retardation without autism and typically developing children, young children with autism more frequently failed to orient to both social and nonsocial stimuli, but this failure was much more extreme for social stimuli (Dawson et al., 1998; Dawson, Toth et al., 2004).

Joint attention. Joint attention refers to the ability to "coordinate attention between interactive social partners with respect to objects or events in order to share an awareness of the objects or events" (Mundy et al., 1986, p. 657). There is a range of joint attention behaviors, which includes sharing attention (e.g., through the use of alternating eye gaze), following the attention of another (e.g., following eye gaze or a point), and directing the attention of another, which are generally demonstrated by typically developing infants by 12 months of age (Carpenter, Nagell, & Tomasello, 1998). Joint attention is fundamentally impaired in autism, present by 1 year of age, and incorporated into the diagnostic criteria for the disorder (APA, 1994; Mundy et al., 1986). In numerous studies, joint attention ability has distinguished preschool children with autism from those with developmental delay and typical development (Bacon, Fein, Morris, Waterhouse, & Allen, 1998; Charman et al., 1998; Dawson et al., 1998; Mundy et al., 1986; Sigman et al., 1992). Joint attention skills are also a good predictor of both concurrent and future language skills in children with autism and typical development (Dawson et al., 1998; Sullivan et al., 2007). Social orienting ability was indirectly related to language ability through its contribution to joint attention skills (Dawson et al., 1998), perhaps because a child's ability to attend to social information contributes critically to his or her acquisition of joint attention skills because such skills require active attention to social cues, particularly those expressed on the face.

Attention to emotional cues. The third core domain of impairment is a failure to attend and respond to others' emotions in a normal manner. Within the first 6 months of life, infants begin attending to the affective displays of others—for example, attending longer and smiling more frequently to a happy face than to a neutral or sad face (Rochat & Striano, 1999). Social referencing, whereby children seek emotional information from an adult's face when presented with a stimulus of uncertain valence, is established by 9 to 12 months of age (Feinman, 1982). By 2 years of age, children begin to respond to another person's distress affectively and prosocially by helping, comforting, and sharing (Rheingold, Hay, & West, 1976; Zahn-Waxler & Radke-Yarrow, 1990). Many but not all children with autism demonstrate a lack of sensitivity to the emotional states of others. When adults display facial expressions of distress, children with autism look less at the adult and show less concern compared to children with mental retardation and typical development (Bacon et al., 1998; Charman et al., 1998; Dawson et al., 1998; Dawson, Toth et al., 2004; Sigman et al., 1992).

Dawson and colleagues used event-related electrical brain potentials (ERPs) to examine whether young children with autism responded differently to distinct emotional expressions. Differential ERPs to distinct facial expressions of emotion have been shown in children (de Haan et al., 1998) and in infants as young as 7 months of age (Nelson & de Haan, 1996). Three- to four-year-old children with autism were shown two pictures of the same face depicting a neutral expression and a prototypic expression of fear (Dawson, Webb et al., 2004). Compared to typically developing children, children with autism exhibited significantly slower early (N300) brain responses and failed to show larger amplitude negative slow-wave responses to the facial expression of fear. Individual differences in N300 latency to the fear faces was associated with performance on behavioral tasks requiring social attention. Moreover, the children with autism displayed aberrant ERP scalp topography in response to the fearful face. The delayed response to the fear face suggests that information-processing speed is compromised, and the abnormal topography suggests a failure of cortical specialization or atypical recruitment of cortical areas.

Motor imitation. The fourth domain of impairment is the ability to imitate others. By 1 year of age, infants are able to imitate actions on objects and gestures, such as waving. Imitation may serve as a basis for social connectedness with others and enable children to differentiate themselves from others (Meltzoff & Gopnick, 1993; Eckerman, Davis, & Didow, 1989; Uzgiris, 1981; Nadel et al., 1999; Trevarthen, Kokkinaki, & Fiamenghi, 1999). Imitation also promotes learning and understanding about others' intentions and goals (Uzgiris, 1999; Kugiumutzakis, 1999) and likely serves as a precursor for the development of a theory of mind (Meltzoff & Gopnick, 1993; Rogers & Pennington, 1991). Imitation also plays a role in symbolic play (Piaget, 1962), peer relationships (Trevarthen et al., 1999), language (Avikainen et al., 2003; Charman et al., 2003), and emotional sharing (Hatfield, Cacioppo, & Rapson, 1994).

Failure to spontaneously imitate others, especially in social play contexts, is a core early impairment in autism (Dawson & Adams, 1984; Dawson & Lewy, 1989; Rogers et al., 1996). Imitation ability discriminates toddlers with autism from those with Mental Retardation or a communication disorder (Stone et al., 1990; Stone, Ousley, & Littleford, 1997). Individuals with autism perform poorly in virtually all aspects of imitation (Rogers et al., 2003), including imitating motor movements (Hertzig, Snow, & Sherman, 1989; Sigman & Ungerer, 1984), facial expressions (Loveland et al., 1994), the style of tasks (Hobson & Lee, 1999), actions involving imaginary objects (Rogers et al., 1996), and vocalizations (Dawson & Adams, 1984). Functional MRI and EEG studies of mirror neurons—which are activated while observing and performing an action—indicate deficits among those with autism during imitation tasks (Dapretto et al., 2006; Bernier et al., in press).

Face processing.   Face-recognition ability is present very early in life. At birth, neonates show the capacity for very rapid face recognition (Walton & Bower, 1993) and a visual preference for faces (Goren, Sarty, & Wu, 1975). By 4 months, infants recognize upright faces better than upside down faces (Fagan, 1972), and by 6 months infants show differential event-related brain potentials to familiar versus unfamiliar faces (de Haan & Nelson, 1997, 1999). On average, face-processing abilities in individuals with autism are consistently impaired. Using high-density ERPs, face recognition abilities in 3- to 4-year-old children with autism, developmental delay, and typical development were examined while children watched images of familiar and unfamiliar faces (mother versus another female), and familiar and unfamiliar objects (toys) (Dawson, Carver et al., 2002). Typical children demonstrated increased amplitudes to novel faces and objects for two ERP components. Children with autism showed the same differential ERP response to objects, but did not show the differential response for faces, indicating children with autism exhibit face-recognition impairments as early as 3 years of age.

By middle childhood, children with autism perform worse than mental age– and chronological age–matched peers on a number of face-processing tasks, including tests of face recognition (Boucher & Lewis, 1992; Boucher, Lewis, & Collis 1998; Gepner, de Gelder, & de Schonen, 1996; Klin et al., 1999) and face discrimination (Tantam et al., 1989). Although typically developing children show better memory performance for faces than nonface visual stimuli, children with autism perform comparably on face and nonface tasks (Serra et al., 2003), or show better performance on nonface tasks (e.g., memory for buildings) than on face tasks (Boucher & Lewis,

1992). Individuals with autism also appear to process faces using abnormal strategies. By middle childhood, typically developing children (a) are better at recognizing parts of a face when the parts are presented in the context of a whole face, (b) perform better when recognition involves the eyes versus the mouth (Joseph & Tanaka, 2003), (c) show a greater decrement in memory for inverted versus upright faces as compared with nonface visual stimuli, and (d) attend to upright faces for longer lengths of time than inverted faces (van der Geest et al., 2002). In contrast, children with autism are better at recognizing isolated facial features and partially obscured faces than typical children (Hobson, Ouston, & Lee, 1988; Tantam et al., 1989) and show better performance on memory for the lower half of the face than the upper half (Langdell, 1978). Studies of visual attention to faces indicate that individuals with autism exhibit reduced attention to the core features of the face, such as the eyes and nose, relative to typical individuals (Klin et al., 2002; Pelphrey et al., 2002; Trepagnier, Sebrechts, & Peterson, 2002).

EARLY ABNORMAL BRAIN DEVELOPMENT IN AUTISM

Individuals with autism have been found to exhibit an atypical pattern of growth in head circumference (HC) characterized by small-to-normal head size at birth followed by an accelerated pattern of growth in HC that appears to begin at about 4 months of age (Courchesne & Pierce, 2005; Dawson et al., 2007; Redcay & Courchesne, 2005; Gillberg and de Souza, 2002). In comparison, although children's HC was larger than normal by 12 months of age, the rate of growth in HC after 12 months was not significantly different than a normative sample, suggesting deceleration after 12 months relative to the first year (Dawson et al., 2007). It is interesting to note that the timing of the onset of accelerated head growth between 4 and 12 months slightly precedes, and then overlaps with, the onset of behavioral symptoms. Perhaps coincidentally, the period after 12 months of age, during which deceleration of rate of head growth was detected, appears to be associated with a slowing in acquisition or actual loss in skills in infants with autism (Dawson et al., 2007).

Structural brain imaging in young children with autism. Results from magnetic resonance imaging (MRI) studies are consistent with the results of HC studies. For example, 2 to 4 year olds with ASD were found to have lager total cerebral volumes than controls, including IQ-matched children with developmental delay, in two MRI investigations (Courchesne et al., 2001; Sparks et al., 2002). This abnormal brain growth appears to be due primarily to excessive enlargement of cerebellar and cerebral white matter and cerebral grey matter, with an anterior-to-posterior gradient of overgrowth (Courchesne et al., 2001). MRI studies have also revealed other abnormalities, especially in medial temporal lobe (MTL) structures such as the amygdala (e.g., Aylward et al., 1999; Schumann et al., 2004). These structures have been strongly implicated in ASD-related symptom expression, particularly social perception and behavior (see Baron-Cohen et al., 2000; Schultz, 2005, for review). Munson et al. (2006) reported amygdala enlargement (relative to total brain volume) in 3- to 4-year-old children with autism was associated with a more severe course during the preschool period.

Chemical brain imaging studies in young children with autism. Brain proton magnetic resonance spectroscopy (^{1}H MRSI) provides a noninvasive method for characterizing tissue-based chemistry and cellular features in vivo. MRI, which is more widely used to investigate ASD than MRSI, is sensitive to changes in tissue water characteristics and defining structure at a macroscopic level, but it is insensitive to much of cellular level organization. An MRSI study of 3- to 4-year-old children with ASD conducted by Friedman et al. (2003) revealed regional and global decreases in NAA, a sensitive marker for neuronoal integrity or neuronal-glial homeostasis, as well as lower levels of other chemicals and prolonged chemical T2 relaxation times. Analyses further demonstrated distribution of these chemical abnormalities was predominately in gray matter tissue (Friedman et al., 2006). Recent longitudinal findings suggest this pattern of chemical alterations generally persists between 3 to 4 and 6 to 7 years of age (Dager, personal communication).

These MSRI findings suggest a pattern of cellular alterations, predominantly affecting gray matter at an early age, that may reflect reduced synapse density perhaps secondary to migratory/apoptotic abnormalities (Fatemi & Halt, 2001), column density/packing abnormalities (Casanova, 2004), and/or active processes such as reactive gliosis and edema (Vargas et al., 2005). In addition, at age 6 to 7 years in the same longitudinal sample, there were new findings of elevated gray matter combined glutamate and glutamine peaks not seen at the earlier age-point (Dager, personal communication). These findings are consistent with the theory that autism is associated with reduced inhibitory balance associated with atypical levels of glutamate (Belmonte et al., 2004).

COMORBIDITY

ASD is associated with several comorbid conditions. Most commonly, ASD may be accompanied by comorbid developmental delay or intellectual disability; however, a significant portion of individuals have average to above-average intelligence. Approximately 40 to 70% of children with ASD are currently estimated to also have intellectual disability or mental retardation (Baird et al., 2000; Chakrabarti & Fombonne, 2001). Given the significant proportion of children who have both ASD and intellectual disability, it is important to consider the child's developmental level and typical developmental milestones when making a diagnosis. Diagnostic criteria also specify that all children with autism must have deficits in communication. Many children with ASD are impaired in formal aspects of language (e.g., complex syntax) similarly to children with specific language impairment (SLI) (Bartak, Rutter, & Cox, 1975; Bishop, North, & Donlan, 1996; Dollaghan & Campbell, 1998; Gathercole & Baddeley, 1990; Tager-Flusberg & Cooper, 1999). Kjelgaard & Tager-Flusberg (2001) found similarities between children with ASD and impaired language to children with SLI, including better vocabulary relative to higher-order language abilities, poor performance on phonological processing, and difficulties in marking tense.

A number of other disorders also co-occur with ASD. Tics, or involuntary stereotyped movements or vocalizations that cause distress to the individual, are reported in 30% of individuals with ASD sampled, with 4.3% meeting criteria for Tourette's Syndrome (Baron-Cohen et al., 1999). Comorbid diagnosis of ASD and Obsessive Compulsive Disorder ranges from 1.5 to 29% (Lainhart, 1999). Mood disorders also co-occur with ASD, with anxiety disorders (Generalized Anxiety Disorder, Agoraphobia, Separation Anxiety, and Phobia) estimated at 7 to 84% and depression ranging from 4 to 58% (Lainhart, 1999). Finally, individuals with autism are at increased risk for developing seizure disorders, with prevalence rates ranging from 5 to 39% (Ballaban-Gil & Tuchman, 2000; Tidmarsh & Volkmar, 2003). Onset is most commonly before 3 years of age or during puberty (11 to 14 years) (Gillberg & Steffenburg, 1987; Goode, Rutter, & Howlin, 1994; Rutter, 1970; Volkmar & Nelson, 1990) and seizures are more common in very low functioning individuals (i.e., IQ of less than 50) and in females (Rutter, 1984; Volkmar & Nelson, 1990).

SEX DIFFERENCES

Autism affects males more commonly than females, with a ratio of 3-4 to 1 (Ritvo et al., 1989; Volkmar, Szatmari, & Nelson, 1993; Yeargin-Allsopp et al., 2003; Zahner & Pauls, 1987). However, affected females are more likely to have comorbid mental retardation in the sever range (IQ < 35) and exhibit more severe symptomatology than males with the disorder (Volkmar et al., 1993). Further, the recurrence risk rate for siblings of females with autism is twice that of siblings of males with autism (Jorde et al., 1990).

CULTURAL CONSIDERATIONS

Autism affects individuals, regardless of socioeconomic level (Fombonne, 1999, 2003; Steffenburg & Gillberg, 1986). Cases of autism are also reported throughout the world including eastern and western Europe (Bujas-Petkovic, 1993; Fombonne et al., 1997) and Asia (Honda et al., 1996).

PROTECTIVE FACTORS

Early interventions targeting the domains of social orienting, joint attention, imitation, and other aspects of language and communication are becoming increasingly available. Early intensive behavioral intervention initiated during the preschool period and sustained for 2 to 4 years has shown a significant impact on outcome in a large subset of children with autism, including significant gains in IQ, language, and educational placement (Faja & Dawson, 2006, for review). Common factors of early interventions include (a) a comprehensive curriculum focusing on imitation, language, toy play, and social interaction; (b) sensitivity to development; (c) supportive teaching strategies; (d) behavioral strategies for reducing interfering behaviors; (e) involvement of parents; (f) gradual transition to more naturalistic environments; (g) highly-trained staff; (h) supervisory and review mechanisms; (i) intensive delivery of treatment (25 hours / week for at least 2 years); and (j) initiation by age 2 to 4 years (Dawson & Osterling, 1997; Green, Brennan, & Fein, 2002: Rogers, 1998; National Research Council, 2001). When these features are present, results are impressive for up to 50% of children.

Recently, intervention approaches targeting toddlers with autism have been developed (Chandler et al., 2002; Drew et al., 2002; Green et al., 2002; Mahoney & Perales, 2003; McGee, Morrier, & Daly, 1999); however, with the exception of Drew et al. (2002), randomized studies of these interventions have not been published. Dawson and Rogers have been investigating the efficacy of the Early Start Denver Model (Smith, Rogers, & Dawson, in press), which is designed to address the unique needs of toddlers with ASD as young as 12 months. We predict that effects of early intervention will be partially mediated by the quality of parent–child interaction. Parent–child interaction is viewed as a *final common pathway* that is influenced both by improvements in parental sensitivity and child behavior.

We hope to demonstrate that very early intervention results not only in significant improvements in behavioral outcome, but also in changes in neural responses to social and linguistic stimuli, as assessed by ERPs to social and linguistic stimuli.

THEORETICAL SYNTHESIS

As previously described, early deviations from normal brain development result in a failure of normal social and communicative development in autism that is apparent early in life. Impairments in social orienting, joint attention, response to emotions, imitation, and face processing are evident by toddlerhood. To help explain this wide range of impairments, all of which involve reduced attention to social input, Dawson and others have proposed the social motivation hypothesis. According to this hypothesis, some of the social impairments evident in autism, such as impairments in face processing, are not fundamental, but rather are secondary to a primary impairment in social motivation or affective tagging of socially relevant stimuli (Dawson et al., 2005; Dawson, Carver et al., 2002; Grelotti, Gauthier, & Schultz, 2002; Waterhouse, Fein, & Modahl, 1996). Evidence of impaired social motivation in young children with autism includes less smiling when looking at their mothers during social interaction (Dawson et al., 1990), less expression of positive emotion during joint attention episodes (Kasari et al., 1990), and failure to show normal preferences for social-linguistic stimuli (Klin, 1991, 1992; Kuhl et al., 2004). There is some evidence that social motivation has a genetic basis in autism, based on data derived from the Broader Phenotype Autism Symptom Scale (BPASS), which was administered to both affected children and family members (Sung et al., 2005). The social motivation trait on the BPASS reflects the degree to which an individual enjoys spending time with others, prefers spending time with people, and feels comfortable in social situations. Sung et al. (2005) found evidence that this trait was heritable in multiplex autism families.

According to the social motivation hypothesis, reduced social motivation results in less time attending to social stimuli, such as faces, the human voice, hand gestures, and so on. Dawson and colleagues hypothesize that social motivation impairments in autism are related to a difficulty in forming representations of the reward value of social stimuli (Dawson, Carver, et al., 2002). One of the primary neural systems involved in processing reward information is the dopamine system (Schultz, 1998; see also Beauchaine & Neuhaus, this volume). Dopaminergic projections to the striatum and frontal cortex, particularly the orbitofrontal cortex, are critical in mediating the effects of reward on approach behavior (Gingrich et al., 2000). Formation of representations of reward value in the orbitofrontal cortex is dependent on input from basolateral amygdala in the medial temporal lobe (Schoenbaum et al., 2003). The dopamine system is activated in response to social rewards, including eye contact (Kampe et al., 2001). In young children with autism, severity of joint attention impairment is strongly correlated with performance on neurocognitive tasks that tap the medial temporal lobe–orbitofrontal circuit (Dawson, Munson et al., 2002). Early dysfunction of the dopamine system, especially in social contexts, may account for the social motivation impairments found in ASD.

OXYTOCIN AND ITS RELATION TO THE DOPAMINE REWARD SYSTEM

Waterhouse et al. (1996) hypothesized that impaired functioning of the oxytocin system flattens social bonding and affiliation in autism. Oxytocin and another peptice, vasopressin, modulate the dopamine reward circuit in social contexts (Pedersen et al., 1994). Several animal studies have shown that vasopressin and oxytocin play important roles in facilitating *social memory*, which has a distinct neural basis from other forms of memory (Ferguson et al., 2000; Ferguson, Young, & Insel, 2002; Nishimori et al., 1996). Both oxytocin and vasopressin appear to facilitate a range of social behaviors, including social affiliation (Witt, Winslow, & Insel, 1992), maternal behavior (Pedersen et al., 1994), and social attachment (Insel & Hulihan, 1995; Winslow et al., 1993). The elegant work of Insel and colleagues allows further speculation regarding the potential genetic basis for impairments in social motivation (see Insel & Fernald, 2004, for a full discussion). Modahl et al. (1998) found that plasma concentration of oxytocin is reduced among children with autism. Kim et al. (2002) found nominally significant transmission disequilibrium between an AVPR1A microsatellite and autism. AVPR1A is a V_{1a} receptor in the brain that mediates action of vasopressin. An association of the oxytocin receptor gene (OXTR) and autism has also been identified (Jacob et al., 2007; Wu et al., 2005). Moreover, intravenous oxytocin administration can reduce repetitive behavior (Hollander et al., 2003) and increase comprehension of affective meaning (Hollander et al., 2007) in individuals with ASD.

EMERGENCE OF SOCIAL BRAIN CIRCUITRY IN THE FIRST YEAR OF LIFE

Dawson and colleagues (2005) proposed a developmental model for the normal emergence of social brain circuitry during early infancy, stressing the key role of the reward system in the development of social brain circuitry. In the model, drawing upon the work of Insel and colleagues, modulation of the dopamine reward circuit by oxytocin is important for shaping the infant's early preference for social stimuli and attention to such stimuli. In normal development, neonates are especially attracted to people, particularly the sounds, movements, and features of the human face (Maurer & Salapatek, 1976; Morton & Johnson, 1991). As early as 6 months of age, typically developing infants match the direction of their mother's head turn to a visible target (Morales, Mundy, & Rojas, 1998), and, by 7 months of age, spontaneously and intentionally orient to naturally occurring social stimuli in the environment. We hypothesize that this occurs, in part, because the infant anticipates pleasure (reward) to be associated with such stimuli (Dawson, Carver et al., 2002), which involves activation of the reward circuit, including prefrontal regions that are involved in forming reward representations (e.g., orbital prefrontal cortex). With increasing experience with faces and voices, which occurs in the context of social interactions, cortical specialization for faces, speech, and other types of social stimuli occurs, involving the fine tuning of perceptual systems. Furthermore, brain regions specialized for the processing of social stimuli (e.g., fusiform gyrus) become increasingly integrated with those involved in reward (e.g., amygdala), as well as regions involved in actions and attention (cerebellum, prefrontal/cingulate cortex). As a result, more complex social brain networks emerge to support more complex behaviors, such as joint attention, intentional communication, and delayed imitation.

IMPLICATIONS FOR AUTISM

One of the earliest symptoms of ASD, lack of *social orienting*, may result in a failure to become an expert face and language processor (Dawson et al., 2005; Grelotti et al., 2002). Because experience drives cortical specialization (Nelson, 2001), reduced attention to people, including their faces, gestures, and speech, may result in a failure of specialization of regions that typically mediate social cognition, and would be reflected in decreased cortical specialization and abnormal brain circuitry for social cognition, resulting in slower information-processing speed (e.g., prolonged latency in electrical brain responses to face stimuli). The abnormal trajectory for brain development in autism is not caused by a simple lack of exposure to social information. Infants with autism, like typically developing infants, are held, talked to, and fed by their parents during face-to-face interactions. However, if the infant with autism finds such interactions less inherently interesting or rewarding, then he or she might not actively attend to faces and voices or perceive social information within a larger social/affective context. Recent research with typical infants suggests that simple exposure to language does not necessarily facilitate the development of brain circuitry specialized for language (Kuhl, Tsao, & Liu, 2003; Kuhl, 2007). Instead, language needs to be experienced by the infant within a social interactive context in order for specialized speech perception to develop. In the case of autism, because the child is not actively attending to the facial and speech stimulation with the social context, his or her early exposure to speech and faces might not facilitate face and speech perception. This prediction is supported by data from 3- to 4-year-old children with autism, who exhibited dramatically different listening preferences from those of typically developing children (Kuhl et al., 2004). Children with autism preferred listening to mechanical-sounding auditory signals (signals acoustically matched to speech and referred to as *sine-wave analogs*) rather than speech (motherese). Preference for mechanical sounds correlated with lower language ability, more severe autism symptoms, and abnormal ERPs to speech sounds, whereas children with autism who preferred motherese were more likely to show differential ERPs to contrasting phonemes. We hypothesize that a failure to affectively tag social stimuli as relevant, and the resultant failure to attend to such stimuli, impedes cortical specialization for face and language brain regions. More complex behaviors requiring integration of social stimuli with volitional movements and attention (e.g., disengagement of attention, joint attention) fail to emerge.

FUTURE DIRECTIONS

Advances in the fields of cognitive and affective developmental neuroscience, developmental psychopathology, neurobiology, and genetics hold promise for discovering the causes of autism and for formulating effective prevention and treatment approaches. At the same time, communication across scientific domains and integration of different types of information at multiple levels of analysis pose new and difficult conceptual and methodological challenges for scientists studying ASD.

A goal of future research will be to clarify the extent of brain and behavioral plasticity as well as the interaction between genetic and environmental vulnerabilities in contributing to risk processes for ASD. Evidence of brain and behavioral plasticity resulting from environmental manipulation with animals, including animal models of genetic, developmental, and degenerative disorders provides an illustration of the future direction of research (see Lewis, 2004, and Nithiananentharajah & Hannan, 2006, for excellent reviews of the enrichment literature). For example, modulation of the genetic expression of neurotransmitter pathways, differential transcription of neurotransmitter-related target genes, and increased neurotrophic factors have been shown to result from environmental enrichment (Pham et al., 2002; Rampon et al., 2000). Evidence of environmental enrichment in two strains of mice that differed in novelty and reward-seeking behavior was found, with enrichment producing increased incentive-seeking in both lines (e.g., Fernandez-Teruel et al., 2002). Finally, maternal nursing and grooming behavior by rats early in development can produce changes in behavioral and hypothalamic-pituitary-adrenal (HPA) stress response that last into adulthood (Liu et al., 1997; Caldji et al., 1998). Interestingly, recent work suggests the mechanism for this change is epigenetic, with maternal behavior directly influencing DNA methylation and chromatin structure (Weaver et al., 2004). Of interest to autism researchers and clinicians are the effects of enrichment on attenuating or reversal of symptoms in animal models where there is an initial vulnerability due to neural insult or deprivation. As a result of standard housing conditions during a critical period, deer mice develop restricted, repetitive motor behaviors, which may parallel those observed in individuals with ASDs. Mice that are exposed to enriched rather than standard environments early in their development do not develop motor stereotypies, but mice exposed later in development do (e.g., Powell et al., 2000; Turner, Lewis, & King, 2003). Finally, enrichment reversed most behaviors associated with a rat model of autism, including the frequency of social behavior and latency to social exploration, sensitivity to sensory input, and anxious behavior during learning tasks (Schneider, Turczak, & Przewlocki, 2006).

In conclusion, although the complexity of autism—both in terms of its etiology and its heterogeneity of symptom expression—pose significant challenges, research focused on identifying autism susceptibility indices, early identification, and early intervention offer real hope for the future. As early identification and intervention become increasingly effective, the new challenge will be translating these scientific findings into social policy. The considerable funding and effort required to implement large-scale early detection efforts and intensive behavioral intervention programs cause legislators and insurance companies pause. Cost-benefit analyses suggest, however, the choice is to pay a lot early or pay more later (Jacobson, Mulick, & Green, 1998; Jacobson & Mulick, 2000). Burdening only families with the financial and emotional cost of helping individuals suffering from autism—or simply failing to provide access to interventions we know can substantially change the lives of individuals—is not a choice our society can ethically defend. Thus, research on strategies to translate scientific findings into meaningful and sustainable community-based efforts will be an increasing focus of the future.

REFERENCES

Adrien, J. L., Lenoir, P., Martineau, J., Perrot, A., Hameury, L., Larmande, C., et al. (1993). Blind ratings of early symptoms of autism based upon family home movies. *Journal of the American Academy of Child and Adolescent Psychiatry, 32*, 617–626.

American Psychiatric Association. (1994). *Diagnostic and statistical manual of mental disorders* (4th ed.). Washington DC.

Asperger, H. (1991). Autistic psychopathy in childhood. In U. Frith (Ed. and Trans.), *Autism and Asperger Syndrome* (pp. 37–92). New York: Cambridge University Press. (Original work published in 1944.)

August, G. J., Stewart, M. A., & Tsai, L. (1981). The incidence of cognitive disabilities in the siblings of autistic children. *British Journal of Psychiatry, 138*, 416–422.

Auranen, M., Vanhala, R., Varilo, T., Ayers, K., Kempas, E., Ylisaukko-oja, T., et al. (2002). A Genomewide screen for autism-spectrum disorders: Evidence for a major susceptibility locus on chromosome 3q25-27. *American Journal of Human Genetics, 71*, 777–790.

Avikainen, S., Wohlschlager, A., Liuhanen, S., Hanninen, R., & Hari, R. (2003). Impaired mirror-image imitation in Asperger and high-functioning autistic subjects. *Current Biology, 13*, 339–341.

Aylward, E. H., Minshew, N. J., Goldstein, G., Honeycutt, N. A., Augustine, A. M., Yates, K. O., et al. (1999). MRI volumes of amygdala and hippocampus in nonmentally retarded autistic adolescents and adults. *Neurology, 53*, 2145–2150.

Bacon, A. L., Fein, D., Morris, R., Waterhouse, L., & Allen, D. (1998). The responses of autistic children to the distress of others. *Journal of Autism and Developmental Disorders, 28*, 129–141.

Bailey A., Phillips W., & Rutter M. (1996). Autism: Towards an integration of clinical, genetic, neuropsychological, and neurobiological perspectives. *Journal of Child Psychology and Psychiatry, 37*, 89–126.

Bailey, A., Le Couteur, A., Gottesman, I., Bolton, P., Simonoff, E., Yuzda, E., et al. (1995). Autism as a strongly genetic disorder: Evidence from a British twin study. *Psychological Medicine, 25*, 63–77.

Bailey, A., Luthert, P., Dean, A., Harding, B, Janota, I., Montgomery, M., et al. (1998). A clinicopathological study of autism. *Brain, 121*, 889–905.

Baird, G., Charman, T., Baron-Cohen, S., Cox, A., Swettenham, J., Wheelwright, S., & Drew, A. (2000). A screening instrument for autism at 18 months of age: A 6-year follow-up study. *Journal of the American Academy of Child and Adolescent Psychiatry, 39*, 694–702.

Ball, L. K., Ball, R., & Pratt, R. D. (2001). An assessment of thimerosal use in childhood vaccines. *Pediatrics, 107*, 1147–1154.

Ballaban-Gil, K., & Tuchman, R. (2000). Epilepsy and epileptiform EEG: Association with autism and language disorders. *Mental Retardation and Developmental Disabilities Research Reviews, 6*, 300–308.

Baranek, G. T. (1999). Autism during infancy: A retrospective video analysis of sensory-motor and social behaviors at 9–12 months of age. *Journal of Autism and Developmental Disorders, 29*, 213–224.

Baron-Cohen, S., Ring, H. A., Bullmore, E. T., Wheelwright, S., Ashwin, C., & Williams, S. C. (2000). The amygdala theory of autism. *Neuroscience and Biobehavioural Reviews, 24*, 355–364.

Baron-Cohen, S., Scahill, V. L., Izaguirre, J., Hornsey, H., & Robertson, M. M. (1999). The prevalence of Gilles de le Tourette syndrome in children adolescents with autism: A large scale study. *Psychological Medicine, 29*, 1151–1159.

Barrett, S., Beck, J. C., Bernier, R., Bisson, E., Braun, T. A., Casavant, T. L., et al. (1999). An autosomal genomic screen for autism. *American Journal of Medical Genetics, 88*, 609–615.

Bartak, L., Rutter, M. L., & Cox, A. (1975). A comparative study of infantile autism and specific developmental language disorder. Vol. I: The children. *British Journal of Psychiatry, 126*, 127–145.

Belmonte, M. K., Cook, E. H., Anderson, G. M., Rubenstein, J. L. R., Greenough, W. R., Beckel-Mitchener, A., et al. (2004). Autism as a disorder of neural information processing: Directions for research and targets for therapy. *Molecular Psychiatry, 9*, 646–663.

Bernier, R., Dawson, G., Webb, S., & Murias, M. (2007). EEG Mu rhythm and imitation impairments in individuals with autism spectrum disorder. *Brain and Cognition, 64*, 228–237.

Bishop, D., North, T., & Donlan, C. (1996). Nonword repetition as a behavioral marker for inherited language impairment: Evidence from a twin study. *Journal of Child Psychology and Psychiatry, 36*, 1–13.

Bleuler, E. (1950). *Dementia Praecox or the Group of Schizophrenias.* (J. Zinkin, Trans.) New York: International Universities Press. (Original work published 1911.)

Bolton, P., MacDonald, H., Pickles, A., Rios, P., Goode, S., Crowson, M., et al. (1994). A case-control family history study of autism. *Journal of Child Psychology and Psychiatry, 35*, 877–900.

Bolton, P., Murphy, M., Macdonald, H., Whitlock, B., Pickles, A., & Rutter, M. (1997). Obstetric complications in autism: Consequences or causes of the condition? *Journal of the American Academy of Child and Adolescent Psychiatry, 36*, 272–281.

Boucher, J., & Lewis, V. (1992). Unfamiliar face recognition in relatively able autistic children. *Journal of Child Psychology and Psychiatry and Allied Disciplines, 33*, 843–859.

Boucher, J., Lewis, V., & Collis, G. (1998). Familiar face and voice matching and recognition in children with autism. *Journal of Child Psychology and Psychiatry, 39*, 171–181.

Bryson, S. E., Clark, B. S., & Smith, I. M. (1988). First report of a Canadian epidemiological study of autistic syndromes. *Journal of Child Psychology and Psychiatry, 29*, 433–445.

Bryson, S. E., Zwaigenbaum, L., Brian, J., Roberts, W., Szatmari, P., Rombough, V., et al. (2007). A prospective case series of high-risk infants who developed autism. *Journal of Autism and Developmental Disorders, 37*, 12–24.

Bujas-Petkovic, Z. (1993). The three-dimensional modeling ability of a boy with autism [Letter to the editor]. *Journal of Autism and Developmental Disorders, 23*, 569–571.

Buxbaum, J. D., Silverman, J. M., Smith, C. J., Kilifarski, M., Reichert, J., Hollander, E., et al. (2001). Evidence for a susceptibility gene for autism on chromosome 2 and for genetic heterogeneity. *American Journal of Human Genetics, 68,* 1514–1520.

Caldji, C., Tannenbaum, B., Sharma, S., Francis, D., Plotsky, P. M., & Meaney, M. J. (1998). Maternal care during infancy regulates the development of neural systems mediating the expression of fearfulness in the rat. *Proceedings of the National Academy of Sciences, 95,* 5335–5340.

Campbell, D. B., Sutcliffe, J. S., Ebert, P. J., Militerni, R., Bravaccio, C., Trillo, S., et al. (2006). A genetic variant that disrupts MET transcription is associated with autism. *Proceedings of the National Academy of Sciences, 103,* 16834–16839.

Cantor, R. M., Kono, N., Duvall, J. A., AlvarezRetuerto, A., Stone, J. L., Alarcon, M., et al. (2005). Replication of autism linkage: Fine-mapping peak at 17q21. *American Journal of Human Genetics, 76,* 1050–1056.

Carpenter, M., Nagell, K., & Tomasello, M. (1998). Social cognition, joint attention, and communicative competence from 9 to 15 months of age. *Monograph of the Society for Research in Child Development, 63,* 1–143.

Casanova, M. F. (2004). White matter volume increase and minicolumns in autism. *Annals of Neurology, 56,* 453.

Centers for Disease Control and Prevention. Prevalence of Autism Spectrum Disorders. Surveillance Summaries, February 9. MMWR 2007; 56 (No. SS-1).

Chakrabarti, S., & Fombonne, E. (2001). Pervasive developmental disorders in preschool children. *Journal of the American Medical Association, 285,* 3093–3099.

Chandler, S., Christie, P., Newson, E., & Prevezer, W. (2002). Developing a diagnostic and intervention package for 2- to 3-year-olds with autism: Outcomes of the frameworks for communication approach. *Autism, 6,* 47–69.

Charman, T., Baron-Cohen, S., Swettenham, J., Baird, G., Drew, A., & Cox, A. (2003). Predicting language outcome in infants with autism and pervasive developmental disorder. *International Journal of Language and Communication Disorders, 38,* 265–85.

Charman, T., Swettenham, J., Baron-Cohen, S., Cox, A., Baird, G., & Drew, A. (1998). An experimental investigation of social-cognitive abilities in infants with autism: Clinical implications. *Infant Mental Health Journal, 19,* 260–275.

Cheh, M. A., Millonig, J. H., Roselli, L. M., Ming, X., Jacobsen, E., Kamdar, S., et al. (2006). En2 knockout mice display neurobehavioral and neurochemical alterations relevant to autism spectrum disorder. *Brain Research, 1116,* 166–176.

Cicchetti, D., & Cohen, D. J. (1995). Perspectives on developmental psychopathology. In D. Cicchetti & D. J. Cohen (Eds.) *Developmental psychopathology. Vol. I: Theory and methods* (pp. 3–22). New York: Wiley.

Coonrod, E. E., & Stone, W. L. (2004). Early concerns of parents of children with autistic and nonautistic disorders. *Infants and Young Children, 17,* 258–268.

Courchesne, E. (1997). Brainstem, cerebellar and limbic neuroanatomical abnormalities in autism. *Current Opinion in Neurobiology 7,* 269–278.

Courchesne, E. (2004). Brain development in autism: Early overgrowth followed by premature arrest of growth. *Mental Retardation and Developmental Disabilities Research Reviews, 10,* 106–111.

Courchesne, E., & Pierce, K. (2005). Brain overgrowth in autism during a critical time in development: Implications for frontal pyramidal neuron and interneuron development and connectivity. *International Journal of Developmental Neuroscience, 23,* 153–170.

Courchesne, E., Karns, C., Davis, H. R., Ziccardi, R., Carper, R., Tigue, Z., et al. (2001). Unusual brain growth patterns in early life in patients with autistic disorder: An MRI study. *Neurology, 57,* 245–254.

Cryan, E., Byrne, M., O'Donovan, A., & O'Callaghan, E. (1996). Brief report: A case-control study of obstetric complications and later autistic disorder. *Journal of Autism and Developmental Disorders, 26,* 453–460.

Dahlgren, S. O., & Gillberg, C. (1989). Symptoms in the first two years of life. A preliminary population study of infantile autism. *European Archives of Psychiatry and Neurological Sciences, 238,* 169–174.

Dapretto, M., Davies, M. S., Pfeifer, J. F., Scot, A. A., Sigman, M., Bookheimer, S. Y., et al. (2006). Understanding emotions in others: Mirror neuron dysfunction in children with autism spectrum disorders. *Nature Neuroscience, 9,* 28–30.

Davidovitch, M., Glick, L., Holtzman, G., Tirosh, E., & Safir, M. P. (2000). Developmental regression in autism: Maternal perception. *Journal of Autism and Developmental Disorders, 30,* 113–119.

Dawson, G., & Osterling, J. (1997). Early intervention in autism: Effectiveness and common elements of current approaches. In M. Guralnick (Ed.), *The effectiveness of early intervention: Second generation research* (pp. 307–326), Baltimore: Brookes.

Dawson, G., & Adams, A. (1984). Imitation and social responsiveness in autistic children. *Journal of Abnormal Child Psychology, 12,* 209–25.

Dawson, G., & Lewy, A. (1989). Arousal, attention, and the socioemotional impairments of individuals with autism. In G. Dawson (Ed.), *Autism: Nature, diagnosis, and treatment* (pp. 49–74). New York: Guilford.

Dawson, G., Carver, L., Meltzoff, A. N., Panagiotides, H., McPartland, J., & Webb, S. J. (2002). Neural correlates of face and object recognition in young children with autism spectrum disorder, developmental delay, and typical development. *Child Development, 73,* 700–717.

Dawson, G., Hill, D., Galpert, L., Spencer, A., & Watson, L. (1990). Affective exchanges between young autistic children and their mothers. *Journal of Abnormal Child Psychology, 18,* 335–345.

Dawson, G., Meltzoff, A. N., Osterling, J., Rinaldi, J., & Brown, E. (1998). Children with autism fail to orient to naturally occurring social stimuli. *Journal of Autism and Developmental Disorders, 28,* 479–485.

Dawson, G., Munson, J., Estes, A., Osterling, J., McPartland, J., Toth, K., et al. (2002). Neurocognitive function and joint attention ability in young children with autism spectrum disorder versus developmental delay. *Child Development, 73,* 345–358.

Dawson, G., Munson, J., Webb, S. J., Nalty, T., Abbott, R., & Toth, K. (2007). Rate of head growth decelerates and symptoms worsen in the second year of life in autism. *Biological Psychiatry, 61,* 458–464.

Dawson, G., Toth, K., Abbott, R., Osterling, J., Munson, J., Estes, A. et al. (2004). Early social attention impairments in autism: Social orienting, joint attention, and attention to distress. *Developmental Psychology, 40,* 271–283.

Dawson, G., Webb, S. J., Wijsman, E., Schellenberg, G., Estes, A., Munson, J., et al.

(2005). Neurocognitive and electrophysiological evidence of altered face processing in parents of children with autism: Implications for a model of abnormal development of social brain circuitry in autism. *Development and Psychopathology, 17, 679–697.*

Dawson, G., Webb, S., Carver, L., Panagiotides, H., & McPartland, J. (2004). Young children with autism show atypical brain responses to fearful versus neutral facial expressions. *Developmental Science, 7, 340–359.*

De Giacomo, A., & Fombonne, E. (1998). Parental recognition of developmental abnormalities in autism. *European Journal of Child and Adolescent Psychiatry, 7,* 131–136.

de Haan, M., & Nelson, C. A. (1997). Recognition of the mother's face by 6-month-old infants: A neurobehavioral study. *Child Development, 68, 187–210.*

de Haan, M., & Nelson, C. A. (1999). Brain activity differentiates face and object processing in 6-month-old infants. *Developmental Psychology, 35, 1113–1121.*

de Haan, M., Nelson, C.A., Gunnar, M.R., & Tout, K.A. (1998). Hemispheric differences in brain activity related to the recognition of emotional expressions by 5-year-old children. *Developmental Neuropsychology, 14, 495–518.*

Devlin, B., Cook, E. H., Jr., Coon, H., Dawson, G., Grigorenko, E. L., McMahon, W., et al. (2005). Autism and the serotonin transporter: The long and short of it. *Molecular Psychiatry 10, 1110–1116.*

Dollaghan, C., & Campbell, T. (1998). Nonword repetition and child language impairment. *Journal of Speech, Language, and Hearing Research, 41, 1136–1146.*

Drew, A., Baird, G., Baron-Cohen, S., Cox, A., Slonims, V., Wheelwright, S., et al. (2002). A pilot randomized control trial of a parent training intervention for pre-school children with autism: Preliminary findings and methodological challenges. *European Child and Adolescent Psychiatry, 11, 266–272.*

Eckerman, C. O., Davis, C. C., & Didow, S. M. (1989). Toddlers' emerging ways of achieving social coordinations with a peer. *Child Development, 60, 440–453.*

Fagan, J. (1972). Infants' recognition memory for face. *Journal of Experimental Child Psychology, 14, 453–476.*

Faja, S. & Dawson, G. (2006). Early intervention for young children with autism. In J. Luby (Ed.), *Handbook of preschool mental health: Development, disorders and treatment.* New York: Guilford.

Falconer, D. S. (1981). *Introduction to quantitative genetics, 2nd edition.* New York: Longman.

Fatemi, S. H., & Halt, A. R. (2001). Altered levels of bcl2 and p53 proteins in parietal cortex reflect deranged apoptotic regulation in autism. *Synapse, 42,* 281–284.

Feinman, S. (1982). Social referencing in infancy. *Merrill-Palmer Quarterly, 28,* 445–470.

Ferguson, J., Young, H., & Insel, T. R. (2002). The neuroendocrine basis of social recognition. *Frontiers in Neuroendocrinology, 23, 200–224.*

Ferguson, J., Young, H., Hearn, E., Insel, T. R., & Winslow, J. (2000). Social amnesia in mice lacking the oxytocin gene. *Nature Genetics, 25, 284–288.*

Fernandez-Teruel, A., Driscoll, P., Gil, L., Aguilar, R., Tobena, A., & Escorihuela, R. M. (2002). Enduring effects of environmental enrichment on novelty seeking, saccharin and ethanol intake in two rat lines (RHA/Verh and RLA/Verh) differing in incentive-seeking behavior. *Pharmacology, Biochemistry, and Behavior, 73,* 225–231.

Folstein, S., & Rutter, M. (1977a). Genetic influences and infantile autism. *Nature, 265,* 726–728.

Folstein, S., & Rutter, M. (1977b). Infantile autism: A genetic study of 21 twin pairs. *Journal of Child Psychology and Psychiatry, 18,* 297–321.

Fombonne, E. (1999). The epidemiology of autism: A review. *Psychological Medicine, 29,* 769–786.

Fombonne, E. (2003). Epidemiology of pervasive developmental disorders. *Trends in Evidence-Based Neuropsychiatry, 5*(1), 29–36.

Fombonne, E., Bolton, P., Prior, J., Jordan, H., & Rutter, M. (1997). A family study of autism: Cognitive patterns and levels in parents and siblings. *Journal of Child Psychology and Psychiatry and Allied Disciplines, 38,* 667–683.

Freeman, B. J., Ritvo, E. R., Mason-Brothers, A., Pingree C., Yokota, A., Jenson, W. R., et al. (1989). Psychometric assessment of first-degree relatives of 62 autistic probands in Utah. *American Journal of Psychiatry, 146,* 361–364.

Friedman, S. D., Shaw, D. W., Artru, A. A., Dawson, G., Petropoulos, H., & Dager, S. R. (2006). Gray and white matter brain chemistry in young children with autism. *Archives of General Psychiatry, 63,* 786–794.

Friedman, S. D., Shaw, D. W., Artru, A. A., Richards, T. L., Gardner, J., Dawson, G., et al. (2003). Regional brain chemical alterations in young children with autism spectrum disorder. *Neurology, 60,* 100–107.

Gathercole, S., & Baddeley, A. (1990). Phonological memory deficits in language disordered children: Is there a causal connection? *Journal of Memory and Language, 29,* 336–360.

Gepner, B., de Gelder, B., & de Schonen, S. (1996). Face processing in autistics: Evidence for a generalized deficit? *Child Neuropsychology, 2,* 123–139.

Gillberg, C., & de Souza, L. (2002). Head circumference in autism, Asperger syndrome, and ADHD: A comparative study. *Developmental Medicine and Child Neurology, 44,* 296–300.

Gillberg, C., & Gillberg, I.C. (1983). Infantile autism: A total population study of reduced optimality in the pre-, peri-, and neonatal period. *Journal of Autism and Developmental Disorders, 13,* 153–166.

Gillberg, C., & Steffenburg, S. (1987). Outcome and prognostic factors in infantile autism and similar conditions: A population-based study of 46 cases followed through puberty. *Journal of Autism and Developmental Disorders, 17,* 273–287.

Gingrich, B., Liu, Y., Cascio, C., Wang, Z., & Insel, T. R. (2000). Dopamine D2 receptors in the nucleus accumbens are important for social attachment in female prairie voles. *Behavioral Neuroscience, 114,* 173–183.

Goldberg, W. A., Osann, K., Filipek, P. A., Laulhere, T., Jarvis, K., Modahl, C., et al. (2003). Language and other regression: Assessment and timing. *Journal of Autism and Developmental Disorders, 33,* 607–616.

Goode, S., Rutter, M., & Howlin, P. (1994). *A twenty-year follow-up of children with autism.* Paper presented at the 13th biennial meeting of ISSBD. Amsterdam, The Netherlands.

Goren, C., Sarty, M., & Wu, P. (1975). Visual following and pattern discrimination of face-like stimuli by newborn infants. *Pediatrics, 56,* 544–549.

Green, G., Brennan, L. C., & Fein, D. (2002). Intensive behavioral treatment for a toddler at high risk for autism. *Behavior Modification, 26,* 69–102.

Grelotti, D., Gauthier, I., & Schultz, R. (2002). Social interest and the development of cortical face specialization; what autism teaches us about face processing. *Developmental Psychobiology, 40,* 213–225.

Hatfield, E., Cacioppo, J. T., & Rapson, R. L. (1994). *Emotional contagion.* Paris: Cambridge University Press.

Hertzig, M. E., Snow, M. E., & Sherman, T. (1989). Affect and cognition in autism. *Journal of the American Academy of Child and Adolescent Psychiatry, 28,* 195–199.

Hobson, P., Ouston, J., & Lee, A. (1988). Emotion recognition in autism: Coordinating faces and voices. *Psychological Medicine, 18,* 911–923.

Hobson, R. P., & Lee, A. (1999). Imitation and identification in autism. *Journal of Child Psychology and Psychiatry, 40,* 649–659.

Hollander, E., Bartz., J., Chaplin, W., Phillips, A., Sumner, J., Soorya, L., et al. (2007). Oxytocin increases retention of social cognition in autism. *Biological Psychiatry, 61,* 498–503.

Hollander, E., Novotny, S., Hanratty, M., Yaffe, R., DeCaria, C. M., Aronowitz, B. R., et al. (2003) Oxytocin infusion reduces repetitive behavior in adults with autistic and Asperger's disrorders. *Neuropsychopharmacology, 28,* 193–198.

Honda, W., Shimizu, Y., Misumi, K., Nimi, M., & Ohashi, Y. (1996). Cumulative incidence and prevalence of childhood autism in children in Japan. *British Journal of Psychiatry, 169,* 228–235.

Hoshino, Y., Kumashiro, H., Yashima, Y., Tachibana, R., Watanabe, M., & Furukawa, H. (1982). Early symptoms of autistic children and its diagnostic significance. *Folia Psychiatrica Neurologica Japan, 36,* 367–374.

Howlin, P., & Moore, A. (1997). Diagnosis of autism: A survey of over 1200 patients in the UK. *Autism, 1,* 135–162.

Insel, T. R., & Fernald, R. D. (2004). How the brain processes social information: Searching for the social brain. *Annual Review of Neuroscience, 27,* 697–722.

Insel, T. R., & Hulihan, T. J. (1995). A gender-specific mechanism for pair bonding: Oxytocin and partner preference formation in monogamous voles. *Behavioral Neuroscience, 109,* 782–789.

International Molecular Genetic Study of Autism Consortium. (1998). A full genome screen for autism with evidence for linkage to a region on chromosome 7q. International Molecular Genetic Study of Autism Consortium. *Human Molecular Genetics, 7,* 571–578.

International Molecular Genetic Study of Autism Consortium. (2001a). Further characterization of the autism susceptibility locus AUTS1 on chromosome 7q. *Human Molecular Genetics, 10,* 973–982.

International Molecular Genetic Study of Autism Consortium. (2001b). A genome wide screen for autism: Strong evidence for linkage to chromosomes 2q, 7q, and 16p. *American Journal of Human Genetics, 69,* 570–581.

Jacob, S., Brune, C. W. Carter, C.S., Leventhal, B.L., Lord, C., & Cook, E.H. (2007). Association of the oxytocin receptor gene (OXTR) in Caucasian children and adolescents with autism. *Neuroscience Letters, 417,* 6–9.

Jacobson, J. W., & Mulick, J. A. (2000). System and cost research issues in treatments for people with autistic disorders. *Journal of Autism and Developmental Disorders, 30,* 585–593.

Jacobson, J. W., Mulick, J. A., & Green, G. (1998). Cost-benefit estimates for early intensive behavioral intervention for young children with autism—general model and single state case. *Behavioral Interventions, 13,* 201–226.

Jamain, S., Quach, H., Betancur, C., Rastam, M., Colineaux, C., Gillberg, I. C., et al. (2003). Mutations of the X-linked genes encoding neuroligins NLGN3 and NLGN4 are associated with autism. *Nature Genetics, 34,* 27–29.

Jorde, L. B., Mason-Brothers, A., Waldmann, R., Ritvo, E. R., Freeman, B. J., Pingree, C., et al. (1990). The UCLA-University of Utah epidemiologic survey of autism: Genealogical analysis of familial aggregation. *American Journal of Medical Genetics, 36,* 85–88.

Joseph, R. M., & Tanaka, J. (2003). Holistic and part-based face recognition in children with autism. *Journal of Child Psychology and Psychiatry, 44,* 529–542.

Kampe, K., Frith, C., Dolan, R., & Frith, U. (2001). Attraction and gaze—the reward value of social stimuli. *Nature, 413,* 589.

Kanner, L. (1943). Autistic disturbances of affective contact. *Nervous Child, 2,* 217–250.

Kasari, C., Sigman, M., Mundy, P., & Yirmiya, N. (1990). Affective sharing in the context of joint attention interactions of normal, autistic, and mentally retarded children. *Journal of Autism & Developmental Disorders, 20,* 87–100.

Kemper, T. L., & Bauman, M. (1998). Neuropathology of infantile autism. *Journal of Neuropathology and Experimental Neurology, 57,* 645–652.

Kim, S. J., Young, L. J., Gonen, D., Veenstra-VanderWeele, J., Courchesne, R., Courchesne, E, et al. (2002). Transmission disequilibrium testing of arginine vasopressin receptor 1A (AVPR1A) polymorphisms in autism. *Molecular Psychiatry, 7,* 503–507.

Kimmel, S. R. (2002). Vaccine adverse events: Separating myth from reality. *American Family Physician, 66,* 2113–2120.

Kjelgaard, M. M., & Tager-Flusberg, H. (2001). An investigation of language impairment in autism: Implications for genetic subgroups. *Language and Cognitive Processes, 16,* 287–308.

Klin, A. (1991). Young autistic children's listening preferences in regard to speech: A possible characterization of the symptom of social withdrawal. *Journal of Autism and Developmental Disorder, 21,* 29–42.

Klin, A. (1992). Listening preferences in regard to speech in four children with developmental disabilities. *Journal of Child Psychology and Psychiatry, 33,* 763–769.

Klin, A., Jones, W., Schultz, R., Volkmar, F., & Cohen, D. (2002). Visual fixation patterns during viewing of naturalistic social situations as predictors of social competence in individuals with autism. *Archives of General Psychiatry, 59,* 809–816.

Klin, A., Sparrow, S. S., deBildt, A., Cicchetti, D. V., Cohen, D. J., & Volkmar, F. R. (1999). A normed study of face recognition in autism and related disorders. *Journal of Autism and Developmental Disorders, 29,* 499–508.

Kolvin, I. (1971a). Psychoses in childhood—A comparative study. In M. Rutter (Ed.), *Infantile autism: Concepts, characteristics and treatment.* Edinburgh: Churchill Livingstone.

Kolvin, I. (1971b). Studies in childhood psychoses: I. Diagnostic criteria and classification. *British Journal of Psychiatry, 118,* 381–384.

Kuehn, B.M. (2007). CDC: Autism spectrum disorders common. *Journal of the American Medical Association, 297,* 940.

Kugiumutzakis, G. (1999). Genesis and development of early infant mimesis to facial and vocal models. In J. N. G. Butterworth (Ed.), *Imitation in infancy* (pp. 36–59). New York: Cambridge University Press.

Kuhl, P. (2007). Is speech learning "gated" by the social brain? *Developmental Science, 10,* 110–120.

Kuhl, P. K., Coffey-Corina, S., Padden, D., & Dawson, G. (2004). Links between social and linguistic processing of speech in preschool children with autism: Behavioral and electrophysiological measures. *Developmental Science, 7,* 19–30.

Kuhl, P., Tsao, F., & Liu, H. (2003). Foreign-language experience in infancy: Effects of short-term exposure and social interaction on phonetic learning. *Proceeding of the National Academy of Sciences, 100,* 9096–9101.

Lainhart J. (1999). Psychiatric problems in individuals with autism, their parents and siblings. *International Review of Psychiatry, 11,* 278–298.

Lamb, J.A., Barnby, G., Bonora, E., Sykes, N., Bacchelli, E., Blasi, F., et al. (2005). Analysis of IMGSAC autism susceptibility loci: Evidence for sex limited and parent of origin specific effects. *Journal of Medical Genetics, 42,* 132–137.

Landa, R., & Garrett-Mayer, E. (2006). Development in infants with autism spectrum disorders: A prospective study. *Journal of Child Psychology and Psychiatry, 47,* 629–638.

Landa, R., Piven, J., Wzorek, M. M., Gayle, J. O., Chase, G. A., & Folstein, S. E. (1992). Social language use in parents of autistic individuals. *Psychological Medicine, 22,* 245–254.

Langdell, T. (1978). Recognition of faces: An approach to the study of autism. *Journal of Child Psychology and Psychiatry, 19,* 255–268.

Levy, S., Zoltak, B., & Saelens, T. (1988). A comparison of obstetrical records of autistic and nonautistic referrals for psychoeducational evaluations. *Journal of Autism and Developmental Disorders, 18,* 573–581.

Lewis, M. H. (2004). Environmental complexity and central nervous system development and function. *Mental Retardation and Developmental Disabilities Research Reviews, 10,* 91–95.

Liu, D., Diorio, J., Tannenbaum, B., Caldji, C., Francis, D., Freedman, A., et al. (1997). Maternal care, hippocampal glucocorticoid receptors, and hypothalamic-pituitary-adrenal responses to stress. *Science, 277,* 1659–1662.

Liu, J. J., Nyholt, D. R., Magnussen, P., Parano, E., Pavone, P., Geschwind, D., et al. (2001). A genomewide screen for autism susceptibility loci. *American Journal of Human Genetics, 69,* 327–340.

Lord, C., Mulloy, C., Wendelboe, M., & Schopler, E. (1991). Pre- and perinatal factors in high-functioning females and males with autism. *Journal of Autism and Developmental Disorders, 21,* 197–209.

Lord, C., Risi, S., DiLavore, P. S., Shulman, C., Thurm, A., & Pickles, A. (2006). Autism from two to nine years of age. *Archives of General Psychiatry, 63,* 694–701.

Lord, C., Shulman, C., & DiLavore, P. (2004). Regression and word loss in autistic spectrum disorders. *Journal of Child Psychology and Psychiatry, 45,* 936–955.

Loveland, K. A., Tunali-Kotoski, B., Pearson, D. A., Bresford, K. A., Ortegon, J., & Chen, C. (1994). Imitation and expression of facial affect in autism. *Development and Psychopathology, 6,* 433–444.

Lucki, I. (1998). The spectrum of behaviors influenced by serotonin. *Biological Psychiatry, 44,* 151–162.

Maestro, S., Muratori, F., Barbieri, F., Casella, C., Cattaneo, V., Cavallaro, M. C., et al. (2001). Early behavioral development in autistic children: The first two years of life through home movies. *Psychopathology, 34,* 147–152.

Maestro, S., Muratori, F., Cavallaro, M. C., Pei, F., Stern, D., Golse, B., et al. (2002). Attentional skills during the first 6 months of age in autism spectrum disorder. *Journal of the American Academy of Child and Adolescent Psychiatry, 41,* 1239–1245.

Mahoney, G., & Perales, F. (2003). Using relationship-focused intervention to enhance the social-emotional functioning of young children with autism spectrum disorders. *Topics in Early Childhood Special Education, 23,* 74–86.

Mandell, D. S., Listerud, J., Levy, S. E., & Pinto-Martin, J. A. (2002). Race differences in the age at diagnosis among Medicaid-eligible children with autism. *Journal of the American Academy of Child and Adolescent Psychiatry, 41,* 1447–1453.

Mars, A. E., Mauk, J. E., & Dowrick, P. W. (1998). Symptoms of pervasive developmental disorders ad observed in prediagnostic home videos of infants and toddlers. *Journal of Pediatrics, 132,* 500–504.

Maurer, D., & Salapatek, P. (1976). Developmental changes in the scanning of faces by young infants. *Child Development, 47,* 523–527.

McCauley, J. L., Li, C., Jiang, L., Olson, L. M., Crockett, G., Gainer, K., et al. (2005). Genome-wide and Ordered-Subset linkage analyses provide support for autism loci on 17q and 19p with evidence of phenotypic and interlocus genetic correlates. *BMC Medical Genetics, 6,* 1.

McGee, G. G., Morrier, M. J., & Daly, T. (1999). An incidental teaching approach to early intervention for toddlers with autism. *Journal of the Association for Persons with Severe Handicaps, 24,* 133–146.

Meltzoff, A. N., & Gopnick, A. (1993). The role of imitation in understanding persons and developing a theory of mind. In S. Baron-Cohen, H. Tager-Flusberg, & D. J. Cohen (Eds.), *Understanding other minds: Perspectives from autism* (pp. 335–366). Oxford, UK: Oxford University Press.

Millen, K. J., Wurst, W. W., Herrup, K., & Joyner, A. L. (1994). Abnormal embryonic cerebellar development and patterning of postnatal foliation in two mouse Engrailed-2 mutants. *Development, 120,* 695–706.

Miller, M. T., & Strömland, K. (1993). Thalidomide embryopathy: An insight into autism? *Teratology, 47,* 387–388.

Modahl, C., Green, L., Fein, D., Morris, M., Waterhouse, L., Feinstein, C., et al. (1998). Plasma oxytocin levels in autistic children. *Biological Psychiatry, 43,* 270–277.

Morales, M., Mundy, P., & Rojas, J. (1998). Brief report: Following the direction of gaze and language development in 6-month-olds. *Infant Behavior and Development, 21,* 373–377.

Morton, J., & Johnson, M. H. (1991). Conspec and conlern: A two-process theory of infant face recognition. *Psychological Review, 2,* 164–181.

Mullen, E. M. (1995). *Mullen scales of early learning.* Circle Pines, MN: American Guidance Service, Inc.

Mundy, P., & Neal, R. (2001). *Neural plasticity, joint attention and a transactional social-orienting model of autism.* (Vol. 23). San Diego, CA: Academic Press.

Mundy, P., Sigman, M., Ungerer, J., & Sherman, T. (1986). Defining the social deficits of autism: The contribution of nonverbal communication measure. *Journal of Child Psychology and Psychiatry, 27,* 657–669.

Munson, J., Dawson, G., Abbott, R., Faja, S., Webb, S. J., Friedman, S. D., et al. (2006). Amygdalar volume and behavioral development in autism. *Archives of General Psychiatry, 63,* 686–693.

Nadel, J., Guerini, C., Peze, A., & Rivet, C. (1999). The evolving nature of imitation as a format for communication. In J. N. G. Butterworth (Ed.), *Imitation in infancy* (pp. 209–234). New York: Cambridge University Press.

Narayan, S., Moyes, B., & Wolff, S. (1990). Family characteristics of autistic children: A further report. *Journal of Autism and Developmental Disorders, 20,* 557–559.

National Research Council (2001). *Educating children with autism.* National Research Council: Committee on Educational Interventions for Children with Autism. National Academy of Sciences. Washington, DC: National Academy Press.

Nelson, C. A. (2001). The development and neural bases of face recognition. *Infant and Child Development, 10,* 3–18.

Nelson, C. A., & De Haan, M. (1996). Neural correlates of infants' visual responsiveness to facial expressions of emotion. *Developmental Psychobiology, 29,* 577–595.

Nishimori, K., Young, L. J., Guo, Q., Wang, Z., Insel, T. R., & Matzuk, M. M. (1996). Oxytocin is required for nursing but is not essential for parturition or reproductive behavior. *Proceedings of the National Academy of Sciences, 93,* 11699–11704.

Nithianantharajah, J., & Hannan, A. J. (2006). Enriched environments, experience-dependent plasticity and disorders of the nervous system. *Nature Reviews Neuroscience, 7,* 697–709.

Ohta, M., Nagai, Y., Hara, H., & Sasaki, M. (1987). Parental perception of behavioral symptoms in Japanese autistic children. *Journal of Autism and Developmental Disorders, 17,* 549–563.

Osterling, J., & Dawson, G. (1994). Early recognition of children with autism: A study of first birthday home video tapes. *Journal of Autism and Developmental Disorders, 24,* 247–257.

Osterling, J. A., Dawson, G., & Munson, J. A. (2002). Early recognition of 1-year old infants with autism spectrum disorder versus mental retardation. *Development and Psychopathology, 14,* 239–251.

Ozonoff, S., Williams, B. J., & Landa, R. (2005). Parental report of the early development of children with regressive autism: The delays-plus-regression phenotype. *Autism, 9,* 461–486.

Pedersen, C. A., Caldwell, J. O., Walker, C., Ayers, G., & Mason, G. A. (1994). Oxytocin activates the postpartum onset of rat maternal behavior in the ventral tegmental and medial preoptic areas. *Behavioral Neuroscience, 108,* 1163–1171.

Pelphrey, K. A., Sasson, N. J., Reznick, J. S., Paul, G., Goldman, B. D., & Piven, J. (2002). Visual scanning of faces in autism. *Journal of Autism and Developmental Disorders, 32,* 249–261.

Pham, T. M., Winblad, B., Granholm, A., & Mohammed, A. H. (2002). Environmental influences on brain neurotrophins in rats. *Pharmacology, Biochemistry, and Behavior, 73,* 167–175.

Philippe, A., Martinez, M., Guilloudbataille, M., Gillberg, C., Rastam, M., Sponheim, E., et al. (1999). Genome-wide scan for autism susceptibility genes. *Human Molecular Genetics, 8,* 805–812.

Piaget, J. (1962). *Play, dreams and imitation in childhood.* (C. Gattegno & F. M. Hodgson, Trans.) New York: Norton.

Pickles, A., Bolton, P., Macdonald, H., Bailey, A., Le Couteur, A., Sim, C-H., et al. (1995). Latent-class analysis of recurrence risks for complex phenotypes with selection and measurement error: A twin and family history study of autism. *American Journal of Human Genetics, 57,* 717–726.

Piven, J., Gayle, J., Chase, G.A., Fink, B., Landa, R., Wzorek, M.M., et al. (1990). A family history study of neuropsychiatric disorders in the adult siblings of autistic individuals. *Journal of the American Academy of Children and Adolescent Psychiatry, 29,* 177–183.

Powell, S. B., Newman, H. A., McDonald, T. A., Bugenhagen, P., & Lewis, M. H. (2000). Development of spontaneous stereotyped behavior in deer mice: Effects of early and late exposure to a more complex environment. *Developmental Psychobiology, 37,* 100–108.

Rampon, C., Jiang, C. H., Dong, H., Tang, Y. P., Lockhart, D. J., Schultz, P. G., et al. (2000). Effects of environmental enrichment on gene expression in the brain. *Proceedings of the National Academy of Sciences, 97,* 12880–12884.

Redcay, E., & Courchesne, E. (2005). When is the brain enlarged in autism? A meta-analysis of all brain size reports. *Biological Psychiatry, 58,* 1–9.

Reznick, J. S., Baranek, G. T., Reavis, S., Watson, L. R., & Crais, E. R. (2007). A parent-report instrument for identifying one-year-olds at risk for an eventual diagnosis of autism: The first year inventory. *Journal of Autism and Developmental Disorders, 37,* 1691–1710.

Rheingold, H. L., Hay, D. F., & West, M. J. (1976). Sharing in the second year of life. *Child Development, 47,* 1148–1158.

Risch, N., Spiker, D., Lotspeich, L., Nouri, N., Hinds, D., Hallmayer, J., et al. (1999). A genomic screen of autism: Evidence for a multilocus etiology. *American Journal of Human Genetics, 65,* 493–507.

Ritvo, E. R., Freeman, B. J., Scheibel, A. B., Duong, T., Robinson, H., Guthrie, D., et al. (1986). Lower Purkinje cell counts in the cerebella of four autistic subjects: Initial findings of the UCLA–NSAC autopsy research report. *American Journal of Psychiatry, 143,* 862–866.

Ritvo, E., Jorde, L., Mason-Brothers, A., Freeman, B., Pingree, C., & Jones, M. (1989). The UCLA–University of Utah epidemiology survey of autism: Recurrence risk estimates and genetic counseling. *American Journal of Psychiatry, 146,* 1032–1036.

Ritvo, E. R., Freeman, B. J., Mason-Brothers, A., Mo, A., & Ritvo, A. M. (1985). Concordance for the syndrome of autism in 40 pairs of afflicted twins. *American Journal of Psychiatry, 142,* 74–77.

Robins, D. L., Fein, D., Barton, M. L., & Green, J. A. (2001). The modified checklist for autism in toddlers: An initial study investigating the early detection of autism and pervasive developmental disorders. *Journal of Autism and Developmental Disorders, 31,* 131–144.

Rochat, P. (1999). *Early social cognition: Understanding others in the first months of life.* Mahwah, NJ: Erlbaum.

Rochat, P., & Striano, T. (1999). Social cognitive development in the first year. In P. Rochat (Ed.), *Early social cognition* (pp. 3–34). Mahwah, NJ: Erlbaum.

Rogers, S. J. (1998). Neuropsychology of autism in young children and its implications for early intervention. *Mental Retardation and Developmental Disabilities Research Reviews, 4,* 104–112.

Rogers, S. J., Bennetto, L., McEvoy, R., & Pennington, B. F. (1996). Imitation and pantomime in high-functioning adolescents with autism spectrum disorders. *Child Development, 67,* 2060–2073.

Rogers, S. J., Hepburn, S. L., Stackhouse, T., & Wehner, E. (2003). Imitation performance in toddlers with autism and those with other developmental disorders. *Journal of Child Psychology and Psychiatry, 44,* 763–781.

Rogers, S., & Pennington, B. (1991). A theoretical approach to the deficits in infantile autism. *Developmental and Psychopathology, 3,* 137–162.

Rogers, S. J., Hall, T., Osaki, D., Reaven, J., & Herbison, J., (2000). The Denver model: A comprehensive, integrated educational approach to young children with autism and their families. In J.S. Handleman & S.L. Harris (Eds.), *Preschool education programs for children with autism* (2nd ed., pp. 95–133). Austin, TX: Pro-Ed.

Rolf, L. H., Haarmann, F. Y., Grotemeyer, K. H., & Kehrer, H. (1993). Serotonin and amino acid content in platelets of autistic children. *Acta Psychiatry Scandinavia, 87,* 312–316.

Rutter, M. (1970). Autistic children: Infancy to adulthood. *Seminars in Psychiatry, 2,* 435–450.

Rutter, M. (1984). Autistic children growing up. *Developmental Medicine and Child Neurology, 26,* 122–129.

Schellenberg, G., Dawson, G., Sung, Y. J., Estes, A., Munson, J., Rosenthal, E., et al. (2006). Evidence for multiple loci from a genome scan of autism kindred: A CPEA study. *Molecular Psychiatry, 11,* 1049–1060.

Schneider, T., Turczak, J., & Przewlocki, R. (2006). Environmental enrichment reverses behavioral alterations in rats prenatally exposed to valproic acid: Issues for a therapeutic approach in autism. *Neuropsychopharmacology, 31,* 36–46.

Schoenbaum, G., Setlow, B., Saddoris, M. P., & Gallagher, M. (2003). Encoding predicted outcome and acquired value in orbitofrontal cortex during cue sampling depends upon input from basolateral amygdala. *Neuron, 39,* 731–733.

Schultz, R. T. (2005). Developmental deficits in social perception in autism: The role of the amygdala and fusiform face area. *International Journal of Developmental Neuroscience, 23,* 125–141.

Schultz, W. (1998). Predictive reward signal of dopamine neurons. *Journal of Neurophysiology, 80,* 1–27.

Schumann, C. M., Hamstra, J., Goodlin-Jones, B. L., Lotspeich, L. J., Kwon, H., Buonocore, M. H., et al. (2004). The amygdala is enlarged in children but not adolescents with autism; the hippocampus is enlarged at all ages. *Journal of Neuroscience, 24,* 6392–6401.

Serra, M., Althaus, M., de Sonneville, L. M. J., Stant, A. D., Jackson, A. E., & Minderaa, R. B. (2003). Face recognition in children with a pervasive developmental disorder not otherwise specified. *Journal of Autism and Developmental Disorders, 33,* 303–317.

Shao, Y. J., Wolpert, C. M., Raiford, K. L., Menold, M. M., Donnelly, S. L., Ravan, S. A., et al. (2002). Genomic screen and follow-up analysis for autistic disorder. *American Journal of Medical Genetics, 114,* 99–105.

Sigman, M., & Capps, L. (1997). *Children with Autism: A developmental perspective.* Cambridge, MA: Harvard University Press.

Sigman, M., Dijamco, A., Gratier, M., & Rozga, A. (2004). Early detection of core deficits in autism. *Mental Retardation and Developmental Disabilities Research Reviews, 10,* 221–233.

Sigman, M., Kasari, C., Kwon, J., & Yirmiya, N. (1992). Responses to the negative emotions of others by autistic, mentally retarded, and normal children. *Child Development, 63,* 796–807.

Sigman, M., & Ungerer, J. (1984). Cognitive and language skills in autistic, mentally retarded, and normal children. *Developmental Psychology, 20,* 293–302.

Smalley, S. L., Asarnow, R. F., & Spence, A. (1988). Autism and genetics. *Archives of General Psychiatry, 45,* 953–961.

Smith, M., Rogers, S., & Dawson, G. (in press). The Early Start Denver Model: A comprehensive early intervention approach for toddlers with autism. In J. S. Handleman & S. L. Harris (Eds.), *Preschool education programs for children with autism,* (3rd ed.). Austin, TX: Pro Ed.

Sparks, B. F., Friedman, S. D., Shaw, D. W., Aylward, E. H., Echelard, D., Artru, A. A., et al. (2002). Brain structural abnormalities in young children with autism spectrum disorder. *Neurology, 59,* 184–192.

Steffenburg, S., & Gillberg, C. (1986). Autism and autistic-like conditions in Swedish rural and urban areas: A population study. *British Journal of Psychiatry, 149,* 81–87.

Steffenburg, S., Gillberg, C., Hellgren, L., Andersson, L., Gillberg, I., Jakobsson, G., et al. (1989). A twin study of autism in Denmark, Finland, Iceland, Norway, and Sweden. *Journal of Child Psychology and Psychiatry, 30,* 405–416.

Stone, J. L., Merriman, B., Cantor, R. M., Yonan, A. L., Gilliam, T. C., Geschwind, D. H., et al. (2004). Evidence for sex-specific risk alleles in autism spectrum disorder. *American Journal of Human Genetics, 75,* 1117–1123.

Stone, W. L., Ousley, O. Y., & Littleford, C. D. (1997). Motor imitation in young children with autism: What's the object? *Journal of Abnormal Child Psychology, 25,* 475–485.

Stone, W., Lemanek, K., Fishel, P., Fernandez, M., & Altemeier, W. (1990). Play and imitation skills in the diagnosis of autism in young children. *Pediatrics, 86,* 267–272.

Sullivan, M., Finelli, J., Marvin, A., Garrett-Mayer, E., Bauman, M., & Landa, R. (2007). Response to joint attention in toddlers at risk for autism spectrum disorder: A prospective study, *Journal of Autism and Developmental Disorders 37,* 37–48.

Sung, Y. J., Dawson, G., Munson, J., Estes, A., Schellenberg, G. D., & Wijsman, E. M. (2005). Genetic investigation of quantitative traits related to autism: Use of multivariate polygenic models with ascertainment adjustment. *American Journal of Human Genetics, 76,* 68–81.

Szatmari, P., Paterson, A. D., Zwaigenbaum, L., Roberts, W., Brian, J., Liu, X. Q., et al. (2007). Mapping autism risk loci using genetic linkage and chromosomal rearrangements. *Nature Genetics, 39,* 319–328.

Tager-Flusberg, H., & Cooper, J. (1999). Present and future possibilities for defining a phenotype for specific language impairment. *Journal of Speech, Language, and Hearing Research, 42,* 1001–1004.

Tantam, D., Monaghan, L., Nicholson, J., & Stirling, J. (1989). Autistic children's ability to interpret faces: A research note. *Journal of Child Psychology and Psychiatry, 30,* 623–630.

Tidmarsh, L., & Volkmar, F. R. (2003). Diagnosis and epidemiology of autism spectrum disorders. *Canadian Journal of Psychiatry, 48,* 517–525.

Trepagnier, C., Sebrechts, M. M., & Peterson, R. (2002). Atypical face gaze in autism. *Cyberpsychology and Behavior, 5,* 213–217.

Trevarthen, C., Kokkinaki, T., & Fiamenghi, G., Jr. (1999). What infants' imitations communicate: With mothers, with fathers, and with peers. In J. N. G. Butterworth (Ed.), *Imitation in infancy* (pp. 127–185). New York: Cambridge University Press.

Turner, C. A., Lewis, M. H., & King, M. A. (2003). Environmental enrichment: Effects on stereotyped behavior and dendritic morphology. *Developmental Psychobiology, 43,* 20–27.

Uzgiris, I. C. (1981). Two function of imitation during infancy. *International Journal of Behavioral Development, 4,* 1–12.

Uzgiris, I. C. (1999). Imitation as activity: Developmental aspects. In J. Nadel & G. Butterworth (Eds.), *Imitation in infancy* (pp. 186–206). New York: Cambridge University Press.

van der Geest, J., Kemner, C., Verbaten, M., & Van Engeland, H. (2002). Gaze behavior of children with pervasive developmental disorder toward human faces: A fixation time study. *Journal of Child Psychiatry and Psychology, 443,* 669–678.

Vargas, D. L., Nascimbene, C., Krishnan, C., Zimmerman, A. W., & Pardo, C. A. (2005). Neuroglial activation and neuroinflammation in the brain of patients with autism. *Annals of Neurology, 57,* 67–81.

Veenstra-VanderWeele, J., & Cook Jr., E. H. (2004). Molecular genetics of autism spectrum disorder. *Molecular Psychiatry 9,* 819–832.

Volkmar, F., & Nelson, I. (1990). Seizure disorders in autism. *Journal of the American Academy of Child and Adolescent Psychiatry, 29,* 127–129.

Volkmar, F. R., Szatmari, P., & Sparrow, S. S. (1993). Sex differences in pervasive developmental disorders. *Journal of Autism and Developmental Disorders, 23,* 579–591.

Walton, G. E., & Bower, T. G. (1993). Amodal representations of speech in infants. *Infant Behavior and Development, 16,* 233–243.

Wassink, T. H., Hazlett, H. C., Epping, E. A., Arndt, S., Dager, S. R., Schellenberg, G. D., et al. (2007). Cerebral cortical gray matter overgrowth and functional variation of the serotonin transporter gene in autism. *Archives of General Psychiatry, 64,* 709–717.

Waterhouse, L., Fein, D., & Modahl, C. (1996). Neurofunctional mechanisms in autism. *Psychological Review, 103,* 457–489.

Weaver, I. C. G., Cervoni, N., Champagne, F. A., D'Alessio, A. C., Sharma, S., Seck, J. R., et al. (2004). Epigenetic programming by maternal behavior. *Nature Neuroscience, 7,* 847–854.

Werner, E., & Dawson, G. (2005). Validation of the phenomenon of autistic regression using home videotapes. *Archives of General Psychiatry, 62,* 889–895.

Werner, E., Dawson, G., Osterling, J., & Dinno, N. (2000). Brief report: Recognition of autism spectrum disorder before one year of age: A retrospective study based on home videotapes. *Journal of Autism and Developmental Disorders, 30,* 157–62.

Wilson, K., Mills, E., Ross, C., McGowan, J., & Jadad, A. (2003). Association of autistic spectrum disorder and the measles, mumps, and rubella vaccine—A systematic review of current epidemiological evidence. *Archives of Pediatrics and Adolescent Medicine, 157,* 628–634.

Winslow, J., Hastings, N., Carter, C. S., Harbaugh, C. R., & Insel, T. R. (1993). A role for central vasopressin in pair bonding in monogamous prairie voles. *Nature, 365,* 545–548.

Witt, D. M., Winslow, J. T., & Insel, T. R. (1992). Enhanced social interactions in rats following chronic, centrally infused oxytocin. *Pharmacology, Biochemistry and Behavior, 43,* 855–861.

Wolff, S., Narayan, S., & Moyes, B. (1988). Personality characteristics of parents of autistic children: A controlled study. *Journal of Child Psychiatry, 29,* 143–153.

Wu, S., Jia, M., Ruan, Y., Liu, J., Guo, Y., Chuang, M., et al. (2005). Positive association of the oxytocin receptor gene (OXTR) with autism in the Chinese Han population. *Biological Psychiatry, 58,* 74–77.

Yeargin-Allsopp, M., Rice, C., Karapurkan, T., Doernberg, N., Boyle, C., & Murphy, C. (2003). Prevalence of autism in a U. S. metropolitan area. *Journal of the American Medical Association, 289,* 49–55.

Yonan, A. L., Alarcon, M., Cheng, R., Magnusson, P. K. E., Spence, S. J., Palmer, A. A., et al. (2003). A genomewide screen of 345 families for autism-susceptibility loci. *American Journal of Human Genetics, 73,* 886–897.

Young, R. L., Brewer, N., & Pattison, C. (2003). Parental identification of early behavioural abnormalities in children with autistic disorder. *Autism, 7,* 125–143.

Zahner, G.E.P., & Pauls, D.L. (1987). Epidemiological surveys of autism. In D. J. Cohen & A. Donnellan (Eds.), *Handbook of autism and persuasive disorders* (pp. 199–207).New York: Wiley.

Zahn-Waxler, C., & Radke-Yarrow, M. (1990). The origins of empathic concern. *Motivation and Emotion, 14,* 107–130.

Zwaigenbaum, L., Bryson, S., Rogers, T., Roberts, W., Brian, J., & Szatmari, P. (2005). *International Journal of Developmental Neuroscience, 23,* 143–152.

CHAPTER 20

Childhood Schizophrenia

ROBERT F. ASARNOW AND CLAUDIA L. KERNAN

HISTORICAL BACKGROUND AND TERMINOLOGICAL AND CONCEPTUAL ISSUES

Cases of childhood psychosis with no apparent brain disease have been reported for at least 200 years (Fish & Ritvo, 1979), antedating Kraepelin's seminal description of dementia praecox. Kraepelin (1919/1971) observed that dementia praecox could begin during childhood and estimated that 6.2% of cases had their onset prior to age 15. Bleuler (1911/1950), who reconceptualized dementia praecox and renamed it Schizophrenia, estimated that 4% of schizophrenic psychoses had their onset prior to age 15. Early child psychiatrists were aware that symptoms of Schizophrenia presented somewhat differently in children than in adults; the construct of childhood Schizophrenia emerged from attempts to diagnose and classify this broad range of disorders.

Indeed, in the 1930s childhood Schizophrenia referred to many different, profound impairments of early onset, paralleling the "numerous expansions and contractions of the concept of schizophrenia" (Kendler et al., 1993, p. 528) in adult psychiatry during the twentieth century. For decades, childhood Schizophrenia was never operationally defined: "Patients were usually defined in a gross way by either brief case descriptions or a list of major symptoms" (Fish & Ritvo, 1979, p. 249). The construct of childhood Schizophrenia included children who today would receive *DSM-IV* (American Psychiatric Association [APA], 2000) diagnoses of Autistic Disorder, Pervasive Developmental Disorder (PDD), Schizophrenia, or Disintegrative Psychosis. Furthermore, there were significant variations among clinicians in how the construct was used. For example, Potter's (1933) criteria included children who today would be diagnosed with a PDD, including autism. Interestingly, a 30-year follow-up (Bennett & Klein, 1966) revealed that the majority of Potter's cases met *DSM* criteria for Schizophrenia. In contrast, the British working party's (Creak, 1963) criteria for "schizophrenia syndrome of childhood" are quite similar to *DSM-IV* criteria for autism and PDD. To further muddy the waters, Kanner's (1949) descriptions of early infantile autism were similar to other descriptions of childhood Schizophrenia.

Bender (Bender & Grugett, 1956) used age of onset to differentiate between two groups of children with Schizophrenia. Children with onsets prior to age 2 were similar to children described by Kanner as having infantile autism. In contrast, children with later onsets had more neurotic, paranoid, and sociopathic symptoms, and tended to manifest Schizophrenia as adults (Fish & Ritvo, 1979). The *DSM-II* (APA, 1968) concept of childhood Schizophrenia was heavily influenced by Kanner and Bender.

Rutter's (1972) landmark work on the classification of psychiatric disorders and Kolvin's (1971) studies of psychotic children resulted in fundamental changes in the conceptualization and diagnosis of Schizophrenia in children. With these newer views, children with Schizophrenia had hallucinations, delusions, and formal thought disorder, whereas children with autism had none of these symptoms (Kolvin, 1971). Children with Autistic Disorder who were followed into adulthood did not have Schizophrenia symptoms (Rutter, 1967). Cogently summarizing, Rutter (1972) concluded the following:

> Childhood schizophrenia has tended to be used as a generic term to include an astonishingly heterogeneous mixture of disorders with little in common, other than their severity, chronicity, and occurrence in childhood. To add to the difficulty, the term has been employed in widely divergent ways by different psychiatrists . . . We must conclude that the term "childhood schizophrenia" has outlived its usefulness. (p. 315)

Thus, reflecting dissatisfaction with the problems with early constructs, in *DSM-III* (APA, 1980), *DSM-III-R* (APA, 1987), and *DSM-IV*, diagnostic criteria for Schizophrenia in children were identical to those used for adults, with minor allowances made for how specific symptoms may be manifested in childhood. The studies cited in this chapter use either *DSM-III*, *DSM-III-R*, or *DSM-IV* criteria to diagnose Schizophrenia in children.

DIAGNOSTIC ISSUES AND *DSM-IV* CRITERIA

The *DSM-IV* states that the essential symptoms of Schizophrenia are "delusions, hallucinations, disorganized speech, grossly disorganized or catatonic behavior, and negative symptoms" (APA, 1994, p. 285). Schizophrenia has been diagnosed reliably in children older than 7 years of age using *DSM-III* and *DSM III-R* criteria (Asarnow, Tompson, & Goldstein, 1994; Russell, Bott, & Sammons, 1989; Spencer & Campbell, 1994). The frequency of core psychotic symptoms in children diagnosed with Schizophrenia using *DSM-III-R* criteria is quite similar to the frequency observed in adults (Russell, 1994). In fact, auditory hallucinations ranged from a prevalence of 80 to 84% of the children investigated in three different studies; delusions were observed in 55 to 63% of the children (Russell, 1994). Note that transient psychotic illness can be misdiagnosed as Schizophrenia in children and adults. Most misdiagnosed children have reactive or brief psychotic episodes in the context of chronic affective or behavioral disorders (Stayer et al., 2004). In such cases, diagnoses of Schizophrenia should not be given.

When one applies *DSM-IV* criteria for Schizophrenia to children, their level of development must be taken into account. It is important to differentiate common childhood phenomena such as imaginary friends, magical thinking, and hypnagogic experiences from true delusions and hallucinations. Hallucinations and delusions in younger children are typically quite simple and unelaborated (Bettes & Walker, 1987; Watkins, Asarnow, & Tanguay, 1988). Children are less likely to experience psychotic symptoms as alien to their experience than adults are, possibly reflecting that (a) the onset of these symptoms is typically quite gradual in children (Russell, 1994) and (b) young children do not have a firm conception as to what normal experiences entail.

The most difficult symptom to diagnose reliably in children and adolescents is *disorganized speech* (Russell, 1994). In the *DSM-IV*, disorganized speech can be manifested as derailment, loose associations, tangentiality, incoherence, and word salad—terms that harken back to Bleuler's descriptions of schizophrenic thought. Applying these criteria to children and adolescents presents special challenges because the cognitive and linguistic processes underlying speech are developing during childhood, with substantial individual differences in the rate of development. For example, Caplan and associates found that both illogical thinking and loose associations are present in many healthy children younger than 7, meaning that overdiagnosing disorganized speech in children is a potential problem (Caplan, 1994a). Such issues may account for the variation in rates of formal thought disorder in children across studies (Asarnow & Karatekin, 1998). In short, without age-appropriate, operational criteria, the diagnosis of formal thought disorder may be unreliable in children.

Social communication has been studied by focusing on the discourse skills used when children organize their sentences during conversations (Caplan, 1994a). These are linguistic devices that enable the listener to follow who and what the speaker is referring to. Children with Schizophrenia speak less than healthy children and show poorer discourse skills than healthy controls. They are also less likely to show conversational repair, the methods used to self-correct during a conversation in order to clarify messages (Caplan, Guthrie, & Komo, 1996).

DIFFERENTIAL DIAGNOSTIC ISSUES

Symptoms of Schizophrenia can occur in other conditions. McClellan and Werry (1994) and Caplan (1994b) discuss guidelines for differentiating these other conditions from Schizophrenia. Making a differential diagnosis involving Schizophrenia in children requires ruling out the following psychiatric conditions: mood disorders, Schizoaffective Disorder, PDDs, communication disorders, Obsessive Compulsive Disorder, Posttraumatic Stress Disorder, dissociative disorders, and medical conditions such as seizure disorders (particularly those involving the temporal lobes), brain tumors, and substance abuse (e.g., PCP, amphetamines, cocaine).

A further differential diagnostic issue is distinguishing between Schizophrenia and a form of *DSM-IV* Psychotic Disorder, Not Otherwise Specified, called *Multidimensionally Impaired Disorder* (Gordon et al., 1994; Kumra et al., 1998). Children with the latter show poor affect regulation and problems with attention and impulse control. These children typically have an earlier age of onset of psychotic symptoms as well as behavioral and cognitive problems than do children meeting *DSM-IV* criteria for Schizophrenia. When such children were followed up 2 to 8 years after the index diagnosis, two broad patterns of outcome were observed. First, almost half developed a Mood Disorder (Bipolar Disorder, Major Depressive Disorder, or Schizoaffective Disorder). Second, in the remainder, psychotic symptoms remitted and disruptive behavior disorders developed. Thus, multidimensionally impaired disorder appears to capture children who do not have Schizophrenia (Jacobsen & Rapoport, 1998).

PREVALENCE

Schizophrenia with onset in childhood is relatively rare. Very large epidemiological studies are therefore required to give a precise estimate of the prevalence of childhood-onset Schizophrenia (COS), but the absence of such investigations has resulted in considerable uncertainty about its rate of occurence.

It is clear that Schizophrenia with onset prior to age 12 is an infrequent occurrence. The prevalence rate of such true COS cases is fewer than 1 in 10,000 (Burd & Kerbeshian, 1987). This figure contrasts with a prevalence rate of 5 to 7 per 1,000 in the general adult population. The prevalence of Schizophrenia increases dramatically once children reach age 13. These results were replicated in two additional samples of children receiving psychiatric treatment in Germany (Remschmidt et al., 1994).

DEVELOPMENTAL PROGRESSION AND PRODROMAL PHASE

The *prodromal phase* refers to a transitional period during which symptoms start emerging prior to the onset of frank psychosis. The period prior to the prodrome is commonly referred to as the *premorbid phase*. As discussed in the following, in COS the boundaries between the premorbid and prodromal phases are frequently unclear, largely because children with Schizophrenia show abnormalities early in their development.

The developmental precursors of COS have been described in a number of retrospective studies, which use archival data and interviews to characterize prepsychotic functioning and symptoms. Children with Schizophrenia are likely to have an insidious onset, with fewer than 5% having an acute onset. In a retrospective study (Remschmidt et al., 1994) of consecutive admissions to a child inpatient facility, children with Schizophrenia showed both positive and negative symptoms years before their first admission. Positive symptoms of Schizophrenia involve an excess of normal functions. They include key *DSM-IV* symptoms of Schizophrenia such as hallucinations and delusions. Negative symptoms involve a decrease in normal functions including social withdrawal and blunted affect. The premorbid peer relationships, school performance, and general adaptation of children with Schizophrenia are worse than those of children who subsequently developed a Depressive Disorder (Asarnow & Ben-Meir, 1988).

A number of independent studies have reported that in a substantial number of children who develop Schizophrenia, symptoms of PDDs are present prior to the emergence of Schizophrenia symptoms. The vast majority of children who subsequently develop Schizophrenia have early histories of speech and language problems (Jacobsen & Rapoport, 1998; Watkins et al., 1988). Histories of gross impairments in language acquisition prior to 30 months of age were found in 72% of children subsequently diagnosed with Schizophrenia. In addition, problems in early motor development were present prior to the onset of psychosis: 28% of the children were hypotonic and 72% had delayed motor milestones or poor coordination (Watkins et al., 1988).

The UCLA COS program (Watkins et al., 1988) identified two somewhat different developmental progressions prior to the first onset of psychotic symptoms. First, children with the most severe speech and language problems prior to 30 months of age often had other autistic or PDD-type symptoms, including a pervasive lack of responsiveness. Subsequently, at ages 6 to 9 years, flat or inappropriate affect, loosening of associations, or incoherence was observed in 71% of this group, but fewer than 10% had developed diagnostically significant hallucinations or delusions. Three years later, however, at ages 9 to 12, 71% had developed diagnostically significant hallucinations or delusions and had their first onset of schizophrenic psychosis.

A second group showed less severe speech and language problems during the first 30 months. They showed fewer psychotic-like symptoms than children with more severe speech and language problems from 6 to 9 years of age. During this age range 82% of this second group were socially impaired and also presented with excessive anxiety, constricted or inappropriate affect, magical thinking, suspiciousness, or hypersensitivity to criticism. They also tended to develop overt psychosis by age 9 to 12. In short, children with more severe speech and language problems had an earlier onset of psychotic symptoms than children with less severe speech and language problems. Yet over time, differences between the two groups decreased, as the frequency of hallucinations and delusions increased in both groups in the 9- to 12-year-old age range (Asarnow, Brown, & Strandburg, 1995).

The National Institute of Mental Health (NIMH) study of COS (Jacobsen & Rapoport, 1998) also observed premorbid histories of speech and language problems and PDD symptoms prior to the onset of Schizophrenia. They found that 60% of their sample met criteria for a developmental speech and/or language problem, while 34% had transient symptoms of PDD prior to the onset of schizophrenic psychosis (Alaghband-Rad et al., 1995). Does this contradict the current view that autism and Schizophrenia are separate disorders? Eight candidate genes for autism were examined in children with Schizophrenia (Sporn et al., 2004). None of these candidate genes were present in children with Schizophrenia with or without a history of PDD. Thus, PDD symptoms in COS children may not be related to autism. In addition, children with a history of PDD symptoms did not differ from children without a history of PDD in gray or white brain volumes at the index diagnosis.

Early histories of delayed acquisition of speech and language, poor motor functioning, and compromised visual/motor functioning have been observed in children who are at risk for Schizophrenia by virtue of having a biological parent with the disorder (Asarnow & Ben-Meir, 1988; Fish et al., 1992). Speech and language delays and poor motor functioning were also found in two British birth cohort studies (Done et al., 1994; Jones et al., 1994). Motor abnormalities may be associated with genetic liability for Schizophrenia because they are found in both medication-free patients and their unaffected first-degree relatives (Rapoport, Addington, & Frangou, 2005).

Clearly, early developmental precursors are present in the vast majority of children who develop Schizophrenia prior to late adolescence, as very few children with Schizophrenia have an acute onset of symptoms. In general, the earlier the onset of Schizophrenia, the earlier and more pronounced the presentation of such developmental precursors. Yet such precursors are not diagnostically specific, as they can also be found in the development histories of individuals with Bipolar Disorder and in children with speech and language disorders. The developmental precursors of COS are likely to reflect early manifestations of the disruptions of neural networks that are central to the pathophysiology of the disorder.

The prodromal phase is marked by a continuation of some of the same features present during middle childhood and the gradual emergence of positive and negative symptoms of Schizophrenia. Common prodromal features are poor peer relations/social isolation, decline in school functioning, inattention/difficulty concentrating, unusual perceptual experiences (illusions), unusual beliefs and thought process, and blunted and/or depressed affect. Typically, the transition from the prodromal phase to psychosis is relatively gradual. Across three studies the average time from onset of nonpsychotic symptoms to a diagnosis of Schizophrenia was from 3 to 5 years (Russell, 1994).

OUTCOME

The essential feature in Krapelin's concept of dementia praecox was the assertion that Schizophrenia is progressive, inevitably eventuating in poor outcomes. Across three follow-up and two retrospective case record studies, most children diagnosed with COS have Schizophrenia or Schizophrenia-spectrum disorders at follow-up, with longitudinal intervals ranging from 5 to 20 years after initial diagnosis. When outcome is defined as remission of Schizophrenia symptoms, the rates of remission range from 3% at an average follow-up of 5 years (Werry, McClellan, & Chard, 1991) to 33% at an average follow-up of 7 years (Asarnow & Tompson, 1999). At very long-term follow-up (about 42 years) only a third of the patients continue to suffer from ongoing psychotic symptoms (Eggers, 2002). This latter finding is consistent with reports on the diminution of psychotic symptoms after 60 years of age in patients with adult-onset of Schizophrenia (Harding et al., 1987).

Whereas symptoms of Schizophrenia tend to remit over time, lifetime diagnoses (reflecting the predominant symptom pattern over time) are stable. Only 4 out of 38 adults followed-up more than 42 years after they were diagnosed with Schizophrenia during later childhood and early adolescence had their diagnoses change at follow-up (Eggers, 2002). There does appear to be considerable variation in adaptive, social, and vocational functioning at follow-up. Twenty eight percent of children with Schizophrenia have relatively good psychosocial outcomes (Asarnow & Tompson, 1999). A 10-year follow-up of children and adolescents with Schizophrenia revealed that 20% had very good or good outcomes as defined by the global assessment of functioning (GAF), while 42% had very poor outcomes and gross impairment (Fleischhaker et al., 2005). A recent 42-year follow-up of consecutive admissions to a child and adolescent psychiatry service yielded similar results (Remschmidt et al., 2007). Children with Schizophrenia are unlikely to be living independently and are highly likely to be in long-term residential care at 15 years postindex diagnosis. They also have low educational attainments and relatively poor work histories (Hollis, 2000).

In general, the outcomes for children with Schizophrenia, particularly those with onset prior to 14 years of age, are generally worse than when onset is in adulthood (Remschmidt & Theisen, 2005). COS appears to be a severe variant of Schizophrenia, which because of early onset interferes with the acquisition of critical adaptive and social skills. Consistent with studies of adults with Schizophrenia, patients with poorer premorbid adjustment (Eggers, 2002; Fleischhaker et al., 2005; Werry & McClellan, 1992) and negative symptoms (McClellan et al., 1999) are the most likely to have poor outcomes.

Stress within the family environment is associated with more negative outcomes in adults with Schizophrenia (Kavanagh, 1992). Even though family factors might appear to have more potential to influence children than adults, there is scant data on the family environments of children with Schizophrenia. The extant data "do present a picture of stress and distress" (Asarnow & Tompson, 1999, p. 10).

Children with Schizophrenia show elevated rates of thought disorder during direct interactions, suggesting that these symptoms are expressed in the family environment (Tompson et al., 1997). Parents of children with Schizophrenia also show elevated levels of thought disorder during the same interaction tasks (Tompson et al., 1997), and elevated levels of communication deviance (Asarnow, Goldstein, & Ben-Meir, 1988), an index of problems establishing and maintaining a shared focus of attention. Distinguishing between the effect of parental behavior on the child with COS versus the effects of the child's behavior on the parents is problematic. Parents of children with Schizophrenia report high levels of burden and disruption (Asarnow & Horton, 1990). Yet it is unclear the extent to which parental thought disorder reflects parental reactions to a disturbed child, shared genetic vulnerability to Schizophrenia, or some other environmental factors (Asarnow, Tompson, & Goldstein, 2000). What is clear is that the family environments of children with Schizophrenia are different from those of children without psychiatric disorders. The functional significance of these differences in family environment have rarely been studied in COS.

In adults with Schizophrenia, returning to homes that are high in expressed emotion is associated with high relapse rates and poor outcomes (Kavanagh, 1992). In contrast to findings with adults there appear to be relatively low levels of parental expressed emotion in families of children with Schizophrenia (Asarnow, Tompson, Hamilton et al., 1994). Expressed emotion does not appear to predict outcome in COS. Clinical observation and the relatively scant literature suggest that family environment appears to have a different quality in COS than adult-onset Schizophrenia. The family environments of children with Schizophrenia are more similar to those of children with a chronic medical condition or a developmental disability than to those of children with a psychiatric disorder with an acute onset, such as depression (J. Asarnow, personal communication). This may reflect the early, insidious onset of the disorder.

SEX DIFFERENCES

There is an excess of boys compared to girls when onset of Schizophrenia is prior to 12 years of age. However, consistent with findings from adult samples (Hafner & Nowotny, 1995), the sex distribution is nearly equal when onset of Schizophrenia is after age 12 (Galdos, Van Os, & Murray, 1993; Werry et al., 1994).

COMORBIDITY

Children with severe psychiatric disorders frequently have comorbid conditions, and this is certainly the case with COS. Studies that have used semistructured diagnostic interviews have reported high rates of comorbidity. Russell et al. (1989) reported that 68% of children with Schizophrenia in the UCLA study met *DSM-III* criteria for another disorder. The most common comorbid diagnoses were Conduct Disorder/Oppositional Defiant Disorder (31%) and atypical depression or Dysthymic Disorder (37%). In children with Schizophrenia the boundaries between (a) negative symptoms such as flat affect and (b) depressive symptoms are often unclear. The high rate of depressive disorders, along with reports that a few cases presenting with Schizophrenia meet criteria for Bipolar Disorder or Schizoaffective Disorder at follow-up, highlights the limitations of cross-sectional diagnoses (Asarnow, Tompson, & McGrath, 2004).

As noted previously, symptoms of autism and PDD frequently occur during infancy and early childhood in children who develop Schizophrenia. However, the risk of Schizophrenia is not elevated in youth with clear Autistic Disorder (Burd & Kerbeshian, 1987; Volkmar & Cohen, 1991), and the observed co-occurrence of the two disorders does not exceed chance levels (Volkmar & Cohen, 1991). Furthermore, candidate genes for autism are not present in children with Schizophrenia and a history of PDD (Sporn et al., 2004), suggesting that PDD in these children may represent a phenocopy.

RISK FACTORS

GENETIC VULNERABILITY

Evidence suggests that genetic factors are strongly implicated in Schizophrenia (Kendler & Diehl, 1993). Every modern study that has used relatively narrow, operationalized criteria for Schizophrenia, personal interviews, made diagnoses of family members blind to proband diagnosis, and used a control group has found that the risk of Schizophrenia in first-degree relatives of patients with adult-onset of Schizophrenia is greater than in relatives of controls. There is also strong evidence for an aggregation of Schizotypal Personality Disorder and limited or mixed evidence for the aggregation of Paranoid, Schizoid, and Avoidant Personality Disorders in the first-degree relatives of patients with adult onset of Schizophrenia. (Kendler, 1997; Kendler & Diehl, 1993; Levinson & Mowry, 1991). In addition, twin and adoption studies suggest that genetic factors are important in the etiology of Schizophrenia (Kendler & Diehl, 1993). Across investigations, the average concordance rates for Schizophrenia are 55.8% among monozygotic twins and 13.5% among dizygotic twins, strongly suggesting heritability for this disorder. Still, that 45% of monozygotic twins who are discordant for Schizophrenia indicates that genes are predisposing factors, but not sufficient by themselves to cause Schizophrenia.

The UCLA Family Study (Asarnow et al., 2001) used modern family history methods to compare the aggregation of Schizophrenia and Schizophrenia-spectrum personality disorders in the first-degree relatives of COS, Attention-Deficit/Hyperactivity Disorder (ADHD), and community control probands. Table 20.1 presents the morbid risk (a statistic that adjusts for how much of the period of risk an individual has passed through) for Schizophrenia and Schizophrenia-spectrum disorders and three other personality disorders in the parents and siblings of the three proband groups. There was an increased lifetime morbid risk for Schizophrenia and Schizotypal Personality Disorder in parents of the COS group compared with parents of the ADHD and community control groups. The parents of COS probands diagnosed with Schizophrenia had an early age of first onset of Schizophrenia (20.8 years). Risk for Avoidant Personality Disorder was also increased in the parents of COS probands compared with parents of community controls. In sum, "the psychiatric disorders that do and do not aggregate in the parents of COS probands are remarkably similar to the disorders that do and do not aggregate in parents of adult onset schizophrenia probands in modern family studies" (Asarnow et al., 2001, p. 586). The relative risk (ratio of risk to relatives of COS and community control probands) of 17 for Schizophrenia in the parents of COS probands is considerably greater than the relative risk of 3 to 6 for Schizophrenia observed in parents in adult-onset Schizophrenia studies, suggesting that that COS is a more familial and possibly more genetic form of Schizophrenia than adult-onset Schizophrenia.

The NIMH Child Psychiatry Branch (Nicolson et al., 2003) replicated and extended these findings by comparing the rates of Schizophrenia-spectrum disorders in parents of probands with COS and adult-onset Schizophrenia and parents of community controls. Parents of COS probands had a significantly higher morbid risk of Schizophrenia-spectrum disorders (24.7%) than parents of probands with adult-onset Schizophrenia (11.4%). Both of these rates were higher than those of parents of community comparison probands (1.5%).

SPECIFIC GENES

Two approaches have been used to identify genes that contribute to susceptibility to Schizophrenia. The first approach, linkage studies, employs hundreds of DNA markers spread across the genome to study families containing individuals with Schizophrenia, in order to identify chromosomal regions containing Schizophrenia liability genes. Once chromosomal regions are identified, fine mapping positional cloning is used to identify genes contributing to susceptibility to Schizophrenia. This approach is entirely empirical, and consequently can yield novel findings. The next step after a putative susceptibility gene is identified is to determine the function of that gene and to elucidate how that function might be involved in the development of symptoms. Population genetic studies have suggested consistently that multiple genes of moderate to small effect contribute to susceptibility to Schizophrenia. In addition, it is likely that there is significant genetic heterogeneity. That is, somewhat different sets of susceptibility genes may be found in different groups of individuals with Schizophrenia.

In studies of adult-onset Schizophrenia, a number of potential susceptibility genes have been identified in multiple linkage studies, including dysbindin, neuregulin-1, DISC1, G72, and the alpha 7 nictotinic receptor subunit. A number of these genes have functions that might be related to certain disease mechanisms in Schizophrenia. One of the unanticipated results of linkage studies of Schizophrenia has been the discovery that almost half of the chromosomal locations linked to Schizophrenia are also linked to Bipolar Disorder. Thus, even though these conditions are separable, there may be some common genetic factors for these two disorders.

A second approach to identifying susceptibility genes for Schizophrenia is a candidate gene approach. Here, genes known to have effects in the pathways through which antipsychotic medications act are studied in patients with Schizophrenia and in family members. A number of genes, including COMT and GRM3, have been identified. In addition, a number of potential susceptibility genes, including GAD1, have been identified by their altered expression in postmortem studies of the brains of patients with Schizophrenia.

The NIMH COS project has used family-based association studies to demonstrate that three of the susceptibility genes identified in studies of adult-onset Schizophrenia are present in COS. Each gene had a specific pattern of correlation with aspects of the clinical phenotype (Rapoport et al., 2005). Polymorphisms in the G72 gene are associated with COS, and COS probands with the risk allele associated with Schizophrenia had a later age of onset and better premorbid adjustment than COS probands without the risk allele (Addington et al., 2004). Dysbindin is associated with COS, and COS probands with the risk allele have poorer premorbid functioning than COS probands without the risk allele. GAD1 was also associated with COS. GAD1 is believed to be involved in the cortical GABA system, which is thought to be altered in Schizophrenia. COS probands with the GAD1 risk allele had an increased rate of loss of frontal gray matter over time, assessed by magnetic resonance imaging (MRI; Addington et al., 2005).

CYTOGENETIC ABNORMALITIES

Cytogenetic, or chromosomal, abnormalities can provide information about potential chromosomal locations that are altered in diseases. Common examples are Down's syndrome and Fragile X. Multiple rare cytogenetic abnormalities have been found in the NIMH COS study. These include one case of Turner's syndrome and four cases of 22q11DS. The 5% rate of 22q11DS in the NIMH-COS study is considerably higher than the estimated rate of 0.36% in four studies that contained 1,100 adult-onset Schizophrenia patients and the rate of 0.025% in the community (Sporn et al., 2004). The 22q11DS deletion syndrome is associated with the Velocardialfacial Syndrome. 22q11DS is associated with an increased rate of cortical gray matter loss during childhood and adolescence in patients who are not yet psychotic (Sporn et al., 2004).

ENDOPHENOTYPES

Endophenotypes are features that lie intermediate to the phenotype and genotype of Schizophrenia (Gottesman & Shields, 1973). In adult-onset Schizophrenia, abnormalities in smooth-pursuit eye movements, neurocognitive functioning, brain structure, brain electrical activity, and autonomic activity show promise as endophenotypes. These abnormalities are probably closer to the biological effects of Schizophrenia genes than are the *DSM-IV* symptoms of Schizophrenia. In addition, these abnormalities exist as quantitative traits, thereby increasing power in linkage and association studies compared to investigations using *DSM-IV* diagnoses.

A number of endophenotypes identified in first-degree relatives of adults with Schizophrenia have also been identified in the first-degree relatives of children with Schizophrenia. The performance of parents of COS, ADHD, and community control probands was compared on three neurocognitive tasks: span of apprehension, degraded stimulus-CPT, and Trail Making Test, which have been shown in prior research to detect impairments in patients with adult-onset Schizophrenia and ADHD. Parents were excluded from the study if they had diagnoses of psychosis. Receiver Operator Characteristic curves show the effect on diagnostic accuracy of various cutoffs for defining neurocognitive abnormality. A combination of scores on the three neurocognitive tests identified 20% of mothers and fathers of COS probands compared to 0% of the mothers or fathers of community control probands. There was diagnostic specificity of neurocognitive impairment: 12% of the mothers of COS probands were identified by a combination of neurocognitive scores compared to 0% of mothers of ADHD children. A cutoff that identified 2% of the fathers of ADHD probands classified 17% of the fathers of COS probands. For fathers, a cutoff identifying 2.5% of ADHD fathers classified 16% of COS fathers. In all, endophenotypes related to neurocognitive impairments can produce a level of diagnostic accuracy that may aid in genetic linkage studies (Asarnow et al., 2002).

Nonpsychotic first-degree relatives of COS patients showed deficits on the Trail Making Test (Gochman et al., 2004) and smooth pursuit eye tracking (Sporn et al., 2005) in the NIMH COS study. In another recent investigation (Ross et al., 2005), COS patients showed impaired response inhibition and spatial accuracy on a delayed oculomotor response task. However, children who were not psychotic but had a first-degree relative with Schizophrenia did not show abnormalities on this task. In general, the adult relatives of patients with Schizophrenia show subtle impairments on some of the same tasks identified as potential endophenotypes in studies of adult-onset Schizophrenia.

CONCLUSIONS REGARDING GENETIC FINDINGS

The finding that putative susceptibility genes for adult-onset Schizophrenia are associated with COS provides support for the biological continuity of adult- and child-onset Schizophrenia (Rapoport et al., 2005). In contrast, there is little evidence that genes associated with autism are present in COS (Sporn et al., 2004). Identifying putative susceptibility genes for Schizophrenia is an important advance but constitutes just a first step in mapping the pathway from gene to the complex behavioral phenotype of Schizophrenia. There is relatively little known about the normal function of putative susceptibility genes for Schizophrenia or how they affect processes related to the development of Schizophrenia. Many of these genes may have multiple functions, which may vary by brain region and developmental stage. The most productive approach to mapping the pathways from gene to disease may entail elucidating pathways to endophenotypes that are more proximal to the effects of susceptibility genes than the clinical symptoms of Schizophrenia.

OBSTETRIC COMPLICATIONS

A meta-analysis of 16 case-control studies and two historical cohort studies found that risk (pooled odds ratio) for the development of Schizophrenia in adulthood was doubled in people with a history of obstetric complications (Geddes & Lawrie, 1995). Patients with Schizophrenia with a history of obstetric complications have an earlier age of onset than patients without a history of obstetric complications. The three types of obstetric complications associated with increased risk for Schizophrenia are (a) pregnancy complications (diabetes, bleeding, etc.); (b) abnormal fetal development (e.g., low birth weight); and; (c) delivery complications (e.g., asphyxia).

Two studies, the NIMH-COS and the Maudsley Early Onset Schizophrenia studies, did not find an increased rate of obstetric complications in COS probands (Rapoport et al., 2005), whereas a Japanese study (Matsumoto et al., 1999) found odds ratios of 6.25 for boys and 2.63 for girls. Obstetric complications do not appear to exert a strong, direct effect on the development of Schizophrenia. Moreover, histories of obstetric complications are found in children with a number of other neuropsychiatric conditions.

Obstetric complications probably constitute one environmental factor that interacts with susceptibility genes for Schizophrenia to set in motion a developmental progression eventuating in the disorder. An example of a gene–environment interaction is that fetal hypoxia is associated with reduced gray matter and increased cerebralspinal fluid in patients with Schizophrenia and their siblings, but has no effect on brain volumes in individuals at low genetic risk (Cannon et al., 1993). The complexity of gene–environment interactions on brain development is compounded by the fact that certain brain regions are more susceptible to environmental effects at different developmental periods (Rapoport et al., 2005; see also Perry, this volume).

PARENT AND FAMILY CHARACTERISTICS

Until relatively recently there was a great deal of interest in the role of parental personality characteristics (e.g., *schizophrenogenic mother*) and parent and family communication patterns (e.g., *double-bind communications*) in the etiology of Schizophrenia. This interest was stimulated initially by psychodynamic theories of personality and psychopathology. There has been scant empirical support for the role of these factors as primary etiological agents in Schizophrenia (Hartwell, 1996).

However, there is intriguing evidence (Tienari et al., 2004) that exposure to certain patterns of communication/family environments may interact with a genetic risk for Schizophrenia to further increase the risk for Schizophrenia-spectrum disorders. In a longitudinal study of children with high genetic liability to Shizophrenia (i.e., those with biological mothers with Schizophrenia) who were adopted at an early age, dysfunctional family rearing environments (based on global ratings) and adoptive parent communication patterns (*communication deviance*) interacted with genetic liability in predicting which adoptees developed a Schizophrenia-Spectrum Disorder (Wahlberg et al., 2004; Wynne et al., 2006). Those reared in adoptive families that provided a dysfunctional rearing environment where parents had high rates of communication deviance were significantly more likely at follow-up to have developed a Schizophrenia-Spectrum Disorder than adoptees reared in adoptive homes that provided more benign psychosocial environments (Wynne et al., 2006). Rearing environment and parental communication patterns in the adoptive homes of children with low genetic liability to Schizophrenia had no effect on the rates of Schizophrenia-spectrum disorders at follow-up.

INSIGHTS INTO PATHOPHYSIOLOGY

Important insights into the disease mechanisms that eventuate in Schizophrenia are provided by a detailed understanding of the brain abnormalities that are central biological features of this disorder. The following sections summarize what is known about brain structure and function in COS.

BRAIN STRUCTURE

Modern quantitative structural brain imaging methods have made it possible to identify brain abnormalities that are not evident by visual inspection of brain images. Quantitative MRI analysis permits the segmentation of the brain into three compartments: (a) gray matter, the somatodendritic tissue of neurons; (b) white matter, myelinated connecting fibers (axons); and (c) cerebrospinal fluid. Gray and white matter segmentation can help determine whether axonal or neuronal loss is primarily responsible for changes in brain volume and organization.

A meta-analysis (Wright et al., 2000) of 58 volumetric MRI studies found that, compared to controls, the mean cerebral volume of adults with Schizophrenia was smaller (98%) whereas the mean total ventricular volume of those with Schizophrenia was greater (126%). The brain regions with the lowest volumes in patients with Schizophrenia were the left amygdala (94%), right amygdala (94%), left hippocampus/amygdala (94%), right hippocampus/amygdala (95%), left parahippocampus (93%), right parahippocampus (95%), and left anterior superior temporal gyrus (93%). A recent meta-analysis of voxel-based morphometric studies found that the left superior temporal gyrus and the left medial temporal lobe were key regions of structural difference in patients with Schizophrenia compared to healthy controls (Honea et al., 2005). *Voxel-based morphometry* is a method for detecting group differences in the density or volume of brain matter.

In patients with COS there is a 9.2% reduction in total brain volume (Frazier et al., 1996), a somewhat greater reduction than is observed in patients with adult-onset Schizophrenia. In contrast to studies of adult-onset

Schizophrenia, four independent cross-sectional studies did not find evidence of hippocampal volume reduction in COS (Rapoport et al., 2005). One study (Taylor et al., 2005) found significant enlargement but another (Matsumoto et al., 2001) found a reduction of the right posterior superior temporal gyrus, an important language center in the brain. Similar to findings in adults, the right anterior cingulate gyrus was larger in COS patients than controls. Anterior cingulate gyrus volumes were relatively smaller in older COS patients than in younger COS patients (Marquardt et al., 2005). In general, COS patients show a greater reduction in brain volumes than adults with Schizophrenia.

Longitudinal data from the NIMH-COS study (Thompson et al., 2001) provide dramatic evidence of progressive changes in brain structure. Over a follow-up period of up to 5 years, healthy control children showed subtle losses of gray matter, at a rate 1 to 2% per year in the parietal lobes, with almost no detectable change in the rest of the brain. In contrast, COS patients showed a progressive loss of brain tissue starting from the back of the brain and spreading forward. There was a loss of up to 3 to 4% per year in some regions of the brain for these patients. Early deficits in parietal lobe regions that support language extended forward into the temporal lobes, sensorimotor and dorsolateral prefrontal cortices, and frontal eye fields. The trajectory of changes in brain structure in COS appears to represent an exaggeration of processes found in normal brain development (Rapoport et al., 2005). These findings highlight the importance of understanding changes in brain structure and function in a developmental context.

NEUROCOGNITION

Starting with Bleuler's seminal descriptions of associative disturbances in patients with Schizophrenia, there has been recognition that cognitive impairments are central deficits in Schizophrenia. Conceptual models and experimental methods from what are now called *cognitive psychology* and *behavioral neuroscience* have been used to elucidate the core cognitive impairments in adults with Schizophrenia. Early studies focused on higher-order cognitive processes such as attention and memory, with the goal of isolating specific stages of information processing and/or subprocesses impaired in Schizophrenia. More recent studies have focused on more elementary cognitive processes that assess more circumscribed neural networks. Inferences about the brain systems underlying impaired performance on cognitive tasks draw upon studies of patients with neurological disease and functional brain imaging studies of patients and controls performing cognitive tasks.

Recent meta-analyses confirm the centrality of cognitive impairments in

Schizophrenia. The presence of cognitive impairments is the most robust finding when Schizophrenia patients are compared to healthy controls. When compared to other neurobiological measures, the average effect sizes for common clinical tests of attention, memory, language, and reasoning are twice as large as for structural MRI and positron emission tomography (PET; Heinrichs, 2004). Although the majority of patients with Schizophrenia show impairments on cognitive tests, there is substantial heterogeneity in their performance. A meta-analysis of data on IQ, memory, language, executive function, and attention from 113 studies (4,365 patients and 3,429 controls) found a consistent trend for adult Schizophrenia patients to perform more poorly than healthy controls in five cognitive domains: IQ, memory, language, executive function, and attention (Fioravanti et al., 2005).

Attempts to isolate specific brain systems that are impaired in Schizophrenia by examining patterns of performance is complicated by the presence of a generalized cognitive impairment. Adults with Schizophrenia perform 1.0 to 1.5 standard deviations below healthy controls on most neurocognitive tests (Bilder et al., 2000). Attempts to identify a circumscribed, specific cognitive deficit must be conducted against this background of a pervasive generalized deficit. Investigators attempt to identify differential deficits (also referred to as *disassociations*) to identify specific cognitive deficits under these conditions. An important methodological issue is that apparent differential deficits observed in patients with Schizophrenia frequently reflect the relative psychometric discriminating power of tasks rather than true differences between cognitive abilities (Chapman & Chapman, 2001). Demonstrating a differential performance deficit requires proving that the control task (the one predicted not to produce deficits in patients) has adequate distributional properties (e.g., no attenuated range) and reliability, comparable to the task hypothesized to detect performance deficits in patients. In the many studies of cognitive functioning in Schizophrenia, relatively few have identified differential deficits not explainable psychometrically.

Like adults with Schizophrenia, COS patients show a generalized cognitive deficit. This is reflected in Full Scale IQ scores (around 85) about one standard deviation below that of healthy controls (Asarnow, Tanguay, Bott, & Freeman, 1987; Rhinewine et al., 2005). Longitudinal analyses reveal that there is an initial steep decline in IQ, from about 2 years prior to 2 years after onset of psychotic symptoms. As with adult-onset Schizophrenia, there does not appear to be a progressive generalized loss of cognitive functioning after this initial decline. This stability of general cognitive functioning in COS, for periods up to 13 years, is noteworthy given chronic illness and related long-term exposure to antipsychotic medications and the concomitant, progressive loss of cortical gray matter (Gochman et al., 2005).

As would be expected given the magnitude of the generalized deficit, COS patients perform poorly on a wide variety of cognitive tasks including tests of attention (Asarnow, Asamen, Granholm, & Sherman, 1994; Rhinewine et al., 2005; Thaden et al., 2006), serial visual search (Asarnow & Sherman, 1984; Karatekin & Asarnow, 1998a), visual and spatial working memory (Karatekin & Asarnow, 1998b), verbal learning and memory (Rhinewine et al., 2005), and executive functioning (R. F. Asarnow et al., 1994; Karatekin & Asarnow, 1999; Rhinewine et al., 2005). The challenge in cognitive studies of COS is not so much identifying tasks that differentiate patients from controls but rather in identifying underlying cognitive processes that can produce such a wide range of performance deficits.

Investigators manipulate both stimulus and processing demands of tasks to isolate the specific cognitive processes underlying impaired performance, providing a basis for making inferences about the brain systems underlying impaired cognition in COS. An example of this approach is a study by Karetekin and Asarnow (1998a), who found that COS patients could deploy their attention broadly, and engage in parallel visual search at the same rate as healthy controls, but had a slower search rate when they had to focus their attention and search displays serially. These results were interpreted as suggesting that patients with COS had difficulty with executive control of selective attention in the service of self-guided behavior.

PSYCHOPHYSIOLOGY

Psychophysiology is the study of how psychological activities produce physiological responses. Historically, most psychophysiologists focused on the physiological responses and organ systems innervated by the autonomic nervous system. More recently, psychophysiologists have focused on the central nervous system, exploring cortical brain potentials such as the many types of event-related potentials (ERPs) and functional neuroimaging (fMRI, PET, and MEG). ERPs use averaging techniques to measure the brain's electrical response recorded from the scalp to sensory stimuli and specific cognitive processing demands. Brain activity is reflected in either positive or negative waves (components) that are typically identified by reference to when the peaks occur relative to stimulus onset. Investigators have attempted to capitalize upon the superior temporal resolution of ERPs to identify the precise stage in cognitive processing where impairments first appear in Schizophrenia.

One of the earliest ERP differences between adult-onset patients and controls is in the P50 component, a positive wave that occurs about 50 milliseconds after stimulus onset in a sensory gating paradigm (*sensory gating* is the blunting of a physiological response to a stimulus by the presentation of another stimulus immediately beforehand). Patients with Schizophrenia show less reduction in P50 after a second stimulus, believed to reflect impaired sensory gating (Freedman & et al., 1983). Mismatch negativity is a negative wave that occurs about 200 milliseconds postonset of infrequent sounds presented within a sequence of repetitive sounds. Mismatch negativity is reduced in adult-onset patients with chronic Schizophrenia and appears to tap sensory memory. The P300 is a positive wave that occurs about 300 milliseconds poststimulus onset when a low probability event is detected and consciously processed. Patients with adult-onset Schizophrenia show reduced P300 amplitudes at midline sites and over the left, but not the right, temporal lobe.

The UCLA COS program (Asarnow et al., 1995; Strandburg et al., 1994) examined ERP components while participants performed tests (e.g., span of apprehension and continuous-performance test) that detect cognitive impairments in COS. A consistent finding was the absence of right-lateralized P1/N1 amplitude in COS patients. Healthy controls typically have larger visual P1/N1 components over the right hemisphere. The absence of this lateralization in COS patients could reflect either differences in the strategic utilization of processing capacity of the hemispheres or right hemisphere processing dysfunction. Across investigations, processing negativity was reduced in COS patients compared to healthy controls and children with ADHD. Processing negativity is a family of negative waves that occur within 400 milliseconds of stimulus onset and is thought to measure the degree to which attentional and perceptual resources are allocated to cognitive processing. Reduced processing negativities is the earliest component in which cognitive processing abnormalities were detected in COS. COS patients showed reduced P300 amplitude. Later components, such as P300, may be the "downstream product of the uncertainty in stimulus recognition created by previous discriminative difficulties, or may be additional neurocognitive deficits" (Asarnow et al., 1995, p. 77). Of note, P300 abnormalities are not specific to Schizophrenia, as they are observed in a number of other disorders.

NEURAL NETWORKS IN SCHIZOPHRENIA

The neuroanatomic and cognitive data in adult-onset Schizophrenia clearly implicate multiple cortical and subcortical structures as well as multiple cognitive processes. What is quite clear is that adult-onset Schizophrenia is *not* a condition where a focal brain lesion results in tightly circumscribed cognitive impairments. Rather, there is a consensus that at least two neural circuits are central to the pathophysiology of Schizophrenia. The first is a front-temporal circuit. As noted previously, the frontal and temporal lobes are the site of some of the greatest anatomic differences between patients with Schizophrenia and healthy controls. These brain regions support working and secondary memory and executive functions, which are both impaired in patients with Schizophrenia. Note that reductions in processing negativities may result from impairments in certain executive functions supported by the frontal lobes that are responsible for the maintenance of an attentional trace (Knight et al., 1981; Michie et al., 1990).

The second is a prefrontal cortical-striatal circuit. This network is implicated in Schizophrenia because it is the target of almost all antipsychotic medications. Antipsychotic drugs block dopamine receptors in the neorcortex and the striatum. The prefrontal cortex partially controls the dopamine reward system that reinforces contextually appropriate stimuli. Abnormalities in reward and motivation (which are key negative symptoms of Schizophrenia) may result when this circuit is compromised. There are a number of recent studies (e.g., Foerde et al., submitted) showing that discrete corticostriatal loops are dysfunctional in Schizophrenia.

COS patients show the same general pattern of neuroanatomic and cognitive findings as patients with adult-onset Schizophrenia. With the exception of the hippocampus, the volume reductions and degree of cognitive impairment appear to be greater in COS than adult-onset Schizophrenia patients.

THEORETICAL SYNTHESIS AND FUTURE DIRECTIONS

For the past 2 decades neurodevelopmental models have provided a useful framework to begin to understand the complex pathways from brain abnormalities to the symptoms of Schizophrenia. Neurodevelopmental models of Schizophrenia were stimulated by data suggesting that abnormalities in brain development start from very early in life, and typically antedate the first onset of psychotic symptoms by many years. An influential neurodevelopmental model by Weinberger (1987) posits that Schizophrenia is "a neurodevelopmental disorder in which a fixed brain lesion from early in life interacts with certain normal maturational events that occur much later" to trigger the onset of psychosis (p. 660). The neurodevelopmental processes that eventuate in Schizophrenia are a result of the interaction of genetic and environmental factors.

The results of the studies of COS previously reviewed in this chapter are broadly consistent with neurodevelopmental models of Schizophrenia. Total brain and gray matter volumes are reduced and ventricles are enlarged in COS (Rapoport et al., 2005). As with adult-onset Schizophrenia, these brain abnormalities are thought to reflect processes beginning during fetal development. Genetic liability to Schizophrenia is expressed behaviorally not only as Schizophrenia, but also in subtle neurocognitive impairments that occur in nonpsychotic relatives of patients and that may be reflected in early language problems. Retrospective studies indicate that COS patients manifest certain neurobehavioral impairments well in advance of the onset of psychotic symptoms. In infancy and early childhood, acquisition of expressive and receptive language is slow and gross motor functioning is impaired. Somewhat later there are impairments in fine motor coordination. These neurobehavioral impairments may be manifestations of the early brain lesions posited by neurodevelopmental models.

It is interesting to note that during middle childhood and adolescence expressive and linguistic language skills are among the least impaired functions in patients with COS. Apparently, early impairments in language functioning are developmental delays rather than static, fixed neuropsychological deficits. Children who develop COS are most likely to be delayed in acquiring skills during infancy and childhood that are at the cusp of development (Asarnow et al., 1995). This constellation of findings highlights the importance of viewing Schizophrenia as resulting from a dynamic developmental process in which the effects of subtle, early biological insults influence how the child responds to normal developmental transitions. The dramatic progressive changes in brain structure in COS previously described may be exaggerations of normal cortical development (Rapoport et al., 2005).

When the same *DSM* criteria that are used to diagnose Schizophrenia are applied to children and adolescents, there is overwhelming evidence of continuity of COS and adult-onset Schizophrenia. Children with Schizophrenia show the same familial aggregation of psychiatric disorders, structural brain abnormalities (with the exception of the temporal lobe), neurocognitive impairments, and psychophysiological abnormalities that are present in adult-onset cases. Although the data are quite limited, COS patients appear to respond to the antipsychotic medications used to treat adults with Schizophrenia (Asarnow & Karatekin, 1998), although they may be less tolerant of these agents (Baldessarini & Teicher, 1995).

The current data suggest that there is an increased familial aggregation of Schizophrenia and Schizophrenia-spectrum disorders, and a greater familial aggregation of neuroanatomical and neurocognitive abnormalities in COS than in adult-onset Schizophrenia. COS may represent a severe, more genetic, and biologically homogeneous form of Schizophrenia in which the biological substrate is more clearly discernable than in adult-onset Schizophrenia. This framework sets the stage for challenging questions. What causes a small number of children to develop Schizophrenia very early in life? What triggers the onset of psychotic symptoms: an exaggeration of normal developmental processes such as pruning, or the failure of protective processes that normally forestall the emergence of psychotic symptoms? Studying COS may provide invaluable insights into the complex neurodevelopmental pathways that eventuate in Schizophrenia.

REFERENCES

Addington, A. M., Gornick, M., Duckworth, J., Sporn, A., Gogtay, N., Bobb, A., et al. (2005). GAD1 (2q31.1), which encodes glutamic acid decarboxylase (GAD-sub-6-sub-7), is associated with childhood-onset schizophrenia and cortical gray matter volume loss. *Molecular Psychiatry, 10,* 581–588.

Addington, A. M., Gornick, M., Sporn, A. L., Gogtay, N., Greenstein, D., Lenane, M., et al. (2004). Polymorphisms in the 13q33.2 gene G72/G30 are associated with childhood-onset schizophrenia and psychosis not otherwise specified. *Biological Psychiatry, 55,* 976–980.

Alaghband-Rad, J., McKenna, K., Gordon, C. T., Albus, K. E., & et al. (1995). Childhood-onset schizophrenia: The severity of premorbid course. *Journal of the American Academy of Child & Adolescent Psychiatry, 34,* 1273–1283.

American Psychiatric Association. (1968). *Diagnostic and statistical manual of mental disorders* (2nd ed.). Washington, DC: American Psychiatric Association.

American Psychiatric Association. (1980). *Diagnostic and statistical manual of mental disorders* (3rd ed.). Washington, DC: American Psychiatric Association.

American Psychiatric Association. (1987). *Diagnostic and statistical manual of mental disorders* (3rd ed., revised). Washington, DC: American Psychiatric Association.

American Psychiatric Association. (1994). *Diagnostic and statistical manual of mental disorders* (4th ed.). Washington, DC: American Psychiatric Association.

American Psychiatric Association. (2000). *Diagnostic and statistical manual of mental disorders* (4th ed., text revision). Washington, D.C.: American Psychiatric Association.

Asarnow, J. R., & Ben-Meir, S. (1988). Children with schizophrenia spectrum and depressive disorders: A comparative study of premorbid adjustment, onset pattern and severity of impairment. *Journal of Child Psychology and Psychiatry, 29,* 477–488.

Asarnow, J. R., Goldstein, M. J., & Ben-Meir, S. (1988). Parental communication deviance in childhood onset schizophrenia spectrum and depressive disorders. *Journal of Child Psychology and Psychiatry, 29,* 825–838.

Asarnow, J. R., & Horton, A. A. (1990). Coping and stress in families of child psychiatric inpatients: Parents of children with depressive and schizophrenia spectrum disorders. *Child Psychiatry & Human Development, 21,* 145–157.

Asarnow, J. R., Tompson, M., Hamilton, E. B., Goldstein, M. J., et al. (1994). Family expressed emotion, childhood-onset depression, and childhood-onset schizophrenia spectrum disorders: Is expressed emotion a nonspecific correlate of child psychopathology or a specific risk factor for depression? *Journal of Abnormal Child Psychology, 22,* 129–146.

Asarnow, J. R., & Tompson, M. C. (1999). Childhood-onset schizophrenia: A follow-up study. *European Child & Adolescent Psychiatry, 8* (S1), 9–12.

Asarnow, J. R., Tompson, M. C., & Goldstein, M. J. (1994). Childhood-onset schizophrenia: A follow-up study. *Schizophrenia Bulletin, 20,* 599–617.

Asarnow, J. R., Tompson, M. C., & Goldstein, M. J. (2000). Psychosocial factors: The social context of child and adolescent onset schizophrenia. *Remschmidt, Helmut.*

Asarnow, J. R., Tompson, M. C., & McGrath, E. P. (2004). Annotation: Childhood-onset schizophrenia: clinical and treatment issues. *Journal of Child Psychology and Psychiatry, 45,* 180–194.

Asarnow, R., & Karatekin, C. (1998). Childhood-onset schizophrenia. In C. E. Coffey & R. A. Brumback (Eds.), *Textbook of pediatric neuropsychiatry* (pp. 617–646). Washington DC: American Psychiatric Press.

Asarnow, R. F., Asamen, J., Granholm, E., & Sherman, T. (1994). Cognitive/neuropsychological studies of children with a schizophrenic disorder. *Schizophrenia Bulletin, 20,* 647–669.

Asarnow, R. F., Brown, W., & Strandburg, R. (1995). Children with a schizophrenic disorder: Neurobehavioral studies. *European Archives of Psychiatry and Clinical Neuroscience. Special Issue: Schizophrenia in childhood and adolescence, 245,* 70–79.

Asarnow, R. F., Nuechterlein, K. H., Fogelson, D., Subotnik, K. L., Payne, D. A., Russell, A. T., et al. (2001). Schizophrenia and schizophrenia-spectrum personality disorders in the first-degree relatives of children with schizophrenia: The UCLA Family Study. *Archives of General Psychiatry, 58,* 581–588.

Asarnow, R. F., Nuechterlein, K. H., Subotnik, K. L., Fogelson, D. L., Torquato, R. D., Payne, D. L., et al. (2002). Neurocognitive impairments in nonpsychotic parents of children with schizophrenia and attention-deficit/hyperactivity disorder: The University of California, Los Angeles Family Study. *Archives of General Psychiatry, 59,* 1053–1060.

Asarnow, R. F., & Sherman, T. (1984). Studies of visual information processing in schizophrenic children. *Child Development, 55,* 249–261.

Asarnow, R. F., Tanguay, P. E., Bott, L., & Freeman, B. J. (1987). Patterns of intellectual functioning in non-retarded autistic and schizophrenic children. *Journal of Child Psychology and Psychiatry, 28,* 273–280.

Baldessarini, R. J., & Teicher, M. H. (1995). Dosing of antipsychotic agents in pediatric populations. *Journal of Child and Adolescent Psychopharmacology, 5,* 1–4.

Bender, L., & Grugett, A. E., Jr. (1956). A study of certain epidemiological factors in a group of children with childhood schizophrenia. *American Journal of Orthopsychiatry, 26,* 131–145.

Bennett, S., & Klein, H. R. (1966). Childhood schizophrenia: 30 years later. *American Journal of Psychiatry, 122,* 1121–1124.

Bettes, B. A., & Walker, E. (1987). Positive and negative symptoms in psychotic and other psychiatrically disturbed children. *Journal of Child Psychology and Psychiatry, 28,* 555–568.

Bilder, R. M., Goldman, R. S., Robinson, D., Reiter, G., Bell, L., Bates, J. A., et al.

(2000). Neuropsychology of first-episode schizophrenia: Initial characterization and clinical correlates. *American Journal of Psychiatry, 157,* 549–559.

Bleuler, E. (1911/1950). *Dementia Praecox, or the Group of Schizophrenias.* (J. Zinkin, Trans.). New York: International Universities Press.

Burd, L., & Kerbeshian, J. (1987). A North Dakota prevalence study of schizophrenia presenting in childhood. *Journal of the American Academy of Child & Adolescent Psychiatry, 26,* 347–350.

Cannon, T. D., Mednick, S. A., Parnas, J., Schulsinger, F., & et al. (1993). Developmental brain abnormalities in the offspring of schizophrenic mothers: I. Contributions of genetic and perinatal factors. *Archives of General Psychiatry, 50,* 551–564.

Caplan, R. (1994a). Communication deficits in childhood schizophrenia spectrum disorders. *Schizophrenia Bulletin, 20,* 671–683.

Caplan, R. (1994b). Thought disorder in childhood. *Journal of the American Academy of Child & Adolescent Psychiatry, 33,* 605–615.

Caplan, R., Guthrie, D., & Komo, S. (1996). Conversational repair in schizophrenic and normal children. *Journal of the American Academy of Child & Adolescent Psychiatry, 35,* 950–958.

Chapman, L. J., & Chapman, J. P. (2001). Commentary on two articles concerning generalized and specific cognitive deficits. *Journal of Abnormal Psychology, 110,* 31–39.

Creak, E. M. (1963). Childhood psychosis: A review of 100 cases. *British Journal of Psychiatry, 109* (Whole No. 458), 84–89.

Done, D. J., Crow, T. J., Johnstone, E. C., & Sacker, A. (1994). Childhood antecedents of schizophrenia and affective illness: social adjustment at ages 7 and 11 (Vol. 309, pp. 699–703).

Eggers, C. (2002). Schizophrenia in childhood and adolescence. Symptomatology, clinical course, etiological and therapeutic aspects. *Z Arztl Fortbild Qualitatssich, 96,* 567–577.

Fioravanti, M., Carlone, O., Vitale, B., Cinti, M. E., & Clare, L. (2005). A meta-analysis of cognitive deficits in adults with a diagnosis of schizophrenia. *Neuropsychology Review, 15,* 73–95.

Fish, B., Marcus, J., Hans, S. L., Auerbach, J. G., et al. (1992). Infants at risk for schizophrenia: Sequelae of a genetic neurointegrative defect: A review and replication analysis of pandysmaturation in the Jerusalem Infant Development Study. *Archives of General Psychiatry, 49,* 221–235.

Fish, B., & Ritvo, E. R. (1979). Psychoses of childhood. In J. D. Noshpitz (Ed.), *Basic handbook of child psychiatry* (pp. 249–304). New York: Basic Books.

Fleischhaker, C., Schulz, E., Tepper, K., Martin, M., Hennighausen, K., & Remschmidt, H. (2005). Long-term course of adolescent schizophrenia (Vol. 31, pp. 769–780).

Foerde, K., Poldrack, R. A., Knowlton, B. J. W., Sabb, F., Bookheimer, S. Y., Bilder, R. M., et al. (submitted). Selective corticostriatal dysfunction in schizophrenia: examination of motor and cognitive skill learning. *Neuropsychology.*

Frazier, J. A., Giedd, J. N., Hamburger, S. D., Albus, K. E., et al. (1996). Brain anatomic magnetic resonance imaging in childhood-onset schizophrenia. *Archives of General Psychiatry, 53,* 617–624.

Freedman, R., & et al. (1983). Neurophysiological evidence for a defect in inhibitory pathways in schizophrenia: Comparison of medicated and drug-free patients. *Biological Psychiatry, 18,* 537–551.

Galdos, P. M., Van Os, J. J., & Murray, R. M. (1993). Puberty and the onset of psychosis. *Schizophrenia Research, 10,* 7–14.

Geddes, J. R., & Lawrie, S. (1995). Obstetric complications and schizophrenia: A meta-analysis. *British Journal of Psychiatry, 167,* 786–793.

Gochman, P. A., Greenstein, D., Sporn, A., Gogtay, N., Keller, B., Shaw, P., et al. (2005). IQ stabilization in childhood-onset schizophrenia. *Schizophrenia Research, 77,* 271–277.

Gochman, P. A., Greenstein, D., Sporn, A., Gogtay, N., Nicolson, R., Keller, A., et al. (2004). Childhood onset schizophrenia: Familial neurocognitive measures. *Schizophrenia Research, 71,* 43–47.

Gordon, C. T., Frazier, J. A., McKenna, K., Giedd, J., et al. (1994). Childhood-onset schizophrenia: An NIMH study in progress. *Schizophrenia Bulletin, 20,* 697–712.

Gottesman, I. I., & Shields, J. (1973). Genetic theorizing and schizophrenia. *British Journal of Psychiatry, 122,* 15–30.

Hafner, H., & Nowotny, B. (1995). Epidemiology of early-onset schizophrenia. *European Archives of Psychiatry and Clinical Neuroscience. Special Issue: Schizophrenia in childhood and adolescence, 245,* 80–92.

Harding, C. M., Brooks, G. W., Ashikaga, T., Strauss, J. S., et al. (1987). The Vermont longitudinal study of persons with severe mental illness. Vol. II: Long-term outcome of subjects who retrospectively met *DSM-III* criteria for schizophrenia. *American Journal of Psychiatry, 144,* 727–735.

Hartwell, C. E. (1996). The schizophrenogenic mother concept in American psychiatry. *Psychiatry: Interpersonal and Biological Processes, 59,* 274–297.

Heinrichs, R. W. (2004). Meta-analysis and the science of schizophrenia: variant evidence or evidence of variants? *Neuroscience & Biobehavioral Reviews, 28,* 379–394.

Hollis, C. (2000). Adult outcomes of child- and adolescent-onset schizophrenia: Diagnostic stability and predictive validity. *American Journal of Psychiatry, 157,* 1652–1659.

Honea, R., Crow, T. J., Passingham, D., & Mackay, C. E. (2005). Regional deficits in brain volume in schizophrenia: A meta-analysis of voxel-based morphometry studies. *American Journal of Psychiatry, 162,* 2233–2245.

Jacobsen, L. K., & Rapoport, J. L. (1998). Research update: Childhood-onset schizophrenia: Implications of clinical and neurobiological research. *Journal of Child Psychology and Psychiatry, 39,* 101–113.

Jones, P., Murray, R., Jones, P., Rodgers, B., & Marmot, M. (1994). Child developmental risk factors for adult schizophrenia in the British 1946 birth cohort. *The Lancet, 344,* 1398–1402.

Kanner, L. (1949). Problems of nosology and psychodynamics of early infantile autism. *American Journal of Orthopsychiatry, 19,* 416–426.

Karatekin, C., & Asarnow, R. F. (1998a). Components of visual search in childhood-onset schizophrenia and attention-deficit/hyperactivity disorder. *Journal of Abnormal Child Psychology, 26,* 367–380.

Karatekin, C., & Asarnow, R. F. (1998b). Working memory in childhood-onset schizophrenia and attention-deficit/hyperactivity disorder. *Psychiatry Research, 80,* 165–176.

Karatekin, C., & Asarnow, R. F. (1999). Exploratory eye movements to pictures in childhood-onset schizophrenia and attention-deficit/hyperactivity disorder (ADHD). *Journal of Abnormal Child Psychology, 27,* 35–49.

Kavanagh, D. J. (1992). Recent developments in expressed emotion and schizophrenia. *British Journal of Psychiatry, 160,* 601–620.

Kendler, K. S. (1997). The genetic epidemiology of psychiatric disorders: A current perspective. *Social Psychiatry and Psychiatric Epidemiology, 32,* 5–11.

Kendler, K. S., & Diehl, S. R. (1993). The genetics of schizophrenia: A current, genetic-epidemioiogic perspective. *Schizophrenia Bulletin, 19,* 261–285.

Kendler, K. S., McGuire, M., Gruenberg, A. M., O'Hare, A., et al. (1993). The Roscommon Family Study. Vol. I: Methods, diagnosis of probands, and risk of schizophrenia in relatives. *Archives of General Psychiatry, 50,* 527–540.

Knight, R. T., Hillyard, S. A., Woods, D. L., & Neville, H. J. (1981). The effects of frontal cortex lesions on event-related potentials during auditory selective attention. *Electroencephalography and Clinical Neurophysiology, 52,* 571–582.

Kolvin, I. (1971). Studies in the childhood psychoses. Vol. I: Diagnostic criteria and classification. *British Journal of Psychiatry, 118,* 381–384.

Kraepelin, E. (1971). *Dementia praecox and paraphrenia* (R. M. Barclay, Trans.). Huntington, NY: Krieger. (Original work published 1919.)

Kumra, S., Jacobsen, L. K., Lenane, M., Zahn, T. P., Wiggs, E., Alaghband-Rad, J., et al. (1998). "Multidimensionally impaired disorder": Is it a variant of very early-onset schizophrenia? *Journal of the American Academy of Child & Adolescent Psychiatry, 37,* 91–99.

Levinson, D. F., & Mowry, B. J. (1991). Defining the schizophrenia spectrum: Issues for genetic linkage studies. *Schizophrenia Bulletin, 17,* 491–514.

Marquardt, R. E. K., Levitt, J. G., Blanton, R. E., Caplan, R., Asarnow, R., Siddarth, P., et al. (2005). Abnormal development of the anterior cingulate in childhood-onset schizophrenia: A preliminary quantitative MRI study. *Psychiatry Research: Neuroimaging, 138,* 221–233.

Matsumoto, H., Simmons, A., Williams, S., Hadjulis, M., Pipe, R., Murray, R., et al. (2001). Superior temporal gyrus abnormalities in early-onset schizophrenia: Similarities and differences with adult-onset schizophrenia. *American Journal of Psychiatry, 158,* 1299–1304.

Matsumoto, H., Takei, N., Saito, H., Kachi, K., & Mori, N. (1999). Childhood-onset schizophrenia and obstetric complications: A case-control study. *Schizophrenia Research, 38,* 93–99.

McClellan, J., McCurry, C., Snell, J., & DuBose, A. (1999). Early-onset psychotic disorders: Course and outcome over a 2-year period. *Journal of the American Academy of Child & Adolescent Psychiatry, 38,* 1380–1388.

McClellan, J., & Werry, J. (1994). Practice parameters for the assessment and treatment of children and adolescents with schizophrenia. *Journal of the American Academy of Child & Adolescent Psychiatry, 33,* 616–635.

Michie, P. T., Fox, A. M., Ward, P. B., Catts, S. V., et al. (1990). Event-related potential indices of selective attention and cortical lateralization in schizophrenia. *Psychophysiology, 27,* 209–227.

Nicolson, R., Brookner, F. B., Lenane, M., Gochman, P., Ingraham, L. J., Egan, M. F., et al. (2003). Parental schizophrenia spectrum disorders in childhood-onset and adult-onset schizophrenia. *American Journal of Psychiatry, 160*, 490–495.

Potter, H. W. (1933). Schizophrenia in children. *American Journal of Psychiatry, 12*, 1254–1270.

Rapoport, J. C., Addington, A. M., & Frangou, S. (2005). "The neurodevelopmental model of schizophrenia: Update 2005": Corrigendum. *Molecular Psychiatry, 10*, 614.

Remschmidt, H., Martin, M., Fleischhaker, C., Theisen, F. M., Hennighausen, K., Gutenbrunner, C., et al. (2007). Forty-two years later: the outcome of childhood-onset schizophrenia. *Journal of neural transmission, 114*, 505–512.

Remschmidt, H., & Theisen, F. (2005). Schizophrenia and related disorders in children and adolescents. *Journal of neural transmission. Supplementum*(69), 121–141.

Remschmidt, H. E., Schulz, E., Martin, M., & Warnke, A. (1994). Childhood-onset schizophrenia: History of the concept and recent studies. *Schizophrenia Bulletin, 20*, 727–745.

Rhinewine, J. P., Lencz, T., Thaden, E. P., Cervellione, K. L., Burdick, K. E., Henderson, I., et al. (2005). Neurocognitive profile in adolescents with early-onset schizophrenia: Clinical correlates. *Biological Psychiatry, 58*, 705–712.

Ross, R. G., Heinlein, S., Zerbe, G. O., & Radant, A. (2005). Saccadic eye movement task identifies cognitive deficits in children with schizophrenia, but not in unaffected child relatives. *Journal of Child Psychology and Psychiatry, 46*, 1354–1362.

Russell, A. T. (1994). The clinical presentation of childhood-onset schizophrenia. *Schizophrenia Bulletin, 20*, 631–646.

Russell, A. T., Bott, L., & Sammons, C. (1989). The phenomenology of schizophrenia occurring in childhood. *Journal of the American Academy of Child & Adolescent Psychiatry, 28*, 399–407.

Rutter, M. (1967). Classification and Categorization in Child Psychiatry. *International Journal of Psychiatry, 3*, 161–187.

Rutter, M. (1972). Childhood schizophrenia reconsidered. *Journal of Autism & Childhood Schizophrenia, 2*, 315–337.

Spencer, E. K., & Campbell, M. (1994). Children with schizophrenia: Diagnosis, phenomenology, and pharmacotherapy. *Schizophrenia Bulletin, 20*, 713–725.

Sporn, A., Greenstein, D., Gogtay, N., Sailer, F., Hommer, D. W., Rawlings, R., et al. (2005). Childhood-onset schizophrenia: Smooth pursuit eye-tracking dysfunction in family members. *Schizophrenia Research, 73*, 243–252.

Sporn, A. L., Addington, A. M., Gogtay, N., Ordoñez, A. E., Gornick, M., Clasen, L., et al. (2004). Pervasive developmental disorder and childhood-onset schizophrenia: Comorbid disorder or a phenotypic variant of a very early onset illness? *Biological Psychiatry, 55*, 989–994.

Stayer, C., Sporn, A., Gogtay, N., Tossell, J., Lenane, M., Gochman, P., et al. (2004). Looking for childhood schizophrenia: Case series of false positives. *Journal of the American Academy of Child & Adolescent Psychiatry, 43*, 1026–1029.

Strandburg, R. J., Marsh, J. T., Brown, W. S., Asarnow, R. F., et al. (1994). Continuous-processing related ERPs in schizophrenic and normal children. *Biological Psychiatry, 35*, 525–538.

Taylor, J. L., Blanton, R. E., Levitt, J. G., Caplan, R., Nobel, D., & Toga, A. W. (2005). Superior temporal gyrus differences in childhood-onset schizophrenia. *Schizophrenia Research, 73,* 235–241.

Thaden, E., Rhinewine, J. P., Lencz, T., Kester, H., Cervellione, K. L., Henderson, I., et al. (2006). Early-onset schizophrenia is associated with impaired adolescent development of attentional capacity using the identical pairs continuous performance test. *Schizophrenia Research, 81,* 157–166.

Thompson, P. M., Vidal, C., Giedd, J. N., Gochman, P., Blumenthal, J., Nicolson, R., et al. (2001). Mapping adolescent brain change reveals dynamic wave of accelerated gray matter loss in very early-onset schizophrenia (Vol. 98, pp. 11650–11655).

Tienari, P., Wynne, L. C., Sorri, A., Lahti, I., Laksy, K., Moring, J., et al. (2004). Genotype-environment interaction in schizophrenia-spectrum disorder: Long-term follow-up study of Finnish adoptees (Vol. 184, pp. 216–222).

Tompson, M. C., Asarnow, J. R., Hamilton, E. B., Newell, L. E., & Goldstein, M. J. (1997). Children with schizophrenia-spectrum disorders: thought disorder and communication problems in a family interactional context. *Journal of Child Psychology and Psychiatry, 38,* 421–429.

Volkmar, F. R., & Cohen, D. J. (1991). Comorbid association of autism and schizophrenia. *American Journal of Psychiatry, 148,* 1705–1707.

Wahlberg, K.-E., Wynne, L. C., Hakko, H., Laksy, K., Moring, J., Miettunen, J., et al. (2004). Interaction of genetic risk and adoptive parent communication deviance: Longitudinal prediction of adoptee psychiatric disorders. *Psychological Medicine, 34,* 1531–1541.

Watkins, J. M., Asarnow, R. F., & Tanguay, P. E. (1988). Symptom development in childhood onset schizophrenia. *Journal of Child Psychology and Psychiatry, 29,* 865–878.

Weinberger, D. R. (1987). Implications of normal brain development for the pathogenesis of schizophrenia. *Archives of General Psychiatry, 44,* 660–669.

Werry, J. S., & McClellan, J. M. (1992). Predicting outcome in child and adolescent (early onset) schizophrenia and bipolar disorder. *Journal of the American Academy of Child & Adolescent Psychiatry, 31,* 147–150.

Werry, J. S., McClellan, J. M., Andrews, L. K., & Ham, M. (1994). Clinical features and outcome of child and adolescent schizophrenia. *Schizophrenia Bulletin, 20,* 619–630.

Werry, J. S., McClellan, J. M., & Chard, L. (1991). Childhood and adolescent schizophrenic, bipolar, and schizoaffective disorders: A clinical and outcome study. *Journal of the American Academy of Child & Adolescent Psychiatry, 30,* 457–465.

Wright, I. C., Rabe-Hesketh, S., Woodruff, P. W. R., David, A. S., Murray, R. M., & Bullmore, E. T. (2000). Meta-analysis of regional brain volumes in schizophrenia. *American Journal of Psychiatry, 157,* 16–25.

Wynne, L. C., Tienari, P., Nieminen, P., Sorri, A., Lahti, I., Moring, J., et al. (2006). I. Genotype-Environment Interaction in the Schizophrenia Spectrum: Genetic Liability and Global Family Ratings in the Finnish Adoption Study. *Family Process, 45,* 419–434.

CHAPTER 21

Eating Disorders

ERIC STICE AND CYNTHIA M. BULIK

HISTORICAL CONTEXT

Eating disorders are psychiatric disturbances involving abnormal eating behaviors, maladaptive efforts to control body shape or weight, and disturbances in perceived body shape or size. Three Eating Disorder syndromes are recognized in the literature: anorexia nervosa, bulimia nervosa, and binge eating disorder. Anorexia nervosa was first recognized as a psychiatric disorder well over a century ago (Gull, 1873), whereas the first published account of bulimia appeared in the late 1970s (Russell, 1979). Although the prevalence of anorexia nervosa has remained relatively stable over time, research suggests that the prevalence of bulimia nervosa increased toward the end of the twentieth century (Wilson, Becker, & Heffernan, 2003). Stunkard (1959) first described binge eating disorder half a century ago among overweight individuals. Despite receiving considerable research attention since the early 1990s, this Eating Disorder has not yet been recognized as a diagnostic entity (American Psychiatric Association [APA], 1994, 2000). Evidence that the prevalence of anorexia nervosa has been relatively stable over time might be interpreted as suggesting that biological processes play a more prominent role in the etiology of this Eating Disorder relative to sociocultural factors. In contrast, evidence that the prevalence of bulimia nervosa has increased over time might be taken to imply that sociocultural factors, such as an increasing abundance of palatable foods and cultural valuation of thinness for girls and women, play a more pronounced role in the etiology of this Eating Disorder.

DIAGNOSTIC ISSUES AND *DSM-IV* CRITERIA

ANOREXIA NERVOSA

Diagnostic criteria for anorexia nervosa include weight loss or failure to gain weight (with weight less than 85% of that expected for height and age), intense fear of gaining weight or of becoming fat despite a low body weight, disturbed perception of weight and shape, an undue influence of weight or shape on self-evaluation or a denial of the seriousness of the illness, and amenorrhea in postmenarcheal females (APA, 1994, 2000). A distinction is made between a restricting type of anorexia nervosa, in which the person does not regularly engage in binge eating or purging (self-induced vomiting or laxative/diuretic use), and a binge-eating/purging type.

Although the diagnostic criteria for anorexia nervosa appear straightforward, they can be challenging to implement for assessors and investigators (Commission on Adolescent Eating Disorders, 2005). In children and adolescents, age- and sex-adjusted norms must be applied. Weight is also adjusted for height using the Body Mass Index (BMI = kg/m^2). Further difficulties are created by the fact that younger individuals and/or those who are not motivated for treatment may deny fear of weight gain, despite engaging in behaviors that suggest its presence.

Reformulating this diagnostic criterion by focusing on observable weight-control behaviors rather than unobservable cognitions could serve to clarify diagnostic decisions. Moreover, fear of weight gain is not a universally expressed feature of anorexia nervosa—with both historical and crosscultural cases failing to display this feature (Striegel-Moore & Bulik, in press). Amenorrhea is also controversial as individuals with and without this symptom do not differ on measures of impairment (Bulik et al., 2000). Moreover, the common yet ill-advised practice of placing amenorrheic individuals on birth control pills to reinstate cycles, and the fact that other forms of birth control can cause functional amenorrhea, can obscure this symptom.

Additional features of anorexia nervosa include a relentless pursuit of thinness and overvaluation of body shape, which usually results in extreme dietary restriction and physical activity (Fairburn & Harrison, 2003). Consequent to semistarvation, individuals become preoccupied with food and exhibit ritualistic and stereotyped eating, such as cutting food into small pieces, moving food around on the plate, and eating foods in a certain order (Wilson et al., 2003). Anorexia nervosa has a very high mortality rate, with causes of death including complications of starvation and suicide (Birmingham et al., 2005).

Common physical symptoms associated with anorexia nervosa include yellowish skin (hypercarotenemia), lanugo (fine, downy hair), hypersensitivity to cold, hypotension (low blood pressure), bradycardia (slow heart rate), and other cardiovascular problems. Purging behaviors may cause enlargement of salivary glands and erosion of dental enamel. Dehydration and electrolyte imbalances from chronic purging may lead to serum potassium depletion and consequent hypokalemia, which increases risk of renal failure and cardiac arrhythmias. Osteopenia may also result from malnutrition and decreased estrogen secretion.

BULIMIA NERVOSA

Bulimia nervosa is marked by recurrent episodes (at least twice weekly for 3 months) of consumption of unusually large amounts of food, coupled with a sense of the eating being out of control; recurrent (at least twice weekly for 3 months) compensatory behaviors to prevent weight gain (e.g., self-induced vomiting, laxative/diuretic abuse, fasting, excessive exercise); and undue influence of weight and shape on self-evaluation (APA, 1994, 2000). If symptoms occur exclusively during a period of anorexia nervosa, the latter diagnosis prevails. During binge episodes, these individuals (and those with binge eating disorder) typically consume between 1,000 and 2,000 calories, often from easily ingestible foods high in fat and sugar content (Walsh, 1993). Bulimia nervosa is often associated with marked feelings of guilt and shame regarding eating behaviors (Wilson et al., 2003). Because of shame and denial, individuals suffer from bulimia nervosa for an average of 6 years before seeking treatment (Fairburn & Harrison, 2003).

Diagnostic criteria for bulimia nervosa can also be difficult to interpret (Commission on Adolescent Eating Disorders, 2005). Binge eating specifies the amount of food typically consumed during a binge episode ("larger than most people would eat"), the duration of the binge episode ("in a discrete period of time"), and subjective experience of the episode ("a sense of a lack of control over eating"). Each of these can be ambiguous. For example, some people may endorse uncontrollable binge eating in a discrete period of time yet still report eating a quantity of food that is not larger than what most people eat. Because many individuals exhibit chaotic eating patterns, it is often difficult to determine whether the eating episodes represent meals at atypical times or whether they represent binge-eating episodes. Others, particularly males, may endorse eating an amount of food that is larger than what most people eat, but deny a loss of control. Compensatory behaviors, such as fasting and excessive exercise, can also be difficult to assess. The frequency and duration criteria (twice weekly for 3 months) have questionable empirical support (Garfinkel et al., 1995). Last, the stipulation that self-evaluation be unduly influenced by weight and body shape is endorsed by a large portion of adolescent girls and can be difficult to separate from general body dissatisfaction. These ambiguities suggest that it might be beneficial to use behavioral criteria for bulimia nervosa, or that clearer decision algorithms should be developed.

Common clinical features of bulimia nervosa include secrecy about the behavior due to shame and guilt. Often parents and peers are unaware of the disordered eating. Individuals with bulimia nervosa are typically in the average weight range. Bulimia nervosa does not appear to be associated with increased mortality (Keel et al., 2003). Additional physical complaints include fatigue, headaches, enlarged salivary glands secondary from recurrent vomiting, and erosion of dental enamel and dentin from gastric fluids. Electrolyte abnormalities (hypokalemia and hypochloremia), resulting from frequent purging, can result in cardiac arrhythmias and arrest. Laxative abuse can lead to dependence and withdrawal and can cause lasting colon damage. These medical disturbances most typically occur among individuals who are engaging in frequent binge-eating and compensatory behaviors; they usually resolve with discontinuation of these behaviors.

BINGE EATING DISORDER

Binge eating disorder is listed in the *DSM-IV* (APA, 1994, 2000) as a provisional Eating Disorder requiring further study, exemplifying an Eating Disorder, Not Otherwise Specified (EDNOS)—a residual category for eating disorders that are not captured by the categories of anorexia or bulimia nervosa. This Eating Disorder involves (a) repeated episodes (at least 2 days per week for 6 months) of uncontrollable binge eating characterized by certain features (i.e., rapid eating, eating until uncomfortably full, eating large amounts of food when not physically hungry, eating alone because of embarrassment, feeling guilty or depressed after overeating); (b) marked distress regarding binge eating; and (c) the absence of regular compensatory behaviors (e.g., monthly vomiting for weight control). If symptoms occur exclusively during episodes of anorexia or bulimia nervosa, the latter diagnoses take precedence.

As with bulimia nervosa, the definition of binge eating is unclear and the frequency and duration requirements are unsupported empirically. Patterns of eating also vary, such as overeating continuously throughout the day (i.e., grazing), underscoring the importance of recording binge-eating days in addition to binge-eating episodes.

Little is known about the clinical features of binge eating disorder, particularly during childhood and adolescence, although obesity is common. Thus, medical complications related to obesity occur, including hypertension, adverse lipoprotein profiles, diabetes mellitus, atherosclerotic cerebrovascular disease, coronary heart disease, colorectal cancer, reduced lifespan, and death from all causes (Fontaine, Redden, Wang, Westfall, & Allison, 2003). Independent of body weight, binge eating confers additional psychiatric and medical risks such as insomnia, specific phobias, daily smoking, alcohol use, and physical pain (Reichborn-Kjennerud, Bulik, Sullivan et al., 2004).

PREVALENCE

Epidemiologic studies using diagnostic interviews suggest that between 1.4 and 2.0% of girls and women and between 0.1 and 0.2% of boys and men experience anorexia nervosa during their lifetimes (Lewinsohn, Striegel-Moore, & Seeley, 2000; Woodside et al., 2001). Subthreshold syndromes occur in 1.1 to 3.0% of adolescent girls (Lewinsohn et al., 2000; Stice, Presnell, & Bearman, 2006). Bulimia nervosa afflicts between 1.1 and 4.6% of girls and women and between 0.1 and 0.2% of boys and men during their lifetimes (Garfinkel et al., 1995; Lewinsohn et al., 2000; Woodside et al., 2001). The prevalence of subthreshold bulimia nervosa is more common and ranges from 2.0% to 5.4% (Lewinsohn et al., 2000; Stice et al., 2006). Despite these sex discrepancies, male athletes may be at elevated risk for eating disorders (Wilson et al., 2003). It is also important to note that the diagnostic criteria for bulimia nervosa may be sex-biased (Anderson & Bulik, 2003). Including strategies that males use to control weight (e.g., protein powders and supplements) and sex-appropriate types of body dissatisfaction (e.g., urges to decrease body fat) could influence estimates of the prevalence of bulimia nervosa in males. Binge eating disorder afflicts between 0.2 and 1.5% of girls and between 0.9 to 1.0% of boys and men during their lifetimes (Hoek & van Hoeken, 2003; Kjelsas, Bjornstrom, & Gotestam, 2004). Community-recruited samples indicate that the prevalence of subthreshold binge eating disorder for adolescent females is 1.6% (Lewinsohn et al., 2000; Stice et al., 2006).

RISK FACTORS, PROTECTIVE FACTORS, AND ETIOLOGIC FORUMLATIONS

ANOREXIA NERVOSA

Although there are numerous theories regarding etiologic processes that promote the development of anorexia nervosa, few prospective studies have investigated factors that predict the onset of anorexia, and no prospective tests of multivariate etiologic models exist. Prospective studies are essential to determine whether a putative risk factor is a precursor, concomitant, or consequence of eating pathology. Numerous risk factors have been implicated in anorexia nervosa, including neurotransmitter dysfunction, negative life-events, low self-esteem, perfectionism, need for control, family dysfunction, internalization of the thin-ideal, premature birth and low birth weight, dietary restraint, childhood sexual abuse, and mood and anxiety disturbances (Fairburn & Harrison, 2003; Wilson et al., 2003; Bulik, Reba et al., 2005). As most of these observations are based on cross-sectional studies, it remains unclear whether these characteristics temporally precede the development of anorexia nervosa.

Nonetheless, three prospective studies have examined risk factors for anorexia nervosa. One suggested that two obstetric complications, premature birth (small for gestational age) and cephalhematoma (a collection of blood under the scalp), were associated with elevated risk for the subsequent development of anorexia nervosa (Cnattingius et al., 1999). These obstetric complications were relatively specific to anorexia nervosa, as they did not predict the onset of psychosis or Schizophrenia (Cnattingius et al., 1999). Subtle brain injuries at birth might result in feeding difficulties that increase risk for later anorexia nervosa. Alternatively, eating pathology in the mothers may result in premature birth and small gestational size of the infants because of malnourishment (Bulik, Reba, et al. 2005). A second study indicated that premorbid neuroticism predicted the onset of anorexia nervosa in twins (Bulik et al., 2006). A third study suggested that girls with the lowest weight and low scores on dietary restraint at age 13 were at increased risk for future onset of threshold or subthreshold anorexia nervosa over a 5-year period (Stice et al., 2006). Of note, such factors as early puberty; perceived pressure to be thin from family, peers, and the media; thin-ideal internalization; body dissatisfaction; depressive symptoms; and low parental and peer support did not predict anorexic pathology onset.

Several studies have investigated predictors of the development of any Eating Disorder, including anorexia and bulimia nervosa (e.g., McKnight Investigators, 2003; Santonastaso, Friederici, & Favaro, 1999). Elevated perceived pressure to be thin, thin-ideal internalization, body dissatisfaction, dieting, and psychological disturbances all predict future onset of any eating disorder, suggesting that these may be general risk factors for eating pathology.

BULIMIA NERVOSA

According to the general sociocultural model of bulimia nervosa, internalization of the socially sanctioned thin ideal for females combines with direct pressures for female thinness, including media-portrayed images of the thin ideal and weight-related teasing, to promote body dissatisfaction, which in turn increases risk for both the initiation of dieting and negative affect, contributing to bulimic pathology (Cattarin & Thompson, 1994; Stice, 2001). Body dissatisfaction, in part based on elevated body mass, is thought to lead vulnerable females to engage in dietary restraint in an effort to conform to this thin ideal, which may increase the likelihood of the initiation of binge eating. Dieting also entails a shift from a reliance on physiological cues to cognitive control over eating behaviors, which leaves the individual vulnerable to overeating when these cognitive processes are disrupted. Body dissatisfaction may also contribute to negative affect, which increases the risk of turning to binge eating to provide comfort and distraction from negative emotional states. An important feature of this general theory is that contextual factors, such as preoccupation with thinness by family members and peers, play an important role in the development of this Eating Disorder.

Consistent with the sociocultural model, a number of factors—thin-ideal internalization, perceived pressure to be thin, body dissatisfaction, dietary restraint, and negative affect—increase risk for future onset of bulimic symptoms and bulimic pathology (Field et al., 1999; Killen et al., 1996; Stice, 2002). Experiments have found that exposure to media images of the thin ideal and thin, attractive peers, particularly those who complain about their weight, results in body dissatisfaction and negative affect (e.g., Stice & Shaw, 1994). Randomized trials have also found that interventions that produce reductions in thin-ideal internalization, body dissatisfaction, body mass, and negative affect have produced expected decreases in bulimic symptoms, but have failed to provide similar support for the role of dietary restraint (reviewed in Stice, 2002). In addition, randomized trials have indicated that assignment to a weight-loss diet results in decreases in binge eating and bulimic symptoms (Klem et al., 1997; Presnell & Stice, 2003). Other risk factors have received support in select studies, such as deficits in social support, substance abuse, and elevated body mass, but still other hypothesized risk factors have not received support in prospective studies, including early menarche and temperamental impulsivity (Stice, 2002).

Early feeding problems may also increase risk for binge-eating and bulimic symptoms. Marchi and Cohen (1990) found that digestive problems and pica (eating nonfood substances) in childhood predicted future bulimic symptoms during adolescence. Initial elevations in body mass and longer duration of measured sucking in infancy predicted emergence of overeating and vomiting during middle childhood (Stice, Agras, & Hammer, 1999).

BINGE EATING DISORDER

The few theories regarding the etiologic processes that promote binge eating disorder overlap conceptually with etiologic theories put forth for bulimic pathology (Vogeltanz-Holm et al., 2000). Prospective studies have provided evidence that initial elevations in body mass, body dissatisfaction, dietary restraint, negative affect, and a tendency to eat in response to negative emotions (emotional eating) increase the risk for future onset of binge eating (Stice, Presnell, & Spangler, 2002; Stice et al., 1998; Vogeltanz-Holm et al., 2000).

Certain patterns emerge from the risk-factor literature. First, the fact that multiple risk factors have been implicated in the development of these disorders provides evidence of equifinality, which posits that multiple pathways may lead to a given psychiatric disorder (von Bertalanffy, 1968). For example, at least three different models of bulimia nervosa have been forwarded: binge eating emerges as a response to dysregulated affect; binge eating emerges secondary to extreme dietary restriction, which increases the reinforcing value of food; and binge eating emerges as part of an array of behaviors (e.g., alcohol use, shoplifting, sexual promiscuity) in individuals high in impulsivity (Stice, 2001; Wonderlich & Mitchell, 1997). Second, certain risk factors that have been identified for eating disorders also predict the onset of other psychiatric conditions. For instance, birth complications, neuroticism, and childhood anxiety increase risk for other disorders, such as mood, anxiety, and externalizing disorders. This pattern of findings is consonant with the notion of multifinality, which posits that the effects of a particular risk factor are qualified by other risk factors operating within the system. Combinations of common and specific risk factors may interact or accumulate, resulting in the final pathway to disease or diseases. For example, an individual with temperamentally high neuroticism could be exposed to an environment that values the societal thin ideal and supports dieting behavior and exercise to achieve low body weight. Engaging in these behaviors at critical developmental periods could lead to a negative energy balance that triggers the underlying genetic predisposition to anorexia nervosa. A similarly neurotically predisposed individual who never diets might later, after experiencing a triggering event, develop an Anxiety Disorder.

GENETIC AND OTHER BIOLOGICAL FACTORS

Research designs that comprise the field of genetic epidemiology, including family, twin, adoption, and molecular genetics studies, have enabled researchers to address a series of increasingly specific questions regarding the contribution of genetic and environmental factors to eating disorders. Family studies address the question of whether a trait or disorder aggregates within pedigrees; however, family studies cannot rule out environmental or social factors as the cause of the observed familial aggregation.

Family studies have shown that eating disorders are strongly familial. Relatives of individuals with anorexia and bulimia nervosa have approximately a 10-fold lifetime risk of having the disorders than relatives of unaffected individuals (Lilenfeld et al., 1997; Strober et al., 2000), and individuals with a family member with binge eating disorder are more than twice as likely to have binge eating disorder themselves compared to those with an overweight or obese relative without binge eating disorder (Hudson et al., 2006). Yet anorexia and bulimia nervosa do not "breed true": There is increased risk for an array of eating disorders in relatives of individuals with specific eating disorders rather than a disorder-specific pattern of familial aggregation (Lilenfeld et al., 1997; Strober et al., 2000). This variegated risk may be in part because individuals commonly cross over between anorexic and bulimic presentations (Wilson et al., 2003).

No adoption studies of eating disorders exist, although the extent to which familial aggregation is due to genes and/or environment has been addressed in numerous twin studies. Such studies capitalize on the fact that monozygotic (MZ; identical) twins share 100% of their genome whereas dizygotic (DZ; fraternal) twins share only 50%. Thus, if members of MZ twin pairs are more frequently concordant for a disorder (both affected) than members of DZ twin pairs, then a genetic contribution is suggested. Further analyses enable more detailed decomposition of liability into genetic, shared environmental, and unique environmental influences. Twin studies have consistently revealed significant genetic contributions to eating disorders, with the remaining variance attributable to unique environmental factors (Bulik et al., 2000). The heritability of anorexia nervosa has been estimated to be between 33% and 84%, and the heritability of bulimia nervosa between 28% and 83% (Bulik et al., 2000; Bulik et al., 2006; Klump et al., 2001; Wade et al., 2000), with the remaining variance in both disorders attributable to individual specific environmental factors, and with negligible impact of shared environmental factors. The broad range of estimates reflects the relatively low prevalence of the traits under study. For a broad definition of binge eating disorder, Reichborn-Kjennerud, Bulik, Tambs, and Harris (2004) reported a heritability estimate of 41%. Individual environmental factors accounted for the rest of the remaining 59% of the variance. In short, there is considerable evidence that risk for eating disorders is influenced by genetic factors.

ASSOCIATION AND LINKAGE STUDIES

Further evidence supporting the role of genes in the pathogenesis of anorexia and bulimia nervosa has emerged from molecular genetics studies. Association studies compare cases of those who display a trait to those who do not display the trait with respect to a candidate gene (or genes) hypothesized to influence the phenotype (eating-disordered behavior). Analyses compare allele or genotype frequencies (Sasieni, 1997) for the two groups. The association approach is optimal when there is prior knowledge of the pathophysiology of a trait that suggests specific candidate genes. More modern approaches (i.e., Whole Genome Association [WGA] studies) do not presuppose prior knowledge or require the selection of candidate genes. In WGA studies, hundreds of thousands to millions of single nucleotide polymorphisms (SNPs) are compared across cases and controls to identify differences. No GWA studies of eating disorders exist.

Linkage studies of eating disorders include large samples of multiplex families or families in which there are multiple individuals affected by the illness under study. (Allison et al., 1998). Anonymous genetic markers scattered across the genome are used to identify chromosomal regions that may contain genes influencing the trait of interest. Linkage studies help narrow the search space within the human genome. Specific genes located under the linkage peaks can be further explored using association approaches.

In terms of association studies, promising areas of research include genes that are known to affect appetite, weight regulation, and mood—with particular emphasis on the serotonin system, which is known to be dysregulated in eating disorders (Kaye et al., 1991). Genetic studies of eating disorders have been reviewed extensively elsewhere (Slof-Op't et al., 2005; Hinney, Remschmidt, & Hebebrand, 2000). Despite efforts to identify associations between candidate genes and eating disorders, genetic research has yielded only sporadic findings, as a result of small samples (yielding inadequate statistical power) and a tendency to report on only one gene or allele while failing to disclose the number of tests performed.

A series of collaborative studies have yielded intriguing linkage results for both anorexia and bulimia nervosa. The first study focused on individuals with anorexia nervosa with at least one affected relative (Grice et al., 2002; Devlin et al., 2002; Bacanu et al., 2005). Narrowing the focus to the classic restricting subtype of anorexia nervosa yielded evidence for a susceptibility locus on chromosome 1 (Grice et al., 2002). Additional analyses incorporating core features of the disorder (drive for thinness and obessionality) revealed several regions of interest on chromosomes 1, 2, and 13 (Devlin et al., 2002).

The first linkage study of bulimia nervosa (Bulik et al., 2003) reported a significant linkage on chromosome 10p when using a broad sample of families with bulimia nervosa, with a second peak on chromosome 14. Subsequent novel approaches designed to further refine the core underlying features (endophenotypes) associated with eating disorders (Bulik, Bacanu et al., 2005; Bacanu et al., 2005) have led to both confirmation of previously observed linkage peaks and identification of additional areas of interest on the genome for anorexia and bulimia nervosa.

In sum, genetic research on eating disorders has recently flourished. A number of multicenter, multinational collaborations have resulted in promising leads in both association and linkage approaches. Human molecular genetics is a rapidly advancing field. New approaches such as GWA studies, in which over 300,000 single nucleotide polymorphisms (SNPs) are genotyped, should help to surpass the confusing parade of small case-control studies focusing on single genes. Collaborative efforts across multiple sites will be necessary to amass the large samples required for GWA.

NEUROENDOCRINE AND NEUROHORMONAL FACTORS

Eating disorders can be viewed as resting at the juncture of disturbances of feeding behavior and impulse control (Simansky, 2005). Several neurotransmitter systems have been implicated in regulating feeding behavior, including serotonergic (cholinergic), histaminergic, and various peptidergic systems (e.g., neuropeptide Y, melanocortin, leptin, orexin and other peptidergic systems; Roth, in press; Yamada et al., 2001). Although hundreds of molecular targets have been implicated in regulating feeding behavior, a smaller number (mostly in the serotonergic and dopaminergic systems) have been linked to psychological and behavioral features of eating disorders such as impulsivity and obessionality (Simansky, 2005). The serotonin pathway has been implicated directly in the expression of eating disorders (Jimerson et al., 1997). In long-term weight-recovered patients with anorexia or bulimia nervosa, levels of 5-hydroxyindolacetic acid (5-HIAA), a metabolite of serotonin, were elevated in cerebrospinal fluid compared to those of healthy controls (Kaye et al., 1991; Kaye et al., 1998). One hypothesis is that hyperserotonergic activity may be a trait marker in eating disorders. Kaye et al. hypothesized that increased brain serotonin activity could predispose to the development of eating disorders and may contribute to the features of eating disorders such as perfectionism, rigidity, and obsessionality.

BRAIN STRUCTURE AND FUNCTIONING STUDIES

A number of structural brain abnormalities have been reported in anorexia nervosa, including gray and white matter loss, increased ventricular size, increased cerebrospinal fluid volume, and enlarged sulci (Golden et al., 1996; Kingston et al., 1996; Swayze et al., 2003). Although many of these abnormalities normalize after weight restoration, the gray matter loss appears to persist (Lambe et al., 1997) and may be related to changes in cortisol levels (Katzman et al.,1996). Wagner et al. (2006) found no differences in CSF volume or gray and white matter volume in individuals with anorexia and bulimia who had recovered, compared with controls. Structural brain changes in bulimia nervosa are less pronounced than in anorexia nervosa. However, cerebral atrophy has been observed in normal-weight individuals with bulimia nervosa (Hoffman et al., 1989).

In terms of functional differences, individuals with both anorexia and bulimia nervosa have globally decreased brain glucose metabolism in the resting state (Frank et al., 2004). Brain imaging studies of individuals with anorexia and bulimia nervosa in both the ill and recovered state have elevated activity of the 5-HT$_{1A}$ receptor in frontal-limbic brain regions (Kaye et al., 2005). This receptor activity is linked negatively to measures of impulse control and behavioral inhibition, which could indicate that an increase in 5-HT$_{1A}$ receptor activity may contribute to the rigid, inflexible, overcontrolled, inhibited behavior found in anorexia nervosa and some forms of bulimia nervosa—many of which exist premorbidly and persist after recovery from the Eating Disorder. Of note, similar findings have emerged among adolescent girls who engage in self-injurious behaviors (see Crowell, Beauchaine, & Lenzenweger, this volume).

DEVELOPMENTAL PROGRESSION

ANOREXIA NERVOSA

Retrospective data suggest that there are two peak periods of risk for anorexia nervosa onset: around age 14 and age 18 (APA, 1994, 2000). These periods correspond to the developmental transitions from grade school to high school and from high school to post high school, which may suggest that developmental stressors can precipitate the onset of anorexia among vulnerable individuals. The fact that eating disorders more broadly tend to emerge after puberty also suggests that hormonal changes or concomitant increases in female gender-role internalization may increase risk for eating pathology, although the relevant mechanisms are unclear.

The course of anorexia nervosa is variable (Wilson et al., 2003; Berkman et al., 2006). Among adolescents with anorexia nervosa, 50 to 70% recover, 20% show improvement but exhibit residual symptoms, and 10 to 20% develop a chronic course (Commission on Adolescent Eating Disorders, 2005). Course of illness is on average 10 years (Strober, Freeman, & Morrell, 1997). Residual symptoms include low weight and disturbances in eating, body image, menstrual, and psychosocial functioning. Relapse is common after discharge from inpatient treatment, occurring in one-third of cases (Strober et al., 1997). Over one-third of patients with the restricting subtype develop bulimia nervosa during the course of illness and approximately one-fourth of individuals with bulimia nervosa develop anorexia over time (Tozzi et al., 2005).

Anorexia nervosa has one of the highest mortality rates of any psychiatric illness. Approximately 6% of patients diagnosed with this disorder die per decade of illness and these patients are 11 times more likely to die than other women of a similar age (Keel et al., 2003; Birmingham, 2005). The most common causes of death are acute starvation and suicide. The suicide rate for anorexia nervosa is 57 times higher than in the general population (Keel, Fulkerson, & Leon, 1997).

Bulimia Nervosa

The peak period of risk for onset for bulimia nervosa is between 14 and 19 years of age for females (Lewinsohn et al., 2000; Stice et al., 2006). Community-recruited samples suggest that bulimia nervosa typically shows a chronic course characterized by periods of recovery and relapse, whereas subthreshold bulimic pathology shows less chronicity (Bohon et al., 2005; Fairburn et al., 2000). One large study that followed a community-recruited cohort of 102 young women with bulimia nervosa for 5 years (Fairburn et al., 2000) found that afflicted individuals often showed marked initial improvement, followed by gradual improvement. By the end of this 5-year study, 15% of participants still met diagnostic criteria for bulimia nervosa, 2% met criteria for anorexia nervosa, and 34% met criteria for EDNOS. This cohort displayed a fluctuating course; each year approximately 33% showed symptom remission and 33% showed relapse. A second study that followed 101 community-recruited adolescent girls with full or subthreshold bulimia nervosa indicated that 54% of the participants with bulimia nervosa recovered over the 1-year follow-up and that 45% of the participants with subthreshold bulimia nervosa recovered (Bohon et al., 2005). Another community-recruited study indicated that 40% of women with bulimia nervosa recovered over a 1-year follow-up (Grilo et al., 2003). Even after recovery, residual symptoms remain including continued impairments in physical and psychosocial functioning (Fairburn et al., 2000). The mortality rate for bulimia nervosa is less than 1% (Keel et al., 1999).

Prospective studies have suggested that both diagnosable and subthreshold bulimia nervosa increase the risk for future onset of depression, suicide attempts, anxiety disorders, substance abuse, obesity, and health problems (Johnson et al., 2002; Stice, Cameron et al., 1999; Stice et al., 2000; Striegel-Moore, Seeley, & Lewinsohn, 2003; Fairburn et al., 2000).

BINGE EATING DISORDER

Prospective data on peak risk periods for the onset of binge eating disorder do not yet exist, although it appears to be somewhat older than anorexia and bulimia nervosa (Commission on Adolescent Eating Disorders, 2005). The symptom of binge eating typically onsets between 16 and 18 years of age (Stice et al., 2006, 1998).

One community-recruited natural history study suggested that binge eating disorder shows a high remission rate over time, with nearly 50% of cases recovering by 6-month follow-up (Cachelin et al., 1999) and 80% of cases recovering by 3- to 5-year follow-up (Fairburn et al., 2000; Wilson et al., 2003). Retrospective data suggest that the mean duration that people suffer from binge eating disorder rivals that for bulimia nervosa (8.1 years); both durations are substantially longer than that for anorexia nervosa (Hudson et al., in press). Moreover, 12-month persistence, defined as 12-month prevalence among lifetime cases, was lowest for anorexia nervosa (0.0%; suggesting differences in severity between clinic cases and community cases) and higher for bulimia nervosa (31%) and binge eating disorder (44%). In addition, binge eating disorder often resolves into a presentation more accurately captured by an EDNOS diagnosis, with individuals continuing to display some residual symptoms, as is the case with other eating disorders.

Little is known about the course and outcome of young-adult binge eating disorder. However, one community-recruited natural history study found that the rate of obesity increased from 20% to 39% over this 5-year study (Fairburn et al., 2000). These findings converge with evidence indicating that binge eating is a risk factor for obesity onset (Stice et al., 2002). Furthermore, low self-confidence, diminished energy level, and discrimination displayed by teachers and peers present significant obstacles to achievement in school and other pursuits among overweight adolescents (Gortmaker, Must, Perrin, & Sobol, 1993).

COMORBIDITY

ANOREXIA NERVOSA

Although considerable research exists on comorbidity with eating disorders, few studies focus on children and adolescents and even fewer on males. However, one study that collapsed across the various eating disorders suggested that men with eating disorders show similar psychiatric comorbidity relative to women with eating disorders (Woodside et al., 2001). Many studies examining comorbidity have used treatment-seeking samples, which are typically biased toward finding elevated comorbidity relative to population levels because each psychiatric condition that an individual has increases the odds of treatment seeking (Berkson, 1946). Nonetheless, these investigations accurately prepare clinicians for comorbid patterns they will encounter. One should also be attentive to whether studies report lifetime comorbidity or concurrent comorbidity.

Studies of community-recruited samples of adolescents indicate that anorexia nervosa shows statistically significant comorbidity with current dysthymia, Bipolar Disorder, Agoraphobia, Simple Phobia, marijuana dependence, and Oppositional Defiant Disorder, but not with current bulimia nervosa, major depression, Conduct Disorder, Attention-Deficit/ Hyperactivity Disorder, other substance use disorders, Social Phobia, Posttraumatic Stress Disorder, Panic Disorder, Obsessive-Compulsive Disorder, or Generalized Anxiety Disorder (Stice & Peterson, in press). Although there appear to be no comparable data from treatment-seeking samples of adolescents with anorexia nervosa, one large study of adults seeking treatment for this disorder also suggested that the current rates of several disorders were elevated relative to prevalence data available from epidemiologic studies of similarly aged participants (e.g., Garfinkel et al., 1995). Herzog, Keller, Sacks, Yeh, and Lavori (1992) found that the rates of current major depression, Obsessive-Compulsive Ddisorder, Panic Disorder, and Phobic Disorder were substantially higher than the lifetime prevalence rates observed in epidemiologic studies. However, Herzog and associates (1992) found that the rates of alcohol and drug use disorders among treatment-seeking adults were lower than the lifetime prevalence rates observed in epidemiologic studies. In terms of lifetime comorbidity, the most common comorbid conditions in adults with anorexia nervosa are major depression and anxiety disorders (Kaye et al., 2004; Walters & Kendler, 1995). Anxiety disorders often predate the Eating Disorder, and depression often persists postrecovery (Kaye et al., 2004; Sullivan et al., 1998).

BULIMIA NERVOSA

Limited data are available regarding psychiatric comorbidity among adolescents with bulimia nervosa. Research with community-recruited samples of adolescents indicate that bulimia nervosa shows statistically significant comorbidity with current major depression, dysthymia, Bipolar Disorder, Agoraphobia, Social Phobia, alcohol dependence, marijuana dependence, and Conduct Disorder, but not with current Simple Phobia, Overanxious Disorder, Panic Disorder, Posttraumatic Stress Disorder, Generalized Anxiety Disorder, Obsessive-Compulsive Disorder, Oppositional Defiant Disorder, Attention-Deficit/Hyperactivity Disorder, or other substance use disorders (Stice & Peterson, in press). One large community-recruited sample of adolescents and adults suggested that, relative to those without bulimia nervosa, those with current bulimia nervosa have much higher current prevalence of major depression, any Anxiety Disorder, Social Phobia, Simple Phobia, Agoraphobia, Panic Disorder, Generalized Anxiety Disorder, and alcohol dependence (Garfinkel et al., 1995). Although there appear to be no comparable data from treatment-seeking samples of adolescents with bulimia nervosa, one large study of adults seeking treatment for this Eating Disorder also suggested that the current rates of several disorders were elevated relative to prevalence data available from epidemiologic studies of similarly aged participants (e.g., Garfinkel et al., 1995). Specifically, Herzog et al. (1992) found that the rates of current major depression and substance use disorders were substantially higher than the lifetime prevalence observed in epidemiologic studies. However, the prevalence of Obsessive-Compulsive Disorder, Panic Disorder, and Phobic Disorder were similar to those observed in epidemiologic studies. Common lifetime comorbid psychiatric conditions among adults with bulimia nervosa include anxiety disorders, major depression, dysthymia, substance use, and personality disorders (Wilson et al., 2003). It remains unclear whether the discrepancies observed across these studies reflect differences in comorbidity across the age span or between clinic- and community-ascertained samples.

BINGE EATING DISORDER

To the best of our knowledge, no studies have examined the prevalence of comorbid psychiatric disorders among children and adolescents with binge eating disorder. One study of nontreatment seeking adults found that women with binge eating disorder did not show significantly higher rates of major depression, Bipolar Disorder, dysthymia, substance abuse or dependence, Panic Disorder, Agoraphobia, Social Phobia, or Obsessive-Compulsive Disorder, relative to weight-matched comparison women (Telch & Stice, 1998). A study of individuals seeking weight-loss treatment indicated that women with binge eating disorder reported significantly higher rates of current major depression relative to weight-matched comparison participants, but that the two groups did not differ in terms of current Bipolar Disorder, Dysthymic Disorder, Posttraumatic Stress Disorder, Agoraphobia, Panic Disorder, Social Phobia, Specific Phobia, or Generalized Anxiety Disorder (Fontenelle et al., 2003). Similar findings emerged from a second study of treatment-seeking individuals with binge eating disorder (Wilfley et al., 2000). The higher rates of comorbidity from the treatment-seeking sample, relative to the nontreatment seeking sample, probably emerged because treatment-seeking samples are biased toward finding elevated comorbidity (Berkson, 1946). These findings should be generalized to adolescents with caution because all of these estimates came from samples of adults.

SEX DIFFERENCES

Research suggests that female:male sex ratios of the prevalence of anorexia nervosa and bulimia nervosa are approximately 10:1 (APA, 1994). For anorexia nervosa, of course, the amenorrhea criterion applies only to women. Although the *DSM* provides no male equivalent, the International Classification of Diseases-10 notes loss of sexual interest and potency as a criterion for anorexia nervosa in males. For bulimia nervosa, the diagnostic criteria are sex-biased. In contrast to women, men tend to present with a greater reliance on nonpurging forms of compensatory behavior such as excessive exercise (Anderson & Bulik, 2003). Considerations of differences in the clinical presentation of bulimia nervosa in men may lead to revised estimates (Anderson & Bulik, 2003). Although binge eating disorder shows a similar sex ratio during adolescence, the distribution across sexes seems to become more balanced by adulthood (Kjelsas et al., 2004). The fact that both anorexia nervosa and bulimia nervosa are more prevalent among girls and women, relative to boys and men, seems to imply that some key difference(s) between the sexes, such as biological factors (e.g., hormonal differences), psychopathology factors (e.g., differences in affective disturbances), or developmental experiences (e.g., greater physical objectification), play a role in the etiology of these two eating disorders.

There is some evidence that homosexual males and males who participate in sports with weight-limit requirements are at elevated risk for developing eating disorders (Wilson et al., 2003). However, very little is known about sex differences in risk factors for eating disturbances or course of eating pathology, owing in large part to the low base rate of these disorders in males.

CULTURAL CONSIDERATIONS

Early stereotypes that eating disorders were confined to upper-middle-class women and girls have generally not been supported in several large studies that have used representative community-recruited samples. In part, this early picture reflects those individuals who were able to seek and afford clinical care (Smolak & Striegel-Moore, 2001). Unfortunately, few epidemiologic data on eating disorders in the United States exist to provide a clear picture of the racial and ethnic distribution of eating disorders and behaviors. Striegel-Moore et al. (2003) explored eating disorders in 2,054 young-adult African American and Caucasian women and reported lower prevalences among the former; no African American women were detected with anorexia nervosa, compared with 1.5% of Caucasian women. Striegel-Moore et al. (2005) noted different patterns of Eating Disorder symptoms across ethnic/racial groups, reporting that binge eating in the absence of purging was more common in African American women, whereas purging in the absence of binge eating was more common in Caucasian women. However, several studies have found no racial or ethnic differences in the prevalence of recurrent binge eating, Eating Disorder symptoms, and risk factors for eating disorders (Smith et al., 1998; Shaw et al., 2004; Stiegel-Moore et al., 2000; Yanovski et al., 1992). One consistent difference that has emerged is that African Americans report less body image dissatisfaction than their White counterparts. There is also evidence that youth who participate in sports with weight requirements or with an extreme focus on appearance are at elevated risk for development of eating disorders because of the emphasis placed on weight and shape within these "cultures" (Wilson et al., 2003). Preliminary data also suggest that there may be increased risk for binge eating disorder in lower socioeconomic classes (Warheit et al., 1993).

SYNTHESIS AND FUTURE DIRECTIONS

It is important to note several controversies in the field and gaps in the literature. First, various researchers and clinicians have suggested that the diagnostic criteria for eating disorders are in need of revision. Some have asserted that the frequency criteria for eating-disordered behaviors (e.g., at least twice-weekly binge-eating episodes per week for bulimia nervosa) are not optimal for delineating clinically meaningful eating pathology (e.g., Garfinkel et al., 1995). This is an empirical question that should be addressed with analyses designed to identify the frequency cut-point with the optimal sensitivity and specificity (signal detection analyses) for key criterion variables (e.g., psychosocial impairment, medical problems, chronicity). The question also remains whether sufficient evidence exists to include binge eating disorder as an Eating Disorder in the next *DSM*. In addition, it will be vital to analyze samples of individuals with EDNOS, in an effort to identify additional Eating Disorder syndromes. Finally, it will be important to conduct large studies on the phenomenology of eating disorders in large representative samples that contain males and females, children, adolescents, and adults, and participants from multiple racial and ethnic groups. Such studies will shed light on sex, developmental differences, and ethnic differences in the manifestation of eating pathology.

Our knowledge of the etiologic and developmental processes that give rise to eating disorders is currently incomplete. Although dozens of psychosocial risk factors have been found to predict future onset of eating-disordered symptoms, almost none have been identified that predict onset of full-syndrome eating disorders. There is a particular dearth of studies on the factors that predict onset of anorexia nervosa. In addition, premorbid biological factors and biomarkers have not yet been identified. Perhaps most importantly, almost no studies have tested integrative models of how psychosocial and biological factors operate together to give rise to eating disorders (i.e., gene–environment correlations and interactions). Prospective studies of high-risk individuals and use of population-based registries may help address these key questions. Without large-scale prospective studies that assess a wide variety of psychosocial and biological factors, our understanding of etiologic processes will not advance. Such studies will also enable documentation of the developmental course of symptom onset of eating disorders and how this relates to the timing of increases in risk factors for eating disorders. Another key gap in the literature is that we know almost nothing of the maintenance factors—either psychosocial or biological—that perpetuate eating-disordered behaviors once they emerge. An improved understanding of risk factors is essential for the design of more effective prevention programs and an improved understanding of maintenance factors is vital for the development of more effective treatment interventions.

Prospective designs are highly valuable, yet vulnerable to third-variable alternative explanations (i.e., that an omitted variable explains the relation between the putative risk factor and the development of eating pathology). Augmenting these approaches with randomized experiments that focus on suspected risk and maintenance factors is a rational complementary strategy. For instance, it may be possible to use randomized prevention trials to effect a lasting reduction in a single putative risk factor (e.g., thin-ideal internalization, negative affect, body dissatisfaction) and test whether there is a consequent reduction in risk for emergence of Eating Disorder symptoms during the period of peak risk for onset of these behaviors among those who receive the preventive intervention relative to those who receive a control intervention (see Howe et al., 2002). It should likewise be possible to use treatment intervention to effect a lasting reduction in a single suspected maintenance factor (e.g., dietary restraint, body dissatisfaction) and test whether there is a significantly greater reduction in symptoms or the prevalence of the disorder among those who receive this treatment relative to those who receive a control intervention. Although the weakness of these experimental trials rests with ecological validity, the convergence of findings from prospective and experimental studies could boost confidence in our etiologic and maintenance models for eating disorders.

Although considerable progress has been made with regard to our understanding of the diagnosis, epidemiology, developmental course, and risk factors for eating disturbances, there are many unanswered questions. We are confident that rigorous and programmatic research that constructively builds upon our current knowledge base will continue to improve our ability to prevent and treat these pernicious psychiatric disturbances.

REFERENCES

American Psychiatric Association. (1994). *Diagnostic and statistical manual of mental disorders* (4th ed.). Washington, DC: American Psychiatric Association.

American Psychiatric Association. (2000). *Diagnostic and statistical manual of mental disorders* (4th ed., text revision). Washington, DC: American Psychiatric Association.

Allison, D. B., Heo, M., Schork, N. J., Wong, S. L., & Elston, R. C. (1998). Extreme selection strategies in gene mapping studies of oligogenic quantitative traits do not always increase power. *Human Heredity, 48,* 97–107.

Anderson, C. & Bulik, C. (2003). Gender differences in compensatory behaviors, weight and shape salience, and drive for thinness. *Eating Behaviors, 5,* 1–11.

Bacanu, S., Bulik, C., Klump, K., Fichter, M., Halmi, K., Keel, P., et al. (2005). Linkage analysis of anorexia and bulimia nervosa cohorts using selected behavioral phenotypes as quantitative traits or covariates. *American Journal of Medical Genetics Part B: Neuropsychiatry Genetics, 139,* 61–68.

Berkman, N. D., Bulik, C. M., Brownley, K. A., Lohr, K. N., Sedway, J. A., Rooks, A., Gartlehner, G. (April, 2006). *Management of Eating Disorders.* Evidence Report/Technology Assessment No. 135. (Prepared by the RTI International-University of North Carolina Evidence-Based Practice Center under Contract No. 290-02-0016.) AHRQ Publication No. 06-E010. Rockville, MD: Agency for Healthcare Research and Quality.

Berkson, J. (1946). Limitations of the application of fourfold table analysis to hospital data. *Biometrics Bulletin, 2,* 47–53.

Birmingham, C., Su, J., Hlynsky, J., Goldner, E., & Gao, M. (2005). The mortality rate from anorexia nervosa. *International Journal of Eating Disorders, 38,* 143–146.

Bohon, C., Muscatell, K., Burton, E., & Stice, E. (2005). *Maintenance factors for persistence of bulimic pathology: A community-based natural history study.* Poster presented at the annual meeting of the Eating Disorder Research Society, Toronto, Canada.

Bulik, C., Bacanu, S., Klump, K., Fichter, M., Halmi, K., Keel, P., et al. (2005). Selection of eating disorders phenotypes for linkage analysis. *American Journal of Medical Genetics Part B: Neuropsychiatry Genetics, 139,* 81–87.

Bulik, C. M., Devlin, B., Bacanu, S. A., Thornton, L., Klump, K. L., Fichter, M. M., et al. (2003). Significant linkage on chromosome 10p in families with bulimia nervosa. *American Journal of Human Genetics, 72,* 200–207.

Bulik, C. M., Reba, L., Siega-Riz, A. M., Reichborn-Kjennerud, T. (2005). Anorexia nervosa: Definition, epidemiology and cycle of risk. *International Journal of Eating Disorders, 37,* S2–S9.

Bulik, C., Sullivan, P., Tozzi, F., Furberg, H., Lichtenstein, P., & Pedersen, N. (2006). Prevalence, heritability and prospective risk factors for anorexia nervosa. *Archives of General Psychiatry, 63,* 305–312.

Bulik, C., Sullivan, P., Wade, T., & Kendler, K. (2000). Twin studies of eating disorders: A review. *International Journal of Eating Disorders, 27,* 1–20.

Cachelin, F. M., Striegel-Moore, R. H., Elder, K. A., Pike, K. M., Wilfley, D. E., & Fairburn, C. G. (1999). Natural course of a community sample of women with binge eating disorder. *International Journal of Eating Disorders, 25,* 45–54.

Cattarin, J. A., & Thompson, J. K. (1994). A 3-year longitudinal study of body image, eating disturbance, and general psychological functioning in adolescent females. *Eating Disorders, 2,* 114–125.

Cnattingius, S., Hultman, C., Dahl, M., & Sparen, P. (1999). Very preterm birth, birth trauma, and the risk of anorexia nervosa among girls. *Archives of General Psychiatry, 56,* 634–638.

Commission on Adolescent Eating Disorders (2005). Defining eating disorders. In D. L. Evans, E. B. Foa, R. E. Gur, H. Hendin, C. P. O'Brien, M. E. P. Seligman, et al. (Eds.), *Treating and preventing adolescent mental health disorders: What we know and what we don't know* (pp. 257–332). New York: Oxford University Press, The Annenberg Foundation Trust at Sunnylands, and the Annenberg Public Policy Center of the University of Pennsylvania.

Devlin, B., Bacanu, S., Klump, K., Bulik, C., Fichter, M., Halmi, K., et al. (2002). Linkage analysis of anorexia nervosa incorporating behavioral covariates. *Human Molecular Genetics, 11,* 689–696.

Fairburn, C. G., Cooper, Z., Doll, H. A., Norman, P. A., & O'Connor, M. E. (2000).

The natural course of bulimia nervosa and binge eating disorder in young women. *Archives of General Psychiatry, 57,* 659–665.

Fairburn, C. G., & Harrison, P. J. (2003). Eating disorders. *Lancet, 361,* 407–416.

Field, A. E., Camargo, C. A., Taylor, C. B., Berkey, C. S., & Colditz, G. A. (1999). Relation of peer and media influences to the development of purging behaviors among preadolescent and adolescent girls. *Archives of Pediatric Adolescent Medicine, 153,* 1184–1189.

Fontaine, K. R., Redden, D. T., Wang, C., Westfall, A. O., Allison, D. B. (2003). Years of life lost due to obesity. *Journal of the American Medical Association, 289,* 187–93.

Fontenelle, L. F., Mendlowicz, M. V., Menezes, G. B., Papelbaum, M., Freitas, W. R., Godoy-Matos, et al. (2003). Psychiatric comorbidity in a Brazilian sample of patients with binge eating disorder. *Psychiatric Research, 119,* 189–194.

Frank, G. K., Bailer, U. F., Henry, S., Wagner, A., & Kaye, W. H. (2004). Neuroimaging studies in eating disorders. *CNS Spectr, 9,* 539–548.

Garfinkel, P. E., Lin, E., Goering, P., Spegg, C., Goldbloom, D. S., Kennedy, S., et al. (1995). Bulimia nervosa in a Canadian community sample: Prevalence and comparison of subgroups. *American Journal of Psychiatry, 152,* 1052–1058.

Golden, N. H., Ashtari, M., Kohn, M. R., Patel, M., Jacobson, M. S., Fletcher, A., et al. (1996). Reversibility of cerebral ventricular enlargement in anorexia nervosa, demonstrated by quantitative magnetic resonance imaging. *Journal of Pediatrics, 128,* 296–301.

Gortmaker, S. L., Must, A., Perrin, J., & Sobol, A. (1993). Social and economic consequences of overweight in adolescence and young adulthood. *New England Journal of Medicine, 329,* 1008–1012.

Grice, D. E., Halmi, K. A., Fichter, M. M., Strober, M., Woodside, D. B., Treasure, J. T., et al. (2002). Evidence for a susceptibility gene for anorexia nervosa on chromosome 1. *American Journal of Human Genetics, 70,* 787–792.

Grilo, C. M., Sanislow, C. A., Shea, M. T., Skodol, A. E., Stout, R. L., Pagano, M. E. et al. (2003). The natural course of bulimia nervosa and eating disorder not otherwise specified is not influenced by personality disorders. *International Journal of Eating Disorders, 34,* 319–330.

Gull, W. W. (1873). Anorexia hysterica (apoepsia hysteria), *British Medical Journal, ii,* 527.

Herzog, D. B., Keller, M. B., Sacks, N. R., Yeh, C. J., & Lavori, P. W. (1992). Psychiatric comorbidity in treatment-seeking anorexics and bulimics. *Journal of the American Academy of Child and Adolescent Psychiatry, 31,* 810–818.

Hinney, A., Remschmidt, H., & Hebebrand, J. (2000). Candidate gene polymorphisms in eating disorders. *European Journal of Pharmacology, 410,* 147–159.

Hoek, H. W., & van Hoeken, D. (2003). Review of the prevalence and incidence of eating disorders. *International Journal of Eating Disorders, 34,* 383–396.

Hoffman, G. W., Ellinwood, E. H., Jr., Rockwell, W. J., Herfkens, R. J., Nishita, J. K., & Guthrie, L. F. (1989). Cerebral atrophy in bulimia. *Biological Psychiatry, 25,* 894–902.

Hudson, J., Hiripi, E., Pope, H., & Kessler, R. (2007). The prevalence and correlates of eating disorders in the National Comorbidity Survey Replication. *Biological Psychiatry, 61,* 348–358.

Hudson, J., Lalonde, J., Pindyck, L., Bulik, C., Crow, S., McElroy, S., et al. (2006).

Familial aggregation of binge-eating disorder. *Archives of General Psychiatry, 63,* 313–319.

Jimerson, D. C., Wolfe, B. E., Metzger, E. D., Finkelstein, D. M., Cooper, T. B., & Levine, J. M. (1997). Decreased serotonin function in bulimia nervosa. *Archives of General Psychiatry, 54,* 529–534.

Johnson, J. G., Cohen, P., Kasen, S., & Brook, J. S. (2002). Eating disorders during adolescence and the risk for physical and mental disorders during early adulthood. *Archives of General Psychiatry, 59,* 545–552.

Katzman, D. K., Lambe, E. K., Mikulis, D. J., Ridgley, J. N., Goldbloom, D. S., & Zipursky, R. B. (1996). Cerebral gray matter and white matter volume deficits in adolescent girls with anorexia nervosa. *Journal of Pediatrics, 129,* 794–803.

Kaye, W. H., Bailer, U. F., Frank, G. K., Wagner, A., Henry, S. E. (2005). Brain imaging of serotonin after recovery from anorexia and bulimia nervosa. *Physiology of Behavior, 86,* 15–17.

Kaye, W., Bulik, C., Thornton, L., Barbarich, B. S., Masters, K., & the Price Foundation Collaborative Group (2004). Comorbidity of anxiety disorders with anorexia and bulimia nervosa. *American of Journal of Psychiatry, 161,* 2215–2221.

Kaye, W. H., Greeno, C. G., Moss, H., Fernstrom, J., Fernstrom, M., Lilenfeld, L. R., et al. (1998). Alterations in serotonin activity and psychiatric symptoms after recovery from bulimia nervosa. *Archives of General Psychiatry, 55,* 927–935.

Kaye, W. H., Gwirtsman, H. E., George, D. T., & Ebert, M. H. (1991). Altered serotonin activity in anorexia nervosa after long-term weight restoration. Does elevated cerebrospinal fluid 5-hydroxyindoleacetic acid level correlate with rigid and obsessive behavior? *Archives of General Psychiatry, 48,* 556–562.

Keel, P. K., Dorer, D. J., Eddy, K. T., Franko, D., Charatan, D. L., & Herzog, D. B. (2003). Predictors of mortality in eating disorders. *Archives of General Psychiatry, 60,* 179–183.

Keel, P. K., Fulkerson, J. A., & Leon, G. R. (1997). Disordered eating precursors in pre- and early adolescent girls and boys. *Journal of Youth and Adolescence, 26,* 203–216.

Keel, P. K., Mitchell, J. E., Miller, K. B., Davis, T. L., & Crow, S. J. (1999). Long-term outcome of bulimia nervosa. *Archives of General Psychiatry, 56,* 63–69.

Killen, J. D., Taylor, C. B., Hayward, C., Haydel, K. F., Wilson, D. M., Hammer, L., et al. (1996). Weight concerns influence the development of eating disorders: A 4-year prospective study. *Journal of Consulting and Clinical Psychology, 64,* 936–940.

Kingston, K., Szmukler, G., Andrewes, D., Tress, B., & Desmond, P. (1996). Neuropsychological and structural brain changes in anorexia nervosa before and after refeeding. *Psychological Medicine, 26,* 15–28.

Kjelsas, E., Bjornstrom, C., & Gotestam, K. G. (2004). Prevalence of eating disorders in female and male adolescents (14–15 years). *Eating Behaviors, 5,* 13–25.

Klem, M. L., Wing, R. R, Simkin-Silverman, L., & Kuller, L. H. (1997). The psychological consequences of weight gain prevention in healthy, premenopausal women. *International Journal of Eating Disorders, 21,* 167–174.

Klump, K. L., Miller, K. B., Keel, P. K., McGue, M., & Iacono, W. G. (2001). Genetic and environmental influences on anorexia nervosa syndromes in a population-based twin sample. *Psychological Medicine, 31,* 737–740.

Lambe, E. K., Katzman, D. K., Mikulis, D. J., Kennedy, S. H., & Zipursky, R. B. (1997). Cerebral gray matter volume deficits after weight recovery from anorexia nervosa. *Archives of General Psychiatry, 54,* 537–542.

Lewinsohn, P. M., Striegel-Moore, R. H., & Seeley, J. R. (2000). Epidemiology and natural course of eating disorders in young women from adolescence to young adulthood. *Journal of the American Academy of Child and Adolescent Psychiatry, 39,* 1284–1292.

Lilenfeld, L., Kaye, W., Greeno, C., Merikangas, K., Plotnicov, K., Pollice, C., et al. (1997). Psychiatric disorders in women with bulimia nervosa and their first-degree relatives: Effects of comorbid substance dependence. *International Journal of Eating Disorders, 22,* 253–264.

Marchi, M., & Cohen, P. (1990) Early childhood eating behaviors and adolescent eating disorders. *Journal of American Academy of Child and Adolescent Psychiatry, 29,* 112–117.

McKnight Investigators. (2003). Risk factors for onset of eating disorders in adolescent girls: Results of the McKnight Longitudinal Risk Factor Study. *American Journal of Psychiatry, 160,* 248–254.

Presnell, K., & Stice, E. (2003). An experimental test of the effect of weight-loss dieting on bulimic pathology: Tipping the scales in a different direction. *Journal of Abnormal Psychology, 112,* 166–170.

Reichborn-Kjennerud, T., Bulik, C., Tambs, K., & Harris, J. (2004). Genetic and environmental influences on binge eating in the absence of compensatory behaviors: A population-based twin study. *International Journal of Eating Disorders, 36,* 307–314.

Reichborn-Kjennerud, T., Bulik, C. M., Sullivan, P. F., Tambs, K., Harris, J. R. (2004) Medical and psychiatric symptoms associated with binge-eating in the absence of compensatory behaviors, *Obesity Research, 12,* 1445–1454.

Roth, B. (in press). *The 5-HT receptors.* Humana Press.

Russell, G. F. M. (1979). Bulimia nervosa: An ominous variant of anorexia nervosa. *Psychological Medicine, 9,* 429–448.

Santonastaso, P., Friederici, S., & Favaro, A. (1999). Full and partial syndromes in eating disorders: A 1-year prospective study of risk factors among female students. *Psychopathology, 32,* 50–56.

Sasieni, P. D. (1997). From genotypes to genes: doubling the sample size. *Biometrics, 53,* 1253–1261.

Shaw, H., Ramirez, L., Trost, A., Randall, P., & Stice, E. (2004). Body image and eating disturbances across ethnic groups: More similarities than differences. *Psychology of Addictive Behaviors, 18,* 12–18.

Simansky, K. J. (2005). NIH symposium series: Ingestive mechanisms in obesity, substance abuse and mental disorders. *Physiology and Behavior, 86,* 1–4.

Slof-Op't, L., Margarita, C. T., van Furth, E. F., Meulenbelt, I. (2005). Eating disorders: From twin studies to candidate genes and beyond. *Twin Research and Human Genetics, 8,* 467–482.

Smith, D. E., Marcus, M. D., Lewis, C. E., Fitzgibbon, M., & Schreiner, P. (1998). Prevalence of binge eating disorder, obesity, and depression in a biracial cohort of young adults. *Annals of Behavioral Medicine, 20,* 227–232.

Smolak, L., & Striegel-Moore, R. H. (2001). Challenging the myth of the golden girl: Ethnicity and eating disorders. In R. H. Striegel-Moore & L. Smolak (Eds.), *Eating disorders* (pp. 111–132). Washington DC: American Psychological Association.

Stice, E. (2001). A prospective test of the dual pathway model of bulimic pathology: Mediating effects of dieting and negative affect. *Journal of Abnormal Psychology, 110,* 124–135.

Stice, E. (2002). Risk and maintenance factors for eating pathology: A meta-analytic review. *Psychological Bulletin, 128,* 825–848.

Stice, E., Agras, W. S., & Hammer, L. (1999). Factors influencing the onset of childhood eating disturbances: A five-year prospective study. *International Journal of Eating Disorders, 25,* 375–387.

Stice, E., Cameron, R., Killen, J. D., Hayward, C., & Taylor, C. B. (1999). Naturalistic weight reduction efforts prospectively predict growth in relative weight and onset of obesity among female adolescents. *Journal of Consulting and Clinical Psychology, 67,* 967–974.

Stice, E., Hayward, C., Cameron, R., Killen, J. D., & Taylor, C. B. (2000). Body image and eating related factors predict onset of depression in female adolescents: A longitudinal study. *Journal of Abnormal Psychology, 109,* 438–444.

Stice, E., Killen, J. D., Hayward, C., & Taylor, C. B. (1998). Age of onset for binge eating and purging during adolescence: A four-year survival analysis. *Journal of Abnormal Psychology, 107,* 671–675.

Stice, E., & Peterson, C. (2007). Assessment of eating disorders. In E. J. Mash & R. A. Barkley (Eds.), *Assessment of childhood disorders* (pp. 751–780). New York: Guilford.

Stice, E., Presnell, K., & Bearman, S. K. (2006). *Risk factors for onset of threshold and subthreshold bulimia nervosa: A 5-year prospective study of adolescent girls.* Submitted.

Stice, E., Presnell, K., & Spangler, D. (2002). Risk factors for binge eating onset: A prospective investigation. *Health Psychology, 21,* 131–138.

Stice, E., & Shaw, H. (1994). Adverse effects of the media portrayed thin-ideal on women, and linkages to bulimic symptomatology. *Journal of Social and Clinical Psychology, 13,* 288–308.

Striegel-Moore, R. H., Franko, D. L., Thompson, D., Barton, B., Schreiber, G. B., & Daniels, S. R. (2005). An empirical study of the typology of bulimia nervosa and its spectrum variants. *Psychological Medicine, 35,* 1563–1572.

Striegel-Moore, R.H., Bulik, C.M. (2007). Risk factors for eating disorders. *American Psychologist, 62,* 181–198.

Striegel-Moore, R. H., Seeley, J. R., & Lewinsohn, P. M. (2003). Psychosocial adjustment in young adulthood of women who experience an eating disorder during adolescence. *American Academy of Child and Adolescent Psychiatry, 42,* 587–593.

Striegel-Moore, R. H., Wilfley, D. E., Pike, K. M., Dohm, F. A., & Fairburn, C. G. (2000). Recurrent binge eating in black American women. *Archives of Family Medicine, 9,* 83–87.

Strober, M., Freeman, R., Lampert, C., Diamond, J., & Kaye, W. (2000). Controlled family study of anorexia nervosa and bulimia nervosa: evidence of shared liability and transmission of partial syndromes. *American Journal of Psychiatry, 157,* 393–401.

Strober, M., Freeman, R., & Morrell, W. (1997). The long-term course of severe anorexia nervosa in adolescents: Survival analysis of recovery, relapse, and outcome predictors over 10–15 years in a prospective study. *International Journal of Eating Disorders, 22,* 339–360.

Stunkard, A. J. (1959). Eating patterns and obesity. *Psychiatric Quarterly, 33,* 284–292.

Sullivan, P. F., Bulik, C. M., Fear, J. L., & Pickering, A. (1998) Outcome of anorexia nervosa. *American Journal of Psychiatry, 155,* 939–946.

Swayze, V. W., II, Andersen, A. E., Andreasen, N. C., Arndt, S., Sato, Y., & Ziebell, S. (2003). Brain tissue volume segmentation in patients with anorexia nervosa before and after weight normalization. *International Journal of Eating Disorders, 33,* 33–44.

Telch, C., & Stice, E. (1998). Psychiatric comorbidity in a non-clinical sample of women with binge eating disorder. *Journal of Consulting and Clinical Psychology, 66,* 768–776.

Tozzi, F., Thornton L., Klump K., Bulik C., Fichter, M., Halmi, K., et al. (2005) Symptom fluctuation in eating disorders: correlates of diagnostic crossover. *American Journal of Psychiatry, 162,* 732–740.

Vogeltanz-Holm, N. D., Wonderlich, S. A., Lewis, B. A., Wilsnack, S. C., Harris, T. R., Wilsnack, R. W., et al. (2000). Longitudinal predictors of binge eating, intense dieting, and weight concerns in a national sample of women. *Behavior Therapy, 31,* 221–235.

von Bertalanffy, L. (1968). *General systems theory.* New York: Braziller.

Wade, T. D., Bulik, C. M., Neale, M., & Kendler, K. S. (2000). Anorexia nervosa and major depression: shared genetic and environmental risk factors. *American Journal of Psychiatry, 157,* 469–471.

Wagner, A., Greer, P., Bailer, U., Frank, G., Henry, S., Putnam, K., et al. (2006). Normal brain tissue volumes after long-term recovery in anorexia and bulimia nervosa. *Biological Psychiatry, 59,* 291–293.

Walsh, B. T. (1993). Binge eating in bulimia nervosa. In C. G. Fairburn & G. T. Wilson (Eds.), *Binge eating: Nature, assessment, and treatment* (pp. 37–49). New York: Guilford.

Walters, E. E., & Kendler, K. S. (1995). Anorexia nervosa and anorexia-like syndromes in a population-based female twin sample. *American Journal of Psychiatry, 152,* 64–71.

Warheit, G., Langer, L., Zimmerman, R., & Biafora, F. (1993). Prevalence of bulimic behaviors and bulimia among a sample of the general population. *American Journal of Epidemiology, 137,* 569–576.

Wilfley, D. E., Friedman, M. A., Dounchis, J. Z., Stein, R. I., Welch, R. R., & Ball, S. A. (2000). Comorbid psychopathology in binge eating disorder: Relation to eating disorder severity at baseline and following treatment. *Journal of Consulting and Clinical Psychology, 68,* 641–649.

Wilson, G. T., Becker, C. B., & Heffernan, K. (2003). Eating disorders. In E. J. Mash

& R. A. Barkley (Eds.), *Child psychopathology* (2nd ed., pp. 687–715). New York: Guilford.

Wonderlich, S. A., & Mitchell, J. E. (1997). Eating disorders and comorbidity: Empirical, conceptual, and clinical implications. *Psychopharmacology Bulletin, 33,* 381–390.

Woodside, D. B., Garfinkel, P. E., Lin, E., Goering, P., Kaplan, A. S., Goldbloom, D. S., & Kennedy, S. H. (2001). Comparison of men with full or partial eating disorders, men without eating disorders, and women with eating disorders in the community. *American Journal of Psychiatry, 158,* 570–574.

Yamada, M., Miyakawa, T., Duttaroy, A., Yamanaka, A., Moriguchi, T., Makita, R., et al. (2001). Mice lacking the M3 muscarinic acetylcholine receptor are hypophagic and lean. *Nature, 410,* 207–212.

Yanovski, S. Z., Leet, M., Yanovski, J. A., Flood, M., Gold, P. W., Kissileff, H. R., et al. (1992). Food selection and intake of obese women with binge eating disorder. *American Journal of Clinical Nutrition, 56,* 975–980.

Author Index

Subject Index

Abused children. *See* Child maltreatment
Acetylcholine, 524–525
Acoustic startle reflex, 42–43
Activation threshold, 254
Active gene-environment correlations, 72–73, 489–490.
    See also Gene-environment (G-E) interaction
Additive genetic effects, 64. *See also* Genetic and environ-
    mental influences, behavioral genetics
Adrenocorticotropic hormone (ACTH), 43–44, 111, 454
Adverse Childhood Experience (ACE) studies, 116
"Advisory on Alcohol Use and Pregnancy," 183. *See also*
    Fetal Alcohol Syndrome (FAS)Age-crime curve, 341
Affective style:
    conceptual models of, 236–238
    EEG asymmetry (*see* Frontal EEG asymmetry)
    future research, 255–257
    overview, 234–236
Alcohol use in childhood and adolescence. *See* Substance
    use in youth
Alcoholic Beverage Warning Label Act, 183. *See also* Fetal
    Alcohol Syndrome (FAS)
Allele, defined, 160
Alpha power, 247
Amygdala, 110, 164–166, 235
Anhedonia, 171–172, 581
Anorexia nervosa. *See* Eating disorders
Antisocial behavior in youth:
    overview, 335–336
    comorbidity, 337
    developmental perspective, 337–338, 380–381
    and sex differences, 338, 339, 341, 346
    and age, 341
    prevalence of, 341
    developmental trajectories of, 338–340, 344–346
    predicting, 341–346
    outcomes of, 346–348
    risk factors of, 348–354
    environmental causes of, 350–354
    gene-environment correlations, 349
    gene-environment interactions, 349–350
    neurophysiological mechanisms of, 354
    and molecular genetics, 355–356
    theoretical synthesis, 356–358
    and Antisocial Personality Disorder, 347 (*see also* Anti-
    social Personality Disorder [ASPD])
Antisocial Personality Disorder (ASPD):
    and Borderline Personality Disorder, 517
    comorbidity and, 387–388
    conceptual issues, 373–376
    cultural considerations, 388–389, 393–394
    developmental progression of, 380–382
    diagnostic issues, 373–376

    etiological formulations, 382–383
        environmental/relationship factors, 385–386,
        390–392
        individual differences, 383–384
        transactional processes, 386–387
    future research, 389–394
    gene-environment interactions, 393
    historical context, 370–372
    and minor physical anomalies, 378–379
    prevalence, 376
    risk factors, 377–379
    and sex differences, 388
    terminology, 373–376, 394
    theoretical synthesis, 389–394
Anxiety disorders:
    behavioral learning processes, 456–460
    biological processes of, 452–456
    and Bipolar Disorder, 561–562
    and comorbidity, 463–464
    conceptual issues, 448–449
    cultural considerations, 464
    developmental progression of, 462–463
    diagnostic issues, 449–450
    and DSM-III, 447, 448
    and DSM-III-R, 447, 463
    and DSM-IV, 448, 449–450, 451, 465
    future research of, 465–466
    historical context, 447–448
    prevalence, 451
    and sex differences, 464–465
    social/interpersonal processes, 460–462
    terminology, 448–449
    theoretical framework of, 451–452
    theoretical synthesis, 465–466
Anxious apprehension, 242
Anxious arousal, 242, 249
Apolipoprotein E (ApoE), 221–222
Apoptosis, 96, 213, 214
Arborization, 96, 217
Aretaeus, 549–550
Arousal, and ADHD studies, 314
Asymmetry score, 247–248
Attention, and ADHD studies, 313–314
Attention-Deficit/Hyperactivity Disorder (ADHD), 8–9,
    11, 16, 63, 133, 139, 142, 187, 192, 194
    and Antisocial Personality Disorder, 387
    and anxiety disorders, 463
    and approach, 317
    and Bipolar Disorder, 561, 562
    and Borderline Personality Disorder, 527
    and brain injury, 211, 216, 223, 224
    Combined Type (ADHD-C), 302, 303, 304, 305, 313, 315